CP

UNITED STATES HISTORY

BY

Ruth Wood Gavian
and William A. Hamm

6 5501 24
70

UNITED STATES
HISTORY

D. C. Heath and Company

MAPS BY Russell Lenz

DRAWINGS BY Marsden Lore

CHARTS BY John Clift

Copyright © 1960 by D. C. HEATH AND COMPANY

No part of the material covered by this copyright may be reproduced in any form without written permission of the publisher. Printed in the United States of America. (6C0)

LIBRARY OF CONGRESS CATALOG CARD NUMBER: 60–5084

CONTENTS

MAPS

CHARTS

KODACHROMES

NOTE ON SUGGESTED READINGS

The purpose of the list of readings which follows each unit is to provide some help in overcoming the limitations of a textbook. Special attention is given to biography and fiction. A star indicates the easier books.

The following suggested readings have been purposely confined to a minimum list of books, both because the general reference works mentioned contain extensive bibliographies, and because, as a matter of sound practice, each class should develop its own list of suitable readings available in the school and the community. These frequently cited books, together with the way each is referred to in chapter activities and unit bibliographies, are as follows:

SOURCE MATERIALS, DOCUMENTS, AND MAPS

Adams, James Truslow (ed.). *Album of American History.* (5 vols.) Scribners, 1949. Referred to as Adams, *Album.*

Commager, Henry Steele (ed.). *Documents of American History.* (5th ed.) Appleton-Century-Crofts, 1949. Referred to as Commager, *Documents.*

———— and Nevins, Allan (eds.). *Heritage of America.* Heath, 1949. Referred to as Commager and Nevins, *Heritage of America.*

Dixon, Robert G. and Plischke, Elmer. *American Government; Basic Documents and Materials.* Van Nostrand, 1950. Referred to as Dixon and Plischke, *American Government Documents.*

Hart, A. B. and Curtis, J. G. (eds.). *American History Told by Contemporaries.* (5 vols.) Macmillan, 1930. Referred to as Hart, *Contemporaries.*

Lord, C. L. and Lord, E. H. (eds.). *Historical Atlas of the United States.* (Rev. ed.) Holt, 1953. Referred to as Lord, *Historical Atlas.*

Nevins, Allan and Weitenkampf, F. *A Century of Political Cartoons.* Scribners, 1944. Referred to as Nevins and Weitenkampf, *Political Cartoons.*

GENERAL REFERENCES

Bailey, Thomas A. *A Diplomatic History of the American People.* Appleton-Century-Crofts, 1958. Referred to as Bailey, *Diplomatic History.*

Beard, Charles A. and Beard, Mary R. *The Rise of American Civilization.* (Rev. ed. 2 vols.) Macmillan, 1949. Referred to as Beard, *American Civilization.*

Bemis, Samuel Flagg. *A Diplomatic History of the United States.* (4th ed.) Holt, 1955. Referred to as Bemis, *Diplomatic History.*

Faulkner, Harold U. *American Economic History*. (6th ed.) Harper, 1949. Referred to as Faulkner, *Economic History*.

Hicks, John D. *American Nation*. Houghton, 1955. Referred to as Hicks, *American Nation*.

Hofstadter, Richard. *The American Political Tradition and the Men Who Made It*. Knopf, 1948. Referred to as Hofstadter, *American Political Tradition*.

Johnson, Allen (ed.). *Dictionary of American Biography*. Scribners, 1946.

Larkin, Oliver W. *Art and Life in America*. Rinehart, 1949. Referred to as Larkin, *Art and Life in America*.

Link, Arthur S. *American Epoch*. Knopf, 1955. Referred to as Link, *American Epoch*.

Lorant, Stefan. *The Presidency*. Macmillan, 1951. Referred to as Lorant, *Presidency*.

Morison, Samuel Eliot and Commager, Henry Steele. *The Growth of the American Republic*. (4th ed. 2 vols.) Oxford, 1951. Referred to as Morison and Commager, *American Republic*.

Schlesinger, Arthur M. *New Viewpoints in American History*. Macmillan, 1922. Referred to as Schlesinger, *Viewpoints*.

———. *Rise of Modern America, 1865–1951*. Macmillan, 1952. Referred to as Schlesinger, *Modern America*.

SERIES

Commager, Henry Steele and Morris, Richard B. (eds.). *The New American Nation*. (N.A.N.) Harper, 1954.

Gabriel, Ralph H. (ed.). *Pageant of America*. (Pageant) Yale University Press, 1925–1929.

Hart, A. B. (ed.). *The American Nation*. (A.N.A.) Harper, 1904–1918.

Johnson, Allen and Nevins, Allan (eds.). *The Chronicles of America*. (Y.C.S.) Yale University Press, 1918–1951.

Schlesinger, Arthur M. and Fox, Dixon R. (eds.). *History of American Life*. (A.L.S.) Macmillan, 1927–1938.

"Methinks I see it now, that one solitary, adventurous vessel, the Mayflower *of a forlorn hope, freighted with the prospects of a future state, and bound across the unknown sea. . . . Suns rise and set, and weeks and months pass, and winter surprises them on the deep, but brings them not the sight of the wished for shore. . . . The awful voice of the storm howls through the rigging. The laboring masts seem straining from their base; . . . the dismal sound of pumps is heard;—the ship leaps, as it were, madly, from billow to billow;—the ocean breaks, and settles with engulphing floods over the floating deck, and beats with deadening, shivering weight, against the staggered vessel. I see them, escaped from these perils, pursuing their all but desperate undertaking, and landed at last, after a five months passage, on the ice clad rocks of Plymouth, —weak and weary from the voyage,— poorly armed, scantily provisioned. . . . without shelter,—without means,—surrounded by hostile tribes."*

EDWARD EVERETT

UNITED STATES HISTORY

TIME LINE

	1445	Portuguese sailors reach Cape Verde Islands
1450		
	1488	Diaz rounds Cape of Good Hope
	1492	Columbus discovers New World
	1498	Da Gama reaches India by rounding Good Hope
1500		
	1513	Balboa discovers Pacific
	1519–22	Magellan expedition circumnavigates the globe
	1521	Cortés conquers Mexico
	1532	Pizarro conquers Peru
	1539	De Soto discovers Mississippi
	1540–42	Coronado explores New Mexico
1550		
	1565	St. Augustine founded by Spanish
	1577–80	Drake circumnavigates the globe
	1588	Spanish Armada defeated
1600		
	1607	Jamestown founded by English
	1608	Quèbec founded by French
	1619	Virginia House of Burgesses
	1620	Mayflower Compact; Plymouth founded
	1643	New England Confederation organized
	1649	Maryland Toleration Act
1650		
	1664	English capture New Netherland
	1676	Bacon's Rebellion
	1688–89	"Glorious Revolution" in England; English Bill of Rights
1700		
	1733	Georgia, thirteenth colony, founded
	1735	Trial of Zenger
1750		
	1754	Albany Congress

UNIT ONE

The Colonial Heritage

★ ★ ★ ★ The discovery of the New World took place as Europe was emerging from the Middle Ages and entering the Modern Age. This was a time of extraordinary change, marked by the growth of commerce and industry, the rise of the middle class, the appearance of independent nation-states, a new interest in science, the invention of printing, the questioning of established authority, and religious unrest. These changes impelled Europeans to explore the whole world and to plant colonies wherever they could find a foothold.

The history of our own nation begins with the settling of the thirteen original English colonies on the Atlantic seaboard. People who emigrated to the colonies, braving the dangers of the voyage and the hardships that awaited them here, were not the ordinary run of human beings. On the contrary, they were people of great courage and determination. They left Europe in protest against religious or political persecution or to escape from poverty and a lack of opportunity. They came here to make a better life for themselves and their children. Had they not been self-reliant and enterprising they would never have come.

The independent spirit of the settlers was encouraged by the conditions they found here. There were innumerable difficulties to be overcome. They had to tame the wilderness and protect themselves from the Indians. They had to produce nearly everything they used. Men, women, and children alike worked hard. They had no respect for those who wished to live without working. A man was judged by his industry, skill, and resourcefulness, not by his family name.

England gave the thirteen colonies a large measure of self-government. This led the colonists to a desire for still more political freedom. The voters took a lively interest in their government. They expected the legislature to protect their rights and keep a watchful eye on the governors sent from England. The colonial legislatures quarreled continually with the governors and often refused to pay them.

Although immigrants brought Old World ways with them, conditions here forced them to make changes in their customs and ideas. Among the small farmers and frontiersmen, a distinctly American society took shape. These people were more optimistic and enterprising than the common people of Europe. The idea that all men are entitled to equal opportunity took firm root in American soil.

CHRISTOPHER COLUMBUS

(Above) *The S.S.* United States *starts on its trans-Atlantic voyage. In contrast* (below) *the small sixteenth-century ships (similar to those used by Columbus) seem like fragile toys. The plowman and the shepherds are typical of European farmers at the time the New World was being explored.*

1. EUROPEANS FIND A NEW WORLD

Changes in Europe Lead to Voyages of Discovery

The modern age is born.

After the Western Roman Empire broke up in the fifth century, western Europe entered a period known to us as the "Middle Ages." The Middle Ages, or the "medieval period" as it is also called, lasted about a thousand years. We often think of the discovery of America as marking the end of the Middle Ages. Although this discovery had tremendous consequences, it did not really usher in modern times. The new age, or modern world, was born gradually during the years, roughly speaking, from 1300 to 1700. We of course live in the modern period and believe it is still to reach its full development.

When Columbus made his famous voyages, the new age was already under way. His achievement was, in fact, made possible because of the changes that were bringing the Middle Ages to a close. These changes include: (1) the expansion of commerce and industry, (2) the growth of nationalism, (3) the development of science, (4) mass production of books, and (5) religious unrest and reform. These changes have continued down to our own day. The first four of them helped prepare the way for the discovery of the New World. All five promoted its settlement by Europeans. We shall discuss the first four here and the fifth in a later chapter.

Commerce and industry expand.

During the Middle Ages the vast majority of Europeans lived by farming. Most of western Europe was covered by great estates, or manors, each controlled by a lord. A typical manor included a castle and a village, surrounded by cultivated land, pastures, and forest. Most of the people on the manor were serfs. They were bound to the land and rarely got a glimpse of the world outside the manor.

Except for a few items like salt and iron, the manor was self-sufficient. An occasional peddler came along with small luxuries which the lord's family might buy—a piece of silk, a dagger of Damascus steel, perfume or spice or medicine from the Orient. The larger towns had annual fairs where local products and also some from far away were offered for sale. Trade was hampered by the difficulties of transportation. Roads were few and in bad weather likely to be impassable. Bridges were rare; travelers either rode their horses through streams or paid to be ferried across. Each lord whose territory the road went through demanded a large toll. Robbers and pirates made travel dangerous either by land or sea. Trade was also hindered by the scarcity of money. Little money was in circulation and few people had a way of earning any. Because of lack of trade, in the

5

VIEW OF VENICE *with bell-tower, church of St. Mark, and ducal palace. The merchant ships in the foreground carried on lively commerce with the Orient. This woodcut was made in 1490.*

first half of the Middle Ages the cities of western Europe that had been developed by the Romans shrank or even disappeared.

In the second half of the Middle Ages, there was more peace and order. Trade expanded and towns grew. More people began to devote their time to handicrafts, such as shoemaking, weaving, or woodworking. In this way they could obtain a cash income. The circulation of money increased along with the expansion of trade and industry.

As towns grew, serfdom declined in the surrounding areas. This came about because the towns lured people from the villages. Many a serf ran away to town. If his lord did not find him for a year and a day he became a free man. Other serfs who were skillful at some handicraft were able to save money enough to buy their free-

dom. They could then pay a cash rent for the land they cultivated instead of working for the lord, or they could move to town.

The Crusades, which began in 1096 and continued for two centuries, played an important part in the expansion of commerce and industry. The Crusaders had to be outfitted for their long journey and supplied along the way. Ships had to be built to carry them and their supplies across the Mediterranean. When they arrived in eastern lands, they found great cities and became acquainted with luxuries that most of them had never dreamed of. On returning home they brought back products of the East as souvenirs —spices, perfumes, paper, silk, cotton, cloth, glassware, carved ivory, knives and swords made of tempered steel, rugs, tapestries, and embroideries.

These things were greatly admired. Before long the demand for them led to a lively trade between Europe and the Near East. Most of this commerce passed through Italian seaports.

The two-way East-West trade brought great riches to the Italian city-states, especially to Genoa and Venice. Wealth poured into the building of palaces, mansions, churches, and city halls. Architects, sculptors, and painters came from near and far to design and decorate splendid buildings. The city-states spent part of their new wealth to build and maintain navies. Wishing a monopoly of the East-West trade, they used their naval power to close the Mediterranean to merchants from other countries.

Nationalism replaces feudalism.

Another change that led to modern times was the rise of nation-states and the decline of feudalism. Before this change, Europeans thought of themselves as belonging to a manor or town, rather than to a nation. A man from Paris would say, "I am a Parisian," not "I am a Frenchman," just as a man from Genoa would say, "I am a Genoese," not "I am an Italian."

1. The feudal system. Feudalism was the system of government and landholding which prevailed in the Middle Ages. It was based on hereditary social classes. A person's rights and opportunities and duties depended strictly upon the class into which he was born. There were noblemen, knights, freemen, and serfs.

All the people living on a manor were dependents and subjects of the lord. In return for his protection they owed him obedience and service. The lord usually received his estate from a more powerful noble to whom he owed certain duties, chiefly to supply a stated number of knights whenever called on. The great nobles received their lands from the king. In return they promised to help him in case of war. A king might raise an army by calling on the great nobles for aid. They in turn would ask nobles who owed them service to come with their men.

Each feudal lord was absolute ruler in his own territory. He made the laws, administered justice, coined money, regulated trade, and gathered taxes. He made treaties with other lords or waged private war upon them as he saw fit. There was constant fighting.

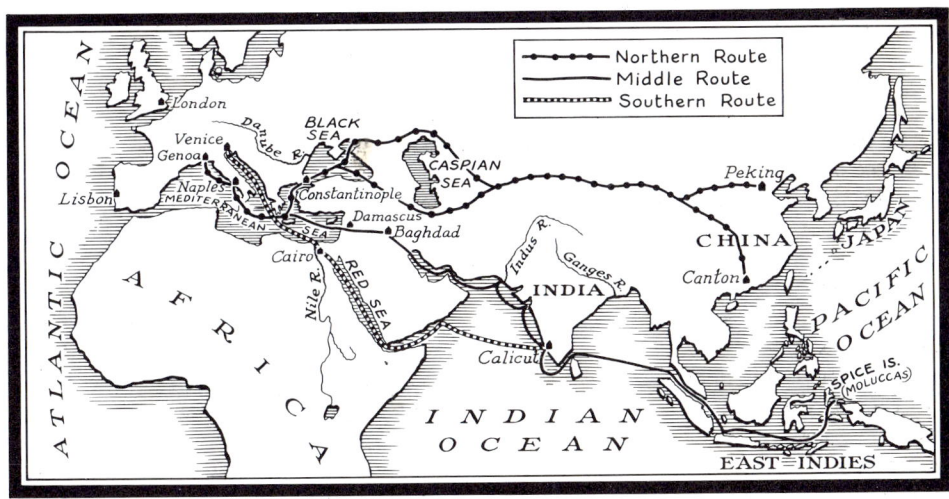

MEDIEVAL TRADE ROUTES

The king was generally too weak to keep the nobles in order. If a group of powerful nobles turned against him, he would lose his throne.

2. *National states.* In the later Middle Ages the kings gained more power, while the feudal lords lost much of theirs. Among the reasons for the increase in royal powers were:

(*a*) The growth of a town-dwelling merchant class, who wished to carry on business without interference by the landed nobles. The first step taken by the merchants was to fight for or purchase their town's freedom from the local lord. The second step was to vote money and military support for the king, to aid him in his struggles with the lords. The merchants preferred the rule of the king because he could give them a single coinage system, a single system of laws and courts, protection against robbers and pirates, and relief from the constant fighting and the oppressive taxes of the nobles.

(*b*) The use of gunpowder, which became common in the 1400's. An armored knight on horseback could be put out of action by a common foot soldier armed with a musket. The castle of a rebellious noble could be battered down by a royal cannon. Thus the knights and lords lost their monopoly of military power.

(*c*) The adoption of national languages in place of local dialects. People who spoke the same language felt that they belonged to a nation. As they told stories of the same heroes and sang the same songs, their sense of belonging together grew. They developed loyalty to their nation and to its king.

(*d*) The growing use of money. So long as taxes were paid in farm products rather than in coin, even a king had little to spend. As the use of money grew, a king could collect enough in taxes to support an army and to maintain government services such as the building and policing of roads.

He might be able to finance voyages of discovery and send colonists to new-found lands.

Toward the end of the Middle Ages five powerful nation-states had emerged—Spain, Portugal, England, France, and Holland. Because of their armed might and wealth, they were ready to expand overseas.

Interest in science develops.

In medieval Europe most of the scientific knowledge possessed by the Greeks and Romans had been forgotten. People were extremely superstitious. They thought that fearsome events like storms, fires, and earthquakes were the work of evil spirits. They also blamed evil spirits for sickness, insanity, and other human ills. They believed that certain days were lucky, others unlucky, depending on the position of the stars and planets.

Until late in the Middle Ages, even scholars took little interest in science. It seemed to them better to devote their time to religious studies than to carry on scientific experiments. They tried to support their opinions by quoting authorities who had written or spoken on the same subject. They took their information and ideas about nature mostly from the writings of the ancient Greek scientist, Aristotle. They did not try to verify what Aristotle said. For instance, Aristotle said an insect has eight legs and nobody thought it necessary to check by looking for himself. The scientific method, which relies on experiment and observation to get at the truth, did not appeal to medieval scholars.

1. *The Renaissance.* Late in the Middle Ages a great intellectual awakening took place in western Europe. It is spoken of as the "Renaissance" or "rebirth." It was a rebirth of interest in nature and human nature after centuries in which religion had been the chief interest. The ideal man had been

the monk who renounced the world and all its pleasures. Now the ideal man was the well-rounded person who enjoyed society and the good things of this life and who cultivated the arts. This shift of attention from life after death to life in this world is known as "secularization." It helped in making science one of the principal influences in the modern age.

The Renaissance was partly the result of contacts with scholars in the Byzantine and Moslem empires. These scholars had preserved and added to the scientific knowledge of the ancient Greeks and Romans. They had made important discoveries in the fields of mathematics, astronomy, chemistry, medicine, geography, and navigation. During the later Middle Ages a number of European scholars went to Byzantine and Moslem cities. They returned home with added knowledge of nature and, still better, an enthusiasm for scientific research. In addition they learned new mathematical skills (like the use of zero and Arabic numerals) and the principles of trigonometry and advanced algebra. These made possible further advances in many fields.

2. Navigation. After 1300 there was great progress in the science of navigation. European sailors had been using a primitive type of compass for over a century. Italian seamen now made the compass more efficient. Better devices for telling time and for measuring latitude and longitude came into use. Italian sailors led the way in preparing maps of coasts and harbors. By 1350 there were accurate "port guides" showing all the Mediterranean coast. Improvements in shipbuilding and seamanship gave men a better mastery of the ocean than they had ever had.

3. Geography. Medieval Europeans knew practically nothing about countries beyond the Mediterranean. After 1300, they began to extend their

(Top) *In this painting, made about 1445,* A SCHOLAR IS SHOWN PRESENTING A BOOK *he has written to the Duke of Burgundy, Philip the Good. The duke's son and a group of monks are interested in this unusual gift.*

(Bottom) THE ASTROLABE, *invented by the Greeks and perfected by the Arabs, was used as an aid to navigation. It helped the mariner to determine his latitude by observing the height of the sun and stars above the horizon.*

9

knowledge of the world. Scholars found old Greek manuscripts and maps lying neglected on dusty shelves in monasteries. Thus they recovered much knowledge of geography. This information was added to as a few daring Europeans traveled to distant places.

Books widen men's horizons.

In the Middle Ages, books were scarce and costly. Each word had to be copied by hand. To copy a long manuscript required months. Laymen rarely owned any books and had little reason to learn to read and write. Even members of the nobility were often illiterate. Except among the clergy few men had book learning.

About the middle of the 1400's Europeans worked out the art of printing from movable type. The making of paper, which was cheaper and less bulky than parchment, had been learned from the Arabs a century or so earlier. By the use of paper and movable type, books could be turned out in large quantities at small expense. Within fifty years hundreds of presses had been built and millions of copies of books had been sold.

THE OBSERVATORY *built by Prince Henry of Portugal. Henry, wearing a broad-brimmed hat, is standing and looking out to sea.*

The intellectual awakening of Europe was speeded up by the mass production of books. Knowledge was no longer confined to the church and the universities. Everywhere in western Europe, ambitious individuals looked for someone who would teach them how to read.

Through reading, people began to learn about the world outside their own village or town. Travel books like *The Book of Ser Marco Polo* were eagerly read. This famous book was written in 1298. The author, a Venetian named Marco Polo, tells of the daring trip to the Far East that he made with his father and his uncle to visit the great Mongol emperor, Kublai Khan. The book was so popular that eighty-five copies were made by hand. A century and a half after its first appearance, it was printed and reached a multitude of new readers. Christopher Columbus was one of them.

Europeans Explore the Earth

Portugal takes the lead.

The Portuguese were the first people of western Europe to establish an independent nation-state (1385). Their country was small and they wished to expand overseas. Prince Henry, a younger son of King John of Portugal, opened the way. For more than forty years he devoted himself to improving the art of navigation and to encouraging exploration of the west coast of Africa. On the southwest tip of Portugal, on a high headland facing the sea, Prince Henry built an observatory and a school of navigation. He invited leading map makers and geographers from all over Europe to work there. Under his direction better maps were drawn and the astrolabe (an instrument for observing the stars) was improved. Portuguese mariners came to his school to be instructed in the art of navigation.

PORTUGUESE ALL–WATER ROUTE TO THE EAST

Year after year Prince Henry sent out ships to explore the western coast of Africa. Little of this region was known when Henry began. According to the ancient Greek maps, Africa did not extend much below the equator. Prince Henry encouraged his sea captains to sail farther and farther south in the hope of rounding the continent. By the time he died in 1460, his seamen had sighted Cape Verde and the Cape Verde Islands, but most of the African coast was still unexplored.

After Henry's death, Portuguese mariners edged farther south. They established supply stations and trading posts along the newly discovered coast. At last Bartholemew Diaz rounded the tip of the continent (1488). Diaz was now sure he could reach the Indies and would have started across the Indian Ocean had his crew not mutinied. (They were terrified to venture so far from the sight of land. Might this vast and unknown ocean not mark the edge of the world?)

The Cape of Good Hope today

11

Ten years later another daring Portuguese sea captain, Vasco da Gama, started from Lisbon with four ships. He was determined to complete Diaz's work of finding an all-water route to the Indies. Columbus, so it was thought, had already reached the Indies. Thus Portugal was in danger of losing to Spain the fruits of nearly a century's exploration. Da Gama rounded the Cape of Good Hope, then skirted the eastern coast of Africa until he reached the Arab port of Malindi. There he hired a pilot to guide his fleet across the Indian Ocean. He came back to Portugal with a cargo of spices and gems worth sixty times the cost of the expedition.

The discovery of an all-water route to the East soon made Portugal wealthy. The cost of transportation by water was far less than by caravan. Trade between Europe and Asia expanded. The Italian monopoly was broken; Portugal had the monopoly instead. Soon Portuguese mariners pushed on to the East Indies and to China, then called Cathay. Like India, these lands were shortly bound to Portugal in a network of trade.

Columbus seeks the Indies.

Columbus was born in Genoa in 1451. He loved the sea and as a youth made voyages to the eastern Mediterranean, to England, and down the African coast. After marrying the daughter of one of Prince Henry's captains, he settled down in Lisbon as a map maker. It was the great period of Portuguese exploration and Columbus was keenly interested in the effort to find an all-water route to the East. For a time he was a sugar buyer in the Portuguese islands off the coast of Africa (the Azores, Cape Verde, and Madeira groups). Here he met navigators who felt sure there were lands still farther west because ocean currents from the west sometimes carried green

branches. Columbus, like other well-informed men of the time, thought the earth was round. He believed the ocean which Marco Polo had seen when he reached the coast of China was the same one which washes the western coast of Europe. In that case, Columbus thought, the best way to reach the East was to sail directly west.

Columbus' idea seemed reasonable to geographers. It was now evident that Africa stretched thousands of miles to the south, although no one had yet reached its southern tip. In addition, the earth was thought to be much smaller than it is. A map drawn by the Italian Toscanelli, a leading geographer, showed Japan at the place actually occupied by Mexico. This map was familiar to Columbus, who wrote Toscanelli and received an encouraging letter from him.

In 1482 Columbus laid his plans before the king of Portugal and asked for ships and men. The king sent a ship out secretly but it soon returned, reporting that Columbus project was foolish. Columbus then tried to get support from Ferdinand and Isabella, the rulers of Spain. They were in the midst of a long, costly war to drive the Moors out of their country and kept Columbus waiting eight years. Finally, after the last Moorish stronghold had fallen, Isabella agreed to help him. The town of Palos was ordered to provide three ships and their crews. Three little caravels, the *Santa Maria*, the *Pinta*, and the *Niña*, were made ready with provisions for a year. To find sailors willing to man them was far more difficult. Columbus finally obtained eighty-eight men.

Columbus sailed from Palos on August 3, 1492. After refitting his ships he left the Canary Islands on September 6. According to his calculations, Japan lay only 2300 miles west of the Canaries. The voyage across the Atlantic was made in a little over five weeks,

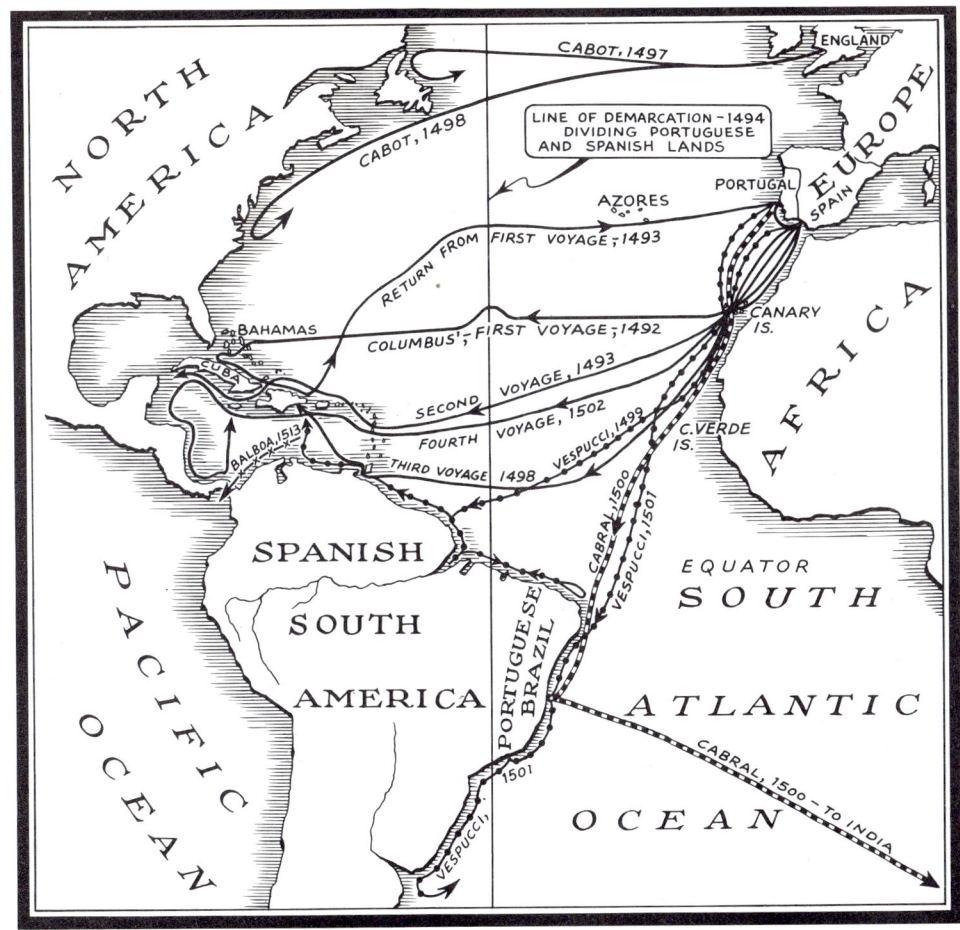

VOYAGES OF COLUMBUS, CABOT, VESPUCCI, CABRAL,
AND BALBOA

but to the fearful sailors it seemed endless. The farther they went, the more frightened they became. They were plotting to throw their admiral overboard and turn about, when signs of land appeared. On October 12, they landed on the gleaming coral beach of one of the Bahamas. Columbus named the island "San Salvador" (Holy Savior) and took possession in the name of Ferdinand and Isabella. Columbus called the native people "Indians," for he felt sure he had found the Indies.

Columbus sailed from one island to another looking for gold and spices. Much to his disappointment, he found no golden-roofed palaces and no

princes clad in silks and jewels, only rude villages and naked savages. At Christmas time, he landed on an island, which he named "Hispaniola" (Little Spain). Here his best ship, the *Santa Maria*, was wrecked. Its timbers were used to build a fort.

Leaving about forty men behind on Hispaniola, Columbus sailed for Spain in mid-January. Three months later, after a stormy voyage, his ship cast anchor at Palos. He received a royal welcome and many honors, including the title "Admiral of the Ocean Sea." Although he brought with him only a few captive red men, some parrots, lizards, and plants, rumors spread

13

COLUMBUS PRESENTING A REPORT *of his voyage to Ferdinand and Isabella. This was the height of his glory.*

over Europe that he had come back with a cargo of gold and precious merchandise.

Columbus continues his search.

The great admiral made three more voyages to the islands he called the Indies. On his second trip, he commanded 17 ships with 1500 colonists aboard. The town which they laid out on Hispaniola became the first permanent settlement of Europeans in the New World. (The garrison left there on the first voyage had been slain by Indians.)

On the third voyage, Columbus steered farther to the south and touched the mainland of South America at the mouth of the Orinoco. Realizing that he saw a continent, he sailed westward along the coast for some 300 miles. Because of trouble among the settlers on Hispaniola, he cut short his explorations to return there.

On his fourth and last voyage, Columbus explored the coast of Central America for about 1200 miles. He and his men suffered terrible hardships and were in constant danger from hostile Indians. He came back to Spain still believing he had found parts of Asia and the Indies. His failure to obtain spices and jewels seemed all the worse because the Portuguese were reaping such huge profits from cargoes brought from India on the route charted by Da Gama. Courtiers jeered Columbus as "the Admiral of the Mosquitoes, who had discovered lands of vanity and delusion as the graves of Castilian gentlemen." Columbus died in poverty and neglect, without knowing he had found a New World.

The Pope draws a line.

When Columbus returned to Europe after his first voyage, the king of Portugal said that the newly discovered islands were part of Guinea. Guinea had been discovered by the Portuguese, and the Pope had approved their claim to it. The Spanish sovereigns now asked the Pope to recognize their discoveries, too. The Pope drew an imaginary line west of the Cape Verde Islands and running from pole to pole. Portugal could claim all new lands east of this Line of Demarcation, and Spain could claim all new lands west of it. At the time (1494) it appeared that Portugal had the advantage, for she got rights to most of Africa and Asia. Later, after it became known that a vast New World had been found, Spain seemed to have the advantage, for all the New World except the eastern portion of Brazil would belong to her. Spain and Portugal respected the Line of Demarcation, but England, France, and the Netherlands paid no attention to it. The French king jibed, "Show me the line in our father Adam's will leaving America to the Spaniards."

Cabot discovers North America.

John Cabot, an Italian navigator, thought he could reach China by sailing westward on a more northerly route than that of Columbus. In 1497 he persuaded the king of England to back his expedition. Showing great courage, Cabot crossed the North Atlantic with one small boat and eighteen men. He landed on the bleak coast somewhere between Labrador and Newfoundland, but the only wealth he found was the fishing banks. The next year Cabot made a second voyage. From the scanty records which are left, we think he explored the coast from Long Island southward, perhaps as far as Florida. He was the first European since the Vikings to sight and explore North America, but he thought he had reached Asia. The tight-fisted Henry VII rewarded him with ten pounds ($50) and a small pension for "discovering a new isle." For nearly a century, the English took no interest in the land Cabot had found.

Cabral claims Brazil for Portugal.

One of the first Portuguese captains to sail for India after Da Gama's historic voyage was Pedro Cabral. He left Lisbon early in 1500 with a fleet of sixteen ships. After reaching the Cape Verde Islands, he deliberately steered far to the west of his course. He sighted the easternmost coast of Brazil, landed there, and claimed it for Portugal. The Portuguese were so excited about Da Gama's new route to the Far East that they paid little attention to Cabral's discovery. Thirty years went by before they began to settle in Brazil.

The new lands receive a name.

Once Columbus proved that land could be reached by sailing west, the "sea of darkness" lost most of its terrors. Many other navigators crossed the Atlantic, some of them authorized to do so and some of them not. Each added something to the picture until at last the outlines of the new lands became clear.

The first to say that a new world had been found was probably Amerigo Vespucci, an Italian merchant. In 1499 he joined a Spanish expedition that explored several hundred miles of the northern coast of South America. Part of this coast had already been explored by Columbus, although few people knew this. Two years later Vespucci went with a Portuguese expedition that sailed down the coast of Brazil for 2000 miles. Vespucci wrote glowing letters which gave the false impression that he had discovered the great unknown mainland. He described it as a "New World, a new fourth part of the globe."

Martin Waldseemüller, who taught in a French college, published a geography in 1507. He included one of Vespucci's letters. Thinking Vespucci had discovered a mainland which Columbus had not seen, Waldseemüller suggested that it be given the name "America." The suggestion caught on. Waldseemüller later tried to correct his mistake, but people were already used to "America" and the name stuck.

For some years the name "America" was applied only to the continent south of the Isthmus of Panama. The region north of the isthmus was still thought to be part of Asia. Gradually explorers showed that another great continent lay north of Panama. Three centuries passed before the size and shape of North and South America were fully known.

A legendary sea monster

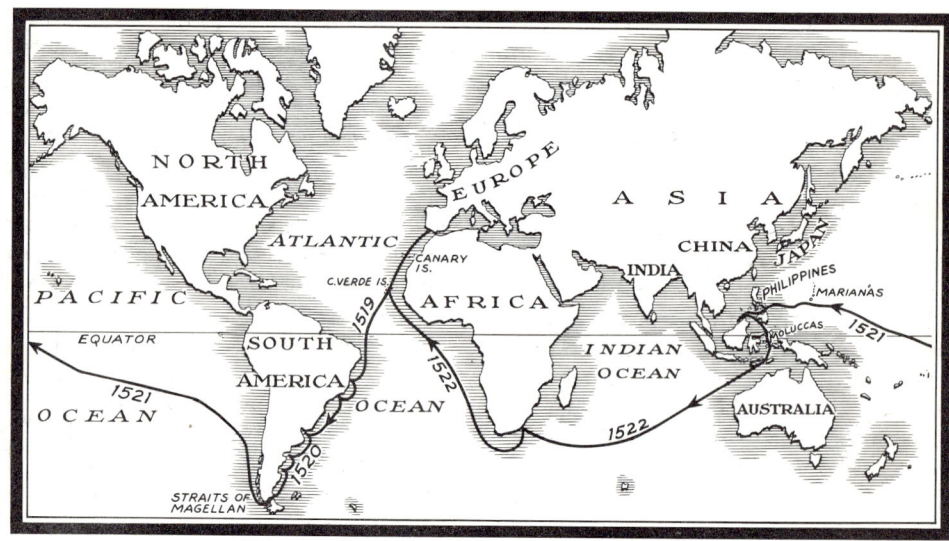

FIRST CIRCUMNAVIGATION OF THE GLOBE

Balboa discovers the Pacific.

Vasco Balboa was governor of a tiny Spanish colony on what we now know as the Isthmus of Panama. The natives told him of a great body of water a short distance away. A boat could sail on this sea to a land far to the south which, said the red men, was rich in gold. With about two hundred men Balboa set out to cross the isthmus (1513). The expedition spent three weeks struggling through forty-five miles of fever-ridden jungles where white men had never trod. When the party reached the other shore, Balboa claimed the sea and all the lands it washed for the king of Spain. Because the ocean (the Pacific) lay south of the isthmus, Balboa named it the "South Sea." At that time no one had any idea of its vast extent.

Magellan's men circle the globe.

The first man to cross the Pacific was Ferdinand Magellan, a Portuguese seaman sailing for Spain. In September, 1519, he left Spain with five rickety ships, aiming to reach the Moluccas, or Spice Islands, by sailing westward. He steered for the "hump" of Brazil, then skirted the coast southward, looking for a strait, or passage, through the continent. Coming to the broad mouth of the Plata, he thought he had found a southwest passage to the East. After sailing up the Plata for days, he saw that it was a great river. He turned back and then continued southward. The sailors mutinied and two of his ships deserted before he found the strait which now bears his name. Passage through this narrow, winding, storm-vexed waterway took thirty-eight days. Emerging at last upon a calm sea, he named it the Pacific.

Fifteen months had gone by since the expedition left Spain. Food was low and the sailors begged him to turn back. Instead of listening, he struck boldly out to the northwest. The distance to be covered proved far longer than he expected. After the last crumb of ship's biscuit was gone, the men ate the rats on board and finally the leather on the rigging. In ten thousand miles the famished sailors saw no land except two desert isles. After ninety-eight days of misery they reached inhabited is-

16

lands (the Marianas). Magellan traded for provisions and pushed on to the Philippines, where he planted the flag of Spain. Here he lost two more ships and was himself killed in a skirmish with the natives. The single remaining ship (the *Victoria*) found the Moluccas, crossed the Indian Ocean, rounded the Cape of Good Hope, and returned to the starting point. It was the first ship ever to circle the globe. The three-year voyage has been described as "the greatest single human achievement on the sea." Though Magellan did not live to complete it, it was his vision, courage, and determination that made it possible.

No other voyage in history added so much to our knowledge of the size and shape of the earth. The voyage proved that (1) the earth is round, (2) it is much larger than had been supposed, (3) a large proportion of its surface is covered by oceans, (4) America is not connected with Asia, at least in the south, and (5) America is not an island continent lying off the coast of Asia.

Magellan's voyage was the climax of thirty-four years of amazing advances in geographical knowledge. From 1488, when Diaz rounded the tip of Africa, until 1522, when the survivors of the Magellan expedition came home, the wide world had been discovered. Three great oceans had been crossed—the Atlantic in 1492, the Indian in 1498, and the Pacific in 1520.

Europeans had left behind the self-contained and narrow life of the feudal village. They had entered the period of great intellectual, social, economic, and political developments that we know as the Modern Age. Now they stood ready to expand over the entire world, taking with them the "secular, inquiring, self-reliant spirit of modern times."

FOR IDENTIFICATION

Vasco Balboa	Magellan
John Cabot	Marco Polo
Pedro Cabral	Prince Henry the
Cathay	Navigator
Columbus	Renaissance
Vasco da Gama	Toscanelli
Bartholomew Diaz	Amerigo Vespucci
Line of Demarcation	Martin Waldseemüller

FOR EXPLANATION OR DEFINITION

astrolabe	medieval
city-state	Middle Ages
Crusades	nation-state
feudalism	secularization
manor	serf

FOR REVIEW

1. What were the chief obstacles to trade and commerce during the feudal period?

2. What events or developments tended to cause the decline of feudalism?

3. Why did the Italian seaports become important commercial centers?

4. What were the chief articles of trade brought from the East?

5. Why did the power of the king tend to increase and that of the feudal lord to diminish during the later Middle Ages?

6. How did the use of money affect feudalism and the growth of the nation-state?

7. What is meant by the Renaissance? What were some of its outstanding characteristics?

17

8. How did the story of the travels and adventures of Marco Polo influence the West?

9. What were the achievements of Prince Henry the Navigator and the Portuguese mariners?

10. How did the voyage of Vasco da Gama affect the city-states of Italy?

11. How did the New World come to receive the name America?

12. What was the Papal Line of Demarcation? What effect did it have?

13. Why did Balboa refer to the Pacific Ocean as the South Sea?

FOR FURTHER STUDY AND DISCUSSION

1. Define and explain the term "commercial revolution." Outline the chief political effects of this revolution.

2. How would you prove that the discovery of the New World was the logical outcome of developments in the fifteenth century?

3. Why were many of the early navigators Italians? Why were these navigators not in the service of Italy?

4. What arguments influenced Columbus to believe that he could reach India and the Spice Islands by sailing westward?

5. What developments during the Renaissance period influenced the discovery and exploration of the New World?

FOR INDIVIDUAL OR GROUP ACTIVITIES

1. Organize a committee to prepare and present to the class a brief annotated bibliography on biographical and fictional books in the school or town library which add color and detail to the events sketched in this chapter.

2. "Magellan's voyage was the climax of thirty-four years of amazing advances in geographic knowledge." On an outline map show the advances in geographic knowledge between 1488 and 1522. Trace the voyages of Columbus, Da Gama, Magellan and his crew.

3. Organize a committee to prepare a floor talk and demonstration on the science of navigation. Have the committee explain latitude and longitude, and how the compass, astrolabe, and sextant assist navigation. Explain why a globe is the only true map. What is a great circle? Explain the meaning of projection. What is a Mercator's projection? What are the advantages and disadvantages of a Mercator's projection? Helpful source: *Life's Picture History of Western Man*, pp. 118–131.[1]

4. As a newspaper reporter write an account of your interview with Columbus upon his return from his first voyage to America. Helpful source: Hart, *Contemporaries*, Vol. I, No. 17.

5. Prepare a floor talk on one of the following: the voyages of the Vikings, the travels of Marco Polo and their influence, the work of Prince Henry the Navigator, the efforts of Columbus to obtain support for his venture, the circumnavigation of the globe by Magellan and his crew.

6. Prepare a dramatic reading of Joaquin Miller's poem on Columbus.

7. Prepare a report on the original peoples of the Americas: where and how they came here and the sort of culture they developed. Helpful source: Morris, *Encyclopedia of American History*.

8. Prepare a report on the explorations in America before Columbus' arrival. Helpful source: Morris, *Encyclopedia of American History*.

---

[1] For other references and for more information about references mentioned in the chapter activities, see pp. xiv and xv.

2. EUROPEANS COME TO LIVE IN THE NEW WORLD

The settlement of America had its origins in the unsettlement of Europe. . . . The settlement of the Atlantic seaboard was the culmination of one process, the breakup of medieval culture, and the beginning of another.———Lewis Mumford

Demolition of houses on the NOTRE-DAME BRIDGE. *Paris, like other places in Europe, was ridding itself of medieval obstructions.*

Spain Builds an Empire in the New World

Spain explores a vast region.

For more than fifty years after the voyages of Columbus, the Spaniards took the lead in exploring the New World. Explorers known as *conquistadores* ("conquerors") led expeditions to America. A few found regions of great wealth in Mexico and Peru, but most of them searched in vain for golden cities that existed only in their imagination.

1. **De León.** Ponce de León (pon'-thā day lay-on') was the first Spaniard to step foot in what is now the United States. In the spring of 1513 he sailed northward from Puerto Rico in quest of a magic fountain that would restore youth to the aged. He found a beautiful peninsula covered with flowers. He named it "Pascua Florida" ("Flowery Easter").

19

2. Cortés. In 1519 Hernando Cortés (côr-tĕz′) landed on the Mexican coast. After founding the town of Vera Cruz, he pushed inland with a force of five hundred men and a few horses, determined to conquer the Aztec Indians. They were a civilized people who built splendid cities, dug canals, wove fine cloth, and worked rich mines of gold and silver. They had developed an accurate calendar and a form of picture writing. They had a considerable knowledge of mathematics and astronomy. Yet the Aztecs could not defend themselves against Spanish cannon. Cortés subdued them and made himself governor of Mexico. A stream of treasure began to flow from Mexico to Spain. It did not stop until the Aztec mines were exhausted.

3. Pizarro. About ten years later (1532–36) Francisco Pizarro led an expedition to Peru and overcame the peaceful Incas. These "Children of the Sun" had the highest civilization of any Indians. To grow crops on the steep mountainsides they built vast stone terraces and extensive irrigation systems. They farmed the land more efficiently than was done in Spain. They had an excellent system of roads. Their magnificent temples to the sun-god were decorated with gold and jewels. But like the Aztecs, their weapons were no match for those of the Spanish. Pizarro plundered and enslaved the Incas. Thousands were worked to death in the mines. The gold and silver they dug was sent by pack train to the coast and then shipped to Spain.

RUINS OF PALENQUE, *Temple of the Sun, built by the Mayans in Yucatán. In some respects the Mayan civilization was more advanced than that of the Aztecs.*

(Top) INCA RUINS AT MACHU-PICCHU, PERU. *This majestic fortress city clings to great granite precipices high in the mountains. The architectural achievements of the Incas are a source of wonderment to all who see them.*

(Bottom) PORTRAIT JUGS MADE BY THE INCAS. *The silver jugs* (on the right) *belong to the early colonial period. The pottery jug* (on the left) *is pre-Inca. They show the amazing skill of the Indian craftsmen.*

Other Spaniards, hoping to find similar treasures, continued the work of exploration. Some pushed southward from Peru, some northward and eastward, until the entire continent of South America had been charted. Meanwhile others—Cabeza de Vaca, Hernando de Soto, Francisco de Coronado, Juan Cabrillo—were exploring Mexico, the coast of California, and what is now the southern United States. Their expeditions gave Spain a claim to much of North America.

New Spain is colonized.

The Spanish lost little time in settling their new possessions. In 1574 the royal geographer reported there were 200 Spanish towns in the Americas, in addition to mining camps and ranches. The Spanish population in these towns was then about 160,000. The great majority of the settlers were men, many of whom married Indian women. Although the Spanish claimed the whole continent of North America, they were not much attracted to the lands north of the Rio Grande. They settled chiefly in Mexico, Peru, Bolivia, and the West Indies.

The land of New Spain was divided into great estates. The Indians who lived on an estate became serfs, who were forced to till the soil, tend the cattle, and work the mines. Five million Indians toiled for the benefit of four thousand Spanish overlords.

New crops are introduced.

The Spanish settlers introduced many Old World crops to the New World, including sugar cane, coffee, cotton, grain (wheat, barley, oats, and rye), and a number of fruits. They also introduced horses, mules, donkeys, cattle, pigs, sheep, and hens. It was a two-way exchange, for the Spanish took a number of New World products to the Old World. Among these were maize, or Indian corn, the white potato, the

sweet potato, all varieties of beans, chocolate, and cocoa, tapioca, vanilla, quinine, cochineal (a dyestuff), tobacco, and mahogany. Some of these new products from America soon came into common use in Europe.

Missionaries labor in New Spain.

The Roman Catholic Church was active in New Spain from the start. A great number of missionaries devoted their lives to converting and teaching the Indians. Thousands of churches and hundreds of monasteries were built. The Church established schools, colleges, libraries, and printing presses. Under Spanish law, the Roman Catholic religion was the only one allowed.

New Spain is ruled despotically.

The provinces of Spanish America were regarded as the personal property of the Spanish king. Governors sent from Spain carried out his orders.

ARCHES OF SANTA INEZ MISSION *in California. This mission dates from the early 19th century.*

INDIAN CIVILIZATIONS AND ROUTES OF SPANISH EXPLORERS

The people had little to say about their government. All trade was strictly controlled by the Council of the Indies in Seville. In making rules for trade the Council acted as if colonies existed only for the benefit of the mother country. The colonists therefore were forbidden to trade with any country except Spain and were not allowed to produce certain things which Spain wished to sell them.

In spite of the despotic government, the Spanish colonies were loyal to the mother country for three hundred years. Then one by one they revolted and established their independence. Today there is not a single Spanish possession in the Western Hemisphere. Nevertheless, nearly everywhere south of the United States except in Brazil, the Spanish language, laws, customs, architecture, and religion endure.

France Builds an Empire in the New World

France claims Canada.

As early as 1500, French fishermen came regularly to the fishing banks off Newfoundland. But when the French learned of the wealth flowing into Spain from America, they were not satisfied with the modest profits from the fisheries. The French king decided to seek a passage to Asia north of the area of Spanish activity. In 1524 he fitted out an expedition led by an Italian captain, Giovanni da Verrazano.

23

Verrazano sailed along the American coast from Carolina to Nova Scotia. "A new land never before seen by man," he called it, not knowing that his countryman, John Cabot, had explored the same coast for England in 1498.

In 1534 a French sea captain, Jacques Cartier (zhak khar-tyay'), undertook the search for a northwest passage to Asia. He sailed along the northern coast of Newfoundland and discovered the Gulf of St. Lawrence. Thinking it must lead to the Pacific, he sailed up the beautiful St. Lawrence River until his way was barred by rapids. Cartier called the land he had found "Canada," from an Indian word meaning "village." He tried to build a town on the site where Quebec now stands, but the attempt failed because the king did not give the settlers enough help. For a long time after that France was too much occupied with fighting Spain and with religious wars at home to try again for a foothold in the New World.

The French establish trading posts.

Meanwhile, French fishermen had started the fur trade. Going ashore on Newfoundland to salt and dry their catch before sailing home, they learned that the Indians were eager to exchange furs for knives, guns, and other articles used by the white men. The trade was so profitable that by the 1580's traders were pushing far up the St. Lawrence to obtain furs from the interior tribes. The traders were daring men who made the wilderness their home. They came to be known as *"coureurs de bois"* (runners of the woods).

A leader in the fur trade, Samuel de Champlain, established the first permanent French colony in America. This was Quebec, where twenty-eight Frenchmen built a fort in 1608. After the first terrible winter only eight remained alive. Champlain explored most of the St. Lawrence Valley and also much of what was to become New England. He won for France the friendship of the powerful Algonquin Indians of Canada but made enemies of the even more powerful Iroquois, who lived in northern New York. One of the trading posts he built became the city of Montreal. Champlain is known as the "Father of New France." He was appointed its first governor. When he died in 1635 there were still only two hundred white men in Canada.

Attempts were made to entice emigrants to Canada, but the severe climate and the long winters discouraged settlers. Of those who did come, the more energetic quickly turned from farming to the fur trade. In their search for pelts the traders scattered over half the continent. Many of them married Indian women and did not return to the French settlements.

MARTYRDOM OF JESUIT MISSIONARIES *in New France, probably drawn by an eyewitness about 1656*

Missionaries spread the Gospel.

Roman Catholic missionaries followed the early French explorers and fur traders. Many were members of the Jesuit order. The priests lived among the Indians, learned their dialects, taught them to read and write, and labored to convert them. As the missionaries went deep into the wilderness, they often faced death from starvation or at the hands of hostile Indians. Some of these priests were tortured to death.

France claims the Mississippi Basin.

One of the missionary-explorers was Father Marquette. While working at a mission station on Lake Michigan, he heard from the Indians of a great river to the south (the Mississippi). He and Louis Joliet (zho-lyay'), a young fur trader, set out in 1673 to explore the river. They went as far south as the mouth of the Arkansas and were convinced that the Mississippi empties into the Gulf of Mexico.

The exploration begun by Marquette and Joliet was completed by Robert Cavelier, Sieur de La Salle. In 1681–82 La Salle led a party of fifty down the Illinois River and then down the Mississippi. After months of hardship they reached the Gulf. La Salle claimed for France all the land drained by the great river and its branches. He called this land "Louisiana," in honor of King Louis XIV. Within a few years his countrymen settled Biloxi on the Gulf, then Mobile, New Orleans, and Natchez.

New France is thinly populated.

The dream of a great and strong French empire in the New World was never realized. Not enough Frenchmen came to New France to hold it. One difficulty was in the system of landholding. The king granted huge estates in New France to nobles, or *seigneurs*. The seigneurs were expected to bring over settlers to work their estates. This semifeudal system did not attract many farmers away from

This section of an old map pictures THE LANDING OF CARTIER IN CANADA *in 1534. The Indians clad in furs and the bears indicate the interest in fur trading.*

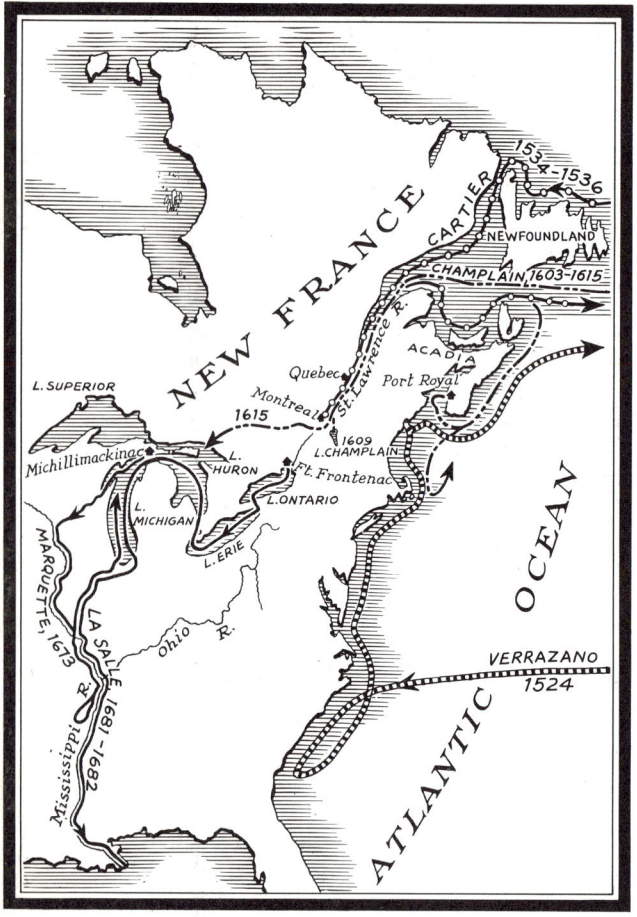

FRENCH EXPLORATIONS

SAMUEL DE CHAMPLAIN. *This navigator, explorer, and colonizer is deservedly known as the "Father of New France."*

The French empire in America stretched from the mouth of the St. Lawrence, westward through the Great Lakes, and southward to the Gulf. By the middle of the 1700's there were no more than 80,000 Frenchmen in all of New France. It was a vast wilderness inhabited by Indians, with only a thin line of mission stations, forts, and trading posts and a few small towns to mark the presence of the French. Because of its sparse population, New France has been aptly described as a "sort of combined trading post and missionary enterprise gilded by dreams of empire."

New France hemmed the English colonists within a narrow strip along the Atlantic. Since there were twenty times as many white people in the English colonies as in New France, they refused to remain hemmed in. In 1763, after the French and Indian War, France was forced to cede most of her New World empire to England (see p. 100). Nevertheless, the French language is still spoken and other elements of French culture are still found in and around Quebec, Montreal, and New Orleans.

France. Another difficulty was the lack of religious freedom. Only Frenchmen who were Roman Catholics were allowed to settle in New France. Had Huguenots (French Protestants) been admitted, the history of New France might have been far different. Half a million Huguenots—7 per cent of the entire French population—fled from France in the period 1675–1700. Many of these people came to North America, but they settled in the English and Dutch colonies. If instead they had poured into Louisiana and Canada, France might have won control of the continent.

SIR FRANCIS DRAKE, *knighted by Queen Elizabeth I for being the first Englishman to sail around the globe*

England Gets Ready to Expand

England becomes mistress of the seas.

In Columbus' day England was a small, poor country.[1] Since it had few ships, its trade with other lands was carried on by foreigners. At that time Spain was superior to England in trade, wealth, and military power. Spain's superiority increased as wealth from its empire in the New World poured in. Spain reached the height of its power in 1580 when Portugal came under the rule of a Spanish king.

By that time England was rapidly gaining strength. One sign of this was the increase in shipbuilding. England's growing foreign trade was now in the hands of Englishmen. Their merchant ships were protected by an expanding navy. English naval vessels were smaller and faster than the clumsy Spanish galleons. English sailors employed a new method of naval warfare. Instead of coming into contact with the enemy ship, boarding it, and fighting hand to

---

[1] In 1707 England and Scotland were united under the name of "Great Britain." When we discuss events after this union took place, we may properly speak of the "British government" and "British people."

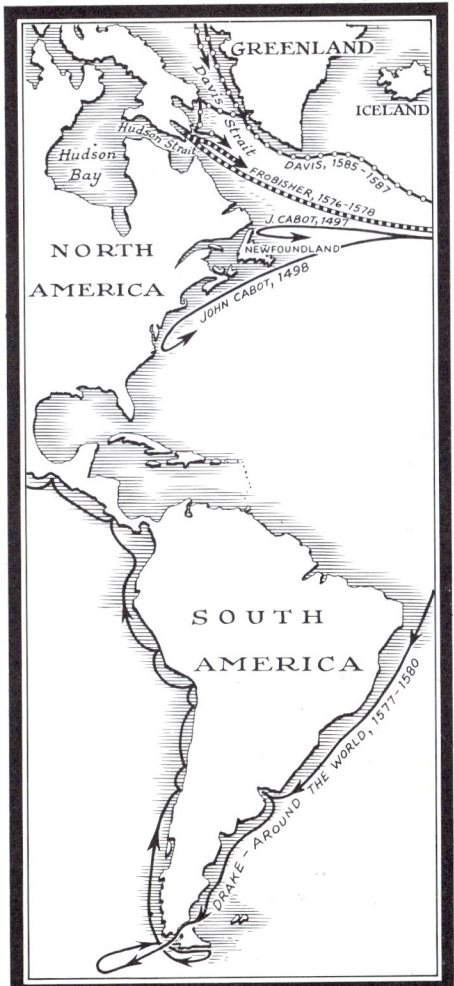

ENGLISH EXPLORATIONS

hand, they disabled the enemy by firing broadsides from a safe distance. Spanish galleons were no match for the English "floating batteries."

As early as the 1560's English sea rovers were capturing Spanish treasure ships and even raiding Spanish ports in the New World. The most daring of the English "sea dogs" was Francis Drake. He made trip after trip to plunder Spanish galleons in the Caribbean.

The king of Spain resolved to put an end to the "sea dogs" and their acts of piracy. In 1588 he sent a great fleet,

27

Queen Elizabeth I painted from life

boastfully described as the "invincible" Armada, to crush the English nation. To his astonishment, the English, aided by a terrible storm at sea, defeated the Spanish Armada. Only about half of the battered Spanish fleet reached home. Spain was never again able to challenge British sea power. In fact, though outwardly Spain was still magnificent, her days as a great nation were drawing to an end.

England's victory over the Armada gave her control of the seas. Spain could no longer prevent her from establishing colonies on the coast of North America. North of Florida the land would belong to the nations which could plant colonies and protect them.

Conditions in England favor expansion.

By 1600 England was better prepared than any other nation to establish a great overseas empire. Let us see why this was the case.

1. Development of commerce and industry. In 1600 the English had moved farther from feudalism than any of the nations on the Continent. Serfdom had disappeared; farmers paid a cash rent for the use of the land. The great landlords had lost most of their

power. Some of the large estates had been broken up into smaller ones. The middle class, consisting of merchants, artisans, businessmen, and bankers, was growing in numbers and influence.

England was well on the way to becoming a bourgeois, or middle class, society. (Because the middle class are dwellers in towns, or *bourgs,* they are spoken of as bourgeoisie.) The spirit of free enterprise was strong. Men could go into business, make money, and rise to positions of influence in the government. A rich businessman might receive a title from the king. There were businessmen in both houses of Parliament. In such a society there would be many persons with the self-reliance, enterprise, and administrative ability needed for establishing a colony.

Businessmen had money to invest. They looked around for opportunities to make more money. They were willing to risk their capital by taking shares in joint-stock companies formed to carry on foreign trade. By 1600 a number of trading companies were in operation. Each one had a charter from the crown giving it a monopoly of trade in some part of the world. (One of these, the British East India Company, eventually got control of most of India and set up its own government there.) "So when the time came to plant permanent settlements in America," wrote the historians, Charles and Mary Beard, "it was not necessary to beg a pittance from the royal treasury to launch epoch-making expeditions. The middle classes were themselves prepared to furnish both leadership and money."

2. The enclosure movement. The growth of the woolen industry in England and on the Continent created a brisk demand for wool. In the 1500's and 1600's most English landlords stopped raising grain and turned to sheep raising, which was more profitable. Sheep raising required far less labor than crop growing, and every

28

THE SPANISH ARMADA *in 1588. The defeat of the Armada left England "mistress of the seas."*

time a farm was converted into a sheep-fold men were thrown out of work. The landlords fenced in, or "enclosed," their fields. They even took away the "commons" on which the tenants had formerly pastured their own livestock. "England is the land," declared a writer of the period, "where sheep eat men."

Thousands of homeless, landless peasants were set adrift to wander over the countryside. Some got work in the towns, but many could not find any new means of livelihood. Harsh laws were passed to curb begging and steal-ing. The prisons filled up with "valiant rogues and sturdy beggars." The existence of unemployment led to the notion that England was overpopulated and must have colonies for her surplus people. England was the only country in Europe with an abundance of men and women used to hard work in the fields and yet cut loose from bondage to the land. These people were willing to brave the perils of going to the New World, and even to bind themselves to work for a period of years to pay the cost of the journey.

29

3. Individualism and nationalism.

As the medieval period in Europe gave way to modern times, profound intellectual, religious, and political changes took place. In discussing the Renaissance we have noted the rebirth of interest in nature and human nature. Another trend was toward *individualism*. Books were becoming plentiful. People were learning to think for themselves and to question established authority. That is, they were becoming individualistic. At the same time nationalism was developing. Many national leaders wished to end the power of the Pope over the political affairs of their countries. The growth of individualism and nationalism led to a revolt against the authority of the papacy. The Protestant movement, or Reformation, was the result.

The forces of individualism and nationalism came to the fore in England during the reign of the Tudors. In 1534 Henry VIII declared the Church of England to be independent of the Pope. He seized the lands owned by the monasteries and divided them among his followers. He did not, however, provide religious liberty for the people. All Englishmen still were compelled to attend and pay taxes to the Church of England. Thus began a long period of religious unrest which sent many Englishmen to the New World seeking to worship God in their own way. (England, unlike France and Spain, allowed people of all religions to emigrate to the colonies.)

Individualism took many forms. One was the remarkable growth of commerce and industry with the accompanying rise of the middle class. Another was the outburst of activity in literature, science, and exploration. The Elizabethan age (1558–1603) produced Shakespeare, Spenser, Francis Bacon, Raleigh, Drake, and other men of genius. It was a time of amazing creativity.

SIR RICHARD GRENVILLE, *one of England's "sea dogs." For his cousin, Sir Walter Raleigh, he led a colonizing expedition to Virginia in 1585. The colonists soon grew discouraged and returned to England.*

The Elizabethan age was also a period of intense nationalism and patriotism. In the words of Shakespeare,

This happy breed of men, this little
  world,
This precious stone set in the silver
  sea,

was overflowing with energy. In these years England flouted the Spanish, made herself mistress of the seas, and launched trading companies to gather profits from the ends of the earth. She was ready to compete with Spain, France, and the Netherlands for foreign trade and for colonies throughout the entire world.

Three Nations Claim North America

In 1600 the only colonies in North America were the Spanish settlements in Florida and in Mexico. North of the Spanish settlements much of the continent was unexplored. The unsettled area was claimed by three nations:

(Above) CAPTURE OF TWO SPAN-
ISH GALLEONS *by three English
ships off Peru*

(Right) *Conference of* SPAN-
ISH AND ENGLISH DIPLOMATS *in
London (1604) to make peace
between their two nations. The
English diplomats are seated on
the right.*

(1) Spain, because the Pope had given her all lands west of the Line of Demarcation and because of the explorations of De Soto, Coronado, Cabrillo, and others. (2) France, because of the explorations of Verrazano and Cartier. (3) England, because of the explorations of John Cabot in 1497, and others (Frobisher, Davis, and Gilbert) who led later expeditions along the Atlantic coast in search of a northwest passage through the continent. Neither England nor France respected Spain's claim to the whole of North America. The seventeenth and eighteenth centuries found all three nations struggling for control of the continent.

Spain had a tremendous start on the others. Until 1588 at least, a Spaniard would have laughed at any sug-

gestion that France and England would be able to establish empires in North America. He would have found it still more ridiculous if anyone had predicted that little England would eventually control most of the continent and that millions of Englishmen would settle there. Yet England was about to begin a great era of colonization. Because of a number of conditions existing in England, such as (1) a strong spirit of free enterprise, (2) a large middle class to furnish leadership and capital for ,overseas ventures, (3) an abundance of farmers cut loose from the land and needing employment, (4) religious unrest, and (5) nationalistic zeal, the English would outdistance other nations in building an overseas empire.

31

FOR IDENTIFICATION

John Cabot
Jacques Cartier
Samuel de
  Champlain
Francisco de
  Coronado
Hernando Cortés
Hernando de Soto
Sir Francis Drake
Huguenots

Louis Joliet
Robert Cavelier, Sieur
  de La Salle
Father Marquette
Francisco Pizarro
Juan Ponce de León
Sir Walter Raleigh
Spanish Armada
Giovanni da Ver-
  razano

FOR EXPLANATION OR DEFINITION

bourgeoisie
conquistadores
coureurs de bois
enclosure

joint-stock company
northwest passage
"sea dogs"

FOR REVIEW

1. Why did Spain take the lead in exploring the New World?

2. What were the achievements of Ponce de León, Cortés, Pizarro?

3. What parts of North and South America were claimed by Spain by the year 1600?

4. What Old World crops and commodities did Spain introduce to the New World; what New World crops did Spain introduce to western Europe?

5. Briefly outline the outstanding characteristics of the Spanish settlements in the New World.

6. How long did Spain keep its colonies in the New World?

7. What were the achievements of Verrazano, Cartier, Champlain, La Salle, and Marquette?

8. Briefly outline the outstanding characteristics of the French settlements in North America. Contrast with the Spanish settlements in this hemisphere.

9. What were some of the exploits and achievements of Sir Francis Drake?

10. What is the significance of the defeat of the Spanish Armada, 1588?

11. What conditions in England toward the close of the sixteenth century tended to favor colonization of the New World?

12. How did the enclosure movement in England affect the settlement of the New World?

FOR FURTHER STUDY AND DISCUSSION

1. How did geographic features and resources influence the areas and the chief characteristics of Spanish and French explorations and settlements?

2. Compare the motives of explorers in the fifteenth and sixteenth centuries with those of explorers in the nineteenth and twentieth centuries.

3. Contrast colonial activities in the sixteenth and seventeenth centuries with the colonial activities of England and France in the nineteenth and twentieth centuries.

4. Contrast Spanish and French treatment of the native population. Helpful source: H. I. Priestley, *The Coming of the White Man, 1492–1848.*

5. Outline in some detail the influence of Christian missionaries in New Spain and New France. Helpful sources: E. G. Bourne, *Spain in America,* and R. G. Thwaites, *France in America, 1497–1763.*

6. Are historians justified in regarding the defeat of the Spanish Armada in 1588 as an important event and date in the history of the world?

FOR INDIVIDUAL OR GROUP ACTIVITIES

1. Prepare a fifteen-minute dramatization of the story of Saint Isaac Joques. Helpful sources: Francis Parkman, *The Jesuits in North America;* T. J. Campbell, *Pioneer Priests of North America;* and Hart, *Contemporaries,* Vol. I, No. 40.

2. On an outline map of the United States indicate the names of ten important states, rivers, or cities that are Spanish in origin, and ten that are French in origin.

3. Prepare a floor talk on the explorations of De Soto or Coronado.

4. Organize four special committees to make special studies and reports on the civilization of the Aztecs, Mayans, Incas, and Pueblos. Helpful sources: W. H. Prescott, *History of the Conquest of Mexico* and *History of the Conquest of Peru*. See also Hart, *Contemporaries*, Vol. I, No. 22.

5. Prepare special floor talks on the work of the Elizabethan "sea dogs," the circumnavigation of the globe by Sir Francis Drake, and the British East India Company.

6. Hold a panel discussion on the meaning and accuracy of the quotation at the beginning of this chapter.

(Right) *Priest with incense burner* FOUND IN A MAYAN BURIAL. *This beautiful statuette probably belongs to the period 700–900* A.D.

(Far right) *Seated woman made of clay shows the great* SKILL OF AN ANCIENT MEXICAN POTTER.

(Below) CAVE DWELLINGS IN MESA VERDE, COLORADO *where Pueblo Indians lived centuries before the Spaniards came.*

3. ENGLAND ESTABLISHES THIRTEEN COLONIES

Virginia Is the First Permanent English Colony

The London and Plymouth companies.

In the closing years of Queen Elizabeth's reign, Sir Walter Raleigh made two attempts to found a colony on Roanoke Island. The first party of settlers (1585) returned to England after a few months. The second group lived at Roanoke a few years, then disappeared. We do not know to this day what became of the "lost colony." These efforts exhausted Raleigh's large fortune. But he never lost faith in the colonization of the great region which he called "Virginia."

In 1606 James I granted charters to two trading companies planning to establish colonies in America. Each received a grant of land for trade and settlement (map p. 35). Each sent out a group of over a hundred settlers in 1607. The Plymouth Company soon failed (see p. 43), but the London Company succeeded in starting the first permanent English colony in the New World.

"Rights of Englishmen" are guaranteed.

The charters given to the Plymouth and London companies laid down rules for colonial government. A council of settlers appointed by the king was to preserve order and regulate trade with the Indians. The Church of England was to be established as the only form of worship. More important, settlers and their descendants were to enjoy "all liberties, franchises, and immunities . . . as if they had been abiding and born within this our Realm of England." In other words, the colonists were to enjoy all the rights and privileges of people living in England. A similar provision was included in the charters of later colonies. England was the only nation that gave settlers in its colonies the same rights as people in the mother country. This helped make the English colonies attractive to settlers from all parts of Europe.

Ever since the Magna Carta (1215), the English had been strug-

34

THE TWO HOUSES OF PARLIAMENT *presided over by the king. The Lords, or upper house, are on a platform close to the throne.*

EARLY LAND GRANTS TO LONDON AND PLYMOUTH COMPANIES

gling to limit the power of their kings. The people had gradually won certain civil liberties, among them: (1) the right of an arrested person to a speedy hearing before a judge, (2) the right of an accused person to trial by jury, and (3) the right of an accused person to confront his accusers. These "rights of Englishmen" were designed to protect them from tyranny and were highly valued. It is no accident that they were guaranteed in the charters issued to the American colonies.

Jamestown is founded.

In the spring of 1607 a group of 104 men sent out by the London Company landed on the shores of Chesapeake Bay. For protection against surprise attacks from the Spanish and from the Indians, they chose a peninsula on the James River for their settlement, Jamestown. It was a poor site, for the nearby marshes teemed with malaria-bearing mosquitoes.

Although the supply of food was running low, the leaders wasted much time the first year in hunting for gold and for a passage to the Pacific. Few of the colonists knew how to grow food or to hunt and fish. Besides, they were soon greatly weakened by attacks of malaria and dysentery. During the first year more than half of them died. The members of the council quarreled among themselves, and the colony would probably have perished had not the young Captain John Smith taken charge. Smith obtained food from the Indians in exchange for trinkets. More settlers and supplies came from England in 1608 and 1609. Sickness, starvation, and Indian attacks continued to take many lives. Only sixty were still alive in the spring of 1610. The miserable remnant were about to abandon Jamestown when a shipload of new settlers and supplies arrived. The settlement was saved, but fantastic hardships were yet to be endured.

Virginia begins to prosper.

Under the original arrangement, most of the colonists were servants and laborers of the company. They were to receive food and shelter, but no wages. All property, including land, belonged to the company. Since all food produced went into a common store, there was little incentive for hard work. In 1611 a new policy was adopted. Each person in the colony over ten years of age received a share in the company and an allotment of land on which to grow food.

The colony needed a product that could be sold abroad at a profit. So far it had exported shingles, clapboards, and other forest products, but these required much labor for a small return. Around 1613 it was discovered that tobacco could be successfully grown and marketed. A young man named John Rolfe found a way of curing tobacco that gave it appeal for Europeans. Tobacco was easy to produce and at that time brought a high price. Soon most of the colonists were occupied in growing tobacco.

By 1619 Virginia had about one thousand settlers, almost all of them men. They lived in a dozen little settlements along the James River. In that year the company sent to the colony ninety English women, all of whom soon found husbands. Another significant event took place the same year. This was the arrival of a Dutch ship whose captain brought twenty Negroes from the West Indies and sold them to planters.

Representative government is started.

In 1619 the managers of the Virginia Company (as the London Company was now known) took an important step. To make their colony more attractive to settlers, they authorized the election of an assembly to help write laws for the colony. Each settlement was asked to elect two representatives. The assembly, known as the House of Burgesses,[1] met with the governor and his council at Jamestown. This was the beginning of representative government in the New World.

A liberal land policy is adopted.

About this time the Virginia Company promised a 50-acre tract of land to each settler who paid his own way across the Atlantic. The settler would receive 50 acres more for every additional person he brought over. This was called the *headright system.* A similar plan was adopted in most of the colonies outside of New England.

Virginia becomes a royal colony.

King James was unfriendly to the Virginia Company because it was controlled by his opponents in Parliament.

---

[1] "Burgess" (or "burgher") was an old English word meaning a free citizen.

(Above) SIR WALTER RALEIGH. *His efforts to found a colony in Virginia failed, yet he aroused the interest of his countrymen in the New World.*

(Right) AN INDIAN CHIEF *painted by John White, who came to Virginia in 1585 with the first settlers sent by Raleigh. The picture on page 36, also painted by John White, shows* INDIAN HUTS *built of bark and mats over a frame of branches. The first English settlers in Virginia and Massachusetts built the same kind of shelters.*

He did not like their independent spirit and liberal ideas. After an Indian massacre in 1622 which cost nearly 350 lives, the king appointed a commission to look into the company's affairs. The commission charged mismanagement, citing the fact that of 14,000 persons sent to Virginia, nearly 13,000 had died of exposure and disease. The company had spent nearly a million dollars with hardly any return to the stockholders. The company's charter was annulled in 1624 and Virginia became a royal colony. This change meant that the governor would be appointed by the king and would rule according to his orders. The assembly was suspended, but four years later Charles I allowed it to resume its meetings. Virginia furnished the pattern by which most of the English colonies came to be governed: a governor appointed by the king; a council or upper house, usually chosen by the governor; and an assembly, or lower house, elected by the freemen of the colony.

Virginia grew slowly until 1649. In that year the English beheaded Charles I and established a republic. Until the "Restoration" in 1660, England was without a king. Meanwhile, thousands of royalists, who had supported Charles, fled to Virginia. Many of the royalist settlers were well to do. They bought and cultivated large estates, or plantations. Before long the rich bottom land along the rivers was all taken up. The small farmers were crowded out and had to settle on the less desirable land farther inland.

Religious Reformers Settle New England

Religious unrest disturbs England.

Ever since the king made himself head of the Church of England (1534), the English nation had been troubled with religious unrest. A minority of the people remained loyal to the Pope and hoped to restore his control over the

STRATFORD, *the great house built by Thomas Lee on his Virginia plantation in the years 1725–30. The H-shaped floor plan, copied from buildings in Shropshire, England, was unusual in the colonies. Stratford has perhaps given more famous men to the nation than any other house in America. From it came* GOVERNORS OF VIRGINIA, SIGNERS OF THE DECLARATION OF INDEPENDENCE, MEMBERS OF THE CONTINENTAL CONGRESS, DIPLOMATS, AND GENERAL ROBERT E. LEE.

English church. Another minority wanted to make the Church of England definitely Protestant. They wished to abolish such practices as the wearing of vestments by the clergy at services and kneeling at the altar rail for communion. They were known as "Puritans" because they sought to "purify," or reform, the church from within. Other reformers withdrew from the Church of England and started new churches. This group was known as "Separatists," or "Dissenters."

Many Separatists believed in the teachings of the Reverend Robert Browne. He held that the church is a community of believers who make a willing covenant with God to worship Him and keep His laws. Any congregation of Christians, he taught, can make their own church and choose their own church officers. This teaching was opposed to an established, or state, church. It was very unpopular with the leaders of the Church of England.

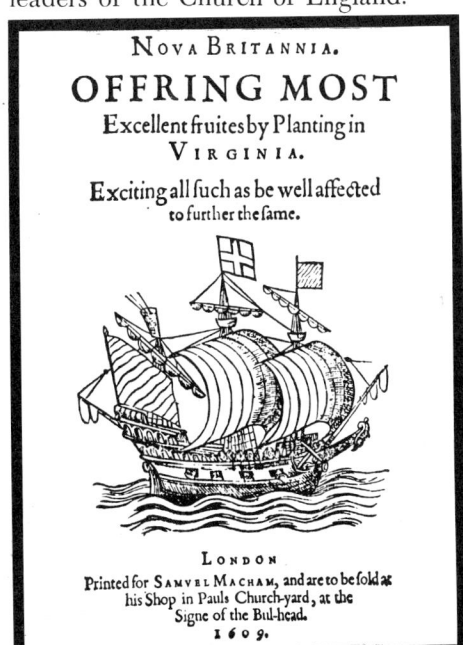

Nova Britannia.

OFFRING MOST

Excellent fruites by Planting in
Virginia.

Exciting all such as be well affected
to further the same.

London
Printed for Samvel Macham, and are to be sold at
his Shop in Pauls Church-yard, at the
Signe of the Bul-head.
1609.

THE TITLE PAGE OF A PAMPHLET *published by the Virginia Company of London in 1609 to attract settlers to Virginia.*

The Pilgrims leave England.

All Englishmen had to attend the Church of England and contribute money to it. Those who did not were fined, thrown into prison, or in some cases, executed. Under James I the Separatists were especially persecuted. In desperation a group of them left England in 1608 and went to Holland, where freedom of worship was permitted. They found it hard to make a living there, and they were unhappy because their children were becoming Netherlanders instead of Englishmen. They longed for another home where "they might more glorify God, do more good to their country, better provide for their posterity, and live to be more refreshed by their labors than ever they could do in Holland."

Some of the Pilgrims, as they came to be called, decided to go to the New World. They got permission from the Virginia Company to settle on its land and finally received a half-way consent from the king. To obtain money for transportation and supplies, they made an agreement with a group of London businessmen. A joint-stock company was formed, with the colonists holding part of the shares. They agreed to work seven years for the company. Meanwhile, the land which they settled and any profits made would belong to the company.

The Mayflower Compact is signed.

In September, 1620, a party of 102 men, women, and children sailed from England in the *Mayflower*. Only a third of them were Pilgrims. The rest were settlers sent over by the new company. After a stormy trip of sixty-five days, Cape Cod was sighted. Although they were far north of the Virginia Company's territory, the weary passengers decided not to sail farther, but to settle at some good site nearby. Since they were outside the limits of Virginia and had no charter of their own, they took steps before landing to provide for the orderly rule of their new community. The leaders drew up a covenant—the famous Mayflower Compact—which was signed by all the men except the servants. It said in part:

In ye name of God, Amen. We whose names are underwritten, the loyal subjects of our dread sovereigne Lord, King James . . . doe by these presents solemnly & mutually in ye presence of God, and one of another, covenant and combine ourselves together into a civill body politick, . . . and by virtue hearof to enacte, constitute and frame such just & equall lawes, ordinances, acts, constitutions & offices, from time to time, as shall be thought most meete & convenient for ye general good of ye Colonie, unto which we all promise due submission and obedience.

Thus the settlers pledged themselves to form their own government and to submit to the will of the majority. This act expressed the basic idea of American democracy—that government depends for its authority on the will of the people. The Compact continued in force until the Plymouth colony was joined to the Massachusetts Bay colony (1691).

Plymouth is founded.

The Pilgrims named their settlement Plymouth. Almost half of the settlers died during the terrible first winter. Yet not one of the survivors returned to England when the *Mayflower* sailed back in the spring. More Separatists came and the colony grew slowly, experiencing much sickness, occasional Indian attacks, and periods of acute food shortage. Gradually they learned to live in the wilderness. "Let it not be grievous to you," wrote friends in England, "that you have been instruments to break the ice for others; the honor shall be yours to the world's end."

The communal system of labor proved unsatisfactory, as it had in Virginia. The fourth season Governor Bradford assigned a parcel of land to each family. The prospect of individual gain was an incentive which led to greater effort to grow food. By 1627 profits from fish and furs enabled the settlers to buy out the London stockholders. This freed them from interference by a group which was not interested in their desire to found a religious community.

Puritans come to Massachusetts Bay.

After Charles I came to the throne in 1625, persecution of the Puritans increased. A group of influential families and clergymen in eastern England decided to establish a Puritan commonwealth in America. They formed the Massachusetts Bay Company, which received a charter early in 1629. The charter of the Massachusetts Bay Company was much the same as other trading company charters. It provided that the members (stockholders) should constitute the "General Court," or assembly, which was to elect a governor, deputy governor, and council each year. The General Court also had power to make such laws for the colony as would not conflict with the laws of England.

A number of the Puritan leaders who wished to emigrate had property and social position. They did not care to go to Massachusetts as dependents of a company in London. For this reason they decided to buy up all the company's stock and carry the charter with them to America. In so doing they transformed the charter of a trading company in England into the constitution for a largely self-governing state.

John Winthrop was chosen governor. In 1630 he sailed for Massachusetts with a band of about a thousand colonists. They founded Boston and several nearby towns. Although 200 died in the first winter, the colonists had a far easier time than those at Jamestown and Plymouth. In the next ten years over 20,000 Puritans came to Massachusetts Bay, including entire congregations with their pastors. The "great immigration" of Puritans continued until civil war broke out in England in 1642. From that time on the colony received few immigrants.

Rule of the "Visible Saints."

One of the first steps in settling a town in Massachusetts was to build a church on the green. All residents were required to attend services, but membership in the Puritan church was limited to a select few. Members were known as "Visible Saints." Only the Visible Saints had a share in the government, for it was intended that the colony be ruled by an *aristocracy of virtue*, consisting of the specially elect of God. Thus church and state were united.

The ministers and church elders tried to control all the affairs of the colony and the private lives of the people as well. They wished their Puritan commonwealth to be a "bulwark against the kingdom of anti-Christ." "We are entered into a convenant with God for this work," preached Winthrop; "He will expect a strict performance." Sober manners, strict observance of the Sabbath, purity of morals, and conformity to the "one true church" were demanded of all who lived in the colony.

When they left England the leaders of Massachusetts claimed to belong to the Church of England. Like other Puritans they wanted to change the church from within. They insisted on "low church" practices, with simple services. No bishop was sent to them, however, and they had to set up their

(Top) JOHN WINTHROP, *founder of Boston and first governor of Massachusetts Bay Colony*

(Lower right) INCREASE MATHER, *president of Harvard College, 1685–1701, and the leading Puritan clergyman for many years*

own church organization. As the Pilgrims had done at Plymouth, each Puritan congregation in Massachusetts chose its own minister and managed its own religious affairs. For this reason they became known as Congregationalists and in time definitely separated from the Church of England.

The Puritans had a great zeal for education. They believed that everyone must read the Bible in order to be godly. Parents were required to see that their children and servants learned to read. The Puritans also insisted that their ministers should be men of learning, able to preach long and scholarly sermons. They established Harvard College in 1636, mainly for the education of clergymen and religious leaders. At the same time they began to establish grammar schools to prepare boys for college. A printing press was

HARVARD COLLEGE *in 1736, one hundred years after its founding*

set up in 1639, and for a generation was the only one in the English colonies.

Rhode Island is founded.

Non-Puritans could remain in the Massachusetts Bay colony as long as they were quiet. If they tried to spread another faith, they were sent away. The Puritan leaders had come to Massachusetts to establish what they considered to be the one true church. To permit rival sects would, in their opinion, endanger souls. It would also threaten the very foundation of their government.

Roger Williams, a young minister at Salem, preached three ideas that alarmed the Puritans: (1) in spite of the royal charter, the land on which the colonists had settled belonged to the Indians; (2) church and state should be separate; (3) the state had no right to interfere with any individual's religious life. Williams was condemned by the General Court and banished. He and his followers fled south. They bought land from the Indians and founded Providence (1636), as "a shelter for persons distressed of conscience." For many years this little

THE THIRTEEN ENGLISH COLONIES

colony of "Rhode Island and Providence Plantations" was the only place in all Christendom where men were free to worship as they chose. Church and state were completely separate. All freemen, whatever their religious beliefs, could vote. The colony prospered as an asylum for religious and political liberty. In 1644 it received a charter from the Puritan government of England granting it practically full self-government. When the king was restored to the throne, he renewed the charter (1663).

Connecticut is founded.

The rich land of the Connecticut Valley early attracted settlers from Massachusetts Bay. The migration began in 1636, when Rev. Thomas Hooker and a large part of his congregation at Cambridge sold their lands and tramped across the wilderness to found Hartford. Other groups soon followed, and several towns were built. Although the Massachusetts Bay colony wished to govern them, they desired to be independent. In 1639 they drew up and adopted the "Fundamental Orders," the first constitution written in America. It created a government like that of Massachusetts Bay but did not require a man to be a church member in order to vote.

After the restoration of the king, Connecticut obtained a royal charter. Like the Rhode Island charter, its terms were remarkably liberal. The freemen were given power to govern themselves, provided that they pass no laws contrary to those of England. Thus Connecticut and Rhode Island were self-governing republics within the British Empire. They remained so until the Revolution.

New Hampshire becomes separate.

In 1607, the same year that Jamestown was founded, the Plymouth Company sent 120 settlers to the Maine coast. They tried to build a town on the Kennebec River. Disease and hunger reduced the colony by half during the first winter. The survivors went back to England, "their former hopes frozen to death." This failure ruined the Plymouth Company. In 1620 its rights were transferred to a new company called the "Council for New England." The Council for New England established a few trading posts and fishing stations in the area that became Maine and New Hampshire. The Council failed to make money and gave up its charter in 1635. Pioneers from the Massachusetts Bay colony soon pushed northward into this region, and that colony claimed the right to govern them. This led to considerable friction. In 1679 the king gave New Hampshire a charter making it a royal colony. Twelve years later Maine was officially united with Massachusetts, under a charter which made Massachusetts a royal colony.

Proprietors Continue the Work of Colonizing

Proprietors receive land and power.

There were a number of wealthy individuals in England who wished to establish colonies at their own expense and who requested grants of land from the king for this purpose. An individual who received land on which to found a colony was known as a *proprietor*. He was given many of the privileges of a feudal lord. He could appoint the governor, the judges, and the officials of his colony. He could make the laws for it, provided that (1) they did not conflict with the laws of England and (2) he obtained the advice and consent of the freemen or their representatives. He could require colonists to pay a tax, or quitrent, for the use of the land (see p. 61). Quitrents were relics of feudalism; they took the place of services once due to the feudal lord. Eventually these taxes were a cause of trouble. Even when the quit-rent was only a token, the payment was irritating to the colonists.

Maryland is founded.

The first successful proprietary colony was Maryland. It was intended as a haven for Roman Catholics, who at the time were persecuted in England. George Calvert, a prominent Catholic and the first Lord Baltimore, was a personal friend of Charles I. The king gave him a large grant of land running from the Potomac River to the 40th parallel (the latitude of Philadelphia). Lord Baltimore named it Maryland, for Queen Henrietta Maria. He died soon after receiving the grant, and his sons, Cecil and Leonard Calvert, carried out his plans for establishing the colony.

Early in 1634 a band of about two hundred settlers led by Leonard Calvert reached the shores of Chesapeake Bay. Upon landing they celebrated Mass. This was the first time a Roman Catholic service had been held publicly in the English colonies. The new-comers chose a high, well-drained spot for their town, which they called St. Mary's. They made friends with the Indians, from whom they purchased land for their settlement. The first year's crops were good and the colony prospered from the start. New settlers flocked in, for Christians of all sects were welcome. Before long, Protestants far outnumbered Roman Catholics.

To protect the Catholics, the second Lord Baltimore got the assembly to pass the Toleration Act (1649). It provided that everyone who professed to believe in the divinity of Jesus Christ should be free to worship in his own way. This did not end religious quarrels, however, for many of the Protestants tried to suppress the Roman

CHARLESTON, SOUTH CAROLINA, *soon after its first settlement. This line engraving was published around 1670.*

Catholic Church. In 1691 the king made Maryland a royal colony, with the Anglican Church as the established, or state, church. Roman Catholics lost their political rights and Lord Baltimore lost all voice in the colony's affairs. When the third Lord Baltimore accepted the Anglican faith, the government of the colony was restored to him (1715). Maryland remained under the control of the Calvert family until the American Revolution.

The Carolinas are founded.

In 1660 Charles II was restored to the English throne. To repay a debt to eight noblemen who helped him regain the crown, the king gave them a huge piece of land lying south of Virginia. The nobles named the land Carolina, in honor of the king. A few hundred people from Virginia had settled in the northern part along Albemarle Sound. The proprietors sent them a governor and authorized an assembly. A steady stream of settlers flowed in, mostly poor frontiersmen from Virginia. Soon this region, which came to be called North Carolina, was covered with small farms.

The settlement of South Carolina began in 1670 with the founding of Charleston. This good harbor, for many years the only one in the South, and the fertile soil brought great prosperity to South Carolina. People of many faiths and nationalities came there, including a number of French Huguenots. First rice and then indigo became the colony's staple products. These were cultivated on large plantations with slave labor. By 1700 Charleston was the largest town in the South and the third largest in the English colonies.

The proprietors stayed in England. Because of their feudal ideas they had one dispute after another with the popular assemblies. The people drove out several governors who tried to collect quitrents. When the assembly of South Carolina proposed to sell land outright to settlers, the proprietors vetoed the act. As a result, the assembly petitioned the king to make South Carolina a royal province. The king agreed and bought out the proprietors. North and South Carolina then became royal colonies (1729).

The Dutch colonize New Netherland.

About the same time that the first settlers of Jamestown were exploring the streams of Virginia in hopes of finding a passage to Asia, the Dutch East India Company hired an English captain, Henry Hudson, to look for a northwest passage. In 1609 Hudson discovered New York Bay. Then he sailed up the river which bears his name until he came to rapids near what is now Albany. He claimed the entire region for the Dutch.

The Hudson River led into the richest fur-bearing country south of the St. Lawrence. Dutch trading posts were soon established at Albany and on Manhattan Island. The Dutch West India Company was organized (1621) to control the fur trade and plant colonies. Little groups of Dutch families settled on Long Island and west of the Hudson. The town of New Amsterdam on Manhattan Island became the capital of New Netherland.

DUTCH AND SWEDISH SETTLEMENTS

45

The company offered a tremendous tract of land on the Hudson River to any of its members who would bring in fifty families at his own expense and settle them on his estate. The *patroon,* or landowner, was to rule over his people much like a feudal lord. The patroon system did not attract many settlers. Later the company gave 200 acres to anyone who would bring in five persons.

The Dutch seize New Sweden.

In 1638 a Swedish trading company made a settlement at what is now Wilmington, Delaware. It was named Fort Christiana for the Swedish queen. Before long other Swedish settlements were planted in the vicinity. The Dutch protested that the Swedes had no claim to this region. When New Sweden was seventeen years old (1655), the Dutch governor of New Netherland, fiery Peter Stuyvesant, led a force against it. The Swedes gave up peacefully and became Dutch subjects.

The English seize New Netherland.

In the closing years of the 1500's, the English helped the Dutch win their independence from Spain. But England and Holland did not remain friends long. The Dutch were successful traders and competed with British merchants in all parts of the world. The rivalry of the two countries for trade and naval power led to armed conflict. They fought three wars between 1652 and 1674 for control of the world's sea lanes.

The English wanted possession of New Netherland because it interfered with a possible union of New England with the other English colonies. Moreover, the Dutch colonists controlled some of the best harbors on the Atlantic coast, as well as a rich fur trade with the Iroquois Indians. Opportunity to seize New Netherland came in 1664 when England and Holland went to war for the second time. Charles II made a present of the Dutch colony to his brother, the Duke of York. The

New Amsterdam, as painted in the 1600's

On the opposite page (top). PENN'S LANDING *on the shores of the Delaware River, as imagined by a nineteenth century painter.*

(Below) PENN SIGNING A TREATY *with the Indians, as imagined by another nineteenth century painter.*

46

Duke sent a fleet of three warships to take possession of it. The people were tired of a government in which they had no part, and the colony surrendered almost without a shot. The English flag now floated from Maine to Florida.

New Jersey is created.

The area taken from the Dutch included what is now New York, New Jersey, Pennsylvania, and Delaware. Soon after receiving his grant, the Duke of York gave the land between the Hudson and the Delaware to two of his followers. The new proprietors, Lord Berkeley and Sir George Carteret, named the province New Jersey.

The two proprietors organized a government with a popular assembly. They granted religious liberty, and many Puritans and Quakers settled there. By 1688 the entire colony had been sold to William Penn and other Quakers. In 1702 New Jersey became a royal province.

Quakers come to the New World.

The Society of Friends, or Quakers, began in England about 1650. Members believed that every person should be guided by the Holy Spirit, or "inner light," within him. They felt no need for ceremony in their religion, or for trained preachers. In their meetings for worshiping God, anyone was free to speak. Believing that all men are equal in the eyes of God, the Friends refused to bow or to take off their hats to anyone, even the king. They thought that slavery was wrong. They held that war is wicked and refused to serve as soldiers. When persecuted they did not fight but offered nonviolent resistance.

In spite of persecution the sect spread rapidly in England and on the Continent. In 1656 the first Quaker missionaries appeared in the English colonies. Severe laws were passed against them in every colony except Rhode Island. In Boston three Quakers were hanged. Such treatment made the Society wish for a colony of its own.

WILLIAM PENN

47

Penn founds Pennsylvania and Delaware.

William Penn was a devoted and gifted young Friend. He had inherited from his father, Admiral William Penn, a claim of 16,000 pounds against Charles II. He asked the king to pay off the debt by giving him land in the New World. In 1681 the king gave Penn a big tract west of the Delaware and named it Pennsylvania.

Penn, like Winthrop, Calvert, and Williams, dreamed of making a city of God in the wilderness. He invited the oppressed of every sect and nationality, so long as they were believers in "one almighty and eternal God." He wished all settlers to be "secure from the abuse of power." "The people must rule," he wrote. He permitted the settlers to elect both houses of the legislature. (In most other colonies the governor appointed the council, or upper house.) The first assembly enacted a "Great Charter," or constitution, for the colony.

Penn made it easy for settlers to get land. Each settler received fifty acres free. Additional land could be rented for a penny an acre or bought on easy terms. Penn gave free land to the settlers who were already in the colony. These included about a thousand Swedes, Finns, and Dutch.

Penn came to the colony in 1682. He planted his capital on the Delaware River and named it Philadelphia, "the city of brotherly love." He laid out broad streets at right angles to one another, expressing the hope that each house would be set in the center of a garden, and that the place might always be a "green country town."

Realizing that his colony needed a seacoast, Penn persuaded the Duke of York to give him three counties west of Delaware Bay (1682). This region became the separate colony of Delaware in 1704, though it was controlled by the Penn family until the Revolution.

Pennsylvania grows rapidly.

Pennsylvania soon became the largest and most prosperous of the English colonies. Penn advertised for settlers both in England and on the Continent. After 1700 a large number of Scotch-Irish came to Pennsylvania and settled on the frontier. They were descendants of Presbyterians who moved from Scotland to Ireland in the early 1600's. Many Germans also came to Penn's colony. Most of these were Mennonites or belonged to other small Protestant sects that were being persecuted in their homeland. The Germans became known as "Pennsylvania Dutch." The colony also attracted a considerable number of Swiss, Welsh, and Irish settlers.

While Penn lived, the colonists enjoyed uninterrupted peace with the Indians. He paid the tribes for land with articles of real value. He made a treaty with them in which it was agreed that any disputes should be settled by peaceful means. Treaties between the Quakers and the Indians were faithfully kept on both sides.

Trouble with the Indians began when the central part of the colony was settled by non-Quakers. For a long time the assembly, which was dominated by Quakers, refused to appropriate money for defense against the Indians. To fight was against Quaker principles. Besides, the assemblymen were sure that the colonists could get along with the Indians by treating them justly. The frontiersmen, however, wanted to drive the Indians westward and, as in every other colony, this led to fighting.

Georgia is settled.

Georgia, the last of the thirteen original colonies, began as a charitable experiment—an attempt by General James Oglethorpe to help worthy men who had been imprisoned for debt. Oglethorpe became concerned

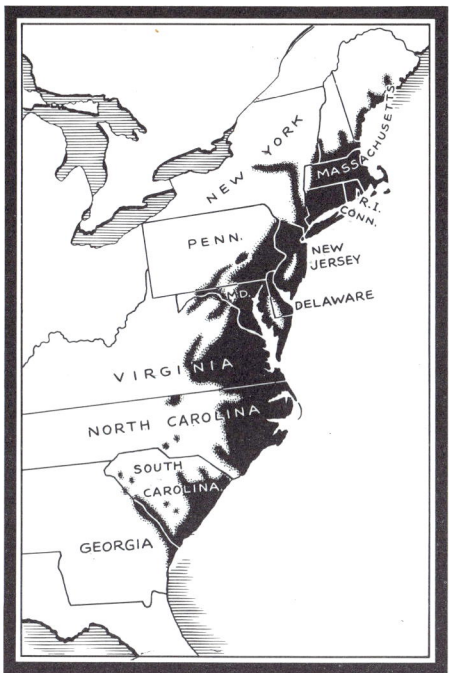

SETTLED PORTIONS
OF THE ENGLISH
COLONIES, 1750

about the plight of debtors in English jails after a friend of his was arrested because of a small debt he could not pay. Confined with prisoners who had smallpox, his friend caught the disease and died. Oglethorpe, who was a member of Parliament, became chairman of a commission to investigate the jails.

He found them to be horrible places. Many prisoners died in jail. Those who lived were broken in health and often in mind. The most pitiable were the prisoners committed for debt. A debtor could not be released until his debt was paid. Unless someone paid it for him, he had to stay in jail the rest of his life. Oglethorpe decided to form a company to pay off the debts of deserving, able-bodied prisoners and settle them in the New World.

He got the backing of twenty prominent men. Together they obtained a grant of land south of the Carolinas. It was named Georgia in honor of the king, George II. The charter said that the proprietors should act as trustees for the colony, and that control should revert to the crown after twenty-one years. Besides offering a refuge to poor debtors, the new colony was expected to serve as a military outpost against the Spanish in Florida and against the southern Indians. Parliament supplied some of the money needed to establish Georgia. It was the only colony assisted in this way.

Oglethorpe was appointed governor and he himself brought the first settlers in 1733. Over a period of years several thousand debtors were helped to migrate to Georgia. The trustees also welcomed Protestants seeking to escape persecution in Europe and offered them religious freedom.

JAMES OGLETHORPE *with a committee of the House of Commons investigating conditions at a London prison, 1729. Painted by William Hogarth.*

The trustees were men of high ideals. They forbade slavery in their colony. They also forbade the importation of hard liquor. Each able-bodied man was to receive fifty acres of land free but no one was to own more than 500 acres of land. Some settlers did not like these restrictions. Learning that people were growing rich in South Carolina by using slaves on rice and indigo plantations, a few Georgians moved there. Others agitated for repeal of the laws against slavery and large landholdings. The trustees reluctantly gave in to these demands. Disappointed in their plans for the colony, they surrendered the charter a year ahead of time. Thus, in 1752, Georgia became a royal province. By that time it had many plantations operated with slave labor.

The Colonists Advance toward Self-government

Englishmen seek more political liberty.

England gave far more liberty to its colonies than any other nation. French and Spanish colonies were ruled by all-powerful royal governors, and settlers had no part in public affairs. On the other hand, all the English colonies had a large measure of self-government. This very fact led to a demand for still greater freedom. The colonists intended to defend all the rights they had and to win more rights if possible. In this they were acting in the same spirit as people in the mother country, who beheaded one tyrannical king (1649) and ousted another (1688).

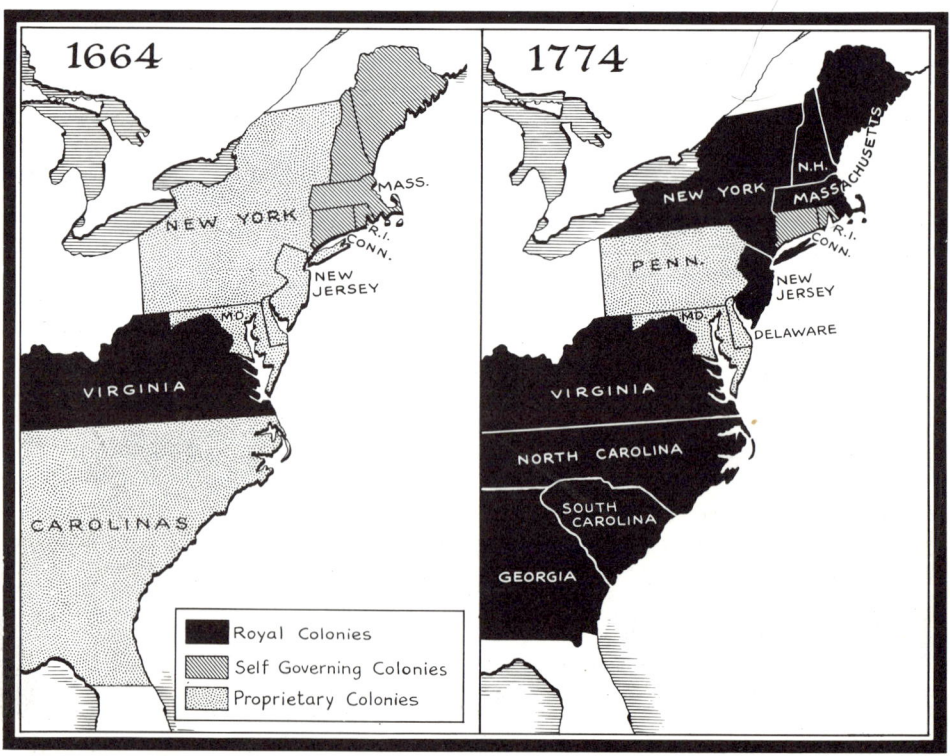

ROYAL, SELF–GOVERNING, AND PROPRIETARY COLONIES

OGLETHORPE *in London presenting a group of Indians to the Lord Trustees of the colony of Georgia, 1734*

Colonies are of three types.

All the English colonies were alike in having a charter; that is, a written grant of privileges from the king. The charter amounted to a constitution, outlining the way in which the colony was to be governed. At first the government was controlled by the commercial company, or the proprietor, that had founded the colony. As time went on, the king wished to have more to say about colonial affairs. One by one he took back eight grants made to companies and proprietors.

When a colony became a royal province, it received a new charter, giving the king more effective control than before. By the time of the American Revolution only three proprietary colonies—Pennsylvania, Delaware, and Maryland—remained. There were also two self-governing colonies—Rhode Island and Connecticut.

The chief difference in the government of the three kinds of colonies was the manner in which the governor was chosen. In the royal colonies he was appointed by the king. In the proprietary colonies he was appointed by the proprietor. In the self-governing colonies he was elected by the voters. Another difference among the three types of colonies was in the governor's powers. These were greatest in the royal and proprietary colonies, where, for example, the governor could veto bills passed by the assembly.

The council is the upper house.

Except in Pennsylvania and Delaware, the governor had a council. Laws passed by the assembly went to the council for its approval. Thus the council acted as the upper house of a two-house legislature. Besides sharing in lawmaking the council advised the governor. It also served as the colony's highest court.

Since the councilmen had much influence, the manner in which they were chosen was important. In the royal colonies and some of the proprie-

51

tary colonies, the governor appointed them. In other proprietary colonies, councilmen were chosen by the proprietor. Only in the self-governing colonies did the voters (or the assembly) elect the council.

Appointed governors meet opposition.

In most of the colonies the governor was appointed, not chosen by the voters. Appointed governors were usually sent from England and did not expect to stay long in America. They seldom understood the problems of the colonists. And many governors tried to get rich through land speculation, the fur trade, or even by the sale of political jobs. Thus the colonists had little reason to like their governors.

The governor was supposed to enforce British laws applying to the colonies. In a proprietary colony he also had to enforce the proprietor's rules. He could hardly carry out his duties without antagonizing the assembly, since it stood for local interests.

The assembly passed bills which expressed the wishes of the voters. Time and again a bill adopted by the assembly was turned down by the governor's council. If not, the governor himself might veto it. The governor vetoed bills which he thought might displease the king or Parliament. In turn the assembly often resisted the governor's efforts to enforce British laws such as those regulating trade and manufacturing. Bitter quarrels between the governor and the assembly were a commonplace.

Assemblies become powerful.

The assemblies had one important weapon which they could use to curb governors who went too far—the power of the purse. By the second half of the colonial period, the assemblies had claimed the right of voting taxes for all purposes, including the governor's salary. If the governor refused to approve bills which the assembly passed, it might keep back all or part of his salary. When threatened with loss of his salary, many a governor gave in.

The assemblies learned to use their power over the purse to cut the governor's authority in all sorts of ways. If a governor asked for money to pay the salaries of new officials whom he wished to appoint, the assembly could say, "All right, provided we can name the men to be appointed." If the governor asked money for official expenses, the assembly could insist on an itemized statement showing how the money would be spent. The assembly might even appoint a committee to supervise the expenditure! Although the governor commanded the military forces, the assembly could through the purse control their use. For instance, the assembly might supply the necessary funds on condition that the soldiers be used only as it directed.

By the mid-1700's the assemblies were able to dominate the government in most of the colonies. "The people have the whole of the administration in their hands," moaned a royal governor of South Carolina. In thus making the assembly supreme, the colonists were merely following the British example. In Great Britain, Parliament had taken over most of the powers of the king. In the royal and proprietary colonies, the assemblies took over most of the powers of the governor. In the self-governing colonies, the governor and his council had always been subject to the voters.

Beginning of a free press.

A few years after the Glorious Revolution (1688–89), Parliament discontinued the censorship of books, pamphlets, and newspapers, and England began to enjoy a free press. (At that time the only other country with a free press was Holland.) In the English colonies, however, the governors often interfered with freedom of the press. James Franklin (Benjamin's older brother) was imprisoned in the 1720's for criticizing the assembly of Massachusetts in his newspaper, *The New England Courant.*

All the colonies had severe laws against libel—the writing or printing of a statement damaging to a person's reputation. A person could be punished for libel even if his statements were true. In 1734 Peter Zenger, publisher of the *New York Weekly Journal,* printed a series of articles attacking the tyrannical policies of the royal governor of New York, William Cosby. Zenger was arrested and put on trial for libel.

Word of the coming trial had reached a noted lawyer, Andrew Hamilton, speaker of the Pennsylvania Assembly. Hamilton was then an old man, but he gladly made the difficult journey from Philadelphia to New York in order to defend Zenger. In court he argued that the articles Cosby complained of told the truth. The chief justice in his turn directed the jury to consider only whether Zenger had published the articles. If he had done so, he was guilty of libel. Then Hamilton made a ringing appeal to the jury in the name of a free press and the right to publish the truth about public officials.

The question before the court . . . is not of small nor private concern. It is not the cause of a poor printer, nor of New York alone . . . It is the cause of liberty, and I have no doubt that . . . every man who prefers freedom to a life of slavery will bless and honor you . . . for securing . . . the liberty of opposing arbitrary [tyrannical] power by speaking and writing truth.

The jury defied the judges and the governor and found Zenger "not guilty." This verdict helped establish the principle that the press has the right to discuss public questions fully and to find fault with officials. Years later Gouverneur Morris spoke of the Zenger trial as "the morning star of that liberty which subsequently revolutionized America."

ANDREW HAMILTON, *the lawyer who defended Peter Zenger. Hamilton helped establish the right of the press to criticize public officials. In his famous charge to the jury, Hamilton declared: "The man who loves his country prefers its liberty to all other considerations, well knowing that without liberty, life is a misery."*

Colonists manage their own affairs.

Parliament sometimes passed laws, such as the Navigation Acts, that affected the colonies. When these measures displeased the colonists, they were evaded. But in general the colonists accepted the right of Parliament to regulate the *external* affairs of the colonies. They also agreed, for the most part, that colonial laws should not conflict with those of England and that the king had a right to veto any which did.

Until the end of the 1600's neither the king nor Parliament showed much interest in the *internal* affairs of the colonies. Most of the time the colonists were left quite free to manage their own affairs. In this way they developed the practice of self-government. Many colonists gained experience as legislators, judges, and public officials. The more they learned of the arts of government, the harder it became to accept any interference from the outside. Later, when the king and Parliament tried to bring the colonies under firmer control, the colonists protested vigorously.

Plain People Struggle against Aristocrats

Right to vote is limited.

When we say that the assembly was elected by the people, we do not mean that every freeman could vote. Actually, only a small minority of the freemen had the ballot. As in England, voters had to be landholders or owners of other property. South of the Potomac the voter generally had to own at least fifty acres of land. In the 1600's voters in most colonies also were required to be members in good standing of an approved church. This meant that Roman Catholics, Quakers, Jews, and atheists were not eligible to vote. Later, many colonies dropped religious qualifications for voting.

Assemblies represent men of wealth.

Membership in the assemblies was limited to the well to do. In South Carolina, for example, an assemblyman had to own five hundred acres of land and ten slaves, or possess other property worth $5000, a large sum in those days. In New Jersey an assemblyman had to own a thousand acres of land. As a rule the assemblymen came from the coastal settlements. They knew and cared little about the needs of wage earners, small farmers, and frontier dwellers. The demands of these people for better protection from the Indians, lower interest rates on mortgages, lower fees for deeds to land, cheaper money, and the like, received scant attention. The assemblymen voted for laws that would advance their own interests.

Conflict between seaboard and frontier.

The ordinary people resented the political power of the seaboard aristocrats and called for reform. The most vigorous demands for reform came from the back country, where men were poor but independent. That is why the struggle between the plain folk and the well to do is sometimes spoken of as a conflict between seaboard and frontier. Occasionally it led to outbreaks of violence.

One such conflict took place in Virginia in 1676, after an Indian massacre. Governor Berkeley refused the request of the frontier settlers for military protection. (His opponents claimed that because he made money from the Indian fur trade, he was unwilling to fight the Indians.) Hoping to change the governor's mind, 500 frontiersmen, small farmers, and wage earners gathered under the leadership of Nathaniel Bacon. They marched on Jamestown, the capital. They demanded that a new assembly be elected, chosen by all freemen regardless of whether they owned property. To this and certain

other reforms the governor agreed. Bacon, however, was more interested in getting a commission authorizing him to lead his men against the Indians. He used force to compel the assembly to enact this commission. The governor signed it with great reluctance, for he believed that the frontiersmen, by violating treaties with the Indians, were responsible for the Indian troubles.

As soon as Bacon and his men had left Jamestown, the governor declared them to be "rebels." Bacon then decided to go back and fight it out with the governor's forces. Berkeley fled and Bacon seized control of the government. Shortly after, he was taken ill and died. The governor subdued Bacon's leaderless forces and returned to the capital. He then proceeded to hang or imprison many of Bacon's followers. When the news of the disturbance reached England, Berkeley was removed from office. "The old fool," said Charles II, "has taken more lives in that naked country than I for the murder of my father." Although the new governor ordered a number of reforms, most of the freemen were still denied the right to vote.

The Thirteen Colonies Remain Separate

Each colony is politically separate.

The English colonies enjoyed a remarkable degree of local home rule.

(Right) SIR WILLIAM BERKELEY, *governor of Virginia from 1642 to 1677. He encouraged silk production, brick making, and the diversification of crops. Recent historical research has enhanced his reputation. It now appears that the main cause of Bacon's Rebellion was the governor's efforts to uphold treaties with the Indians and to save friendly tribes from extermination. Bacon, on reexamination of the facts, emerges more as a trouble-maker and rabble-rouser than a hero-reformer.*
(Left) "BACON'S CASTLE," *so called because it was seized and occupied by one of Bacon's rebel garrisons*

Each settled most of its problems in its own way. The only central government with authority over all the colonies was three thousand miles away. Because each colony was used to running so many of its own affairs, proposals to unite with other colonies were not welcomed.

Yet the colonists had many common traditions. For the most part they spoke the same language, observed the same customs, and held the same ideas about political justice. In each colony they developed very similar institutions for carrying on the general government—that of the colony as a whole. And they all feared common dangers—the French, the Indians, and the loss of their liberties. But most of the time the colonies had little to do with one another. Each had more trade with England or the West Indies than with the other mainland colonies. Difficulties of travel and communications tended to keep each colony isolated from the rest.

Attempts at union fail.

As early as 1643, Massachusetts Bay, Plymouth, Connecticut, and New Haven (which was then a separate colony) formed the New England Confederation. For over forty years delegates from these colonies met occasionally to discuss common affairs. The Confederation broke up when it was no longer needed for defense against the Indians. In a few other cases adjoining colonies co-operated in fighting Indians, but no lasting organization was set up.

In 1686 James II attempted to unite the New England colonies under one government known as the Dominion of New England. He appointed Sir Edmund Andros governor-general and gave him dictatorial power. When James II was driven from the throne two years later, the colonists promptly put Andros in jail. The new sovereigns, William and Mary, dissolved the Dominion. They did, however, combine Plymouth, Maine, and Massachusetts.

In 1754, because war with the French and their Indian allies seemed to be near, commissioners from seven northern colonies met at Albany, New York. The meeting is known as the "Albany Congress." The aim of the group was to form an alliance with the six Iroquois Nations and to plan for united military action. The Albany Congress considered a possible union of all the colonies for purposes of defense. A plan proposed by Benjamin

Franklin for such a union was unanimously accepted. But none of the colonial assemblies approved it. This did not surprise Franklin, for he wrote:

It is not likely, in my opinion, that any of them [the assemblies] will act upon it so far as to agree to it, or to propose any amendments to it. Everybody cries, "A union is absolutely necessary," but when they come to the manner and form of union, their weak noddles are perfectly distracted.

Nevertheless, the French and Indian wars that broke out three years later drove the colonies into close co-operation. A permanent union was not to be long delayed.

Colonial practices have come down to us.

Many features of colonial government were continued after the American Revolution. Among these were the written constitution, the two-house legislature, the veto power of the governor, control of the purse by the people's representatives, and freedom of the press.

In addition, the great body of English law known as *common law* was transplanted to the colonies. Common law rests on custom and court decisions rather than on the acts of a legislature. In deciding a case, judges use the common law to settle points not covered by legislation. Most of our ideas concerning justice and the rights of the individual came down to us in the common law. Later, these principles formed the basis for our written law.

(Upper right) *The hall of the* HOUSE OF BURGESSES *in colonial Williamsburg*

(Lower right) GOVERNOR'S MANSION AT WILLIAMSBURG, *the early capital of Virginia. Restoration of colonial Williamsburg was a gift to the American people from John D. Rockefeller, Jr.*

Puritan mother and child

FOR IDENTIFICATION

Albany Congress	Mayflower Compact
Bacon's Rebellion	James Oglethorpe
William Bradford	William Penn
Duke of York	Pilgrims
Fundamental Orders	Puritans
of Connecticut	Captain John Smith
House of Burgesses	Peter Stuyvesant
Maryland Toleration	Roger Williams
Act	Peter Zenger

FOR EXPLANATION OR DEFINITION

charter	"power of the purse"
common law	proprietor
debtor's prison	quitrent
headright system	representative assembly
indentured servant	royal colony
patroon	written constitution

FOR REVIEW

1. How did the charters to the London and Plymouth companies provide for the government of the colonies?

2. What were the "rights of Englishmen" included in the charters?

3. Where and when was the first English colony started? Describe the hardships suffered by the early settlers. How were they met?

4. What is the significance of the establishment of the House of Burgesses, 1619?

5. How did religious unrest in England influence the settlement of the colonies? Describe the settlement of Plymouth.

6. What is the significance of the Mayflower Compact?

7. How were Rhode Island, Connecticut, and New Hampshire settled? In what important respect did Rhode Island differ from Massachusetts?

8. What was a proprietary colony? Name three proprietors and the colonies they founded.

9. Briefly describe the Swedish settlements on the Delaware and the Dutch settlements in New York. How did these settlements come under the control of England?

10. State the religious beliefs of the Quakers. What were the outstanding characteristics of the proprietary colony of Pennsylvania?

11. Under what circumstances were the Carolinas and Georgia founded?

12. (a) Name the three types of colonial government. (b) In what way were the three types alike? (c) What were the chief differences?

13. (a) How was the colonial governor chosen? (b) What were his chief powers?

14. (a) What rights were claimed by the colonial assemblies? (b) Why was it difficult for the assembly to have its way? (c) How did colonial assemblies sometimes force a governor to carry out their wishes?

15. (a) What action led to the arrest of Peter Zenger? (b) On what grounds did the jury vote to free him? (c) How did this case help the growth of the spirit of self-government?

16. (a) Why was there friction between the people on the seaboard and the people in the "back country"? (b) What did Nathaniel Bacon demand? (c) What was the outcome of Bacon's Rebellion?

17. (a) What conditions tended to keep the colonies separate from one another? (b) What conditions tended to bring them together?

18. (a) What was the New England Confederation? (b) What was the Dominion of New England?

19. (a) What was the purpose of the Albany Congress of 1754? (b) What happened to Franklin's Plan of Union?

1. (a) Why did the feudal system of land-holdings fail to develop in the colonies? (b) To what extent did the patroon system in New York and the quitrent system in some of the other colonies resemble the feudal system?

2. (a) The first amendment to the Constitution states that "Congress shall make no law respecting any establishment of religion, or prohibiting the free exercise thereof." How does this compare with early colonial practices in Massachusetts, Virginia, Rhode Island, and Maryland? (b) Outline the story of the Maryland Toleration Act of 1649. (c) Briefly describe the careers of Anne Hutchinson and Roger Williams.

3. (a) In what respects was the colonial period one of experimentation with democracy? (b) What were the chief democratic features of colonial government? (c) What colonial practices were not "democratic" according to twentieth century standards? (d) What features of colonial government had an enduring influence on American government?

4. Colonial assemblies by controlling the purse strings were frequently able to accomplish reforms. What clauses in the American Constitution are based on this colonial practice? Can you cite any recent instances when Congress or your state legislature resorted to this device?

FOR INDIVIDUAL OR GROUP ACTIVITIES

1. Organize the class into thirteen committees. Assign to each the study of one of the colonies. Prepare for exhibit charts and tables outlining the development of each colony: its beginnings, outstanding leaders, geographic features and resources, government, important cities, and significant events. Helpful sources: Morris, *Encyclopedia of American History*, and Hart, *Contemporaries*, Vol. I.

2. Prepare a radio script on how New Amsterdam became New York; or send a news dispatch to a London newspaper describing the event.

3. Investigate and report on the basis of Virginia's claim to land in the vicinity of the Great Lakes and of Massachusetts' claim to Maine.

4. Prepare biographic sketches of William Penn, Lord Baltimore, James Oglethorpe, Governor Winthrop, Peter Stuyvesant.

5. Report on or dramatize the work of the first representative assembly in America. Helpful source: Hart, *Contemporaries*, Vol. I, No. 65.

6. Have a member of the class write a short story about the Charter Oak of Connecticut. Helpful source: Hart, *Contemporaries*, Vol. I, No. 12.

7. Organize three committees to make special reports on the New England Confederation, the Dominion of New England, and the Albany Congress. Helpful sources: Commager, *Documents*, Nos. 18 and 31; Morris, *Encyclopedia of American History*; and Hart, *Contemporaries*, Vol. I, Nos. 122, 135, 136.

KING JAMES I *succeeded to the English throne in 1603 on the death of Queen Elizabeth I.*

The whole idea of colonization, as worked out by the English in America, was new. . . . There were no precedents for plantations, properly so called, in which homes were erected, tillage begun, domestic life cultivated, and the means wherewith to continue a separate social and economic life brought into being.

——Charles M. Andrews

4. THE COLONISTS MAKE A LIVING

Farming Is the Chief Occupation

Land ownership is widespread.

In England nearly all the land belonged to landlords. Attempts to establish this system of landholding in the colonies were not very successful. Land was plentiful, and the colonists saw no reason why they should pay rent for it.

1. Freeholders. In New England the colonial legislatures controlled the land. Each group desiring to establish a town asked the legislature for a grant. Upon receiving it, the town meeting distributed the land among the settlers. A green, or common, was reserved in the center of town. Each man received

a house lot near the common. The town frequently kept pasture land which all the settlers could use. The remaining land was divided, each settler receiving a share of the upland, the meadowland, and the marshland. These communities were very different from the scattered farms in the southern colonies.

In New England the settlers became absolute owners of their farms. That is, they were freeholders. There were some freeholders in each of the other colonies also.

2. The quitrent system. In the proprietary colonies, the proprietors of-

HOUSE OF A PROSPEROUS NEW ENGLAND FAMILY *built about 1660 at Farmington, Connecticut. The small windows, long roof line, and overhang are typical of houses built in this period.*

fered settlers large grants of land subject to a yearly quitrent. The first Lord Baltimore, for instance, granted 1000 acres to individuals who brought over five settlers. Each holder of a thousand-acre tract was supposed to pay sixteen shillings a year to Baltimore. Proprietors also granted land in small tracts to individual settlers.

In the royal colonies, too, much of the land was granted subject to a quitrent. Often a large landholder had to pay the king only a token, such as one beaver skin yearly for each thousand acres. Large landholders usually divided their property into small parcels and collected quitrents from the settlers.

The settlers tried to evade payment of quitrents. Sometimes there were violent outbreaks against the rent collectors, known as "rent wars." To avoid these difficulties many large landholders sold land outright. Others gave up the attempt to collect quitrents. With the American Revolution the payment of quitrents ceased.

3. Squatters and pre-emption laws. On the frontier many of the settlers were "squatters," with no legal right to the land they occupied. If an owner wanted his land, the squatters could be dispossessed by force. When this happened, it caused great bitterness. About 1750 Pennsylvania passed a pre-emption law, allowing squatters the first chance to buy at the regular purchase price the land they had cleared. To satisfy frontiersmen most of the other colonies in time adopted a similar law.

Clearing the land is hard work.

Untouched or virgin forest covered the land east of the Mississippi. To clear his land of trees was the first task of the pioneer farmer. If time was short, he might kill the trees by cutting off a girdle of bark. He could then plant Indian corn or other coarse crops under the leafless branches. The next winter he would cut down the dead trees. Then he and his neighbors would roll the giant trunks into piles to be burned. By pouring water through the ashes, his wife could obtain potash for making soap.

In New England much of the land was strewn with rocks left by glaciers. To make room for crops, the rocks had to be removed, so they were piled to make walls or rolled into gullies. Each season more stones came to the surface, and the backbreaking toil went on for generations.

Farming methods are crude.

During the colonial period, agriculture was held back by crude tools and poor methods of work. Most of the farmer's tools were the same kind that had been used elsewhere for thousands of years, including the axe, spade, hoe, fork, sickle, and flail. The colonist's plow and harrow were usually made of wood.

Animals helped do some tasks. Oxen were used more generally than horses for farm work. They were cheaper than horses and could stand more hardships.

But horses are faster, and for this reason farmers who could afford to do so used horses.

The average farmer had scarcely heard of improved breeds of livestock and improved varieties of plants. He knew little about how to feed livestock in winter. His cows yielded no milk and his hens laid no eggs in winter. A few farmers, who had more learning or money than the rest, experimented with new tools and methods. Thomas Jefferson was one of these. Among other things he developed an iron plowshare. Yet it did not come into wide use for a number of years because most farmers believed it would poison the land.

Most farms are small.

In every colony small or family-size farms were the most common. These were worked by the farmer's family, assisted, perhaps, by one or two indentured servants or Negro slaves. The farmer grew a variety of crops and livestock, chiefly for his family's use. When farm work was slack, the men and boys busied themselves with hunting, trapping, fishing, cutting firewood, making shingles, boiling maple sap, making shoes, and like activities. The women and girls helped with the outdoor work, spun thread and wove cloth, made the family clothes and the household linens, molded candles, made soap, and did scores of other household tasks. With all this hard work, the family on the average small farm produced little beyond its own needs and saw little, if any, cash. The typical small farm was, therefore, *a subsistence farm.*

Southerners develop plantation system.

The soil and climate of the coastal, or tidewater, region from Chesapeake Bay south was well suited for plantations. These large farms used gang labor to grow a great quantity of one crop for sale. In Virginia and Maryland the staple, or cash, crop was tobacco. In South Carolina and Georgia it was rice or indigo. The plantations also grew most of their own food and produced many other things for their own use. The typical planter had from fifty to a hundred slaves, but some had several hundred.

The wealthy planters were far outnumbered by small farmers who had only a few slaves or, more often, none at all. But the planters held all the political offices and controlled public affairs. They were also the social and intellectual leaders of their communities. They built beautiful mansions and

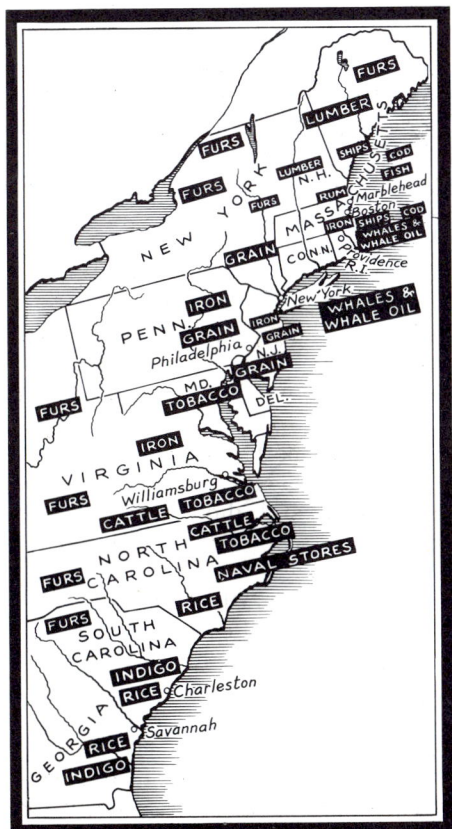

COLONIAL PRODUCTS
AND RESOURCES

decorated them with furniture, silver, and textiles from England. They also imported fine clothes, books, musical instruments, coaches, and other luxuries. A planter usually had his agent in England select the goods and pay for them out of the money due from the sale of his cash crop.

The large planters bought the tobacco, rice, or indigo produced by smaller planters in the neighborhood. They shipped both what they purchased and what they grew themselves to agents in London and Liverpool. The planters had to take whatever the buyer across the sea was willing to pay. They had no way of knowing whether their agent returned the full selling price, less his commission, or whether he kept part of it for himself. A similar suspicion arose in connection with purchases made by the agent. He might easily make more than a fair commission on the things he bought for a planter. Indeed, the planters often accused their agents of "selling cheap and buying dear."

Mixed farming prevails in the Middle Colonies.

In New York, Pennsylvania, New Jersey, and Delaware the climate and soil were well suited for mixed farming. (In mixed farming a variety of crops and livestock are raised, rather than a single staple.) Because they produced so much wheat, corn, oats, and barley, these colonies were spoken of as the "Bread Colonies." They also produced a surplus of livestock and shipped salted and smoked meat abroad.

Many farms in the Middle Colonies, particularly in New York, were large. The work was done chiefly by indentured servants. Some of the huge estates in New York were cultivated by tenant farmers. The tenants gave part of their crops to the landlord in payment for the use of the land.

(Above) "THE VOYAGEURS." *This spirited painting of fur traders was done in 1846 by Charles Deas, an American artist.*

(Right) PLAN OF A NEWLY CLEARED FARM IN AMERICA (*from an old print*). *Note the different types of fences (log fence, worm fence, post and rail fence), the dwelling house and wings, the log house, the barracks or Dutch barn, and the barn roofed with shingles.*

Other Industries Develop

Farmers try to obtain a cash income.

One of the farm family's hardest problems was to get cash to pay for items not produced at home. The owner of a plantation or a large estate usually could obtain a money income by raising a cash crop for export. The small farmer often could grow no more than his family needed. In the winter, or whenever farm work did not take all his time, he tried to earn money by trapping, cutting lumber, or in some other way. These nonfarm activities were especially important in New England, where the returns from farming were meager.

Farmers living inland found it difficult to get their products to market unless they lived near a navigable stream. Only the most valuable products, in a form easy to transport, could be carried overland. Surplus grain was either fed to livestock, which could be driven to market, or made into whiskey, which could be carried by pack horse. Pioneers living near the frontier usually were too far from market to sell anything except furs and skins.

Fur trade flourishes.

One of America's greatest natural resources was furs. Fur-bearing animals were numerous wherever there was virgin forest. Frontiersmen used furs and skins for clothing and blankets, just as Indians did. Both frontiersmen and Indians exchanged furs and skins for manufactured articles.

From the beginning the fur trade was one of the chief businesses in each of the colonies. Profits were enormous because the Indians would accept trinkets, cloth, and rum in exchange for valuable pelts. Traders also supplied the Indians with firearms and ammunition without thought to the safety of settlers in the back country.

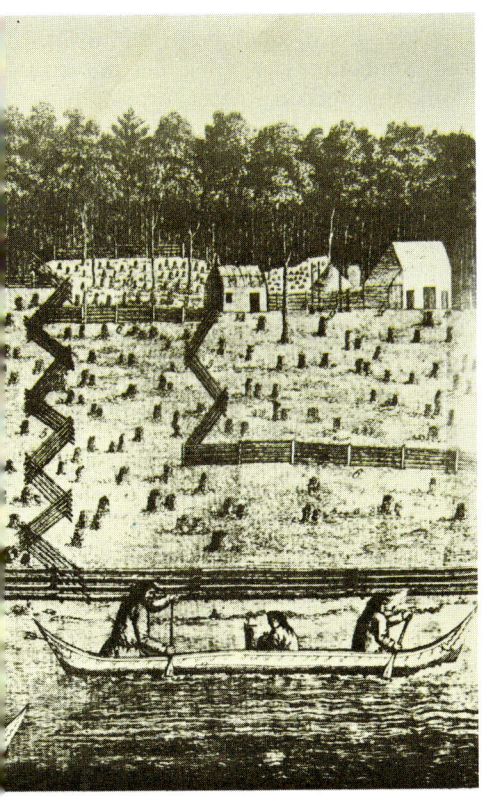

65

Forest products are in demand.

There was a large market for forest products on both sides of the Atlantic. The growing English navy needed a supply of naval stores—masts, spars, tar, pitch, rosin, and turpentine. England preferred to buy these from her colonies rather than from foreign countries. To increase the production of naval stores in the colonies, Parliament offered a bounty to the producer, which was paid in addition to the market price. The best trees for masts and spars were New England white pines. Tar, pitch, rosin, and turpentine were produced chiefly from the yellow pines of the Carolinas.

A large quantity of forest products was used at home. Shipyards took the greatest amount. The fishing industry and the rum industry used much lumber for barrels. In addition, lumber was needed for all kinds of buildings.

Lumber mills run by water power were built on nearly every stream. Such mills were especially numerous in New England. By 1720 there were over seventy sawmills on one small river in New Hampshire.

Fishing is a leading industry.

From the beginning fishing was important to colonists living near the coast. Close to shore were clams, oysters, scallops, lobsters, smelts, shad, alewives, and sardines. These were abundant and easily taken.

The Grand Banks are shallow fishing grounds that stretch in an arc from Long Island to Newfoundland. John Smith, who explored the New England coast in 1614, said truly that the fisheries were worth more than the gold mines of South America. Fishing soon became a leading New England industry. In every seaport town, land was assigned the fishermen for drying, salting, and packing fish. By 1700 New Englanders were shipping 10,000,000 pounds of fish a year.

Whaling became important late in the colonial period. Whales furnished oil for candles and lamps, whalebones for corsets, and ambergris for making perfume. At first many whales were caught near the shores of southern New England. Every village along the coast had watchers to report the appearance of a whale in the waters offshore. In time whales stopped coming in so close, and it was necessary to make long voyages in search of them. Colonial whalers from New Bedford and Nantucket frequently spent months in the Arctic and the South Atlantic.

Shipbuilding employs many artisans.

The building of ships for fishing and commerce was a leading industry along the northern coast, especially in New England. Nearby forests provided oak for timbers and boards, pine or fir for masts, and pitch, tar, and turpentine. From the farms came hemp for rope, while nearby mines supplied iron for chains and anchors. In scores of busy shipyards swift and beautiful vessels were built, at half the cost of similar ships from English yards. By the 1750's New England was launching some seventy new ships a year, New York and Pennsylvania forty-five, and the colonies to the south, forty.

Many American ships were sold abroad, chiefly in England. It is estimated that one third of the vessels flying the British flag in 1775 had been built in American shipyards. Most of these craft were of small size; they would hardly average 100 tons each.

Whaling scene painted by Benjamin F. West

Manufacturing is done by hand.

As we have seen, the average colonist lived on a fairly self-sufficing farm. He had little ready money and was unable to purchase manufactured goods imported from Europe. He either made the things he could not do without or bought them with his produce from a local craftsman.

At first manufacturing was carried on only during the farm slack season, and every farmer had to be a "Jack-of-all-trades." Gradually some began to specialize in making one kind of article. For example, a man who was especially good at making shoes might make them not only for his own family but also for some of his neighbors. Later he might begin to spend all his time in making shoes.

By the 1700's nearly all the colonies had a variety of small manufacturing businesses, including gristmills, sawmills, distilleries, tanneries, hat shops, shoeshops, woolen mills, ironworks, and blacksmith shops. Often the shop was in the owner's house or on his farm. The work was usually done by the owner, assisted by one or two indentured servants and perhaps a few young apprentices who worked for their keep. These businesses remained small because of the lack of skilled workers. Goods were made mostly for people that lived nearby. The better grades of furniture, tools, cloth, and clothing were usually imported from abroad. Toward the end of the colonial period, however, there were artist craftsmen who made articles of fine design and quality.

The colonial legislatures tried to encourage manufacturing. They offered premiums, or bounties, for the production of such items as iron, salt, silk, and woolen cloth. For example, Pennsylvania allowed 2 pence a gallon for rum exported. Sometimes the legislature appropriated money to pay the cost of building a mill. To get skilled workmen to migrate to America the lawmakers offered land grants. They also regulated wages, and prices and quality of certain manufactured goods.

Colonial Commerce Becomes Important

Colonial commerce is far-flung.

Over the years trading towns gradually developed in the colonies. They were located at points where goods could be brought in or sent out by water, for land transportation was extremely difficult. The largest commercial centers were Boston, Philadelphia, New York, and Charleston. There were also many smaller trading ports.

There was some trade between the thirteen colonies, but trade with the West Indies and Europe was far more important. The colonists carried on a lively trade with the West Indies. The West Indian planters specialized in growing sugar; they imported nearly all their foodstuffs and manufactured goods. American traders brought them great quantities of dried

67

KING'S COLLEGE, *established by royal charter in 1754, was rechartered thirty years later as Columbia College. In pre-Revolutionary days a medical school was added, which, during the early days of the Revolution, was used as a military hospital.*

ALEXANDER HAMILTON'S *education at King's College was interrupted by the Revolutionary War. When the war began he entered the army and in a short time was made captain.*

fish, grain, salt meat, lumber, naval stores, and some manufactures. In exchange they received sugar and molasses to be carried to England or made into rum in New England distilleries.

The southern colonies sent most of their surplus products direct to England. Ships sailing from Baltimore, Charleston, Savannah, and other southern ports carried tobacco, rice, indigo, pitch, tar, and turpentine. On the return trip they carried English manufactured goods to the same colonies.

The triangular trade develops.

In addition to the direct trade with the West Indies and with England, there were three-legged, or triangular, trade routes. These developed because the West Indies and England did not need all of the products which New England and the Middle Colonies had to sell.

Lack of money hinders colonial commerce.

The merchant-shipowner who conducted any kind of triangular trade usually came back home not only with a cargo but with gold and silver. The money represented his profit from the enterprise. Many colonial merchants grew wealthy and built fine homes in the seaport towns.

"Hard money" (gold and silver) was scarce in the English colonies. They had no gold or silver mines. The only way they could obtain gold and silver was to sell more goods abroad than they imported. But colonial exports consisted mainly of foodstuffs and raw materials. These did not bring enough to pay for the manufactured goods which were imported. Any gold or silver that came into the colonies had to be shipped out again to European merchants and bankers.

Because of the scarcity of money, the colonists fell back on barter, that is, exchanging goods for goods. They also used such articles as wampum, hides,

wheat, corn, cattle, and tobacco for money. The great difficulty in using articles of this type for money was that they had no fixed value. Uncertainty as to what they were worth delayed every transaction.

Paper money does not solve problem.

The colonies began to issue paper money in an attempt to get around the difficulties due to the lack of hard money. Paper money was used to pay the expenses of the government. When a colony issued paper money it declared that its treasurer would sometime, somehow redeem the paper for gold or silver. When a large amount of paper money was in circulation, people doubted its value. Yet the law made it "legal tender," which meant it had to be accepted in payment for goods or debts.

At times so much paper money was issued that its value fell, and as a result the prices of goods rose. In other words, there was a period of "inflation," in which money became cheap and goods became dear. Creditors, many of whom were English merchants, objected to accepting cheap money in payment for debts. On the other hand, debtors liked cheap money, for they found it an easy way to pay

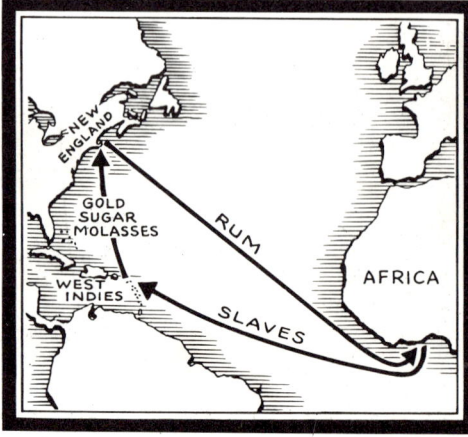

COLONIAL TRADE ROUTES

their debts. Farmers liked cheap money because it led to higher prices for their products and also because they were usually in debt to moneylenders and merchants.

Parliament was under pressure from British merchants and bankers to protect them from cheap colonial money. Finally (1764) Parliament forbade the colonies to issue any more paper money except in case of emergency.

England Regulates Colonial Business

England follows the mercantile theory.

An economic doctrine known as *mercantilism* shaped the attitude of European nations toward their colonies. This doctrine assumes that: (1) a nation should be self-sufficient, producing everything needed for peace or war, and (2) a nation's power and wealth depend largely on the amount of gold and silver it owns. A country which lacked deposits of precious metals could obtain them in two ways: (1) by working mines in other parts of the world, or (2) by building up a *favorable balance of trade.* An English economist of the 1600's said, "We must ever observe this rule: to sell more to

strangers yearly than we consume of theirs in value." If England exported to other countries goods worth more than the goods these countries sold to England, they would have to send gold or silver to make up the difference. Thus England would have a favorable balance of trade.

Englishmen expected the mother country to have a favorable balance of trade with its colonies. This condition was sure to result so long as England supplied the colonies with manufactured goods and bought from them only food and raw materials. Under this policy the colonies had to ship gold and silver to England to pay the balance or go into debt to English creditors. It was England's favorable balance of trade with the colonies that drained them of "hard" money and forced them to issue paper money.

Colonies benefit the mother country.

According to the mercantile theory, colonies were valuable possessions. They were expected to benefit the mother country in a number of ways:

1. By providing gold and silver.
2. By supplying food and raw materials, which could not be produced at home.

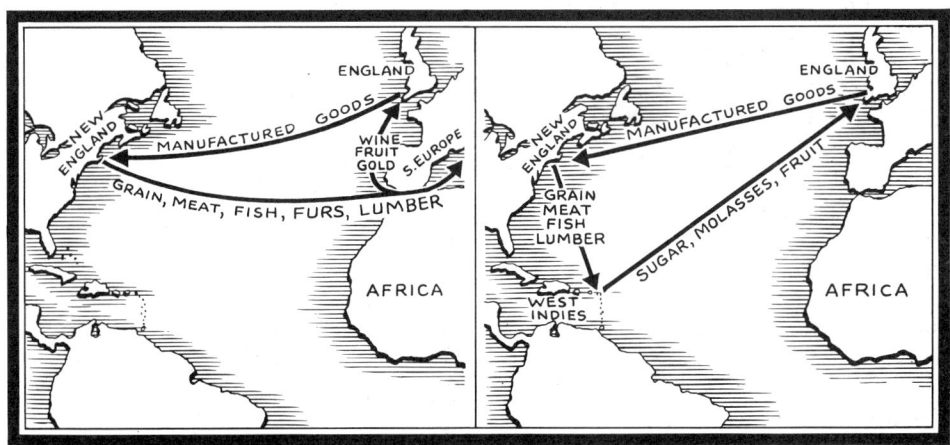

COLONIAL TRADE ROUTES

3. By furnishing a market for manufactured goods. This would stimulate the growth of industry in the mother country. People mistakenly thought that a colony would buy more manufactured goods if it had no manufactures of its own.

4. By encouraging the growth of a large merchant fleet. A merchant fleet would be a training school for the navy and would strengthen the navy in time of war.

5. By providing naval bases. This was especially important to England, with its large navy and world-wide trade.

England built an empire to obtain the benefits which the mercantile theory promised. So did other European states. Each nation adopted laws to control economic activities within its empire. Let us see how England tried to insure that its colonies would contribute as much as possible to its wealth and power.

The Navigation Acts cause irritation.

Under the laws of the United States today only American ships can carry products from one American port to another. The coast trade is a privilege reserved for American citizens. Yet long ago when Parliament passed similar laws, many Americans were displeased.

In 1651 Parliament restricted all trade within the empire to ships built and owned in England or the colonies. In addition, three fourths of every ship's crew had to be of English nationality. These laws greatly benefited the empire's shipbuilders and shipowners. A powerful merchant fleet flying the English flag was soon plowing the seas. The laws did not please American exporters, including farmers who raised things for sale abroad. They felt that the freight rates they had to pay were higher because there was no competition from foreign ships.

Another navigation act passed in 1660 stated that certain exports from the colonies, known as "enumerated articles," could be sent only to places in the British Empire. At first only five products were enumerated. But the list was increased from time to time until finally most of the raw materials produced in the colonies were included. The colonists felt that in limiting the market for their exports, Parliament was limiting their profits too.

An act passed in 1663 provided that all foreign goods bound for the colonies must be shipped from England. There import duties were collected. English merchants then re-exported the goods to the colonies. The extra handling and middlemen's profits raised the price of goods to the colonists.

By restricting colonial trade to English ships and English ports, the Navigation Acts made it easier for the Royal Navy to guard ships bound to or from the colonies from pirates and privateers. These were real dangers, but the Americans preferred to take their chances in order to trade directly with foreign countries. The colonists protested vigorously against the acts of 1660 and 1663 and often disobeyed them.

The Sugar and Molasses Act is ignored.

In 1733, in order to benefit the sugar growers of the British West Indies, Parliament passed what is known as the Sugar and Molasses Act. It required Americans to pay a heavy duty on molasses, rum, and sugar imported from the French and Dutch West Indies. Americans thought the act unreasonable, since the British West Indies did not produce enough sugar and molasses to supply the rum distilleries of New England. The distillers felt they could not stay in business if compelled to pay the duties on non-British sugar and molasses. So they took to smuggling. British customs officials in New England did not try very hard to enforce the law. Some accepted bribes from the smugglers in return for letting them alone.

Parliament limits manufacturing.

Small quantities of American manufactured products gradually began to go from one colony to another, to the West Indies, and to England. Thus they came into competition with goods made in England. When this happened, English manufacturers complained. Parliament then passed laws to limit manufacturing in the colonies. In 1699 the colonists were forbidden to send woolen goods beyond their own town or county boundaries. In 1732 they were forbidden to export hats or send them from one colony to another. This step was taken because the colonists could make beaver hats cheaper than the English hatters and were gaining the hat market from them. The growth of the colonial iron industry disturbed English ironmakers. To satisfy them Parliament passed an act in 1750 forbidding the colonists to enlarge or build rolling mills and steel furnaces. All these laws were intended to prevent colonial manufactures from competing with English manufactures in England and abroad and even in the American colonies. But as the laws were not carefully enforced, they had little effect.

The mercantile system benefits the Empire.

In making laws which restricted colonial commerce and manufacturing, the members of Parliament did not feel any ill will toward the colonies. They tried to consider the welfare of the empire as a whole. They encircled the entire empire with a wall of economic and military protection. Within this area, all business enterprise of whatever nature was to be in the hands of the king's subjects.

At the same time, the statesmen in London believed that the economic interests of the mother country were more important than those of her colonies. They thought that the mother country suffered loss if the products of its colonies went to other nations, or if the colonies bought from other nations goods which the mother country could supply. It was their plain duty, so they thought, to prevent this loss.

We should remember that colonial businessmen enjoyed a number of real advantages under British laws. Several important colonial products were given favored treatment in British markets— that is, smaller duties were charged on them than on similar products from foreign countries. Also, Parliament paid bounties to the colonists for the production of twenty-four raw materials, including supplies needed by the navy, such as lumber, hemp, and pitch. Then too the British navy carried on a continual fight against pirates. Without this protection American commerce with the West Indies and with Europe would have been impossible.

Mercantilism is a source of friction.

In spite of the advantages the mercantile system gave them, the colonists found it irritating. They were apt to overlook the advantages and to emphasize the disadvantages. They talked about their "natural right" to engage in honest enterprise as they saw fit. Many of them ignored the restrictions Parliament laid down. The stronger the colonies became, the more they resented being treated as the "tail to England's economic kite." When Parliament, in the dozen years following the defeat of France (1763), insisted that the trade laws be enforced, the colonists challenged the right of Parliament to control their affairs. The friction which developed during those years was one of the principal causes of the American Revolution.

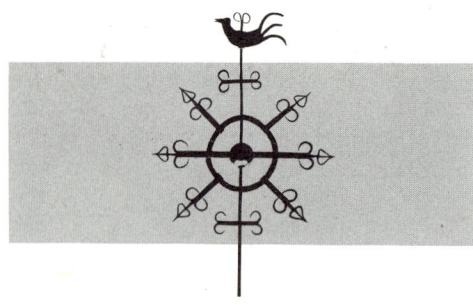

FOR EXPLANATION OR DEFINITION

artisan	legal tender
"Bread Colonies"	mercantilism
cash crop	naval stores
enumerated articles	plantation system
favorable balance	pre-emption laws
of trade	squatter
freeholder	subsistence farm
hard money	triangular trade

FOR REVIEW

1. Explain the system of landholding that developed in the colonies.

2. How did the pioneer farmer clear his land of trees?

3. What kind of tools were used by the colonial farmer?

4. What kinds of work were done on colonial farms by men and boys? By women and girls?

5. (a) Describe the plantation system in the southern colonies. (b) What were the staple crops? (c) How did the planters market these crops?

6. (a) Which colonies raised grain for export? (b) Why did frontier farmers convert their extra grain into whiskey?

7. Describe farming conditions in the Middle Colonies.

8. What forest products were in great demand?

9. Why and how did many New Englanders turn to the sea for a living?

10. What types of small manufacturing developed in the colonies?

11. How did the colonial legislatures endeavor to encourage manufacturing?

12. Enumerate the chief articles of colonial commerce.

13. (a) Why did the colonists find it difficult to secure "hard money"? (b) Why did the issuance of paper money fail to solve their difficulties?

14. (a) Explain the "mercantile theory of trade." (b) How were the colonies expected to benefit the mother country?

15. (a) What was the purpose of the English Acts of Trade and Navigation? (b) How did they help or hurt colonial commerce and industry?

16. (a) State the provisions of the Sugar and Molasses Act of 1733. (b) What was its purpose? (c) State objections to it.

17. (a) What advantages did the British laws give to colonial businessmen? (b) Why did the operation of the mercantile system become a source of friction between England and the colonies?

FOR FURTHER STUDY AND DISCUSSION

1. What is meant by the statement: "There was a natural division of work between the old country and the new"?

2. Does the United States today seek to maintain a favorable balance of trade?

3. Why did England encourage colonial production of pig iron but oppose production of finished iron products?

FOR INDIVIDUAL OR GROUP ACTIVITIES

1. Assuming that you were a colonial exporter, prepare a five-minute comment on the Navigation Acts.

2. Assign committees to prepare a special report on the whaling industry of New England and the tobacco, indigo, and rice industries of the South.

3. If you were a colonial representative in England, what representations would you make to the British government concerning the Navigation Acts? If you were a member of Parliament, what reply would you make?

4. Present a report to the class on colonial currency. Helpful source: L. M. Hacker, *The Shaping of the American Tradition.*

Baltimore, Maryland, in 1752, from a sketch by John Moale

5. AN AMERICAN SOCIETY EMERGES

The Europeans, on coming to America, left behind them, in large part, the traditions of the past, the institutions and customs of their fatherland; they built a society which has analogies with those of Europe, but which at bottom is radically different.——Alexis de Tocqueville, 1835

England's Colonies Are Rapidly Peopled

Colonial population grows rapidly.

In 1700 the English colonies contained about 300,000 settlers. Seventy-five years later the population had increased to between 2,500,000 and 3,000,000. This tremendous growth was due partly to a high birth rate and partly to immigration. Though the people had settled all along the Atlantic seaboard, the good trading centers were the first towns to become heavily populated.

During the colonial period and for a long time afterward, American families were large. Families of eight, ten, or twelve children were rather common. Children helped in the hard work of the home and the farm. Thus the more numerous they were, the more likely the family was to get ahead. The custom of early marriage also favored large families. Even though many children died in infancy, the average family raised more children than is the case today. It is estimated that at least two thirds of the colonists at the time of the Revolution were not immigrants but descendants of earlier comers.

Immigrants came for various reasons.

Some people came from Europe to the English colonies in search of religious freedom. Among them were Pilgrims, Puritans, Quakers, German and Swiss Mennonites, Huguenots, Roman Catholics, and Jews. Some came as officials, ministers of the Gospel, or missionaries to the Indians. Some came for love of adventure. Others came to escape political persecution. The largest number came in the hope of making a better living. The custom of giving the newcomer fifty or one hundred acres of land attracted the poor working people and peasants of Europe. Here they could become independent; in Europe it was practically impossible to reach that goal.

Crossing the Atlantic was perilous.

Immigration to America was held back by the cost and dangers of the journey. At best the trip from Europe required six to eight weeks; if storms drove the ship from its course, the voyage might last three or four months. There were no regular lines of ships, no regular dates of sailing, and no laws to regulate fares or protect the safety and health of the passengers. The traveler, after making a bargain with the sea captain for passage, had to wait in port, possibly for several weeks, until the ship was ready to sail and winds were favorable. Meanwhile, he was using up his money and the store of food he had bought for the journey.

Ships were small and completely lacking in comfort. Sanitary arrangements were crude. The sick and the well lived, slept, and ate in a crowded hold. The supply of fresh water, always very limited, became dangerously low if the journey was prolonged by lack of wind or by stormy weather. Contagious diseases frequently broke out. It was not unusual for half or more of those on board to die from smallpox, measles, or dysentery. Young children, weak mothers, and the sick were almost sure to perish under the hardships of a long voyage.

Poor people came as indentured servants.

Many farmers and plantation owners were so eager for laborers that they paid the cost of the voyage for immigrants who would work for them a period of years. In exchange for their passage adults had to serve from three to seven years; children, until they came of age. The contract between master and servant was known as an *indenture;* this gives us the phrase "indentured servant." About one third of the immigrants to the English colonies came as indentured servants.

The terms of the indenture were harsh, and the servant little better off than a slave. But when the time of servitude was up, he was free. He usually received a suit of clothes and some farm implements from his master. Most colonies allowed fifty acres of land to each freedman. Many freedmen became prosperous farmers or mechanics. Others remained day laborers.

Most indentured servants came here gladly, but some adults and children were carried here against their will and forced to become servants. Kidnapers stalked the streets of London and other seaports in the British Isles. They made a business of hustling their victims into ships bound for America. Upon arrival here the captain delivered his unwilling passengers to whoever would pay him most.

Some indentured servants came from English prisons. To avoid the expense of keeping offenders in prison, the authorities frequently sentenced them to be transported to America. Some were in prison because of their religious or political ideas, many because of debts, others because of very minor offenses, a few because of serious crimes. Those sent to America had to serve masters in the colonies for a term of years, usually seven, and were then given their liberty. Some 50,000 prisoners were brought to the American colonies. They were known as "His Majesty's Seven-Year Passengers."

Slave merchants brought in Negroes.

Until after 1700 white indentured servants were more numerous than Negro slaves. The colonists from Maryland southward, however, gradually came to depend on slave labor, especially on the plantations. Throughout the 1700's the importation of slaves increased rapidly.

Negro slavery existed in all of the colonies, but three fourths of the slaves were in the five southern colonies—Maryland, Virginia, North Carolina, South Carolina, and Georgia. Slave labor drove free labor from the plantations. As indentured servants gained their freedom and as new immigrants arrived, they avoided the plantation regions. They settled in the northern colonies, or else pushed beyond the plantation area in the South, to make homes on the frontier.

The Frontier Is a Melting Pot and a Leveler

Life on the frontier is hard and bare.

The differences between life in America and life in Europe were greatest in the back country and on the frontier. At the outset the frontier was the coastal strip itself. The colonists had to adjust themselves to the wilderness or die. They learned from the Indians how to grow corn, to make bark houses, canoes, and snowshoes, to find game, to tan skins and shape them into clothes and moccasins, to clear the land by girdling trees, and to use the native plants for food and medicine. They had to be hunters, fishermen, farmers, and all-round craftsmen. Everyone—man, woman, and child—had to work hard. There was little time for idleness or recreation or cultural pursuits. Gradually, as a group of settlers got well established, life became easier and more comfortable. Yet by our standards it was still a life of toil.

Meanwhile, just beyond their settlement, newcomers were going through a similar struggle to subdue the wilderness. Whoever they were, and wherever they settled, the first settlers, or pioneers, lived much the same kind of life.

The coastal plain is settled.

As the population grew, the frontier was pushed westward and northward. The river valleys were settled first and then the hillier and less fertile land in between. By 1775 most of the land as far west as the Appalachians was occupied, and settlers were trickling through the first highlands. In the Carolinas and Georgia, the Piedmont (the plateau between the coastal plain and the Appalachians) was only partly settled. There were still great tracts of virgin forest lying between the river valleys. Yet even here frontiersmen had penetrated the mountains and settled in what is now Kentucky and Tennessee.

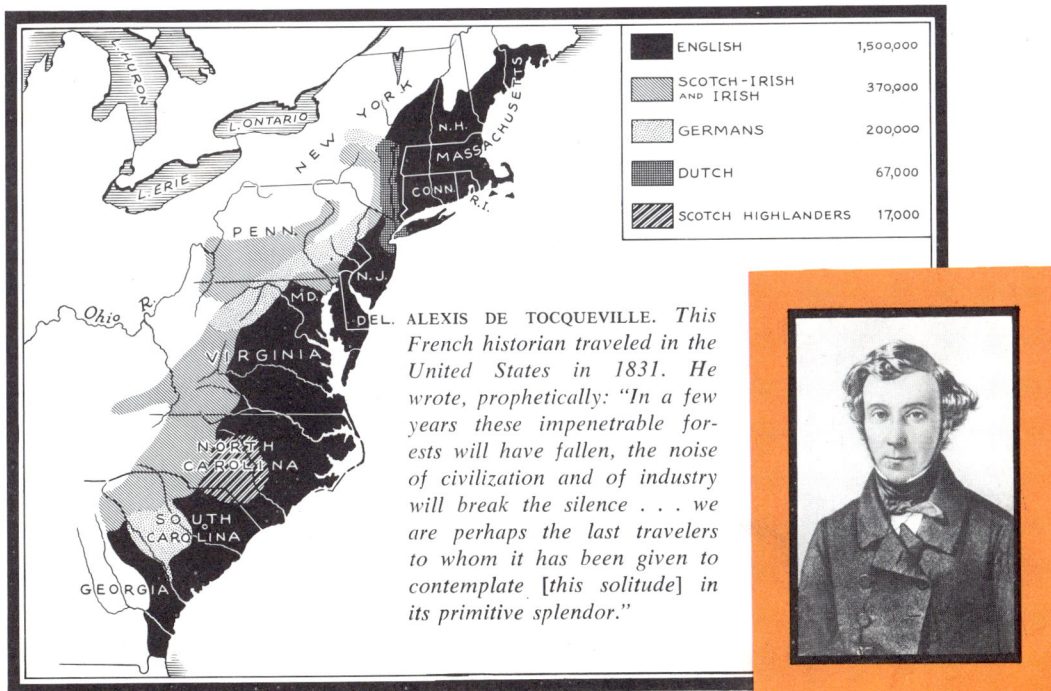

ENGLISH	1,500,000
SCOTCH-IRISH AND IRISH	370,000
GERMANS	200,000
DUTCH	67,000
SCOTCH HIGHLANDERS	17,000

ALEXIS DE TOCQUEVILLE. *This French historian traveled in the United States in 1831. He wrote, prophetically: "In a few years these impenetrable forests will have fallen, the noise of civilization and of industry will break the silence . . . we are perhaps the last travelers to whom it has been given to contemplate* [this solitude] *in its primitive splendor."*

NATIONAL ORIGINS OF WHITE SETTLERS

Interior of a mansion, Philadelphia, 1761

Marble-topped mahogany mixing table

Walnut and gilt mirror

The frontier becomes a melting pot.

In the beginning every settler was a pioneer. Later immigrants had a choice—they could go to an area already settled or to the frontier. The frontier attracted three groups: (1) adventurous young men from the older settlements, (2) new immigrants who were too poor to buy land in the older settlements, and (3) indentured servants who had completed their terms of service. In New England the frontier was settled, as a rule, by young people of English stock, usually of the Puritan faith, who moved west or north from the coastal settlements. Elsewhere people of many nationalities and religions mingled on the frontier.

The frontier fosters democracy.

Down the whole length of the frontier, people lived in much the same way. All were poor and all had to rely on their own efforts. All faced the same difficulties and dangers. All had about the same opportunities. A man was judged by his courage, strength, skill, resourcefulness, and his neighborliness in time of trouble. Differences in nationality, religious belief, and social position counted less than anywhere else in the world.

The spirit of democracy which developed on the frontier was not forgotten when a region grew out of its frontier stage. The small farmers, who made up nine tenths of the white population of the colonies, usually owned their own land and believed they were just as good as anyone else. They considered farming as a dignified way of life. However poor they might be, they were independent and filled with self-respect.

Living Conditions Vary

Social classes are based on wealth.

In Europe society was divided into hereditary social classes. Those who

COLONIAL ELEGANCE

worked with their hands were looked down upon. There was little chance for a poor man to rise above the class into which he was born. Rich businessmen had less prestige than big landholders with an ancient family name. Europeans brought the class system with them to America. But here it was easier to rise from one class to another. "Birth," wrote Benjamin Franklin, "cannot be carried to a worse market than that of America, where people do not inquire concerning a stranger, 'What is he?' but 'What can he do?'"

The upper class in the colonies lived much like people of similar means and social standing in England. The men occupied themselves in business, in managing plantations and estates, in government, military affairs, or in the professions. But colonial aristocrats were far more likely to be self-made men than were English aristocrats. The colonial aristocracy was based on wealth, not birth. Men who made fortunes in commerce or land speculation were constantly moving into it.

The great middle class of colonists consisted chiefly of small farmers. It also included small businessmen, sea captains, minor officials, overseers, clergymen, and skilled craftsmen. Members of this group did not have much time for cultural activities. Nor did they have money enough to copy the upper class in dress, houses, and recreation. Yet some of them made a fortune and climbed into the upper class.

The lowest class included unskilled laborers, indentured servants, and Negroes. Most Negroes, being slaves, had no chance to rise in the social scale. Nor did a freed Negro have much hope of becoming really independent. White freedmen and laborers, if young and strong, could usually save enough money after a while to become farmers on the frontier. Then, like their neighbors, they might through their own efforts move up in social standing.

Oak cradle, 17th century

Painted pine and oak cabinet, early 18th century

New England kitchen

COLONIAL SIMPLICITY

(Above) PORT ROYAL PARLOR, *Winterthur Museum. Port Royal was a house built in 1762 in Frankford, near Philadelphia, by Edward Stiles, a prosperous West India merchant.* (Far left) THE ENTRANCE HALL *of the Corbit house, Odessa, Delaware (1772).* (Left) A BEDROOM *of a New York 18th century house now in the Winterthur Museum.*

Homes are of various styles.

The first settlers had to be content for a time with crude shelters such as bark houses, lean-tos, and thatched huts. As soon as possible these were replaced with more substantial houses. Most pioneers built a one-room log cabin, with a huge stone fireplace at one end to cook the meals and furnish warmth and light. Oiled paper let in daylight through one or two wall openings. These were protected at night with heavy wooden shutters. A ladder led to a low loft, where some of the household slept.

As time passed, prosperous families put up larger, more attractive houses, with glass windows and a fireplace in every room. In New England, houses were usually built on a frame of beams, with clapboards on the outside and wood paneling on the inside. In the Middle Colonies the Dutch and German settlers preferred houses of stone or brick. In the South the planters often built a very large log house, lined it with paneling, and covered the outside with clapboards. During the 1700's splendid mansions were built in the growing towns.

Furnishings reflect wealth.

A farmer's house usually contained only plain homemade furniture. The floors were bare except for small homemade rugs. Tableware consisted of wooden, earthen, and pewter dishes, and pewter spoons. Among the customary furnishings were a spinning wheel, loom, churn, candle mold, and several sizes of iron kettles.

The houses of the wealthy were beautified with carved or painted woodwork and with wallpaper, floor coverings, draperies, and upholstered furniture. Their dining rooms contained china, glass, and fine silver. As a rule, these articles were either imported or copied from English models.

This elaborate 18TH CENTURY DOORWAY *was made for a Massachusetts tavern.*

Clothing is usually homemade.

Most of the colonists dressed plainly in coarse, heavy clothing, which was made at home out of homespun material. Shirts and underwear were made of linen. Breeches, skirts, and work clothes were often made of linsey-woolsey, a coarse mixture of wool and linen. Deerskin, buckskin, and lambskin were also much used for outer garments, particularly on the frontier. Stockings might be knitted from worsted or cotton or made from cloth. Shoes were heavy, with double soles. In summer most of the farming people went barefoot.

From the beginning the well to do ordered fine fabrics (silks, cottons, wool broadcloth, linens) and clothes from England. They desired to be in the latest fashion and to possess many changes of costume. The love of costly clothes kept many planters in debt to English merchants.

81

The farm family provides its own food.

Food was plentiful in colonial households, and the housewife then was acquainted with most of the meats, vegetables, and fruits that we use today. The greatest difficulty was in keeping perishable foods. Except in cold weather, meat and fish had to be used at once, or else smoked, salted, or pickled. The winter diet was heavy and rather tiresome. It consisted of meat, fish, pies, puddings, dried and preserved fruit, pickled or salted vegetables, dried beans and peas, and a few vegetables that can be kept in a storage pit. Corn was the principal cereal. The only bread used in most homes was corn bread.

The colonists were great hunters and fishermen. Deer, wild turkeys, geese, pigeons, rabbits, and squirrels were always to be found. In the streams and ponds were many kinds of fish; in the bays were oysters; and along the shores were lobsters, crabs, and clams. Because meat and fish were so abundant, several varieties were commonly served at a single meal.

The small farmer could rarely afford to buy spices, coffee, tea, cocoa, cane sugar, and other imported luxuries. For sweetening he and his family depended mainly on maple sugar and on honey. For seasoning they used herbs. Substitutes for tea were made from herbs. Many families, especially those in the back country, produced or caught everything that went on their tables except salt.

The colonists used alcoholic beverages freely. Beer and cider were made in most homes. Apple and peach brandy, cherry cordial, and rum were also widely used. Rum was especially popular among deep-sea fishermen and others exposed to severe weather.

Amusements are simple.

Life in the colonies, except for the few who achieved wealth, was hard and serious. For adults, and even for children, there was little time for pleasure. In fact, the religious beliefs of many were against amusement for its own sake. Recreation most often took the form of a change of occupation. For example, the farmer went hunting, trapping, or fishing, or joined his neighbors in a harvesting or husking bee or a barn- or house-raising.

A log-rolling was one kind of work bee. When a farmer had cut down trees and was ready to drag them from the land to clear a field, his neighbors came to help him. While the men rolled the heavy logs into a pile to be burned, the women barbecued a steer or a pair of deer over an open fire and prepared piles of corn bread. After dinner there were sports such as shooting contests, wrestling, and foot races. These were followed by country dances like the Virginia reel.

Baptisms and weddings gave people a chance for feasting, drinking, and seeing each other. Church services, court sessions, and in New England the annual town meeting, also served to bring people together and give them an opportunity to exchange news and gossip.

The county fair was an important social occasion, although its main purpose was trade. Fairs were held in all the colonies, except in New England, where they were frowned upon. Fairs usually lasted three days and featured horse racing and cockfighting. Much of the entertainment was provided by traveling performers such as jugglers, acrobats, and puppeteers.

Planters and other members of the upper class had more elaborate social pleasures than the ordinary colonist. Their big houses were often filled with company. They gave brilliant balls and parties. They spent much time playing cards, racing horses, and fox hunting. George Washington, like other planters, was proud of his horses and his hounds. His diary tells us that he went fox hunting fifteen times in January and February, 1769. Thus we see that members of the colonial aristocracy patterned their social life upon that of the English gentry.

City life resembles that in England.

By the early 1700's a number of colonial seaports had become thriving commercial centers. All had many well-to-do families who lived in beautiful homes and were acquainted with the best European thought and culture. By 1750 the four largest cities—Boston (population, 16,000), Philadelphia (13,-000), New York (13,000), and Charleston (8,000)—were as elegant as almost any city in England or France.

We would not think them elegant. Most of the streets were unpaved. Refuse was not collected but was thrown into the streets, where roaming hogs ate what was edible. There were no sewers. People obtained water from open wells, which were so polluted as to cause many cases of serious illness. Since most of the buildings were of wood, the fire hazard was great. When a building caught fire, the neighbors fought the blaze with water carried in buckets. If the flames spread, houses had to be blown up to prevent the loss of the entire town. There was no police force. A military watch made the rounds by night, carrying a lantern for light.

Family life is closely knit.

In colonial America the members of the family group depended on one another far more than is the case today. Most of their activities, whether economic or social, centered in the home. The home was important for religious observances, such as family worship, and for education, since many children had no instruction except from their parents. There was little social life outside the home. Moreover, the family cared for its members in sickness and old age. Apart from his family, a free individual had no security, for there were very few institutions to care for the sick and the needy.

Not many persons could support themselves except as part of a family group, unless they were willing to be servants. A farmer had to have the help of his wife and children. A shopkeeper, too, could not get ahead without the combined labor of himself, his wife, and his children. A widow and her children sometimes carried on a farm or a business, but a single woman could not do so. Since marriage was the road to economic independence, men and women married young and promptly remarried if the marriage partner died.

SHIPBUILDING *along the East River, New York, early 1700's*

Young people choose their own mates.

In Europe upper- and middle-class marriages were generally arranged by the parents. In America marriages were not usually arranged by parents, except among the upper class. In America it was easy for young people to get a start and this encouraged them to marry for love. Courtship, however, was carried on in the presence of the girl's family and thus required their consent.

Children are strictly brought up.

Children had none of the freedom they enjoy today. While they were probably loved as much then as now, parental love was expressed differently. Caresses were not often given. Everyone believed that "children should be seen and not heard," and "to spare the rod is to spoil the child." Prompt obedience was demanded.

In most families children from an early age were kept busy helping their parents and had little time for play. When ten or twelve years of age, a boy might be placed as an apprentice to learn a trade. His hours of work and duties would be the same as an adult's. At the same age the daughter of poor parents might be placed as a domestic servant. She would work all her waking hours in return for her keep.

Colonists Are Deeply Religious

Nearly all of the white settlers were Christians. While they were divided into numerous denominations, each with its own doctrines and forms of worship, they had many common beliefs. The only non-Christians were a small number of Jews who lived in the larger seaports. They too shared many of the ideas and values of the Christians, since Christianity was derived from Judaism. Among the basic ideas of our Judaic-Christian heritage is the supreme worth and dignity of the individual human being. Every man is precious. All men are sons of the same Father, members of one human family. It is a man's duty to do justice, to be generous, to help the unfortunate, to show mercy to the weak, to be honest and truthful, and to love his neighbor as himself. A man must strive to do good and to make the good prevail in his family and wherever he is.

The colonists did not always agree, any more than we do today, as to how these great ethical principles are to be applied. Yet the Judaic-Christian tradition helped to unite people of different classes, sects, and nationality. Moreover, these principles inspired some to fight injustice and exploitation and to stand up for the rights of the underprivileged. The effort to build a more democratic society, which has continued to our own day, is based upon man's loyalty to these ideals.

Religious customs are observed.

Those who came to the New World to escape religious persecution were people to whom religion meant a great deal. Such a group were the Puritans, who settled in New England. The Puritans insisted on regular church attendance, daily reading of the Bible, family prayers, and a God-fearing life. The Sabbath was strictly observed. Unnecessary labor on the Sabbath was forbidden, and the Lord's day was supposed to be spent in going to church, praying, and reading the Bible. Puritans did not play cards, dance, or attend the theater. They had very strict ideas about courtship and marriage. Young and old were expected to live a "godly, righteous, and sober life."

All groups who had been persecuted for their beliefs took their religion seriously, though few were quite so strict as the Puritans. In addition to going to Sunday and to midweek church services (if a church was with-.

in reach), many families held devotions at home. At the beginning of every meal the head of the family, or an honored guest, offered prayers. After breakfast, and again before bedtime, the family gathered for a reading of the Scriptures and for prayers. If there were servants or slaves in the household, they too attended the devotions.

Nine colonies have a state church.

An established, or state, church receives part of its support from public taxation. In Massachusetts, New Hampshire, and Connecticut, the Puritan, or Congregational, church was established. In New York, Maryland, Virginia, North and South Carolina, and Georgia, the Anglican church was established, although the Anglicans were soon outnumbered by members of other sects. In four colonies—Rhode Island, Pennsylvania, New Jersey, and Delaware—church and state were entirely separate. These colonies were the first places in the Western world to put all churches on an equal footing.

Freedom of worship grows.

For many years freedom of religion was severely limited in most colonies. In those with a state church, only members of that church had the right to vote and to hold office. Clergymen of other faiths were often barred from conducting public services. Several colonies, moreover, tried to keep Roman Catholics, Quakers, Jews, and unbelievers from settling within their borders.

Rhode Island was the only colony with complete religious freedom. Settlers there could worship as they wished. A man's political rights did not depend upon his religious beliefs. All kinds of believers were welcome, even those with no religion. Pennsylvania and Delaware, under the leadership of William Penn, offered almost as much religious liberty as Rhode Island. Penn

TOURO SYNAGOGUE *at Newport, Rhode Island, was built in the 1700's.*

in his colonies gave political rights to all who professed belief in God.

In 1689 Parliament passed the Toleration Act granting freedom of worship in England to nearly all Protestants. Soon after, most of the colonies passed a similar act. This was a big step forward. By the end of the colonial period there was more religious freedom in the thirteen colonies than anywhere else in the world. Most of the colonies, however, still barred Roman Catholics, Unitarians, and Jews from voting and holding office. Even after the Revolution a long time passed before every state gave them full political rights.

Intellectual Interests Grow

The chief motive for education was religious.

In the 1600's the average colonial parent was satisfied if his children learned to read the Bible and knew the elements of their religion. At that time the chief motive for education was religious. Protestants believed firmly that everyone should read the Scriptures for himself. Education was generally left to the home and the church. Many parents taught their children at home.

Orphans were bound out as apprentices and were instructed by their masters. If parents or guardian neglected a child's education, he was likely to grow up in ignorance. In some denominations, however, the clergymen saw to it that all the children in their flocks learned to read.

A colonial schoolmaster and pupils

The early colonial schools were parish schools, intended to teach a particular religious faith and supported by members of that faith. This was true from one end of the colonies to the other. Wherever there were enough people of a given denomination to support a school, one was pretty sure to be started.

Education was most widespread in the Puritan colonies, and there the schools were partly supported by taxation. Since their church and state were closely united, the Puritans found it natural to spend public funds on their schools. In 1647 the Massachusetts legislature passed what has been called the most important school law in American history. The act required that every town having fifty families provide an elementary school, and every town having one hundred families provide also a Latin grammar school to prepare boys for Harvard College. Thus Massachusetts made education a community responsibility. Each of the other Puritan colonies soon adopted a similar law.

Nonchurch education appears.

In addition to parish schools, other kinds gradually appeared. One type, the neighborhood or "field" school, was supported by a group of neighbors who joined together to hire a teacher for their children. The school might be held in a home or in a building put up on a piece of waste land (an "old field"). The teacher might be a man who traveled from place to place on horseback, finding work for a few months wherever he could.

In more thickly settled communities, most children started their education in a "dame school." In the dame school a housewife, for a small fee, taught children to read and count. The dame school met in her kitchen. Some children went on from the dame school to a "school of the three r's," or "writing school," where they learned to write and do arithmetic. Boys preparing for college continued their education in a Latin grammar school, where they studied Latin, Greek, mathematics, and religion. The Latin school was often conducted by a minister in his home.

Another kind of private school, the academy, appeared late in the colonial period in some of the larger towns. The academy was the forerunner of the modern high school. In addition to the classics its pupils could study English,

French, bookkeeping, surveying, and navigation. Unlike the Latin school, the academy took girls as well as boys.

Apprenticeship is one type of education.

Parents who wished a son to learn a skilled trade, such as carpentry or shoemaking, bound him out as an apprentice when he was eleven or twelve. He went to live in his master's family and worked for his master until he reached twenty-one. In addition to teaching the boy his trade, the master was expected to teach him enough reading, writing, and figuring to enable him to practice the trade with skill and understanding.

Colleges are founded to train ministers.

Colleges were established in several of the colonies. The first was Harvard, founded at Cambridge, Massachusetts, in 1636. The second was the College of William and Mary, founded at Williamsburg, Virginia, in 1693. Six other colleges were established before the Revolution. All except one were chiefly interested in preparing young men for the ministry. The exception was the Academy of Philadelphia, founded by Benjamin Franklin in 1751. It gave particular attention to English, the sciences, geography, government, and history—subjects which received little or no attention in other colonial colleges.

Books offer the means of self-education.

Many poor people who came to America developed a hunger for education. If they knew how to read, they had the key to unlock the intellectual treasures of the ages. Travelers from Europe who came here during the 1700's were impressed by the amount of reading that was done. They noted that the common people were more alert than those of the same rank in Europe and more likely to be able to read.

Yet most Americans were too poor to buy books. The only books possessed by the average family were the Bible or Book of Common Prayer, a cookbook, and a few old almanacs. A few wealthy men had private libraries of a thousand or more volumes. Benjamin Franklin started the first subscription library in the colonies (1732); anyone might read in the library room, and those who helped support the library might take books out. Subscription libraries were soon opened in other cities. By the time of the Revolution several cities also had public libraries.

Newspapers are eagerly read.

During the 1600's the only newspapers seen in the colonies were occasional papers brought from London. In 1704 a weekly newspaper of four small pages began to appear in Boston. It was not long before papers appeared in other towns. Newspapers were usually owned and printed by the same person. For foreign news the papers depended on personal letters from abroad supplied by their readers. Most of the space was given to essays copied from English publications. Poor and dull as they seem to us, colonial newspapers had a wide influence. The average circulation was only a few hundred copies. However, each copy had a large number of readers. Many who did not subscribe to a paper went to the nearest tavern to read it. By 1775 there were about forty colonial newspapers. That year saw the birth of the first colonial daily.

Almanacs are popular.

A kind of publication familiar to nearly all the colonists was the almanac. It was a curious combination of facts about history and the sun, moon, and tides, observations on the weather, jokes, puzzles, interest tables, and advice on farming. Some newspaper owners published an almanac yearly. Few families were too poor or too far from town to have at least one. The most

WITCHCRAFT TRIAL *in Salem Village, 1692. The accusers, most of them young girls, are writhing, screaming, swooning. The defendant, George Jacobs, the white-haired man at lower right, was hanged.*

famous of the colonial almanacs is Franklin's *Poor Richard's Almanac,* prized for its witty sayings, proverbs, and common-sense advice.

The postal system is established.

The development of a postal system gradually linked the colonies together intellectually. As early as 1672 postriders carried mail between Boston and New York, making the round trip about once each month. A postal service was established between Boston, New York, and Philadelphia in 1691, but the mails were infrequent and no one knew when they could be expected. As late as 1760 there were only eight mails a year from Philadelphia to towns south of the Potomac. In the mid-1700's the British government set up a postal system serving all the colonies. Fairly regular mail routes connected the larger towns. For twenty

years Benjamin Franklin served as deputy postmaster-general for the colonies. He reduced postal rates and encouraged the circulation of newspapers and magazines.

Superstition is widespread.

In colonial times the people generally followed the changes of the moon in planting their crops and held firmly to hundreds of other superstitions. Many believed that demons existed and thought that men and women might bargain with them to obtain magic powers. A witch was one supposed to have contact with a demon, who gave the power to cause injury to livestock and to persons. This notion had caused terrible persecutions in Europe for centuries. In 1692 at Salem, Massachusetts, a hundred and fifty persons were accused of witchcraft and imprisoned. Twenty of them were executed. Some of the more prominent of the witch hunters later realized their error and made public apology for it. There was no further persecution of witches in the colonies after this outbreak.

Medical science is in its infancy.

Against sickness and death the colonists were almost helpless. Disease germs had not been discovered, and people thought that sickness was due to such things as night air, bad blood, witchcraft, and evil spirits. Nothing was known about correct diet and very little about hygiene and sanitation. Epidemics were frequent in every community. It is probable that nearly half the children died before reaching their tenth year. Deaths of mothers in childbirth were common. A large proportion of mothers died of exhaustion while their youngest children were still small. Against these disasters people depended on primitive medicines and on treatments, such as sweating and bleeding, which often hastened death. As late as

1799 George Washington, during his last illness, was drained of two quarts of blood.

Physicians had little opportunity in America for training. Many had merely served an apprenticeship to a physician, tending his office, helping him prepare medicines, and going with him sometimes on home visits. After serving the required period, the apprentice set out for himself, usually with very little knowledge of the human body. A physician who tried to perform an autopsy was likely to be prevented by an angry crowd. About 1750 signs of a change in attitude toward medical service could be seen in the larger towns. At this time the physicians in Philadelphia and New York began to take their apprentices into laboratories where human bodies were dissected. In 1765 a medical school, the first in America, was established in Philadelphia.

The scientific method gains ground.

In the later colonial period scientific research attracted a small but growing number of men. Because colonial colleges neglected science, Americans seeking training in science usually went abroad to study. Some, however, like the Quaker farmer, John Bartram, were self-taught. Bartram won recognition in Europe as the world's greatest "natural botanist." David Rittenhouse of Pennsylvania became known overseas as an astronomer and mathematician. John Mitchell of Virginia won eminence in agriculture, botany, and medicine. The most famous American scientist of the colonial period was Benjamin Franklin. In 1743 he and other learned men founded the American Philosophical Society. Its purpose was to promote the applied sciences and scientific experiment. The Society opened a library where Americans could consult the latest European works of science. It encouraged the founding of museums of natural history and held conferences of scientists. The world of science and the machine was starting on its way.

DR. WILLIAM GLEASON, *a Connecticut physician, takes the pulse of an unseen patient.*

The American Character

Americans differ from Europeans.

By 1775 a distinctly American society was taking shape. At some points it was much like English society. The wealthy merchants and planters lived much as the merchants and landed gentry in England lived. But the great majority of Americans—the small farmers and frontiersmen—were quite different from the plain people of Europe. They were more independent and self-respecting. All of them were expecting to get ahead by hard work and enterprise. They resented the wealthy aristocrats on the plantations and in the cities. They wanted to build a society in which every man might rise from the bottom to the top of the ladder. The idea that all are entitled to equal opportunity was becoming a part of the American character.

Americans are optimistic and enterprising.

The abundance of land and the absence of a hereditary class system helped produce a distinctly American character. No matter how poor he might be, the immigrant felt he had chances here for a good future. St. John Crevecoeur, a French gentleman who came to the colonies about 1769, wrote:

The rich stay in Europe, it is only the middling and poor that emigrate. . . . Everything tends to regenerate them; new laws, a new mode of living, a new social system—here they become men. . . . A European, when he first arrives, seems limited in his intentions as well as his views; but he very suddenly alters his scale. He no sooner breathes our air than he forms new schemes, and embarks on designs he never would have thought of in his own country. . . . He begins to feel the effects of a sort of resurrection; hitherto he had not lived, but simply vegetated; he now feels himself a man, because he is treated as such; the laws of his own country had overlooked him in his insignificancy; the laws of this cover him with their mantle. Judge what an alteration there must arise in the mind and thoughts of the man! He begins to forget his former servitude and dependence, his heart involuntarily dilates and glows, and its first swell inspires him with those new thoughts which mark an American.

Religious and cultural toleration grows.

Especially in the later colonial period, people of different religions and nationalities mingled freely. While there was some discrimination against non-Protestants, nearly every faith was protected under the British flag. The majority of the colonists had learned that different sects could and should get along peaceably. There was also a spirit of cultural toleration. People of different nationalities—English, Irish, German, French, Swedish, Dutch—intermarried. Thus tolerance was becoming one of the marks of an American.

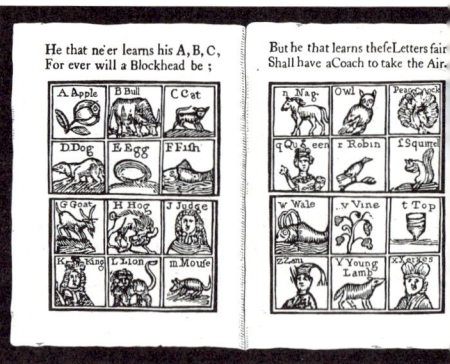

Colonial primer

FOR IDENTIFICATION

American Philosophical Society
Anglican Church
John Bartram
Congregational Church

Benjamin Franklin
Judaic-Christian tradition
John Mitchell
David Rittenhouse

FOR EXPLANATION OR DEFINITION

almanac
apprenticeship
coastal plain
dame school
indentured servant

Latin grammar school
log rolling
Piedmont
state-supported church
subscription library

FOR REVIEW

1. What racial stocks were represented in the colonies? In what area did the non-English racial stocks predominate?

2. (a) Describe the characteristics of frontier life. (b) Who were attracted to the frontier? (c) Why did a spirit of democracy develop on the frontier?

3. (a) Why did the rigid European class system fail to take root in America? (b) What social classes did develop?

4. (a) Describe a typical log cabin. (b) Describe the house a prosperous New England farmer might build to replace a log cabin. (c) Describe the house a prosperous merchant or planter might build.

5. (a) How did most of the colonists obtain their clothing? (b) What materials were commonly used for clothing? (c) How did the well to do obtain their clothing?

6. (a) Compare the food of the colonists with ours. (b) What imported foods used

by all classes today were familiar only to the well to do in colonial times?

7. (a) Why did most of the colonists seldom enjoy amusement for its own sake? (b) How did they meet the need for sociability?

8. (a) Name the four largest cities in 1750. (b) Describe a colonial city, contrasting it with a modern city.

9. (a) What are some of the essentials of the Judaic-Christian tradition? (b) What was the leading religious faith in New England? (c) Discuss the influence of religion on family life.

10. (a) What is meant by a state church? (b) In which colonies was there a state-supported church? (c) Why did freedom of worship develop slowly? (d) What were some evidences of the growth of tolerance in the colonies?

11. (a) Why was there a large degree of literacy among the New England colonists? (b) What were the provisions of the Massachusetts school law of 1647? (c) Describe various kinds of colonial schools. Which one was most like a modern high school?

12. (a) Name and locate the first two colleges in the colonies. (b) How did the Academy of Philadelphia differ from other colleges?

13. (a) What books were likely to be found in a colonial home? (b) Describe a colonial newspaper; an almanac.

14. Describe the growth of the colonial postal system.

15. (a) What did the colonists think were the causes of sickness? (b) How did the average colonial doctor get his training?

16. (a) Where did colonial scientists receive their training? (b) How did the American Philosophical Society stimulate the development of science?

FOR FURTHER STUDY AND DISCUSSION

1. Why was slavery more prevalent in the South than in the New England or Middle Colonies?

2. What culture there was in colonial America was not created by the colonists but was brought with them from the Old World. How did the conditions of frontier life influence cultural development?

3. What is meant by the phrase "a classless society"? To what extent did social and economic conditions among the colonies tend to promote the development of a classless society? Has this tendency continued in the United States?

4. To what extent did conditions in the New World tend to foster an interest in science?

5. To what extent are superstitions as prevalent today as in colonial times?

6. Can you find in Crèvecoeur's description of American society a partial explanation of the American Revolution?

7. In what respects was a distinctly American society beginning to take shape by the time of the American Revolution?

FOR INDIVIDUAL OR GROUP ACTIVITIES

1. Arrange an exhibit illustrating colonial dress, art, recreation, and architecture.

2. Prepare a list of the more important colonial writers and their works. Helpful sources: Merle Curti, *The Growth of American Thought;* Hart, *Contemporaries,* Vol. II, Nos. 90–96; E. S. Slosson, *The American Spirit in Education;* and B. Perry, *The American Spirit in Literature.*

3. Assign a special committee to report on the influence of Franklin on: (a) colonial newspapers and magazines and (b) colonial scientific and cultural development. Helpful sources: Benjamin Franklin, *Autobiography* and Carl Van Doren, *Benjamin Franklin.*

4. The influence of the Puritan tradition has often been the subject of controversy. Assign two small committees to study the Puritan influence and have them report to the class in the form of a twenty-minute debate. Helpful source: George M. Walder, ed., *Puritanism in Early America.*

5. Report to the class on H. W. Longfellow's *The Courtship of Miles Standish.*

6. Prepare a three-column chart—Education, Amusements, Religion—which will contrast conditions in Massachusetts, Pennsylvania, Virginia.

UNIT ONE REVIEW

HIGH POINTS

1

Changes in Europe that ushered in the Modern Age also made possible the discovery and settlement of the New World. These changes included (1) the expansion of commerce and industry, (2) the growth of nationalism, (3) the development of science, (4) the mass production of books, and (5) the unrest in religious thinking. Europeans were emerging from the narrow self-contained life of the feudal village. They were becoming curious about other lands. They were eager for products of the East, which were brought by caravan to Mediterranean ports and distributed by Italian merchants throughout Europe.

2

By the end of the 15th century Portuguese explorers had reached India by sailing around Africa and across the Indian Ocean, and Columbus had discovered America while seeking to reach India by sailing westward from Europe. Later explorers proved that North and South America lay between Europe and the Indies. During the 16th century explorers claimed extensive portions of the Americas for Spain, Portugal, France, England, and Holland.

3

The discovery of America led to the greatest migration in human history. In this migration European ways of living and thinking were transplanted to the Americas. During the same period Europeans also established colonies and spheres of influence in Asia and Africa. The migrants carried with them the scientific knowledge and the commercial, industrial, and political developments which characterize the Modern Age. These Western ideas are still revolutionizing society in all parts of the world.

4

England won control of the seas from Spain in 1588 and soon afterward began to establish colonies in the West Indies and along the Atlantic coast of North America. Between 1607 and 1733 thirteen English colonies were started on the mainland. Unlike Spain and France, England gave her colonies a large measure of political, religious, and economic freedom.

5

Attempts to develop feudal estates worked by tenants did not succeed in the English colonies. Land ownership was widespread. A large proportion of the colonists were small, self-sufficient farmers. They were coming to believe that all men are equal and should have equal opportunities.

6

At first the thirteen colonies had more ties with England than with one another. Toward the end of the colonial period they began to be drawn closer together by coastal trade, by the establishment of a general postal system, by the circulation of colonial newspapers, and by the growing awareness of common needs and interests.

7

English institutions and English law became thoroughly established in all the colonies. Many non-English settlers came, mostly after 1700, but they adopted the English language and outlook. The emerging American society was strongly influenced by English traditions.

8

The class system was weaker in the thirteen English colonies than anywhere

else. A proud family name counted far less than in Europe. American aristocracy was based on wealth, not birth.

QUESTIONS

Before you attempt to formulate answers to the following questions, leaf through the pages of the text, pausing to note the paragraph headings and to examine the maps, charts, and illustrations. At the end of each chapter, examine once again the items you were asked to identify, define, or explain. Look up those with which you are unfamiliar. In somewhat the same way skim through your notebook. If you have difficulty with any of the questions, read the appropriate portions of other books.

1. Make an outline of the ideas or events you would include in an article for the school newspaper to support the statement that the discovery of America in 1492 was the logical outcome of developments in Europe in the fifteenth century.

2. a) Why did Spain take the lead in the colonization and settlement of the New World?

b) What parts of the present United States came under the influence of Spanish and French exploration and settlement?

c) How did the colonial activities of Spain and France in the sixteenth and seventeenth centuries influence the history of the United States in the eighteenth and nineteenth centuries?

3. a) Describe the chief geographic features of that portion of the United States embraced by the original thirteen colonies.

b) How did these geographic features influence colonial economic and political life?

4. a) Make a list of the important economic and political ideals, institutions, and traditions that the colonists brought with them from the Old World to the New.

b) How were these ideals and institutions adopted and modified by the colonists during the seventeenth and eighteenth centuries?

c) Which of these ideals and institutions have had an enduring influence upon the development of the United States?

5. How did political and religious developments in England in the seventeenth century influence the development of the colonies?

6. a) Religious beliefs, motives, and experiences were a powerful factor in the development of Spanish, French, and English settlements. Make a list of the outstanding developments in the colonial period which you think would support this statement.

b) In what respects did colonial religious experiences influence subsequent American history?

7. a) How did conditions of frontier life influence scientific and cultural development in the colonies?

b) What were the opportunities for school and college education in the colonies in the eighteenth century?

8. a) In what respects was colonial America an "outpost" of Europe?

b) Contrast the differences among the Spanish, French, and English colonies as regards: areas each controlled, occupations, relations with the Indians, government, and relations with the mother country.

c) Using the headings "System of Landholding," "Social Classes," and "Op-

portunities for Individual Advancement"
compare life in the colonies with that in
England during the eighteenth century.

9. Benjamin Franklin, one of the greatest
men of the colonial period, was born in
Boston in 1706 and died in Philadelphia
in 1790. His life almost spans the eighteenth century. He is often referred to as
the "many-sided" Franklin. Without emphasizing Franklin's services as a diplomat
or member of the Constitutional Convention, use the story of his life and achievements as the basis for a feature news article which will describe social, cultural,
literary, and scientific progress in the colonies during the eighteenth century.

SUGGESTED READINGS

(See note, pages xiv, xv.)

SOURCE MATERIALS, DOCUMENTS,
AND MAPS

Commager, *Documents.*
° Commager and Nevins, *Heritage of Amer-
ica.*
Hart, *Contemporaries,* Vols. I and II.
Lord, *Historical Atlas.*

GENERAL REFERENCES

° Andrews, C. M. *Colonial Folkways.* Yale
University Press, 1919. (Y.C.S.)
° Andrews, C. M. *Fathers of New England.*
Yale University Press, 1919. (Y.C.S.)
Beard, *American Civilization,* Vol. I.
Cheyney, Edward P. *European Background
of American History.* Harper, 1904.
° Fisher, Sydney G. *The Quaker Colonies.*
Yale University Press, 1919. (Y.C.S.)
° Goodwin, M. W. *Dutch and English on the
Hudson.* Yale University Press, 1919.
(Y.C.S.)
Hicks, John D. *The Federal Union.* 2nd ed.
Houghton Mifflin, 1952.
° Johnston, Mary. *Pioneers of the Old South.*
Yale University Press, 1918. (Y.C.S.)
Larkin, *Art and Life in America.*
Morison and Commager, *American Repub-
lic,* Vol. I.

Morris, *Encyclopedia.*
Underhill, Ruth M. *Red Man's America.*
University of Chicago Press, 1953.
Wertenbaker, Thomas J. *The First Ameri-
cans, 1607–1690.* Macmillan, 1927.
————. *The Founding of American Civili-
zation: The Middle Colonies.* Scribner's,
1938.
Willison, George F. *Saints and Strangers.*
Reynal and Hitchcock, 1945.
° Wissler, Clark, Skinner, C. L., and Wood,
W. *Adventures in the Wilderness.* Yale
University Press, 1925. (Pageant)

BIOGRAPHY

Brockuniar, Samuel H. *The Irrepressible
Democrat: Roger Williams.* Ronald, 1940.
° Crouse, Anna E., and Crouse, Russel. *Peter
Stuyvesant of Old New York.* Random
House, 1954.
Flenley, Ralph. *Samuel de Champlain,
Founder of New France.* Macmillan, 1925.
° Foote, A. E., and Skinner, A. W. *Explorers
and Founders of America.* American Book,
1907.
Galt, T. F. *Peter Zenger, Fighter for Free-
dom.* Crowell, 1951.
° Kjelgaard, J. A. *The Explorations of Pere
Marquette.* Random House, 1951.
° Lawson, Marie. *Pocahontas and Captain
John Smith.* Random House, 1950.
Leighton, M. *The Sword and the Compass.*
Houghton Mifflin, 1951. (John Smith)
Morison, Samuel E. *Admiral of the Ocean
Sea.* Little, Brown, 1942. (This is a classic
biography of Columbus.)
° ————. *Christopher Columbus, Mariner.*
Little, Brown, 1955. (Based on the above
but, on the whole, more interesting to the
high school student.)
Smith, Bradford. *Bradford of Plymouth.*
Lippincott, 1951.
Thwaites, R. G. *Father Marquette.* Apple-
ton, 1902.
Walsh, R. J. *Adventures and Discoveries of
Marco Polo.* Random House, 1953.

NOTE: Consult Johnson, *The Dictionary of
American Biography* (Scribner, 1946) and
also Morris, *Encyclopedia of American History,* which contains a number of informative
biographical notes, including sketches of William Bradford, Captain John Smith, Roger
Williams, Anne Hutchinson, Jonathan Ed-
wards, and others mentioned in this unit.

FICTION

The fiction titles listed here and at the end of other units scarcely begin to hint at the wealth of material which can be effectively used to enrich and illuminate the understanding of the past.

* Cather, Willa. *Shadows on the Rock.* Knopf, 1931. (Colonial Quebec, Count Frontenac)

* Cooper, James Fenimore. *The Last of the Mohicans.* Dutton, 1906. (Indian fighting in northern New York)

Hawthorne, Nathaniel. *The House of the Seven Gables.* Dutton, 1907. (Old Salem)

———. *The Scarlet Letter.* Dutton, 1907. (Puritan Massachusetts)

Hough, Emerson. *The Mississippi Bubble.* Grosset, n.d. (New France)

Irving, Washington. *Diedrich Knickerbocker's History of New York.* Harcourt, Brace, 1927. (A kindly satire)

* Johnston, Mary. *Croatan.* Little, Brown, 1923. (First settlers in Virginia)

* ———. *1492.* Little, Brown, 1922. (Columbus)

* ———. *The Slave Ship.* Little, Brown, 1924. (Slave trade in Virginia)

* ———. *To Have and To Hold.* Houghton Mifflin, 1900. (Life on a Virginia plantation)

Kingsley, Charles. *Westward Ho!* Burt, 1891. (Rivalry of England and Spain; the Spanish Armada)

Parker, Sir Gilbert. *The Seats of the Mighty.* Appleton, 1913. (Frontenac)

* Pyle, Howard. *Jack Ballister's Fortunes.* Century, n.d. (Early Virginia)

* Singmaster, Elsie. *The Magic Mirror.* Houghton Mifflin, 1934. (The Germans in Pennsylvania)

* Skinner, Constance L. *Roselle of the North.* Macmillan, 1927. (Early fur trade)

Sublette, Clifford M. *The Bright Face of Danger.* Little, Brown, 1926. (Bacon's Rebellion)

TIME LINE

1750		
	1754	Albany Congress; French and Indian War begins
	1755	Braddock's defeat
	1759	Battle of Plains of Abraham
1760		
	1763	Treaty of Paris ending French and Indian War
	1765	Stamp Act Congress
	1767	Townshend Acts
1770		
	1772	Committees of correspondence
	1773	Boston Tea Party
	1774	Intolerable Acts: First Continental Congress
	1775	Lexington and Concord; Second Continental Congress
	1776	Declaration of Independence
	1777	Battle of Saratoga
1780		
	1781	Yorktown; Articles of Confederation ratified
	1783	Treaty of Paris ending the Revolutionary War
	1786	Virginia Statute of Religious Liberty
	1787	Northwest Ordinance; Constitutional Convention
	1789	Washington inaugurated
1790	1790	The first census: population 3,929,000

UNIT TWO   *Americans Form a New Nation*

★ ★ ★ ★ The people of the thirteen colonies were used to governing themselves with very little interference from across the sea. Like all English people, they loved liberty and wanted self-government. When Parliament, in the reign of George III, tried to tighten its controls over the colonies, it met unexpected resistance. With every attempt Parliament made to enforce its control, colonial resistance increased. In the short span of a dozen years from 1763 to 1775, open rebellion broke out. The measures which England took to overcome the rebellion drove the colonists to declare their independence.

The thirteen newly formed states called themselves the United States of America. Yet they were not really united. Each of the thirteen insisted on the rights of an independent nation. The first central government of the United States, the Continental Congress, had a difficult time. The states gave it so little power that it could hardly raise an army or keep it in the field. The government which took its place, the Confederation Congress, was scarcely any stronger. Nevertheless, with the aid of England's foes, the new nation somehow won its six-year struggle for independence.

With the end of the war the states were even less willing to give up any of their rights. The nation still faced grave problems both at home and abroad. Action was necessary, yet the Confederation Congress lacked power to act. Efforts to strengthen the government got nowhere until 1787. Then Congress called a convention to revise the Articles of Confederation. The gifted men who attended the convention ignored the Articles and produced a completely new constitution.

This Constitution set forth a remarkably effective plan of federal government. It allowed the states to keep a large degree of independence, yet gave the central government the authority needed to act on matters of national concern. After a hard fight the Constitution was ratified, and the new plan of government went into effect. As the years passed, it successfully met one test after another. Moreover, it proved flexible enough to meet constantly changing conditions. Today, after nearly two centuries, the Constitution still serves our nation well.

(Above) CHIEFS OF THE SIX NATIONS (*the Iroquois Confederacy*) *at a council with Sir William Johnson at Johnson Hall, Johnstown, New York, in 1774.*

(Left) SIR WILLIAM JOHNSON (*1715–1774*) *from a portrait c. 1750. This British official came to America as a youth of twenty-three and settled in the Mohawk valley. So successful was he in dealing with the Indians that Governor Clinton of New York appointed him Colonel of the Six Nations. Later he was made superintendent of Indian affairs.*

The Revolution was in the minds and hearts of the people. . . . Its causes should be . . . sought in the history of the country from the first plantation in America.

———John Adams

Washington as a young officer

6. THE COLONISTS RESIST IMPERIAL CONTROL

Great Britain Wins New France

National rivalries are world-wide.

While colonizing the New World, the major European nations—Great Britain, France, Spain, Portugal, and the Netherlands—were also planting colonies in Africa and Asia. They regarded each colonial area as a prize worth fighting for. Hence, in their efforts to establish and hold an empire, these nations engaged in almost continual warfare.

Late in the 1600's a series of Anglo-French wars began. With some years of intermission, they lasted for over a century. The first three began in Europe but led to fighting between the English and French colonies. The fighting here in America brought no decision. The fourth war, which we call the "French and Indian War," started in the colonies and spread to Europe and India. It settled the question of whether the French or the British would control North America.

Fighting breaks out in the Ohio Valley.

The French and Indian War began in a struggle for possession of the Ohio Valley. Both British and French fur traders had entered the area. When the British government gave a grant on the Ohio River to a group of Virginia land speculators, the French became alarmed. They started (1753) to build a chain of forts from Lake Erie to the Ohio. Virginia's governor sent George Washington, then twenty-one years of age, to tell the French to leave. Instead, the French built additional forts, among them Fort Duquesne at the forks of the Ohio River. In 1755 a regiment of British regulars led by General Braddock tried to capture Fort Duquesne but failed miserably.

This battle marked the beginning of years of fierce fighting between Great Britain and France. The Algonquin Indians sided with the French. Hoping to drive out the British, who were steadily taking their land, these Indians carried on savage attacks against frontier communities. The Iroquois, however, fought with the British.

The British colonies had no cannon or other war equipment, but they supplied thousands of men, most of them dressed in their own homespun and carrying their own weapons. While these colonial fighting men were brave and hardy, they were not a match for the well-trained and well-equipped French regulars. The French and their Indian allies would easily have won the war in America had it not been for the British army and navy.

The tide turns.

For a few years the war went badly for the British. But in 1758 they won important victories at Louisburg, a naval base close to the Gulf of St. Lawrence, and Fort Frontenac, controlling the approach to Lake Ontario. The French then had to abandon Fort Duquesne, which was renamed Fort Pitt and later, Pittsburgh. The climax of the war came when General James Wolfe took Quebec from the French. This battle ended effective resistance by the French in North America.

British histories speak of 1759 as the "wonderful year." It brought British successes in America, Europe, the Mediterranean, and the Far East. Yet the war continued for several years. Spain, fearful of British victory, entered the war as an ally of France in 1762. Finally, defeated on all fronts, France was compelled to make peace.

The Treaty of Paris enlarges the British Empire.

The war closed officially in 1763 with the Treaty of Paris. England obtained most of India and all of North America east of the Mississippi, except New Orleans. France lost practically all her possessions in India and in America. Spain had to give up Florida. To compensate Spain for its losses, France gave this ally New Orleans and all of Louisiana west of the Mississippi.

The colonists feel more secure.

So long as the French held Canada and the Mississippi Valley, the English colonies needed British protection. Once the French had been driven out, however, the colonists felt that they could protect themselves. The French minister forecast that the colonies would "shake off their dependence" on the mother country "as soon as Canada was ceded" by France. A dozen years after the signing of the Treaty of Paris, the colonists did indeed begin fighting for their independence. "With the triumph of Wolfe at Quebec," wrote a noted English historian, "began the history of the United States."

BATTLE *of Quebec, 1759*

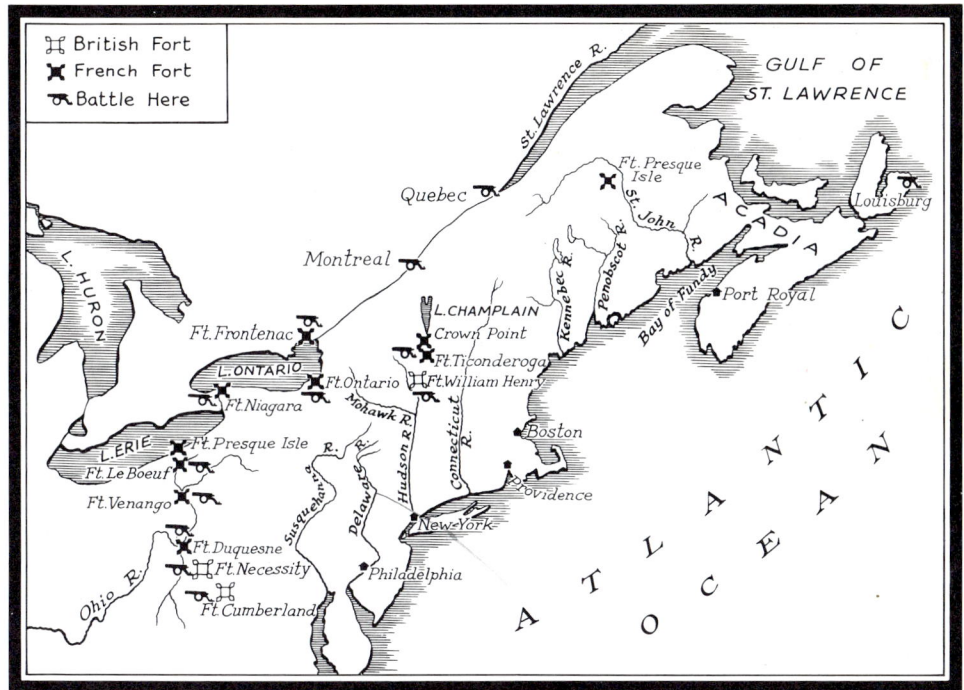

FRENCH AND INDIAN WAR

Scaling the steep banks of the St. Lawrence, GENERAL JAMES WOLFE *(above) and his men defeated the French under the command of* MAJOR GENERAL MONTCALM *(right). Both generals were mortally wounded in the fierce battle.*

Britain Faces the Problem of Governing the Colonies

The British are displeased.

Some of the colonies had been generous in supplying men and money to carry on the French and Indian War. Others refused to give any aid. Each colonial assembly did as much or as little as it pleased. Furthermore, when the assemblies voted money, they insisted on spending it as they thought best. Maryland, for instance, refused to let her troops serve under the British commander in chief. The British were still more displeased by colonial trade with the enemy. The sale of American food and other provisions to French forces in Canada had, it was said, prolonged the war by three years. To Englishmen it seemed plain that a firmer policy was needed in dealing with the colonies.

PONTIAC

Immediate problems must be met.

After the war the English government was faced with three immediate problems in regard to the colonies:

1. The Indian problem. The colonists needed stronger defenses against the Indians. In 1763 Pontiac, chief of the Ottawa tribe, united with other chiefs in a powerful effort to drive the British from the continent. The Indians destroyed most of the British forts. Fortunately British regulars arrived in time and Pontiac's war collapsed.

Still the British feared that another Indian uprising might come at any time. Since the colonists did not provide well for their own defense, the British government thought that 10,000 of its regular soldiers should be kept in the colonies. To maintain these men would cost £300,000 ($1,500,000) a year. Parliament wanted the colonists to pay at least a third of the cost.

2. The question of debt and taxation. The French and Indian War had doubled the British debt. Interest on the debt was a heavy burden for the mother country. Since the colonists received most of the benefits from the French and Indian War, should they not help pay the interest on the war debt? This suggestion seemed reasonable to the English, because their landowners were already taxed from 20 to 30 per cent of their incomes.

3. Enforcement of the trade and navigation acts. The acts regulating trade and navigation in the colonies had never been strictly enforced (see p. 72). Smuggling was widespread; most English officials in the colonies winked at it, and some accepted a share in the profits. It was reported to Parliament in 1763 that the American revenues from customs amounted to less than £2000 a year, and cost £7000 to collect. Parliament thought something must be done to stop this loss.

George III increases royal authority.

All three problems called for closer supervision of the colonies. The policy of stricter control was encouraged by George III. His father and grandfather had let Parliament and the cabinet run the country and they had left the colonies to do much as they pleased. But George had been brought up by his mother with the oft-repeated instruction, "George, be a king." When he came to the throne in 1760, he set about gaining as much power as he could. He chose cabinet ministers who would do his bidding. He used his influence to secure the election to Parliament of members of the Tory party, who would support him. The king backed up their attempts to bring the colonies under the rule of Parliament.

The Colonists Protest the British Program

The Grenville Acts irritate the colonists.

George Grenville became British prime minister in 1763. Upon his advice Parliament passed a series of acts affecting the colonies. Each act was objectionable to some group of colonists. The measures which most displeased the Americans were:

1. The closing of the frontier. To avoid trouble with the Indians, Grenville issued the Proclamation of 1763, closing lands west of the Appalachians to settlers (see map, p. 103). Pioneers who had settled in the Indian country were "forthwith to remove themselves." No one but the British government was to buy land from the Indians. Fur traders had to have a license. The proclamation was most unpopular in the colonies and was not obeyed.

2. The Currency Act, 1764. The colonies were forbidden to issue paper money. This measure particularly angered those who imported English goods. Its purpose was to protect English merchants from cheap colonial money (see p. 70).

3. The Sugar Act, 1764. To obtain money to help meet the expense of protecting the colonists, Parliament passed the Sugar Act of 1764. New duties were placed on several products that had been duty-free. The number of enumerated articles which could be sold only in England was enlarged. To lessen the temptation for smuggling, the old rates on molasses were reduced. In addition the Sugar Act gave customs officials new powers to help them

KING GEORGE III *at seventy years of age, sad and confused. His critics accused him of the loss of the American colonies.*

NORTH AMERICA AFTER
THE TREATY OF PARIS, 1763

capture smugglers. Smuggling became harder but did not stop.

4. *The Quartering Act, 1765.* To reduce the cost of keeping English soldiers in America, the colonists were required to furnish the troops with supplies and living quarters. Payment for these services was to come from the government of the colony where the troops were stationed. The colonists objected to this measure because they thought the troops had been sent to keep them in order.

5. *The Stamp Act, 1765.* British ministers proposed a Stamp Act requiring that stamps must be bought and placed on all legal documents, pamphlets, newspapers, and playing cards. These tax stamps had been used for many years in England, and people there were accustomed to them. Such taxes were thought to fall chiefly upon the more prosperous and not to be a heavy burden to anyone. The colonists strongly objected to this proposal.

Grenville told colonial agents in London that the colonies must raise more money to help support the army. He gave the colonists a year to suggest a more satisfactory method than the stamp tax. He got no reply, for the colonists thought that Parliament had no right to tax them at all. Accordingly, the Stamp Act was passed.

The Stamp Act is repealed.

The Stamp Act caused more anger than any other part of the Grenville program. Secret societies called "Sons of Liberty" were formed in every colony. Stocks of stamped paper were burned. Stamp sellers were threatened with violence, and the homes of some of them were destroyed by mobs. Very few stamps were sold.

The Massachusetts assembly asked each colony to send delegates to a congress to protest the Stamp Act. The New Hampshire assembly refused to send delegates, and in Virginia, North Carolina, and Georgia the governors refused to call the assembly for the purpose of choosing delegates. Representatives from the remaining nine colonies met in New York City in October, 1765. The meeting was known as the Stamp Act Congress. After eleven days of debate the delegates passed a resolution denying the right of Parliament to tax the colonies without their consent. This action showed that at last most of the colonies were developing the ability to stand together.

The merchants of New York, Philadelphia, and Boston agreed to buy no more English goods until the Stamp Act was repealed. The boycott, or refusal to buy goods, was known as "nonimportation." British merchants soon felt the pinch and urged repeal of the act. Parliament repealed it early in 1766. News of the repeal caused loud rejoicing in the colonies. Nonimportation was abandoned. In New York and Virginia statues were erected to George III as a "restorer of liberty." Yet the colonists had not won their claim to be taxed only with the consent of their own legislatures.

The Townshend Acts renew the quarrel.

Parliament's efforts to raise revenue in the colonies began again in 1767 under a new Chancellor of the Exchequer, Charles Townshend. Since the colonists would not submit to an *internal* tax, such as the stamp tax, Townshend decided to rely on *external* taxes, or import duties. Accordingly, duties were placed on glass, paper, lead, paints, and tea. The revenue raised in this way was to be used to pay the salaries of governors, judges, and other appointed officials, thus removing them from the control of the assemblies. Customs officers were given power to search the homes of any colonists suspected of smuggling and to try suspects without a jury. Americans were furious over these measures. Were their homes and places of business to be searched whenever a royal officer saw fit? And were their assemblies to lose all power over colonial officials appointed by the king? To add to the colonists' fear and anger, Parliament suspended the assembly of New York for refusing to obey the Quartering Act.

Again the colonies flamed with protests, pamphlets, and meetings. Samuel Adams of Boston was the most active in stirring up opposition. He inspired the Massachusetts assembly (1768) to send a Circular Letter to the assemblies of the other twelve colonies denouncing the Townshend Acts and calling for resistance to them. For this defiance the royal governor of Massachusetts dissolved the assembly. When assemblies in other colonies endorsed the Circular Letter, they too were dissolved.

Once more the colonists turned to nonimportation to force Parliament to listen. Colonial merchants agreed not to buy British goods. The boycott cut British imports in half.

The Boston Massacre leaves deep scars.

Customs officers in Boston were attacked by mobs. To protect them and enable them to do their work, two regiments of British soldiers were sent there in 1768. This made the citizens of Boston very angry. Whenever soldiers appeared in the streets, hoodlums pestered them by name-calling and sometimes by throwing rubbish at them. This nagging went on for eighteen months, until it provoked a riot called the "Boston Massacre" (March 5, 1770), in which five citizens were killed. Under the leadership of Samuel Adams a town meeting was held the next day. Those present demanded that the governor order the removal of the troops. He did so, but he could not repair the damage done to relations with the mother country. The incident aroused a new storm of indignation.

Parliament gives in.

On the very day of the Boston Massacre, the British government decided to repeal all the duties imposed by the Townshend Acts, except the tax on tea. This was to be kept as a sign that Parliament had the right to impose taxes on the colonies. The colonists now resumed trade with Britain but formed societies whose members agreed not to drink dutied tea.

Committees of correspondence fan the flames of liberty.

A small group of radicals led by Samuel Adams kept on stirring up opposition to any interference by Parliament in colonial affairs. They now claimed that Parliament had no right to make laws for the colonies. However, they were not yet demanding complete independence. What they

To the PUBLIC.

THE Senſe of the City relative to the Landing the India Company's Tea, being ſignified to Captain Lockyer, by the Committee, nevertheleſs, it is the Deſire of a Number of the Citizens, that at his Departure from hence, he ſhould ſee, with his own Eyes, their Deteſtation of the Meaſures purſued by the Miniſtry and the India Company, to enſlave this Country. This will be declared by the Convention of the People at his Departure from this City; which will be on next Saturday Morning, about nine o'Clock, when no Doubt, every Friend to this Country will attend. The Bells will give the Notice about an Hour before he embarks from Murray's Wharf.

By Order of the COMMITTEE.

NEW YORK, April 21ſt, 1774.

A NOTICE *protesting the landing of the India Company's tea. It was published by the New York Committee of Correspondence.*

EVENTS LEADING TO THE AMERICAN REVOLUTION

	BRITISH ACTION	COLONIAL REACTION
1733	Molasses Act passed	Smuggling became widespread
1750	Manufacture of ironware forbidden	
1763	Proclamation of 1763 closed frontier	Not obeyed
1764	Sugar Act, Currency Act passed	
1765	Quartering Act, Stamp Act passed	Sons of Liberty destroyed stamps
		Stamp Act Congress
		Nonimportation agreement
1766	Stamp Act repealed	Rejoicing in colonies
1767	Townshend Acts; new efforts to stop smuggling	Nonimportation revived; customs offic attacked by mobs
1768	British troops sent to Boston	Massachusetts' Circular Letter to other colon
		Pestering of troops; Boston Massacre, 1770
1770	Repeal of Townshend duties except tax on tea	Burning of the customs schooner *Gaspée*, 17
	Quartering Act expired	Committees of correspondence active
1773	Tea Act passed	Tea ships not allowed to unload
		Boston Tea Party
1774	Intolerable Acts	First Continental Congress met
1775	American ports closed	Lexington and Concord, April 1775
		Second Continental Congress convened May
		Washington appointed commander in chief
		Battle of Bunker Hill, June 17
1776	Siege of Boston	*Common Sense* published, January
	British evacuated Boston and occupied New York	Declaration of Independence, July 4, 1776

wanted was the right of the colonies to make all their own laws—the kind of independence enjoyed today by members of the British Commonwealth.

The more determined patriots organized committees of correspondence to exchange ideas and plans of action. Samuel Adams was the principal leader in this movement. In 1772 he got the Boston town meeting to appoint a committee to write to other towns in the province. Soon every town in Massachusetts had a similar committee.

Other colonies also set up committees of correspondence. The Virginia Burgesses appointed an intercolonial committee of eleven men, including Thomas Jefferson and Patrick Henry. The exchange of letters kept the public informed about any unwelcome activities of the British government. A Tory writer declared later:

This was the source of rebellion. I saw the small seed when it was implanted . . . I have watched the plant until it became a great tree.

The Tea Act leads to the Boston Tea Party.

Tea drinking had so fallen off in the colonies that the British East India Company was in great financial difficulties. The company's warehouses in England were full of tea. Hoping to help out, Parliament excused it from paying the usual export duty on tea (12 pence a pound). It would have to pay only the tax of 3 pence a pound on tea imported into the colonies. Lord North, the Tory prime minister, hoped the colonists would be so pleased at the low price of tea that they would gladly pay the small tax.

The company sent over a number of ships but nowhere were they kindly received. At Charleston the tea was locked up in a warehouse and sold three years later for the benefit of the Revolution. At Philadelphia and New York the tea ships were not allowed to unload; they carried their cargo back to England. In Boston two mass meetings resolved that the tea must be sent back to England. The governor refused to permit this. Then a group of "Sons of Liberty" disguised as Indians boarded the tea ships and dumped £18,000 worth of tea into the harbor. The town officials made no effort to prevent this lawless act, which became known as the "Boston Tea Party."

Parliament passes the "Intolerable Acts."

As a result of the Boston Tea Party, Parliament passed four acts to punish the colonies. Two of the acts affected all the colonies, while two singled out Massachusetts for special punishment. (1) One act provided that royal officers in America, accused by the colonists of serious offenses, could be tried in England. The colonists objected to this act because their complaints against the accused might not be given a full hearing across the sea. (2) Another act gave the governor of any colony power to force the citizens to quarter (house) soldiers in their homes in case of need. This would make it easier to use troops to compel obedience to the king. (3) A third act forbade the people of Massachusetts to hold town meetings. (4) Finally, the port of Boston was closed to all trade until payment should be made for the tea that had been destroyed. British warships were stationed in the harbor to prevent goods from going in or out. Business came to a standstill, and the people of Boston suffered unemployment and want. These four measures, passed in 1774, were known in the colonies as the "Intolerable Acts."

A fifth measure, the Quebec Act, which came the same year, was not intended as a punishment for any colony. But the colonists found it just as intolerable as the other four. This act widened the boundaries of Quebec southward to the Ohio River. It recognized the right of Canadians to make full use of the French language and to keep their Roman Catholic religion.

The English colonists did not want a great Catholic, French-speaking province north and west of them. They also objected to its autocratic form of government. The strongest objections arose because the act wiped out the claims of four colonies to the Ohio country.

Massachusetts resists.

The Intolerable Acts left the colonists no choice except to resist or submit. Parliament expected that they would soon give in. To make clear that submission was expected, four British regiments were sent to Boston, and their commander, General Gage, was made governor of Massachusetts. The inhabitants showed no sign of yielding.

Die Einwohner von Boston werfen den englisch-ostindischen Thee ins Meer am 18. December 1773.

"The inhabitants of Boston THROWING THE INDIA COMPANY'S TEA INTO THE SEA *on December 16, 1773." (Translation.) This event was famous abroad for many years.*

107

The soldiers were unsafe outside the cover of the fleet and the barracks. Fires broke out in stacks of straw intended for their bedding; farmers would not sell them food; workmen refused to build them shelters. After five months Gage advised that the four acts be suspended until a force large enough to conquer the whole of New England could be brought to America. He said that it would take no less than 20,000 men. King George understood the situation correctly, for he wrote, "The die is cast; the colonists must either submit or triumph."

The First Continental Congress meets.

The punishment of Massachusetts created a bond of sympathy among the colonies. Cities near and far sent supplies for the relief of Boston's poor. Pamphlets pointing out that Massachusetts was suffering in the common cause appeared everywhere. The day on which the port of Boston was closed (June 1, 1774) was observed in Philadelphia and Virginia as a day of mourning. For proclaiming a day of mourning, the governor of Virginia suspended the House of Burgesses. The members then met at a nearby tavern and called upon all the colonies to hold a congress to consider their united interests.

A few weeks later, the first Continental Congress met at Philadelphia. Fifty-six delegates were present, representing all the colonies except Georgia. For seven weeks the discussions went on behind locked doors.

Two ideas were generally accepted: (1) that there was a united America, and (2) that the Congress should act for it. In regard to what should be done, two plans divided the delegates. One group wished to create a union of the colonies, this union to have a president and the privilege of making its own laws. Had this plan been adopted, and had England allowed it, the colonies would have remained in the Empire. A second group of delegates favored a declaration of rights and grievances and an "Association," or agreement, to resist England by stopping trade with her. The views of this group won out.

A famous paper known as the "Declaration of Rights and Grievances" was drawn up. It listed the rights claimed by the colonists and named thirteen acts of Parliament which violated these rights. Repeal of these acts was asked. Congress also adopted an "Association" not to import or use British goods. To enforce it, committees of inspection were appointed to publish the names of any merchants who broke the nonimportation agreement. The Congress hoped that by this means Great Britain would be forced to give in. The members adjourned in October, after deciding to meet again on May 10, in case the British did not heed their protests.

English feelings are mixed.

The Association proved so effective that in 1775 the import trade from Great Britain was cut about 95 per cent. Early that year a large number of English businessmen begged Parliament to repeal the thirteen acts displeasing to the colonists. Several outstanding English statesmen also spoke in favor of the colonies, urging Parliament not to drive them further into rebellion. "We cannot, I fear," said Edmund Burke in Parliament, "falsify the pedigree of this fierce people, and persuade them that they are not sprung from a nation in whose veins the blood of freedom circulates. . . . An Englishman is the unfittest person on earth to argue another Englishman into slavery." Englishmen agreed, however, that the action of the Continental Congress in adopting the Association was an act of rebellion. The king and most members of Parliament believed that rebellion should be firmly put down by armed force.

ADVANTAGES IN THE REVOLUTION

BRITISH ADVANTAGES	AMERICAN ADVANTAGES
Strong navy which was able to blockade our ports and to protect troop and supply ships	Colonists were fighting on their own soil, for their own homes
Regular army well trained, well equipped, with experienced officers	Had many brave privateers
Strong central government able to raise money to carry on war	Were excellent guerrilla fighters
Large number of factories which could turn out war materials	Many Americans had rifles, whereas British had only muskets
One third of American colonists were loyal to the king	Received foreign aid throughout the war
	Had a great leader—George Washington

Armed Resistance Begins

The colonists prepare to fight.

War appeared likely, and the colonies began to get ready for it. Companies of volunteers began to drill. Committees of safety were organized. Royal governors reported these activities to the home government but were powerless to stop them.

During the winter of 1775, Massachusetts Patriots were particularly active. Every town organized a company of militia and appointed officers to train the men. One quarter of each company were "minutemen," pledged to meet at a minute's notice. Stores of provisions and munitions were collected at Worcester and Concord. General Gage decided to seize the stores at Concord and to arrest Samuel Adams and John Hancock, Patriot leaders who were hiding in Lexington.

PAUL REVERE, *the Boston silversmith and patriot, painted by Copley. The beautiful* "LIBERTY BOWL" *was made by him in honor of the House of Representatives of Massachusetts Bay for their courage in resisting the British Government.*

The first blows are struck.

On the night of April 18, 1775, a thousand British redcoats left Boston for Lexington. Warned by the midnight ride of Paul Revere and William Dawes, the Lexington militia gathered to meet the foe. When the British entered the town at dawn, their way was barred by sixty men lined up on the village green. The British ordered them to withdraw, but they refused. The little band was quickly swept aside, leaving eight killed and ten wounded. The British were too late to capture Hancock and Adams but marched on to Concord in time to destroy a small quantity of military stores. On their way back to Boston they were shot at from every hill and stone wall.

The news from Lexington and Concord went swiftly from one end of the colonies to the other. Everywhere it led to patriotic demonstrations and more vigorous preparations for war. Sixteen thousand militiamen from all over New England gathered outside Boston, ready for battle. They began a siege which lasted until the British removed their forces from Boston eleven months later.

Early in May a small band of Vermont patriots, led by Ethan Allen, sur-prised and captured Fort Ticonderoga. Without firing a shot these "Green Mountain Boys" took possession of a large quantity of ammunition and guns. Then they seized Crown Point, which opened the way to Canada.

The following month brought the bloody Battle of Bunker Hill. During the night of June 16 the New England militiamen fortified a hill a mile or so from Boston. The next day General Gage sent a force of regulars to dislodge them. Twice the colonials turned back the attackers with heavy losses. When the Redcoats charged a third time, the Americans had to retreat.

The Second Continental Congress meets.

Three weeks after the clashes at Lexington and Concord, the Second Continental Congress met in Independence Hall, Philadelphia. It faced a situation which could not be ignored—the people of Massachusetts were in arms against the king's troops. Many delegates urged the Congress to try once more a loyal petition to the king. Many others believed that the time for petitions was past and urged that men and supplies be sent to the camps around Boston. A few argued that the colonies should declare their independence.

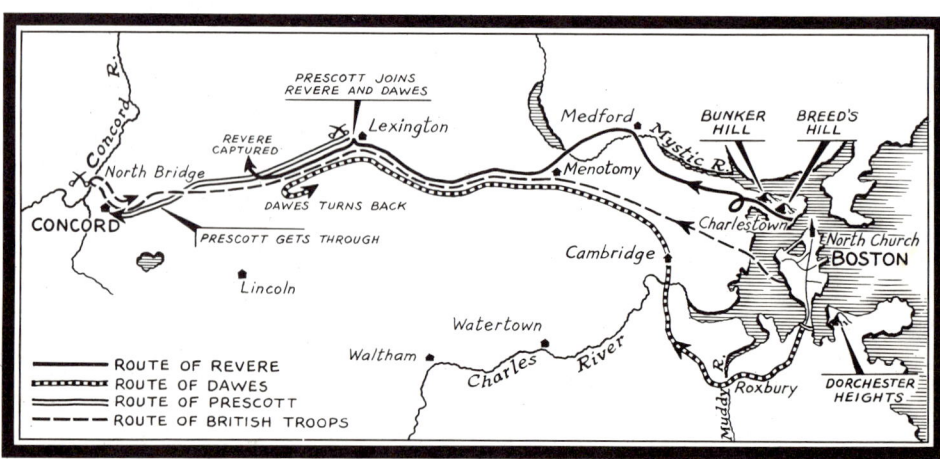

FIRST SHOTS OF THE REVOLUTIONARY WAR

110

"The Affair at North Bridge" from a painting. This episode at Salem, Massachusetts in February, 1775 was ONE OF THE FIRST INSTANCES OF ARMED RESISTANCE *to British soldiers in the American colonies.*

The Congress took a middle course. A respectful petition was sent to the king. (Some called it the "olive-branch" petition.) The Congress also urged the several colonies to prepare to defend themselves. It adopted as its own the army of New Englanders camped in a semicircle around Boston and appointed a Virginian, Colonel George Washington, as commander in chief of the Continental forces.

The Congress provided for a postal system and a system of money and credit. In this and in other ways it began to perform some of the tasks of a central government for all the colonies. Events were to keep the Congress in session for many years.

The British take harsh measures.

For months the majority of the colonists waited hopefully for the king's reply to the "olive-branch" petition. The king refused to receive the petition. Instead he proclaimed that the colonists were rebels. He hired twenty thousand Hessians to put down the revolt (see p. 116). Parliament closed all American ports, forbidding ships to enter or leave them. "It throws thirteen colonies out of the royal protection," said John Adams, "and makes us independent in spite of supplications and entreaties." As further signs that the British would not yield to colonial demands, the towns of Falmouth, Maine, and Norfolk, Virginia, were burned. These actions convinced many of the colonists that separation from England was the only way out.

Thomas Paine calls for independence.

Early in 1776 there was published a stirring pamphlet which boldly called for complete independence. This was *Common Sense* by Thomas Paine, a young Englishman who had recently come to Philadelphia. It gave the arguments for independence in a simple, lively style. A monarchy is an absurd form of government, wrote Paine, and George III nothing but a "Royal Brute." It is foolish, he said, for a great nation to remain under the control of an island across the ocean. If America were a separate nation it could trade with the whole world. It would also avoid being drawn into European wars. Moreover, Paine said, America is the only home left for human liberty.

Common Sense put into words what many were thinking. It was read far and wide. It helped persuade the undecided and the wavering that the thirteen colonies ought to separate from England.

British authority in the colonies ends.

Ties with the mother country were snapping. In April Congress opened colonial ports to all nations. A month later Congress advised the colonies to establish independent governments, as several had done already. Royal governors and other royal officials took refuge on British ships.

The colonies declare their independence.

In June, Richard Henry Lee, of Virginia, placed a motion before Congress saying that "these United Colonies are, and of right ought to be, free and independent states." The motion was adopted.

A committee was then chosen by Congress to draw up the Declaration of Independence. Thomas Jefferson wrote the first draft, which was approved by the other members of the committee with few changes. The Declaration was adopted on July 4, 1776. This famous document is based on English political ideas. It sets forth the reasons for separating from England.

We hold these truths to be self-evident: That all men are created equal; that they are endowed by their Creator with

THE SECOND CONTINENTAL CONGRESS *voting independence at Independence Hall, Philadelphia.*

certain unalienable rights; that among these are life, liberty, and the pursuit of happiness. That, to secure these rights, governments are instituted among men, deriving their just powers from the consent of the governed, that, whenever any form of government becomes destructive of these ends, it is the right of the people to alter or to abolish it, and to institute a new government, laying its foundation on such principles, and organizing its powers in such form, as to them shall seem most likely to effect their safety and happiness.

In addition to this immortal statement of human rights, the Declaration lists the grievances of the colonies. These could leave no doubt what they desired from a government. The last paragraph repeats Lee's motion and pledges the members of Congress to defend the independence of the United States with their lives, their fortunes, and their sacred honor.

The Declaration clears the air.

The war was no longer merely an effort to force the British government to recognize American rights but a fight for independence. Every American now had to make up his mind whether to support the revolution or the king. About one third of all the colonists regarded the Declaration as an act of treason to the king. Taking the name of "Loyalists," they refused to have any part in the "rebellion." Most of the Loyalists belonged to the upper, or privileged, class.

Those who received the news of the Declaration with rejoicing came mostly from the less privileged classes —frontiersmen, small farmers, small tradesmen, wage earners. They hoped that the Revolution would bring them political and economic freedom. Many others, privileged and underprivileged alike, were saddened at the cutting of the ties with the mother country. Yet now that they had to make a choice they took the American side.

The hated stamp

FOR IDENTIFICATION

Samuel Adams	Fort Duquesne
Ethan Allen	George Grenville
Boston Massacre	Intolerable Acts
Boston Tea Party	Thomas Paine
Bunker Hill	William Pitt
Common Sense	Pontiac
Declaration of Rights	Quebec Act
and Grievances	Charles Townshend
Declaratory Act	General James Wolfe

FOR EXPLANATION OR DEFINITION

boycott	internal tax
committees of	nonimportation
correspondence	"olive-branch" petition
external tax	

FOR REVIEW

1. What were the causes of the French and Indian War?

2. Why did the governor of Virginia send George Washington to the Ohio?

3. What events in America hastened the conflict between England and France?

4. What is the significance of the victory of Wolfe at Quebec?

5. State terms of the Treaty of Paris, 1763, affecting the American colonies.

6. How did the French and Indian War change the attitude of the colonies toward England?

7. (a) What were the problems facing England in regard to the colonies after the French and Indian War? (b) What was George III's policy in colonial affairs?

8. (a) What was the purpose of the Proclamation of 1763 closing the frontier? (b) How was it received by the colonists?

9. What did Parliament hope to accomplish by the Sugar Act of 1764? By the Currency Act of 1764?

10. What was the purpose of the Quartering Act, 1765? The Stamp Act of 1765?

113

11. (a) What action was taken by the Stamp Act Congress of 1765? (b) What action did Parliament take?

12. What were the Townshend Acts?

13. What was the purpose of the Massachusetts Circular Letter drafted by Samuel Adams, 1768?

14. (a) Why were British soldiers sent to Boston in 1768? (b) How were they treated? (c) What were the effects of the Boston Massacre, 1770?

15. How did the colonists endeavor to keep the various sections of the country informed of developments?

16. (a) What were the chief provisions of the Intolerable Acts of 1774? The Quebec Act of 1774? (b) How did the Intolerable Acts help to bind the colonies together?

17. What action was taken by the First Continental Congress?

18. Why did the British march to Lexington and Concord? What happened?

19. (a) What were the first actions taken by the Second Continental Congress? (b) What steps did it take that show it was acting as a central government for all the colonies?

20. (a) What motion did Richard Henry Lee place before the Congress? (b) What were the reasons for the Declaration of Independence? (c) What basic principles of government and human rights does it set forth? (d) What were its effects?

FOR FURTHER STUDY AND DISCUSSION

1. (a) What were the essential elements in the problem of imperial control of the colonies? (b) How was this problem affected by the French and Indian War?

2. (a) Why did the colonists object to the Proclamation of 1763? (b) Does it deserve to be regarded as the most important of all the acts that contributed to the American Revolution?

3. Was resistance to the Stamp Act illegal, revolutionary? Give your reasons.

4. Discuss colonial efforts to bring about a change in Parliamentary policy in 1774 and 1775. Compare with methods used to secure repeal of the Stamp Act.

5. In 1775 the Second Continental Congress declared, "We have not raised armies with ambitious designs of separating from Great Britain." How can you reconcile this statement with the Declaration of Independence in the following year?

6. Select four or five of the grievances against George III mentioned in the Declaration of Independence, and give specific examples which illustrate these grievances.

7. Explain the doctrine of equality announced in the Declaration of Independence.

8. Note the quotation from John Adams at the beginning of this chapter. What arguments would you advance in support?

FOR INDIVIDUAL OR GROUP ACTIVITIES

1. Assume that you were a newspaper editor in England in sympathy with the policy of the government in the period 1763–76. Write the headlines you would use to report the Stamp Act Congress, the Boston Tea Party, the meeting of the First Continental Congress, the Battle of Lexington and Concord, the Declaration of Independence. What headlines would you use to report the same events if you were a newspaper editor in Boston in sympathy with the colonial cause?

2. As a farmer living in the "back country," write a letter to the *Pennsylvania Gazette*, stating your views on the Proclamation of 1763.

3. James Otis' "Speech against Writs of Assistance," 1761, is in Commager, *Documents*, No. 32. Prepare a brief summary of his argument. What is the significance of Otis' contention that "an act against the Constitution is void"?

4. Organize two committees, one supporting Parliament and one supporting the colonists. Have these committees prepare for exhibition contrasting posters or cartoons on major events mentioned in this chapter.

5. Dramatize the meeting of the Second Continental Congress. Illustrate the conflicting points of view of its members.

6. Prepare an assembly program about the revolutionary period, using famous speeches, poems, or articles.

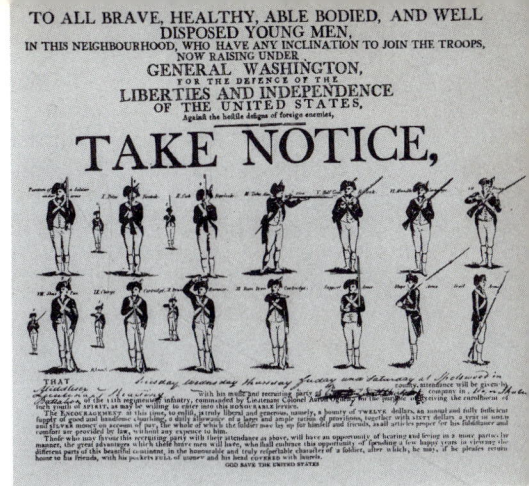

These are the times that try men's souls. The summer soldier and the sunshine patriot will, in this crisis, shrink from the service of his country; but he that stands it now deserves the love and thanks of men and women.

——Thomas Paine, *The Crisis*

7. THE THIRTEEN COLONIES WIN THE WAR FOR INDEPENDENCE

The Opponents Are Not Evenly Matched

Congress seeks and obtains foreign aid.

To declare independence is one thing; to win it in battle, quite another. From the first, Americans realized they were no match for the mighty British Empire. Unless they could get foreign help, victory could hardly be expected. Three months before the Declaration of Independence Congress sent an agent to Europe to seek aid. Spain and France, smarting from their recent defeat by the British, answered the American call for help. They secretly shipped military supplies to the revolting colonists.

The British have important advantages.

With ten times the wealth and three times the population of the thirteen colonies, Great Britain was a powerful foe. At first most British leaders thought it would not take long to subdue the Americans. The British had the following advantages:

1. A strong navy. This enabled the British (a) to blockade American ports and (b) to protect their troop ships and supply ships. The Americans had a very small navy.

2. A well-equipped, well-trained, well-disciplined regular army, led by experienced officers. The American troops lacked both equipment and training. They heartily disliked to take orders. A large number of their officers had no military experience.

3. A strong central government with full authority to raise money and to carry on the war. The Americans had a Continental Congress without any authority. It was really not a legislature but a conference of ambassadors from thirteen independent states. It could not raise money by taxation, and the states usually turned a deaf ear to its requests for money.

4. A large number of factories able to turn out every kind of war material. The colonies had few factories, for the British restrictions and the scarcity of labor had held back the growth of manufacturing.

115

5. The co-operation of American Loyalists. At least a third of the colonists were loyal to the king, while another third did not care which side won. Thousands of Americans joined the royal army. New York furnished more soldiers to George III than to George Washington. In every colony there were Loyalists who opposed the efforts of the Patriots to carry on the war.

The British also have handicaps.

The British also had a few disadvantages. In contrast to the American Patriots, the English people were half-hearted in their support of the war. They did not regard the colonists as enemies. Those who opposed the king at home believed that in resisting him the Americans were fighting the cause of all Englishmen. Many British officers resigned their commissions rather than fight the colonists. When more troops were needed, few Englishmen volunteered. So the king hired thousands of fighting men from German princes. These Hessians and Brunswickers had no interest in the war. When the Americans offered them free land, they deserted in large numbers.

British lukewarmness toward the war even reached the high command. Sir William Howe, who was commander in chief of the British forces in America in the early years of the war, did not try to crush the rebels. He had opposed the harsh measures that brought on the war. After war began he still hoped that the Americans could be persuaded to give up their demand for independence.

Another handicap of the British was the necessity of moving troops and supplies a distance of three thousand miles in sailing ships. The journey never took less than five weeks and often took twelve. Many soldiers were weakened by the long voyage and some died on the way.

The greatest handicap of the British was the fact that in order to win they had to conquer a vast territory. While they could readily seize American shipping and occupy the coastal towns, they could not advance far inland without being cut off from their base of supplies. When hard pressed the British could withdraw only to the sea. The Americans could withdraw to the Appalachians, where they were safe from attack.

Colonial advantages.

In addition to geographical advantages, the Americans had other factors on their side:

1. They were used to the climate.
2. They knew the lay of the land.
3. They were fighting on their own soil and for their own homes.
4. The typical volunteer was a farmer. He excelled in wilderness fighting and guerrilla warfare.
5. Many American soldiers used rifles, which had better range and accuracy than the smoothbore muskets used by the British.
6. The Americans received foreign aid throughout the war.
7. The Americans had a great leader, George Washington. He became a symbol of national resistance, giving his countrymen courage in the long periods of adversity. Two modern historians say of him in their book:

He proved all in all to the patriot cause, its best guide and support. He can be criticized on narrow military grounds. He never handled an army larger than a modern division, he made many missteps, he was defeated again and again. Yet, taking command at forty-three, he became the soul of the war. This Virginia planter and frontier colonel was its informing spirit because of his unflagging patriotism, his calm wisdom, his serene moral courage; because in the gloomiest hours he never lost his dignity, poise, or decision; because he knew how to combine enterprise and caution; because his integrity, elevation, and magnanimity never failed, his fortitude never faltered.[1]

Progress of the War to 1777

Washington takes command.

In June, 1775, Washington accepted the position of commander in chief with the understanding that he would receive no pay for his services. He took command at Cambridge two weeks after the Battle of Bunker Hill and found the colonial militia "a mixed multitude of people under very little discipline, order, or government." The men were poorly armed and without supplies. They were thinking about going home. Washington began at once to develop them into a real fighting organization.

Attempts to conquer Canada fail.

American leaders thought the Canadians would gladly throw off the British yoke and join the American cause. Congress sent two expeditions north in the autumn of 1775. The first one, led by General Richard Montgomery, took Montreal. A second expedition, led by General Benedict Arnold, marched through the Maine wilderness to help Montgomery attack Quebec. In the fierce fighting at Quebec on the last day of the year, Montgomery was killed and Arnold wounded. After spending the winter outside Quebec, the Americans were forced to retreat to Crown Point. The hope of Canadian help had proved vain, and the attempt to conquer Canada was given up.

The British evacuate Boston.

Early in 1776 the guns captured at Ticonderoga arrived in Cambridge. In March, Washington's forces seized and fortified Dorchester Heights, just south of Boston. General Howe, who was

now in command of the British forces, saw that he could not hold the city. He and his army sailed to Halifax, Nova Scotia, taking with them hundreds of Loyalists.

Patriots win early contests in the South.

The British met another setback in the early months of 1776. Loyalists were numerous in the Carolinas and with their aid the British hoped to occupy both colonies. A large group of Loyalists headed toward Wilmington, North Carolina, to co-operate with a British fleet which was on its way there. They were met and beaten at Moore's Creek by a Patriot force. The British commander now realized he had little

ABRAHAM WHIPPLE. *This Rhode Island naval officer, with a party of fifty men, attacked and burned the British schooner* Gaspée *in June, 1772. The* Gaspée, *while trying to enforce revenue laws, had run aground.*

---

[1] Quoted by permission from *Pocket History of the United States* by·Allan Nevins and Henry Commager, Pocket Books, Inc. p. 91.

chance of success in North Carolina. He decided to attack Charleston, South Carolina. Patriots had built a log fort to defend Charleston. Their cannon did so much damage to the British fleet that it went back to New York (June 28, 1776). The South was saved from further invasion for two years.

Patriot successes in the South and at Ticonderoga and Boston encouraged those who wanted to cut loose from the British Empire. By June, as we have noted, a Congressional committee was at work on the Declaration of Independence (see p. 112).

The British seize New York.

After the British left Boston, Washington expected them to attack New York. He shifted most of his troops to Manhattan and Brooklyn. Companies of raw recruits from nearby states joined his army until it numbered between twenty and twenty-five thousand men. It was probably the largest force Washington ever commanded, but it had little equipment and was poorly prepared for battle.

General Howe landed on Staten Island in July. His brother, Admiral Richard Howe, brought a strong fleet with 150 transports to support him. General Howe now had 32,000 men. In August he surprised and shattered part of the American forces in the Battle of Long Island. Washington had no choice but to withdraw his army as rapidly as possible. Pursued by the British, the Americans retreated, first from Long Island, then from Manhattan, and finally across New Jersey to Pennsylvania. Thousands were taken prisoner. Thousands more went home because they were discouraged or their terms of enlistment had expired.

Washington appeals for a regular army.

Thus far the Americans had no regular army. The fighting was done by state militia who enlisted for terms of three, or at most, six months. By the time the men had some experience, their enlistment was over. Many were small farmers. If their families were not to starve, they had to go home from time to time to help with the plowing and harvesting. Others were frontiersmen whose families might be massacred by Indians during their absence. It is not surprising that desertions were common or that when the militiaman's brief term of enlistment ended, he usually hurried home. Near the end of 1776 Washington complained to Congress that his volunteers "come in, you cannot tell how; go, you cannot tell when; and act, you cannot tell where; consume your provisions, exhaust your stores, and leave you at last at a critical moment." He appealed for the organization of a regular army, under the control of Congress and looking to Congress for its pay.

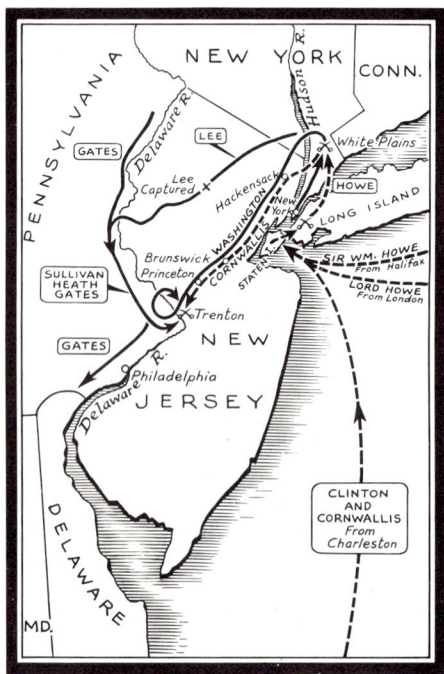

THE WAR IN THE CENTER, 1776

118

THE BATTLE OF PRINCETON, *January 3, 1777. Victory here and at Trenton restored the patriots' shattered morale.*

Washington gains a brilliant victory.

Howe had possession of New Jersey. When he offered pardon to New Jersey patriots who would declare their loyalty to the king, 2700 accepted. The people of Philadelphia expected their city to be occupied any day. The Patriot cause seemed hopeless.

In this black hour Washington suddenly turned north. Late on Christmas night, 1776, with what was left of his army, he crossed the ice-filled Delaware River. After a quick march, he fell upon the Hessians at Trenton. Taken completely by surprise, the enemy was driven from the town with heavy losses. A few days later Washington made a surprise attack on Princeton, where he defeated three British regiments. Having recovered most of

the state of New Jersey, Washington went into winter quarters at Morristown.

These victories restored American courage and greatly strengthened the country's faith in Washington. Yet try as it might, Congress could not raise an adequate army. Few men were willing to enlist for a term of one or two years. This is not hard to understand. No provision was made for the families of men in service and no pensions were paid for men who fell in battle. Much of the time, too, Congress lacked money to pay its soldiers or even to clothe and feed them. Throughout the war Washington had to depend chiefly on state militiamen. This meant building an army over and over from raw recruits.

119

The British lose the Battle of Saratoga.

The year 1777 was to prove the most important of the war. The British worked out a careful plan for driving a wedge through New York state from Canada to the Atlantic. Their purpose was to separate New England from the rest of the states. General Burgoyne, with an army of 8000 men, was to come down from Canada by Lake Champlain and the upper Hudson Valley. Colonel St. Leger was to come with another force from Canada by way of Lake Ontario. At the same time General Howe was to proceed from New York up the Hudson to Albany to join his forces with those of Burgoyne and St. Leger. With New England cut off and the great Champlain-Hudson route in their hands, the British thought the rebellion could quickly be ended.

The elaborate scheme ended in complete failure. St. Leger was de-

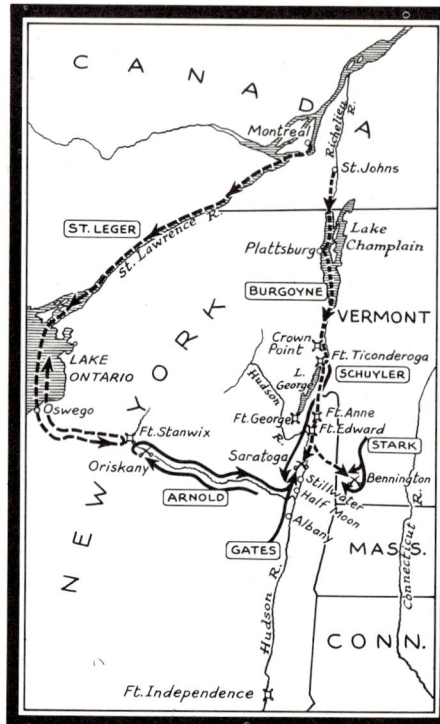

THE SARATOGA CAMPAIGN, 1777

(Left) GENERAL JOHN BURGOYNE. *The British plan for a three-pronged attack to isolate New England demanded flawless liaison between the forces commanded by St. Leger, Howe, and Burgoyne.*

(Below) *Burgoyne's camp on the Hudson River near Albany*

feated at Oriskany, New York. Burgoyne's army made painfully slow progress through the rough, wooded country between Lake Champlain and the Hudson River, with the result that his supplies of food ran short. Meanwhile, about 20,000 Americans, chiefly short-term militiamen from New England and New York, gathered to meet him north of Albany. No help came from Howe, who had gone to capture Philadelphia at the very time he should have advanced up the Hudson to aid Burgoyne. Burgoyne tried to push on, although his men were on half rations. He suffered heavy losses in several fights. Unable either to retreat or to advance, he surrendered at Saratoga (October 17, 1777). This disaster to the British proved to be the turning point of the war. Yet hard, discouraging years for the Patriots still lay ahead.

Howe takes Philadelphia.

Instead of going to meet Burgoyne, Howe had embarked from New York with his main force and sailed up Chesapeake Bay. Washington guessed that he intended to attack Philadelphia and moved south to meet him. After bitter fighting at Brandywine Creek, Howe occupied Philadelphia, and the Congress fled to York, Pennsylvania.

Washington moved his defeated army to Valley Forge, some thirty miles west of Philadelphia. He and his men suffered hardships all winter. Congress had no funds to pay for supplies and foodstuffs; the paper money it issued was almost worthless. Hungry and poorly clad, the army dwindled until, again, less than 5000 men were left.

The Revolution Becomes Part of a World War

The French become our allies.

Ever since the Declaration of Independence the French and Spanish had been giving secret aid to the Americans. The French wanted to help the revolting colonies for three reasons:

1. They desired revenge on England for earlier French defeats.

2. They hoped for trade advantages with the United States.

3. They hoped to recover lost territory in the Mississippi Valley.

When news of Burgoyne's surrender at Saratoga reached Paris in December, the French felt reasonably sure that the Americans could win. They decided to recognize the independence of the United States and give it open military aid. In February, 1778, France and the United States signed a treaty in which each nation promised to make war on the enemies of the other and not to make a separate peace. At once Great Britain and France were at war. After entering the war France greatly increased its aid to the American cause.

Parliament tries to end the war.

The British prime minister, Lord North, was disturbed by the French alliance. Under his leadership Parliament passed the Conciliatory Acts (March, 1778) offering the Americans everything they had asked for before their Declaration of Independence. The acts of Parliament they had objected to would be repealed if they would remain in the empire. Had the offer come sooner, it might have been accepted. Coming after the Battle of Saratoga and the French alliance, it was too late.

Spain and Holland enter the war.

A year later Spain joined France in war against Great Britain. Holland, long a secret enemy of the British, also entered the war. Great Britain could not give her full attention to crushing the revolt in North America. She was forced to use much fighting strength in defending her own shores and her trading privileges in Africa and India.

Individual Europeans help our cause.

The American struggle for independence stirred the sympathy of Europeans who loved liberty. Many private citizens in France and Holland lent money to the United States. Other Europeans crossed the ocean to offer their services as officers. Lafayette, a young French nobleman, came in 1777, serving with distinction until the end of the war. Baron von Steuben came from Poland in 1778 to train the army. He became a valued advisor to Washington and spent his own fortune for the American cause. Kosciusko, a distinguished Polish engineer, served here throughout the war. Baron De Kalb from Bavaria and Count Pulaski from Poland died here in battle for the American cause.

War on the sea.

At the outbreak of the war the Americans had almost no navy. During the siege of Boston, Washington had guns placed on some fishing schooners. These converted vessels seized several British ships carrying military stores to Boston. By 1777 the Continental navy consisted of thirty-four small vessels, but at the end of the war only seven were in commission. In addition there were a few small state navies. Probably the best-known American naval hero was John Paul Jones.

Hundreds of British merchantmen were captured by American privateers. A privateer was an armed ship, privately owned, with a government license to capture enemy vessels. When the captured ship was sold, the profits were divided between owner and crew.

After France entered the war her navy played an important part in defeating the British. The French fleet based in the West Indies was a constant threat to British warships in American waters. This threat kept the British from continuing their close blockade of American ports. Soon American ships were going in and out of their home ports almost at will. The help given by the French fleet made possible the victory at Yorktown, which brought the war to a close.

Clark wins in the West.

To keep as many Americans as possible from joining Washington's army, the British encouraged the Indians to attack frontier settlements. The Indians got ammunition and guns from British forts in the territory north of the Ohio River. In 1778 George Rogers Clark made a daring plan to seize these forts. Leading an expedition of 175 Virginians, he sailed down the Ohio and took Kaskaskia, Cahokia, and Vincennes. Colonel Henry Hamilton, the British governor for the Northwest, came from Detroit in December and retook Vincennes. Clark then gathered about 150 men at Kaskaskia and set out for Vincennes. Because of an untimely flood the men had to wade many miles in icy water up to their waists and sometimes up to their necks. To add to their sufferings, provisions gave out. After eighteen terrible days they reached the fort at Vincennes and forced the surprised Hamilton to surrender. With this victory Clark's men were in possession of the great Northwest.

The war shifts to the South.

Until 1778 practically all the fighting had been in the North. After 1778 it was nearly all south of the Potomac. Sir Henry Clinton, the new British commander in chief, believed that most of the people in the South were Loyalists. He planned to detach Georgia, the Carolinas, and Virginia from the other colonies one by one.

GENERAL GEORGE ROGERS CLARK

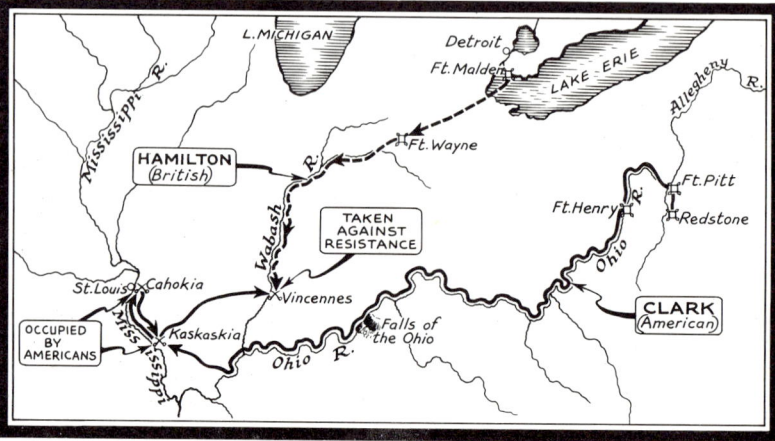

FIGHTING IN THE WEST, 1778–79

GENERAL NATHANAEL GREENE

LORD CORNWALLIS

PRINCIPAL THRUSTS AND BATTLES OF THE REVOLUTIONARY WAR

Late in 1778 British ships appeared off Savannah, Georgia, and captured the town. Patriot officials and militia were driven from the state and a colonial government set up. The British accomplished little more until May, 1780, when they took Charleston, the richest seaport in the South. Cornwallis, who was in command of the British southern campaign, then began to march north through the interior of the Carolinas. He expected to be joined by thousands of Loyalists. Instead, Patriot guerrillas sniped at his men. A large detachment of his army was captured by frontiersmen at the Battle of King's Mountain (October 7, 1780). His advance was stopped altogether at the Battle of Guilford Court House in North Carolina (March, 1781). Cornwallis then withdrew to the coast.

Cornwallis is trapped at Yorktown.

Cornwallis next tried to conquer the rich state of Virginia. He boasted that he would drive out "that boy" Lafayette and his small force. Cornwallis was unsuccessful and returned to the coast with his army worn out and reduced in numbers. He established himself at the mouth of the York River on Chesapeake Bay. Here he threw up fortifications and called for reinforcements.

At this time Washington, with about 6000 American soldiers, waited near New York watching Clinton. Count Rochambeau, with about 5000 French soldiers, was at Newport, Rhode Island. Washington, on learning that Cornwallis was at Yorktown, saw his chance. He sent a swift ship to the West Indies to beg Comte de Grasse to bring the French fleet to Chesapeake

SURRENDER OF LORD CORNWAL-
LIS *at Yorktown, October 19,
1781. Painted by John Trumbull.*

Bay. Rochambeau with his army joined Washington on the Hudson, and the two leaders pretended to be making ready to besiege New York City. Then they suddenly marched south and laid siege to Yorktown. The French fleet already had possession of the entrance to Chesapeake Bay and easily drove off the British fleet when it arrived from New York to rescue Cornwallis. Cornwallis' 7500 men were surrounded by 16,000 enemies. Considering his situation hopeless, Cornwallis surrendered on October 19, 1781.

There were still about 30,000 Brit-

ish soldiers in New York and the southern seaport towns. George III wished to continue the war, but his people were tired of the struggle. Parliament voted to make peace with the colonies (March, 1782). Soon after, peace talks began in Paris.

The British recognize our independence.

The British government tried hard to arrange a peace without granting American independence. Neither Congress nor any of the states would agree to such an arrangement. France and Holland also refused it. Once the Brit-

ish gave in on this main point, they made generous terms. England acknowledged the thirteen states, each by name, to be free and independent. She recognized the Great Lakes as the northern boundary and the Mississippi as the western boundary of the new nation. She returned Florida to France's ally, Spain. England agreed that the Americans could continue to share the fisheries on the Newfoundland and Canadian coasts, just as they had before.

Great Britain asked the United States to arrange for the payment of debts owed by Americans to Brit-

ish merchants. The British also asked that all property taken from the Loyalists be returned to them. The American commissioners explained that the states controlled these matters and that Congress could do no more than recommend that the states give satisfaction. The British commissioners accepted this suggestion. Hence the treaty included a promise to remove all barriers to the collection of British debts in American courts. It also pledged Congress to advise the states to restore the property of the Loyalists. The British promised, for their part, to restore or

125

ports
N.W.

UNITED STATES

NORTH AMERICA AFTER
THE TREATY OF PARIS, 1783

pay for all goods and slaves seized by their army during the war.

The final treaty of peace was signed at Paris on September 3, 1783.

The Revolution inspires other nations.

The United States in 1783, with a population of 3,500,000, was a small nation compared with some of the European nations. But the Revolution meant more than the entrance of a small nation into the world. It meant the birth of a nation whose ideals were equal opportunity, individual liberty, and government by the consent of the governed. Although these ideals were not at once or fully put into practice, they were to prove an inspiration for generations to come.

The Revolutionary War was the first example of a successful revolt by a colonial people. It led Great Britain

to treat her remaining colonies more generously. It encouraged the Spanish and Portuguese colonies to fight and win their national independence early in the 1800's.

The French Revolution, which began in 1789, was the child of the American Revolution. The French Declaration of the Rights of Man affirms the same ideals as our own Declaration of Independence. The influence of both declarations has been felt in many parts of the world right down to our own time. The unrest which we see in colonial lands today springs from the desire of all men everywhere for their right to "life, liberty, and the pursuit of happiness."

FOR IDENTIFICATION

Burgoyne	Treaty of Paris, 1783
George Rogers Clark	Valley Forge
Conciliatory Act	Vincennes
Saratoga	Yorktown

FOR EXPLANATION OR DEFINITION

blockade	Patriots
Loyalists	privateer

FOR REVIEW

1. What advantages did the British have? What disadvantages?

2. What advantages did the colonists have? What disadvantages?

3. How did geographic features influence the conduct of the war?

4. In what ways did Washington find militiamen unsatisfactory? What solution did he recommend? What difficulties did Congress have in raising a regular army?

5. Trace the movements of Washington from the evacuation of Boston to Morristown, New Jersey.

6. What was the purpose of the British drive from Canada in 1777? Why did this drive fail?

7. Why did France decide to help the colonies?

8. What other European nations entered the war against England? Why?

126

9. What individual Europeans helped the colonies? State the services of each.

10. State the services of John Paul Jones.

11. (a) How did frontier settlements suffer during the war? (b) How did George Rogers Clark win the Northwest?

12. (a) What is the significance of the military campaigns in the South? (b) How was Cornwallis trapped at Yorktown?

13. State the terms of the Treaty of Paris, 1783, with regard to the thirteen colonies, the northern boundary, the Newfoundland fisheries, the payment of American debts, and property taken from Loyalists.

14. What was done with Florida at the end of the war?

15. What effect did the American Revolution have in Europe? Elsewhere?

FOR FURTHER STUDY AND DISCUSSION

1. France contributed ships, money, and men. Arrange these in order of their importance and defend your arrangement. Report on the extent of French financial assistance to the colonies.

2. Did the victories of George Rogers Clark have any influence on the making of the peace treaty? (Consult other accounts before forming an answer.)

3. Evaluate the services of George Washington as commander in chief.

4. Vergennes, the French Minister of Foreign Affairs, is reported to have exclaimed, "The English buy the peace, rather than make it." What did he mean? Helpful source: Hart, *Contemporaries*, Vol. II, No. 216.

5. What features of the Treaty of Paris do you think were likely to be a source of future difficulties with England?

6. Why is the American Revolution an important event from the point of view of world history? Helpful source: Hart, *Contemporaries*, Vol. II, No. 217.

FOR INDIVIDUAL OR GROUP ACTIVITIES

1. Many interesting events of the Revolutionary War, because of limitations of space, are but briefly mentioned or are omitted from the text: the story of Nathan Hale, the exploits of John Paul Jones, the story of Benedict Arnold and Major André, the work of Robert Morris and Haym Salomon in financing the war, the activities of Benjamin Franklin and Silas Deane in France, the fighting in the South. Assign committees to investigate these topics and submit a brief report.

2. By means of biographical sketches of men like Lafayette, von Steuben, Pulaski, Kosciusko, John Barry, John Paul Jones, Daniel Morgan, Charles Lee, and others, prepare a review of the main events in the War of Independence.

3. Prepare a pictorial chart of the American advantages at the outbreak of the American Revolution.

4. Assign special committees to report on the fighting in the West Indies, and the contributions of Spain and Holland to the winning of the war.

5. Read Kenneth Roberts' novel *Oliver Wiswell*, dealing with Loyalists during the Revolutionary War. What sidelights on the war does this novel reveal?

LANDING OF THE FRENCH ARMY *under Count Rochambeau at Westport, Rhode Island, in July, 1780.*

Religion, morality, and knowledge being necessary to good government and the happiness of mankind, schools and the means of education shall forever be encouraged.——Northwest Ordinance of 1787

Cleveland, Ohio, in 1800

8. THE NATION EXPERIENCES A CRITICAL PERIOD

The Revolution Brought Important Changes

The Revolution as a social movement.

The revolt against Great Britain was accompanied by far-reaching changes in American society. A more democratic social order was emerging. The common people had taken to heart the ringing phrases of the Declaration of Independence: "All men are created equal . . . They are endowed by their Creator with certain unalienable rights . . . among these are life, liberty, and the pursuit of happiness." Aroused by the stirring events of the Revolution, more and more of the people began to take part in discussing public affairs. They called for an end to special privilege based on birth and wealth. Among other changes they demanded the right to vote.

State governments are created.

Separation from England brought immediate gains in political democracy. The thirteen colonies became thirteen independent states. Eleven of them held conventions which drew up new constitutions. (Only in Connecticut and Rhode Island, which had been self-governing colonies, were the old charters considered to be a suitable base for state government.) Many of the men who framed the new constitutions were called "radicals" by the conservatives of that time. These "radicals" insisted on giving the people more voice in the government than they had under the colonial charters. Among the changes they won were these:

1. Stronger popular control. Governors were now responsible to the people rather than to the Crown. In five states the governor was elected by popular vote; in the other eight, he was elected by the legislature. In all states the upper house of the legislature was chosen either by the people or by the lower house.

2. Increased representation of frontier sections. In several states the long-slighted western counties received more representation in the legislature.

3. More safeguards against tyranny. The state constitutions sharply limited the power of the governor. In nine states he was granted no veto power. Except in four states, his term was to be a single year. Frequent elections were provided in order that the officials and representatives could be changed whenever the voters felt a change was needed. In addition to these safeguards, a number of the new constitutions included a bill of rights guaranteeing freedom of speech and press, freedom from unwarranted search and seizure, and the right of trial by jury.

4. *Broader suffrage.* In most of the colonies voting had been restricted to a small class. During and after the Revolution the qualifications for voting were considerably lightened. While four states restricted voting to landholders, the amount of land required was generally small. In Virginia, for example, it was twenty-five acres of settled land. Pennsylvania, New Hampshire, and Georgia gave the suffrage to all men who paid a poll tax. Other states limited voting to persons who paid a property tax, but the property could be personal, such as tools or furniture or livestock.

Religious freedom is increased.

During the Revolution the movement to separate church and state gained strong support. The Anglican Church was disestablished in all six states where it had formerly received public aid. Separation of church and state was not achieved so quickly in the three states where the Congregational Church was established.

When the Anglican Church was disestablished in Virginia, some argued that all denominations should receive state aid. Others, including Thomas Jefferson, argued that the government should support no church. After a long struggle, the Virginia legislature adopted Jefferson's Statute of Religious Liberty (1786). It declares:

No man shall be compelled to frequent or support any religious worship, place, or ministry whatsoever, nor shall he be enforced, restrained, molested, or . . . otherwise suffer on account of his religious opinions or belief: but . . . all men shall be free to profess, and by argument to maintain, their opinions in matters of religion.

Speaking of this Statute, James Madison said that "in Virginia was extinguished forever the ambitious hope of making laws for the human mind."

The principles expressed in the Statute of Religious Liberty eventually were to have great influence in the United States and in other democratic countries. For a time, however, several of the states did not fully accept them. For example, in three states only Protestants could be elected to the legislature. But before many years went by such restrictions were seen to be a denial of liberty of thought and conscience and were abolished.

The number of landowners is increased.

During the Revolution the states seized the lands of the Crown, the proprietors, and the rich Loyalists. Much of this land was broken up into small parcels and sold to farmers or given to veterans. The quitrent system was abolished. In addition, the laws of inheritance were changed so that all children might have an equal share in their father's land. (Under the English law of *primogeniture*, which had been followed in the southern colonies, the eldest son inherited all his parents' land.) All these changes in the land system increased the number of small landowners.

Other changes emphasize human rights.

The new respect for individuals led to better treatment of criminals. Laws setting the death penalty for minor offenses were repealed. Four states changed laws that put poor debtors in jail. Soon after the Revolution a society was formed in Philadelphia to work for improvements in prisons. At that time prisons were places of horror. It was a long time, however, before they were much changed.

In the late 1700's there was a growing belief that slavery was wrong. In 1775 Philadelphia Quakers organized the first antislavery society in the world. Jefferson tried to include in the Declaration of Independence a statement that slavery was a violation of the "most sacred rights of life and liberty." Nearly all the states prohibited the importation of slaves from abroad. In addition, most of the northern states abolished slavery or arranged for the gradual freeing of slaves within their borders. Virginia made it easier for masters to set their slaves free, and quite a few slaveowners did free their Negroes.

Thus we see that a start was being made at putting into effect the noble principles of the Declaration of Independence. These high ideals gave to America a priceless heritage. Yet by 1783 the democratic revolution was only in its beginning. "The American war is over," wrote Benjamin Rush of Philadelphia, "but this is far from the case with the American revolution. On the contrary, nothing but the first act of the great drama is closed."

The Independent States Form a Confederation

Articles of Confederation are ratified.

Between 1775 and 1781 the Continental Congress served as the national government. It had no official powers, but the war was on and it had to act. It created a Continental army and navy. It adopted the Declaration of Independence. It made agreements with the Indians and with foreign countries. It asked the states for contributions of money and supplies.

The members of Congress wanted to have its powers put down on paper and approved by the states. A committee of congressmen was appointed in June, 1776, to draw up a plan for uniting the states into a confederation, or league. Late the next year Congress submitted this plan of union, or constitution, to the states. The plan, known as the Articles of Confederation, did not go into effect until the war was almost over. The long delay was caused by a dispute over western land claims.

Six of the states—Massachusetts, Connecticut, Virginia, North Carolina, South Carolina, and Georgia—claimed

	STEPS TOWARD UNION	COLONIES
1643–1684	New England Confederation	4
1686–1689	Dominion of New England	7
1754	Albany Congress (Franklin's Plan)	7
1765	Stamp Act Congress	9
1772–1776	Committees of correspondence	13
1774	First Continental Congress	12
1775	Second Continental Congress	13
		STATES
1781–1789	Articles of Confederation	13
1785	Mt. Vernon Conference	2
1786	Annapolis Convention	5
1787	Constitutional Convention	12
1787–1790	Federal Constitution ratified	13
1789	Federal Constitution placed in operation	13

large areas west of the Appalachians because their original charters granted them lands "from sea to sea." New York also claimed western lands because of a treaty with the Iroquois Indians. The other six states had no such claims. Maryland refused to approve the Articles of Confederation unless all claims to western lands were ceded to the new government. Since the consent of every state was necessary before the Articles could go into effect, Maryland finally won its point. In 1780 New York agreed to cede its claims. A few months later, Virginia offered to sacrifice its claims. Maryland then ratified the Articles and they went into effect March 1, 1781. Thus, through the insistence of one state, the lands west of the Appalachians became a national domain.

The Articles create a weak central government.

The Articles of Confederation announced a "perpetual union" and a "firm league of friendship" between the states. Each state was to retain its "sovereignty, freedom, and independence." The Articles intentionally made the central government weak. The government was headed by a one-house Congress in which each state had an equal voice. No matter of importance could be settled unless at least nine of the states agreed.

Congress was given the power to declare war and to maintain armed forces. It could make treaties but could not compel the states to observe them. It could borrow money but could not levy taxes to repay the loan. Congress depended on the states to enforce any

American soldier of the Revolution in his buckskin clothing

WESTERN LANDS AFTER STATES GAVE UP CLAIMS

laws it might enact. It could not punish lawbreakers. Moreover, it had no right to collect duties on imports or to regulate commerce.

Congress had the greatest difficulty in getting funds to support the government and the armed forces. From 1781 to 1783, for example, Congress asked the states for $10,000,000, but they furnished only $1,500,000. Government officials and members of the armed forces seldom received their pay. The interest on the national debt was unpaid. The treasurer borrowed money until no one would lend the government another dollar.

Congressional leaders were not blind to the weaknesses of this "league of friendship." Congress appealed to the states in vain for power to levy a small duty on imports. Congress also begged for power to regulate commerce; this, too, was refused. A change in the Articles required the consent of all the states. To every suggestion that the Articles be amended, one state at least said "no." Because of this situation Washington described the Confederation as "a rope of sand."

Why were the states so unwilling to strengthen the national government? There were several reasons. *First,* there was the strong loyalty felt by the people of a state to their state government. The state governments had been in operation since the first settlement of the country. The people regarded their state assemblies as their own mouthpiece, for in endless squabbles with royal governors the legislatures had stood for liberty. *Second,* there was the fear that the central government might interfere with the people's liberties. The war had been fought to end interference by Parliament; interference by Congress was equally unwelcome. *Third,* there was scarcely any feeling of national unity now that the war had been won. Communication and commerce between states was slight. Travel

was extremely difficult. Most people, except soldiers, still had never been outside their own state.

Foreign nations make difficulties.

The diplomats whom Congress sent abroad met a cold reception. The new republic had hardly a friend in the world. Every European king hoped it would collapse. Even our ally, France, hoped we would remain so weak that we would do as she said.

The Spaniards, who held Florida, the land west of the Mississippi, and the Mississippi's mouth, made no secret of their ill will. They interfered with our use of the Mississippi. They claimed that Florida included most of what is now Alabama and Mississippi. They maintained posts in this area and stirred up the Indians who lived there to attack American settlers. Efforts to make an agreement with Spain came to nothing.

Great Britain did not take the trouble to send us an ambassador. It refused to make a trade treaty, saying that thirteen different treaties would be necessary. It also refused to withdraw from military and fur-trading posts in the Northwest Territory. The British excuse was that the states, contrary to the Treaty of Paris, had not returned the property taken from the Loyalists and had interfered with the collection of debts owed to English merchants. Congress had no power to make the states observe the treaty.

Most shameful of all, the pirates of Algiers, Tunis, Morocco, and Tripoli interfered with our commerce in the Mediterranean, stealing our ships and holding our citizens for ransom. The British navy no longer protected our commerce. Congress could not stop these crimes, for it was too poor to build a navy. It was plain that the United States could never win the respect of other nations so long as its government had so little power.

132

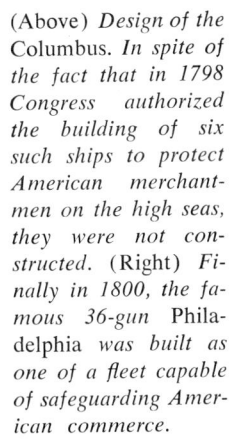

(Above) *Design of the Columbus. In spite of the fact that in 1798 Congress authorized the building of six such ships to protect American merchantmen on the high seas, they were not constructed.* (Right) *Finally in 1800, the famous 36-gun Philadelphia was built as one of a fleet capable of safeguarding American commerce.*

The states quarrel with one another.

The weakness of the Confederation was also shown by quarrels between the states. Connecticut and Pennsylvania nearly went to war over a boundary dispute. An argument over the frontier between Vermont and New York resulted in the calling out of troops. Several states made commercial war upon one another. Connecticut laid duties on imports from Massachusetts. Pennsylvania laid duties on goods from Delaware and New Jersey. New York taxed all imports from other states and charged a fee for every out-of-state boat which landed on its shores. Such signs of ill will between the states led to a fear that the Confederation would soon fall apart.

A depression creates social unrest.

After the war came several years of hard times. Great Britain closed its ports in the West Indies to American

133

vessels. The loss of the West Indies market hurt American shipowners, sailors, merchants, and all who had formerly produced goods for the West Indies. Manufacturing, which had boomed during the war to supply our military needs, fell off sharply. As a result there was much unemployment in the towns.

Of all the troubles suffered during the postwar depression, the one which bothered the most people was the scarcity of money. The paper money issued by Congress and by the states during the war had become entirely worthless. The soldiers went home, as Washington said, "without a farthing in their pockets." Gold and silver money became very dear; that is, only a little money could be obtained by selling a large quantity of goods. Prices and wages dropped.

In 1785 and 1786 there was much suffering, especially among small farmers and wage earners. Thousands who owed money lost their property or were imprisoned for failure to pay what they owed. In many cases the money had been borrowed when a dollar was worth little; now when dollars were worth a great deal, payment was very difficult. For example, a farmer who had borrowed a hundred dollars when this sum was worth ten bushels of wheat might have to sell a hundred bushels of wheat when the time came to pay his debt.

The poorer people demanded that the state governments print paper money to revive trade and make easier the payment of their debts. They also asked for "stay" laws to delay or prevent the courts from seizing property for the nonpayment of debts. In seven states, where a paper-money party came into power in 1786, paper money was issued. Since no one really knew what it was worth, creditors did not wish to accept it. Some of the states passed laws requiring creditors to take

paper money in full payment for debts. Others passed laws to protect debtors from losing their homes and tools. Men of wealth complained that these laws were unjust. They wanted to strengthen the central government so that it could protect their interests.

Shays's Rebellion causes alarm.

In Massachusetts the legislature refused both to issue paper money and to delay the collection of debts through the courts. To make matters worse, the legislature levied poll taxes and land taxes, which fell heavily on the small farmer. Many had no money to pay their taxes or the interest on their mortgages. Their farms were sold for taxes or foreclosed by the mortgage-holder. When the farm brought less than the mortgage and the farmer could not pay the balance, he might be sent to jail. In 1786 the farmers in the western part of the state rebelled. They released debtors from prison and broke up sessions of the courts where cases against debtors were being tried. Early in 1787, under the leadership of a captain of the Revolutionary army, Daniel Shays, the farmers tried to break into an arsenal at Springfield in order to get muskets and cannon. The governor sent troops, and the uprising was put down. Similar disturbances occurred in Vermont and New Hampshire. Conservative men feared that the trouble might spread and that the states might not be able to keep order. They thought the only remedy was to strengthen the central government.

A Wise Plan Is Adopted for the Territories

The Confederation might have broken up except for one thing—the possession of a rich national estate, or domain, consisting of the western lands. Common ownership of these valuable lands bound the states together. Only by staying in the Union could a state benefit from this property. Even more important, the existence of a national domain encouraged the growth of nationalism. Everyone who crossed the Appalachians entered a land belonging to the entire nation. For protection he must turn to the Confederation, not to his native state. Far-sighted citizens of the original states found a common interest in planning the development of the West. They looked forward to admitting many new states to the Union and believed that the United States would become a great nation.

Congress plans settlement of the West.

In the Land Ordinance of 1785 Congress outlined a method for settling the West. Government surveyors were to lay the land out in "townships" six miles square. Every township was to be divided into 36 sections, each of one square mile or 640 acres. In each township, one section was to be set aside for the support of public schools. This provision, which made millions of acres of land available as an endowment for public schools, reflected the growing demand for education. In addition, four sections of each township were to be set aside as a bounty for veterans of the Continental army. The remaining sections were to be sold at public auction for not less than one dollar an acre. A purchaser must take an entire section. The sale of land, it

was hoped, would furnish money to pay the expenses of the Confederation and to retire part of the war debt. Since few pioneers could afford to buy a whole section, this feature of the law caused bitter complaints and was eventually changed.

The Northwest Ordinance.

The most important act passed by the Congress of the Confederation was the Northwest Ordinance (1787) providing for the government of the Northwest Territory. The Ordinance stated that Congress should appoint from the landholders of the region a governor and judges. When there were five thousand free men in the territory, there should also be a governor's council and an elected house of representatives. When there were sixty thousand inhabitants, the voters might adopt a constitution, establish a state, and ask for admission to the Union.

LAND ORDINANCE OF 1785

SECTION *640 acres*

HALF SECTION *320 acres*	
QUARTER SECTION *160 acres*	

←——— *one mile* ———→

TOWNSHIP

VETERANS

36	30	24	18	12	6
35	29	23	17	11	5
34	28	22	16	10	4
33	27	21	15	9	3
32	26	20	14	8	2
31	25	19	13	7	1

←——————— *six miles* ———————→

135

This act gave the world a new principle for the government of colonies. The settlers of the West would not remain subjects of the original thirteen states. Instead they would have some share in their own government almost from the beginning. Later they would form states that were equal with the original thirteen. Carrying out this principle, the thirteen states have added thirty-seven others to the Union.

The Movement for a Stronger Union

The majority of voters feared a strong central government and believed that their state legislature was the best bulwark against tyranny. Yet even before the Articles of Confederation went into effect, some Americans wished to give Congress more power. They foresaw that the new government would be too weak to command respect at home and abroad. As time went on, more people came to this way of thinking. Washington wrote in a letter to the state governors in 1783:

There must be lodged somewhere a supreme power, without which the Union cannot be of long duration and everything must very rapidly tend to anarchy and confusion.

Washington kept on urging a stronger union in speeches and in letters to leaders in each of the states.

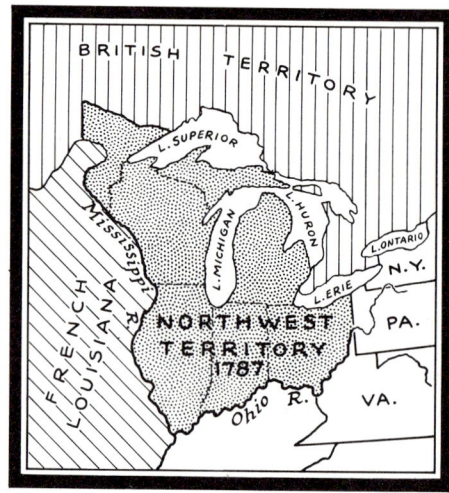

THE NORTHWEST TERRITORY

The Mount Vernon Conference, 1785.

Washington was more interested in the country beyond the Appalachians than most men of his time, for he saw that this region would soon fill with settlers. He pointed out that unless the East and West were connected by ties of trade they might easily break apart.

After returning to his home, Mount Vernon, in 1783, Washington gave most of his time to plans for improving transportation between Virginia and Maryland and the West. Maryland and Virginia long had disagreed over navigation rights on the Potomac. In 1785, at Washington's suggestion, the two states appointed commissioners to work out an agreement. The commissioners met at Mount Vernon. They drew up a pact, which was later approved by the two state legislatures. The commissioners also discussed plans for a canal connecting the Potomac and the Ohio. On this, Pennsylvania and Delaware would have to be consulted. Washington suggested that the four states might also consult together about reducing the trade barriers between them. The idea grew, and the Mount Vernon Conference ended its work by proposing that all the states be invited to take part in

Mount Vernon, George Washington's plantation home on the Potomac

a conference on navigation and trade. Such a conference, it was hoped, would convince the people of the need for greater co-operation between the states and for a stronger central government.

The Annapolis Convention, 1786.

A few months later the Virginia assembly invited all the states to send delegates to a meeting at Annapolis to consider trade and navigation problems. Nine states named delegates, but when the convention met (September, 1786) only five states were represented. The gathering could not accomplish the purpose for which it was called. Yet it did something which proved of far greater importance. At the suggestion of Alexander Hamilton the delegates urged Congress to call a convention to meet in Philadelphia the following year for the purpose of considering changes in the Articles of Confederation.

Congress calls a convention.

When the plan of the Annapolis commissioners was placed before Congress in October, it was not approved. Congress felt that no other body but itself had the right to recommend changes in the Articles. Soon afterward, however, all the troubles we have described seemed to come to a head. Several of the states were in the grip of the paper-money party; debtors rioted in Vermont and New Hampshire; Shays's followers carried on civil war in Massachusetts. Moreover, the western settlers were talking of leaving the Union unless the United States government could persuade Spain to give them the free use of the Mississippi. In February, 1787, the New York legislature blocked an amendment to give Congress the power to collect a duty on imports. Among men of wealth and influence there was a growing belief that republican government was a failure. Some said openly that the country would be better off with a king.

In this dangerous hour the Virginia legislature made a bold and statesmanlike move. It chose a delegate to the proposed convention at Philadelphia. Because that delegate was George Washington, the news was greeted with joy throughout the land. All at once people began to speak well of the idea of holding a convention. New Jersey, Pennsylvania, North Carolina, and Delaware appointed delegates. Congress decided to fall into line by sending out a formal call for a convention. All the remaining states except Rhode Island then made plans to take part.

FOR IDENTIFICATION

Annapolis Convention	Northwest Ordinance
Land Ordinance	Northwest Territory
Mount Vernon Conference	Virginia Statute of Religious Liberty

FOR EXPLANATION OR DEFINITION

amendment	poll tax
cede (cession)	primogeniture
confederation	property tax
critical period	"stay" laws
national domain	suffrage

FOR REVIEW

1. What changes made in the constitutions of the state governments during the war advanced political democracy?

2. How did the Revolution advance the cause of religious freedom?

3. What changes in the land system took place as a result of the Revolution?

4. What social changes can be traced to the revolutionary period?

5. How did the Revolution help unite the people of the different states? Why did this feeling of unity tend to disappear after the war?

6. What were the Articles of Confederation? Why was their ratification delayed?

7. (a) What powers did Congress have under the Articles of Confederation? (b) What important powers did it lack?

8. What were the chief weaknesses of the Articles of Confederation?

9. Why did the Articles of Confederation provide that amendments to it would require the consent of all the states?

10. Why did the states delay so long in creating a stronger government?

11. What events illustrate that the government of the Confederation did not command respect abroad?

12. What types of disputes developed between the states during the government of the Confederation?

13. Explain how the unlimited issuance of paper money affects a creditor. A debtor. What is meant by a "stay" law?

14. What conditions led to Shays's Rebellion? What did the rebellious farmers do? How did Shays's Rebellion help prepare the way for a stronger central government?

15. What were the provisions of the Land Ordinance of 1785?

16. What were the provisions of the Northwest Ordinance of 1787? Why did Daniel Webster assert that few laws have produced "more distinct, marked, and lasting" effects?

17. Why did Washington hope to bind the East and West together? How?

18. What was the purpose of the Mount Vernon Conference? What states were represented? What proposals did it make?

19. What was the purpose of the Annapolis Convention? Why did it fail? What important action did the convention take?

20. What action of the Virginia legislature led to the calling of a convention to revise the Articles of Confederation?

FOR FURTHER STUDY AND DISCUSSION

1. Among the important powers which the Constitution gives to Congress are the power to tax and the power to control commerce. What events during the "critical period" explain these provisions of the Constitution? Why did the Constitution forbid the states to issue paper money?

2. (a) Why were speculators in western lands interested in securing the passage of the Northwest Ordinance? Would this group be interested in the establishment of a strong central government? Why or why not? (b) Would the attitude of the settler be different from that of the speculator from whom he purchased his land? Why or why not? (Consult other books for material concerning Manasseh Cutler and the Ohio Company.)

3. (a) In passing the Northwest Ordinance was Congress in effect establishing a "colonial policy"? (b) How has the Northwest Ordinance affected the growth of the United States? (c) Has the United States applied the policy of the Northwest Ordinance to territories that are not contiguous to the United States?

FOR INDIVIDUAL OR GROUP ACTIVITIES

1. Assign two students to read and report on Jameson, *The American Revolution Considered as a Social Movement.* Students might consult also the chapter on the "Decline of Aristocracy in America" in Schlesinger's *New Viewpoints in American History.*

2. Prepare posters and cartoons which illustrate the weaknesses of the Articles of Confederation.

3. (a) Write a radio script on Shays's Rebellion, outlining the grievances which caused it, the demands that were made, the alarm it caused, and its final results. (b) Request a committee of three to suggest other events or movements in American history that are comparable.

4. Is there any similarity between the problems involved in establishing a more perfect union in 1787, and the problems involved in developing an effective international organization today? Helpful source: Van Doren, *The Great Rehearsal.*

5. Jefferson, our minister to France during the years 1785–89, wrote: "We are the lowest and most obscure of the whole diplomatic tribe." Assign a committee to read about foreign affairs under the Articles of Confederation and report briefly on our difficulties with England, France, Spain, and the Barbary pirates. Helpful source: Bailey, *Diplomatic History.*

JAMES MADISON

The example of changing a constitution by assembling the wise men of the state instead of assembling armies will be worth as much to the world as the former examples we have given them.——Thomas Jefferson

Independence Hall

9. OUR FEDERAL CONSTITUTION IS MADE AND RATIFIED

The Constitutional Convention Plans a Federal Union

The states send outstanding men.

The convention called to revise the Articles of Confederation met at Philadelphia in May, 1787. Its work took nearly four months to complete. All the states except Rhode Island were represented.

The state legislatures vied with one another in sending their most distinguished men. Of the fifty-five delegates who attended the meetings, eight had been signers of the Declaration of Independence. Nearly all had been active in the Revolution as members of Congress, military officers, or public officials. Seven were or had been state governors.

The delegates were exceptionally well educated, over half being college graduates. The majority were lawyers. There were also wealthy landowners and businessmen, and a scattering of professors, physicians, and clergymen. Small farmers, wage earners, and frontier settlers were not represented. Yet as events proved, this rather one-sided group acted wisely for the good of the whole people.

Leading members of the convention.

Washington was chosen as the presiding officer. Although this meant that he could not enter into the debate, his opinions were sought after.

139

James Madison of Virginia, a scholar in the field of government, took a leading part in the convention's work and often is referred to as the "Father of the Constitution." He made careful notes of the proceedings day by day. These notes were published after all the delegates had died, as Madison's *Journal of the Constitutional Convention*. It is our chief source of information concerning the convention.

Pennsylvania sent the aged Benjamin Franklin, whose wit and homely common sense kept the members in good humor during the most trying hours. From the same state came the brilliant lawyer James Wilson. With his keen understanding of constitutional law, Wilson was the most useful member of the convention after Madison. Gouverneur Morris, a third Pennsylvanian, became chairman of the Committee on Style and was largely responsible for the final arrangement and wording of the Constitution.

ALEXANDER HAMILTON

Alexander Hamilton, one of the most forceful advocates of a strong national government, was a member of the New York delegation. Since he was outvoted by the other New York delegates, who did not share his views, his attendance was irregular. His greatest service was in explaining and defending the Constitution after it was submitted to the states.

William Paterson of New Jersey and Luther Martin of Maryland turned out to be the staunchest representatives of the interests of the small states. Martin was also a champion of paper money and the only delegate who spoke up for the small farmers and debtors. He refused to sign the Constitution because of the clauses which forbid the states to issue paper money and to impair contracts.

The convention discards the Articles.

Although the convention had been called for the sole purpose of recommending changes in the Articles of Confederation, most delegates believed that a new plan of government must be developed. The convention therefore simply threw aside the Articles and decided to write a wholly new constitution. The delegates were well aware that the task would be difficult and that they would often disagree. To make easier the reaching of agreements and to reduce pressure from special interest groups, what went on in the meetings was kept secret.

In a discussion of what sort of constitution would be approved by the people, many of the delegates said that it would have to be a weak one. They thought the people were not ready for a thoroughgoing reform. Washington gravely broke into the discussion to give his own view.

It is too probable that no plan we propose will be adopted. Perhaps another dreadful conflict is to be sustained. If, to please the people, we offer what we ourselves cannot approve, how can we afterward defend our work? Let us raise a standard to which the wise and the honest can repair. The event is in the hand of God.

These words carried great weight. They changed the tone of the convention from politics to statesmanship.

Agreement on the fundamentals.

The problem facing the convention was to create a national government strong enough to work but not too strong to be adopted. If the new plan was to win the approval of the voters, it must not go too far in weakening the power of the states. As the delegates debated the problem, a large majority found that they agreed on certain basic ideas. There was agreement, for example, on these aims: (1) A truly *national* government must be established in place of a confederacy. (2) This government should have the authority to enforce its laws. (3) The new Congress must have the power to legislate on all matters of national concern; this would include the power to tax, to regulate foreign and interstate commerce, to coin and borrow money, and to defend the country on land and sea. (4) The new government must have three branches—legislative, executive, and judicial. (5) The debts of the Confederation must be paid. (6) Property rights should be protected both from mobs and from radical legislation such as that favored by the paper-money party. (7) Restraints must be laid on the state governments. Disputes among the delegates had to do mainly with how these purposes could be accomplished.

Three major differences appear.

One of the major disagreements in the convention resulted because the states were unequal in area, wealth, and population. The combined population of five states (Virginia, Massachusetts, Pennsylvania, North Carolina, and New York) was almost twice that of the remaining eight. The five with the largest population, together with Georgia, were also the states having the greatest area and land values. It is not surprising, then, that the small states were fearful that the large ones would control the new national government.

A second question dividing the delegates was whether the national government or the state governments should be higher in power. The experiences of the Confederation had shown the necessity for a stronger central government. Yet many people still believed each state should be sovereign, that is, supreme. A sovereign state, they thought, should make all its own laws, except on a few matters that could not possibly be handled by each state independently. The small states were more anxious to keep their sovereignty than the larger ones, fearing that a powerful national government

BENJAMIN FRANKLIN

in which they had little influence might act in ways that would injure their interests.

A third difference among the delegates was in their attitude toward democracy. Should the new constitution enable the masses of people to control the government, or should it give control to men owning a substantial amount of property? Most of the delegates were afraid of democracy, believing that the common people were inclined to be rash and lawless. Alexander Hamilton, arguing in favor of a life term for senators, said:

All communities divide themselves into the few and the many. The first are rich and wellborn, and the other the mass of people who seldom judge or determine right.

We see this aristocratic point of view reflected in various decisions of the convention, such as the indirect election of the President and the senators.

Two plans of union are debated.

The most serious conflict of the convention arose over two general plans of union. These are now called the Virginia and New Jersey plans, or the "large-states plan" and the "small-states plan." The Virginia plan was largely the work of Madison. It called for a strong central government, with an executive committee of three persons, one from each section. Congress was to have two houses, and the states were to be represented either according to their population or their wealth.

Paterson of New Jersey declared that his state would never accept this proposal. "She would be swallowed up." Wilson of Pennsylvania replied:

Are not the citizens of [my state] equal to those of New Jersey? Does it require one hundred fifty of the former to balance fifty of the latter? . . . If the small states will not confederate on this plan, Pennsylvania [will] not confederate on any other.

Paterson offered the New Jersey plan, which provided for increasing the powers of the existing Congress and adding an executive and a judiciary. Each state was to continue to have equal representation. Under this plan a small state would have as much voice in the Union as a large one.

The "Great Compromise" solves the problem of representation.

The two plans were debated for weeks. The most difficult question to settle was how the states were to be represented in the new government. At times there seemed no hope of reaching an agreement. James Wilson insisted that the small states having only a minority of the people of America ought to give in to the large states. A Delaware delegate replied:

The large states dare not dissolve the Confederation. If they do, the small ones will find some foreign ally of more honor and good faith, who will take them by the hand and do them justice.

The delegates from the small states pleaded that at least the upper house of Congress should give an equal voice to each state. This would guarantee the small states against being swamped by their large neighbors. Rather than wreck the convention, the large states finally gave in. At the suggestion of Roger Sherman of Connecticut, the convention adopted the "Connecticut Compromise," also known as the "Great Compromise." It was agreed to have two houses in Congress—the House of Representatives, in which the states are represented according to their population, and the Senate, in which they are represented equally. The members of Congress vote individually, not as part of a state delegation. Without this compromise the Constitution would never have been drafted. The rest of the work of the convention was comparatively easy.

142

DIFFERENCES BETWEEN THE ARTICLES OF CONFEDERATION AND THE CONSTITUTION

ARTICLES OF CONFEDERATION	THE CONSTITUTION
1. A loose confederation of states	1. A strong union of people
2. No executive (laws to be executed by committees of Congress)	2. Executive powers given to President
3. Congress could not levy taxes	3. Congress has power to levy taxes on individuals
4. Congress had no power to control commerce	4. Congress can regulate foreign and interstate commerce
5. One vote in Congress for each state	5. Two votes in Senate for each state; representation in House according to population
6. Important measures required ⅔ vote (9 states) in Congress	6. Laws are passed by simple majority vote, subject to presidential veto, which Congress can override by ⅔ vote
7. Amendment only by consent of all the states	7. Amendment by consent of ¾ of states
8. No federal courts; Congress itself tried to settle disputes between states	8. The Supreme Court and other federal courts
9. Congress could not compel obedience to its enactments	9. Federal government has power to enforce laws by coercion of individuals

The delegates decide on a federal union.

The Articles of Confederation declared that "each state retains its sovereignty, freedom, and independence." While the average American still wanted his state to be sovereign, most of the delegates hoped to reduce the powers of the states in order to set up an effective national government. It was decided to form a *federal* government—one in which the states keep important powers while the central government also has much power. This would require each state to delegate or surrender part of its sovereignty to the central government. The functions and powers of the central government would have to be carefully defined. They must also be limited, or the plan would be rejected by the voters.

Federal laws are to apply to individuals.

Having agreed on a federal union, the delegates had to solve another basic problem: How should the new national government enforce its powers? Under the Confederation the states had paid little attention to the wishes of Congress. What was to save the new government from the same fate? The delegates discussed the possibility of using federal troops to compel a state to obey a law passed by Congress. But this was not favorably received, for it would mean civil war and would quickly break up the Union.

As the discussion went on the delegates found a solution: *the federal government should have the power to act directly on the people within the states.* It can, for example, collect taxes from

143

individuals without calling on the states. It can try in its own courts and punish those who break federal laws or disobey the Constitution. In matters of federal concern the people must obey the federal government and it can compel them to do so. This is the essence of the Constitution and the secret of its success.

The regulation of commerce is agreed upon.

In the states south of the Potomac —Virginia, North Carolina, South Carolina, and Georgia—farming was the only industry. All the other states were interested in commerce as well as in farming. While delegates from the commercial states were in favor of giving Congress the power to regulate foreign and interstate commerce, those from the four southern states were not. The southern delegates feared that if Congress could regulate commerce, it might favor the commercial states. A compromise was arranged which gave Congress the power to regulate commerce, but forbade it: (1) to impose a tax on articles exported from any state and (2) to give preference to the ports of one state over those of another.

A compromise is reached on taxation.

If Congress were given the power to tax, might it not treat large and small states unequally? Delegates from the small states argued that Congress should impose no taxes without a two-thirds vote of its members. As such a rule would enable a small group of congressmen to hold up any tax bill, it would almost amount to denying Congress the right to levy taxes. The difficulty was overcome by an agreement that (1) all taxes should be the same throughout the United States, and (2) all direct taxes (such as head taxes and land taxes) should be apportioned among the states according to population. The delegates from the small states then agreed that a tax bill could be passed by a simple majority.

The slave-trade clause.

Except in the far South, slavery had been gradually dying out. In New England it had almost disappeared. In Maryland and Virginia there was a strong party in favor of abolition (doing away with slavery). In North Carolina the abolition movement was gathering strength. But in the rice and indigo swamps of South Carolina and Georgia slavery was still considered necessary. Some of the southern delegates feared that Congress might stop the slave trade. To satisfy them Congress was forbidden for twenty years to interfere with the bringing in of slaves or to levy an import tax of more than ten dollars on each slave brought in (Art. I, Sec. 9, of the Constitution).

The three-fifths rule.

Southern delegates proposed that slaves should be counted in deciding the number of representatives for each state. But they did not wish to have the slaves counted when direct taxes were apportioned among the states. Northern delegates wished to include slaves in figuring taxation but not in figuring representation. The convention readily agreed that five slaves should count as three persons in figuring both the number of representatives and the amount of direct taxes.

How should the President be chosen?

One of the most puzzling questions that came before the convention was the method of choosing the President. What share should the people have in his election? Should each state have equal weight in choosing him or should the states having more people be given more weight? Since a conservative and aristocratic group controlled the convention, it was quickly decided that the people should not vote directly for the

President. After much debate the convention agreed that the President should be selected by electors, chosen as the legislature of each state might think best. To please the large states, the number of electors from each state was made equal to the number of its representatives and senators.

The federal government is given limited powers.

The powers of the federal government were carefully listed or enumerated (Art. I, Sec. 8). Among these *delegated* powers are the right to lay taxes, to borrow money, to coin money, to fix weights and measures, to regulate foreign and domestic commerce, to raise and support an army, and to declare war. Congress was also given the power to "make all laws which shall be necessary and proper for carrying into execution the foregoing powers." This is known as the *"elastic clause"* or the *"implied powers clause."* To prevent confusion, certain powers were denied the states (Art. I, Sec. 10). The states are not to coin money, to issue bills of credit (that is, paper money), to lay duties on imports, to enter into treaties, or to impair or weaken the validity of contracts (as, for example, by preventing the collection of debts). Many of the difficulties that had arisen during the Confederation were due to these very actions by the states.

Certain powers granted to the federal government are not denied to the states. For example, the states as well as Congress may levy taxes. Powers which can be exercised by both the nation and the states are known as *concurrent powers*. In general all the powers given the federal government in Section 8 of Article I and not denied the states in Section 10 are concurrent powers.

All other powers are reserved to the states.

The convention intended that all powers not granted to the federal government and not prohibited to the states should be considered as reserved to the states. To make this absolutely certain, the Tenth Amendment was added in 1791. All the powers of local government are thus left to the states. The states are to decide who shall vote and how. The states are responsible for schools, local courts, policing, the incorporation of banks and stock companies, the care of bridges, roads, canals, and many other matters.

Despite the care taken by the convention in dividing powers between the nation and the states, many cases have arisen where it was not clear whether the power to do a certain thing belongs to the federal or to the state governments. Such cases often come before the Supreme Court.

At the CONSTITUTIONAL CONVENTION *of 1787 Washington was the presiding officer and the guiding spirit of the remarkable group of delegates.*

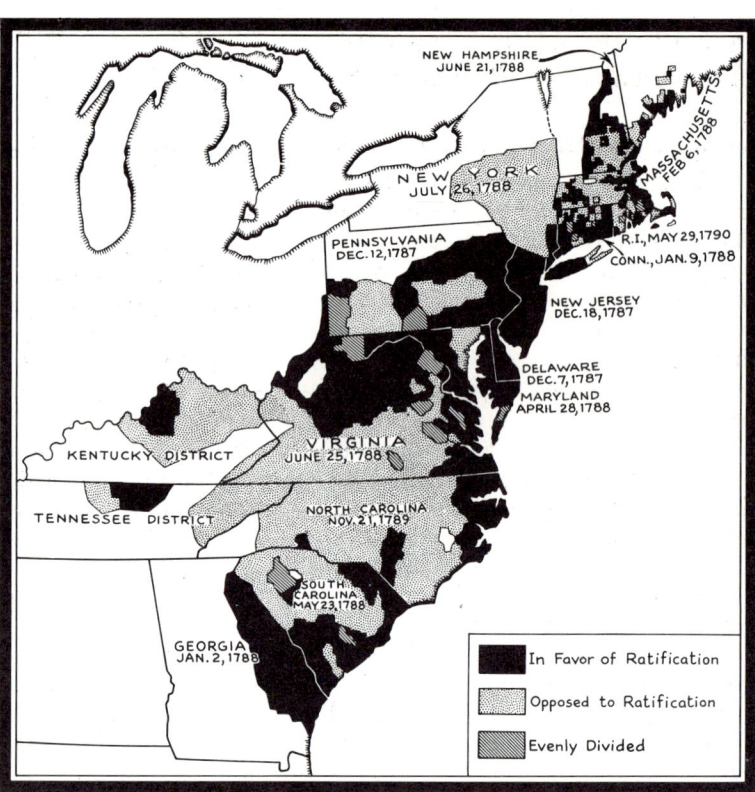

In the map:

NEW HAMPSHIRE
JUNE 21, 1788

MASSACHUSETTS
FEB. 6, 1788

NEW YORK
JULY 26, 1788

R.I., MAY 29, 1790

CONN., JAN. 9, 1788

PENNSYLVANIA
DEC. 12, 1787

NEW JERSEY
DEC. 18, 1787

DELAWARE
DEC. 7, 1787

MARYLAND
APRIL 28, 1788

KENTUCKY DISTRICT

VIRGINIA
JUNE 25, 1788

TENNESSEE DISTRICT

NORTH CAROLINA
NOV. 21, 1789

SOUTH CAROLINA
MAY 23, 1788

GEORGIA
JAN. 2, 1788

VOTE ON RATIFICATION OF THE CONSTITUTION

■ In Favor of Ratification

▨ Opposed to Ratification

▨ Evenly Divided

The Constitution can be changed.

The delegates realized that the Constitution was not perfect and that changes might become necessary. Article V gives two ways of proposing an amendment and two ways of ratifying it. The consent of three fourths of the states is necessary before an amendment can take effect. Here the framers overrode the sovereignty of the states. One exception—and only one—was made to the right of three fourths of the states to bind the rest against their wills: "No state, without its consent, shall be deprived of its equal suffrage in the Senate."

The amending process is slow and difficult. One fourth of the states plus one can block a change desired by the rest. Thus, although some 2700 amendments have been introduced in Congress, only 22 have been adopted.

The convention adjourns.

In September, 1787, after nearly four months of wearisome work, the convention held its last meeting. Only three of the forty-two delegates present refused to sign. Franklin expressed the views of the others in his usual happy manner. "I confess," he said, "that there are several parts of this Constitution which I do not at present approve, but I am not sure that I shall never approve them." Pointing to the half sun painted in gold on the back of Washington's chair, he remarked:

I have often . . . in the course of the session and the vicissitudes [changes] of my hopes and fears as to its issue, looked at that behind the President, without being able to tell whether it was rising or setting; but now, at length, I have the happiness to know it is a rising, and not a setting sun.

In Spite of Strong Opposition the Constitution Is Ratified

A new method of ratification is provided.

The Constitution placed so many limits on the sovereignty of the states that the framers feared it would not be accepted. Some state legislatures had refused to approve any increase in the powers of the old Congress. Would they not refuse to approve the new plan of government? How then could it be put into effect?

The framers decided to ignore the rule in the Articles of Confederation that said changes in the government must be approved by the legislatures of all thirteen states. The framers recommended to the Confederation Congress that it ask each state legislature to call a special convention, elected by the voters, to pass upon the Constitution. Then the framers wrote into the Constitution the provision that when nine states had approved it, it should go into effect for these states, no matter what the other four decided (Art. VI). This was a revolutionary proposal and a master stroke. It made possible a peaceful revolution by which a new government replaced the Confederation.

Two parties arise.

As soon as the Constitution was published, people divided into two groups—the *Federalists,* who wished its adoption, and the *Antifederalists,* who did not. Both parties had strong, able leaders. The Federalists included nearly all the men of wealth—the merchants, industrialists, holders of government bonds, and professional men. They had tried for a long time to strengthen the central government. The Antifederalists included two large groups: (1) those who feared a strong government remote from the people and the weakening of their state government, and

(2) those who favored paper money and laws to protect debtors. Most people were Antifederalists at the start.

Doubts trouble the people.

Heated arguments went on wherever people gathered. There were serious questions to be thrashed out. Would the proposed central government oppress the people with heavy taxes? Would it drag them into foreign wars? Might not a President with such powers become a tyrant? Might not the senators become a new aristocracy? Why were the liberties of the people not mentioned—had the convention been more interested in protecting property than human rights? Would the new government reduce the states to mere figureheads? Why did the Constitution begin with the words "We, the people," instead of "We, the states"? These are but a few of the doubts expressed by the Antifederalists.

Federalist writers answer doubters.

Defenders of the Constitution flooded the country with pamphlets, newspaper articles, and letters. The best remembered are eighty-five long articles written by Alexander Hamilton, James Madison, and John Jay. They appeared in New York newspapers and helped win that state. Many of the articles were reprinted in the newspapers of other states where the conventions had not yet voted. The articles were later gathered together in a famous volume called *The Federalist.*

Nine states ratify the Constitution.

Except for Rhode Island, the small states were the most eager to ratify. Their leaders were pleased with having won the fight for equal representation in the Senate. Delaware, New Jersey, and Georgia ratified unanimously, and Connecticut approved by a wide margin. The first large state to act was

Pennsylvania, where the well-organized Federalists hurried the calling of a convention before the Antifederalists had time to organize their supporters. The Federalists won, however, only after agreeing to recommend ten amendments to the Constitution.

The sixth state to ratify was Massachusetts. Here the contest was close and bitter. When the convention first met, the Antifederalists were in the majority. The Federalists proposed that the convention ask for twelve amendments. This device won the support of Samuel Adams and other waverers. The Constitution was then approved by a narrow margin. Every state but one which ratified after Massachusetts recommended similar amendments.

The next to vote were Maryland and South Carolina, where the Federalists won easily. New Hampshire, which had waited to see what her great neighbor, Massachusetts, would do, became the ninth state to ratify.

In no state was there a harder fight than in Virginia. The Antifederalists pointed out that the Constitution gave to the President and Congress more power than the king and Parliament had ever exercised over the colonies. They argued that the states would be enslaved and individual liberty destroyed. After three weeks of debate the Federalists brought forward forty amendments, promising that Congress would submit them to the states. The Constitution was then approved by a slim margin.

By this time (June, 1788) every state but New York, North Carolina, and Rhode Island had ratified. The Constitution was now certain to go into effect. Yet without New York the new nation would be divided in the middle and perhaps hopelessly handicapped. When the New York convention met in June, two thirds of its members were opposed to the Constitution. Governor George Clinton led the Antifederalists.

After a month of fiery debate Alexander Hamilton persuaded Clinton to change sides. The threat that the eastern part of the state would join the Union even if it had to break away from the rest of the state brought victory by a close vote.

North Carolina did not ratify until November, 1789, several months after Washington was made President. Rhode Island held out until May, 1790, when Congress threatened to treat it as a foreign nation.

DOLLY MADISON

FOR IDENTIFICATION

Antifederalist	New Jersey plan
The Federalist	William Paterson
Great Compromise	Virginia plan
Alexander Hamilton	James Wilson
James Madison	

FOR EXPLANATION OR DEFINITION

concurrent powers	implied powers
delegated powers	judiciary
direct tax	legislative
elastic clause	ratification
elector	sovereign
executive	three-fifths rule

FOR REVIEW

1. What groups were represented at the Philadelphia Convention? What groups were not represented?

2. Which of the thirteen states did not send delegates?

3. Why were the convention proceedings kept secret? How do we know what went on?

4. Name at least six fundamental issues on which the delegates agreed. Three on which they disagreed.

5. Why did the small states fear they would be overshadowed by the large ones?

6. What is meant by a sovereign state?

7. Why did some of the delegates fear democracy?

8. State the main difference between the large-states and the small-states plans.

9. What was settled by the "Great Compromise"? Explain why the large states at last gave in.

10. What is meant by the statement that the delegates decided to form a *federal* government?

11. What did this decision involve regarding the powers of the federal government and the powers of the states? What did it involve concerning the enforcement powers of the federal government?

12. What compromise was reached on the power to regulate commerce? The power of taxation?

13. What is the slave-trade clause? Why was it included?

14. Why did the convention resort to the device of having the President chosen by electors? How is the number of electors for each state determined?

15. Why were the powers of the federal government enumerated? Name some of the powers *delegated* to the federal government in Article I, Section 8.

16. What powers were denied to the states in Article I, Section 10?

17. Explain what is meant by *concurrent powers* and *reserved powers*. Give illustrations of each.

18. How may the Constitution be amended? Is every part of it subject to amendment?

19. What method was provided for the ratification of the Constitution? Why may the provision be described as revolutionary?

20. What arguments did the Antifederalists use against ratification? How did the Federalists answer these arguments?

21. What does *The Federalist* include?

22. Describe the fight over ratification in Massachusetts, Virginia, and New York.

23. Which states did not ratify the Constitution until after Washington's inauguration as the first President?

FOR FURTHER STUDY AND DISCUSSION

1. How did the Constitution correct the defects of the Articles of Confederation?

2. "So far as the structure of the government was concerned, the Constitution was a bundle of compromises" (Beard). What were these compromises?

3. Using the *World Almanac,* find which states have the largest and the smallest populations. Why do these states have the same number of senators? Is this undemocratic? Should the Constitution be changed? If so, how?

4. It is sometimes argued that the President should be elected by direct popular vote. In opposition to this proposal, it has been said that the present method tends to emphasize the "federal character" of our government. Explain this statement.

FOR INDIVIDUAL OR GROUP ACTIVITIES

1. Imagine yourself to be a member of the Constitutional Convention. Prepare a brief speech in defense of the Great Compromise or the compromise on taxation.

2. Examine a copy of *The Federalist.* Report on its organization and purpose. Why is it regarded as one of the most important works on government ever written?

3. Write a sketch on Madison. Should he be called the "Father of the Constitution"?

4. Arrange for the exhibit of original posters or cartoons which will illustrate the points on which the delegates were in substantial agreement, the compromises they found it expedient to accept, and the struggle over ratification.

5. Write a report on how the Bill of Rights came to be added to the Constitution.

6. Imagine the class to be a state ratifying convention. Have various class members represent different social and economic groups, e.g. merchants, lawyers, manufacturers, bankers, farmers, and laborers. Debate the ratification of the Constitution. Helpful source: McLaughlin, *The Confederation and the Constitution.*

THE PRESIDENT REPORTS *to a joint session of Congress on what he thinks needs to be accomplished in the year ahead.*

We the People *of the United States, in order to form a more perfect Union, establish*

insure domestic Tranquility, provide for the common defence, promote the general Welfare, and secure the Blessings of Liberty to and our Posterity, do ordain and establish this Constitution for the United States of America.

Article I.

Section 1. *All legislative Powers herein granted shall be vested in a Congress of the United States, which shall consist of a Senate or of Representatives.*

Section 2. *The House of Representatives shall be composed of Members chosen every second Year by the People of the several States, and in each State shall have Qualifications requisite for Electors of the most numerous Branch of the State Legislature.*

No Person shall be a Representative who shall not have attained to the Age of twenty-five Years, and been seven Years a Citizen of the U and who shall not, when elected, be an Inhabitant of that State in which he shall be chosen.

Representatives and direct Taxes shall be apportioned among the several States which may be included within this Union, according to their Numbers, which shall be determined by adding to the whole Number of free Persons, including those bound to Service for a Term of Years, and each not taxed, three fifths of all other Persons. The actual Enumeration shall be made within three Years after the first Meeting of the Congress of the U and within every subsequent Term of Ten Years, in such Manner as they shall by Law direct. The Number of Representatives shall not exceed thirty Thousand, but each State shall have at Least one Representative; and until such enumeration shall be made, the State of New Hampshire entitled to chuse three, Massachusetts eight, Rhode Island and Providence Plantations one, Connecticut five, New York six, New Jersey four, Per eight, Delaware one, Maryland six, Virginia ten, North Carolina five, South Carolina five, and Georgia three.

The federal system, perhaps the greatest of all American contributions, solved the crucial problem of preserving the benefits of local autonomy over matters of a local nature and the benefits of centralized authority over matters of a national character.——Henry Steele Commager

10. THE CONSTITUTION OUTLINES OUR FEDERAL SYSTEM

The Constitution Is the Supreme Law of the Land

The Constitution is the supreme law of the land.

The Constitution established the framework within which our nation has developed since 1789. In order to understand the ways in which our country has grown, let us examine the main features of this great document.

Governmental powers are divided.

The thirteen states, as we have seen, were willing to surrender to the national government only certain definite powers. The national government is, then, one of *limited,* or *delegated,* powers. The word "delegated" tells us that these powers were given to the national government by the states. All other powers are reserved to the states. These are often spoken of as *reserved, retained,* or *residual* powers.

The Constitution provides a federal, or dual, system of government, in which both national and state govern-ments exercise authority over the people. Simple as it may seem, the working out of the federal system was a great contribution to the art and science of government. Our Constitution furnishes a pattern which has influenced every federal government set up since it appeared.

While the federal government has a limited sphere of action, within that sphere it is supreme. The Constitution, together with the federal laws and treaties made under it, is declared to be "the supreme law of the land" (Art. VI, Sec. 2). The judges in every state, as well as the federal judges, are bound to uphold the Constitution, "anything in the constitution or laws of any state to the contrary notwithstanding." This means that state legislation in conflict with the Constitution or with federal laws and treaties is null and void. Furthermore, all state officials must swear to support the Constitution.

151

The federal government has expanded.

The fathers of the Constitution knew that great changes were bound to come in American affairs. They wished Congress to be able to deal with them as might best serve the purposes of the Union. These purposes were set forth in the preamble: "to form a more perfect union, establish justice, insure domestic tranquility, provide for the common defense, promote the general welfare, and secure the blessings of liberty to ourselves and our posterity."

Besides granting Congress specific powers, the Constitution gives it two general powers. One of these is the power to raise and spend money for "the general welfare of the United States." The other, stated in the "elastic clause," is the power to make all laws which shall be necessary and proper for carrying out the specified powers of Congress. Many a conflict has raged over these lines. Congress has repeatedly changed its views as to what is "necessary and proper," and what is demanded for the "general welfare." With the rise of industry and the growth of cities, Congress has enacted legislation which the founders of our nation could not have imagined, such as laws to regulate railroads and broadcasting, to conserve our natural resources, and to provide social security. Each new type of law is sure to be laid before the Supreme Court in a test case. The Court then has to decide whether the given act of Congress is constitutional. On some questions the Court has reversed itself in a later decision, usually after a change in its membership. Over the years the Court's decisions have let the federal government gradually expand its sphere of action.

The federal government's three branches.

The men who framed the Constitution were determined to protect the nation from a military dictator or a small group of individuals who might try to seize control. For this reason they divided the powers of the federal government among three separate branches—the legislative, to make the laws; the executive, to see that the laws are carried out; and the judicial, to administer justice and protect the rights of individuals.

The framers of the Constitution also made sure that no political party or faction could get possession of all three branches of government at a single election. This was accomplished by providing different terms of office and different ways of selecting key officials. Members of the House of Representatives are elected for a term of two years. Senators are elected for a term of six years. Since the terms of one third of them expire every two years, the entire membership of the Senate is not subject to election at any one time. The President is elected for a term of four years, while federal judges are appointed for life. Thus the men who hold important federal posts cannot be swept from office all at once.

Each branch checks the other two.

The framers of the Constitution feared that popular pressure upon the government might lead to hasty and ill-considered action. One way they took to prevent this was to give each branch checks upon the other two.

1. Checks on the executive branch. The executive branch is subject to many checks. (a) Any of its actions may be reviewed in the courts if a citizen brings suit. (b) Without money provided by Congress no agency can continue its work. (c) In filling important offices the President must get the approval of the Senate. (d) A treaty requires a two-thirds vote of the Senate to ratify it or make it legal. (e) The President may be removed from office by Congress. To do this the House of Representatives impeaches him, that is, brings charges against him. The Senate

CHECKS AND BALANCES

How the President Checks:

How the Congress Checks:

How the Supreme Court Checks:

CONGRESS

PRESIDENT	recommends laws
approves appointments	vetoes laws
frames laws	calls Congress in special session
overrides presidential veto	appoints federal officers
ratifies treaties	negotiates treaties
approves expenditures	executes laws
can impeach and try President	

PRESIDENT

can declare a presidential policy
to be unconstitutional

SUPREME COURT

appoints judges

grants pardons

SUPREME COURT

approves appointments

can impeach judges

establishes new courts

CONGRESS

determines constitutionality of laws

interprets laws

interprets treaties

Legislative

Judicial

Executive

tries him. If found guilty, he would be removed from office.

2. Checks on the legislative branch. The President may recommend the passage of laws, may call Congress in special session, and may veto bills passed by Congress. His veto can be set aside by a two-thirds vote of both houses. The judicial branch checks Congress by its power to decide what each law means, and also by judging whether a law is constitutional.

3. Checks on the judicial branch. This branch is the most nearly independent. Yet Congress controls the number of judges and fixes their salaries. Judges are appointed by the President with the approval of the Senate. The House of Representatives may impeach a judge, and if the Senate finds him guilty, he is removed from office. Another check on the judiciary is the President's power to pardon those convicted in federal courts.

Because of the controls that each branch has upon the others, our federal government is often said to be a system of "checks and balances." This system prevents any one branch from becoming too powerful or interfering unduly with the rights of property and individuals. Though the system often causes delay, this was the intention of the framers. In highly controversial matters delay may be desirable. In time of national emergency delay could be dangerous. Congress in such cases can grant temporary powers to the President.

The Constitution protects property rights.

Madison wrote in one of his *Federalist* papers that the first object of government is to protect property. The Constitution contains various clauses which safeguard property holders.

1. Restrictions on the right of eminent domain. Every nation claims the right of *eminent domain*—that is, the

right of taking private property for public purposes, as for a highway or a military post. The Fifth Amendment forbids Congress to take private property without just compensation to the owner and without due process of law.

2. Restrictions on the power to tax. The framers of the Constitution feared that the power to tax might be used to favor one section or group of people more than another. They therefore provided that direct taxes must be apportioned among the states according to their population. Indirect taxes (such as an excise) must be uniform throughout the United States, and Congress is forbidden to levy export taxes (Art. I, Sec. 9). Restrictions are also placed on the right of the states to levy taxes on imports or exports (Art. I, Sec. 10).

3. Restrictions on paper money, legal tender, and impairment of contracts. The framers of the Constitution particularly desired to prevent the states from passing laws that favor debtors at the expense of creditors (see p. 134). Accordingly, the Constitution forbids the states to issue bills of credit (paper money) or to make anything but gold or silver coin legal tender in payment of debts. The states are also forbidden to pass laws which impair the obligation of a contract (such as laws interfering with the foreclosure of mortgages) (Art. I, Sec. 10).

The Constitution protects civil rights.

The members of the Constitutional Convention left to the states the main responsibility for protecting civil, or personal, rights. They nevertheless adopted a number of safeguards to individual liberty.

1. Both the federal government and the states are forbidden to pass *ex post facto* laws and bills of attainder (Art. I, Secs. 9, 10). An *ex post facto* law is one that makes a person liable to punishment for an action which was not con-

sidered a crime when it was committed, or which increases the severity of the punishment for a previous act. A *bill of attainder* is a legislative act decreeing punishment for a person without a trial. These two types of laws had been common in Britain, where the dominant party in Parliament used them to punish its opponents.

2. The federal government may not suspend the writ of *habeas corpus* except in cases of rebellion or invasion when the public safety may require it. The writ of *habeas corpus* is intended to prevent unjust imprisonment. By obtaining a writ of this kind, a person who has been arrested can compel the authorities to bring him into court without delay. Those responsible for his imprisonment must prove in open court that there are lawful reasons for holding him. Otherwise the judge will order his release.

3. Persons accused of breaking a federal law are entitled to trial by jury. In order that the defendant may more readily obtain witnesses, the trial must be held in the state in which the crime was committed (Art. III, Sec. 2).

4. Treason is limited to two offenses only: (a) making war against the United States (that is, attempting to overthrow the government by force) and (b) giving aid and comfort to its enemies. To be found guilty of treason a person must have himself performed an act aimed at overthrowing the government (not merely talked of such an act), and the act must be testified to by two witnesses (unless he confesses it in open court). The family and descendants of a person convicted of treason shall not be made to suffer for his crime (Art. III, Sec. 3). The Constitution makers defined treason so carefully because they wished to prevent abuses that had arisen in Great Britain.

As we have learned, many Americans were dissatisfied with the original Constitution on the ground that it did not go far enough in protecting the "rights of man." Seven of the ratifying conventions urged that amendments be added to keep the federal government from interfering with the rights of the individual. This was done when the first ten amendments, known as the "Bill of Rights," were ratified in 1791.

The Bill of Rights.

No part of the Constitution is more highly prized than the Bill of Rights. So long as it is observed, the federal government cannot oppress the people. Here are the principal rights listed in the first eight amendments:

1. Freedom of religion.

2. Freedom of speech and of the press.

3. Freedom of assembly and of petition for the righting of grievances.

4. Freedom to keep and bear arms.

5. Freedom from quartering of soldiers in homes in time of peace.

6. Freedom from unreasonable search and seizure of persons and property.

7. Guarantee that indictment for crime shall be by a grand jury only.

8. Freedom from double jeopardy (being tried again for an offense for which one has been tried and found not guilty).

9. Freedom from self-incrimination (being compelled to be a witness against oneself) in a criminal case.

10. Guarantee that no one shall be deprived of life, liberty, or property without due process of law.

11. Security of private property. It shall not be taken for public use without just compensation.

12. Guarantee of a fair, speedy, public, and local trial.

13. Guarantee of a jury trial in criminal cases.

14. Freedom to confront and question accusers when on trial.

15. Guarantee of counsel (an attorney) when on trial for crime.

16. Freedom from excessive bail and fines and from cruel and unusual punishment.

The free press of a free people

Many of these rights are designed to prevent the punishment of innocent persons and to give each person *equality before the law*. All of them together are a bulwark against tyranny, protecting the many from the few and the few from the many.

The Constitution and these first eight amendments mention the most cherished rights gained by the people in the long struggle for self-government. But there are others which are not listed. Amendment IX declares that the listing of certain rights is not to be taken to mean that others do not exist. Amendment X follows closely on the thought in Amendment IX. It states that the powers not delegated to the United States and not prohibited to the states are reserved to the states or to the people. This amendment states positively a basic principle: *in a republic the people are the source of all governmental powers*. They may delegate these powers or may forbid their use. They keep certain powers in their own hands, notably public opinion, which they can express through free speech, a free press, free assembly, and the right of petition.

The "due process" clause.

The Fifth Amendment states that no one shall "be deprived of life, liberty, or property without due process of law." Due process includes the various legal safeguards won by Englishmen over the centuries. So far as criminal law is concerned it means the rights listed in items 6–16 above. This amendment limits the federal government, not the states. The Fourteenth Amendment, adopted in 1868, places the same restrictions on the states.

As a result of court interpretation, the Fifth and Fourteenth Amendments have become our most important safeguards of the rights of persons and of property. Since a corporation is considered a person in the eyes of the law, its property is also protected by these amendments. For a time the due process clause was a stumbling block in the way of social legislation, such as workmen's compensation and minimum wage laws. The courts ruled that such measures deprived employers of their property without due process of law (see p. 311). Gradually the courts accepted a different view and ruled that property rights, like civil rights, are not absolute. The federal and state governments may limit personal and property rights in the interest of public health, safety, and morals, or for the sake of the general welfare.

Good relations among the states.

Article IV has to do with relations between the states and between the states and the federal Union. The first section declares: "Full faith and credit shall be given in each state to the public acts, records, and judicial proceedings of every other state." For instance, a marriage contracted in one state is valid in any other state. Section 2 says: "The citizens of each state shall be entitled to all privileges and immunities of citizens in the several states." This means that a citizen of any state may enter or carry on business in another state and enjoy the same protection as if he were living in his own state. Under another clause a person who has committed a crime in State A and fled to State B is usually turned over, or extradited, to the police of A upon request of A's governor.

Section 3 provides that Congress may admit new states to the Union. It may not form a new state by taking part of the land belonging to an existing state, without that state's consent. Congress was given power to make all needful rules for the territories and other property of the United States.

Under Section 4 the United States guarantees every state a republican form of government. This implies that

156

(Above) COLONIAL COVERLET *with a patchwork Star of Bethlehem design and appliquéd chintz peacocks*

(Right) COLONIAL PENNSYLVANIA GERMAN PIE PLATE. *The inscription reads, "The plate is made of clay; when it breaks the potter laughs."*

157

the people of a state shall have the power to make their own laws and choose their own government officers. However, the Constitution leaves each state free to decide which of its people may vote. Not until the Fifteenth Amendment was adopted in 1870 did the nation limit the freedom of the states to bar any group from voting.

The United States guarantees to protect each state against invasion and against domestic violence. If a rebellion or other disturbance breaks out within a state, the legislature or governor may ask the President to send an armed force to deal with it. In writing these provisions, the framers had in mind the outbreaks of violence in Massachusetts and several boundary disputes in which a state had been invaded by militiamen from a neighboring state.

The unwritten Constitution.

Reading the Constitution does not tell us how it actually works. Various practices which it does not mention have grown up and become part of our political machinery. The whole political party system is an example. Custom, not the Constitution, is responsible for holding a national convention of each party to select nominees for President and Vice-President. The committee system by which Congress does most of its work rests on custom. The power of the Supreme Court to declare acts of Congress or of the state legislatures unconstitutional is not expressly stated in the Constitution. It was claimed by the Court very early in its history and became a custom.[1] These and other practices have developed with the times. They are almost as binding as the Constitution itself. For this reason they are often considered as the *unwritten* Constitution.

[1] The Supreme Court claimed this power on the basis that the Constitution is the supreme law of the land (see Art. VI, Sec. 2).

The Constitution has proved flexible.

The United States has grown from a nation of less than 4 million to one of over 170 million, from 13 states to 50, from a nation without influence abroad to a world leader. Through all these tremendous changes the Constitution has continued to serve the nation well. That it has endured so long is a great tribute to the genius of the men who wrote it. It is also proof of the capacity of the American people for self-government. They have made the Constitution a living document. It is the duty of every citizen who believes in democracy to know the Constitution, to uphold its principles, and to maintain as unalienable the rights which it has transmitted to us.

FOR IDENTIFICATION

Bill of Rights	Fourteenth
elastic clause	Amendment
Fifth Amendment	

FOR EXPLANATION OR DEFINITION

bill of attainder	"full faith
checks and balances	and credit" clause
committee system	impeach
double jeopardy	reserved powers
due process	residual powers
eminent domain	separation of powers
excessive bail	unconstitutional
ex post facto law	unwritten constitution
extradition	writ of *habeas corpus*

FOR REVIEW

1. Explain in detail the division of powers between the nation and the states.

2. State the purposes of the Union according to the preamble of the Constitution.

3. Name two general powers given to the federal government. Who decides what these powers include?

4. How did the framers of the Constitution prevent a party from getting control of all three branches of the government at a single election?

5. Explain the principle of separation of powers. What is meant by a system of checks and balances? Name the checks on each branch.

6. Give specific illustrations of how the Constitution protects private property.

7. Give illustrations of how the Constitution protects personal or civil rights.

8. What is the Bill of Rights? Enumerate the rights guaranteed to the people.

9. State the provisions of the Ninth and Tenth Amendments.

10. (a) Why is the Fifth Amendment particularly important? (b) What is the relation of the Fourteenth Amendment to the Bill of Rights?

11. How have court decisions influenced the meaning of the Constitution?

12. How did the Constitution provide for harmonious relations among the states? Consult Article IV.

13. Illustrate how custom and practice have influenced the American system of government. What is meant by the *unwritten* Constitution?

FOR FURTHER STUDY AND DISCUSSION

1. In what respects has the Constitution changed? How can the Constitution change without formal amendment?

2. Does the Constitution, in addition to outlining a form of government, also endorse an economic philosophy?

3. Personal rights and property rights are not absolute, but relative. Explain.

4. "What the laws mean in practice, and what the public officials do, depend in the last analysis on the social and economic pressures behind them." Explain.

5. Examine Section 1 of the Fourteenth Amendment. What special privilege does the first sentence confer upon persons born or naturalized in the United States? Do the remaining sentences restrict or increase the power of the states? Of the federal government? Explain.

6. How and why is the federal judiciary now taking a more active part in the government of the United States than in the early period of our history? Name an amendment to the Constitution that extended widely the jurisdiction of the Supreme Court and explain why the amendment had this effect.

7. What proposals have been made to limit the authority of the Supreme Court? Debate the merits of these proposals.

FOR INDIVIDUAL OR GROUP ACTIVITIES

1. Prepare a chart to illustrate the various steps by which a bill becomes a law. Helpful source: Dixon and Plischke, *American Government, Basic Documents and Materials*, pp. 87–100.

2. Hold a panel discussion which will contrast the merits of the British system of cabinet government, which makes the executive dependent on the legislative branch, and the American system in which the executive is independent of the legislature. Helpful source: Dixon and Plischke, *American Government, Basic Documents and Materials*, pp. 1–21.

3. Keep a record, as your study of our history unfolds, of the instances when the doctrine of states' rights became a matter of political controversy or debate.

4. List in parallel columns the changes made in the original Constitution. Use these headings: *By Amendment* and *By Custom*.

5. Read and report on the chapter "The Founding Fathers: An Age of Realism" in Hofstadter, *The American Political Tradition*.

HIGH POINTS

1

The question of whether France or Great Britain should control the thirteen British colonies was settled as a result of the French and Indian War. In that struggle France lost nearly all its possessions in North America. Since the thirteen colonies no longer needed the mother country's help for defense against the French, they became impatient of any British restraints.

2

The British in turn were displeased with the Americans for their actions during the war with France and for their widespread violation of the trade and navigation acts. Britain also wished the colonists to pay part of the cost of the war and of the cost of the British army stationed in America to defend them from the Indians. Under George III the British government adopted a stricter policy toward the colonists. The Americans, who were used to governing themselves with very little interference from across the sea, protested vigorously. From 1763 to 1776, as Parliament tried to assert its authority over them, relations between the colonies and the mother country grew more and more strained.

3

The First Continental Congress (1774) declared that the colonies had exclusive power to legislate on their own internal affairs. The Congress demanded the repeal of thirteen acts of Parliament which violated this principle. Meanwhile, the Congress called upon the colonists to stop the importation of British goods. The British government replied that the colonies were in rebellion and made preparations to use force. Three and a half years later the British vainly offered the colonists all they had asked for.

4

Fighting broke out in Massachusetts in the spring of 1775. The struggle began as a war for the "rights of Englishmen" and the redress of grievances. Yet in shortly over a year it became a war for independence. Both in America and in England the people were divided in their attitude toward the war. Both sides suffered from a lack of wholehearted public support. Without Washington's forceful leadership, the American army would not have stayed in the field. Fortunately, the Patriots continued the struggle, and foreign aid came in time to save their cause. In 1783 Great Britain recognized the independence of the thirteen colonies.

5

From 1776 until 1789 the new nation suffered from the lack of a strong central government. The thirteen sovereign states were but loosely united in a league of friendship, under the Articles of Confederation. The establishment of a national domain through the cession to the nation of the western land claims helped to hold the states together. In adopting plans by which new states could be formed from this domain, Congress gave the world a new principle for the government of colonies.

6

Discontent with the weaknesses of the Confederation, especially on the part of businessmen and other men of substantial property, led to the calling of the Philadelphia Convention. The delegates were convinced that the thirteen state legislatures would never give unanimous consent to the amendment of the Articles of Confederation. The Convention therefore wrote a completely new plan of government, the federal Constitution, and provided that it would go into effect if ratifying conventions in nine states approved

it. Despite much opposition, the Constitution was ratified. Its adoption ended the Confederation and amounted to a bloodless revolution.

7

The Constitution solved for the first time anywhere some of the chief practical problems of federal government. A leading English statesman called it "the most wonderful work ever struck off at a given time by the brain and purpose of man." It furnished the pattern for a strong federal republic in which the member states keep some of their sovereignty. Many other countries have copied from it in writing their own constitutions.

QUESTIONS

1. (a) Explain the meaning of the statement that the French and Indian War brought an end to "a century of salutary neglect." What is the significance of the adjective "salutary"? (b) List and explain four actions of the English government in the period 1763–65 which displeased the colonists. What actions did the colonists take to show their displeasure?

2. Reread the Declaration of Independence carefully, noting that it submits "facts to a candid world" to prove that "the history of the present king of Great Britain is a history of repeated injuries and usurpations, all having in direct object the establishment of an absolute tyranny over these states." (a) Describe "the facts" which justify at least six of the charges that the Declaration makes against the king of England. (b) What clauses or provisions of the Constitution may be traced to the ideas expressed in the Declaration?

3. Compare the terms of the Treaty of Paris (1763) ending the French and Indian War and the terms of the Treaty of Paris (1783) ending the Revolutionary War.

4. What were the chief weaknesses of the Articles of Confederation? How were these weaknesses corrected by the Constitution?

5. State the provisions of the Northwest Ordinance of 1787 and explain why this law is regarded as extremely important in American history.

6. Why is the Revolutionary War regarded as a great *social* and *political* movement?

7. (a) State the main points on which the delegates to the Constitutional Convention agreed, and the points on which they disagreed. How were the disagreements compromised? (b) Why is the compromise over representation referred to as the "Great Compromise"?

8. Why is the government of the United States known as a *federal* government?

9. Review the period 1754–87 by outlining the services of each of the following: Samuel Adams, Benjamin Franklin, George Washington, Thomas Paine, Thomas Jefferson, James Madison, Alexander Hamilton.

SUGGESTED READINGS

SOURCE MATERIALS, DOCUMENTS, AND MAPS

Amherst Series: *The Declaration of Independence and the Constitution.*

161

Commager, *Documents.*

° Commager and Nevins, *The Heritage of America.*

Dixon and Plischke, *American Government Documents.*

The Federalist. (Annotated edition) Macmillan, 1948.

Franklin, Benjamin. *Autobiography.* Modern Library, 1944.

Hart, *Contemporaries,* Vols. II and III.

Lord, *Historical Atlas.*

Paine, Thomas. *Common Sense.* Liberal Arts, 1953. (American Heritage Series)

GENERAL REFERENCES

Alden, John R. *The American Revolution, 1775–1783.* Harper, 1954. (N.A.N.)

Bailey, *Diplomatic History.*

Beard, *American Civilization.*

Beard, Charles A. *An Economic Interpretation of the Constitution of the United States.* Macmillan, 1935.

———. *The Republic.* Viking, 1943.

° Becker, Carl L. *The Eve of the Revolution.* Yale University Press, 1918. (Y.C.S.)

° ———. *The Declaration of Independence.* Harcourt, Brace, 1922.

Corwin, Edward S. *The Constitution and What It Means Today.* Princeton, 1924.

° Farrand, Max. *The Fathers of the Constitution.* Yale University Press, 1921. (Y.C.S.)

° ———. *The Framing of the Constitution of the United States.* Yale University Press, 1913.

Fiske, John. *The Critical Period of American History, 1783–1789.* Houghton, 1902.

Gipson, L. H. *The Coming of the Revolution, 1763–1775.* Harper, 1954. (N.A.N.)

Hofstadter, *American Political Tradition.*

Larkin, *Art and Life in America.*

McLaughlin, Andrew C. *The Confederation and the Constitution, 1783–1789.* Harper, 1905. (A.N.S.)

Miller, John C. *Origins of the American Revolution.* Little, Brown, 1943.

———. *Triumph of Freedom, 1775–1783.* Little, Brown, 1948.

Morison and Commager, *American Republic,* Vol. I.

Nettels, Curtis P. *The Roots of American Civilization.* Crofts, 1938.

Ogg, Frederic A. *Builders of the Republic.* Yale University Press, 1927. (Pageant)

° ———. *The Old Northwest.* Yale University Press, 1919. (Y.C.S.)

Parkman, Francis. *The Battle for North America.* Doubleday, 1948.

Schlesinger, Arthur M. *New Viewpoints in American History.* Macmillan, 1922.

Van Doren, Carl. *The Great Rehearsal.* Viking, 1948.

Wallace, Willard. *Appeal to Arms.* Harper, 1951.

Wood, William, and Gabriel, Ralph H. *The Winning of Freedom.* Yale University Press, 1927. (Pageant)

° Wrong, George M. *Washington and His Comrades in Arms.* Yale University Press, 1921. (Y.C.S.)

BIOGRAPHY

Axelrod, Jacob. *Patrick Henry, the Voice of Freedom.* Random House, 1947.

Bowen, Catherine D. *John Adams and the American Revolution.* Little, Brown, 1950.

Bowers, Claude G. *The Young Jefferson.* Houghton, 1945.

° Cousins, Margaret. *Ben Franklin of Old Philadelphia.* Random House, 1952.

° Fisher, Dorothy Canfield. *Paul Revere and the Minute Men.* Random House, 1950.

Harlow, R. V. *Samuel Adams, Promoter of the Revolution.* Holt, 1923.

Lodge, Henry Cabot. *George Washington.* Houghton, 1891.

° Mayer, Jane. *Betsy Ross and the Flag.* Random House, 1952.

° Nicolay, Helen. *The Boy's Life of Washington.* Century, 1932.

° ———. *The Boy's Life of Lafayette.* Harper, 1920.

° ———. *The Boy's Life of Benjamin Franklin.* Appleton-Century, 1935.

° ———. *The Boy's Life of Alexander Hamilton.* Century, 1927.

° Richards, L. E. *Abigail Adams and Her Times.* Appleton, 1917.

° Sperry, Armstrong. *John Paul Jones.* Random House, 1953. (Landmark)

Van Doren, Carl. *Benjamin Franklin.* Viking, 1938.

° White, Stewart Edward. *Daniel Boone, Wilderness Scout.* Doubleday, 1946.

FICTION

Bacheller, Irving. *In the Days of Poor Richard.* Bobbs-Merrill, 1926. (The beginning of the Revolution)

162

° Boyd, James. *Drums.* Scribner, 1926.) North Carolina during the Revolution; John Paul Jones)

Churchill, Winston. *The Crossing.* Macmillan, 1927. (Clark, Boone, Jackson, Sevier)

———. *Richard Carvel.* Macmillan, 1927. (Maryland and England before the Revolution; John Paul Jones)

Cooper, James Fenimore. *The Spy.* Garden City, 1942. (A spy for Washington)

Dyer, W. A. *Sprigs of Hemlock.* Century, 1931. (Shays's Rebellion)

° Edmonds, Walter D. *Drums along the Mohawk.* Jarrolds, 1938.

° Forbes, Esther. *Johnny Tremain.* Houghton 1943. (Boston in the Revolution)

Ford, P. L. *Janice Meredith.* Grosset, 1941. (A romance introducing Major André)

° Gross, W. L. *Jack Gregory.* Crowell, 1923. (Surrender of Cornwallis)

° Hart, W. S. *A Lighter of Flames.* Crowell, 1923. (Patrick Henry)

° Holbrook, Stewart. *America's Ethan Allen.* Houghton, 1949.

Mason, F. Van Wyck. *Three Harbours.* Grosset & Dunlap, 1944.

Mitchell, S. W. *Hugh Wynne, Free Quaker.* Century, 1922. (A thrilling novel introducing Lafayette, André, and others)

Morrow, Honoré. *Let the King Beware.* Morrow, 1936. (A Tory returns to England)

Roberts, Kenneth. *Arundel.* Doubleday, 1930. (Arnold's expedition against Quebec)

———. *Northwest Passage.* Doubleday, 1937. (The exploration and settlement of the Northwest)

———. *Oliver Wiswell.* Doubleday, 1940. (A presentation of the Tory point of view)

———. *Rabble in Arms.* Doubleday, 1933. (A sequel to *Arundel*)

° Sabatini, Rafael. *The Carolinian.* Houghton, 1925. (The struggle between loyalists and patriots)

° Thompson, M. *Alice of Old Vincennes.* Grosset, 1908. (A romance involving the exploits of George Rogers Clark)

(Top) FRENCH SNUFFBOX *of tortoise shell with copper gilt, decorated with a print of Voltaire, Rousseau, and Franklin. Late 18th century.*

(Right) CHINESE WALLPAPER *used in a Philadelphia home in 1768. This imported landscape paper was painted by hand and mounted on linen.*

TIME LINE

1790	1789	Washington inaugurated
	1791	Bill of Rights
	1793	Proclamation of Neutrality
	1795	Jay and Pinckney treaties
	1797	Adams inaugurated
	1798	Alien and Sedition Acts; Virginia and Kentucky resolutions
1800		
	1801	Jefferson inaugurated
	1803	Louisiana Purchase
	1804	Lewis and Clark expedition begins
	1807	Embargo Act
	1809	Embargo Act repealed; Nonintercourse Act
1810		
	1812–14	War with England
	1814	Hartford Convention; Treaty of Ghent
	1816	Protective tariff
	1817	Monroe inaugurated
	1819	Florida purchased from Spain
1820	1820	Fourth census: population 9,638,000
	1823	Monroe Doctrine
	1825	John Q. Adams inaugurated

164

UNIT THREE   *The National Government Grows Stronger*

★ ★ ★ ★ Our Constitution outlined the new government of the United States. Yet the document was only an outline and left many details to be worked out. The first Congress and the first President, George Washington, had to decide how to put the Constitution into effect. The decisions they made gave the young republic a good start. Yet for some years no one knew whether the new nation would be strong enough to last. President Washington felt that the government was seriously endangered by party strife.

Strong differences of opinion developed on such important questions as how the federal government should get money to pay its expenses, whether it should assume the debts of the states, whether it should charter a central bank, and whether it should allow free criticism of Congress and the administration. There was even argument as to whether a state might nullify an act of Congress. Two political parties arose. The Federalists, led by Alexander Hamilton, and the Democratic-Republicans, led by Thomas Jefferson, took opposite sides on the leading issues. The Federalists, who were more conservative than their opponents, held office until 1800. They shaped the nation during its most formative years. Long after they lost control of Congress and the Presidency, their ideas continued to dominate the Supreme Court.

Almost from the start our nation's leaders had to deal with difficult foreign problems. Great Britain, France, Spain, and even the little Barbary states in North Africa ignored American rights. The United States was hardly twenty-three years old when it went to war with England. This struggle, known as the War of 1812, showed that the United States was determined to be treated with respect. The war strengthened the feeling of national unity.

During the first ten years after the war, our federal government became more vigorous. The people were more willing than they had been earlier to let Congress take action to promote the general welfare. At the same time the United States showed a new firmness in dealing with other nations. The peak of national feeling came in 1823 when President Monroe announced the famous policy known as the Monroe Doctrine.

WASHINGTON'S TRIUM-
PHAL ARRIVAL *in New
York City, April 1789,
for his inauguration.
Along the frontiers of
the new nation pioneers
were starting settlements
that would, in time, rival
in importance the already
established cities of the
east coast.*

The preservation of the sacred fire of liberty and the destiny of the republican model of government are justly considered, perhaps, as *deeply*, as *finally*, staked on the experiment entrusted to the hands of the American people.——George Washington

President George Washington

11. FEDERALISTS LAUNCH THE NEW NATIONAL GOVERNMENT

The New Government Begins

Washington becomes President.

Arrangements were made for launching the new government in the spring of 1789. Washington's name was on everyone's lips, and when the electoral college met, he was chosen unanimously for President.

In mid-April Washington left his beautiful home on the Potomac to go to New York, the temporary capital. In every village and town the people gathered to cheer him. Children sang by the roadsides; bridges were decorated with evergreens and flowers; banquets were given for him at every halting place. As he approached the city of New York, he was saluted by thirteen guns. On April 30, before a vast throng, George Washington took the oath of office as our first President.

What the country was like.

When Washington became President the United States had almost four million people. Its area was one third its present size. All the land west of the Mississippi and the entire shore of the Gulf of Mexico belonged to Spain.

There were only five cities with a population of over 10,000. Most Americans lived in small villages or on farms or plantations, surrounded by forests. A Frenchman who journeyed through the seaboard states a few years later (1796) wrote that he scarcely traveled for more than three miles together through open and cleared land. "Compared with France the entire country is one vast wood."

Communications were slow and poor. Roads were impassable much of the time. In 1776 it had taken twenty-nine days for news of the Declaration of Independence to reach Charleston. News traveled no faster in 1789.

The westward movement was gaining in volume. By 1789 more than 100,-000 people had crossed the Appalachians and settled in the fertile valleys of the Ohio and the Cumberland. Kentucky and Tennessee would soon be admitted as new states. Because the country west of the Appalachians was so vast and so remote, well-informed Europeans thought it would break off from the Union.

167

The new government is an experiment.

In his inaugural address Washington said that the American republic was an experiment. At that time even its strongest supporters wondered if it would last. At least half of the people had opposed ratification of the Constitution. Fortunately, the new government was in the hands of its friends. Many members of the first Congress had helped frame the Constitution or had worked for its adoption. When filling important positions, Washington took care to select men who wanted the new government to succeed. They helped him and Congress to create the necessary "machinery" for carrying on the government.

When the Confederation went out of existence, it left behind a dozen clerks, an empty treasury, and a huge debt. There were no federal laws, courts, or law-enforcement officers. Moreover, the Constitution provided only the broad outline for the new government. The first President and first Congress had to work out methods of putting the Constitution into effect. The wisdom of their decisions might determine whether the federal Union would live or die.

Congress establishes executive departments.

The Constitution mentions executive departments but leaves Congress to decide what the departments shall be. The first Congress created a Department of State, a Department of War, and a Department of the Treasury, each headed by a secretary. Congress also created the office of Attorney General, to handle the legal business of the government, and that of Postmaster General, to run the postal service.

To head the departments Washington picked men of ability and experience. He chose the brilliant young lawyer, Alexander Hamilton, for Secretary of the Treasury, then the most important post in the government. He called on Thomas Jefferson to be Secretary of State.

The Cabinet develops.

The Cabinet was not mentioned in the Constitution. It says merely that the President "may require the opinion, in writing, of the principal officer in each of the executive departments, upon any subject relating to the duties of their respective offices" (Art. II, Sec. 2). Washington relied heavily on the advice of the department heads. Soon they came to be known as the President's Cabinet. Congress made them responsible only to the President.

Congress sets up federal courts.

The Constitution said that the judicial power was to be vested in "one Supreme Court and in such inferior [lower] courts as Congress may from time to time establish." The judges were to be appointed by the President and confirmed by the Senate. In the

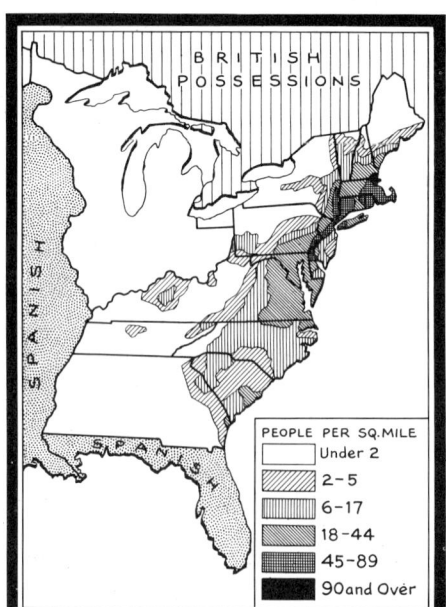

DISTRIBUTION OF UNITED STATES POPULATION, 1790

168

Judiciary Act of 1789 Congress provided that the Supreme Court should consist of one chief justice and five associate justices—a number which has been changed several times since. The act also set up three circuit courts and thirteen district courts.

The Judiciary Act provided that all disputes over the meaning of the Constitution, federal laws, and treaties shall be settled by the Supreme Court. This power of the Supreme Court is known as "judicial review." Without it each state could have placed its own interpretation on federal laws and treaties.

Congress passes a tariff act.

To pay its expenses and the interest on the public debt, the new government had to impose taxes. But what kind of taxes? Ever since the Stamp Act of 1765, the people had opposed taxation by the central government. Congress decided to place duties of from 5 to 10 per cent upon most kinds of imports. The purpose of the tariff act was (1) to support the government and (2) to encourage American manufacturers. The act also helped shipowners by allowing a discount of 10 per cent on goods imported in American ships.

Congress submits the Bill of Rights.

As we mentioned earlier, a number of states had ratified the Constitution with strong recommendations for changes (see p. 148). During its first session Congress submitted twelve amendments to the states. Ten of them were ratified. These ten, known as the Bill of Rights, became part of the Constitution in 1791.

Hamilton's Program Strengthens the National Government

The public debt is to be paid in full.

As Secretary of the Treasury, Hamilton solved many difficult financial problems. Soon after entering the Cabinet he sent to Congress a brilliant "Report on the Public Credit." It contained three recommendations concerning the war debts owed by the nation and the states:

1. The foreign debt of $12,000,000, owed chiefly to the French and the Dutch, should be paid in full.

2. The domestic debt (about $44,000,000 with the unpaid interest) should be paid in full. This amount had been borrowed by the United States from its own citizens during the war. The interest on it had never been paid.

3. The federal government should assume, or take over, the unpaid war debts of the states, amounting to about $21,000,000.

Everyone agreed to paying the foreign debt, but a vigorous fight developed over the domestic debt. Most of the loan certificates were no longer in the hands of the original holders, since speculators had bought them up for as little as 15 cents on the dollar. Some congressmen argued that the certificates held by speculators should be redeemed at their market value, which had gone up to 25 cents on the dollar. But Congress adopted Hamilton's recommendation—to pay the full face value of the certificates.

The proposal for assumption of the *state* war debts aroused even more opposition. A few states had paid off a large portion of their debt and did not want to be taxed to help states which had paid little or nothing on their debt. Besides, most of the state bonds had passed into the hands of speculators for a few cents on the dollar. When the assumption bill was brought to a vote in the House, it failed to carry by two votes. But Hamilton would not admit defeat. He got the necessary votes by means of a clever bargain.

It happened at this time that Congress had before it the question of where to locate the national capital.

Virginia, which was against the assumption of state debts, was eager to have the capital on the Potomac River. Many other states were less concerned about the location of the capital than about having the federal government take over their debt. Hamilton saw his chance to arrange a bargain between the two sides. The Virginia congressmen agreed to vote for assumption of the state debts in return for a promise by other congressmen to vote to locate the national capital on the Potomac. This kind of political arrangement is known as *logrolling*—"You help roll my log and I'll help you roll yours." Logrolling is still practiced today.

The entire debt is "funded."

The total debts came to about $75,000,000. Since the federal government did not have the money to pay this sum, Hamilton proposed that the debt be "funded." Accordingly, the old bonds and certificates issued by the Confederation Congress and by the states were called in. In exchange for them the treasury issued new long-term bonds of the same face value, on which it promised to pay interest regularly. Such a procedure, by which a short-term loan is converted to one of long term, is known as "funding."

The whiskey excise leads to a rebellion.

To help pay the interest on the huge public debt, Hamilton recommended an excise, or tax, of 25 cents a gallon on whiskey. The money was to be collected at the stills. Congress adopted this recommendation. A storm of opposition immediately broke out in the back country of Pennsylvania, Virginia, and North Carolina, where the sale of whiskey was the farmers' only source of cash. Here the farmers commonly made their grain into whiskey, since grain was too bulky to be carried to market on horseback. To have to pay a tax on whiskey seemed to them most unfair. To collect the tax government officers had to enter the still owner's property and measure the whiskey on hand—a procedure which was greatly resented.

Because of the protests, Congress removed the tax from the product of the smaller stills. This action quieted the farmers of Virginia and North Carolina. In Pennsylvania, however, resistance continued. In four western counties of the state the farmers held meetings, refused to pay the tax, appointed committees of safety, and threatened violence to tax collectors and to any who obeyed the law. Similar actions had forced Parliament to repeal the hated stamp tax (see p. 104). When federal officers tried to arrest the leaders of the movement, riots occurred. Some of the farmers were wounded and one was killed. Mobs forced a federal officer to flee for his life.

This defiance of the federal government has come to be known as the "Whiskey Rebellion." A force of a thousand soldiers could easily have restored order, but the President, strongly urged by Hamilton, planned to show the strength of the federal government. Fifteen thousand militia from Virginia, Maryland, and Pennsylvania were sent into the rebellious area. Messengers went ahead to persuade the people to submit, and there was no bloodshed. Eighteen leaders were arrested, but only two were convicted, and they were soon pardoned by the President.

Congress charters the first Bank of the United States.

In 1789 there were only three banks in the entire country, one each at Philadelphia, New York, and Boston. Additional banks were needed to care for the nation's growing industry and commerce. Hamilton thought there should be a central bank chartered by the federal government, with branches in different parts of the nation. Such a

THE CITY OF WASHINGTON IN 1800. *The inserted memorandum from John Adams directs the "Several Heads of Departments" to move official papers and books to the new capital "for the dispatch of business" by June fifteenth.*

bank would provide a safe place for depositing public funds. The Treasury could borrow from it as need arose, pledging expected income from taxes. If branches of the bank were established in the principal cities, the Treasury could use checks to transfer funds from one part of the country to another. This would be safer and easier than shipping gold. Even more important, the bank would issue bank notes. These would provide a sound, uniform currency that would circulate in all parts of the country. A sound currency was one of the nation's greatest needs.

Hamilton persuaded Congress to pass a bill chartering the Bank of the United States. The bank was to be privately owned and managed. The federal government was to subscribe one fifth of its capital and to name one fifth of its directors. One fifth of the profits would be paid into the Treasury.

Jefferson, speaking for believers in states' rights, urged Washington to veto the bank bill. He argued that the proposed bank would be too powerful and would have an unfair advantage over banks chartered by the states. Furthermore, the Constitution does not say that Congress may charter a bank. In Jefferson's view, it was unconstitutional for Congress to use a power not specifically given to the federal government.

This way of thinking is known as the doctrine of *strict construction* or *specific powers.*

Hamilton replied that the Constitution does not *forbid* the federal government to charter a bank. He called attention to the "elastic clause," which says Congress may make laws "necessary and proper" for carrying out the powers which are listed. Among the listed powers of Congress are collecting taxes, paying debts, borrowing money, and regulating the currency. Hamilton argued that the chartering of a national bank was a necessary and proper way of using these listed powers. He also insisted that Congress has the right to use powers *implied* in the powers actually granted. This is the doctrine of *loose construction* or *implied powers.* Washington accepted Hamilton's argument and signed the bank bill.

The central office of the bank was established in Philadelphia. In time branches were opened in eight other cities from New Hampshire to Georgia. The bank's notes circulated everywhere and were accepted at full face value. Having a uniform currency in all states made business transactions easier.

Hamilton advocates a protective tariff.

In a famous "Report on Manufactures" Hamilton urged Congress to adopt a protective tariff with rates so high that foreign goods would be shut out. Such a tariff would encourage American manufacturing, which was then in its infancy. The growth of manufacturing, said Hamilton, would make the country self-sufficient, give employment to women and to children "of a tender age," attract immigrants, and widen the demand for farm products. Hamilton wished to place high duties on all foreign goods which could be produced here.

Jeffersonians were against a protective tariff. They said it would hurt farmers by raising the price of manufactured goods and by making it harder to sell their surplus crops abroad. Merchants and shipowners argued that they too would be hurt by a protective tariff. Since it would raise prices, the tariff was also unwelcome to consumers. Although Congress increased the duties on a number of items (1792), it did not adopt Hamilton's high tariff policy.

Hamilton succeeds in his aims.

Hamilton had designed his financial program to make the national government strong and to gain for it the support of men of wealth. In both aims he was successful. The government now had all the revenue it needed and its credit was excellent. It had proved its ability to enforce an unpopular law, the whiskey tax. It had also taken various steps to encourage business and commerce. Bondholders, stockholders in the Bank of the United States, manufacturers, and merchants stood firmly behind the new government.

Differing Interests Give Rise to Political Parties

National political parties develop.

The Constitution says nothing about political parties. The framers of the Constitution hoped that the strife caused by parties could be avoided. They did not appreciate the value of an opposition party in keeping a government from having all its own way.

The parties which appeared during the contest over ratification did not last long. The Antifederalists accepted the decision of the country and made no attempt to overthrow the Constitution. But the nation soon divided again into two camps, one that approved Hamilton's program and one that opposed it.

The group supporting Hamilton were called *Federalists,* because of their belief in a strong central govern-

QUARRELS IN CONGRESS. *Here is one artist's interpretation of the arguments going on in Congress.*

ment. They thought a strong government was needed to protect property rights and to maintain order. They included nearly all of the important businessmen, large planters, holders of government bonds, and speculators in western lands. Socially most Federalists belonged to the upper class.

Those who opposed Hamilton's program were, for the most part, farmers, pioneers, shopkeepers, and wage earners. They thought that Hamilton's policies favored the few at the expense of the many. They feared that a strong federal government would destroy their liberties. They gradually turned to Thomas Jefferson as their spokesman. They began to call themselves "Democratic-Republicans" or "Republicans," to show that they were against monarchy, aristocracy, and privilege. This new party was the ancestor of the modern Democratic party. It should not be confused with the modern Republican party, which began in the 1850's.

The Federalists heaped accusations on the Republicans and the Republicans answered in the same spirit. Republican newspapers denounced almost everything the Federalists did. Even Washington was criticized without mercy. Stung by such attacks, Washington once exclaimed, "I would rather be in my grave than in the Presidency."

Republicans organize local clubs.

The people who opposed Hamilton's program were more numerous than those who favored it. But they were not used to taking part in politics. Jefferson and his friend James Madison set about to correct this. They helped start Republican societies in all parts of the country. These clubs encouraged people who felt dissatisfied with the government to work for a change. The clubs prepared lists of candidates for office. They got out the vote on election day. They kept in touch with similar societies in other localities. They raised money to start newspapers friendly to their views. In these ways they built up the influence of their party.

We know today that local political clubs are necessary for two-party government. The Federalists, however, were unhappy over the growth of an opposition party. They considered the Republicans little better than mutineers and thought that their societies were subversive. They accused Jefferson of deliberately stirring up the Pennsylvania farmers to rebel. This was untrue. The Federalists never understood the value of party opposition. As we shall see in the next chapter, this led to their downfall.

First United States Bank, 1791

FOR IDENTIFICATION

Bank of the United States	Federalists
	Alexander Hamilton
Democratic-Republicans	Judiciary Act
	Whiskey Rebellion

FOR EXPLANATION OR DEFINITION

assumption   inaugural
bank note   logrolling
Cabinet   loose construction
capital   revenue
excise   specific powers
funding   strict construction
implied powers   tariff

FOR REVIEW

1. Describe conditions in the United States at the time of Washington's inauguration.

2. What were some of the problems facing the new government in 1789?

3. Who were two of the first members of Washington's Cabinet?

4. What courts did the first Congress establish?

5. Why were the first ten amendments added to the Constitution?

6. What did Hamilton propose concerning the foreign and domestic debts? Why did opposition develop? What bargain did Hamilton make concerning the location of the national capital?

7. Explain what is meant by "funding the debt."

8. What kind of tax is an excise? Why did some object to the tax on whiskey?

9. How did Washington deal with the "Whiskey Rebellion"?

10. Why did Hamilton urge that Congress charter the Bank of the United States?

11. Was the first Bank of the United States a private corporation? Why is the note-issuing privilege important? What control did the government have over the bank?

12. Why did Jefferson oppose the chartering of the bank?

13. Explain the meaning of the terms: elastic clause, implied powers, loose construction, strict construction. Quote the elastic clause (see Art. I, Sec. 8, of the Constitution).

14. Why did Hamilton urge the adoption of a protective tariff policy?

15. What were Hamilton's principal achievements as the first Secretary of the Treasury?

16. Contrast the views of Hamilton and Jefferson about the federal government, the tariff, the encouragement of manufacturing, and the elastic clause.

17. What groups supported Hamilton? What groups supported Jefferson?

18. How did the first political parties begin to develop?

FOR FURTHER STUDY AND DISCUSSION

1. In what respects was the government of the new nation "undemocratic"?

2. What actions of the new government established precedents which have become features of our unwritten constitution?

3. How would the assumption of state debts by the national government tend to strengthen the national government?

4. Why did Jefferson refer to the members of Congress who supported Hamilton's program as a "corrupt squadron"?

5. What were the political motives back of Hamilton's financial program? Explain how the creation of the first Bank of the United States was in keeping with Hamilton's political ideals.

6. State your reasons for agreeing or disagreeing with Hamilton's tariff theories. Does it make any difference whether you think of conditions as they were in 1789 or as they are today?

7. Give reasons for your agreement or disagreement with Hamilton's political theory that men of substance and property must be won over to the support of the national government.

8. Would you have been a supporter of Hamilton or of Jefferson? Why?

FOR INDIVIDUAL OR GROUP ACTIVITIES

1. Make a special report on the question of ceremonials and titles, the suppression of the "Whiskey Rebellion," or the "deal" concerning the location of the capital.

2. Find examples of the bitter partisan attacks made by Federalists and Republicans. Contrast with partisan attacks today.

Observe good faith and justice towards all nations; cultivate peace and harmony with all.
——George Washington

George Washington, from a miniature by Charles W. Peale

12. FOREIGN PROBLEMS PERPLEX THE NEW NATION

Washington Avoids Foreign Entanglements

Washington accepts a second term.

Dismayed by the growing party strife and weary of the cares of office, Washington wished to retire after one term. He was eager to return to Mount Vernon and to the life of a country gentleman. Hamilton and Jefferson urged him to serve a second term for the good of the nation. He reluctantly agreed. Again he was unanimously elected.

Washington stayed in office mainly because of what he described as "the delicate posture of our foreign affairs." Our relations with Great Britain, Spain, and France were embarrassing. The British still held a chain of fur-trading posts within our boundaries. The Spanish still refused to let our shipping pass freely through New Orleans. Our old ally, France, was already at war with Austria and Prussia and would probably soon be at war with Great Britain. If we allowed ourselves to be drawn into the conflict we might lose our independence. In times so threatening, Washington's advisers told him that he must remain at the helm.

Americans take sides in the French Revolution.

The French Revolution had begun in 1789. At first Americans rejoiced that the French were following our example in rising up against tyranny. They hailed the great French Declaration of the Rights of Man. When European kings sent armies into France for the purpose of crushing the revolution, Americans waited anxiously for news. Each victory won by the citizen army of France was celebrated here, especially in Republican circles. It became the fashion among Republicans to drop titles and to speak of "Citizen Smith," "Citizeness Jones," and "Citizen Judge."

As time went on, the revolution in France grew increasingly violent and bloody. The king and queen and thousands of nobles were beheaded on the guillotine. Hamilton and his followers were terribly shocked. They thought the revolution was leading to the overthrow of law and order and to mob rule. They lost all sympathy with the common people of France. This was not true of Jefferson and his followers.

They thought the suffering through which France was passing was the price it must pay to win freedom.

France and Britain go to war.

Early in 1793 war broke out between France and Great Britain. Britain joined a coalition of European powers which was formed to restore the French monarchy and prevent the spread of the revolution. Opinion in the United States became more sharply divided. The Federalists had strong commercial ties with the British. Besides, they were disgusted by the radicals who had come to power in France. The Federalists therefore sided with the British. The Republicans, on the other hand, hoped for a French victory. It seemed to them Great Britain was an enemy of human rights. The more reckless partisans on each side wanted the United States to enter the war.

Washington proclaims our neutrality.

The newly formed French Republic sent a minister, Edmond Genêt, to ask the United States to open its ports to French naval vessels and privateers. He landed at Charleston (April, 1793) and was welcomed enthusiastically by Republicans all the way to Philadelphia. Even before presenting himself to the President, he began to license privateers. He also hired Americans to attack Spanish Florida and Louisiana.

President Washington was neither pro-French nor pro-British. He believed that the United States needed time to set its own house in order and that it was too weak to risk taking part in a foreign war. He intended to avoid war at all costs. With the approval of his entire Cabinet, Washington issued a proclamation of neutrality declaring that the United States would take no part in the conflict. He warned American citizens against helping any nation at war.

Genêt goes too far.

The proclamation was a bitter disappointment to the pro-French faction. Their scathing criticism of the President led Genêt to think that the public did not approve of neutrality. He therefore appealed directly to the people and to Congress for aid to France. This action angered the Federalists and even caused many Republicans to turn against him. Genêt continued to fit out privateers and to act in other ways as if America were French soil. When he had been here four months, Washington asked the French government to recall him. A new French minister arrived and Genêt was relieved of his post. Genêt was afraid to return to France. Washington allowed him to stay here and he later became an American citizen.

THE STORMING OF THE BASTILLE, *July 14, 1789.*
To the common people of France this massive prison was the symbol of tyranny.

THE TWO POLITICAL PARTIES, 1793–1800

FEDERALISTS (*Hamilton*) FAVORED:	REPUBLICANS (*Jefferson*) FAVORED:
Powerful national government	Weak national government (states rights)
Loose construction of the Constitution	*Strict* construction of the Constitution
A strong central bank	State banks only
Protective tariff	Tariff for revenue only
Help to business interests and investors	No special favors to business and investors
An expanding bureaucracy	Reduction in number of federal officeholders
Rule by the "best people"	Extension of democracy
Restrictions on free speech and press (Alien and Sedition Acts)	Freedom to criticize government (Virginia and Kentucky resolutions)
The British in foreign relations	The French in foreign relations

Difficulties with Great Britain.

With a large pro-French faction shouting that we should fight for France, the President found it hard to preserve our neutrality. Neutrality was all the more difficult because of Great Britain's attitude toward the United States. Not only did the British still hold a chain of military and trading posts on our soil in the Northwest, but they had built one additional fort there. British officials continued to sell liquor and firearms to the Indians in that area. When the United States complained, Great Britain replied that we had not carried out the agreement in the Treaty of Paris regarding debts owed by Americans to British citizens. The fact is, however, that the British wanted to keep the valuable fur trade of the Northwest.

To make matters worse, the British seized scores of American ships bound for the French West Indies. They imprisoned the American crews or forced them to serve in the royal navy. Fearing that we would have to fight the British, Congress authorized the fortification of harbors and other defensive measures. The situation was tense. The governor of Canada told the Indians of the Northwest that Great Britain and the United States would soon be at war and that the Indians could recover their lands if they helped the British.

Republicans propose an embargo.

Jefferson and other Republican leaders favored an embargo against British goods. They hoped this would force Great Britain to listen to American complaints. But merchants and shipowners were against any such measure. In spite of the seizure of some American ships, they were making large profits from wartime trade. Hamilton sided with them. He pointed out that 90 per cent of our imports came from Great Britain. If we shut these imports out, the federal government would lose most of its revenue. Moreover, he warned, an embargo might provoke the British to declare war. With Hamilton's help, the Federalists succeeded in defeating a bill calling for an embargo.

Jefferson resigns from the Cabinet.

Hamilton and Jefferson differed on so many important questions that they could not work together. Each attacked the other in the press. They became personal as well as political enemies. Washington tried in vain to make peace between them. At the end of 1793 Jefferson left the Cabinet and returned to Monticello, his estate in Virginia. He resigned because he thought Washington was too much under Hamilton's influence and was even leaning on Hamilton for advice in foreign affairs. In retirement Jefferson conducted an immense correspondence with Republican leaders. His purpose was to build up the party.

Jay makes a treaty with Britain.

In the hope of preventing war, Washington decided to send a special envoy to London. John Jay, Chief Justice of the Supreme Court, was selected to go. In negotiations that lasted from June to November, 1794, Jay made the best terms he could get.

Great Britain was fighting to the death with France. The British refused to stop seizing American ships bound for French ports, but did promise to pay for seized cargoes of foodstuffs. They would not stop taking off our ships sailors whom they claimed to be British subjects. They also refused to give American ships full privileges of trading with the British West Indies. As to differences arising out of the Treaty of 1783 both sides agreed to settle them by arbitration; that is, by discussion between British and American commissioners. The British gave in on only one matter of immediate importance: they promised to withdraw from the western posts within two years. Britain probably yielded this from fear that otherwise we might fight.

When Jay's treaty was published (March, 1795), a storm of criticism broke out in Congress and in the press.

Angry Republicans burned images of Jay. When Hamilton spoke in defense of the treaty in New York, he was stoned. Washington did not like the treaty, but he knew there was no hope of making a better one. He threw his influence behind it, securing the Senate's approval by a bare two-thirds vote. The pro-French faction criticized him, yet his action postponed war with England for many years and gave the new nation time to gain strength.

Troubles with Spain are adjusted.

Settlers beyond the Appalachians had only one way of sending their products to market—to float them down the Mississippi to New Orleans and there transfer them to ocean-going vessels. Yet when the goods reached New Orleans, the Spanish authorities demanded such heavy taxes that there was no profit. As if this were not enough, Spain refused to accept the southwestern boundary of the United States established in the Treaty of Paris.

The Westerners believed that the people of the East cared nothing for their difficulties; they became so dissatisfied, in fact, that they talked of setting up a government of their own. Washington was well aware of the danger that the West might leave the Union. "A touch of a feather," he wrote, "would turn them [the Western states] either way." In 1795, since all efforts to reach an understanding with Spain had failed, Washington decided to send a special envoy to Spain. He chose for the job Thomas Pinckney.

Now that Great Britain had made a treaty with the United States, the Spanish government changed its attitude. It feared that the two nations might form an alliance which would threaten the safety of Spanish possessions in America. Spain, therefore, decided to listen to American complaints. Pinckney was able to obtain all that he had been sent to ask, and everything

THE TREATY OF GREEN-VILLE. *In return for the land ceded by the Indians, General Anthony Wayne, representing the United States, promised to pay them 20,000 dollars' worth of goods immediately, and an annuity forever.*

that Spain had been refusing for the past twelve years. Spain granted us the free use of the Mississippi and the right to land goods at New Orleans free of duty while awaiting ocean-going ships. (This is called the "right of deposit.") The southwestern boundary dispute was also settled.

Victory over Indians of the Northwest.

Settlement of the Northwest had been delayed by trouble with the Indians. Twice, in 1790 and 1791, the tribesmen defeated American troops which were sent to subdue them. The Indians demanded that a large part of the Northwest Territory be made into an independent Indian nation. The President ordered General Anthony Wayne to subdue the Indians. Wayne trained an army and won a decisive victory in the Battle of Fallen Timbers. A year later (1795) Wayne and the Indians drew up the Treaty of Greenville. It gave most of Ohio and part of Indiana to the United States. As a result, settlement of this area went forward rapidly.

Washington retires.

The three treaties concluded in 1795—with Great Britain, Spain, and the Indians of the Northwest—made Americans feel more secure. The Spanish and British no longer controlled part of our soil. The threat of war had receded. The new government was fairly launched, and Washington felt he could safely lay down the burdens of his office. For personal reasons he refused to be considered for a third term.

As his second term neared its close, he issued his famous Farewell Address. In this affectionate message he warned his countrymen against sectionalism, saying that the Union should benefit all sections—North and South, East and West. He criticized the violent spirit shown by the pro-British and pro-French factions. He spoke of the "baneful effects of the spirit of party," saying it was "the interest and duty of a wise people to restrain it." Thinking of our alliance with France, he warned against *permanent* alliances with any foreign nation, and said: "We may safely trust to temporary alliances for extraordinary emergencies." He urged the new nation to use its geographic isolation to develop peacefully into maturity and strength. "If we remain one people under an efficient government," he said, "the time is not far off when we may defy injury from any other nation."

179

PRESIDENT WASHINGTON AT FORT CUMBERLAND, *Virginia,*
reviewing some of the thousands of troops he had called
to suppress the Whisky Rebellion (see p. 170). Though
his action was unpopular among western farmers, Wash-
ington was determined to enforce the laws of the new
republic.

Difficulties with France Disturb John Adams' Term

The Federalists elect John Adams.

The election of 1796 was the first to be contested by two parties. The Federalists in Congress met together in a party caucus [1] and agreed to support John Adams for President and Thomas Pinckney for Vice-President. They passed over Hamilton since he had no popular following. The Republican congressmen also held a caucus and chose Thomas Jefferson as their candidate for President, with Aaron Burr of New York as his running mate.

Adams was elected President with 71 electoral votes, while Jefferson, his opponent, became Vice-President with 68. The election of a President and Vice-President of opposite parties happened because the Constitution then stated that the man receiving the largest number of electoral votes would become President and the man receiving the next largest, Vice-President.

Adams is respected but not popular.

John Adams had been in the public service ever since 1774, when Massachusetts sent him to the First Continental Congress. During the Revolution and the Confederation period, he served as a minister in Europe. He was Vice-President during Washington's administration. Adams was able, upright, and patriotic, but he lacked the qualities of a popular leader.

Adams admired Washington and hoped to continue the same policies. For this reason Adams kept most of Washington's Cabinet officers. This

[1] The *caucus,* or conference of party leaders to decide policy, was not provided for in the Constitution or by any law. In theory the electors might have ignored the action of the caucuses. Instead, they pledged themselves in advance to support their party candidates.

proved to be a mistake. Although Hamilton was no longer in the Cabinet, its members looked to him for instructions rather than to Adams. Since Hamilton was no friend of Adams, the Cabinet often worked against the President.

Adams sends three envoys to France.

Ever since our proclamation of neutrality in 1793, relations with France had been growing worse. French disappointment at our refusal to give them aid turned to anger when we accepted Jay's treaty with Great Britain. Since the treaty allowed the British to keep on seizing foodstuffs bound from the United States to France, the French thought that we had taken sides against them. In revenge they seized American ships carrying food to Great Britain. By June, 1797, the French had confiscated over three hundred American ships. While England also hurt our commerce, France injured it far more.

At this time we had no representative in France. Washington had recalled James Monroe in 1796. His successor, Charles C. Pinckney, had been appointed, but the French government refused to receive him. (He was the brother of Thomas Pinckney and was strongly pro-British.) News that Pinckney had been asked to leave France reached here soon after Adams became President. Adams sent John Marshall and Elbridge Gerry to join Pinckney. Since Gerry was pro-French, Adams hoped the three envoys would be received.

The XYZ affair.

Talleyrand, the French Secretary of Foreign Affairs, treated the American envoys with contempt. He refused to receive them unless they agreed to make him a personal gift of $240,000 and to arrange a large loan to France. They replied to his go-betweens, "No, not a sixpence," and left the country early in 1798. When Adams heard of

A PAIR OF FRENCH VASES *showing Washington and Lafayette. For several years after the American Revolution the friendship between the United States and France was expressed in various art forms.*

JOHN ADAMS

this, he told Congress: "I will never send another minister to France without assurance that he will be received, respected, and honored as the representative of a great, free, powerful, and independent nation." Adams sent Congress the dispatches from our envoys, in which Talleyrand's go-betweens were referred to as "Mr. X, Mr. Y, and Mr. Z." Hence the episode became known as the "XYZ affair."

After this, few Americans expressed any pro-French leanings. Republicans joined with Federalists in the cry, "Millions for defense, but not one cent for tribute." A new song, "Hail, Columbia," expressing pride in the United States, became popular almost overnight.

We fight an undeclared naval war.

Congress got ready to protect American rights by force. A Department of the Navy was created. Our small navy was made ready to fight.

Congress authorized capture of armed French ships. In the next two years eighty-five were seized by American warships and privateers. The British "lent" us guns and ammunition. Our undeclared naval war with France lasted from 1798 to 1800.

Adams puts country before party.

A strong wing of the Federalist party, led by Hamilton, hoped that France would declare war on the United States. Adams knew he would never be re-elected if he opposed Hamilton. Yet he acted with characteristic courage. Against the advice of his Cabinet, he sent three peace commissioners to France. The French government promised to receive them respectfully. Hamilton and his friends were furious.

While the American envoys were on the way, Napoleon set himself up as dictator of France. He was glad to settle the quarrel with the United States in order to give all his attention to fighting in Europe. A new treaty between France and the United States was completed (September, 1800). The two governments promised to return all naval vessels they had captured, and the United States gave up its claim for damages to American commerce. The agreement prevented war. By making friends with Napoleon, it helped to clear the way for the purchase of Louisiana.

Adams, by his independence of character and personal courage, had done a great service to his country. Yet he was not re-elected (see p. 187). Though he never again held public office, he had no regrets and years later suggested as his epitaph: "Here lies John Adams, who took upon himself the responsibility of the peace with France in the year 1800."

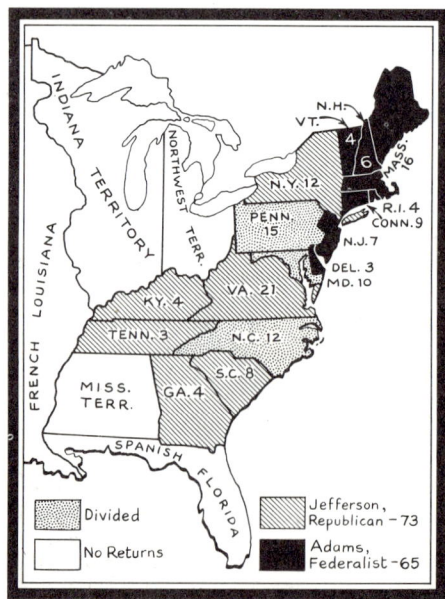

PRESIDENTIAL ELECTION, 1800

Mistakes Lead to Downfall of the Federalists

Federalists pass Alien and Sedition Acts.

In the summer of 1798 the Federalists in Congress saw a chance to weaken the Republican party. They passed a series of four laws known as the "Alien and Sedition Acts." Because war with France seemed likely, Federalist congressmen claimed that these laws were necessary to protect the country from internal enemies.

1. The Naturalization Act stated that an alien must reside in the United States fourteen years before he could become a citizen. Previously only five years was required. Since most immigrants supported the Republican party, the real reason for this measure was obvious.

2. The Alien Act required all foreigners to register with the federal government and allowed the President to deport without trial any whom he thought "dangerous to the peace and safety of the United States." This act caused great anxiety and resentment among aliens, especially if they had been critical of the Federalist administration. President Adams did not deport a single alien, but two shiploads of French immigrants left the country for fear of what might happen.

3. The Alien Enemies Act gave the President power to deport or imprison aliens in time of war almost at will.

4. The Sedition Act authorized heavy penalties for those who tried to hinder the operation of the government or who publicly criticized it. Twenty-five persons were arrested for criticizing the government and ten were convicted, most of them Republican editors and printers.

Those sent to prison were generally considered martyrs in the cause of freedom. Many showed them honor.

Matthew Lyon, a Vermont editor, was jailed for criticizing the President in his newspaper. He paid a fine of $1000 and served four months in jail. He was re-elected to Congress while serving his sentence. After his release Lyon's admirers accompanied him to Philadelphia in a constantly changing procession twelve miles long.

merely the agent of the states, which have given it certain responsibilities, (4) the individual states have the right to judge whether the federal government has exceeded its powers. Kentucky claimed that if a state considers a federal law to be unconstitutional, it has the right to declare the law null and void and to refuse to obey it.

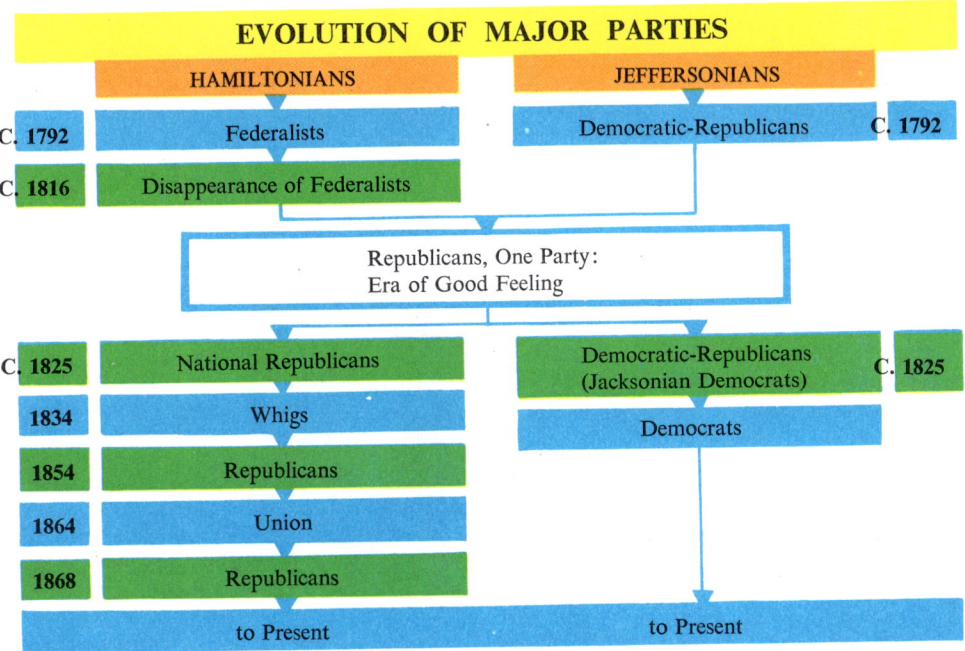

EVOLUTION OF MAJOR PARTIES

HAMILTONIANS — JEFFERSONIANS

C. 1792 Federalists — Democratic-Republicans C. 1792

C. 1816 Disappearance of Federalists

Republicans, One Party: Era of Good Feeling

C. 1825 National Republicans — Democratic-Republicans (Jacksonian Democrats) C. 1825

1834 Whigs — Democrats

1854 Republicans

1864 Union

1868 Republicans

to Present — to Present

Kentucky and Virginia pass resolutions.

Republican party leaders protested against the Alien and Sedition Acts, claiming that they destroyed free speech and the free press. The Republican-dominated legislatures of Kentucky and Virginia passed resolutions condemning the acts as unconstitutional and asking for their repeal. These resolutions are important because they outlined the *compact*, or *states' rights*, theory of the Constitution. According to this theory: (1) the Union is a voluntary association of equal and sovereign states, (2) the Constitution is a compact, or agreement, between the states, (3) the federal government is

The Supreme Court soon insisted that it alone had the power to settle a dispute between a state and the federal government. But those who believed in states' rights were dissatisfied. They said the Supreme Court was almost certain to decide in favor of the federal government. Debate over the right of nullification has never completely died down.[1]

---

[1] Although the issue was thought to have been finally settled in the War between North and South, nullification was again threatened when the Supreme Court ruled against segregation in the public schools (see Chapter 46).

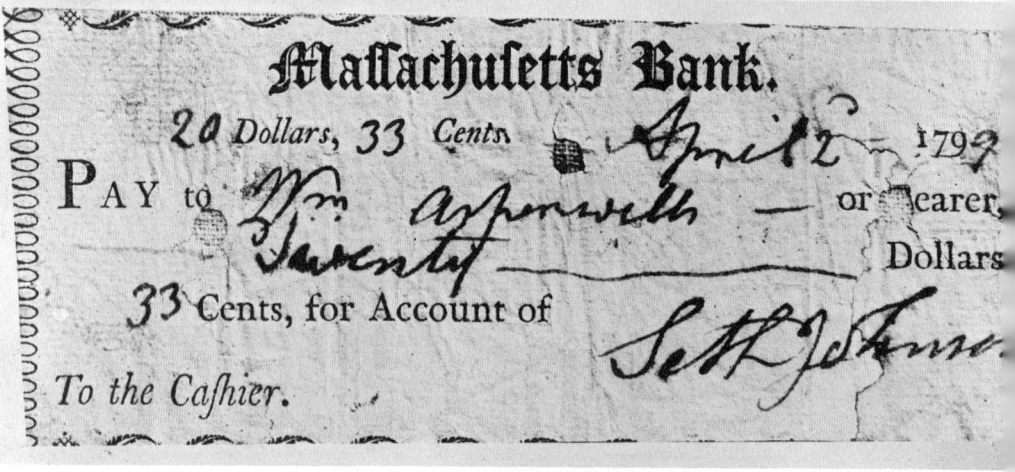

AARON BURR

THOMAS JEFFERSON

The Massachusetts Bank in 1799 had been in business for fifteen years. It was the first bank to serve Boston and today is still in operation as the First National Bank of Boston.

Republicans win election of 1800.

By 1800 the country was ripe for a change. The issues had been developing for nearly ten years: (1) The Federalists stood for loose construction of the Constitution and a strong national government. The Republicans favored strict construction and strong state governments. (2) The Federalists wished to further the economic interests of the manufacturers, investors, and merchants, most of whom lived in the North. The Republicans wished to promote the interests of the agricultural South and West. (3) The Federalists

distrusted the masses of the people, believing in control by the upper class. The Republicans believed in liberty, equality, and democracy. They stood firmly behind the Bill of Rights.

Again the Republicans nominated Thomas Jefferson of Virginia and Aaron Burr of New York. As running mate for President Adams, the Federalists nominated Charles C. Pinckney of South Carolina. Thus we see that the custom of choosing candidates for President and Vice-President from different sections of the country was established early in our history.

After a bitter campaign, the Republicans won the election by a few votes. However, both Jefferson and Burr had the same number of votes. This meant that the House of Representatives, where Federalists were still in control, had to choose which of the two would be President. The result was a tie which continued for weeks. Hamilton, who respected Jefferson and despised Burr, persuaded a few of the Federalists not to vote. This broke the deadlock and allowed Jefferson to be chosen on the thirty-sixth ballot.

The Twelfth Amendment is adopted.

The election again called attention to the need for a change in the manner of electing a President. The new Congress passed the Twelfth Amendment, providing that the electors were to cast separate votes for President and Vice-President. Thereby the strongest party would be able to elect both of these officials. The amendment was ratified and went into effect in 1804.

Federalists keep control of the courts.

The Federalists had lost control of the executive and legislative branches of the government. They still controlled the judiciary, for the judges were nearly all Federalists and had been appointed for life. A few days before the end of his term Adams appointed John Marshall as Chief Justice of the Supreme Court. For thirty-four years Marshall was to interpret the Constitution according to Federalist principles (see pp. 226–228).

During the closing days of Adams' term, Congress passed a Judiciary Act. It created sixteen circuit courts, each with a judge, marshal, prosecutor, and clerk. The President promptly appointed Federalists to these positions. The Republicans scornfully called these officials "midnight judges," because Adams was still at work signing their commissions on his last night in office.

The Federalists deserve credit.

When the Federalists took office in 1789 the new United States government was only a plan on paper. The Federalists put the Constitution into operation by organizing the executive branch and creating a judicial system. They arranged to pay off the war debt of the national and state governments. They chartered the Bank of the United States, which helped the government transact its business and which created a sound national currency. They helped build up manufacturing and commerce.

By skillful diplomacy they preserved peace and kept the country from being drawn into European wars. They smoothed out serious difficulties in our relations with Great Britain, France, and Spain. They forced the Indians to cede much of the Northwest. They admitted three new states to the Union—Vermont (1791), Kentucky (1792), and Tennessee (1796). When they turned the administration over to the Republicans in 1801, the United States was a "going concern." The Federalists had served the country well for twelve years but they never regained control.

Why did the Federalists lose control?

If the Federalists achieved so much, why were they not able to stay in power? First, the split between Hamilton and Adams weakened the party. Second, Jefferson and Madison had united the opposition into a strong new party. Third, and most important, the Federalists did not sympathize with the common people. They followed policies which benefited special interests—the commercial, investing, and manufacturing classes—and they kept the government in the hands of men of wealth. In the Alien and Sedition Acts, the Federalists tried to stifle criticism. The common people wanted a greater voice in the government. They looked to the Republican party and its leader, Jefferson, to give it to them.

Abigail Adams, wife of John Adams and mother of John Quincy Adams

FOR IDENTIFICATION

John Adams	John Marshall
Alien and Sedition Acts	Pinckney's treaty
	Talleyrand
Aaron Burr	Treaty of Greenville
"Farewell Address"	Virginia and Kentucky
"Citizen" Genêt	resolutions
Jay's treaty	XYZ affair

FOR EXPLANATION OR DEFINITION

caucus	nullification
embargo	proclamation
guillotine	of neutrality
"midnight judges"	right of deposit

FOR REVIEW

1. Why was Washington willing to accept a second term but not a third?

2. How did Americans feel about the French Revolution in its early stages? After it became violent?

3. What was the attitude of each political party toward the war between France and England?

4. How did Washington deal with the actions of "Citizen" Genêt?

5. Why did Washington issue the proclamation of neutrality? What groups were opposed to neutrality?

6. Why did Jefferson resign from Washington's Cabinet?

7. (a) What were our grievances against England? (b) Why did Hamilton oppose an embargo of British goods?

8. (a) Why did Washington send Jay to England? (b) What were the provisions of the Jay treaty? (c) How was Jay's treaty received in the United States? (d) Why did Washington support the treaty?

9. (a) Describe our grievances against Spain. (b) How were they settled?

10. What were the terms of the Treaty of Greenville, 1795?

11. Why is Washington's Farewell Address an important state paper?

12. How did it happen that a President and a Vice-President of opposite political parties were elected in 1796?

13. (a) What were our grievances against France? (b) Why did Adams send three envoys?

14. (a) What was the XYZ affair? (b) What is the origin of the saying "Millions for defense, but not one cent for tribute"? (c) Describe the undeclared naval war with France, 1798–1800.

15. (a) How did President Adams put country above party? (b) What were the consequences to him? (c) What were his strengths and weaknesses as President?

16. How did Napoleon's rise to power affect relations between the United States and France?

17. What were the Alien and Sedition Acts? Why were they passed? How did these laws hurt the Federalists?

18. What were the Virginia and Kentucky resolutions? Explain the compact theory of the Constitution.

19. State the issues in the campaign of 1800.

20. (a) What part did Hamilton play in the election of 1800? (b) Why did that election lead to adoption of the Twelfth Amendment? (c) What are its provisions?

21. Summarize the accomplishments of the Federalist party.

22. Why did the Republican party triumph over the Federalists?

FOR FURTHER STUDY AND DISCUSSION

1. Why was the West an important factor in determining the foreign policy of the new nation?

2. Using the Jay treaty as an example, investigate and report on the role of the House of Representatives in the making of treaties. Helpful sources: the Constitution, Art. II, Sec. 2, and Hart, *Contemporaries*, Vol. III, No. 97.

3. Summarize the substance of Washington's Farewell Address. Do you think his

advice concerning foreign affairs was sound? Do you think the general outlines of his policy should be pursued today? In what respect, if any, have Washington's views been misrepresented and distorted? Helpful source: Commager, *Documents*, No. 100.

4. Is the pursuit of a policy of "isolation" related to the existence of a "frontier"? State the reasons for your opinion.

5. Explain what is meant by the "third term" tradition. To what extent was this tradition a factor in the elections of 1912 and 1940?

6. Since Jefferson was nominated by a party caucus, it has been suggested that this method of nomination made him the chosen leader of Congress as effectively as a choice of prime minister in England makes that official the leader of Parliament. Explain this statement. Should the President be the leader of his party in Congress? Is he usually?

7. Prepare a brief biographical sketch of Hamilton's political activities from 1800 till his death in the duel with Aaron Burr in 1804. How did Hamilton's death affect the fortunes of the Federalist party?

8. "The Virginia and Kentucky resolutions expressed a point of view concerning the nature of the federal government that was not finally determined until the surrender of Lee at Appomattox." Explain the meaning of this statement. Helpful source: Commager, *Documents*, Nos. 102, 103, 104. Note also the point of view expressed by other states in reply to the Virginia and Kentucky resolutions.

FOR INDIVIDUAL OR GROUP ACTIVITIES

1. Have a small committee prepare a report on the controversy over the authorship of Washington's Farewell Address.

2. Hold a mock session of Washington's Cabinet to discuss the desirability of issuing the proclamation of neutrality of 1793.

3. Prepare a chart for bulletin board display headed *Federalists* and *Democratic-Republicans*. On it summarize the point of view of both parties on financial policy, foreign policy, theories concerning the nature of the federal government, and the doctrine of implied powers. On the same chart indicate the leaders of each party, and the groups and sections from which each party drew its chief support.

4. Write a brief story of "Citizen" Genêt's career as an American citizen.

5. Write a newspaper editorial criticizing the Alien and Sedition Acts, or criticizing the Virginia and Kentucky resolutions. Have some member of the class prepare a cartoon to accompany each of these editorials. Helpful source: Hart, *Contemporaries*, Vol. III, No. 100.

6. Prepare a brief account of the background of the writing and singing of Joseph Hopkinson's "Hail, Columbia." Arrange for a dramatic reading or singing of the song. Helpful source: Hart, *Contemporaries*, Vol. III, No. 100.

7. On March 4, 1801, the *Columbian Centinel*, a Boston newspaper, Federalist in sympathy, published an interesting summary of the record of the administrations of George Washington and John Adams. You will find this in Hart, *Contemporaries*, Vol. III, No. 105. Read and discuss.

(Above) TALLEYRAND

(Right) NAPOLEON

I have sworn upon the altar of God eternal hostility against every form of tyranny over the mind of man.——Thomas Jefferson

13. THOMAS JEFFERSON SERVES AS PRESIDENT

A New Party Comes to Power

The election of Thomas Jefferson in 1800 brought the new Republican party to power. Jefferson liked to speak of this election as a "revolution." He felt that it marked a return to the principles expressed in the Declaration of Independence—equality, personal liberty, and popular government. The new party placed full confidence in the common sense and goodness of the people. It disagreed with the Federalist doctrine that only the upper class can be trusted to rule.

Jefferson champions democracy.

All his life Jefferson was a foe of special privilege. In Virginia he had fought to disestablish the church, to abolish primogeniture, to give land to the landless, and to provide free elementary education. He also urged the gradual freeing of the slaves. During the Confederation period he took a leading part in persuading Virginia to cede its western land claims to the nation, although its claims were stronger than those of any other state. The Land Ordinance of 1787, providing a way for new regions to advance from colonies to states, was largely his work. He and James Madison drew up the influential Virginia Bill of Rights.

Jefferson grew up on a frontier farm in Virginia. Here he absorbed the democratic ideas of his backwoods neighbors. When he spoke of the American people he meant the farmers and pioneers. "Those who labor in the earth," he wrote, "are the chosen people of God if ever He had a chosen people." Jefferson hoped America would remain a land of small farmers, able to speak their minds and stand up for their rights. "Cultivators of the earth," he said, "are the most valuable citizens. . . . they are tied to their country and wedded to its liberty and interest by the most lasting bonds."

Jefferson takes office in the new capital.

The federal government had moved from Philadelphia to Washington in the summer of 1800. Jefferson was the first President to be inaugurated in the new capital. At that time Washington was a shabby village. Only one wing of the Capitol was ready for use. The White House was unfinished, the principal staircase not even begun. The streets were rough, muddy lanes, hacked through the brush. Gouverneur Morris remarked sarcastically: "We want nothing here but houses, cellars, kitchens, well-informed men, amiable women, and other trifles of that sort to make our city perfect."

The inaugural ceremony was very simple, as Jefferson wished it to be. The incoming President did not follow the custom of riding in a coach drawn by four or six horses. He walked from his simple boarding house to the Capitol and there took the oath of office.

A great inaugural address.

At his inauguration Jefferson quietly delivered one of the finest addresses ever made by an incoming President. He pleaded with the Federalists to forget the bitter feelings they had shown during the campaign. Good citizens, he pointed out, must recognize the right of the majority to rule, although the majority must not oppress the minority. Political intolerance is as bad as religious intolerance. Republicans and Federalists, he declared, should unite as Americans in preserving the Union and developing the country's resources.

But every difference of opinion is not a difference of principle. We have called by different names brethren of the same principle. We are all Republicans, we are all Federalists. If there be any among us who would wish to dissolve this Union or to change its republican form, let them stand undisturbed as monuments of the safety with which error of opinion may be tolerated where reason is left free to combat it.[1]

He went on to speak of the blessings enjoyed by Americans—separation by a wide ocean from the havoc of European wars; land enough for "the thousandth and thousandth generation"; a religion, practiced in various forms, but teaching "honesty, truth, temperance, gratitude, and the love of man."

Finally, he stated the essential principles of our government on which his program would be based. The government should "restrain men from injuring one another [and] leave them otherwise free to regulate their own pursuits." It should preserve the rights of the states and give equal and exact justice to all. It should seek honest friendship with all nations, but entangling alliances with none. The civil authority should be supreme over the military. The national debt should be paid and public expenditures reduced. Both agriculture and commerce should be encouraged. Education should be widespread. The right to personal freedom, freedom of the press and of religion, and trial by juries fairly selected should be safeguarded.

Democratic customs are introduced.

Although Jefferson was a man of wealth and refinement, he liked simplicity and thought it suited a republican government. He abolished several Old World customs which had been dear to the Federalists. He gave up the formal weekly receptions held by Washington and Adams. He discouraged the use of titles of honor, like "Excellency." Instead of traveling about in a coach he rode horseback or walked. He dressed simply and even went to market to buy supplies for his table.

He wished everyone to feel welcome in the White House and in the

---

[1] See Commager, *Documents*, No. 186, 187.

191

offices of the government. To him the poorest citizen was as worthy of respect as the highest officer. The White House during Jefferson's stay there was as open to visitors as his spacious home in Virginia had been.

In yet another way, Jefferson departed from Federalist customs. He stood firmly for freedom of speech and of the press. Although opposition newspapers abused him without letup, he made no effort to silence them. Under his leadership Congress gave reporters desks on the floor of both houses, with the right to report everything that went on. Reporters had formerly not been permitted to comment on happenings in Congress.

Jefferson hopes to unite the country.

The new President had wide popular support in all sections, yet he was feared and distrusted by the Federalists. He hoped to win many of these men over to support Republican principles. To quiet Federalist fears that the South would control the new administration, Jefferson chose two department heads and the Postmaster General from New England. He picked a fellow Virginian, James Madison, to be Secretary of State. Albert Gallatin of Pennsylvania was appointed Secretary of the Treasury.

When Jefferson began his presidential term, jobs in the federal government were held entirely by Federalists, many of them bitterly hostile to Jefferson. His followers urged him to discharge all Federalists. This he refused to do, but he did dismiss twenty officials appointed by Adams after the election. Jefferson said it is not fair for a defeated President to make appointments that will continue after he has left office. Similarly, the so-called "midnight judges," who had not yet received their commissions when Jefferson took office, did not get them. As time went on and vacancies occurred in federal jobs, Republicans were appointed. Jefferson said his aim was to have an equal number of officeholders from each party.

Some Federalist laws are repealed.

The Republicans promptly repealed the hated excise on whiskey, thus carrying out a promise they had made before the election. The Naturalization Act was changed to permit a foreigner to become a citizen in five rather than fourteen years. The much-criticized Alien and Sedition Acts were allowed to expire. The fines already collected under these acts were refunded and the men imprisoned were set free. The Judiciary Act of 1801 was repealed and a new one passed which set up six circuit courts instead of sixteen. Yet for the most part, the government structure built by the Federalists was left unchanged.

The national debt is reduced.

Under the Federalists the national debt had grown to 80 million dollars. The Republicans had promised to reduce the debt. Soon after taking office, Secretary of the Treasury Gallatin outlined a program for paying off the entire debt in sixteen years. He cut government expenditures and persuaded Congress to increase tariff duties slightly. In eight years he slashed the debt to 52.5 million dollars, in addition to providing 15 million for the purchase of Louisiana. His thrifty policies pleased the people. Gallatin has gone down in history as one of the ablest men ever to fill the position of Secretary of the Treasury.

The Tripolitan War, 1801–1805.

Jefferson always opposed war when it could be avoided. Yet when necessary he defended American rights by force, as in the undeclared war against Tripoli. Tripoli was one of four Barbary states in North Africa whose rulers

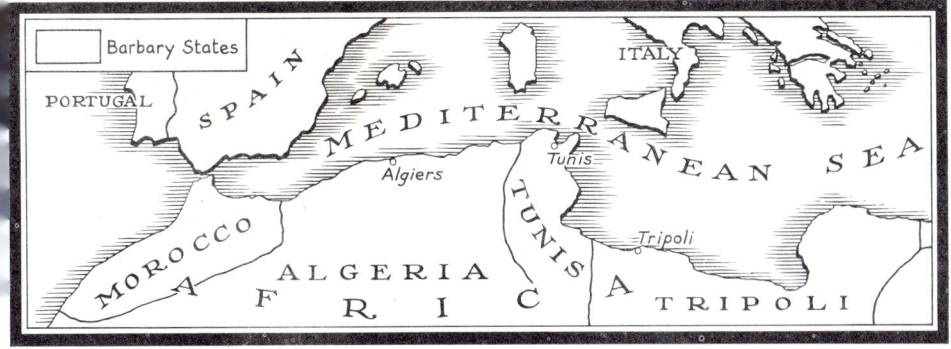

BARBARY STATES

"BOMBARDMENT OF TRIPOLI." *Of Commodore Edward Preble's several bombardments of Tripoli against the Barbary pirates the most important occurred on August 3, 1804.*

had long been in the habit of seizing ships which passed their shores. Between 1790 and 1800 our State Department sent more than two million dollars to buy off the pirates. During those years the United States was too weak to follow a bolder policy.

Jefferson decided it was time to try force. Before he could do so, the ruler of Tripoli, dissatisfied with the payment he was receiving, declared war on the United States. Then Jefferson, using his authority as commander in chief, sent a squadron of warships to the Mediterranean. For four years our little navy gave a good account of itself as it struggled with the difficult problems of war in a distant sea.

In 1805 the ruler of Tripoli promised to stop interfering with American ships, and the Tripolitan War came to an end. Our victory had a good effect on the rulers of the other Barbary states, even though we continued to pay tribute to them until 1816. Meanwhile the Republicans, who had been inclined to think the navy a useless extravagance, looked upon it with more favor and increased its strength.

Federal money is spent for roads.

One of the greatest needs in the settled areas of the United States was for transportation facilities. In the older states private companies were being chartered to build toll roads, toll

When Jefferson offered to buy NEW ORLEANS *for 10 million dollars it was a busy and important port. Today it is extremely important to our commerce. The huge grain elevator shown here forms part of a business which exports more grain than any other place in the United States.*

bridges, and toll canals. The states usually gave these companies the right of way (the land on which the road was built) and part of the cost of construction. The people in the new states of Kentucky, Tennessee, and Ohio could not raise enough by taxes to build the needed transportation facilities. Nor would private companies build these facilities, which would be unprofitable because of the thin population of these states. The settlers therefore looked to the national government for help.

Ever since the early days of Washington's administration, statesmen had disagreed on whether the national government had the power to improve harbors, build roads, or make other "internal improvements." The argument centered around the "general welfare" clause of the Constitution and the clause authorizing Congress to establish post roads. In the past, Jefferson had taken the view that the federal

government was limited to powers enumerated in the Constitution (the doctrine of *strict* construction). As President, however, he often took a broader view, adopting the Federalist policy of *loose* construction (see pp. 171–172). Such was the case in this instance.

The demand for federal aid to make internal improvements came largely from the small farmers. Jefferson, who was always sympathetic to their needs, felt that the desired aid should be given. Congress responded by setting aside for the building of highways in the West, part of the money received from the sale of public lands. In 1808 Congress authorized the building of a road from Cumberland, Maryland, to Wheeling in the western part of Virginia. This highway, known as the National, or Cumberland, Road, was begun in 1811. It was gradually extended to Illinois, and proved extremely important to settling the West.

Gallatin recommends a far-sighted plan.

With Jefferson's approval, Gallatin drew up plans for a national network of roads, canals, and river and harbor improvements. He recommended that canals be cut across Cape Cod and other peninsulas along the Atlantic coast. The East and the West, he said, should be knit together by roads connecting Atlantic coastal rivers with tributaries of the Ohio. He suggested that the federal government spend twenty million dollars over the next ten years to aid these projects. At this time (1808), Congress did not show much interest in his report.

The Louisiana Purchase Doubles Our Territory

Napoleon acquires Louisiana.

Settlers were moving westward in an unending stream. A few thousand had crossed the Mississippi into Louisiana, a great area which then belonged to Spain. Many Americans believed that sooner or later the United States would acquire Louisiana. They knew that Spain was weak and could not long oppose the expansion of the United States.

Late in 1800 Napoleon Bonaparte persuaded the king of Spain to cede Louisiana back to France. Napoleon promised never to deed the territory to another power. When rumors of this secret deal reached Jefferson, he was alarmed. The mighty Napoleon would be a dangerous neighbor. His plans to build a world empire were well known. By taking possession of Louisiana he would not only block expansion of the United States beyond the Mississippi, but also would be in a position to seize American territory between the Mississippi and the Appalachians.

Jefferson warns France.

Jefferson instructed Robert Livingston, our minister to France, to tell the French government that if France took possession of Louisiana, the friendship between the two nations would be destroyed. He wrote:

There is on the globe one . . . spot, the possessor of which is our natural and habitual enemy. It is New Orleans, through which the produce of three eighths of our territory must pass to market. . . . The day that France takes possession of New Orleans . . . we must marry ourselves to the British fleet and nation.

Jefferson tries to buy New Orleans.

Late in 1802 Spanish officials in New Orleans withdrew the right of deposit. The action was contrary to the Treaty of 1795 (see pp. 178–179). It was a heavy blow to our Western settlers. They believed that Napoleon had ordered it and that he intended also to deny them the use of the Mississippi River. The Westerners demanded action. They talked angrily of seizing New Orleans if the United States failed to protect their interests. This would mean war with France.

Jefferson hoped to avoid war. He told Livingston to ask the French to sell us a tract of land on the lower Mississippi for use as a port. Jefferson sent his friend James Monroe to Paris to assist Livingston. Monroe was instructed to offer as high as ten million dollars for New Orleans and the Floridas, if the Floridas were included in the French territory. Should Napoleon refuse to sell us at least a port, the two envoys were to try to make an alliance with England. "On the event of this mission," Jefferson said solemnly, "depend the future destinies of this Republic."

Napoleon sells all of Louisiana.

Unexpected developments helped our commissioners. The French had just lost the island of Santo Domingo and with it the naval base needed to defend Louisiana. Napoleon saw he could not hold Louisiana in case of a British or American attack. Besides, he was about to renew the war with Great Britain and he urgently needed money. Moreover, he wished to forestall an Anglo-American alliance. Abruptly Napoleon offered the United States the whole of Louisiana for fifteen million dollars. Livingston and Monroe were astonished by the offer. They realized that the territory was a wonderful bargain. They had no instructions to buy an empire, but their courage was equal to the occasion, and they accepted.

Federalists protest the purchase.

According to the agreement with Napoleon, the inhabitants of Louisiana were to be admitted into the Union as soon as possible. This meant that new states would be created by the method provided in the Northwest Ordinance. Angry protests burst from the Federalists. They feared that an increase in the number of western states would make it impossible for the Federalist party to return to power. The country might be permanently controlled by planters and farmers, and the Republican party

might stay in office forever. The Federalists forgot their former interest in loose construction, and claimed that the Constitution gave the United States no authority to buy additional territory.

Constitutional scruples are cast aside.

Jefferson was pleased with the amazing bargain made by Livingston and Monroe, but he was also troubled. Did the federal government have power to purchase territory? Could the territory be made part of the Union without an amendment to the Constitution? Jefferson believed not. He drafted an amendment to remove any doubts about the legality of the agreement with France.

The amendment to legalize the purchase never was passed, however. Ratification would have taken a long time and Napoleon was dropping hints that he might sell Louisiana to Spain instead. Jefferson decided not to wait. He sent the amendment to the Senate, where it was promptly approved. In the general rejoicing that greeted the treaty, few congressmen cared whether or not it was constitutional.

ROBERT R. LIVINGSTON. *As minister to France he alerted Jefferson to the possibility of buying the Louisiana Territory.*

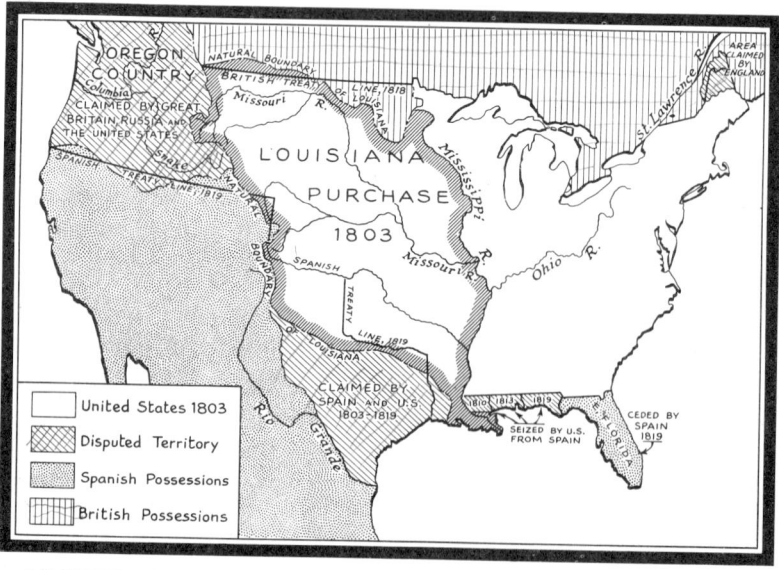

UNITED STATES AFTER THE LOUISIANA PURCHASE

196

Importance of the Louisiana Purchase.

The Louisiana Purchase more than doubled the area of the United States. The territory consisted of nearly a million square miles, dazzlingly rich in natural resources. It has been a source of immense wealth to the United States.

The purchase gave the United States full possession of the Mississippi Valley, with its great river system and the valuable port of New Orleans. For the first time "the Father of Waters went unvexed to the sea." The danger that the Westerners would leave the Union was ended.

An immense region had been opened for fur traders, land speculators, and pioneers. Eventually fifteen states, in whole or in part, were carved out of it. To this day, farming has been the principal occupation in most of the territory. Its settlement enabled the farmers of the nation to control the country for decades.

Without Louisiana the United States could not have acquired Oregon, Texas, and California. With it, there was little doubt that the nation would eventually expand to the Pacific. Since Florida was now cut off from the other Spanish possessions in North America, it seemed certain that Florida too would become part of the United States. In the words of Henry Adams:

The annexation of Louisiana was an event so portentous as to defy measurement. It gave a new face to politics and ranked in international importance next to the Declaration of Independence and the adoption of the Constitution.

The uncertain boundaries of Louisiana.

Exactly how large the new territory was, no one knew. Whether it included West Florida and Texas was not at all clear. Its northern boundary was also indefinite. According to the treaty of purchase, the United States obtained "the colony or province of Louisiana with the same extent it now has in the hands of Spain, and that it had when France possessed it [prior to 1763]." Uncertainty as to the boundaries of the land we had bought was to disturb our relations with Spain for years.

The Lewis and Clark expedition.

Jefferson's interest in science had led him years earlier to suggest that the United States explore the vast region beyond the Mississippi River. A few weeks after the purchase of Louisiana he obtained $2500 from Congress for this purpose. To lead the expedition Jefferson selected two young Virginians —his secretary, Meriwether Lewis, and William Clark, a younger brother of the Revolutionary hero George Rogers Clark. Both Lewis and Clark had much experience in frontier life. Their instructions were to make scientific observations and to establish friendly relations with the Indians. At that time the Indians of the area sold their furs in Canada. Jefferson hoped that Americans could obtain this profitable trade. He also hoped to strengthen our claim to Oregon.

In May, 1804, the explorers started up the Missouri with forty-three men. They spent the first winter in what is now North Dakota. The next spring they found passes through the Rockies. They followed the Columbia River all the way to the Pacific, which they reached in November, 1805. By this time they had covered four thousand miles, carefully mapping and describing the country. They were the first Americans to cross the continent.

For a time on the return trip the expedition split into two groups to explore the Yellowstone River and other branches of the Missouri. The explorers returned to St. Louis in September, 1806. They had endured great hardships but had lost only one man. Their maps and reports were invaluable. The natural wonders they described amazed the public, but the *New York Gazette*

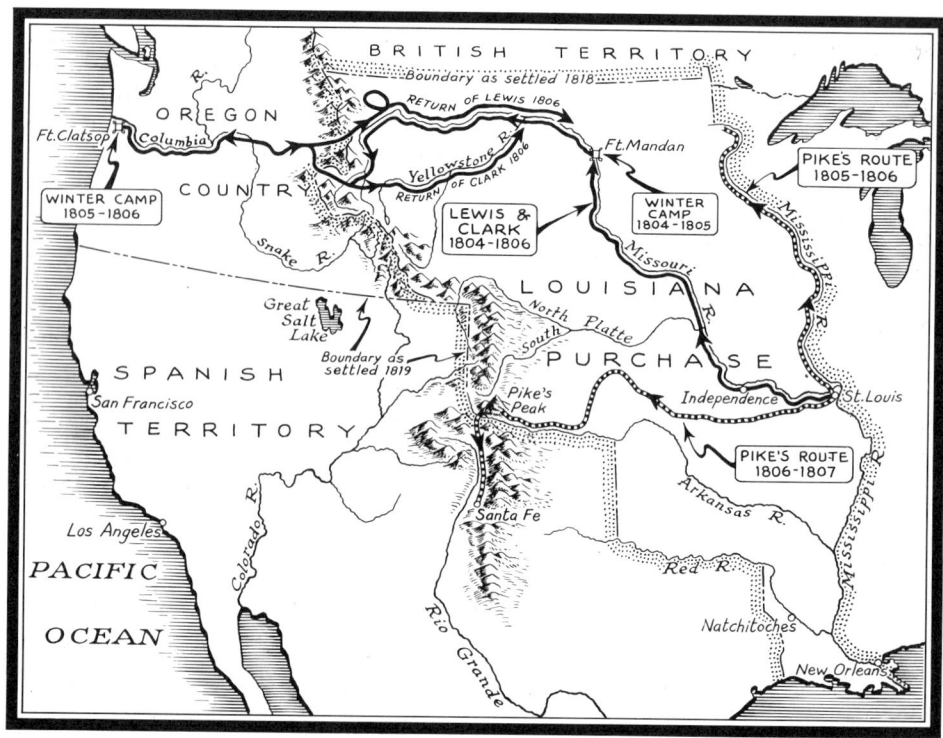

EXPEDITIONS OF LEWIS AND CLARK, AND OF PIKE

predicted the region would probably never be traveled through again.

Pike explores the Southwest.

Another expedition, led by Lieutenant Zebulon Pike, set out in the summer of 1805 to trace the Mississippi to its source. The next summer Pike was sent to explore the Arkansas River region and the Southwest. Pike discovered the Royal Gorge of the Arkansas and the mountain peak in Colorado which bears his name. Like Lewis and Clark, he brought back with him valuable observations of the climate, the animal and plant life, and the Indian tribes. The exploits of Lewis and Clark and Pike awakened public interest in the region beyond the Mississippi.

Secession of the Northeast is planned.

A group of New England Federalists objected strongly to the creation of states from the Louisiana territory.

They wished to keep the region of Louisiana in the condition of a colony rather than to increase the number of Western states. When the Senate ratified the Louisiana treaty with a clause promising to admit the people of Louisiana to the Union, these Federalists were bitter. Led by Senator Thomas Pickering of Massachusetts, they made secret plans to take New England and New York out of the Union. They hoped to set up a northern confederacy. The plotters persuaded Vice-President Aaron Burr to desert the Republican party and run for governor of New York in 1804 on the Federalist ticket. If elected, Burr was to detach his state from the Union and become president of the proposed confederacy.

Hamilton exposed the plan and thereby spoiled Burr's chances of winning the election. As a result, Pickering's conspiracy broke down. To get revenge, Burr challenged Hamilton to a duel. At the signal to fire Hamilton shot into the air, but Burr shot to kill. Dueling was against the law, and Burr fled from New York charged with murder.

Foreign Relations Trouble Jefferson's Second Term

Jefferson is re-elected.

Throughout his first term as President, Jefferson's popularity grew. On the whole his program had pleased all sections. He had lifted the national honor by fighting the pirates of Tripoli. He had promoted land settlement by buying land from the Indians and helping them move westward. The new naturalization law encouraged immigration. The national debt was being rapidly paid off. The area of the country had been doubled. The nation was prosperous. Road building was going forward everywhere. Federalist leaders might grumble that the nation was being ruined by the Republicans, but the people did not believe it. In the election of 1804 Jefferson was re-elected by a huge majority.

Britain and France seize American ships.

Jefferson's second term was marked by difficult foreign problems. France and Great Britain were again locked in a life-and-death struggle. The British ruled the sea, but Napoleon ruled most of Europe. Unable to defeat him on land, Britain hoped to blockade him into giving up. The British issued a series of Orders in Council, directing all neutral ships bound for ports controlled by Napoleon to stop first at an English port and secure a license. These rules were intended to prevent contraband (articles necessary for war) and foodstuffs from reaching Napoleon and his allies. Napoleon replied by declaring he would seize any ship which stopped at any British port.

The United States claimed that as a neutral it had the right to trade with either side. When neither the French nor the British paid any attention, there was little our government could do except protest. Our navy was far too small to defend our commerce. Between 1803 and 1812 the British captured 917 American merchant ships, while Napoleon captured 558. The French seized fewer than the British only because the French had less sea power.

Despite the capture of a great many American ships, our trade with the warring countries increased. Both sides needed American foodstuffs and were willing to pay high prices for them. If one ship in three got to its destination and back again, the profits made up for the loss of the other two.

The British seize our sailors.

Even more irritating than interference with our trade was the British practice of impressing, or seizing, sailors from our ships. Britain was in great need of sailors for its navy. Yet the men of its fleet were so ill-fed, ill-treated, and ill-paid that crews could not be obtained by voluntary enlistment. For centuries the British navy had relied on forced labor. Press gangs went about the ports of Great Britain seizing men to serve as sailors. The harsh discipline and miserable food and quarters led many of them to desert at the first opportunity. They were particularly glad to sign up on American ships, which offered better food, higher pay, and fairer treatment than those of any other nation.

When an American ship was in British waters, all agreed that the authorities had a right to remove British deserters. But the British did not stop with this. They claimed the right of searching our vessels wherever they found them and taking off British subjects. British warships often cruised just outside American ports, stopping all

The west front of MONTICELLO. *Jefferson designed the structure of his beautiful hilltop home, Monticello ("little mountain" in Italian). His plans were influenced by the principles of Palladio, a renowned Italian architect.*

(Above) LA ROTONDA, *designed by Andrea Palladio (16th century, Italy) and visited by Jefferson in the 18th century.* (Right) POPLAR FOREST *in Bedford County, Virginia, was designed by Jefferson as a retreat from the activities at Monticello.*

ships coming in or going out. In many cases it was difficult for British officers to tell whether a sailor was an Englishman or an American. Moreover, American naturalization papers were not accepted, for the British insisted that no one born under their flag could become a citizen of another country. Thousands of sailors born in the United States or naturalized in our courts were taken by the British. France also practiced impressment and refused to recognize American naturalization papers. However, hardly any French citizens served on our ships, and France did not find it worth while to search for them.

The "Chesapeake Affair."

Anger against Great Britain was raised to fever pitch in 1807 by an attack on an American naval vessel. A British man-of-war, the *Leopard*, stopped an American frigate, the *Chesapeake*, a few miles out of Norfolk, Virginia, claiming that British deserters were aboard. When the American captain denied there were deserters and refused to allow a search, the *Leopard* fired three broadsides into the *Chesapeake*, wounding eighteen sailors and killing three. Officers of the *Leopard* then boarded the *Chesapeake* and took four so-called deserters.

Jefferson issued a proclamation ordering British warships to stay out of American waters. He instructed our minister in London, James Monroe, to ask reparations for the damage to the *Chesapeake* and to demand once more that the impressment of American seamen be stopped. The British government was willing to discuss our claim for damages but would not yield on the question of impressment.

Congress embargoes foreign trade.

The act of firing on an American warship and taking persons off by force was an outrage. President Jefferson would have had the American people

with him had he asked Congress to declare war. But Jefferson hated war as a method of settling disputes. Besides, he thought the country unable to bear the burden of war with a nation as powerful as Great Britain. Such a war might even cost our independence. He decided to try "peaceable coercion."

Believing that our exports were necessary both to Britain and to France, he reasoned that if we cut off trade with those countries, they would be forced to come to terms with us. Before the Revolution our nonimportation measures had compelled Parliament to repeal the Stamp Act and the Townshend Acts. With this in mind Jefferson recommended an act forbidding American ships to sail for a foreign port. Congress passed this Embargo Act (December, 1807) by large majorities in both houses.

The Embargo Act is a failure.

The Embargo Act did not have the effect intended. Napoleon looked upon it as helpful to him. His navy was so weak that he could not keep American ships from sailing to British ports. Hence he was glad to have the American government do this for him. In addition Napoleon now claimed that any American ships which found their way into European harbors were British ships in disguise. So he captured them. As for Great Britain, the embargo had no effect at all on its policy; the British refused to move from the position they had taken. Perhaps they would have come to terms had not their crops been unusually large in 1808 and had they not obtained much American produce that was smuggled across the border into Canada.

Although the embargo did cause some hardship in the West Indies and in parts of England, the worst results were in the United States. Shipowners and merchants who obeyed the law faced ruin. About 150,000 men (mostly sailors, bookkeepers, and longshoremen) lost their jobs. Farm prices tumbled. Hard times spread throughout the country. New England Federalists held town meetings to demand repeal of the Embargo Act. A new movement for secession got under way. Jefferson confessed later that "I felt the foundation of the government shaken under my feet by the New England townships." He had kept the nation out of war, but the people were unwilling to pay the price. Just before he left office Congress repealed the Embargo Act.

Jefferson retires.

Although Jefferson could easily have been re-elected, he refused a third term. Believing that in a democracy officials should be changed frequently, he wished to follow Washington's example in serving only two terms. Besides, he was heartily weary of office.

Leaving the White House to his friends, James and Dolly Madison, Jefferson retired eagerly to Monticello and the life he loved. Here he spent much of his time in writing letters and advising government leaders. His and Washington's dream of a national university had not been realized. At the age of seventy-five he launched a campaign for a state university in Virginia and finally persuaded the legislature to appropriate $300,000. A site was chosen in Charlottesville, the geographic center of the state, a few miles from Monticello. Jefferson was appointed first head of the university. He himself laid out the campus, designed the buildings, selected the faculty, and outlined the curriculum. Science, agriculture, political science, and modern languages were raised to a position of importance beside the classics.

Near the end of his life Jefferson wrote the inscription for his tombstone, not mentioning the high offices he had held in the state and national governments. It tells us the things by which this great man wished to be remembered.

Here was buried Thomas Jefferson, Author of the Declaration of Independence, of the Statute of Virginia for Religious Freedom, and Father of the University of Virginia.

Late 18th century woodblock used for printing calico

FOR IDENTIFICATION

Barbary states	Robert Gray
Aaron Burr	Meriwether Lewis
Chesapeake affair	Orders in Council
William Clark	Zebulon Pike
Albert Gallatin	Tripolitan War

FOR EXPLANATION OR DEFINITION

contraband	internal
Cumberland Road	improvements
embargo	press gangs
impressment	right of search

FOR REVIEW

1. Why is the election of 1800 sometimes referred to as the "revolution of 1800"?

2. (a) What points did Jefferson emphasize in his first inaugural? (b) How do these points reflect Jefferson's devotion to democratic ideals?

3. What caused the war with Tripoli? What did it accomplish?

4. (a) Why did Westerners want the national government to help with building roads and waterways? (b) How did Congress respond to this demand? (c) What program of internal improvements did Gallatin recommend? (d) How did these recommendations of the Republicans conflict with their earlier theories concerning the Constitution?

5. (a) What circumstances prompted Napoleon to sell the Louisiana territory?

203

(b) What prompted the United States to buy? (c) How did the Louisiana Purchase influence American history?

6. What did the purchase of Louisiana have to do with "loose" or "strict" construction of the Constitution? Why did the Federalists now adopt the doctrine of "strict" construction?

7. What was accomplished by the Lewis and Clark expedition?

8. What areas were explored by Zebulon Pike? State the results.

9. What were the reasons for Jefferson's popularity at the end of his first term?

10. (a) Explain the plot to set up a northern confederacy. (b) What led to the duel between Burr and Hamilton?

11. How did England and France interfere with our commerce?

12. Explain the practice of impressment. Why did it cause resentment in America?

13. Describe the *Chesapeake-Leopard* affair. How did it affect American public opinion?

14. (a) How did Jefferson seek to avoid war? (b) What was the effect of the embargo on England? On France? (c) How did the embargo affect American shippers? (d) What was the attitude of the Federalists toward the Embargo Act?

15. (a) What were the major events of Jefferson's presidency, 1801–1809? (b) For what three accomplishments did Jefferson wish to be remembered?

FOR FURTHER STUDY AND DISCUSSION

1. "Fundamentally the triumph of Jefferson in 1800 marked another milestone in the great contest which had long raged and which continued to rage between capitalism and agrarianism." Explain the reasons for this interpretation of Jefferson's election in 1800.

2. (a) What were the causes for westward migration in the early years of the nineteenth century? (b) What problems did westward migration create for both the states and the national government? (c) How did these problems affect the policies of the Republicans? (d) What similar problems are present today?

3. Explain the meaning of Jefferson's statement that "the day France takes possession of New Orleans we must marry ourselves to the British fleet and nation." Does this statement reveal a change in point of view on the part of Jefferson? Helpful source: Tallant, *The Louisiana Purchase* (Landmark).

4. Why did political tension develop between Jefferson and Burr, and between Hamilton and Burr?

5. Why is Albert Gallatin considered one of our great Secretaries of the Treasury?

FOR INDIVIDUAL OR GROUP ACTIVITIES

1. Prepare an outline map showing the boundaries of the United States in 1801, the route of the National, or Cumberland, Road, the boundaries of the Louisiana Purchase, the routes of the Lewis and Clark expedition, and the explorations of Zebulon Pike.

2. Report on the origins and the findings of the Lewis and Clark expedition. Helpful source: Neuberger, *The Lewis and Clark Expedition.*

3. Prepare a similar report on the explorations of Zebulon Pike.

4. (a) Read Jefferson's first inaugural (see Commager, *Documents,* No. 106) and outline its major ideas. (b) Indicate how Jefferson's program as outlined in the inaugural differed from that of the Federalists.

5. Report on the "Tripolitan War," the New England "Conspiracy," the Burr "Conspiracy," and Burr's trial for treason.

6. (a) Write a news article on the duel between Hamilton and Burr. (b) Write an editorial on the duel.

7. Write a letter to a friend in England explaining the point of view of Americans about England's interference with the rights of neutrals. Then write a reply, setting forth the point of view of England.

8. Prepare an editorial for a Republican newspaper defending the embargo; or one for a Federalist newspaper criticizing it.

9. Outline Jefferson's ideas on political, educational, and religious freedom.

O say, can you see by the dawn's early light
What so proudly we hailed at the twilight's last gleaming?
Whose broad stripes and bright stars through the perilous fight,
O'er the ramparts we watched were so gallantly streaming!
——Francis Scott Key

HENRY CLAY, *speaker of the House under Madison*

14. THE WAR OF 1812 COMPLETES OUR INDEPENDENCE

The United States Struggles to Remain Neutral

Madison is elected President.

In 1808, Jefferson used his influence in the Republican party to secure the nomination of James Madison, his friend and Secretary of State. Madison easily won, for the South and West were loyal to the Republican party. Like Washington and Jefferson, Madison was a Virginia planter. Like them he had spent many years in the service of his state and his country. Madison had taken an important part in writing the constitution of his state and in the movement to establish a stronger Union. For his work in the federal Constitutional Convention, he is known as the "Father of the Constitution."

A new trade policy—nonintercourse.

After Congress repealed the unpopular Embargo Act, it passed a milder measure, the Nonintercourse Act, in its place. This law permitted trade with all foreign ports except those under British or French control. It stated that trade would be reopened with Britain and France when these powers stopped violating our neutral rights. While our foreign trade revived somewhat, the Nonintercourse Act did not keep the warring countries from interfering with our ships.

In 1810 Congress replaced the Nonintercourse Act by a strange measure known as the Macon Act. This law reopened our trade with all countries for one year. At the same time it promised Great Britain and France that if either of them gave up its restrictions on our commerce, we would stop all trade with the other, i.e., its enemy.

Madison falls into a trap.

Napoleon saw in the Macon Act a chance to trick the United States into taking sides against the British. He sent word (August, 1810) that in three months France would repeal the decrees which hurt our commerce, provided the British took a similar action.

Madison took the French offer at face value. He gave the British three months to drop their objectionable Orders in Council (see p. 199). When the British refused to do so, Congress forbade trade with Great Britain and its colonies. Thus Napoleon tricked the United States into joining his paper blockade. However, France kept on seizing American ships.

The War Hawks Push the Nation into War

Expansionists want war.

Many settlers in the West and South wanted the United States to seize Canada and Florida. Canada looked attractive because of its rich fur trade. Florida was important because it commanded the outlets of rivers running into the Gulf of Mexico. Moreover, so long as Florida was in Spanish hands it provided a refuge for runaway slaves. Frontiersmen thought that the Spanish in Florida and the British in Canada stirred up the Indians in the United States and supplied them with arms. For all these reasons, the expansionists argued, we ought to take Canada and Florida. They hoped we would go to war with Great Britain and its ally, Spain.

The British are blamed for Indian troubles.

Under the Treaty of Greenville (1795) the Indians of the Northwest had been promised possession of a large tract of forest "as long as the sun shall climb the heavens or the waters shall run in the streams." Yet for fifteen years white settlers had been moving into this land, spoiling it for hunting. In this way the forest Indians were being steadily pushed westward toward the plains, a region in which they did not know how to live.

In 1810 General William Henry Harrison, governor of the Indian Ter-

ritory, prepared to occupy a stretch of land along the Wabash River. The land had been recently "purchased" from some Indians. It was the home of the Shawnees, a peaceful agricultural tribe. Tecumseh, chief of the Shawnees, demanded that the land be returned, on the ground that the Indians who signed the treaty of purchase had no authority to sell lands belonging to the whole tribe. "The Indians were once a happy race," Tecumseh told Harrison, "but are now made miserable by the white people, who are never contented but always encroaching. They have driven us from the great salt water, forced us over the mountains, and would shortly push us into the lakes. But we are determined to go no further."

Chief Tecumseh saw that individual tribes could not oppose the white man's advance. The Indians' one hope lay in a confederacy of all the Indians east of the Mississippi. Tecumseh and his brother, the Prophet, traveled among the tribes, urging them not to cede any more land to the whites and not to drink the white man's liquor, which was destroying them.

In 1811 Tecumseh went south to bring the southern tribes into his confederacy. During Tecumseh's absence, Harrison marched 800 soldiers into the Wabash Valley. The Prophet attacked them with a force of about 400 warriors. After a fierce battle and heavy losses, Harrison drove the Indians off and burned their village, Tippecanoe.

Rightly or wrongly, many Westerners believed that British officials in Canada were backing Tecumseh's confederacy. These Westerners insisted that their homes would never be safe from the Indians so long as Canada was in British hands.

War Hawks gain power in Congress.

Meanwhile a change had taken place in Congress. In the election of

Sinking of HMS Java *by the* Constitution, *December 29, 1812. The* Constitution *won the name* "OLD IRONSIDES" *when English shots failed to penetrate its oaken sides.*

1810 frontier sections sent to Congress a group of fiery young Republicans who clamored for war. John Randolph, a Virginian with long service in Congress, dubbed this group the "War Hawks." Among them were two men who were to influence American politics for two generations—Henry Clay of Kentucky and John C. Calhoun of South Carolina. When Congress met the next November Henry Clay was chosen Speaker of the House. He at once appointed War Hawks to the principal committees.

Soon the House Committee on Foreign Affairs, most of whose members were War Hawks, issued a report urging war on Great Britain. The report said that Canada should be seized to make up for losses inflicted on American shipping and to prevent the British from stirring up the Indians along the frontier. The report stated that Canada could be easily conquered,

since the Canadians were discontented with British rule.

John Randolph attacked the report in a sarcastic speech. He suggested that the War Hawks had their eyes on the Canadian fur trade. He doubted that the British were responsible for the troubles with the Indians, saying that the frontiersmen had given the Indians more than enough cause to fight. He ridiculed the recklessness of the war "boys" and their failure to consider the cost of the war. "It seems this is to be a holiday campaign—there is to be no expense of blood and treasure on our part—Canada is to be subdued by the principle of fraternity."

The Federalists were strongly against the report. Said Congressman Stowe of New York: "We are told that commerce must be protected. From whom does this come? Have the ship-owners asked for your assistance? Are there any petitions from merchants on

207

THE WAR OF 1812

your tables? No. . . . . It is remarkable that this spirit of protecting commerce has come from the interior. It is not from the shipowners, but from the men furthest removed from ships."

Was war necessary?

Our minister to London, William Pinckney, left there in disgust early in 1811. If he had remained at his post, we would have known that leading British statesmen were urging concessions toward the United States. In 1812 Madison wished to send special envoys to London to make one more try for

peace, but the War Hawks persuaded him not to do so. As it turned out, this was a tragic mistake.

Great Britain did not want war with the United States. Weakened by nearly twenty years of war with France, Britain needed all its strength to win that struggle. For months Englishmen had been asking their government to give in to the United States. Finally, on June 16, two days before our declaration of war, the Prime Minister announced that the restrictions to which the United States objected would be repealed. Had there been a cable in those days, war might have been avoided.

War is declared.

On June 18, 1812, Congress declared war on England. The vote showed a sharp division of opinion—79 to 49 in the House, and 19 to 13 in the Senate. Practically all of those who voted for the war were Republicans, and practically all of them lived west or south of New York state. The vote made it perfectly plain that the commercial and shipping interests did not want war.

While the desire of many Americans for Canada was perhaps the main reason for war, there is no question that the United States had definite grievances against Great Britain. President Madison stated these in his war message to Congress: (1) impressment of American sailors, (2) the hovering of British war vessels on our coast, (3) the restrictive Orders in Council, (4) the Indian uprising of 1811, which Madison said was prompted by the British. We also had good reasons for fighting France, but the War Hawks overlooked this in their eagerness to fight Great Britain.

Commercial interests oppose the war.

News of the declaration of war was greeted joyously in frontier sections. In the Northeast, however, it was received coldly. Shipowners had been making huge profits in spite of the loss of many ships. The British navy would now sweep our commerce from the sea. Moreover, the war would help Napoleon in his attempt to conquer Great Britain and the whole of Europe. The governor of Massachusetts proclaimed a day of mourning. When Congress asked for 100,000 militiamen, New York and the New England states at first refused to let their militia serve outside their own boundaries. Farmers in these states sold provisions to the British armies in Canada. The merchants and bankers of the Northeast would not subscribe to the national loans. It was Mr. Madison's war, they said, and he could pay the bills.

Madison is re-elected.

The presidential election of 1812, in which Madison was re-elected, was a kind of referendum on whether the country should continue the war. The voting reflected the same sectional division as that on the declaration of war five months earlier. Those who favored the war voted for Madison. Those who declared themselves "Friends of Union, Peace, and Commerce" voted for the Federalist candidate, DeWitt Clinton of New York. Clinton carried Delaware and every state east of Delaware except Vermont. If he had carried Pennsylvania, which he lost by a few votes, he would have won the election.

The War Ends in a Draw

The nation is unprepared for war.

When war began the regular army consisted of only 6700 men, mostly located at frontier posts from which they could not be withdrawn. A new army had to be recruited, trained, and equipped. The lack of experienced officers was an enormous handicap to our side. Short enlistments also interfered with developing a trained, seasoned army. Among other mistakes, Congress failed to place one general in supreme command of all our forces.

The nation's revenue, which came largely from duties on imports, dropped sharply as soon as the war began. Congress was unwilling to vote new taxes. Loans proved difficult to raise, for many of the well-to-do people of the Northeast opposed the war. Moreover, the Bank of the United States, which could have helped to float a loan, had ceased to exist in 1811. Thus the Treasury had a hard time paying its bills.

The invasion of Canada fails.

The war party thought it would be easy to take Canada. Henry Clay boasted to Congress, "The militia of Kentucky alone are competent to place Montreal and upper Canada at your feet."

Canada had less than 500,000 people, while the United States had nearly 8 million. The Canadians did not want to join the United States, and they fought hard. They had the help of several thousand British regulars and several thousand Indians. Their greatest protection was the wilderness which lay between their settlements and ours.

In 1812 three American expeditions were sent to invade Canada. One column, or force, of 2000 men surrendered to the British at Detroit without a battle. This gave the British control of the entire Michigan country and left the frontier open to Indian raids. Another column of 4000, chiefly New York militia, failed when three fourths of the men refused to cross the Niagara River into Canada. The third column, which had been sent against Montreal, also failed because the men would not leave American soil. Our soldiers did not lack courage, but they were poorly equipped and did not have the discipline which comes with training. Then, too, they believed that militia could not be called upon to serve outside the United States.

We regain the Northwest.

In 1813 the nation was cheered by a brilliant victory on Lake Erie. Commodore Oliver H. Perry built a small fleet at Erie, Pennsylvania, for the purpose of clearing Lake Erie of British ships. Then he sailed west across the lake toward Detroit. When he neared Put-in-Bay, a fierce battle took place. To the astonishment of the British, their squadron was destroyed. Perry reported: "We have met the enemy and they are ours."

Perry's victory (September 10, 1813) forced the British to leave Detroit. As they retreated, an American force led by General William Henry Harrison pursued them a short distance into Canada. The British were overtaken and defeated in the Battle of the Thames River. The death of the great Indian leader, Tecumseh, in this battle ended the Indian confederacy.

Americans fight well on the sea.

At the beginning of the war our navy consisted of less than 20 frigates and sloops. Yet American naval officers and seamen were among the best in the world. In a series of single-ship actions, the Americans defeated equal or heavier British vessels. They destroyed or captured 254 naval and merchant ships before the war ended. The navy was assisted by nearly 500 privateers, which captured over 1300 enemy ships. Privateering helped to shorten the war.

The British blockade our coasts.

During 1813, however, the mighty British navy practically drove the American navy off the seas and established a tight blockade of the United States. Our commerce practically stopped. The entire country felt the effects of the blockade. Farmers grew crops which they could not sell and paid high prices for things they had to buy. Receipts from customs duties fell to almost nothing, and the United States government could not pay its bills. Merchants and shipowners became more strongly opposed to the war than ever.

Renewed attacks on Canada fail.

New American efforts to take Montreal in 1813 ended in failure. A final attempt to invade Canada in the summer of 1814 also failed. Our forces withdrew from Canada in July after the hard-fought Battle of Lundy's Lane near Niagara Falls.

210

OLIVER HAZARD PERRY. *From a painting by John W. Jarvis. By winning control of Lake Erie, Commodore Perry gave American negotiators at Ghent a chance to make good their claims to the Northwest.*

The British take the offensive.

Napoleon was overthrown in 1814. The British were then able to send reinforcements to Canada. Late in August over 10,000 British veterans started from Montreal, invading the United States along the Lake Champlain route, just as Burgoyne had done in 1777 (see p. 120). The British commander wished to get control of the lake, on which the British and the Americans each had a small fleet. The British expected an easy victory, since heavy guns gave their ships double the fighting strength of the American ships. But the young American commander, Captain Thomas Macdonough, handled his ships so well that he won the day. With the waterway in American hands, the British had to retreat. New York and New England were saved from further attack.

For months before this defeat the British had kept full control of our coast and were able to land raiding parties almost anywhere they liked. They had raided a number of coastal villages and forced others to give ransom. They had "annexed" eastern Maine to Canada. In August (1814) a British fleet entered Chesapeake Bay and landed 4000 men. This army advanced inland to Washington without meeting serious opposition. Our government fled, and the British burned the public buildings in revenge for destruction of public buildings in Toronto during an American raid a year earlier. The British then returned to their ships and moved on Baltimore. Here they met determined and well-organized resistance. After bombing Fort McHenry, which guarded the city, and landing troops, they were forced to withdraw. It was during this battle that Francis Scott Key was inspired to write "The Star-Spangled Banner." After the fighting at Baltimore, the British made ready to attack New Orleans. They hoped to seize that city and detach the Mississippi Valley from the Union.

Jackson becomes a national hero.

Meanwhile, in 1813, the Creek Indians joined the war on the side of the British. They seized Fort Mims on the lower Alabama River and killed several hundred settlers. A few months later Andrew Jackson, at the head of 3000 Tennessee volunteers, defeated the Indians at Horseshoe Bend. He forced them to sign a treaty giving up most of their land.

In the fall of 1814 Jackson seized the fort of Pensacola in Spanish Florida, which the British intended to use as a base for attacking New Orleans. The War Department then sent Jackson to defend New Orleans with a force of 5000 frontiersmen hastily called from the Southwest. As the Americans threw up breastworks, some 8000 British veterans advanced from the coast across the swamps. On January 8, 1815, as the British charged over open ground before the city, they met withering rifle fire. Twice they rallied, and each time they were driven back. Jackson's great victory smashed the invasion and made him the hero of the war.

The Treaty of Ghent.

Had the commanders only known, the Battle of New Orleans need not have been fought. A peace treaty had been signed at Ghent, Belgium, two weeks earlier on Christmas Eve, 1814.

Peace negotiations had started in August, when five able Americans (John Quincy Adams, Albert Gallatin, Henry Clay, Thomas Bayard, and Jonathan Russell) met British representatives at Ghent. Both sides badly wanted peace. The British public, after twenty-two years of war in Europe, was thoroughly sick of fighting. The United States was almost bankrupt, its navy and merchant fleet were bottled up, and Federalist leaders in the Northeast were talking of joining the British. Negotiations dragged, for the two peace commissions disagreed on everything except a desire to end the fighting. After five months of discussion they arranged a "peace without victory." The treaty said nothing about impressment of seamen or the rights of neutral shipping; these had become dead issues with the end of the war in Europe. The treaty said that conquered territory should be returned. (However, West Florida, which we had taken from the Spanish, remained in our hands.) It was agreed that the Northwest boundary dispute and the problems of trade, furs, and fishing rights should be settled by arbitration.

New Englanders propose constitutional changes.

From the start many New Englanders had opposed the war. They blamed the conflict on the desire of the South and the West for more territory, a desire they did not share. If Canada and Florida were added to the Union,

the farmers would have still more power in the national government. The big merchants and manufacturers of the Northeast feared that Congress would ignore their interests. Some Federalist leaders wanted New England to secede from the Union rather than submit to domination by the South and the West.

In October, 1814, the Massachusetts legislature invited the other New England states to send delegates to a convention "to deliberate upon the dangers to which the eastern section of the Union is exposed by the course of the war." Soon after, twenty-six Federalists, representing five states, met at Hartford, Connecticut. After a secret session lasting three weeks, a report was issued. In words similar to those of the Kentucky and Virginia resolutions of 1798, the report set forth the right of a state to nullify, or disregard, an act of Congress.

THE BURNING OF THE CITY OF WASHINGTON *by the British, August, 1814. After setting fire to the Capitol, the White House, and other public buildings the British moved on to attempt the destruction of Baltimore.*

The report called for seven amendments to the Constitution, each of them intended to protect New England from unwelcome federal policies. The changes proposed were: (1) to require a two-thirds vote of Congress for admitting a new state to the Union, declaring war, or placing restrictions on foreign commerce; (2) to prohibit naturalized citizens from holding federal office; (3) to protect individuals from military conscription; (4) to limit embargoes to no more than 60 days; (5) to put an end to the "three-fifths rule," by which Negro slaves were counted in apportioning representation in Congress; (6) to limit the President to a single term; (7) to prohibit any President from being succeeded by another from the same state.

Three members of the Hartford Convention were sent to present these demands to the President and Congress. When the delegates reached Washington, news had just come of the signing of the peace treaty. Amid the rejoicing nobody would take their proposals seriously. Nothing came of their mission.

Results of the War of 1812.

According to the peace treaty, nothing had been changed by the war. The treaty did not even mention the grievances that led the United States to declare war. As a military event, moreover, the war was indecisive. Yet the effects of the conflict on the United States were far-reaching:

1. The power of the Indians east of the Mississippi was broken. The Canadian hope of forming an Indian buffer state in the Northwest was gone. The Creeks in the old Southwest had been subdued and settlement of this area could now go forward rapidly.

2. The blockade led to an increase in manufacturing.

3. The Federalist party was discredited. People were disgusted by the selfishness and lack of patriotism shown throughout the war by many Federalists, who refused to buy war bonds and talked of taking their states out of the Union. The convention at Hartford was so ridiculed that the very name "Federalist" became a term of contempt.

4. The Republicans, who had formerly opposed a strong national government, learned that a government must be strong in order to defend itself. The calamities of the first two years of the war had shown the need for a stronger navy, a larger regular army, and a central bank.

5. Despite the discontent in the Northeast, the conflict strengthened the feeling of national unity. All Americans felt pride in the naval victories and in the British defeat at New Orleans. The fact that men of different states had again fought side by side added to the sense of unity.

6. Americans turned their backs on Europe. From 1789 to 1815 the national government had been greatly concerned with foreign affairs. The long struggle between France and Great Britain had created many problems for the young United States and had led us into two wars. After 1815 Americans could occupy themselves mainly with affairs at home. For the next century isolation from Europe was to be the nation's fixed policy. That is why the War of 1812 is sometimes described as our "second war for independence."

FOR IDENTIFICATION

Henry Clay
William Henry Harrison
Francis Scott Key
Lake Erie

Thomas Macdonough
Oliver H. Perry
Tecumseh
Tippecanoe
Treaty of Ghent

FOR EXPLANATION OR DEFINITION

arbitration commission
Hartford Convention
Macon Act

Nonintercourse Act
paper blockade
privateer
War Hawks

FOR REVIEW

1. (a) What was the purpose of the Nonintercourse Act? How did it differ from the Embargo Act? (b) What offer was made by the Macon Act? (c) How did Napoleon take advantage of it?

2. How did troubles with the Indians in the Northwest and in the South serve as a prelude to the War of 1812?

3. Who were the War Hawks? Who was their leader? Why were they eager for war with England?

4. What were the reasons for the War of 1812 as outlined by President Madison in his war message to Congress?

5. How did commercial and shipping interests feel about the war?

6. How did the Northeast show its opposition to the war?

7. Account for the failure of our efforts to take Canada.

8. What was accomplished by the American navy? By American privateers?

9. What were the effects of the British blockade?

10. How was the British invasion from Canada blocked?

11. What event inspired the writing of our national anthem?

12. How did Andrew Jackson become the great hero of the War of 1812?

13. What were the terms of the Treaty of Ghent? What is meant by arbitration?

14. What was the Hartford Convention?

15. What were the principal results of the War of 1812?

FOR FURTHER STUDY AND DISCUSSION

1. (a) Why didn't the War of 1812 have the wholehearted support of all the sections? (b) In general, what was the attitude of the North? South? West?

2. What justification is there for the statement that "agrarian cupidity, not maritime right" urged the war? What, besides "agrarian cupidity," was a factor?

3. Could the War of 1812 have been avoided? Explain.

4. Were the actions of those opposed to the war treasonable?

5. How did the War of 1812 affect the Federalist and Republican parties?

6. Do you agree that the War of 1812 was inconclusive from a military and diplomatic point of view? Explain.

7. Explain why the delegates to the Hartford Convention supported each of the resolutions summarized on pp. 213–214.

8. Account for the fact that the "sectional war of 1812" resulted in a great upsurge of national confidence and pride.

FOR INDIVIDUAL OR GROUP ACTIVITIES

1. Prepare floor talks, using maps, on the principal military engagements of the War of 1812. Include American attempts to invade Canada, English thrusts from Canada, the English attack upon Washington and Baltimore, and the achievements of Andrew Jackson.

2. Make a brief report on *The Naval War of 1812* by Theodore Roosevelt.

3. Arrange in parallel columns the essential principles of the Virginia and Kentucky resolutions and of the Hartford Convention. Helpful source: Commager, *Documents*, Nos. 102, 103, 115.

4. Read aloud to the class the poem "Old Ironsides," by Oliver Wendell Holmes, and tell the story of the *Constitution*. Helpful source: Hansen, *Old Ironsides, the Fighting "Constitution."*

5. Prepare, for bulletin board display, ten newspaper headlines which summarize the major events of the War of 1812.

6. Prepare a summary of the commerical and industrial effects of the War of 1812.

215

"FOURTH OF JULY CELEBRATION *in Center Square, Philadelphia, 1819"* by *John Lewis Krimmel. Another birthday for the young and growing nation is celebrated here and throughout the land.*

> The constitution and laws of a state, so far as they are repugnant to the Constitution and laws of the United States, are absolutely void. These states are constituent parts of the United States. They are members of one great empire—for some purposes sovereign, for some purposes subordinate.
>
> ——John Marshall

15. NATIONALISM CONTRIBUTES TO AN ERA OF GOOD FEELING

The Republicans Adopt a Nationalistic Program

A surge of nationalism follows the War of 1812.

Ever since this country's beginning most Americans had felt a stronger tie of loyalty to their own state than to the Union. The spirit of nationalism, or devotion to the nation as a whole, had developed slowly. It was greatly strengthened by the War of 1812. Americans in every state and section now saw the need for an adequate central government. They worked together to correct national weaknesses revealed by the war. They condemned as narrow, selfish, and unpatriotic the antinationalist attitude shown by many Federalists during the war.

The "revolution of 1800," which had brought Thomas Jefferson into power, was based on widespread distrust of a strong central government. But events since 1800, especially the war with England, had taught the Republicans that a strong central government was necessary and that it need not destroy liberty. The old Republicans had opposed a standing army, fearing it might lead to dictatorship by a military class, as in so many other countries. They had thought that a navy was a useless expense. Now all Americans agreed that the nation should be armed.

The change in Republican ideas could be seen in Madison's annual message to Congress in 1815. This former upholder of states' rights called for new warships, a standing army, national aid for building roads and canals, a protective tariff, and the re-establishment of a national bank. Congress carried out these recommendations. As a New England congressman remarked, the Republicans were "out-Federalizing Federalism." The spirit of nationalism had triumphed over the spirit of localism and states' rights.

Second Bank of the United States.

The new attitude of the Republicans was clearly shown by their chartering of the second Bank of the United States. The first Bank of the United States had been established in Washington's administration after bitter debate between the followers of Hamilton and of Jefferson (see p. 171). When the bank's charter ran out in 1811, the Republicans refused to issue a new charter, since they then favored state-chartered banks. During the next few years the banking business was left in the hands of three hundred state banks, each of which issued its own paper money. The value of this flood of paper currency was so uncertain that merchants found it hard to carry on business. The state banks could not provide the nation with a uniform currency (one having the same value in all parts of the country). In 1816 Congress authorized the establishment of the second Bank of the United States. It was similar to the first bank, but its capital was to be three and a half times larger. In return for a twenty-year charter the bank paid the federal government $1,500,000. President Madison signed the bank bill without argument, although in 1791 he had led the fight in Congress against chartering the first bank.

A protective tariff is adopted.

During the period of the embargo, nonintercourse, and the War of 1812, the flow of manufactured goods from Great Britain to the United States was cut off. To provide needed items, many factories were built here, most of them in the Northeast. Much American wealth that formerly had been invested in foreign commerce was put into manufacturing. Soon American manufacturers built up a good market.

When the war ended, British merchants tried to recapture the American market. Their warehouses were bulging with goods. They offered these goods in America at prices well below what was asked for American-made products. Our manufacturers, fearing they would be driven out of business, called on Congress to raise the duties on imports. A bill for this purpose was presented to Congress.

Northern importers and shipowners were against the bill since it would reduce trade between the United States and Europe. On the other hand, the Republicans, once firmly opposed to a protective tariff (see p. 172), now voted for it. They thought it would cause factories to spring up in all parts of the country.

Henry Clay of Kentucky argued for the bill as part of an "American system" of high tariffs and internal improvements (roads, canals, and the like). He wanted the revenue from the tariff to be used for internal improvements in the West. He said that the "American system" would benefit all sections of the country. In 1816 Congress passed the tariff act.

The question of internal improvements.

To strengthen the nation and tie all parts of it together, roads, bridges, and canals were greatly needed. Everyone agreed on the need, but not on how to pay for them. The question was: Should internal improvements be paid for by the federal government or by the states and local communities? Many of the older Republicans thought that the federal government had no power to make internal improvements.

The younger Republicans did not accept this view. Shortly before Madison was to leave the presidency John C. Calhoun, of South Carolina, introduced what is known as the "bonus bill." It provided that the $1,500,000 which the government was to receive for chartering the second Bank of the United States should be used for building roads and canals. Congress passed the bonus bill by a close vote. Madison vetoed it. While he heartily approved of its purpose, he thought it went beyond the powers of Congress.

Incoming President James Monroe, also a Republican, agreed with Madison. He, too, told Congress that a constitutional amendment was needed to give the federal government power to make internal improvements. Yet opposition from the East, particularly New England, prevented such an amendment. Thus for many years the building of canals and roads, except the National Road (see pp. 193–194), was left to the individual states and to private companies.

Party strife almost disappears.

In 1816 the Republican candidate for President, James Monroe, had won an easy victory over the Federalist candidate, Rufus King of New York. The 1816 election was the last time the Federalists put up a presidential candidate. Their once proud party was nearly dead.

James Monroe was the fourth and last of the "Virginia dynasty" of Presidents. He was also the last of the revolutionary generation to occupy the White House. Soon after his inauguration he made a tour of the North and West. Everywhere he received an enthusiastic welcome. The *Columbian Centinel,* a Federalist paper which had appeared with a black border the day of Jefferson's inauguration in 1801, spoke of Monroe as the herald of "an era of good feeling." The phrase has been used ever since in describing the eight years of Monroe's presidency. It was a tribute to the new feeling of national unity.

The country was pleased with the new nationalistic policies of the Republicans. Now that they had become so much like the early Federalists, political parties seemed to be a thing of the past. The absence of party feeling was shown in the presidential election of 1820. James Monroe, running for a second time, received all the electoral votes but one. That was cast by an elector who felt that only one man, George Washington, deserved the honor of a unanimous vote for President.

Foreign Policy Reflects Growing National Strength

A great Secretary of State.

Among the reasons for the absence of party strife during Monroe's administration was the skillful conduct of foreign affairs. The Secretary of State, John Quincy Adams, won new respect

JAMES MONROE

JOHN QUINCY ADAMS

Avenue of young trees leading to the Capitol, Washington, D. C.

for the United States in its dealings with other nations. A son of John Adams, the second President, he had spent eighteen years abroad, most of them in the diplomatic service. At different times he had been minister to the Netherlands, Prussia, Russia, and Great Britain. This lengthy experience, combined with his remarkable ability and intense patriotism, made him one of the greatest Secretaries of State the country has ever had.

Relations with Britain improve.

When Madison became President both the United States and Great Britain were building warships on the Great Lakes. Knowing that this naval race was costly and dangerous, Madison instructed Adams to propose disarmament. The two governments then agreed to limit their armed vessels on the Great Lakes to four small ships to be used against smugglers. The resulting Rush-Bagot Treaty of 1817 was the first example in history of naval disarmament. It led at once to better feelings between the United States and Great Britain.

Four commissions set up under the Treaty of Ghent worked out other agreements between the United States and Great Britain. A commercial treaty, concluded in 1815, opened the ports of both countries to the ships of the other on equal terms. (However, Americans could not trade with the British West Indies, and Britishers could not trade from port to port along our coast.) A treaty completed in 1818 dealt with fisheries, with the northern boundary of the Louisiana Purchase, and with conflicting claims to Oregon. In regard to fisheries, the British government renewed the privileges it had given our fishermen in 1783. They were allowed to take fish along the coasts of Canada and Newfoundland and to land on unsettled portions of these coasts to dry and cure their catch. In regard to the Louisiana Purchase the two nations agreed that the forty-ninth parallel should be its northern boundary.

Under the same treaty the Oregon country was left open to the citizens of both the United States and Great Britain for ten years. Oregon was a vast region extending from Spanish California to Russian Alaska. American and British fur-trading companies were just beginning to enter the area. Since no agreement could be reached in 1818 as to dividing Oregon, the United States and Great Britain decided to occupy it jointly. In 1827 they agreed to continue the period of joint ownership indefinitely. (For the final settlement in 1846, see p. 339.)

We acquire Florida.

The Louisiana Purchase included a small stretch of land on the Gulf coast. Its boundaries were not clearly stated in the purchase treaty, and Jefferson claimed that it included West Florida. In 1810 and 1813 President Madison took possession of sections of West Florida (see pp. 212–213). The United States wanted all of West Florida (the Florida panhandle), since it contained the mouths of several important rivers which flowed from our cotton belt to the Gulf of Mexico. The United States also wanted the peninsula of Florida. If it belonged to us we could get rid of the smugglers, pirates, runaway slaves, and hostile Indians who lived there.

Under the Pinckney Treaty of 1795 (see p. 178), Spain had promised to keep the Indians from annoying us, but she was too weak to carry out the promise. Creek Indians, who had taken refuge in Florida after the Battle of Horseshoe Bend (see p. 212), kept crossing the border and attacking settlers in Georgia and Alabama. General Andrew Jackson was ordered to punish the Indians. In 1818 he not only pursued them into Spanish territory but seized and held the principal Spanish forts. He also executed two British traders, Arbuthnot and Armbrister, who had aided the Creeks.

The general's high-handed actions might easily have led to war with Great Britain and with Spain. Britishers talked angrily of fighting unless the United States apologized for the "murder" of Arbuthnot and Armbrister. But Secretary of State Adams persuaded the British government to take no action. Spain asked the United States for reparations. Adams sent a blunt note in return. He demanded that Spain either place a force in Florida adequate to keep order there or cede the province to the United States.

Spain was having trouble at home and in its colonies and could not send more soldiers to Florida. In 1819, therefore, Spain agreed to cede Florida to the United States. In return the United States promised to pay the claims of American citizens against Spain, which amounted to five million dollars. At the same time an agreement was drawn up regarding the western border of Louisiana. Spain gave up its claim to Oregon, and the United States gave up its claim to Texas. The surrender of Texas was a disappointment to Adams, yet he knew the Spanish ambassador had to have something to show in return for dropping Spanish claims to Oregon. At the time Texas was regarded as of doubtful value, and besides, our claim to it was questionable. Within a few years, however, Westerners began to demand the "reannexation" of Texas.

Adams protests the Russian advance.

The farsighted Adams saw that the United States must have an outlet upon the Pacific. For this reason he wanted to put a stop to Russian advances in North America. Russian fur traders had pushed through Siberia and across Bering Strait into Alaska late in the 1700's. During the War of 1812 the Russian-American Fur Company had built a fortified village on Spanish territory near San Francisco Bay. In 1821 the Czar announced that the Pacific

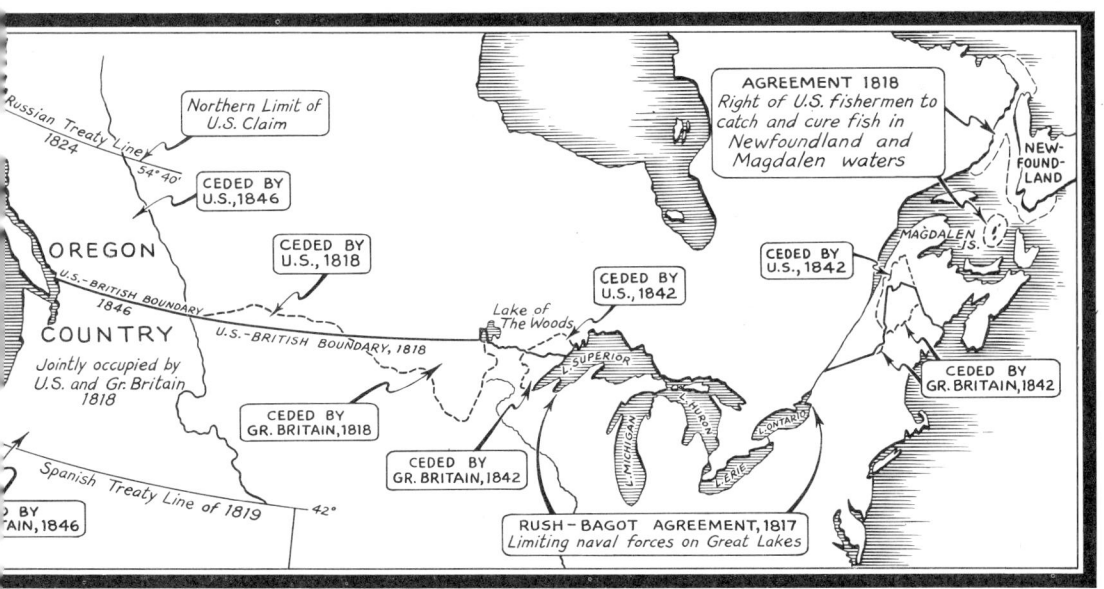

AGREEMENTS WITH GREAT BRITAIN

FORT WALLA WALLA *on the Oregon Trail. This was the Hudson Bay Company's post for trade with the Nez Percé Indians. Pioneers to the Northwest found a welcome haven here.*

coast as far south as the parallel of 51° was Russian territory. Neither the United States nor England was willing to accept the Russian claim. In a letter to the Russian ambassador (July, 1823), Adams announced that "the American continents are no longer subjects for any new European colonial establishments." The Russian question was settled a year later (see p. 223).

We fear for Latin America.

More alarming than the Russian advance was the danger that European nations might interfere in Latin America. Between 1810 and 1823 nearly all the Spanish colonies in America had declared their independence and set up republics. European rulers were alarmed at the growth of the republican spirit in the world. They knew that if it were allowed to grow unchecked, their crowns would soon be in danger. To put down republican uprisings everywhere, Austria, France, Prussia, and Russia formed a league, called the Quadruple Alliance. The four rulers of the Alliance first took steps to crush democratic movements in Spain and Italy. Then in 1823 they talked of a plan to help Spain to reconquer its American colonies.

The four rulers reckoned without public opinion in the United States. Our people had rejoiced at each victory won by Latin American patriots. Many had sent financial aid, and some had given military service to the revolutionists. The new republics had adopted constitutions based on our own. Our government had recognized most of them in 1822. It felt bound to help them keep their hard-won independence.

The British suggest joint action.

The British had developed a profitable trade with the new republics. This would stop if Spain reconquered them, for Spain would not permit its colonies to trade with other countries. Therefore the British also hoped to discourage the Quadruple Alliance from interfering in America. George Canning, the British foreign minister, proposed (August, 1823) that the United States and Great Britain join in warning the Alliance to stay out of the Americas. He further suggested that both countries pledge themselves not to acquire any part of Spain's former possessions.

President Monroe's first impulse was to agree. The most powerful nation in the world was offering us what amounted to an alliance. Monroe consulted Jefferson and Madison, and they approved of joint action with Great Britain to protect Spain's former colonies. In addition, Madison and certain other Republican leaders proposed that the United States and Great Britain join in helping the patriots in Greece, who were then fighting for freedom from Turkey. The rebellion of the Greeks had particularly aroused American sympathies. Money and arms for the Greeks had been collected in churches throughout the United States.

Adams insists on separate action.

Secretary of State Adams, on the other hand, believed the United States ought to act by itself. He knew that Great Britain would in any case prevent the Quadruple Alliance from interfering in South America. Furthermore, he thought we ought not to meddle in European affairs.

One important advantage of separate action instead of joint action with the British was that the United States avoided making a promise not to acquire Texas, California, or Cuba.

The Monroe Doctrine.

Monroe and his Cabinet accepted the views of the Secretary of State. The foreign policy of John Quincy Adams thus became the Monroe Doctrine. It was announced in the President's annual message to Congress in December, 1823. The purpose of the Monroe Doctrine was to keep the American continents for the Americans. It included the following ideas: (1) the Western Hemisphere was not open to further colonization by European powers; (2) European powers were warned not to interfere with the political affairs of any portion of the Western Hemisphere, for such interference would be regarded as "dangerous to our peace and safety"; (3) the United States would not interfere with the existing colonies of any European power; (4) the United States would not participate in purely European affairs.

UNITED STATES SQUADRON *sailing the Mediterranean in 1825*

"CARAVAN EN ROUTE," *by Alfred J. Miller. In 1837 the American Fur Company's outfit headed west. Stretched out for miles came the galloping horsemen, while the long line of wagons followed slowly.*

"INDIANS APPROACHING FORT BENTON" *by* CHARLES WIMAR

The last statement meant that we would not help the Greeks in their rebellion against Turkey or interfere with the internal affairs of any European country.

The Monroe Doctrine was a success. This was partly due to the fact that the British supported it. Under threat of war England compelled France to promise not to attack the Spanish colonies. Austria, Russia, and Prussia could not make war in Latin America without the help of the French fleet, so they, too, gave up the idea. The following year Russia signed a treaty with the United States in which she dropped all claims to territory south of the parallel 54° 40'. The Monroe Doctrine had accomplished the purpose for which it was announced.

The Monroe Doctrine was not a law. It was merely an opinion expressed by the President of the United States. Yet it has survived to this day as a basic part of American foreign policy. It was the high-water mark of the new nationalism which grew out of the War of 1812. It showed how far American pride, self-confidence, and independence had developed.

Supreme Court Strengthens the National Government

Marshall dominates the Court.

Shortly before leaving office in 1801, President John Adams appointed John Marshall of Virginia to the post of Chief Justice. Although Marshall was a cousin of Thomas Jefferson, the two men were far apart in their political views. Marshall was a staunch Federalist. His legal decisions rested on two basic ideas: (1) that the federal government, not the states, should be supreme, and (2) that private property should be considered sacred.

Marshall served as Chief Justice from 1801 until his death in 1835. For thirty-four years his personality dominated the bench. Although he was but one member of the Supreme Court, his strong, logical mind and his powers of persuasion won the other members to his way of thinking. Dissenting opinions were rare. Republican Presidents appointed states' rights Republicans as associate justices, hoping to offset Marshall's views. It did not work. In time the Republican judges became "Marshallized" by his interpretations of the Constitution.

Power of judicial review.

Ever since the adoption of the Virginia and Kentucky resolutions, which declared that a state has the power to decide whether an act of Congress is constitutional, men had argued the question as to where lay the final authority. Did the state courts or the federal courts have the last word in deciding what is the law of the land? Led by Chief Justice Marshall the Supreme Court, in a series of decisions, asserted its authority to pass on the constitutionality of a law. This view of the Court as final authority was first set forth in the case of *Marbury* vs. *Madison* (1803).

In this case, in the name of the entire Court, Marshall declared unconstitutional a portion of the Judiciary Act of 1789. Since the Constitution is the supreme law of the land, Marshall argued, it limits the powers of Congress. If Congress could ignore its limitations, then the Constitution would disappear. The courts must therefore declare null and void any legislative act which is contrary to the Constitution. "It is emphatically the province and duty of the judicial department to say what the law is." This is the principle, or idea, of *judicial review*. It is not stated in the Constitution.

The decision shocked President Jefferson and other Republican leaders. They denied that the framers of the

Constitution meant to make the judiciary branch more powerful than the legislative and executive branches. The final authority, they insisted, should rest with the people's elected representatives, not with judges who are neither chosen by the voters nor made accountable to them. Jefferson said that Marshall had made the Constitution "a mere thing of wax in the hands of the judiciary, which they may twist and shape in any form they please." However, Marshall's view prevailed.

wished to appeal to the United States Supreme Court, but the highest court in Virginia ruled that its decision was final. The United States Supreme Court then asserted its authority and overruled the Virginia court. In this and other cases Marshall swept aside the argument that the decision of a state court is final in disputes arising under state law. To prevent endless confusion, the final judgment must rest in the federal Supreme Court. Thus the Supreme Court assumed the right of

DARTMOUTH COLLEGE. *This is the earliest known print showing Dartmouth Hall (1784) and the College Chapel (1790). Notice the students playing cricket.*

In a second case (*Fletcher* vs. *Peck*, 1810) the Supreme Court set aside an act of a state legislature. The Court held that an act of the Georgia legislature violated Article I, Section 10, of the Constitution. Marshall wrote the opinion, which said a state is not sovereign but "a part of a large empire . . . a member of the American union, and that union has a Constitution . . . which imposes limits to the legislatures of the several states."

Martin vs. *Hunter's Lessee* (1816) was a case which had been tried in the state courts of Virginia. The loser

judicial review not only of acts of Congress and acts of state legislatures but also of decisions made by state courts.

A charter is held to be a contract.

Dartmouth College had been chartered by George III in colonial days. In 1816 the New Hampshire legislature decided to bring the college under state control. A new charter was issued and new trustees appointed. The old trustees refused to turn over their records and funds. They engaged Daniel Webster, a Dartmouth graduate, to plead their case. When *Dartmouth* vs.

227

JOHN MARSHALL, *Chief Justice of the United States from 1801 to 1835*

Woodward reached the Supreme Court, Marshall wrote a decision supporting the old trustees. He argued that a charter is a contract. Since the Constitution forbids the states from impairing the terms of a contract, the college could not be brought under state control.

This decision protected private schools, colleges, and other chartered institutions from political interference. Its most far-reaching effect, however, was in protecting business corporations from regulation by state legislatures. At that time businesses were just beginning to organize as corporations. Once a business had been chartered by a state legislature, Marshall held that it was immune to regulation. His view prevailed for many years. Not until long after his death did the Supreme Court rule that a state legislature may alter a charter when necessary to protect public health, safety, and morals.

Loose construction upheld.

In *McCulloch* vs. *Maryland* (1819), the problem of whether the Bank of the United States was constitutional reached the Supreme Court. The state of Maryland had laid a tax on a branch of the bank, and the treasurer of the branch, McCulloch, had refused to pay it. In deciding the case the Supreme Court ruled on two questions: (1) Has Congress power to create a bank? (2) Have the states power to tax a bank created by Congress?

Marshall's decision was one of the most important that the Supreme Court has ever handed down. He ruled that Congress has the power to charter a bank under the "necessary and proper" clause of the Constitution. This clause, he said, authorized any action "appropriate" to carrying out the powers specifically granted to Congress. Thus he supported Hamilton's view that the Constitution gives Congress a wide range of implied powers.

The Court denied the right of a state to tax the bank. If a small tax could be set, a large one could be set also, and the bank could be taxed out of existence. The power to tax involves the power to destroy, argued Marshall, and if a state has the power to destroy, it can make useless the power of Congress to create. But the Constitution is the supreme law of the land, and no state can have power to destroy what the federal government has the power to create. Therefore a state may not tax any agency of the federal government.

In the case of *Gibbons* vs. *Ogden* (1824), Marshall placed the broadest possible interpretation upon the power of Congress to regulate commerce. The state of New York had granted Robert Fulton and his associates a monopoly of steamboat transportation on the Hudson. The Supreme Court ruled that this monopoly was unconstitutional because it interfered with the power of Congress to regulate interstate commerce. Marshall defined interstate commerce to include not only the exchange of goods but most other interstate activi-

(Above) *Two chiefs of the Kansas Indians, 1821*
(Right) YOUNG OMAHAW, *War Eagle, Little Missouri, and Pawnees.*

Nobility of the forest and the plains, they had built a way of life—language, beliefs, tribal government, and love of land.

ties. He declared that anything affecting interstate commerce may be regulated by Congress. In the twentieth century this interpretation has enabled the federal government to control broadcasting, the telephone industry, the transmission of electric power, and other activities not foreseen when the Constitution was written.

Marshall's influence still endures.

As Lord Bryce pointed out, the Constitution at the time it was adopted was "rather a ground plan than a city." Marshall filled in this ground plan. Becoming Chief Justice at a time when there were scarcely any precedents to guide the federal courts, he created a large body of precedents. During his

229

long years in office the Supreme Court handed down over eleven hundred opinions. Nearly half of them were written by Marshall himself. Many of his opinions dealt with clear constitutional issues. His reasoning was so logical and so sharp that it was nearly always accepted by other judges. Although some of the principles he laid down have been modified by later decisions, on the whole his interpretations of the Constitution have endured.

Marshall laid the foundation of American constitutional law. His greatest contribution was to establish the Supreme Court as the final authority on what the Constitution means. In this way he gave a strength and steadiness to the federal government that would have been impossible had either the states or Congress been the final authority.

In so strengthening the government Marshall defeated Jefferson's attempts to limit the influence of the judiciary. Marshall also attacked the whole Republican doctrine of states' rights. For this he was charged by Republicans with being an enemy of democracy and too much concerned with the rights of property. Jefferson objected to many of Marshall's views and particularly to the way in which he steadily enlarged the power of the federal government at the expense of the states. Yet today it is generally realized that Marshall did more perhaps than any other statesman to build a lasting national union out of a loose collection of states. His legal opinions were truly described by his biographer as "the mighty cable woven by him to hold the American people together as a united and imperishable nation."

JOHN C. CALHOUN

FOR IDENTIFICATION

John Q. Adams
John C. Calhoun
Dartmouth vs.
  Woodward
Fletcher vs. *Peck*
Gibbons vs. *Ogden*
Marbury vs. *Madison*
Martin vs. *Hunter's
  Lessee*

McCulloch vs.
  Maryland
Monroe Doctrine
Rush-Bagot
  agreement
Second Bank
  of the United States
West Florida

FOR EXPLANATION OR DEFINITION

American system
bonus bill
internal
  improvements
judicial review

"necessary and
  proper" clause
protective tariff
state-chartered banks
"Virginia dynasty"

FOR REVIEW

1. What Federalist principles were adopted by the Republicans after the War of 1812?

2. (a) Why was the charter of the first Bank of the United States allowed to expire? (b) What was the effect on the currency? On business? (c) When and for how long was the second Bank of the United States chartered?

3. What is a protective tariff? What groups favored and which ones opposed the Tariff of 1816? What was the attitude of Henry Clay to the Tariff of 1816?

4. (a) What was Calhoun's argument for a national program of internal improvements? (b) Why did President Madison veto Calhoun's bill? (c) Why was the Constitution not amended to authorize Congress to make internal improvements?

5. (a) What was meant by the term "era of good feeling"? (b) How did Monroe's re-election in 1820 show the absence of partisanship?

6. How did our relations with Great Britain improve while John Quincy Adams was Secretary of State? What were the terms of the Rush-Bagot agreement?

7. What claims did the United States have to West Florida? How did Andrew Jackson's actions in Florida tend to hasten a settlement of the Florida question?

8. How and when did the United States acquire Florida? What boundary disputes were settled by the Florida purchase treaty?

9. (a) What conditions led to the writing of the Monroe Doctrine? How was it issued? (b) Outline the main points of the Monroe Doctrine. (c) What made the success of the Monroe Doctrine possible?

10. (a) Why is the chief-justiceship of John Marshall (1801–1835) of great importance in American history? (b) Why did Jefferson try to lessen Marshall's influence? (c) How did Marshall's decisions affect the powers of the Supreme Court? Those of the national government? Those of the state governments?

11. State the significance of the decisions of the Supreme Court in each of the following: *Marbury* vs. *Madison, Fletcher* vs. *Peck, Martin* vs. *Hunter's Lessee, Dartmouth* vs. *Woodward, McCulloch* vs. *Maryland,* and *Gibbons* vs. *Ogden.*

FOR FURTHER STUDY AND DISCUSSION

1. Compare the second Bank of the United States, 1816–36, with the first Bank of the United States, 1791–1811.

2. Outline the reasoning by which Marshall established the principle of judicial review in the case of *Marbury* vs. *Madison.* Do you agree or disagree with the statement that the logic of Marshall's argument in this case is flawless?

3. (a) Should internal improvements be undertaken at the expense of the federal government, or should the states and local governments finance them? Helpful sources: Hart, *Contemporaries,* Vol. III, No. 131; Commager, *Documents,* Nos. 116, 125. (b) How did the discussion of this question in 1816–17 involve theories of the nature of the federal government? (c) Are there any evidences that the question of internal improvements is a matter of controversy in the twentieth century?

4. Why is *McCulloch* vs. *Maryland* considered to be one of the most important judicial decisions in our history?

5. How did the decision in *Gibbons* vs. *Ogden* tend to increase the power of the national government?

FOR INDIVIDUAL OR GROUP ACTIVITIES

1. Report on the part played by Adams, Clay, Jefferson, Monroe, and others in the formulation of the Monroe Doctrine.

2. Investigate and report on the activities of Andrew Jackson in Florida. Should Jackson have been reprimanded? How did the question of Jackson's censure influence later political developments? Helpful sources: Bailey, *Diplomatic History,* pp. 168–172; James, *Andrew Jackson: The Border Captain.*

3. Prepare brief biographical reports on each of the following: Simón Bolívar, José de San Martín. Helpful source: Whitridge, *Simón Bolívar, the Great Liberator.*

4. Write a brief radio newscast of President Monroe's tour of New England. Helpful source: Dangerfield, *The Era of Good Feelings.*

The United States Branch Bank at 15 Wall Street. THIS ORIGINAL FAÇADE, *built in 1822–24, was moved uptown and is now the façade of the American wing of the Metropolitan Museum of Art.*

HIGH POINTS

1

In the period from 1789 to 1824, the federal government outlined in the Constitution became a going concern. Many basic policies were worked out for the conduct of domestic and foreign affairs.

2

Two political parties soon developed. The Federalists, led by Alexander Hamilton, stood for government by the upper class, that is, by men who, because of wealth or profession, were leaders in their community. The Republicans (or Jeffersonian Democrats), led by Thomas Jefferson, stood for states' rights and government by the people. The Federalist party lost many of its supporters when it adopted Alien and Sedition Acts to curb freedom of speech and of the press. By 1816 this party had practically ceased to exist.

3

The election of 1800, in which the Republicans came to power, was called a revolution by the incoming President, Thomas Jefferson. The party of the farmers and planters had taken control from the party of the merchants and manufacturers. The Republicans gave more attention than the Federalists to the needs of settlers west of the Appalachians.

4

The nation's territory was more than doubled by purchase of Louisiana (1803) and purchase of Florida (1819).

5

The futile and indecisive War of 1812 settled nothing, although it gave us a national anthem and a number of new national heroes. Nevertheless, it marked a turning point in our relations with Great Britain. Despite ill feelings left by the armed struggle, machinery was created for the peaceable settlement of disputes between the two nations. The Rush-Bagot Treaty of 1817, which provided for disarmament on the Great Lakes, led to a new era in our relations with Canada.

6

The young nation had been too weak to obtain the respect of foreign governments. Until 1815 our chief problems had to do with foreign affairs. The disregard of our neutral rights by European belligerents stopped only when the Napoleonic wars ended. After that the United States was able to adopt a policy of isolation from Europe.

7

A new sense of national unity was evident in Madison's second term. It was seen in a general willingness to strengthen the nation's defenses, to establish the second Bank of the United States, and to adopt a protective tariff. This feeling of unity continued to gain strength under President Monroe and his able Secretary of State, John Quincy Adams.

8

Partly because of the example of the United States, the desire for self-government was growing among oppressed peoples in Europe and in Latin America. Americans sympathized with their struggles and some gave tangible aid. In the period 1810–23 republics were established in most parts of Latin America. Our desire to protect the independence of these sister republics was expressed in the Monroe Doctrine.

9

The Monroe Doctrine (1823) stated that we would not interfere in European

affairs and warned European powers that they must not establish any new colonies in the Western Hemisphere or interfere with the existing governments there. Monroe spoke for a nation of ten million people which was becoming conscious of its strength.

10

Under Chief Justice John Marshall, a staunch Federalist, the Supreme Court assumed the right to pass on the constitutionality of the acts of Congress and of the executive, the acts of state legislatures, and the decisions of state courts. The judiciary thus became the most powerful of the three branches of the federal government.

11

In interpreting the Constitution, the Supreme Court adopted the doctrine of implied powers, or loose construction. This greatly strengthened the federal government at the expense of the states.

QUESTIONS

1. (a) Why did political parties develop? (b) Who were the leaders of the first political parties? (c) How did the Federalists differ from the Republicans? (d) What did the Federalists accomplish during their twelve years in power, 1789–1801?

2. (a) Account for the fact that foreign affairs were extremely important in the first thirty years of our history. (b) State the background and significance of each of the following: The Jay Treaty; the undeclared naval war with France; the Louisiana Purchase; the War of 1812; the Rush-Bagot agreement; the Florida Purchase; the Monroe Doctrine.

3. Compare the services and accomplishments of Jefferson and Hamilton. Show that the differences between Hamilton and Jefferson on specific issues reflected a fundamental difference in political philosophy.

4. Indicate how the Republicans in power pursued policies that they criticized when not in power.

5. What constitutional questions were involved in the following: The chartering of the first Bank of the United States; the "Whiskey Rebellion"; the Virginia and Kentucky resolutions; the purchase of Louisiana; Calhoun's "bonus bill" for internal improvements.

6. (a) How did the presidential elections of 1796 and 1800 lead to a demand for an amendment to the Constitution? (b) State the provisions of the Twelfth Amendment.

7. Explain the gradual disappearance of the Federalist party.

8. Formulate the doctrine of implied powers or loose construction.

9. What were some important social and economic changes between 1789 and 1825?

10. Explain how each of the following promoted nationalism: The Louisiana Purchase, the War of 1812, Clay's "American system," Marshall's decisions, and the Monroe Doctrine.

11. (a) Of the five Presidents during the period under review (Washington, John Adams, Jefferson, Madison, and Monroe) why are Washington and Jefferson regarded as outstanding? (b) Describe the character and services of the other three. (Read the interesting essay "A Yardstick for Presidents" in Schlesinger, *Paths to the Present*.)

12. How did the growing West influence issues and policies in the period 1789–1825?

13. "Eighteen hundred and fifteen is a turning point in American as in European history; and a point of divergence between them. Up to that time the development of the United States had been vitally affected by European forces . . . with the peace of Ghent, America turned her back on the Atlantic. Every serious difficulty under which the young republic had labored since the War of Independence dropped out of sight." Outline the major points you would develop in an essay to support this quotation.

14. (a) Under what circumstances did the United States obtain possession of Florida? (b) What problems were solved and created by the purchase of Florida, 1819?

15. (a) What is the historical background of the Monroe Doctrine? (b) What part did John Quincy Adams play in its formulation? (c) State the essential principles of the Doctrine. (d) What were the effects of the Monroe Doctrine at the time? On subsequent American foreign policy? (e) In what way is the Monroe Doctrine an expression of nationalism?

16. (a) How did John Marshall, as Chief Justice of the Supreme Court, contribute to the development of nationalism? (b) What is meant by the doctrine of judicial review? (c) Explain the significance of the decisions of the Supreme Court in *Marbury* vs. *Madison*, *McCulloch* vs. *Maryland*, *Fletcher* vs. *Peck*, *Martin* vs. *Hunter's Lessee*, *Gibbons* vs. *Ogden*.

SUGGESTED READINGS

SOURCE MATERIALS, DOCUMENTS,

AND MAPS

Amherst Series: *Hamilton and the National Debt.*

Botkin, B. A. *A Treasury of American Folklore.* Crown, 1944.

Commager, *Documents*, Nos. 90–120.

Commager and Nevins, *The Heritage of America.*

Lord, *Historical Atlas.*

Nevins and Weitenkampf, *Political Cartoons.*

GENERAL REFERENCES

Bailey, *Diplomatic History.*

Basset, John S. *The Federalist System, 1789–1801.* Harper, 1906. (A.N.S.)

Beard, *American Civilization*, Vol. I.

Beirne, Francis F. *The War of 1812.* Dutton, 1949.

Bowers, Claude G. *Jefferson and Hamilton; The Struggle for Democracy in America.* Houghton, 1925.

Channing, Edward A. *The Jeffersonian System, 1801–1811.* Harper, 1906. (A.N.S.)

° Corwin, Edward S. *John Marshall and the Constitution.* Yale University Press, 1921. (Y.C.S.)

Dangerfield, George. *The Era of Good Feelings.* Harcourt, Brace, 1952.

° Davis, Julia. *No Other White Men.* Murray, 1940. (The Lewis and Clark expedition)

Faulkner, *Economic History.*

Ford, Henry J. *Washington and His Colleagues.* Yale University Press, 1918. (Y.C.S.)

° Forester, C. S. *The Barbary Pirates.* Random House, 1953.

————. *The Age of Fighting Sail.* Doubleday, 1956.

Hicks, John D. *The Federal Union.* Houghton, 1952.

Johnson, Allen. *Jefferson and His Colleagues.* Yale University Press, 1921.

Krout, J. A., and Fox, D. R. *The Completion of Independence, 1790–1830.* Macmillan, 1944. (A.L.S.)

Morison and Commager, *American Republic*, Vol. I.

° Neuberger, Richard L. *The Lewis and Clark Expedition.* Random House, 1951.

Perkins, Dexter. *Hands Off; A History of the Monroe Doctrine.* Little, Brown, 1941.

Pratt, Fletcher. *The Heroic Years: Fourteen Years of the Republic, 1801–1815.* Random House, 1934.

° Tallant, Robert. *The Pirate Lafitte and the Battle of New Orleans.* Random House, 1951.

BIOGRAPHY

Adams, James Truslow. *The Living Jefferson*. Scribner, 1936.

Bakeless, John. *Lewis and Clark, Partners in Discovery*. Morrow, 1947.

Briggs, Berta N. *Charles William Peale, Artist and Patriot*. McGraw-Hill, 1952.

° Brown, John Mason. *Daniel Boone*. Random House, 1952.

° Mayer, Jane. *Dolly Madison*. Random House, 1954.

° Moses, Belle. *John Marshall*. Appleton-Century, 1938.

° Nicolay, Helen. *The Boy's Life of Alexander Hamilton*. Century, 1927.

° ———. *The Boy's Life of Thomas Jefferson*. Appleton-Century, 1933.

Padover, S. K. *Jefferson*. Harcourt, Brace, 1942.

Schachner, Nathan. *Aaron Burr, a Biography*. Stokes, 1937.

———. *Alexander Hamilton*. McGraw-Hill, 1952.

° Seymour, Flora. *Meriwether Lewis, Trail Blazer*. Appleton-Century, 1937.

° Van Loon, H. W. *Thomas Jefferson*. Dodd, Mead, 1943.

Whitney, Janet. *Abigail Adams*. Little, Brown, 1947.

° Whitridge, Arnold. *Simón Bolívar*. Random House, 1954.

FICTION

Atherton, Gertrude. *The Conqueror*. Lippincott, 1943. (Alexander Hamilton)

———. *Rezanov*. Modern Library, 1919. (Russian colony in California)

Bacheller, Irving. *D'ri and I*. Grosset and Dunlap, 1935. (Impressment and the War of 1812)

Churchill, Winston. *The Crossing*. Grosset & Dunlap, 1904. (Clark's campaign and the Louisiana Purchase)

° Finger, Charles J. *When Guns Thundered at Tripoli*. Holt, 1937. (Tripolitan War)

° Forester, C. S. *Captain from Connecticut*. Little, Brown, 1941. (War of 1812)

° Hale, Edward Everett. *The Man without a Country*. Little, Brown, 1906. (The famous story of a man who renounces his country)

° Hawthorne, Hildegarde. *Westward the Course*. Longmans, 1946. (Lewis and Clark)

Kingsley, Sidney. *The Patriots*. Random House, 1943. (A play involving Washington, Hamilton, Jefferson, and others)

Kummer, Frederic A. *Torch of Liberty*. Winston, 1941. (Alien and Sedition Acts)

° Marshall, B. G. *Old Hickory's Prisoner*. Appleton, 1925. (War of 1812)

° Meader, S. W. *Who Rides in the Dark?* Harcourt, Brace, 1937. (Stagecoach days)

° Meigs, Cornelia L. *As the Crow Flies*. Macmillan, 1943. (Louisiana Purchase)

Page, Elizabeth. *The Tree of Liberty*. Farrar, Straus, 1939. (The growth of the United States; Jefferson and others)

Pidgin, C. F. *Blennerhassett*. Clark, 1902. (Burr's attempt to win an empire)

° Roberts, Kenneth. *Captain Caution*. Collins, 1953. (War of 1812)

° ———. *Lively Lady*. Doubleday, 1931. (The capture of an American privateer by the British)

———. *Lydia Bailey*. Doubleday, 1947. (War with Tripoli)

° Seawell, Molly E. *Decatur and Somers*. Appleton, 1908. (Tripolitan War)

° Shepard, Odell. *Holdfast Gaines*. Macmillan, 1954. (Tecumseh, Jackson, Lafitte)

° Sperry, Armstrong. *All Sails Set*. Lane, 1946. (Maritime history of New England in the early nineteenth century)

° Stackpole, E. A. *Privateers Ahoy!* Morrow, 1937. (War of 1812)

Silver coffee urn designed by Thomas Jefferson

TIME LINE

1790	1790	Slater brings factory system to America
	1793	Whitney's cotton gin
1800		
	1807	Fulton's steamboat *Clermont*
	1818	National Road completed
1820	1820	Missouri Compromise
	1821	First public high school
	1825	Erie Canal completed
	1828	Tariff of Abominations: Railroad construction begins
	1829	Jackson inaugurated
	1830	Webster-Hayne debate
	1831	*Liberator* started; McCormick reaper invented
	1832	South Carolina ordinance of nullification
	1833	Compromise tariff
	1837	Van Buren inaugurated; Mann starts educational reforms
1840	1841	Harrison inaugurated; Tyler, first Vice-President to succeed to the presidency
	1842	Webster-Ashburton treaty
	1844	Morse perfects telegraph; Goodyear vulcanizes rubber
	1845	Polk inaugurated
	1846	Mexican War begins; Oregon boundary settled; Howe's sewing machine; Hoe's cylinder press
	1848	Mexican War ended; women's rights convention

UNIT FOUR   *Democracy Makes Important Gains*

★ ★ ★ ★ The willingness to put the welfare of the nation before that of any state or section—that is, the spirit of nationalism—flourished for a few years after the War of 1812. Then the spirit of sectionalism gradually came to the fore. Sectional interests began to seem more important than national interests. Sectionalism was shown in bitter quarrels in Congress over the tariff, the Bank of the United States, internal improvements, and the extension of slavery. By 1850 the sharpest difference between the sections had to do with slavery. This unit deals with events in the quarter of a century preceding 1850, when the forces of sectionalism and nationalism were about equally balanced.

During this period the West, because of its growing population, gained more influence in Washington. By 1828 the West was able to send one of its own sons, General Andrew Jackson, to the White House. From that time on the section was to have an increasing voice in national affairs. In fact, political leaders in both the North and the South began to seek the support of the West.

The period from 1825 to 1850 was remarkable not only for sectional wrangling but for the advance of the Industrial Revolution. These years saw more economic and social changes than any previous quarter of a century. Manufacturing and commerce grew. Steamboats and locomotives came into use. Farm machinery was introduced. A shift from subsistence farming to commercial farming got under way. Immigrants came here in ever-growing numbers. Towns grew into cities.

In the same years a literary awakening took place. American writers created poetry, essays, fiction, and history of real stature. Some of these works were praised by European critics, who saw that American culture could no longer be ignored.

The period is also known for the spread of democratic ideas and for reforms which benefited the common people. The reform movement was based on the belief that all human beings should have equal opportunity to develop their capacities. The spread of public schools was one of the principal achievements of the period. For the first time schools were within the reach of most of the nation's boys and girls.

237

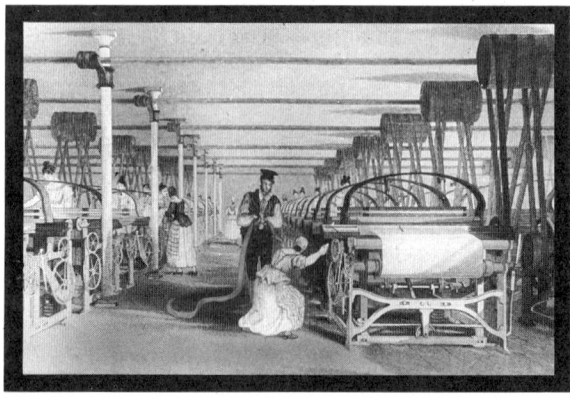

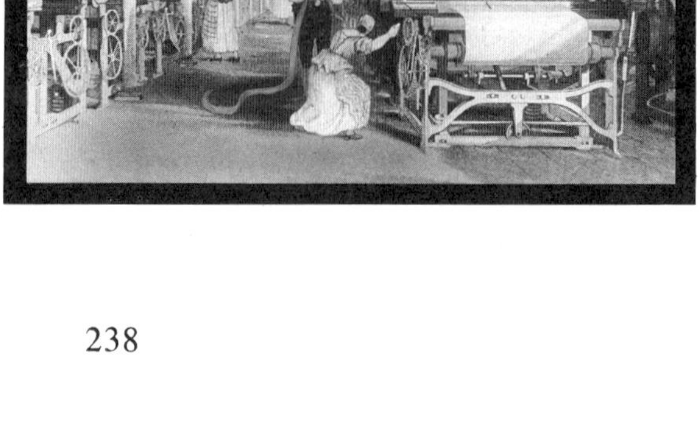

(Above) ELI WHITNEY GUN FACTORY, about 1826. From a painting by William Giles Munsen.

(Left) Weaving room in SLATER'S FACTORY. This room was equipped with Cartwright machinery. Here, in 1793, was the first factory for making cotton cloth in the United States.

Nature says to every individual man, your rights are all
held by the tenure of reverence for the same rights in
all other men.——John Quincy Adams

16♦ THE SPIRIT OF SECTIONALISM BECOMES STRONG AGAIN

outline

Economic Differences Add to Sectional Rivalries

The "Era of Good Feeling" did not last long. Sectional rivalries developed which made political harmony impossible. By the middle of the 1820's the three sections—the Northeast, the South, and the West—were struggling against one another for control of the national government. Each was conscious of its own economic interests and wanted to advance them even at the expense of other sections.

The current of nationalism, so pronounced just after the war, was soon checked by the countercurrent of a narrow sectionalism. Sectionalism grew because each section was developing a different type of economy (see map p. 243). Factories were multiplying in the Northeast. Cotton plantations were spreading over the South and the South itself was expanding westward. The old Northwest was rapidly filling up with small farms cultivated by their owners. The resulting clash of interests and ideals led eventually to civil war.

Interests of the Northeast Shift to Manufacturing

The Industrial Revolution begins.

The change from making goods by hand to making goods by machine and from production in the home to production in the factory is known as the *Industrial Revolution*. This change began in England in the middle 1700's with the invention of machines for spinning and weaving and with the development of a workable steam engine. By 1775 England's Industrial Revolution was well under way. Soon English textile manufacturers captured most of the world market for woolen goods.

To hold this market England tried to keep the new manufacturing methods from spreading to other countries. Parliament banned the export of machines or plans and models of machines. Workmen familiar with the machines were forbidden to leave England.

Several English mechanics managed to come to America and set up from memory the spinning jenny and the power loom. The most famous of these immigrants was Samuel Slater, who is called the "father of the American factory system." In 1790 Slater built a mill in Rhode Island for manufacturing cotton thread. Other spinning mills were soon started, and by 1812 there were almost three hundred.

The first power loom in the United States was built by Francis Lowell in 1814. That same year Lowell started a cotton factory at Waltham, Massachusetts. It was the first factory in the

239

world where spinning and weaving were done under the same roof. Similar factories were erected at several places on the Merrimack River and on scores of smaller streams in New England and eastern New York. Cotton cloth now came into everyday use.

Before long many other products were being made in factories, using machines turned by water power or by steam power. But the coming of the factory did not stop manufacture at home or in small shops using hand methods. Farm families continued to make many of the things they needed. On the plantations the slaves were kept busy during the winter in spinning, weaving, making their own clothes, and producing articles for plantation use. As late as 1850 a great deal of manufacturing was still carried on by hand methods throughout the country.

Eli Whitney devises the system of interchangeable parts.

Although the American Industrial Revolution started with English inventions, it was carried forward by American inventions. Probably no invention was more important than the system of interchangeable parts. This system was worked out by Eli Whitney, owner of a gun shop near New Haven. In those days the parts for each gun were made one at a time and then carefully assembled by a craftsman, who worked on the parts until they would fit together. A part taken from one gun might not fit any other gun. Whitney decided to use machine tools to stamp or shape identical parts. He obtained a government contract in 1798 to produce 10,000 rifles in two years, an unheard-of number. He produced the rifles by making 10,000 identical barrels, 10,000 identical triggers, and so on. Since the parts were made to precise measurements, they required no hand finishing to make them fit together. Hence they could be assembled

rapidly. Furthermore, a gun could be easily repaired by using spare parts.

The system of interchangeable parts greatly reduced the cost of various other articles made of a number of parts, such as clocks.

The Northeast develops manufacturing.

The factory system grew much faster in the Northeast than in other sections. Perhaps the most important reason for this was the fact that Northerners had more money to invest in factories—money they had made in commerce, shipbuilding, and banking. Moreover, Northern investors had business experience. The Northeast had still other advantages for manufacturing. A cheap source of power was at hand in the streams and waterfalls of New England and in the coal fields of Pennsylvania. The necessary raw materials were either produced locally or were readily brought in by water. A good labor supply, consisting of surplus farm youth and of immigrants from Europe, was available. In New England particularly, the land could not support the growing families, and factory employment was welcomed.

The Industrial Revolution produces great changes.

The rise of the factory system in the United States had far-reaching effects. Among these were the following:

1. Existing cities in the Northeast grew rapidly. New cities, like Lawrence, Lowell, and Fall River, appeared on water-power sites.

2. Two new social classes appeared—the industrialists who owned the factories and the laborers who worked in them.

3. Factory workers suffered from low wages, long hours, and unhealthy living and working conditions. Slums multiplied as these people crowded into cheap tenements close to their places of work.

4. The growth of cities brought an increased market for farm products.

5. Better transportation facilities, including canals, railroads, and steamboats, were built to supply the cities with food and raw materials.

6. The industrialists made great profits from manufacturing. They used part of the money to expand their businesses. Much of the money went into bank deposits in Eastern cities.

7. Eastern bankers lent money in all parts of the country. In the words of a Western congressman, "All the flourishing cities of the West are mortgaged to this money power."

8. What is known as the business cycle appeared. This term refers to the alternation of periods of prosperity and depression; that is, after a period of prosperity comes a period of depression, then recovery, then prosperity, depression, and so on.

9. Manufactured goods became cheaper and more abundant.

The Northeast makes demands in Congress.

Commercial interests—merchants, importers, shipowners, shipbuilders—had long been the most important group in the Northeast. They tried to encourage trade with foreign countries. For many years Daniel Webster was their spokesman in Congress. In 1816, therefore, he protested strongly against the adoption of a protective tariff, since it was likely to discourage trade. Again in 1824, when a new tariff bill was being considered, he spoke against any increase in duties. By 1828, however, Webster believed that manufacturing had become more important to his section than commerce. Therefore he voted in favor of a high protective tariff. His action was a sign that the commercial interests of the North would soon lose their control. From then on Congress paid increasing attention to manufacturers.

Factory owners believed that laws which helped manufacturing would help the whole nation. They asked for a high protective tariff to keep out manufactured goods made abroad. They wanted sound money and a national bank. They wanted to encourage immigration in order to increase the labor supply.

At first the factory owners tried to discourage the westward movement because it took laborers away from manufacturing districts. They did not favor free homesteads for Western settlers or any other plans for helping the poor man get a farm in the West. As time passed they changed their minds about these matters, for they saw that the West would furnish a market for manufactured products. They began to back up Westerners in their demand for better means of transportation. Much later they supported the proposal for giving settlers free land in the West.

Cotton and Slavery Determine the Interests of the South

A huge demand for cotton develops.

As we have noted, the use of power-driven textile machinery reduced the price of cotton cloth. Now more and more people in all parts of the world could afford to buy it. To supply the increased demand the textile mills bought all the raw cotton they could find. This drove up the price of cotton.

Whitney invents the cotton gin.

Despite the higher prices cotton production in the United States did not rise much at first. Unfortunately the sea-island, or long-staple, variety of cotton, which was easy to get ready for market, could be grown only in the hot, damp regions along the coast. The variety which could be grown almost everywhere in the South—the upland variety—had short fibers which clung to the seed. So much labor was required to separate the fiber from the seed that production of this kind of cotton did not pay. Eli Whitney was in Georgia for a short time in 1793 and became interested in the problem. After a few weeks of experimenting he invented a cotton gin that would clean upland cotton and greatly speed production. With a gin operated by hand a man could produce 50 pounds of fiber a day; without it, he could produce but a single pound. When the gin was turned by water power or steam, one man's daily output might be as much as 1000 pounds.

Cotton production expands tremendously.

The use of the cotton gin made upland cotton a profitable crop. By 1800 cotton production in the United States was 40 million pounds a year. This was twenty times as much as it had been only ten years earlier. Nearly all this cotton was grown in the Carolinas and Georgia.

Later, as the soil became exhausted, the cotton planters moved to newly cleared land farther west. By 1840, about one third of the cotton came from states west of the Alleghenies. At that time the annual production of cotton had reached 175 million pounds. From then on production doubled or tripled in every decade. Most of the increase came from the Gulf states and Arkansas.

Cotton changes the Southern attitude toward slavery.

During the revolutionary period many Americans in both the North and the South had opposed slavery. The states north of Delaware abolished slavery early, freeing the slaves within their borders either all at once or gradually (see p. 130). Antislavery sentiment was also strong in Delaware, Maryland, and Virginia. In 1787 Southern congressmen were among those who voted for the Northwest Ordinance, which banned slavery north of the Ohio.

At this time slave labor was not profitable except in the rice fields of South Carolina and Georgia. By 1798 even these states forbade the importation of slaves. Some Southerners freed their slaves. Many Southerners favored laws for gradual emancipation.

Hope for the emancipation of slaves in the South faded out a few years later, however, with the enormous expansion of cotton growing. In fact, as cotton growing expanded, so did the demand for slaves. Raising the crop required a large amount of hand labor, and the need for labor was spread over a large part of the year. Most of the work could be done by women and children as well as by men. Moreover, the work could be done in gangs. Thus slaves could be used profitably in raising cotton. It was, in fact, an ideal plantation crop.

As early as 1803 South Carolina repealed its laws against the slave trade. Most Southerners came to regard slavery as necessary to their prosperity. Instead of apologizing for the slave system they argued that it was a good thing for both whites and Negroes. In time they refused to listen to anyone with a different opinion of their "peculiar institution."

The South has other crops too.

By the 1830's cotton and sugar cane were the two leading Southern crops. Sugar cane thrived in Louisiana. Tobacco was the leading cash crop in Virginia, North Carolina, Kentucky, and Tennessee. Rice was important in a few coastal areas. In addition to a cash crop nearly every farmer raised some crops for home use. The South, however, did not grow all its own food. Many planters preferred to use as much of their land as possible for a cash crop and to buy staples like corn and bacon.

242

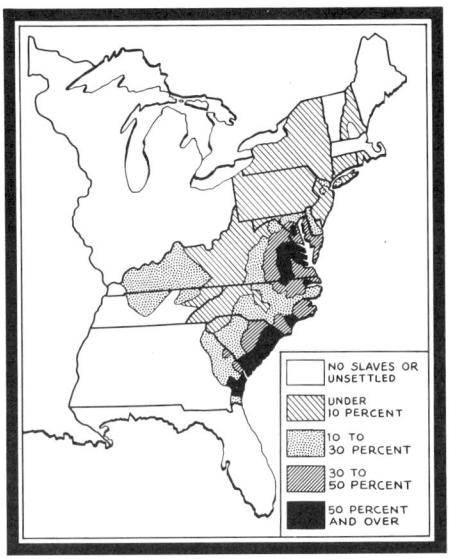

PROPORTION OF SLAVES
TO POPULATION, 1790

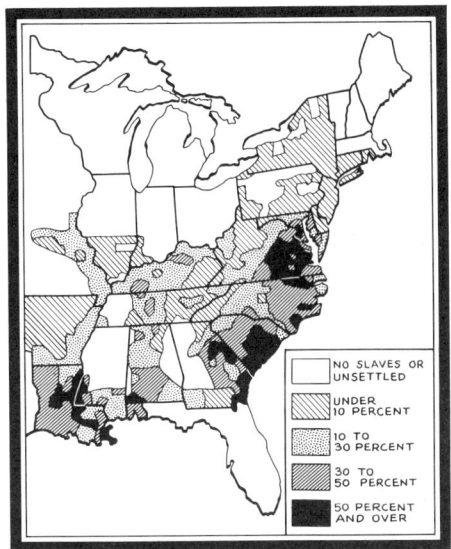

PROPORTION OF SLAVES
TO POPULATION, 1820

Much flour, corn, and cured meat came in from the Northwest.

Class distinctions are well marked.

Southern society was divided into distinct classes. At the top of the pyramid were a few thousand great planters. They owned from fifty to several hundred slaves each, and employed white overseers to supervise them. Most of the great planters were active in public affairs. As a group they dominated the political, social, and economic life of the South. Many of them served in Congress.

Next to the great planters came a larger group, the middle and small planters, who owned from ten to fifty slaves. They had less leisure than the great planters, for they gave personal attention to managing their estates and to training and supervising their slaves.

Most of the white people in the South were small farmers. They occupied the less desirable land, farther from the rivers and less fertile than the land cultivated by the planters.

Some of them owned a few slaves, but the great majority had none. Some did not even own land but rented it. These farmers grew a variety of crops and livestock, mainly for their own use. Because it was difficult for them to get their products to market, as a rule they had very little money. The lowest group among them were referred to as "poor white trash." They scratched a bare living from worn-out land and were looked on as shiftless and "no account." Yet today we know that these people were victims not only of worthless soil but of malaria, hookworm, and malnutrition.

On the same level with the small farmers were the poor and middle-class whites of the towns and cities. The South had few large towns, since it lived by farming rather than commerce or industry. However, Baltimore and New Orleans ranked among the nation's five leading cities.

At the bottom of the social pyramid were the slaves and a much smaller number of free Negroes. The economic

243

lot of a free Negro was often no better than that of a slave.

The South makes demands in Congress.

Like the Northeast and the West, the South wished Congress to advance its own particular interests. To understand the struggle which developed between North and South we should keep in mind the following points:

1. Southerners, except a few who owned factories, opposed a protective tariff, since it increased the price of manufactured goods. So long as the South depended on Europe and the Northeast for manufactures, it wished to buy them at low cost. Furthermore, the South sold most of its cotton and tobacco abroad and believed that the tariff hurt its foreign markets.

2. The South lacked capital and was heavily in debt to Northern bankers. It disapproved of the second Bank of the United States, preferring to do business with banks under its own control.

3. Southerners generally were against federal aid for building roads and canals. The planters relied on rivers for transportation and did not care to be taxed for internal improvements.

4. Southerners were eager to see the territory of the United States expand, but they wanted land suited for plantations. Texas and California looked far more desirable to them than Oregon.

5. The planters were against proposals for giving land to Western settlers, for this would hasten the settlement of areas unsuited to slavery. When such areas were admitted to the Union, they would come in as free states, and the slave states might be outnumbered in Congress.

6. Fear of being outvoted in Congress led the South to advocate states' rights and a strict construction of the Constitution.

The West Steadily Gains Population and Influence

The Old West fills up rapidly.

The term "Old West" is sometimes used in speaking of the area between the Appalachians and the Mississippi. In 1800 only one in twenty Americans lived in this region. Only two states west of the Appalachians had then been admitted to the Union—Kentucky (1792) and Tennessee (1796). In 1820 one in every four Americans lived west of the mountains. By then six more states had joined the Union. So many people moved west that by 1850 half of the nation's population lived west of the Appalachians. By that time, too, a small number had settled west of the Mississippi.

Where the settlers came from.

The great bulk of the Western settlers were native-born Americans. Some

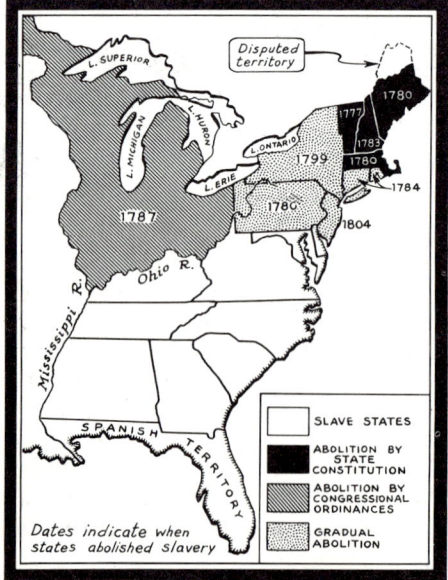

PROGRESS OF ABOLITION, 1800

had been poor wage earners and day laborers back East, but most were farmers who went west in search of richer land. Many left the thin and rocky soils of New England. Others left the worn-out soil of Virginia, the Carolinas, and Georgia.

THE SUSQUEHANNA RIVER *at Northumberland. Both river and canal formed part of Pennsylvania's great transportation system.*

Our dwellings, our schoolhouses, and churches will have mouldered to ruins, our graveyards will be overrun with shrub oak; and [there will be left] but here and there a wretched hermit, true to his paternal soil, to tell the tale of other times.

How settlers went west.

Most of the Western settlers had followed river valleys across the Appalachians. With the completion of the Erie Canal in 1825 this became the principal route.

In 1818 the National Road was completed from Cumberland on the

Easterners complain of the westward movement.

When conservative Easterners realized that a great many industrious heads of families were going west, they complained of "plots to drain the East of its best blood." Pamphlets were distributed far and wide describing the hardships of frontier life and advising people not to go west. But nothing could stop the westward movement so long as there was good, cheap land to be had at the end of the journey.

Whole communities were emptied of people. This caused one New Englander to lament:

Potomac to Wheeling on the Ohio. The road was carefully graded and had a surface of crushed stone and gravel. There were then few improved roads, and most of these were toll roads. The National, or Cumberland, Road was free to all. In the next twenty years the road was extended nearly to St. Louis. It was soon crowded with settlers going west. When they reached the Ohio or some other river flowing westward, they either paid for passage down the river or built a boat (usually a flatboat or a raft) to carry the party and their belongings.

Many settlers traveled westward in a canvas-covered Conestoga wagon, drawn by four or six oxen or horses. In it the travelers stowed their provisions, clothing, blankets, kettles, tools, seeds, medicines, and everything that they expected to need and for which they could find room. The women and young children rode in the wagon. The men and boys walked beside it, often driving a cow and a few sheep.

Other travelers could not afford such a large wagon. Instead they used a cart drawn by two horses or oxen, or even one. Some had only a pack horse. Others went on foot, their few belongings in a wheelbarrow, in a handcart, or in a pack on their backs.

At night the travelers usually camped by the roadside. The more prosperous slept in taverns when possible. Here the traveler might have to share a bed with two or three strangers or even sleep on the floor. The journey at best was long and hard. Bad weather, an accident to the horses or to members of the party, illness, or hostile Indians might make it a nightmare. As a rule several families traveled together for safety's sake and for companionship.

How settlers got their land.

At first the government sold its Western lands only in large tracts to land companies and wealthy individuals. These purchasers resold the land in small parcels, usually at a price much higher than they had paid for it. In 1796 Congress authorized the government to sell its lands in tracts of 640 acres (one square mile) at $2.00 an acre. Few settlers could raise the money for a tract of this size. In 1800, therefore, Congress provided for the sale of tracts of 320 acres, with four years to pay. Even these terms could not be met by the average person, and the demand for a more liberal policy continued. It came mainly from Easterners who hoped to settle in the West. In 1820 Congress passed an act permitting the sale of parcels of 80 acres at $1.25 an acre. Many settlers could now afford to buy land directly from the government, and the westward movement grew.

"BEDDING DOWN FOR THE NIGHT," *from a painting by Benjamin F. Reinhart*

Squatters receive pre-emption rights.

Some frontiersmen saw no reason why they should pay either a land company or the government for the land they needed. Others were too poor to pay for land. Thus many a man became a "squatter"; that is, he simply marked off a few acres in the wilderness, built a cabin, and cleared some land for crops. Unfortunately sooner or later the government or other owner of the land would sell it. Then the squatter would have to move on.

Many a squatter considered that he had a better right to his clearing than anyone else. Had he not spent endless labor on it while in constant danger from the Indians? Squatters often fought those who tried to remove them from their homes. To check such disorder when a new area was opened for sale, Congress sometimes gave *pre-emption* rights to the settlers already there. This meant that the squatter had the first chance of buying his holding and that he could buy it for the minimum price of $1.25 an acre. In 1830 Congress provided that pre-emption rights should be given every time that government lands were placed on sale.

Westerners have trouble obtaining money and credit.

Money was always very scarce in newly settled areas. Because it was so difficult to get their products to market the settlers lacked a cash income. Thus they had to live on what they could produce themselves. To buy land or machinery or livestock, they needed credit. Yet credit was hard to obtain and a high rate of interest was charged for all loans.

One of the hardest problems settlers faced was getting enough cash to pay interest and installments on their debts. Nearly all settlers were in debt for their land, either to the government or to private sellers. Of those who bought land from the government on time payments, very few were able to make their payments when due. To avoid further trouble, Congress in 1820 decided to do away with selling land on credit. But private owners continued to sell land on credit. When the settler could not pay the interest or installments, he lost his farm.

New areas pass through three stages.

The first comers to the wilderness were pioneers. Many of them were single men. The typical pioneer lived mainly by hunting and trapping. He was a squatter and often did not expect to stay long in one place. He was satisfied with a small cabin or even a lean-to. He usually had a garden patch and a pig or two. Such men blazed the trails and held back the Indians.

The second stage in the settlement of a new area began when farmers moved in with their families. Instead of a cabin, they built a log house with glass windows, a good chimney, and two or three rooms. Instead of using a spring, they dug a well. They bought land and cleared one field after another. They and their neighbors made roads, put up rough bridges over the streams, and organized local government. They might hire a teacher and open a school. Traveling preachers came now and then to hold church services for them.

As the region grew more thickly settled and land values rose, a third stage began. Most of the earlier settlers sold out one by one and moved west to newer and cheaper lands. Their places were taken by a more prosperous type of farmer, willing to pay for cleared land. These farmers built larger barns, then better houses of bricks or boards. They farmed more skillfully, as they had to do if they were to make money from high-priced land. Meanwhile, storekeepers, mechanics, and professional men began to move in. The crossroads hamlets developed into villages. Before long, some of them became cities.

The frontier influences American ideas.

The frontier has had a great influence upon American ideas and customs. Here are some of the attitudes of the frontiersman which are still commonly held by Americans:

1. Equality. On the frontier all men were independent; no man had to work for somebody else. All were considered equal if they could swing an ax, plow a field, or shoot Indians. A man's ancestry or nationality was of little importance. What mattered was his own ability and character.

2. Optimism. The frontier, with its unused soil and untouched mineral resources, was a land of opportunity. The poorest man might get ahead. Westerners were filled with hope for the future and confident that their children would be better off than their parents.

3. Rugged individualism. Because they believed that if they worked hard they would succeed, the Western settlers were ambitious and energetic. They were impatient of anything that might limit a man's chances to make money; they wanted freedom from government regulation. This is the idea of "rugged individualism."

4. Democracy. The frontiersman hated aristocracy and special privilege. He believed in the rule of the people. As the states west of the Appalachians came into the Union, most of them gave the privilege of voting and holding office to all white men. This example led the rising labor organizations in the East to demand the same benefits. Before long the seaboard states did away with any property and religious qualifications which kept white men from voting and holding office.

The plantation system also moves west.

The leveling influence of the frontier lasted longer in the Northwest than

Artists of the early 19th century have left us with vivid paintings of people and activities of the period. (Above) "WILLIAM HOWARD SMITH," *age five, by Joseph Whiting Stock.* (p. 249 upper) "SHOOTING FOR THE BEEF," *by George Caleb Bingham.* (p. 249 lower) "RINGING THE PIG," *by William Sidney Mount.*

249

in the Southwest. Beginning about 1815 cotton planters moved into the rich valleys of Alabama, Mississippi, Louisiana, and Arkansas. Most of them came from plantations farther east where the soil had been exhausted. They came with scores—sometimes hundreds—of slaves, herds of horses and cattle, and long wagon trains of goods. They bought land already cleared, and the frontiersmen who had cleared it moved farther west or settled on rougher lands not suited to plantations. The class system which the planters brought with them was altogether opposed to the democratic ideas and customs of the frontiersmen.

were the same as on the western frontier. Again, there were rising towns and cities along the Ohio River. A factory owner in Cincinnati was as likely to demand a protective tariff and a liberal immigration policy as a factory owner in New Haven. Small farmers were numerous in each section and most of them were likely to need easier credit and better transportation.

No section was a solid unit in its demands, and the West least of all. There were really two Wests—the Northwest, which was closed to slavery, and the Southwest, which was not. Wherever slavery existed the planters formed the ruling class and wished the

TRADING POST *at Bellevue, Nebraska. At such posts as this efforts were made to reduce friction between the Indians and the westward-moving white hunters and traders.*

The West consists of two distinct parts.

In discussing sectional interests we should keep in mind that the sections overlapped. For example, there were frontier areas in northern New England where the needs of the people

slave system to be protected and extended. Usually when we speak of the South we mean the whole area where the plantation system was found. This, of course, includes the Southwest. Yet for some purposes we lump Southwest and Northwest together as the West.

The West demands more influence.

The entire West was eager for a greater voice in the national government. By about 1820 people in the new states were asking why the original states should continue in control. Were Presidents to be chosen only from Virginia and Massachusetts? Why should not a President come from the West? As new states were added to the Union, the West gained influence in national affairs. Its leaders won recognition from the rest of the country. Kentucky's Henry Clay, for example, was chosen Speaker of the House in 1811. In 1825 he became Adams' Secretary of State. Another Westerner, Andrew Jackson of Tennessee, nearly won the Presidency in 1824. Four years later he did become President—the first one from west of the Appalachians. Westerners celebrated his election with great enthusiasm.

The Northwest makes demands of its own.

The people of the Northwest needed a market for their surplus farm products. They urged federal aid for building roads, canals, and railroads. Like the South, they opposed the bankers of the East. They thought state banks would provide more credit, under easier terms than the Bank of the United States. They wanted more people in the West, so they asked Congress to encourage immigration from Europe. They also asked for a liberal land policy, to make it easy for poor men to obtain land.

The Sections Struggle for Control of Congress

Missouri seeks admission to the Union.

The sharpest conflict between the sections had to do with the extension of slavery into the territories. It flared up suddenly in 1819 after Missouri applied for admission to the Union as a

The First Cotton Gin

slave state. Although slaveholders controlled the territory, only 10,000 slaves lived within its borders. Northerners tried to force Missouri to become a free state. When the bill for admission of Missouri was introduced, General James Tallmadge, a representative from New York, offered an amendment. It provided that no more slaves could be brought into Missouri and that all children of slaves born after the date of admission should be free upon reaching the age of twenty-five. The amendment passed the House but was rejected in the Senate. Congress adjourned in March, 1819, with the Missouri bill deadlocked.

The Missouri question is hotly debated.

The dispute over the admission of Missouri provoked angry discussion all over the country. Through the summer and autumn of 1819 public meetings were held, and state legislatures met to adopt resolutions on the subject. Feelings were so intense that some people predicted disunion or even civil war. "This momentous question," wrote Jefferson, "like a fire bell in the night, awakened and filled me with terror. I considered it at once as the knell of the Union."

Whether Missouri should be admitted with or without slavery seemed important for several reasons:

1. There were an equal number of states in the Northern, or free-soil, section, and in the Southern, or slaveholding, section. This meant that each section had an equal number of senators. However, the population of the free states was increasing much faster than that of the slave states. Already the North had more representatives in Congress than the South. This made Southern leaders the more anxious to keep the balance in the Senate.

2. Congress had not passed any law regarding slavery in the Louisiana Purchase. Louisiana had been admitted with slavery. There were already a large number of slaves in the Arkansas Territory. If Missouri were admitted as a slave state, would not slavery spread through all the rest of the territory bought from France? Northerners agreed that this must be prevented. Otherwise the South, allied with slaveholding states yet to be created, would have permanent control of the national government. Besides, there was a growing belief in the North that slavery was a moral wrong and should be confined to states where it already existed. Another argument for keeping slavery out of the rest of the Louisiana Purchase was that this region should be a place where poor men could go and establish themselves as farmers. Poor men did not prosper in places where there was slavery.

3. Southerners insisted that every state had the constitutional right to decide whether slavery should be allowed within its borders. If Congress interfered with slavery in Missouri, they argued, Congress might try next to interfere with slavery in the older states of the South. Northerners answered that Congress had the power to exclude slavery from the territories. To this, Southerners replied that the territories were owned by all the states in common. Therefore, Southerners had as much right to move into a territory with their property, including slaves, as Northerners. When Southerners attacked the Tallmadge amendment, they felt they were defending their sacred constitutional rights. A Georgia senator, W. C. Cobb, told Tallmadge he had "kindled a fire which all the water of the ocean cannot put out, which only seas of blood can extinguish."

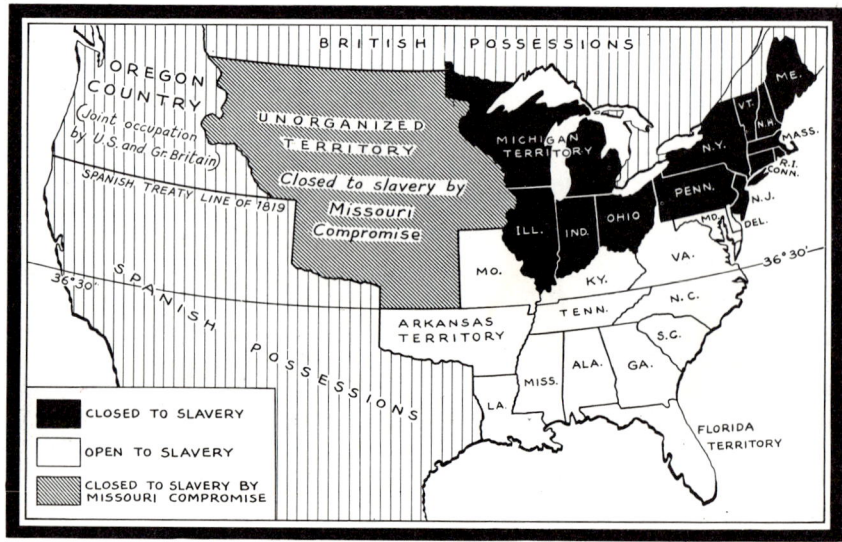

THE MISSOURI COMPROMISE, 1820

The Missouri Compromise is adopted.

At the end of 1819 Maine asked to enter the Union as a free state. (It had just separated from Massachusetts with that state's consent.) This offered a chance to end the deadlock over Missouri. After a long debate a compromise was arranged: Maine was to be admitted as a free state and Missouri as a slave state. It was agreed that in the rest of the territory purchased from France slavery should be barred north of the parallel 36° 30'. The compromise was passed in 1820, through the influence of Henry Clay, Speaker of the House. He was ever afterward known as the "Pacificator."

The Missouri Compromise made free soil of four fifths of the territory in the Louisiana Purchase. Why did Southern congressmen agree to it? One reason was the belief that the grass-lands north and west of Missouri were useless for farming. Much of the region was thought to be a desert. Another reason was the desire of responsible men in both North and South to end the threat of disunion.

The dispute over the extension of slavery was shelved for a time. But the compromise was only a truce. John Quincy Adams called it the "preamble to a great and tragic volume," and added, "The seeds of the Declaration of Independence are yet maturing."

John Quincy Adams Has an Unhappy Administration

"Favorite sons" seek election in 1824.

The Missouri Compromise temporarily restored the Era of Good Feeling. Monroe was re-elected in 1820 without opposition. The country seemed so harmonious that John Marshall said Monroe's administration "was not darkened by a single cloud." Yet sectional rivalry came to the surface again in the presidential election of 1824.

JOHN QUINCY ADAMS

The Republican party was the only one in the field. The congressional caucus chose William H. Crawford, then Secretary of the Treasury, as the official candidate. Crawford, an upland planter from Georgia, was favored by Monroe. A number of state legislatures, which objected to the caucus method of selecting candidates, put forward their own "favorite son." New England supported John Quincy Adams, the gifted and experienced Secretary of State. Tennessee enthusiastically endorsed her military hero, Andrew Jackson, who was then in the Senate. Kentucky named her brilliant statesman and orator, Henry Clay, then Speaker of the House. All four candidates were nationalist in their point of view.

When the electoral college met, Jackson received 99 votes (32 less than a majority), Adams 84, Crawford 41, and Clay 37. Since no candidate had a majority, the House of Representatives had to make the final choice. As provided in the Twelfth Amendment, the President would be chosen from the three highest candidates. Realizing he was out of the race, Clay threw his support to John Quincy Adams. With Clay's help, Adams won the election on the first ballot. Representatives of 13 states voted for Adams, 7 for Jackson, and 4 for Crawford.

Adams is falsely charged with corruption.

Jackson took his defeat bitterly. He believed that Clay had robbed him of the election. When Adams appointed Clay to be Secretary of State, Jackson

253

men charged that the two had made a "corrupt bargain." Clay, as the story went, had used his influence for Adams because Adams had promised to make him Secretary of State. The charge was untrue. Clay would have supported Adams in any case, for he believed Adams to be far better qualified than Jackson. Moreover, Clay was an appropriate choice for Secretary of State. Jackson, however, believed the charge as long as he lived. He resigned from the Senate in 1825 and spent the next three years fighting Adams. His followers kept accusing Adams of corruption. For example, when Adams bought a billiard table and a chess set for the White House, paying for them himself, he was accused of buying "gaming tables and gambling furniture" at public expense. By constant repetition many people came to believe the charges. Yet in reality Adams was a man of great public spirit and unbending honesty.

Adams outlines a nationalistic program.

Adams was a man of rare vision, who looked far into the future. He was well aware of the revolutionary changes that were taking place in manufacturing and in farming. In his inaugural address he endorsed a nationalistic program. He insisted that Congress had ample powers to pass laws needed for the general welfare. Congress should, he said, actively promote economic and intellectual improvements. He recommended federal aid for building roads and other transportation facilities. Like Washington and Jefferson, he urged Congress to found a national university and institutions for scientific research. He believed that the public domain, if wisely and honestly managed, would furnish revenue for these purposes for all time to come. The land, forests, and minerals owned by the nation should, he declared, be held in trust and used for the common good.

His ideas on conservation were way ahead of his time. They offended land speculators and land grabbers, some of whom were members of Congress.

Adams is a poor politician.

John Quincy Adams was devoted to the public welfare. Yet like his father, President John Adams, he was never popular. Although both men loved their country deeply, they did not win the nation's affection.

Adams was not a good party man. He might have used his control over federal jobs to obtain support in Congress, but this he scorned to do. He would neither reward friends nor punish enemies. He refused even to reply to the slanders spread by Jackson's men.

A good politician must be willing to make compromises. He needs to find the middle ground where men of various views can get together in order that they may agree on a course of action. Adams was not flexible enough to do this. He stubbornly held to the principles he thought right. For example, he tried to protect the rights of Indians in Georgia to the remnant of their lands, which they held under federal treaty. His efforts angered Georgians and citizens of other states where Indian tribes still owned land. Adams lost his hope of re-election by repeatedly taking an unpopular stand on important issues.

Jackson and his friends fought Adams at every turn. They were able to block nearly everything he suggested. They split the Republican party in two. The Jackson group took the name *Democratic* Republicans, or Democrats. They claimed to represent the common people. Adams' supporters called themselves *National* Republicans. They were much like the old Federalist party, for they believed in a strong national government and a protective tariff. Jacksonians charged them with caring only for the rich.

The Tariff Act of 1828 angers the South.

In 1816 all sections of the nation had agreed on a tariff act that was openly protective. Before long, however, Southerners decided that the tariff hurt their interests. They wished to return to a tariff for revenue only. In spite of their opposition, Congress adopted a new tariff act in 1824. It raised the duties on hemp, wool, flax, iron ore, and other raw materials produced chiefly in the North and West.

Factory owners asked for still higher rates on manufactures. To satisfy them, a new tariff bill was introduced in 1828. Southern congressmen decided on a trick which they hoped would defeat it. They joined with Westerners in asking for higher rates on everything, particularly on raw materials. The trick failed. In spite of the high duties on raw materials, to which factory owners objected, most congressmen from the Northeast voted for the bill. It passed by a small margin.

Jackson men had voted for the tariff bill, expecting to embarrass Adams in an election year. He would lose the South if he signed the bill, and he might lose the Northeast if he vetoed it. As John Randolph said, the tariff "had nothing to do with manufactures except the manufacture of a President." After much thought Adams signed, and thereby lost many votes in the South and West.

Southerners referred to the Tariff of 1828 as the "Tariff of Abominations." The duties, which averaged 49 per cent, were the steepest the country had ever had. They were bound to result in much higher prices for manufactured goods. The planters said they would go without rather than pay more for the products of Northern factories. South Carolinians asked whether it was worth while to stay in a Union in which one section could oppress another. Some Southerners even urged their representatives to resign from Congress.

Jackson wins the election of 1828.

The campaign of 1828 really began in 1824 with the charge that Jackson had been cheated of the Presidency. His friends built up a strong party organization. Jackson was presented as the people's champion, while Adams was denounced as a foe of the people, a waster of the people's money, and one who had bought his own election. By 1828 feelings on both sides were extremely bitter. Instead of discussing the issues, each party waged a campaign of mudslinging.

Jackson had been the idol of the West ever since the Battle of New Orleans. The frontiersmen lovingly called him "Old Hickory." He was also popular among city wage earners. He was one of the plain people, and the plain people throughout the nation wanted him for President. All the Western and Southern states gave their electoral votes to Jackson, as did Pennsylvania. Adams trailed far behind. Calhoun was re-elected Vice-President.

The popular vote was the largest yet cast, for several of the original states had recently abolished property and taxpaying qualifications for voting. The newly enfranchised voters were poor men, and they were for Jackson. Nevertheless, Adams received 44 per cent of the popular vote.

Sectionalism is in the saddle.

By 1828 little remained of the national unity that had been so evident during Monroe's eight years of office. Even in Monroe's two terms sectionalism was never absent. It led to a crisis over the admission of Missouri. In 1824 it made the election a contest between four favorite sons. By the time Adams entered the White House in 1825, sectional feelings were so strong that Congress did not support his nationalistic program. The country paid little attention to his farsighted proposals for the general welfare. The various sections

255

thought more of their own than the nation's interests. In fact, Adams' term has been called the "Era of Hard Feeling."

The strongly protective Tariff of 1828 enraged the South and helped Jackson win the election. Since he was a cotton planter, Southerners hoped he would work for their interests. They waited to see what he would do about the tariff. They had no intention of being dominated by the Northeast, and they were already alarmed by its growing power in Congress. The tariff dispute shows that by 1828 sectional hostility had become a serious threat to national unity.

FOR IDENTIFICATION

Conestoga wagon
Democratic
  Republicans
Francis Lowell
Missouri Compromise
National Republicans

Samuel Slater
Tallmadge
  amendment
Tariff of
  Abominations

FOR EXPLANATION OR DEFINITION

"corrupt bargain"
cotton gin
factory system
"favorite son"
frontier

Industrial Revolution
interchangeable parts
pre-emption
rugged individualism
squatter

FOR REVIEW

1. Why did sectionalism gradually replace nationalism?

2. What is meant by the Industrial Revolution? How did England try to prevent the spread of the Industrial Revolution?

3. When and where did power spinning and power weaving begin in the United States?

4. What great contribution did Eli Whitney as a gun manufacturer make to the Industrial Revolution in the United States?

5. (a) Why did the factory system develop chiefly in the Northeast? (b) What were some of the effects of the rise of the factory system in the United States?

6. What were the economic results of Whitney's invention of the cotton gin?

7. (a) What were the attitudes of the North and the South toward slavery in the early years of the Republic? (b) Why did the expansion of cotton production change the Southern attitude toward slavery?

8. What demands did the South make on Congress?

9. What is meant by the "Old West"? Where did settlers of the "Old West" come from? Why did Easterners complain of the movement to the West?

10. Describe the routes used by settlers in going to the West.

11. What was the policy of the federal government toward the sale of public land through 1820?

12. What is a squatter? What rights did Congress give squatters when government lands were placed on sale?

13. (a) Why was money scarce in newly settled areas? (b) Why did most settlers go into debt? (c) Why did Congress in 1820 forbid the sale of government land on credit?

14. (a) Describe the three main stages of settlement in new areas. (b) What were some of the attitudes of the frontier which influenced American ideas?

15. (a) What important difference developed between the Northwest and the Southwest? (b) How did frontier interests sometimes overlap? (c) What were the chief political demands of the West?

16. (a) Why did the application of Missouri for admission as a state start a bitter controversy? (b) What was the Tallmadge amendment? (c) Why were Southerners so angry over this amendment?

17. State the provisions of the Missouri Compromise. What were the effects of the Compromise?

18. (a) Who were the candidates for the Presidency in 1824? How were they nominated? (b) Why was the House of Representatives called upon to elect the President in 1824? (Review the election of

1800 and the Twelfth Amendment to the Constitution.) (c) What criticism did the supporters of Andrew Jackson make against John Q. Adams and Henry Clay?

19. (a) What were the main features of President Adams' nationalistic program? (b) Why did Adams run into trouble in carrying out his program? (c) Into what two groups did the Republican party split during the administration of John Q. Adams, 1825–29?

20. (a) What were the main features of the Tariff Act of 1828? (b) Why did the South refer to it as the "Tariff of Abominations"? (c) How did the enactment of this tariff affect the presidential election of 1828?

21. (a) Describe the main features of the election of 1828. (b) Why was the popular vote so large? (c) Account for the success of Andrew Jackson in this election.

FOR FURTHER STUDY AND DISCUSSION

1. Compare the differing demands in Congress of the West, South, and Northeast. What were the reasons for the differences? Helpful source: Krout and Fox, The Completion of Independence, 1790–1830 (A.L.S.)

2. How did the cotton gin affect Southern economic life? Why did it contribute to the demand for expansion?

3. Why did the South become the defender of the institution of slavery?

4. How did the "leveling" influence of the frontier affect social and political conditions in the "new" West?

5. (a) Discuss whether the chief factors involved in the controversy over the admission of Missouri were economic, political, or humanitarian. (b) Using a map, indicate the effect of the Missouri Compromise on the question of slavery in the Louisiana Purchase territory. (c) Under what circumstances was the law declared unconstitutional? (See p. 359.)

6. (a) Why did the enactment of a tariff law frequently weaken party harmony? (b) Why did the protective tariff receive some Southern support in 1816 and serious Southern opposition in 1828? (c) Explain the meaning of Randolph's statement that the purpose of the Tariff of 1828 was "the manufacture of a President." Helpful source: Amherst Series, The Great Tariff Debate, 1820–1830.

7. How do you account for Calhoun's shift of opinion on the question of the tariff? How do you account for Webster's shift of opinion? Did Calhoun and Webster lead or follow the opinions of their respective states?

8. Why did the administration of John Q. Adams become an "Era of Hard Feeling"?

FOR INDIVIDUAL OR GROUP ACTIVITIES

1. Make a chart showing the chief inventions of the Industrial Revolution between 1730 and 1830. Give inventors and dates, and state how each invention was used. Helpful sources: Kier, The Epic of Industry (Pageant); Kaempffert, ed., A Popular History of American Inventions, Vol. I.

2. Exhibit maps and pictures which illustrate the movement to the Mississippi.

3. Organize a small committee to look up and report on various readings on the settlement of the trans-Appalachian West. Using these reports as background, prepare a thirty-minute radio or television script for presentation to the class. Helpful sources: Commager and Nevins, The Heritage of America, pp. 251–300; Brown, Daniel Boone; Holbrook, Davy Crockett.

4. Assume that the class is the Senate or House of Representatives in session in 1820 to debate the Missouri Compromise. Have two pupils attack the Compromise from the Northern point of view; have two attack it from the Southern point of view; and have two pupils urge its adoption.

5. Draw and exhibit cartoons which reflect contrasting points of view on westward migration, the Missouri Compromise, the Tariff of Abominations, and the election of 1828.

6. Submit an outline report of President Adams' First Annual Message to Congress. Helpful source: Commager, Documents, No. 130.

7. Prepare a campaign speech or editorial urging the election of Adams in 1828 and another urging the election of Jackson.

257

There are no necessary evils in government. Its evils exist only in its abuses. If it would confine itself to equal protection, and, as Heaven does its rains, shower its favors alike on the high and the low, the rich and the poor, it would be an unqualified blessing.——Andrew Jackson

17. ANDREW JACKSON RISES TO POWER WITH THE WEST

Jackson Represents the Humbler Classes of Society

Jackson's election is a "revolution."

The election of 1828, like that of 1800, is often spoken of as a "revolution." Both brought to the Presidency a man who wanted to serve the common people. But the revolution of 1828 was a far greater overturn than that which placed Jefferson in the White House. Jacksonian democracy was more democratic than the Jeffersonian variety in several respects: (1) In 1800 only a minority of men could vote, but by 1828 most states had given the ballot to all white adult males. (2) Jefferson distrusted propertyless workers, fearing that they could be easily swayed by demagogues or rabble-rousers. When he spoke of "the people" he usually meant the independent farmers. In the years since his term of office, the laboring class had increased in numbers and political importance. The Jackson party depended on attracting laborers as well as farmers. (3) Jefferson and his political associates were scholars and aristocrats, while Jackson and his associates were mostly self-made men with little formal education. (4) The West had risen to power, with its belief in equal opportunity and its dislike of special privilege. Henceforth no party could elect a President without the support of the West.

Jackson is a man of the people.

Unlike the Presidents who preceded him, Andrew Jackson was born in poverty and received little formal education. He grew up in a rough region on the Carolina frontier. After working three years in a lawyer's office, he was, when not quite twenty, admitted to the bar. He moved to Nashville, a frontier settlement in Tennessee, where he was soon appointed public prosecutor for a large district. Later he served successively as Tennessee's first representative in Congress, as a United States senator, and as a judge in the supreme court of Tennessee. During the War of 1812 he won fame as an Indian fighter. When he defeated the British at the Battle of New Orleans, he became a national hero.

Jackson was the first President since John Adams who had not served as Secretary of State. When Jackson took office, he knew little about the problems of running a government or of dealing with foreign countries. Yet he made one of our most outstanding Presidents. He had great courage and independence of character, was honest and sincere, and his heart was completely with the common people. In his own words he represented "the humbler members of society—its farmers,

GENERAL ANDREW JACKSON

mechanics, and laborers who have neither the time nor the means" of securing favors from the government.

Jackson's inauguration.

On the day of Jackson's inauguration (March 4, 1829), ten thousand visitors crowded into Washington, some from hundreds of miles away. Eager throngs watched the tall, erect, gray-haired veteran pass on foot from his inn to the Capitol. After the ceremony a witness said that "countrymen, farmers, gentlemen, mounted and dismounted, boys, women, children, black and white," rushed pell-mell to the White House to greet their hero. It was the people's day, and they joyfully packed the President's home. Jackson was pushed against a wall, and those nearest him had to link arms to prevent him from being crushed. It is said that some stood in muddy boots on the satin-covered furniture trying to get a glimpse of him. Refreshment tables laden with cut glass and china were upset. "I never saw such a mixture," wrote Justice Story. "The reign of King Mob seemed triumphant."

Jackson adopts the spoils system.

Many of the people who flocked to the inauguration were looking for government jobs. One of them said: "I am ashamed of myself, for I feel as if every man I meet knew what I came for." "Don't distress yourself," said another, "for every man you meet is on the same business." Those who had worked for Jackson's victory expected a reward for their services. They wanted the President to adopt the spoils system.

The spoils system, by which a victorious party fills government jobs on the basis of party service, was already well known in state politics. The Democrats had found the system effective in building up a strong party organization in New York and Pennsylvania.

Jackson saw additional reasons for redistributing federal offices. From colonial days onward, federal offices had been fitted with persons from the "better families." Once appointed, a man could usually expect to hold his job for life and perhaps pass it on to his son. "Office," Jackson told Congress, "is considered as a species of property, an engine for the support of the few at the expense of the many." He favored the principle of *rotation in office*, that is, of short terms to give more persons a chance to hold office and to prevent the growth of a permanent officeholding class. He thought that one man had as much right to a government job as another. He believed that official duties could be made "so plain and simple that men of intelligence may readily qualify for their performance."

Recent studies show that the number of persons removed by Jackson was exaggerated by his opponents. According to the most careful estimate, between a fifth and a tenth of all federal officeholders were dismissed during his eight years as President. Under some later Presidents the percentage of removals was considerably higher.

Jackson is a "strong" President.

Jackson had remarkable qualities of leadership, which he used in the

259

name of the people. He believed that the people had chosen him to be their spokesman. He fought vigorously for what he thought they wanted, without regard to the opinions of Congress and the Supreme Court. Jackson vetoed more acts of Congress than all previous Presidents, and once he refused to enforce a Supreme Court decision.

Jackson's strength as President lay in his ability to win wide support for his policies. His veto messages were written to explain his position to the public. Jackson made the office of

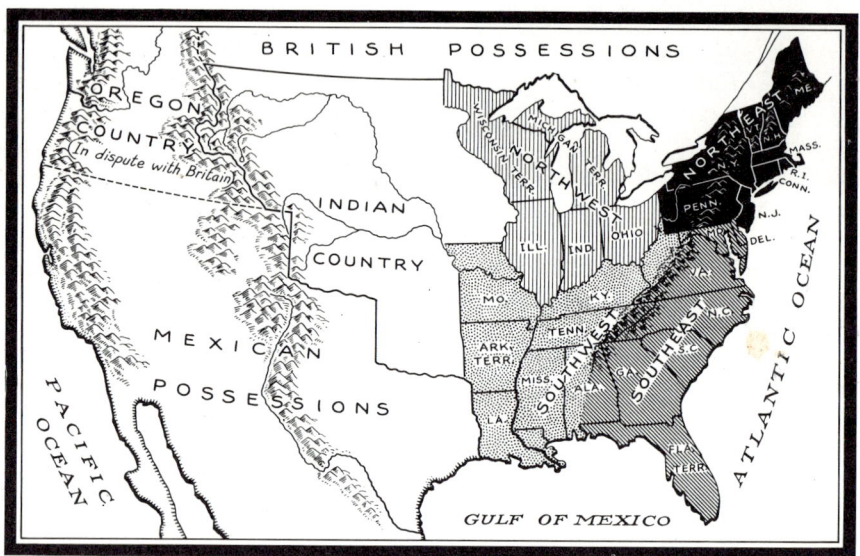

SECTIONS OF OUR COUNTRY WHEN JACKSON WAS PRESIDENT

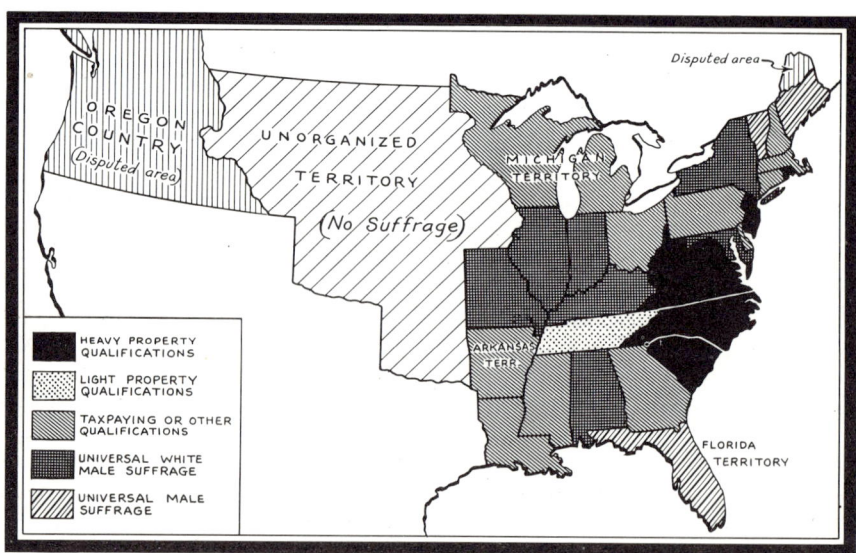

MALE SUFFRAGE, 1830

260

President far more important than it had been up to that time. Like Abraham Lincoln, Theodore Roosevelt, and Woodrow Wilson, Jackson is described as a "strong" President. Because of his vigorous leadership his enemies called him "King Andrew."

Jackson Meets the Threat of Nullification

Calhoun champions states' rights.

We have noted the anger of the South over the Tariff of 1828. South Carolina led the opposition. That state had grown poor mainly because of a land-destroying system of cotton culture, but the planters blamed the decline on the tariff. Because they regarded the Tariff of 1828 as abominable, they talked of leaving the Union.

Late in 1828 the South Carolina legislature approved a statement called the "South Carolina Exposition and Protest." Vice-President John C. Calhoun had written it, in the hope of bringing about a tariff reduction. The "Exposition and Protest" attacked the tariff as "unconstitutional, unequal, and oppressive." It revived the theory of nullification, first outlined thirty years earlier in the Kentucky and Virginia resolutions (see p. 185). According to this theory, each state had the right to decide for itself whether an act of Congress was unconstitutional. In case a state decided in the negative, it could declare the act null and void (of no effect) within its borders. Advocates of nullification believed each state should be completely sovereign in domestic affairs.

Although Calhoun was arguing for states' rights, he loved the Union. He believed it could be held together only by preventing one section from taking advantage of another. The right of nullification, he thought, was necessary to check sectional tyranny. If the nation accepted this right, Congress would refrain from making a law which was likely to be nullified by any state. There would then be no danger, Calhoun thought, that any state would leave the Union.

The South seeks alliance with the West.

Southerners in Congress saw that they could not get a lower tariff without Western votes. In a senatorial debate in 1829–30, Robert Y. Hayne of South Carolina tried to win Western support. He attacked a bill, introduced by a Connecticut senator, to limit for a time the sale of public lands. Westerners also objected to this bill, claiming that it was an attempt by New England manufacturers to keep workers from going west. Hayne proposed an alliance between the South and the West, since both were agricultural sections. Southern congressmen, he said, would vote for cheap lands in the West if Western congressmen would join them in voting for a tariff for revenue only.

Hayne then condemned the increase in federal powers and asserted, "The very life of our system is the independence of the states." He declared it was unconstitutional for Congress to pass a law harmful to one section or intended to build up one section at the expense of another. Further he agreed with Calhoun on the right of a state to nullify any act of Congress which the state considered to be unjust.

Webster replies to Hayne.

Senator Daniel Webster of Massachusetts presented the North's answer. His long, impassioned speech is considered one of the greatest of American orations. Webster denied that the Union was a compact of states and that the federal government was a mere instrument for doing the will of the states. The *people*, he said, not the states, made the Union. It is "the people's Constitution, the people's govern-

WEBSTER'S REPLY TO HAYNE, *January 26, 1830. This debate, which began as a simple question of politics, soon became a battle of ideas in which the conflicting beliefs of North and South were etched deeply in the minds of all the listeners.*

ment, made for the people, made by the people, and answerable to the people." If Congress exceeded its powers, he continued, there were remedies in appeals to the Supreme Court, in constitutional amendments, and in frequent elections. The doctrine of nullification was absurd. If first one state and then another could ignore this or that law to suit its convenience, the government of the Union would be a mockery.

In closing, Webster spoke in high praise of the Union: "While the Union lasts we have high, exciting, gratifying prospects spread out before us, for us and our children." He expressed the fear that before his death the country would be drenched in the blood of civil war. In an eloquent conclusion Webster pleaded that Americans take as their motto "Liberty and Union, now and forever, one and inseparable."

During the next generation Webster's ringing words continued to echo in the North and West. They were repeated on special occasions, such as school graduations and Fourth of July celebrations. They established in the hearts of the people a new idea of the value of the Union. One of those who treasured Webster's vision was Abraham Lincoln, who read the speech in a Louisville paper shortly before his twenty-first birthday. Little did he realize that he would take up the burden, a generation later, of preserving the Union of which the Massachusetts statesman spoke with such deep feeling.

Jackson toasts the Union.

Vice-President Calhoun and other Southerners in Washington counted on Jackson's sympathy. Soon after the Webster-Hayne debate they arranged a banquet to celebrate Jefferson's birthday, at which they hoped the President would publicly take their side. On the printed menu were twenty-four toasts, many of them referring to states' rights and nullification as true Jeffersonian principles. As Chief Executive, Jackson was called on first. Rising to his full height and looking Calhoun straight in the eyes, Jackson said deliberately: "Our Federal Union—it *must* and *shall* be preserved!" Everyone present knew that the President had challenged the South Carolinian. The Vice-President tried to save the situation. Waiting until everyone sat down, he offered a second toast: "The Union—next to our liberty, the most dear!" After a slight pause he added: "May we all remember that it can only be preserved by respecting the rights of the states and distributing equally the benefits and burdens of the Union."

This dramatic incident, lasting but a minute or two, emphasized two opposing ideas of the nature of the Union. The states'-rights doctrine, as stated by Calhoun and Hayne, may have been nearer to the intent of the framers and ratifiers of the Constitution. However, the doctrine of federal supremacy, as stated by Webster and upheld by Jackson, was coming to be accepted by the majority of the people in the North and the West.

South Carolina nullifies the Tariff of 1832.

In the summer of 1832 Congress passed a new tariff bill. Although duties were reduced to an average of 36 per cent, it was still a high tariff. The South was greatly disappointed. The South Carolina legislature called a convention, which declared the new tariff act to be unconstitutional and "not binding upon this state." The people were told not to pay customs duties within South Carolina's borders after February 1, 1833. If the United States should use force to collect, South Carolina would leave the Union. The governor called

for volunteers, and companies began to drill. The state appeared close to an armed conflict with the United States. Some of the extremists had medals struck with the inscription, "John C. Calhoun, First President of the Southern Confederacy."

Jackson prepares to use force.

The President was determined to preserve the Union and enforce its laws. In a spirited proclamation to the people of South Carolina (December 10, 1832), he attacked the idea of nullification and declared: "The laws of the United States must be executed. . . . Those who told you that you might peaceably prevent their execution deceived you; they could not have deceived themselves. Disunion by armed force is treason."

Jackson sent warships to Charleston. At his request Congress began debate on a "force bill" giving the President power to use the army and navy to enforce the tariff act. No one doubted that the President intended to compel the state of South Carolina to obey the law.

A compromise tariff is adopted.

Meanwhile (December, 1832) Calhoun had resigned the Vice-Presidency to enter the Senate. His hope that other Southern states would co-operate with South Carolina on nullification had come to nothing. Therefore he was anxious to compromise. He supported a compromise tariff worked out by Henry Clay. Clay's tariff bill called for lowering the rates gradually over a period of nine years. In 1842 they would be about the same as under the Tariff of 1816, with none above 20 per cent. Satisfied that the compromise tariff was going through, South Carolina repealed its act of nullification. Congress passed both the new tariff bill and the force bill on the same day (March 1, 1833). Then, to save its face, South Carolina passed another measure nullifying the Force Act.

Each side claimed victory—South Carolina for proving that a single state could make Congress lower the tariff, and the nationalists for getting Congress to adopt the Force Act. But in reality nothing had been settled. "The nullifiers intend to blow up a storm on the slave question next," Jackson wrote to a friend. His words came true. Clay himself years later (in the last days before his death in 1852) expressed doubts about the wisdom of the compromise he had put through in 1833. Would it have been better, he asked, if at that time force had been used against the nullifiers?

Georgia defies the Supreme Court.

Jackson did not always uphold the authority of the federal government. In regard to the Cherokee Indians he upheld the state of Georgia against the Supreme Court.

When Jackson took office, the fate of the Indians was still unsettled. John Adams, Thomas Jefferson, and others had believed we should civilize the Indians and let them keep part of their land. Jackson, on the other hand, like most other frontiersmen, had no respect for Indians. He believed they should be driven off lands wanted by white men. In the old Northwest exactly that policy was followed; the white settlers advanced along a wide front, pushing the Indians steadily westward. But in the South, the white men settled chiefly along the great rivers, leaving five powerful Indian tribes on the lands in between. These tribes were accepting the Christian religion and taking up most of the white men's ways. Consisting of the Creeks, Choctaws, Chickasaws, Seminoles, and Cherokees, they were known as the "Five Civilized Tribes." The Cherokees, for example, were excellent farmers and stock raisers. They lived in Georgia in neat wooden houses surrounded by orchards. They built roads, kept inns, and made cotton and woolen cloth. They had an alphabet and kept written records. They had a constitution and a government much like ours. The United States had recognized them in treaties as an independent nation.

All went smoothly until the people of Georgia decided they wanted the Cherokee lands. Then the state authorities announced that the Indians must move. The Cherokees appealed to the courts. The Supreme Court, under John Marshall, ruled that the Cherokees were a nation and that the laws of Georgia did not apply to them. Georgia refused to obey the Supreme Court decision and began to remove the Indians by force. This action was just as serious as South Carolina's refusal to obey the tariff law. Yet President Jackson did nothing about it. He is reported to have said, "John Marshall has made his decision; now let him enforce it."

Alabama and Mississippi followed Georgia in taking steps to get rid of the Indians. Since the President would not protect them, the Indians had to give in. They sold their land to the federal government and moved westward. Congress set aside for them a large section of land in what is now Oklahoma, promising that this reservation should never be taken from them. By 1837 practically all of the Indians east of the Mississippi had been moved to reservations west of that river.

The second Bank of the United States.

Another issue on which Jackson sided with one section against another was that of a national bank. The second Bank of the United States had been chartered in 1816. At that time the need for a central bank was plain. The bank provided a safe depository for federal funds and a sound national currency.

By Jackson's time the bank had twenty-nine branches located throughout the nation. It was the largest corporation in the country and one of the largest in the world. One fifth of the bank's stock was owned by the federal government; one fifth of its board of directors were appointed by the government. Although all federal funds were deposited in the bank, about half its deposits were those of businessmen. It lent money to other banks, to businessmen, and when necessary to the federal government. Its bank notes, or promises to pay, were cheerfully accepted throughout the nation and even in foreign countries. These notes made up about one fourth of the nation's currency.

Nicholas Biddle of Philadelphia had become president of the bank in 1823. He managed it so skillfully that he won the praise of Albert Gallatin. Not only did Biddle make money for the stockholders, but he tried to operate the bank in the public interest. For example, he insisted that the state-chartered banks, most of which borrowed from the central bank, keep ample reserves of gold and silver. He discouraged them from reckless lending and from issuing too many bank notes. This was a valuable service to the nation, but it aroused opposition from several sources.

The second Bank has many enemies.

Several hundred banks had been chartered by state legislatures. Naturally the owners of these banks were jealous of the Bank of the United States. They called it the "monster" or the "octopus." For the federal government to put all its money in a single bank, they argued, was unfair. They also hated the bank for interfering with the way they ran their own banks.

In the Democratic party were two groups of people who opposed the second Bank of the United States. One, the "hard-money men," thought that gold and silver were the only honest currency. They wanted to put an end to the right of all banks to issue paper money. This right, they felt, enabled bankers to make profits without useful work. The other group wanted easy credit and plenty of paper money. They wished to free their local banks from the restrictions imposed by a central bank.

Dislike of the bank was especially strong in the West. Very few of the bank's stockholders were Westerners, yet most of its profits came from lending money there. Westerners thought it unfair for wealthy stockholders living in the East and in Europe to make money from poor Western farmers. Many Westerners did not realize that the capital needed to develop new communities and new enterprises could come only from more wealthy areas, and that it must be paid for by those who used it.

JOHN ROSS, A CHEROKEE CHIEF, *opposed the cession of Indian lands to the state of Georgia.* (Below) *The Ross home*

NICHOLAS BIDDLE. *As president of the Second Bank of the United States, Biddle made it a force in the national economy.*

turned it with a lengthy veto message. The bank, he wrote, was a monopoly deriving huge profits from lending money belonging to the federal government. The profits went to a few hundred wealthy Easterners and foreigners. Furthermore, the bank had tremendous powers over the nation's economy. It might use these powers to influence elections and control public affairs. "It is easy to conceive," wrote Jackson, "that great evils to our country and its institutions might flow from such a concentration of power in the hands of a few men irresponsible to the people."

Jackson vetoes the Recharter Bill.

Jackson was a hard-money man. He distrusted all banks, but especially the Bank of the United States, because it stood for the Eastern "money power." To him the so-called money power was the greatest foe of democratic government. He thought he could strike a blow at this power by destroying the bank. He attacked the bank in each of his annual messages to Congress.

Late in 1831 the National Republicans held a convention and nominated Henry Clay as their candidate for President.[1] Clay thought the bank would be a fine campaign issue. He persuaded Biddle to apply for a renewal of the bank's charter, although the old one would not expire until 1836. Congress passed the Recharter Bill in 1832 and sent it to the President. Jackson re-

---

[1] In the election of 1832 all the candidates for President and Vice-President were nominated by national conventions. The congressional caucus was never used again for this purpose.

BORN TO COMMAND.

OF VETO MEMORY.

HAD I BEEN CONSULTED.

KING ANDREW THE FIRST.

Jackson, as a cartoonist saw him

The voters settle the issue of the bank.

"This worthy President," Biddle said angrily, "thinks that because he has scalped Indians and imprisoned judges, he is to have his way with the bank. He is mistaken." Biddle threw all the bank's influence into the election campaign. As Clay hoped, the recharter bill became the chief issue. The Na-

266

tional Republicans pointed out the great usefulness of the bank and accused the Democrats of stirring up the poor against the rich. The ordinary people, however, knew little about banking and they believed that Jackson was defending them from the money kings. In the 1832 election "Old Hickory" won a sweeping victory.

Jackson took his re-election as a mandate from the people to cut all ties between the government and the Bank of the United States. He ordered the Treasury Department to deposit no more funds in the bank after October 1, 1833, and gradually to withdraw the funds already there. Some eighty state banks were selected to receive the federal funds. Jackson's foes called these the "pet banks."

The country suffers from lack of a central bank.

With the loss of federal deposits, the bank rapidly declined in wealth and influence. It could no longer act as a brake on the state-chartered banks. Most of these now made loans and issued bank notes with little regard for safe banking principles. Only the insiders knew whether a bank could make good on its notes. Creditors therefore often refused to accept paper money, or accepted it only at a discount. Yet the banks were so profitable that hundreds of new ones sprang up. Congressman Thomas Hart Benton of Missouri, a hard-money man, complained: "I did not join in putting down the Bank of the United States to put up a wilderness of local banks."

Jackson tries to check speculation.

The early and middle 1830's were years of unusual prosperity. Many people were moving west. Immigrants were pouring in from Europe. Industries were growing rapidly. In the East railroads were under construction. Roads and canals were being built in all parts of the country. Stock in these new enterprises was eagerly bought by those who had the money.

Prices were going up. This fact led many people to buy land as a speculation, that is, in the hope of selling it soon at a higher price. Most of the speculators borrowed money to pay for their purchases. Sales of government land increased by leaps and bounds.

The state-chartered banks did nothing to discourage speculation and too much borrowing. Instead they encouraged both by issuing more and more paper money. As a result, prices soared still higher. Finally, in the summer of 1836, Jackson became alarmed. To check the speculation in land and the excessive issue of bank notes, he sent his famous "Specie Circular" to government land agents. The circular instructed them to take nothing but specie—gold and silver—in payment for public lands. Land sales fell off at once. The circular weakened the public's confidence in the banks. The bright bubble of speculation was about to burst.

Jackson retires.

When the election of 1836 came around, Jackson was more popular than ever. "General Jackson may be President for life, if he wishes," wrote one of his political opponents. But Jackson was in his seventieth year and in poor health. He was eager to go home to the "Hermitage" and did not want another term. Refusing to run for re-election, he threw his support to his closest adviser, Martin Van Buren of New York.

Few Presidents have accomplished so much as Jackson. He won every important contest of his administration. This was possible because he kindled the imagination of the plain people and kept their support. In fact, Jackson was the most forceful and influential political leader the nation had in the years between the presidencies of Jefferson and Lincoln.

Van Buren's Term Is Marked by Unrest

The Whig party arises.

During Jackson's second term his opponents formed a new party called the Whigs. The name was suggested by a New York editor who felt that all opponents of "King Andrew" should unite, as the Whig party in England had done to lessen the authority of George III. The new party included several groups having little in common except dislike for Jackson. The largest consisted of National Republicians, led by Henry Clay of Kentucky and Daniel Webster of Massachusetts. They wanted a high tariff, a central bank, and a strong national government.

Van Buren is elected.

Jackson's great popularity assured the election of his chosen successor, Van Buren. "The little magician," as Van Buren was called, carried fifteen states.

For the only time in our history the choice of Vice-President was thrown into the Senate. Van Buren's running mate, Colonel R. M. Johnson of Kentucky, was chosen on the first ballot.

A terrible depression begins in 1837.

When Van Buren took office the country was entering a long period of hard times. The principal cause of it was the wild speculation in roads, canals, land, and industry which had gone on during Jackson's second term. Hundreds of banks had rashly assisted speculation by lending money on easy terms. State governments had borrowed heavily to assist private companies in the building of toll roads, canals, and railroads. British and European investors had joined in the speculation, buying American stocks and bonds and land, for they thought the United States was "the country with a future."

The "Specie Circular" pricked the bubble. Land buyers asked banks to redeem their notes in gold and silver. The weaker banks soon had to suspend specie payments and by the end of May, 1837, all the banks had done so. Foreign investors became alarmed and sent back the bonds they had bought, demanding to be paid in specie. Many states could not redeem their bonds. Two states repudiated their bonds altogether.

No one wanted to accept paper money and there was far too little specie in the country for ordinary business needs. Prices dropped disastrously. Unable to meet their obligations, many business houses went into bankruptcy. More than six hundred banks failed, including some of the "pet banks" which had federal funds on deposit. Nine tenths of the factories in New England closed. Work on canals and railroads ceased. Unemployment brought terrible suffering to Eastern wage earners. In the winter of 1838 there were food riots in the cities.

In those days practically everybody thought a depression was an act of nature like a tidal wave or a tornado. Few people had any idea of the steps which might be taken to pull the country out of bad times. It is worth noting that Nicholas Biddle believed a central bank having large resources could check a depression. His ideas for providing an ample money supply and for overcoming a contraction of credit are now accepted practices. Yet they were not tried in the United States until the Federal Reserve system was created in 1913.

Subtreasuries are set up.

Congress met in special session in October, 1837. Though there was no federal debt, the government had no money to pay its expenses. Therefore Congress instructed the Treasury to issue ten million dollars in short-term notes. But where should the notes be deposited? Since state-chartered banks had proved unsafe for federal deposits, President Van Buren proposed an independent treasury system. Subtreasuries would be created in six or eight cities to keep and pay out public money. The Whigs fought this proposal, for they wanted to re-establish the Bank of the United States. However, the Independent Treasury Act was adopted in 1840.

Relations with Great Britain are strained.

British investors were understandably indignant because two American states had repudiated their bonds. Another source of friction with Great Britain was the aid given by American citizens to a rebellion which broke out in Canada in 1837. At that time many unemployed Americans living along the border joined the rebel forces. Mobs emptied several American arsenals and gave their contents to the Canadians. A rebel leader, William L. Mackenzie of Toronto, fled to Buffalo, where he established headquarters for a time. Such violations of American neutrality were resented by the British. In December, 1837, a party of Canadian Loyalists rowed across the Niagara River and destroyed a small American steamer, the *Caroline,* that was engaged in carrying supplies to the rebels. In the fight one American was killed and several were wounded. Americans along the border demanded war. President Van Buren issued a proclamation urging Americans to observe the neutrality laws and asking those who had joined the rebels to return home. Although he sent a strong protest to the British government over the sinking of the *Caroline,* American jingoes, or extreme nationalists, accused him of tamely yielding to Great Britain.

The following year the Maine boundary dispute flared up again. An

MARTIN VAN BUREN, *Secretary of State under Jackson, and eighth President of the United States. Inheriting Jackson's office, but not his popularity, Van Buren faced four years of opposition, depression, and growing discontent with his policies.*

269

area of 12,000 square miles lying north of the Aroostook River was claimed by both the United States and Great Britain. Attempts to settle the dispute by arbitration had failed. When Canadian lumberjacks entered the area in the winter of 1838–39, the governor of Maine ordered them to leave. They fell back to New Brunswick, where more Canadians joined them. Maine called out the militia and threatened to fight the "invaders." Congress voted $10,000,-000 and authorized the President to call 50,000 volunteers if necessary. Instead, to the disgust of the hotheads, Van Buren wisely sent General Winfield Scott to arrange a truce between Maine and New Brunswick. The truce avoided bloodshed and made it possible to settle the dispute by negotiation a few years later (see p. 274).

Van Buren declines to annex Texas.

Another problem which became troublesome during Van Buren's administration was whether Texas should be admitted to the Union. In 1836 (while Jackson was President), Texas had revolted against Mexico and asked to be annexed to the United States. (See pp. 335–36 for the full story of the revolution.) Northerners opposed annexation, because Texas had slavery and was large enough to make half a dozen states. While Jackson did want to annex it, he did not wish to stir up a sectional quarrel which might prevent the election of his friend Van Buren. After the election—on his last day in office—Jackson recognized the independence of Texas. The Lone Star Republic then formally petitioned Congress for annexation. Van Buren took no action, however. In the first place he was opposed to the admission of more slave states. Moreover, Mexico threatened to declare war if we annexed Texas. Thus Van Buren sharply disappointed the expansionists. They wanted Texas even if it meant war.

There is little "hidden" persuasion in this Whig campaign flag.

The Whigs Win a Hollow Victory

"Tippecanoe and Tyler too."

In 1840, Jackson and other Democratic leaders backed Van Buren for re-election and put up a strong fight in behalf of the party. Most unjustly, however, Van Buren was blamed for the hard times which prevailed throughout his term. His peace-loving foreign policy also cost him popularity with some groups of voters. In addition, Whig newspapers constantly pictured him as a wealthy man with snobbish habits. For example, he was said to eat with gold spoons, dress himself before costly French mirrors, and put cologne on his whiskers.

The managers of the Whig party looked around for a candidate who would please the common people. They turned aside from Henry Clay, the founder of the party. They preferred someone whose views were less well known, believing that such a candidate would satisfy more groups of voters. Whig leaders wanted a Westerner in order to attract the farm vote. A military hero, they knew, always appeals to the voters. In General William Henry

Harrison of Ohio, they found just the candidate they wanted. His political opinions were hazy, and for this reason he would not offend any important group of voters. Harrison had beaten the Indians at Tippecanoe in 1811 and had served with honor in the War of 1812. To catch Southern votes, the Whigs nominated John Tyler of Virginia for Vice-President. Tyler was a states'-rights man, an anti-bank man, and a low-tariff man. His only bond with the Whigs was his hatred for Jackson. This fact did not worry the Whig leaders. The vice-presidency was not a position of power. They had no idea Tyler would ever become President.

Nicholas Biddle, who thought a Whig victory would mean recharter of the Bank of the United States, advised the Whig managers: "Let him (Harrison) say not one single word about his principles or his creed—let him say nothing—promise nothing. Let no committee, no convention, no town meeting ever extract from him a single word about what he thinks now or will do hereafter." This advice was followed. The Whig leaders did not prepare a party platform. Catch phrases such as "Tippecanoe and Tyler too," "Harrison, two dollars a day, and roast beef," and "Van, Van, is a used-up man" were more useful than a platform.

Clay's friends were greatly disappointed that he had not been nominated. One of them said sneeringly that old General Harrison, if given a pension and a barrel of hard cider, would be content to retire to a log cabin. A Democratic newspaper dubbed Harrison the "log-cabin candidate." The Whigs thereupon turned the tables on the Democrats. They boasted that their candidate was a man of the people and they pretended that he lived in a log cabin. (Actually Harrison came from a well-to-do family and was a man of considerable means, while Van Buren had been born poor.) At every politi-

WILLIAM HENRY HARRISON, *ninth President of the United States*

cal meeting the Whigs displayed a log cabin, a jug of cider, and a coonskin cap to show their candidate's love of the simple life. They treated those who came to the meetings from barrels of hard cider. "Oh, know ye the farmer of Tippecanoe?" sang the crowds.

Let Van from his coolers of silver drink wine,
And lounge on his cushioned settee.
Our man on his buckeye bench can recline,
Content with hard cider is he.
The iron-armed soldier, the true hearted soldier,
The gallant old soldier of Tippecanoe!

The Whigs put on the jolliest election campaign America has ever had. "Tippecanoe and Tyler too" won by a huge majority. The Whigs also gained control of Congress. The people seemed to forget that the Whig party was supported by the rich and wellborn, the Eastern "money power" which they hated. Their old leader, Jackson, had done what he could to help Van Buren. He felt that Van Buren's defeat was the defeat of Jacksonianism.

The Liberty party makes its bow.

A new party appeared in 1840 but obtained only 7000 popular votes. This was the Liberty party, dedicated to the abolition of slavery. It grew rapidly and eventually split the Whig party into fragments.

(Above) *Junction of Erie and Champlain canals*

(Left) DANIEL WEBSTER *at his farm. In party politics Webster was as unyielding as the New England soil from which he sprung, but when sectionalism threatened to split the nation he rose above partisan demands and fought tirelessly for the preservation of the union.*

Tyler succeeds Harrison.

Just one month after his inauguration President Harrison died—worn out from the strain of meeting swarms of office seekers. For the first time in our history a Vice-President stepped into the vacant office of the President. The Whig leaders found themselves in a curious position. They had expected to pull the strings for the easygoing Harrison; instead they had to deal with John Tyler, a strong-willed Virginian who disliked most of their policies. As has been pointed out, he was no Whig but an anti-Jackson Democrat. While he retained all the members of Harrison's Cabinet, Tyler intended to do his own thinking. Harrison's death had robbed the Whigs of their victory.

Tyler and the Whig leaders disagree.

Henry Clay had declined Harrison's offer to appoint him Secretary of State, for he wished to remain in the Senate. At a special session of Congress which met a few weeks after Harrison's death, Clay outlined a legislative program. It called for repeal of the Independent Treasury Act, restoration of the bank, a higher tariff, and distribution of money from land sales for use by the states in making internal improvements. The program was a revival of Clay's American system (see p. 218). "Tyler dare not resist me," Clay said hopefully. "I will drive him before me."

Tyler signed a bill repealing the year-old Independent Treasury Act (see p. 269). He also accepted a higher tariff. He refused to accept the distribution scheme and he twice vetoed a bank bill. Disgusted with Tyler's opposition, Clay resigned from the Senate (1842) to devote himself to the next presidential campaign. Soon after, to show their displeasure with Tyler, all members of the Cabinet except Daniel Webster resigned. Webster, who was Secretary of State, stayed in hopes of bringing about better relations with Great Britain.

JOHN TYLER, *tenth President of the United States. He was described by his enemies as a Democrat in Whig's clothing and his rejection of most Whig policies pointed out the great weakness of a party whose unity was based on opposition rather than agreement on basic principles.*

The Maine boundary dispute is settled.

Webster was then engaged in trying to settle the Maine boundary dispute. Lord Aberdeen, a friend of the United States, had recently become British foreign secretary. Aberdeen sent Lord Ashburton, a personal friend of Webster, to Washington. The two men reached an agreement which gave the United States a little more than half of the disputed territory. They also agreed on the boundary running from Lake Superior west to Lake-in-the-Woods (see p. 213). Soon after the Webster-Ashburton Treaty was ratified in 1842, Webster also resigned from the Cabinet. Two years later he returned to the Senate.

Hatbox

FOR IDENTIFICATION

Nicholas Biddle
Cherokees
Exposition and Protest
Five Civilized Tribes
independent treasury
  system
Webster-Ashburton
  Treaty
Webster-Hayne
  debate
Whigs

FOR EXPLANATION OR DEFINITION

Compromise Tariff
  of 1833
force bill
nullification
"pet banks"
removal of deposits
Specie Circular
spoils system
states' rights

FOR REVIEW

1. Why is the election of 1828 considered a revolution? Compare with the election of 1800.

2. How did Jackson's preparation for the Presidency differ from that of earlier Presidents? Briefly sketch the career of President Jackson.

The Democratic party changes character.

Tyler filled his Cabinet with anti-Jackson Democrats. For Secretary of State, he picked John C. Calhoun. Under Calhoun's leadership, control of the Democratic party passed to the Southern planters. The preservation of states' rights became the Democratic slogan. The party's immediate goal was the annexation of Texas and other territory suitable for the plantation system.

The annexation of Texas became the leading issue in the presidential election of 1844. From then until 1861, the nation was torn by controversy over the extension of slavery. Before taking up that story we shall pause for a look at ways of living and thinking in the first half of the 1800's.

★ ★ ★ ★ ★

3. What is the spoils system? Did Jackson originate the spoils system?

4. (a) Why did Southerners object to the Tariff of 1828? (b) What was the South Carolina Exposition and Protest? (c) Outline the arguments of the Exposition and Protest.

5. How did the sections line up over the resolution to limit sale of Western lands?

6. State the arguments developed by Senator Hayne in his famous debate with Webster. Give the arguments developed by Webster in his reply to Hayne.

7. (a) When did South Carolina decide to nullify the tariff law of 1828? Why did it delay until this time? (b) What did South Carolina intend to do if the United States enforced the tariff law within its borders? (c) What did Jackson do? What did South Carolina do? (d) What were the provisions of the Compromise Tariff of 1833? (e) What was the force bill? (f) Did South Carolina abandon the idea of nullification?

8. Compare Jackson's attitude toward the Indians with that of Jefferson.

9. (a) How did Georgia defy the Supreme Court in removing the Cherokees?

274

(b) Why did Jackson permit Georgia to ignore the Supreme Court decision?

10. (a) What were the advantages of the second Bank of the United States? (b) What were the arguments against a central bank?

11. (a) Since the bank's charter did not expire till 1836, why did the question of rechartering it come up in 1832? (b) Summarize Jackson's arguments for vetoing the recharter bill. (c) What were the results of the election of 1832?

12. (a) Why did Jackson order the withdrawal of government funds from the bank? (b) Why were some state banks referred to as "pet banks"?

13. Describe the boom that preceded the panic of 1837.

14. What was the purpose of Jackson's Specie Circular? What were its effects?

15. How did the National Republicans come to be known as the Whigs?

16. What were the causes of the depression of 1837?

17. What were the important features of the independent treasury system?

18. (a) Why did our relations with Great Britain become strained during Van Buren's administration? (b) What action did Van Buren take? (c) How and when was the Maine boundary dispute settled?

19. (a) How and when did the question of the annexation of Texas develop? (b) Why did the question of Texas annexation provoke controversy? (c) What action did Van Buren take?

20. (a) Why did the Whigs select General Harrison rather than Clay as their presidential candidate in 1840? (b) Who was the Whig vice-presidential candidate? (c) Briefly describe the election of 1840. (d) Why is the Whig victory in 1840 referred to as a "hollow" victory?

21. (a) On what issues did Clay and President Tyler disagree? (b) How did the character of the Democratic party change during President Tyler's administration? (c) What serious issue began to develop during Tyler's presidency?

FOR FURTHER STUDY AND DISCUSSION

1. How did Jacksonian democracy differ from Jeffersonian democracy? Helpful sources: A. M. Schlesinger, Jr., *The Age of Jackson;* Hofstadter, *The American Political Tradition,* pp. 18–68; Schlesinger, *New Viewpoints in American History,* pp. 200–220.

2. How does the election of a man like President Jackson illustrate the development of democracy?

3. To what extent was the Democratic party of Jackson a farmer-labor party?

4. Distinguish between the practical and theoretical reasons for opposition to the second Bank of the United States. Which were valid and which not? Helpful source: Amherst Series, *Jackson versus Biddle.*

5. How did the deposit of federal funds in "pet banks" tend to encourage speculation? Distinguish between "pet banks" and wildcat banks.

6. Contrast the arguments of the "Exposition and Protest" and Webster's reply to Hayne. Which of these arguments do you consider the more logical? Which is the more accurate, historically? Which is more necessary from the point of view of national development?

7. Briefly summarize the politics of tariff legislation from 1816 through 1833.

8. Why did President Jackson and Vice-President Calhoun become enemies?

9. What sections or interests did Jackson offend by his attitude toward the bank, the tariff, and internal improvements?

10. How did economic conditions influence the elections of 1836 and 1840?

11. How did President Harrison's death influence political developments?

12. Indicate the similarity, if any, of the "Exposition and Protest" to the Virginia and Kentucky resolutions and to the Hartford Convention.

13. Compare the presidential campaign of 1840 with the most recent campaign.

FOR INDIVIDUAL OR GROUP ACTIVITIES

1. In *New Viewpoints in American History,* Professor Schlesinger has three in-

teresting essays which help to illuminate the Jacksonian era and place it in perspective: "The Decline of Aristocracy in America," pp. 72–103; "The Significance of Jacksonian Democracy," pp. 200–220; and "The States' Rights Fetish," pp. 220–245. Report on these essays to the class.

2. One of the most interesting, penetrating, and significant books on American democracy by a foreign observer is De Tocqueville's *Democracy in America*, originally published in 1835. Your class might review the modern edition of the book edited by Phillips Bradley. Note the editor's introduction and evaluative essay.

3. Have two members of the class prepare dramatic readings of important passages in the speeches of Hayne and Webster in their famous debate.

4. Read and report on Jackson's analysis of the powers and duties of the President in reply to a Senate resolution that he had assumed authority and power not conferred by the Constitution. Helpful source: Hart, *Contemporaries*, Vol. III, No. 162.

5. Prepare an exhibit of posters, cartoons, illustrations, and newspaper headlines which reviews the dramatic and colorful events of Jackson's presidency.

6. Here are some suggestions for short stories, news articles, or dramatic sketches: A meeting of the "kitchen cabinet"; the toasts of Jackson and Calhoun at the Jefferson Day dinner; a conversation between Biddle and Clay on their strategy to have the bank rechartered; the celebration of Jackson's inauguration in 1829; Biddle's advice to Harrison in the campaign of 1840; the Whig campaign in 1840; Clay's resignation from the Senate.

7. Assume that the Compromise Tariff of 1833 has been passed and the smoke of battle cleared. Write an editorial on the struggle and on its significance.

8. Prepare a series of radio broadcasts, reviewing the careers of Clay, Webster, and Calhoun. Include the measures they sponsored, the issues on which they agreed or disagreed, and the services they performed for their country.

9. Investigate and report on the policy of the federal government toward the Indians in the period 1825–40.

"RUSTIC DANCE AFTER A SLEIGH RIDE" *from a painting by William Sidney Mount*

The American is a new man, who acts upon new principles; he must therefore entertain new ideas, and form new opinions.——*Jean de Crèvecoeur*

18. AN AMERICAN CULTURE DEVELOPS

American Writers Win International Recognition

A literary awakening.

The Revolution brought us political independence from England, but cultural independence was still to be achieved. For a long time after the war Americans looked to Europe for leadership in literature, the fine arts, and science. This was to be expected in a new land where only a few people had the wealth and leisure for cultural pursuits. Moreover, opportunities for training in both the arts and sciences were poor. On this side of the ocean, would-be artists, writers, and scientists had to overcome so many obstacles that most of them gave up and turned to surer ways of earning a living.

Europeans read Irving, Cooper, and Bryant.

The first American writer to be widely read abroad was Washington Irving. His *Diedrich Knickerbocker's History of New York* (1809) was translated into many languages. It is a comical account of Dutch rule in the Hudson Valley and a satire on the Jeffer-

sonians. In 1815 Irving departed for Europe, where he lived for seventeen years. During his stay in England he wrote the *Sketch Book* (1819), consisting of essays and legendary tales, such as "Rip Van Winkle" and "The Legend of Sleepy Hollow." The *Sketch Book* became a best-seller on both sides of the ocean. Because of its elegant yet simple style, it was used abroad for almost a century as a first reader for students of the English language. Irving wrote a number of other books. In the 1820's and 1830's he was considered America's leading man of letters.

James Fenimore Cooper won international acclaim for his novel *The Spy* (1821), telling of the Revolutionary War. His most famous works, the "Leatherstocking" series of novels, were different from anything yet written. They dealt with the life of pioneers and Indians on the American frontier. Cooper also wrote novels about sailors. Like Irving, Cooper lived in Europe for a number of years. As each new book came from his pen it was promptly published in America and in the leading cities of Europe.

Another American writer whom Europeans recognized was the young poet William Cullen Bryant. His fame began in 1817, when the *North American Review* published his poem "Thanatopsis" on the theme of death. Written a few years before, when Bryant was only seventeen, it was the first great poem by an American. Two English critics hailed his "To a Waterfowl" as the best short poem in the language.

Most of Bryant's poems had nature as their theme. In 1825 the "father of American poetry," as Bryant was called later, left his home in western Massachusetts to settle in New York. For nearly fifty years he edited the *New York Evening Post*, promoting reforms, fighting special privilege, and stimulating the discussion of ideas.

The South claims Poe and Simms.

The greatest writer produced by the South during this period was Edgar Allan Poe (1809–1849). He won lasting fame for his poems, short stories, and literary criticism. His tales of horror, such as "The Pit and the Pendulum" and "The Fall of the House of Usher," and his detective stories, such as "The Gold Bug" and "The Murders in the Rue Morgue," set a standard which has seldom been equaled. Poe's poetry is noted for its melancholy, fantastic images, and verbal music.

What Cooper did for the region of his boyhood, central New York, William Gilmore Simms did for the Carolinas and Georgia. He wrote eighty-seven books, mostly historical romances of the Revolution and the frontier. He also wrote poetry.

New England has a "Golden Day."

The literary awakening bore its richest fruit in New England. Few nations have witnessed such a literary outpouring as that which took place in and around Boston during the middle third of the century. The period has been called New England's "Golden Day." Much of the writing was inspired by two movements—Unitarianism and Transcendentalism. The Unitarians preached that all men can become good and that God is a loving Father who cares for the individual. The Transcendentalists taught that men should rely on their own insight rather than on an outside authority to tell them what is wrong or right. After Ralph Waldo

(Top) LYDIA HUNTLEY SIGOURNEY, *an editor of* Godey's *Lady's Book, was well known in her time for her sentimental writings.*

(Left) JAMES FENIMORE COOPER, *an outstanding interpreter of the American frontier*

(Right) EDGAR ALLAN POE, *though unrecognized by his countrymen in his lifetime, has since been acclaimed as one of America's master-writers.*

Emerson's *Nature* appeared in 1836, most New England writers were greatly influenced by the spirit of Transcendentalism.

Emerson was the leader of the Transcendentalists. After serving six years as a Unitarian minister in Boston, he resigned to spend his time lecturing and writing. In the quiet of his little white cottage in Concord, he wrote essays and poems that stressed the worth and unlimited possibilities of each individual. To live nobly, Emerson said, a man must be free to seek the truth and must be independent in spirit. "Whoso would be a man must be a nonconformist. . . . Nothing is at last sacred but the integrity of your own mind." A man should be self-reliant, Emerson believed, in his search for the highest values. "Let man stand erect, go alone, and possess the universe." One should not strive for material goods, he said, for then "Things are in the saddle and ride mankind."

Emerson's closest friend was the peculiar genius, Henry Thoreau. Wishing to make himself independent of money and possessions, Thoreau built a hut on Walden Pond near Concord, where he lived like a hermit for two years. His best-known volume, *Walden* (1854), describes the wild life he observed while living in the woods and gives his reflections on man and society. Thoreau was little known in his lifetime but has since been recognized as a powerful social critic. His antislavery convictions led him to refuse to pay taxes during the Mexican War. For this he went to jail. Thoreau believed it is man's duty to do the right as he sees it even when it means disobeying the law. His essay on "Civil Disobedience" inspired Gandhi many years later in his campaign of passive resistance to free India from British control.

Many other New England writers rose to fame during this period. Nathaniel Hawthorne, another friend of Emerson's, is regarded as the father of the American psychological novel. His masterpiece, *The Scarlet Letter* (1850), deals with the problem of sin. Richard H. Dana is remembered for a stirring narrative, *Two Years Before the Mast* (1840), which was written to get justice for the common sailor. The Quaker poet, John Greenleaf Whittier, used his pen mainly in the fight against slavery. His masterpiece, "Snow-Bound," however, is an idyll of rural New England home life. Henry Wadsworth Longfellow was the most beloved American poet in his own day. Such poems as "Evangeline," "The Song of Hiawatha," "The Courtship of Miles Standish," "The Children's Hour," and "A Psalm of Life" were once familiar to all American school children. James Russell Lowell was noted as a literary critic. He also wrote poetry and humorous sketches, in some of which he attacked slavery, intemperance, and war. Like Longfellow and Lowell, the physician Oliver Wendell Holmes was a Harvard University professor. He wrote whimsical essays, biography, psychiatric novels, hymns, and verse. Among his best-known poems were "Old Ironsides," "The Wonderful One-Hoss Shay," "The Last Leaf," and "The Chambered Nautilus."

During the "Golden Day" New Englanders produced many scholarly works in history and biography. Jared Sparks, George Bancroft, Richard Hildreth, and John Palfrey are remembered for their important contributions to American history. William H. Prescott is noted for his dramatic *Conquest of Mexico* and *Conquest of Peru,* and for his lives of Ferdinand and Isabella. John L. Motley achieved fame with his *Rise of the Dutch Republic.* Francis Parkman, whose books are among the most delightful of all histories, wrote a magnificent series on the struggle between France and England for North America.

(Left to right) WALT WHITMAN, JAMES RUSSELL LOWELL, HENRY DAVID THOREAU
(Below) JOHN GREENLEAF WHITTIER (left) *and* RALPH WALDO EMERSON (right)

THE POOR VOTER ON ELECTION DAY

The proudest now is but my peer,
The highest not more high;
To-day, of all the weary year,
A king of men am I.
To-day alike are great and small,
The nameless and the known;
My palace is the people's hall,
The ballot-box my throne!

Who serves to-day upon the list
Beside the served shall stand;
Alike the brown and wrinkled fist,
The gloved and dainty hand!
The rich is level with the poor,
The weak is strong to-day;
And sleekest broadcloth counts no more
Than homespun frock of gray.

To-day let pomp and vain pretence
My stubborn right abide;
I set a plain man's common sense
Against the pedant's pride.
To-day shall simple manhood try
The strength of gold and land;
The wide world has not wealth to buy
The power in my right hand!

While there's a grief to seek redress,
Or balance to adjust,
Where weighs our living manhood less
Than Mammon's vilest dust,—
While there's a right to need my vote,
A wrong to sweep away,
Up! clouted knee and ragged coat!
A man's a man to-day!

      John Greenleaf Whittier

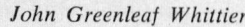

The Old Manse, Concord

NATHANIEL HAWTHORNE

"By the rude bridge that arched the flood . . ." the famous Revolutionary battle was fought.

Whitman and Melville win tardy recognition.

Two of the greatest American writers of the period were almost ignored in their own lifetime. Walt Whitman was a Brooklyn (N. Y.) newspaperman of eccentric personality. His *Leaves of Grass* appeared in 1855. Few critics appreciated it at the time, although Emerson wrote to its author, "I find it the most extraordinary piece of wit and wisdom that America has yet contributed." In verse which lacks stanzas, rhyme, and sometimes regular meter, Whitman expressed his faith in the common man. His remedy for the evils he saw in society was more democracy. "Whoever degrades another degrades me." Although his work is uneven in quality, much of it has now become world-famous.

Herman Melville was born in New York City, and at eighteen went to sea. While still a youth he began writing novels based on his adventures aboard ship and among the natives he found on islands in the South Seas. His finest work, *Moby Dick* (1851), tells of its hero's search for a fierce white whale. The book is an allegory of man's struggle with himself. Misunderstood and neglected while its author lived, *Moby Dick* is today considered one of the masterpieces of American literature.

The reading habit grows.

When Jackson was elected President, only a small number of Americans had the habit of reading. But before twenty years had passed, the average man and woman were reading as they had never done before. In part this change resulted from the growing number of free schools. In part it was due to the increasing use of whale-oil lamps, which made it easier for people to read in the evening after work was done. In part it was due to improved methods of printing, which led to cheaper newspapers and magazines.

In 1833 Benjamin A. Day, a New York City printer, decided to publish a newspaper which workingmen could afford and would wish to read. Other daily papers sold for eight to ten dollars a year, a price beyond the reach of most people. Day planned to sell his paper, the *New York Sun,* for a cent a copy. He saw that he could make money only if the paper had a large enough circulation to attract advertisers. So he made his paper interesting to ordinary people having little education. Within three years the *Sun* had a daily sale of 27,000 copies, while the most successful of the older New York papers had a sale of only 1700 copies.

Day's plan was quickly copied by other editors. In 1835 James Gordon Bennett started the *New York Herald.* In 1841 a former Vermont printer's apprentice, Horace Greeley, founded the *New York Tribune.* During the next thirty years the *Tribune* was probably the most influential paper in the country. Greeley made it the champion of abolition, labor organization, women's rights, free homesteads, and other reform movements. In 1851 the *New York Times* made its bow. By this time penny papers were being printed in the smaller cities as well.

As the demand for reading matter grew, hundreds of weekly and monthly magazines appeared. Many lasted for only a few months. As one died, another sprang up in its place. The most popular and successful magazine of the period was *Godey's Lady's Book.* In addition to such light magazines were a great number devoted to religion, temperance, abolition, and science.

Before Jackson's time hardly any American writer could support himself with his pen. But as the army of readers grew, hundreds found it possible to earn a living from writing. Many who wrote regularly for newspapers and magazines turned to the writing of books in their spare time.

"THE PRESIDENT'S HOUSE." *This sketch by James Hoban won first prize in a competition held in 1792 for the proposed federal buildings in Washington.*

In Other Arts the Period Is Less Creative

The drama gains popularity.

In colonial days the theater was frowned upon by most religious groups, and few theaters existed. In Massachusetts and Pennsylvania the giving of stage plays was forbidden. After the Revolution, American playwrights argued that the drama could serve to win support for the Republic. One of the most earnest was William Dunlap, who wrote and produced plays on patriotic American themes.

With the coming of the steamboat and the railroad, the number of theaters grew. Traveling companies were organized to carry the drama even to the small towns. Along the Ohio and the Mississippi, showboats brought the theater to the people. Both European and American plays were shown. Many dealt with American history, such as the events and personages of the Revolution, the battle over the Bank of the United States, the dispute over the Maine boundary, or Indian wars. *Rip Van Winkle* was often given. The noble Indian and the Negro comic were favorite characters. A temperance play, *Ten Nights in a Bar-Room*, became popular in the 1850's. At the same time

Uncle Tom's Cabin was shown on practically every stage in the North and was instrumental in arousing sympathy for slaves.

By the 1820's it had become the custom for leading English actors and actresses to make American tours. Some of them, like Joseph Jefferson and Junius Booth, settled in America to become actor-managers. In most theatrical companies a large proportion of the professionals were of English birth and training. Yet by the mid-century at least two Americans, Edwin Booth (Junius' son) and Charlotte Cushman, were becoming celebrated abroad.

Painting and sculpture develop slowly.

In the early 1800's America had several excellent portrait painters. Among them were John Singleton Copley, Gilbert Stuart, Charles Willson Peale, Rembrandt Peale, and John Trumbull. Interestingly enough, most of these men had studied in England under another American, Benjamin West. Their paintings of the great men of the Revolution and the early Republic are well known. Trumbull, a colonel in the Revolutionary War, also painted historic scenes, such as "The Battle of Bunker Hill," "The Signing of the Declaration of Independence," and "The Surrender of Cornwallis at Yorktown."

283

(Above) *This portrait of James Peale by his brother Charles Willson Peale (1741–1827) demonstrates the painter's objectivity and realism.*
(Below) THE GOLD-DOMED MASSACHUSETTS STATE HOUSE *is a monument to the genius of Charles Bulfinch. It shows the classic spirit of American architecture at this period.*

These pictures, reproduced in color by the new lithographic process, soon appeared in public buildings and private homes. They helped arouse pride in the new nation.

In the first half of the nineteenth century hundreds of artists traveled up and down the countryside earning a living by painting portraits. There was a great demand for miniatures—small portraits on ivory. After the introduction of the camera in the 1840's, painters of portraits found it far harder to support themselves.

About 1825 several painters began trying to put on canvas the beauties of the American landscape. Earlier artists had shown little interest in the landscape except as a background for an historic or a religious event. Most of the landscape painters of the years 1825–50 were self-taught and had faulty technique, yet some of their work has great charm. They are spoken of today as the "Hudson River School," because that river was one of their favorite subjects.

Meanwhile other artists began to paint scenes of everyday life. Perhaps the first of these genre painters, as they are called today, was William Sidney Mount. Another genre painter, George C. Bingham, of Virginia and Missouri, is noted for his vigorous pictures of frontier life. (See pp. 248–49, 276.)

The history of American sculpture began with Horatio Greenough of Boston, who went to Rome to study in 1825. One of his works is a statue of Washington in a Roman toga, done according to the classical style then popular in Europe. About the middle of the century Americans developed a more original, realistic style of sculpture. A good example is the statue of Andrew Jackson on horseback made in 1853 by Clark Mills. This was the first equestrian statue in America. Some of the best sculpture of this period consists of wooden figureheads for ships carved by forgotten craftsmen. (See p. 311.)

Architecture reflects European styles.

In the late colonial and the post-Revolutionary period, the English style of architecture known as "Georgian" was popular in America. Among the best examples of it are the mansions built by Samuel McIntire (1757–1811) for the wealthy merchants of Salem, Massachusetts. Many of these stately houses are still standing. They are square houses, three stories high, with a wide central hallway running from front to back. They are noted for their beautiful doorways and interior details.

Charles Bulfinch of Boston studied abroad and then became a professional architect. He planned the Massachusetts and Connecticut statehouses, with their imposing porticos and golden domes. Many of the simple but handsome churches to be seen in New England are of Bulfinch design. From 1817 until its completion in 1830 he was the architect of the national capitol in Washington.

Thomas Jefferson, a skillful architect as well as a statesman, preferred the classical form of architecture. This was inspired by Greek and Roman models. Jefferson's own home, Monticello, has classical columns, dome, and portico. The plantation houses he designed for his friends also show the classical influence. He based his design for the state capitol of Virginia on a Roman temple. Jefferson designed the University of Virginia, still considered one of the most beautiful groups of college buildings in the world (see illus. pp. 200–201).

About 1840 the dignified Georgian, Roman, and Greek styles went out of fashion. The Gothic style came in. With its pointed windows, colored glass, and elaborate cornices, it was better suited to a church than to a family dwelling. The "gingerbread" mansions built after the middle of the 1800's show touches of Gothic influence.

(Above)   *Top of chest designed and carved by* SAMUEL McINTYRE, *a famous craftsman of the "Adams" style.*
(Below) CHARLES BULFINCH *designed the carvings on these arches in the Derby House at Salem, Massachusetts.*

285

Music, too, is borrowed from Europe.

Music developed even more slowly in America than did the other arts. In colonial times few people had time to learn an instrument, and there was very little music except singing. The first musical society in the colonies was founded in Charleston in 1761. In 1786 William Billings, a tanner, organized a singing society at Stoughton (Mass.) which is still in existence.

Lowell Mason did more than anyone else to encourage congregational singing in churches. He collected hymns and set them to music, often using tunes written by the great German composers. Also he promoted musical education by establishing the Boston Academy of Music (1832). Six years later he succeeded in having music introduced into the Boston schools.

Little music was written in America until late in the 1800's. American songs were generally set to European tunes. Stephen Foster was one of the first Americans to write original melodies for his songs. His "Old Folks at Home" (1851) became popular at once.

German immigrants to the United States contributed enormously to the development here of an appreciation of music. Wherever a group of Germans settled, musical activities were sure to become a feature of the community life. It was a German, Gottlieb Graupner, who founded the first genuine orchestra in the United States. Known as the Boston Philharmonic Society, it began its activities about 1810. Five years later Graupner helped to launch Boston's still famous Handel and Haydn Society, a group of singers who produce oratorios. After 1845, when thousands of German intellectuals came here to escape persecution, a large number of orchestras, bands, singing societies, and music schools were established. Fine music from then on ceased to be the privilege of the few.

286

Americans Contribute to Scientific Advance

American scientists study natural history.

The young republic also leaned heavily on Europe in the field of science. American scientists purchased books and equipment abroad. Some of them studied in Europe, since American colleges neglected research. The study of science was encouraged by two learned societies, the American Philosophical Society, founded by Benjamin Franklin in 1743 (see p. 89), and the American Academy of Arts and Sciences, founded by John Adams at Boston in 1780. Both societies collected and published scientific writings and both maintained libraries.

In the first half of the 1800's, natural history was the favorite field of American scientists. Among the most picturesque American naturalists was John James Audubon. Audubon came to the United States from France in 1803. He spent many years observing and painting the wild birds in various parts of the country. One of his great works, *Birds of America*, contains remarkably exact likenesses of nearly 500 species. He began a similar study of American four-footed animals which his sons completed after his death.

Asa Gray (1810–1888) became one of the world's leading botanists. He described and classified a vast number of American plants. His scheme of classification is still used by botanists. As a teacher at Harvard and a writer, Gray helped popularize the study of botany.

Among other Americans who made important contributions to science in the first half of the century were Matthew Maury and Joseph Henry. Maury, a naval officer, founded the science of oceanography. In one of his researches he used a large number of ships' logs to study winds and ocean currents. Then he prepared tables showing the winds and currents to be expected at various seasons in all parts of the ocean. These tables, first published in 1847, were of immense value to navigators. While Maury pioneered in oceanography, Joseph Henry worked in the new field of electromagnetism. He improved the electromagnet. He discovered the principles underlying the telegraph and made possible its invention by Samuel F. B. Morse.

Scientific institutions are founded.

The growing interest in science led to the establishment of schools devoted entirely to science and technology. The first ones were the Rensselaer Polytechnic Institute at Troy (New York) and the Franklin Institute at Philadelphia. Both were founded in 1824.

In 1829 an Englishman, James Smithson, left his fortune to the United States government "to found an establishment for the increase and diffusion of knowledge among men." Congress hesitated to accept the gift until 1846. Then, through the efforts of John Quincy Adams, the Smithsonian Institution was chartered. Joseph Henry, its first director, made it a leading center for scientific research.

Americans contribute to medical science.

During this period the best medical schools were in Europe. There was little medical research, and most of that was done in Europe. Yet Americans made some important contributions to medical science.

An American surgeon, William Beaumont, made careful observations of the secretions and action of the stomach. His findings, published in 1833, were of world-wide importance. They completely changed existing theories of the physiology of the stomach.

Americans also were the first to use the new gases, nitrous oxide (laughing gas) and ether, to relieve the pain of surgery. Dr. Horace Wells, a Vermont

ASA GRAY

MATTHEW FONTAINE MAURY

dentist, used laughing gas in 1844 in the extraction of teeth. Two years later Dr. W. T. G. Morton, a Boston dentist, employed ether in tooth extraction. Dr. John C. Warren then arranged for the use of Morton's discovery in an operation at the Massachusetts General Hospital. The demonstration, which was observed by a number of physicians, was one of the most important events in the history of medicine. Later it became known that a Georgia physician, Dr. Crawford W. Long, had used ether in operations as early as 1842.

Americans encourage applied science.

Europeans criticized American scientists for their failure to develop "pure" science. Instead of making studies that might lead to the discovery of new principles, American scientists usually worked on practical problems. For this reason they contributed much to technology but little to basic science. The astonishing advances in American technology were made possible in most cases by basic research done in Europe.

Perhaps Americans should have done more work in scientific theory. Yet they led in harnessing science for man's physical comfort and well-being. By lowering the cost of agricultural and industrial products and by reducing drudgery, practical science promised to bring the common man a healthier and happier life.

The Spirit of Democracy Is Seen in Religious Activities

New religious teachings become popular.

In the first half of the 1800's Americans had a spiritual awakening. It was stimulated by new religious ideas that gave more hope to the average man and woman. People turned away from the Calvinistic teachings of a stern, unforgiving God who has predestined all but a few of the elect to suffer everlasting punishment. Instead many listened to the teaching of the Universalist, John Murray, that "every individual shall in due time be separated from sin and rendered fit to associate with the denizens of heaven." Many turned away, too, from the teaching that human nature is evil, and accepted the idea that man is essentially good and capable of developing godlike qualities of character. This idea, which was made popular by Emerson and many other Transcendentalists, encouraged all sorts of reform efforts and acts of social service.

Protestant sects multiply.

In this period laymen increasingly wanted a share in the management of their churches. The churches which flourished were those in which the local congregation was largely self-governing. Local leaders sometimes took their followers out of the denominational fold and established a new sect. The Baptists, for instance, divided into some twenty sects. The Methodists, Presbyterians, Quakers, and Congregationalists also split. About half the Congregational churches, for example, became Unitarian. In addition, entirely new sects sprang to life, such as the Adventists and Mormons.

Circuit riders preach to frontier dwellers.

Some sects, especially the Methodists and the Baptists, were active in the West. They sent traveling ministers, called "circuit riders," to frontier areas. The circuit rider, though often poorly educated, was full of religious zeal. He gave away Bibles and religious leaflets and urged daily Bible reading and family prayers. He called the people to repent their sins and lead a righteous life, promising that the repentant could be redeemed. Little churches soon dotted the regions where the circuit riders traveled.

Revivals become the custom.

By 1800 certain of the traveling preachers, known as "revivalists," had begun to attract great throngs in the West. People flocked from miles around to hear them speak, at open-air camp meetings which lasted for days. The fiery preaching, the singing of stirring gospel hymns, and public confessions and testimonials, aroused worshipers to a high pitch of emotion. Some were moved to hysterical outbursts, in which they shook, fell on the ground, rolled, and wept or laughed by turns. Despite some emotional excesses, the revivals brought religious inspiration to countless thousands. Among the most famous revivalists were the Methodists, Francis Asbury and Peter Cartwright, and the Presbyterian, Charles G. Finney. Their work was not confined to the West. Revival meetings were held in Eastern cities as well. To this day revivals are a feature of many Protestant sects.

Separation of church and state is completed.

As we have noted, most states had stopped giving financial support to any church during or soon after the Revolution (see p. 129). Massachusetts, however, did not abolish taxes to support the Congregational Church until 1833. By this time in all the states nearly all religious qualifications for public office had disappeared. Sects which maintained schools tried to get tax support for them and sometimes did so. But by 1850 it was generally understood that taxes would be used only for the support of public schools and these must be nonsectarian. All sects had come to stand equal before the law.

The missionary spirit is strong.

Beginning early in the 1800's, American Protestant missionaries went to India, China, Africa, and Hawaii. Others worked among the American Indians. Wherever they went, the missionaries put the language of the natives into writing and translated the Scriptures into the native tongue. They also started schools and hospitals as rapidly as they could get funds. In 1848 an Episcopalian bishop, George Doane, expressed the missionary spirit of his time in a stirring hymn:

> Fling out the banner! Heathen lands
> Shall see from far the glorious sight,
> And nations crowding to be born,
> Baptize their spirits in its light.

Roman Catholic missionaries also worked in Asia, Africa, and among the American Indians. Their activities, however, were directed from Rome. Therefore, although some were Americans, they are not described as American missionaries.

The churches foster several services.

During the nineteenth century the idea that an individual may find salvation through good works came to be widely held. The duty of the religious to help others was more emphasized than it had been for centuries. One result was the growth of philanthropy. Well-to-do people and even those of small means contributed generously to missions and to charitable agencies.

An annual meeting of the SOCIETY OF FRIENDS *in Indiana*

Francis Bowen, a Harvard economist, wrote in the 1850's: "The sums which are contributed here by individuals for the support of schools, colleges, churches, missions, hospitals, and institutions of science and beneficence, put to shame the official liberality of the oldest and wealthiest governments in Europe."

Before this period Quakers had been the only denomination to show much interest in social reform. Now other denominations became interested in social questions. Preachers and their congregations took part in the temperance movement, the effort to improve the care of prisoners and the insane,

and—in the North—the antislavery crusade. Preachers sometimes lost their churches as a result of taking too strong a stand on a public question. Congregations sometimes split over these questions. The bitter controversy over slavery split the Methodist, Baptist, and Presbyterian churches into Northern and Southern branches.

The churches took on new activities. They established Sunday schools and young people's societies. City churches built parish houses for social gatherings. Some denominations built hospitals, orphanages, and homes for the aged. Thus the churches were developing the idea of social service and were becoming concerned with the care of the body and the mind as well as with the care of the soul.

Wooden weathervane

FOR IDENTIFICATION

John James Audubon	Washington Irving
George Bancroft	Dr. Crawford W. Long
Dr. William Beaumont	Henry W. Longfellow
James Gordon Bennett	James Russell Lowell
William Cullen Bryant	Lowell Mason
Charles Bulfinch	Matthew Maury
James Fenimore Cooper	Herman Melville
John Singleton Copley	Samuel F. B. Morse
Richard H. Dana	Dr. W. T. G. Morton
Benjamin Day	John Lothrop Motley
Ralph Waldo Emerson	Francis Parkman
Stephen Foster	Edgar Allan Poe
Asa Gray	William H. Prescott
Horace Greeley	William Gilmore Simms
Nathaniel Hawthorne	Gilbert Stuart
Joseph Henry	Henry Thoreau
Oliver Wendell Holmes	Dr. Horace Wells
	Benjamin West
	Walt Whitman
	John Greenleaf Whittier

FOR EXPLANATION OR DEFINITION

Calvinism	Smithsonian
circuit riders	Institution
genre painters	Transcendentalism
Godey's Lady's Book	Unitarianism
revivals	Universalism
showboats	

FOR REVIEW

1. Why did literature, the fine arts, and science develop so slowly in America?

2. Who were among the first American writers to achieve foreign recognition? Name some of their important works.

3. What were the sources of the novels of James Fenimore Cooper?

4. What writers represented the South in the first half of the nineteenth century?

5. (a) What is meant by Unitarianism? Transcendentalism? How did these movements influence literature? (b) What ideals were emphasized by Emerson? By Thoreau? (c) How did Thoreau influence Gandhi?

6. Name some of the important works of Hawthorne, Longfellow, and Holmes.

7. What fields of historical research attracted the attention of Bancroft, Parkman, Prescott, and Motley?

8. What two writers of the mid-nineteenth century achieved tardy recognition? Describe their work.

9. (a) What important changes in newspaper publication were introduced by Benjamin Day? (b) Describe the work of Horace Greeley.

10. Trace the growth in popularity of the drama. What did English actors contribute?

11. (a) Why did painting and sculpture develop slowly? (b) Name some of the famous American portrait painters of the early nineteenth century. (c) What were characteristics of the "Hudson River School"? (d) What invention lessened the demand for portrait painters?

12. Outline some of the main characteristics of Georgian, classical, and Gothic architecture. What contributions did Thomas Jefferson and Charles Bulfinch make to American architecture?

13. How did Lowell Mason and Gottlieb Graupner promote the enjoyment of music? What did German immigrants contribute?

14. (a) Name two societies which encouraged the study of science. Who founded each? (b) State the scientific achievements of Audubon, Gray, Maury, and Henry.

15. When and where were the first American schools devoted to science and technology established? Tell of the founding of the Smithsonian Institution.

16. For what medical research did Dr. Beaumont receive recognition?

17. Distinguish between "pure" and "applied" science. What were some of the early achievements of Americans in the field of applied science?

18. (a) What were the main features of the spiritual awakening of the early nineteenth century? (b) When was the separation of church and state completed? (c) Describe the work done by missionaries. (d) What social service activities began to interest ministers and their congregations?

FOR FURTHER STUDY AND DISCUSSION

1. How do you account for the fact that the flowering of American culture began in the Northeast?

2. How did literature reflect the new America?

3. Why is the introduction of the cheap newspaper a factor in the growth of American democracy?

4. Why is it claimed that Emerson's philosophy of "the divine self-sufficiency of the individual" reflected the social and economic environment of his times?

5. Explain the meaning of Emerson's statement: "The appearance of character makes the state unnecessary."

6. How do you account for the fact that Whitman and Melville achieved great recognition in later generations?

7. How is the generous support of charitable agencies by the public related to democratic ideals?

FOR INDIVIDUAL OR GROUP ACTIVITIES

1. Make a selection for class reading of representative poems of Longfellow, Holmes, Whittier, Poe, and Whitman. Prepare short biographies of these men, endeavoring to emphasize the distinctive characteristics and influence of each. Helpful sources: Morris, *Encyclopedia;* Brooks, *The Flowering of New England* and *The World of Washington Irving;* Perry, *The American Spirit in Literature.*

2. Prepare book reviews on the following: Dana, *Two Years Before the Mast;* Cooper, *The Spy* or *The Last of the Mohicans;* Hawthorne, *The House of the Seven Gables;* Holmes, *Autocrat of the Breakfast Table;* Poe, *The Gold Bug* or *Murders in the Rue Morgue;* Simms, *The Partisan.*

3. Hold a panel discussion dealing with Emerson's essay "Man the Reformer" and Thoreau's "The Duty of Civil Disobedience," which you will find in Commager, *Living Ideas in America,* pp. 451–453 and pp. 379–384. See Amherst Series, *The Transcendentalist Revolt against Materialism;* also Krout and Fox, *The Completion of Independence 1790–1830,* pp. 332–370.

4. Prepare an exhibit to illustrate early nineteenth-century art, music, architecture, drama, and literature in the United States.

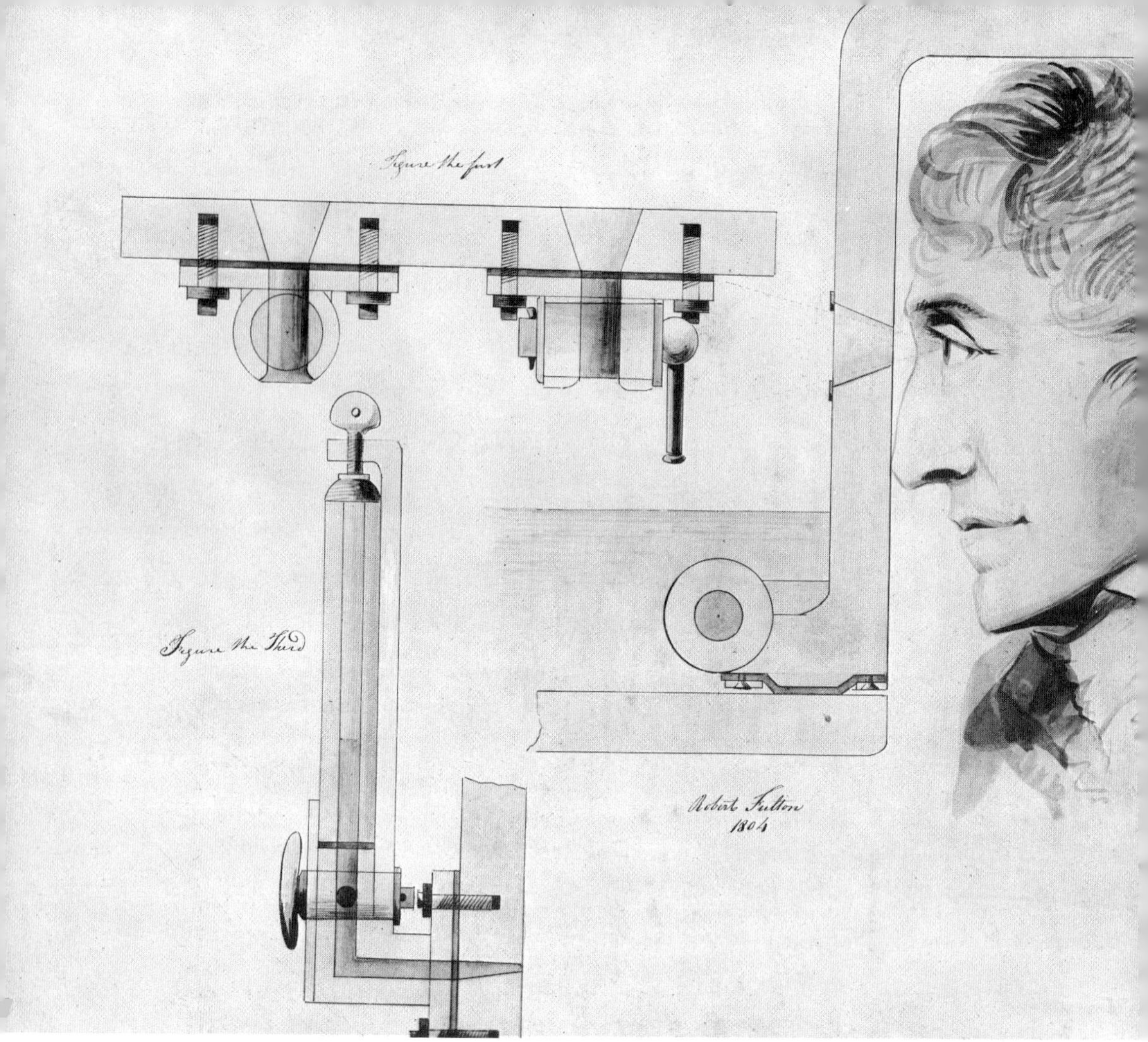

(Top) *In this self-portrait and design, done around 1804,* ROBERT FULTON *demonstrated his advanced ideas of submarine warfare. The detail at left shows the submarine window reinforced against water pressure; the bathometer below measured depth.*
(Below) *Fulton's steamboat, the* Clermont

America is a land of wonders, in which everything is in constant motion and every change seems an improvement. . . . No natural boundary seems to be set to the efforts of man; and in his eyes what is not yet done is only what he has not yet attempted to do.
——Alexis de Tocqueville

19. ECONOMIC AND SOCIAL CHANGES GAIN MOMENTUM

Transportation and Communication Are Improved

On both sides of the Atlantic the Industrial Revolution went hand in hand with amazing changes in transportation and communication. In fact, the growth of industry depended on faster ways of moving goods and sending messages. Americans were particularly interested in improving transportation and communication because of the vast size of their country.

Steamboats come into use.

The first American to experiment with propelling a boat by steam was John Fitch of Connecticut. As early as 1785 he tried out a crude model. Robert Fulton of Pennsylvania was the first American to show that a steamboat could be a commercial success. His *Clermont,* a wood-burning side-wheeler, made a trial run from New York to Albany in 1807. The next summer the *Clermont* made regular trips.

In 1811 and 1812 steamboats were launched on the Mississippi. The first boat to steam from Pittsburgh to New Orleans could not return because the river current proved too strong. More powerful steamers were built and by 1819 about sixty of them were operat-

ing regularly on the Ohio and Mississippi. By 1830 the number had grown to two hundred. Steamships soon plied the smaller rivers in the Mississippi Valley as well as the main streams. The growing commerce made New Orleans a seaport second only to New York.

River steamboats were broad and low, with a shallow draft. Some had three decks and palatial accommodations for passengers. Even so, travel was hazardous. Boiler explosions and fires were frequent, especially when rival captains engaged in races. Ships often went aground on sand bars or were caught by submerged trees. By 1850 a thousand Mississippi steamers had been lost. When Charles Dickens traveled on the Mississippi (1842), he remarked: "It always conveyed that kind of feeling to me which I should be likely to experience if I had lodgings on the first floor of a powder mill." In spite of the risks to life and cargo, the steamboat provided cheap and rapid transportation. It greatly hastened the development of the West.

Many highways are built.

Beginning in the 1790's there was lively interest in the building of toll

293

roads, or turnpikes (see p.194). In the next thirty years hundreds of turnpike companies were chartered. They built over 4000 miles of roads. State governments also built toll roads. The most important highway to the West was the Cumberland Road built by the federal government (see p. 194). Use of this road was free. It was soon crowded with settlers going west.

Canals are dug.

The next important step in developing commerce between East and West was the digging of canals. Although a few short canals were built before 1800, the era of canal building in the United States really began in 1817 when work started on the Erie Canal. American engineers had no experience with a project of this size and difficulty. Yet in seven years they completed a waterway of 363 miles, running from Albany on the Hudson River to Buffalo on Lake Erie. Locks were built to overcome an ascent of 617 feet and a descent of 42 feet. When the canal was ready for traffic in 1825, a newspaperman wrote: "They have built the longest canal in the world, in the least time, with the least experience, for the least money, and to the greatest public benefit."

Within ten years the cost of the canal was repaid from the tolls charged for its use. Shippers gladly paid the tolls, for the cost of sending a ton of goods overland from Buffalo to Albany was about eight times the cost of sending it on the canal. Cheap freight rates encouraged the rapid settlement of the region around the Great Lakes. The newborn commerce of this area poured into the canal. Buffalo, which had been only a village, became an important city almost overnight. Other busy towns grew up along the canal. New York City doubled its population within a decade, outdistancing Philadelphia as America's leading city.

The success of the Erie led to canal building on a grand scale. New York developed a network of 800 miles of canals, and Pennsylvania, a network of 954 miles. Ohio built two canals that crossed the entire state, linking Lake Erie with the Ohio River. Indiana, Illinois, and Wisconsin also built canals to connect the Great Lakes with the Mississippi. Many shorter canals were dug in the East and the Old Northwest. The South built fewer canals, for it was well supplied with rivers. By 1850 the canal building era came to an end. By then railroads were faster and could be used the year round. Soon most of the canals fell into disuse.

Steam railroads are built.

At the very time that canals were being dug, the steam railroad was introduced. Inventors in England, France, and the United States had been experimenting with railroads for many years. For power they tried horses, sails, and stationary engines. The first steam locomotive in the United States was probably the one built by Colonel John Stevens in 1825. It ran on a private circular track in Hoboken, New Jersey.

The businessmen of Baltimore, eager to get their share of trade with the West, organized the Baltimore and Ohio Railroad Company in 1827. A line twelve miles long was opened in 1830. At first the cars were pulled by horses but within a few months the company decided to use steam for power. In 1852 the road reached Cumberland, 178 miles west of Baltimore. Meanwhile, other companies had built short lines between most of the cities along the Atlantic coast.

The early railroads were quite unlike those of today. Except in coal-mining areas, the locomotives burned wood, and showers of sparks often started fires along the tracks. The rails were of wood, capped with iron strips, which often got loose and stopped the

294

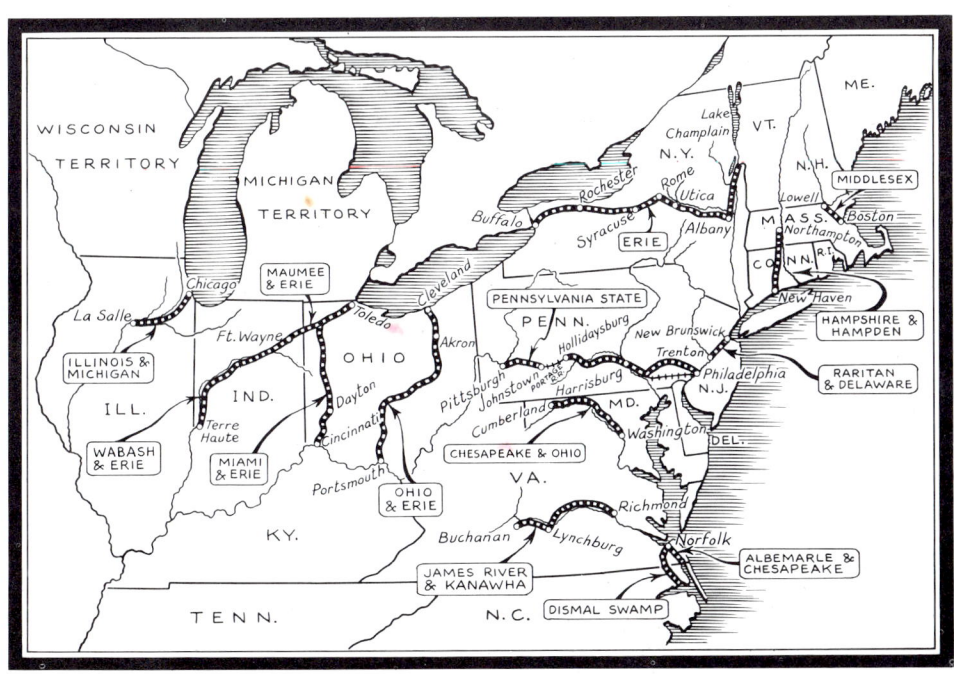

TRAVEL ROUTES IN 1833

Map 1 labels (Travel Routes in 1833):

BRITISH POSSESSIONS

OREGON TERRITORY

INDIAN COUNTRY

SPANISH POSSESSIONS

ATLANTIC OCEAN

GULF OF MEXICO

Columbia River · Lewis and Clark · Missouri R. · Yellowstone · RETURN OF CLARK · Snake R. · OREGON TRAIL · North Platte · South Platte · Omaha · CALIFORNIA TRAIL · Sacramento · OLD SPANISH TRAIL · Denver · Independence · SANTA FE TRAIL · St. Louis · Colorado · Santa Fe · Albuquerque · Los Angeles · Gila R. · Pecos R. · Red R. · Canadian R. · Brazos R. · Colorado R. · Rio Grande · Arkansas R. · Memphis · Nashville · Natchez · NATCHEZ TRACE · Baton Rouge · New Orleans · Mobile · Montgomery · Augusta · Savannah · Charleston · Fernandina · Raleigh · Richmond · Washington · Cumberland · CUMBERLAND ROAD · Baltimore · Philadelphia · Pittsburgh · New York · New Haven · Providence · Boston · Portland · Albany · Buffalo · Cleveland · Columbus · Cincinnati · Indianapolis · Vandalia · Ohio R.

Legend:
- Major Highways
- Major Canals
- Cumberland Road
- Natchez Trace
- Major Trails
- Route of Lewis and Clark Expedition

Map 2 labels (Principal Canals, 1840):

WISCONSIN TERRITORY · MICHIGAN TERRITORY · Lake Champlain · ME. · VT. · N.Y. · N.H. · MIDDLESEX · Lowell · MASS. · Boston · Northampton · R.I. · CONN. · New Haven · HAMPSHIRE & HAMPDEN · Rochester · Rome · Utica · Syracuse · ERIE · Albany · Buffalo · Cleveland · MAUMEE & ERIE · Chicago · La Salle · Ft. Wayne · Toledo · Akron · OHIO · PENNSYLVANIA STATE · PENN. · Hollidaysburg · Johnstown · Pittsburgh · PORTAGE · Harrisburg · New Brunswick · Trenton · Philadelphia · N.J. · RARITAN & DELAWARE · ILLINOIS & MICHIGAN · ILL. · IND. · Dayton · Cincinnati · Terre Haute · WABASH & ERIE · MIAMI & ERIE · Portsmouth · OHIO & ERIE · Cumberland · MD. · Washington · DEL. · CHESAPEAKE & OHIO · VA. · KY. · Buchanan · Lynchburg · Richmond · Norfolk · ALBEMARLE & CHESAPEAKE · JAMES RIVER & KANAWHA · DISMAL SWAMP · TENN. · N.C.

PRINCIPAL CANALS, 1840

295

train. Locomotives were so light in weight that they could be derailed by striking a cow. Going up or down a steep grade was impossible and even a slight grade caused trouble. One locomotive had a pair of mechanical legs which were made to drag when going downgrade. Cables and stationary engines were used to drag trains up a hill. Another difficulty arose from the fact that each company used tracks of a different gauge (distance between the rails). Thus the trains of one company could not run over the tracks of another. A traveler going by rail from Albany to Buffalo in the 1840's had to make seven changes. A standard gauge did not come into general use until after the War between North and South.

Gradually inventors solved all the practical problems of railroading. Year by year the equipment was improved with such devices as brakes, headlights, cowcatchers, and steel rails. Travel by train grew safer and faster. Everybody did more traveling, including millions who had never traveled before.

Rails connect the East and West.

A number of Eastern cities, jealous of New York's enormous trade moving over the Erie Canal, built rail lines to the West. In 1834 the state of Pennsylvania completed a combination of railroads and canals running from Philadelphia to Pittsburgh. The canal boats were dragged across the Alleghenies on a portage railroad, which was operated by means of stationary engines and endless ropes. For twenty years this railway was one of the wonders of America.

(Above) *Crossing the inclined planes of the* ALLEGHENY PORTAGE RAILWAY *in 1834. This linking of canals and rails into a single system helped make Pennsylvania an important industrial state.*
(Below) *A Black Ball Line packet ship*

In 1842 Albany and Buffalo were joined by rail. The same year a line from Boston to Albany was completed. In 1852 the Pennsylvania Railroad reached Pittsburgh. The next year, after the state of Pennsylvania at last granted a right of way across its southwest corner, the Baltimore and Ohio reached Wheeling. By this time the South also had a western road, running from Charleston and Savannah to Atlanta and thence to Chattanooga. Yet in miles of track and volume of traffic, the North was still far ahead of the South.

The telegraph revolutionizes communication.

A struggling American artist, Samuel F. B. Morse, was the inventor of the first practical telegraph. In 1835 he developed an electrical instrument for sending messages over a wire. The messages were transmitted as dots and dashes, using the code he had invented.

In 1838 Morse asked Congress to grant him $30,000 for building an experimental telegraph line between Washington and Baltimore. For several years Congress did not act, since many congressmen thought the telegraph was the scheme of a crank. Morse almost starved waiting for a bill to be presented to Congress and then waiting for its passage. In 1844 the line was ready. Morse, sitting at his telegraph key in the Supreme Court chamber, tapped out the first message, "What hath God wrought!"

Morse offered his invention to the United States government for $100,000, but Congress did not accept. He then organized a company to build a line from New York to Philadelphia. The telegraph proved so useful that many companies entered the field. By 1860 they had spread a network of lines over most of the nation.

The development of the underwater cable was the next great step in

SAMUEL F. B. MORSE, *artist and inventor*

communication by telegraph. Morse laid a cable under New York harbor in 1842. Englishmen laid a cable under the English Channel in 1850. Cyrus W. Field, a New York merchant, made several attempts to lay one across the Atlantic. After repeated discouragements, Field managed to connect Ireland and Newfoundland by cable in 1858. The cable worked for only a month before the insulation burned out. Field raised money for another cable, and in 1866 his efforts were crowned with success.

Packet ships sail the Atlantic.

A packet ship is one that carries mail, freight, or passengers regularly between two ports. An American company, the Black Ball Line, was the first in the world to send ships across the Atlantic on a regular schedule. It announced that beginning in January, 1818, a fast ship would sail for Liverpool each month at a given day and hour. When the time came for the first trip the packet, *James Monroe*, had only seven passengers and a light cargo. Instead of waiting for days or weeks, as the custom was, to make up a cargo, the captain "stood down the harbor at exactly the hour appointed." Punctuality and speed quickly attracted the best-paying freight and passenger traffic to the Black Ball Line. Within a few years many other American companies adopted the same plan.

Clipper ships make fabulous speed records.

To meet the demand for more speed, American shipbuilders developed the clipper. These slender, sharp-prowed ships carried a great spread of sail. They were the fastest and most beautiful sailing ships ever built.

The first true clipper was the *Rainbow,* launched at New York in 1845. On her maiden voyage she sailed to China for a cargo of tea and was back in New York only 7 months and 17 days later. On her next trip she knocked a full month off that record, an achievement never bettered by any other sailing ship.

Donald McKay, who moved to the United States from Nova Scotia as a youth, built the finest of all the clipper ships in his East Boston yards. The *Flying Cloud,* which he completed in 1851, twice made the trip from New York to San Francisco around Cape Horn (15,000 miles) in 89 days. The *Lightning,* on her maiden voyage in 1854, established a record of 436 miles in 24 hours. This figure was not surpassed by any ship for a generation.

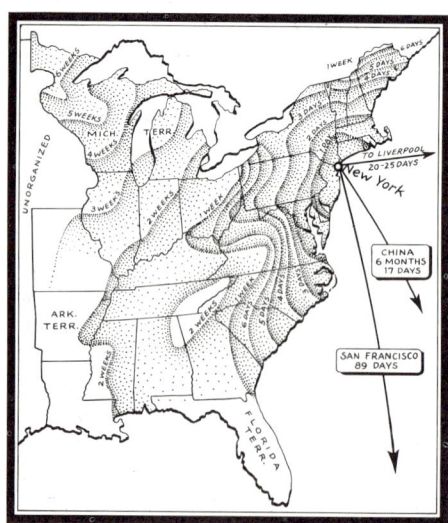

RATES OF TRAVEL
FROM NEW YORK, 1830

Steamships drive out sailing ships.

The development of ocean-going vessels powered by steam began when the *Savannah* crossed the Atlantic to England in 1819. The *Savannah* was primarily a sailing ship, with a steam engine and paddle wheels for use in the harbor or when there was no wind on the sea. Nearly a generation went by before another American steamship crossed the Atlantic. While American shipbuilders concentrated on improving the sailing ship, the British developed the ocean-going steamship. A Nova Scotian, Samuel Cunard, founded his famous transatlantic steamship line in 1840. Ten years later an American, E. K. Collins, started a rival line. For several years the Collins line received a subsidy from the federal government. When Congress withdrew the subsidy in 1858, the line went out of business.

Clippers could compete with the early steamships, which were wooden side-wheelers. In fact these first steamships had to carry so much coal to run their engines that when possible they saved fuel by using auxiliary sails. More efficient steamships with iron hulls, screw propellers, and improved engines came into use late in the 1850's. These spelled the doom of the clipper. Except on the long run from England to Australia, steamships shortly replaced clippers. At the same time American supremacy in shipbuilding passed to the British, for they could build iron ships cheaper than we could. After about 1860 our shipbuilding declined and our merchant marine dwindled.

An Agricultural Revolution

The market for farm products expands.

The growth of manufacturing at home and abroad increased the demand for American farm products, especially for cotton, wool, leather, meat, and grain. This encouraged farmers to

298

(Top) CAIRO, ILLINOIS, *a leading Mississippi port. Here the steamboat and the raft—the new and the old—worked side by side helping America grow.*
(Right) *By 1853, as this poster shows, refrigerator cars were bringing sea food to the inland consumer.*

produce for the market instead of just for their own use. Yet there were many farmers who could not get their products to market.

Commercial farming increases.

Every time a new highway, bridge, canal, or railroad was built, the farmers in that area rejoiced. Better means of transportation meant that they could cease to be *subsistence* farmers and could become *commercial* farmers. Unlike the subsistence farmer, the commercial farmer produces a substantial amount for sale. Commercial farming became more important year by year, but subsistence farming did not disappear. Even today there are some subsistence farmers.

Better farming methods are introduced.

The growth of markets led to a greater interest in up-to-date ways of farming, such as the rotation of crops and the use of barnyard manure to enrich the soil. Agricultural societies spread information about the new methods. One of the first of these societies had been organized at Philadelphia as early as 1785. Many others soon came into being. Their members consisted of prosperous and well-educated "gentlemen-farmers."

Beginning around 1810, many of the agricultural societies held annual livestock shows and fairs. To attract exhibitors, prizes were awarded for the best animals and the best farm products. To attract the public, such entertainment as community singing, athletic events, orations, horse racing, and other events might be provided. The agricultural fair helped to interest the less wealthy farmers in improved seeds and livestock and new methods of husbandry.

The farmer and his wife could also find new ideas in magazines. The first one especially for farm dwellers, the *American Farmer*, began publication in 1819. About 400 different farm journals had appeared by 1860. Though most of them did not last long, a few are still published today. Their articles and advertisements led many farm families to adopt more modern ways of farming and homemaking.

Farm machinery is invented.

Until about 1800 scarcely anything had been done to improve farm implements since ancient times. Farmers used crude wooden plows and harrows to prepare the soil. They sowed grain or grass by scattering the seed from their hands. The great majority still reaped the grain with a sickle. They threshed it either with a flail or by the tramping of work animals. Crops that required cultivation they hoed by hand. With these primitive tools and methods a family could grow little beyond its own needs, even though the women and children toiled in the fields along with the men.

The 1800's brought many changes in farm implements. The first important tool to be improved was the plow. The problem was to make a plow that could cut and turn the soil cleanly, that would not become clogged with earth, and that would not break against stones or roots. Jefferson had designed an iron plow before 1800. However, it broke easily. In 1819 Jethro Wood a New York blacksmith, patented an iron plow which could be repaired by replacing the parts. Experiments with steel plows came next. In 1837 John Deere of Illinois perfected a light, strong, steel plow that would cut the tough prairie sod. Within twenty years his factory was turning out hundreds of plows a month. Equipped with Deere's plows, settlers for the first time began moving into the Great Plains.

Reaping grain by hand

Seventeenth-century plow with iron tip

Deere's plows in a contest

Early McCormick reaper

From hand reaping and plowing with oxen to the tractor-drawn gang plow (left) to the giant combine (above) that cuts and threshes at one time: INDUSTRIAL PROGRESS IN AGRICULTURE.

More startling improvements took place in reaping. In George Washington's time a farmer using a hand sickle could cut half an acre of wheat a day if he worked hard. With a cradle, which came into use in the early 1800's, he might cut two acres a day. During the same years the scythe replaced the sickle for cutting grass. Several inventors here and in England tried to develop a horse-drawn reaper. The first to become a commercial success was patented by Cyrus McCormick of Virginia in 1834. It could reap five or six acres of grain in one day. Soon McCormick added a device to rake the grain as the knives cut it. Then a seat was added for the driver. Next came an attachment to bind the grain into bundles. Useful as the machine was, for several years McCormick found scarcely any buyers for it. Then he realized that the best market was in the West, and he built a factory in the young prairie town of Chicago. In the year 1848 he sold 500 reapers and from then on sales went up rapidly.

Threshing machines were used in America soon after 1800, but they were not very satisfactory. In the year 1837 two Maine farmers, the Pitts brothers, patented an improved model operated by two horses. By the 1850's the same inventors had made a machine that threshed, separated, and cleaned the grain.

About the same time mowing machines and horse-drawn rakes came into use for making hay. An iron harrow with steel teeth replaced the wooden harrow in preparing plowed land for seeding. The horse-drawn hoe, or cultivator, and the horse-drawn seed drill were also introduced.

Thus by 1850 an agricultural revolution was going forward. Like the Industrial Revolution, it raised the output of the worker and lightened his labor. Small farmers were slow to adopt machinery.

More People Live in Cities

Cities expand.

The growth of industry attracted people to the cities. At the same time, the rising productivity of the farmers meant that fewer people were needed in rural areas to produce the nation's food. In 1800, 6 per cent of the nation's population was "urban"—that is, living in places with 2500 people or more. By 1850 the number of urban dwellers was 15 per cent of the total population.

City life is improved.

We moderns would find life in the cities of 1800 uncomfortable. Except in Philadelphia, even the main streets were unpaved or only roughly paved with cobblestones. While some cities had begun to enjoy whale-oil lamps for street lighting, in 1800 there were no water mains or sewer pipes. Few individuals ventured out of their homes at night, for there were no policemen to protect them. Fire fighting was left to volunteers. People threw their garbage into the streets, where pigs, hens, and dogs disposed of most of it.

Gradually, city people came to realize that their local government had to take over certain responsibilities that had formerly been left to individuals. Street lighting was among the first of these new municipal functions. The provision of a safe water supply followed. One of the first municipal water works was that of New York, which was built after the city was ravaged with cholera and yellow fever in 1832. It was not until 1845 that New York added a police force to its system of night watchmen. By this time in the larger cities the government was taking on the responsibility for water supply, sanitation, and police and fire protection.

Homes become more comfortable.

In the second quarter of the 1800's new comforts and conveniences could

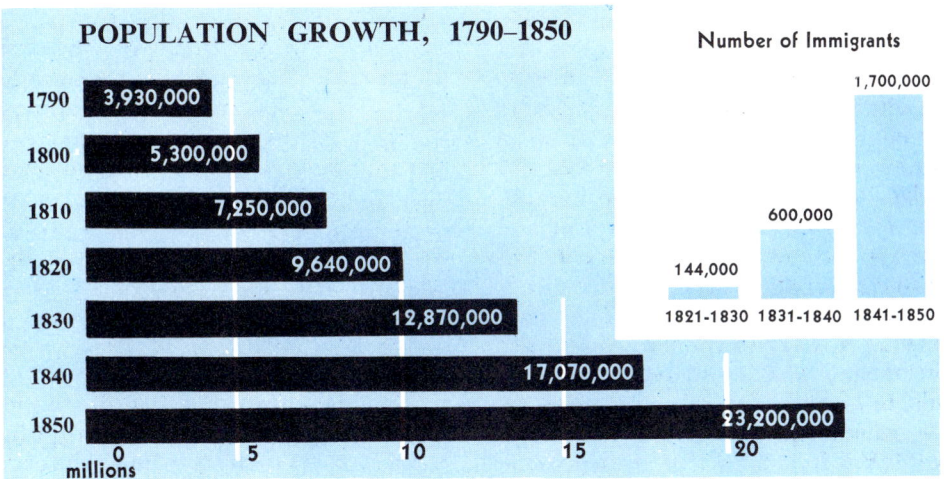

POPULATION GROWTH, 1790–1850

Year	Population
1790	3,930,000
1800	5,300,000
1810	7,250,000
1820	9,640,000
1830	12,870,000
1840	17,070,000
1850	23,200,000

0 5 10 15 20
millions

Number of Immigrants

Period	Number
1821-1830	144,000
1831-1840	600,000
1841-1850	1,700,000

be found in homes, especially in the cities. New methods of heating were coming into use. All through the Northeast, kitchen fireplaces had been closed and iron ranges had taken their place. In cities coal was replacing wood as a fuel. Hot-air furnaces were being installed in public buildings, churches, and the houses of the well to do.

Lighting was also improved. It is said that this generation was born by candlelight and died by oil lamps. The lamps burned whale oil or lard, for petroleum had not yet come into use. By 1850 gaslights were replacing whale-oil lamps for lighting city streets.

The kitchen was changed not only by the new cookstove but by new kitchenware. In place of heavy copper and iron utensils, tinware made its appearance. Tinware was so cheap that most housewives could afford a good supply of pots and pans.

Wallpaper, once found only in the homes of the well to do, now was made cheaply in American factories. As a result it was coming into common use. Carpets, too, were being made in America at a price that middle-class people could afford. They were rapidly taking the place of homemade rag rugs. Spring-construction furniture made its appearance. Rocking chairs became popular. The doorbell was taking the place of the door knocker. The invention of photography enabled the poor as well as the rich to have their portraits made. By 1850 homes often contained photographs of the family.

Immigration Alters American Life

The number of immigrants to the United States rose rapidly during the second quarter of the 1800's. In 1830 only 3 per cent of our people were foreign-born, but in 1850 the figure was 10 per cent. The newcomers came largely from the British Isles and Germany.

Why immigrants came.

Before 1830 the United States offered little to unskilled laborers and poor tenant farmers from Europe. Jobs were scarce and land was too expensive. Then the picture changed. The boom of the 1830's, with its feverish building of canals and railroads and the growth of industry, created many jobs for the unskilled. Another cause of the rise in immigration was the Pre-emption Act of 1830, which encouraged poor men to settle on the public land in hopes of being able to purchase it at some future time (see p. 247). America looked all the more attractive because the Industrial Revolution in England and Germany was robbing thousands of craftsmen of their means of livelihood. At the same time the packet lines were making it easier to come to America.

In the 1840's a series of bad crop years drove many English, Scotch, and German peasants to come here. Ireland suffered a famine in 1846 in which one in every five of the people died. To escape starvation nearly a million Irish peasants came to the United States.

Unsuccessful revolutions in Germany and elsewhere in Europe in the early 1830's and again in 1848–49 caused still others to flee to America. Many well-educated German liberals fled during these years. Among them were distinguished scientists and hundreds of professional musicians.

Immigrants settle in the North.

Since poor men found little chance to get ahead in the South, few immigrants went there. Instead they arrived in northern ports and remained in the North. Many immigrants, particularly the Irish, landed with empty pockets and therefore stayed in the city where they landed. However, many were hired in gangs to dig canals or build railways. After these jobs were finished the immigrants generally went to some nearby factory town to seek work. German immigrants were more likely to arrive with some cash. Many of these went to Buffalo, Cleveland, Detroit, Cincinnati, St. Louis, and Milwaukee. A still larger number bought land in rural areas.

Immigrants meet opposition.

As the foreign-born became more numerous, they met with considerable hostility from the natives. Some groups of immigrants were more resented than others, depending mainly on whether they were non-English, whether they were willing to work for lower wages than Americans, and whether they were Roman Catholic.

IMMIGRANTS, *arriving in New York. These newcomers had left behind them a continent plagued by wars, revolutions, and famine.*

Most of the newcomers were un-educated and unskilled. Often they had spent everything they had to get to America and they had to accept any job they could find. They frequently took work as strikebreakers, thus defeating the efforts of other wage earners to obtain higher pay and better working conditions. The bitter feeling that resulted sometimes led to street fights.

The Irish were the chief target for attack. Not only were they very poor, but they were of the Roman Catholic faith. Most Americans in those days deeply distrusted the Roman Catholic Church. They knew little about it, for in 1815 only one in a hundred Americans was a member. In the 1830's, when Irish immigrants first began coming in any number, an anti-Catholic drive started. A Boston mob destroyed a convent school. In other cities, too, Roman Catholic churches and convents were sometimes damaged or destroyed.

Anti-Catholic and antiforeign feeling reached its height in the early 1850's, when the so-called "American party" was organized to oppose foreigners and Roman Catholics. Most people called it the "Know-Nothing party" because when asked about their purposes, members would reply, "I know nothing." The Know-Nothings demanded that immigration be restricted and that the naturalization period be changed from five years to twenty-one years. They tried to prevent the election of Roman Catholics to public office. They also tried to discourage recent immigrants from voting. The antiforeign movement did not attract the majority of Americans. It collapsed when the slavery issue took the center of the stage.

Immigrants seek communities of their countrymen.

Immigrants struggling against prejudice and insecurity tended to cling together for aid and comfort. If possible they settled near their countrymen and tried to preserve their own culture. The Germans, for example, formed German-speaking communities, established their own schools, clubs, and churches, and published their own newspapers. New York City in 1851 had seven foreign-language papers—four German, one French, one Italian, and one Spanish. Although adult immigrants might cling to their old customs, their children rapidly became Americanized. In the public schools these boys and girls learned to speak English and to get along with people of various backgrounds and religions. When they grew up and established homes of their own, they considered themselves to be, and were accepted as, Americans.

FOR IDENTIFICATION

Clermont	Robert Fulton
John Deere	"Know-Nothings"
Cyrus W. Field	Cyrus McCormick
John Fitch	Samuel F. B. Morse
Flying Cloud	John Stevens

FOR EXPLANATION OR DEFINITION

agricultural revolution	packet ships
canal era	portage railway
clipper ships	standard gauge
	turnpike

FOR REVIEW

1. What contributions did Fitch and Fulton make to the development of the steamboat?

2. (a) When did steamboats become important on the Mississippi? (b) Describe steamboat transportation on the rivers of the West. (c) What were some of the economic and political effects of the river steamboat?

3. (a) When was the Erie Canal built? (b) What were the end points of the canal? (c) Outline the economic and political effects of its construction.

4. (a) Describe the beginnings of steam locomotion. (b) Describe the early Baltimore and Ohio Railroad. (c) What were

305

some of the difficulties of early railroad transportation? How were they overcome?

5. Tell the story of Morse's invention of the telegraph. Tell of the development of the underwater cable.

6. (a) Describe the era of the packet and the clipper. (b) Tell the story of the development of ocean-going vessels powered by steam. (c) Why could the clipper compete with early steam-powered ocean-going vessels?

7. (a) How did improvements in transportation affect farming? (b) What is meant by *subsistence* farming? *Commercial* farming?

8. (a) What improvements were made in farming methods and in farm implements in the early nineteenth century? (b) Describe the McCormick reaper. (c) What other improvements in farm machinery had been developed by 1860?

9. What were the effects of the agricultural revolution?

10. (a) Why did cities begin to grow in number and in population? (b) What were some of the discomforts of city life? How were they overcome?

11. List the improvements made in the American home in the period 1800–1850.

12. (a) Why did an increasingly large number of immigrants come to the United States between 1830 and 1860? (b) What parts of Europe did most of the immigrants come from? (c) Where did they settle?

13. (a) Why was there hostility to the immigrant? (b) Why were the Irish immigrants the chief target for attack?

14. Who were the Know-Nothings? What were their demands?

FOR FURTHER STUDY AND DISCUSSION

1. How did Pennsylvania seek to overcome the advantages that the Erie Canal gave to New York? Helpful sources: Faulkner, *American Economic History;* Hulbert, *Paths of Inland Commerce.*

2. How are improvements in transportation and agriculture, the rise of the factory system, and the growth of cities interrelated? Helpful source: Fish, *The Rise of the Common Man,* pp. 62–108.

3. Discuss the effects of the river steamboat on New Orleans and St. Louis; the effects of the Erie Canal on New York City. Helpful sources: Faulkner, *American Economic History,* pp. 209–294; Hulbert, *Paths of Inland Commerce.*

4. (a) Account for the opposition to the immigrant in the 1840's. (b) Why has a similar opposition been evident at other periods of our history? (c) Does a comparable opposition exist today? Helpful sources: Wittke, *We Who Built America;* Fish, *The Rise of the Common Man,* pp. 109–136; Orth, *Our Foreigners;* Amherst Series: *Immigration, An American Dilemma.*

5. Compare the hardships of the pioneers who went west with the hardships of immigrants to the United States.

FOR INDIVIDUAL OR GROUP ACTIVITIES

1. On a large outline map, trace and label the important turnpikes, canals, and early railroads. Helpful source: Lord, *Atlas.*

2. Prepare a list with dates of important improvements in agriculture in the period 1800–1850; and a comparable list with dates of important industrial inventions. Helpful source: Wilson, *American Science and Invention, A Pictorial History.*

3. Plan a picture exhibit of transportation, agricultural, and industrial developments in the first half of the nineteenth century.

4. Prepare reports on the four selections in Hart, *Contemporaries,* Vol. III, ch. 24: The First American Steam Railroad; Boat, Stage, Railroad, and Canal, 1832–1833; Dickens' account of travel in 1842; and Morse's account of the first telegraph line, 1844.

5. (a) Report on the essays: "The Influence of Immigration" in Schlesinger, *New Viewpoints in American History,* pp. 1–22; "The Role of the Immigrant" in Schlesinger, *Paths to the Present,* pp. 51–72. (b) Compare the ideas expressed in these essays with those in the pamphlet written by the inventor Samuel F. B. Morse, "Imminent Dangers to the Free Institutions of the United States through Foreign Immigration:" Hacker, *The Shaping of the American Tradition,* pp. 391–394.

20. REFORMERS SEEK A FULLER LIFE FOR ALL

Brook Farm

An Age of Reform Begins

The years from about 1825 to 1850 are often spoken of as the "age of reform." It was an age of change. The growth of industry, the concentration of people in cities, and the inflow of immigrants created new problems. Americans became aware that many of their fellow citizens were living in poverty and that many children were growing up without schooling. Other evils, such as drunkenness, imprisonment for debt, and slavery, began to attract attention. Public-spirited men and women agitated against these evils and formed societies to combat them.

It was easy for Americans to believe in reform. Democracy rests on the belief that men can create a better society by using their reason and by working together. Democracy also teaches that every individual has an equal right to life, liberty, and the pursuit of happiness. Whatever denies these rights therefore should be attacked.

Reformers use democratic processes.

Persons who wanted to bring about a reform of any kind did not have to work alone. They usually joined with other citizens to promote the desired change. When Alexis de Tocqueville came to the United States from France in 1831, he was astonished by the number of civic organizations he found here. He wrote:

In no country in the world has the principle of association been more successfully used, or applied to a greater number of objects, than in America. . . . In the United States associations are established to promote the public safety, commerce, industry, morality, and religion. There is no end which the human will despairs of attaining through the power of individuals combined in a society.

The success of civic associations was partly due to the fact that so many Americans were familiar with demo-

307

cratic methods. They knew how to form an organization, to nominate and elect a slate of officers, to consider a motion, and to run a meeting. Even more important was the right to freedom of speech, press, and assembly. Americans could generally express their discontents openly and agitate for reform without fear of imprisonment.

More Educational Opportunities Are Provided

Public education is neglected.

The founders of the United States had clearly seen the need of widespread education. They realized that self-government could succeed only if the citizens were informed of their rights and responsibilities. Washington advised Congress to found a national university. Thomas Jefferson planned a great system of public schools for Virginia and until his death worked to have it adopted. In 1785 Congress began the practice of giving land to new states to encourage the establishment of schools and universities (see p. 135). Some of the older states set up school funds to help local authorities to establish schools. Yet in most places the taxpayers were then unwilling to support education at public expense. The school funds were soon spent or diverted to other uses. The land grants were hastily sold for a small price. Little was done to carry out the educational plans of the fathers of the Republic.

When the age of reform began, education was still considered to be the responsibility of parents and churches. In all parts of the country parents who could afford to do so sent their children to private schools, which were supported by tuition fees. Except in New England, there were few public schools. Even public schools were only partly supported by taxation. Parents who sent their children to a public school had to pay part of the cost of schooling if they were able. In New York, Philadelphia, and Baltimore, charitable societies conducted schools for poor children. Yet in those cities as elsewhere, a large number of boys and girls did not go to school because their parents were too proud to accept charity. In New York in 1820, nearly half of the children went uneducated.

Free public schools are demanded.

In the second quarter of the nineteenth century the movement to establish a tax-supported public school system got under way. It was led by clergymen, teachers, and other members of the middle class. They wanted free public schools primarily to help the underprivileged. The movement was strongest in New England, where the idea of the perfectibility of man— i.e., that all men can become godlike— was popular. Labor organizations in the Northeast joined in the fight, insisting that all children had an equal right to an education.

Opposition to public schools came mainly from three sources: (1) private schools, (2) churches which conducted schools, and (3) owners of property, who objected to paying higher taxes. Most of this last group sent their own children to private schools and thought that taxation to support public schools was unjust. The newspapers generally spoke for the taxpayers. They argued that free education was "socialistic," and that poor children should go to schools run by charitable agencies. Some said the poor were better suited to their station in life without an education. Others pointed to the poor quality of the existing public schools to prove that education should be left in private hands.

Public elementary schools spread.

The opponents of public education could not stop the educational

308

awakening. In the period from 1825 to 1850 many communities established public schools for the first time. Most were just for the elementary grades. However, the principle of full public support was not yet accepted. Most public schools were still partly financed by fees or "rates" paid by the parents. The big cities led the way in making the public schools entirely free. Later (between 1850 and 1870) the states passed laws doing away with "rates" in all public schools within their borders.

The educational awakening leads to better schools.

Along with the campaign for free public schools was a drive to lengthen the school term and to improve the teaching. At that time most schools were ungraded and had only one room. They were open only three or four months of the year. Lincoln's school days all told did not exceed twelve months, yet his boyhood experience was typical of country boys throughout the nation.

Many teachers had little education; none had special training for teaching. All were poorly paid. The public thought that the duties of a teacher could be handled by any honest, industrious person. Learning meant memorizing out of books; the work of the teacher was to hear pupils recite their lessons and whip them when they could not. The dunce's stool, the fool's cap, and the birch rod were in daily use. In fact these instruments of punishment and a few old textbooks were the only teaching aids found in most classrooms.

A handful of educational pioneers campaigned for a longer term and better methods of teaching. Among them were Horace Mann of Massachusetts, Henry Barnard of Connecticut and Rhode Island, and Calvin Stowe of Ohio. Through their efforts the first state normal schools for training teach-

ers were established, teachers' associations were formed, and teaching began to be considered a profession. Under their leadership the idea that a public school should be maintained at the lowest possible cost was gradually given up. To raise the standards of education cities began to employ a superintendent of schools and many states created the office of superintendent of schools.

Much remains to be done.

At the mid-century many rural children in the South and West still had no school within reach. Most schools were conducted in crude, uncomfortable one-room buildings. Attendance was irregular. Even in the cities many children did not attend school because they were employed. Nowhere was school attendance required, until Massachusetts adopted a compulsory attendance law in 1852. The law said that children from eight to fourteen years of age must attend school for twelve weeks each year.

Public high schools are founded.

The earliest public high school in the United States opened in Boston in 1821. Six years later Massachusetts passed a law requiring every town of 500 families to provide a tax-supported high school. One by one the larger cities in other parts of the nation started public high schools. The first high schools were for boys only, but gradually girls were accepted too. For a long time most people felt that secondary education was only for the well to do. Throughout the 1800's the majority of boys and girls of high school age were too busy helping their parents to have time to go to school.

Girls win more opportunities for education.

In colonial times girls did not go to grammar schools or to academies. After the Revolution some private academies began to admit girls, and other academies especially for girls were opened. The girls who attended academies were from well-to-do families. Usually they were taught little except music, embroidery, French, and drawing. Until 1833 no college admitted women, but here and there a rich girl studied college subjects with a tutor.

A few women leaders insisted that girls ought to have the same educational opportunities as boys. Among them were two New Englanders, Emma Willard and Mary Lyon. In 1821 Mrs. Willard opened an academy for girls at Troy, New York, where girls could have solid academic training. This academy, still in existence, is now called the Emma Willard School.

Mary Lyon, while still a schoolgirl, vowed she would start a seminary, or college, for women that was as good as those open to men. When she was sixteen, she began teaching school for seventy-five cents a week and board. She studied college subjects in her spare time. For years she tried to interest prominent people in starting a college for women. Although she was ridiculed on every side, she finally collected $68,500. She used the money to build Mount Holyoke Female Seminary, which opened in 1837.

In 1836, the Georgia Female College at Macon, now known as Wesleyan College, was chartered. It was the first college in the world to grant degrees to women. By 1860, sixty or more so-called women's colleges had been established. Very few of them actually deserved the name.

Coeducational colleges also began to appear. Oberlin College, founded in 1833, was the first college in the world to admit both men and women. Antioch College, also in Ohio, became coeducational in 1853. The first state university to admit women students was Iowa, which opened in 1855 as a coeducational institution.

HORACE MANN

The Ladies Hall at OBERLIN COLLEGE

Schools for the handicapped are opened.

The needs of the blind, deaf, and disabled were naturally neglected at a time when many normal boys and girls had no chance for schooling. Yet here and there were individuals who felt that handicapped children ought to have the chance for an education. The first school for deaf mutes was opened by a minister at Hartford, Connecticut, in 1817. Kentucky started the first state school for the deaf five years later. In 1832 the first schools for the blind were opened privately in Boston and New York. Ohio founded the first state school for the blind (1837). Other states gradually established schools for the handicapped. In this way one more portion of the population received the opportunity for self-improvement.

310

ANTIOCH COLLEGE, AT YELLOW SPRINGS, OHIO.

(Above) *This striking wood carving of a woman with her Bible on the stern of a whaling brig (1845) indicates the increasing importance of* WOMEN IN AMERICAN CULTURE.

(Below) ANTIOCH COLLEGE, *Yellow Springs, Ohio. A pioneer in co-education, Antioch had women teachers as well as women students.*

Workingmen Urge Reforms

Workers begin to organize.

Even before the Declaration of Independence, skilled artisans in the large towns sometimes joined together in benevolent societies. Local craft unions began to appear in the early days of the republic. Composed of the members of a single skilled trade, such as carpenters, printers, or tailors, these early unions were weak and did not last long. Employers fought unions by hiring nonunion labor, by forming employers' associations, and by asking the courts to declare unions illegal. In 1806 the Philadelphia Journeymen Cordwainers were tried for criminal conspiracy after a strike for higher wages. The court ruled that the work-

ers had no right to strike or take common action against their employers. In so doing they were "conspiring against fair trade . . . for the mere combination to raise wages is an offense against common law." The union was fined and went bankrupt. It was the first of several unions to be tried for conspiracy and found guilty.

In the 1820's the courts tried a new series of labor cases. On the whole the unions received a more sympathetic hearing. By 1827 it was understood that workers have the right to combine. However, the courts still regarded strikes, boycotts, and picketing as unlawful. The unions therefore put most of their efforts into political activity, hoping to obtain laws more favorable to wage earners.

Unions make political demands.

Unions grew rapidly during the years when Andrew Jackson was in the White House. There were some fifty labor newspapers in this period, and from their pages we learn what the unions wanted:

1. Equal suffrage for all white men who are citizens (By 1828, every state, except Rhode Island, had granted equal suffrage. There it was not granted until 1843, after a rebellion led by Thomas W. Dorr.)
2. The right of labor to organize, strike, and bargain collectively
3. Free and equal public education
4. Dissolution of monopolies, particularly the Bank of the United States (destroyed in 1836)
5. Free homesteads in the West: the public domain to be given to actual settlers
6. The ten-hour work day
7. Abolition of imprisonment for debt
8. Regulation of factories and mines to protect health and safety
9. Restriction of child labor
10. Exemption of wages and tools from seizure for debt
11. Payment of wages in cash instead of in products
12. Abolition of compulsory militia service
13. Mechanic's lien laws, requiring that wages be paid before any other claims against an employer
14. Abolition of competition from prison labor
15. Abolition of slavery (This demand became strong about mid-century.)

Workers make some gains.

During the age of reform workingmen won some of their political demands. Their success was made possible largely because they had won the right to vote. We should remember, however, that the workers were never alone in their reform efforts. Everything that labor asked for was supported by some of the more privileged people. The workingmen's desire to improve their condition fitted into the prevailing spirit of reform. Apart from equal male suffrage and the growth of public schools, the chief gains they made in this period were these:

1. The right to strike is recognized. In 1842 the Supreme Court of Massachusetts handed down a decision recognizing the right of labor unions to exist and even to strike for the closed shop.[1] The court declared that a combination of persons is not a criminal conspiracy unless it seeks to accomplish a criminal purpose or uses criminal methods. In other states labor unions still had to fight for recognition of their right to strike, but the Massachusetts case set a valuable precedent.

2. Imprisonment for debt is abolished. One of the most inhuman customs of the time was imprisonment for debt. Anyone who failed to pay a debt, even of a few cents, could be sent to jail. He must stay there until the debt was paid. Meanwhile he might have to depend on charity for food, fuel, and blankets. The jails were crowded with poor debtors, some of them women with nursing babies or little children. The first state to do away with imprisonment for debt was Kentucky (1821). Others gradually followed.

3. Some workers win the ten-hour day. The hours of work in factories and shops followed the custom of the farm, where everyone labored from sunrise to sunset, or from "can see to can't see." By the mid-1830's most unions in the building trades had won the ten-hour day. In 1836 President Jackson established it in national shipyards. His successor, Martin Van Buren, extended it to all employed on federal public works. In 1847 New Hampshire became the first state to place factory workers on the ten-hour day. Within ten years six other states followed.

---

[1] In a closed shop the employer may not hire nonunion workers.

However, these pioneer laws had loopholes and were not very effective.

4. A few states limit child labor. The majority of factory workers were children, some of them as young as six. In 1842 Massachusetts and Connecticut prohibited children under twelve from working more than ten hours a day. Seven years later, Pennsylvania fixed the minimum age of workers in commercial establishments at thirteen years. For a long time not much effort was made to enforce these laws.

5. Mechanic's lien laws. By 1840 nearly every state gave the worker first claim against the property he made or repaired. This meant that the mason and carpenter who built a house, for example, could collect their wages before the man who sold the building materials could collect what was due him.

Labor organizations rise and fall.

With every downswing of the business cycle, labor unions decline. During the terrible depression from 1837 to 1845 the labor movement was practically wiped out. It flourished again in the early 1850's as several national unions arose. In 1857 another depression settled over the nation, and the labor movement was almost crushed. The development of strong, permanent unions was still far in the future.

Idealists Form Co-operative Communities

Co-operative communities are advocated.

Beginning in colonial times, various small religious sects had experimented with co-operative communities. Such communities were based on the belief that Christians should own everything in common and should share equally in the labor and the benefits of community life. While some of these experiments succeeded for a time, they rarely lasted long. Individual owner-ship proved more attractive than communal ownership. Yet a few philosophers and writers, known as Utopian socialists, held that all land and industries ought to be owned in common.

With the coming of the Industrial Revolution in Europe and America, the Utopian socialists won more converts. Wage earners were interested, since industrialism was bringing them great hardships, such as excessively long hours, unhealthy or dangerous working conditions, and low wages. At the same time, many of the owners of industry were making big profits. The socialists claimed that it was private ownership of land and industry—i.e., the means of production—that led to such exploitation and injustice. They said the remedy lay in public ownership of the means of production. They proposed to start small co-operative communities where their ideas could be demonstrated.

Robert Owen founds New Harmony.

Among the Utopian socialists was Robert Owen, a wealthy British manufacturer. In the early years of the century he had created a model mill town at New Lanark, Scotland. His efforts there convinced him that the happiest community would be one where everybody worked for the benefit of all. He hoped to establish such communities in various parts of the world. He planned to set up model villages of about a thousand inhabitants each, in which each family would be allotted a house and an acre or two of land. Work was to be divided into such departments as (1) farming and manufacture, (2) home industry, (3) commerce, and (4) literature, science, and education.

On a visit to America in 1825 Owen bought a prosperous co-operative village started ten years earlier by the Harmony Society, a German sect. The village consisted of about 160 dwellings, a church, schoolhouse, silk fac-

tory, woolen mill, sawmill, brickyard, distillery, dye works, and 30,000 acres of land. The "industrious and well disposed of all nations" were invited to join in the new way of life. Over a thousand people came, among them leading scientists and educators. Unfortunately, there were also incompetents, idlers, and crooks. Some colonists worked; some did not. Quarrels arose. Within three years the experiment had to be abandoned.

Frances Wright founds Nashoba.

At least eleven new co-operative communities were started about the same time as New Harmony. One of these, Nashoba, was founded by a Scotswoman, Frances Wright. She bought 2000 acres of land near Memphis and a group of slaves to work it. Her idea was to have the slaves buy their freedom with the profits from their labor. She wanted to show that Negroes would work without being forced to do so if they had an incentive. She also expected to prove that Negroes could safely be given their freedom if they were properly prepared for it. "Swamp fever," poor management during her absence, and discord among the white members of the Society, led her to give up the experiment after five years. The slaves were freed, however, and transported to Haiti.

(Top) *An artist's conception of Robert Owen's planned settlement at* NEW HARMONY, *Indiana. Below is the settlement as it looked in reality.*

On page 307 is a picture of BROOK FARM *in Massachusetts showing the original farmhouse, the cottage (called the Eyrie) and the Pilgrim House. The remains of the community house, destroyed by fire in 1846, are visible in front of the Eyrie. This setback put the community into debt and hastened the end of the experiment.*

Hard times result in new experiments.

The terrible suffering among jobless city dwellers in the late 1830's and early 1840's aroused new interest in co-operative living. "We are all a little wild here," wrote Ralph Waldo Emerson to Carlyle, "with numberless projects of social reform. Not a reading man but has a draft of a new community in his pocket." About forty new co-operative communities sprang to life during these years. With the return of better times in the late 1840's, most of them broke up.

Transcendentalists establish Brook Farm.

The best-known co-operative was Brook Farm, founded near Boston in 1841. Among its members were Nathaniel Hawthorne, Charles A. Dana, Bronson Alcott, Margaret Fuller, and other noted Transcendentalists. Each member owned an equal share in the enterprise and helped with the work of the farm, the shops, and the school. The residents discussed, wrote, played, and sang, and for a time were happy with their experiment. A destructive fire in 1846 hastened the end of this remarkable venture. Hawthorne's novel *The Blithedale Romance* describes his experience at Brook Farm.

Icarians, too, try to create Utopias.

Another depression in the 1850's brought a new crop of experiments. These were inspired by a French book, *A Voyage to Icaria*, describing a socialist Utopia. The author led several hundred so-called Icarians to America in 1848. The longest life of any Icarian colony was twenty years. By the time the last one failed in 1898, there was little interest in co-operative villages.

Reformers Campaign Against Various Evils

The treatment of prisoners improves slowly.

During the age of reform, as we have noted, the cruel practice of imprisonment for debt was abolished. Humanitarians also tried to improve the treatment of criminals. Many states reduced still further the number of crimes punishable by death. Maine abolished the death penalty altogether (1837). Most states did away with such punishments as the pillory, branding, and flogging. Yet prisoners generally were confined under conditions which

broke down their health and sanity. Because of bad food, crowding in dark, unsanitary cells, overwork, and brutal treatment, prisoners had a very high death rate. In some states the prisons were run by contractors who made money by working the inmates twelve to fifteen hours a day in their workshops and by feeding them very little. Conditions were somewhat better where public officials operated the prisons and provided work for the inmates.

Prison reformers, finding it difficult to arouse sympathy for adult prisoners, put most of their effort into securing better treatment of young offenders. At that time the young and old, the hardened criminals and first offenders, were thrown into the same prisons. Reformers urged that juvenile delinquents and first offenders be kept in separate institutions. With money given by charitable citizens, a House of Refuge for juvenile delinquents was opened in New York in 1825. Similar houses were opened the next year in Boston and Philadelphia, and later on in other cities. In 1847 Massachusetts established the first publicly supported institution for juvenile delinquents. Twenty years later New York became the first state to provide a special prison for young adults who were first offenders.

Dorothea Dix fights for the insane.

Dorothea Dix was a Massachusetts Quakeress who spent most of her life trying to improve the treatment of prisoners, paupers, and the insane. On visiting a jail in Cambridge in 1841, she was shocked by the conditions she found there. Criminals, idiots, and insane persons were crowded together in an unheated room. After inspecting the plight of the insane in other Massachusetts jails and almshouses, she sent a petition to the legislature. Her petition asked the state to provide special institutions for the mentally ill, where they might receive proper care. "I have

315

DOROTHEA DIX

Signing a pledge of temperance

seen . . . insane persons confined . . . in cages, closets, cellars, stalls, pens!" she wrote, adding that many were "chained, naked, . . . and lashed into obedience."

She appealed for private contributions. With this financial aid, she traveled over 60,000 miles in eight years, visiting almost every state. Everywhere, she went into prisons and poorhouses and reported what she found. In one state after another she addressed the legislature, usually persuading it to establish a hospital for the insane. She then went to Europe to continue her work.

The temperance crusade is started.

At this period hard drinking was usual among all classes and occupations. Whiskey was considered a necessity for those engaged in physical labor. Drunkenness was common. The churches began a crusade against drinking. By 1830 the temperance movement was well under way. It was strongest in New England and in states where many New Englanders had settled. Ohio was the first state to restrict the sale of liquor (1830); Maine was the first to prohibit its sale entirely (1846). Within a dozen years thirteen states fol-

lowed Maine's example by passing laws which strictly regulated or prohibited the sale of liquor.

One argument against strong drink was the injury it did to the human system. Another argument—that it reduced the workman's efficiency—was first heard about 1830. That year the superintendent in charge of building the Baltimore and Ohio Railroad told his workmen not to drink—an action which attracted much attention. The most common argument against drinking, however, was the religious one that drinking led people into sin.

A movement for women's rights begins.

Custom and the common law kept women in an inferior position. Girls were ruled by their fathers. When they married, they were ruled by their husbands. The husband could do as he pleased with his wife's property; he had a right to any wages she might earn and to any other income she might receive. He could make all decisions concerning their children.

During the Jacksonian Era women began to rebel against their lack of freedom. They asked for greater educational opportunities and for changes in the laws regarding property. In 1839 Mis-

316

MARY LYON

sissippi granted married women control over their own property. By 1851 seven states had passed similar laws.

Women still had no part in the government. Most Americans were shocked when a woman spoke on a public platform. Such women as Frances Wright, Dorothea Dix, Emma Willard, and Mary Lyon were insulted and ridiculed for speaking in public. Women abolitionists found it necessary to fight for their own rights as well as for the rights of the slaves.

In 1840 eight American women were sent as delegates to an antislavery convention in London. Admittance to the convention was refused merely because they were women. The rejected delegates, led by Elizabeth Cady Stanton and Lucretia Mott, organized a women's rights convention when they returned to America. The first in the history of the world, the convention met at Seneca Falls, New York, in 1848. In a Declaration of Sentiments which became famous, the delegates said that men *and women* are created equal and women should have equality with men in education, in earning a living, in voting, and in the eyes of the law. Newspapers belittled the declaration with scornful headlines such as "The Reign of the Petticoats" and "Insurrection among Women." Most men either laughed at or condemned the whole movement, but such men as Whittier, Emerson, William Lloyd Garrison, and Wendell Phillips supported it. The Seneca Falls Convention of 1848 was the opening gun in a struggle that was to last a century. Even today women do not have full legal equality with men, and only a small number have succeeded in reaching high positions in politics, government, and business.

Americans organize to oppose war.

The Quakers had always said that war was the greatest of all evils. After 1800 other Christians here and in Europe took up the cause, believing that war is contrary to Christ's teachings. Peace societies were formed in New England during the War of 1812 and soon spread into other states. In 1828 they combined to form the American Peace Society. It was led by William Ladd, a Maine sea captain and farmer. During the Jacksonian period the peace movement grew. It urged disarmament, arbitration of disputes, and a federation of the nations of the world. Ladd pleaded for a permanent world court and a congress of nations to meet at fixed periods. The ideas expressed in his *Essay on a Congress of Nations* (1840) were widely circulated during the first World War. Today, as you know, we have both a world court and a congress of nations (the U. N.).

The approach of war between the North and the South divided the peace advocates. Some Northerners, including Abraham Lincoln, urged that war be avoided by compensating slaveowners for gradually freeing their slaves. Others bitterly opposed compensation; their hatred of slavery was so strong they preferred to stamp it out by force. When war finally came, the peace movement was temporarily forgotten.

317

The Antislavery Cause Arouses Great Bitterness

The emancipation movement begins.

In the early years of the Republic, Southerners as well as Northerners joined antislavery societies. The emancipation movement was especially strong in Virginia. Washington said: "Not only do I pray for it [emancipation] on the score of human dignity, but I can clearly foresee that nothing but the rooting out of slavery can perpetuate the existence of our Union." Jefferson, Madison, Monroe, George Mason, Patrick Henry, and other Virginians expressed similar feelings.

At this period slaveowners often set free their favorite slaves, and some, including Washington, arranged in their wills for freeing all their slaves. Jefferson freed his slaves before his death. Yet most white people objected to having free Negroes in their communities. This feeling was as strong in the North as in the South. In both sections free Negroes had a hard time, for white workmen usually refused to work with Negroes. Moreover, many Southerners feared that free Negroes would help the slaves to revolt. After a plot by a free Negro of Charleston was discovered (1822), most of the Southern states passed laws to discourage the freeing of slaves.

Colonization in Africa is tried.

A number of leading Southerners thought the solution to the problem was to send the freed Negroes to Africa. In 1817 the American Colonization Society was formed for this purpose. Congress appropriated $100,000 for the society's work. The society set up the Negro republic of Liberia but could persuade few American Negroes to go there. Most of those who did go died of tropical diseases. Plainly colonization in Africa would not solve the problem.

Even before the colonization experiment failed, Southerners had lost interest in freeing the slaves. The reason was that cotton had become the leading Southern crop, and planters needed all the slaves they could get (see p. 242). The price of slaves increased rapidly. In 1800 a first-class field hand brought $400 to $500; by 1850 such a slave was worth from $1500 to $2000. At these prices few masters could afford to free a slave. If forced to free their slaves without compensation, the planting class would become bankrupt.

Abolition is demanded.

While sentiment for emancipation was losing ground in the South, it was growing stronger in the North. Northern humanitarians could not long close their eyes to the evils of the slave system. At first the antislavery movement was led by men of moderate views. These men favored gradual emancipation, usually with colonization of the freed Negroes, and strict enforcement of the laws forbidding the importation of slaves. Among these leaders was a gentle Quaker, Benjamin Lundy of Ohio. In 1821 Lundy gave up his prosperous saddler's trade to spend his life in the antislavery crusade. For the next fourteen years he published a weekly journal, *The Genius of Universal Emancipation*. He traveled widely, speaking against slavery wherever he could get a hearing.

After 1830 more militant leaders came to the fore. Because they demanded immediate abolition of slavery, they are known as "abolitionists." The most extreme was a penniless young printer, William Lloyd Garrison of Massachusetts. He called slavery a crime and slaveholders heartless brutes. The first issue of his newspaper, the *Liberator*, appeared on New Year's Day, 1831. His spirit is shown by a statement in the first issue:

318

I will be as harsh as truth and as un-compromising as justice. On this subject [slavery], I do not wish to think, or speak, or write with moderation. No! No! Tell a man whose house is on fire to give a mod-erate alarm . . . tell the mother to grad-ually extricate her babe from the fire into which it has fallen; but urge me not to use moderation in a cause like the present. I am in earnest—I will not equivocate—I will not excuse—I will not retreat a single inch—and I will be heard.

Through the pages of the *Liberator* and through thousands of public speeches, Garrison continued to be heard until slavery was finally abol-ished. While Garrison was the best-known abolitionist, many others were equally devoted if less fanatical.

In 1833 Garrison and others formed the American Antislavery So-ciety. After that the abolition move-ment grew steadily. It was spurred by the progress of antislavery forces abroad. The British Parliament in 1833 provided for emancipation of slaves throughout the empire, with compensa-tion for their owners. By 1850 all Latin-American countries, except Brazil and Cuba, and all European countries had abolished slavery.

The "Underground Railroad."

Congress had passed a Fugitive Slave Act in 1793. Its sole object was to allow the slaveowners to recover a runaway slave with the least cost and inconvenience. Northerners who hated the slave system defied this law by helping runaways to escape to Canada. A secret society for this purpose devel-oped, possibly as early as 1804. About 1831 the organization began to be re-ferred to as the "Undergound Rail-road." The homes of trusted persons willing to aid fugitives were known as "stations." Hiding by day and traveling by night, the slaves were guided by "conductors" from one station to an-other until they reached safety. The most successful conductor was proba-bly Harriet Tubman, who herself es-caped from slavery in 1849. Going South again and again, always at the risk of her life, she managed to bring out over three hundred of her people. One estimate puts the total number of runaways helped by the underground system at 75,000.

"THE UNDERGROUND RAILWAY," *from the painting by C. T. Webber*

Abolitionists arouse bitter opposition.

In both the North and the South abolitionists met persecution. In the South it became impossible to speak publicly against slavery. (However, as late as 1831 the Virginia legislature discussed and almost passed a proposal for gradual emancipation with compensation for slaveowners.) Southern abolitionists, like James G. Birney of Kentucky and the Grimké sisters of Charleston, South Carolina, were forced to go North to escape the wrath of their neighbors. Even in the North antislavery meetings were frequently broken up and speakers stoned. In 1835 a Boston mob destroyed the office where the *Liberator* was published and dragged Garrison through the streets. He narrowly escaped death. Often printing shops which published abolition papers were wrecked. In 1837 Elijah Lovejoy, a minister who published an abolition journal in Illinois, was killed by a mob. Violence against Negroes became common in the North. In New York City, for example, mobs attacked Negro quarters, destroying property and taking life. In New Hampshire three hundred men destroyed a Negro schoolhouse. Such outrages strengthened the abolition movement. Thousands joined it because they felt it had become the cause of human liberty.

Nat Turner leads a slave uprising.

Southerners had long dreaded a revolt of the slaves. They reminded one another that there had been a slave uprising on the island of Haiti in 1804, when all the whites had been killed or banished and the Negroes had set up a republic. Since that time Southern white men had feared that something similar might take place in the South, especially in regions where there were more slaves than whites.

A local uprising did occur in 1831. Led by a Negro preacher named Nat Turner, it was a revolt against the slaveowners of Southampton County, Virginia. Nearly sixty white people were killed. Southerners believed that the revolt was inspired by propaganda from the North. They asked Northern legislatures to forbid abolition societies and to have all abolition literature destroyed. President Andrew Jackson himself tried to have Congress make it unlawful to mail antislavery literature. Although such a law was not adopted, Southern postmasters confiscated and burned all such literature they found.

The Southern states passed laws intended both to stop runaways and to make another slave uprising impossible. Slaves were forbidden to leave their master's land without a pass. They were forbidden to assemble, even for worship, unless white men were present. Negroes were forbidden to preach. Some of the states made it a crime to teach Negroes, whether slaves or freemen, to read or write. Some states banished their free Negroes; others made it difficult for free Negroes to stay free.

Southerners defend slavery.

Soon after 1830 Southerners stopped apologizing for the slave system as a "necessary evil." Instead they began to praise it as a "positive good." Slavery, it was argued, was not only in the best interests of the social order but also in the best interests of the Negroes. It was said to be a means of civilizing and Christianizing them. Southerners also pointed out that they took care of the slaves in sickness and old age, while under the wage system many business concerns left their workers to look out for themselves when injured, sick, or too old to work. Moreover, slaves need not fear hard times, while free workers might lose their jobs when business was bad. Slaves were better off and more contented, Southerners claimed, than white wage earners in the North.

320

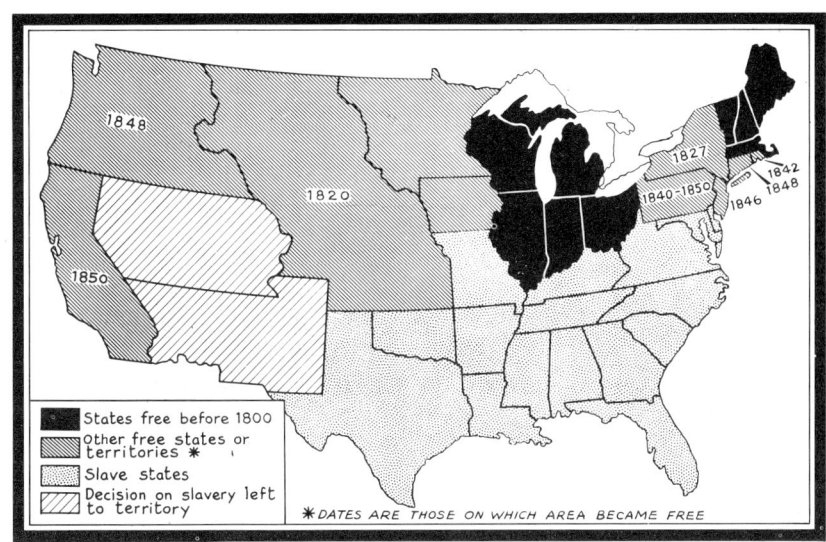

PROGRESS OF ABOLITION, 1850

John Quincy Adams fights the "gag" rule.

Abolitionists sent many petitions to their representatives in Congress, asking that slavery be abolished in the District of Columbia. The main purpose of the petitioners was to keep the slavery question before the public. This, of course, was what proslavery men wished to avoid. Those favoring slavery would, in fact, have stopped all antislavery talk if they could.

In 1836 the proslavery men got Congress to pass a "gag" resolution, providing that antislavery petitions should be laid aside without being read or printed and that no further action should be taken on them. This was a clear violation of the First Amendment, which guarantees the right to petition the government.

John Quincy Adams, formerly President and now a member of the House of Representatives, protested that the "gag" resolution was unconstitutional. He fought to have the resolution repealed. The abolitionists sent him petitions by the hundreds, and he presented them all. Whenever the regular hour for petitions arrived, Adams was at his desk in the House, a pile of petitions before him. He would rise with words like these: "I have a request from citizens from the town of ———— praying for the abolition of slavery in ————." The Speaker's hammer would fall and Adams would be declared out of order. He would take another paper from the pile, begin with the same words, and be cut off in the same manner. He stopped only when he reached the bottom of the pile. He kept this up for eight years, until at last the friends of slavery saw that the "gag" resolution was making friends for the abolitionists. The rule was repealed late in 1844.

The antislavery drive weakens other reform efforts.

As the antislavery drive grew, it distracted people's attention from other public issues. Most reformers came to think that no evil was so pressing as human bondage. Until this evil was overcome, other reforms could wait. After 1850 the energy previously spent on a variety of causes was poured into the attack on slavery.

321

Despite their increasing activity, the abolitionists never attracted the majority of Northerners to their side. Most Northerners, however, did come to feel strongly that slavery should not be extended beyond its existing boundaries. Questions relating to the extension of slavery continued to rock the nation until the end of the War between the North and South.

The Spirit of Reform Is Still with Us

The idea of reform shapes our culture.

Although we may smile at some of the proposals made during the age of reform, this period had a lasting influence on our history. Private organizations, such as antislavery societies, labor unions, missionary boards, and charitable agencies, did a great deal to educate the public and to awaken the public conscience. Numerous welfare movements got started during these years and have continued ever since.

In building up organizations and promoting causes, the reformers of this period helped to establish reform as a major American pattern. They taught Americans to examine their institutions in the light of democratic principles, religious ideals, and the faith that all men have divine capacities. They made "the greatest good of the greatest number" the test of every established institution or proposed reform. Though individual reform movements have sometimes failed, the idea of reform has remained as one of our strongest traditions. In their book *U.S.A. The Permanent Revolution,* the editors of *Fortune* write:

The history of the United States begins with a revolution . . . not merely a revolution against Britain but a revolution in human affairs.' . . . It was—and is—the revolution of the human individual against all forms of enslavement.

An unknown artist's conception of a PRE-WAR PLANTATION. *The great house, surrounded by slave quarters and work buildings, dominates the scene, while down below a ship waits at the dock for loading.*

A child of the period

FOR IDENTIFICATION

Henry Barnard	Mary Lyon
James G. Birney	Horace Mann
Dorothea Dix	Lucretia Mott
William Lloyd	Robert Owen
Garrison	Elizabeth Cady
Grimké sisters	Stanton
William Ladd	Nat Turner
Elijah Lovejoy	Emma Willard
Benjamin Lundy	Frances Wright

FOR EXPLANATION OR DEFINITION

abolition	*The Liberator*
academy	mechanic's lien
American Peace	New Harmony
Society	normal schools
Brook Farm	seminary
closed shop	Seneca Falls
co-operative	Convention
communities	Underground
emancipation	Railroad
"gag" resolution	Utopian socialist
humanitarians	utopias

FOR REVIEW

1. Why are the years 1825–50 referred to as an "age of reform"?

2. What methods were used by reformers?

3. What was the condition of education and the schools in the first third of the nineteenth century?

4. What were some of the arguments against free public schools?

5. What groups led the fight for free public schools?

6. Who was Horace Mann? Henry Barnard? What reforms did they introduce?

7. When were the first public high schools established? *MASS State Tou*

8. (a) What contributions to educational progress were made by Emma Willard and Mary Lyon? (b) Why is the founding of Mount Holyoke Female Seminary an important milestone in education?

9. (a) What political and economic reforms were demanded by labor organizations? (b) What important gains were made by labor in the period 1825–50? (c) Explain what is meant by a mechanic's lien law.

10. What were the aims of the "Utopian socialists"?

11. (a) Describe the co-operative community established by Robert Owen at New Harmony, Indiana. (b) Describe the Brook Farm Community. (c) Describe the community founded by Frances Wright. (d) Who were the Icarians?

12. Why was there a need for prison reforms? What changes were made in the treatment of criminals?

13. To what did Dorothea Dix devote her life? How did she go about her great work?

14. (a) Where did the temperance movement develop its strongest support? (b) State the arguments against the use of strong drink.

15. (a) What conditions led women to demand more freedom? (b) Describe the purpose and importance of the Seneca Falls Convention of 1848.

16. Describe the early peace movement.

17. (a) What were the early steps in the emancipation movement? (b) Explain the work of the American Colonization Society. (c) Why did Southerners lose interest in the emancipation movement?

18. (a) Name the newspapers published by Benjamin Lundy and William Lloyd Garrison. (b) In what respect did these men differ on the question of the abolition of slavery? (c) What was the objective of the American Antislavery Society?

19. Describe the work of the "Underground Railroad." Who was Harriet Tubman?

20. Why did the abolitionists arouse bitter opposition? How and where did this opposition manifest itself?

21. Describe Nat Turner's revolt in 1831. How did it affect the abolitionists' cause?

22. What arguments did the Southerners use to defend slavery?

23. What was the "gag" resolution? How did John Quincy Adams succeed in having it repealed?

24. How did the antislavery movement affect other reform movements?

25. What important American tradition is illustrated by the variety of reform movements in the period 1825–50?

FOR FURTHER STUDY AND DISCUSSION

1. "Humanitarian striving was a characteristic of the new democratic spirit." What are the evidences of humanitarian striving? Why is it referred to as a characteristic of the new democracy? Was the agitation over slavery a manifestation of the "democratic spirit"?

2. Why was the abolitionist movement of Garrison unpopular in the North?

3. Prepare brief biographical sketches and estimate the value of the work of the following: Dorothea Dix, Horace Mann, Henry Barnard, William Lloyd Garrison, Mary Lyon, Emma Willard, Lucretia Mott, Elizabeth Cady Stanton, Robert Owen.

4. How did the development of labor unions promote the growth of democracy?

5. (a) Compare the major items with which labor unions were concerned in the 1820's with those with which they are concerned at the present. (b) Indicate those items which have been of continuing interest to labor unions. (c) Which items benefit society as a whole?

6. Investigate and report on the "utopian" experiments at New Harmony, Brook Farm, and elsewhere. Suggest reasons for their failure. Are there any similar proposals today for the reform of society?

7. Compare the life of a boy or girl in 1840 with that of a boy or girl today as regards educational opportunities, amusements, clothing, responsibilities in the home, occupational opportunities.

FOR INDIVIDUAL OR GROUP ACTIVITIES

1. Read and report on the description of a Shaker village at Lebanon, Ohio. Helpful source: Commager and Nevins, *Heritage of America*, No. 95.

2. Discuss De Tocqueville's comments on the institution of slavery. Helpful source: Bradley, ed., *De Tocqueville's Democracy in America*, Vol. I, pp. 370–397.

3. Write an article for the school newspaper on the career and influence of Wendell Phillips. Helpful source: Hofstadter, *The American Political Tradition*, Chapter VI, "Wendell Phillips: The Patrician as Agitator."

4. Use the following for a class or assembly program of dramatic readings: the plea of Dorothea Dix to the Massachusetts legislature, the Seneca Falls Declaration of Women's Independence, Garrison's statement of principles in the first issue of the *Liberator*, the extemporaneous speech of Wendell Phillips on the murder of Elijah Lovejoy. Helpful sources: Commager and Nevins, *Heritage of America*, Nos. 91 and 92; Hart, *Contemporaries*, Vol. III, No. 174; Commager, *Documents*, Nos. 149, 163, 172; Commager, *Living Ideas in America*, pp. 376–379. A chairman or narrator might be selected to prepare brief introductions for these selections.

5. Hold a panel discussion of the ideas advanced by Horace Mann in defense of public education. Helpful source: Commager, *Documents*, No. 173.

6. Prepare a radio script on the operation of the Underground Railroad. Helpful sources: Commager and Nevins, *Heritage of America*, Nos. 108, 109, 110; Hart, *Contemporaries*, Vol. III, No. 183.

7. Analyze and discuss the merits of the proslavery arguments. Helpful source: Hart, *Contemporaries*, Vol. III, Nos. 169, 173, 175.

HIGH POINTS

1

The current of nationalism, which had reached its height not long after the War of 1812, was soon checked by the opposing current of sectionalism. Each section— North, South, and West—was developing a different type of economy and culture. What each needed from the national government differed somewhat from the needs of the other two. The sections disagreed over the protective tariff, federal aid for internal improvements, public land policy, the Bank of the United States, and the extension of slavery into the territories. The last-named question aroused by far the bitterest conflict; it was settled temporarily by the Missouri Compromise (1820).

2

In the election of 1824 only one party was active, the old Democratic Republican party founded by Jefferson and Monroe. John Quincy Adams was elected President. Sectional and partisan feelings were so strong during his term that Congress did nothing to advance his farsighted program for economic and intellectual improvements and for conservation. Had he been more of a politician, he might have won attention for his program. Although a great statesman and patriot, Adams knew little about practical politics.

3

While Adams was President, the Republican party split into two—the National Republican party, which was much like the former Federalist party, and the Democratic party, which was like Jefferson's old party. The Democrats elected Andrew Jackson of Tennessee for two terms as President and his close friend, Martin Van Buren of New York, for one term. Jackson and Van Buren wished to represent the common people, including the small farmers, the pioneers, and the growing number of Eastern wage earners. Jackson exercised strong leadership, thus making the office of President more important than it had been before.

4

Jackson's victory over the second Bank of the United States was considered by his followers as a defeat of the dreaded Eastern money power. Unfortunately, in their hatred of monopoly and special privilege, Jackson's party did not realize the need for a central bank which could exercise control over local banks. The destruction of the Bank of the United States opened the way for feverish speculation in land and canals. The speculative boom, which was financed by the paper money issued by state-chartered banks, soon collapsed. The panic of 1837 and several years of hard times followed.

5

While the young republic grew in area, population, and wealth, it was also growing in culture. After 1820, American writers, particularly Irving, Cooper, Bryant, Poe, and Emerson, won favorable attention both at home and abroad. Three others who began writing before the middle of the century—Thoreau, Melville, and Whitman—were neglected during their lifetime. Yet by the 1840's a number of American writers were earning a living with their pens.

6

New England had an extraordinary period of literary activity during the middle third of the century. Poets, philosophers, novelists, historians all contributed to New England's "golden day." Ralph Waldo Emerson was the leader of the most influential group of writers, the Transcenden-

talists. He called men to reform society so that every individual might develop the divine spark within him. Emerson's influence on American thought is still powerful.

7

The arts of drama, architecture, painting, sculpture, and music developed slowly in the United States. In these fields Americans depended heavily on European models and looked to Europe for training and inspiration.

8

American scientists described and classified plants, birds, insects, and rocks. They preferred to work on practical problems, and they collected much valuable information on nature's visible forms. Thus Americans contributed more to applied science than to scientific theory.

9

The Industrial Revolution came to the United States from England at the close of the 1700's. It set in motion a vast series of economic and social changes. Among them were the rapid growth of cities, increased immigration from Europe, the appearance of the business cycle, loss of security for millions of former farm dwellers, and the mass production of many types of goods.

10

Paralleling the Industrial Revolution and helping it advance were revolutions in agriculture, in transportation, and in means of communication. Each of these revolutions was made possible by an endless chain of inventions, some of which were worked out here and others in Europe.

11

Interest in social reform was particularly widespread in the years from 1825 to 1850. Religious and intellectual leaders battled against ignorance, poverty, drunkenness, cruelty, and exploitation. Laboring men joined in the fight for free public schools, free homesteads for Western settlers, and the right of labor to organize and to strike. Considerable progress was made along a wide front, but by 1850 reformers were concentrating their efforts in the fight against slavery.

12

The years from 1800 to 1850 saw remarkable developments in American life and thought. The great changes that ushered in and accompanied the Modern Age, discussed in Chapter 1, were much in evidence. These changes—the growth of commerce and industry, the widening of men's horizons to include the nation rather than a single community, the rise of science, the mass production of books—were opening new opportunities and presenting new challenges to Americans of the nineteenth century.

QUESTIONS

1. Why did the question of the admission of Missouri precipitate a political crisis? State the main features of the Missouri Compromise.

2. (a) Describe the beginnings of the Industrial Revolution in the United States. (b) What important changes in agriculture and transportation accompanied the Industrial Revolution?

3. (a) Describe the settlement of the trans-Appalachian West. (b) How did economic changes affect social and political developments?

4. (a) How did the interests of the commercial and manufacturing Northeast differ from those of the South and West? (b) How did the interests of the different sections influence national politics?

5. (a) Why has the term "Era of Good Feeling" been applied to Monroe's administration? (b) What caused the development of factions within the Republican party? (c) Compare the presidential election of 1824 with that of 1800. (d) Who were the outstanding leaders of the Democrats? Of the Whigs?

6. In what respects did "Jacksonian democracy" differ from "Jeffersonian democracy"?

7. (a) Why did the tariff become a subject of political and sectional controversy after 1816? (b) Account for the fluctuation in tariff rates between 1816 and 1833.

8. Outline the arguments of the South Carolina Exposition and Protest. Compare with the arguments advanced by Senators Hayne and Webster in their famous debate, with the Virginia and Kentucky resolutions, and with the opposition to the Supreme Court decision (1954) on segregation in the public schools (see Chap. 46).

9. (a) Why did the question of the re-chartering of the second Bank of the United States become an important issue in Jackson's administration? (b) Explain Jackson's point of view on this issue, and describe his actions in dealing with it.

10. Describe the various ways in which "humanitarian striving" manifested itself during the Jacksonian era.

11. What notable results were achieved by the young republic in science, education, and literature?

12. Trace the development of antislavery sentiment before 1850.

13. Summarize the achievements and influence of each of the following: John Quincy Adams, Andrew Jackson, Henry Clay, Daniel Webster, John C. Calhoun, Horace Mann, Ralph Waldo Emerson.

SUGGESTED READINGS

SOURCE MATERIALS, DOCUMENTS, MAPS

Amherst Series: *The Great Tariff Debate, 1820–1830.*

———. *Jackson versus Biddle; The Struggle Over the Second Bank of the United States.*

———. *The Transcendentalist Revolt Against Materialism.*

———. *The Turner Thesis Concerning the Role of the Frontier in American History.*

Commager, Henry Steele, *Documents.*

———. *Living Ideas in America.* Harper, 1951.

° Commager and Nevins, *Heritage of America.*

Hart, *Contemporaries,* Vol. III.

Lord, *Historical Atlas.*

Nevins and Weitenkampf, *Political Cartoons.*

GENERAL REFERENCES

° Adams, Samuel Hopkins. *The Erie Canal.* Random House, 1953.

Bailey, *Diplomatic History.*

Beard, *American Civilization.*

Bemis, *Diplomatic History.*

Bradley, Phillips (ed.). *Alexis de Tocqueville's "Democracy in America."* Vintage, 1945.

Brooks, Van Wyck. *The Flowering of New England.* Dutton, 1941.

———. *The World of Washington Irving.* Dutton, 1944.

° Corwin, Edward S. *John Marshall and the Constitution.* Yale University Press, 1921.

Dangerfield, George. *The Era of Good Feelings.* Harcourt, Brace, 1952.

DeVoto, Bernard. *Across the Wide Missouri.* Houghton, 1947.

° Dodd, William E. *The Cotton Kingdom.* Yale University Press, 1919.

Dulles, Foster R. *Labor in America.* Crowell, 1949.

Faulkner, *Economic History.*

° Faulkner, Harold U., and Starr, Mark. *Labor in America.* Harper, 1949.

Fish, Carl R. *The Rise of the Common Man.* Macmillan, 1927. (A.L.S.)

Hicks, John D. *The Federal Union.* Houghton, 1952.

Hofstadter, *American Political Tradition.*

° Hulbert, Archer B. *The Paths of Inland Commerce.* Yale University Press, 1920.

Kaempffert, W. B. *A Popular History of American Invention.* Scribner, 1924.

Krout, J. A., and Fox, D. R. *The Completion of Independence, 1790–1830.* Macmillan, 1944. (A.L.S.)

Larkin, *Art and Life in America.*

Lorant, *Presidency.*

MacDonald, William. *Jacksonian Democracy, 1829–1837.* Harper, 1906. (A.N.S.)

Morison and Commager, *American Republic,* Vol. I.

° Ogg, Frederic A. *The Old Northwest.* Yale University Press, 1919.

° ———. *The Reign of Andrew Jackson.* Yale University Press, 1919.

° Orth, Samuel P. *The Armies of Labor.* Yale University Press, 1919.

° Perry, Bliss. *The American Spirit in Literature.* Yale University Press, 1918.

Schlesinger, Arthur M. *New Viewpoints in American History.* Macmillan, 1922.

Schlesinger, Arthur M., Jr. *The Age of Jackson.* Little, Brown, 1947.

Slosson, Edwin E. *The American Spirit in Education.* Yale University Press, 1921.

Stone, Irving. *They Also Ran.* Doubleday, 1945.

Turner, Frederick J. *The Frontier in American History.* Holt, 1921.

Wittke, Carl. *We Who Built America; The Saga of the Immigrant.* Prentice-Hall, 1939.

BIOGRAPHY

Chambers, Wm. R. *Old Bullion Benton,* Little, Brown, 1956.

Coit, Margaret D. *John C. Calhoun: American Portrait.* Houghton, 1950.

° Hill, Ralph N. *Robert Fulton and the Steamboat.* Random House, 1954.

° Holbrook, Stewart H. *Davy Crockett.* Random House, 1955.

James Marquis. *Andrew Jackson; Portrait of a President.* Bobbs-Merrill, 1937.

° Kiernan, John, and Kiernan, Margaret. *John James Audubon.* Random House, 1954.

Lutz, Alma. *Emma Willard, Daughter of Democracy.* Houghton, 1929.

Mann, Mary Peabody. *Life of Horace Mann.* Walker, Fuller, 1865.

Mayo, Barbara. *Henry Clay.* Farrar, Straus, & Cudahy, 1953.

Nicolay, Helen. *Andrew Jackson, The Fighting President.* Century, 1929.

Tharp, Louise H. *The Peabody Sisters of Salem.* Little, Brown, 1950.

° Whitridge, Arnold *Simón Bolívar.* Random House, 1954.

FICTION

Adams, Samuel Hopkins. *Canal Town.* World, 1945. (Erie Canal)

———. *The Gorgeous Hussy.* Houghton, 1934. (Social conditions in the age of Jackson)

Bacheller, Irving. *The Light in the Clearing.* Bobbs-Merrill, 1917. (Politics and religion in the Jackson era)

Benét, Stephen Vincent. *The Devil and Daniel Webster.* Farrar and Rinehart, 1937. (New England)

Breslin, Howard. *The Tamarack Tree.* McGraw-Hill, 1947. (The Whig party, Webster, Harrison)

° Edmonds, Walter D. *Rome Haul.* Macmillan, 1938. (Erie Canal)

Eggleston, Edward. *The Hoosier Schoolmaster.* Judd, 1892.

Eggleston, George C. *The Last of the Flatboats.* Lothrop, 1900.

Greene, Homer. *Picketts Gap.* Macmillan, 1907. (Early railway problems)

Hawthorne, Nathaniel. *The Blithedale Romance.* Dutton, 1926. (Brook Farm)

Judson, Clara. *Reaper Man.* Houghton, 1948. (Cyrus McCormick)

McCarter, M. *Winning the Wilderness.* McClurg, 1914. (Building the National Road in Kansas)

Moore, J. T. *Hearts of Hickory.* Cokesbury, 1926. (Early career of Andrew Jackson)

Morrow, Honoré. *Black Daniel.* Morrow, 1931. (Daniel Webster)

Nicholson, Meredith. *The Cavalier of Tennessee.* Bobbs-Merrill, 1928. (Later career of Andrew Jackson)

° Nolan, Jeanette C. *Patriot in the Saddle.* Messner, 1945. (Story of Andrew Jackson)

Quick, Herbert. *Vandemark's Folly.* Bobbs-Merrill, 1922. (Traffic on the Erie Canal)

° Snedeker, Caroline D. *The Beckoning Road.* Doubleday, 1929. (An experiment in community living)

° ———. *The Town of the Fearless.* Doubleday, 1931. (Robert Owen and New Harmony)

Stone, Irving. *The President's Lady.* Doubleday, 1951. (Rachel and Andrew Jackson)

° Twain, Mark. *The Adventures of Huckleberry Finn.* Dodd, Mead, 1953. (Life along the Mississippi)

TIME LINE

1800

    1805   Lewis and Clark reach Pacific

1820

    1821   Santa Fe Trail

    1836   Texas independence gained

    1840   Sixth census—population 17,069,000
    1842   Oregon Trail
    1844   China opened to America trade
    1845   Polk inaugurated; Texas annexed
    1846   Mexican War begins; Oregon boundary settled
    1847   Mormons settle Great Salt Lake Valley
    1848   Treaty of Guadalupe Hidalgo; gold discovered in California
    1849   Taylor inaugurated; California gold rush

1850   1850   Fillmore succeeds to Presidency; Compromise of 1850
    1853   Pierce inaugurated; Gadsden Purchase
    1854   Kansas-Nebraska Act; Republican party organized; Perry opens
                Japan to West; Ostend Manifesto
    1857   Buchanan inaugurated; Dred Scott decision; business panic
    1858   Lincoln-Douglas debates
    1859   John Brown's raid
    1860   Eighth census—population 31,443,000; Lincoln elected; South
                Carolina secedes
    1861   Southern Confederacy formed; Lincoln inaugurated; Fort Sumter
    1862   Emancipation Proclamation issued
    1863   Gettysburg
    1865   Appomattox; Lincoln assassinated; Johnson succeeds to Presidency;
                Thirteenth Amendment
    1867   Reconstruction Act; Alaska purchased
    1868   Fourteenth Amendment; Johnson impeached and acquitted
    1869   Grant inaugurated

1870   1870   Fifteenth Amendment

UNIT FIVE   *The Expanding Nation Divides and Unites*

★ ★ ★ ★ As manufacturing became ever more important to the North and cotton growing more important to the South, the interests of the two sections grew further and further apart. Each wanted to control the national government so that its own interests might be favored. When the South saw that it was losing strength in Congress, the idea of leaving the Union gained favor. The only alternative that Southern leaders would accept was to increase the number of slave states in the Union by annexing land suited to slavery. Southerners therefore pressed eagerly for the annexation of Texas, and they fought enthusiastically to obtain New Mexico and California from Mexico.

After the Mexican War the South insisted that all of the huge territory ceded by Mexico should be open to slavery. The North wanted to bar slavery from the whole area. The quarrel was temporarily stopped by the Compromise of 1850. Despite this compromise, the conflict over slavery soon broke out again. The repeal of the Missouri Compromise of 1820 angered many people in the North and led to civil war in Kansas. Antislavery men accused the "slave lords" of planning to establish slavery in all the territories and declared that the Supreme Court itself supported these plans. As the 1850's drew to a close, tension reached the breaking point. The North became determined that not even one more slave state should be added to the Union. Acts of violence increased. The "irrepressible conflict" of two civilizations was at hand.

The victory of the Republican party and the election of Lincoln in 1860 meant that the North had at last gained control of the national government. The states of the deep South promptly seceded from the United States and set up an independent government known as the Confederate States of America. When Lincoln refused to let the Confederate states leave the Union, there began four years of hard fighting. This struggle, which we speak of as the War of the Confederate States for Independence or the War between North and South, was very costly to both sides. It left the South completely exhausted. Furthermore, the abolition of slavery meant that the South had to rebuild its social and economic system.

The Southern states were compelled to return to the Union on any terms they could get. President Lincoln wished the terms to be as easy as possible, but he was assassinated before he could carry out his plans. Congress then took charge and forced the South to pass through ten terrible years of so-called "reconstruction."

331

JOHN JACOB ASTOR

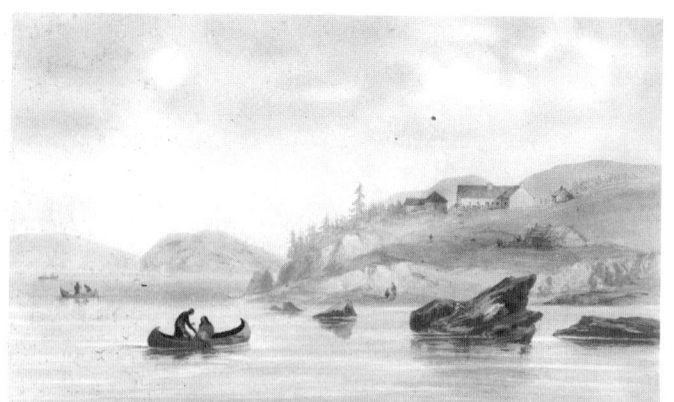

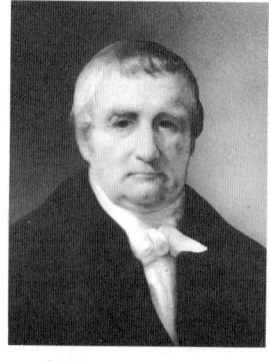

(Above) ASTORIA, *the trading post set up at the mouth of the Columbia River. Astor extended his fur trade from the Great Lakes to the Pacific, and from there to the Hawaiian Islands, China, and India.*

(Below) "THE TRAPPERS," *from a painting by William Ranney*

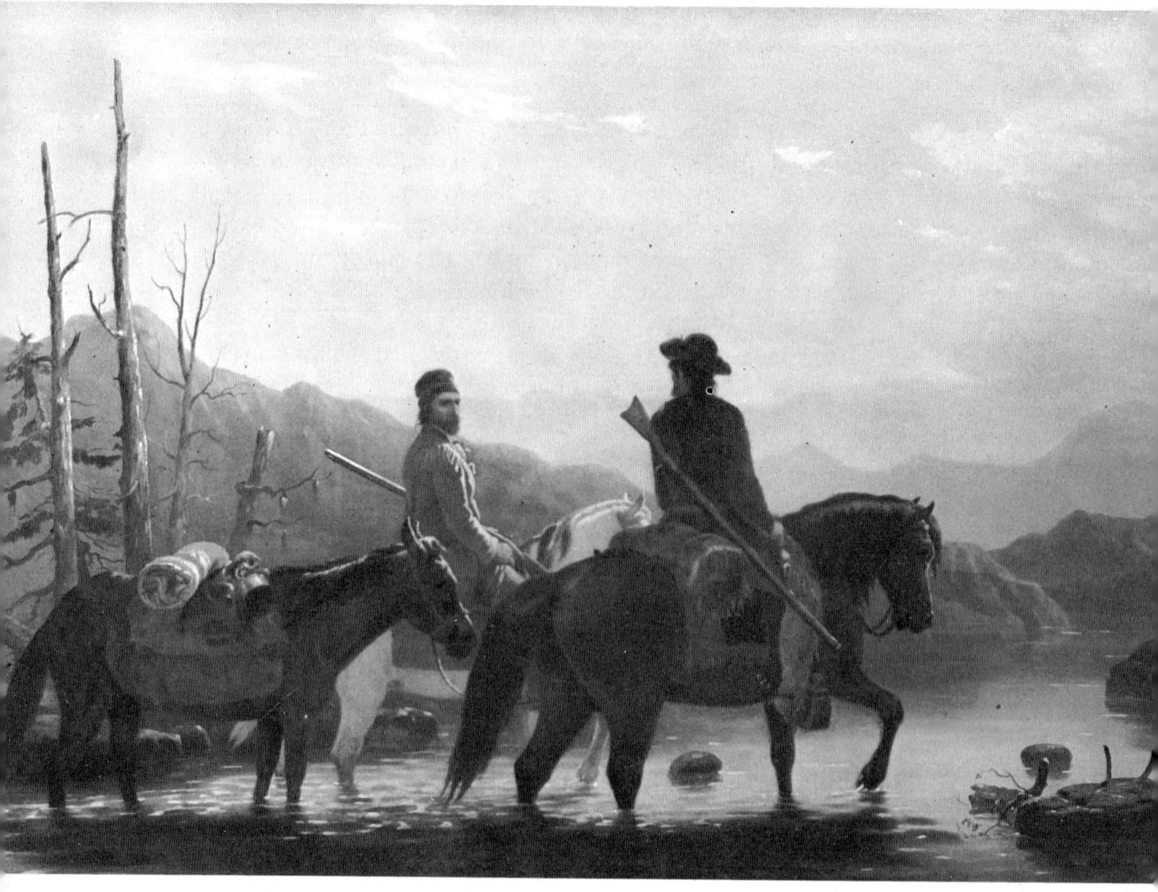

HENRY CLAY

21. THE UNITED STATES EXPANDS TO THE PACIFIC

American Settlers Enter the Far West

Explorers and traders open the Far West.

The story of the settling of the vast country west of the Mississippi is full of colorful episodes. One of the first of these has to do with the exploring expedition sent out by Jefferson in 1804. Led by two young army officers, Meriwether Lewis and William Clark, the expedition, you will remember, went up the Missouri River, crossed the Rockies, and followed the Columbia River all the way to the Pacific (see p. 197).

The expedition opened up a vast new section to American fur traders. Clark himself, immediately after his return from Oregon, helped organize the Missouri Fur Company. Soon afterward John Jacob Astor established branches of his American Fur Company in the Northwest. In 1811, Astor sent a ship around Cape Horn to set up a trading post, Astoria, at the mouth of the Columbia. A few years later a St. Louis fur trader, William Ashley, organized the Rocky Mountain Fur Company. This was the first company to employ trappers rather than to depend on buying furs from the Indians. One of Ashley's men, Kit Carson, became famous as a scout and Indian fighter.

The Far Southwest was then part of Mexico. Americans did not enter it to any extent until after 1821, when Mexico won her independence from Spain. That year an energetic Missouri trader, William Becknell, got together a pack train, which he led nearly eight hundred miles over rough, dangerous country from Franklin, Missouri, to Santa Fe. He sold his goods to the Mexicans at a handsome profit and the following year he took a wagon train to Santa Fe. Other traders followed the route he had marked out, known as the Santa Fe Trail. For protection they traveled together in wagon caravans. Trade with Santa Fe soon awakened American interest in the Southwest.

American missionaries go to the Northwest.

The Indians on the Columbia River, after learning something about the Christian religion from British fur traders, sent four men all the way to St. Louis (1831) to ask that preachers be sent them. The Methodist Church was first to answer their call. Quickly raising funds, it sent two ministers and a teacher to the Northwest in 1834. They built a mission house in the fertile and beautiful Willamette Valley. Two years later a group of Congregational and Presbyterian missionaries came. They were led by a physician, Dr. Marcus Whitman. In 1840, Father Pierre De Smet founded Roman Catholic missions in the Oregon country. Besides teaching the Christian faith, the missionaries showed the Indians how to raise crops and build homes. The missionaries wrote enthusiastic letters to their friends in the East, describing the rich soil and fine climate of Oregon. Before long many Easterners decided to move there.

The journey to Oregon is long and hard.

Most of those going to Oregon followed a route which came to be known as the Oregon Trail. Starting at Independence on the Missouri River, the trail led across plains and mountains, then down the Columbia to the Pacific coast, a total distance of some 2000 miles. The first large party of settlers, numbering about 120, successfully made the long dangerous journey over the trail in 1842.

Settlers bound for Oregon over the trail traveled in ox-team caravans. On good days they might cover twenty-five miles; on bad days, five to ten. The long lines of covered wagons got into motion at dawn. At nightfall they camped in a circle, the wagons on the outside, the people and animals within. All night long, guards watched for prowling Indians and wild beasts. The journey from Independence required five or six months. Often oxen and mules wore out and prized possessions had to be left by the way. Feeble members of the party died on the journey and were buried in unmarked graves.

The courage called for on the journey is suggested in this description written by a man who made it in 1843:

The way lies over trackless wastes, wide and deep rivers, rugged and lofty mountains, and is beset with hostile savages. Yet whether it were a deep river with no tree upon its bank, a rugged defile where even a loose horse could not pass, a hill too steep for him to climb, or a threatened attack of an enemy, they [the travelers] are always found ready and equal to the occasion and always conquerors.

Some settlers preferred to go to Oregon by sea. They could go around Cape Horn, a voyage of six or seven months, or they could sail to the Isthmus of Panama, cross that narrow strip of land, and then take another ship up the coast to Oregon. The trip across the isthmus was made partly by land and partly by water. The distance was only sixty miles but because of the dense jungles required a week. Many who attempted to cross the isthmus died of tropical diseases before they could reach the Pacific.

The ownership of Oregon is still undecided.

Although thousands of Americans were settling in Oregon, it did not yet belong to the United States. Since 1818 the United States and Great Britain had owned the region together (see p. 220). There had been several attempts to divide the territory, but the two nations could not agree on the boundary. The United States wished the dividing line to be the 49th parallel, while Great Britain wished it to be the Columbia River. Now that the territory was being settled, the boundary question had to be decided.

By 1843 there were three or four thousand Americans in Oregon, most of them in the Willamette Valley. That year some of the leaders met in a barn to organize a government for the region. They adopted laws to be in force "until such time as the United States of America should take over the territory." This action stirred Congress to debate the Oregon question. The views of the different sections of the country rang through Senate and House. Western congressmen wanted to make Ore-

AM CLARK

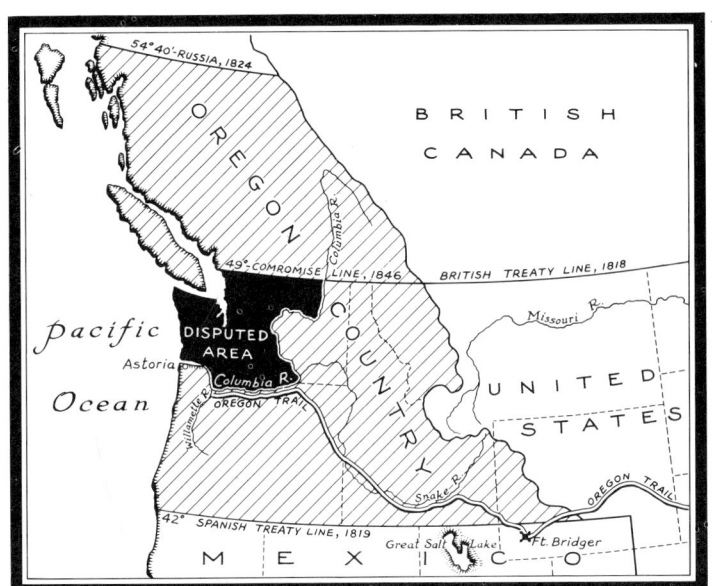

MERIWETHER LEWIS

OREGON BOUNDARY DISPUTE

gon part of the United States. Eastern and Southern congressmen were cool to the proposal. Some feared it might lead to war with England. Others thought that a territory so far away as Oregon could not become a state but must remain a colony. A senator from South Carolina asked: "What do we want with this territory? . . . To talk about constructing a railroad to the western shore of this continent shows a wild spirit of adventure which I never expected to hear . . . in the Senate of the United States." The wealth of the Indies, he added, would not build a railroad across the deserts and mountains lying between the Mississippi and the Pacific.

Texas Becomes Independent

The question of whether the United States would annex Texas was more pressing than the future of Oregon and was debated with far more emotion. It became a leading issue in the 1844 presidential election. Let us see why.

Americans settle Texas.

As we have noted, the boundaries of the Louisiana Purchase were uncertain. Americans claimed that Texas was included, but Spain denied it. In 1819, when the United States persuaded Spain to sell Florida, the State Department agreed to a western boundary which gave up our doubtful claims to Texas (see p. 221). This action angered many Westerners, who resolved to get the Texas country back whenever it could be done "with peace and honor." Other Americans decided to settle in Texas anyway.

A little over a year after the treaty with Spain, an American, Moses Austin, received permission from the Spanish government to bring three hundred American families to Texas to settle there and become Spanish citizens. Under the leadership of Austin's son Stephen a thriving community was established. In the meantime, Mexico had become free from Spain (1821). The Mexican government, wishing to speed up the settlement of Texas, in 1825 offered large tracts of land to

335

individuals who agreed to bring in at least two hundred families. One receiving such a grant was known as an *empresario*. Soon nearly all of Texas had been parceled out, mainly to Americans. The empresarios sold land for only 12½ cents an acre, while the cheapest land in the United States was then ten times as much. Within ten years about 20,000 Americans, mostly from Southern states, settled in Texas.

SAM HOUSTON

ANTONIO LOPEZ
DE SANTA ANNA

Texas becomes the "Lone Star Republic."

The Mexican government was weak, inefficient, and constantly changing. Presidents, congresses, and dictators appeared and disappeared. A policy adopted by one set of officials was ignored by the next. Yet each succeeding government wanted to keep Texas.

As more Americans moved to Texas, Mexico began to fear it would lose this valuable province. The United States had twice tried to purchase the territory (in 1827 and 1829), and Texans were already showing their impatience with certain laws. Hoping to strengthen Mexico's hold on the province, Mexican officials tried to restrict immigration. They also tried to put an end to slavery. In 1829 the Mexican president declared that slavery was abolished. The Texans protested so vigorously, they were allowed to keep their slaves. The next year Mexico prohibited almost all American immigration and further importation of slaves. However, the government was too weak to enforce either law. From 1830 on the Texans and Mexicans grew farther apart and Texan resentment grew. Most Texans now expected Texas to become part of the United States. In the fall of 1835, when a new Mexican dictator, Santa Anna, tried to strengthen his rule over Texas by sending soldiers there, the Texans rebelled.

In two months Texas volunteers drove the last Mexican soldier across the border. Santa Anna himself then swept northward with an army. Meeting small bands of armed revolutionists, he crushed one after another. The Texans were beginning to lose heart when an heroic event restored their courage. An old fortified mission chapel, the Alamo at San Antonio, was held by about 180 Texans commanded by Colonel William Travis. Nearly 3000 Mexicans led by Santa Anna closed in around them. Travis and his men refused to surrender. After a thirteen-day siege all but six had fallen at their posts. They were captured and shot by Santa Anna. The fate of the defenders of the Alamo aroused all Texans. Their battle cry became "Remember the Alamo!"

Less than two months later the little Texas army, led by General Sam Houston, succeeded in taking revenge. In the Battle of San Jacinto (April 21, 1836) the Texans almost destroyed Santa Anna's forces. Santa Anna himself was captured. When he signed a treaty agreeing to the independence of Texas, he was allowed to return to Mexico. In September Sam Houston was elected president of the new "Lone Star Republic." Texas sent petitioners to Washington asking to enter the Union or to be recognized as an independent nation.

COLONEL
WILLIAM TRAVIS

THE ALAMO, *at San Antonio*

Should Texas be annexed?

The South wanted to annex Texas at once. Texas was large enough to make at least half a dozen slave states. If Texas were annexed, the South believed it would control the Senate for a long time to come, and perhaps always. Without Texas the balance between slave states and free states in the Senate would soon be lost. On the other hand, it was because Texas had slavery that many Northerners opposed annexation. A third group, the "expansionists," said it was "manifest destiny"—something that had to be—for the United States to control the continent to the Pacific. The expansionists said we must not only have Texas but much more besides.

The debate went on for years. In 1837, you will remember, President Andrew Jackson recognized the independence of Texas, but President Van Buren let the question of annexation ride. Van Buren did not favor adding new slave states to the Union and, besides, he would not risk war with Mexico (see p. 270). President John Tyler felt differently. When he thought the time was ripe, he had a treaty of annexation drawn up. It was sent to the Senate in April, 1844. The Senate rejected it a few weeks later by a decisive majority.

Several Southerners voted against it because they doubted that the Constitution allowed the President to annex a foreign nation to the Union. All Northern senators voted against it.

As a whole, the South was deeply disappointed when the Senate did not ratify the treaty of annexation. Why should the North grow continually stronger by the addition of new free states, while the South was not permitted to grow? Rather than be controlled by a Congress in which the North would have the majority, should the South not secede from the Union? A leading South Carolina newspaper declared in a headline, "Disunion, the only remedy." But Calhoun, the best-known Southern leader, advised patience.

We Acquire Texas and Oregon

Expansion becomes an election issue.

In 1844 former President Van Buren and the great Kentuckian, Henry Clay, were expected to be rival candidates for the presidency. Then, just before the party conventions in May, the two met and published separate letters opposing annexation. This courageous act cost Van Buren the Democratic nomination. "Old Hickory," still powerful in the party, was an expansionist. He turned away from his old friend Van Buren and threw his support to James K. Polk, former governor of Tennessee. Polk was the first example of a "dark horse"[1] candidate for President. He was known to favor expansion, and expansionists had control of the convention. They boldly declared for the "reoccupation of Oregon and the reannexation of Texas." To minimize the slavery issue, they urged taking the whole of Oregon as far north as Alaska, that is, to latitude 54° 40′. Their slogan, "Fifty-four forty or fight," was of course a threat to fight Great Britain.

Henry Clay was unanimously chosen by the Whigs. It was his third try for the nation's highest office. He traveled widely, speaking to immense audiences. Fearing that he would lose the South, Clay tried to explain away his earlier opposition to annexing Texas. He wrote letters saying he would be glad to see Texas annexed if it could be done "without dishonor, without war, with the common consent of the Union, on just and fair terms." This juggling displeased the antislavery men in his own party and probably cost Clay the election. The Liberty party, with an antislavery platform, drew enough votes from Clay to place New York State in the Democratic column. Had Clay received New York's electoral votes, he would have been elected.

Texas is annexed.

Although the popular vote in the election was actually very close, President Tyler in his last annual message to Congress said that a "majority of the people" had declared in favor of immediate annexation. Knowing that the

---

[1] The term "dark horse" is borrowed from racing. An unexpected and little-known candidate is said to be like a horse which comes up from behind and wins a race.

Senate still would not ratify a treaty of annexation, he recommended that Congress pass a joint resolution to annex Texas. Such a resolution would need only a simple majority vote of both houses, rather than a two-thirds vote. After a long debate and by a close margin, both houses approved the joint resolution which admitted Texas as a state. It provided also that, with the consent of Texas, four other states might be formed from the territory. Texas was to retain its public lands and its debts. The United States was to negotiate with Mexico concerning a disputed Texas boundary. President Tyler signed the measure just before he left office.

The offer of annexation reached Texas none too soon. The Lone Star Republic was considering an offer from Great Britain to guarantee its independence and to make it a large loan. Part of the loan must be used to purchase and free the slaves owned by Texans. Texas decided to accept the American terms and was admitted to the Union late in December, 1845. Mexico, which had never recognized the independence of Texas, then broke off diplomatic relations with the United States.

President Polk's four aims.

A few years ago a poll of prominent American historians listed Polk as one of the "near-great" presidents of the United States. Yet most Americans know very little about him. Only forty-nine when elected, he was the youngest man to occupy the White House up to that time. A pleasant, dignified, and unassuming man, he had made a good record as speaker of the House and in two terms as governor of Tennessee. While President he threw all his energies into carrying out four purposes: to lower the tariff, to re-establish the independent treasury system (see p. 269), to settle the Oregon boundary question, and to acquire California.

The last two were much more difficult than the others, but in the end Polk accomplished all four.

The Oregon question is settled.

Although Polk had been elected on a platform calling for all the Oregon territory, he knew our claim to the entire region was unreasonable. Therefore, he pressed the British to accept the 49th parallel as the boundary. They still wished the Columbia River to be the boundary. After Congress voted to end joint occupation and to erect forts in Oregon, the British gave in. A treaty fixing the boundary at 49° north latitude was signed in June, 1846. The treaty also gave the British all of Vancouver Island and the right to navigate the Columbia River. Americans in the Oregon region were disappointed that part of it was to belong to England, but the rest of the country was satisfied.

Polk tries to buy the Southwest.

Before the Oregon question was settled, Polk had tried to persuade Mexico to sell California and if possible the region then called New Mexico. The whole vast area had fewer than 20,000 white inhabitants, and many of these were Americans. There were no signs that colonists from Mexico would people the region in the near future, if ever. Furthermore, Mexico had been unable to establish an effective government there and was too weak to defend it. California, in fact, might already have come under the control of a European power had the United States navy not been on guard. Why then, thought Polk, should Mexico not be willing to sell both California and New Mexico to the United States?

Late in the fall of 1845, therefore, he sent John Slidell as special minister to Mexico. Slidell was instructed to settle the Texas boundary dispute and to offer up to $30,000,000 for California and New Mexico. The United States was so unpopular with the Mexican people, however, that their government would not receive our minister. Even if he had been received, no responsible Mexican official would have dared suggest the sale of two fifths of his nation's territory. After vainly waiting in Mexico City for weeks, Slidell came home.

INDEPENDENCE ROCK, *Wyoming, a famous camp site on the trails to Oregon and California.*

We Fight Mexico and Obtain the Pacific Southwest

Hostilities begin.

Our relations with Mexico had been strained for years, not only because of Texas but because of arguments over American claims against Mexico. The claims were for injuries to American citizens and damages to their property during revolutionary uprisings within Mexico. Mexico had further angered the United States in 1835 by executing without trial a group of twenty-two Americans, on the charge that they were plotting a revolution. At the same time, Mexico also had reason to complain. Residents of our country had encouraged revolution in Texas and had furnished men and money to the revolutionists. Moreover, hundreds of Americans had settled in California and the province of New Mexico and were already talking of setting up an independent government there.

What finally led to war was the Texas boundary question. Mexico claimed that the southern boundary of Texas was the Nueces River, while Texas for years had claimed the Rio Grande as its boundary. Now that Texas was part of the United States, Polk supported the Rio Grande claim. When he learned that Slidell's mission was a failure, Polk took a step which shows how a President can maneuver the country into war. He ordered General Zachary Taylor to occupy the disputed territory between the two rivers. After Taylor crossed the Nueces, Mexico declared that a state of war existed and sent its troops across the Rio Grande to attack Taylor's forces. Skirmishes took place between the Mexican and American soldiers. As soon as Polk learned of these actions, he sent a war message to Congress saying that Mexico had invaded our territory and shed American blood. Congress declared war on May 12, 1846.

We take possession of New Mexico and California.

A few days later Colonel Stephen Kearny was instructed to occupy New

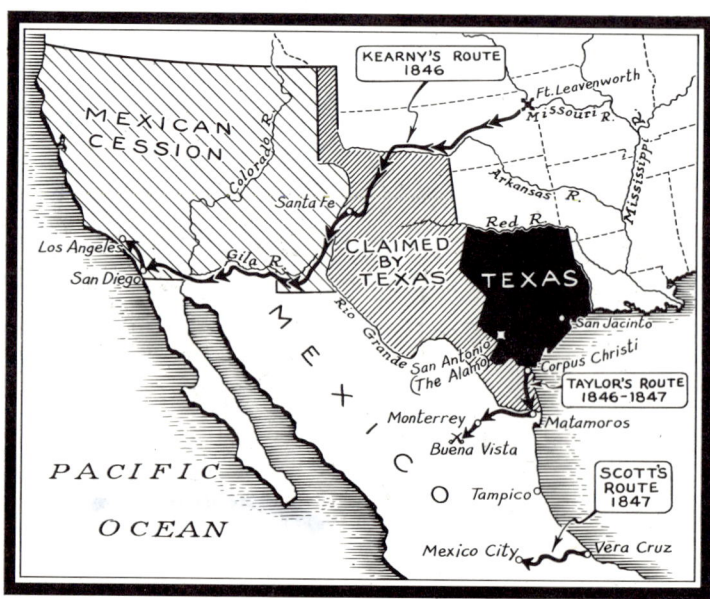

MAJOR CAMPAIGNS IN MEXICAN WAR

340

Mexico and California. In the summer of 1846 he led 1800 men on the long march from Fort Leavenworth on the upper Missouri to Santa Fe. Entering Santa Fe without resistance, Kearny set up a temporary American government. With 300 men he then hurried across the desert to California. On the way they met the scout Kit Carson bearing news that California was already in American hands. In June, as Carson reported, the Americans in the Sacramento Valley, led by Colonel John C. Frémont, had revolted. They had proclaimed the Republic of California and hoisted a white flag with a bear and a star on it. As soon as they learned that the United States and Mexico were at war, they took down the bear flag and ran up the Stars and Stripes. Frémont's forces were supported by an American naval squadron, which had been waiting off the coast with instructions to seize the harbors if war began. When Kearny reached California, the remaining resistance was quickly put down.

Mexico is defeated.

Meanwhile, General Taylor had invaded northern Mexico. In September, 1846, after a stubborn battle, he had captured the fortified city of Monterrey. In February, 1847, at Buena Vista, Taylor defeated an untrained Mexican force several times larger than his own.

Early that spring an army commanded by General Winfield Scott landed near Vera Cruz on Mexico's eastern coast. They captured that seaport and then marched westward through the mountains to the capital. After a hard-fought campaign, Scott took Mexico City in September 1847. With the loss of their capital, the Mexicans were ready to make peace.

The peace treaty.

The peace terms were signed at Guadalupe Hidalgo outside of Mexico City early in 1848. Mexico acknowledged our title to Texas, New Mexico, and California, an area even greater

These three wealthy young men from Los Angeles, of Spanish birth and American education, represent the cultural mixing that took place during the 1850's in California.

341

than the Louisiana Purchase. Mexico also accepted the Rio Grande as the boundary of Texas. In return the United States agreed to pay Mexico $15,000,000 and to assume claims of American citizens against Mexico amounting to over $3,000,000. Much of the land ceded by Mexico was desert, and some Americans wondered whether it was worth the price paid for it.

Although Mexico gave up nearly half of its territory, this did not satisfy the extreme expansionists. Two members of the Cabinet, including James Buchanan, Secretary of State, wanted to take all of Mexico. Polk, however, took only what he had originally offered to buy.

Was the Mexican War justifiable?

Although a large majority of Congress had voted to declare war against Mexico, there had been considerable opposition to the war in the North. Some had come from Whigs aiming to discredit the Democratic administration. Much of it expressed honest objections to acquiring territory that would probably be open to slavery. Other opposition was based on the belief that Mexico had been goaded into attacking the United States. Abraham Lincoln, a young country lawyer serving his only term in Congress, presented the latter view when he offered the famous "Spot Resolution." In it he challenged the President to name a spot on American soil where Mexicans had shed American blood. James Russell Lowell called the war a plot to get "bigger pens to cram slaves in."

Had Polk been more patient, the Texas boundary question could doubtless have been settled peaceably. On the other hand, could bloodshed have been avoided in California and New Mexico, had they remained under Mexican control? More than 100,000 immigrants, mostly Americans, had settled there by 1850. Probably they would have gone there even if it were still part of Mexico and probably they would have insisted on joining the Union. Mexico would doubtless have tried to put down their rebellion by force, as it did in Texas, and would have failed. A more reasonable government in Mexico might have realized in 1845 that it could not hold its distant provinces and might have accepted Polk's offer to buy them.

Those who justify the war have to admit that it was unfortunate. In the republics south of the Rio Grande it left fear and hate that lasted for generations. In the United States it multiplied the tension between North and South. Disputes over whether the newly acquired territory should be open or closed to slavery soon threatened the nation with disunion.

The Gadsden Purchase.

In 1853 the United States acquired more Mexican land. We paid Mexico $10,000,000 for a narrow strip of land lying on the southern border of New Mexico. This "Gadsden Purchase," as it is known, was needed to insure the best route for a railroad across the southern Rockies to the Pacific coast. The strip was small compared to what we got after the war for $18,000,000, and critics of the war described the payment as "conscience money." This purchase rounded out the present boundaries of the United States.

The Mormons settle Utah.

One of the most unusual communities in the history of American pioneering was founded during the Mexican War. This was the Mormon colony in the valley of the Great Salt Lake. The Mormons were a religious group, started in 1830 in western New York by Joseph Smith. Young Smith announced that he had found sacred writings, *The Book of Mormon*, inscribed on golden plates. He called his organization the "Church of Jesus Christ of Latter Day Saints" and rapidly won a large number of followers. Because the Mormons were abolitionists and because of their religious beliefs, they suffered persecution. Pushed by hostile neighbors, the Mormons moved in a group from New York to Missouri and then to Illinois. There they built a prosperous city, Nauvoo. When the Mormon church gave its approval to plural marriage, a mob of non-Mormons killed Smith and his brother. Soon after, the Mormons were driven from Illinois.

In 1847, led by Brigham Young, they moved into the Great Salt Lake Valley, in the area that was about to be ceded to the United States. Here the Mormons found a healthful climate and land that was fertile but dry. They dug irrigation ditches up and down the valley and converted the desert into productive farmland. For their capital they built beautiful Salt Lake City. They sent missionaries to the Eastern states, to Great Britain, and to Europe, to win converts who would settle in Utah. Within three years 11,000 people had settled there and Utah was organized as a territory.

A gold rush quickly populates California.

In January, 1848, just two weeks before the signing of the treaty ending the Mexican War, gold was discovered in the Sacramento Valley. When they heard the news, Californians dropped whatever they were doing and hurried to the gold fields. By early summer a thousand men were busy washing gold. With nothing but a shovel and a pan, a man could make from $10 to $100 a day. One miner made $4500 in a few weeks; a schoolboy carried home over $3000 after less than two months' work. Sometimes an individual found a single nugget worth thousands of dollars.

A Californian has given us a vivid picture of what happened:

BRIGHAM YOUNG, *Mormon leader and colonizer*

SUTTER'S MILL, *where gold was discovered*

"IN AUBURN RAVINE." *News of gold brought women as well as men to California.*

343

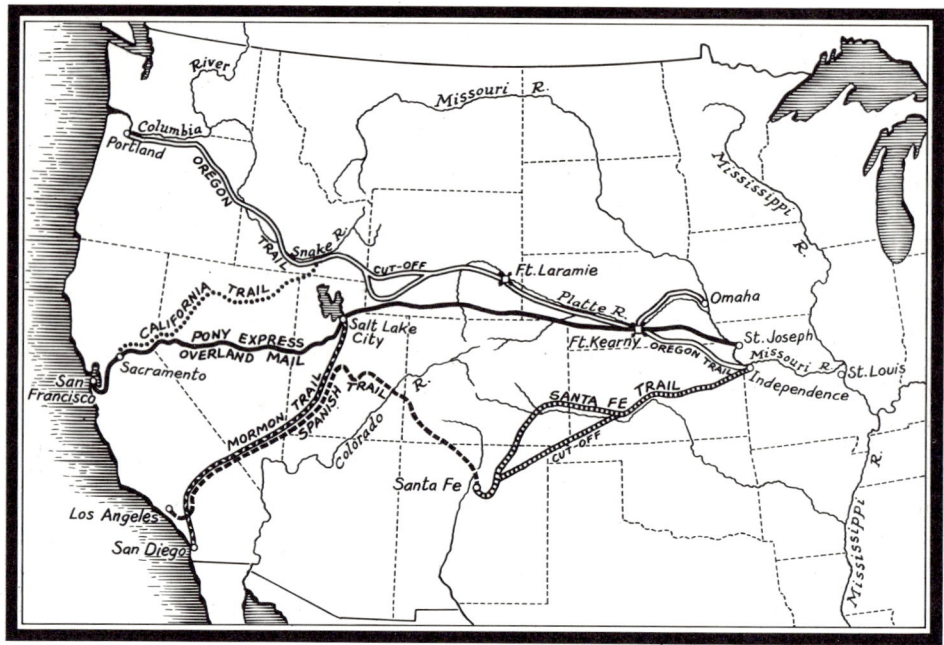

MAIN ROUTES WEST BEFORE 1860

Settlements were completely deserted; houses, farms, and stores abandoned. Ships, deserted by their sailors, crowded the bay of San Francisco; soldiers deserted wholesale; churches were emptied; town councils ceased to sit; merchants, clerks, lawyers and judges, and criminals everywhere flocked to the foothills.

The news reached the East in the fall of 1848. At once people from every walk of life prepared to leave for California. Most of these people went overland by the Santa Fe Trail. Soon the deserts were littered with the skeletons of their horses and oxen, their abandoned prairie schooners and baggage, and the graves of those who perished of sickness or thirst. Others went across the pestilence-laden Isthmus of Panama, then battled for a place on a little steamer plying up the coast. The safest and easiest but the most costly way was the long, long voyage around South America.

The greatest rush of gold seekers was in 1849, and the "Forty-niners" are

famous in song and story. The following is part of a song celebrating the gold rush:

I'll scrape the mountains clean, old girl.
I'll drain the rivers dry.
I'm off for California, Susannah, don't you
    cry.
Oh, Susannah, don't you cry for me.
I'm off to California with my washbowl on
    my knee.

As thousands poured into California, the seaport towns and the mining camps grew like mushrooms. Prices rocketed. Rooms rented for unheard-of prices. In 1849 a tent in San Francisco rented for $40,000 a year; a pick or shovel sold for $10 to $50. In the mining camps flour and potatoes sold for $1.00 a pound, sugar and coffee for $4.00 a pound. Wages were set by the amount of gold one could pan in a day. Carpenters got $20 a day; clerks, from $300 to $500 a month. These high prices and wages continued for several years in the more remote camps.

The Compromise of 1850 Temporarily Saves the Union

The Wilmot Proviso.

The question of slavery in the territories, which had been settled by the Missouri Compromise in 1820, was reopened early in the Mexican War. During a debate in Congress David Wilmot of Pennsylvania offered a resolution to shut out slavery from any territory that might be obtained from Mexico. The resolution is known as the *Wilmot Proviso*. It passed the House in 1846 and again in 1847, but was defeated both times in the Senate. The attempt to pass the Wilmot Proviso has been called "the turning point in the history of the slavery struggle." Its passage by the House, in which Northerners were a majority, showed that the North had made up its mind not to permit the extension of slavery.

Should the Southwest be open or closed to slavery?

The acquisition of California and New Mexico at the end of the war sharpened the debate on the extension of slavery. Slavery did not exist in either region at the time, for it had been forbidden by Mexican law. Furthermore, since most of the territory was unsuited for plantations, slavery probably would not be profitable there. Few Americans realized this, however, and they discussed with ever-growing bitterness whether slavery would be permitted in the new territory.

There were four proposals for dealing with the question:

1. To divide the new territory into slave and free areas by continuing the Missouri Compromise line of 36° 30′ to the Pacific. President Polk favored this solution.

2. To exclude slavery from the whole Mexican Cession. This was the solution offered in the Wilmot Proviso.

3. To open the whole territory to slavery and to give slaveowners federal protection from interference by antislavery men.

4. Popular sovereignty—letting the people of a territory decide whether to permit slavery within its borders. Senator Lewis Cass of Michigan urged this method of meeting the problem. Popular sovereignty meant that every territory would be open to slaveholders at the start. When a territorial government was set up, the settlers would vote whether their particular territory was to be slave or free.

JAMES K. POLK

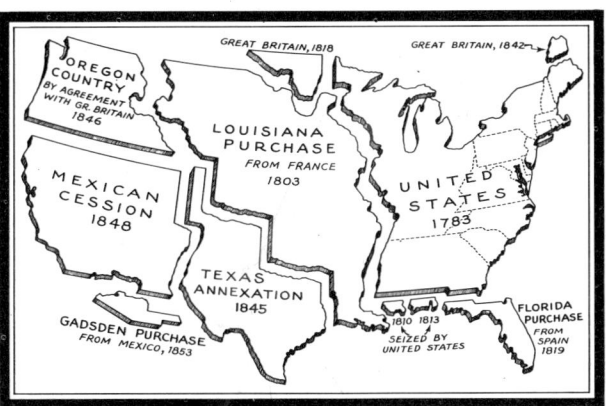

TERRITORIAL GROWTH OF THE UNITED STATES

The question was still unsettled when Polk's term came to an end.

Zachary Taylor becomes President.

Polk had declared when elected that he would serve only one term. Perhaps he could not have won another, yet few Presidents have accomplished more than he did.

In the 1848 presidential campaign each party had the problem of how to hold both its Northern and Southern members. Since the Democrats were stronger in the South, they chose a Northerner, Lewis Cass, as their presidential candidate. Their platform said nothing about slavery. The Whigs, who were strongest in the North, named a Southerner, General Zachary Taylor. "Old Rough and Ready," as he was known to veterans of the Mexican War, came from Louisiana and owned 300 slaves. The Whigs did not draw up any platform, for fear it might offend some important group of voters. They counted on Taylor's popularity as a military hero to lead the party to victory.

The effort of the major parties to dodge the slavery issue led to the formation of the Free Soil party. The Free Soilers declared that the nation should not extend or encourage slavery but should limit, localize, and discourage it. They insisted that slavery was a *local* institution, protected only by the laws of the slave states. Their slogan was "Free Soil, Free Speech, Free Labor, Free Men." Unlike the earlier Liberty party (see p. 271), the Free Soil party did not ask the abolition of slavery. Its object was not to interfere with slavery where it already existed but to keep it from being extended. The Free Soilers nominated former President Martin Van Buren. He did not carry a single state, but by splitting the Democratic vote in New York he caused Cass to lose the election. "Old Rough and Ready," the Whig candidate, won by a narrow margin.

California seeks admission to the Union.

After the discovery of gold there, California was rapidly settled (see p. 343). Its people needed an orderly government, yet the slavery question kept Congress from agreeing how to set it up. Late in 1849 the Californians took matters into their own hands. They drew up a constitution which barred slavery. Then they elected a governor and a legislature and asked for admission to the Union. The new Congress would have to take action.

Congress faces five serious questions.

The new Congress, which met in December, 1849, was a brilliant gathering. In the Senate were the great trio of debaters, Daniel Webster, Henry Clay, and John Calhoun, now almost at the end of their lives. Besides them were a number of rising young leaders, some with strong antislavery views.

The leading questions before Congress all had to do with slavery:

1. Should California be admitted to the Union with the free-soil constitution its people had approved? In 1849 there were fifteen free and fifteen slave states. The admission of California would upset the balance in the Senate. Southern extremists threatened to secede if the North got control of the Senate.

2. Should slavery be permitted in the rest of the Mexican Cession?

3. Should the Texans be allowed to push their western boundary into New Mexico far beyond the boundary of the old Spanish province of Texas?

4. Should slave markets be barred from the District of Columbia? Abolitionists had demanded this for years.

5. Should the Fugitive-Slave Act, passed in 1793 and disregarded in the North, be replaced by a law with teeth?

Sectional feeling in Congress and in the nation had never been so bitter. The members of the House voted sixty-nine times before they could agree on

SAN FRANCISCO IN 1851. *With the discovery of gold San Francisco mushroomed overnight. From a quiet town of 900 in 1848 it became a bustling city of 10,000 in 1849.*

a Speaker. People doubted that the Union would hold together much longer.

Clay suggests a compromise.

Clay was now seventy-three years old and racked with consumption. He had won election to the Senate, after an absence of seven years, in order to work out some compromise which might save the Union. Early in the session (January, 1850) he outlined his plan for adjusting the differences between North and South. Asserting that secession from the Union would mean war—a war that would be "ferocious and bloody, implacable and exterminating"—he called upon both sections to show a spirit of compromise. His plan had five main provisions, covering each of the important problems before Congress: (1) California should be admitted as a free state; (2) Congress should organize two territorial governments in the rest of the Mexican Cession (Utah and New Mexico), leaving the people of each territory to decide

whether to prohibit slavery; (3) Texas should be paid $10,000,000 for its claim to part of New Mexico; (4) the slave trade (but not slavery) should be abolished in the District of Columbia; (5) Congress should pass an effective fugitive-slave law. For the next seven months Congress, and the entire nation, argued over Clay's proposals.

Calhoun and Webster take opposite sides.

On March 4, Calhoun, also desperately ill of consumption, appeared in the Senate to attack the suggested compromise. He was so weak that his speech was read for him. Calhoun declared that the South had nothing to compromise or concede. Unless the North stopped its antislavery propaganda, honestly enforced the fugitive-slave law, and gave the South equal rights in the new territories (that is, allowed slavery in all of them), the South was bound to secede. He pointed out that the cords which held the sections together were fast breaking.

347

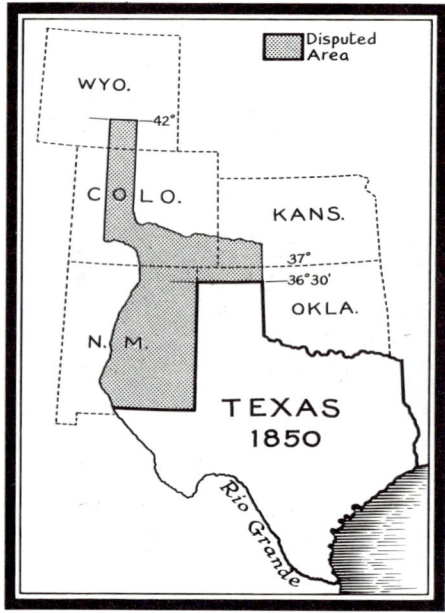

TEXAS AND THE COMPROMISE
OF 1850

Three days later Calhoun tottered into the Senate to hear Daniel Webster's reply. If the Massachusetts statesman spoke against the compromise, it would surely be defeated. The galleries were packed when Webster rose to make his last great speech. "I wish to speak today," he began, "not as a Massachusetts man, but as an American. . . . I speak today for the preservation of the Union."

Although Webster had strongly opposed the extension of slavery, he supported the compromise because he saw that the Union was in great danger. He declared that slavery would never gain a foothold in the new territories, since their soils and climate were not suited to it. "I would not take pains uselessly to reaffirm an ordinance of nature nor to re-enact the will of God. I would put in no Wilmot Proviso for the mere purpose of a taunt or a reproach." He said the abolitionists had done no good and much harm by their extreme views. The South had a

right to insist that the fugitive-slave law be strictly enforced. At the same time he rebuked Southerners who said that slavery was superior to the free labor system. He warned Calhoun that secession would lead to war. "There can be no such thing as peaceable secession. Disruption of the Union . . . must produce war, and such a war as I will not describe."

Webster's seventh of March speech was denounced by antislavery groups. Abolitionists called him a "Benedict Arnold" and a "fallen angel." They said he had betrayed his principles in order to get Southern support in the coming presidential election. Many with more moderate views approved his stand, hoping that compromise would heal the breach between the sections. Northern businessmen distributed 200,000 copies of his speech.

The Compromise of 1850.

President Taylor, although he was a Southerner, opposed the extension of slavery. He used his influence against the compromise, saying that each point should be decided separately on its own merits. In July, Taylor suddenly died. His successor, Millard Fillmore of New York, actively supported the compromise. Congress then adopted each of Clay's proposals, and they became law. Clay and Webster, with their followers, had for the time being saved the Union from disaster.

Effects of the Compromise of 1850.

It was not easy to say which side had fared the better in the Compromise of 1850. The admission of California looked like an important gain for the North, since it gave the free states a majority in the Senate. The question of slavery in New Mexico and Utah was left in doubt, but nature had already decided that slavery would not succeed there. The settlement with Texas meant that New Mexico was

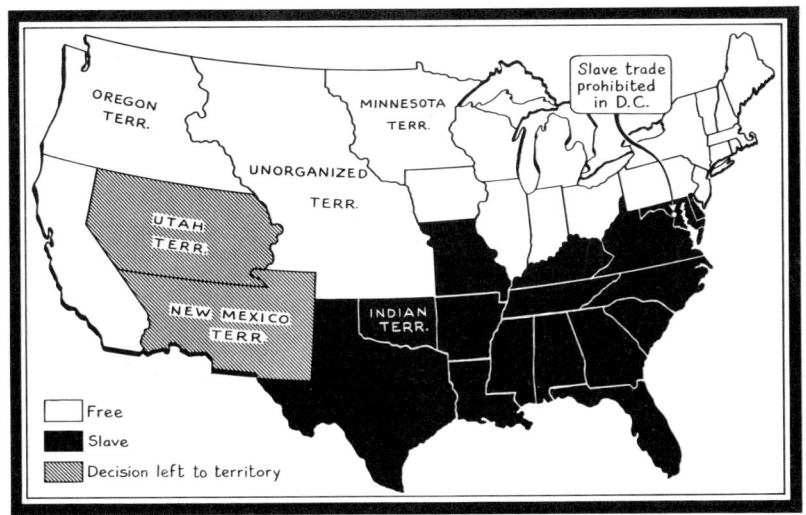

SLAVERY AFTER THE COMPROMISE OF 1850

larger than it would otherwise have been. The closing of the slave markets in Washington only meant their removal to nearby Virginia. This satisfied both sides. The abolitionists could no longer say that the trade in human beings went on under the very shadow of the national Capitol.

The new Fugitive-Slave Act seemed to be an important victory for the slaveholders. They could now use federal courts and federal officers to help them get back a runaway slave. Anyone who aided a slave's escape was liable to a heavy fine and six months' imprisonment. A Negro accused of being a runaway slave was denied a jury trial and could not testify in his own defense. The magistrate before whom he was brought received twice as large a fee for handing him over to the man who claimed him as for declaring him to be a free Negro. Many Northerners considered the law to be most unjust and continued their underground activities. Emerson wrote in his diary, "I will not obey it."

The compromise may have delayed war between the sections for ten years. Meanwhile the North grew rap-idly in population, wealth, and industry. It also became more united. By 1861, when war broke out, the North had the power to preserve the Union by force. This was not true in 1850.

Franklin Pierce becomes President.

The desire for harmony was shown in the election of 1852. The Democrats praised the compromise and promised to enforce the Fugitive-Slave Act. They pledged the party to "resist all attempts at renewing, in Congress or out of it, the agitation of the slavery question." They had a hard time to agree on a candidate who could please both North and South. Finally, on the forty-ninth ballot, they nominated a man "without a record" and "without an enemy" —General Franklin Pierce of New Hampshire.

The Whigs, already losing strength in the South, dared not take a strong stand. They promised to maintain the compromise until time showed changes to be necessary. Like the Democrats, they condemned further agitation over slavery. Choosing a candidate gave them equal trouble. The Whigs passed over President Fillmore, Daniel Web-

349

ster, and Henry Clay, since their support of the new Fugitive-Slave Act displeased so many Northerners. On the fifty-third ballot they nominated another hero of the Mexican War, General "Fuss and Feathers" Winfield Scott of Virginia.

The popular vote was close. Nevertheless, Pierce carried twenty-seven states, while Scott carried only four. The Free Soil party polled but 5 per cent of the popular vote. Four years earlier it had polled 10 per cent. The drop in the Free Soil vote was another sign of the nation's wish to forget the quarrel over slavery.

Spaniards in California. A hacienda owner and his wife pause in their ride to talk with an overseer.

FOR IDENTIFICATION

John Jacob Astor	Stephen Kearny
Moses Austin	Liberty party
Kit Carson	Lone Star Republic
Lewis Cass	Mormons
Millard Fillmore	Franklin Pierce
"Forty-niners"	James K. Polk
Free Soil party	Winfield Scott
John C. Frémont	Zachary Taylor
Sam Houston	Brigham Young

FOR EXPLANATION OR DEFINITION

Compromise of 1850	"reannexation of
"dark horse"	Texas"
"Fifty-four forty or	"Remember the
fight"	Alamo"
joint resolution	"reoccupation of
manifest destiny	Oregon"
popular sovereignty	Wilmot Proviso

350

FOR REVIEW

1. Name the explorers who opened up the Far Northwest. What was their route?

2. How did Americans become interested in the Far Southwest?

3. How did missionaries help in settling Oregon?

4. Describe the journey of an ox-train caravan to Oregon.

5. Why did Congress hesitate to make Oregon a part of the United States?

6. (a) Why did many Americans buy land in Texas rather than in the United States? (b) When and why did Mexico prohibit the immigration of Americans to Texas? (c) Why did Texans disregard Mexican laws? (d) How did the Lone Star Republic come into being?

7. (a) Why didn't President Van Buren annex Texas? (b) Why didn't the Senate ratify the treaty of annexation when President Tyler submitted it in 1844? (c) What was the attitude of the South toward the annexation of Texas?

8. (a) Why did Democratic leaders choose a "dark horse" for their candidate in 1844? (b) Why did Whig leaders try to avoid the issue of annexing Texas and Oregon in 1844? (c) How do you account for Clay's defeat and Polk's election?

9. How did President Polk succeed in settling the Oregon question in 1846?

10. (a) What incident led to the war between the United States and Mexico? What was the "Spot Resolution"? (b) State the terms of the treaty of Guadalupe Hidalgo. (c) What was the Gadsden Purchase?

11. Who founded the religious group known as Mormons? What is the correct name of the Mormon church? Why were the Mormons driven from Illinois? How did they use the land?

12. (a) When and where was gold discovered in California? (b) How did the news of this discovery affect people in California and in the East? (c) Describe the three routes to the West used by "Forty-niners."

13. (a) What was the Wilmot Proviso? (b) Why has it been called the "turning point" in the struggle over slavery?

14. Name the presidential candidates in 1848. What was the program of the Free Soil party? How did this third party influence the election of 1848?

15. (a) State the issues that confronted Congress in 1850. (b) Outline the provisions of Clay's Compromise of 1850. (c) What was the point of view of Calhoun toward the Compromise of 1850? (d) What arguments did Webster use in its defense?

16. (a) What parts of the Compromise of 1850 favored the South? What parts favored the North? (b) What were the effects of the compromise?

17. Explain the difficulty in selecting presidential candidates in 1852.

18. Briefly describe the presidential campaign of 1852. How did this campaign reflect the national mood for harmony?

FOR FURTHER STUDY AND DISCUSSION

1. How did the issue of expansion become involved with the issue of slavery?

2. Why do you agree or disagree with the statement that American expansion to the Pacific was a form of imperialism? Helpful source: Stephenson, *Texas and the Mexican War* (Y. C. S.).

3. Explain the arguments involved in using the campaign slogans "Reannexation of Texas" and "Reoccupation of Oregon."

4. Why did Polk and his party abandon the idea of "Fifty-four forty or fight"?

5. Criticize or defend President Polk's actions preceding the declaration of war with Mexico. Helpful sources: Bemis, *Diplomatic History*, pp. 232–240; Bailey, *Diplomatic History*, pp. 262–271; Hart, *Contemporaries*, Vol. IV, Nos. 10, 11, 14.

6. Distinguish between the Liberty party and the Free Soil party.

7. Discuss the soundness of the argument advanced by Webster in his seventh of March speech in behalf of the Compromise of 1850. Helpful source: Hart, *Contemporaries*, Vol. IV, Nos. 19, 20, 21, 22.

8. (a) Why was the Compromise of 1850 regarded as a "final" solution of the slavery question? (b) Why is the compromise sometimes referred to as a "sectional truce" and "businessman's peace"?

FOR INDIVIDUAL OR GROUP ACTIVITIES

1. (a) Prepare charts which summarize the essential facts concerning the elections of 1844, 1848, and 1852. (b) Write editorials in which you urge the voters to support your choice of candidates: Polk or Clay in 1844; Taylor, Cass, or Van Buren in 1848; Pierce or Scott in 1852.

2. Read to the class excerpts from *The Biglow Papers* to illustrate Lowell's views on Texas, California, and the Mexican War.

3. Report on: Slidell's mission to Mexico, defense of the Alamo, the Battle of San Jacinto, Scott's capture of Mexico City, the discovery of gold in California. Helpful sources: Commager and Nevins, *Heritage of America*; Hart, *Contemporaries*, Vol. IV; Stephenson, *Texas and the Mexican War*; White, *The Forty-niners*.

4. Prepare a radio playlet for class or assembly presentation on the dramatic debate in the Senate on the Compromise of 1850. Helpful sources: Rhodes, *History of the United States since the Compromise of 1850*; Schurz's biography of Clay; Fuess's biography of Webster; von Holst's biography of Calhoun; Johnston and Woodburn, *American Orations*, Vol. II.

5. Write an article for the school newspaper on the theme: Polk is "undeservedly one of the forgotten men of American history." Helpful source: Schlesinger, *Paths to the Present*, ch. 5.

6. Prepare a book report on Nevins, *Frémont, Pathfinder of the West*.

7. On outline maps illustrate: (a) the boundary dispute between Texas and Mexico, (b) the Oregon boundary dispute and its settlement, (c) the principal events of the Mexican War, (d) the Gadsden Purchase, (e) the status of slavery in the states and territories west of the Mississippi after the Compromise of 1850. Helpful source: Lord, *Historical Atlas*.

8. Prepare editorials or cartoons for a Mexico City newspaper and a South Carolina newspaper of 1848 on the outbreak of the war with Mexico.

9. Hold a panel discussion on: (1) the causes and results of the Mexican War, (2) the causes and results of the Compromise of 1850.

THE ERA OF GREAT PLANTATIONS *produced many homes such as Oak Alley* (above) *in Louisiana. Here central halls invited every breeze, while overhanging galleries gave protection from sun and rain.*
Beneath the great oaks of a plantation home long rows of slave cabins stood in grim contrast to the splendor of the great house only a few hundred yards away.

No sir, you dare not make war on cotton. No power on earth dares make war upon it. Cotton is king.——Senator J. K. Hammond

22. SECTIONAL DISCORD LEADS TO DISUNION

Growing Economic Differences between North and South

Economic progress is rapid.

The ten-year period from 1850 to 1860 (except for the panic of 1857) was one of bustling activity. The great flood of gold from California was exchanged for goods or invested in enterprises of all sorts. This activity pushed prices up and led to a new era of prosperity. Manufacturing expanded. The building of highways, telegraph lines, and railroads boomed.

Railroads spread over the Midwest.

Although transportation by canal and by river was at its peak in the 1850's, the railroad was soon to become the chief means of transportation. Before 1850 about 9000 miles of track had been laid. By 1860 there were 30,000 miles. The greater part of the increase was in the Middle West, where thousands of new farms were being settled. Chicago became the center of a network of rail lines.

In these years many short rail lines were consolidated under a single management. Some of the larger systems, like the Pennsylvania, took over hundreds of small railroad companies in order to create trunk lines connecting East and West. By 1856 railroads from the East reached ten places on the Mississippi. Beyond the Mississippi railroads were in process of construction.

Railroads bind East and West together.

For years New Orleans was the great commercial center of the Mississippi Valley. Most of the products of the West went down the Mississippi on their way to the markets of the world. The railroads changed this, for Western products began to go by rail to Atlantic seaports. New Orleans declined in importance. Chicago became the center of the trade in grain and livestock. From Chicago products moved east by rail or over the Great Lakes and the Erie Canal by freight boats. The growing trade between East and West helped to make the two sections more aware of their common economic interests.

Manufacturing expands in the North.

The output of American factories doubled in value between 1850 and 1860. Western farmers demanded steel plows, reapers, seed drills, threshers, and other machines. The building of railroad and telegraph lines and new factories called for iron, steel, and copper products. The growing cities needed an ever-increasing supply of food and manufactures. Meat packing, canning, flour milling, and the manufacture of textiles were becoming more important. In addition, several new industries were started. One of these was

353

the production of ready-to-wear clothing and shoes, made possible by the invention of the sewing machine. Another was the production of rubber goods, made possible by Goodyear's invention of the vulcanizing process.

Most of the increase in manufacturing took place in the North. By 1860 the value of manufactured goods produced in the South was only 8 per cent of the total for the nation. There are several reasons why manufacturing grew so much faster in the North. The North had more water power, a larger supply of skilled labor, a greater number of experienced managers, and more capital available for investment in industry. The wealth of the South was tied up in land and slaves. Furthermore, the ownership of a plantation carried far more prestige in the South than the ownership of a business. In the North, on the other hand, men with capital to invest could win prestige as merchants, builders, manufacturers, and bankers.

Population increases faster in the North.

In 1800 the North and the South were about equal in population. By 1860 the North had nineteen million people, while the South had only twelve and a half million, including about four million slaves. Population grew more rapidly in the North because more immigrants settled there, establishing themselves in the growing factory towns. Few immigrants went South, because they would have to compete with slave labor.

The South faces economic problems.

Southerners realized that their section was less prosperous than the North. For this they blamed Northern businessmen. Southerners sold their export crops—cotton and tobacco—to Northern merchants, or consigned them to Northern commission men. In either case they felt that Northerners were

getting rich at their expense. They also resented their dependence on Northern factories and felt that they had to pay too much for manufactured products.

To remedy these grievances, Southern leaders had various proposals. One of the most common was to do away with the protective tariff in hopes of encouraging foreign imports and thus lowering the price of manufactured goods. Under Democratic leadership, Congress cut the tariff in 1846 and again in 1857. Another idea was to boycott Northern manufactures and use homemade articles instead. A third proposal was to ship cotton and tobacco direct to Europe instead of through New York. In addition, Southern journals urged parents to send their sons and daughters to schools and colleges in the South. There was also much talk about secession from the Union. Few Southerners thought that the abolition of slavery might be a remedy.

Slaveholding Is Confined to a Small Class

Most Southerners are not slaveowners.

In discussing the differences between North and South, we should keep in mind that the great majority of Southerners did not own slaves. It is estimated that only 1 in 4 Southern families in the 1850's had any slaves. Half of the slaveowning families had less than five slaves. Only about 11,000 families had fifty or more slaves. The figures given in the census of 1860 are shown in the graph. Along with the concentration of slaveholding went a concentration of wealth. According to one estimate a thousand families received close to half of all the income received in the South.

When Northerners spoke of the "slave power" they had in mind the political influence of the great planters. The small farmers, who far outnum-

354

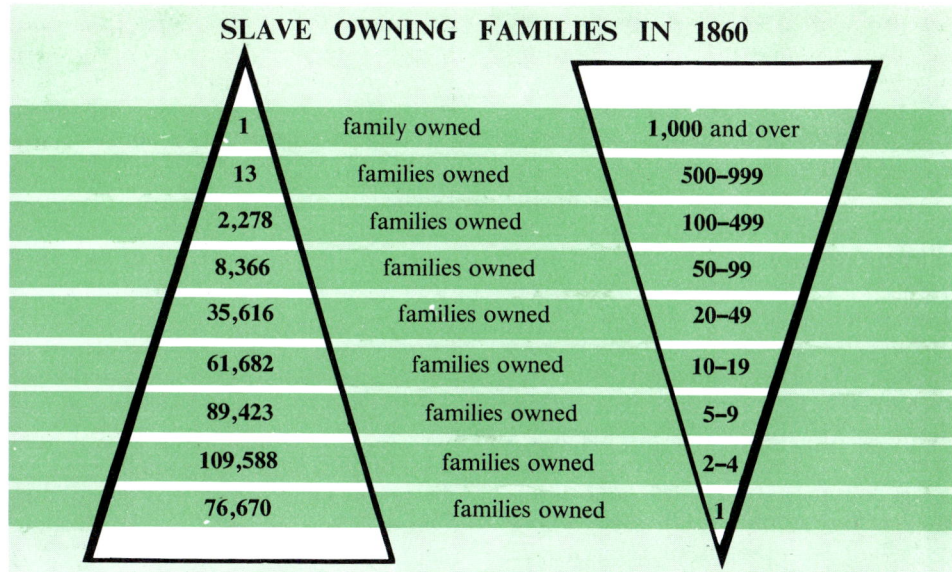

SLAVE OWNING FAMILIES IN 1860

1	family owned	1,000 and over
13	families owned	500–999
2,278	families owned	100–499
8,366	families owned	50–99
35,616	families owned	20–49
61,682	families owned	10–19
89,423	families owned	5–9
109,588	families owned	2–4
76,670	families owned	1

bered the planters, took little part in politics. They looked up to the planters and did not dispute their right to manage public affairs. Thus the great planters held in their hands a concentration both of wealth and of power.

Most slaves live in the deep South.

Slaveholding was more important in some parts of the South than in others. In the 1850's half the slaves in the United States lived in five states— South Carolina, Georgia, Alabama, Mississippi, and Louisiana. Half the people in these states, called the deep South, were slaves. They were used chiefly in growing cotton, sugar cane, and rice. Most of the larger plantations were in the river valleys, where slaves made up nine tenths of the population.

The proportion of slaves to the total population was much smaller in the upper South—Virginia, Maryland, North Carolina, Tennessee, and Kentucky. Here the land was wearing out through continual tobacco growing, so that farming was no longer very profitable. For this reason, it did not pay to use first-class slaves that could be sold for high prices in the cotton belt. Be-

sides, the slave population increased so rapidly that there was not enough work for all of them in the upper South. As a result slaveowners in this section sold unneeded slaves "down the river" to the cotton planters of the lower South.

Slave smuggling increases.

With the westward -march of the plantation system, the demand for slaves grew and their price went up. In the 1850's the planters in Mississippi, Louisiana, Arkansas, and Texas pressed Congress to reopen the African slave trade. Congress did not do so and the smuggling of slaves increased. In 1859 nearly a hundred ships sailed from New York to engage in smuggling slaves. So long as there was plenty of fertile land suitable for plantations, slavery was a means to wealth and power. The slave smugglers therefore found a ready market for their wares.

Small farmers too defend the slave system.

When so few Southerners owned slaves, we might ask why nearly all Southern whites defended the slave system. One reason was their belief

355

that Negroes were an inferior race who had to be kept under control. Most Southerners, whether slaveholders or not, thought slavery was the only way by which the two races could live side by side. Another reason was the ambition of nearly every small farmer in the South to become a slaveowner. A farmer who possessed a family of slaves had more social standing and could make more money than one who did not. He dreamed of moving to the new cotton lands in the West and making a start as a planter. He knew that this was the way to wealth and privilege. So, even if he had no slaves, he defended his constitutional right to hold them. He was fiercely proud of being a Southerner and he resented any criticism of the South's "peculiar institution"—the slavery system.

Americans Take Interest in the Caribbean and the Far East

The United States tries to buy Cuba.

After the Mexican War some American leaders talked of the destiny of the American flag to float over the entire continent. The expansionist spirit was especially strong in the South. A New Orleans journal declared in 1848: "We have New Mexico and California. We *will* have old Mexico and Cuba!" That year President James Polk offered Spain $100,000,000 for Cuba, but the Spanish government replied it would rather see the island sink beneath the sea. This refusal did not quiet Southern demands for the "Pearl of the Antilles." After the balance between free and slave states was lost in 1850, Cuba looked all the more tempting. Slavery was well entrenched there.

Like Polk, President Franklin Pierce was an expansionist. Shortly after he entered the White House he offered $130,000,000 for Cuba. When Spain again refused to sell, Pierce instructed our minister to Spain to talk with our ministers to Great Britain and France on the best way to "detach" Cuba from the mother country. The three diplomats, Pierre Soule of Louisiana, James Buchanan of Pennsylvania, and John Mason of Virginia, met at Ostend, Belgium, in the summer of 1854. They drew up a report to the State Department, saying that the possession of Cuba was necessary for the peace of the United States. If Spain would not sell it, then "by every law, human and divine, we shall be justified" in taking it by force. The report somehow got to the newspapers before it got to Washington. Although not an official statement, enemies called it the "Ostend Manifesto." A storm of criticism both here and abroad forced the Secretary of State to deny having anything to do with it. The Democratic party, however, continued to urge the purchase of Cuba.

Filibusters receive Southern support.

The desire for land suited to plantations inspired groups of armed adventurers, or *filibusters*, in efforts to seize land south of the border. Hot-headed members of well-known Southern families took part in or gave aid to these lawless expeditions, hoping that the lands taken would be annexed to the United States. In 1849, 1850, and 1851 a Spanish general, Narciso López, three times obtained men, money, and arms in the South for attempts to stir up revolution in Cuba. On the third try López and fifty of his followers, mostly Americans, were captured and executed by the Spanish. In 1853 William Walker, an American, led a small force which tried to obtain control of Lower California and northern Mexico. Later Walker went to Nicaragua with sixty-five followers and for a brief time established himself as president. President Pierce actually recognized his

356

government. The fact that prominent Southerners supported the filibusters aroused great anger in the North. Abolitionists charged that the planters were plotting to add much additional slave territory to the United States.

Trade treaties with China and Japan.

A less controversial form of expansion was shown in the Far East. Americans first became interested in the Far East soon after the Revolutionary War, when New England merchantmen started to trade with China. For many years Canton was the only Chinese port open to foreigners, but in 1842 Great Britain forced China to open several other ports. The United States obtained the right to trade in these ports in 1844. It also received the privilege of *extraterritoriality*. This meant that American citizens in China were governed only by American law and could be tried only by American officials. Other nations obtained similar privileges, for China was too weak to refuse.

After 1844 American trade with China grew. American clipper ships soon carried most of the tea exported from China. More and more American missionaries went there. Of 150 Protestant missionaries in China in 1851, 88 were from the United States.

Japan allowed foreigners to enter but one port, Nagasaki, and that was open only to the Dutch. Shipwrecked Americans and others who landed in Japan were harshly treated. Shortly before his term of office was over, President Millard Fillmore sent Commodore Matthew C. Perry with a small fleet to Tokyo. Arriving there in the summer of 1853, Perry brought a friendly letter from the President urging Japan to open its ports for trade. He left Tokyo after ten days, saying he would return in a few months with a larger squadron. When he came back, early in 1854, he brought a miniature telegraph and steam railroad and other presents that aroused great interest in the marvels of the modern age. Impressed by the gifts as much as by fear of Perry's fleet, the Japanese agreed to make a trade treaty. The treaty started Japan on the way to becoming a modern nation. Within a few years Japan ceased to be an isolated feudal state. Determined to build up its strength, it adopted Western ways.

"JAPANESE TRAIN CROSSING BRIDGE," *from a print by an unknown Japanese artist. The clipper ships in the background signify the end of Japanese isolation from the Western world.*

(Above) HARRIET BEECHER STOWE. *The title page* (right) *from a Welsh translation of her novel,* Uncle Tom's Cabin, *demonstrates the world-wide appeal of its anti-slavery message.*

The Sectional Quarrel Flares Up Again

In 1850 the majority of Americans were satisfied with the compromise worked out by Clay (see p. 347). They believed the quarrel between the sections was ended. Northern businessmen were particularly pleased that the threatened storm had blown over. Much of their business was done in the South and they wanted Southern good will. "Cotton thread holds the Union together," wrote Emerson. Yet the political truce over slavery lasted hardly four years.

The Fugitive-Slave Act creates tension.

The new fugitive-slave law offended many people in the North. They refused to take part in catching runaway slaves. The Underground Railroad became more active than ever. Mobs sometimes freed captured Negroes from officers taking them back to slavery. News of such happenings caused angry protests from the South.

Ten Northern states passed "personal liberty" laws, which had the effect of nullifying the Fugitive-Slave Act. These "personal liberty" laws forbade state officials to help capture runaway slaves, prohibited the use of state and local jails for confining them, and provided that the slaves should have a jury trial before removal from the state. By this time antislavery feeling in the North had become so strong that a jury was unlikely to send a captured Negro back to his master.

Uncle Tom's Cabin.

Despite the activities of antislavery societies, millions of Northerners knew or cared little about the hard lot of the slave. They were jarred out of their indifference by a book published in 1852, which gave the world a tragic story of human suffering under the slave system. This book was *Uncle Tom's Cabin,* by Harriet Beecher Stowe. Mrs. Stowe lived in Cincinnati, where she helped runaway slaves and heard their pitiful tales. Yet she had friends in Kentucky who were planters, and she tried to do justice to the many slaveholders who were as kind to their slaves as the system itself would permit. The one brutal character in the novel, Simon Legree, was a hired overseer from the North. When the pious Uncle Tom ran away, he was caught by bloodhounds and whipped to death by Legree. Abolitionists criticized Mrs. Stowe for showing the favorable aspects of slavery, while Southerners complained that she greatly exaggerated its evils. *Uncle Tom's Cabin* went through many editions. Changed into a play, it had countless performances here and abroad. Perhaps no other book ever aroused such a storm of emotion. When Mrs. Stowe visited the White House during the War between North and South, President Lincoln greeted her as "the little woman who brought on" the war. Still, by itself a book could hardly produce a war. Let us see how events in the nine years after the publication of *Uncle Tom's Cabin* actually led to war between the sections.

The Kansas-Nebraska Act.

In his first message to Congress (December, 1853), President Franklin Pierce spoke of the repose the country had enjoyed since passage of the Compromise of 1850. He declared he would allow nothing to disturb that repose if he had power to prevent it. Yet seven weeks later he approved a law which, in effect, destroyed all the compromises worked out between the North and South since Missouri asked to enter the Union (see p. 251). This law was the Kansas-Nebraska Act, sponsored by Stephen A. Douglas, a Democratic senator from Illinois.

Douglas' bill provided for making two territories, Kansas and Nebraska, from that part of the Louisiana Purchase which lay north of 36° 30'. Slavery had been barred from it forever by the Missouri Compromise of 1820. Efforts to organize Kansas and Nebraska as territories had failed because pro-slavery members of Congress were no longer satisfied with that compromise. The Kansas-Nebraska bill repealed the Missouri Compromise and left the people of each territory to decide whether it should enter the Union as a free or a slave state. This was according to the principle of "popular sovereignty," which had been applied to New Mexico in the Compromise of 1850 (see p. 347). After a hard fight lasting several months, Douglas put the bill through and it became law in May, 1854.

The passage of the Kansas-Nebraska Act opened to slavery an area of 500,000 square miles, larger than all the free states east of the Rockies put together. The act ended the hope that slavery would die out or could be limited to the states where it already existed. Northerners now feared that slavery would spread into all the territories. Then the "slave power" would probably get permanent control of the national government. The "slave lords" might even be able to put through a constitutional amendment opening every state in the Union to slavery.

Horace Greeley wrote in the *Tribune* that the act would make more abolitionists in three months than abolition orators could make in fifty years.

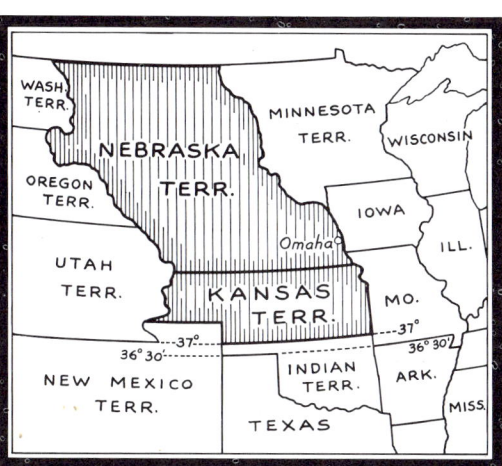

THE KANSAS–NEBRASKA ACT

"It is at once the worst and best bill on which Congress ever acted," declared Senator Charles Sumner of Massachusetts. The worst "because it extends slavery," and the best because it "annuls all past compromises with slavery and makes all future compromises impossible."

A new Republican party is formed.

Many people in the North thought the time had come to form a new party to resist the expansion of slavery. At a a convention held at Jackson, Michigan, in July, 1854, the new party was organized. It took the name "Republican." Their platform asked for repeal of the Kansas-Nebraska Act and the Fugitive-Slave Act and for abolition of slavery in the District of Columbia. In the fall election, the new party won many seats in Congress. The election returns showed that the Whig party had fallen apart. Many Northern Whigs had joined the Republicans, while the remaining Southern Whigs had gone over to the Democrats.

"Bleeding Kansas."

As soon as the Kansas-Nebraska Act was passed, proslavery and antislavery men began a struggle for the control of Kansas. Each group sent settlers there. It was not well adapted to slavery, and the free-soil settlers were soon in a majority. In March, 1855, an election was held to choose members of the territorial legislature. So many proslavery men crossed the river from Missouri to cast illegal votes in Kansas that a proslavery legislature was elected. The free-soil men refused to recognize this legislature and a few months later formed a government of their own. Congress would have to choose which government to recognize.

Guerrilla fighting broke out in what was then described as "bleeding Kansas." In the spring of 1856, "border ruffians" from Missouri and proslavery Kansans sacked the town of Lawrence, center of the free settlers. In revenge a New England abolitionist, John Brown, and seven others murdered five proslavery men. Armed clashes continued until federal troops restored order. Before the miniature civil war was stopped, much property was destroyed and over two hundred lives were lost. Far from solving the problem of slavery in the territories, popular sovereignty had only made it worse.

Violence occurs in Congress.

Tempers were almost as strained in Congress as in Kansas. In May, 1856, Charles Sumner made a violent speech denouncing the "crime against Kansas." Sumner's tirade contained insulting references to several proslavery senators. He particularly attacked Senator A. P. Butler of South Carolina, who was absent because of illness. Two days later Butler's nephew, Representative Preston Brooks, came to the Senate chamber late in the day, found Sumner sitting at his desk, and beat him over the head with a heavy cane until he collapsed. Motions to expel or censure Brooks did not pass, but he resigned his seat. The people of his district promptly reelected him with only six dissenting votes. Sumner was not able to return to the Senate for more than three years.

James Buchanan is elected President.

In 1856 the Republican convention met at Philadelphia. It had no delegates from the South. Its platform denounced the Ostend Manifesto and demanded that Kansas be admitted to the Union as a free state. A popular military hero, Colonel John C. Frémont of California, was nominated for President.

The Democratic convention tried to please both sections. Because the party needed Northern votes, the delegates wanted a Northern man to head the ticket. They passed over President Pierce and Senator Douglas, fearing that neither could carry the North. They chose James Buchanan of Pennsylvania, then minister to Great Britain. In his campaign speeches Buchanan insisted that his party represented the whole nation. Buchanan swept the South and won the election, but Frémont carried eleven out of sixteen Northern states. For a new party the Republicans had done remarkably well.

The Drift toward Disunion

The Dred Scott decision.

Buchanan had been in the White House only two days when the Supreme Court handed down a decision which became a milestone in the great antislavery struggle. It concerned the famous Dred Scott case. Dred Scott was a slave whose master had taken him from Missouri into territory where slavery was forbidden by the Missouri Compromise. After two years Scott was brought back to Missouri. In 1846, with the approval of his owner and with the aid of antislavery lawyers, Scott sued for freedom, claiming that residence in free territory had made him free.[1]

The courts of Missouri denied Scott's plea, saying that he was not a citizen and had no right to bring suit. Then his owner sold Scott to a citizen of New York in order that he might bring suit in the federal courts, since the federal courts may try cases between citizens of different states. After several years the case reached the Supreme Court. In a 7 to 2 decision, prepared by Chief Justice Taney, the Supreme Court ruled that (1) a Negro was not a citizen and therefore could not bring suit and (2) that a slave did not become free when taken into free

ROGER B. TANEY, *Chief Justice*

territory. Going still further, the Court declared that neither Congress nor a territorial legislature could prohibit slavery in a territory. Therefore the Missouri Compromise had been unconstitutional. This meant that a constitutional amendment would be necessary to keep slavery out of the territories. In view of the number of slave states, such an amendment could not pass.

Southerners rejoiced over the Court's findings. Many Northerners refused to accept the decision. The poet-editor William Cullen Bryant wrote:

Hereafter, if this decision shall stand for law, slavery, instead of being what the people of the slave states have hitherto called it, their peculiar institution, is a Federal institution . . . the shame of all the states; . . . wherever our flag floats, it is the flag of slavery . . . it should be dyed black. . . . Are we to accept these new readings of the Constitution. . . ? Never, never!

The decision was a hard blow to the Republican party, since its basic purpose was to keep slavery from spreading. Abraham Lincoln, a rising party leader in Illinois, said that the Republicans would do their best to get the Court to overrule the decision. This might be done by appointing new judges, should a Republican be elected President.

---

[1] This idea, or principle, was accepted in the British Isles. In 1772 the highest British court decided that as soon as a slave set foot on the soil of the British Isles, he became free. To have the principle recognized here would be a triumph for the antislavery movement.

The panic of 1857 strengthens the Republican party.

One event after another added to the nation's unrest. Soon after the Dred Scott decision a business panic began. Banks failed and factories shut down. Work on new railroad lines stopped. In the large cities hungry wage earners rioted. The panic followed a period of heavy speculation and overbuilding, but high-tariff men blamed it on the low tariff then in effect. When the Democratic administration refused to raise the rates, high-tariff men joined the Republican party.

Hard times strengthened the demand for free homesteads in the West. Labor leaders told workingmen to "Vote yourself a farm." This slogan also appealed to small farmers in the East trying to make a living on inferior land. Proslavery men were against free homesteads, which would quickly people the territories with small farmers and add free states to the Union. Democratic opposition to a homestead law drove many workingmen and small farmers into the Republican party. They felt that the "slave power" was running the Democratic party for its own interests.

Abraham Lincoln runs for senator.

In 1858 the author of the Kansas-Nebraska Act, Stephen Douglas, stood for re-election as senator from Illinois. He was a Democrat, a noted speaker, and one of the outstanding men of his time. When President Buchanan tried to have Kansas admitted as a slave state, against the wishes of a majority of the people living there, Douglas broke with him. This courageous act, which made Douglas unpopular in the South, showed that he sincerely believed in popular sovereignty.

To run against Douglas, Republican leaders in Illinois chose Abraham Lincoln. He had become famous in the Midwest through a speech at Peoria during the 1854 election campaign. Speaking of the repeal of the Missouri Compromise, he said it was wrong, for all national laws should carry out the idea held by the fathers of the Republic —that slavery was to be restricted and finally abolished. He declared too that popular sovereignty as applied to slavery was wrong, for slavery in a territory was the concern of the entire United States. There was no more excuse for permitting slavery to go into free territory, he said, than for reviving the African slave trade. At the same time he could appreciate the difficulties of getting rid of slavery where it was already established. "I surely will not blame them [the Southerners] for not doing what I should not know how to do myself. If all earthly power were given me, I should not know what to do as to the existing institution."

When Lincoln accepted the nomination as senator, he made another great speech. Every American is familiar with a portion of it:

A house divided against itself cannot stand. I believe this government cannot endure permanently half slave and half free. I do not expect the Union to be dissolved—I do not expect the house to fall— but I do expect it will cease to be divided. It will become all one thing or all the other. Either the opponents of slavery will arrest the further spread of it, and place it where the public mind shall rest in the belief that it is in the course of ultimate extinction; or its advocates will push it forward till it shall become alike lawful in all the States, old as well as new, North as well as South.

The Lincoln-Douglas debates.

As part of his campaign Lincoln challenged Douglas to a series of debates on the issues of the day. Each debate drew crowds of people, many riding for miles to hear "Honest Abe" and the "Little Giant." Newspapers throughout the country printed excerpts from their speeches.

Douglas attacked Lincoln for his "house divided" speech, saying it was "a plea for a war of the sections." He called Lincoln's words "abolition ravings." Praising his own doctrine of popular sovereignty, he said again and again, "I do not care whether slavery is voted up or voted down." Douglas also endorsed the Dred Scott decision.

In a debate at Freeport, Lincoln asked Douglas whether the people of a territory could lawfully bar slavery within their boundaries before they had a state constitution. If Douglas said "yes," his answer would be in conflict with the Dred Scott decision and would anger the South. If he said "no," he would anger his friends in the North. Douglas avoided saying "yes" or "no." He answered that slavery had a legal right in the territories, but that it could not exist where the people did not want it, since their legislatures would not pass laws giving police protection. This "Freeport doctrine" offended the South and cost Douglas any chance of being elected President two years later. However, he won the senatorship by a narrow margin. Lincoln, although he lost the election, gained a national reputation through the debate.

A small Southern farmer condemns slavery.

A book written by Hinton R. Helper, a native of North Carolina, was published anonymously in 1857. Entitled *The Impending Crisis in the South and How to Meet It*, it called on Southerners who owned no slaves to throw off the domination of the "lords of the lash." Helper contrasted the prosperity and rapid progress of the North with the backwardness of the South. He declared that the slavery system doomed the non-slaveholding whites to "galling poverty and ignorance." The book was banned in the South, but the Republicans distributed it widely in the North. It was useful as propaganda against the "slave power."

John Brown's raid.

Late in 1859 an act of violence by a Northern abolitionist brought the South close to the breaking point. John Brown, who had taken part in the fighting in Kansas (see p. 360) and had brooded for years over the evils of slavery, decided that the time had come for the slaves to strike for their freedom. Believing that God had chosen him for the task, he planned to set up a Negro republic on American soil. With eighteen followers he seized the arsenal at Harpers Ferry, Virginia, and offered arms to the slaves in the surrounding countryside. The next day he was captured by a small federal force. After a fair trial Brown was condemned and hanged for treason. He died willingly for what he believed, bearing himself to the very end with remarkable dignity. Radical members of the anti-slavery party hailed him as a martyr and a hero. Southerners were horrified by Brown's act, for there was nothing they dreaded more than a slave revolt. They feared that other abolitionists would come into the South to set the slaves against their masters. They were angrier than ever against the North.

The Democratic party splits in two.

When the Democratic convention met in 1860, the party members were sharply divided. Southern extremists, led by Senator Jefferson Davis of Mississippi, wanted the party to ask Congress to guarantee slavery in any territory where the legislature refused to give police protection. Such a demand was a strange one to come from the party of states' rights. Douglas led the fight against the proposal, for it would force slavery upon the people of a territory against their will. The convention split in two. The Northern delegates nominated Douglas for President; the Southern delegates nominated John Breckinridge of Kentucky. Both groups favored the acquisition of Cuba.

ABRAHAM LINCOLN,
from a photograph by Matthew Brady

The Republicans nominate Lincoln.

The Republicans chose Lincoln as their candidate, passing over Senator Seward, their best-known leader. While asking that slavery be kept out of the territories, they promised not to interfere with it in the states where it existed. They condemned the fanatical John Brown and rebuked efforts to reopen the African slave trade. They promised a protective tariff, a better banking system, free homesteads for settlers, a Pacific railway, and federal aid for improving rivers and harbors. The Republican program meant a strong central government and federal aid to industry and commerce. It alarmed the South as much as the demand that slavery be kept out of the territories. Southern leaders said openly that if the Republicans won the election, the South would secede.

A new party, the Constitutional Union, was organized for this campaign. It nominated John Bell of Tennessee on a platform urging that the Union be preserved. It won many votes in every Southern state, particularly in those areas where the small farmers lived. However, it carried only three states— Virginia, Kentucky, and Tennessee.

WILLIAM H. SEWARD, *Secretary of State under Lincoln. He defined the struggle between slavery and antislavery groups as an "irrepressible conflict."*

JOHN C. BRECKINRIDGE

Lincoln wins the election of 1860.

In the South the campaign was a struggle between Breckinridge and Bell. In the North it was a struggle between Lincoln and Douglas. While Lincoln got but 40 per cent of the popular vote, he carried every free state except New Jersey. This gave him a majority in the electoral college. The Republican party had at last broken the political alliance between the South and West, which had kept the Jeffersonians and then the Democrats in power for so long.

South Carolina and the Gulf states secede.

Had the people of the South been asked to vote on secession, it is probable that the majority would have voted "no." They were not asked. A group of South Carolina extremists were largely responsible for secession. They believed that if one state should secede and ask for the support of its neighbors, it could not be refused.

The South Carolina legislature was in session when the news of Lincoln's election flashed over the wires. It called for a special convention, which met December 17, 1860. After only three days' debate, the convention voted to

STEPHEN A. DOUGLAS, *the "Little Giant"*

365

JEFFERSON DAVIS

secede. Leaders in some of the neighboring states protested that this step should not have been taken by one state acting alone. However, within six weeks Georgia, Florida, Alabama, Mississippi, Louisiana, and Texas also seceded from the Union.

The Confederate States are organized.

In February, 1861, at a convention held in Montgomery, Alabama, the seven seceding states formed the "Confederate States of America." As president they chose Jefferson Davis of Mississippi. Davis had resigned from the Senate when his state seceded from the Union. The Confederacy adopted a constitution like that of the United States in most respects. It gave less power to the central government, however, and more to the individual states.

President Davis was authorized to raise an army and to secure a foreign loan. A tax was levied on cotton for export. Agents were sent abroad to seek help from European nations. Commissioners were also sent to Washington to work out a treaty and to arrange for the surrender of federal property located in the Confederacy.

Why did secession occur?

It should not be thought that the main reason for secession was fear that slavery would be abolished. The Republican platform pledged the party not to interfere with slavery where it already existed. Lincoln had said again and again that he had no intention of interfering with slavery in the slave states. If Congress wanted to abolish slavery, it could do so only by a constitutional amendment. Since an amendment must be approved by three fourths of the states, the South could easily block it. It is clear, then, that slavery did not stand in serious danger from the national government.

Secession was the result of a long struggle for control of the national government by two sections with opposing economic interests. The triumph of the Republican party meant that at last the North had gained control. By stopping the spread of slavery into the territories, the North would prevent the formation of any new slave states. Southern leaders feared that in the future the North would always hold the reins of the national government. Already the North had six more senators than the South and twice as many representatives. Rather than give in, the secessionists preferred to form an independent nation. They saw a bright future for the Confederacy. They did not expect war with the North, but if it came, they felt sure of an early victory.

FOR IDENTIFICATION

John Bell	Hinton R. Helper
John Breckinridge	Matthew C. Perry
John Brown	Dred Scott
James Buchanan	Harriet Beecher
Jefferson Davis	Stowe
Stephen A. Douglas	Charles Sumner

366

FOR EXPLANATION OR DEFINITION

"bleeding Kansas" Kansas-Nebraska Act
Constitutional Union Lincoln-Douglas de-
  party   bates
extraterritoriality Ostend Manifesto
  filibusters panic of 1857
Freeport doctrine "Pearl of the Antil-
Harpers Ferry   les"
Impending Crisis *Uncle Tom's Cabin*

FOR REVIEW

1. (a) State the evidences of rapid economic progress in the decade 1850–60. (b) Contrast the economic progress of the North and South in this decade. (c) Why didn't the North and the South grow at the same rate? (d) How did the South react to Northern economic expansion?

2. (a) How did the deep South differ from the upper South in regard to the principal crop, the proportion of slaves in the population, and the prices paid for slaves? (b) Name the five states of the deep South.

3. Why did small farmers in the South defend the institution of slavery?

4. What efforts did the United States make to acquire Cuba? Why? What was the Ostend Manifesto?

5. (a) What trading privileges did the United States acquire in China? (b) How and when was Japan opened to American trade? What were the results to Japan?

6. How did the fugitive-slave law and the Underground Railroad create tension between the North and South?

7. What effect did Mrs. Stowe's *Uncle Tom's Cabin* have on the North?

8. (a) State the provisions of the Kansas-Nebraska Act. (b) Why did this law cause anger in the North?

9. What led to the formation of the Republican party? What was its attitude toward the abolition of slavery?

10. (a) How did antislavery men work to keep Kansas free soil? (b) How did proslavery men from Missouri work to get control of Kansas? (c) How did it happen that Kansas had two different territorial governments at the same time?

11. Why did Brooks attack Senator Sumner? What were some of the results?

12. Who were the presidential candidates in the campaign of 1856? What showing did the new Republican party make?

13. (a) What did antislavery leaders hope to accomplish by having Dred Scott sue for his freedom? (b) On what grounds did Scott sue for his freedom in the Missouri courts? Why did the courts of Missouri refuse to hear his case? (c) How did lawyers succeed in getting the case of Scott into the federal courts? How did the Supreme Court rule? (d) What was the effect?

14. (a) What were some of the causes and results of the panic of 1857? (b) How did the agitation for "free homesteads" affect the two political parties?

15. (a) Why did Lincoln oppose the repeal of the Missouri Compromise? The principle of popular sovereignty? (b) What was the occasion of the Lincoln-Douglas debates?

16. (a) How did Douglas answer Lincoln's question at Freeport? (b) What were the immediate and the long-range results of the Lincoln-Douglas debates?

17. What was the theme of Helper's *Impending Crisis*? How did the South react to this book?

18. Tell the story of John Brown's raid and its results.

19. (a) What proposal at the Democratic national convention of 1860 caused the party to split? (b) Who became the presidential nominee of the Southern faction? Of the Northern faction?

20. What were the main planks in the Republican platform of 1860? How did the South feel about this program?

21. What did the Constitutional Union party stand for? Who was its presidential nominee? Where did it win votes?

22. What did the South Carolina legislature do upon hearing the news of Lincoln's election? How did other states react?

23. When and where were the "Confederate States of America" formed? Who became the President of the Confederacy?

24. Why did the South secede?

FOR FURTHER STUDY AND DISCUSSION

1. How did the nation's continued increase in population tend to affect the political power of the South? Helpful source: Cole, *The Irrepressible Conflict,* ch. I.

2. How did railroad construction in the 1850's influence the outcome of the War between North and South?

3. "Peaceable secession might have been achieved in 1850." What is the basis for this opinion? Why could not peaceable secession have been achieved in 1860? Helpful source: Kelly, *Lincoln and Douglas; the Years of Decision.*

4. Account for the choice of Lincoln as the Republican candidate in the campaign of 1860 and for his election.

5. How did the Dred Scott decision affect the political aspects of the slavery controversy? Helpful source: Hart, *Contemporaries,* Vol. IV, Nos. 41–45.

6. Why did the provisions of the Kansas-Nebraska Act renew the slavery struggle? What was the Emigrant Aid Society and why was it formed? Helpful source: Hart, *Contemporaries,* Vol. IV, Nos. 36–39.

7. On an outline map, illustrate the areas affected by the Compromise of 1850 and the Kansas-Nebraska Act.

8. Compare the South Carolina Ordinance of Nullification and Ordinance of Secession. Helpful source: Commager, *Documents,* Nos. 143 and 198.

9. How did the South defend secession? Helpful source: Hart, *Contemporaries,* Vol. IV, Nos. 54, 55, 58, 61, 62.

FOR INDIVIDUAL OR GROUP ACTIVITIES

1. (a) Study and report on the chief differences between the Constitution of the Confederate States and the federal Constitution. Explain the reasons for these differences. (b) Discuss whether there are any features of the Confederate Constitution worthy of consideration by the American people today. Helpful source: Commager, *Documents,* No. 201.

2. Make a list of the specific events or incidents which helped to prepare men's minds, North and South, for armed conflict. In parallel columns list the economic, social, and political causes of secession.

3. *Uncle Tom's Cabin* and *The Impending Crisis* are frequently cited as having had considerable influence on the course of events in 1860 and 1861. Prepare brief reports on each of these books.

4. Study and report in some detail on the trouble in Kansas and John Brown's raid. Discuss the influence of each.

5. Prepare brief biographical sketches of Harriet Beecher Stowe and her brother Henry Ward Beecher.

6. Prepare a series of dramatic readings for class or assembly presentation; for example, Lincoln's "house divided" speech; Lincoln-Douglas debates; John Brown's last speech. Helpful source: Commager, *Documents,* Nos. 186, 187, 189.

7. Report on Beale's essay, "What Historians Have Said about the Causes of the Civil War" in Sheehan, *The Making of American History.*

The Civil War is the crux of our history. You cannot understand any part of our past, from the convening of the Constitutional Convention down to this morning, without eventually
arriving at the Civil War.——Bernard De Voto

ABRAHAM LINCOLN

23. THE CONFEDERATE STATES FIGHT
FOR INDEPENDENCE

The Firing on Fort Sumter Precipitates War

Buchanan takes no action.

The winter of 1861, before Lincoln
took office, was a time of doubt and in-
decision. Should force be used to bring
the seven seceded states back into the
Union, or should the North follow the
advice of the abolitionists, and let them
go in peace?

President Buchanan did not know
how to deal with the crisis. He was too
easygoing to take a firm stand. Besides,
he had usually favored the Southern
point of view. Three members of his
Cabinet were secessionists, yet he did
not dismiss them. In his annual message
to Congress he denied that a state has
the right to leave the Union: "Secession is neither more nor less than revolution." At the same time he said that
neither he nor Congress had any power
to force a state to stay in the Union.
His attitude was very different from
that of Jackson in 1833 (see p. 263).

A compromise is sought.

Meanwhile in Congress men
searched feverishly for a compromise
that might save the Union. The most
important plan was offered by Senator
John J. Crittenden of Kentucky, successor to Henry Clay. It called for amendments to the Constitution: (1) reviving
the Missouri Compromise line of
36° 30' and extending it to the Pacific;
(2) guaranteeing that Congress would
not interfere with slavery in the slave
states and the District of Columbia;
(3) pledging the federal government to
pay for fugitive slaves if not recovered.
The Republicans, backed by President-
elect Lincoln, turned down this plan.
While they were ready to protect slavery where it existed, they were not willing to allow it in any territory whatsoever. Lincoln opposed the Crittenden
compromise on the ground that it would
be followed by Southern attempts to

obtain slave territory in Cuba and below the Mexican border. This would surely lead to new threats of disunion.

The Confederacy seizes federal property.

During the winter the seceded states took over the forts, arsenals, post offices, and other United States property within their borders. President Buchanan made no effort to stop them. In taking over federal property, Confederate officials met no resistance except at Fort Sumter in Charleston Harbor. The commander, Major Anderson, refused to give up the fort. He asked Buchanan for reinforcements, and a small merchant ship was sent with men and supplies. When Confederate guns at the harbor entrance fired upon the ship, it turned back. Buchanan took no further action. Northerners showed little anger over the incident. They seemed discouraged and leaderless.

Lincoln pleads for patience.

The whole country waited anxiously to learn what the incoming President intended to do. In his inaugural address Lincoln tried to calm Southern fears, while making clear that he would maintain the Union. He said he must hold and possess the forts and other property of the United States in the South and collect the customs duties, but "beyond what may be necessary for these objects, there will be no invasion—no using of force against, or among, the people anywhere." He promised not to interfere with slavery, directly or indirectly, in the states where it existed. He would work to enforce the fugitive-slave law.

Physically speaking, he pointed out, the states could not separate. "We cannot remove our respective sections from each other, nor build an impassable wall between them." The sections must remain face to face, and political and commercial relations must continue. Would these relations be more satisfactory after separation than before?

Lincoln closed with an appeal to the Southern people:

In your hands, my dissatisfied fellow countrymen, and not in mine, is the momentous issue of civil war. The government will not assail you. You can have no conflict without being yourselves the aggressors. You have no oath registered in heaven to destroy the government, while I have the solemn one to "preserve, protect, and defend it."

The deciding step is taken.

The day after his inauguration Lincoln was shown a letter from Major Anderson in Fort Sumter saying that his provisions would be exhausted in a few weeks. If provisions were sent, the Confederacy might consider it an act of war. Rather than take the risk, most of the Cabinet thought that Anderson should be ordered to withdraw from the fort.

Lincoln considered the question for nearly a month. Confederate representatives came to Washington with an offer to buy Fort Sumter and all other federal property in the seceded states, but Lincoln would not see them. Finally he made up his mind about Sumter—supplies would be taken to Anderson. He sent word of this to the governor of South Carolina. The Confederacy then called on Major Anderson to surrender. When he refused, the fort was shelled until he and his men gave up. Thus began four years of bloody conflict.

Both sides call for volunteers.

On April 14, 1861, when the news from Charleston flashed through the North, the people seemed to forget all their differences in a cry for revenge. The next day Lincoln issued a call for volunteers to put down what he called the "insurrection." Men responded quickly and in greater numbers than the President asked. Jefferson Davis also called for volunteers, and thousands rushed to the Confederate colors. The "irrepressible conflict" had come.

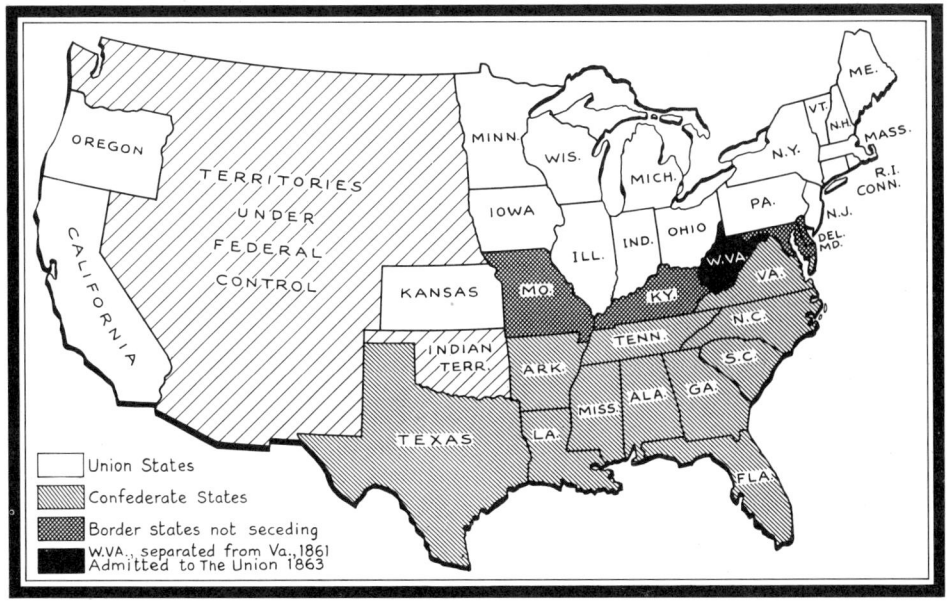

THE UNITED STATES IN 1861

Union States
Confederate States
Border states not seceding
W.VA., separated from Va.,1861
Admitted to The Union 1863

Four more states leave the Union.

Up to this time eight slave states in the upper South had not seceded. In each of them two parties were struggling for control—the secessionists and the Unionists. Once it became clear that Lincoln would use force against the seceded states, the four middle slave states—Arkansas, Tennessee, North Carolina, and Virginia—joined the Confederacy.

Virginia's action deprived the Union of the services of the ablest commander in the country—Robert E. Lee. Lincoln had already offered him command of the Union army. Lee hated slavery and had freed his own slaves. He loved the Union, which he had served for thirty-two years. Still he felt that he could not fight against his own state, his relatives and his neighbors. With deep regret he resigned his commission in the United States Army and accepted one in the Confederate army. He became a tower of strength to the Confederacy.

West Virginia is formed.

A bitter division of opinion developed in Virginia, and the western counties refused to follow the rest of the state. They held a convention at Wheeling, declared that they represented the wishes of the people of Virginia, and voted to stay in the Union. At a later convention they organized the state of West Virginia, which was admitted to the Union in 1863. Lincoln approved this action as a war measure, although the Constitution forbids the division of a state without its consent.

Four slave states remain in the Union.

In Missouri the Unionists and secessionists fought a civil war of their own, but the state did not secede. The governor of Kentucky declared that his state would take no part in the war—that is, it would remain "neutral." Lincoln's tact kept Kentucky in the Union, and tens of thousands of her citizens enlisted in the Union army. However,

371

several thousand other Kentuckians served in the Confederate army.

In Maryland the secessionist party was strong. If Maryland seceded, Washington would be surrounded and might become the Confederate capital. However, United States military authorities occupied Baltimore and Annapolis, where they arrested secessionist leaders. The secession movement collapsed. Maryland was saved for the Union. The fourth slave state to stay in the Union was Delaware. This state's legislature voted unanimously to reject secession.

On both sides loyalties are divided.

Neither side had the united support of its people. The Confederate army, as well as the Union army, included volunteers and officers from every state, both North and South. Sometimes a single family had members fighting on opposite sides. This kind of family tragedy was frequent in the border states.

Democrats in the North broke up into two groups—the "war" Democrats and the "peace" Democrats. The first group, led by Stephen A. Douglas, supported Lincoln and his war policy. The "peace" Democrats believed that the Union could be restored by negotiation rather than war. These "Copperheads," as they were called, formed secret societies, including the Knights of the Golden Circle, Order of American Knights, and Sons of Liberty. They were particularly numerous in southern Ohio, Illinois, and Indiana. Some Copperheads destroyed draft records, led draft riots, and encouraged Union soldiers to desert. Some conspired with Confederate agents eager to separate the Northwest from the Union. The South too had secret societies which gave aid and comfort to the enemy.

Neither side is well prepared.

When the war began neither the United States government at Washington nor the Confederate government at Richmond was ready for a large-scale military effort. Armies had to be raised and trained. Officers had to be chosen. Munitions and other supplies had to be furnished in huge quantities. Both sides had to obtain funds to carry on the war, for their treasuries were almost empty.

The North has greater resources.

In men and resources the North had definite advantages.

1. Man power. The Union had more than three times as many white men of military age as the Confederacy. In addition the Union permitted Negroes to serve as soldiers, and about 300,000 of them did so.

2. Industries. Practically all the iron, steel, textile, and munitions plants in the country were in the North. After the first year of the war the North produced nearly everything needed for its army and navy. The South, while it had a few factories at the outset and managed to start some new ones during the war, could not produce anywhere near enough manufactured goods to supply its armed forces.

3. Transportation. The North possessed far better transportation facilities than the South. Most of the Northern rail lines had been connected into systems. In the South, most of the lines were short and disconnected. Furthermore, when Southern railroad equipment wore out under heavy wartime use, it could not be replaced. The Confederacy was also inferior to the Union in canals, river steamboats, and improved highways. This fact bothered the invaders as well as the defenders.

4. Ships. Practically all the warships and merchant ships of the United States were in Union hands. The navy blockaded Southern ports, helped take important points on the coast and on the rivers, and captured a large number of Confederate blockade runners.

The South has other assets.

Not all the advantages were on the side of the North. When war began, the South felt sure of victory.

1. Military leaders. The Confederacy had many able officers of high rank who resigned from the United States Army to serve their own state. The South was also better supplied with minor officers than the North. All young men of the planter class knew how to ride and to use arms. A large proportion of them had gone to military schools. Many of them had seen service in the Mexican War.

2. Interior lines. Since an attacking force must be larger than a defending force, the Confederate army did not need as many men as the Union army. It did not have to invade and conquer the North. All it needed to do was to fight long and hard enough to persuade the people of the North that victory would cost more than it was worth.

3. A long coast line. The South had about 3550 miles of coast. This long coast made effective blockade unlikely.

4. Hopes of foreign aid. Confederate leaders fully expected to receive aid from Great Britain and France. These countries depended on the South for raw cotton. Rather than have thousands of cotton mills shut down, would they not help the Confederacy break the blockade? Further, would they not prefer to trade with an independent South which would not have a protective tariff? If Britain and France had helped, the Confederacy probably would have won, just as with foreign aid the thirteen colonies had won their freedom eighty years before.

5. Greater moral appeal. The Confederacy was fighting for independence. In this cause many Southerners would count no sacrifice too great. The United States, on the other hand, seemed to be fighting to force unwilling states to remain in the Union.

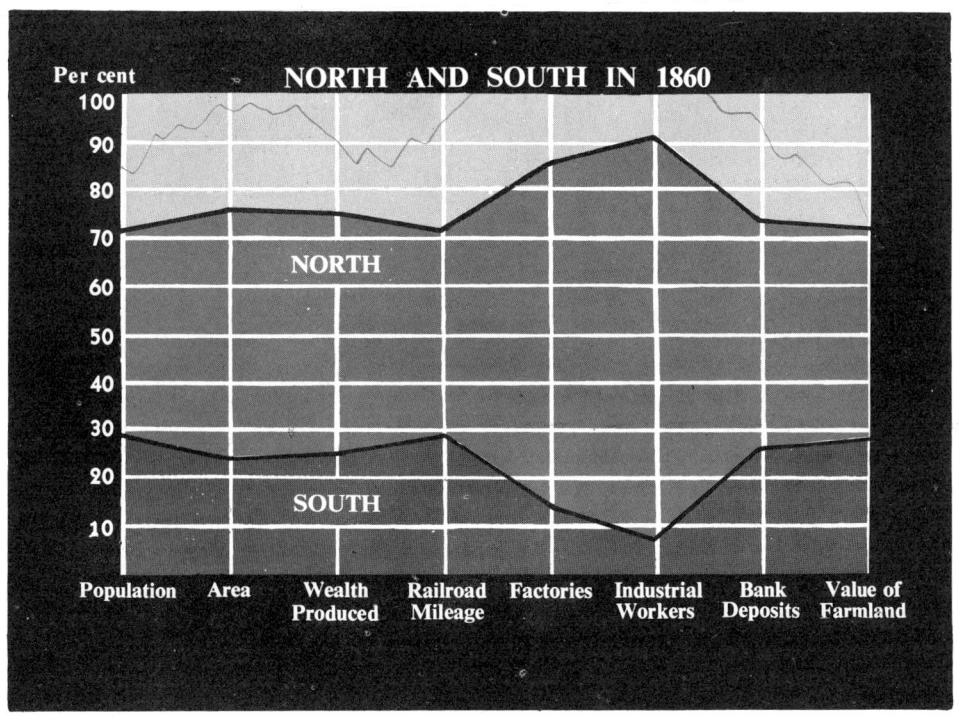

NORTH AND SOUTH IN 1860

Lincoln exalts the Union.

Lincoln's task was to convince the people of the North that saving the Union was a great cause. To him, as to Jackson, Clay, and Webster, the Union was a symbol of popular government. Lincoln constantly expressed this idea. He wanted every American to feel that his dignity as a citizen in a free republic depended on the fate of the Union. If the Union were destroyed, the enemies of freedom would be the only gainers. "We must settle this question now," he said, "whether in a free government the minority have the right to break up the government whenever they choose. If we fail it will go far to prove the incapability of the people to govern themselves."

Lincoln was able to save the Union because he inspired millions of his countrymen with the belief that it was worth fighting for. Without his moral leadership, the people of the North might have decided to let the seceding states leave the Union.

Both Sides Have Trouble Getting Soldiers and Funds

Both sides have to draft soldiers.

At first there was a rush of volunteers in both North and South. When it appeared that the war would last a long time, enlistments dropped. The Confederacy, with less than a third as many white men as the Union states, started to draft men in April, 1862.

Almost a year later the United States Congress passed the first national conscription act. It applied to all able-bodied citizens from 20 to 45 years of age. Names were drawn by lot. Any man whose name was drawn could be excused from service by paying $300 or by furnishing a substitute. The poor naturally grumbled at a law which enabled the well to do to escape military service. Draft riots broke out here and there. The worst was in New York City, where about five hundred people were killed before order was restored.

The Confederate draft was equally unpopular. Because those owning or overseeing fifteen slaves were exempted, poorer men objected that it was a "rich man's war and a poor man's fight." The draft was also thought to be an injury to states' rights. President Jefferson Davis was denounced as a foe of liberty. Several governors refused for a time to let draftees leave their states. The governor of Georgia declared that no act of the United States government before Georgia seceded had struck a blow at constitutional liberty so severe as the Confederate draft. South Carolina asserted the right of nullification as loudly as it had done in 1832 (see p. 263).

President Lincoln combats subversion.

In wartime the President of the United States always exercises unusual powers. Lincoln was no exception. During the War between North and South, he used such strong measures to curb subversive activity that he was severely criticized. No doubt some of his agents did go too far.

At the very beginning of the war Lincoln suspended the writ of habeas corpus in parts of Maryland. Military officers there arrested persons suspected of disloyalty and put them in military prisons without a regular trial. Innocent people suffered along with the guilty. For instance, a loyal mayor of Baltimore was held prisoner over a year.

On the same day that Congress passed the Draft Act, it authorized the President to proclaim martial law and suspend the writ of habeas corpus "whenever the public safety may require it." Lincoln used these powers to keep the Copperheads from antiwar activities (see p. 372). During the entire war federal agents arbitrarily arrested over 13,500 persons. They also suspended between 300 and 400 newspapers for a time. To critics who condemned these actions, Lincoln replied with a question:

Must I shoot a simple-minded soldier boy who deserts, while I must not touch a hair of a wily agitator who induces him to desert?

In 1866 the Supreme Court heard the case of a Copperhead named Milligan who had been condemned to death by a military court in Indiana. The Court set aside the sentence because Milligan had been denied trial by jury in an area where the civilian courts were open. The Court held that even in time of war:

. . . martial law can never exist where the courts are open. . . . It is the birthright of every American citizen, when charged with crime, to be tried and punished according to law. . . .

The Confederacy has financial trouble.

The Confederacy had great difficulty in raising money to pay for the war. It tried a direct tax on property. It also sold its bonds at home and abroad. Since the amount obtained in these ways was far short of the need, paper money was issued. Tons of paper bills came from the printing presses. This money had no security. By 1863 twenty-two paper dollars would buy only one gold dollar, and by 1865 sixty-one paper dollars were needed. The Confederate government kept going by paying its bills with paper money and by collecting some of its taxes in produce.

The North too prints paper money.

Although its resources were far greater, the government of the United States also had trouble in paying its bills. About one fourth of the money it spent during the war came from taxes. Excise taxes were placed on nearly everything—food, clothing, tobacco, alcoholic beverages, manufactured products, luxuries, railroad tickets, advertisements. For the first time a federal in-

come tax was adopted. In addition, there was a sharp increase in the tariff. By 1864 duties averaged 47 per cent, the highest level yet.

The United States government was more successful than the Confederacy in selling bonds. Yet it too paid some of its bills by issuing unsecured paper money—that is, paper money not backed by gold or silver. "Greenbacks," as they were called, changed in value with Union victories and defeats. They were worth only 39 cents on the dollar in the dark summer of 1864. When the war ended they were worth 67 cents.

The South Seeks Foreign Aid

The North blockades the South.

One of President Lincoln's first acts after the fall of Fort Sumter was to order a blockade of Southern ports. At that time our navy was small and consisted chiefly of old wooden sailing ships. The Navy Department hurriedly bought and built several hundred ships for blockade duty. By 1863 the blockade had greatly reduced Southern commerce. Cotton exports fell to a trickle, depriving the South of its chief source of wealth. Lack of money and the increasingly tight blockade made it almost impossible for the South to keep its armies supplied.

The Virginia fights the Monitor.

At the outset of the war the Norfolk navy yard was partly destroyed by federal forces and left to the Confederacy. A half dozen ships of war were sunk, among them the steam frigate *Merrimac*. The Confederacy had the *Merrimac* raised. Its sides were then covered with armor and an iron ram fastened to its bow. Union naval officials heard that the *Merrimac* was being armed and ordered John Ericsson to design a ship to meet it. He built the *Monitor*, with a small, nearly flat, iron hull and a revolving gun turret.

CITY POINT, VIRGINIA, *was important to both the Union and the Confederacy because of its strategic location on the James River.*

The test of strength came in March, 1862, when the *Merrimac* (renamed the *Virginia*) steamed out of Norfolk Harbor. She easily destroyed several Union vessels which were blockading the port. Then she met the *Monitor*, which had rushed there to protect the Union fleet. The battle which followed was the first ever waged between ironclads. After pounding one another for several hours without doing much damage, each retired, claiming victory. The *Merrimac* had poor engines and never fought again. The battle proved the value of ironclads. Northern shipyards soon built many ships like the *Monitor*. Meanwhile the Confederacy tried to buy ships abroad and to obtain other foreign aid.

France and England favor the South.

In the early years of the war, the United States had trouble in keeping Great Britain and France from aiding the Confederacy. In both countries the governing classes sympathized with the Southern cause. As aristocrats, they admired the great planters and feared the extension of democracy. They ridiculed Lincoln for his humble background. Besides, they had practical reasons for hoping the South would win. French and British merchants looked forward to an independent South, because it would place no tariff on their products. Napoleon III desired to weaken the United States in order to further his own ambitions in Mexico (see p. 398). He wished France to recognize the Confederacy if Britain would do so too.

The Trent affair angers the British.

Late in 1861 an incident occurred which brought the United States and Great Britain close to an open break. A Union warship stopped the English mail steamer *Trent* and took as prisoners two Confederate diplomats who were on their way to Europe. The action was wildly applauded in the North but provoked great wrath in England. The British government protested that its rights as a neutral had been violated. Lincoln released the two prisoners, explaining that Great Britain was defending one of the rights of neutral ships which we ourselves had defended in the War of 1812.

The South buys warships abroad.

Since the Confederacy could neither build nor equip warships, it ordered them from British shipyards. To conceal their destination, orders were placed in the names of foreign firms. In 1862 three cruisers built for the Confederacy, the *Florida*, the *Shenandoah*, and the *Alabama*, slipped out of British ports. Before they were sunk or captured, they destroyed 257 Yankee merchantmen. As a neutral, Britain had no right to allow warships for either side to leave its shores or use its ports. Therefore the United States sent England a bill for the ships sunk by the three cruisers. This bill, known as the *Alabama* claims, was settled in 1872.

In the summer of 1863 a British firm was at work on several ironclad war vessels ordered by the Confederacy. They were ramming vessels, or rams, designed to break the Union blockade. Ambassador Charles Francis Adams laid the evidence before the British government, and the rams were kept in port. The Confederacy then tried to buy rams secretly in France. When the news leaked out, Napoleon felt obliged to stop the deal. This ruined Confederate hopes to end the blockade.

The South loses European support.

The Emancipation Proclamation, issued in September, 1862, was taken to mean that the North was fighting to abolish slavery and not merely to preserve the Union. The effect on public opinion in Great Britain and France was felt at once. The public in both countries wanted the Union to win. British workingmen, although a great many were unemployed because of the scarcity of cotton, held mass meetings demanding that no help be given to the South. In a famous letter, Lincoln thanked the millworkers of Manchester, England, for their support of the Union.

The chance that the Confederacy could get recognition from European countries ended in 1863 when the Union gained several military victories. By that time Europeans no longer expected the Confederacy to win the war. Recognition looked like a bad risk.

The First Two Years of War Are Indecisive

War plans of each side unfold.

When the conflict broke out neither Northern nor Southern military leaders had worked out a plan for waging war. Before long, however, the leaders on each side knew what they had to accomplish in order to win. The aims of the United States were:

1. To cut off Southern exports and imports by means of a coastal blockade
2. To hold the border slave states in the Union
3. To dishearten the Confederacy by the early capture of Richmond, its capital
4. To split the Confederacy by seizing control of the Mississippi River
5. To destroy Southern railroads and factories

LINCOLN MEETS McCLELLAN *at the Headquarters of the Army of the Potomac.*

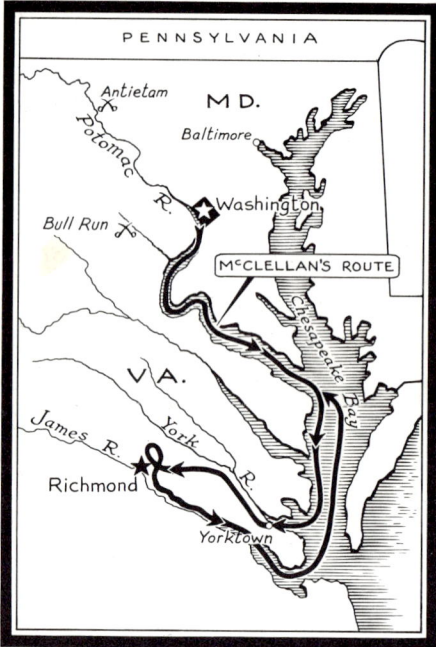

PENINSULAR CAMPAIGN, 1862

The aims of the Confederacy were:

1. To keep its ports open
2. To bring the border slave states (Maryland, Delaware, Kentucky, Missouri) into the Confederacy
3. To dishearten the North by capturing Washington and a few leading cities in Maryland and Pennsylvania

From the start Union forces took the offensive. Most of the Confederate troops were used for defense only. Before the struggle ended the fighting forces had met in over a thousand engagements. About a hundred and fifty of the clashes were big enough to be called "battles."

The war in the East, 1861–62.

The Union armies carried on two principal campaigns, one east and one west of the Appalachians. The chief purpose of their eastern activities was to destroy the Southern forces protecting Richmond. The story of this campaign is a long tale of Union blunders and defeats. Repelling one Union attack after another, Confederate armies prevented the capture of Richmond until the last days of the war. Their victories were due mainly to the brilliant generalship of Robert E. Lee and T. J. ("Stonewall") Jackson. Again and again they defeated Union forces much larger than their own. Their tactics are still studied by military leaders.

In the summer of 1862 Lee carried the war into the North in hopes of adding Maryland to the Confederacy. With 60,000 men, he marched through that state, calling on the people to rise to the South's defense. Some welcomed him, but others refused even to sell him provisions. At Antietam his advance was stopped by Union forces led by General George McClellan. Although the battle was a draw, Lee retreated to Virginia, and the North went wild with joy.

Lee's withdrawal from Maryland had two important results: (1) It kept the British and French from recognizing the Confederacy and forcing the Union to accept a negotiated peace. (2) President Lincoln, who had been waiting for favorable news before doing so, published the Emancipation Proclamation (see p. 387). After that the common people of Europe sided strongly with the Union.

The war in the West, 1861–62.

The Union campaign in the West was far more successful than that in the East. Its aims were (1) to block Confederate attempts to take Kentucky and Missouri, and (2) to gain control of the Mississippi.

General Ulysses S. Grant helped drive the Confederates out of Kentucky in 1861. Early the next year he captured Fort Henry and Fort Donelson near the Tennessee-Kentucky line. The Confederates then had to give up the important city of Nashville, and Union troops advanced to the southern

"FARRAGUT AT THE MISSISSIPPI FORTS," *from a painting by Joffray. After three days of bombardment, Admiral David Farragut passed the forts with his fleet and entered New Orleans. The capture of this city, a center of river and ocean commerce, was a victory of strategic importance.*

boundary of Tennessee. Here (April 6–7, 1862), raged one of the fiercest fights of the entire war—the terrible Battle of Shiloh, or Pittsburg Landing, in which 25,000 men were killed or wounded. The Confederates fell back to Corinth, a railroad center in northern Mississippi. They were driven out of Corinth a few weeks later.

Meanwhile, a Union fleet commanded by Admiral David Farragut steamed up the Mississippi River. After knocking the river forts to pieces, Farragut captured New Orleans, the largest Confederate city. Next, a fleet of Union gunboats moving down the Mississippi captured Memphis. By mid-June, Vicksburg was the only point on the Mississippi left in Confederate hands. If Vicksburg could be taken the entire river would be under Union control, and the Confederacy would be cut in two. The remainder of 1862 brought little gain to either side.

A Turning Point Is Reached

The North is discouraged.

In the North the year 1863 opened in deepest gloom. The Eastern campaign had led to one defeat after another. Voluntary enlistments had fallen so low that in March Congress was obliged to pass a draft law. Grant and his men had spent months in Mississippi but seemed to make no progress in the attempt to take Vicksburg. Letters criticizing Grant poured into the White House, and Lincoln said sadly, "I think Grant has hardly a friend except myself." "Peace" Democrats were urging peace on almost any terms. The French emperor, Napoleon III, was trying to get the British prime minister to join him in recognizing the Confederacy as an independent nation. Defeat of the Union forces looked certain. But the tide was about to turn, bringing three important victories—Vicksburg, Gettysburg, and Chattanooga.

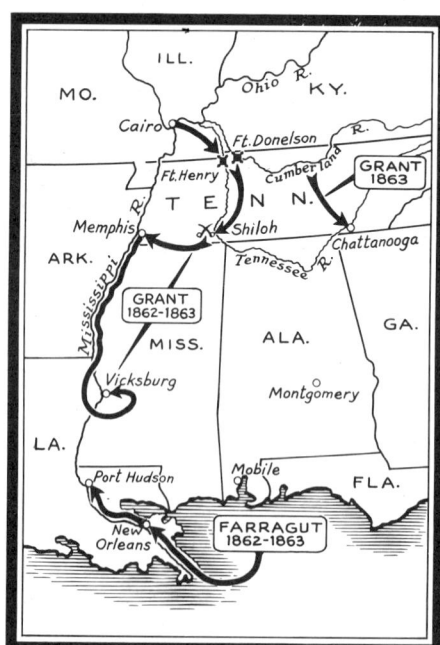

MISSISSIPPI RIVER
AND TENNESSEE CAMPAIGNS

380

Grant captures Vicksburg.

In April, with the aid of a fleet of gunboats, Grant succeeded in surrounding Vicksburg. He then began to starve and shell the city into submission. To escape bombardment, the people took refuge in caves and cellars. They killed horses and mules for food. On July 4 the city surrendered. This victory gave the Union control of the Mississippi. Texas, Arkansas, and Louisiana were completely cut off from the other Confederate states.

The South loses a great general.

While Grant was besieging Vicksburg, the Army of the Potomac, commanded by General Joseph Hooker, prepared to attack Lee once more. Hooker had 130,000 men, while Lee had only half as many. But Lee's military skill and that of his assistant, "Stonewall" Jackson, made up for the small size of their forces. In the forest around Chancellorsville, Virginia, Lee sprang a trap on Hooker. After three days of fighting (May 2–5, 1863), Hooker fell back with a heavy loss of men. This was "Stonewall" Jackson's last battle, for he was mortally wounded when his own men fired upon him by mistake. By his death the Confederacy suffered a stunning blow, and Lee lost the man whom he called his "right arm."

Lee is stopped at Gettysburg.

After the Battle of Chancellorsville, Lee decided to invade the North for the second time. His plan was to move swiftly through the Shenandoah Valley into Pennsylvania, seize Harrisburg, then turn east and come down upon

"STONEWALL" JACKSON

Baltimore and Washington. If he succeeded in taking these cities, the North might be willing to make peace.

The Army of the Potomac, now commanded by General George Meade, went north into Pennsylvania. On July 1, it met Lee's army at Gettysburg. A desperate three-day battle took place. On the third day Lee risked everything by ordering General George E. Pickett to head a charge against the Union center. In the face of a withering fire, 15,000 men in gray charged across a mile-wide plain and up the slope of Cemetery Ridge. Less than a hundred managed to reach the crest. The next day, July 4–the very day that Vicksburg surrendered–Lee's weakened army began its retreat. In the Battle of Gettysburg Lee had lost 28,000 men.

Gettysburg had been the high tide of Confederate hopes; the tide was now clearly running out. However, Lee's army had not been destroyed. General Meade did not interfere with it on its way back to Virginia. Meade's failure to prevent Lee's escape and perhaps to end the war disturbed President Lincoln. "We had them within our grasp," Lincoln said to his secretary. "We had only to stretch forth our hands and they were ours."

Grant conquers Tennessee.

During the rest of 1863 the heaviest fighting was in southeastern Tennessee. Union leaders hoped to capture Chattanooga, a busy railroad junction and one of the three most important strategic points in the South (the others being Vicksburg and Richmond). A Union force of 70,000 men led by General W. S. Rosecrans approached Chattanooga early in September. Twelve miles from the city it met a strong Confederate force led by General Bragg. Here the Battle of Chickamauga was fought, and 36,000 men were killed or wounded in two days. The Union forces escaped capture by fleeing into Chattanooga. Bragg then laid siege to the city. Grant was placed in command of all the Union forces in the West and sent to the rescue. Assisted by General William T. Sherman, Grant drove the besiegers from their positions. Chattanooga and all of Tennessee were now in Union hands. This gave the Union army control of the mountain passes into Georgia.

GENERAL ULYSSES S. GRANT *at Cold Harbor, June, 1864*

Grant becomes supreme commander.

Lincoln had finally found the general he was looking for—one "who would take the responsibility and act." He put Grant at the head of all the Union armies. Grant arrived in Washington for the first time in his life on March 8, 1864, a "short, round-shouldered man in a very tarnished uniform." He took charge of the Army of the Potomac and began to hammer at Lee's lines.

The MONITOR *and the* MERRIMAC *fought the world's first engagement between ironclads. This reproduction of an old lithograph is not altogether accurate. Of the wooden naval frigates shown only the* MINNESOTA *(right) was present; the other two had been disposed of by the Confederate ironclad the day before.*

"SUBMARINE TORPEDO BOAT H. L. Hunley GUARDED BY A REBEL SENTINEL" *by* CONRAD WISE CHAPMAN. *The Confederates'* Hunley *was the first submarine to sink an enemy warship. Here, in a Charleston dock, she is being overhauled in preparation for the successful attack in which she went down.*

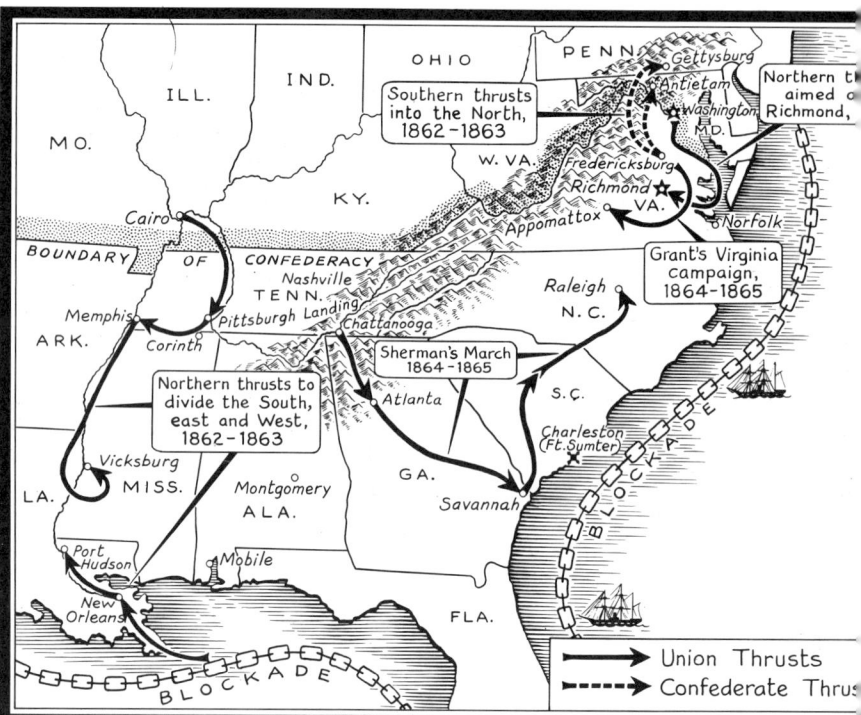

PRINCIPAL THRUSTS IN THE WAR
BETWEEN NORTH AND SOUTH

Sherman marches to the sea.

Grant gave Sherman chief command in the West and ordered him to march from Chattanooga to Atlanta. Atlanta was the chief industrial city in the South. It had numerous rolling mills, ironworks, and munitions plants. It was also a railroad center. Its loss would greatly hurt the Confederacy.

Sherman began his drive in May, 1864, with an army of 100,000 men. Opposing him was an army of 60,000 led by the able Joseph E. Johnston. In a series of flanking movements, Sherman forced Johnston to fall back. Sherman took Atlanta early in September, burning whatever might be of value to the enemy. Then he moved onward to the sea, destroying nearly everything in a belt of land sixty miles wide. He estimated that the property destroyed was worth $100,000,000.

Grant's Virginia campaign.

While Sherman was marching through Georgia, Grant was moving toward Richmond. In forty days of fighting in a marshy woodland known as the "Wilderness," he lost 55,000 men, almost as many as in Lee's entire army. In June Grant moved his army across the James River and laid siege to Petersburg, a railroad junction twenty miles south of Richmond. Here the two armies fought nine months of trench warfare.

Lincoln is re-elected.

By the summer of 1864 the North was thoroughly war-weary. Hundreds of thousands of men had died of wounds or disease. Victory still seemed far in the future. Lincoln was nominated for a second term on a no-com-

384

promise war platform. For his running mate the convention chose Andrew Johnson of Tennessee. Johnson was a staunch Unionist, whom Lincoln had appointed as military governor of Tennessee.

The Democrats nominated General George B. McClellan on a platform calling for immediate steps towards peace. McClellan's election would probably have meant a cease fire. This could have been obtained only by recognizing the independence of the Confederate States, for until the very end of the war its leaders refused to consider any other peace terms.

Lincoln thought it "extremely probable" that he would lose the election, but three Union successes that summer saved the day. In addition to Sherman's entrance into Atlanta, there was the capture of Mobile by Admiral Farragut and a victory in the Shenandoah Valley by General P. H. Sheridan. These successes, said Secretary of State William H. Seward, "knocked the bottom out of the Chicago [Democratic] platform." Lincoln received 2,-200,000 votes to McClellan's 1,800,000— a bare majority of the popular vote. However, Lincoln carried every Union state except New Jersey, Delaware, and Kentucky. As he said, the people had decided "not to swap horses while crossing the stream."

The Confederacy collapses.

Just before Christmas, 1864, Sherman occupied Savannah. A few weeks later he turned northward through the Carolinas, taking three cities and causing even more destruction than in Georgia. The Confederates were not able to offer any serious resistance. As they retreated, they destroyed railroads and bridges to slow his advance.

On April 2, 1865, Grant took Petersburg. This forced Lee to abandon Richmond. Lee hoped to take his half-starved army to North Carolina to join Johnston. When he reached the village of Appomattox, about eighty miles west of Richmond, he found Grant with 62,000 men directly in his path. Lee had only 27,000 men, of whom less than 10,000 were armed. There was nothing to do but surrender. On April 9, 1865, the two commanders met at Appomattox Courthouse to discuss the terms.

Grant's generous terms pleased the Southern people. The Confederate officers and men were to go free on condition that they should not fight again. Officers were to keep their side arms and horses, and men in the cavalry and artillery who owned their horses were to keep them "for the spring plowing." Soon after, the other Confederate armies also surrendered, and the war was over.

"There is a true glory . . . the glory of duty done . . ." Lee after Appomattox.

The South is exhausted.

In the final days of the war the Confederacy had but ·200,000 soldiers in the field. These were half starved, half clad, with the scantiest of arms and munitions. Opposed to them the United States had a million men in the field, well fed, well clothed, and abundantly equipped. Besides, the United States had two million reserves, while the Confederacy had no reserves.

The South was completely exhausted. Great parts of it lay in waste. Some of the chief Southern cities had been burned. Most of the railroads and bridges had been destroyed. Food was scarce, and in Richmond and other cities near the coast, civilians were starving. Because of the tight blockade, neither soldiers nor civilians could obtain medical supplies and manufactured goods. The worthlessness of Confederate bonds and paper money added to all the other hardships. Toward the end of the war a spool of thread cost $25, a quart of milk $4, a pound of sugar $75, a pair of shoes $150. By the time Lee surrendered, nearly everyone in the South was bankrupt and in want.

The nation mourns its dead.

The War between North and South was the most terrible war in all history up to that time. Nearly 618,000 men were killed in battle or died of wounds or disease. This is 1 in 4 of those who took part. On the Union side about 360,000 soldiers died during the conflict. On the Confederate side about 258,000 soldiers perished. Disease claimed twice as many soldiers as were killed in action or died from wounds. In proportion to its white population, the Confederate loss was three times as heavy as that of the North.

The custom of Memorial Day, or Decoration Day, was begun in the South to honor the Confederate dead. The Northern states soon made it a legal holiday for honoring those who died for the Union. Now we observe Memorial Day to honor those who died in all our wars.

The Union is supreme.

In losing the war the Southern states lost all hope of forming an independent nation. That the Union was supreme over the individual states was no longer in doubt. The question of whether a state had the right to secede from the Union had been settled. The United States had become an "indestructible Union of indestructible states."

Slavery Is Abolished

Congress acts against slavery.

When eleven Southern states seceded and took their representatives out of Congress, the Republican congressmen took steps to restrict slavery. First, Congress freed the slaves in the District of Columbia, paying $300 compensation for each. Then it prohibited slavery in every territory, in defiance of the Dred Scott decision. Next (July, 1862), Congress declared that any captured slaves whose masters were serving the Confederacy should be set free.

Abolitionists criticize Lincoln.

Lincoln was severely criticized here and abroad because he did not make abolition a war aim. But he knew that to do so would drive the border slave states from the Union. Lincoln worked to have the slaves freed gradually by voluntary action of the states, with federal compensation to slaveholders. To his last day he favored compensation, saying that the blame for slavery rested on the North as well as the South. Most of the Republican members of Congress, however, were against compensation.

From the onset of the war, a group of radical Republicans, led by Horace Greeley of the *New York Tribune*,

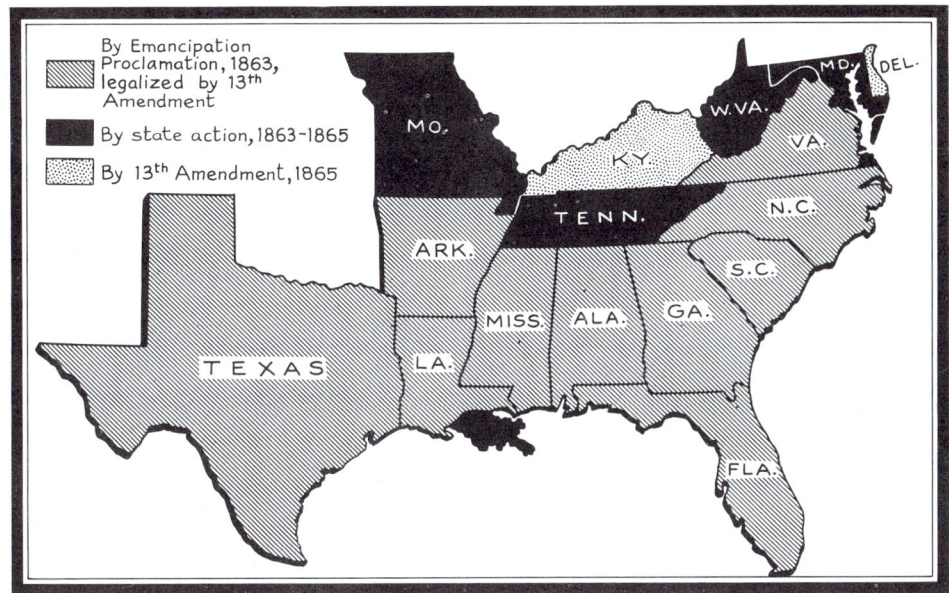

EMANCIPATION OF SLAVES

clamored for immediate emancipation. Replying to Greeley in August, 1862, Lincoln stated his position clearly:

My paramount object in this struggle is to save the Union, and is not either to save or destroy slavery. If I could save the Union without freeing *any* slaves, I would do it: and if I could save it by freeing *all* the slaves, I would do it; and if I could save it by freeing *some* and leaving others alone, I would also do that. What I do about slavery and the colored race I do because I believe it helps to save this Union.

The Emancipation Proclamation.

At the time this famous letter was printed, Lincoln had already written the Emancipation Proclamation. Because the Union forces had met a long series of defeats, to publish it then would have looked like a last desperate bid for foreign support. The President therefore waited for a Union victory. After Lee's retreat from Maryland in September, 1862 (see p. 378), Lincoln announced that on January 1, 1863, all slaves in the areas still in rebellion would be free, then and forever. The order applied only to places still behind the Confederate lines. As these were conquered, the slaves would be free. Thus for the first time abolition became the stated goal of the North.

The Proclamation had three aims: (1) to weaken the South through the loss of the slaves; (2) to gain the support of the abolitionists, who up to this time had opposed the war; and (3) to win the support of the British people. The last aim was the most important.

At that time the British government was considering whether to take steps to break the blockade. Cotton mills in England were closing down for lack of cotton, and there was great suffering in the manufacturing districts. The millowners wanted the government to recognize the Confederacy as an independent nation and to insist on trading with it. After the Emancipation Proclamation most of the British sided with the Union. This fact, and the improving prospects of Union victory, meant that England would do nothing to help the Confederacy (see p. 377).

The South moves toward emancipation.

In three of the five slave states which remained in the Union, state conventions ordered emancipation. West Virginia ordered it in 1862, Missouri in 1863, and Maryland in 1864. Near the end of the war three Confederate states which had come under Union control—Tennessee, Louisiana, and Arkansas—also passed laws to free the slaves within their borders. At this time General Lee and President Jefferson Davis both urged that slaves be taken into the Confederate armies with the promise of freedom when their service was over. In the closing weeks of the war the despairing Confederate government offered to free all the slaves in return for aid from England and France.

The Thirteenth Amendment.

Soon after the Emancipation Proclamation, Lincoln suggested an amendment to the Constitution to end slavery forever in any part of the United States. After a long dispute Congress approved the measure in January, 1865, and sent it to the states for ratification. It was quickly ratified by all the Union states except Delaware and Kentucky, and by eight former Confederate states. Before the year's end it became the Thirteenth Amendment to the Constitution. Southern slaveowners lost several billion dollars' worth of slave property for which they received no compensation. The slavery question was settled, but in its place was another no less difficult—the race problem—which has troubled the nation ever since.

FOR IDENTIFICATION

David G. Farragut	George B. McClellan
Ulysses S. Grant	*Merrimac*
"Stonewall" Jackson	*Monitor*
Robert E. Lee	William T. Sherman

FOR EXPLANATION OR DEFINITION

Alabama claims	Fort Sumter
blockade	Gettysburg
border states	greenbacks
conscription	Pickett's charge
Copperheads	Thirteenth Amend-
draft riots	ment
Emancipation Procla-	writ of habeas corpus
mation	

FOR REVIEW

1. What was President Buchanan's attitude toward the seceded states?

2. State terms of the Crittenden compromise. Why did Lincoln oppose it?

3. Outline the program advocated by Lincoln in his first inaugural address.

4. What was Lincoln's decision in regard to Fort Sumter? What was the result?

5. (a) Name the four "middle" slave states. (b) Why did they secede? (c) Explain how West Virginia came into being.

6. Name the four border slave states which remained in the Union.

7. Who were the Copperheads? How did they interfere with the Union war effort?

8. (a) Compare the North and the Confederate States as to man power, industries, and transportation facilities. (b) State the advantages which the South had.

9. How did Lincoln's moral leadership and his concept of the Union strengthen the Northern cause?

10. Why did both sides resort to conscription? What were some of the effects of the draft both in the North and in the South?

11. (a) What is meant by martial law? (b) Why was Lincoln criticized for suspending the writ of habeas corpus? (c) Why is the Milligan case significant?

12. Compare the attempts of the North and the South to finance the war.

13. (a) What was the purpose of the Northern blockade of Southern ports? (b) What is the significance of the battle between the *Monitor* and the *Merrimac*? (c) How did the South obtain aid in its efforts to break the blockade? (d) Why did the South lose European support?

14. (a) What was the aim of the Union armies in the East? (b) What was Lee's aim in invading Maryland in 1862? What was the outcome of this invasion? (c) What were the aims of the Union campaign in the West? (d) What gains had been made by the close of 1862?

15. Why was the capture of Vicksburg (July, 1863) important?

16. (a) What was the purpose of Lee's second invasion of the North? (b) Why is the battle of Gettysburg referred to as the "turning point" in the war?

17. Why did Sherman's march to the sea leave bitter memories in the South?

18. (a) Who were the presidential candidates in 1864? (b) Why was Lincoln doubtful about his re-election? (c) What military events probably helped him win?

19. What terms of surrender did Grant impose upon Lee at Appomattox?

20. Describe conditions in the Confederacy in the final months of the war.

21. After secession what actions did Congress take to restrict slavery?

22. Explain Lincoln's attitude on abolition.

23. State the provisions, purpose, and timing of the Emancipation Proclamation.

24. What steps did the South take in the direction of emancipation?

25. State the provisions of the Thirteenth Amendment. When was it proposed and ratified? Why was it necessary?

FOR FURTHER STUDY AND DISCUSSION

1. How important was the Northern blockade in determining the outcome of the war? Helpful sources: Cole, *The Irrepressible Conflict*, pp. 386–389; Faulkner, *Economic History*, pp. 350–355.

2. What were the weaknesses of the draft system? Helpful sources: Hicks, *Federal Union*, pp. 630–631; Randall, *The Civil War and Reconstruction*, pp. 405–419.

3. Why is the Emancipation Proclamation referred to as a "war measure"? Helpful source: Randall, *The Civil War and Reconstruction*, pp. 489–503.

4. Why was there a movement within his party to prevent Lincoln's renomination? Helpful source: Randall, *The Civil War and Reconstruction*, pp. 618–621.

5. How would you prove that Lincoln was an outstandingly great President? Helpful source: Hofstadter, *American Political Tradition*, pp. 93–136.

FOR INDIVIDUAL OR GROUP ACTIVITIES

1. On a series of outline maps indicate the following: The free states, the states of the Confederacy, and the slave states which did not secede; the military campaigns in the East, the West, the South. Prepare charts or tables which compare the North and South as regards total population, industrial and military strength.

2. Prepare a series of dramatic readings on the War between North and South, sketching the background of each selection. Helpful sources: Commager and Nevins, *Heritage*, and Commager, *Documents*.

3. Make a collection of songs and poems popular during the war. Use the most interesting for a school assembly program.

4. Many of Lincoln's phrases and stories have become famous. Prepare a collection of Lincoln quotations and Lincoln stories.

5. Report on the decision of the Supreme Court in the Milligan case and its application to recent problems.

6. Report on: Sherman's march through Georgia, Jefferson Davis, Clara Barton, the work of the Sanitary Commission. Helpful source: Boylston, *Clara Barton, Founder of the American Red Cross*.

7. Read Whitman's "O Captain! My Captain!" and Hawthorne's sketch of Lincoln in Commager and Nevins, *Heritage*.

8. Have members of the class report on chs. 1, 2, 6, and 14 of Hendrick, *Statesmen of the Lost Cause*.

Tyranny and despotism can be exercised by
many more rigorously, more vigorously, and more
severely than by one.——Andrew Johnson

24. RECONSTRUCTION IS A TRAGIC ERA

Lincoln and Johnson Favor a Lenient Reconstruction Policy

Lincoln plans reconstruction.

Throughout the war Lincoln had been studying how to rebuild, or reconstruct, the Union. He saw the difficulties that would face the nation when the war was over. He wanted to restore friendly relations between North and South as quickly as possible.

Late in 1863 Lincoln announced his plan for bringing the seceded states back into the Union. He would pardon those individuals who had aided the Confederacy if they took an oath of allegiance to the United States. As soon as 10 per cent of the voters of a state had taken this oath and formed a loyal government, he would recognize it. He said that according to the Constitution, Congress should decide when members from the seceded states might resume their seats. Three states—Louisiana, Arkansas, and Tennessee—were then under military governors appointed by Lincoln. These states accepted Lincoln's terms and set up loyal governments during 1864. Congress refused to seat their representatives. Lincoln knew then that he faced a hard struggle with Congress.

Radicals sponsor a stiffer plan.

The Republicans in Congress had split into two groups—the conservatives, or moderates, who backed President Lincoln, and the so-called "Radicals," or extremists, who opposed him. The latter had made trouble for Lincoln from the beginning of his term in their zeal to abolish slavery and to punish the Southerners. It was not surprising then that they did not accept his plan for reconstruction.

As a substitute for Lincoln's plan, which the Radicals considered too lenient, they passed the Wade-Davis Bill. This measure gave Congress the right to control reconstruction. It required a *majority* of the voters of a seceded state to take an oath of allegiance to the United States before a legal state government could be organized. No one who had held a state or Confederate office during the "rebellion," and no one who had voluntarily borne arms against the United States, could take part in organizing the new government. Such persons would not even be allowed to vote. The bill came to Lincoln for his signature in July, 1864, at the end of the congressional session. He killed it with a "pocket" veto.

Lincoln pleads for moderation.

On March 4, 1865, when the war was nearing its end, Lincoln gave his second inaugural address. He pleaded for forgiveness and good will. His closing words belong among the noblest examples of American literature.

With malice toward none, with charity for all, with firmness in the right as God gives us to see the right, let us strive on to finish the work we are in; to bind up the nation's wounds, to care for him who shall have borne the battle, and for his widow and his orphan; to do all which may achieve and cherish a just and lasting peace among ourselves and with all nations.

Lincoln's charity toward the defeated South was shown soon after in the liberal terms of surrender offered to the defeated Confederate armies. General Lee expressed an equally statesmanlike attitude. He wrote:

The war being at an end, the Southern states having laid down their arms, and the questions at issue between them and the Northern states having been decided, I believe it to be the duty of everyone to unite in the restoration of the country and the re-establishment of peace and harmony.

News of Lee's surrender reached Washington on April 9. Lincoln turned once more to the problem of reconstruction. On April 14 he met his Cabinet to discuss what was to be done for the South. He spoke kindly of Lee and other Confederate leaders. He rejoiced that Congress was not in session and that he would have a chance to restore the states to their proper place in the Union before it met again.

Lincoln's death grieves the nation.

On the evening of April 14 the President attended the theater. A half-crazed actor, John Wilkes Booth, stole into the President's box and shot him through the head. Lincoln never spoke again. When he died a few hours later, Secretary of War Stanton said prophetically: "Now he belongs to the ages." The whole country mourned. As the funeral train bore his body home to Springfield, Illinois, thousands gathered at every stop to pay their respects to the dead President.

ABRAHAM LINCOLN. *The strain of war leaves no man unmarked. Compare this picture with the one on page 364.*

The loss to the nation from Lincoln's death can never be estimated. He was the one man who might possibly have curbed the hatred and party selfishness which followed the war, who might have reunited North and South with the least delay and the least suffering. Long afterward Jefferson Davis said: "Next to the destruction of the Confederacy, the death of Abraham Lincoln was the darkest day the South has known." Lincoln's death meant more than the loss of his leadership. It meant that the North felt new hatred for the South. Northerners thought his murder was the result of a Confederate plot to overthrow the United States government. They shouted for revenge.

Andrew Johnson becomes President.

The man who succeeded Lincoln —Vice President Andrew Johnson—was self-educated. Born in a log hut in North Carolina and left fatherless when three years old, he grew up in ignorance and poverty. At the age of ten he became a tailor's apprentice. After running away from his master, he settled in Greeneville, Tennessee, where he worked at his trade. He married, and his wife taught him how to write. In time young Johnson saved enough to start a tailor shop. By his mid-thirties he owned land and slaves and was regarded as Greeneville's first citizen. He became the leader of the small farmers of eastern Tennessee and rose from one political office to another. When the war came, Johnson was a United States senator, the only senator from a seceded state who remained loyal to the Union. President Lincoln appointed him military governor of Tennessee, a difficult and dangerous post. In 1864 he was nominated for Vice President, although he was a Democrat, because Lincoln wanted a Southerner on the ticket.

Johnson was honest, fearless, and intelligent. He fought for what he believed to be right, but he had little of Lincoln's skill in guiding public opinion. At times he hurt his own cause by using violent language to his political enemies.

Johnson forms new state governments.

The new President followed Lincoln's plans for reconstruction except in minor details. He appointed a temporary governor for each of the Southern states. He pardoned large numbers of Confederates so that they might take part in forming loyal state governments. Each state held a convention which repealed its act of secession. Then its white citizens elected a governor and a legislature. When the new legislature approved the Thirteenth Amendment, Johnson considered the state to be back in the Union. All the states but Texas completed these steps by the time that Congress met in December, 1865.

Johnson urged each of the new state governments to give the vote to Negroes able to read and write or possessed of property. He did not, however, make this a condition for recognizing the state as restored to the Union. Like Lincoln, he believed that the Southerners should be left to solve their problems in race relations gradually. The new state governments did not give the vote to any Negroes. They insisted on the principle of white supremacy. This was stated by the governor of Mississippi: "Ours is and ever shall be a government of white men."

The freedmen suffer severely.

At the end of the war the South was in economic ruin. A great number of the white people were penniless. The plantation system had broken down. Over three million Negroes had been set free suddenly, without any preparation for freedom. The great majority were illiterate and unskilled and had no property of any kind.

In the deep South the former slaves were worse off than they had been under slavery. The luckiest were those who stayed with their former masters, for at least they had food and shelter. Thousands of Negroes took to the roads, wandering aimlessly from place to place, living on what they could find. Other thousands swarmed into the cities, where they lived under horribly crowded conditions. Diseases swept the Negro quarters. In some communities one fourth to one third of the Negroes died from disease or starvation within two or three years.

The Negroes of the upper South got along better, since there were not so many of them in proportion to the white population. Most of them soon

"TEACHING THE FREEDMEN," *from an engraving by J. T. Trowbridge*

managed to find work, although the wages were miserably low. Many worked just for their "keep."

The sufferings of the Negroes would have been greater had not Congress in the last days of the war created the Freedmen's Bureau. The Bureau gave food and medicine to the ex-slaves and helped them find work or rent land. The director of the Bureau, General Oliver O. Howard, was a man of the finest character, but some of the subordinate agents were dishonest or incompetent. For a number of reasons the Bureau came to be greatly disliked by white Southerners. Most of its activities came to an end in 1869.

"Black codes" anger the North.

One of the first tasks of the state legislatures created under Johnson's guidance was to make a set of laws to govern the freedmen. These "black codes," as they were called, gave Negroes many of the rights of white citizens, such as the right to own personal property, to sue and be sued, to make contracts, and to marry persons of their own race. They were not allowed to vote, to hold office, to sit on juries, to serve in the militia, or to carry arms. In some states they were forbidden to own land and to testify in court cases involving whites. In some states, also, it was made difficult for a Negro to enter any occupation except farming or domestic service.

Laws were passed to keep Negroes from becoming tramps and to force them to work steadily. For example, Negro workers had to make long-term agreements or contracts with their employers. If they quit the job before the contract ended, they could be fined. Furthermore, any Negro not having lawful employment was liable to a fine for "vagrancy." Usually a Negro was unable to pay a fine. In that case the court bound the Negro out to a white man who would pay his fine in return for a certain number of days of work. Dependent Negro children were bound out to whites as apprentices, until they came of age.

Many people in the North thought the "black codes" were "slavery in disguise." Most Southerners, however, looked at these laws as necessary to preserve social order. They felt that the Northerners who condemned the "black codes" did not understand the problems due to emancipation.

Johnson Has a Stormy Administration

Congress rejects Johnson's work.

President Johnson, in his first annual message to Congress (December, 1865), announced that the Union had been restored. Representatives from all the former Confederate states except Texas were then in Washington ready to take their seats in Congress. Both the Senate and the House refused to admit them. Congress, led by Radical Republicans, had turned its back on Johnson's plan for reconstruction. There were several reasons for the rejection.

1. Desire to reduce the President's power. Always during a war the President's powers are increased. When the war is over, Congress seeks to regain control. In 1865 Congress felt that the time had come to take the reins again.

2. Demand for punishment of the South. Many people in the North believed that Johnson's program was too generous to the former Confederate states—that they should not be allowed to return to the Union without punishment for their disloyalty. The leader of the Radicals, Congressman Thaddeus Stevens of Pennsylvania, thought the South should be treated as a "conquered province."

3. Protection of the Negro. To some of the Radicals, especially to Congressman Stevens and Senator Charles Sumner, protection of the Negro was all-important. They feared that slavery was being revived under the "black codes." They believed that if Negroes could vote, legislators and officials would pay more attention to their rights. Stevens went further than most Radicals in urging that the lands

of the former slaveholders be taken from them and divided among the freedmen. He thought it was simple justice to give the freedmen land on which to make a living. Little was done, however, to provide the freedmen with land.

4. Republican control of national affairs. The Republicans wanted to stay in power. They saw that once the seceded states were back in the Union, the Democrats would again be in the majority. The South would have more seats in the House and more votes in the electoral college than ever before. (The three-fifths rule, by which five slaves counted as three persons, had reduced the number of representatives from the South. As freedmen the Negroes counted the same as whites.)

To keep the Democrats from winning control of the national government, the Republicans wished to delay in restoring the Confederate states to the Union. Meanwhile, they would try to shift some of the Southern states into the Republican column. This could be done by giving the vote to the Negroes, who would naturally support the party which had set them free. Since the President's plan of reconstruction did not accomplish this, the Radicals would make their own plan. The Radicals had the strong backing of Northern industrialists and bankers. These men feared that, if the Democrats returned to power, they would lower the tariff, do away with the national banking system, and wipe out other laws helpful to business which the Republicans had passed.

The Fourteenth Amendment is submitted.

In 1866 Congress passed another amendment to the Constitution with the understanding that every Confederate state must ratify it before seeking admission to the Union again. This was the Fourteenth Amendment. It begins: "All persons born or naturalized in the

United States . . . are citizens of the United States and of the State wherein they reside." This simple sentence sets forth one of the most important results of the war. It declares that there is such a thing as United States citizenship, and that a person born or naturalized in the United States is a citizen of the United States as well as of the state wherein he resides. Its chief purpose was to give United States citizenship to Negroes.

The amendment goes on to forbid any state from interfering with the rights of United States citizens. No state shall "deprive any person of life, liberty, or property, without due process of law," nor "deny to any person . . . the equal protection of the laws." This section was written to protect the Negro. It has been used chiefly to protect corporations from state interference (see p. 525).

The second section was intended to force the Southern states to allow Negroes to vote. It threatens to reduce the state's representation in Congress if the state deprives any of its adult male citizens of the right to vote, except for taking part in rebellion or crime. The penalty has never been enforced.

The third section was aimed at Confederate leaders. It barred from state or federal office anyone who had violated his oath to support the Constitution. The fourth section says that neither the United States nor any state shall pay the debts of the Confederacy and that no payment shall be made for the loss or emancipation of any slave.

The amendment was a harsh dose for the South. Tennessee ratified it, believing it must take the bitter medicine. Congress then seated Tennessee's representatives and senators. The other ten Confederate states refused to accept the amendment. They thought they could block ratification by holding out, since they were more than one fourth of the total number of states.

Congress compels the South to accept.

The Republican majority in Congress dealt harshly with the ten Confederate states which had rejected the Fourteenth Amendment. Early in 1867 a severe Reconstruction Act was passed. Johnson vetoed it, but Congress passed it over his veto. It swept away the civil governments built up under the President's guidance and placed the ten unreconstructed states under military rule. The ten states were divided into five military districts, each under a major-general of the United States Army. The generals were to preserve order and supervise the elections.

The Reconstruction Act offered a way of escape from permanent military rule. Each state was to hold a convention to frame a new constitution. Whites who had aided the Confederacy were not permitted to vote for delegates to the convention, but Negroes could do so. The convention was to write a constitution giving Negroes the right to vote. When a new state government had been organized and the Fourteenth Amendment had been ratified, the state would take its former place in the Union. This plan, by giving the vote to Negroes and taking it away from most of the whites, was expected to assure Republican control of these ten Confederate states.

The ten states failed to call constitutional conventions. Congress then passed three additional reconstruction acts. These required the military commanders to enroll voters and to provide for the writing and adoption of a new constitution. A total of 703,000 Negroes and 627,000 whites were registered as voters. Negro voters were in the majority in five states. By 1868 seven of the states had ratified the amendment and it became part of the Constitution.

Southern white people objected strongly to the congressional program of reconstruction. Northerners who helped to carry out the program in the South were described as "carpetbaggers." Southern whites who helped them were known as "scalawags." In each of the ten states carpetbaggers got control of the new government.

Radicals curb the Supreme Court.

Meanwhile, the Radicals in Congress wished to make Congress the most powerful branch of the government. They passed an act forbidding the Supreme Court to hear cases arising under the reconstruction acts. This was done for fear the Supreme Court would declare the acts unconstitutional.

The Radicals humiliate Johnson.

The Radicals disliked Johnson because he objected to their plan for reconstruction. They went out of their way to shame him. They undid everything he had done to reconstruct the South. Then they took control of the army out of his hands and gave it to General Grant. This action denied the President any authority over the ten states which Congress had placed under military rule. Next, the Radicals tried to prevent Johnson from removing their ally, Edwin Stanton, from the position of Secretary of War.

Stanton did all he could to obstruct Johnson's policies by working behind his back. When Johnson asked him to resign, he refused. To prevent Stanton's removal, Congress passed a Tenure of Office Act (1867), making it a "high misdemeanor" for the President to dismiss a federal officer without the consent of the Senate. This robbed Johnson of an important power held by every previous President.

Johnson is impeached.

The President thought the Tenure of Office Act was unconstitutional. He defied Congress by removing Stanton. Johnson's enemies seized upon this action as an excuse for impeaching him

ANDREW JOHNSON

—that is, bringing him to trial. They expected to remove him from the Presidency.

The Constitution says that the President may be impeached for high crimes and misdemeanors in office. In reality Johnson's only offense was his opposition to Congress's program of reconstruction. His enemies drew up a long list of charges against him, and early in 1868 the House of Representatives impeached him. He was then tried before the Senate. If he was found guilty, it would mean that any future President who was unpopular with Congress could be removed.

The trial lasted nearly two months. The President was defended by five distinguished lawyers, including the Attorney General. Johnson did not appear before the Senate, although he was summoned. On the advice of his lawyers he remained at the White House, attending to his official duties. The case against him was purely political.

397

This became more and more clear as the trial went on. The President's enemies tried by bribery and threats to secure the two-thirds majority necessary to convict him. They needed thirty-six votes, but with all their efforts they could obtain only thirty-five. Every Democrat in the Senate voted "Not guilty," but only seven Republican senators had the courage to do so. No other President of the United States has ever been impeached. The nation has accepted the principle that the President cannot be removed for opposing the majority of Congress.

The United States buys Alaska.

In foreign relations Johnson and his able Secretary of State, William H. Seward, made a good record. When Russia in 1867 suddenly offered to sell Alaska to the United States, Seward did not hesitate. He arranged a treaty by which we bought Alaska for $7,200,-000. At the time the value of the territory was unknown and many thought Seward was foolish to buy it. Yet the Senate promptly ratified the treaty out of gratitude to Russia for having sent its fleet to American waters in 1863. The visit of the Russian fleet was considered a friendly gesture to the United States and a warning to France and Great Britain against helping the South.

Johnson forces the French out of Mexico.

Napoleon III of France took advantage of the War between North and South to conquer Mexico and set up a puppet state there. He persuaded an Austrian prince, Maximilian, to become emperor. The United States protested that France had violated the Monroe Doctrine, but took no other action until the Confederacy was defeated. To those who criticized his policy, Lincoln replied we could fight but one war at a time.

President Johnson sent 50,000 troops to the Mexican border and asked Napoleon to withdraw his forces from Mexico. War with France seemed possible. It was avoided by Seward's skillful diplomacy. In 1867 Napoleon called his troops home and left Maximilian to his fate. Despite the pleas of the United States for mercy, the prince was shot.

Radical Reconstruction Fails

Grant is elected President.

The 1868 Republican convention met at Chicago while Johnson's impeachment trial was still in progress. General Grant was chosen to head the Republican ticket. Leaders of the party thought he would make an ideal figurehead, for he knew nothing about politics. He had never held public office and only once in his life had taken the trouble to vote. He was enthusiastically supported by his former soldiers and by other Northerners who gave him credit for saving the Union.

The Democrats nominated former Governor Horatio Seymour of New York. They condemned the Radical program of reconstruction, demanded an end of military rule in the South, and applauded President Johnson.

Seven Confederate states were re-admitted to the Union before the November election. These were Alabama, Arkansas, Florida, Georgia,[1] Louisiana, North Carolina, and South Carolina. All but two (Louisiana and Georgia) went Republican. Grant won a decisive victory in the electoral college (214 to 80), but had only a bare majority of the popular votes.

The Fifteenth Amendment.

The strength shown by the Democrats in 1868 alarmed Republican lead-

---

[1] Congress refused to seat the representatives from Georgia because the state legislature did not seat Negro members who had been duly elected. The state was returned to military rule until 1870, when it was restored to the Union.

ers. If the reconstructed states should stop Negroes from voting, the Democrats would win the next election. To prevent this, the Radicals framed the Fifteenth Amendment and sent it to the states. Its purpose was to make Negro suffrage permanent in the South. At the same time, it gave the ballot to Negroes in twenty Northern states where they did not have it.

The amendment declares that "the right of citizens to vote shall not be denied or abridged by the United States or any state on account of race, color, or previous condition of servitude." A state might still deny its citizens the right to vote on some other ground—for instance, not paying poll taxes, not owning property, or not passing an educational test. By setting up such requirements, Southern whites were later able to keep most Negroes from voting.

When the Fifteenth Amendment was sent to the states, four states were still under military rule—Georgia, Mississippi, Texas, and Virginia. Congress required them to ratify both the Fourteenth and the Fifteenth Amendments. They did so. The Fifteenth Amendment became part of the Constitution in 1870. The same year the four states were taken back into the Union.

White politicians control Negro voters.

Most of the suddenly freed slaves could neither read nor write. They knew nothing of the world outside the plantations on which they worked. They were not in any way prepared to share in the government. Many looked to their old masters for guidance and advice and would have supported the Democratic party, as their masters did, had they been left alone. The Republicans took care to prevent this. They organized the Negroes into secret political clubs called "Union Leagues." By 1868 nearly every freedman belonged to one of these clubs.

The purpose of the Leagues was to control the Negro vote. New members were required to take an oath to vote for League candidates. They were taught that the Republicans were their friends, while the Democrats were enemies seeking to deny their rights. They were warned not to listen to their former masters.

The Union League clubs were led by white politicians. Some were genuinely interested in the welfare of the Negroes. Others were willing to use the Negroes for their own purposes.

Carpetbaggers rule the South.

After the governments established by President Johnson were wiped out by Congress, new ones were set up. The old officeholding class was now barred from voting or holding office. The voters were Negroes and poor whites without political experience. Control passed into the hands of the carpetbaggers. Most of the high offices in the state and local government were held by these Northerners. Minor offices were held by scalawags and Negroes.

It is sometimes said that Negroes controlled the carpetbag governments. This is a myth. While Negro voters actually had a majority in five states for two or three years, they voted as white politicians told them to. Their ballots were inspected by white men before being put in the ballot boxes. Furthermore, only in South Carolina and Louisiana did Negroes ever have a majority in the state legislature. High offices went only to white men. Negroes who held public office generally took orders from a white political "boss," for Negroes were not expected to be independent.

Taxes rise alarmingly.

The carpetbag governments were often inefficient and wasteful. For example, the state of Florida decided to build a railroad from Jacksonville to Pensacola. The legislature authorized a bond issue of $2,800,000. After the bonds were sold and various "commissions" had been paid, the state got $1,400,000. When 19 miles of railroad had been built, it was learned that all the money was gone.

Similar stories could be told of all the reconstructed states while they were ruled by carpetbaggers. The states borrowed heavily to pay for the rebuilding of railroads destroyed in the war and for new railroad lines. Prices were inflated and money did not go far. Most of these states floated bonds through Northern banks at a discount of from 50 to 75 per cent. Taxes rose from two to fourteen times what they had been before the war. Thousands of taxpayers could not meet their taxes and lost their houses and lands. Business staggered beneath its tax burden. The taxpaying class blamed the high taxes on the carpetbaggers, charging them with extravagance, waste, and corruption.

In this period there is no doubt many government officials and legislators were corrupt. They worked hand in hand with dishonest businessmen who were willing to pay handsomely for government contracts and other favors. Business and political ethics had sunk to the lowest levels in our history. "Corruption is the fashion," said a carpetbag governor of Louisiana. "I do not pretend to be honest, but only as honest as anybody in politics." In one term he pocketed half a million dollars. Deplorable as his attitude was, at the time it was all too common in the North as well as in the South.

Carpetbaggers do some good.

Southern Democrats hated the rule of the carpetbaggers. We should not forget, however, that much useful legislation was passed during the brief period of carpetbag control. Community services were organized, such as hospitals, orphanages, almshouses, and asylums for the insane. Prison reforms were started. Imprisonment for debt was abolished. Dueling was outlawed. Some of the legal discriminations against women were removed, giving them more control of their property and earnings. The tax system, which had favored the rich, was improved by spreading the cost of government more equally. Even more important was the establishment of many free public schools, some of which were for Negroes. These changes made the South less feudalistic and more democratic than it had ever been.

The Ku Klux Klan.

The Southern whites naturally wanted to regain control of their state and local governments. As long as Congress kept federal troops in the South to protect Negro voters and support the carpetbag governments, Southern white men could not act openly. So they formed secret societies to frighten the Negroes and discourage them from voting, and also to drive out the carpetbaggers. The most noted of these organizations was the Ku Klux Klan.

The Klan started in Tennessee in 1866 and quickly spread over the entire South. Its leaders were prominent Confederate officers. Most of its members were Confederate veterans. In 1867 the hundreds of local Klans united in the "Invisible Empire of the South," with General Nathan Forrest as "Grand Wizard." The Klan's weapon was terror. Klansmen, dressed in white robes and hoods, would appear suddenly in the night to punish those who disobeyed its orders. Klansmen broke up meetings of the Union League, whipped Negro politicians and Negro militiamen, and tarred and feathered carpetbaggers and scalawags.

Rash, cruel men got control of some of the local Klans, with the result

400

that moderate men dropped out. Such Klans were often guilty of frightful outrages against defenseless Negroes. Then, too, criminals took advantage of the hood to rob and murder. In 1869 General Forrest ordered all Klans to disband. Some of them refused to break up. Congress than passed a series of force bills to stamp out the organization and to protect Negroes from violence. By 1872 the Klan had disappeared.

Home rule is restored.

It was now clear that Negroes would not be allowed to vote in most Southern communities unless federal troops were kept there to protect them. Northerners were tired of using force. They began to say that the Negro was the Southerner's problem. The more liberal-minded Republicans in Congress joined with Democrats to restore home rule in the Southern states. In 1871 Congress gave nearly all the former Confederates the right to vote. The next year Congress restored the right to hold office to all but some five hundred Confederate leaders.

In one Southern state after another the Democrats regained control. This was easiest in the upper South, where whites outnumbered Negroes. In the deep South the Democrats frightened Negroes away from the polls or stuffed ballot boxes so that the Republicans could not win an election. By 1876 only three Southern states —South Carolina, Florida, and Louisiana—were still controlled by the Republicans. In these states federal troops supervised the elections. In 1877 President Hayes removed the last federal troops from the South. This meant the end of carpetbag rule and Radical reconstruction.

The Solid South rejects the Republicans.

Republican efforts to control the South caused hatred which lasted for generations. White men in the South remembered the twelve years of reconstruction (1865 to 1876) more bitterly than the four years of war. Those states which passed through military reconstruction voted Democratic in every presidential election until 1928. In that year four of these states went Republican rather than vote for a "wet" and a Roman Catholic (see p. 658). They returned to the Democratic fold in succeeding elections until 1952, when three of them went for Eisenhower. The devotion of the South to the Democratic party has given the region the label "Solid South."

Two members of the KU KLUX KLAN *in their disguises*

"PRISONERS FROM THE FRONT" *from a painting by Winslow Homer (dated 1866). As an artist-correspondent assigned to the Army of the Potomac, Homer drew many scenes of army camp life. The young officer in the painting was Colonel Francis C. Barlow of the 61st New York Volunteers.*

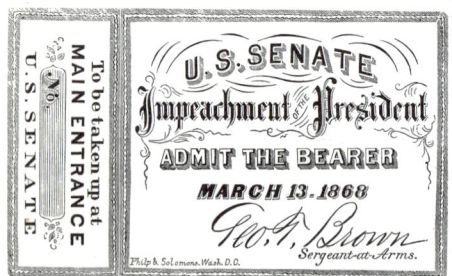

Facsimile of ticket of admission to the impeachment trial

FOR IDENTIFICATION

John Wilkes Booth	William H. Seward
Andrew Johnson	Edwin Stanton
Maximilian	Thaddeus Stevens

FOR EXPLANATION OR DEFINITION

"black codes"	Radical Republicans
carpetbaggers	scalawags
Freedmen's Bureau	Solid South
impeachment	ten per cent plan
Ku Klux Klan	Tenure of Office Act
military reconstruction	Union Leagues
	Wade-Davis bill

FOR REVIEW

1. (a) Outline Lincoln's plan for bringing the seceded states back into the Union. (b) What action of Congress prevented the carrying out of his plan? (c) Outline provisions of the Wade-Davis bill.

2. Why did Jefferson Davis consider Lincoln's death a blow to the South?

3. (a) Tell the story of Andrew Johnson's early life. (b) Why was he chosen military governor of Tennessee? (c) Why was he nominated for Vice President in 1864?

4. What was Johnson's plan of reconstruction?

5. (a) Describe the condition of the Negroes after the war. (b) Explain the work of the Freedmen's Bureau.

6. State the main restrictions placed upon the freedmen by the "black codes." What were "vagrancy laws"? Why did Northerners object to both the "black codes" and the "vagrancy laws"?

7. List the reasons why Congress rejected Johnson's plan of reconstruction.

8. (a) Summarize the provisions of the Fourteenth Amendment. (b) State the purpose or intent of each part of the amendment. (c) What clause or section of the amendment has never been enforced?

9. How were the Southern states compelled to accept the Fourteenth Amendment?

10. (a) How did the "Radicals" in Congress undertake to limit the authority of the Supreme Court and the President? (b) Why did President Johnson remove Stanton as Secretary of War? (c) What was the Tenure of Office Act?

11. (a) On what grounds was President Johnson impeached by the House of Representatives? (b) According to the Constitution, for what reasons may the President be impeached? (c) What is the significance of President Johnson's acquittal?

12. Tell something of Johnson's record in the field of foreign relations.

13. Name the candidates and issues in the presidential campaign of 1868.

14. (a) Why were the Republican leaders eager to give the Negroes the vote? (b) State the provisions of the Fifteenth Amendment.

15. Why did the Republicans organize the Negro voters into "Union Leagues"?

16. (a) Describe carpetbag rule in the South. (b) Why did taxes rise sharply under the carpetbaggers? (c) What useful reforms were inaugurated during the period of carpetbag rule?

17. (a) Why did Southerners form secret societies during this period? (b) Name the most famous of these secret organizations. (c) Describe its purposes and methods. (d) How was it finally stamped out?

18. Why was Radical reconstruction given up? Describe the restoration of home rule in the former Confederate states.

FOR FURTHER STUDY AND DISCUSSION

1. Who had the right to determine the conditions for the readmission of Southern states—the President or Congress? Why?

2. If Booth had missed, would Lincoln have experienced the same difficulties with Congress that Johnson did?

3. How might the readmission of Southern states weaken the influence of the Republicans? How did they hope to avoid this?

4. (a) How does the Fourteenth Amendment tend to limit the power of the states? How does it tend to increase the power of the Supreme Court? (b) Was the South justified in its opposition to the amendment? (c) Account for the fact that the provision for reducing a state's representation under certain conditions has not been enforced. Helpful sources: Commager, *Documents*, Nos. 252, 253, 272, 273; Hart, *Contemporaries*, Vol. IV, No. 152; Randall, *The Civil War and Reconstruction*, pp. 734–740.

5. How did the Fourteenth Amendment tend to strengthen the position of the economic groups that won the War between North and South?

6. (a) Is the "Solid South" a result of the "Radical" Republican program of reconstruction or a result of Democratic policies prior to the War between North and South? Why? (b) How may the continued economic and industrial transformation of the South affect political conditions?

7. (a) What is the respective jurisdiction of the House of Representatives and the Senate in cases of impeachment? (b) Distinguish between the *real* and the *alleged* reasons for Johnson's impeachment.

FOR INDIVIDUAL OR GROUP ACTIVITIES

1. Prepare a chart listing important dates and events in the history of reconstruction from 1864 to 1877. Helpful source: Morris, *Encyclopedia*, pp. 246–253.

2. Report on the reconstruction program in one state. Include an account of the social and economic reforms attempted during reconstruction as well as evils and abuses. Helpful sources: Commager, *Documents*, Nos. 246, 247, 250, 254; Amherst Series, *Reconstruction in the South*, pp. 16–62; Commager and Nevins, *Heritage*, Nos. 184, 185, 186.

3. Arrange for an exhibit of cartoons, with appropriate captions, on the major events in the history of reconstruction.

4. Write a short essay comparing the conflict between Johnson and Congress with that between Jackson and Congress.

5. (a) Have four or five members of the class write out short explanations of how they would have voted on Johnson's impeachment, or (b) assign to a small committee the task of preparing a radio script on the highlights of Johnson's impeachment.

6. Write brief biographical sketches of Thaddeus Stevens, Edwin Stanton, and Horace Greeley.

7. Prepare a book report on Booker T. Washington's autobiography, *Up from Slavery*.

8. Hold a panel discussion on the significance of the Fourteenth Amendment.

9. Prepare a television or radio script on the story of a Republican senator who sacrificed his career in politics rather than vote "guilty" in Johnson's trial. Helpful source: Kennedy, *Profiles in Courage*.

HIGH POINTS

1

In the 1840's the United States expanded to the Pacific. The first step was the annexation of Texas. Next, Great Britain consented to divide Oregon along the 49th parallel. Then Mexico, after military defeat by the United States, ceded California and the huge province of New Mexico. The Gadsden Purchase (1853) of a small strip of land along the border of New Mexico gave the United States its present continental boundaries. At this time some Americans felt that it was "manifest destiny" for the United States to acquire Cuba, old Mexico, and Central America. These lands looked especially attractive to Southerners wishing to add more slave states to the Union.

2

The addition to the United States of the great tract of land ceded by Mexico led to bitter disputes over the extension of slavery. Most Northerners were against the spread of slavery into new territories. The slaveholders, however, demanded the right to move with their slaves into any territory. In 1850 the nation came close to breaking up over this issue. A compromise adopted in that year held the Union together for one more decade, but the terms satisfied neither side.

3

In 1854 the Missouri Compromise was repealed. In the territories which that agreement had closed to slavery—Kansas and Nebraska—the principle of popular sovereignty was now applied. Fighting broke out in Kansas, as proslavery men struggled with antislavery men for control of the territorial government. Another blow to the North was the Dred Scott decision of 1857, in which the Supreme Court ruled that slavery could not be kept out of a territory. This decision aroused fear in the North that slavery would spread into all the territories. As a result many Northerners joined the Republican party, which had been organized in 1854 to oppose the spread of slavery.

4

Southerners feared the triumph of the Republican party because (a) it intended to limit slavery to the states where it already existed, and (b) it had a nationalistic program that the South regarded as contrary to its interests. When the Republicans won the presidential election of 1860, South Carolina promptly seceded from the Union. Six Gulf states soon followed South Carolina. Four more states left the Union when President Lincoln called for volunteers to put down the "rebellion." Lincoln was able to keep the four border slave states from seceding.

5

Lincoln decided that the United States must fight to bring the seceded states back into the Union. As he pointed out, separation of the North and the South was physically impossible. The incident which began hostilities was the Confederate attack on Fort Sumter in Charleston Harbor. The North had more men and far larger economic resources than the South. Nevertheless, the war lasted four years and cost both sides a heavy price in blood and treasure. By the end of the conflict much of the South lay in waste and most of its people were in want.

6

The Emancipation Proclamation, which went into effect on January 1, 1863, indicated that if the North won the war, slavery would be abolished. The Proclamation at once reduced Confederate chances of securing foreign aid. The Thirteenth

Amendment was adopted in 1865 to end slavery forever in all parts of the United States.

7

Lincoln and his successor, Andrew Johnson, planned to restore the former Confederate states to the Union swiftly, leaving each state to deal with the problems arising from emancipation. The Radical Republicans rejected the Lincoln-Johnson program of reconstruction largely because (1) they feared the return of slavery in disguise, and (2) they wanted to insure Republican control of the Southern states and of the national government. They insisted on giving the vote to Negroes and denying the vote to most Southern white men.

8

When ten of the former Confederate states refused to ratify the Fourteenth Amendment, they were placed under military rule by Congress. All ten had to ratify the Fourteenth Amendment, and four, the Fifteenth Amendment also. These amendments were intended to guarantee full civil and political rights to Negroes.

9

In most Southern communities Negroes voted only so long as federal troops gave them protection. Even the presence of federal troops did not guard them from the Ku Klux Klan and other secret organizations determined to maintain white supremacy. The last federal troops were withdrawn in 1877. By that time the Democrats had regained control of every former Confederate state.

10

The South suffered great hardship during the period of political reconstruction. The section was impoverished by the war and by losing the capital that had been invested in slaves. Its difficulties were increased by "carpetbag" government, which was often inefficient and corrupt. Race relations were a serious problem, for neither whites nor Negroes were prepared for the system of free labor.

11

Radical Republicans tried to remove President Andrew Johnson from office because he opposed their plan of reconstruction. Their failure to remove him saved the constitutional principle of separation of powers. It kept Congress from making the executive branch the mere servant of the majority party.

QUESTIONS

1. (a) Indicate on an outline map the territory acquired by the United States as a result of the following: The annexation of Texas; the settlement of the Oregon boundary dispute; the Mexican Cession; the Gadsden Purchase. (b) Indicate on the map the earlier acquisition of territory by the United States.

2. (a) What were the reasons for America's expansion to the Pacific? (b) Was this expansion "imperialistic"? (c) List the outstanding leaders in American expansion, and indicate the major contribution of each.

3. (a) How did the issue of expansion become involved with the issue of slavery? (b) Why did the Mexican Cession lead to a dispute between North and South? (c) How did the Compromise of 1850 temporarily settle this dispute? (d) Indicate the parts played by Clay, Calhoun, and Webster in the Compromise of 1850.

407

(e) Why was the compromise regarded at the time as a "final solution" of the slavery question?

4. (a) Why did the Kansas-Nebraska Act of 1854 rekindle the controversy between North and South? (b) How did the Supreme Court decision in the Dred Scott case contribute to the conflict? (c) What differences in point of view were crystallized as a result of the Lincoln-Douglas debates? (d) How did the Free Soil party differ from the Liberty party? The Republican party from the Free Soil party?

5. (a) What economic and political considerations caused the South to become alarmed at the growth of the Republican party? (b) How did the presidential campaign of 1860 reflect the differences of opinion that prevailed throughout the country? (c) Why did the South secede after Lincoln's election? (d) Describe the situation which led to the outbreak of hostilities between North and South.

6. (a) How did economic progress during the 1850's give the North an advantage over the South in 1860 which it had not had in 1850? (b) How did the North and South compare in advantages and disadvantages at the start of the war?

7. (a) What effect did the Emancipation Proclamation have upon the war? (b) Why is the battle of Gettysburg considered the turning point in the struggle? (c) Why is the outcome of the War between North and South referred to as the triumph of nationalism and industrialism?

8. (a) What was the Lincoln-Johnson program of reconstruction? (b) Why was this program opposed by the Radical Republicans? (c) Outline the features of the congressional plan of reconstruction.

9. (a) Explain the circumstances under which the Thirteenth, Fourteenth, and Fifteenth Amendments were added to the Constitution. (b) What is the relationship of the Fourteenth Amendment to the Bill of Rights?

10. Tabulate the social, economic, and political effects of the war and reconstruction upon the South; upon the North.

11. What facts would you emphasize in defense of the opinion that the War between North and South was a "conflict of two civilizations bound together like twin enemies in a trap of their own making"?

SUGGESTED READINGS

SOURCE MATERIALS, DOCUMENTS, AND MAPS

Adams, *Album*. Vols. II and III.

Amherst Series: *Slavery as a Cause of the Civil War*.

———. *Reconstruction in the South*.

Angle, Paul (ed.). *The Lincoln Reader*. Rutgers University Press, 1947.

Commager, Henry Steele (ed.). *The Blue and the Gray*. 2 vols. Bobbs-Merrill, 1950.

———. *Documents*.

Hart, *Contemporaries*. Vol. IV.

Lord, *Historical Atlas*.

Nevins, Allan (ed.). *American Press Opinion*. Heath, 1928.

Nevins and Weitenkampf, *Political Cartoons*.

GENERAL REFERENCES

° Adams, Samuel Hopkins. *The Pony Express*. Random House, 1950. (Landmark)

° ———. *The Santa Fe Trail*. Random House, 1951.

Bowers, Claude G. *The Tragic Era*. Houghton, 1929.

Buck, Paul H. *Road to Reunion, 1865–1900*. Little, Brown, 1937.

Catton, Bruce. *Glory Road*. Doubleday, 1952.

———. *Mr. Lincoln's Army*. Doubleday, 1951.

———. *A Stillness at Appomattox*. Doubleday, 1953.

———. *This Hallowed Ground*. Doubleday, 1956.

Cole, A. C. *The Irrepressible Conflict, 1850–1865*. Macmillan, 1934. (A.L.S.)

Craven, Avery. *The Coming of Civil War*. Scribner, 1942.

De Voto, Bernard. *The Year of Decision*. Houghton, 1950.

° Dodd, William E. *The Cotton Kingdom*. Yale University Press, 1919. (Y.C.S.)

Eaton, Clement. *A History of the Old South*. Macmillan, 1949.

° Fleming, Walter L. *The Sequel of Appomattox*. Yale University Press, 1919. (Y.C.S.)

° Kantor, MacKinlay. *Gettysburg*. Random House, 1952.

° ———. *Lee and Grant at Appomattox*. Random House, 1950.

° Kelly, Regina Z. *Lincoln and Douglas; the Years of Decision*. Random House, 1954.

° Kjelgaard, James A. *The Coming of the Mormons*. Random House, 1953.

Leech, Margaret. *Reveille in Washington*. Harper, 1941.

Lorant, *Presidency*.

Macy, Jesse. *The Anti-Slavery Crusade*. Yale University Press, 1919. (Y.C.S.)

Morison and Commager, *American Republic*.

Nevins, Allan. *Ordeal of Union*. 2 vols. Scribner, 1948.

Parkman, Francis. *The Oregon Trail*. Modern Library, 1949.

° Pratt, Fletcher. *The Monitor and the Merrimac*. Random House, 1951.

Riegel, R. E. *America Moves West*. Rev. ed. Holt, 1947.

Stampp, K. M., *The Peculiar Institution: Slavery in the Ante-Bellum South*. Knopf, 1956.

° Stephenson, Nathaniel W. *The Day of the Confederacy*. Yale University Press, 1919. (Y.C.S.)

° ———. *Texas and the Mexican War*. Yale University Press, 1921. (Y.C.S.)

° Stewart, George R. *To California by Covered Wagon*. Random House, 1954.

° White, Stewart Edward. *The Forty-Niners*. Yale University Press, 1918. (.Y.C.S.)

° Wiley, Bell I. *The Life of Johnny Reb*. Bobbs-Merrill, 1943.

° ———. *The Life of Billy Yank*. Bobbs-Merrill, 1952.

BIOGRAPHY

° Boylston, H. D. *Clara Barton, Founder of the American Red Cross*. Random House, 1955. (Landmark)

° Carter, Hodding. *Robert E. Lee and the Road to Honor*. Random House, 1955.

Hale, William H. *Horace Greeley; Voice of the People*. Harper, 1950.

James, Marquis. *The Raven, a Biography of Sam Houston*. Bobbs-Merrill, 1953.

° Johnson, W. W. *Sam Houston, the Tallest Texan*. Random House, 1953.

° Kuhn, Ferdinand. *Commodore Perry and the Opening of Japan*. Random House, 1955.

McCormac, Eugene I. *James K. Polk*. University of California Press, 1922.

Nevins, Allan. *Frémont: The West's Greatest Adventurer*. Harper, 1928.

——— (ed.). *Polk; The Diary of a President, 1845–1849*. Longmans, 1929.

° North, Sterling. *Abe Lincoln: Log Cabin to White House*. Random House, 1956.

Ross, Ishbell. *Angel on the Battlefield*. Harper, 1956.

Sandburg, Carl. *Abraham Lincoln*. Harcourt, Brace, 1954.

Stryker, Lloyd P. *Andrew Johnson: A Study in Courage*. Macmillan, 1936.

Todd, Helen. *A Man Named Grant*. Houghton, 1940.

FICTION

° Allee, Marjorie H. *Susanna and Tristram*. Houghton, 1929 (Underground Railroad)

Allen, T. D. *The Doctor in Buckskin*. Harper, 1951. (The Whitmans in Oregon)

° Boyd, James. *Marching On*. Scribner, 1927. (Viewpoint of a non-slaveholding Southerner)

Cable, George. *John March, Southerner*. Scribner, n.d.

° Cather, Willa. *Death Comes for the Archbishop*. Knopf, 1927. (Early New Mexico)

Churchill, Winston. *The Crisis*. Macmillan, 1927. (The War between North and South; Lincoln)

° Crane, Stephen. *The Red Badge of Courage*. Appleton, 1925. (Chancellorsville)

Ehrlich, Leonard. *God's Angry Man*. Simon and Schuster, 1932. (John Brown)

Glasgow, Ellen. *The Voice of the People*. Doubleday, 1922. (Virginia during Reconstruction)

Guthrie, A. B. *The Way West*. Sloane, 1949. (From Missouri to the West)

Hough, Emerson. *Fifty-four Forty or Fight*. Bobbs-Merrill, 1909. (Struggle for Oregon)

Kantor, MacKinlay. *Long Remember*. Coward-McCann, 1934. (Gettysburg)

° Mitchell, Margaret. *Gone with the Wind*. Macmillan, 1936. (Georgia during and after the war)

Stone, Irving. *Immortal Wife*. Doubleday, 1948. (Story of Frémont)

° Young, Stark. *So Red the Rose*. Scribner, 1934. (The South during and after the war)

TIME LINE

	1859	First oil well, Titusville, Pa.
1860		
	1861	Morrill Tariff Act
	1862	Homestead Act; Morrill Land-Grant College Act
	1863	National Banking Act
	1866	Transatlantic telegraph cable
	1867	First elevated railway; Granger movement begins
	1869	Grant inaugurated; first transcontinental railroad; Knights of Labor
1870		
	1873	Business panic; silver demonetized
	1876	Bell's telephone
	1877	Hayes inaugurated
	1878	Bland-Allison Act
	1879	Resumption of specie payment; Edison's incandescent lamp
1880	**1880**	Tenth census—population 50,155,000; Tuskegee Institute established
	1881	Garfield inaugurated, assassinated; Arthur succeeds to Presidency
	1883	Pendleton Act
	1885	Cleveland inaugurated; linotype machine
	1886	American Federation of Labor
	1887	Interstate Commerce Act; Electoral Count Act
	1889	Harrison inaugurated
1890	**1890**	McKinley Tariff; Sherman Antitrust Act
	1892	Homestead strike
	1893	Cleveland inaugurated; panic
	1894	Wilson-Gorman Tariff; Pullman strike
	1897	McKinley inaugurated; Dingley Tariff; first subway

410

UNIT SIX   *Modern America Emerges (1865—1900)*

★ ★ ★ ★   The America we know today took shape in the thirty-five years between Appomattox and 1900. Whether we are thinking of ways of living or ways of working, it was a time of rapid change. Among the most spectacular changes was the growth of our population and the settlement of the vast area west of the Missouri River. So quickly was the Great West settled and so quickly were new states created that by 1896 the Union had forty-five states. By then there was no longer any good land which a settler could obtain free. Still the westward movement went on.

Another spectacular change was the growth of industry, which was greatly speeded by the War between North and South. While industry grew faster in the North, before the end of the century the South too was becoming industrialized. In both sections there was a drop in the proportion of people engaged in farming. As workers moved into commerce and manufacturing, cities grew rapidly.

Industrialization brought startling changes in ways of living. People began to have more comforts and more leisure. More Americans went to high school and to college. There were more public libraries and art galleries, more books, more periodicals—in short, more opportunities for culture. Both the fine arts and scientific research received greater attention than ever before.

The rise of big business was another change that took place in this period. Little factories were combined into great industrial plants. Short railroad lines were joined to form great railroad systems. As corporations grew larger, those who controlled them gained political power. The public began to fear that big business would rule the nation. Congress responded by passing a law to check the growth of the trusts. Despite this law, business kept on getting bigger.

Throughout this period labor conditions were very unsatisfactory. Workingmen tried to win better conditions, but their gains were small since there were always more workers than jobs. Farmers too were discontented. They asked for laws to protect them from monopolists. In an effort to get the government to pay more attention to their woes, workingmen and farmers at times united in a third-party movement. The political history of this period is marked by the rise and fall of third parties.

411

Lazell, Perkins and Co., iron manufacturers at Bridgewater, Massachusetts, c. 1860.
This was the largest iron works in New England at the time, with 28 buildings and
five coal-burning steam engines supplementing the water wheels. THE INTRODUCTION
OF COAL AS A SOURCE OF POWER *freed the manufacturer from his dependency on*
woodlands and waterways. He could build his factory anywhere along the railroad
line that would be attractive to labor.

The millionaires who are in active control started as poor boys and were trained in that sternest but most efficient of all schools—poverty.

———Andrew Carnegie

25. THE INDUSTRIAL REVOLUTION CONTINUES

The War Spurs Industrial Expansion in the North

The North enacts its own program.

When the Republican party came to power in 1861, it was pledged to a high tariff, land grants to aid railroads, free farms for Western settlers, and a reform of banking and currency. This nationalistic program was supported by Northern businessmen. It could hardly have been written into law had the Southern states not seceded and taken their representatives out of Congress. When this happened, Congress speedily adopted the whole program.

1. A steep protective tariff. The tariff rate had been dropping ever since 1832, when South Carolina threatened to nullify the "Tariff of Abominations" (see p. 263). Before Congress passed the Morrill Tariff Act (1861) to raise the duties, the average duty was 12 per cent. By the end of the war it had risen to 47 per cent. This tariff wall protected the Northern manufacturers against practically all competition from abroad. Although one reason for adopting the high rates was to raise money for the war, the war's end did not bring lower rates. No real reduction of the tariff came until 1913, when Woodrow Wilson became President.

2. Free land for homesteads and railroads. In 1862 Congress passed the Homestead Act. It permitted the head of a family to obtain 160 acres of public land merely by building a dwelling on it and working it for five years. Before the good land was gone, several hundred thousand families got free farms. Beginning in 1862 Congress also voted vast tracts of land as subsidies to transcontinental railroads.

3. A system of national banks. Since the destruction of the Bank of the United States by Andrew Jackson, the nation had been without a uniform currency. Banks were chartered by the states, and each bank issued its own brand of paper money. In 1861 there were seven thousand kinds of bank notes in circulation, and almost as many kinds of counterfeit notes. Only an expert could tell what a piece of paper money was worth.

In 1863 Congress passed the National Banking Act. It had two objects: (1) to create a market for government bonds to finance the war, and (2) to give the country a sound, uniform currency. Under this law and its amendments any bank choosing to accept fed-

413

eral regulation could get a charter as a "national bank." A national bank could buy government bonds, deposit them with the treasury at Washington, and issue bank notes up to 90 per cent of the value of the bonds. By lending its notes to borrowers, a national bank could earn double interest on its capital.

In 1865 Congress drove the notes of state banks out of circulation by placing a 10 per cent tax on them. A year later 80 per cent of all the banks had accepted federal regulation and had obtained a national charter.

The adoption of the Republican program meant that the policies of Hamilton had triumphed over those of Jefferson. What the planters had feared from the Republicans had come to pass. A revolution had taken place—a new class had come to power. Manufacturers and bankers, instead of landowners, now controlled the reins of government. They could stay in command as long as they had the support of the Western farmer.

The war stimulates Northern business.

The war brought a period of prosperity to the North. Business boomed as manufacturing, transportation, and commerce expanded to meet the needs of the United States Army and Navy.

The war placed heavy demands on Northern railroads. Thousands of miles of new track were laid. Connecting links, double tracks, and bridges were built. War needs led Congress to vote federal aid for building a railroad to the Pacific. Although work on the first transcontinental railroad began during the war, it was not completed until 1869 (see p. 420).

To supply the United States Army with food, clothing, guns, and ammunition, mass production was needed. The first large packing houses were built to fill army orders for meat. Canning factories were erected to produce canned products for the army. Scores of new woolen mills were built to make army blankets and cloth for uniforms. The manufacture of ready-to-wear clothing, then in its infancy, suddenly expanded to produce items needed by soldiers in carload lots. Shoe factories equipped with power machinery sprang up to fill huge army orders for shoes. The production of farm machinery, like that of factory machinery, leaped ahead. The strong demand for farm products and the drain of men into the army led farmers to buy reapers, mowers, and other farm machines as fast as these could be turned out.

The war stimulated every type of industry in the North. Many new plants were built to make machines for farms and factories, railroad equipment, ships, and guns. The need for iron led to the opening of scores of iron mills. War also helped the mining industry, for the expanding railroads and war industries called for large quantities of coal, iron, copper, and lubricating oil.

The Industrial Revolution Spreads West and South

Expansion continues after the war.

For several years after the war, Northern industry continued its rapid growth. Thousands of businessmen who had made fortunes from army contracts invested their wealth in new factories. Plenty of workers could be found among the hundreds of thousands of immigrants pouring into the country each year. Also these people became customers for manufactured products. The West was filling up at the same time, creating a demand for farm machinery, manufactures of all kinds, and more railroads. The five years after Appomattox saw more rails laid, more lumber sawed, more houses built, more coal, iron, silver, and copper mined, more flour milled, and more cotton cloth woven than any previous five years in the nation's history.

European leaders thought that the return of a million Union soldiers to civilian life in 1865 would cause hard times. They were mistaken. The Union soldiers had little trouble finding jobs. Many went into the factories, oil fields, and mines, or into railroading. Others claimed a free homestead in the West and settled down to farm. Except in the South the country enjoyed prosperity until the panic of 1873. After six years of hard times, business picked up again and another period of industrial expansion began.

A broad basis for industrial growth.

The rapid industrial progress of the United States was not an accident. It was a natural result of the fact that our country had everything required for large-scale industries—varied natural resources, an abundant labor supply, money to invest, a market for industrial products, able scientists and inventors, skillful managers, and a government eager to encourage private business.

1. Natural resources. Few nations are so richly blessed with natural resources as the United States. Its stimulating climate, numerous harbors, navigable rivers; its great water power; its forests; its immense stores of coal, oil, natural gas, iron, copper, lead, zinc— all these set the stage for the development of industry. In 1860 the nation's mineral resources and much of its forest were still almost untouched.

2. Labor supply. After the War between North and South our population continued to grow rapidly, partly because of the high birth rate and partly because of immigration. Every year we had a million and a quarter more people. They could not all go into farming, for the use of machinery was raising the output of farm workers and reducing the demand for farm labor. Most of the additional people went to

the cities, where they were willing to work for any wage they could get.

3. Money to invest. The rapid growth of industry demanded capital— that is, money to invest in buildings, machinery, railroads, and raw materials. Much of the capital needed soon after the War between North and South was supplied by Northern bankers and manufacturers out of the huge profits they made during the war. More of it came from Europe. European investors had faith in the United States and its future. They were willing to lend money to our businessmen at fairly low rates of interest.

4. A market for industrial products. The United States furnished a broad and growing market. High tariffs kept out foreign competition. The businessman had the whole country for his market.

5. Able scientists and inventors. Americans are a practical people. They have been quick to apply scientific discoveries to everyday affairs. Searching for ways to save labor, they have improved numberless machines and ways of making things. Inventions made before the War between North and South, such as the sewing machine, the telegraph, a safe process for canning food in tins, and the Bessemer process for making steel, launched important new industries. After the war the rate of invention was faster. The typewriter, refrigerator car, telephone, phonograph, dynamo, incandescent lamp, and the internal combustion engine were among the important inventions made between 1865 and 1900.

6. Skillful managers. To succeed, a business needs skillful management. The good manager must be at once practical and imaginative, careful and daring. He sees and makes use of opportunities which others neglect. In the United States after the war many able men were attracted to the field of business management.

7. Government aid. Our national government has always tried to encourage private business. For instance, the patent system gives an inventor complete control of his invention for a period of years. During and after the War between North and South, businessmen were given many advantages by the national government. The tariff was raised again and again. Enormous grants of public land were made to railroad companies. Large tracts of land covered with timber or known to contain minerals were sold to individuals and companies for as little as a dollar or two an acre. Cattlemen grazed their herds and lumbermen cut trees on the public lands. Many Americans grew rich from these valuable privileges.

State and local governments were as eager as the national government to encourage business. They voted gifts of money and land to railroad companies. They gave *franchises* to railroad, water, electric, telephone, and gas companies. (A franchise permits a company to use public ways for its lines, pipes, or other facilities, and protects it from competition.) In addition, state legislatures issued charters to corporations. These charters gave them various privileges, including the right to do business anywhere in the United States. All these government benefits did a great deal to stimulate private enterprise.

Industry moves westward.

The growth of industry was not limited to the East. Manufacturing had begun to develop in the Midwest even before the war. After the war, manufacturing continued to increase, particularly in the states bordering the Great Lakes. Factories also began to grow up in the Pacific Coast states. The bulk of the nation's industries, however, still were located east of the Mississippi and north of the Ohio.

Industrialization comes to the South.

Under the slavery system, wealthy Southerners had put their money into slaves rather than industry. Thus in 1860 there were not more than forty textile mills in the South and these were small. At this time the South had only 8 per cent of the nation's factory workers. Ten years later even fewer factories existed, as many machines wore out or were destroyed during the war.

In the 1870's, however, manufacturing in the South began to increase. In many villages in the hill country, leaders scraped up enough money to start a small factory run by water power. Cotton mills, flour mills, lumber mills, furniture shops, and tobacco factories gradually became numerous. The factories drew workers chiefly from the poor whites of the foothills and mountains. They were willing to work 72 to 75 hours a week for extremely low wages. Any wages looked attractive to a family which had been trying to exist on rough or worn-out land. Entire families flocked to the mill villages. Usually they were hired as a family unit and everyone except the youngest children was expected to work.

Mining too expanded. Great coal beds were opened in the Appalachian regions, from Maryland to Alabama. Immense deposits of iron ore were found, all the way from Virginia through northern Alabama to Arkansas. Birmingham, which was a cotton field in 1870, became a booming iron center during the next twenty years. By that time the South was producing one fifth of the nation's pig iron.

By 1900 the South had established almost all forms of industry. Its manufactured products were worth over four times as much as in 1860. Yet Northern industries had increased with equal speed. Thus the South still produced only 8 per cent by value of the nation's total manufactures. Most Southerners continued to live by farming.

Faster Transportation and Communication Aid Industry

Remarkable improvements in transportation and communication accompanied the growth of industry. Mass production was made possible, in fact, by cheaper and faster ways of moving raw materials and finished goods. Swifter means of communication also aided the industrial advance. Easy communication helped businessmen to manage complicated modern enterprises and to serve customers over a wide area.

The first transcontinental railroad.

Beginning in 1849, with the rush to the California gold fields, there was much talk of the need for a railroad to the Pacific. To build it, congressmen agreed federal aid was necessary, but they could not agree on the route. Southerners wanted the road to start from New Orleans or Memphis. Northerners wanted it to start from some point in the North. After the Confederate states seceded, the problem was simplified. In 1862 Congress decided on a route starting from Omaha, Nebraska.

The Pacific Railway Act of 1862 gave charters to two railroad companies —the Union Pacific and the Central Pacific. The Union Pacific was to build westward from Omaha, and the Central Pacific eastward from Sacramento. For each mile of road built Congress promised the companies ten square miles of the public land along their right of way. Congress also lent the companies from $16,000 to $48,000 a mile according to the roughness of the country. The two companies raced toward their meeting point to see which could build more miles and collect more of the government bounty.

The Central Pacific company faced harder construction problems than did its rival. In the first 125 miles it had to climb over 7000 feet through the Sierra Nevada mountains. Every rail, car, locomotive, and piece of machinery had to be carried around Cape Horn or across the Isthmus of Panama. Roadways had to be blasted over mountains, and bridges built over gorges. In one sixty-mile stretch in the Sierras fifteen tunnels were bored. Most of the work was done by 10,000 coolies whom the company brought in from China.

Building the first transcontinental railroad

These five MODERN GOLIATHS *give the railroads the power and the speed so essential in the modern age.*

Compare the giant 20th century locomotives (above) with the painting at right, which shows a transcontinental express of the Central Pacific Railroad in the 1890's passing through the forty miles of snowsheds in the Sierra Nevadas. The snowsheds provided not only cover for the tracks but also depots, section houses, and homes for families of railroad people, who worked on the line. The Chinese, as shown in the painting by Joseph Becker, were employed as section hands and cooks. Snowshed men, employed by the "railroad barons" as maintenance crews, telegraphers, and so forth, were usually immigrants from Europe.

The Union Pacific built its railroad with the labor of Irish immigrants and ex-soldiers of the Union and Confederate armies. As the men crossed the Indian-troubled prairies, they worked with their rifles in easy reach. To house the workers, a huge construction camp moved forward as they advanced—a "city on wheels." The engineer in charge has left us an interesting summary of the problems the railroad builders faced:

At one time we were using at least ten thousand animals, and most of the time from eight to ten thousand laborers. The bridge gangs always worked from five to twenty miles ahead of the track, and it was seldom that the track waited for a bridge. To supply one mile of track with material required about forty cars, as on the plains everything . . . had to be transported from the Missouri River. . . . Our Indian troubles commenced in 1864 and lasted until the tracks joined at Promontory. . . . At that time every mile of road had to be surveyed, graded, tied, and bridged under military protection.

The two railroad lines met in Utah on May 10, 1869, and the entire country celebrated the great event. As the last spike was driven into place, the telegraph carried the strokes to the major cities of the country. A wonderful feat of engineering had been accomplished.

Other Far Western lines are built.

The first railroad line to the Pacific was hardly finished before others were started. Within fifteen years seven different lines had entered the Rockies, and three—the Southern Pacific, the Northern Pacific, and the Santa Fe—had reached the coast. All but one (the Great Northern) received land grants from the federal government of a value that was often more than the cost of construction. In addition the railroads asked for, and received, lavish gifts of money or land from the states, towns, and counties which they crossed.

Great railroad systems are formed.

The combining of short rail lines into unified railroad systems was much needed. For example, freight going from New York to Chicago by rail had to be unloaded seventeen times, carted across towns, and reloaded into other trains. Shortly after the war Commodore Vanderbilt bought the separate lines on this route and combined them into the New York Central Railroad system. By modernizing the equipment and track and by making it unnecessary to change trains, he cut in two the hours required to travel from New York to Chicago by rail. In creating the New York Central, Vanderbilt did not hesitate to bribe legislatures and judges, to sell stock to the public for twice its value, and to take advantage of inside information to win huge sums on the stock exchange. He increased his personal fortune from $10,000,000 to $104,000,000 in twelve years. One writer has described his methods as those of a "robber baron," yet he helped to open up a continent. What he did was soon repeated by other railroad leaders in all parts of the country.

Railroads improve their service.

Between 1860 and 1900 the railroads became more efficient, safe, and comfortable. Steel rails, introduced in 1863, gradually replaced iron rails. Iron bridges supplanted wooden ones, and in turn were rebuilt with steel. By 1886 practically all railroads had changed to a standard gauge, or width, of track, (4 feet, 8½ inches). After this change a railroad car owned by one company could run on the tracks of any other company.

The Westinghouse air brake came into use in the 1870's. Brakemen no longer had to apply the brakes to each car separately, for the new device set the brakes on every car at once. About the same time interlocking block signals were introduced. The automatic car

420

coupler replaced the dangerous link-and-pin coupler. State legislatures passed laws to hasten the adoption of these and other safety devices.

The spark-belching, wood-burning engines, still widely used in 1860, gradually gave way to coal burners. Heavier and larger passenger cars with vestibules supplanted the flimsy boxlike cars of an earlier day. In passenger cars gas lamps and steam heat replaced swaying kerosene lamps and wood-burning stoves. Meanwhile, sleeping cars and dining cars came into use on the main lines.

Standard time zones are established.

In 1883 the railroads adopted four standard time zones—Eastern, Central, Mountain, and Pacific—each one hour apart. Before that there were about one hundred different local times. Philadelphia time, for example, was five minutes slower than New York time and five minutes faster than Baltimore time. The adoption of standard time zones was a great convenience to travelers and railroad men.

Railroads become our biggest business.

For fifty years after the War between North and South the building and operation of railroads was the nation's biggest business. Vast sums of money and enormous quantities of labor and raw materials were poured into the industry. When railroad construction was booming the country enjoyed prosperity. When it slowed down, the country suffered from hard times.

During these postwar years the whole nation was covered with a network of rails. In 1865 there were 35,000 miles of railroad, practically all of it east of the Mississippi. Railroad mileage had doubled by 1873, when a severe panic checked further construction for a time. Then came another tremendous burst of construction, which lasted until the panic of 1893. By 1900 the country had 193,000 miles of road—almost a third of the world's total.

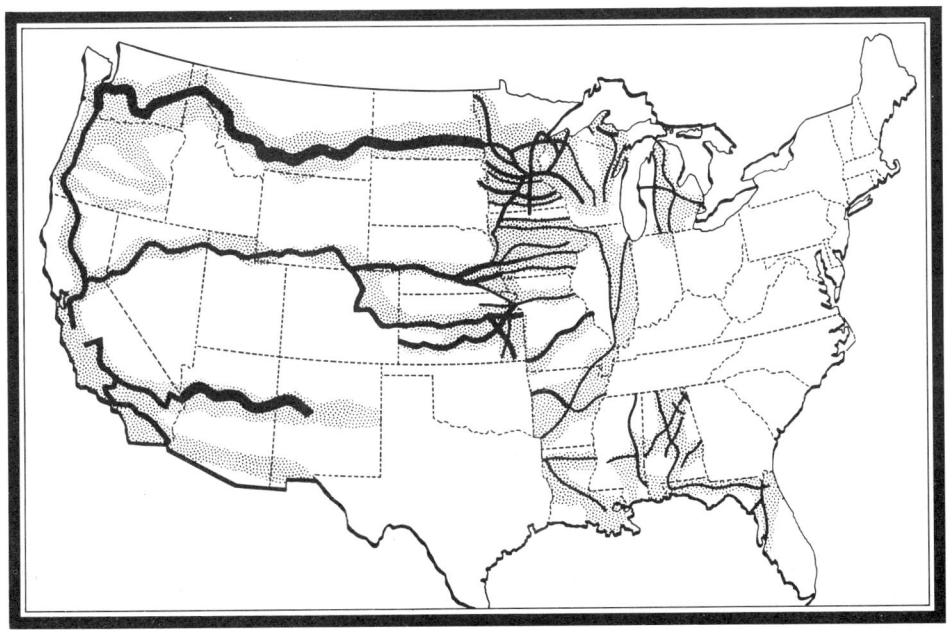

LAND GRANTS TO RAILROADS

421

Better communication helps business.

The building of a telegraph line from Washington to Baltimore in 1844 marked the beginning of a revolution in communication. The value of the telegraph in the safe and efficient operation of railroads was seen at once. Within a few years every railroad station was equipped with telegraph instruments; every railroad line was paralleled with a telegraph line. Before long, too, the telegraph proved to be a great help to businessmen in buying and selling in distant markets. It transformed the business of the stockbroker, enabling him to quote latest prices to customers in all parts of the country. The telegraph also brought remarkable changes to the newspaper business. For example, it made possible the rise of news-gathering services like the Associated Press and the United Press.

Cyrus Field succeeded in laying the first transatlantic telegraph cable in 1866 (see p. 297). That same year the second Atlantic cable was laid. Soon all the continents were linked by under-seas communications. The cable helped greatly in the development of foreign trade. Later it made world-wide news services possible.

In 1876 a Scotch immigrant, Alexander Graham Bell, exhibited the first practical telephone. Within twenty years nearly a million telephones were in use. The telephone enabled businessmen to serve customers in a wider area than ever before.

The invention of the typewriter was another important step in improving communication. The first typewriter to be commercially successful was patented in 1868. Businessmen and others found the machine a great convenience. Before the end of the century it came into common use.

Improvements in printing and papermaking were another part of the revolution in communication. The linotype machine for setting and casting type was invented in 1885. About the same time a practical process for making paper from wood pulp was developed. These and other inventions cut the cost of printing. Newspapers, magazines, and books became cheaper and more plentiful.

Better postal service also played a part in promoting easy communication. Until 1863 everyone went to the post office to get his letters. In that year free delivery of mail was started in the larger cities. In 1887 carrier service was given to all towns with 10,000 or more people. Free rural delivery began ten years later.

Industry seeks a nationwide market.

As transportation and communication improved, industrialists looked for bigger markets. They sent salesmen far and wide. They bought advertising space in magazines with a national circulation. By offering more attractive products or lower prices, they took business away from local shops and craftsmen until many of these were forced out of business. Local slaughterhouses, for example, gradually disappeared as meat packing became a big business. The local shoemaker stopped making shoes, since he could not compete with the big shoe factory. The local miller lost out because his customers liked the finer and whiter flour made in great mills equipped with the latest machinery. In time, most kinds of small-scale manufacturing for a purely local market almost ceased.

New methods of distribution appear.

Before the days of mass production there were two kinds of stores: (1) the shop, where goods of a particular kind were made and sold, and (2) the general store, where foodstuffs and a variety of other goods were sold. As manufactured articles became abundant, merchants developed new types of stores.

The first chain of grocery stores was started by George Gilman, a New York tea importer. When the nation was rejoicing over the completion of the Union Pacific Railroad in 1869, Gilman took the name "Great Atlantic and Pacific Tea Company." In twelve years the company had a hundred stores. The F. W. Woolworth Company, founded in 1879, developed the first chain of variety stores.

Mail-order catalogs were another new development. In 1872 Montgomery Ward and Company began to sell goods from a mail-order catalog. Sears, Roebuck and Company followed in 1886. Most of the mail orders came from rural areas. The more prosperous farmers gladly sent away for many articles formerly made on the farm.

The department store appeared first in large cities. It was something like a general country store but on a much larger scale. In 1876 John Wanamaker opened one of the first department stores in the country at Philadelphia. Six years later Marshall Field started one in Chicago.

The distribution of goods in places far from where they were made led to a new emphasis on packaging. Individual packages came into use for many items formerly sold in bulk. As early as 1900 the manufacture of boxes, tins, bottles, and other containers had become an important industry.

Corporations Become Big and Powerful

Many small businesses combine.

At the close of the War between North and South most businesses were small. For instance, hundreds of companies were drilling oil in Pennsylvania. In that state alone were more than two hundred oil refineries. Seventy-five companies were making mowers and reapers in the state of New York. Fifty companies were making salt in Michigan. By 1900 the picture was different. Except in the field of retailing, small companies did but a minor part of the total business of the country. One giant concern, or a few of them, might control an entire industry. For example, the International Harvester Company made almost all the farm implements, while the Standard Oil Company did a large part of the oil refining.

Grain elevators at the Grand Depot Grounds, Chicago, 1866

Most businesses adopt corporate form.

As businesses grew bigger and adopted mass production methods, they also changed their form of organization. In Lincoln's time the typical business was owned by one individual or by a partnership. A partnership enables two or more persons to pool their money and skill to carry on a business for profit. Should the business fail, however, or should one of the partners withdraw or die, each partner is *liable*, or responsible, for all debts of the business. A corporation, on the other hand, has rights and liabilities distinct from those of the persons composing it. A man who invests in a corporation is not responsible for its debts. If it fails, he will lose only as much as he has invested in it. Because of this *limited liability*, the corporate form is better suited to large enterprises than is the partnership. By 1900 most businesses of any size had taken the corporate form, and nearly three fourths of all manufacturing was done by corporations.

A corporation must have a charter.

Individuals who seek to form a corporation must obtain a charter, or certificate of incorporation, from a state government. At first a special act of the legislature was necessary. Now all the states have laws outlining the steps to be followed by those who wish to incorporate. When these steps are completed, a state agency issues the charter. The charter recognizes the corporation and gives it the right to conduct a certain kind of business. In the eyes of the law the corporation is an artificial legal person. It can do many things which an individual can do.

A corporation chartered in one state may do business in all other states. The state which charters a corporation may require it to pay certain fees and taxes. To obtain this revenue some states have made the procuring of a charter very easy.

Stockholders own the corporation.

A corporation starts out with a certain amount of capital stock. The price for which the shares can be sold depends chiefly on the actual or expected success of the corporation in making profits. The stockholder hopes that the business will prosper so that he will receive dividends on his shares. The value of the stock is closely related to the prosperity of the business.

Once a year the stockholders meet to elect the directors and officers of the corporation. Generally each share of common stock carries one vote. The great majority of small stockholders do not attend stockholders' meetings. Either they do not vote or they sign proxies giving one of the officers of the corporation the right to vote for them.

Corporations often combine.

Corporations engaged in the same business often join together to avoid competition. The trend toward combination of business began soon after the War between North and South. Several forms of combination are, or have been, used.

1. The pool. In the early days of large-scale production, from about 1877 to 1887, the arrangement most commonly used was the pool. The managers of several competing corporations agreed to divide the territory or the business in such a way that each could make a profit. Pooling was most commonly used by rival railroads.

A pooling arrangement worked only so long as the members kept their promises. If one of them broke the agreement, the others could not take him to court. In 1887 the Interstate Commerce Act declared that pooling was illegal for railroad companies.

2. The trust. In 1882 the Standard Oil Company worked out a form of combination known as a "trust." The stockholders of about forty separate oil companies turned over their stock and their votes to a board of nine trustees. In exchange the stockholders received a share in the earnings of the trust. Other industries saw the advantage of the trust organization and adopted it. In every case the trust sought to do away with competition and to establish control over the industry.

In 1890 Congress passed the Sherman Antitrust Act, making trusts illegal. Lawyers, however, found other ways for businesses to combine. Today the term "trust" is used to mean any large business combination which controls an industry.

3. The holding company. While Congress was still discussing the antitrust bill, a substitute for the trust was found. This is the *holding company.* New Jersey was the first state to make it legal. Before long several other states adopted a similar provision.

A holding company is one which owns a controlling interest in other companies. The Pennsylvania Company, for example, was formed to hold the stock of railroads in the Pennsylvania Railroad system. Other well-known examples of the holding company are the American Telephone and Telegraph Company and the General Motors Corporation.

4. The merger. This is the consolidation of two or more companies. One company absorbs the others by buying their physical assets. Mergers have gone on at a rapid rate for nearly a century. In 1953 for the first time Congress placed restrictions on mergers.

Why do businesses combine?

The combining or consolidation of business first became important in the 1860's and has continued ever since. Combination was a natural development. Big business could take advantage of the changes in transportation and communication that were opening up a nation-wide market. Big business could afford to use specialized laborsaving machinery. It could hire specialists to manage each of its activities. It could make a fuller use of by-products. Big business had another advantage in being able to pay for research and for national advertising.

A large business often, but not always, produces at a lower cost per unit than the small business. Lower costs are a legitimate advantage. In addition a big business may be able to take unfair advantage of competitors and consumers. A big concern might receive special discounts from transportation companies and raw material suppliers. Again it might sell its product in one locality at less than cost until it had driven local competitors to the wall. It might bribe legislators to pass laws for its special benefit. If unfavorable legislation was passed, it might bribe law-enforcement officials not to enforce it. It might influence the press by threatening to withhold advertising and by other kinds of financial pressure. These unfair practices were common until passage of the Clayton Antitrust Act in 1914.

Oil and Steel Show How Great Industries Develop

The oil business suddenly expands.

The swift growth of the oil business is an example of the way in which large-scale enterprise develops. Petroleum had long been used as a medicine. In 1850 a Pittsburgh druggist began distilling it to make a lamp fuel called "kerosene." At that time petroleum was collected in small quantities from oil seeps or skimmed from creeks. The first oil well was sunk in 1859 at Titusville in northwestern Pennsylvania. This started a rush of oil prospectors to the region. Wooden oil derricks sprang up by the hundreds. Farm land under which oil was found jumped in value from a few dollars an acre to

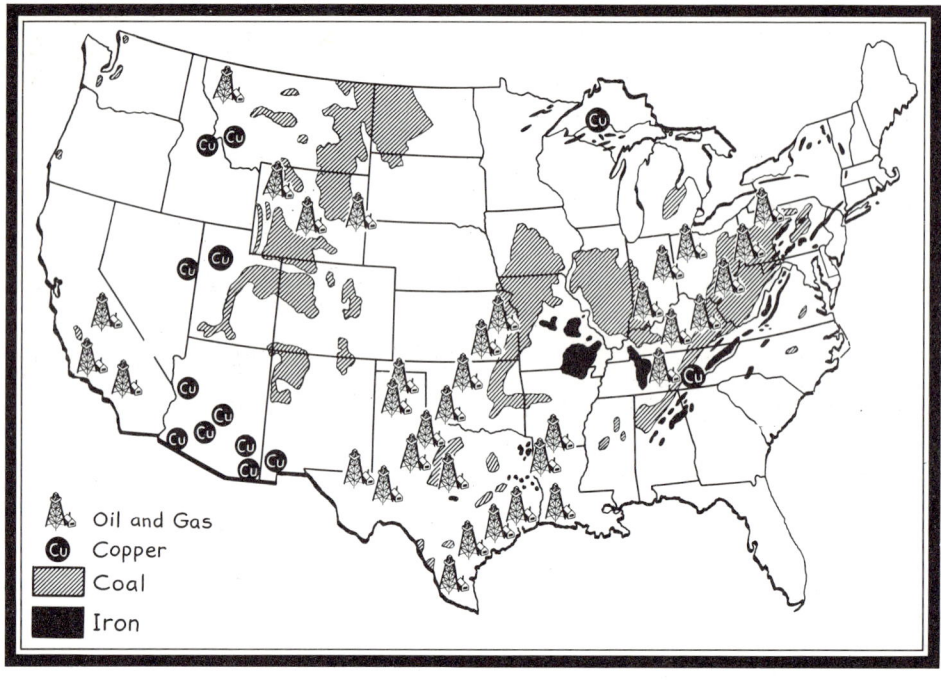

MINERAL RESOURCES

hundreds of dollars a square foot. New towns grew up almost overnight. By 1865 oil refining had become one of the nation's leading industries.

Kerosene was cheaper than whale oil and gave a better light than candles. All over the world it soon became the principal material for lighting. A new use was found for it about 1880, when a safe kerosene stove was perfected. Housewives found cooking with kerosene much more satisfactory in hot weather than cooking with coal or wood. Meanwhile, some of the by-products of kerosene manufacture, such as lubricating oils, vaseline, and paraffin wax, were in great demand. Gasoline, another by-product, had little use until the automobile age.

Rockefeller enters the oil business.

When the first oil well was drilled, John D. Rockefeller was a bookkeeper in Cleveland, Ohio. That year, at the age of nineteen, he and a partner started a small produce commission business. They made money out of war contracts and in 1862 invested $4000 in an oil refinery. Within eight years Rockefeller's firm, the Standard Oil Company of Ohio, was the largest refining company in Cleveland.

The oil refiners were engaged in cutthroat competition and Rockefeller made up his mind to gain control of the industry. One of his weapons was the secret rebate, or discount, on railroad charges. In 1872 he persuaded the railroads running out of Cleveland to pay a large rebate on oil shipped by the Standard Oil Company. He even got the railroads to pay him a rebate on the oil they carried for his rivals. The railroads also gave him copies of way-bills which told where his competitors were selling their oil and at what price. To escape ruin, most of his rivals sold their businesses to Rockefeller.

Within a few years Rockefeller had control of 95 per cent of the nation's refineries, pipe lines, and oil storehouses. As we have noted (p. 424), his companies were combined into the Standard Oil trust. The trust entered the business of drilling and pumping oil. Within ten years it was master of the oil business from well to consumer. Having no competition to speak of, it could set prices to suit itself. It had, that is, become a *monopoly*. In 1892 it changed its form to a holding company.

In 1895 the wealth of the Standard Oil Company exceeded $238,000,000. About half was invested in physical assets—oil wells, gas wells, pipe lines, and buildings. The rest was invested in securities, chiefly the stock of railroad companies and banks. Standard Oil had a controlling interest in several of these other businesses. It had brought under one management: (1) raw materials, (2) factories, (3) transportation facilities, and (4) banking facilities. In 1911 the Supreme Court divided the Standard Oil Company into thirty-eight separate companies. The same group of men, however, had a controlling interest in each of them.

Carnegie becomes the steel king.

As Rockefeller's name stands out in the story of oil, that of Andrew Carnegie stands out in the story of steel. Carnegie, who was born in Scotland in 1835, came to America a poor boy. At thirteen he worked in a cotton mill, earning $1.20 for a 72-hour week. At seventeen he was a telegraph clerk; two years later he was private secretary to the president of the Pennsylvania Railroad. When only twenty-two he became a district traffic manager for the Pennsylvania. Before he was thirty he had an income of forty to fifty thousand dollars a year from investments in oil wells and in companies making railroad cars. In 1865 he decided to put all his time and money into the iron busi-

JOHN D. ROCKEFELLER, SR., *in 1914, after his retirement from active management of the Standard Oil Company.*

ness. Within a few years he organized, or bought into, companies that made iron bridges, rails, and locomotives.

About this time two new methods of making steel—the Bessemer process and the open-hearth process—were developed. These produced steel far more cheaply than the older methods. Steel began to replace iron for many purposes. In 1875 Carnegie set about building the largest steel mill in the country. Soon it was turning out more steel than all the other American mills put together. He sold steel to his railroad friends, and they gave him secret rebates on all his shipments. Gradually he bought up most of his rivals. Year by year his holdings grew. He acquired coal mines, coke companies, iron mines, and a fleet of steamboats to carry the iron ore from Minnesota to Lake Erie. By controlling all the resources and facilities needed in making steel, he was able to produce at a lower cost than any of his competitors.

427

The United States Steel Corporation.

By 1900 the Carnegie company was producing one fourth of all the steel made in the United States. With the help of a high tariff and cheap labor, it made a profit of $40,000,000 a year. Carnegie was an old man. Since he wanted to retire and give away his money, he agreed to sell his holdings. The banking firm of J. P. Morgan and Company arranged to combine the Carnegie company and its larger rivals into the United States Steel Corporation. The new company did 60 per cent of the country's steel business.

Carnegie and Rockefeller give to public welfare.

After his retirement Carnegie devoted his time to the wise spending of his huge fortune. He declared, "Where wealth accrues honorably, the people are always silent partners." He believed it the duty of a man of wealth to live modestly and, after providing for his family's legitimate needs, to use all his money for the public welfare. Before Carnegie died in 1919 he had given away nearly $350,000,000. It was spent for educational purposes, such as building public libraries, endowing colleges, providing pensions for college teachers, and promoting international peace. Rockefeller's gifts were even larger. The many endowments that he set up are used for education, medical research, and public health work. In their benefactions both men were guided by what Carnegie called the "gospel of wealth."

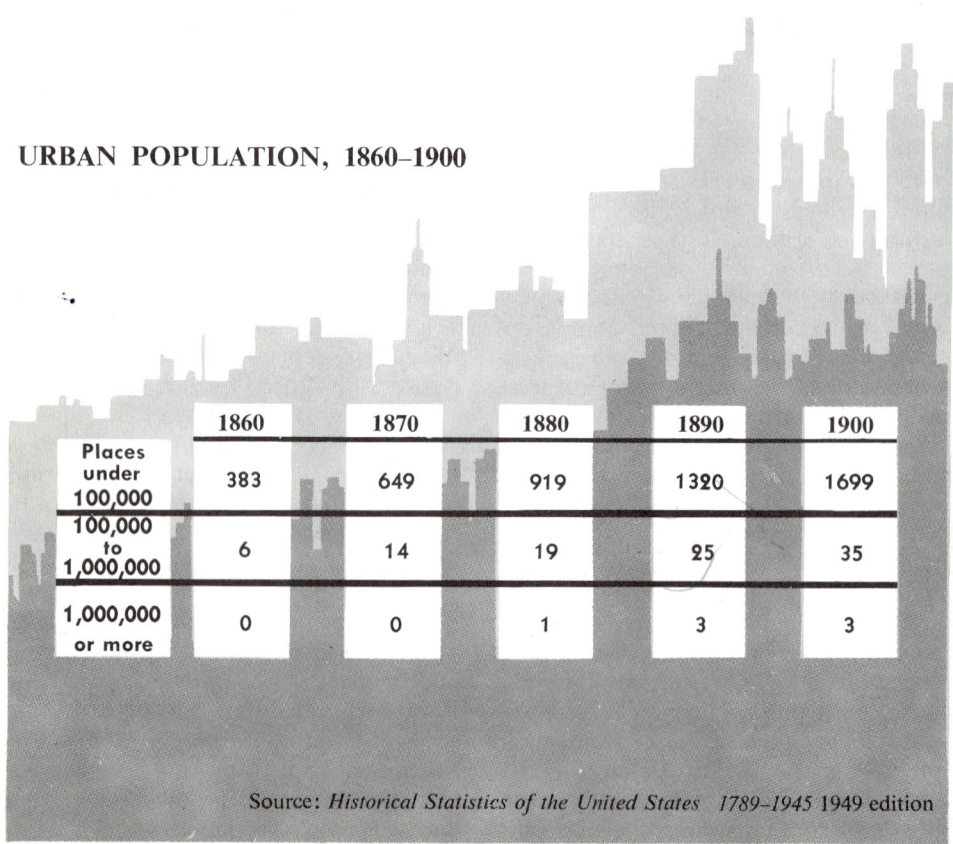

URBAN POPULATION, 1860–1900

	1860	1870	1880	1890	1900
Places under 100,000	383	649	919	1320	1699
100,000 to 1,000,000	6	14	19	25	35
1,000,000 or more	0	0	1	3	3

Source: *Historical Statistics of the United States 1789–1945* 1949 edition

428

Industrialization Brings Benefits as Well as Problems

By 1900 the United States had become the world's leading industrial nation. It was in the midst of an economic revolution marked by the growing use of machines, large-scale production, and the consolidation of business. This revolution was transforming American life.

Industrialization creates problems.

One of the most obvious effects of industrial growth was the concentration of population in cities, with many people living in slums. Industrialization also made for widespread insecurity. The wage earner had no land and was dependent for a livelihood on conditions beyond his control. Unable to save from his meager wages, he was haunted by fear of unemployment. This was no imaginary fear, for the business cycle, with its alternating periods of prosperity and depression, was becoming more pronounced.

Industrialization centered vast wealth in the hands of a few men. What is more important, it gave these men power over millions of workers and consumers. They could use their power to keep wages down and prices up, to crush attempts of labor to organize, and to dictate to state legislatures and even to Congress itself. Even those who showed great generosity in disposing of their fortunes were usually against laws to improve working and living conditions. Such laws, they argued, interfered with free enterprise.

Large-scale business meant a loss of close personal contact between worker and employer. Millions no longer worked for themselves or for someone they knew, but for a large corporation. The directors and officials of the corporation were not likely to know the employees or how they lived. The owners of the corporation—its stockholders—had even less knowledge of the men and women who worked for it.

Industrialization produces benefits.

Industrialization had good effects as well as bad. It added enormously to the nation's wealth and income. It used machines and power to lessen human drudgery. It was reducing the length of the work day, giving the worker more leisure time. It made travel and communication easier and cheaper than ever before. It made more goods available at lower cost, bringing a wide variety of comforts within reach of the average family. Andrew Carnegie called this "triumphant democracy."

★ ★ ★ ★ ★

FOR IDENTIFICATION

Alexander Graham Bell	J. P. Morgan
	John D. Rockefeller
Andrew Carnegie	Commodore Cornelius
Cyrus Field	Vanderbilt
Marshall Field	F. W. Woolworth

FOR EXPLANATION OR DEFINITION

coolies	merger
dividends	monopoly
franchise	Morrill Tariff Act
"gospel of wealth"	National Banking Act
holding company	stock
Homestead Act	time zones
limited liability	trust

FOR REVIEW

1. (a) State four economic "planks" in the Republican platform of 1860. (b) How did the Republican party carry out its promises?

2. Explain the operation of the Homestead Act.

3. (a) What were the reasons for the National Banking Act of 1863? (b) How did Congress stop the issuance of notes by state banks?

4. How did the War between North and South affect: (a) transportation; (b) the slaughtering industry; (c) the clothing and shoe industry; (d) the farm machinery

industry; (e) the iron and steel industry; (f) the mining industry?

5. Why was there little serious unemployment after the War between North and South?

6. State the reasons for America's great industrial growth in the period 1865–1900.

7. What were the chief sources of labor and of capital in the period 1865–1900?

8. What industries developed in the South in the period 1865–1900?

9. (a) Tell the story of the building of the first transcontinental railroad. (b) How did the federal, state, and local governments help in the building of transcontinental railroads?

10. How did Commodore Vanderbilt organize the New York Central?

11. List improvements made in railroad service in the period 1865–1900.

12. How did the invention of the telegraph and the telephone aid in the growth of business enterprise?

13. What improvements were made in printing and papermaking?

14. How did the development of a nationwide market affect small-scale manufacturing?

15. What changes took place in the method of distribution from 1865 to 1900?

16. Define a partnership; a corporation.

17. How does a corporation obtain its charter? What are the advantages of the corporate form of organization?

18. Why did competing corporations tend to combine? Explain the term "pool."

19. What was the meaning of the term "trust" in the 1880's and 1890's? What is the meaning of the term today?

20. (a) List a few economic advantages that may result from large-scale business consolidations. (b) What are some of the evils which may result?

21. Tell the story of the development of the oil industry. How did John D. Rockefeller obtain control of the industry?

22. (a) How did Andrew Carnegie become one of the leaders in the steel industry? (b) Tell the story of the organization of the United States Steel Corporation. (c) How did Carnegie use his wealth?

23. Summarize the benefits and problems resulting from industrialization.

FOR FURTHER STUDY AND DISCUSSION

1. How are each of the following related to the industrial growth of the United States: natural resources, transportation, inventions, corporations, the growth of cities? Helpful source: Faulkner, *American Economic History*, pp. 407–429.

2. (a) Why does modern business prefer the corporation to other forms of organization? (b) How did corporations try to avoid the evils of cutthroat competition? (c) Explain the difference between the pool, the trust, and the holding company. Helpful source: Faulkner, *American Economic History*, pp. 431–440.

3. (a) Explain what is meant by a rebate. (b) Why did railroads grant rebates to the Standard Oil Company? (c) Why was the granting of rebates regarded as an evil? Helpful source. Faulkner, *American Economic History*, pp. 440–443.

FOR INDIVIDUAL OR GROUP ACTIVITIES

1. (a) Trace on an outline map the routes of the main transcontinental railroads. (b) Prepare a chart indicating the railroad mileage by decades, 1830–1900. Helpful source: Lord, *Historical Atlas*, p. 208. (c) Exhibit pictures to illustrate improvements in railroad operation and travel.

2. Prepare book reports on Howells, *The Rise of Silas Lapham;* Norris, *The Pit* and *The Octopus;* and Ford, *The Honorable Peter Sterling.*

3. Report on the chapter "The Foundations of the Modern Era" in Schlesinger, *New Viewpoints in American History.*

4. Prepare biographical sketches of the following: Alexander Graham Bell, Andrew Carnegie, Jay Cooke, James B. Duke, Thomas A. Edison, Cyrus W. Field, Marshall Field, Edward H. Harriman, James J. Hill, Cyrus H. McCormick, J. Pierpont Morgan, John D. Rockefeller, Leland Stanford, Cornelius Vanderbilt, George Westinghouse.

One example of modern American industrial growth is shown in this picture of the Baton Rouge oil refinery (Standard Oil Company [New Jersey]), Baton Rouge, Louisiana. What has made such growth possible at this particular location? Consider the accessibility of oil resources, the possibilities for transportation, and the type of business organization.

A great city is that which has the greatest men and women.——Walt Whitman

26. URBANIZATION CHANGES WAYS OF LIVING AND THINKING

More People Live in Cities

The expansion of manufacturing and trade led to a remarkable growth of cities. In 1860 only 1 American in 6 lived in a place having 10,000 or more people, but by 1900, 1 in 3 did so. At the same time the number living in large cities was climbing. By 1900 the United States had 77 cities with 50,000 or more people. The growth of cities is called *urbanization*. It accompanied the Industrial Revolution.

How the cities got their people.

The cities drew many of their people from the farms. It became the custom for most of the farmers' sons and daughters to go to the city to earn their living. If a farmer had poor land, all his boys and girls were likely to leave home for the city. In this period thousands of farms in the Northeast were given up. Soon nothing remained of them but cellar holes surrounded by clumps of lilacs, tumble-down buildings, scrubby orchards, and pastures growing up into forest. In some hilly parts of New England whole villages were gradually abandoned.

The cities also attracted millions of immigrants from Europe. Between 1860 and 1900 nearly 15,000,000 foreigners

came to the United States, most of them settling in factory and mining towns in the Northeast. At the end of the century about 14 per cent of the total population was foreign-born. In a few of the largest cities the proportion was 50 per cent or more.

Cities Improve Their Facilities

Cities pave their streets.

In the 1880's the streets of our large cities were either badly paved or not paved at all. Cobblestones and granite blocks were the favorite paving materials in the East, while wood blocks were popular in the Midwest. Streets so constructed soon became rough and uneven. Toward the end of the century brick, asphalt, and macadam pavements began to replace the cobblestones. Many years passed before even the large cities thought it necessary to pave all their streets. Smaller cities did not pave their streets until well into the present century.

Fine bridges are built.

Since most large cities are intersected by waterways, either ferries, bridges, or tunnels are necessary. The

Broadway, New York City, in the 1860's, with THE ELEVATED RAILWAY *invented by John Randel, Jr.*

John Roebling's BROOKLYN BRIDGE

art of bridge building made giant strides after 1865. The steel arch bridge across the Mississippi at St. Louis, opened in 1874, is a monument to the genius of James B. Eads, first engineer in the American Hall of Fame. In building the foundations Eads used construction methods never before attempted. Brooklyn Bridge, opened in 1883, is a monument to another great engineer. It was erected by John Roebling, a German-American. The longest suspension bridge ever built up to that time, it is a structure of remarkable beauty. Eads and Roebling solved many problems of bridge design and construction. As a result their successors were able to put up bridges under even more difficult conditions.

Electric street railways flourish.

In the 1850's and 1860's horse-drawn streetcars became a familiar sight in the larger cities. A faster means of transportation was needed. For many years inventors had been trying to develop an electric railway. The electric motor had been designed, but was little used because of the high cost of battery-produced current. Electric railways became feasible when Charles Brush, a young Ohio engineer, made a practical dynamo, or generator (1876). The dynamo produced current far more cheaply than could batteries.

A number of short electric trolley lines were built in the 1880's and by 1890 nearly eight hundred companies were in the business. Horse-drawn cars soon disappeared from most cities. Trolley lines were quickly extended into areas where horsecars had never reached. Because the trolleys enabled people to live farther away from their work, the population of the suburbs climbed.

Elevated lines and subways are built.

The first elevated railway was opened in New York City in 1867. "Els" were built in Brooklyn and Kansas City in the 1880's. Chicago's "el" was opened in 1893. The first elevated trains were drawn by small steam locomotives, which scattered cinders and ashes on people in the streets below. Boston's "el," opened in 1901, was the first on this side of the Atlantic to be operated by electricity.

In the middle 1890's the city of Boston built a subway. The city of New York opened its first subway in 1904. Subways eventually replaced most of the elevated lines.

Street lighting is improved.

In 1879 Charles Brush lighted the public squares of Cleveland with arc lights. Arc lights were much brighter than gas or oil lamps, and the Brush system quickly spread. Arc lights made city streets safer and pleasanter and encouraged people to go about after dark.

Fire protection is strengthened.

Until late in the century fire was a constant worry to city dwellers, since they realized it could easily spread over most of a city. In 1871 a large part of Chicago was destroyed by fire. A year later Boston had a bad fire. After these disasters all our city governments gave more thought to fire prevention. They passed laws requiring builders to use fire-resistant materials and more careful methods of building. Strict rules were drawn up for electric wiring. Fire-fighting methods were improved by adopting the fire alarm signal box, the water tower, the fireboat, and the

chemical engine. Most cities that still had volunteer fire departments now hired full-time firemen instead.

Waste removal is difficult.

In 1879 a noted engineer said that proper sewage disposal was "the great unanswered question of the day." At that time nearly all cities had open sewers, which caused foul odors and spread disease. Only the largest cities had underground sewers. Sewers emptied into nearby lakes, rivers, and harbors. Open sewers have now almost disappeared, but the emptying of sewage into nearby bodies of water is still a common practice.

In large cities on the coast, garbage was carried in scows and barges a few miles out to sea and emptied on an outgoing tide. Other cities arranged with farmers to collect it for feeding swine. To get rid of nearby piggeries and to avoid the spread of a dangerous parasite, trichina, which is often present in garbage-fed swine, some cities put up furnaces to burn garbage.

Attention is given to pure water.

City dwellers once got water from wells in their back yards, but by the mid-1800's, the larger cities had water mains serving the majority of their people. At first little attention was given to making the water supply safe. Often the water was piped from a lake or river into which sewage was poured. Typhoid fever and other diseases carried by dirty water caused much loss of life. Many a city learned the importance of pure water only after suffering a terrible epidemic. Toward the end of the century cities began to filter or chlorinate their water supply to purify it.

City governments take on new duties.

The improvements we have been discussing, except those in transportation lines, were made by city governments. This points to an important

PER CENT OF PEOPLE LIVING IN ———

year	FARM AND COUNTRY	PLACES OF 10,000 OR MORE
1790	97%	3%
1860	85	15
1900	68	32
1920	58	42
1940	52	48
1950	46	54

Source: *Statistical Abstract*, 1958

434

trend: the *increasing responsibilities* of city governments. Cities had to assume many tasks which in the country or the village were left to individuals, such as providing water, street lighting, waste disposal, and police and fire protection. *Laissez faire,* the idea that the government should interfere as little as possible, was giving way to the idea that the government must take action to advance the public welfare.

Many City Dwellers Enjoy New Comforts and Leisure

New comforts and conveniences appear.

During the last third of the century, the homes of the more prosperous city dwellers became more comfortable and convenient than ever before. Years later these new comforts and conveniences spread to people living in the country. In time almost everyone, even the poor, would have some of them.

1. Lighting. In the 1860's and 1870's kerosene lamps were widely used. In the larger cities prosperous families were installing gas lights. When Edison produced a successful electric incandescent lamp (1879), the electric lighting of homes began. By the end of the century most people in large cities had either gas or electricity.

2. Heating. In the sixties, the ordinary home was heated by stoves, while the more prosperous had hot-air furnaces. Radiators, heated by steam or hot water, were introduced in the seventies, mostly in office and apartment buildings. By 1900 many middle-class homes had some sort of central heating.

3. Telephones. When first shown at the Philadelphia Exposition in 1876, the telephone was considered a toy. Businessmen soon realized its value, however. At first telephones were used only in stores and offices, but by 1900 they were found in many homes.

Women have more leisure.

Factories gradually took over much of the work once done in the home. City housewives no longer did any spinning or weaving. While they still did a great deal of sewing, they now had the help of the sewing machine. City women let the canning factories do most of their canning and let the bakeries and biscuit factories do part of their baking. By this date commercial laundries were fairly common; they served families who could afford to send the washing out.

Middle-class city women began to have considerable time for their own enjoyment. Many used their leisure in church work, others in women's clubs of various kinds. By 1890 there were so many women's clubs that a national organization—the General Federation of Women's Clubs—was formed to link them together. Club work helped train women to take a more active part in public affairs. This in turn led many to feel that women should have the right to vote.

The amusement business expands.

City people had more time for recreation than farm people. For those with money to spend, a great variety of amusements was available. The amusement business—which is now one of our biggest industries—began to grow rapidly soon after the War between North and South.

Many new theaters were opened. Almost every fair-sized city had a stock company which remained at the same theater, giving a long series of different plays. Also about two hundred road companies traveled from place to place. The blackface minstrel show was so well liked that in the early 1880's there were thirty or more traveling minstrel companies. In the 1890's the variety, or vaudeville, show, with its succession of songs, dances, acrobatic stunts, trained-animal acts, and the like, became very

435

popular. Musical plays and operettas also drew large audiences.

Circuses gained favor in this period, mainly because of new features introduced by the famous American showman, P. T. Barnum. As part of his show he brought together freaks and curiosities—giants, dwarfs, and strange animals from the ends of the earth. He was the first to conduct circus performances in two rings, and the first to transport his show by rail instead of by wagon. His circus was so successful that other circus men copied his ideas. In the 1890's about forty or more different circuses were touring the United States.

The Cincinnati Red Stockings, 1869

The amusement park was popular for holiday outings. Most such parks were sponsored by trolley car companies. The attractions might include a lake for boating and bathing, picnic grounds, swings, a deer park, theater, dance hall, roller coaster, merry-go-round, and the like.

During these same postwar years, commercialized sport grew into an important business. Baseball was the first sport to draw great throngs of spectators. A professional ball club was organized in Cincinnati in 1869. Soon after, professional baseball spread over the nation. Horse racing, prize fighting, and football also attracted large numbers of spectators.

"The Velocipede," from a lithograph published in 1869

Bicycling becomes a fad.

Bicycling was a popular sport for men as early as 1880, when the League of American Wheelmen was formed. Ladies rode on tricycles, which were much steadier and safer than the high-wheeled bicycle then in use. When the modern "safety-type" bicycle was introduced from England about 1890, the sport really came into its own. By 1893 a million bicycles were in use. Many people went to and from work on wheels. Others used their bicycles for pleasure trips into the country. There

436

were thousands of bicycle clubs. Members often got together on Sunday for a hundred-mile run. Few cyclists could have guessed that the noisy "horseless carriages," which passed them now and then, would soon cause bicycles to go out of fashion.

Secret societies attract millions.

Secret fraternal orders grew tremendously in the last third of the century. A few, such as the Masons and the Independent Order of Oddfellows, came here from England. The Masons influenced many similar organizations. Among the well-known societies which started here are the Knights of Pythias, the Elks, the Moose, the Red Men, and the Knights of Columbus.

Fraternal orders promote good-fellowship among their members and may provide sickness and death benefits. Some maintain orphanages, homes for the aged, and hospitals—chiefly for members and their dependents. In addition, such orders have done much charitable and educational work. They reached the peak of their popularity in the 1920's. Since then they have been weakened by the movies, the automobile, the radio, and television.

Urbanization Brings Problems

Extremes of wealth and poverty exist.

The number of wealthy persons grew with the rise of big business. In 1860 there were probably only three millionaires in the country. By the end of the century there were at least 3800. The country's wealth was multiplying and it was passing into the control of a small number of people. In 1900, according to one estimate, 10 per cent of the population owned 90 per cent of the nation's wealth. Another estimate tells us that 1 per cent of the people owned over 50 per cent of the wealth. These figures show that the nation had changed since 1831, when a French observer, Alexis de Tocqueville, said that nothing he found here struck him "more forcibly than the general equality of conditions among the people."

The new rich parade their wealth.

Many Americans, especially the newly rich, liked to spend money in showy ways, in what social scientists call "conspicuous consumption." They built mansions in the most fashionable parts of the big cities and in resorts such as Newport (R. I.) and Bar Harbor (Me.). They filled their houses with costly furnishings and with antiques and works of art collected for them in Europe and Asia. They gave lavish parties, which were reported in the society pages of the newspapers. The public liked to read of their doings and to follow the same living patterns whenever they could.

The city poor live in slums.

A few blocks from the "Gold Coast" of any large city were slums. Here the poor lived in crowded, unsanitary tenements. In this period a typical tenement building in New York was five or six stories high. Except for a ten-foot-square back yard the building covered the entire lot. Many of the rooms had no windows or windows that opened on a sunless, ill-smelling airshaft. All the families on a floor shared one cold-water faucet and one water closet. Several families might live in a single flat. Most slum dwellers were unskilled laborers, working for low wages. Many were recent immigrants who came without money or education. Others were chronically sick or disabled.

Diseases spread quickly in the slums because of crowding, filth, and the presence of rats, flies, and other vermin. The death rate in the tenement section of New York City was over three times that of the city as a whole. While many upper- and middle-class people felt that slum dwellers

AMERICAN AMUSEMENTS *of the late 19th century were many and varied, simple and complex. The quiet picnic under the trees on a hot summer day in New England is shown in the painting "A Pic Nick" by Jerome P. Thompson* (right). *The thrilling circus that moved from one section of the country to another is shown in the painting "Bareback Riders" by W. H. Brown* (lower right). *The vast playground for New York City's masses of people—Coney Island—offered everything from a dip in the Atlantic to "A Trip to the Moon." The painting* (below) *of Steeplechase Park by Leo McKay gives some idea of the variety of attractions that drew people of all ages for a holiday at Coney.*

were to blame for their poverty, all agreed that the slums should be cleaned up. A few of the largest cities passed tenement-house laws requiring landlords to make their buildings fit to live in. These laws were poorly enforced. The idea that a property owner had the right to do as he pleased with his own property was so strong that it stood in the way of enforcement.

The liquor problem is attacked.

The saloon was a sort of poor man's club, and slum neighborhoods had more saloons than the better neighborhoods. Drunkenness was so widespread among the poor that many reformers thought it the biggest obstacle in the fight against poverty. Indeed, to the average citizen the prevalence of hard drinking among the poor proved that their poverty was their own fault.

The temperance movement, which had lost ground during the conflict over slavery, was revived after the war. In 1869 the oldest of our third parties—the National Prohibition party—was organized. Five years later a group of religious women founded the Women's Christian Temperance Union. With a branch in almost every town, it soon became a real force in public affairs. The W.C.T.U. insisted that school children be taught the bad effects of alcohol. By the end of the century every state required instruction in temperance. In spite of these efforts the liquor business continued to flourish.

Reformers showed that liquor, vice, and crime were linked. Saloons often became hangouts for the worst elements in a community, who turned them into gambling dens and worse. Saloonkeepers paid the police for protection. The liquor business was, in fact, one of the main sources of corruption in city politics. The Antisaloon League of America, established in 1895, soon won the support of millions of thoughtful men and women. For many years it fought the saloon as the destroyer of the home and the ally of crime and corrupt politics.

Settlement houses help the poor.

Slums developed in every industrial country. Leading English writers and clergymen for some years had called attention to the appalling conditions among the poor people of London. Some of these reformers went to live among the poor to learn about their difficulties and to discover how best to help them. This was the beginning of the settlement house movement.

The first settlement house, Toynbee Hall, was opened in a London slum in 1884. The next year a settlement known as the Neighborhood Guild opened its doors in a New York slum. By the close of the century the United States had nearly a hundred settlement houses. Let us describe the best-known, Chicago's Hull House, as an example of all the rest.

Jane Addams founds Hull House.

If you were to list America's great women, you would probably give Jane Addams a place near the top. The daughter of a millowner in an Illinois town, she early took an interest in the lives of the millworkers. She decided while still in her teens to devote her life to helping the poor. After she graduated from college she worked for a time at Toynbee Hall. Then she came home and bought Hull House, a decaying mansion in the midst of a Chicago slum. She invited a number of college students and college instructors to live there with her. In return they gave part of their time to work with the poor people of the neighborhood.

The most desperate need seemed to be a daylong nursery for children whose mothers worked. Hull House provided one. It also offered a variety of recreational activities for young and old, another crying need in a slum area.

JANE ADDAMS

Clubs for all age groups were started. The settlement house made a special effort to combat the influence of the 250 saloons in the neighborhood. It offered the men a meeting place and a program of activities. Since most of the people in the area were foreign-born and eager to learn American ways, classes were given in such subjects as English, American history and government, hygiene, cookery, sewing, and child care. The house ran a penny savings bank and an employment bureau. The idea was to help the people to help themselves.

In time the residents of Hull House persuaded the city government to correct various evil conditions in the slums. Through their efforts, for example, more attention was given to cleaning the streets and alleys and to inspecting tenement houses. Also at their urging, the city provided some playgrounds and parks. Other reforms called for action by the state government. Hull House residents led in getting the state legislature to pass laws to prevent child labor and to improve working conditions.

Jane Addams directed Hull House for forty-six years until her death in 1935. Her influence was felt all over the United States and beyond its borders. Those who lived at Hull House gained a new understanding of the lives of industrial workers. Some of them have founded settlement houses in other cities. Many have worked for better laws and better law enforcement.

Help is given the sick poor.

Dispensaries where the poor could get medicine and medical advice could be found in a few cities before 1800. Sooner or later dispensaries were started in most cities. They were supported by contributions from the public.

Another service to the sick poor began in 1886, when visiting nurse associations were organized in Boston and Philadelphia. Trained nurses went to the homes of the needy sick, to tend the patient and to instruct members of the family in caring for him. This service proved so valuable that soon nursing associations were organized in other cities. Today visiting nurse services are no longer limited to the poor.

Hospitals are transformed.

Until about a century ago hospitals were places of terror where infection spread from one person to another. A patient was far safer at home. Only the destitute, or those with no one to tend them, went to a hospital. Many communities had no hospital except a "pesthouse"—a place where persons with dangerous diseases could be isolated.

Vital discoveries in the medical field were made during the 1860's and 1870's by Louis Pasteur and other European scientists. They proved that many diseases are caused by germs and that the spread of germs from one person to another can be controlled. In 1865 an English surgeon, Joseph Lister, showed that the infection of wounds could be prevented. These and other discoveries freed hospitals from their old dangers. They became places of recovery instead of short cuts to death. More hospitals

441

were built. Until the end of the century, however, few but the poor were cared for in hospitals.

Americans Enjoy Better Education

The common schools move forward.

The last third of the century saw great advances in public elementary education, particularly in the North. School buildings were improved. Except in one-room schools, pupils were now grouped by grade. The school year was lengthened. Teachers used less corporal punishment and made more effort to help pupils learn. Schoolbooks became more attractive. Maps, globes, and other teaching aids began to come into use. The curriculum was broadened in many places to include nature study, hygiene, drawing, and manual training. In some cities kindergartens were added to the public schools.

Public high schools develop rapidly.

At first many taxpayers felt it was wrong to use public funds to support a high school. A citizen of Kalamazoo, Michigan, brought suit to prevent the city from spending money for instruction beyond the elementary grades. The state supreme court ruled against the taxpayer (1872). Similar cases reached the supreme court in other states during the next ten years. The courts agreed that a community may tax itself for secondary education if it chooses.

The number of public high schools increased from about 300 in 1860 to nearly 5000 in 1900. At that time high schools still were found only in cities and large towns. Yet one in nine boys and girls between 14 and 17 years of age was enrolled in a public or a private school.

Some places provide free textbooks.

In 1885 the United States Commissioner of Education felt obliged to state publicly that the practice of providing free textbooks for pupils in the public schools is not "communistic." The plan had begun in New York City a few years before, and Massachusetts had just made it obligatory throughout the state. By the end of the century ten states in the North and West required local school boards to furnish free textbooks, while ten other states permitted them to do so. To supply texts free was an important forward step, since many families could not afford to buy the books for their children. School attendance went up as soon as free textbooks were available.

Rural education lags behind.

The thin population and lack of wealth delayed educational progress in rural areas. Many children lived out of reach of a school. Others attended irregularly or not at all, because their help was needed at home. The rural school usually kept open only three or four months in the year. It was ungraded, and often its teachers were poorly qualified. These facts help us

(*Above*) *DR. BENJAMIN RUSH, signer of the Declaration of Independence and father of American mental hygiene. Beginning in 1783 at the Pennsylvania Hospital, Dr. Rush initiated improvements in the treatment of the insane as well as instigated social reforms, advocating temperance and condemning capital punishment. His great-great grandson, DR. ALEXANDER RUSH (right) stands in the same amphitheater in which his famous ancestor once stood. The engraving (below) is a view of the House of Employment, the Alms House, and Pennsylvania Hospital in Philadelphia about 1767.*

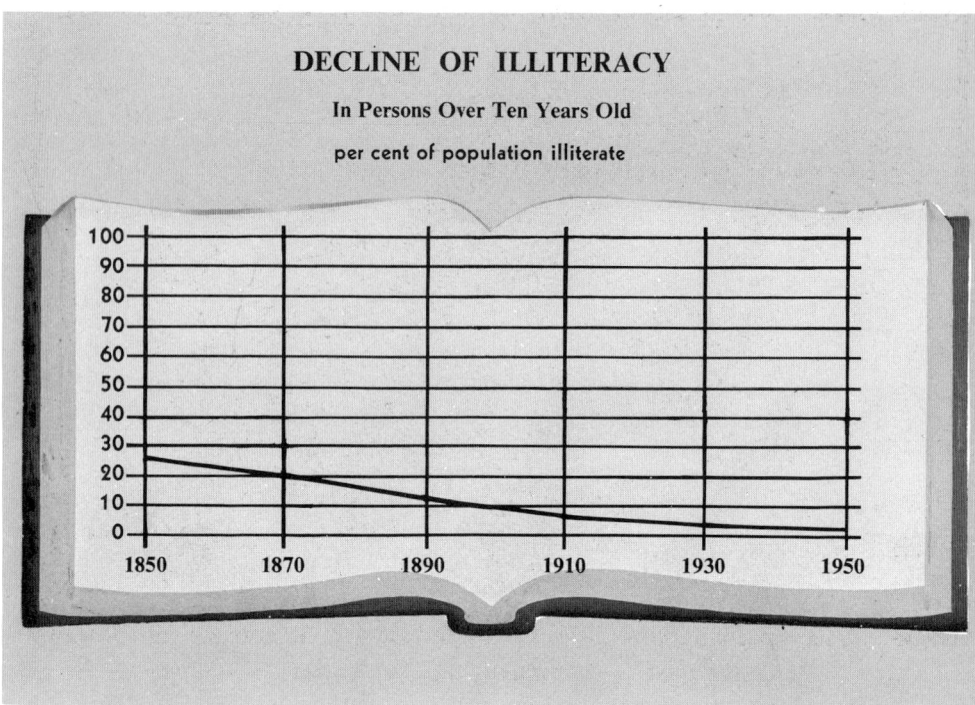

DECLINE OF ILLITERACY

In Persons Over Ten Years Old

per cent of population illiterate

| | 1850 | 1870 | 1890 | 1910 | 1930 | 1950 |

understand why many rural people of this period had little or no education.

The South struggles against obstacles.

The South was almost entirely rural. In addition it had handicaps that the North and West did not have: (1) The war had destroyed most wealth in the South. (2) The idea of public responsibility for education was not yet so fully accepted there as in other sections. Among upper-class Southerners the assertion might still be heard that "it is robbery to tax one man to educate another man's children." (3) The provision of separate schools for each race was costly, particularly where the population was thin. Many a rural district could hardly support one school, let alone two.

In spite of these handicaps, the South did make educational progress, especially in providing elementary schools. Gifts of Northern philanthropists helped. The largest gift before 1900 was made by George Peabody, who set up a fund of two million dollars to encourage public elementary education for both races. "This I give to the suffering South," he declared, "for the good of the whole country." The trustees used the income of the fund to train Southern teachers and improve Southern school buildings.

The freedmen seek education.

At the close of the War between North and South at least 90 per cent of the freedmen were completely illiterate —unable to read or write. They were eager for education. Many felt they could die happy if they could only learn to read the Bible. Northern churches sent hundreds of teachers to instruct the freedmen and provided money to build scores of schools. Every year, as more schools were opened for them, the number of Negro students grew. By 1900 the percentage of illiterate Negroes had been cut in two.

444

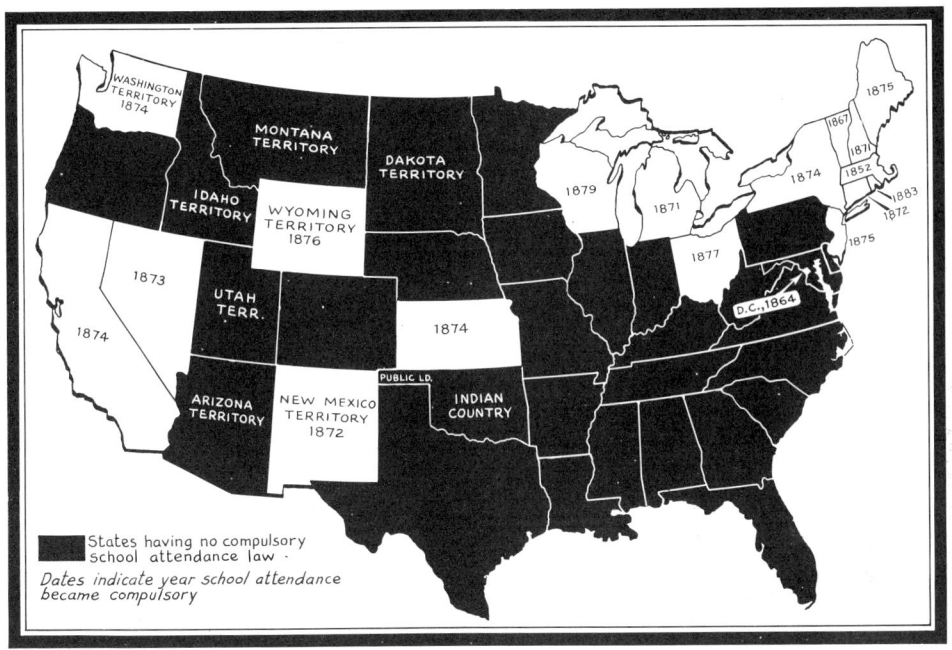

COMPULSORY SCHOOL ATTENDANCE, 1880

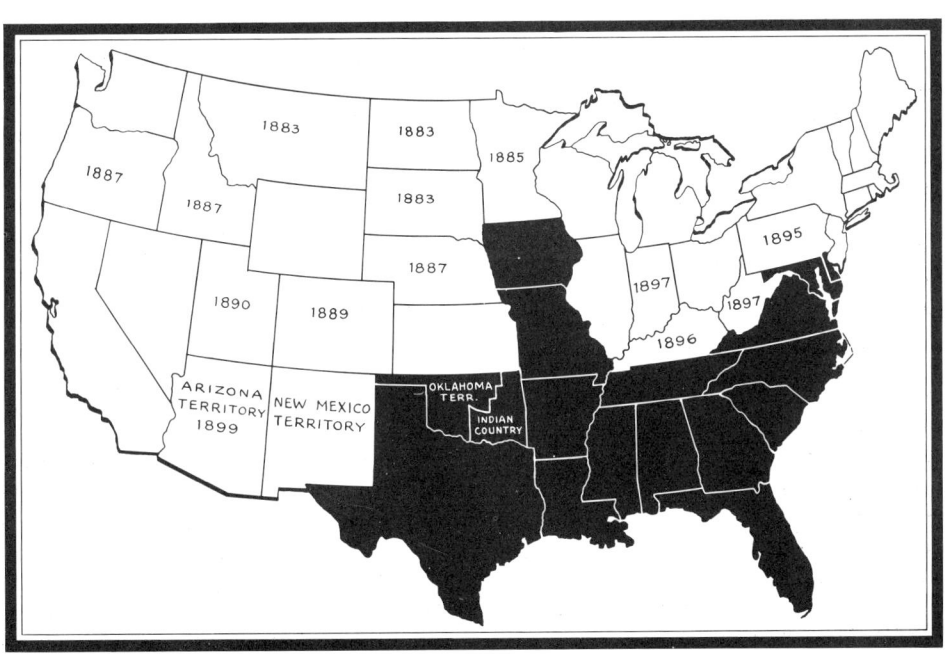

COMPULSORY SCHOOL ATTENDANCE, 1900

445

Negroes were not satisfied merely to learn the "3 R's." Slowly more advanced schools were provided. One of the first and still the best-known was Hampton (Virginia) Institute, which opened in 1868. Its founder, General Samuel Armstrong, had commanded Negro troops during the war and later served with the Freedmen's Bureau. Believing that the Negro race could rise through vocational education, he obtained money from the American Missionary Association to build the school. One of the first graduates of Hampton, Booker T. Washington, founded Tuskegee Institute in southern Alabama (1881). How this penniless young Negro, with the gifts of other poor Negroes and friendly white people, built a school and made it a great institution for the betterment of his race, is an inspiring story. You may read it in his autobiography, *Up from Slavery*.

More students attend college.

By 1900 we had almost five hundred colleges, twice as many as in 1860. What is more, the proportion of young people going to college had risen. As the new century began, 4 per cent of the population between 18 and 21 years old was in college.

The number of women students rose remarkably as more women's colleges were founded, and as a large number of colleges for men decided to admit women also. By 1900, 70 per cent of the colleges were *coeducational*—that is, they took both men and women students. Professional schools such as those for the study of medicine, law, and architecture, gradually opened their doors to women. By using these new opportunities, women were to gain more independence and also a greater voice in public affairs.

Congress encourages science education.

In 1862 Congress passed the Morrill Land-Grant College Act. It gave land to each state and territory to endow a college for the study of subjects related to agriculture and the mechanic arts. The act strengthened the existing state universities and led to the founding of many others. Even more important, it encouraged the colleges to pay more attention to science. Land-grant colleges soon developed strong departments in both pure and applied science. Their example was followed by other colleges which had formerly neglected science. As colleges trained more scientists, research in medicine and other fields expanded.

Free public libraries multiply.

Our country was the first in the world to establish free, tax-supported libraries. The same region that produced Horace Mann and the educational awakening (p. 309) produced the public library movement. It grew out of the same faith in democracy and the perfectibility of man. The movement was firmly launched by a Massachusetts law of 1851 permitting towns to establish public libraries. Shortly afterwards, the great Boston Public Library came into being. By the century's close, we had 6000 public libraries, counting only those with at least 300 books. Many public libraries began when generous individuals left their private libraries to the community or gave money for a library building. Andrew Carnegie provided buildings for over 2000 public libraries, but most of them were not erected until after 1900.

Literature and the Fine Arts Advance

Many new writers appear.

In the middle third of the century the literary center of the nation was New England. After 1870 New England's leadership was challenged by new writers from other sections. They helped Americans become aware of the size of their country and its variety.

Writers react to industrialization.

The writers of this period saw the swift rise of industry and the growth of cities. They felt the conflict between urban and rural ways of living. Yet each reacted to conditions in his own way. Some writers tried to preserve a picture of the pre-industrial civilization that was passing away. Some saw the gathering ills of an industrial civilization and tried to warn against them. Others turned their backs on the conditions they did not care to see and penned romances.

Local-color writers picture rural life.

Many writers in this era recorded the life and atmosphere of the section they knew best. Because of their concentration on a particular locality, they are known as "local-color" authors. We can mention only a few.

1. The Far West. Perhaps the most picturesque of the new sectional literature had to do with the Far West. Bret Harte wrote humorous and sentimental tales of the mining camps. Harte was a New Yorker who moved to California as a youth soon after the gold rush. He liked to show vagabonds as more admirable than conventional people. His best-known stories are "The Luck of Roaring Camp" and "The Outcasts of Poker Flat."

Joaquin Miller went to Oregon with his parents in a covered wagon. At seventeen he ran away from home and took up a wandering, adventurous life. His many volumes of poetry and prose reflect his experiences as a miner, Indian fighter, pony-express rider, and frontier lawyer. *Pacific Poems* and *Songs of the Sierras* are his most popular works.

Helen Hunt Jackson wrote stories of the old Spanish missions in California and of Indian life. Her most famous

SAMUEL L. CLEMENS *as he was at 18 before he left Hannibal, Missouri to start his life of adventure and later when he became known as* MARK TWAIN.

EDWARD BELLAMY'S *idea of Utopia appealed to the optimistic spirit of nineteenth century America.*

HENRY *and* WILLIAM JAMES, *one a novelist, the other a philosopher, increased the intellectual stature of nineteenth century America.*

work, *Ramona* (1884), is a tragic novel whose theme is the white man's unjust treatment of the Indian.

2. *The South.* No section had so many local-color writers as the South. Thomas Nelson Page is one of a host of postwar authors who wrote romantically of plantation life in the days of slavery. Many of his stories are in Negro dialect. George W. Cable wrote sketches of Creole life in old New Orleans. Mary N. Murfree has preserved for us the life of the people of the Tennessee mountains. James L. Allen wrote novels and short stories with a Kentucky background.

Joel Chandler Harris is the member of this group who is most certain of lasting fame. When his first volume of Uncle Remus tales was published in 1880, he at once gained a wide audience. These animal legends, which Harris put together from stories told him by plantation Negroes, are full of wisdom, fun, and pathos. Br'er Rabbit, who always manages to outwit Br'er Fox and Br'er Wolf, is loved by millions of readers here and abroad.

3. *New England.* Louisa May Alcott's novels give us a warm and tender picture of family life in a small Massachusetts village. *Little Women*, which appeared in 1869, still sells well the world over. It was followed by *Little Men, An Old-Fashioned Girl, Eight Cousins*, and *Rose in Bloom*. These stories were immensely popular for over half a century.

Sarah Orne Jewett wrote of a lovely and serene life in Maine. *The Country of the Pointed Firs* (1896) is one of her best works. Mary Wilkins Freeman is known for character studies of rural New Englanders. Her collections of short stories entitled *A Humble Romance* (1887) and *A New England Nun* (1891) are outstanding.

4. *The Midwest.* The greatest of the local-color writers was Samuel L. Clemens (Mark Twain). He spent his boyhood in Missouri, in surroundings which he later immortalized in *The Adventures of Tom Sawyer* (1876), *The Adventures of Huckleberry Finn* (1885), and *Life on the Mississippi* (1883). In addition to works of local color, Clemens wrote travel books, such as *Innocents Abroad;* historical novels, such as *The Prince and the Pauper* and *A Connecticut Yankee at King Arthur's Court;* and the idealistic study, *Personal Recollections of Joan of Arc.* A satirical novel, *The Gilded Age* (1873), which he wrote with Charles Dudley Warner, deals with political corruption and loose business morals in the days of President Grant. It reveals Clemens as a severe critic of unfair business practices and social injustice.

Howells leads in realistic fiction.

Realism is an effort to depict life as it is, without prejudice or glamor. William Dean Howells, through his writings and his influence as editor of the *Atlantic Monthly* (1871–81), became the leader of the realistic school of fiction in this country. Born in Ohio, as a young man he went to live in the East. He was deeply interested in the social, economic, and ethical problems of his time. In more than fifty books he described the life and character of middle-class Americans. In *The Rise of Silas Lapham* (1885), he tells of a self-made millionaire, country-bred and honest, whose family tried to enter the aristocratic society of Boston.

Another realist, Henry James, went to England to live. His novels are profound psychological studies of the American upper middle class. His portrayal of American women shows that he admired their mental ability and independence.

A realist who dealt with the hardships of farm life was Hamlin Garland. As a boy he experienced the drudgery and loneliness of pioneer living. In 1891 he published the first of a series of harsh sketches of Midwestern farm life, *Main-Travelled Roads.*

Social critics win attention.

Toward the end of the century many writers expressed their concern over the evils that industrialism had brought in its train. One of these was the economist, Henry George, who tried to explain why poverty was increasing at a time when the nation was growing richer. George thought the cause was the private ownership of land (including natural resources, such as timber, water power, and minerals). As a remedy he urged that all taxes be removed from labor and the products of labor, and that all the revenues needed to operate our government be obtained from taxes on land. This proposal became known as the "single tax." George's book, *Progress and Poverty* (1879), went through more than a hundred editions.

Between 1880 and 1900 over forty American authors wrote books describing an ideal society or Utopia. The most widely read was Edward Bellamy's *Looking Backward, 2000–1887.* The hero wakes up in the year 2000 in the city where he had lived in 1887. The city has become far more healthful, beautiful, and comfortable. Poverty, ignorance, and crime have disappeared. All business is owned by the city, yet the government is completely democratic. Each citizen is free to choose his own occupation. In order to obtain plenty of volunteers for the harder and less interesting jobs, wages and hours are adjusted until these jobs become as attractive as any others.

The society pictured by Bellamy appealed to many Americans. They formed hundreds of clubs to work for "Nationalism," as Bellamy's system was called. His followers even started a short-lived Nationalistic party.

Most of the other Utopias described in this period resembled Bellamy's in broad outline. It is interesting to note that the authors of these books did not consider themselves to be radicals. Rather they had an unlimited faith in the power of democratic government to cure all evils. Today we are more aware of the difficulties in creating an ideal society. Also, we do not think that abolishing private enterprise would bring us nearer to Utopia.

Interest in the fine arts grows.

As wealth accumulated, the fine arts received more attention. In 1865 the United States had almost no public art galleries. Five years later, through the generosity of wealthy art lovers, three large galleries had been founded —the Corcoran Gallery in Washington, the Metropolitan Museum of Art in New York, and the Museum of Fine Arts in Boston. Within a few more years art galleries were opened in Chicago, St. Louis, Detroit, Milwaukee, Minneapolis, Cincinnati, and other cities. Another sign of the growing interest in art was the opening of art schools. At the same time, too, more Americans were going abroad to study art.

American painters win fame.

In the closing years of the nineteenth century a number of American painters were doing outstanding work.

George Inness is regarded by many as the greatest of American landscape painters. He had marked skill in rendering light. Another American painter who received international applause was James M. Whistler. He declared that what matters in painting is not the subject but the way it is translated into color and form. One of his most famous paintings is the portrait of his mother, which he exhibited in 1871 under the title "Arrangement in Gray and Black."

Winslow Homer loved to paint landscapes and scenes of life along the Maine coast and in Florida and the Bahamas. His canvases and water colors

"THE AGNEW CLINIC" *by* THOMAS EAKINS. *Dr. D. Hayes Agnew was one of the greatest surgeons and anatomists of his time (1818–1892). He was professor of surgery for many years at the University of Pennsylvania. Eakins, commissioned by Agnew's students to do this portrait of the great doctor, painted his largest and most ambitious work.*

"SNAP THE WHIP" *by* WINSLOW HOMER. *At one time Henry James described Homer as "almost barbarously simple." In speaking of himself as an artist Homer said, "When I have selected the thing carefully, I paint it exactly as it appears."*

are hung in leading museums throughout the United States.

Albert P. Ryder lived completely in the world of his imagination. He never painted the actual but used nature's themes—clouds, trees, ocean, the moon—in shadowy fantasies that express his feelings. His work evokes a lonely and poetic mood.

Thomas Eakins made pictures of people—doctors, athletes, singers, actresses, businessmen, and humble workers. He painted exactly what he saw. Neglected in his lifetime, he is now considered to be one of the greatest American artists.

Good and poor sculpture is produced.

After the War between North and South most communities put up monuments to honor their soldier dead. Usually the monument consisted of warriors on horseback or on foot. Some of this statuary had little artistic merit, but some excellent work did appear.

Perhaps the foremost American sculptor was Augustus Saint-Gaudens (1848–1907). Irish-born and European-trained, he loved his adopted country and was able to express its ideals. His statues of Farragut and Sherman in New York and of Lincoln in Chicago set new artistic standards for public monuments. His memorial for Mrs. Henry Adams in Rock Creek Cemetery, Washington, "The Peace of God," is considered by some critics to be the greatest sculpture America has yet produced. Daniel Chester French (1850–1931) is another American sculptor who created many important monuments. He is best known for the heroic marble statue of Lincoln in the Lincoln Memorial at Washington.

Architecture worsens, then improves.

By 1850 the classical style of architecture had gone out of fashion. More elaborate styles came in. Buildings were decorated with turrets, pinnacles, gables, and all sorts of ornamental gewgaws. Even business structures, such as railroad stations and stores, were often decorated without regard for their purpose.

Louis H. Sullivan, who began his work as an architect in Chicago in the 1870's, insisted that "form follows function." He meant that the form of a building should be determined by its use. He had no patience with false fronts and meaningless decoration. He showed what he meant when he designed business structures, such as the Wainwright Building in St. Louis and the Transportation Building at the Chicago's World Fair of 1893. His ideas had world-wide influence, especially in the design of buildings for business and public uses.

Americans led the way in developing the "skyscraper." It was made possible by new building materials, such as steel girders, concrete, and plate glass, as well as by the invention of the elevator. The first skyscraper, built in Chicago in 1884, had only ten stories. A twenty-nine-story structure was erected in New York in 1898. At the time, this was considered an amazing achievement.

Chicago World's Fair inspires city planning.

In 1893 a World's Fair was held in Chicago to celebrate the four hundredth anniversary of the discovery of America. The planning committee engaged the services of America's most noted landscape architect, Frederick L. Olmstead, designer of New York City's splendid Central Park. The nation's leading architects, sculptors, painters, and engineers were also called to help. They designed and built a spacious White City on the shore of Lake Michigan.

Millions of Americans visited the fair. Probably all who saw it went home with the desire to improve their surroundings. In any event, the fair inspired city officials to plan ahead, so that their communities could be made beautiful with boulevards, parks, lakes, and wooded stretches. Although these plans were to take a long time to fulfill, they promised a new day for Americans living in cities. The time was coming when cities would be designed for the health, safety, and enjoyment of all their people, when the slums would be torn down, when healthful and attractive housing would be recognized as a basic human need. Nineteenth-century Americans who wrote about Utopia, like their millions of readers, dreamed of such cities. Today we are on the way to achieving them.

A nineteenth century traffic problem

FOR IDENTIFICATION

Jane Addams	William Dean Howells
Louisa May Alcott	George Inness
Edward Bellamy	Henry James
Charles Brush	John Roebling
Samuel L. Clemens	Augustus Saint-
Joel Chandler Harris	Gaudens
Bret Harte	Booker T. Washington
Winslow Homer	James M. Whistler

FOR EXPLANATION OR DEFINITION

Antisaloon League	slums
fraternal orders	temperance movement
"Gilded Age"	tenements
Hampton Institute	Tuskegee Institute
land-grant colleges	urbanization

FOR REVIEW

1. (a) Why did cities grow in number and size in the period 1865–1900? (b) What were the chief sources of the city population?

2. How was transportation within the city improved during the 1880's and 1890's?

3. Describe conditions in the average city in the 1880's in regard to: (a) transportation facilities; (b) street lighting; (c) sewage disposal; (d) water supply; (e) fire protection.

4. (a) What improvements were made in the lighting and heating of homes in the 1880's and 1890's? (b) What improvements were made in plumbing facilities?

5. How was the work of the city housewife made easier?

6. Account for the growth of women's clubs in the period 1865–1900.

7. (a) What important changes in the amusement business developed with the growth of cities in the period 1865–1900? (b) What contribution did P. T. Barnum make to the amusement industry?

8. Describe the bicycle fad of the period.

9. Account for the growth of fraternal orders. What social work did they perform? Name several of these orders.

10. Explain the term "conspicuous consumption." What are some evidences of "conspicuous consumption" in the 1890's?

11. Explain the terms "slum" and "tenement." Why did New York City find it necessary to pass a tenement-house law?

12. Account for the organization of the National Prohibition party, 1869; the Women's Christian Temperance Union, 1874; and the Antisaloon League, 1895.

13. (a) Describe the work of Jane Addams at Hull House. (b) Why did settlement houses increase in number and influence?

14. (a) What social services were developed for the sick poor? (b) How were hospitals made safer?

15. (a) What important advances were made in public education in the period

453

1865–1900? (b) Why did rural areas lag behind the cities in the improvement of educational facilities? (c) What special difficulties faced the South? What educational progress was made there?

16. Why is the Morrill Land-Grant College Act of 1862 sometimes referred to as one of the most important educational laws ever passed?

17. (a) Explain how the literature of the period 1865–1900 reflected social changes. (b) Name six writers of this period whose literary fame still endures. (c) What is meant by "local-color" writers?

18. What did Henry George regard as the basic cause of poverty? What remedy did he propose?

19. What were the signs of growing interest in the fine arts? Tell something of the work of leading painters and sculptors of the period.

20. What was the great contribution of Louis H. Sullivan to architecture?

21. What were some of the long-range effects of the Chicago World's Fair, 1893?

FOR FURTHER STUDY AND DISCUSSION

1. How did the growth of cities affect the lives of each of the following groups: the well to do, the middle class, the poor?

2. What new responsibilities were city governments forced to assume as cities grew in size?

3. How did the growth of cities influence elementary, secondary, and college education? Public libraries?

4. (a) What social evils accompanied the growth of cities? (b) What efforts were made to correct these evils? Helpful source: Nevins, *Emergence of Modern America* (A.L.S.), pp. 318–334.

5. How did urbanization affect the following: (a) literature; (b) recreation; (c) architecture?

6. Contrast conditions in American cities in 1830 and 1880.

FOR INDIVIDUAL OR GROUP ACTIVITIES

1. (a) Investigate and report on the growth of population in the city in which you live, or the one nearest to your home, or the largest city in your state. (b) Prepare a short talk for presentation to the class on the geographic and economic factors which led to the founding and development of the city you select.

2. Plan an exhibit of pictures which illustrate styles, homes, home furnishings, and recreation in the years 1865–1900. Helpful source: Davidson, *Life in America*, Vol. II.

3. Collect and exhibit pictures which illustrate the Centennial Exposition, 1876, and the Chicago World's Fair, 1893. Helpful source: Davidson, *Life in America*, Vol. II.

4. Report on the development of various sports in the period 1865–1900. Helpful sources: Schlesinger, *The Rise of the City* (A.L.S.); Davidson, *Life in America*, Vol. II; Krout, *Annals of American Sport*.

5. Report on the chapter "Biography of a Nation of Joiners" in Schlesinger, *Paths to the Present*.

6. Prepare book reports on each of the following: Addams, Jane, *Twenty Years at Hull House* and *The Second Twenty Years at Hull House*; Riis, Jacob, *How the Other Half Lives*; Washington, Booker T., *Up from Slavery*.

7. Write short essays on the influence of *Progress and Poverty* by Henry George, and *Looking Backward* by Edward Bellamy. Helpful sources: Morison and Commager, *American Republic*, Vol. II, pp. 368–370; Hacker, *The Shaping of the American Tradition*, pp. 710–717; Curti, *The Growth of American Thought*, pp. 614–617, 628–629.

8. Prepare charts and maps which illustrate the growth of public schools. Helpful sources: Morison and Commager, *American Republic*, Vol. II; Lord, *Historical Atlas*.

As long as there are big corporations,
there will be big unions.

——M. C. Smith

SAMUEL GOMPERS

27. THE RISE OF THE LABOR MOVEMENT

Labor Conditions Were Poor

Industrial progress brings hardships.

The growth of industry and the rise of big business produced wealth for some people. Yet for a long time it brought little benefit to wage earners. They did not gain much in wages. In some ways they were worse off than in the old days of small-scale industry. They no longer had personal contact with their employers. They no longer used their own simple tools but worked on costly machines which they could never hope to own. They no longer lived on farms but in big cities. Unemployment from any cause soon reduced them to misery.

Hours were long and wages low.

In the 1860's most workers in industry had an 11-hour day and a 6-day week. Workers in textile mills, ironworks, and on the railroads commonly worked from 72 to 84 hours a week. Skilled workmen were glad to get $2.00 a day. Common laborers got from $1.00 to $1.25 a day. Women workers earned less; they toiled in factories and shops for, at most, $3.50 to $4.00 a week. Children got from 50 cents to $2.00 a week.

Employment was irregular.

Fear of unemployment has haunted wage earners since the beginning of the Industrial Revolution. Unemployment may be *seasonal, technological,* or *general.* In some occupations, such as canning and the garment trades, the workers experience *seasonal* unemployment. In practically all occupations the introduction of new machines may bring *technological* unemployment. The workers who are displaced by machines often cannot find other jobs for a long time. Since their old skills are no longer needed, they may have to take jobs at lower pay. When a period of hard times comes, nearly all employers lay off workers. Then unemployment becomes *general.*

We do not have any exact figures of the amount of unemployment in the years from 1865 to 1900. In the depression years following the panics of 1873 and 1893, hundreds of thousands of men were jobless. Even in good years there were not enough jobs for all who wanted them. The stream of immigrants from Europe and the movement of native-born Americans from the farms to the city flooded the labor market. The supply of unskilled labor always outran the demand.

Industrial accidents were numerous.

Little was done to protect workers from accidents. Machines rarely had safety devices. Factories were poorly lighted. Accidents to workers in factories, mines, and on the railroads were frequent. When an accident took place, it was usually considered to be the worker's fault. Under the common law the employer did not have to pay the injured worker, if he or any of his fellows was in any way to blame for the accident.

Work places were often unhealthful.

Industrial workers often toiled in surroundings that endangered their health. Sanitary arrangements were crude, and the presence of a large number of workers in one place favored the spread of infection. Besides, in mines and in many factories workers were exposed to dust, steam, or fumes while on the job. As a result, these workers had a high rate of tuberculosis. The worst health conditions were found in sweatshops in the clothing industry. In these small, crowded, unsanitary places, women and children, the aged, and the disabled toiled long hours (sometimes 15 or more a day) at incredibly low pay. They did handwork, like making artificial flowers or finishing garments, and were paid by the piece. Many slum dwellers in large cities turned their own dwellings into sweatshops. Here every member of the family worked from early till late to earn a bare existence.

Industrial feudalism appears.

Wage earners in coal-mining areas and in Southern textile districts often lived in a village owned by the company for which they worked. The workers rented their houses from the company and did their buying in the company store. Frequently, in fact, wages were paid in the form of scrip—certificates which could be used as money only in that village. If a worker protested against the rent he paid for his house or the prices he paid in the company store, he might lose his job and be evicted as well. The owners of such a company town had powers like those of a feudal lord, for they even controlled the local government. Workers living there resented their lack of freedom. Resentment developed even in the well-designed model towns which some employers created for their workers.

Labor gets little sympathy.

In this period few leaders of opinion and few statesmen gave thought to the troubles of the wage-earning class. It was widely believed that the government should not interfere between employers and employees. Low wages were held to be due to an oversupply of workers—a condition which could not be helped. The common belief was that unemployment was the workers' own fault, and that even in hard times, deserving men could always find jobs. If workers crowded into unhealthy slums, that too was their own fault. The industrious and capable would, it was thought, climb the ladder from poverty to independence.

National Labor Unions Emerge

Early trade unions come and go.

From the early days of the Republic, workingmen had tried to organize. For the most part their unions were weak, small, and short-lived (p. 313). During Andrew Jackson's presidency, labor unions grew in number and strength. They went to pieces, you will remember, when the panic of 1837 threw a great number of men out of work. From that time until the end of the century, unions sprang up when times were good and all but died out during hard times.

The first national unions appeared in the 1850's, but only one survived the panic of 1857. In the 1860's at least thirty-one national unions were organized, each one representing workers in a single craft, or trade. A few of these, such as the Brotherhood of Locomotive Engineers, have continued to the present day.

The first national industrial union.

In 1869 a group of poor garment cutters in Philadelphia launched the "Noble Order of the Knights of Labor." To protect members from being blacklisted by employers, the doings of the order and even its name were at first kept secret. The Knights aimed to unite all labor into one big union. They welcomed all toilers—skilled and unskilled, men and women, white and Negro, farmers, white-collar workers, clergymen, teachers, and shopkeepers.

The Knights tried to promote the interests of farmers as well as wage earners. They also sponsored co-operative workshops, owned and managed by workers. They urged government ownership of railways, telegraph lines, water works, and other utilities. They demanded the eight-hour day, the stopping of child labor, equal pay for men and women, the shutting out of Chinese immigrants, and the adoption of income and inheritance taxes. They relied chiefly on educational and political methods rather than collective bargaining to gain what they wanted.

During the first ten years, the Knights attracted only 10,000 members. After the order dropped its secret features (1881), membership climbed. By 1886 it had reached 700,000, consisting mostly of unskilled workers. Unfriendly newspapers referred to the head of the Knights, Terence V. Powderly, as the "labor czar" and said he would soon be more powerful than the President. Yet the Knights of Labor declined as quickly as it had risen.

The decline of the Noble Order of Knights of Labor was due partly to the loss of some large-scale railway strikes in 1886. Partly it was due to public disfavor arising from the Haymarket affair (see p. 460). Finally, it was due to the difficulty of holding skilled and unskilled labor in the same union. Most of the skilled workers in the Knights joined a new organization—the American Federation of Labor.

Birth of American Federation of Labor.

A new labor organization began to take shape in 1881 when six prominent craft unions established a national federation. In 1886 it took the name "American Federation of Labor" (A.F. of L.) and elected full-time paid officers. Samuel Gompers was chosen president at a salary of $1000 a year. Under his practical, hardheaded leadership the Federation soon became so firmly established that it was able to weather the hard times that hit with the panic of 1893. As Gompers pointed out, this was noteworthy, for "in every previous industrial crisis the trade unions were literally mowed down and swept out of existence." By 1900 the Federation had 550,000 members, and included some 70 per cent of all union workers.

The A.F. of L. differed greatly from the Knights of Labor. (1) It rejected the idea of one big union and stood for the organization of skilled workers into self-governing trade, or craft, unions. (2) It limited membership to workingmen. (3) It worked for immediate, day-to-day gains for its members, not for sweeping economic reforms. It did not sponsor co-operatives or urge government ownership. (4) It emphasized collective bargaining rather than a political and educational program.

Gompers dominates the A.F. of L.

For forty years the man who stood out above all others in the American

THE SHOEMAKERS' STRIKE *in Lynn, Massachusetts, in 1860. Eight hundred women, preceded by the city guards and a band, led the workmen's protest march through the snow.*

Federation of Labor was Samuel Gompers. His father, a London cigar maker, came to this country with his family in 1863. Samuel went to work in his father's trade at the age of thirteen and soon became active in the cigar makers' union. He had no schooling, but was eager to learn. In the cigar factory he found a chance to develop his mind through reading and discussion. He wrote long afterwards:

It was the custom of the cigar makers to chip in to create a fund for purchasing papers, magazines, and books. Then while the rest worked, one of our members would read to us for perhaps an hour at a time, sometimes longer. In order that the reader might not be the loser financially, each one of the other men in the shop gave him a definite number of cigars. I had a habit of saving any interesting magazine or newspaper articles to read to my shopmates. Others did the same. . . .

Gompers took an active part in organizing the A.F. of L. and served as president until his death in 1924. He advised the Federation's member unions to put all their efforts into raising wages, shortening hours, and getting better working conditions, rather than into idealistic schemes for making over society. He urged each union to build up a large reserve fund from dues, so it would not go to pieces in case of a strike or a depression. Under Gompers' guidance the Federation gradually won important gains for skilled workers.

Labor unions face many obstacles.

Throughout the nineteenth century most workers did not belong to a union. Enormous difficulties stood in the way of labor organizations.

1. Scarcity of able leaders. The kind of men who make effective leaders of labor unions could usually earn far more by going into business for themselves or by working up into an executive position in industry. Also, as long as free land could be had, the bolder and more capable workmen—the possible leaders—were apt to go west and become farmers, leaving other workmen leaderless.

2. Public opposition. Most people outside the wage-earner class were hostile to unions. During a strike a large section of the public regularly sided with the employer, believing that he had the right to hire and fire workers as he chose and to offer whatever wages he chose. Most people, including many wage earners, opposed the union demand for the *closed shop*—that is, a shop in which only union members are permitted to work.

3. Immigration. There was a constant flood of immigrants eager for jobs and willing to work for any wages. Immigrants were so poor that they could not refuse jobs as strikebreakers. Then, too, they could not be easily organized because of language difficulties, religious differences, and the grudges felt by some nationalities toward others.

4. Race prejudice. The unfriendly attitude of white workers toward Negro workers weakened the labor movement. Skilled white workers generally insisted on keeping Negroes out of their local unions. White workers often called strikes to force the dismissal of Negro workers. As a result Negroes willingly served as strikebreakers when given the chance.

5. *The growing number of women workers.* Women worked for smaller wages than men, even when doing the same work. Employers used them instead of men whenever possible. Yet women took little interest in labor unions, for most of them did not expect to remain wage earners long.

6. *Opposition of employers.* The greatest difficulty of all was the belief of the average employer that he had a right to run his business as he pleased. He had no patience with the idea that he should bargain with representatives chosen by his employees. He was likely to discharge any of his men who tried to form a union. He might even plant spies among his workers to report any "troublemakers."

Industrial Strife Is Widespread

Both sides develop weapons.

In the long struggle between capital and labor each side has used certain weapons against the other. Labor's main weapon is the *strike*. This is the refusal to work until demands are granted. To prevent the use of strikebreakers, or "scabs," the strikers picket the place of work; that is, they stand at the entrances to persuade strikebreakers not to enter. Another of labor's weapons is the *boycott*. This is the refusal to buy or handle the product of a certain employer. Employees of companies which have dealings with a struck plant may refuse to handle products of that plant. The boycott has occasionally brought ruin to an employer, and sometimes the courts have forced unions to pay heavy damages.

When a strike is called, the employer may close his plant and refuse to deal with his employees except on his own terms. This is the *lockout*. Following a lockout the employer may bring in strikebreakers to run his plant.

The blacklist and the "yellow-dog" contract have been much used to discourage workers from joining a union. The blacklist contains the names of men discharged for trying to start a union or for stirring up labor troubles. It was often sent all over the country to other employers in the industry. Once blacklisted, a man might never be able to get another job unless he changed his name. The "yellow-dog" contract is an agreement made by a worker when he is hired that he will not join a union. In 1935 Congress made both the blacklist and the "yellow-dog" contract illegal.

Violence occurs in labor disputes.

So long as employers refused to recognize the right of workers to organize and to bargain collectively for better terms, labor disputes often led to violence. Workers frequently beat up strikebreakers. Sometimes they damaged the employer's property. The Molly Maguires, a secret society of Pennsylvania coal miners, used terror in fighting oppressive working and living conditions. They not only destroyed property but injured or murdered a number of mineowners and others. The society was active in the early 1870's, until a Pinkerton detective made his way into the inner circle. As a result the leaders were brought to trial and ten were hanged. The society then broke up. Labor leaders strongly condemned its tactics. They saw that violence could only bring harm to the labor movement.

Employers, too, used violence. Labor organizers frequently were beaten up and ordered to leave town. During strikes corporations sometimes hired thugs to commit acts of violence which could be blamed on the strikers. Thus public opinion was turned against the strikers and the company had an excuse for demanding the use of troops.

Strikes become frequent.

Industrial progress brought a long and bitter struggle between capital and labor. Workingmen wanted a larger share in the wealth created by their toil, shorter hours, and safer, healthier working conditions. Employers resisted these demands and fought unions "tooth and nail."

Strikes became increasingly frequent. How many took place before 1881 we do not know. Between 1881 and 1900 nearly 24,000 strikes occurred. The most spectacular strikes in this period were the railroad strike of 1877; the strike at the McCormick Harvester works in 1886, which led to the Haymarket riot; the Homestead strike of 1892; and the Pullman strike of 1894. These are worth our attention as examples of the fierce conflict between big business and labor unions. In this struggle the government and the courts generally took the side of the corporations.

Soldiers break a nationwide railway strike.

With the rise of big business, labor disputes were apt to affect thousands of workers. The first labor dispute on a national scale was the railroad strike of 1877. Before the strike firemen and brakemen earned from $30 to $40 a month. They averaged only four days' work a week and had to spend a good part of their wages for room and board at distant stations. When four big Eastern railway lines suddenly ordered a 10 per cent cut in wages, the workers struck. The strike spread until 100,000 men in fourteen states had walked out.

The strike quickly led to violence. Strikers tried to prevent the movement of trains by new crews. The governors of ten states called out the militia to preserve order. In some twenty railroad centers the appearance of soldiers led to clashes in which strikers and bystanders were killed or wounded. Angry mobs then destroyed railroad property worth millions of dollars. The governors of four states asked for federal troops to curb the rioters. This was the first strike in which the army was used. The troops quickly broke the strike and the workers had to accept the wage cut.

The Haymarket affair.

In the spring of 1886 a strike at the McCormick Harvester Company in Chicago was met by a lockout. Police broke up a meeting of the strikers. When stones were thrown at the officers, they fired into the crowd and killed four men. The next day some 1500 people gathered at Haymarket Square to protest the shooting. The meeting was orderly. When it was nearly over a company of police directed the crowd to scatter—thus for the second day in succession interfering with the right of free speech. Someone threw a bomb, killing a policeman and wounding others. Street fighting then broke out. Many

"THE HOMESTEAD RIOT," *from a picture in* Harper's Weekly, *July 16, 1892*

people were hurt and ten, including six policemen, were killed.

No one knows to this day who threw the bomb. Eight German anarchists were rounded up and put on trial for murder. (Anarchists are persons who want to do away with government.) Some of the arrested men had advocated violence in speeches or writings, and the judge held that in consequence "somebody, not known, did throw the bomb." Under this ruling the eight defendants were convicted of murder, not because of any acts but because of their beliefs. One killed himself, four were hanged, and three received life sentences. Six years later Governor John P. Altgeld pardoned the three survivors, saying they had not had a fair trial. For this he was savagely denounced in many newspapers.

Although the Knights of Labor were not responsible for the Haymarket affair, they were blamed for it. A great fear of anarchism seized the nation. For many years the opponents of labor organizations took advantage of this fear by accusing unions of anarchist tendencies.

The steelworkers' union is crushed.

In 1892 employees of the Carnegie Steel Company at Homestead, Pennsylvania, went on strike against a wage cut. Company officials determined to destroy their union. They got ready to operate the plant with nonunion men, hiring 300 armed guards to protect them. The guards were supplied by the Pinkerton Detective Agency. A battle resulted between strikers and guards, with deaths on each side. The governor of Pennsylvania sent 8000 state militia to the aid of the steel company, and the plant started up again with nonunion labor. Less than a fourth of the strikers were rehired and the union was completely broken.

Poor labor conditions continued in the steel mills for many years. The workday was twelve hours long until after World War I. Wages remained relatively low. The majority of steelworkers were immigrants from eastern Europe, helpless to win better conditions. The steel companies defeated every effort to unionize their workers until 1937.

Cleveland breaks the Pullman strike.

The winter of 1893–94 was a terrible one for labor. One in every six wage earners was unemployed. Bands of jobless men wandered over the country. Many companies ordered wage cuts because of the hard times. In April the Pullman Company ordered a 20 per cent wage slash in its car works. The men asked the company to arbitrate— that is, to lay the question before a board of judges. This George M. Pullman refused to do, although the mayors of fifty American cities urged him to consent. A strike in the car works followed.

The American Railway Union, led by Eugene V. Debs, backed up the strikers by ordering its members not to work on trains carrying Pullman cars. In order that the strike should not interfere with the mails, the union asked the railroad companies not to attach Pullman cars to mail trains. The companies, however, insisted on attaching Pullman cars to every train carrying mail. When strikers refused to move the trains, railroad officials protested to President Grover Cleveland that this was an interference with the United States mails.

The Attorney General then obtained a court order, or *injunction*, forbidding all strike activities. When Debs and six other union leaders ignored the injunction, they were charged with contempt of court and sent to prison for six months. Without them the strike would probably have collapsed for lack of leadership. Meanwhile, however, mobs in Chicago had stopped a number

"LONGSHOREMEN'S NOON," *by John George Brown. This scene was painted at the time when American labor was beginning to make itself felt as a force in American life. Here on the docks is a group of longshoremen listening to one of their fellows.*

462

"STEELWORKERS—NOONTIME," *by Thomas Pollock Anshutz. By 1900 the steadily growing steel industry was beginning to recognize the bargaining rights of its workers. While some gains for labor had been made there were still many to be won in the years ahead.*

of trains and had destroyed much railroad property. President Cleveland sent federal troops there "to protect the mails." Soon trains were running under military guard and the strike was broken. The governor of Illinois, John P. Altgeld, who thought the strikers' cause was just, protested the President's action. Altgeld insisted that he could have restored order by using the militia. He argued that the President has no constitutional right to send federal troops into a state without the consent of its governor.

A powerful antilabor weapon.

After the Pullman strike the injunction was used regularly in labor struggles. The employer would ask a court to forbid the union or its leaders from acting in certain ways likely to injure his business or property. The court would usually issue an order forbidding the actions feared by the employer. Anyone who disobeys an injunction is in "contempt of court" and may be sentenced to prison without a jury trial. The injunction could be used to prevent such actions as striking, urging others to strike, collecting money to further a strike, and even the meeting of strikers. In 1932 this powerful weapon against labor was limited by passage of the Norris–La Guardia Anti-Injunction Act.

Labor Makes Some Gains

Bureaus of labor are created.

The struggles of the unions gradually led the public to take more interest in labor conditions. In 1869 the Massachusetts legislature set up a bureau of labor statistics. A few years later Congress created a federal Bureau of Labor Statistics. By 1900 most states had similar bureaus. All of them collected and published information on wages, hours, industrial accidents, strikes, and other labor matters. Their

publications showed that the growth of industry had produced serious labor problems, among them low wages, irregular employment, child labor, a high rate of industrial accidents and industrial diseases, and continual disputes between capital and labor. People began to realize that these conditions were harmful to the whole nation.

Some companies adopt enlightened labor policies.

Corporation officials thought it their duty to keep labor costs as low as possible. In time some of them saw that poor labor conditions were expensive and persuaded their boards of directors that more attention should be given to the welfare of employees. In 1880 the Baltimore and Ohio Railroad became the first American firm to provide its employees with benefits in case of injury or death and with old age pensions. Two years later the Pillsbury Flour Mills adopted a profit-sharing plan. During the next decade over a hundred firms started sharing profits. Other companies built model towns to take their employees out of the slums. Labor and its leaders, however, disapproved of company-owned towns.

A few labor laws are passed.

Individual employers could go only so far in improving the condition of their workers. To go farther might increase their cost of production above that of competitors. One firm, for example, could not afford to raise wages or shorten hours very much unless its competitors did the same. To get this action, laws regulating labor conditions were needed. Yet attempts to pass such laws met fierce opposition. Most people still believed in the principle of laissez-faire—the idea that the government should let business alone.

In spite of the strong opposition, a number of states did pass laws to protect labor. Some of these laws regulated

A child working in a cotton mill at the turn of the century

labor conditions in mines, laundries, and sweatshops. Others required safety devices on power saws and other dangerous machinery. Some regulated housing. Such laws were often poorly enforced, yet they were signs of a new attitude toward labor. They prepared the way for stronger legislation in the twentieth century.

The states also made a little progress in protecting women and children in industry. By 1900 twelve states limited the hours of women workers. Four states prohibited the employment of women at night. Twenty states prohibited the employment of young children at night. Some of these early laws now seem very timid. For instance, one state forbade the employment at night of girls under 12 years of age. The real evils of child labor had scarcely been touched.

Laws attempting to limit the workday of men did not succeed. The courts held that such laws were unconstitutional because they interfered with the individual's freedom of contract. As late as 1900, 70 per cent of industrial workers labored sixty or more hours each week.

Labor wins curbs on immigration.

By 1880 nearly a third of a million immigrants came here every year. Within a few years the figure rose to nearly a million. The United States, it was thought, had room for all who wished to come. Steamship companies sent agents all over Europe to persuade people to come to America. Western railroad companies, with land to sell, did the same thing. Large corporations made contracts with laborers who wished to come to America. The cor-

465

poration paid the laborer's fare, and the laborer promised to work for the corporation for a certain period of time. Unskilled Chinese laborers by the tens of thousands, for example, were brought in under contract to build railroads in the West.

Labor leaders saw that their efforts to raise wages and improve working conditions would not get far so long as the country was flooded with poor immigrants eager to take any job. First the labor unions demanded that the Chinese be shut out, and in 1882 Congress passed an act excluding Chinese laborers.

Next the unions called on Congress to stop the practice of bringing in laborers under contract. Congress did so in 1885. Still the flood of immigrants increased. Labor leaders then asked that immigrants unable to read and write be shut out. This request was opposed by employers and many others.

Labor's gains are far from ideal.

By 1900 labor had made notable gains, but compared with today, labor conditions were still poor. Although more workers than ever before belonged to unions, most workers remained unorganized. By 1900 certain craft unions had won the 8-hour day. In industry the 10-hour day was replacing the 11- and 12-hour day. Yet bakers commonly worked 84 hours a week, as did horsecar drivers, hotel employees, store salesmen, and many others. Wages had gone up throughout the country. By 1900 in the North the most highly skilled workers received $3 a day; unskilled men got $1.50 a day. The average earnings of all American wage earners were something like $400 or $500 a year. Prices were less than a third as high then as they are today. Yet most American workers found their wages barely enough to support even a small family. In 1900, then, labor still had a hard struggle ahead.

JOHN P. ALTGELD

FOR IDENTIFICATION

John P. Altgeld	Eugene V. Debs
American Federation of Labor	Samuel Gompers
	Knights of Labor
Anti-Injunction Act	Terence V. Powderly
Chinese Exclusion Act	

FOR EXPLANATION OR DEFINITION

blacklist	Molly Maguires
boycott	Pullman strike
closed shop	strikebreaker
company town	sweatshop
contempt of court	technological
craft union	unemployment
injunction	"yellow-dog" contract
lockout	

FOR REVIEW

1. In what ways were wage earners worse off during the early decades of America's industrial growth than before?

2. Describe labor conditions and wages in the 1860's.

3. Define three types of unemployment.

4. What was the general attitude of the government and leaders of public opinion toward labor unions, low wages, working conditions, and industrial accidents during the 1870's and 1880's?

5. Describe the ups and downs of early labor organizations.

466

6. With regard to the Knights of Labor, indicate: (a) the reasons for secrecy during its early years; (b) the groups it welcomed to membership; (c) the things it demanded; (d) the reasons for its decline.

7. (a) Describe the beginnings of the American Federation of Labor. (b) How did the A.F. of L. differ from the Knights of Labor in organization, aims, and accomplishments? (c) Describe the work and influence of Samuel Gompers.

8. What were the chief obstacles to the development of strong and successful labor unions in the period 1865 to 1900?

9. Explain the strike, the boycott, and picketing as weapons of labor.

10. Explain the lockout, blacklist, "yellow-dog" contract, and injunction as weapons of the employer.

11. Why were labor disputes frequently accompanied by violence? What methods did large employers of labor use to break up unions and strikes?

12. (a) Describe the railway strike of 1877 and the way it was finally settled. (b) Describe the Haymarket affair and its effects. (c) Describe the Homestead strike of 1892 and its outcome.

13. (a) What caused the Pullman strike of 1894? (b) On what grounds did President Cleveland intervene in this strike? (c) On what grounds did Governor Altgeld protest the use of federal troops?

14. What benefits resulted from the formation of state and federal bureaus of labor?

15. State the nature of early state laws regulating labor conditions. On what grounds did the courts declare some of these labor laws unconstitutional?

16. (a) How did some employers encourage immigrants to come to the United States? (b) Why did labor leaders demand laws to restrict immigration? (c) What success did they have in the 1880's?

17. Describe labor conditions in 1900.

FOR FURTHER STUDY AND DISCUSSION

1. (a) Why did the labor union movement fail to attract large numbers of workers in the period 1865–1900? (b) Briefly contrast labor union membership in 1900 with labor union membership today.

2. Why was the American Federation of Labor stronger and more successful than the Knights of Labor? Helpful source: Orth, *Armies of Labor* (Y.C.S.).

3. What is meant by the phrase "government by injunction"?

4. Why do many employers work for laws to improve labor conditions?

5. (a) What was the attitude of Samuel Gompers toward labor unions and partisan politics? (b) State your reasons for agreeing or disagreeing with Gompers on this point.

FOR INDIVIDUAL OR GROUP ACTIVITIES

1. Prepare brief biographical sketches of Uriah S. Stephens, Terence V. Powderly, Samuel Gompers, and Eugene V. Debs. Helpful sources: Madison, *American Labor Leaders;* Morris, *Encyclopedia.*

2. Organize committees to investigate and report on each of the following: (a) the Molly Maguires and the use of Pinkerton detectives; (b) the Baltimore and Ohio strike of 1877; (c) the Haymarket affair, 1886; (d) the Homestead strike, 1892. Helpful sources: Orth, *The Armies of Labor* (Y.C.S.); Adamic, *Dynamite; The Story of Class Violence in America;* Morison and Commager, *American Republic,* Vol. II, pp. 160–166; Beard, *American Civilization,* Vol. II, pp. 227–236.

3. Write a letter to a newspaper commenting on Governor Altgeld's pardon of the Haymarket "anarchists." Helpful source: Commager and Nevins, *Heritage of America,* No. 225.

4. Hold a panel discussion on the conflicting points of view of President Cleveland and Governor Altgeld concerning the use of federal troops in the Pullman strike, 1894. Helpful sources: Commager, *Documents,* No. 334; also Amherst Series, *The Pullman Boycott of 1894,* which contains the injunction, the decision of the Supreme Court, and statements by Cleveland, Altgeld, and others.

Western America is one of the most interesting subjects of
study the modern world has seen. . . . A vast territory, won-
derfully rich in natural resources of many kinds . . . thrown
open to a vigorous race with . . . modern science at its command. . . .——James Bryce, 1893

28. THE FRONTIER PERIOD
COMES TO A CLOSE

The Great West Is Occupied

Settlement of the Great West is swift.

In 1860 the vast region west of the
Missouri River was, for the most part,
a wilderness. Known as the "Great
West," it included half the area of the
United States.

Why had this huge area been so
long unsettled by white men? The answer lies in its climate and topography.
A portion of it—the Great Plains—was a
land of scanty rainfall and frequent periods of drought. The Great Plains had
few trees and few navigable streams.
Although covered with grass, it had
long been known as the "Great American Desert." Beyond the plains was a
broad stretch of high mountains and
plateaus. Much of this region actually
was a desert. When the frontier reached
the Great Plains, it leaped fifteen hundred miles to the Pacific coast.

In 1860 the Great West was still
the land of the Indians. Thirty years
later a startling change had taken place.
The Indians were shut into reservations; the vast herds of buffalo on which
they lived had been wiped out; five
railroads had pushed across the prairies
and the mountains to the Pacific; five

million farmers had settled on the land;
and the frontier line was gone.

Miners Are Attracted

Prospectors explore a large area.

The first frontier of the Great West
was that of the miners. As we noted
(p. 344), the gold rush of 1849 brought
throngs of pioneers to California. When
gold that could be gathered by washing gravel (that is, placer mining) began to give out there, prospectors
swarmed over the mountain-plateau
region from Canada to Mexico.

In 1858 gold was found in the foothills of the Rockies near Pikes Peak.
The rush of the "fifty-niners" brought
over 100,000 gold seekers to that area.
They soon learned that placer mining
did not pay there. The precious minerals were embedded in quartz, and expensive machinery was needed to mine
them. Many who had come westward
with the slogan "Pikes Peak or Bust"
painted on their wagons changed it to
"Busted, by Gosh!" and went back east.
Enough stayed, however, to organize
the territory of Colorado in 1861.

SALT RIVER, ARIZONA, *1904. In the Far West many settlers stripped the soil of minerals and left a wasteland, as shown here. Later, when the Roosevelt Dam was completed this land became productive.*

Late in the fifties gold and silver were discovered in Carson Valley on the western edge of Utah territory. By 1861, .because so many people had poured into the region, the territory of Nevada was carved out of Utah. The Comstock lode, the richest known silver deposit in the world, between 1860 and 1890 yielded $340,000,000. Tunnels were dug deeper and deeper into the solid rock to reach the ore.

The 1860's saw gold rushes to Idaho, Montana, Wyoming, the Black Hills of South Dakota, New Mexico, and Arizona. A new discovery of gold or silver anywhere soon brought thousands of fortune hunters. Within a few weeks a city of tents and huts would rise near the "diggings." When the surface deposits gave out, most of the people left. Some moved on where rumors of new discoveries called them; others returned, perhaps empty-handed, to the East.

Miners make and enforce laws.

The early mining camps had to make their own laws. As soon as a group of miners came together in a promising spot, they formed a mining district and elected officers. Since they were on the public land, they drew up regulations fixing the size and number of claims. To hold a claim a man must record it and must work it a given number of days each year. Disputes were settled in a miners' court, an open meeting of miners.

To curb the lawless, vigilance committees were formed. Their members were known as "vigilantes." In Montana, vigilantes broke up a large gang of outlaws that had terrorized the mining communities, hanging twenty-one desperadoes in one month (January, 1864). Most of those caught by the vigilantes were criminals. Yet, under this rough-and-ready method of law enforcement, little time was spent in determining the guilt or innocence of the accused. Since the usual legal safeguards of a fair trial were absent, vigilante justice was often nothing but lynch law.

As a new mining area was settled, the different communities soon joined together to form a territorial government and to ask Congress for recognition. This habit of self-government so

469

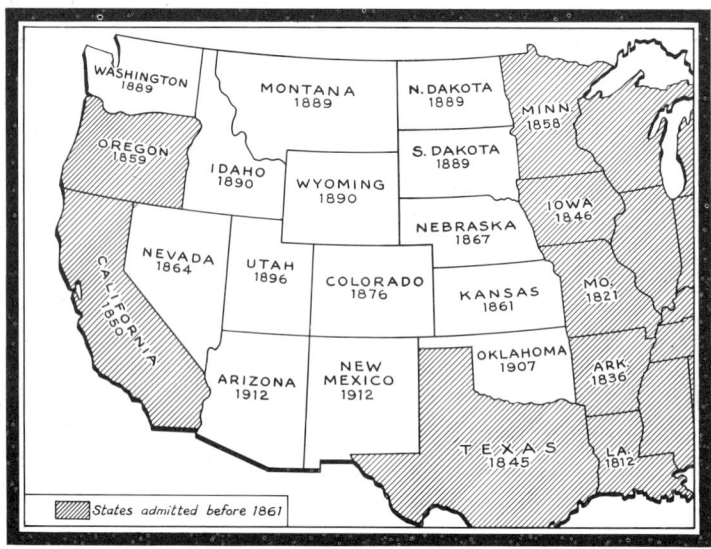

STATES OF THE GREAT WEST

impressed a European visitor to the West that he wrote:

Making governments and building towns are the natural employments of the migratory Yankee. . . . Congregate a hundred Americans anywhere beyond the settlements and they immediately lay out a city, frame a state constitution, and apply for admission to the Union, while twenty-five of them become candidates for the United States Senate.

Other metals are discovered.

The nation's growing industries called for copper, lead, zinc, iron, and other base metals. Thus mineral deposits which the seekers of gold and silver ignored often proved more valuable than the precious metals. The greatest copper deposits in the world were found at Butte, Montana, in the 1860's. Here the vast Anaconda mines are located. Enormous quantities of copper also were discovered in Utah, Nevada, and Arizona. Rich deposits of ore containing silver and lead were found in Colorado in 1876, and for a time Colorado led the world in the production of lead. Since then, many

other minerals have been found in the mountains of the Great West. Some of these, such as molybdenum and uranium, were unknown to prospectors of the nineteenth century.

Cattlemen Range the Great Plains

The buffalo are killed off.

While prospectors and miners were moving into the mountain-plateau region, cattlemen began to move into the Great Plains. This area stretched from the Rio Grande to Canada and from Kansas, Nebraska, and the Dakotas to the Rockies. The millions of buffalo that roamed over the grasslands were replaced by beef cattle. The Indians gave way to cattlemen and farmers.

When the railroads first crossed our country, the buffalo grass on the Great Plains supported great numbers of buffalo. It is estimated that just after the War between North and South there were about 15,000,000 of these beasts in the United States. The size of the herds was often almost unbelievably large. One train, for example, passed through a single herd for a hundred and twenty miles.

The building of railroads across the plains meant the end of the buffalo. Passengers shot them from the train windows for the pleasure of seeing them kick. Professional hunters shot them for their skins. Even when the price of buffalo skins dropped so low that it did not pay to skin the animals, the destruction went on. Most of the buffalo were just left to lie where they dropped, food only for coyotes and insects. During the early 1850's, millions were killed each year. By 1881 only a few remained.

The Indians are subdued.

The settlement of the Great Plains brought on twenty-five years of warfare with the Indians (1862–1886). Again and again they were driven from lands that had been promised them in solemn treaties. Always they were pushed into less desirable lands. If they fought the whites, they were certain to be defeated and savagely punished. Yet fight they did. In these years there were literally thousands of skirmishes between Indians and federal troops.

The destruction of the buffalo was a final, tragic blow for the Plains Indians. It meant their destruction too. Their tent coverings, boat coverings, bow strings, clothing, and food all had come from these animals. Now starvation stared the Indians in the face. At last, in return for food, they had to give up their freedom and accept the terms offered by the federal government.

A new Indian policy was adopted in 1887 when Congress passed the Dawes Act. It offered farms and citizenship to Indians who stopped living in tribes. More than half the Indians accepted this offer and became naturalized citizens. The remainder were removed to reservations, where poverty was their lot. Even today the Indians on most reservations live in want.

Texans organize the "long drive."

Cattle raising on a large scale had begun in Texas in Spanish times. Spanish cowboys worked out the methods for handling cattle on the open range—roping, branding, and the yearly "round-up" to identify the calves. Many of our words associated with cattle raising, such as ranch, lariat, broncho, corral, rodeo, are of Spanish origin. The sturdy Texas longhorn descended from cattle brought to America from Spain.

Before the Texans revolted from Mexico in 1836, they had a "beef trail" over which cowboys drove cattle to market in New Orleans. Later they sometimes drove cattle as far as Chicago, New York, and San Francisco. When the railroads reached St. Louis, in the 1850's, Texans began to drive cattle there to be shipped east in livestock cars. The drive to St. Louis was a dangerous journey of seven or eight hundred miles and took over two months. On the way the cowboys had to cross rivers, defend their herds from

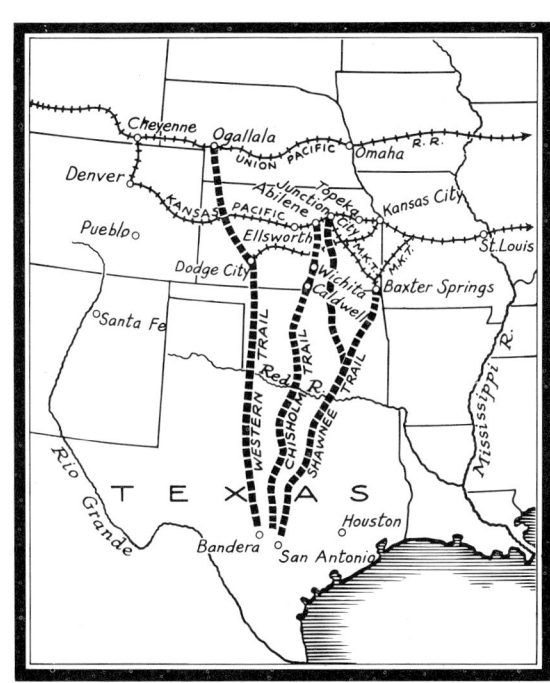

CATTLE TRAILS

A Montana cowboy

It's a whoop and a yea, get along my little
    dogies,
  For camp is far away.
It's a whoop and a yea and a-driving the
    dogies,
  For Wyoming may be your new home.

Before long, stockmen found that
they could winter cattle in the North,
for the animals would paw through the
snow to reach the nourishing grass un-
derneath. Cattle raising spread all over
the Great Plains and into the mountain

cattle thieves, stop stampedes among
the frightened cattle, and fight roving
bands of Indians. After the war, as the
railroads pushed westward, shipping
points were established in Kansas. The
hoofs of thousands of Texas cattle
pounded out trails to each of these
"cow towns." The most famous was the
Chisholm Trail, ending at Abilene.

The "Cattle Kingdom" expands northward.

As the buffalo were killed off and
as the Plains Indians were penned into
reservations, the cattle industry spread
from Texas as far north as Canada.
Buyers searched Texas for herds of
young beef animals, hired cowboys to
drive them north in the early spring,
and fattened them on free grass in the
public domain. In a good season the
cattle sold, after fattening, for four or
five times what they had cost. Memories
of this colorful business come to us in
songs such as the "Texas Lullaby":

472

valleys. Still in the North it was a risky business. After an unusually heavy snow or a sleet storm that formed a hard crust, the cattle sometimes died by thousands from hunger. In time cattlemen learned that they must provide hay for such emergencies.

Cattle barons rule the open range.

At first anyone with a few dollars could start a herd by buying some cows and calves and turning them out to graze on the public land. But after a few years, the big cattlemen and cattle companies, by fair means or foul, got control of the ranges. Ignoring the land laws, they fenced in water holes and streams or enclosed huge tracts of the range. In this way they drove out small competitors. They also waged continual war on the sheep raisers, who had moved in and whose flocks ruined the pasture for cattle. Cattlemen frequently clubbed herds of sheep to death or stampeded them over a cliff.

As the West grew, FREE-ROAMING LONGHORNS (left) *were fenced in to make pasture for sheep* (below, left) *and* FARM LAND *for the homesteader* (below).

473

For some twenty-five years these "cattle barons" ruled the land of the blue sky and the prairie grass. Meanwhile, small farmers, or "nesters," began to settle along the streams on homesteads given them by the federal government. The enraged stockmen tore down the homesteaders' fences, threatened violence, and sometimes killed those who insisted on staying. The homesteaders, however, had the federal government behind them. President Cleveland ordered the stockmen's illegal fences cut down and the grasslands thrown open for settlement. This brought the "cattle frontier" to an end.

By 1890 most of the cattlemen and sheepmen had moved onto lands too dry for any use but pasture. They dug wells and erected windmills to provide water for themselves and their stock. They bought and fenced grazing lands.

Farmers Settle the Great Plains

The Great Plains attract farmers.

Within a single generation after the War between North and South farmers flocked into the Great Plains. They settled most of the land suited for crop growing, as well as much that was not. For several reasons farmers were now willing to settle in this region.

1. Desirable land in other sections had already been occupied and could be bought only for a good price. On the Great Plains the best land was $1.25 an acre; poorer land could be obtained free from the government. The Homestead Act of 1862 granted 160 acres free to a man or woman who would live on it and cultivate it for five years. Settlers eagerly set out their claims. Later it was realized that a farm of 160 acres was much too small to support a family on the semiarid land of the Great Plains, but this fact was not known at the time.

2. Machinery for driving wells and pumping water was now available. In the East farmers could get water from streams, springs, or shallow wells. On the plains few streams or springs ran all the year round; farmers had to drive deep wells and to pump underground water to the surface. When the machinery for this was developed and turned out cheaply by mass production after the war, people could live even in the drier parts of the plains. Well diggers traveled through the region drilling wells for stockmen and farmers. Once water was found, a windmill was put up to pump the water to the surface where it could be used.

3. Barbed wire fencing was introduced. On the plains the lack of materials for building fences was a serious obstacle to farmers. Trees were scarce, and there were no rocks. Smooth wire strung on posts did not hold livestock. The problem was solved by the invention of barbed wire. Put on the market in 1874, it quickly came into wide use. It spelled the doom of the open range, for farmers could now fence in their crops and defy the stockmen.

4. A network of railroads was built. More than anything else, the railroads speeded settlement of the West. Once a line was built, prospective settlers knew they could get their crops to market. Moreover, the pioneer could ride to his new land in comparative comfort and safety instead of risking life and limb going there by wagon. Finally, the railroads attracted settlers by extensive advertising.

Railroads advertise for settlers.

Most of the railroads in the West had received land grants along their right of way. The railroads wished to sell these lands to settlers in order to gain future business. They published maps and pamphlets which described their territory in glowing terms. They sold tickets at bargain rates to those going to look over the land. They offered free transportation to the West to the land purchaser and his family. Their salesmen and advertising covered not only the United States but the whole of Europe. At one time a single road—the Northern Pacific—sent 800 agents abroad to sell land. As a result, immigrants poured into the country.

Life on the last frontier is hard.

In addition to struggling with the Indian and the cowboy, the settler on the Great Plains had to struggle with nature. The climate was marked by extremes of temperature. North of Oklahoma the winters brought terrible blizzards and long periods of bitter cold. The summers brought long hot spells when even the nights were torrid. In some years plagues of grasshoppers swarmed over the plains, eating every green thing in their paths and killing the crops. Prairie fires, once started, might sweep over the plains for days.

Drought was a still worse disaster. On the eastern border of the plains region rainfall averages 30 to 40 inches a year, while near the Rockies it is only 10 inches a year. On the plains a period of a few years when the rainfall is satisfactory is always followed by a series of dry years. When drought comes, crops die. Water for livestock and even for human beings becomes scarce. At such times, with no water for housecleaning or washing, the wife of many a settler begged him to go back east. After the drought and grasshopper plague of 1874, thousands left their farms. Sometimes they chalked a message on the sides of their grimy covered wagons—"Going back to our wife's folks" or "In God we trusted; in Kansas we busted." Again in the late eighties, drought drove thousands of the desperate settlers to abandon their farms. The abandoned areas were always resettled by newcomers when the dry years were over.

A SOD HOUSE *in Custer County, Nebraska, c. 1887*

Another hardship of life on the Great Plains resulted from the lack of trees. Lumber was costly because it had to be brought from a distance. Instead of log cabins the early settlers lived in dugouts or sod houses, or a combination of both. The dugout was a room dug in the side of a hill or ravine. A sod house took more time to build but was much more comfortable. It was made of strips of sod like big bricks, with wooden door frames and window frames set in the walls.

Loneliness was almost harder to bear than the heat and dust and toil. From one year's end to another the pioneer might see only a dozen faces. In winter, when deep snows blocked the roads for weeks, the farmhouse seemed like a prison. Far from neighbors, a long way from a town, beyond reach of a doctor, the farmer's wife sometimes lost her mind.

The Frontier Period Ends

Oklahoma is settled.

In Jackson's time the rich lands of Oklahoma were set aside as a permanent reservation for the civilized Indian tribes (see p. 264). Fifty years later, when most of the West had been settled, land-hungry white men demanded the right to settle on the

475

Indian lands. The federal government bought most of the territory from the Indians. It was to be thrown open to settlement on April 22, 1889. Crowds gathered on the border waiting for the signal to enter. At noon, upon the blast of a bugle, the rush began. On horseback, on foot, and in every kind of vehicle, the people hurried for the best locations. At nightfall on the first day Oklahoma had 50,000 white settlers. The next year Oklahoma was organized as a territory. By the end of the century Oklahoma's white population had reached 400,000, and the Indians had only a few small reservations left.

The states are completed.

The rapidity with which the Great West was settled is truly astonishing. After 1860 pioneers poured in from the Midwest, the East, the South, and Europe. By 1900 about 1 in every 7 Americans lived in the western half of the United States.

The Great West was quickly organized into territories and states. As you see by the map, eleven states were admitted between 1861 and 1896. Oklahoma entered in 1907. Five years later, with the admission of New Mexico and Arizona, the 48 continental states were complete.

The good public lands are used up.

In 1860 the United States had over a billion acres of land in the public domain. This was more than half the area of the entire nation. By 1950 the public domain had been cut to 24 per cent of our land area. About half of this reduction took place in the years from 1860 to 1900.

We should not fall into the common error of thinking that most of the public domain was given away to homesteaders. Almost four times as much of the public land has been sold or granted as has been given away under the homestead acts. The land grants went chiefly to the states for educational purposes or to the railroads. In turn the states and the railroads sold most of their grants to settlers.

To get free land, a settler had to go back twenty to forty miles from a railroad. Since the railroads ran through river valleys, the land they had to sell was richer, more level, and better watered than most of the free land. Those who had the money therefore found it far better to buy land than to claim a free homestead. This explains why only one tenth of the new farms in the West started between 1862 and 1892 were acquired as free homesteads.

The frontier comes to an end.

In 1890 the superintendent of the Census announced that the frontier was gone. He explained that it was no longer possible to draw a line between the edge of settlement and the wilderness. Soon after this announcement, a noted American historian, Frederick J. Turner, pointed out that the disappearance of the frontier marked the close of a remarkable period. Here are a few lines from his most famous article:

Since the days when the fleet of Columbus sailed into the waters of the New World, America has been another name for opportunity, and the people of the United States have taken their tone from the incessant expansion which has not only been open but has even been forced upon them . . . each frontier did indeed furnish a new field of opportunity, a gate of escape from bondage to the past. . . . What the Mediterranean Sea was to the Greeks, breaking the bond of custom, offering new experiences, calling out new institutions and activities, that, and more, the ever retreating frontier has been to the United States directly, and to the nations of Europe more remotely. And now, four centuries from the discovery of America, at the end of a hundred years of life under the Constitution, the frontier has gone, and with its going has closed the first period of American history.

476

14. In what ways did Professor Turner consider the era of the frontier to be a remarkable period in American history?

FOR IDENTIFICATION

Chisholm Trail   Great Plains
Comstock lode   Homestead Act
Dawes Act

FOR EXPLANATION OR DEFINITION

barbed wire   "long drive"
buffalo   mining frontier
cattle frontier   open range
cow towns   placer mining
"fifty-niners"   vigilantes

FOR REVIEW

1. Describe the location and topography of the Great Plains.

2. Compare conditions west of the Missouri in 1860 with those in 1890.

3. Describe the miners' frontier.

4. Explain the work of vigilance committees. Why is it described as "lynch law"?

5. Why did mining become big business?

6. Why was the destruction of the buffalo a tragedy for the Plains Indians?

7. What new Indian policy was established by the Dawes Act, 1887?

8. What is the origin of many of the words associated with cattle raising?

9. What developments brought an end to the "cattle frontier"?

10. (a) Why did the Great Plains at last attract settlers? (b) What inventions were necessary for settlement of the Great Plains? Why? (c) How did railroad companies aid in settling the Great Plains?

11. What hardships did the settlers on the Great Plains have to endure?

12. Describe the settlement of Oklahoma.

13. Why did the majority of the settlers buy land rather than claim a free homestead under the Homestead Act of 1862?

FOR FURTHER STUDY AND DISCUSSION

1. How did the settlement of the "West" after 1865 differ from the settlement of the "West" from 1800 to 1865?

2. How did the development of mining contribute to wiping out the frontier line?

3. Why was there a conflict between "cattle king" and homesteader? What was the outcome of the struggle?

4. Account for the present popularity of motion picture "westerns."

5. What difficulties encountered by the homesteader of the late nineteenth century were overcome in the twentieth century? In what respect do some of the difficulties still persist in the plains region?

FOR INDIVIDUAL OR GROUP ACTIVITIES

1. Prepare book reports on the following: Helen Hunt Jackson, *Ramona;* Edna Ferber, *Cimmaron;* O. F. Rölvaag, *Giants in the Earth;* Willa Cather, *O Pioneers!;* Owen Wister, *The Virginian;* Walter Clark, *The Ox-Bow Incident.*

2. Make a brief report on the career of "Buffalo Bill"—William F. Cody.

3. Read and summarize Professor Turner's article on "The Significance of the Frontier in American History." Helpful sources: Heffner, *A Documentary History of the United States,* pp. 164–177; Amherst Series, *The Turner Thesis concerning the Role of the Frontier in American History.*

4. Try your hand at preparing a short story, dramatic sketch, or radio program to show what happens when individuals take the law into their own hands. Try illustrating the conflict between cattle king and nesters; try describing a "ghost town."

5. Have one committee prepare a collection of pictures on the settlement of the Great Plains, and another committee prepare a collection of poems or folklore stories that illustrate the cattle frontier or the miners' frontier. Helpful sources: Davidson, *Life in America;* Botkin, *A Treasury of American Folklore.*

477

Agitation prevents rebellion, keeps the peace, and secures progress.——Wendell Phillips

29. THE AGRICULTURAL REVOLUTION CREATES PROBLEMS

outline

Farming Changes Greatly

The share-crop system develops.

During the years 1860–1900, as the Industrial Revolution gathered speed, an agricultural revolution was also going forward. In most sections the greatest change was the rising output per farm worker, made possible by labor-saving machinery and modern methods. In the South, where half the nation's farmers lived, the biggest change was in the labor system. There, the freeing of the slaves meant that Southerners had to work out a new labor system.

After the war the planters had land to be farmed but no money to pay wages. The freed Negroes had no money to buy or rent the land but they were willing to work. To get farming going again, planters asked their former slaves to stay on the old place and work in return for food, shelter, and a share of the crop. Many Negroes accepted these share-crop offers. However, they objected to working in gangs, as they had done as slaves. Hence the planters divided their land into small parcels and gave each worker one parcel to farm by himself. In time not only Negroes but landless whites became share croppers.

The share-crop agreements became fixed by custom. In addition to land, the landlord furnished the tenant with a cabin, tools, seed, and a mule. The tenant gave his own labor and that of his family and, out of the returns from his half of the crop, he paid half the cost of fertilizer, ginning, and baling. If the tenant had his own mule and tools, his share was larger.

The crop-lien system retards progress.

Unless he had an unusually good crop, the share cropper earned very little for his year's work. Long before the next harvest he had to buy on credit or borrow money to keep his family going. As security he pledged his growing crop—that is, he gave a *lien*, or mortgage, on the crop to the lender. The lender was usually a local merchant. In many cases he was the landlord as well. When the crop was sold and the debts were paid, the share cropper was lucky if he had anything left. Often he remained in debt from

478

A demonstration of the advantages of a DIVERSIFIED CROP *at the Tuskegee Institute Conference of Negro Farmers in 1915*

one year to another. As he had no right to move while he was in debt, he was not a free man. For many years the average Negro share cropper was, in fact, hardly as well off as he had been under slavery, and in many parts of the deep South he was scarcely more free.

Under the crop-lien system the lender often insisted that the debtor use all his land, except a small garden patch, for cotton. Cotton was more certain of a good yield and a good price than other crops. Besides, the lender wanted to sell the debtor flour, corn meal, and salt pork. Thus the crop-lien system discouraged farmers from diversifying their crops or even raising much of their own food. As a result share croppers had a very poor diet and could not be efficient workers. In spite of this, some white and some Negro share croppers managed to save money and buy land of their own.

Cotton growing expands and prices fall.

For several years after the war the South produced less cotton and other products than formerly. As order was gradually restored, production increased. By 1880 the cotton crop equaled that of 1860. Twenty years later it was nearly twice as large. The increase was due mainly to the westward expansion of the cotton belt. A great number of the new cotton farms were started in Texas.

Meanwhile cotton production was also increasing in Egypt, India, and other cheap-labor areas. The result was that cotton prices went down in the 1880's and remained low. If American growers had lowered their costs by using machinery, they might have maintained their profits. The small size of most cotton farms, however, as well as the share-crop labor system, stood in the way. Diversification of crops would

479

have helped offset the low price of cotton. Here the crop-lien system and the ignorance of the typical small farmer stood in the way. With the spread of the boll weevil in the 1890's, cotton growers in some areas were forced to grow other crops. Thus in time the boll weevil was seen to be a blessing in disguise.

Use of farm machinery grows.

Outside the South, the use of farm machinery was rising rapidly. In 1899 the Patent Office reported that up to that time it had issued nearly 66,000 patents for farm implements and machines. This figure reflects the lively interest of American farmers in devices to save labor. The use of these devices steadily raised the average output per farmer. For example, in 1830 the growing and harvesting of a bushel of wheat took over 3 hours of human labor. By the end of the century only 10 minutes was needed. The reduction was made possible by the use of the gang plow, seed drill, and the combine. The combine reaped, threshed, cleaned, and bagged the grain in one continuous operation. The largest of these machines was drawn by forty horses and could harvest up to 70 or 80 acres in one day.

In almost every branch of farming, machinery was introduced. Shortly before the War between North and South the mowing machine, horse-drawn rake, hay drier, and mechanical hay fork came into use, reducing by four fifths the time needed to harvest a ton of hay. After the war the corn planter, potato planter, fertilizer drill, manure spreader, corn sheller, cream separator, incubator, and a hundred other machines began to lighten the farmer's toil. Small farmers and others without money were of course slow to adopt machinery. Even today, when there is such an abundance of machinery, some farmers struggle along using hand tools.

The use of farm machinery made it possible for the farmer to feed the growing number of city dwellers. When Jackson was President, 80 per cent of the population lived and worked on farms, but by 1900 less than 40 per cent were farmers. By 1950 the proportion had dropped to 15 per cent.

Mechanization brings problems.

The introduction of machinery brought problems that farmers had never known before. Formerly farm equipment was simple and cheap. Frequently the farmer made it himself. Once he had it, it might last a lifetime. Now the farmer needed expensive equipment, which must be replaced every few years. Without it he could not compete with farmers who were well-equipped, because their output was so much greater. A farmer also needed more land than formerly, since machines do not pay for themselves on a small farm. In most areas good land was no longer to be had at low cost. A farmer therefore had to invest considerable money just to get started. Many went into debt to buy machinery.

Science helps the farmer.

Agricultural science developed faster in this period than ever before. Biologists produced new varieties of plants and better breeds of livestock and poultry. (Luther Burbank's work as a plant breeder is especially noteworthy.) Soil chemists developed new fertilizers and more efficient methods of soil management to preserve moisture and fertility. Entomologists discovered ways to control many insect pests. Microbiologists found ways to control a number of plant and animal diseases. The work of these scientists enabled each farmer, as well as each acre of land, to produce more.

The federal and state governments did much to encourage scientific farming. An important step was taken by

480

Congress in 1862 when it passed the Land-Grant College Act (see p. 446). The same year Congress set up the Bureau of Agriculture "to acquire and diffuse . . . useful information on subjects connected with agriculture . . . and to distribute new and valuable seeds and plants." The states also began to set up agricultural bureaus. In 1887 Congress appropriated money to establish an agricultural experiment station in each state. Every year since that time, both Congress and the states have set aside funds for agricultural research.

New methods of marketing appear.

One aspect of the Agricultural Revolution was the development of new ways of marketing farm produce. The introduction of the refrigerator car in the 1870's was especially important. Refrigeration made it possible to send fresh meat to all parts of the United States and to other countries. The refrigerator car encouraged dairying, since it could carry fluid milk from the farm to the city. It also led farmers in the Far West and the South to grow perishable fruits and vegetables for shipment to all parts of the country. The growth of the canning industry also helped farmers to supply a distant market. The canning of condensed and evaporated milk, for example, gave dairy farmers living far from cities a market for their milk. Taken together, refrigeration and canning made possible a great expansion in the production of meat, milk, fruit, and other perishables.

Farmers depend on market conditions.

The change from subsistence to commercial farming began in any area after canals or railroads were built there. The change went on throughout the century, as small, self-sufficient farms gave way more and more to farms of larger size producing for the market.

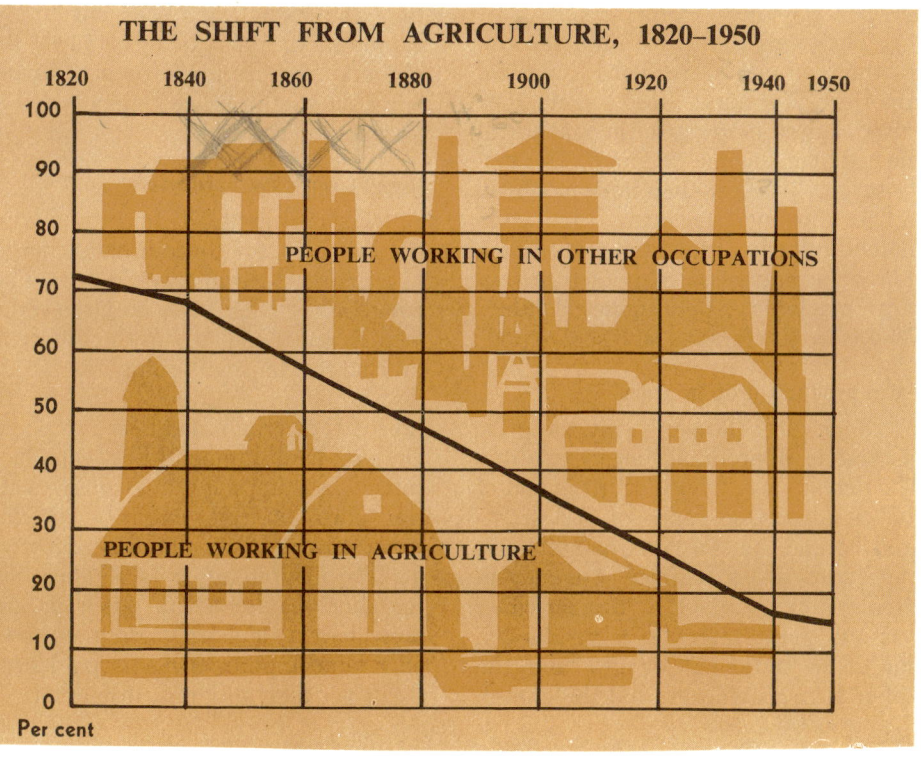

THE SHIFT FROM AGRICULTURE, 1820–1950

The commercial farmer concentrated his efforts on one or more cash crops and bought what his family needed.

Such specialization made for far greater efficiency. Yet it was not an unmixed blessing. To make a living, the commercial farmer had to cultivate more land than the self-sufficient farmer. To compete with other commercial farmers, he had to use machinery and up-to-date methods. Often he was forced to borrow heavily for land and equipment. He also became dependent on market conditions. If the demand for his crop was high, he made money, while the self-sufficient farmer just made a living. If prices fell, on the other hand, the sale of the commercial farmer's crop might not bring enough to meet family expenses, to say nothing of taxes, interest, and the cost of growing another crop.

Farmers Are Discontented

Farmers' problems increase.

The years from 1865 until the end of the century were hard ones for American farmers. Each year they raised larger crops, yet their share of the national income declined. The majority got little for their toil and lived in fear of losing their farms. They complained bitterly against the middlemen, railroad companies, manufacturers of farm machinery, and money lenders. Why were the farmers so discontented?

Farm products drop in price.

Soon after the war's end, the price of American products began to drop. The decline lasted until near the end of the century. One cause of the drop—and the one that farmers thought most important—was a scarcity of money in circulation (see p. 485). Another cause was the great increase in production due to the settlement of new land, the use of farm machinery, and the growth

of agricultural science. Production was expanding faster than the market. Businessmen could combine to limit output and keep up prices, but farmers could not combine. Each farmer produced as much as he could and sold it for what it would bring.

The surplus of staple crops was sold abroad, chiefly in Europe. But these markets also received exports of other agricultural countries. American grain, for example, competed with grain from Russia, Canada, Australia, and Argentina. American cotton competed with ever-increasing supplies from India and Egypt. Any change in crop prices on the world market was reflected in prices at home.

Manufactured goods are high.

While prices received by the farmer were falling, many of the prices he had to pay did not go down. In fact, some prices rose. As trusts got control of various industries, they limited domestic competition. Since at the same time the high tariffs shut out foreign competition, the prices of farm machinery, fertilizer, kerosene, barbed wire, shoes, and other items needed by farmers all were high.

Freight rates are burdensome.

Farmers generally had to pay high freight rates, for the railroads charged as much as the traffic would bear. They commonly gave rebates to large industrial shippers, making up the difference in charges to small shippers. Besides discriminating between shippers, the railroads discriminated between places. On long-haul shipments between places served by competing lines or by water transportation, rates might be cut close to actual cost. Then the difference was made up by charging far higher rates for short hauls, where the rail company had a monopoly. Farmers living near noncompetitive points paid heavily to get their products to market.

482

Middlemen take a large slice.

Farmers also paid high charges to the middlemen who helped them market their crops. The corporations owning the grain elevators, stockyards, and other storage facilities at terminals generally had a monopoly and could charge what they liked. In the 1860's, it was estimated, farmers west of the Mississippi paid middlemen 50 cents out of each dollar for grain sent to Atlantic ports. Since freight cost as much more, the farmer got little for himself. Sometimes the grain brought less than the cost of getting it to market.

Interest payments crush many.

If a farmer had to borrow money, he could not get it so cheaply as a merchant or a manufacturer. In the West he paid 10 to 20 per cent interest. In the South he might pay 30 to 50 per cent. Many a farmer's family went in rags because the interest on borrowed money took every cent they could earn. Thousands lost their farms every year because they could not keep up the payment of interest on their mortgages. A Nebraska editor complained:

> There are three great crops raised in Nebraska. One is a crop of corn, one a crop of freight rates, and one a crop of interest. One is produced by farmers who by sweat and toil farm the land. The other two are produced by men who sit in their offices and behind their bank counters and farm the farmers.

Repayment of debts is difficult.

A fall in the price of farm products brought disaster to many a farmer who had debts. For example, the money he borrowed when his wheat was worth a dollar a bushel might have to be repaid when wheat was worth fifty cents a bushel. If he could not meet his debt when due, he would probably lose his farm and become a laborer or a tenant farmer. Loss of their farms threatened millions of farmers, for nearly half of America's farm owners had mortgages on their property.

Farmers Organize to Solve Their Problems

Granger movement sweeps the West.

Farmers gradually saw that they must organize. In 1867 a group of clerks in the Bureau of Agriculture, led by Oliver H. Kelley, started a national secret society for farmers and their wives. This new order was called the "Patrons of Husbandry," or more commonly the "Grange." Its purpose was to break down the isolation of farm life and create opportunities for farm families to get together. The order grew rapidly during the hard times of the early seventies, for farmers wanted a chance to meet to discuss their problems. Soon there were Granges in nearly every state. The movement was strongest in the grain-growing region of the Upper Mississippi Valley.

The Grangers establish co-operatives.

Economic distress among Grangers led them to organize co-operatives. A co-operative enterprise is owned by its members. In running its affairs each member has one vote. Any profits are divided among members once a year, according to the amount of business each has done with the co-operative.

Between 1870 and 1875 the co-operative fever spread through the West. Many Granges organized co-operative stores for their members. On farm equipment they saved at least 30 per cent. When the big makers of farm machinery refused to sell to co-operatives, the Grangers bought several small factories for making farm equipment. Hundreds of co-operative marketing associations, creameries, grain elevators, and warehouses were formed to reduce middlemen's charges. In some areas co-

A FARMERS' CO-OPERATIVE *grain mill near Statesville, North Carolina. As the sign on the mill shows, a co-operative both belongs to and serves the farmers who own it.*

operative insurance companies and loan agencies were set up. When well-managed, the co-operatives often saved members a great deal of money. Yet the more successful the co-operatives were, the more fiercely they were fought by their enemies. Railroad companies, for example, stopped supplying cars to co-operative grain elevators. Banks might foreclose the mortgages of farmers who dealt with co-operatives. Thus most of the co-operatives soon had to close.

Grangers demand curbs on monopolies.

Although the purpose of the order was social and educational, many of the Granges turned early to political action. They demanded laws to correct abuses by railroads and grain elevators and to regulate their services and their rates. The legislatures of a number of Midwestern states responded by passing what were known as "Granger laws."

Regulation of public utilities is upheld.

The big corporations refused to obey the "Granger laws," saying that the government had no right to interfere with their business. Their lawyers argued that state regulation of rates violated the Fourteenth Amendment by depriving the corporation of its property without due process of law. They asked the Supreme Court to declare the Granger laws unconstitutional.

In 1876 the Supreme Court upheld the Granger laws in a series of cases. The most far-reaching decision (*Munn vs. Illinois*, 1876) had to do with an Illinois law fixing charges for the storage of grain in warehouses or elevators. The Supreme Court based its decision on the right of the state, in the exercise of its police power, to regulate common carriers, ferries, inns, and the like. The court declared that:

Property does become clothed with a public interest when used in a manner to make it of public consequence and affect the community at large. . . . When private property is devoted to public use, it is subject to public regulation.

In effect, grain warehouses and elevators were declared to be *public utilities* and therefore subject to public regulation.

The Interstate Commerce Act.

The railroads fought the Granger laws until most of them were repealed. Meanwhile, railroad lawyers kept bringing cases before the Supreme Court in which they challenged the decision in *Munn* vs. *Illinois*. In two cases decided in 1886 the railroads won a sweeping victory. In the Santa Clara case, the Court said that the Fourteenth Amendment does apply to corporations. If a state sets rates too low to permit a reasonable profit, said the Court, a corporation is deprived of its property without due process of law. In the case of *Wabash* vs. *Illinois*, the Court ruled that a state may not fix rates on commerce that crosses state lines. Since most railroad traffic does cross a state line, this decision made the states almost helpless to regulate railroads.

By the time these decisions were handed down (1886), the Granger movement had lost its strength. Other farm organizations had developed, however, and they urged Congress to take action in regard to railroads. The next year the Interstate Commerce Act was passed. It applied only to railroads passing through more than one state.

This law forbade railroads (a) to give rebates, (b) to discriminate between persons or localities in fixing rates, (c) to charge a higher rate per mile for short hauls than for long, and (d) to pool their traffic. The act required railroads to publish their rates and give advance notice of any changes. To supervise the railroads the act created the Interstate Commerce Commission. The Commission was given power to investigate but little to act. While it could issue orders, it could make the railroads obey only by bringing them into court. Court rulings usually took the teeth out of its recommendations. All manner of shady practices continued until Congress, years later, gave the Interstate Commerce Commission enough power to be effective. While the Interstate Commerce Act of 1887 was weak, it was at least a beginning in the regulation of railroads by the federal government.

Farmers demand cheap money.

The Grangers had centered their political activity in a crusade against the railroads. Meanwhile, another proposal for curing the farmers' ills began to attract attention. This plan called for expanding the supply of money in order to raise prices. To understand why farmers thought this would help, we should keep in mind that the value of money changes according to the quantity in circulation. Increase the quantity in relation to the amount of goods and services available, and the dollar drops in value. Prices therefore go up. Decrease the quantity of money without decreasing the supply of goods and services, and the dollar is worth more. Prices therefore go down. We may express the relationship in an equation:

$$\text{Prices} = \frac{\text{Quantity of money in circulation}}{\text{Quantity of goods and services}}$$

Since farmers wanted higher prices, they wanted to increase the money supply.

For a generation after the War between North and South, however, the money supply did not expand, although production went up enormously. Relative to population, the supply of money actually shrank. In 1865, after the currency had been inflated by a wartime issue of $400,000,000 in greenbacks, there were $31 in circulation for every person in the country. By 1895 per capita circulation was only $17. The drop in the money supply was an important reason, though not the only one, for the drop in farm prices.

Farmers join the Greenback movement.

In the late 1860's the Treasury began to retire the paper money, or greenbacks, issued during the war. As a result the greenbacks at once became scarcer and more valuable. Farmers, many of whom had borrowed these paper dollars during the war

485

when they were worth as little as 40 cents in gold or silver, protested the change in money values. Why, they asked, should they have to pay their debts with dollars worth more than those they had borrowed? Why should the Treasury, by contracting the currency, benefit creditors at the expense of debtors?

For ten years "hard money" men and "soft money" men fought over the question of greenbacks. Bankers and others with money to lend claimed that the only sound or honest money was gold or silver, or notes exchangeable, dollar for dollar, for gold or silver. Congress listened to the "hard money" men and in 1875 passed the Resumption Act. It said that the Treasury would redeem in gold all greenbacks presented to it after January 1, 1879.

Farmers and other debtors formed the Greenback party to fight for repeal of the Resumption Act. The party also tried to get Congress to issue more greenbacks. "Inflate the currency," argued a Greenbacker, "and you raise the price of my steers and at the same time pay off the public debt." In the election of 1878 the Greenback party obtained over a million votes. It did not succeed in having the Resumption Act repealed or in getting a larger supply of greenbacks. Still it did persuade Congress to leave the greenbacks outstanding (about $347,000,000) in circulation.

Farmers did not give up the struggle for cheaper money. In the 1880's and 1890's they joined a movement for unlimited, or free, coinage of silver. They also went on demanding curbs on monopolies. How they continued their fight for better conditions is told in the next chapter.

FOR IDENTIFICATION

Granger movement
Greenback party
Interstate Commerce Commission
Oliver H. Kelley

Munn vs. Illinois
Patrons of Husbandry
Resumption Act
Wabash vs. Illinois

FOR EXPLANATION OR DEFINITION

commercial farming
co-operatives
crop-lien
diversification

farm tenancy
"hard money"
share cropper
subsistence farming

FOR REVIEW

1. Why did the share-crop system develop in the South?

2. What was the crop-lien system? Why did it tend to retard agricultural progress?

3. Why did cotton prices decline in the 1880's?

4. Why did the practice of crop diversification develop slowly in the South?

5. (a) List ten laborsaving farm machines. (b) What problems developed with the mechanization of the farm?

6. How did the use of farm machinery affect the proportion of the population living on the farms? The size of farms? The sum needed to start and run farms?

7. How did agricultural science help farm production? What did the federal government do to encourage scientific farming? What did the states do?

8. Describe the important changes in the marketing of farm products after 1865.

9. Summarize the advantages and disadvantages of specialized farming.

10. (a) Explain the reasons why farmers were discontented in the period 1865–1900. (b) What proposals did the farmers advocate to improve conditions? (c) Describe the Granger movement and what it accomplished in the period 1867–76.

11. (a) What is a co-operative? (b) What advantages does it bring its members?

12. (a) Why did farmers demand that railroads and grain elevators be regulated? (b) State the decision of the Supreme Court in Munn vs. Illinois.

13. (a) What was the decision of the Supreme Court in the case of *Wabash* vs. *Illinois*? Why did this decision lead to the passage of the Interstate Commerce Act of 1887? (b) State the chief provisions of this law. What were its weaknesses?

14. (a) Why did the farmers demand "cheap money"? (b) Review instances in our earlier history of the same demand.

15. (a) What were the demands of the Greenback party, 1875–84? (b) Why did many farmers and debtors support it? (c) What other "cheap money" proposal did the farmers support at a later date?

FOR FURTHER STUDY AND DISCUSSION

1. How are debtors affected by rising prices? By declining prices? How are creditors affected? (Review the story of Shays's Rebellion, p. 134.)

2. What was at issue in the case of *Munn* vs. *Illinois*? State the argument of the Court. Helpful source: Commager, *Documents*, No. 294.

3. (a) What was the issue in the case of *Wabash* vs. *Illinois*? (b) Describe the "short and long haul" abuse in this case. (c) Summarize the argument and suggestions of the Court. Helpful source: Commager, *Documents*, No. 314.

4. Although the Interstate Commerce Act of 1887 was weak and ineffective, it is commonly regarded as an important milestone in federal legislation. Why?

5. Summarize the ideas advanced by the Grangers in 1873 and 1874. Helpful source: Commager, *Documents*, No. 287.

FOR INDIVIDUAL OR GROUP ACTIVITIES

1. Arrange a picture exhibit on the development of farm machinery. Helpful source: Davidson, *Life in America*.

2. Prepare short sketches of the careers and accomplishments of Luther Burbank and George Washington Carver.

3. Deliver floor talks on the social activities and influence of the Grangers and on the workings of a co-operative. Have a special committee prepare a chart of statistics on co-operatives today. Helpful sources: Buck, *The Agrarian Crusade* (Y.C.S.); *The World Almanac*.

4. Compare farm problems and issues of the period 1870–1900 with farm problems and issues today. Helpful source: Buck, *The Agrarian Crusade* (Y.C.S.).

"CORNHUSKING." *As the painting shows, this tradition had both economic and social advantages—the farmer got his work done and the young people had a chance to meet one another.*

Great wealth and lavishness were the keynotes of NINE-TEENTH CENTURY WEALTH. Mrs. William Astor's art gallery ballroom (above) and W. K. Vanderbilt's marble palace in Newport demonstrate the opulence of the "Gilded Age."

Modern politics is a struggle not of men but of forces.——Henry Adams

30. POLITICAL DISCONTENT PRODUCES POPULISM

A Low Moral Tone Prevailed in Business and Politics

Opportunities are dazzling.

The swift economic changes that took place after 1865 offered businessmen and speculators many chances to get rich. A billion acres of the public domain, much of it covered with virgin forest and some of it rich in minerals, could be bought for a song or obtained free. The rapidly growing population provided both a market for industry and an abundant labor supply. The expanding cities clamored not only for industrial products but for water, sewer, and gas systems, for paved streets and street lights, for streetcar lines, and new public buildings. Throughout the country, every community stood ready to offer money and other gifts to any railroad company which would run a line through it. In addition, rich rewards were open to those who could combine competing businesses into large and powerful units.

Success is measured in wealth.

In this period ambitious young men more often went into business than into politics. The successful businessman was more honored than the political leader. The admiration that the prewar generation gave to men like Clay, Calhoun, and Webster now went to men like Vanderbilt, Rockefeller, and Carnegie. Success was measured more and more by the acquisition of wealth.

In the scramble for wealth those with the fewest scruples had the advantage. Fortunes were won more quickly and surely by unfair methods than by honest service to the public. Some businessmen were "robber barons" who got ahead by crushing their competitors, by oppressing their employees, by selling watered stock for a price far above its real value, by manipulating the stock market, by fraudulent claims to public land, and by corrupt deals with public officials. Such men felt no moral obligation to the public. Their business activities seemed to them a strictly private affair.

Businessmen seek government favors.

All levels of government—municipal, state, and national—must purchase supplies and make contracts for constructing public works. In addition, all levels of government make laws that help or hurt businessmen. Officeholders who can award a contract, vote for a law affecting business, or overlook a law violation are courted by businessmen. Corruption arises when the office-holder accepts any sort of bribe, such as money, gifts, entertainment. In fact, the source of political corruption is the desire of citizens for special favors.

In the generation after 1865 political corruption flourished. It was found in many parts of the country and at all levels of government. It was worst in the large cities, where officials had new responsibilities, such as water supply and street paving, and had to handle ever greater funds. The opportunities for graft in a large city are illustrated by the story of the Tweed Ring.

The Tweed Ring rules New York.

William M. Tweed, a poor book-keeper, was elected alderman in New York City in 1851. Within a few years he became leader of the Democratic organization, Tammany Hall. He placed himself and three friends in important posts in the city government. This "Tweed Ring" gained full control of city funds.

Tweed's power, like that of any political "boss," depended on his ability to "deliver the vote." As leader of Tammany Hall, he befriended as many voters as possible. Tammany served the workingman as a social club and a welfare agency. It met immigrants when they landed, found jobs for them, and helped them get their naturalization papers. In case of hard times Tammany got aid for its members. It frequently provided picnics and outings at no cost. Thus it won favor and votes among the poor. In addition Tammany could count on the votes of those who worked for the city, those who received contracts from the city, and those who held licenses from the city. All these people stood to lose if Tammany lost an election.

On election day Tammany's precinct leaders would make sure that all its friends went to the polls. Were victory in doubt, the precinct leaders would pack the ballot boxes in favor of Tammany candidates. This was done by hiring voters to vote several times under different names.

The Tweed Ring used its power to enrich itself. Franchises were sold, contracts were sold, jobs were sold, licenses were sold, tax favors were sold. In addition the Ring robbed the city of at least thirty million dollars in padded charges on city purchases. For a court-house designed to cost $250,000, the city paid sixty times as much. The bill for carpets alone was $300,000, and most of the carpets went to a hotel owned by Tweed's son.

The Tweed Ring was over in 1871 when the *New York Times* Harper's Weekly exposed it. Tweed was brought to justice, but most of his confederates escaped punishment. Within three years Tammany Hall again controlled the city. Its leaders no longer indulged in the open plunder that led to Tweed's downfall. Yet New York, like other big cities, continued to suffer from political corruption.

Corruption on the state level.

A congressional investigating committee reported in 1873:

> The country is fast becoming filled with gigantic corporations wielding and controlling immense aggregations of money and thereby commanding great influence and wealth. It is notorious in many state legislatures that these influences are often controlling.

In this period, railroad companies commonly tried to dominate state legislatures and state courts. When Jay Gould and Cornelius Vanderbilt were fighting for control of the Erie Railroad, both gave bribes to state senators and judges. Later, Gould said he had obtained control of the legislatures of four states.

Corruption on the national level.

National politics is usually cleaner than state and local politics. In the postwar period, however, corruption reached into Congress and even into the Cabinet. The most notorious example came to light in 1872. The directors of the Union Pacific had organized themselves into a construction company named the Crédit Mobilier. They charged the Union Pacific over three times as much for building the road as it really cost. To block an investigation by Congress, Congressman Oakes Ames, one of the organizers of the Crédit Mobilier, sold shares of stock at half price to other congressmen. Ames even lent them money to buy the stock. When the facts came out, Ames was censured by Congress.

On the opposite page, A POLITICAL BARBECUE *in New York City.* (Left) WILLIAM M. ("BOSS") TWEED *and* (below) CORNELIUS VANDERBILT.

The Major Parties Straddle the Real Issues

Republicans dominate national politics.

The Republicans had come to power in 1861 by winning the support of Western farmers and Northern businessmen. The party emerged from the war with new strength and popularity. It had saved the Union and put an end to slavery. In addition, its economic policies pleased large numbers of voters (p. 413). For many decades it would dominate national politics most of the time.

The Democratic party recovers.

The Democratic party, which had been the controlling party since 1800, was weakened by the war. It had lost the support of Western farmers. Outside the South the Democratic party was handicapped by the charge of disloyalty. Its Southern members were blamed for secession. Its Northern members were blamed because so many of them had opposed the war. For a long time after the war Republican orators harped on the charge of disloyalty. This was described as "waving the bloody shirt."[1]

Yet the Democratic party soon began to recover. It could count on the votes of workingmen in most of the large Northern cities. (A few cities, such as Philadelphia, were Republican strongholds.) After the withdrawal of federal troops from the South in 1877, it could also count on carrying every state that had undergone Radical reconstruction (see p. 401). Its candidate for President won a majority of the popular vote in four out of nine elections between 1868 and 1900. However, it won a majority of the electoral vote in only two. Although the Democrats rarely elected a President, they often had a majority in the House of Representatives.

Both parties try to please businessmen.

Republican leaders consisted mostly of businessmen and other men of wealth. They held firmly to the idea that what is good for business is good for the country. They believed the government should actively help business by such means as tariffs and subsidies, but otherwise should leave it alone.

While the Republicans were regarded as the party of business, the Democrats still claimed to be the party of farmers and workingmen. However, as Southern manufacturing and commerce grew, the Democratic party gained members from the business class. In fact the party looked to this class for leadership and for financial support. As a result the party gave up its historic stand against national banking and government aid to business. Democratic congressmen might argue in favor of a low tariff, but they usually voted for a high tariff when it gave protection to industries in their districts.

Both parties obtained campaign funds from wealthy businessmen. In return contributors expected tariff protection and other favors. Big corporations often contributed to both parties. The sugar trust, for example, supported the Democrats in a Democratic state and the Republicans in a Republican state. It did so expecting that the men elected to office would take care of its interests.

The major parties differ but little.

Every four years each party drew up a platform stating its views and its program. Since each party had to please at least three groups of voters—businessmen, farmers, and wage earners—it could not take a firm stand on issues that divided them. Platform writers

---

[1] The phrase originated when Congressman Ben Butler showed the House of Representatives a nightshirt stained with the blood of a flogged carpetbagger.

492

tended to avoid the real issues or to use high-sounding phrases that meant little. The two parties differed less on principles than on strategy. Strategy depended on whether the party was in or out of office. The "in party" gloated on its record. The "out party" accused the "ins" of corruption and cried, "Turn the rascals out!"

James Bryce, the English statesman who visited our country in the 1880's, wrote in his book, *The American Commonwealth*:

Neither party has any clear-cut principles . . . Both certainly have war-cries, organization, interests enlisted in their support. But those interests are in the main the interests of getting and keeping the patronage of the government.

Third parties demand reforms.

In the years from 1870 to 1896 there was great unrest among farmers and laborers. They made up a left, or radical, wing in each of the major parties. When they could not get the conservative, or right, wing to listen to their demands, they were likely to desert to a third party. In each presidential campaign from 1872 on, one or more minor parties appeared. They asked for reforms such as a larger supply of money, regulation of railroads, laws to protect wage earners, reduction of the tariff, and inheritance and income taxes. They condemned the old parties as tools of big business. Most of the minor parties began in a period of hard times and faded away when conditions improved. Their lack of financial backing kept them from making much headway.

A Series of One-Term Administrations Does Little

Our political history in the years from the death of Lincoln to the death of McKinley is unimpressive. It was a period in which Congress refused to accept presidential leadership. Some Presidents, including Johnson, Hayes, Arthur, and Cleveland, tried to guide the nation and were blocked by Congress. Others were satisfied to let Congress determine the nation's course. No President who served in this period achieved much. Little was done to find solutions to the problems of the period.

Grant is a failure as President.

General Grant was unfamiliar with the ways of politicians. In making appointments he took advice from party leaders who cared little for the public welfare. Many of those he appointed turned out to be dishonest or incompetent. Grant even chose unscrupulous men for posts in the Cabinet. The President's brother-in-law was involved in a plot to corner the gold supply of the country. After a one-day panic known as "Black Friday" (September 24, 1869), the country learned that the President himself had been duped into helping the plotters.

A group known as "Liberal Republicans" tried to prevent Grant's re-election in 1872. The Liberals called for purifying the government, for lower tariffs, and for an end to the policy of punishing the South. They held a convention and nominated Horace Greeley for President. The Democrats also nominated Greeley. Grant, however, easily won re-election.

With the exception of Harding's term as President (see p. 654), we have had no administration so smirched by corruption as was Grant's. In Grant's second term frauds came to light in one executive department after another. One of the most heartless was the illegal sale of trading posts in the Indian Territory. The traders cheated the Indians and paid the Secretary of War for the privilege. The President's personal secretary was involved in a Whiskey Ring, which robbed the Treasury of

HAMILTON FISH

would not pay, Sumner said the United States should seize Canada. This threat was greatly resented by the British. Secretary of State Fish lessened the tension by dropping the claims for indirect damages. Great Britain then expressed regret for the escape of the *Alabama* and other vessels. She agreed to let an international court decide how much she owed in direct damages. The court, which included one representative each from the United States, Great Britain, Italy, Brazil, and Switzerland, awarded us $15,000,000 in gold for the *Alabama* claims. We, in turn, were told to pay $7,430,000 for British claims against our government. The settlement, known as the Geneva Award, cleared the air and led to better feelings between the two nations.

a million dollars a year in taxes. These are but two of many cases of wrongdoing by men close to the President.

Relations with Great Britain improve.

Almost the only achievements of Grant's administration were in foreign affairs. The Secretary of State, Hamilton Fish, was among the ablest we have ever had. To him goes the credit for negotiating the Treaty of Washington (1871), a milestone in our relations with Great Britain. By this treaty Britain and the United States agreed to submit their disputes to arbitration.

Among the questions to be settled was a disputed boundary line in Puget Sound, the right of Americans to fish in Canadian waters, and claims of British subjects for war damage. The worst quarrel had to do with damage done to United States shipping by the *Alabama* and other Confederate cruisers built in British shipyards (see pp. 376–77). Charles Sumner, chairman of the Senate Committee on Foreign Relations, claimed that Great Britain owed us more than two billion dollars for direct and indirect damages. If the British

Graft and hard times are 1876 issues.

The panic of 1873 ushered in five years of hard times. The Republicans, who had taken credit for prosperity, now got the blame for the depression. The Democrats won most of the midterm elections of 1874 and expected to win the Presidency in 1876. They nominated Governor Samuel J. Tilden of New York. Tilden had led the fight against the Tweed Ring and other grafters in his state. The Republicans also named a reformer, Governor Rutherford B. Hayes of Ohio.

The Democrats made reform their chief talking point. They also demanded the recall of federal troops from the South. Republican orators "waved the bloody shirt" as usual, urging men to "vote as they shot." The campaign was a quiet one in the North. In some of the Southern states violent disorders broke out over efforts to frighten Negro voters away from the polls.

The election of 1876 is disputed.

When the election returns were in, the nation suddenly found itself facing a crisis. Tilden had a clear majority of

494

the popular votes and 184 electoral votes that were sure. He needed 185 to win. Hayes had 165 votes that surely belonged to him. Twenty electoral votes were in doubt. Nineteen of these came from South Carolina, Florida, and Louisiana, which were still under military control. These states had sent in two sets of returns, one favoring the Democrats and one the Republicans. The other doubtful vote came from Oregon. To win, Hayes needed *all* of these doubtful votes, while Tilden needed but one of them.

The Constitution is silent as to who shall pass upon disputed returns. Congress could not agree, for the Senate was Republican and the House Democratic. The nation grew more and more uneasy as the date for inaugurating a President drew near. At last a way was found out of the deadlock. Congress set up an electoral commission consisting of eight Republicans and seven Democrats. After long deliberation, the commission decided it could not go behind the returns certified by the state authorities.[1] Since in each case the state authorities were Republican, all of the disputed votes went to Hayes.

Regardless of his own feelings, Hayes had no choice but to accept the commission's findings. Two days later he took the oath of office. No disturbance marred the event. A controversy which in many countries would have provoked a revolution had been peacefully settled. This was a tribute to Hayes and Tilden. Throughout the months of uncertainty, both had placed the good of the nation first. It was also a tribute to the American people.

---

[1] While the decision caused anger at the time, its wisdom was gradually accepted. Ten years later Congress passed the Electoral Count Act, requiring the states to settle all disputes as to their presidential electors. Congress was directed to accept only those electoral returns which bear the governor's seal.

The last federal troops leave the South.

In his inaugural address Hayes announced his motto: "He serves his party best who serves his country best." To carry out this motto he repeatedly offended the leaders of his own party. Shortly after taking office, the new President withdrew federal troops from South Carolina and Louisiana. The Republican governments in those states promptly collapsed. Since the Republican government in Florida had already fallen, the Democrats were now in control in all the former Confederate states. Radical reconstruction had ended and the Solid South had begun (p. 401). From that time on, the federal government made no effort to enforce the Fifteenth, or Negro suffrage, Amendment in the South.

Hayes backs civil service reform.

The civil service is made up of the officials, clerks, and others who man the executive branch of the government. Under the "spoils system" which then existed, the party in power filled these jobs with faithful party workers. Jobholders had to show their loyalty to the party by giving a percentage of their salary to its campaign funds and by spending a good part of their time doing party work. The system made for wastefulness, inefficiency, and corruption. To cite one example, Hayes found that the New York customhouse had two hundred men on the payroll who were doing no work whatever for the government. They had been appointed at the request of the New York Republican boss, Senator Roscoe Conkling.

Hayes was the first President who seriously tried to get rid of the spoils system. He filled his Cabinet with men who believed in civil service reform. He told them that appointments and promotions were to be made strictly on the basis of merit. He issued an order to all federal employees saying that they were not to take part in political

495

campaigns. Also, their salaries were not to be assessed for campaign expenses. These policies angered the Republican "old guard," who called themselves "Stalwarts." They sneered at Hayes as a "half-breed" Republican and fought his reform efforts.

Congress refused to pass a civil service law. If the merit system replaced the spoils system, jobholders would be chosen by examination and not upon recommendation by a congressman. Why should congressmen give up the patronage that helped them stay in office? Civil service reformers saw that they must stir up public opinion. They formed societies to work for the merit system at all levels of government.

The silver question arises.

During most of Hayes's term the country suffered from a severe business depression. Wage earners and farmers were extremely discontented. Nationwide railroad strikes in 1877 led to riots and the first use of federal troops to settle a labor dispute (see p. 460). Low prices for farm products drove farmers into the Greenback movement (see p. 485). When Congress made greenbacks redeemable in gold and refused to issue more of them, farmers demanded free, or unlimited, coinage of silver. This was another way to expand the currency.

Silver and gold had been recognized as money since the first days of the Republic. In 1834 the ratio between the two metals was fixed at 16 to 1. Later the value of silver went up in relation to gold, so that silver was worth less as money than in some other form. Then the silver miners sold all their silver to the silversmiths instead of bringing it to the mint to be coined. Silver dollars disappeared from circulation. In 1873 Congress voted to stop coining silver dollars; that is, silver was "demonetized." A year or two later

new silver mines, such as the Comstock lode, flooded the market with silver. Mineowners began to speak of demonetization as the "crime of '73." They clamored for the government to "remonetize silver" at the old ratio of 16 to 1. Silver was no longer worth so much, however, and Congress did nothing for a while.

The Bland-Allison Act.

The Greenback party backed up the miners' demand for free coinage of silver. In 1878 the silverites won a partial victory when Congress passed the Bland-Allison Act. The act directed the Treasury to buy not less than two nor more than four million dollars' worth of silver each month. Silver dollars were to be coined at the ratio of 16 to 1, although silver was still not worth that much. President Hayes vetoed the bill. He said it was dishonest for the government to make dollars which would be worth only 90 cents in gold. After much debate Congress finally passed the bill over his veto.

The Bland-Allison Act was in force for twelve years. The Treasury bought only the minimum amount of silver required by the act, and no inflation of the currency resulted. Neither the mineowners nor the farmers were satisfied. But business revived in 1879, and agitation for free silver died down for a few years.

Garfield is elected President.

Hayes gave the country an honest and courageous administration. Yet his efforts to reduce the evils of the spoils system antagonized Senator Conkling and other important party leaders and kept Hayes from being renominated in 1880. The Stalwarts, led by Conkling, tried to nominate Grant for a third term but failed. After a long deadlock, a "dark horse"—James A. Garfield of Ohio—was nominated. His running mate was Chester A. Arthur, a friend of Conkling's. In selecting Arthur, the Stalwarts showed their contempt for President Hayes, who had removed Arthur from his post as collector of customs in New York.

To oppose Garfield the Democrats named General Winfield S. Hancock. The newly formed Greenback-Labor party also had a candidate. Garfield won the Presidency with a safe majority of electoral votes, but his popular majority was under 8000.

Garfield is assassinated.

Garfield was the last of our presidents who was born in a log cabin. He had worked his way through college, taught school, been president of Hiram College, held the post of Major General in the Union army, and served in Congress from 1863.

Garfield was a friend of Hayes and displayed the same independence. He challenged Senator Conkling by filling important jobs in New York State without consulting him. Since senators regarded federal jobs in their state as their property, the President's action enraged Conkling. Garfield angered the Stalwarts still more by ordering an investigation of contracts for the delivery of mail on "star routes" in the West.[1] Much fraud was uncovered and those responsible for it were tried.

In July, only three months after he took office, Garfield was shot by Charles Guiteau, a demented office seeker. After Garfield's death in September, Vice-President Arthur took over his office.

Arthur works for civil service reform.

When Arthur became President, reformers expected the worst. As collector of the port of New York, he had given jobs to a large number of Conkling's henchmen. Would he continue to take orders from Conkling? The new President surprised the nation by devoting himself to reform. In his annual messages to Congress he urged that federal jobs be filled by competitive examination. He also discouraged the practice of "shaking down" federal employees to obtain campaign funds.

The murder of Garfield awakened the people to the need for a better method of filling federal jobs. In 1883 Congress passed the Pendleton Act. It forbade the assessment of federal employees for political contributions. It provided for a nonpartisan civil service commission of three members. The commission was to hold competitive examinations for the "classified service"—those offices which the President placed under the merit system. Arthur put one federal job in eight on the classified list. Each succeeding President has added other jobs to the list until about 75 per cent of the total have been classified.

Civil Service examinees

---

[1] Star routes were roads where the mail was carried under contract by a driver.

The Democrats return to power.

Arthur was too colorless to win public enthusiasm. Besides, he had offended the Stalwarts. When the Republican convention met in 1884, therefore, Arthur was dropped. The nomination went instead to James G. Blaine, a well-known politician from Maine. Blaine had served many years in Congress and had been Garfield's Secretary of State. His brilliant and magnetic personality attracted a large number of followers. Yet his record in Congress left doubts about his honesty. The reformers in his party refused to support him. They were promptly nicknamed "mugwumps"—an Indian word for "big chiefs"—because they thought themselves better than the rest of their party.

The Democrats nominated Governor Grover Cleveland of New York. Cleveland was the son of a poor country minister. He had studied law while working in a Buffalo law office. After passing his bar examination he went into politics. As sheriff of Erie County and later as mayor of Buffalo, he was a relentless foe of corrupt politicians. In 1882 he was elected governor of New York and became nationally known for his fearlessness and honesty. The leaders of Tammany Hall hated him. "We love him for the enemies he has made," said his friends.

The campaign of 1884 was one of the most disgraceful in our history. Ignoring any real issues, opponents accused both candidates of personal weaknesses. The vote was very close. By winning New York, Cleveland won the election. For the first time since 1856 the Democrats had elected a President.

Cleveland stands for honest government.

Cleveland believed sincerely that "public office is a public trust." He worked hard for what he considered to be the public welfare. "The Presidency," he said, "is the people's office."

By this he meant that the President should serve the whole people rather than special interests and groups.

The Democrats had been out of office for twenty-four years. Deserving party servants swarmed to Washington to seek jobs. Cleveland was strongly opposed to the spoils system and spent a great deal of time selecting good men for office. When he reappointed a Republican as postmaster of New York, party leaders howled. He angered them still more by doubling the jobs to be filled by competitive examination.

Cleveland was the first President to fight for conservation. He ordered an investigation of dishonest occupation of public lands. His Secretary of the Interior, L. Q. C. Lamar, recovered 81 million acres that were illegally occupied by cattle ranchers, railroads, timber companies, and squatters on Indian reservations.

Cleveland also made a determined effort to stamp out frauds in the granting of pensions to disabled Union veterans. Congress had the habit of passing private bills granting pensions to individuals unable to qualify under regular laws. Unlike earlier Presidents, Cleveland examined these bills with care. He vetoed 233 out of more than 700 passed during his administration. For this he was unjustly charged with "weighing the merits of the veterans in an apothecary's scale." He also vetoed a general pension bill to give a pension to every dependent veteran who had served three months.

Cleveland urges tariff reduction.

The high tariffs adopted during the War between North and South brought in more money than the government needed. Congress spent the surplus on public buildings and river and harbor improvements. Every congressman tried to get a share of the money for his district. The result was seen in extravagant "pork-barrel" bills.

Cleveland sent messages to Congress urging that the tariff be lowered, "to relieve the people of unnecessary taxation . . . and prevent the accumulation of a surplus in the Treasury to tempt to extravagant waste." The tariff then in force, he said, added many millions to the cost of living. While the tariff brought immense profits to manufacturers, he pointed out, wages were no higher in protected industries than in those without protection. A bill providing slightly lower duties passed the House but was ignored by the Senate.

Benjamin Harrison is elected.

In the campaign of 1888 the Democrats renominated Cleveland. The Republicans nominated former Senator Benjamin Harrison of Indiana, grandson of the Whig President, William Henry Harrison. The main issue was the tariff. The Republicans insisted that American prosperity depended on high rates. They collected a record-breaking campaign fund. Although Cleveland got 100,000 more popular votes, Harrison won by an electoral vote of 233 to 168.

Congress dominates Harrison's term.

Unlike Cleveland, Harrison did not try to influence Congress. He let the leaders of Congress shape the policies of the administration. For the first time in fifteen years the Republicans had a majority in both houses. They passed the Dependent Veteran Pension bill vetoed by Cleveland, nearly doubling the annual cost of pensions. They made large appropriations for warships and coastal defense, lighthouses, harbor improvements, and public buildings. Federal expenditures for one year reached $1,000,000,000 for the first time. When the Democrats denounced the "billion-dollar Congress,"

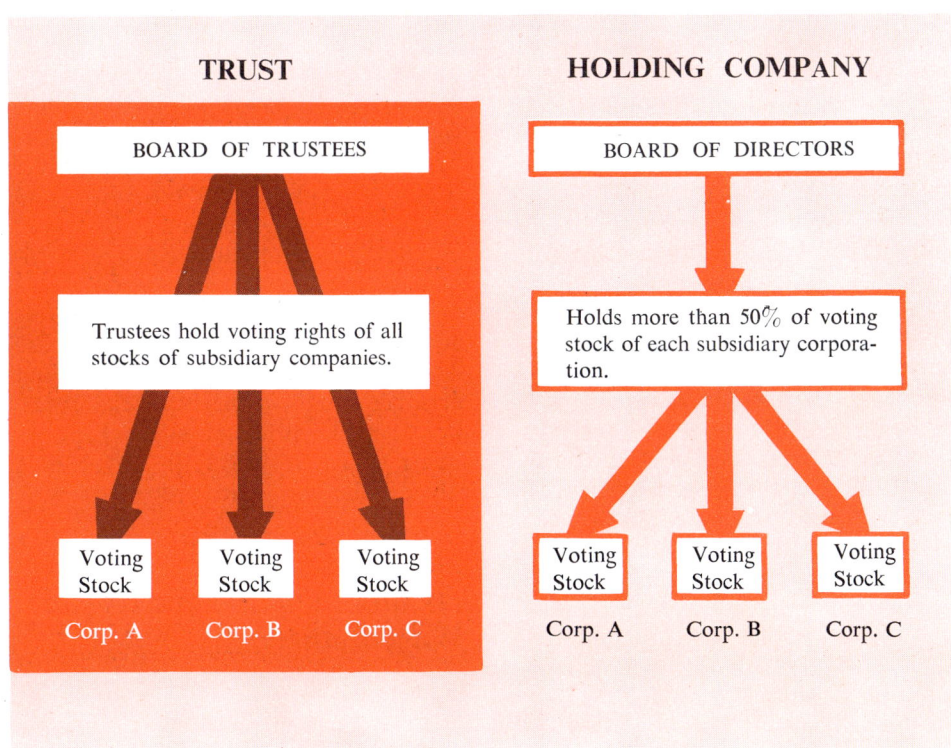

TRUST

BOARD OF TRUSTEES

Trustees hold voting rights of all stocks of subsidiary companies.

Voting Stock — Corp. A

Voting Stock — Corp. B

Voting Stock — Corp. C

HOLDING COMPANY

BOARD OF DIRECTORS

Holds more than 50% of voting stock of each subsidiary corporation.

Voting Stock — Corp. A

Voting Stock — Corp. B

Voting Stock — Corp. C

Speaker of the House Reed replied that this was a "billion-dollar country." This same Congress in 1890 adopted three other laws of far-reaching influence.

1. The Sherman Antitrust Act. Protests against monopolies were getting louder. In the 1870's the complaints had come from small businessmen who were being crushed to the wall and from farmers who had to pay high freight rates. During the eighties the public had begun to complain that the trusts were raising prices and making unreasonable profits. Some states had compelled the trusts to break up. But a trust broken up in one state might incorporate in another where the laws were less strict and go on doing business exactly as before. Federal regulation seemed to be necessary.

The first step in federal regulation of big business had come in 1887, when Congress passed the Interstate Commerce Act (see p. 484). This act applied only to railroads. The public demanded a law aimed at all kinds of big business.

In 1888 President Cleveland told Congress that "corporations which should be carefully restrained . . . and servants of the people, are fast becoming the people's masters." Both the Republican and Democratic parties claimed to be against monopolies. Finally, in 1890, Congress passed the Sherman Antitrust Act. It declared that "every contract, combination . . . or conspiracy in restraint of trade" is illegal. Because the terms "a combination," "conspiracy," and "restraint" were hard to define, the act proved a weak weapon against the trusts. They quickly found a way to get around the act. The great combinations simply changed their form from trust to *holding company* (p. 425). In 1895 the Supreme Court ruled that the Antitrust Act did not apply to holding companies. Thereafter combinations became more numerous and more powerful.

2. The McKinley Tariff. Soon after Congress met in 1890, William McKinley of Ohio, chairman of the House Ways and Means Committee, introduced a tariff bill. It raised the duties on practically every article produced in the United States. Duties were even placed on farm products like wheat, corn, and potatoes, of which we had a large surplus and which, therefore, we were not likely to import. After a long fight Secretary of State Blaine succeeded in having a *reciprocity* clause added to the tariff bill. It provided that countries opening their markets to our exports could ship tea, coffee, hides, spices, drugs, molasses, and raw sugar to the United States without having to pay a duty on them. The clause was intended to build up our trade with the countries of Latin America.

3. The Sherman Silver Purchase Act. Six new Western states had come into the Union in 1889 and 1890. Their senators refused to vote for the McKinley Tariff unless a bill was passed to help the silver miners. Since the Bland-Allison Act of 1878, the Treasury had been buying $2,000,000 worth of silver each month. But the output of silver was still climbing and the price continued to fall. Farmers and miners were clamoring for unlimited coinage of silver. To quiet them and to get votes needed to pass the tariff bill, Congress adopted the Sherman Silver Purchase Act. It more than doubled the amount of silver bought monthly by the Treasury. Yet the price of silver kept on going down. By 1893 the silver in a silver dollar was worth only 60 cents.

Populism Unites Farmers and Wage Earners

Farmers' Alliances call for reforms.

During the late 1880's farm prices reached the lowest level in many years.

500

World markets were flooded with grain and cotton. Wheat dropped to 50 cents a bushel, cotton to 6 cents a pound. Corn was so cheap in the Midwest that farmers burned it for fuel. Railroad rates, interest rates, and tax rates remained high. No matter how hard they toiled, most farmers got into debt and stood in continual danger of losing their farms.

These conditions led to a new protest movement among farmers. They formed clubs known as Alliances. The Northern Alliance was particularly strong in Kansas, Nebraska, Iowa, Minnesota, and the Dakotas. The hard-pressed farmers of the "middle border" joined it by the hundreds of thousands. The Southern Alliance covered the cotton and tobacco belt. Like the Grange, the Alliances provided social and educational programs which helped break down the isolation of farm life. The Alliances held farmers' institutes, conducted circulating libraries, and published hundreds of newspapers and magazines for farmers. In addition the Alliances set up co-operatives—stores, creameries, cotton warehouses, grain elevators, and an insurance company. Most of these ventures collapsed, as earlier ones had done, because of lack of capital, inexperienced management, and the hostility of banks and railroads (see p. 484). Just as the Grange had done in the 1870's, the Alliances turned to political action. Believing that big business controlled both the state and federal governments, they tried to elect legislators who would represent the farmer. They called for a broad program of reform.

Conservatives ridiculed their demands and spoke of Alliance members as "hayseed socialists." Yet the Alliances grew so rapidly that Congress had to listen to them. The Interstate Commerce Act, the Sherman Antitrust Act, and the Sherman Silver Purchase Act were passed partly because of Alliance pressure. These acts did not satisfy the Alliances. They thought the Interstate Commerce Act and the Sherman Antitrust Act were much too weak. They wanted free, or unlimited, coinage of silver. They had also asked for a lower tariff, but Congress had once again raised the rates.

The summer and fall of 1890 a political whirlwind swept the West and South. Crowds of farmers and wage earners gathered at picnic grounds and in schoolhouses, churches, and public halls to hear Alliance speakers. In Kansas, where the storm was fiercest, the most popular speaker was Mary Lease. She declared: "Wall Street owns the country. It is no longer a government of the people, by the people, and for the people, but a government of Wall Street, by Wall Street, and for Wall Street." She expressed the feeling of a multitude of the common people, and they flocked to hear her.

The People's party is organized.

The elections of 1890 sent more than a score of Alliance men to Congress and hundreds to the state legislatures. Western farm leaders were encouraged by this success. They decided to invite labor and reform groups to join them in forming a new political party. In May, 1891, over 1400 delegates met in Cincinnati. They included Knights of Labor, Greenbackers, silverites, single taxers, disciples of Edward Bellamy (see p. 449), and Alliance members. They organized the People's party, commonly known as "Populists." A second convention met at Omaha on Independence Day, 1892, to adopt a platform and nominate a presidential ticket. Following the custom of the major political parties, the Populists chose a war veteran as their standard-bearer. He was General James B. Weaver, an Iowan who had run for President on the Greenback-Labor ticket in 1880.

The Populists draw up a platform.

The platform adopted at the Omaha Convention has become a famous historical document. Its preamble blasted both the major parties and painted a dismal picture of the country.

We meet in the midst of a nation brought to the verge of moral, political, and material ruin. Corruption dominates the ballot box, the legislature, the Congress, and touches even the ermine of the bench. . . . The newspapers are largely subsidized and muzzled; public opinion silenced; business prostrated; our homes covered with mortgages; labor impoverished; and the land concentrating in the hands of the capitalist. The urban workmen are denied the right to organize for self-protection; imported pauperized labor beats down their wages; a hireling standing army, unrecognized by our laws, is established to shoot them down [1] . . . The fruits of the toil of millions are boldly stolen to build up colossal fortunes for a few. . . .

The new party, the preamble stated, sought to restore the government to the "plain people." The platform summarized the demands of farmers and wage earners:

1. A flexible currency system, controlled by the government, not the banks
2. An increase in the amount of money in circulation
3. Government loans at 2 per cent on nonperishable farm products and on farm real estate
4. A graduated income tax
5. Public ownership and operation of railroads, telegraphs, and telephones
6. A reduction of the tariff
7. Postal savings banks
8. Prohibition of land ownership by aliens and large speculators
9. Restriction of immigration
10. The eight-hour day for governmental and industrial workers
11. Prohibition of the use of private armies in labor disputes
12. The direct election of senators
13. A single term for President and Vice-President
14. Adoption of the secret ballot

In the East the Populist platform was regarded as extremely radical. Yet within a generation most of the planks were put into effect. This illustrates the chief function of minor parties in our political system—to arouse interest in proposed reforms.

Cleveland is elected again.

In their 1892 convention the Republicans nominated President Harrison on the first ballot. The Democrats put up former President Grover Cleveland. The tariff was the main issue of the campaign. The violent strike in the steelworks at Homestead that summer (p. 461) cast doubt on the Republican claim that a high tariff helped the workingman. Steel was a highly protected industry, yet steelworkers had very poor labor conditions.

The Populists made a good showing, polling over a million votes. They captured the 22 electoral votes of Colorado, Idaho, Kansas, and Nevada, and they elected several men to Congress. The Populist movement so split the Western Republicans that the Democrats easily won the election. For the first time since 1860 Democrats controlled both houses of Congress as well as the Presidency.

A severe depression strikes.

During the next four years various events deepened the popular unrest. Cleveland was hardly in the White House when the country found itself in the grip of the panic of 1893—probably the worst it had yet suffered. Business firms crashed, banks failed, factories shut down, mortgages were foreclosed. Thousands of unemployed walked the streets looking for jobs that

---

[1] This phrase refers to the armed guards used by the Carnegie Company to break the Homestead strike (see p. 461).

did not exist. City soup kitchens served long lines of hungry people.

Populists thought the panic resulted from a scarcity of currency. Business leaders thought just the opposite. They blamed the panic on the large government purchases of silver, which were draining the Treasury's gold reserves. Cleveland called a special session of Congress to repeal the Sherman Silver Purchase Act. His action convinced the silverites that he was a tool of Wall Street. More loudly than ever they asked for free coinage of silver.

The government took no further action to cure the depression. Cleveland, like other conservative men of his day, thought the storm had to blow itself out. For two years conditions grew worse. Farm prices fell still lower and there were still more wage cuts and unemployment.

The jobless ask Congress for work.

Jacob S. Coxey, a well-to-do reformer, thought of a plan to publicize the needs of the jobless. In 1894 he led a few hundred unemployed men to Washington to ask Congress to create jobs by building roads and other public works. When he tried to make a speech on the Capitol steps, Coxey was arrested and his followers driven away.

In a written protest Coxey said that persons seeking favors for corporations were welcome in the committee rooms of Congress, while the way had been barred to him and the needy unemployed. Unfortunately for the unemployed, most people outside the wage-earning group thought the men of "Coxey's Army" were vagabonds deserving no sympathy. The march resulted only in new bitterness among the jobless.

The same year saw a wave of strikes, most of them due to wage cuts. Cleveland's handling of the Pullman strike (see p. 461), aroused fierce resentment among workmen. They were shocked to discover that the Sherman Antitrust Act, which appeared powerless to break up monopolies, could be used to smash strikes.

Cleveland fails to get tariff reform.

In his first message to Congress, Cleveland asked for a new tariff to replace the McKinley Act. "A tariff for any other purpose than public revenue," he declared, "is public robbery." By a very large majority the House passed the Wilson tariff bill. It cut duties on manufactured goods and put many items on the free list. The bill was greatly changed in the Senate. Most senators, including some of the Democrats, were determined to protect industries in their own state. They added over six hundred amendments. The resulting measure, known as the Wilson-Gorman Act (1894), was almost as protective as the McKinley Tariff. Cleveland refused to sign the bill and it became law without his signature.

Supreme Court voids the income tax.

The same year, to make up for a slightly lower tariff and to soothe popular discontent, Congress levied a 2 per cent tax on incomes above $4000. Conservatives fought the income tax. A senator from Ohio called it "socialism, communism, devilism." A senator from New York said professors and socialists had caused the people to demand this dangerous kind of tax. In 1895 the Supreme Court, by a vote of 5 to 4, declared the income tax unconstitutional.[1] Speaking for the Court, Mr. Justice Field said:

The present assault upon capital is but the beginning. It will be but the steppingstone to others larger and more sweeping, till our political conditions will become a war of the poor against the rich.

---

[1] It violated the "direct tax" clause, Art. I, Sec. IX, para. 4, of the Constitution.

GROVER CLEVELAND

The Court's action reversed a unanimous decision in 1881 upholding the wartime income tax. To the Populists this seemed clear proof that the Court, and the rest of the government, was on the side of the wealthy. The party faced the presidential election of 1896 strong and determined. This time, they thought, a Populist might win the election.

The Republicans nominate McKinley.

In the campaign of 1896, Republican leaders decided to take a firm stand for a higher tariff and against free silver. They chose as their candidate Governor William McKinley of Ohio. He was well liked in Congress. The public knew him chiefly as the author of the McKinley Tariff of 1890, the highest ever adopted up to that time. His ideas were conservative. He called Populism "a sudden, dangerous, and revolutionary assault upon law and order." Nothing is worse, he said, than attempts "to array class against class, the classes against the masses, section against section, labor against capital, the poor against the rich, or interest against interest."

McKinley owed his nomination to the efforts of Marcus A. Hanna, a Clevelander said to be "the owner of more oil wells, street railways, aldermen, and legislators than any other man in Ohio."

Hanna had gone into politics years before to obtain franchises and other favors for his vast business enterprises. Now he wanted to be a "President-maker." He was a warmhearted man and got real pleasure from promoting his friend McKinley. Hanna spent a year and a half of his time and more than $100,000 of his own money in getting McKinley nominated. He then took charge of McKinley's campaign.

The Democrats nominate Bryan.

When the Democratic convention met, there was an angry debate over the money question. "Silver" Democrats wanted to make free silver the chief issue of the campaign. They were opposed by Cleveland and other "gold" Democrats from the Northeast.

WILLIAM JENNINGS BRYAN

Among the delegates was a Nebraska lawyer, William Jennings Bryan, then only thirty-six years old. With all his heart he believed in free silver and in the Populist cause. He made a speech to the convention that excited the delegates to a frenzy and united all but a handful behind the free-silver plank. In his words the fight for free silver was a "cause as holy as the cause of liberty, the cause of humanity." It was a contest, Bryan said, between the idle holders of idle capital and the toiling millions. He pleaded for the little businessman, the wage earner, the

504

miner, the farmer. His concluding words are well known:

You shall not press down upon the brow of labor this crown of thorns. You shall not crucify mankind upon a cross of gold.

The delegates went wild. The hall shook with their cheers. Next day they nominated the young Nebraskan on a platform calling for free silver, an income tax, protective labor laws, and tariff reduction.

The Populists also nominate Bryan.

The Populists made a fatal mistake by delaying their convention until after those of the two major parties. When they met, the Democrats had stolen their loudest thunder—free silver. If they threw their support to Bryan, he had a good chance of victory. This, however, would merge their party with the Democratic party. If they nominated a candidate of their own, their party might be kept together, but the silver vote would be split and McKinley would surely be elected. They faced a difficult decision.

Most of the thirteen hundred delegates were poor men. Some had walked a long distance to save railroad fare. Others used up their small store of money before the long convention was over and suffered for want of a suitable sleeping place and adequate food. Many had grown old in the service of various reform groups and minor parties. After days of discussion the convention decided to support Bryan. This resulted in the end of their organization.

Bryan, the "Great Commoner."

The youthful Bryan was an attractive figure. Taller and broader than most men, with coal-black hair, black flashing eyes, a determined mouth, he looked like one born to command. A great orator, he was also gifted with a beautiful speaking voice. His speeches were rich in quotations from the Scriptures. Quick-witted and fearless, he won the devotion of millions of plain people. He knew their problems, for he had grown up on an Illinois farm, attended a country college, and settled in Nebraska to practice law. Faithful to democratic ideals and devoted to the public interest as he saw it, he won the title the "Great Commoner."

A history-making campaign.

Free silver was the most talked-of issue of the campaign. Yet the real issue was the belief that Bryan stood for the rights of the plain people. Silver and gold were merely symbols—silver, of the prairies and villages; gold, of big business and the "money power." Bryan said "This is not a contest for the supremacy of one of two metals—it is not a miners' campaign." The fight, he believed, was to save the people from being controlled by Wall Street.

Like the campaign of 1800 to elect Jefferson and that of 1828 to elect Jackson, this was a struggle between two different economic classes—"a battle between the Western plow-holder and the Eastern bondholder." The battle split the Democratic party wide open. Cleveland and the other "gold" Democrats refused to support Bryan. The Republican party too divided along sectional lines, for Western Republicans, like Western Democrats, favored free silver.

The campaign was the most bitter, hard-fought, and expensive of any up to that time. Mark Hanna collected a huge campaign fund from businessmen and bankers who feared the election of Bryan. The money provided an army of speakers, an ocean of pamphlets printed in twenty languages, and numberless parades and mass meetings. McKinley stayed at home in Canton, Ohio, speaking from his front porch to the crowds who came on excursion trains to hear him. Bryan spoke of McKinley's listeners as "worshipers at the shrine of the golden calf." Republican leaders called Bryan an anarchist, a blasphemer, and a lunatic.

The Democrats, too, employed speakers and published pamphlets, but their campaign fund was small. In the main they depended on their candidate's own efforts. Bryan went directly to the people. Riding in hot, dusty day coaches, he crisscrossed twenty-nine states, speaking eight and ten times a day. Everywhere he attracted throngs. Those who heard him could never forget the experience.

McKinley wins the election.

The shrewd Hanna, seeing that the election would be close, saved his trump cards to the end. Just before the election, manufacturers put up notices that should Bryan win, they would close their doors. At the same time bankers warned farmers that if Bryan won, their mortgages might not be renewed. Undoubtedly these threats led many of Bryan's supporters to vote for McKinley.

DAWSON CITY, *the Yukon, during the gold rush*

The popular vote was large and close, but McKinley received most of the electoral votes. The Democrats did not carry a single state in the Northeast and Midwest. Besides electing the President, the Republicans won a majority of the seats in the House of Representatives and the Senate. They had control of all branches of the government.

The tariff is boosted again.

In his first inaugural address McKinley urged a higher tariff. He called a special session of Congress, which passed the Dingley Tariff (1897). The duties averaged 57 per cent. This was the highest tariff we had yet had. The captains of industry were in the saddle, and they looked forward to greater wealth and power than ever before.

The silver question is forgotten.

The nation's excitement over the silver question soon waned. The depression lifted and prosperity returned. This was partly due to a large increase in the world's production of gold. New gold mines were discovered in Alaska, South Africa, and Australia. Besides, a new and cheap process was invented for extracting gold from inferior ore. With the increase in the gold supply, the price of gold fell. This caused the price of silver, farm products, and other goods to rise. Farmers and miners stopped asking the government to buy silver. Reformers turned their attention to other questions that were perhaps more important in the long run.

Meanwhile, foreign affairs came to the forefront. McKinley had been in office only a year when the United States went to war with Spain (see p. 571). The country shortly acquired overseas possessions and these brought many new problems. Bryan ran against McKinley in 1900 and lost by a wide margin. Free silver had become a dead issue.

The reform movement goes on.

Although the People's party was defeated in 1896, the reform movement did not die. Ten years later Theodore Roosevelt was to take up the same battle that the Populists had fought. The next unit will tell what the reform movement accomplished in the twenty years before World War I.

★   ★   ★   ★   ★

FOR IDENTIFICATION

Alabama claims	Benjamin Harrison
Chester A. Arthur	Rutherford B. Hayes
James G. Blaine	William McKinley
Bland-Allison Act	McKinley Tariff
William J. Bryan	Pendleton Act
Grover Cleveland	Sherman Antitrust Act
Farmers' Alliances	Samuel J. Tilden
Hamilton Fish	Tweed Ring
James A. Garfield	James B. Weaver
Marcus A. Hanna	Wilson-Gorman Tariff

FOR EXPLANATION OR DEFINITION

"billion-dollar Congress"	Liberal Republicans
civil service reform	merit system
classified list	"mugwumps"
Coxey's Army	Populism 
Crédit Mobilier	reciprocity
demonetization of silver	"Stalwarts"
Electoral Count Act	"star route" frauds
free silver	Tammany
"half-breeds"	"waving the bloody shirt"

FOR REVIEW

1. Summarize the opportunities for acquiring wealth in the period 1865–1900.

2. What sort of favors or privileges do businessmen seek from governments—national, state, and local?

3. (a) What are the chief causes of political corruption? (b) Describe the operations of the Tweed Ring. (c) Explain the Crédit Mobilier scandal and how Oakes Ames tried to prevent its investigation.

4. How did the Republicans gain and keep control of national politics for so long?

5. (a) In general, what economic and sectional groups supported the Republicans? The Democrats? (b) Why did businessmen sometimes contribute to the campaign expenses of both parties?

6. Why were several third parties started in the period 1870–1900?

7. Why is Grant commonly regarded as a weak President? Mention scandals that were revealed during his administration.

8. How did the Treaty of Washington (1871) improve our relations with Great Britain? How did it arrange for the settlement of the *Alabama* claims?

9. (a) Who were the candidates in the presidential campaign of 1876? What were the issues? (b) Why were the election results disputed? How was the dispute settled? Can such a dispute happen again?

10. What actions or policies of President Hayes offended the leaders of his party?

11. (a) Why did the silver question become an important issue in the 1870's? (b) Why did Congress "demonetize" silver in 1873? (c) Why did farmers support silver miners in urging the unlimited coinage of silver? (d) What were the terms of the Bland-Allison Act?

12. (a) Who were the candidates in the presidential campaign of 1880? (b) What caused Garfield's death? (c) What effect did it have on public opinion?

13. How did Chester A. Arthur's actions as President compare with those of his earlier career?

14. State the terms of the Pendleton Act, 1883. How was it carried out?

15. (a) Why did some Republicans refuse to support Blaine in 1884? (b) Briefly describe the early career of Grover Cleveland. (c) What was Cleveland's attitude toward the Presidency?

16. (a) What were Cleveland's major policies and accomplishments during his first administration, 1885–89? (b) Who defeated Cleveland in his second campaign for the Presidency, 1888?

17. State the provisions of the Sherman Antitrust Act of 1890. Why was this law ineffective against the trusts?

18. Describe the McKinley Tariff of 1890. Explain the "reciprocity" clause.

19. What were the provisions of the Sherman Silver Purchase Act, 1890?

20. (a) Why did Farmers' Alliances grow in number and influence in the late 1880's? (b) What political action did the Alliances demand? (c) What important federal laws were passed partly as a result of pressure from the Alliances?

21. (a) Account for the origin of the Populist party in the 1890's. (b) What groups supported this party? (c) List some of the demands of the Populist party as expressed in their platform of 1892.

22. Why was Cleveland successful in his third campaign for the Presidency, 1892?

23. (a) How did Populists explain the panic of 1893? How did business leaders explain it? (b) What did Cleveland do to cure the depression?

24. What was Coxey's purpose in leading the unemployed to Washington? What was the result of his action?

25. (a) Why did Cleveland veto the Wilson-Gorman Tariff of 1894? (b) On what grounds was the income tax provision of this law declared unconstitutional?

26. (a) What were the main arguments advanced by Bryan in his famous "Cross of Gold" speech? (b) Contrast the campaigns conducted by McKinley and by Bryan in 1896. (c) What role did Marcus A. Hanna play in this campaign? (d) What were the fundamental issues in this campaign?

27. Why did agitation over "free silver" almost disappear during McKinley's first administration?

FOR FURTHER STUDY AND DISCUSSION

1. In an essay on this period of our history, Hofstadter uses the title "The Spoilsmen: an Age of Cynicism." Is this title justified? Helpful source: Hofstadter, *American Political Tradition*, pp. 164–185.

2. "Neither Jackson nor Cleveland understood the social changes that made their times periods of class and sectional conflict." Compare the Jackson and Cleveland eras as regards "class and sectional conflict." Give reasons for your agreement with or disagreement with the quotation.

3. Why did farmers find it difficult to force Congress to take action on their demands?

4. How would each of the following tend to affect prices: an increase in the volume of business; government issue of a large quantity of paper money (greenbacks); free coinage of a cheaper metal than gold; the unchecked issuance of bank notes which circulate as currency; the extension of bank credit?

5. How are the opposition to the "resumption of specie payment," the demand for greenbacks, and the demand for "free silver" related to one another?

6. Study the list of the demands of the Populists on page 502. Which of these demands were considered "radical" at the time? Which are no longer so considered?

7. Why is the campaign of 1896 sometimes referred to as the first really important political campaign after the War between North and South? Helpful source: Amherst Series, *William Jennings Bryan and the Campaign of 1896.*

FOR INDIVIDUAL OR GROUP ACTIVITIES

1. Report in some detail on each of the following: Tweed Ring, Crédit Mobilier, "star route" frauds, Whiskey Ring.

2. Read James Russell Lowell's "Centennial Ode" and explain the allusions to corruption in that biting satire.

3. Report on the conditions of the civil service system in your city, county, and state today. State the reasons why you think the principles of the merit system should or should not apply to all but a few elective and appointive positions.

4. Report on Hanna's methods of conducting the campaigns of 1896 and 1900.

5. Select portions of the Populist party platform of 1892 and Bryan's "Cross of Gold" speech and present them as dramatic readings to the class. Helpful source: Commager, *Documents*, Nos. 325, 342.

6. Many of Thomas Nast's cartoons have been frequently reproduced. Select six of these cartoons for classroom display and prepare short paragraphs explaining each.

HIGH POINTS

1

The period from 1865 to 1900 saw far-reaching changes in the American economy. Manufacturing expanded at a tremendous rate, especially in the Northeast. Little mills turned by a water wheel gave way to immense plants driven by turbines or engines. While the little mills had produced for a nearby market, the plants which replaced them sought a nationwide market. The spread of railroads to all parts of the country made it possible for a company to sell its products over a far wider area. Mass production together with transportation by rail was making more and better goods available to more people.

2

The rise of giant corporations created great uneasiness. Small businessmen threatened by unfair methods of competition, and farmers forced to pay high freight rates and high prices for manufactures, demanded laws to curb monopolies. When state legislatures passed such laws, the courts frequently sided with the corporations. Likewise, when Congress passed a law to regulate railroads and another to limit trusts, the courts made interpretations which tended to shield the corporations. Nevertheless, these laws were a start in regulating big business.

3

Urbanization went hand in hand with industrialization. Young people from the farms and an ever-increasing stream of immigrants from Europe flocked to the cities. The rapid growth of cities intensified the problems of housing, sanitation, poverty, and crime prevention. Reformers such as Jane Addams helped arouse the public to the shocking living conditions in slum areas.

4

Opportunities for education became more widespread. Many communities built public high schools. Colleges opened their doors to women. Science courses and scientific research received more attention. A large number of public libraries and art galleries were established, partly or wholly by private gifts.

5

Literature and the fine arts attracted a steadily growing interest. Many writers were concerned over the problems created by the spread of industrialization and the growth of cities. Painters, sculptors, and architects gradually turned away from European models to express their own ideas.

6

Labor conditions were poor. In this period wage earners did not benefit very much from the advance of science and industry. Their efforts to organize were sternly dealt with by employers. Only the strongest unions were able to survive. Strikes were often broken by state militia or federal troops. The government policy of unrestricted immigration created a surplus of labor and kept wages low. A few states passed laws to protect employed women and children, but as a rule these laws were not strictly enforced.

7

This period saw the occupation of the Great West. The Indians were driven into small reservations; the buffalo were killed off, and transcontinental railroads were built. By 1890 the map no longer showed a frontier line, although the westward movement has never stopped.

8

The Agricultural Revolution progressed rapidly. It was marked by growing use of

509

farm machinery, advances in agricultural science, a shift from subsistence to commercial farming, a rising output per farm worker, and the tendency of farmers to specialize. These changes made farming a business which required a considerable investment.

9

The price of farm products declined so much between 1865 and 1896 that many farmers could not meet expenses. Hundreds of thousands lost their farms through foreclosure and tax sales. Farmers formed organizations to agitate for laws to protect their interests. When the major political parties ignored their demands, farmers joined minor parties. In the Populist movement farmers sought to make an alliance with wage earners. The Populists urged a program of reform which frightened many of the wealthy. Although populism was fiercely denounced at the time, Congress has since made most of the changes the Populists asked for.

10

In political affairs the period 1865–1900 was not very creative, probably because the ablest men went into business rather than politics. Little was accomplished in solving the problems resulting from industrialization. Yet two political achievements deserve mention. (1) The Great West was carved into territories and by 1896 all but three (Oklahoma, New Mexico, and Arizona) had become states. (2) A beginning was made in taking the federal civil service out of politics and placing it under the merit system.

QUESTIONS

1. Tabulate the important economic and social changes that took place in the United States between 1865 and 1900.

2. (a) What have been the chief factors in promoting America's industrial expansion? (b) How did the War between North and South tend to speed up industrialization? (c) What outstanding inven-

tions contributed to America's industrial growth? (d) What new developments in transportation and communication brought about important changes?

3. (a) Why did business make increasing and extensive use of the corporate form of business organization? (b) List in parallel columns the good and bad effects resulting from the beginnings of big business enterprise. (c) How did state legislatures seek to check some of the evils of big business? (d) Explain the reasons for passage of the Interstate Commerce Act of 1887 and the Sherman Antitrust Act of 1890. (e) What part did the Supreme Court play in the effort of the states and the federal government to regulate big business?

4. (a) How did industrialization lead to urbanization? (b) List a few of the problems that developed as a result of the rapid growth of cities. How were some of these problems met in the period 1865–1900?

5. How did urbanization and industrialization affect the status of women? Education? The arts?

6. Why do social and political institutions respond slowly to industrial and economic change?

7. (a) List the chief sources of the labor supply which built our railroads, factories, and cities. (b) What were the chief reasons for labor unrest in the period 1865–1900? (c) What difficulties did labor have to overcome in developing strong labor organizations? (d) Describe the start of the American Federation of Labor.

8. (a) What were the chief developments and characteristics of the agricultural revolution, 1865–1900? (b) How did the agricultural and industrial revolutions influence the "closing of the frontier"? (c) How has the occupation and settlement of the West affected American life?

9. Why were farmers discontented in the period 1865–1900? What different measures did they use or advocate to improve their condition?

10. (a) How did new conditions and new problems affect the fortunes of the major

political parties? (b) List the minor political parties that developed between 1865 and 1900 and some of the measures they advocated. (c) Describe the disputed election of 1876; the election of 1884. (d) How did President Cleveland become unpopular with members of his own party?

11. Describe the platform and influence of the Populist party. Which of the "radical" demands of the Populists have since been generally accepted?

12. What were the issues and who were the candidates in the presidential campaign of 1896? Why is this campaign regarded as the first significant campaign after that of 1860?

13. List the most important developments in foreign affairs in the period 1865–1900.

14. Explain how the careers of the following reflect some of the outstanding issues and developments of the period: John D. Rockefeller, Andrew Carnegie, Samuel Gompers, "Boss" Tweed, Grover Cleveland, William Jennings Bryan, Thomas Nast, Bret Harte, Jane Addams, John Peter Altgeld, Thomas Edison.

SUGGESTED READINGS

SOURCE MATERIALS, DOCUMENTS, AND MAPS

Adams, *Album*, Vols. III and IV.

Amherst Series: *The Turner Thesis concerning the Role of the Frontier in American History.*

———. *Democracy and the Gospel of Wealth.*

———. *John D. Rockefeller—Robber Baron or Industrial Statesman?*

———. *The Pullman Boycott of 1894—The Problem of Federal Intervention.*

———. *William Jennings Bryan and the Campaign of 1896.*

Commager, *Documents.*

* Commager and Nevins, *Heritage of America.*

Hart, *Contemporaries.* Vol. IV.

Lord, *Historical Atlas.*

Nevins and Weitenkampf, *Political Cartoons.*

GENERAL REFERENCES

Addams, Jane. *Twenty Years at Hull House.* Macmillan, 1910.

———. *The Second Twenty Years at Hull House.* Macmillan, 1930.

Allen, Frederick L. *The Lords of Creation.* Harper, 1935.

Beard, Mary R. *Short History of the American Labor Movement.* Macmillan, 1942.

Billington, R. A. *Westward Expansion: A History of the American Frontier.* Macmillan, 1949.

Binkley, W. E. *American Political Parties; Their Natural History.* Knopf, 1943.

* Buck, Solon J. *The Agrarian Crusade.* Yale University Press, 1920. (Y.C.S.)

* Burlingame, Roger. *Engines of Democracy: Inventions and Society in Mature America.* Scribner, 1940.

* ———. *March of the Iron Men: A Social History of Union through Invention.* Scribner, 1946.

Cochran, T. C., and Miller, W. *Age of Enterprise: A Social History of Industrial America.* Macmillan, 1942.

Davidson, M. B. *Life in America.* Houghton, 1951.

Dulles, Foster R. *America Learns to Play: A History of Popular Recreation, 1607–1940.* Appleton-Century, 1940.

* Faulkner, Harold U., and Starr, M. *Labor in America.* Harper, 1949.

* Ford, Henry J. *The Cleveland Era.* Yale University Press, 1920. (Y.C.S.)

Gabriel, Ralph H. *Toilers of Land and Sea.* Yale University Press, 1926. (Pageant)

Handlin, Oscar. *The Uprooted: The Epic Story of the Great Migrations that Made the American People.* Little, Brown, 1951.

* Hendrick, Burton J. *The Age of Big Business.* Yale University Press, 1919. (Y.C.S.)

Hicks, John D. *American Nation.*

———. *The Populist Revolt.* University of Minnesota Press, 1931.

* Hough, Emerson. *The Passing of the Frontier.* Yale University Press, 1918. (Y.C.S.)

Kaempffert, W. B. *A Popular History of American Invention.* Scribner, 1924.

* Keir, Malcom. *The Epic of Industry.* Yale University Press, 1926. (Pageant)

* ———. *The March of Commerce.* Yale University Press, 1927. (Pageant)

* Krout, J. A. *Annals of American Sport.* Yale University Press, 1929. (Pageant)

Larkin, *Art and Life in America.*

Link, *American Epoch.*

* Moody, John. *The Masters of Capital.* Yale University Press, 1919. (Y.C.S.)

* ———. *The Railroad Builders.* Yale University Press, 1919. (Y.C.S.)

Nevins, Allan. *The Emergence of Modern America, 1865–1878.* Macmillan, 1927. (A.L.S.)

* Orth, Samuel P. *The Armies of Labor.* Yale University Press, 1921. (Y.C.S.)

* ———. *The Boss and the Machine.* Yale University Press, 1919. (Y.C.S.)

* ———. *Our Foreigners.* Yale University Press, 1920. (Y.C.S.)

Perry, Bliss. *The American Spirit in Literature.* Yale University Press, 1918. (Y.C.S.)

* Reynolds, Quentin. *Custer's Last Stand.* Random House, 1951.

Riegel, R. E. *America Moves West.* Rev. ed. Holt, 1947.

Riis, Jacob. *How the Other Half Lives.* Scribner, 1890.

Schlesinger, Arthur M. *The Rise of the City, 1878–1898.* Macmillan, 1933. (A.L.S.)

Shannon, Fred A. *The Farmer's Last Frontier: Agriculture, 1860–1897.* Farrar and Rinehart, 1945.

* Slosson, Edwin E. *The American Spirit in Education.* Yale University Press, 1921. (Y.C.S.)

Sullivan, Mark. *Our Times,* Vols. I and II. Scribner, 1926–27.

Tarbell, Ida. *Nationalizing of Business, 1878–1898.* Macmillan, 1936.

* Thompson, Holland. *The Age of Invention.* Yale University Press, 1921. (Y.C.S.)

* ———. *The New South.* Yale University Press, 1920. (Y.C.S.)

Turner, Frederick J. *The Frontier in American History.* Holt, 1921.

* Washington, Booker T. *Up from Slavery.* Doubleday, Page, 1901.

Webb, Walter P. *The Great Plains.* Ginn, 1931.

Wittke, Carl. *We Who Built America: The Saga of the Immigrant.* Prentice-Hall, 1939.

BIOGRAPHY

Allen, Frederick L. *The Great Pierpont Morgan.* Harper, 1949.

Bryan, Florence. *Susan B. Anthony, Champion of Women's Rights.* Messner, 1947.

* Clark, Graves G. *Thomas Alva Edison.* Aladdin, 1950.

Croly, Herbert D. *Marcus Alonzo Hanna,* Macmillan, 1912.

* Davis, Royce M. *The Boy's Life of Grover Cleveland.* Harper, 1925.

* de Kruif, Paul. *Seven Iron Men.* Harcourt, Brace, 1929.

Fuess, Claude M. *Carl Schurz.* Dodd, Mead, 1932.

* Garst, Doris S. *The Story of Buffalo Bill.* Bobbs-Merrill, 1938.

Hale, William H. *Horace Greeley, Voice of the People.* Harper, 1950.

Hibben, Paxton. *The Peerless Leader, William Jennings Bryan.* Farrar and Rinehart, 1929.

Nevins, Allan. *Grover Cleveland: A Study in Courage.* Dodd, Mead, 1932.

Werner, Morris R. *Bryan.* Harcourt, Brace, 1929.

Winkler, John. *Incredible Carnegie.* Vanguard, 1931.

———. *John D.; A Portrait in Oils.* Vanguard, 1929.

* ———. *Morgan the Magnificent.* Doubleday, 1932.

FICTION

* Aldrich, Bess Streeter. *A Lantern in Her Hand.* Appleton-Century, 1934. (Pioneer life in Nebraska, 1864–1900)

Bacheller, Irving. *The Handmade Gentleman.* Harper, 1909. (New York in the time of Vanderbilt and Carnegie)

Cather, Willa. *Death Comes for the Archbishop.* Knopf, 1927. (New Mexico and Arizona)

* ———. *My Ántonia.* Houghton, 1926. (Immigrant farmers)

Churchill, Winston. *Coniston.* Macmillan, 1927. (Political corruption)

* Clark, Walter V. *The Ox-Bow Incident.* Random House, 1940. (Nevada in the 1880's)

* Ferber, Edna. *Cimarron.* Doubleday, 1930. (Oklahoma land rush)

Ford, P. L. *The Honorable Peter Sterling.* Holt, 1910. (The career of Cleveland)

* Harte, Bret. *The Luck of Roaring Camp.* Houghton, 1919. (California mining camps)

* Howells, William Dean. *The Rise of Silas Lapham.* Houghton, n.d. (Story of a self-made man)

* Jackson, Helen Hunt. *Ramona.* Little, Brown, 1916. (Indian missions)

Norris, Frank. *The Octopus.* Garden City, 1901. (Farmers *vs.* railroads)

512

——. *The Pit.* Garden City, 1903. (Speculation on Chicago wheat market)

* Rölvaag, O. E. *Giants in the Earth.* Harper, 1927. (Norwegian settlers in South Dakota)

* Tarkington, Booth. *The Magnificent Ambersons.* Doubleday, 1918. (Changes in a Midwestern city)

Wharton, Edith. *The Age of Innocence.* Appleton, 1920. (New York City in the 1870's)

White, William Allen. *A Certain Rich Man.* Macmillan, 1926. (Big business)

Wister, Owen. *The Virginian.* Macmillan, 1902. (Wyoming, 1874–90)

A loggers' trestle over CEDAR RIVER CANYON, *Washington*

TIME LINE

1900	1900	Socialist party enters national politics; Robert M. LaFollette and the "Wisconsin idea" (1900–1906)
	1901	Roosevelt succeeds to Presidency: New York Tenement House Law
	1902	Coal strike; Newlands Reclamation Act; "trust busting" begins; initiative and referendum; first workmen's compensation law
	1903	"Muckraking era," 1903–1910; recall and direct primary introduced; Department of Commerce and Labor
	1904	Steffens' *The Shame of the Cities*
1905	1905	Industrial Workers of the World organized
	1906	Sinclair's *The Jungle*; Meat Inspection Act; Pure Food and Drugs Act; Hepburn Act
	1908	Conservation Conference; Brandeis' defense of Oregon ten-hour law for women
	1909	Taft inaugurated; Payne-Aldrich Tariff
1910	1910	Mann-Elkins Act
	1911	"Rule of reason" decision
	1912	Progressive party organized; first minimum wage law
	1913	Wilson inaugurated; parcel post; Federal Reserve Act; Department of Labor established
	1914	Federal Trade Commission; Clayton Antitrust Act; World War I begins
	1916	Federal Farm Loan Act; Adamson Act
	1917	Smith-Hughes Act; United States enters World War I; Selective Service Act
	1918	Armistice
	1919	Treaty of Versailles; Eighteenth Amendment
1920	1920	Fourteenth census—population 105,710,000; Nineteenth Amendment

UNIT SEVEN

The Progressive Movement

★ ★ ★ ★ Reform is part of the American way of life. Sometimes the demand for reform is stronger than at other times. By 1896 popular discontent was so great that a wave of reform like that in Andrew Jackson's time swept over the country. Just as in his day, the people were calling for a greater voice in the government. To get it they found they had to destroy the power of the political boss. They also insisted that business be regulated in the public interest. Among other things, they wanted control over railroad rates, control over labor conditions, and protection for consumers.

The period from 1896 to 1916 is often spoken of as the "Progressive Era." In these years the reform movement was carried forward by progressives in both major parties. It began with the election of forceful young progressives to state and local office. Under their leadership improvements were made in state and city government. In addition laws were passed to promote the general welfare in various ways, as by restricting child labor, limiting the hours of women workers, inspecting tenement houses, and regulating the rates charged by public utilities companies.

Some of the needed changes called for federal action. When Theodore Roosevelt became President, he used his high office to promote reform. His successors in the White House, William Howard Taft and Woodrow Wilson, also worked for reform. During the administrations of these three men, Congress passed a number of measures for which progressives had been asking. These laws gave the federal government new power over business and banking, extended federal protection to consumers, and recognized the rights of labor unions.

The Progressive Era also brought two important amendments to the Constitution. One provided for the direct election of senators and thereby made the Senate more responsive to the needs of the people. The other, authorizing a federal income tax, gave the world an example of a peaceful revolution. Congress proceeded to adopt a graduated income tax and soon the federal government was getting most of its revenue from such taxes. The nation had indeed changed since the days when persons urging an income tax were thought to be dangerous radicals.

Poverty, overcrowding, and tenement living led to vice and corruption in the large cities of industrial America. As the situation grew worse, men arose who denounced the lack of ethics which had produced such evil. WALTER RAUSCHENBUSCH (left), *a minister of the Social Gospel, believed that the answer lay in applying Christian ideals to economics and social reform. In this way such places as Bandit's Roost in New York City* (below) *would give way to what he called the "golden city of peace."*

31. A NEW ERA OF REFORM ARRIVES

Progressives Attack Corruption and Injustice

The Progressive Era begins.

Bryan called the campaign of 1896 "the first battle." It marked the defeat of the Populist party but not of its program. A new period of reform known as the "Progressive Era" was beginning. Reform was made necessary by a host of evils—child labor, sweatshops, slums, the poor distribution of wealth, the concentration of economic power, unfair tax laws, the waste of natural resources, the corruption of government, and others.

The demand for reform came from civic organizations, such as the National Child Labor Committee and the League for Industrial Democracy, as well as from labor unions and farmers' groups. It was heard in all political parties. Not since the 1830's and 1840's had there been so many voices calling for reform.

Clergymen preach the "social gospel."

The reform movement drew its inspiration mainly from two sources: (1) the American dream of freedom and equal opportunity for all; and (2) basic Judaic-Christian teachings (see p. 84). Among those who worked for reform were pastors and laymen of all faiths.

Within the Christian faith, certain clergymen preached what is called the "social gospel," based on the teaching "I am my brother's keeper." Believing that religious principles should be applied to business and industry, they denounced men who got rich by disregarding the welfare of their employees and the public. Two books on the social gospel were widely read: *In His Steps* (1896) by Charles Sheldon and *Christianity and the Social Crisis* (1907) by Walter Rauschenbush.

In the early 1900's several denominations appointed commissions to study working and living conditions among industrial workers. Their reports helped educate church members and the general public to the need for reforms. The Federal Council of the Churches of Christ in America, organized in 1908 and representing thirty-three Protestant bodies, stood for the social gospel. Its platform called on the churches to work for the following program of reform:

1. Conciliation and arbitration in industrial disputes
2. Protection of the worker from dangerous machinery and occupational diseases
3. Abolition of child labor and the protection of women in industry

517

4. Gradual reduction of the hours of labor, with work and leisure for all
5. Release from employment one day in seven
6. Living wages in every industry; the highest wage that each industry can afford; and the most equitable division of the products of industry that can ultimately be devised
7. Recognition of the Golden Rule and the mind of Christ as the supreme law of society and the sure remedy for all social ills

The effort to apply Christian principles to industrial problems was not limited to Protestant leaders. As early as 1891 Pope Leo XIII had called attention to the rights of workingmen in his encyclical letter *De Rerum Novarum* (On the Condition of the Working Classes). In the United States, Archbishop John L. Spalding took an active part in promoting better industrial conditions. Another Roman Catholic reformer was Father John Ryan, whose book *A Living Wage* (1910) called attention to the misery of a large class of ill-paid workers.

Popular writers stir public opinion.

Even before the Progressive Era began, popular writers had been telling of the need for reform. We have mentioned Henry George's *Progress and Poverty* (1879) and Edward Bellamy's *Looking Backward, 2000–1887*. These books led millions of people to think about ways of improving society.

Another influential book was *How the Other Half Lives* (1890), by Jacob Riis, a young reporter for the *New York Sun*. He pictured the disease, crime, and misery in the overcrowded slums of New York. Newspapermen in other cities made similar reports. Gradually the nation came to realize that city dwellers had grievances just as serious as those of the farmers.

In 1894 a Chicago newspaperman, Henry D. Lloyd, published a volume entitled *Wealth against Commonwealth*, showing how trusts destroyed competitors and bribed public officials. In other writings Lloyd called attention to abuses in mines and factories.

In the early 1900's several young novelists wrote powerful stories about the evils they saw around them. *The Octopus*, by Frank Norris, told of the struggle between the farmers and the railroads. *The Pit*, by the same author, showed how the farmers suffered from the activities of speculators in the Chicago grain market. Upton Sinclair's novel, *The Jungle*, exposed the horrible conditions in Chicago packing plants. Jack London's novels laid bare the suffering of sailors and unskilled workers.

FRANK NORRIS

A New Englander, Winston Churchill, in *Coniston* and *Mr. Crewe's Career*, pictured the corruption of New Hampshire politics by railroad companies.

During the same years popular magazines began to print articles about dishonesty in business and politics. In 1902 and 1903 *McClure's* published a series of articles by Ida Tarbell, telling of the ugly methods used by the Standard Oil Company in crushing its rivals. At the same time *McClure's* ran a series by Lincoln Steffens called "The Shame of the Cities." Steffens showed how politicians in many cities were growing rich by selling franchises and other favors to public utility companies. The public liked these writings, and other magazine editors hastened to supply articles of the same type. For instance, *Everybody's Magazine* brought out a series on the beef trust and another on the stock market. *Collier's* bared frauds in the advertising of patent medicines and described the adulteration of food. *Cosmopolitan* printed one of the most shocking and important series of articles, *The Treason of the Senate.* The author, David G. Phillips, proved that some senators served the big corporations rather than the public.

education, labor conditions, the regulation of business within state borders, and most other matters of social welfare. In each state the reformers naturally turned first to their state legislature for action. When the people became thoroughly aroused and when they had a strong leader, they usually got the laws they demanded.

LINCOLN STEFFENS

JACK LONDON

Writers of this type of material came to be known as "muckrakers." They aroused public opinion and deepened and strengthened the whole reform movement. By 1912, however, muckraking went out of fashion. The magazines that had exposed so many evils came under the control of more conservative men.

The states point the way.

Under our Constitution the states are responsible for local government,

A reform tried in one state might be copied by other states and later, perhaps, by the national government. The states led the way. They also served as training schools for national leaders. Men who cleaned up politics in their own state often were sent to Congress, and sometimes even to the White House. Three of our Presidents since 1900—Theodore Roosevelt, Woodrow Wilson, and Franklin D. Roosevelt —became known as Progressives while serving as governors of their states.

519

Both parties include Progressives.

In the 1890's most reformers belonged to the Populist party or to the Bryan wing of the Democrats. By the turn of the century a large number of Republicans, especially in the Middle and Far West, also were clamoring for reform. By 1911 Progressives or reformers were so numerous in the Republican party that they hoped to capture control of it. We should keep in mind, therefore, as we consider the progressive movement, that it was broader than any party.

Reform governors win distinction.

Among the founders of the progressive movement was John Peter Altgeld, Democratic governor of Illinois from 1893 to 1897. His term of office was notable for pioneer labor legislation, antitrust activity, civil service and tax reform, and the improvement of prisons and mental hospitals. That he had the courage to take an unpopular stand was shown when he pardoned the Haymarket anarchists (see p. 461). His battle against the transportation and gas monopolies of Chicago cost him election for a second term.

Robert M. La Follette, Republican governor of Wisconsin for three terms (1900 to 1906), made his state the most progressive in the Union at that time. Under his forceful leadership, the legislature created commissions to regulate the railroads and other public utilities and to fix their rates on the basis of what their physical assets were worth.[1] La Follette secured passage of an inheritance tax, workmen's compensation act, and laws to limit the working hours of women and children. He set aside

state forest reserves and water-power sites for the people's benefit. He strengthened the state university and used its teachers as advisors in all phases of the state government.

Reform governors were elected in several other states during the Progressive Era. Joseph W. Folk served as governor of Missouri (1905–09) after successfully prosecuting a ring of corrupt St. Louis politicians. Charles E. Hughes became governor of New York (1907–10) after conducting a probe of life insurance companies in that state. As governor, Hughes obtained passage of laws regulating life insurance companies in order to protect policyholders. Hiram Johnson, who served as governor of California (1911–17), fought the railroad companies that dominated politics in that state. He managed to push through a broad program of economic and political reforms.

Political Reforms Give the People More Control

Power of the political boss is checked.

Leaders of the progressive movement thought that political corruption was at the bottom of most of the evils of their time. Corruption occurred when private interests tried to control the government for their own advantage (see p. 491). The success of their efforts depended on the help of local political leaders, known as "party bosses." The alliance of private interests and political bosses was called the "invisible government."

Progressive leaders saw little hope of achieving other reforms unless they could check the political boss. Here are the more important reforms made for this purpose.

1. The merit system. One way of weakening the political boss is to take away his power over government jobs. This can be done by adoption of the

---

[1] The utility companies fought this principle for fixing rates, which held them to a reasonable return on their actual investment. When La Follette became a United States senator he persuaded Congress to adopt a Valuation Act (1913), applying this principle on a national basis to railroad rates.

520

merit system. Under this system most government employees are chosen through competitive examination and once appointed cannot be removed except for misconduct or inefficiency. The merit system was adopted first in New York and Massachusetts in the eighties. As we have noted (see p. 497), the first federal employees came under the merit system in 1883. By the end of the Progressive Era (1916) only nine states had adopted it.

2. *The Australian, or secret, ballot.* Formerly each party prepared its own ballot, using a distinctive color. When the voter dropped his ballot into the ballot box, anyone in the polling place could tell what party he was voting for. Those who bought votes could easily make sure that their purchases were delivered. An employer could check on how his workmen voted. To make voting secret, and the voter free to vote as he wished, Massachusetts adopted the Australian ballot (1888). This ballot is furnished by the government and contains the names of the candidates of all parties. The voter marks and casts his ballot in complete secrecy. By 1900 nearly all the states used the Australian ballot.

3. *The direct primary.* In the old days local candidates were nominated in little meetings held by the party boss of the district. State and national candidates were chosen at conventions by an inner circle, or "ring," of bosses. Unless favored by the inner circle of his party, no one had a chance of being nominated. The remedy was sought in the direct primary. Under this system, nominations are made by vote of party members at a primary election held in advance of the general election. Any citizen may run for any office (except President and Vice President), provided a certain number of voters sign a petition to place his name on the ballot at the primary election. Wisconsin was the first state to adopt the direct primary. By 1918 every state but four had followed Wisconsin's example. Unfortunately, the average citizen does not take the trouble to vote in the primary. Some states have therefore returned to the old system of nomination at party meetings.

4. *Direct legislation.* The *initiative* and the *refendum* give the voters direct control over the passage of new laws. Under the initiative any bill may be placed before the people at an election upon the petition of a certain percentage of the voters. If a majority of them vote for the bill, it then becomes a law. The initiative has value when a legislature refuses to pass a measure favored by the people. The referendum allows citizens who disapprove of an act already passed by the legislature to get up a petition requiring that it be submitted to popular vote. South Dakota adopted the initiative and referendum in 1898. Nearly half the states and most cities have since adopted these devices.

5. *The recall.* This device enables the people to remove an official before his term expires. Whenever a certain number of voters are dissatisfied with an official, they may sign a petition requiring him to stand for a new election. If defeated, he cannot serve any more of his term. The recall was introduced in the United States in 1903 when Los Angeles wrote it into the city charter. Today the recall is provided for state officers in one fourth of the states and for city officials in more than a thousand cities. It is seldom used.

6. *Direct election of United States senators.* For many years cynics had spoken of the Senate as a "rich man's club." Although elected by state legislatures, senators were in fact chosen at party caucuses, which were often controlled by party bosses behind the scenes. Frequently, therefore, a senator did not truly represent the people. The Populists, and later the Progressives, demanded the election of senators by

popular vote. To effect this change, a constitutional amendment was needed. As early as 1893 the House of Representatives favored such an amendment, but the Senate refused to concur. Conservatives denounced the proposal as an "assault on the Constitution."

By 1910 twenty-eight states, mainly in the West and South, had devised ways for selecting senators of the people's choice. The action of these states changed the make-up of the Senate, with the result that at last it approved an amendment providing for the direct election of senators. The states quickly ratified it, and in 1913 it went into effect as the Seventeenth Amendment.

7. *The nonpartisan ballot.* Reformers argued that local officials should be chosen without regard to their membership in national parties. There is no Republican or Democratic way of running a police department, a school system, or a waterworks. City officials should therefore be selected for their knowledge of municipal affairs and not because of their views on the tariff or on foreign policy. These arguments led many cities (1) to change the date for electing local officials to a different day from that on which state and national officials are elected, and (2) to adopt a nonpartisan ballot in which the party of the candidates does not appear.

Improvements in city government.

Most of our large cities were badly governed when the Progressive Era began. Political bosses controlled appointments to office, the purchase of supplies, and every other city activity. They were growing rich from graft. City government was so complicated that the voters never knew who was responsible for inefficiency and corruption in the different departments. The solution, reformers decided, was to "elect only a few men and hold them responsible for city affairs." This idea was carried out in many cities by (1)

adopting a one-house legislature, or council, in place of the cumbersome two-house system, and (2) giving the mayor power to appoint the chief officials. Under the resulting *strong-mayor type* of government, the voters could hold the mayor to account when any department was poorly run.

Galveston, Texas, introduced a new type of city government in 1901. A terrible storm and flood had destroyed most of the city, and the citizens decided they must have a strong, efficient government to take charge of reconstruction. They abolished the mayor and council scheme and put the government of the city in the hands of five commissioners. By 1920 more than four hundred cities had followed Galveston's example. Under the *commission type* of government, each commissioner has full control of one department. He appoints the officials in his department and the citizens hold him responsible for its work. One of the commissioners serves as mayor for ceremonial duties.

A few years after Galveston's experiment, another type of city government was introduced. It is known as the *city manager plan.* The council, which is elected by the people, appoints a manager to take charge of city business. When the voters choose good councilmen, and the councilmen select a competent and honest manager, this plan produces excellent results. It has become very popular.

In order to change its form of government, a city must first have permission from the state legislature. Permission may be hard to get, for in every state the majority of legislators are persons from small communities, who usually do not understand the needs of large cities. Members of state legislatures often block reforms in city government and even interfere actively in city affairs. This situation has led many cities to try to get "home rule"—the

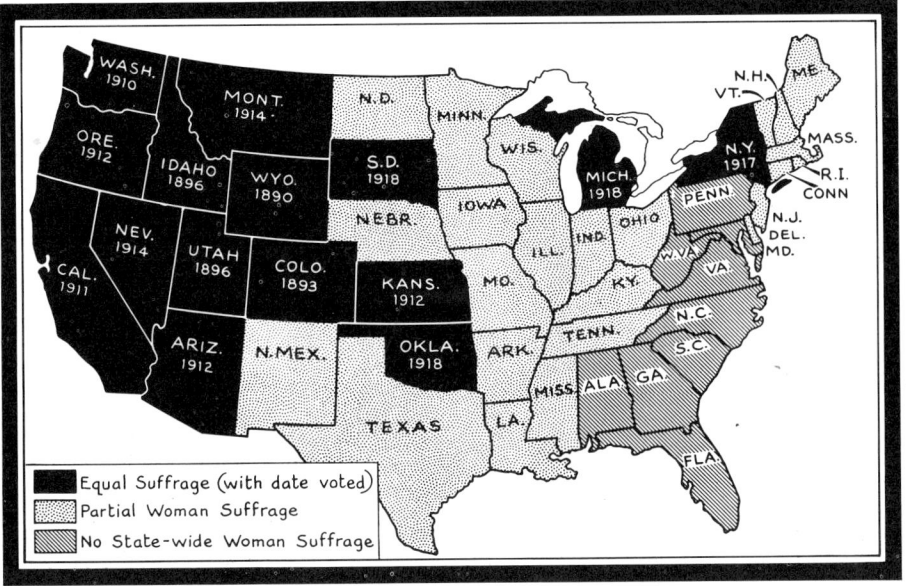

WOMAN SUFFRAGE (1919) BEFORE THE 19TH AMENDMENT

CARRY NATION, *hatchet and Bible in hand. In New York the men paraded for women's suffrage.*

right to make their own charters, or constitutions, and to manage their own affairs. Missouri (1875) was the first state to give its big cities home rule. Nearly half the states now allow cities of a certain size to write their own charters. Experience has shown that home rule is extremely important to a big city. Without it, the best efforts of reformers often fail.

Women win the suffrage.

Women took an active part in the reform movement. All over the country they organized women's societies to work for this or that reform. Some worked for the cause of temperance,

523

that is, for control of the sale of liquor; others for changes in city government, for labor laws, public health, pure food, or prison reform. In most states they made slow progress because they did not have the right to vote. In correcting this injustice the West led the way. The territory of Wyoming gave women the right to vote in 1869. Colorado adopted woman suffrage in 1893; Idaho and Utah did so three years later. The next victory came in the state of Washington in 1910. Nearly every year after that, one or more states gave women full or partial suffrage. Meanwhile the "suffragists" worked for an amendment to the federal Constitution giving the women of every state the right to vote. The Nineteenth, or Woman Suffrage, Amendment was added to the Constitution in 1920.

The States Seek to Control Private Enterprise

Laissez faire is challenged.

As we have pointed out, the idea that government should leave business alone (*laissez faire*) was commonly accepted in the 1800's. Jefferson expressed it when he said that the powers of government should be exercised only to protect the life, property, and freedom of the individual. The saying, "That government is best which governs least," reflects the same idea. Most Americans firmly believed that the individual had the right to manage his own economic affairs without interference by the government. With free competition between individuals, the law of supply and demand would, it was thought, automatically regulate the economy. Since wages, profits, interest, and rent would be determined by free competition, everyone taking part in economic activity would, it was claimed, receive a just reward for his contribution. Therefore, the govern-

ment need not and should not interfere in business affairs.

In reality, laissez faire was more talked about in theory than it was actually practiced. Businessmen did not wish the government to be *neutral*. Instead they looked for government favors in the way of land grants, subsidies, protective tariffs, patent rights, and franchises. Businessmen protested only when the government placed restrictions on them for the sake of consumers or workers.

After the rise of big business, the idea of laissez faire became considerably less popular. Small businessmen demanded laws to curb the trusts. Consumers asked protection against monopolistic prices, fraudulent advertising, impure foods, and injurious drugs. Workingmen asked for laws compelling employers to install safety devices on dangerous machinery. Workingmen also called for restrictions on child labor and on the number of working hours. However, those whose profits would be affected usually denounced such proposals as contrary to free enterprise.

Public utilities are regulated.

The first attempts to control big business in the public interest began before the Progressive Era. We have mentioned the Granger laws (see p. 484), the Interstate Commerce Act (see p. 485), and the Sherman Antitrust Act (see p. 500). These measures did not accomplish their purpose. The task of bringing big business under control therefore was taken up by leaders of the progressive movement.

Since the regulation of interstate railways was up to Congress, the states turned their attention to other public utilities. During the Progressive Era most of the states established public utility commissions to regulate the rates and practices of electric light plants, water works, telephone companies, gas companies, and street railways. A few commissions were fairly successful. More often they proved no match for the powerful companies they were supposed to regulate. In many cases the rulings of state commissions were set aside by the courts as contrary to the due process clause in the Fourteenth Amendment (see p. 484).

Cities resort to public ownership.

Some reformers—among them Governor John P. Altgeld of Illinois, Mayor Samuel M. Jones of Toledo, and Mayor Thomas L. Johnson of Cleveland—insisted that public ownership of the utilities was the only way to secure fair rates. They argued that efforts at regulation did not work well and that the utility companies continued to bribe officials and newspapers. The utility companies fought government ownership, arguing (1) that government should not compete with private enterprise, and (2) that government officials would not run any business so efficiently as it could be run by private enterprise. Yet hundreds of cities bought water works and electric light plants. Today most cities own water works but not electric plants.

Tenement houses are regulated.

Another type of business which seemed to need regulation was housing. Bad housing was a problem in every large city. In New York City in 1890 it was found that half a million persons lived in rickety wooden tenements five or six stories high. A typical tenement house had fourteen rooms to the floor, only four of which had direct sunlight. Ten years later conditions were still worse, due to the rapid growth of population. Governor Theodore Roosevelt appointed a Tenement House Commission, which declared that New York had "the most serious tenement house problem in the world." To prevent the building of new slums,

This boy working in a glass factory was a victim of the social evils of his day which prompted the progressive movement.

the legislature then passed a model tenement house law (1901). This measure regulated the size of rooms, air space, light, and sanitary arrangements for all *new* buildings in large cities of New York State. Other states one by one passed similar laws.

Child labor is restricted.

As industrialization went on, more and more children were employed in factories and mines. In 1900, of every five children between the ages of ten and fifteen, one was a wage earner. Individuals who knew the misery of these young workers formed the National Child Labor Committee in 1904 to work for the restriction of child labor. The movement was strengthened by John Spargo's book, *The Bitter Cry of the Children* (1906). Spargo wrote of scenes he had actually observed—children kept awake during the long night in a cotton mill by having cold water dashed in their faces; little girls in canning factories snipping beans for sixteen hours a day in the rush season; ten-year-old "breaker" boys bent for ten hours a day over a dusty coal chute, picking sharp slate out of the fast-moving coal; and tots in city tenements toiling until late at night over artificial flowers.

Shocked by these revelations, state legislatures passed new child labor laws or improved their old ones. By 1914 every state but one had some minimum age limit for child workers. Most states forbade the employment of children in mines and quarries and also limited the workday of children employed in factories. Yet in a few states it was legal for children of twelve to work in factories for as long as ten hours a day. Where child labor was permitted, factory owners were at an advantage, since their labor costs were lower. The solution of the child labor problem called for federal action.

Workmen's compensation laws.

By 1900 most states had adopted sanitation and safety rules for mines and factories. Here again, however, enforcement was often weak. The accident rate among industrial workers was extremely high. Each year some 500,000 Americans were killed or injured at their work. Industrial accidents and industrial diseases were a major cause of poverty among wage earners' families.

A number of governors appointed commissions to study the problem. As a result, eleven states adopted workmen's compensation laws in 1911 and all but six states did so by 1921. Under a compensation law the question of who is to blame for the worker's injury is not asked. The worker is entitled to be compensated for an injury (whether accident or disease) arising out of his employment. The cost of industrial injuries is charged to industry. To make certain that benefits will be paid when due, the employer is required to carry insurance or to set aside a fund for compensation.

Today every state has a workmen's compensation law. Yet the coverage and the benefits paid differ widely from state to state. Many workers still lack real protection and some are not covered at all.

The Courts Veto Much Social Legislation

How far does police power go?

Social legislation (as we may term labor laws and other statutes to promote the general welfare) is passed by the states under their *police power* This is the right of a state to protect the people's health, safety, morals, and welfare. Often the police power interferes with the property rights of individuals by placing limits on their use of property. In large cities, for instance, one may not keep livestock in his yard or store explosive or flammable chemicals where he sees fit or do his own electric wiring. While the courts have upheld many laws that interfere with private property, they have rejected many more as not a proper and reasonable use of the police power. The rejected legislation is usually declared to deprive a person of liberty or property "without due process of law." Any such deprivation is forbidden by state constitutions and by the Fifth and Fourteenth amendments to the United States Constitution.

Whether any new law is a proper and reasonable use of the police power or whether it interferes unduly with property rights is open to argument. Even the justices of the Supreme Court frequently disagree on such questions. In certain instances, after changes in the membership of the Supreme Court, an earlier decision has been reversed.

The courts check social legislation.

The courts acted as a powerful brake on the reform movement from the 1870's, when the Granger laws were passed, until the days of the New Deal sixty years later. Again and again laws designed to protect workers or consumers or the poor were found unconstitutional. For example, in 1885 the highest court in New York State set aside an act to stop the manufacture of cigars in tenement houses, writing:

It cannot be perceived how the cigar maker is to be improved in his health or his morals by forcing him from his home and its hallowed associations and beneficent influences to ply his trade elsewhere.

Young Theodore Roosevelt, who had sponsored the bill in the New York legislature after inspecting tenement rooms where whole families and their lodgers ate, slept, and rolled cigars, wrote in his *Autobiography:*

The judges who rendered this decision were well-meaning men. They knew nothing whatever of tenement house conditions . . . or of the life and labor of three fourths of their fellow citizens in great cities. . . . This decision completely blocked tenement house reform legislation in New York for a score of years.

Laws imposing an income tax or fixing public utility rates or providing workmen's compensation were often rejected as an assault on property rights. An Ohio court undid an act providing allowances to the needy blind on the ground that "innumerable cases may clamor for similar bounties, and it is doubted that any line could be drawn short of an equal distribution of property." Laws to protect labor were frequently overruled as interfering with the worker's freedom of contract. The Illinois supreme court, for example, threw out an act limiting the hours of women workers to 48 a week on the ground that women should have the same liberty of contract as men (1895). A few years later the highest New York court rejected an act to ban night work by women, declaring it an arbitrary interference with the right of an adult female to work at any time of day that suits her. The United States Supreme Court sometimes overruled social legislation that had been upheld by a state court. In 1905, for instance, the Supreme Court found unconstitutional a New York law limiting the very long working hours in bakeries.

Louis Brandeis, the "people's lawyer."

Louis Brandeis was a successful corporation lawyer in Boston. In 1896, when he was forty, he resolved to devote at least half his time to serving without fee as a lawyer for the people. His plan was to fight against monopolies and to work for laws to protect consumers and working people. In Boston he defended the public interest in a series of utility cases. In New York he took part in the sensational insurance investigation conducted by Charles Evans Hughes. Brandeis next persuaded the Massachusetts legislature to establish a low-cost system of savings bank life insurance. (The system was later copied in neighboring states.) Then, in the years from 1907 to 1914, he appeared as counsel for the people in a series of cases heard by the Supreme Court. Four cases tested the constitutionality of state laws to limit the hours of women workers. Brandeis prepared for these cases by collecting evidence to show that long hours of work hurt the health of women workers, caused accidents, and injured the whole community. One case (*Muller* vs. *Oregon*, 1908) dealt with a law to establish a minimum wage for women. Brandeis offered evidence to prove that women workers need this protection and without it the community suffers. The Court considered these facts and

found the laws to be within the state's police power.

Brandeis pioneered in presenting the Court with facts as to social conditions instead of arguments based entirely on legal precedents. His briefs grew out of his theory of a *living law*—one that keeps pace with changing conditions. This theory is said to have opened a new era in the practice of American constitutional law. Thereafter few judges set a law aside without listening to evidence as to the conditions which the law was designed to correct.

Reformers seek national legislation.

Reformers soon learned that action on the city and state level was not enough. The solution of many of the nation's problems, such as the regulation of interstate commerce and the raising of labor standards, called for national action. After the turn of the century a growing number of reformers worked for federal laws and, if needed, amendments to the Constitution. Advocates of various reforms joined with like-minded people in national organizations. Many young progressives ran for Congress, where they kept up a battle for reform. By 1916, two Constitutional amendments and a sheaf of important new federal laws had been adopted. In the next two chapters we shall learn how three Presidents—Theodore Roosevelt, Taft, and Wilson—served the progressive movement.

United States Supreme Court

FOR IDENTIFICATION

Louis D. Brandeis	Frank Norris
Charles E. Hughes	Jacob Riis
Robert M. La Follette	Upton Sinclair
Henry D. Lloyd	Ida M. Tarbell

FOR EXPLANATION OR DEFINITION

Australian ballot	police power
city manager plan	public utility
commission	commissions
government	recall
De Rerum Novarum	referendum
direct primary	Seventeenth
initiative	Amendment
invisible government	social legislation
laissez faire	woman suffrage
"muckrakers"	workmen's
Nineteenth	compensation laws
Amendment	

FOR REVIEW

1. List the problems that received serious attention during the Progressive Era.

2. (a) What reforms were advocated by religious leaders? (b) Explain the meaning of the term "social gospel."

3. How did novelists contribute to the reform movement? Magazine writers?

4. Name some of the muckrakers and the subjects on which they wrote.

5. Why were reforms usually begun by the states rather than by Congress?

6. (a) Name three Presidents who achieved reputations as Progressives while state governors. Name three other progressive governors who achieved fame in national politics. (b) List some of the reforms sponsored by Robert M. La Follette as governor of Wisconsin.

7. Explain the Australian ballot and the reasons for its adoption.

8. What reforms were introduced to weaken the influence of the political boss?

9. Explain the operation and purpose of the direct primary. What is its weakness?

10. Explain the initiative, the referendum, and the recall.

528

1. Describe the movement for the direct election of senators.

2. (a) Why were cities badly governed at the turn of the century? (b) What reforms were introduced to improve mayor-council governments?

3. Describe the commission type of city government; the city manager plan.

4. (a) How does a city get permission to change its form of government? (b) What is meant by "home rule" for cities?

5. Where did women first win the right to vote? When was the Constitution amended to give women this right?

6. Explain the meaning of the term "laissez faire." In what sense was laissez faire more talked about as an ideal than actually practiced? Why did the idea of laissez faire lose its popularity?

7. What was the first industry which Congress tried to regulate and control?

8. (a) Why did states establish public utility commissions? (b) Why did some cities resort to public ownership of public utilities?

9. Describe the movement for the abolition of child labor.

20. What were the reasons for the introduction of workmen's compensation laws?

21. (a) Explain the meaning of the legal term "police power." (b) Why did the courts consider some social legislation was not a proper use of police power? (c) Describe some of the laws that the courts once declared were improper uses of the states' police power. (d) How did Brandeis contribute to the practice of constitutional law?

22. Why did reformers seek national legislation?

FOR FURTHER STUDY AND DISCUSSION

1. Discuss the quotation from Herbert Croly at the beginning of this chapter.

2. What is the relationship of the Progressive movement to the Populist revolt?

3. How did the social legislation of the early nineteenth century affect the doctrine of laissez faire?

4. Why was the Progressive movement concerned with political as well as social reforms?

5. Compare the reforms advocated and achieved during the Jackson Era with those advocated and achieved during the Progressive Era.

6. Discuss whether the state and local laws enacted during the Progressive Era weakened or strengthened free enterprise.

7. On what legal or constitutional grounds did the courts tend to check the social reforms urged by Progressives? On what grounds did the courts gradually begin to sustain the constitutionality of the social reform program of the Progressives? Helpful source: Hart, Contemporaries, Vol. V, Nos. 101, 102, 103, 111, 112.

8. Explain the working of the direct primary in your state, county, or city. How is either the initiative or referendum used in your state today? Helpful source: Hart, Contemporaries, Vol. V, No. 99.

9. Why are woman suffrage, the direct election of senators, and the income tax amendment regarded as essential phases of the Progressive movement?

10. Describe the type of government your city has today.

FOR INDIVIDUAL OR GROUP ACTIVITIES

1. Prepare a short book report on one of the following: Sinclair, The Jungle; Churchill, Coniston; Norris, The Pit or The Octopus; Sheldon, In His Steps.

2. Arrange an exhibit of cartoons illustrating the Progressive Era.

3. Prepare biographical sketches of Hiram Johnson, Robert M. La Follette, Charles Evans Hughes, John P. Altgeld.

4. Prepare a research paper on whether or not the direct primary, initiative, and referendum as actually practiced and applied today have fulfilled the high hopes of their early advocates.

5. Report on the ways in which your city or state today actively uses its police power to "promote the general welfare."

6. Write an essay on the influence of Louis D. Brandeis on the idea of what is proper use of police power.

ROOSEVELT *as a young man during his stay in the West. The knowledge of nature he gained at this time aided him in later years when he fought for a worth-while conservation program.*

A man who is good enough to shed his blood for his country is good enough to be given a square deal afterward. More than that no man is entitled to, and less than that no man should have.

——Theodore Roosevelt

32. THEODORE ROOSEVELT AND TAFT FURTHER REFORMS

The Progressive Movement Finds a National Leader

Big business prospers under McKinley.

In the campaign of 1896, you will remember, discontented groups—farmers, workingmen, small businessmen—supported Bryan. His defeat and the election of the conservative McKinley dealt a blow to the reform movement.

During McKinley's administration, big business grew faster than ever. The census of 1900 showed 185 trusts, which together turned out 14 per cent of the nation's industrial products. The first billion-dollar company, the United States Steel Corporation, was founded in 1901. About the same time five companies making farm implements combined in the huge International Harvester Company. Combinations also took place in the fields of banking, railroading, and mining. McKinley considered the growth of big business a sign of progress.

Prosperity returned during McKinley's first term. Prices rose and business boomed. The Republican party took the credit for bringing back good times. This, and the easy victory in the Spanish-American War, insured Republican success in the next election.

McKinley is re-elected.

In 1900 the Democrats nominated Bryan again. This time they tried to make imperialism the chief issue of the campaign (see p. 573). They also endorsed their platform of 1896 (see p. 505) and called for curbs on monopolies. The Republicans nominated President McKinley, choosing as his running mate young Governor Theodore Roosevelt of New York. Taking the "full dinner pail" as their slogan and predicting hard times if Bryan were elected, the Republicans won the contest.

The Social Democratic party (later known as the Socialist party) first entered national politics in the 1900 election. Their platform called for public ownership of land, railroads, telegraph and telephone lines, power plants, banks, and factories. They wished to carry out this program gradually and peacefully by securing an amendment to the Constitution. Eugene V. Debs, who became a Socialist as a result of his imprisonment during the Pullman strike (see p. 461), headed the Social Democratic ticket. The Socialist Labor party, which was smaller and more radical than the Social Democratic party, also had a presidential candidate. Together the two Socialist parties polled only about 100,000 votes.

A reformer becomes President.

In September, 1901, six months after beginning his second term, McKinley was shot. Theodore Roosevelt, the Vice-President, became the nation's chief executive.

Roosevelt has been described as "the most dynamic and colorful personality to enter the White House since the days of Jackson." His interests and experiences were remarkably varied. Born of an old and well-to-do New

York family, he was educated at Harvard and at Columbia University Law School. After graduation he served three terms in the New York legislature. Roosevelt then spent two years on a ranch in North Dakota, where he gained knowledge of the West and its problems. His books and articles on ranching, wild life, and American history soon attracted attention. In 1889 President Harrison named him to the Civil Service Commission. After five years in Washington, Roosevelt left to head the New York City police force. Two years later (1897) McKinley made him Assistant Secretary of the Navy. When the Spanish-American War began, Roosevelt resigned to lead a volunteer regiment, the "Rough Riders." The publicity he obtained during the war led to his election as governor of New York in 1898.

In every office Roosevelt showed outstanding courage, honesty, and ability. As governor he annoyed Republican Boss Platt by fighting for taxes on corporation franchises. To get Roosevelt out of New York politics, Platt proposed his nomination for Vice-President, an office in which he might soon be forgotten. The leaders of the party would hardly have agreed to nominate Roosevelt had they thought he would become President. In fact, Marcus Hanna privately deplored his nomination, saying "There is only one life between that madman and the White House."

Theodore Roosevelt was a born leader. His vitality and enthusiasm, his ability to dramatize himself, and his gift for coining vivid phrases won him followers wherever he went. He was interested in everybody and made friends with all sorts of people. He had sympathy for all classes and races—rich and poor, white, yellow, and black. Like Andrew Jackson, he won the trust of the plain people. Soon after he became President, people began to speak of him affectionately as "Teddy" or "T.R.",

and children named their toy bears "Teddy" in his honor.

Roosevelt is a masterful President.

Roosevelt often said that our Presidents are of two types: (1) those like Jackson and Lincoln who assert their leadership in the name of the people; and (2) the average kind who allow Congress to dominate the national government. Roosevelt took his inspiration from Jackson and Lincoln. Instead of waiting for Congress to send him bills, he told the lawmakers what he wanted. He rallied support for his program by means of fighting speeches. He used his skill in practical politics to win the support of party leaders. At times his use of the appointing power secured passage of the measures he wanted. He wrote in his autobiography:

I did not usurp power, but I did greatly broaden the use of the executive power. I caused to be done many things not previously done by the President and the heads of the executive departments. In other words, I acted for the common well-being of all our people, whenever and in whatever manner was necessary, unless prevented by direct constitutional or legislative prohibition.

Roosevelt calls for a "square deal."

In his first message to Congress (December, 1901), Roosevelt said the government must find a way to protect workers, consumers, small businessmen, and investors. He said that large-scale business is here to stay. We should not try to destroy it, but should try to make it serve the public good. Believing there are good trusts as well as bad ones, he said, "We draw the line against misconduct, not against wealth." The biggest corporation, like the humblest private citizen, must be made to obey the law. By weeding out evil business practices, said the President, government regulation can insure a "square deal" for capital, labor, and the public.

532

Roosevelt's message offended the champions of laissez faire and rugged individualism. They considered him a radical. In reality he was an enlightened conservative. He did not want to overturn the economic system but to preserve it by making necessary reforms.

Roosevelt acts as "trust buster."

The Sherman Antitrust Act had been effective only as a weapon against labor unions. It did not halt the formation of giant holding companies. By 1904, forty-eight companies owned 40 per cent of all the capital used for manufacturing in the United States.

The great power exercised by these monopolies was a threat to consumers, workers, and farmers. The beef trust, for example, dictated the prices of livestock and meat and fought the attempts of its employees to organize. The tobacco trust kept down the price of raw tobacco to the grower, kept up the price to consumers, and held wages close to the hunger level. In addition, some trusts resorted to downright fraud. The Industrial Commission, as it reported to Congress in 1900, uncovered a number of such practices. The sugar trust, for one, had robbed the federal government by tampering with customs scales. It had cheated local governments by diverting water from public reservoirs through secret mains to avoid paying for it. The trusts seemed to be above the law and more powerful than Congress. Years later Roosevelt wrote:

When I became President, the question of the *method* by which the United States government was to control the corporations was not yet important. The absolutely vital question was whether the government had power to control them at all.

Roosevelt made up his mind that the corporations could be brought under control. Soon after becoming President he declared: "We have the power, and we shall find out the way."

Early in 1902 Roosevelt ordered the Attorney General to start an antitrust suit against the Northern Securities Company, a powerful railroad holding company. Wall Street was surprised and angry, for the Supreme Court had already decided that the Sherman Antitrust Act did not apply to a holding company (see p. 425). Would the Supreme Court now reverse itself? For two years business leaders waited to find out. Then by a vote of 5 to 4 the Court declared the Northern Securities Company to be an illegal combination. Roosevelt said of the decision:

The Northern Securities suit is one of the great achievements of my administration. . . . Through it we emphasized the fact that the most powerful men in this country were held accountable before the law. . . . The success of the Northern Securities case definitely decided the power of the government to deal with all great corporations.

He attacked other combinations, among them the oil, chemical, and meat-packing trusts. Before his administration closed, no less than forty-four antitrust suits were under way.

Roosevelt pressed Congress to strengthen the Antitrust Act. He also urged that corporations engaged in interstate business be required to obtain a federal charter. Congress did not approve either of these recommendations. It did, however, create a Department of Commerce and Labor (1903), with a Bureau of Corporations to investigate the "organization, conduct, and management of corporations." The reports of this bureau helped the Department of Justice to enforce the antitrust law.

Roosevelt steps into the coal strike.

The President soon took part in another kind of contest with big business, this time against the coal trust.

The miners of anthracite (hard) coal had serious complaints. Their earnings were small and usually were paid in scrip (i.e., certificates good only in high-priced company stores). Miners had to live in cheaply built company houses. Their work was dangerous, and no compensation was paid in case of death or injury. In 1902 the United Mine Workers asked for recognition of their union, a nine-hour day, a 20 per cent increase in wages, and guarantees that the coal dug would be fairly weighed. The operators refused to discuss these demands because they were determined not to take part in collective bargaining. In May, 1902, 140,000 miners went on strike. When their leader, John Mitchell, offered to submit the dispute to arbitration, the mine operators declared: "We will give no consideration to any plan for arbitration or mediation or to any interference by a third party." The spokesman of the operators wrote, in reply to a letter urging him to end the strike:

The rights and interests of the laboring man will be protected and cared for, not by the labor organizers, but by the Christian men to whom God, in His infinite wisdom, has given control of the property interests of the country.

As the strike dragged on, a coal shortage developed. The price of coal went up from $5.00 a ton to $30.00. Since city people in the East depended on hard coal to heat their homes, they begged that the strike be ended. The mine operators urged the President to prosecute the United Mine Workers under the Antitrust Act and to send soldiers to the coal districts to protect strikebreakers. Instead, Roosevelt let it be known he might use soldiers to take over the mines unless the operators came to an agreement with the miners. Meanwhile, Secretary of War Elihu Root had a conference with J. P. Morgan, head of the banking firm which indirectly controlled most of the mines. Morgan persuaded the operators to back down. The President then appointed a commission to mediate the dispute. The miners went back to work while the commission held an inquiry. In the end the miners received a 10 per cent raise and the nine-hour day. Their union was not recognized until 1916.

The President's action in the coal strike set a precedent. It showed that the powers of the federal government could be used to protect *both* sides in an industrial dispute. Newspapermen here and abroad praised the President. The London *Times* said:

In a most quiet and unassuming way the President has done a very big and entirely new thing. We are witnessing not merely the ending of the coal strike, but the definite entry of a powerful government upon a new sphere of operation.

Holmes is appointed to the Supreme Court.

To fill a vacancy on the Supreme Court, Roosevelt called Oliver W. Holmes. Holmes had been a judge of the Massachusetts Supreme Court for twenty years and its Chief Justice for three years. His opinions in certain labor cases had shown that he placed human rights above property rights. When Holmes took the oath of office in Washington (December 8, 1902), a new chapter opened in American constitutional law.

Holmes believed that the Constitution was not intended to be a strait jacket. He thought it should be interpreted in such a way as to permit changes that the majority of the people feel are demanded by new social conditions. "The present," he said, "has a right to govern itself so far as it can." He often warned against the use of the Fourteenth Amendment to prevent the states from making experiments with new kinds of legislation. The chief value of the federal system, he said, is that it permits experimentation in forty-

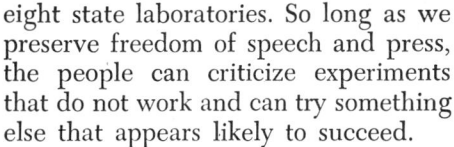

(Above) JUSTICE OLIVER WENDELL HOLMES, *the minority of one, whose opinions later became those of the majority.*

(Above and right) ELIHU ROOT *and* J. P. MORGAN. *Their cooperation helped end the great coal strike and set in motion a new era of government participation in labor disputes.*

eight state laboratories. So long as we preserve freedom of speech and press, the people can criticize experiments that do not work and can try something else that appears likely to succeed.

Holmes served on the United States Supreme Court for thirty years. In hundreds of cases he found himself in a minority of one or two. He became known as the "great dissenter," because of the noble language in which he set forth his dissenting opinions. As the years went by, almost all of his dissents came to be accepted as good law.

Roosevelt is re-elected.

Roosevelt cultivated the support of both conservative and progressive leaders of his party. When the Republican National Convention met in 1904, he was nominated unanimously.[1] In spite of his activities in prosecuting trusts, big business gave lavishly to his campaign fund.

---

[1] Although four earlier Vice-Presidents (Tyler, Fillmore, Johnson, and Arthur) had succeeded to the Presidency on the death of their chiefs, none had won his party's nomination for the ensuing term.

The Democrats turned away from the twice-defeated Bryan and nominated a conservative New York judge, Alton B. Parker. The Democratic platform charged the Republican administration with being "spasmodic, erratic, sensational, spectacular, and arbitrary." Hoping to win support from businessmen, the Democrats dropped their demand for an income tax.

Roosevelt was at the peak of his popularity. His vigorous foreign policy, as well as his trust-busting activities, pleased the public. He won election by a wide margin. He then announced he would not be a candidate again.

Congress strengthens the I.C.C.

After becoming President in his own right, Roosevelt was bolder in his recommendations for reform. His biggest fight was to bring the railroads under control. The railroad companies owned one tenth of the nation's wealth. They were so powerful that neither state legislatures nor Congress had succeeded in regulating them (see p. 484).

535

Farmers and others demanded more effective regulation. Some reformers urged the government to buy and operate the railroads. Roosevelt did not favor this proposal. Instead he asked Congress to strengthen the Interstate Commerce Commission. After a long struggle in the Senate, Congress passed the Hepburn Act of 1906. This law gave the Interstate Commerce Commission authority over companies operating pipe lines, railway express service, sleeping cars, refrigerator cars, ferries, and storage and other facilities at railway terminals. The act required railroad companies to divorce themselves from the ownership of coal fields. The I.C.C. was authorized to inspect the accounts kept by all carriers and to require them to follow uniform accounting methods. In this way Congress made it difficult for the companies to hide rebates and bribes. The act also prohibited railroad companies from giving passes to any persons except their employees. This meant that the companies could no longer bribe public officials and newspapermen by supplying free passes to them and their families. The I.C.C. was given power to reduce unreasonable rates, but reductions would not go into effect unless approved by the courts.

In the same year Congress passed an Employers' Liability Act, requiring the railroads to pay compensation to workers injured on the job. Congress also passed a law requiring the railroads to adopt certain safety appliances. These acts gave the government real power over the railroads. Still stronger laws would be passed within a few years (see p. 606).

The Pure Food and Drug Act.

The food and drug industry was next to feel President Roosevelt's "big stick." For several years chemists in state and federal agencies had been investigating the adulteration of foods.

(A food is *adulterated* when it contains impurities.) They found that harmful substances called *preservatives* were commonly mixed with meat, preserves, milk, and butter, in order to keep them from spoiling. Injurious coal-tar dyes were often added to candy, baked goods, canned goods, and preserves. In addition, experts knew that many widely advertised patent medicines contained narcotics or other dangerous drugs. The states were trying to regulate the sale of food and drugs, but the job was too big without help from the federal government. Year after year a pure-food and drug bill had been introduced into Congress but it never passed. Manufacturers had always fought the proposal as "socialistic" and "destructive of liberty."

In his annual message to Congress in 1905, Roosevelt urged the passage of a national pure-food and drug act. Shortly after, a bill was introduced to require truthful labeling of food and drugs and to prevent the sale of diseased meat, spoiled food, and food containing harmful preservatives and dyes. A number of senators opposed the bill on the ground that it interfered with the "liberty" of the consumer. Finally, in 1906, the bill passed. While it corrected many abuses, it was too weak to stop them completely. In 1938 Congress passed a more effective law—the Pure Food, Drug, and Cosmetic Act.

The Meat Inspection Act.

In the spring of 1906 Roosevelt read *The Jungle*, best-selling novel by Upton Sinclair, which told of conditions in the great meat-packing plants. T.R. at once appointed a commission to investigate. The commission reported to him secretly that the reality was even worse than Sinclair's description. Roosevelt then urged Congress to pass a bill requiring federal inspection of places where meat is packed for interstate commerce. When the packers succeeded in blocking the bill, the President made public a part of the commission's report. Congress then passed the Meat Inspection Act (1906), saying that no meat may be shipped from one state to another unless approved by a federal inspector. The familiar words "Government inspected and passed" stamped on meats and printed on the labels of canned meat are there because of this law.

Roosevelt pushes conservation.

In all of his annual messages to Congress, Roosevelt called attention to the need for conserving our natural resources. Conservation, he declared, was one of the nation's most vital problems. The forests, mineral lands, and water-power sites still left in the public domain should not be given away or "sold for a song." Instead they should be held in trust for the benefit of the entire nation. During his administration nearly 150 million acres were set aside as national forests. Eighty million acres of mineral land and one and a half million acres of water-power sites were also withdrawn from sale. In his determination to save what was left of the national heritage, Roosevelt had the Attorney General sue companies that had obtained large tracts of the public land by fraud. As a result the government recovered much land. Believing that the public lands should benefit the whole nation, not just a few users, Roosevelt started the practice of charging a fair rental for the privilege of grazing sheep and cattle on the public domain. To care for the national forests he persuaded Congress to create the Forest Service. He appointed Gifford Pinchot, a crusader for conservation, as director.

Roosevelt did a great deal to educate the public to the importance of conservation. He constantly discussed the problem in popular articles and speeches. In 1908 he called the state governors to the White House for a conference on conservation. This meeting created so much interest that soon nearly every state set up a conservation commission. Following the conference Roosevelt appointed a National Conservation Commission, headed by Gifford Pinchot. Its duty was to make an inventory, or list, of the country's natural resources and to recommend a program for conserving them. Thus T.R. helped build a new public attitude toward natural resources.

A reclamation program is launched.

In 1902 Congress passed the Newlands Reclamation Act, providing federal funds for irrigation of desert lands in the West. The irrigated lands were to be sold to settlers on a ten-year payment plan. Under this act Roosevelt started no less than twenty-seven irrigation projects. By 1920 over twenty million acres of seemingly worthless desert had been transformed into gardens and orchards. Among the irrigation projects built under the Newlands Act are the Roosevelt Dam in Arizona, the Coolidge Dam on the Gila River, the Hoover Dam on the Colorado River, and the Grand Coulee Dam on the Columbia River. These projects supply water for irrigation, produce hydroelectric power, and promote flood control.

T.R. chooses his successor.

By 1908 Roosevelt had served two terms—one as McKinley's successor and one in his own right. He had given the country an example of strong presidential leadership, not only on the domestic front but also in foreign affairs (see p. 582). He had voiced the desires of the common people as no other President since Lincoln had done. In so doing he had vastly strengthened the reform movement. Having won the affection of millions of his countrymen, he could doubtless have had another term for the asking. Instead he stuck to his

Tunnel Vista in BRYCE CANYON NATIONAL PARK, *Utah. The wealth of a country cannot be measured solely by what is taken from the earth. What endures is important too. The men who realized this, men like Roosevelt and Pinchot, left us not only a heritage of beauty but a memorial to those who conquered the wilderness.*

Theodore Roosevelt and the Scottish naturalist John Muir. The efforts of the conservationists helped mature us as a nation. We were no longer despoilers but actively sought the preservation of what we had and the rebuilding of what we had lost.

1904 decision not to run again. He asked the Republicans to nominate as President his old friend, William Howard Taft, then serving as Secretary of War. The Democrats nominated Bryan for the third and last time. With Roosevelt's backing, Taft easily won the election.

The Republican Party Splits

President Taft lacks political glamor.

Taft had been in public office since early youth. As a federal judge, then as governor of the Philippines, and later as Roosevelt's Secretary of War, he had shown outstanding ability. He was a man of high principles and unquestioned patriotism. Unlike his energetic predecessor, he was cautious, slow-moving, deliberate. He had none of Roosevelt's showmanship. By contrast with Roosevelt, the public found him tame. Although his personality was genial, he failed to win the affection of the people.

Furthermore, Taft's view of the Presidency was different from Roosevelt's. The President, he thought, should be a balance wheel rather than a mainspring in the mechanism of federal government. Taft was unwilling to use any powers not specifically given him under the Constitution or in acts of Congress. Nor did he try to arouse public opinion to support his policies.

Taft steers a middle course.

The progressive or "insurgent" wing of the Republican party had been gaining strength since the turn of the century. Throughout Taft's term the progressives fought to capture control of the party from the conservative or "Old Guard" wing. Taft hoped to work with both groups as Roosevelt had done, but he lacked T.R.'s political skill. Soon he lost progressive support.

Taft was more conservative than Roosevelt. For advice he constantly turned to conservative leaders in Congress. Yet he was not a "standpatter." He saw that reforms were necessary to keep the socialists and other radicals from gaining ground. "If the tyranny and oppression of an oligarchy of wealth cannot be avoided," he said, "then socialism will triumph, and the institution of private property will perish."

The Payne-Aldrich Tariff.

Since 1897, when the Dingley Tariff was adopted, the cost of living had gone up 40 per cent, while wages had risen less than 20 per cent. Progressives claimed that the tariff benefited big manufacturers without bringing corresponding benefits to consumers and wage earners. Moreover, said progressives, by shutting out foreign competition the tariff encouraged the growth of trusts.

Shortly after his inauguration, President Taft called Congress into special session and asked it to reduce the tariff. In taking this step he showed more courage than Roosevelt, who had avoided the tariff issue as "political dynamite." The House promptly passed a bill with lower duties but, as in Cleveland's time, the Senate restored all the important duties to the old level or a still higher one. When the resulting Payne-Aldrich Tariff was sent to the President, progressives urged him to veto it. Yet in spite of the bill's faults, Taft signed it because it created a tariff commission. This new agency was to gather figures on the cost of production here and in other countries and to investigate the effect of the tariff on competition in each industry. Taft hoped the reports of the tariff commission would furnish a scientific basis for rate-making. Congress, however, gave no heed to the commission's reports. Progressives felt that on the tariff question the President had weakly surrendered to the Old Guard.

540

Progressives cut the Speaker's power.

The leader of the Old Guard Republicans, "Uncle Joe" Cannon of Illinois, had been Speaker of the House since 1903. He was opposed to all reforms, for he said that half of all ideas for change were useless and the other half were dangerous! Under the rules of the House, Cannon could and did act as a dictator. He appointed all the committees. As a member of the Rules Committee, he was able to stifle bills he did not favor. As presiding officer of the House, he had the right to grant or deny recognition to any member wishing to take part in debate. Political opponents called him the "Czar," because he gave them so little chance to be heard.

In the spring of 1910 insurgent Republicans joined with Democrats in a bitter fight to curb "Uncle Joe's" authority. The power to appoint committees was given back to the House. The Speaker was denied membership on the Rules Committee. These changes made the House of Representatives more responsive to public opinion.

The Taft administration is fruitful.

In his quiet, undramatic way, Taft accomplished more than he was given credit for at the time. In one term his Attorney General, George Wickersham, brought almost twice as many antitrust suits as had been brought in Roosevelt's two terms. Taft extended the merit system to thousands of postal employees. He added to the national forests. When Congress authorized the reservation of mineral lands, Taft withdrew fifty-nine million acres of coal lands from sale. He was the first President to reserve petroleum lands. He managed the executive departments efficiently and urged Congress to adopt the budget system.

Congress enacted a long list of constructive measures during Taft's presidency, some of which he proposed.

For the first time a small tax was laid on corporation earnings (1909). While Congress refused Taft's request for an inheritance tax, at his suggestion Congress submitted to the states a Constitutional amendment to permit the federal government to tax incomes. Congress also sent the states an amendment for the direct election of United States senators. The Mann-Elkins Act (1910) increased the powers of the Interstate Commerce Commission. Several laws recommended by the National Conservation Commission were adopted. In addition to giving the President authority to reserve mineral lands and water-power sites, these laws permitted him to buy land in the Appalachians for national forests. The Campaign Expense Publicity Act required that campaign expenditures for candidates to Congress be made public. The Radio Act required that passenger vessels be equipped to send wireless messages. Congress created the Postal Savings Bank (1910). The parcel post system, long demanded by farmers, was started. A Bureau of Mines was set up in the Department of the Interior to promote conservation and to work for mine safety. The Children's Bureau was

President Taft and his family in the first official White House automobile. Young Robert, seated in front of his father, seems to think of it as a solemn occasion.

established (1912) "to investigate and report on all matters pertaining to the welfare of children." A separate Department of Labor was created (1913), "to foster, promote, and develop the welfare of wage earners."

All the measures named had Taft's approval. But all of them were pushed through by a combination of Democrats and insurgent Republicans. Thus the public saw President Taft not as a leader of the reform movement but as one who accepted reforms which others had fought for.

T.R. returns from Africa.

At the beginning of Taft's term, Roosevelt had gone abroad—in order, as he said, to give the President a free hand. He spent nearly a year in Africa shooting big game. Then he toured Europe, where he was honored by some of the leading universities and entertained by kings. The American public eagerly read stories of his adventures in the newspapers, which reported everything he did and said. His followers, disappointed in President Taft, began to hope that T.R. would come back to take up the fight against privilege. A popular ditty said:

Teddy, come home and blow your horn,
The sheep's in the meadow, the cow's in the corn.
The boy you left to tend the sheep
Is under the haystack fast asleep.

Upon Roosevelt's return in the summer of 1910, he and Taft were less friendly than before. Roosevelt blamed Taft for the deep split in the Republican party and tried vainly to bring the warring groups together. T.R. soon found that the progressive tide was rising. "The whole country is insurgent," a friend wrote to him.

T.R. preaches the "New Nationalism."

During the campaign of 1910, Roosevelt toured the West, speaking in behalf of progressive Republican candidates. He recommended the direct primary, the initiative, the referendum, and the recall. He even advocated the recall of judicial decisions. This meant that when a state court found a state law to be contrary to the state constitution, the voters could demand a referendum on the question. To conservatives this proposal seemed dangerously radical. No state has tried it even yet.

At Osawatomie, Kansas, Roosevelt made a famous speech on the "New Nationalism." The national government, he declared, must have power to protect the whole people. It must bring the great corporations under control. It must regulate the terms and conditions of labor in the interests of the common good. The executive, not the courts, should be regarded as the "steward of human welfare." He attacked the courts for being more concerned with property than human rights, and quoted Lincoln's words, "Labor is the superior of capital and deserves much higher consideration." He endorsed graduated taxes on inheritances and incomes, a comprehensive workmen's compensation act, laws to regulate the labor of women and children, and strict supervision of all corporations engaged in interstate business. Thus T.R. was pointing in the direction of a stronger national government, and to regulating and taxing private property for the benefit of the whole people. Conservative newspapers denounced the speech as an "assault on organized institutions." Men of property began to desert to the Democratic party.

La Follette and Roosevelt become rivals.

Early in 1911 a group of insurgent congressmen organized the National Progressive Republican League. They hoped to win control of the Republican party and to nominate Senator Robert La Follette of Wisconsin as the party's next candidate for President.

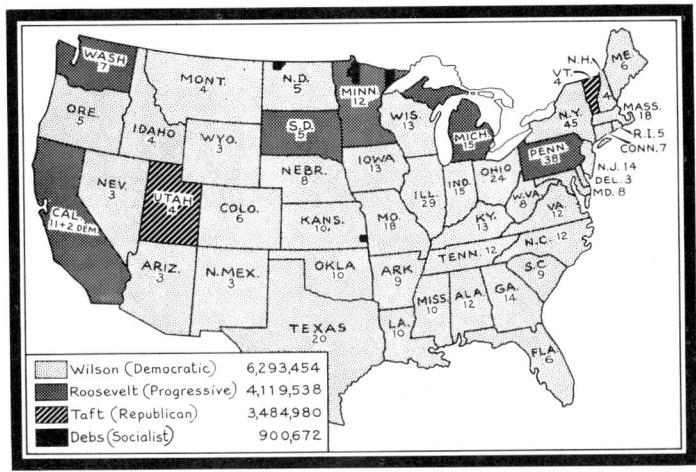

Wilson (Democratic)	6,293,454	
Roosevelt (Progressive)	4,119,538	
Taft (Republican)	3,484,980	
Debs (Socialist)	900,672	

PRESIDENTIAL ELECTION, 1912

They expected Roosevelt to support their plans, for he had said many times that he would not run for a third term. T.R., however, could not play second fiddle to anyone else. He referred to certain League members as extremists and in other ways undermined La Follette's leadership. Early in 1912 T.R. announced, "My hat is in the ring," meaning he would be a candidate. Roosevelt's decision to run split the progressive Republicans.

Taft is renominated.

The majority of Republican voters would doubtless have preferred Roosevelt to Taft as their party's candidate. Taft, however, had the advantage of being in office. As President he could promise patronage and thus control the party machinery. When the Republican convention met in June, 1912, Taft was renominated on the first ballot. Roosevelt called the action "theft." He asked his followers to form a new party.

The Progressive party is organized.

A few weeks later Roosevelt's supporters met to organize the Progressive party and name him as their candidate. When Roosevelt arrived to accept the nomination, he told reporters he felt like a "bull moose." The new party then took the bull moose as its symbol.

The Progressive, or Bull Moose, party adopted the most significant platform since the Populist platform of 1892 (see p. 502). It began with a list of political reforms: there should be direct primaries; the direct election of United States senators; the short ballot; the initiative, referendum, and recall; woman suffrage; the recall of state judicial decisions; a nationwide presidential primary; full publicity for campaign contributions and expenditures; and an easier method for amending the Constitution. In the economic field the platform called for a revised currency system, an inheritance tax, and control of big business in the public interest. The platform also endorsed certain reforms thought necessary to bring about social justice, including jury trial for contempt cases arising out of labor disputes; abolition of child labor; minimum wage laws; the eight-hour day; safety and health codes for places of employment; workmen's compensation; unemployment insurance; old age insurance; and others. Although this platform seemed radical at the time, a large part of its aims were achieved within a generation.

The Democrats name Woodrow Wilson.

The split in the Republican party gave the Democrats an excellent chance of victory. At the Democratic national convention, conservatives and liberals struggled for control. Bryan was still the most influential member of the party. Defying conservative Democrats from Wall Street and from Tammany Hall, he threw all his strength to Woodrow Wilson, the liberal governor of New Jersey. Wilson was nominated on the forty-sixth ballot. Bryan, who had never been able to win the Presidency himself, had named the next President.

The campaign of 1912.

Of the four parties which took part in the campaign of 1912, three—Progressives, Democrats, and Socialists—had platforms which called for sweeping reforms. Even the Republican platform was more progressive than usual.

The campaign was mainly a contest between Roosevelt and Wilson. Wilson received the regular Democratic vote, while the Republican vote was divided between Roosevelt and Taft. Taft carried only two states, Roosevelt six, and Wilson forty. The popular vote was a better measure of party strength. Taft received 23 per cent of the total ballots cast, Roosevelt, 27 per cent, and Wilson, 42 per cent. In addition to winning the Presidency, the Democrats won majorities in both houses of Congress. Thus for the second time since 1856 they controlled both the executive and legislative branches of the government.

The nation's unrest was shown in the large vote for the three reform candidates—Wilson, Roosevelt, and Debs. Together they obtained over three fourths of the popular vote. Debs, running for the fourth time on the Socialist ticket, got over 900,000 votes, or 7 per cent of the total. This was twice as many as he received in 1908. Only once since then, in 1920, has the Socialist party done so well.

★ ★ ★ ★ ★

FOR IDENTIFICATION

Joseph G. Cannon	Alton B. Parker
Hepburn Act	Payne-Aldrich Tariff
Justice Oliver	Pure Food and Drug
Wendell Holmes	Act
Mann-Elkins Act	Theodore Roosevelt
Meat Inspection Act	William Howard Taft
John Mitchell	Woodrow Wilson

FOR EXPLANATION OR DEFINITION

adulteration	Northern Securities
"Bull Moose" party	case
conservation	Old Guard 540
"full dinner pail" 535	Postal Savings Bank
insurgents 540	recall of judicial
National Conservation	decisions
Commission	reclamation
"New Nationalism"	"square deal" 537
	standpatter

FOR REVIEW

1. What are some of the evidences of business prosperity during McKinley's administration?

2. Describe the presidential compaign of 1900. What new party appeared?

3. (a) How did Roosevelt happen to become the vice-presidential candidate in 1900? (b) Discuss the qualities that made Theodore Roosevelt so popular. (c) How did Roosevelt secure support for his legislative program?

4. What was Roosevelt's attitude toward industrialism and the trusts?

5. (a) How did Roosevelt enforce the Sherman Antitrust Act? (b) What is the significance of the Supreme Court decision in the Northern Securities case, 1904?

6. Compare Roosevelt's record as a "trust buster" with that of Taft.

7. (a) What were the issues involved in the anthracite coal strike of 1902? (b) How did Roosevelt bring about a settlement of this strike? (c) What is the significance of his action?

544

8. Briefly describe the career and influence of Justice Oliver Wendell Holmes. Why is he known as the "great dissenter"?

9. Describe the presidential campaign of 1904.

10. How did the Hepburn Act of 1906 strengthen the Interstate Commerce Commission?

11. (a) What was the need for the Pure Food and Drug Act, 1906? The Meat Inspection Act, 1906? (b) What arguments were used against the passage of the Pure Food and Drug Act?

12. Why did Roosevelt champion the cause of conservation? What steps did he take to promote conservation?

13. What is the significance of the Newlands Reclamation Act, 1902?

14. Describe the presidential campaign of 1908.

15. In what respects did Taft differ from Roosevelt?

16. On what grounds did Taft support the Payne-Aldrich Tariff? Why did his support of the tariff cause factions to develop in the Republican party?

17. Who were the "insurgents"? How did the "insurgents" and the Democrats limit the power of the Speaker of the House?

18. (a) List the important laws passed during Taft's administration, 1909–13. (b) Discuss whether the laws show that Taft deserves to be remembered as an able and progressive President. (c) Why did Roosevelt criticize Taft?

19. Why did Roosevelt describe his program as "the New Nationalism"?

20. (a) Why did Roosevelt and La Follette become rivals? (b) How did this rivalry affect the National Progressive Republican League? (c) Describe the origin of the Progressive or "Bull Moose" party in 1912. (d) What were the chief planks in its platform of 1912?

21. How did the split in the Republican party lead to Wilson's election in 1912?

22. What actions of President Taft caused him to lose the support of the progressive elements in the Republican party?

FOR FURTHER STUDY AND DISCUSSION

1. Why is it comparatively easy for a President to secure his own nomination or the nomination of a friend?

2. How did the Speaker of the House of Representatives become one of the most powerful officials in the national government? Investigate and report on the revolt against Speaker Cannon. Helpful sources: Ogg and Ray, *Introduction to American Government*, pp. 312–324; Ogg, *National Progress* (A.N.S.).

3. Compare the actions of Cleveland in the Pullman strike with those of Theodore Roosevelt in the coal strike of 1902.

4. Contrast the progressivism of Theodore Roosevelt with that of Robert M. La Follette. Helpful source: Hofstadter, *American Political Tradition*, pp. 206–207.

5. In his policy toward trusts, was Theodore Roosevelt a leader and formulator of opinion or did he merely follow or modify a public opinion which others had created? Helpful sources: Hofstadter, *American Political Tradition*, pp. 206–207; Amherst Series, *Roosevelt, Wilson, and the Trusts*.

6. State why you would have voted for Taft, Roosevelt, or Wilson in 1912.

FOR INDIVIDUAL OR GROUP ACTIVITIES

1. Select short passages from Roosevelt's writings or speeches and present them as dramatic readings to the class.

2. Exhibit, with brief explanations, a series of political cartoons illustrating various phases of Roosevelt's career.

3. Write the script for a five-minute radio newscast on one of the following: The split between Roosevelt and Taft; the Bull Moose Convention of 1912; the Democratic Convention of 1912. Helpful sources: Commager and Nevins, *Heritage of America*, Nos. 235, 236; Link, *Woodrow Wilson and the Progressive Era*, pp. 1–25; Steffens, *Autobiography*; Roosevelt, *Autobiography*; Sullivan, *Our Times*.

4. Read the dissenting opinion of Mr. Justice Holmes in the Northern Securities case. Summarize his arguments for the class. Helpful source: Commager, *Documents*, No. 363.

The President is at liberty . . . to be as big a man as he can.
His capacity will set the limit. He has no means of compelling
Congress except through public opinion.
——Woodrow Wilson

33. WILSON ADVOCATES THE NEW FREEDOM

A Democratic President Charts a Program of Reform

An idealist in politics.

Woodrow Wilson was the first Southerner to reach the White House since Andrew Johnson. Born in Virginia in 1856, he had spent his boyhood in Georgia and the Carolinas. His father was a Presbyterian minister, who taught him that man's duty is to battle unceasingly for the right. Wilson's religious upbringing influenced everything he did and thought. All his life he was an idealist who would not compromise with wrong.

After practicing law for a short time and writing a scholarly book on American government, Wilson decided to be a college teacher. He was a brilliant lecturer, and students flocked to his courses. In 1902 he was made president of Princeton. He promptly began a campaign to raise scholarship standards. He also worked to make the university more democratic. His fight against exclusive clubs for rich students attracted public attention.

As early as 1906, Colonel George Harvey, a New York publisher, suggested Wilson for the Presidency. Harvey was looking for a conservative leader who could replace Bryan as the head of the Democratic party. In 1910, when Wilson was about to resign from Princeton because of conflict with the trustees, Harvey secured his nomination as governor of New Jersey. Wilson campaigned vigorously and won the governorship by a big majority. Then, to the surprise of the political bosses who nominated him and helped him win, he set to work to clean up politics.

Up to this time the reform movement had made little progress in New Jersey. Under Wilson's leadership the legislature defied the bosses and passed important reform measures, including the direct primary, a corrupt practices act to regulate campaign contributions, workmen's compensation, and a plan for regulating public utilities. Wilson became known as the most progressive governor in the East. In 1911, as an aspirant for the Presidency, he made a speaking tour through the West. The next year, with the support of Bryan, Wilson won the Democratic nomination for President.

Wilson preaches the "New Freedom."

Wilson was a remarkable public speaker. Since early youth he had dreamed of "swaying men to great purposes by the power of eloquence." Those who listened to him felt his deep sincerity, fairness, and high purpose.

In his 1912 campaign for the Presidency, Wilson preached the "New Freedom." Its theme was "equal and exact justice for all." He promised that his administration would be run in the interest of the many, not the few. By attacking monopoly and special privilege, the government would restore equality of opportunity. "Law in our day," he said, "must come to the assistance of the individual . . . to see that he gets fair play. . . . Freedom today is more than being let alone."

Wilson outlines his program.

Wilson's first inaugural address, March 4, 1913, reflected his idealism and spirit of dedication. He began by asking the meaning of the recent Democratic victory. "The success of a party means little except when the Nation is using that party for a large and definite purpose." That purpose, he declared, was unmistakable: to do away with evils that had come along with the good from our industrial achievements.

Wilson named the chief things that ought to be changed:

1. A tariff which cuts us off from our proper share in the commerce of the world, violates the just principles of taxation, and makes the government a facile instrument in the hands of private industry;

PRESIDENT WOODROW WILSON

PRESIDENT WOODROW WILSON *attending Flag Day exercises, June 1914. At left,* WILLIAM JENNINGS BRYAN *and* JOSEPHUS DANIELS; *at extreme right,* FRANKLIN DELANO ROOSEVELT.

547

2. A banking and currency system based upon the necessity of the government to sell its bonds fifty years ago, and perfectly adapted to concentrating cash and restricting credits;
3. An industrial system which, take it on all its sides, financial as well as administrative, holds capital in leading strings, restricts the liberties and limits the opportunities of labor, and exploits without renewing or conserving the resources of the country.

Wilson declared that the government should be "put at the service of humanity" in safeguarding the health and welfare of its people. These were fine-sounding phrases, but could a college professor with little experience in politics manage to get them written into law?

Wilson's view of the Presidency.

Like Andrew Jackson and Theodore Roosevelt, Wilson gave the nation an example of strong presidential leadership. He believed it is the President's duty to propose legislation and to work actively for its passage. Wilson also thought that the President should lead his party and make it an instrument for serving the entire people. By battling vigorously for his ideas, he made himself the real head of his party. When necessary he threatened to withdraw patronage from Democratic congressmen who opposed him. To a great degree he kept the support of both conservative and progressive Democrats.

The tariff is reduced.

The new President lost no time in attacking what he called "the triple wall of privilege"—the tariff, the trusts, and the banking and currency system. Shortly after his inauguration he called a special session of Congress. When it met he addressed it in person instead of sending a written message to be read by a clerk. This was a return to the custom followed by Washington and John Adams. It made plain Wilson's desire for closer co-operation between the President and Congress.

Wilson's first message to Congress dealt only with the tariff. He urged repeal of the Payne-Aldrich Act. High protection, he argued, was the "mother of trusts." We should abolish special privilege and artificial advantage of every kind, he said, and put our producers "under the necessity to be efficient, economical, and enterprising."

Following Wilson's message, the House passed the Underwood bill, reducing many duties and dropping some altogether. When the Senate took up the measure, swarms of lobbyists appeared. (A *lobbyist*, you remember, is a person who tries to persuade members of a legislature to vote in a certain way. Frequently the lobbyist goes to work on a congressman by getting people in his district to send him letters or make him personal visits.) Under pressure from the lobbyists, the senators got ready to make over the Underwood bill by the well-known method of logrolling. The senators from sugar-growing sections, for example, promised to vote for a high duty on plate glass if the senators from sections where plate glass was manufactured would vote for a high duty on sugar. In this way each senator arranged to get what he wanted for his own district.

Wilson did not intend to let the lobbyists write the new tariff bill. He took action in a way no other President had ever tried. He wrote a public letter pointing out that lobbyists were at work to prevent a reduction of the tariff. He said that the people at large have no lobby to protect their interests. The letter was like a bombshell. The Senate felt obliged to appoint an investigating committee. For a while the lobbyists were checked. The Senate then passed the House bill with few changes. For the first time since 1857, the average duty was lowered.

Although economists praised the Underwood-Simmons Tariff as a step toward freer trade, it was far from a free-trade measure. It still gave substantial protection to American manufacturers. While it placed about a hundred items on the free list, these were products which no longer needed protection. Rates were lowered on almost a thousand items, chiefly raw materials and foodstuffs.

A tax is placed on incomes.

It was thought that reduction of the tariff might mean some loss of revenue. To make up for this, Congress adopted a tax on incomes. The rates were graduated, ranging from 1 per cent on the first $3,000 a year of taxable income to 6 per cent on that part of an individual's income above $500,000. The adoption of a federal income tax was possible because the Sixteenth, or Income Tax, Amendment had been added to the Constitution earlier in the year.[1] The amendment was a great victory for the progressive movement. Within a few years the income tax was to supply most of the revenue of the federal government.

Congress Improves Our Banking and Currency

Monetary reform is needed.

The farmers had been demanding banking and currency reform for years. When the country suffered a severe money panic in 1907, bankers and businessmen agreed that changes were necessary. In 1908 Congress appointed a National Monetary Commission, head-

---

[1] By this time a large number of states had begun to lay graduated taxes on incomes. The adoption of the Sixteenth Amendment meant that the people, acting through Congress and their state legislatures, had *recalled* a Supreme Court decision which said Congress could not levy an income tax.

ed by Senator Aldrich, to examine the whole problem. After four years of study the commission reported. It found four chief faults with the banking and currency system:

1. *The currency was not elastic.* In other words, it did not expand or contract in response to the business needs of the country. The amount of money in circulation changed very little because it was based on the amount of gold and silver in the Treasury and on a small supply of United States bonds held by national banks. Every fall, when crops were going to market, there was a scarcity of money, interest rates rose sharply, and panics often resulted. Partly because money was "tight," farmers could not get credit and had to sell their crops as soon as harvested.

2. *The currency lacked mobility.* Two thirds of the nation's banks kept their surplus funds in New York City banks. The concentration of idle cash in New York encouraged speculation on the stock exchange. Meanwhile, the rest of the country had too little money for the needs of businessmen and farmers.

3. *The banks lacked stability.* Most of the nation's 25,000 banks were small ones serving local needs. State laws required banks to keep on reserve a certain proportion of the money received from deposits. Yet each bank had only its own reserve. It would have to close if a "run" developed, that is, if too many depositors tried to draw out their accounts at once.

4. *There was no central bank.* Unlike other industrial countries, we had no central bank to control banking practices and to regulate credit.

To overcome these difficulties, Senator Aldrich backed a plan put forward by the big bankers. They wanted a powerful central bank under their own control, a successor to the first and second Bank of the United States. The Bryan Democrats refused to hear of this solution. The Democratic party had always opposed a central bank under private control.

The Pujo Committee reports.

Reformers had long suspected the existence of a "money trust." In 1911 Woodrow Wilson, then governor of New Jersey, said: "The great monopoly in this country is the money monopoly. So long as it exists, our old variety and freedom and individual energy are out of the question." One year later, the House of Representatives appointed a committee, headed by Congressman Pujo, to investigate the bank and money problem.

In 1913, just before the close of President Taft's term, this committee issued a sensational report. It showed that the directors of three large New York banks held 341 directorships in 112 big corporations. These companies were in fields vital to the whole economy, such as railroading, shipping, insurance, coal, copper, iron, and steel. Leading banks in other large cities also held many directorships in large companies. By means of such interlocking directorates, a small number of bankers had power over all parts of the nation's economic life. The Pujo Committee concluded that the big bankers had far too much control over credit. Its report strengthened opposition to the Aldrich plan.

The Federal Reserve Act.

Shortly after his election, Wilson and his advisors began work on a substitute plan for banking reform. To pass, there must be a compromise between what the big bankers wanted and what progressives in both parties wanted. When introduced into Congress in June, 1913, the plan became known as the "Glass-Owens" bill. In the long struggle for its enactment, Wilson took an active part. It became law in December, 1913, and is now called the "Federal Reserve Act." It is generally considered the greatest peacetime achievement of Wilson's administration.

The new law divided the country into twelve districts, each having one Federal Reserve Bank, which serves as a central bank for its district. All twelve banks are governed by a small Federal Reserve Board chosen by the President. The Board also appoints one third of the directors in each regional bank.

All national banks are *required* to join the Federal Reserve system, and all other banks are *permitted* to join. Each member bank subscribes to the stock of the Federal Reserve Bank in its district. Thus each Federal Reserve Bank is owned by its member banks. The Federal Reserve Banks are "bankers' banks," doing business only with other banks.

Benefits from the new system.

The Federal Reserve system has helped the entire nation. Here are the chief advantages it gave:

1. *The currency is elastic.* The Federal Reserve system puts money into circulation or takes it out of circulation according to the needs of businessmen and farmers, which are reflected in their use of credit. The method is simple. A member bank which has lent its available funds on mortgages or promissory notes can take this "commercial paper" to a Federal Reserve Bank and sell or exchange it for Federal Reserve notes. When the borrower pays back his loan, the money is withdrawn from circulation. Thus the supply of money increases or decreases with changes in the demand for money.

2. *The currency is mobile.* One Federal Reserve Bank may borrow from another. In this way heavy seasonal demands for currency in any section of the country are readily cared for. By making possible the quick flow of credit from one district to another, the Federal Reserve system has particularly helped the South and the West.

3. *Banks are more stable.* Formerly any bank would fail if depositors started a run when most of its assets were "frozen"—that is, tied up in loans that could not be promptly collected. Banks in the Federal Reserve system are not likely to fail because they can quickly get money in exchange for mortgages and promissory notes.

4. *Speculation can be discouraged.* When a businessman borrows a thousand dollars from his local bank on a promissory note, the bank deducts the interest in advance. This is known as *discounting* a note. If the banker sells the note to the Federal Reserve Bank, the process is known as *rediscounting* because the note is discounted a second time, usually at a lower rate. The Federal Reserve Board fixes the rediscount rate. By lowering the rate the Board makes rediscounting more profitable. By raising the rate it discourages rediscounting, and this in turn discourages member banks from lending money. When there is overconfidence and excessive speculation, the Board may raise the rate. The rediscount rate is one of the best tools we have to help smooth out the ups and downs of the business cycle.

The Federal Reserve Act worked so well that private bankers soon became its staunch supporters. Yet for twenty years most of the state banks remained outside the Federal Reserve system. The great boom during the 1920's and the disastrous panic of the 1930's showed that further banking reforms were needed (see p. 691).

Congress helps farmers to borrow.

Since colonial times farmers had been demanding cheaper credit. The Federal Reserve Act had two provisions designed especially to help farmers. First, it gave national banks the right to lend money on farm mortgages. The mortgage had to be paid within five years and could not exceed 50 per cent of the value of a farm. Second, the act allowed Federal Reserve Banks to rediscount notes secured by harvested crops.

FEDERAL RESERVE DISTRICTS, 1914

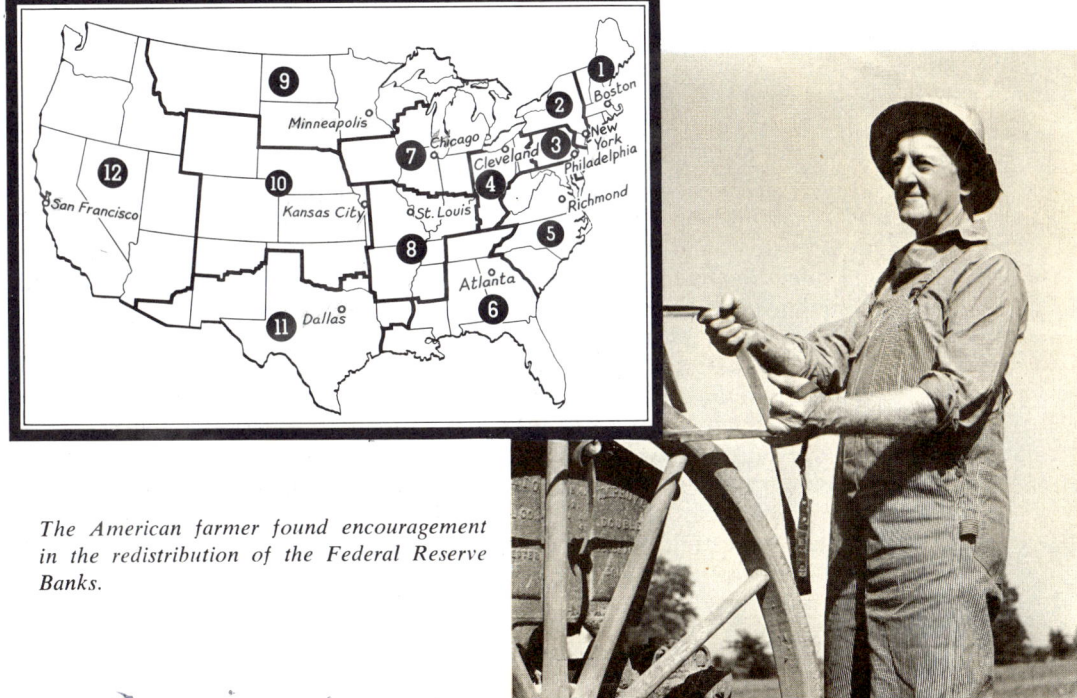

The American farmer found encouragement in the redistribution of the Federal Reserve Banks.

In 1916 Congress went much further in meeting the credit needs of the farmers. Under the Federal Farm Loan Act, twelve regional Federal Land Banks were set up to write mortgages on farm property. Land bank mortgages bear not over 6 per cent interest and must be paid off gradually over a period of thirty-three years. While land banks write only a small fraction of all farm mortgages, their competition has led other lenders to improve their terms.

The Bonded Warehouse Act (1916) made it easier to get loans on harvested crops. This measure provided for the licensing and bonding of warehouses. Receipts issued by a bonded warehouse for crops such as grain, cotton, tobacco, and wool can be used as security, or collateral, for loans. The act made it possible for farmers to hold their staple crops off the market in the hope of getting a higher price for them later in the season.

Congress Strengthens the Antitrust Laws

Wilson asks for new antitrust laws.

President Roosevelt and President Taft had done their best to enforce the Sherman Antitrust Act. About a hundred suits had been brought against corporations which had obtained, or sought to obtain, a monopoly. Because of the attitude of the courts, however, little was accomplished. Only a few corporations were found guilty of restraining trade. Meanwhile, big business continued to get bigger. In 1911 the Supreme Court had laid down its famous "rule of reason," declaring in effect that the Sherman Act prohibited only the *unreasonable* restraint of trade. The decision discouraged those who had looked to the Sherman Act to restore free competition.

Reformers now felt that "trust busting" was hopeless. Instead of trying to break up monopolies already formed, it seemed better to stop the formation of new ones. "We propose to prevent private monopoly by law," declared Wilson, "to see to it that the methods by which monopolies have been built up are impossible." He said that Congress should outlaw monopolistic practices "item by item."

As soon as Congress wound up its work on the tariff and the banking system, the President asked for laws to regulate all forms of big business except those already under the supervision of the Interstate Commerce Commission and the Federal Reserve Board. Congress spent most of 1914 considering this legislation, then passed both the Clayton Antitrust Act and the Federal Trade Commission Act.

The Clayton Antitrust Act.

The new antitrust law was more specific than the earlier one. It forbids the following practices *if they tend to destroy competition or create a monopoly:*

1. Price discrimination or price cutting for the purpose of "freezing out" a competitor.

2. "Tying" contracts, by which a manufacturer or distributor seeks to keep a retailer from dealing in the products of a competing manufacturer or distributor. Under a "tying" contract a retailer who buys from manufacturer X may not sell a competing product from manufacturer Y.

3. Purchase by one corporation of stock in another if the purchase tends to lessen competition.

4. Interlocking directorates among banking and business corporations above a certain size.

In addition to forbidding the practices listed, the Clayton Act made corporation directors personally responsible for violations. (Under the Sherman Act corporation directors could not be punished for its violation.) The Clayton Act also said that a competitor who is injured by unfair practices may obtain an injunction to stop these practices and may sue the offender for triple damages. This provision was intended to make it easier for the small businessman to get help before the large corporation had destroyed his business.

The Federal Trade Commission Act.

To help enforce the Clayton Act, Congress set up the Federal Trade Commission (F.T.C.). The commission has five members appointed by the President. Its duties are to investigate the business practices of corporations doing business across state lines and to hear complaints of unfair methods of competition. The F.T.C. accomplishes nearly all its work without going to the courts. By holding conferences with representatives of an industry, it works out rules of fair play to govern business practices in that industry. It then orders firms which break these rules to stop doing so. If the firm continues the unfair practice, the F.T.C. may appeal to the courts. Some of the practices considered unfair are misbranding of goods, bribery, adulteration of goods, false advertising, and false statements about competitors. The F.T.C. also disapproves of too close an imitation of a competitor's trade name or package by a rival company.

The purpose of the Federal Trade Commission is to help businessmen obey the law rather than punish them for disobeying. The commission has power to readjust or reorganize a business charged with violating the antitrust laws. In this way it has reduced the number of antitrust suits.

Did the new antitrust laws succeed?

The F.T.C. has raised the standards by which interstate businesses are conducted and has checked a large number of unfair practices. But the consolidation, or merging, of competing businesses has not slowed down. One reason is that the courts make it difficult to show that any given merger has "lessened competition" and lessened it "unreasonably." Another reason is that the Clayton Act contained a major loophole. It did not forbid a merger brought about when one firm bought the physical assets (i.e., land, buildings, and equipment) of another. In 1950 Congress forbade such a purchase if it substantially lessens competition.

Other Forward Steps Are Taken

The Clayton Act helps labor unions.

Wilson's New Freedom brought several benefits to workingmen. The Clayton Antitrust Act declared that "the labor of a human being is not a commodity or article of commerce" and that "nothing in the antitrust laws shall be construed to forbid the existence and operation of labor . . . organizations." These clauses meant that unions could no longer be prosecuted by federal authorities as "conspiracies in restraint of trade." The Clayton Act gave still more help to labor by forbidding federal courts to issue injunctions in labor disputes except to prevent "irreparable damage to property." The act said that injunctions were not to be used to interfere with peaceful strikes, picketing, and union meetings. In case an injunction was issued, strike leaders were not to be sent to jail for contempt of court without a jury trial. Samuel Gompers, president of the American Federation of Labor, hailed these parts of the Clayton Act as "labor's Magna Carta." Yet in spite of the Clayton Act the use of injunctions in labor disputes went on much as before, for conservative judges felt it their duty to prevent any possible injury to property.

Seamen win protection.

Jack London's novels had shown the harsh life of the common sailor. In

1915, after twenty years of struggle, the Seamen's Union got Congress to pass a law to improve safety standards and working conditions on American merchant ships. Since the measure was sponsored by Senator La Follette, it is known as the La Follette Seamen's Act. Among other much needed reforms the act provided that desertion from the American merchant marine was no longer a crime.

time and a half for overtime for workers on interstate railroads, prevented the strike. Another provision of the act gave the President power to take over and operate the railroads if military needs required such action.

Congress tries to abolish child labor.

In 1916 Congress passed a law forbidding the shipment across state lines of (1) goods from factories employing

By 1916 the movement to abolish child labor had achieved some success in many states. Here, PRESIDENT WILSON *signs the Child Labor Law of 1916.*

Railroad workers get eight-hour day.

In 1916, the railroad brotherhoods demanded an eight-hour day with time and a half for overtime work. When the railroad managers rejected these demands, a nationwide railroad strike was threatened. President Wilson tried unsuccessfully to mediate the dispute. When his efforts were refused, the President persuaded Congress to act. The Adamson Act was quickly passed. The new law, giving an eight-hour day and

children under fourteen and (2) products from mines and quarries employing children under sixteen. Two years later the Supreme Court by a 5 to 4 vote found the act to be an invasion of states' rights and therefore unconstitutional. The next year Congress passed a new measure to accomplish the same purpose by placing a tax on the products of child labor. This too was declared unconstitutional on the ground that the purpose was not to raise revenue but to restrict child labor. Years later the Supreme Court decided that Congress might regulate child labor (see p. 699).

Justices Brandeis and McReynolds.

President Wilson made two appointments to the Supreme Court. Both men served on that bench for many years and both became noted, but for opposite reasons. Attorney General James C. McReynolds, a native of Kentucky, was elevated to the Court in 1914. He had taken part in a number of antitrust suits and was thought to be a strong foe of monopoly. After becoming an associate justice, his views turned conservative. He wrote more opinions finding laws unconstitutional than any other justice. Progressives were relieved when he finally retired in 1941.

In 1916 Wilson named Louis D. Brandeis, also a Kentuckian, to the Supreme Court. The "people's lawyer" was well known as an enemy of special privilege and a champion of social justice. He was an authority on interstate commerce and had fought brilliantly for the right of the states to enact social legislation (see p. 527). Conservatives firmly opposed his confirmation. After a long investigation, the Senate finally approved Brandeis for associate justice.

Brandeis, like Justice Holmes, believed that law has to adapt itself to the needs of a changing society. The two justices upheld the right of the states to pass laws designed to meet new social and economic needs. In such cases Brandeis and Holmes often found themselves in a minority of two. After 1937, when the membership of the Court changed from conservative to liberal, Brandeis usually agreed with the majority. By then his dissenting opinions and the reasoning back of them were accepted by most of his fellow justices.

Congress extends federal activities.

The services of the federal government were notably increased by laws passed during Wilson's administration. In addition to those we have discussed, a few more should be mentioned.

The Smith-Lever, or Agricultural Extension, Act (1914) offered the states federal grants-in-aid for the promotion of better methods of farming and homemaking. In accepting a grant the state agreed to match it with an equal sum. In each state the money enabled the college of agriculture or the state university to establish an "extension service" to take scientific knowledge to farm people. The extension service employs county agricultural agents, home demonstration agents, and boys' and girls' club agents to carry on this important educational work.

The Federal Highway Act (1916) provided grants-in-aid to the states for building roads. The demand for this measure came from automobilists, then few in number, and from farmers, who needed better roads in order to get their crops to market. The same year Congress passed the Alaska Railway Act, authorizing construction of a railroad system in Alaska, to be federally owned and operated.

The Smith-Hughes Act (1917) offered the states grants-in-aid for vocational education in agriculture and home economics. With the aid of these grants, many communities added vocational departments to their high schools. In fact, the Smith-Hughes Act brought about a great expansion of vocational education.

Wilson is re-elected.

The reform wave reached its crest in 1914. It began to recede after war broke out in Europe. By election time in 1916 Americans were much more concerned about foreign affairs than in further reform at home.

The Democrats renominated President Wilson. The platform praised the new banking and antitrust laws and the new laws to benefit farmers and wage earners. Campaign speakers soon found, however, that audiences responded best to the slogan "He kept us out of war."

Roosevelt hoped the Republicans would nominate him. Instead they chose Charles Evans Hughes, who resigned from the Supreme Court to run. Roosevelt refused to run on the Progressive ticket because so many Progressive leaders were determined to keep the United States out of the war. Instead of helping the Progressives, Roosevelt tried to get all his followers back into the Republican party. He criticized the President severely for not going to the defense of Belgium and for writing notes to Germany instead of fighting when Germany violated our neutral rights. Both Roosevelt and Hughes attacked Wilson for his Mexican policy (see p. 593).

On election night it appeared that Mr. Hughes had been elected. The early morning papers even announced his victory. A few hours later, when returns from outlying districts came in, it was learned that Hughes had lost California and with it the election. The popular vote was 9 million for Wilson and 8.5 million for Hughes. Wilson drew a much larger percentage of the popular vote than he had in 1912.

Two amendments to the Constitution.

Wilson's program of reform could be carried little farther because of the gathering war clouds. In fact, the Progressive Era is said to have ended in 1916, a few months before the United States declared war on Germany. Yet two amendments added to the Constitution in 1919 and 1920 may be considered as fruits of the Progressive Era.

We have already noted the long struggle for woman suffrage, which came to an end in 1920 when the Nineteenth Amendment was ratified. The Eighteenth, or Prohibition, Amendment was ratified a year earlier. It followed an even longer struggle.

The prohibition movement began during the Jackson Era. After the War between North and South, it gathered strength. By 1900 seven states, all of them rural, were "dry," and many other states had "local option." (Local option means that any town or county in the state may prohibit the sale of alcoholic beverages within its boundaries.) By 1917 nearly all rural areas and small towns were dry. During World War I Congress stopped the manufacture of alcoholic beverages to conserve grain. It also sent the states an amendment to the Constitution prohibiting the manufacture, sale, or transportation of intoxicating beverages. The amendment was promptly ratified.

Wilson's domestic achievements.

In the four years of his first term, Wilson obtained more legislation of long-range importance than any President since Lincoln. His achievements were made possible because of the support he received from progressives in both parties. Yet it was his strong leadership of Congress and of public opinion that got his program written into law. As a noted opponent said, for a man thought to be a mere theorist, Wilson had accomplished "the most astonishing practical results."

FOR IDENTIFICATION

Adamson Act	Federal Highway Act
Agricultural Extension Act	Federal Reserve Act
Nelson W. Aldrich	Federal Trade Commission Act
Bonded Warehouse Act	Charles Evans Hughes
Clayton Antitrust Act	La Follette Seamen's Act
Federal Farm Loan Act	Pujo Committee
	Smith-Hughes Act

FOR EXPLANATION OR DEFINITION

collateral
commercial paper
Eighteenth
    Amendment
elastic currency
graduated income tax
grants-in-aid
interlocking
    directorate

lobbyist
local option
logrolling
mobile currency
"money trust"
"New Freedom"
rediscount rate
"rule of reason"
"tying" contracts

FOR REVIEW

1. Briefly describe Woodrow Wilson's career prior to his nomination for President.

2. (a) In what ways was Wilson well prepared for the Presidency? In what ways was he not prepared? (b) Why is Wilson regarded as a strong President?

3. What program of action did Wilson outline in his first inaugural?

4. (a) What do lobbyists do when a bill they are interested in is under consideration? (b) Give an example of logrolling in Congress. (c) How did Wilson try to weaken the influence of tariff lobbyists?

5. Compare the Underwood-Simmons Tariff of 1913 with the Payne-Aldrich Tariff of 1909.

6. (a) Why did Congress adopt a tax on incomes? (b) What were the early rates?

7. (a) What weaknesses in our currency and banking system were reported by the National Monetary Commission? (b) What reform was supported by Senator Aldrich?

8. What important facts about banking were revealed by the Pujo Committee?

9. (a) Outline the structure of the Federal Reserve system. Explain the terms "Federal Reserve Bank" and "member banks." (b) How does the Federal Reserve system provide for an elastic currency? For a mobile currency? (c) How can the Federal Reserve Board discourage speculation?

10. Explain the Federal Farm Loan Act and the Bonded Warehouse Act. How did these laws help the farmer?

11. What was the "rule of reason" decision of the Supreme Court in antitrust cases? What were its effects?

12. What were the chief antitrust features of the Clayton Antitrust Act, 1914? Why did it not halt business mergers?

13. (a) Describe the organization and functions of the Federal Trade Commission. (b) Name some practices which the F.T.C. considers "unfair."

14. What important labor clauses did the Clayton Antitrust Act contain?

15. State key provisions of the La Follette Seamen's Act; of the Adamson Act.

16. Describe two laws passed by Congress during Wilson's administration to regulate child labor. What happened to these laws?

17. Briefly describe the work and influence of Justice Louis D. Brandeis.

18. State the provisions of the Agricultural Extension Act, the Federal Highway Act, and the Smith-Hughes Act.

19. Describe the presidential campaign of 1916. What was the most important issue? Why?

20. Outline the main steps in the struggle which led to the adoption of the Eighteenth (Prohibition) Amendment.

FOR FURTHER STUDY AND DISCUSSION

1. How did Wilson's "New Freedom" differ from Theodore Roosevelt's "New Nationalism"? Helpful sources: Link, *Woodrow Wilson and the Progressive Movement*; Amherst Series, *Roosevelt, Wilson, and the Trusts*; Hofstadter, *American Political Tradition*; Hart, *Contemporaries*, Vol. V.

2. Compare the purposes, provisions, and accomplishments of the Sherman Antitrust Act of 1890 with the Clayton Antitrust Act of 1914. Helpful source: Faulkner, *Economic History*, pp. 447–454.

3. (a) Contrast the work of the Federal Trade Commission with the work of the Interstate Commerce Commission. Helpful source: Faulkner, *Economic History*. (b) Why has there been a tendency for Congress to create independent administrative boards and commissions?

4. How did the antitrust legislation of 1914 help the small businessman?

557

5. Compare the rates of the 1913 income tax law with those in effect today.

6. (a) Explain what is meant by a bank's reserve; by the name "Federal Reserve system." (b) Explain the process of discounting and rediscounting. (c) Why are Federal Reserve notes *elastic?* Why are they *sound?* (d) How can the Federal Reserve Board control the amount of commercial paper discounted? Helpful source: Hart, *Contemporaries*, Vol. V, No. 73.

7. Why did not the United States imitate the policy of England and France and create a strong central bank?

8. Summarize the gains made by labor during Wilson's administration.

FOR INDIVIDUAL OR GROUP ACTIVITIES

1. Prepare sketches of the careers of Louis D. Brandeis and Charles Evans Hughes.

2. Report the colorful details of the following: Wilson's struggle with the political machine in New Jersey; Wilson's fight for the Underwood Tariff; the controversy over the nomination of Mr. Brandeis to the Supreme Court; the close vote in California in the presidential election of 1916.

3. Read and report on the essay "Woodrow Wilson—The Conservative as Liberal" in Hofstadter, *American Political Tradition*, pp. 238–282. Compare with the same author's interpretation of Theodore Roosevelt. Select quotations to read aloud.

4. Prepare an essay supporting or criticizing Gompers' claim that the Clayton Antitrust Act was "labor's Magna Carta."

5. Prepare tables of significant dates and events to show the status of labor in 1895, in 1915, and today.

6. Plan an exhibit of political cartoons which illustrate Wilson's governorship of New Jersey and his first term as President.

7. Write short editorials on each of the following: lobbies, good and bad; the "rule of reason"; the work of the Pujo Committee; the Adamson Act.

CHARLES EVANS HUGHES   LOUIS D. BRANDEIS

GREAT NORTHERN GRAIN ELEVATORS, *Superior, Wisconsin. Here the farmer's produce is stored for future needs. The capacity is 12,000,000 bushels.*

HIGH POINTS

1

The Progressive Era (1896 to 1916) brought many reforms. The era began with corrective laws by states and cities. Some reforms were intended to put an end to the corrupt alliance of political bosses and private interests—the so-called "invisible government." Other reforms were intended to correct evils arising from the growth of industry. Since the states lacked power to regulate businesses engaged in interstate commerce, federal laws also were needed. Under three Presidents—Theodore Roosevelt, Taft, and Wilson—Congress enacted much corrective legislation. The reform movement reached its height during Wilson's first term and practically came to an end when the country entered World War I.

2

The progressive movement gave the people more control over the nomination and election of officials. This resulted from electoral improvements, such as the secret ballot, direct primary, corrupt practices laws requiring publicity for campaign expenditures, and the shift to popular election of United States senators. The initiative, referendum, and recall, woman suffrage, and new types of city government also enlarged the people's influence. The political boss did not disappear, but his power was reduced.

3

To a considerable extent the progressive movement changed the attitude of big business. Business leaders no longer ignored public opinion, as in the 1880's and 1890's. Instead, many of them tried to win approval by showing that they were serving the public and by giving thought to the welfare of their workers.

4

By the end of the Progressive Era, the principle that business could and should be regulated by government was widely accepted. The large corporations had been taught that they could not do as they pleased. Few trusts had been dissolved, but the Federal Trade Commission had begun to correct abuses in their methods of doing business.

5

There was a growing tendency for the states to use their police power to promote the public welfare. During the Progressive Era the states adopted much social legislation to protect the health, safety, morals, and welfare of their people. This legislation often interfered with property rights and some of it was thrown out by the courts. Yet the idea was growing that human rights must be placed before property rights.

6

Largely through the efforts of Theodore Roosevelt, the need for conserving natural resources was recognized. Both state and federal governments took action to protect the public lands from wasteful exploitation. The chief steps were the establishment of state and national forests and the withdrawal from sale of water-power sites and certain mineral lands owned by the nation.

7

The adoption of the Sixteenth, or Income Tax, Amendment (1913) was perhaps the greatest landmark of the progressive movement. Only eighteen years earlier the Supreme Court had thrown out a federal income tax law, denouncing it as an attack on capital. By 1913 the idea of apportioning taxes according to ability to pay was generally accepted as just. Con-

gress adopted graduated income and estate taxes, as did most of the state legislatures.

8

The reform movement reached its height during the first term of Woodrow Wilson. His chief peacetime achievement was the creation of the Federal Reserve system. It gave the nation a flexible and mobile money supply. Twelve regional Reserve Banks under the Federal Reserve Board met the nation's need for centralized banking under public control.

9

Under Presidents Theodore Roosevelt, Taft, and Wilson, the federal government extended its activities. Besides controlling the money supply and the banks in the Federal Reserve system, the federal government began to protect consumers from impure and wrongly labeled foods and drugs, to regulate labor conditions on ships and on railroads, and to supervise all corporations doing business across state lines. In addition, through federal grants-in-aid, the states were encouraged to build highways, to provide educational services for farmers and homemakers, and to establish vocational courses in secondary schools. The old fear of a strong national government seemed to be passing away.

QUESTIONS

1. What were the reasons for the agitation by progressives in the opening years of the twentieth century? How was the public prepared to support reform?

2. (a) Why did cities and states lead in the introduction of reform measures? (b) What political reforms were introduced to curb the power of the "boss" and the "machine"? (c) What reforms were effected by the sixteenth, seventeenth, and nineteenth amendments to the Constitution?

3. (a) What social legislation in the states and the nation improved the position of the consumer and the worker? (b) What is meant by the doctrine of "police power"? How did the Supreme Court's interpretation of this doctrine influence the progressive movement? (c) What influence did Louis D. Brandeis and Oliver Wendell Holmes have on the progressive movement?

4. List some governors and mayors identified with reforms and indicate their special contribution.

5. Describe the legislation which strengthened the Interstate Commerce Commission in the period 1900–1916.

6. (a) Review the provisions of the Sherman Antitrust Act of 1890. (b) What did Presidents Roosevelt and Taft do to enforce this act? (c) How was the Clayton Antitrust Act of 1914 an improvement over the Sherman Act? (d) How and why did the Clayton Act deal with the subject of labor?

7. (a) State the purposes and function of the Federal Trade Commission. (b) What have been the accomplishments of this Commission? (c) The Interstate Commerce Commission and the Federal Trade Commission were among the first regulatory and supervisory agencies set up by the federal government. Make a list of other federal regulatory commissions or bodies that are functioning today.

8. How did Theodore Roosevelt promote the cause of conservation?

9. List the progressive measures sponsored by President Taft. Why did his support of the Payne-Aldrich tariff cause him to lose favor? What other actions of President Taft caused him to lose popularity?

561

10. How did Wilson's actions with regard to the Underwood Tariff Act reveal his conception of the Presidency?

11. What defects in our monetary and banking system were corrected by the Federal Reserve Act of 1913? How were these defects corrected?

12. How did the Wilson administration help the farmer and the laborer?

13. What reforms were promoted by using the principle of federal "grants-in-aid"?

14. The Progressive Era virtually came to an end with Wilson's second inauguration. Did it come to an end because of World War I, or because the major objectives of the progressive movement had been achieved?

15. Compare the Progressive Era, 1900–1916, with the Jacksonian era.

SUGGESTED READINGS

SOURCE MATERIALS, DOCUMENTS, AND MAPS

Adams, *Album.*

Amherst Series: *Roosevelt, Wilson, and the Trusts.*

——. *Democracy and the Gospel of Wealth.*

——. *Immigration—An American Dilemma.*

Commager, *Documents.*

° Commager and Nevins, *Heritage of America.*

Davidson, M. B. *Life in America.* Houghton Mifflin, 1951.

Dixon and Plischke, *American Government Documents.*

Hacker, Louis M., and Zahler, H. S. (eds.). *The Shaping of the American Tradition.* Columbia University Press, 1947.

Hart, *Contemporaries.*

GENERAL REFERENCES

° Allen, Frederick L. *The Big Change: America Transforms Itself, 1900–1950.* Harper, 1952.

° Bassett, John S. *Makers of a New Nation.* Yale University Press, 1928. (Pageant)

Beard, *American Civilization,* Vol. II.

Binkley, W. E. *American Political Parties; Their Natural History.* Knopf, 1945.

Chamberlain, John R. *Farewell to Reform.* Liveright, 1932.

Dulles, Foster R. *Labor in America.* Crowell, 1949.

Faulkner, Harold U. *Economic History.*

——. *The Decline of Laissez Faire, 1897–1917.* Rinehart, 1951.

——. *The Quest for Social Justice, 1898–1914.* Macmillan, 1931. (A.L.S.)

Hicks, *American Nation.*

Hofstadter, Richard. *The Age of Reform; From Bryan to F. D. R.* Knopf, 1955.

——. *American Political Tradition.*

° Howland, Harold. *Theodore Roosevelt and His Times.* Yale University Press, 1921. (Y.C.S.)

Link, Arthur S. *American Epoch.*

——. *Woodrow Wilson and the Progressive Era, 1910–1917.* Harper, 1954. (N.A.S.)

Morison and Commager, *American Republic,* Vol II.

Ogg, Frederic A. *National Progress, 1907–1917.* Harper, 1918. (A.N.S.)

Regier, Cornelius C. *The Era of the Muckrakers.* University of North Carolina Press, 1932.

Schlesinger, *Modern America.*

Seymour, Charles. *Woodrow Wilson and the World War.* Yale University Press, 1921. (Y.C.S.)

Steffens, Lincoln. *Autobiography.* Harcourt, Brace, 1931.

——. *The Shame of the Cities.* Smith, 1948. (reprint)

Sullivan, Mark. *Our Times,* vol. 3. Scribner, 1930.

Wish, Harvey. *Contemporary America.* Harper, 1945.

BIOGRAPHY

Bell, Herbert C. F. *Woodrow Wilson and the People.* Doubleday, 1945.

Bolles, Edmund Blair. *Tyrant from Illinois: Uncle Joe Cannon's Experiment with Personal Power.* Norton, 1951.

Bowers, Claude G. *Beveridge and the Progressive Era.* Houghton Mifflin, 1932.

Dodd, William E. *Woodrow Wilson and His Work.* Smith, 1932.

A FLYING BOAT *of 1914 vintage. This plane, powered by a 75-horsepower motor, gave air service between Tampa and St. Petersburg, Florida.*

° Hagedorn, Hermann. *Boy's Life of Theodore Roosevelt.* Harper, 1922.

———. *The Roosevelt Family of Sagamore Hill.* Macmillan, 1954.

La Follette, Robert M. *Autobiography.* La Follette's Magazine, 1913.

Mason, Alpheus T. *Brandeis, a Free Man's Life.* Viking, 1946.

Mowry, George E. *Theodore Roosevelt and the Progressive Movement.* University of Wisconsin Press, 1946.

Pringle, Henry F. *Theodore Roosevelt.* Harcourt, Brace, 1931.

———. *The Life and Times of William Howard Taft.* Farrar and Rinehart, 1939.

° Riis, Jacob. *The Making of an American.* Macmillan, 1902.

White, William A. *The Autobiography of William A. White.* Macmillan, 1946.

FICTION

Adams, Henry. *Democracy, An American Novel.* Holt, 1925. (Corruption in Washington)

Atherton, Gertrude. *Senator North.* Dodd, Mead, 1914. (Political problems)

Churchill, Winston. *Mr. Crewes' Career.* Macmillan, 1927. (Corporations in politics)

° Hobart, Alice T. *Oil for the Lamps of China.* Bobbs-Merrill, 1933. (Big business in China)

Quick, Herbert. *The Hawkeye.* Bobbs-Merrill, 1923. (Politics in Iowa)

Sinclair, Upton. *The Jungle.* Vanguard, 1926. (Picture of misery in Chicago)

Updegraff, Robert R. *Captains in Conflict.* Shaw, 1927. (Big business, 1890–1914)

Wilson, Charles M. *Rabble Rouser.* Longmans, 1936. (Arkansas politics)

TIME LINE

	1867	Alaska purchased; Midway taken over by U.S. Navy
	1898	War with Spain; Philippines, Guam, and Puerto Rico acquired; Hawaii annexed
	1899	Open Door policy; Hague Peace Conference
1900	1900	Boxer rebellion
	1901	Hay-Pauncefote Treaty
	1903	United States acquired Panama Canal Zone
1905	1905	Roosevelt mediates Russo-Japanese War
	1907	Second Hague Peace Conference
	1909	Taft inaugurated
1910		
	1912	Marines sent to Nicaragua
	1913	Policy of "watchful waiting" toward Mexico
	1914	Panama Canal opened; outbreak of World War I
1915	1915	Sinking of *Lusitania*
	1916	Virgin Islands purchased
	1917	United States enters World War I
	1918	The Armistice is signed
	1919	Treaty of Versailles
1920	1920	Senate rejects League of Nations
	1921	Harding inaugurated

UNIT EIGHT *The United States Becomes a World Power*

★ ★ ★ ★ Toward the end of the nineteenth century, we Americans began to show more interest in the world beyond our borders. Our businessmen wanted to find foreign markets for manufactured goods. Our investors wanted to invest money abroad. These men saw that other great powers were gaining colonies and spheres of influence in Asia and Africa, and many of them felt the United States too ought to expand overseas. Yet the majority of Americans at that time thought the possession of colonies was contrary to our traditions.

A long series of disturbances in Cuba led to the Spanish-American War. As a result of that conflict the United States gained possession of Puerto Rico and the Philippines. At the same time we annexed the Hawaiian Islands at the request of their people. Five years later we bought land on which to build the Panama Canal. These events gave the United States an empire. In harmony with democratic ideals, Congress prepared our possessions for self-government. In the case of the Philippines, we prepared the people for independence.

During the early years of the present century the United States started to play a more active role in world affairs. Our government used its influence to preserve the independence of China, to end the Russo-Japanese War, and to keep France and Germany from fighting over Morocco. In our own hemisphere we kept European powers from intervening in Latin America and we tried to promote cooperation between all the republics. We also took part in peace conferences at The Hague and helped to establish the Hague Permanent Court of Arbitration. We made treaties with a large number of nations, binding them and the United States to settle disputes by peaceful means.

When war swept over Europe in 1914, the United States wanted to stay out. Nevertheless, most Americans hoped the Allies would win. Finally, after repeated violations of our neutral rights, we declared war on Germany. With a speed that astonished the Germans, the United States raised an army and transported it overseas. With our help, the tired Allies won the war.

At the war's end the United States was in a position to take the leadership in world affairs. President Wilson worked to establish the League of Nations, which he hoped would be strong enough to maintain peace throughout the world. Many Americans, however, wanted the United States to return to its old policy of isolationism. They succeeded in keeping us out of the League of Nations. By turning our backs on the League and on Europe, some think we lost the peace.

SIBERIA

ASIA

ALASKA
1867

CANADA

PACIFIC
OCEAN

UNITED
STATES

PUERTO RICO
1898

MIDWAY
·1867

WAKE
·1898

·HAWAIIAN IS.
1898

PHILIPPINES
1898

·GUAM
1898

PALMYRA
1912

CANAL ZONE
1903

HOWLAND &
BAKER·
1857

·JARVIS
1857

SOUTH
AMERICA

SAMOA IS.
1899

INTERNATIONAL

DATELINE

UNITED STATES POSSESSIONS IN 1914

The question is no longer whether or not we shall play
our part in the world but whether we shall play it well
or ill.——Theodore Roosevelt

34. THE UNITED STATES GAINS AN EMPIRE

The United States Gets Footholds in Faraway Places

Industrialism encourages imperialism.

In the years from 1870 to 1914 the major European nations and Japan took part in a scramble for colonies and "sphere of influence"[1] in so-called "backward" areas. European powers gained control of most of Africa. The Dutch took Indonesia. The European powers and Japan carved China into spheres of influence. In addition, Japan took Korea and Formosa. By 1914 practically all the undeveloped lands in the Eastern Hemisphere were dominated by colonial powers.

The new burst of imperialism after 1870 was due chiefly to industrialization. Industrial nations wanted to control "backward" areas for economic reasons: (1) as sources of raw materials, (2) as markets for industrial products, and (3) as places to invest industrial profits. These nations had navies and armies equipped with modern weapons. They could easily conquer and control the natives in a land without modern industry. Accordingly, those countries which were most industrialized were the most likely to acquire an empire.

[1] The phrase "sphere of influence" was coined to describe an area in which a foreign power had control of trade and natural resources.

The United States becomes interested in overseas possessions.

As long as our nation had plenty of undeveloped land in the West, few Americans were interested in getting colonies overseas. In 1867 Secretary of State Seward had hard work to persuade Congress to buy Alaska (see p. 398), even though the price was less than two cents an acre. At that time Congress refused to buy the Virgin Islands and the Dominican Republic. Toward the end of the century, however, when the Western lands had been settled, American leaders began to give more thought to the possibility of obtaining overseas possessions.

This change of attitude was partly due to national pride. Other nations were building empires. Would they soon surpass the United States in wealth and power? To prevent this, should we not join the race for colonies? People began to say that it was the "manifest destiny" of the United States to expand beyond its continental boundaries.

The new interest in empire was strengthened by the rapid growth of American production. The United States had more farm products, minerals, and manufactures than its people

567

could buy. American exports tripled between 1870 and 1900. Could we sell still more abroad if we owned colonies and placed them behind our tariff walls?

Moreover, some Americans had money to invest, and wished to invest it abroad. They thought that since the United States was now well supplied with capital, investments in less developed areas would be more profitable than at home.

First steps toward empire.

To provide harbors and coaling stations for American ships, the United States Navy had already taken possession of a number of small islands in the Pacific. In 1867, for instance, an American naval officer planted our flag on the uninhabited Midway Islands—tiny dots of land a thousand miles west of Hawaii. Five years later another naval commander visited one of the Samoan Islands, about 5000 miles southwest of California. He made arrangements with a native chieftain for American control of the splendid harbor of Pago Pago on the island of Tutuila. In 1889, by agreement with Great Britain and Germany, the United States got outright possession of all the Samoan Islands except the two largest, which went to Germany. By that time we had over fifty little islands in the central and South Pacific. Many years later some of these became useful as air bases and radio stations.

We annex the Hawaiian Islands.

The fertile and beautiful Hawaiian Islands lie about 2000 miles southwest of California. As early as the 1790's, ships owned by New England merchants began to stop in Hawaii on the way to the Far East. In 1820 the first band of American missionaries went to the islands, where they won many natives to the Christian faith. Before long, American whalers were using the islands as a base, and hundreds of American planters were settling there to raise sugar. Honolulu became in many ways like a New England town.

In 1842 Secretary of State Daniel Webster announced that the Monroe Doctrine applied to Hawaii and that no foreign power would be allowed to interfere with Hawaiian affairs. His announcement shows that it was thought necessary even then to keep the islands from falling into the hands of a power that might be hostile to the United States. As time went on the Kingdom of Hawaii gave the United States special trading privileges and the use of Pearl Harbor for a naval base.

Early in 1893 American residents led a revolt against the established native government. After setting up a republic, they asked that Hawaii be annexed to the United States. (In a similar way Americans in Texas had revolted against Mexico in 1836 and petitioned for annexation.) President Harrison had a treaty of annexation drawn up, but before the Senate could ratify it, Cleveland succeeded Harrison as President. Cleveland was suspicious about the revolution and sent a special commissioner to Hawaii to look into it. The commissioner reported that the revolutionists had had the help of United States Marines. He also reported that the native Hawaiians did not wish annexation. Cleveland then withdrew the treaty. Republicans were angered by this action, which they called a "betrayal of American interests." When McKinley became President, he drew up a new treaty. On finding that he could not get the necessary two-thirds vote in the Senate to ratify it, McKinley asked Congress for a joint resolution. (This device, requiring only a majority vote, had been used in the case of Texas half a century earlier.) In 1898, during the Spanish-American War, Congress voted to annex the Republic of Hawaii.

The United States Fights a War to Free Cuba

Revolutions sweep Cuba.

Cuba and Puerto Rico were the last remnants of a once mighty Spanish empire in the New World. Their closeness to our shores made them important to our safety. Our government therefore had always kept an eye on them. Before the War between North and South some Americans talked of getting control of Cuba. A few Southerners even took part in expeditions designed to free the island from Spain (see p. 356).

In the years from 1868 to 1878 Cuban patriots fought for independence. American sympathizers gave them money and supplies. At one time President Grant considered sending troops to Cuba to stop the bloodshed and destruction of property. Finally, the Spanish authorities put down the rebellion. Unrest continued, for the island was exploited without mercy for the benefit of the mother country. Spain took $25 out of every $26 collected in taxes. The Cubans had no voice in their government. Moreover, most of them were very poor.

In 1895 the Cubans started another war against Spain. The immediate cause of the outbreak was a fall in the price of sugar, which in turn was due to our Wilson-Gorham Tariff (1894). Cuban sugar planters left their fields idle, creating widespread unemployment. The people blamed the government for their sufferings. Soon the whole island was in revolt. Gomez, leader of the rebels, ordered them to destroy plantations, tear up railways, and burn factories. He hoped this destruction would force the United States to intervene, since much of the property belonged to American investors.

In 1896 Spain tried to put down the rebellion by sending General Weyler to Cuba as governor. Weyler locked up hundreds of thousands of Cuban civilians in concentration camps to keep them from giving aid to the rebels. Most of the prisoners were women and children. The camps were horribly unclean and overcrowded, and the prisoners had little food. Within a few months half of them perished from disease and hunger.

Cleveland and McKinley protest.

When news came of the suffering in the concentration camps, many Americans felt that the United States should go to the aid of the Cubans. President Cleveland sent a protest to the Spanish government. When McKinley became President, he did the same thing. In answer the Spanish government pointed out that the rebels were getting arms illegally from the United States and asked the President to shut off this aid.

Propaganda for American intervention.

American sympathy for the Cubans and dislike for Spain were magnified by what is known as the "jingo press." At the time, two publishers—William Randolph Hearst of the *New York Journal* and Joseph Pulitzer of the *New York World*—were having a race to secure readers. Their reporters hunted for stories to startle and attract the public. Often they "doctored" the news to make it more exciting. The trouble in Cuba seemed made to their order. They played up stories of Spanish cruelty and called General Weyler a "human hyena," a "mad dog," a "butcher."

Judging from newspaper sales, the American people liked the sensational methods of Hearst and Pulitzer. The circulation of their so-called "yellow journals" climbed and climbed. Other papers began to imitate their methods and buy their stories. Thus the clamor for war with Spain spread over the whole country.

569

Spain makes concessions.

In 1897 a more liberal government came to power in Spain. It recalled Weyler, sent a more merciful governor in his place, and promised to give Cuba self-government. This did not satisfy the Cubans, for they wanted full independence. However, the new governor set to work to improve conditions on the island, and the revolution seemed to be dying down.

"Remember the Maine."

Early in 1898, there was a riot in Havana between revolutionists and loyalists. Soon afterwards our government sent the battleship *Maine* to Havana harbor on what was described as a friendly visit. The real purpose was to protect American lives and property in case of further rioting. Loyal Spaniards resented the sending of the battleship. It looked to them like a threat from the United States to use force to help the revolutionists.

For several weeks the *Maine* lay at anchor in Havana. Then, on the night of February 15, 1898, she suddenly blew up, with a loss of 260 officers and men. The captain of the vessel, realizing that Americans would think Spain had blown up the ship, telegraphed to Washington: "Public opinion should [wait] until further report." Public opinion did not wait, for the "yellow journals" claimed that Spain had deliberately blown up our battleship. A typical headline in the *Journal* shrieked, "The warship *Maine* was split in two by an enemy's secret infernal machine." From one end of the country to the other the cry arose, "Remember the *Maine!*" Congress unanimously voted money to make the army and navy ready for war.

The facts about the sinking of the *Maine* are still unknown. American investigators, who examined the hull, reported that the explosion was due to an underwater mine. Spanish authori-

An example of YELLOW PRESS *performance*

NAVAL OFFICERS THINK THE MAINE WAS DESTROYED BY A SPANISH MINE

ties insisted that the explosion took place inside the ship. We shall probably never know exactly what did produce the explosion. Today it seems unthinkable that the Spanish government had anything to do with it, for Spain was trying to avoid war with the United States. It is possible that the rebels were responsible, believing that destruction of the ship would lead the United States to declare war on Spain.

War is declared.

President McKinley and his Cabinet still hoped to settle the Cuban problem by diplomacy. Three weeks after the sinking of the *Maine*, the President asked Spain to close the concentration camps and to arrange a truce. The Spanish cabinet agreed to close the camps at once. It also promised to prepare Spanish public opinion for a truce. Our minister to Madrid cabled: "I hope that nothing will be done to humiliate Spain, as I am satisfied that the present government is going . . . as fast and as far as it can."

Meanwhile, McKinley was savagely criticized for his patience. One critic, Theodore Roosevelt, said, "McKinley has no more backbone than a chocolate éclair." Congressmen in both parties urged war to free Cuba and revenge the *Maine*. One explained this attitude by saying: "Every congressman has two or three newspapers in his district—most of them written in red ink . . . and shouting for blood."

The pressure for war became so strong that McKinley could no longer resist it. He wrote a message asking Congress for authority to use the army and navy to restore order in Cuba. The day before sending the message, he received a note from Spain promising to stop the fighting in Cuba and to call a Cuban parliament. Perhaps McKinley had lost faith in Spanish promises. At any rate he did not make the note public and he barely mentioned it to Con-

PRESIDENT WILLIAM McKINLEY

gress. For this lack of frankness he has been severely blamed.

On April 19, 1898, just a few days after hearing the President's message, Congress voted to use our armed forces to make Cuba free and independent. At the same time, in the famous Teller Resolution, Congress stated that the United States had no intention of annexing Cuba.

Dewey blockades Manila.

At first the public considered the war a crusade to help the Cubans win their liberty. But there were men in high places who wanted the United States to seize Spanish possessions, especially the Philippines. One of these was Theodore Roosevelt, Assistant Secretary of the Navy. A few weeks before war began, Roosevelt had ordered Commodore George Dewey to take our Asiatic squadron to Hong Kong. After war was declared, Dewey received orders to proceed to the Philippines and destroy or capture Spain's Pacific fleet. On May Day, 1898, Dewey won the Battle of Manila Bay, destroying the Spanish men-of-war with the loss of only one American sailor and with no damage to our ships. Dewey then blockaded Manila. When American troops arrived in August, they easily took the city.

571

Cuba and Puerto Rico give up.

Soon after war was declared, a Spanish squadron commanded by Admiral Cervera started across the Atlantic. Wild rumors spread that American coastal cities might be bombarded. Learning that our Atlantic fleet was on the lookout for him, Cervera took refuge in the Cuban harbor of Santiago. Soon after, his ships were bottled up by the American fleet.

In mid-June a force of 17,000 Americans commanded by General William Shafter landed near Santiago. Our troops captured the forts defending the city one by one. On July 1 the important San Juan Hill was taken. Theodore Roosevelt, who had resigned from the Navy Department to help organize the regiment known as "Rough Riders," won fame in this battle.

Admiral Cervera knew that when Santiago fell his ships would be bombarded from the heights above the bay. He determined to make a dash for freedom, that the fleet might at least go down fighting. The Spanish vessels were completely outclassed and our ships destroyed them one after another as they left the harbor. Ten days later Santiago surrendered, and Spanish resistance in Cuba practically ceased. American troops, under General Miles, then occupied Puerto Rico, almost without opposition.

The war ends.

Late in July Spain asked for peace. A truce was signed on August 12, a few hours before the American army occupied Manila. The war had lasted 109 days. It had cost the United States 2926 lives. Of these men 361 had died in battle or from wounds; the others died of disease.

The peace treaty was written at Paris. Spain had already agreed to give up all claim to Cuba and to cede Puerto Rico and Guam (a small island in the Pacific) to the United States.

Spain did not want to give up the Philippines. Her representatives argued that we had taken only the city of Manila and had taken it after the signing of the armistice. Finally, Spain yielded the Philippines for $20,000,000.

When the treaty was sent to the Senate, there was a long and heated debate in regard to the Philippines. Many senators denounced the plan to annex these distant islands. They said it was tyranny to take over millions of unwilling people. Besides, it was against the spirit of the Declaration of Independence for the United States to rule lands which must always remain colonies. In addition, they argued, the United States would have to keep up a powerful navy to defend them. This would be expensive and might lead to foreign wars.

Other senators claimed that it was our duty to carry civilization and Christianity to the Filipinos. They pointed out that if we returned the islands to Spain, it was likely that either Japan or Germany would soon seize them. In that case the islanders might never gain their freedom. It was also argued that the islands would be a convenient base for trade with China and other parts of the Far East.

The disputes in the Senate went on for weeks. Ratification of the treaty looked doubtful. Then William Jennings Bryan, the popular Democratic leader, came to Washington. He urged his followers to support the treaty so that the United States could end the war, get control of the Philippines, and grant the Filipinos independence. The treaty was finally ratified with only one vote to spare.

The war has important results.

The brief Spanish-American War marked a turning point in our history.

1. The nation now faced the difficult problem of ruling colonies.
2. It now had a stake in the Far East.

3. Since the United States must be ready to defend its distant possessions, the army and navy had to be strengthened.
4. The nation saw the necessity for building a canal across the isthmus connecting North and South America. The need for the canal was brought home when the battleship *Oregon*, ordered from the Pacific coast to Cuba early in the war, required sixty-eight days to make the journey.
5. Americans felt more friendly to Great Britain. The British had celebrated American victories almost as their own and had discouraged other powers from going to the aid of Spain. Henceforth the British and the Americans were to co-operate increasingly in world affairs.
6. Americans now realized that their country was a world power—one which had influence far beyond its borders.

Our Possessions Create New Problems

Anti-imperialists lose the battle.

When rejoicing quieted down after our easy victory over Spain, Americans saw that almost overnight their country had become an empire. We had acquired far-flung possessions inhabited by people of diverse tongues, races, and religions. What was the United States to do with these dependencies? Should they be kept permanently as colonies? Should they be prepared for admission into the Union as states? Should they be given their independence? The Filipinos were already in revolt against American rule. The fact that our soldiers were trying to subdue people who wanted to be independent shocked many Americans in both parties.

In the presidential campaign of 1900 the leading issue was how to deal with our new possessions. Most Republican leaders thought we should keep them and rule them as colonies. President McKinley insisted we were liberators, not oppressors, of the native peoples. "Don't haul down the flag!" be-

came the Republican rallying cry. Bryan, the Democratic candidate, wanted the Philippines and Puerto Rico to be made independent as soon as possible. The Democratic platform took a firm stand against imperialism, asserting that "no nation can long endure half republic and half empire." McKinley was elected by a larger majority than in 1896. The anti-imperialists had lost the battle.

Did the Constitution follow the flag?

A puzzling question soon arose in regard to our dependencies. Were their citizens to have the same liberties and privileges that the Constitution gives to citizens of the United States? In other words, did the Constitution follow the flag? In a series of decisions known as the "insular cases," the Supreme Court ruled that the Constitution did not completely apply to overseas possessions. Their people would have full civil rights only if Congress granted them. Furthermore, Congress might levy duties on imports from the dependencies. Soon, however, Congress gave free trade to our possessions and gradually it gave them full civil rights.

The Filipino revolt is suppressed.

The possession which created the most problems for the United States was the Philippines. This group of 7000 islands lies 500 miles off the coast of China. Only 400 of the islands are inhabited. When they came under American control they had 7 million people.

Spain ruled the Philippines for four hundred years, yet did little to improve the lot of the common people. In 1896 they revolted. To stop the revolt Spain promised reforms, but the promises were not kept. When Admiral Dewey took Manila in 1898, rebel leaders proclaimed a republic. A few months later, when they found that the United States did not intend to set the islands free, they again took up their fight for freedom. Led by the daring Emilio Aguinaldo, Filipino guerrillas for months resisted a force of 60,000 Americans. With the capture of Aguinaldo in 1901, the revolt came to an end.

Civil government is organized.

In 1901 military control of the Philippines ended. A commission of five Americans, headed by Judge William Howard Taft, was given the task of setting up a civil government. President McKinley told the commission to be guided in all matters by the best interests of the native people. The commission carried out its work with great tact and skill.

The next year Congress passed the Philippine Act. Under it the people were made "citizens of the Philippine Islands," with most of the rights of American citizens except the right of trial by jury. Beginning in 1907 the Filipinos were given a legislature. They elected the lower house, while a commission appointed by the President acted as the upper house. By 1913 Filipinos held a majority of places on the commission.

The Jones Act promises independence.

Gradually the United States was preparing the Filipinos for independence. In 1916 the Democratic majority in Congress pushed through the Jones Act. It provided a bill of rights for Filipinos. It authorized the Filipinos to elect both houses of their legislature. The Jones Act also declared that it was the purpose of the United States to recognize the independence of the Philippines, "as soon as a stable government can be established."

The Republicans, who returned to power in 1920, thought that the granting of independence should be postponed. Some felt that the islands were necessary to the United States as a commercial base in the Far East. Others argued that the Philippines were too weak to protect themselves without American help. Still others pointed out that Philippine prosperity depended on free trade with the United States, which would be lost if the Philippines were independent. These arguments had such weight that Presidents Harding, Coolidge, and Hoover firmly opposed setting any date for giving the islands their independence. Meanwhile, many Filipino leaders insisted that the islands had a stable government and should be set free.

Beginning in 1929 new arguments in favor of independence were heard in the United States. (1) Possession of the islands had not increased our trade with China and other parts of the Far East. (2) The cost of administering, fortifying, and defending the islands was a heavy expense. (3) Military and naval experts pointed out that in case of war in the Pacific the defense of the Philippines would be difficult. If we had to place a fleet in Philippine waters, we would weaken the defense of Hawaii, our west coast, and the Canal Zone. (4) Many Filipinos were coming to California. Labor unions wished to put an end to this immigration by making the Philippine Islands foreign territory. (5) Philippine sugar, tobacco, and coconut oil competed with American products, yet Congress felt an obligation to admit Philippine imports duty-free. If the Philippines were a foreign country, Congress would be more likely to shut out their products. These arguments could be summed up by saying that imperialism in the Philippines did not pay. There was also a growing belief that we had finished our task of preparing the Filipinos for self-government and that we had no right to refuse them their freedom.

The Philippines become free.

In 1934 Congress passed an act providing that the Philippines should become independent on July 4, 1946.

(upper left) UNIVERSITY OF MANILA

(lower left) PAGO PAGO, *the largest town* *American Samoa*

(right) A FILIPINO "LUMBERJACK" *climbs* *towering coconut palm.*

Meanwhile the islands were to be self-governing except in foreign affairs. The Filipinos quickly accepted this plan. They held a convention and adopted a constitution for the Commonwealth of the Philippines. In 1935 they made Manuel Quezon their first president.

Congress realized that the new commonwealth would need time to adjust itself to the loss of the American market. The Philippine Independence Act provided, therefore, that a certain amount of Philippine sugar, coconut oil, and other products would be admitted duty-free each year until 1946. Faced with the loss of the free American market, many Filipinos were not so sure as formerly that independence would be good for the islands.

The Philippine Commonwealth was attacked and conquered by Japan early in 1942 (see p. 742). Filipino guerrillas helped us reconquer the islands in 1944 and 1945. On July 4, 1946, the Stars and Stripes were lowered and the new Philippine Republic was born.

The United States continues to help.

Congress granted the Philippines more than six hundred million dollars for reconstruction after the war. Congress also passed the Bell Act, providing for eight years of free trade between the United States and the Philippines, with gradually rising tariffs for the next twenty years. The Philippine Congress, realizing that American protection was necessary, agreed that we could maintain army, navy, and air bases in the islands.

Americans may take pride in what the United States did for the Philippines while they were under its control. Between 1898 and 1935 the Philippines made more progress than had been made in the previous three centuries. Under Spanish rule modern improvements were almost unknown, while most of the people lived in hopeless poverty. Under American rule highways, railroads, and telephone and telegraph systems were built. Fine public buildings were erected. Thousands of free public schools were opened. The number of people unable to read and write dropped from 85 per cent to 37 per cent. Modern methods of agriculture were introduced, greatly increasing the output of farms and plantations. Many large estates were broken up into small farms. Foreign trade increased to six times what it had been. The people had more to eat and wear and better houses in which to live. Some of the most important improvements were made in the field of public health. In order to control the many diseases spread by impure water, safe water was provided for every community. Smallpox was wiped out by vaccination. By these and other health measures sickness and death rates were cut so much that the population doubled.

Perhaps the best thing we did was to help the Filipinos become a nation capable of self-government. We made this possible by educating the people and allowing them to take responsibility for their government. Along with our language they learned our ideas of democracy and the rights of the common man. As a result of our encouragement and their own desire for self-rule, they made themselves ready for independence in the short space of about thirty-five years.

Other Dependencies Become Self-governing

Hawaii.

Mark Twain spoke of the Hawaiian group as "the loveliest fleet of islands that lies anchored in any ocean." The islands are famous for their scenery, pleasant climate, and the good will of their people. While most of the best land is used for sugar and pineapple plantations, there are also a great many small farms. Most Hawaiians speak English.

As we have noted, Hawaii was annexed to the United States in 1898 at its own request. From then on all persons born in Hawaii have been citizens of the United States. In 1900 Congress made Hawaii an *incorporated territory*. Thus it became part of the United States and all sections of the Constitution applied to it and its citizens. Hawaii had a popularly elected legislature of two houses. Like other territories its governor was appointed by the President. In 1959 Hawaii was granted statehood.

Alaska.

For thirty years after the purchase of Alaska, neither the public nor Congress paid much attention to it. The discovery of rich gold deposits in 1898 brought an influx of settlers. In 1906 Congress granted the voters of Alaska the right to send a delegate to the House of Representatives. Six years later Congress provided for a territorial legislature, thus giving the people more voice in their government. In 1912 Alaska became an incorporated territory and in 1959 it joined the Union as the forty-ninth state.

Alaska is our last frontier. With an area twice that of Texas, its population in 1950 was 129,000, or about one inhabitant to every four square miles. Scientists tell us that Alaska could support at least five million people. It is rich in minerals, lumber, furs, and fish. About half the territory is suitable for grazing, and in some sections crops can be grown. The climate is like that of Norway and Sweden.

An airport at ANCHORAGE, ALASKA. *These planes are mostly local craft used for transporting men and supplies into the rugged back country.*

A HOUSING PROJECT *located in Santurce, Puerto Rico. Civic leaders have had many such projects built to meet the needs of the rapidly growing cities.*

Puerto Rico.

This beautiful island in the West Indies is smaller than any of our states except Delaware and Rhode Island. When ceded to the United States, it had nearly a million people. Since then, despite emigration, its population has more than doubled. Puerto Rico, with about 650 people per square mile, is one of the most densely populated places in the world.

Puerto Ricans on the whole accepted the rule of the United States willingly. Since the people had had no experience in self-government and since most of them were illiterate, Congress could not make them self-governing at once. Under the Foraker Act of 1900 Puerto Rico was made an *unincorporated territory*. This meant that the island was not a part of the United States but a possession. Hence some parts of the Constitution did not apply to it. The Puerto Ricans were allowed to elect representatives to the lower house of their legislature, while the President of the United States appointed the governor and the upper house.

In 1917 Congress passed the Jones Act. This made the Puerto Ricans citizens of the United States. It also gave them the right to elect the upper house of their legislature. Truman was the first President to select a native Puerto Rican for governor (1946). The next year Congress agreed to let the people of Puerto Rico elect their own governor. On July 4, 1952, Puerto Rico achieved "home rule." On that day a new constitution, written and adopted by the people, went into effect. It declares Puerto Rico to be a "commonwealth" and a "free associate state" with the United States of America.

The new constitution was approved by an overwhelming majority of Puerto Ricans, yet a small group still demand full independence from the United States. Others hope that their island will become a state of the Union. Statehood would have serious disadvantages, for the money collected in Puerto Rico for federal taxes would then go to the United States Treasury. Today it is spent on the island for roads, schools, irrigation, and other projects for the benefit of the people.

Under the American flag Puerto Rico made striking advances in health, education, transportation, and irrigation. In the first fifty years the death rate was cut in half, which resulted in a rapid growth of population. Illiteracy dropped from 77 per cent in 1898 to 25 per cent in 1950. The Spanish culture and traditions have been retained, but all Puerto Rican school children must learn English as well as Spanish.

In recent years Puerto Rican leaders have pushed a program of economic development. By offering low taxes and cheap labor they have attracted factories from the United States. They are also trying to make the island a popular vacation spot for American tourists. Their efforts have gradually created more jobs, but population continues to grow faster than the opportunities for employment. That is why thousands of Puerto Ricans come to the United States each year to look for work.

Non-self-governing territories.

In addition to territories that are fully self-governing, the United States has a few other small possessions. Among these are the Canal Zone, American Samoa, Guam, and the Virgin Islands. We bought the Virgin Islands from Denmark in 1917 because we feared that Germany might take them and endanger the Panama Canal. Since 1927 the people of the Virgin Islands have been citizens of the United States. They are largely self-governing. In 1950 the people of Guam became American citizens and received limited self-government. Besides giving the people of our possessions as much voice in their government as is practicable, Congress has spent money generously to improve their welfare. Thus the United States has tried to be a wise trustee and not an exploiter of dependent areas.

FOR IDENTIFICATION

Emilio Aguinaldo	Pago Pago
Admiral Cervera	Joseph Pulitzer
Commodore George Dewey	Manuel Quezon Santiago
William Randolph Hearst	William Seward General William Shafter
Jones Act	Teller Resolution
Manila Bay	Virgin Islands
Midway Islands	

FOR EXPLANATION OR DEFINITION

anti-imperialists	joint resolution
commonwealth	manifest destiny
concentration camps	"Remember the *Maine*"
imperialism	"Rough Riders"
incorporated territory	spheres of influence
insular cases	Teller Resolution
jingo press	unincorporated territory

FOR REVIEW

1. Explain the point of view that industrialization tends to produce imperialism.

2. How and when did the United States become interested in overseas possessions?

3. What did most Americans think of Seward's plan to buy the Virgin Islands, the Dominican Republic, and Alaska?

4. Show that Alaska was well worth the price paid for it.

5. How did the United States obtain the Midway Islands? Of what use are they?

6. Why did we take control of Pago Pago in Samoa?

7. How and when did Americans become interested in the Hawaiian Islands?

8. Why was President Cleveland reluctant to annex Hawaii? How and when did the United States obtain control of Hawaii?

9. Why did American planters once want the United States to get control of Cuba?

10. (a) What conditions aroused American sympathy for the Cubans in 1896? (b) What reply did Spain make to McKinley's protest against conditions in Cuba?

579

11. Why was the battleship *Maine* sent to Havana? What happened to it? How did this help bring about the war?

12. How did the "jingo press" influence popular opinion about Spain and Cuba?

13. (a) Why has McKinley been criticized for his war message to Congress? (b) How did Congress respond to this message?

14. What were the major military engagements of the Spanish-American War?

15. What were the terms of the peace treaty with Spain?

16. What arguments were used to support and oppose annexation of the Philippines?

17. State the principal results, direct and indirect, of the Spanish-American War.

18. What was the chief issue in the presidential campaign of 1900? Which side did the Republicans take? The Democrats?

19. What important question was decided by the Supreme Court in the insular cases?

20. Describe the location, population, and resources of the Philippine Islands.

21. (a) Why did the Filipinos rebel against the United States? (b) Who was their leader? (c) What were the arguments against granting independence to the Filipinos at that time?

22. (a) What arguments in favor of Philippine independence were advanced in the 1930's? (b) State the main features of the Philippine Independence Act. (c) Outline the progress made in the Philippines while they were an American colony.

23. (a) Describe the social and economic conditions in Hawaii. (b) Describe the climate and resources of Alaska.

24. Contrast the government of Puerto Rico before and after July 4, 1952.

25. (a) Describe social and economic conditions in Puerto Rico today. (b) Why have large numbers of Puerto Ricans migrated to the mainland?

26. How and why did the United States acquire the Virgin Islands?

27. Explain the aim of the United States in the Virgin Islands, the Canal Zone, and the small islands we own in the Pacific.

FOR FURTHER STUDY AND DISCUSSION

1. Defend or criticize McKinley's policy toward events in Cuba. Helpful source: Bailey, *Diplomatic History*, pp. 494–510.

2. Was the Spanish-American War a cause of the emergence of the United States as a world power? If so, why? Helpful source: Kennan, *American Diplomacy, 1900–1950*; Dulles, *America's Rise to World Power* (N.A.N.).

3. Do you agree or disagree that America's acquisition of the Philippines was a mistake? Helpful sources: Bemis, *Diplomatic History*, pp. 463–475; Amherst Series, *American Imperialism in 1898*, pp. 70–103; Bailey, *Diplomatic History*, pp. 511–526; Morison and Commager, *American Republic*, Vol. II, pp. 336–341.

FOR INDIVIDUAL OR GROUP ACTIVITIES

1. On an outline map of the Pacific, locate the following: Midway Islands, Guam, Samoa, Hawaii, Pearl Harbor, the Philippines, Manila.

2. On an outline map of the Caribbean locate the following: Key West, Cuba, Havana, San Juan, Santiago, Puerto Rico, Virgin Islands.

3. Prepare book reports on the following: Millis, *The Martial Spirit*; Mahan, *The Influence of Sea Power on History*.

4. Assume that you were a member of the peace commission. Write a brief memorandum advocating or criticizing the annexation of Puerto Rico and the "purchase" of the Philippines.

5. As an example of American humor at the time of the Spanish-American War, select and read to the class selections from Finley Peter Dunne. Helpful source: Ellis (ed.), *Mr. Dooley at His Best*.

6. Report on the decision of the Supreme Court in the insular cases. Helpful source: Commager, *Documents*, No. 352.

7. (a) Using an encyclopedia and recent editions of the *World Almanac* and *Information Please Almanac*, prepare floor talks on Alaska and Hawaii today. (b) Then, report on the steps taken to make Alaska and Hawaii states of the Union.

35. THE UNITED STATES EXTENDS ITS INFLUENCE

The United States Champions the Open Door in China

The Chinese Empire is carved up.

At the turn of the century we had only 2 per cent of China's trade but our businessmen hoped for more of it. Unfortunately, the government of China was falling apart. It was too weak to defend itself or to keep order. In 1895 Japan forced China to give up Formosa and the Ryukyu Islands. Soon after, France added more Chinese territory to French Indochina, while Britain enlarged Burma at China's expense. In 1898 and 1899 Germany, France, Russia, and Britain each obtained from China the "lease" of an important seaport. With the lease of a seaport went economic control over a vast area. As the European powers developed their spheres of influence it appeared that the United States might be shut out of the Chinese market.

Hay announces the Open Door policy.

Our government wished to stop the dismemberment of China and to protect American trade. In 1899 John Hay,

581

McKinley's Secretary of State, sent notes to all the powers concerned with China, asking them to maintain there an "Open Door" policy. This meant that merchants of all nations should be treated equally in China, even in leased territories and spheres of influence. Great Britain approved of this Open Door policy, for she already had 80 per cent of China's trade. The other powers agreed only halfheartedly. Early in 1900 Secretary Hay declared that the Open Door policy was in effect. His statement was, however, more hopeful than accurate. Time was to show that most of the powers gave lip service to the principle of the Open Door but did not intend to put it into practice.

The Boxers attack foreigners.

In 1900 a Chinese secret society known as the "Boxers" led an uprising against foreigners. The Boxers wanted to put an end to the Westernizing of China. They destroyed property belonging to foreigners and murdered over two hundred of them, mostly missionaries and their families. In Peking, Boxers surrounded the foreign legations, where nine hundred foreigners had taken refuge. An international army of European, Japanese, and American troops went to the rescue.

Secretary Hay feared that the other great powers would use the Boxer uprising as an excuse to seize more Chinese territory. He stated that it was the purpose of the United States to uphold the territorial integrity (wholeness) of China. This statement had the desired effect. The only penalties imposed on China were the punishment of the Boxer leaders and the payment of damages for injuries and losses suffered by foreigners during the uprising.

Our share of the damages, or indemnity, was twenty-four million dollars, which was more than our actual loss. At the suggestion of President Roosevelt, Congress returned most of the money to China. This friendly action won the good will of the Chinese people. China used the money to create a fund for sending Chinese students to American colleges.

Russia and Japan fight.

Japan was rapidly becoming a modern industrial nation. It needed foreign markets and access to raw materials. Most of all it needed room for its expanding population. Japan therefore looked around for colonies. Manchuria, a rich northern province of China, was especially tempting. Japan also wanted the independent Kingdom of Korea, control of which seemed necessary to Japanese security. Russia, however, stood in Japan's way.

Russia already had a sphere of influence in Manchuria. In addition, Russia wanted Korea. As a result of this clash of interests, early in 1904 Japan and Russia went to war. American sympathies were with Japan. We admired the Japanese for becoming Westernized so rapidly. We disliked the czar's government, because it was backward and because it persecuted minorities. Moreover, President Roosevelt and his advisors thought a Japanese victory would prevent the Russians from becoming too powerful in the Far East.

After a year of fighting, Russia was facing revolution and Japan was nearly bankrupt. The Japanese government secretly asked President Roosevelt to serve as mediator between Japan and Russia. When the czar agreed to talk peace, Roosevelt arranged a peace conference at Portsmouth, New Hampshire. During the negotiations the Japanese were persuaded to give up their demand for a money indemnity. The Russians ceded half of the island of Sakhalin, gave up their claims in southern Manchuria, and withdrew from Korea. Japan was now dominant in the Far East.

Our Relations with Japan Become Less Friendly

We sign a pact with Japan.

The United States and Japan had been friends ever since Commodore Perry's visit there in 1854 (see p. 357). After the Russo-Japanese War, however, tension developed. The United States took note of Japan's growing strength. American leaders feared that Japan meant to extend its influence in the Far East, especially in China. Sensational journalists here and in Europe harped on the "yellow peril"—the danger which they said existed that the yellow race would overwhelm the white race.

To ease the tension, the Root-Takahira Agreement was signed at Washington (1908). Both Japan and the United States agreed to respect each other's possessions in the Pacific, to uphold the Open Door in China, and to support China's independence and territorial integrity. The United States recognized that Japan had special interests in Manchuria and left it free to annex Korea.

Immigration leads to bitterness.

Japanese immigration to the Pacific coast states was a source of friction between our country and Japan. In 1906 the San Francisco Board of Education expressed the attitude of many Californians toward the Japanese by barring Japanese pupils from the public schools. When the Japanese government protested, President Roosevelt persuaded the school board to change its rule. Meanwhile, Californians were demanding that Japanese immigrants be excluded from the United States. (Chinese immigrants had been excluded since 1882.) T.R. hoped to keep Congress from passing an exclusion act, since it would be sure to hurt the pride of a sensitive nation. In 1907 he got the Japanese government to make a "gentlemen's agreement," by which it promised to keep laborers from emigrating to the mainland of the United States. Still the Californians were not satisfied. In 1913 they passed a law to prevent all Orientals from buying farms or leasing them for more than three years. A few other states passed similar laws. The federal government could not interfere, although these laws created bitter feelings in Japan.

Japan attempts new conquests.

Since 1902 Japan had been a military ally of Great Britain. When Britain went to war with Germany in 1914, Japan also declared war. Japan seized the peninsula of Shantung, which had been a German sphere of influence in China. Japan also took from Germany the Caroline, Marianas, and Marshall islands in the South Pacific. There were about 1400 of these little islands, with a total area of some 830 square miles. A Japanese admiral called them "natural aircraft carriers." (They proved useful to Japan in her attempt to win control of the Pacific in the 1940's.)

In 1915 Japan insisted that China agree to twenty-one demands. These were intended to turn all China into a Japanese sphere of influence. The United States protested, and China took courage to resist. Japan then postponed most of the demands "for further discussion." Once again the United States had shown a desire to protect the independence of China.

The United States Digs a Canal at Panama

Early talk of a canal.

From the time when Balboa crossed the Isthmus of Panama and discovered the Pacific Ocean (1513), men dreamed of digging a canal across this narrow strip of land. The United States first showed its interest in such a canal in 1846, the year when the Oregon question was settled and when we seized California. Having suddenly reached the Pacific, the nation needed an easy water route from the East to the West. Hence a treaty was drawn up with Colombia, to which the isthmus belonged, giving the United States a right of way across it. Soon after, gold was discovered in California, and the "Forty-niners" started their famous rush to the "diggings." The journey overland by wagon or around Cape Horn by ship was long and dangerous. People realized that a canal across the isthmus was greatly needed.

About this time the British became interested in a possible canal route through Nicaragua. Tension developed, for the United States did not wish Great Britain to control the proposed canal. The British sent a special envoy to Washington to work out an agreement. The Clayton-Bulwer Treaty (1850) resulted. By this pact the United States and Britain agreed that any canal connecting the two oceans that either might build should be controlled by both. Further, the canal should not be fortified and should be open to the use of all nations. No canal was dug then, however. After the transcontinental railroads were built, our interest in a canal lagged.

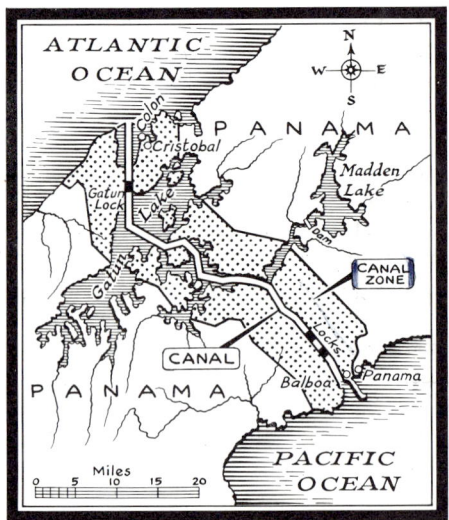

THE PANAMA CANAL

A French company begins work.

In the early 1880's a private French company started digging a canal across Panama. Americans became somewhat alarmed, and President Hayes declared that "the policy of this country is a canal under American control." His statement did not discourage the French company. Its head was Ferdinand de Lesseps, who had won world-wide praise as the builder of the Suez Canal. Lesseps appointed an advisory board of distinguished Americans. In addition he sold some of the stock in his company to Americans. The result was that objections to the project died down.

Lesseps figured that the canal would cost 170 million dollars. Unfortunately, construction proved more difficult than he expected. After some five years of work he had spent nearly 300 million dollars and had completed only about one third of his task. The greatest problem was tropical diseases. Thousands of engineers and workmen died every year from yellow fever and malaria. It looked as if the work could not be completed until medical science found ways to control these plagues.

Statue of FERDINAND DE LESSEPS *at Port Said, Egypt*

Unable to raise any more money, the company went bankrupt and digging stopped.

American interest revives.

When the French company failed, no group was more disappointed than our Western farmers. For years they had been complaining of railroad freight rates. They believed that cheap water transportation from coast to coast would force the railroads to lower their rates.

American manufacturers too were eager to have the canal completed. More and more they looked on the whole United States as their market. Cheaper transportation would help them to sell goods in all sections of the country.

After the United States obtained Hawaii and the Philippines, the need for a canal was plain to nearly everyone. Our businessmen saw new trade opportunities in the Far East. To make the most of them called for a short, cheap route from the Atlantic to the Pacific. Besides, a canal would help us defend our new possessions. Unless a canal were dug, the United States would have to build and maintain two navies—one in the Atlantic and one in the Pacific.

The Hay-Pauncefote Treaty.

American military leaders insisted that a canal ought to be entirely under our control. Also, it should be fortified. Yet these requirements could not be met under the terms of the Clayton-Bulwer Treaty. Our Secretary of State, John Hay, took up the problem with the British ambassador at Washington. A new agreement, the Hay-Pauncefote Treaty, was approved in 1901. In the new pact the British government agreed that the United States might build, control, and fortify a canal so long as all nations could use it on equal terms.

Congress selects a route.

The canal could be dug either through Panama or Nicaragua. The French Panama Company, which was eager to sell its rights and equipment to the United States, naturally wanted Congress to decide in favor of the Panama route. However, Nicaragua is nearer to the United States. Besides, engineers said it would be easier and cheaper to dig a canal through Nicaragua than through Panama. In January, 1902, the House of Representatives voted in favor of the Nicaragua route. In May, when a Nicaraguan volcano chanced to become active, the Senate decided in favor of the Panama route. Congress then agreed to pay the French Panama Company forty million dollars. The President was instructed to arrange with Colombia for control of a strip of land across Panama. If Colombia's terms were unsatisfactory, the canal was to be built across Nicaragua.

Panama breaks away from Colombia.

For a strip of land six miles wide across Panama, the United States offered to pay Colombia ten million dollars at the start and a yearly rent of $250,000. Colombia refused the offer. The rights of the French Panama Company would expire in a little more than a year, and its property would then belong to Colombia. By waiting, Colombia hoped to obtain the forty million dollars which the United States was willing to pay for the French company's property.

Roosevelt was in a hurry to start digging the canal before the next election. The French company too wanted immediate action. Furthermore, leaders in Panama feared that if there were a delay, the canal would be built in Nicaragua instead. The idea occurred to all of them that Panama might declare itself an independent nation and then accept the terms offered by the United

States. Panama once had been independent, and since joining Colombia had tried several times to secede. Panama would gladly try again if the United States would give it protection.

While Panamanian leaders and officers of the French company organized a small army in Panama, President Roosevelt sent several warships there with orders to prevent the landing of Colombian troops. As soon as the American vessels reached Panama (November 3, 1903), the tiny republic proclaimed its independence. Three days later it was recognized by our State Department. Only fifteen days after the bloodless revolution the Hay–Bunau-Varilla Treaty was signed, by which the United States guaranteed the independence of Panama. In return for a strip of land ten miles wide, we agreed to pay Panama ten million dollars down and $250,000 every year. The French company received forty million dollars, as agreed upon earlier.

Roosevelt's so-called "cowboy diplomacy" probably speeded up the building of the canal by at least a few months, but it put the United States in a bad light. The American minister to Colombia said that the friendly relations existing between the two countries were "changed suddenly and unexpectedly when President Roosevelt denied to Colombia the right to land troops upon her own soil to suppress a threatened revolt." Roosevelt's action not only offended Colombia but also aroused distrust throughout Latin America. In 1921, after Roosevelt's death, the United States paid Colombia twenty-five million dollars. This was a way of saying "We are sorry."

The Canal Zone is made healthy.

United States Army engineers began work on the canal in 1904. Their first task was to provide safe living and working conditions in a rainy, tropical land, where disease constantly threatened all the inhabitants. Fortunately, medical science had advanced since the French company had tried to dig the canal. Colonel William Gorgas of the Army Medical Corps did a remarkable job as health officer of the Canal Zone. To prevent yellow fever and malaria, mosquitoes had to be controlled. He ordered the screening of living quarters and the draining of swamps where mosquitoes breed. To prevent typhoid, he saw to it that water and food supplies were safe from contamination. Gorgas succeeded in making the Canal Zone the healthiest strip of land under tropical skies, with a death rate actually lower than in an average city in the United States.

The canal is completed.

Excavation stopped in 1905 while engineers argued whether the plan for a lock canal should be given up in favor of a sea level canal. The debate was settled months later when Congress voted for a lock canal. In 1907 Colonel George W. Goethals was placed in charge of the project. After that, progress was very rapid. No engineering problem was too hard for him to solve. When rock slides filled Culebra Cut as fast as it was dug, he went right on digging until the slides stopped. He was most considerate of the welfare of the thousands of men who worked under him. He had a high standard of honesty and permitted no politics in filling positions and no graft in buying supplies. Although the canal and its fortifications cost almost half a billion dollars, the taxpayers got all they paid for.

The cutting of the canal is one of the greatest works of engineering ever attempted. Thirty-five thousand men labored on it for ten years. A mountain was removed at Culebra Cut. Another mountain was built to dam the Chagres River and form Gatun Lake. Huge locks were built to lift vessels eighty-

COLONEL WILLIAM C. GORGAS

MAJOR WALTER REED

(Below) CULEBRA CUT, *Panama Canal. Here the sweating laborers dug with pick and shovel; drills and dynamite pierced through the stone; and powerful steam shovels cleared the way for the great canal.*

five feet and lower them again to sea level. The vast undertaking has been called "the greatest liberty man has ever taken with nature." The canal was opened to ships in August, 1914, just at the beginning of World War I.

The canal proves its value.

The Panama Canal has greatly helped the commerce of the United States and other countries, particularly those of the Western Hemisphere. The great ditch shortened the distance by water from New York to San Francisco by 8000 miles. Also it has increased the usefulness of our navy and in this way strengthened the defenses of the entire Western Hemisphere.

Do we need another canal?

The possibility that an enemy might succeed in making the canal useless has caused military leaders to urge the building of a second one. In 1914 we paid Nicaragua $3,000,000 for a perpetual right of way for a canal. In 1939 Congress considered the question of building a Nicaraguan canal but voted against it. Instead Congress directed that another set of locks be built for the Panama Canal, to provide a third set in case the two old ones should be damaged. Work on the new locks was begun but never completed. Since locks can be easily made useless, engineers have proposed the digging of a sea level canal, but no action has been taken in the matter.

We Try to Promote Inter-American Co-operation

The Pan American Union is launched.

In 1889 the first Pan-American Conference met in Washington. All but one of the twenty-one republics in North and South America sent delegates. The conference agreed to form an International Union of American Republics, to encourage peace, commerce, and friendship between its members. (The title was changed in 1910 to the Pan American Union and in 1948 to the Organization of American States.) The organization has permanent headquarters in Washington and each member country pays a share of its expenses. It is a clearinghouse for information about the American republics and works for greater co-operation among them. Conferences of its twenty-one members are held every few years, each time in a different country.

Pan-Americanism fails.

Development of co-operation between the United States and the Latin American republics and among the latter has not been easy. Several reasons may be given.

1. The Latin American nations feel a closer relationship to Europe than to the United States or to each other. They are bound to Europe by ties of culture and trade.

2. Travel and communication between the Latin American countries and between them and the United States has always been difficult. The lofty Andes Mountains and the dense tropical jungles interfere with travel by land. Besides, the lack of capital has delayed the building of railroads, highways, and telephone lines to connect the various countries.

3. Differences in language, religion, and customs exist. For instance, neither Spanish nor English is understood in all parts of North and South America. The Brazilians speak Portuguese. In Paraguay and in several other areas most of the people speak an Indian tongue. In a few places in Latin America, German or Italian is the principal language heard.

4. Latin American distrust of the United States is of long standing. It began when we seized New Mexico and California during the Mexican

War. Distrust of the United States reached its height between 1905 and 1925. In those years Latin Americans said that the Monroe Doctrine was not a shield to protect them but rather a cloak for "Yankee imperialism." They used this term to describe our frequent interference in the affairs of the countries around the Caribbean Sea.

By the late 1920's our State Department realized the need of a new approach to our neighbors. To win their friendship we must treat them as equals rather than as children. Our leaders stopped using the term "Pan-Americanism," because south of our border it had come to be thought merely a fancy name for "imperialism." Instead, they spoke of "Inter-American co-operation." The phrase became a reality with the development of the Good Neighbor policy.

Caribbean America Becomes Our Sphere of Influence

Our Caribbean policy.

The flags of sixteen nations fly over the mainland and islands that make up the region known as Middle, or Caribbean, America. Twelve are the flags of republics, while four fly over possessions of the United States, Great Britain, France, and the Netherlands. The United States has always had an interest in Caribbean America. Since the beginning of the present century this interest has greatly increased.

Through the years the United States has developed certain ideas, or principles, that guide our dealings with these Caribbean neighbors. *First*, of course, is the Monroe Doctrine, originally stated in 1823. *Second* is the principle that all possible canal routes through Central America shall be controlled by the United States. We have made treaties with Central American countries to assure us that no corpora-

tion and no country except the United States shall be allowed to dig a canal across them. *Third* is the principle that no outside nation shall use force against any country of the Western Hemisphere for the purpose of collecting debts or protecting property owned by its citizens. This idea is an extension of the Monroe Doctrine. How the principles have been applied follows.

Cuba and the Platt Amendment.

In 1898, when the long civil war in Cuba ended, the island was damaged and disorganized. An American military government was set up. Under the able direction of General Leonard Wood, a public school system was established and hospitals, roads, bridges, and railways were built. Even more important was the attack on yellow fever. A group of American army doctors, headed by Dr. Walter Reed, tested and proved the theory of a Cuban doctor that yellow fever is carried by a mosquito. The terrible disease was then stamped out in Cuba by destroying the breeding places of mosquitoes.

Congress had promised that Cuba should be independent and prepared to honor its word. In 1901 the Cubans held a constitutional convention and adopted a constitution much like ours. Since Congress feared that Germany might try to get control of Cuba, Congress required the Cubans to write into their constitution the so-called Platt Amendment. The amendment said: (1) that Cuba should not weaken its independence by any treaty with a foreign power, or by borrowing more money abroad than it could easily pay back; (2) that the United States should have the right to intervene when necessary to restore order and to protect Cuba's independence; (3) that the United States should have the right to buy or lease naval stations on the Cuban coast. These restrictions made Cuba an American protectorate.

Early in 1902 our military government withdrew, leaving the Cuban government in full charge of the island's affairs. For four years everything went well. Then stormy times began. The United States sent in soldiers four times (1906, 1912, 1917, and 1920) to restore order and protect American property. Cuban patriots hated this interference. Other Latin American states criticized us for meddling in Cuban affairs. In 1934, as part of the "Good Neighbor policy," President Franklin D. Roosevelt canceled the Platt Amendment. However, the United States kept one naval base on the island.

Venezuela has debt troubles.

Our growing interest in the Caribbean was shown in the Venezuelan crisis of 1901–1902. Venezuela was heavily in debt to German, English, and Italian investors. The dictator-president, Cipriano Castro, refused either to pay the debts or to submit them to arbitration. To frighten Castro, Germany, Great Britain, and Italy sent warships to blockade Venezuelan ports. Although the blockade had the silent approval of our State Department, the American public regarded it as a violation of the Monroe Doctrine.

After the Germans sank two Venezuelan gunboats and shelled a town, Castro agreed to arbitration. The European powers continued the blockade until President Theodore Roosevelt persuaded them to let the Hague Tribunal settle the dispute. It was now evident that the people of the United States would not tolerate any efforts by other powers to "spank" our Latin American neighbors.

T.R. enlarges the Monroe Doctrine.

The countries of Latin America objected to the blockade of Venezuela much more than we did. In 1902 the foreign minister of Argentina, Luis Drago, proposed that the use of force by any state to collect a debt owed by another state be declared illegal. Drago argued that bankers who lend money to a foreign country make the terms hard enough to justify the risk they take. Therefore their government has no obligation to collect their loans.

Although the "Drago Doctrine" was applauded throughout Latin America, President Roosevelt did not fully agree with it. He feared that it would encourage reckless borrowing. In his annual message to Congress in 1904, he said it was the duty of the United States to intervene in the affairs of a neighbor republic in case of long-continued wrongdoing or failure to pay debts. His statement came to be known as the "Roosevelt corollary" to the Monroe Doctrine. It meant that the United States might force its neighbors to pay their bills in order to prevent any outside power from doing so.

We intervene in Santo Domingo.

Roosevelt first put his corollary into effect in 1905 by taking charge of the finances of Santo Domingo, or the Dominican Republic. At the time this little country was bankrupt because of a series of revolutions. It owed money to European and American creditors and could not even pay the interest. There were rumors that European powers intended to seize Dominican customhouses.

Secretary of State Hay persuaded the Dominican president to give the United States control of its customhouses. Part of the money we collected was to be turned over to the Dominican government for its regular expenses and the rest used to pay off its debts. An American financial advisor was appointed. He quickly succeeded in doubling the country's revenues and cutting in half the claims of foreign creditors. With the customhouses in American hands, revolution was less profitable than before. The Dominican Republic enjoyed several years of peace and progress before trouble broke out again.

New disorders began in 1911 with the murder of the Dominican president. Five years later the country was still without a state government. President Woodrow Wilson sent Marines there late in 1916. The Marines ruled the country for eight years. During this time schools and roads were built and sanitary conditions were improved. Yet the people resented martial law and censorship. In 1924 the United States withdrew its troops and returned the government to the Dominican people. Our financial supervision of Dominican affairs continued until 1940.

Taft tries "dollar diplomacy."

Roosevelt's foreign policy was known as the "big stick" because of his motto "Speak softly and carry a big stick." His successor, President Taft, adopted a policy known as "dollar di-

plomacy." It meant (1) using the State Department to promote the sale of American goods abroad and (2) encouraging Americans to invest money abroad. Taft tried particularly to en-

JOHN HAY

THE UNITED STATES IN THE CARIBBEAN

courage Americans to invest in the Caribbean republics. Investments there would tend to keep European investors out of these lands and thus remove one cause for possible European intervention.

American bankers and businessmen, however, did not care to invest money in countries where lives and property were unsafe. Thus when fighting broke out in Cuba, Honduras, the Dominican Republic, and Nicaragua, Taft sent American forces to restore order. As soon as the disturbance was over, our troops were withdrawn.

Nicaragua becomes a protectorate.

At the time Taft was in the White House, Nicaragua had passed through one revolution after another and was heavily in debt. Taft thought the country would become more orderly if its finances were straightened out. A new dictator had just come to power there. Taft let him know that his government would not be recognized by the United States until it got a loan from American bankers to pay off its European creditors. Taft further insisted that Nicaragua should have an American financial advisor.

In spite of American financial help, in 1912 another revolution began. Nicaragua's president called on the United States for help and Taft sent 2500 Marines. Because disturbances continued, a small American force remained in Nicaragua nearly all the time until 1933. Nicaraguan guerrillas fought our soldiers as long as they stayed.

Wilson intervenes in the Caribbean.

When Woodrow Wilson became President, he was opposed to all forms of imperialism. He announced that the United States would not use its armed forces to protect investments by Americans in other lands. Although Mr. Wilson believed that the Latin American countries should enjoy complete independence, he soon found that he could not abandon the Roosevelt corollary. In fact, he interfered more than Roosevelt and Taft had done in Caribbean affairs.

Wilson continued the occupation of Nicaragua, which Taft had begun. As already noted, Wilson sent Marines to the Dominican Republic and placed that country under our military rule (see p. 591). When civil war broke out in Cuba in 1917, he sent Marines there. He also arranged the purchase of the Danish West Indies, or Virgin Islands (1917). By that time it was clear that the Caribbean had become an American lake.

Haiti had been torn with revolution since 1911. Terrible disorders broke out in 1914 and 1915, and in both years Wilson sent Marines to protect American lives and property. In 1916 Haiti agreed to let the United States supervise its finances and its police.

Under American occupation Haiti enjoyed more peace and prosperity than ever before. Roads, sewers, water systems, schools, and hospitals were built. For the first time the health of the people received attention. As a result of changes in the prisons, the death rate of prisoners dropped from 65 per cent a year to less than 2 per cent. In spite of these improvements, many Haitians wanted the Americans to leave. Through the nineteen years of occupation, more than two thousand Haitians were shot for resisting American officials. President Herbert Hoover made preparations to restore control to the people. The last Marines left Haiti in 1934.

Revolution in Mexico.

The largest Caribbean republic is Mexico. Civil war broke out there in 1911. For more than a quarter of a century afterwards the country was torn with strife. Americans watched the struggle with concern. They did not like to see so much disorder in a bordering country. Furthermore, some 50,000 Americans were living in Mexico at the time, and Americans had invested nearly a billion dollars there.

To understand the civil war, we must look back over Mexican history. Between 1877 and 1911 Mexico was ruled by a cruel tyrant, Porfirio Díaz. Crushing all opposition, he ran the country for his own benefit. Vast areas of land which belonged to the Indian villages or to the nation were given to his personal friends. Thus the villagers became landless *peons,* scarcely better off than slaves. Díaz gave away the nation's mineral resources to rich foreigners, who in turn helped him to stay in power. The foreigners, chiefly Americans, Britishers, and Germans, invested money to develop the mines and oil fields. When the managers of these enterprises could not get enough laborers because of the long hours and miserable wages that prevailed, Mexican officials supplied them with slave laborers. Huge profits were made, but the Mexican people did not benefit from them. It was truly said, "Mexico is rich, but the Mexicans are poor."

Late in 1910 Francisco Madero organized a revolt against Díaz. Madero, who came from a cultivated and well-to-do family, wished to restore constitutional government. For several months the United States let him use New Mexico as a base. In May, 1911, Díaz fled from Mexico; that fall Madero became president. He allowed Mexican workers and peons to organize and took away some of the privileges enjoyed by foreign businessmen. Madero had been in office little more than a year when his enemies, led by the reactionary General Huerta, started a rebellion against him. Too late, President Taft shut off the export of arms to the rebels. In February, 1913, Madero was overthrown and murdered. Huerta then became dictator.

Wilson tries "watchful waiting."

Although other nations quickly recognized the Huerta government, the United States refused to do so. President Wilson announced a new principle to guide American foreign relations—the United States would not recognize governments founded on force. Wilson hoped the Huerta government would collapse. "My ideal," he said, "is an orderly . . . government in Mexico; but my passion is for the submerged 85 per cent of the people who are now struggling for liberty."

Civil war soon started between Huerta's followers and the Constitutionalists (those who had followed Madero). President Wilson sent his own representative to Mexico City to urge Huerta to resign. Huerta scornfully refused. Then Wilson lifted the arms embargo so that the Constitutionalists might get arms from the United States. For this and for not recognizing Huerta, the President was savagely criticized at home and abroad. Businessmen with investments in Mexico backed Huerta because they wanted order restored as quickly as possible. They made fun of Wilson's policy of "watchful waiting," which they claimed was prolonging the civil war.

In April, 1914, Wilson learned that a German ship was on its way to Vera Cruz with munitions for Huerta. To prevent delivery of the cargo, Wilson ordered American warships to seize the port. This action cost the lives of eighteen Americans and nearly two hundred Mexicans. War fever swept both the United States and Mexico. At this point Argentina, Brazil, and Chile (the "ABC powers") offered to mediate the quarrel. Wilson gladly accepted their offer. When the mediators sided with the United States, Huerta thought it wise to leave Mexico. Carranza, leader of the Constitutional party, then declared himself president. Wilson recognized him and called our troops out of Vera Cruz. All Latin America was glad that we had let other Latin American states help in settling the dispute.

An expedition is sent against Villa.

Carranza was no sooner in office than one of his former lieutenants, Pancho Villa, led a revolt against him. After a year of bloody fighting Villa retired to the mountains in northern Mexico, where he lived as a bandit chief. Since he blamed the United States for Carranza's victory, he wanted revenge. Early in 1916 a band of his followers killed eighteen American citizens, whom Carranza had asked to help operate the mines. American newspapers now angrily demanded that we "clean up" Mexico. A few weeks later Villa raided a town in New Mexico, killing seventeen more Americans. President Wilson then sent General Pershing into Mexico with 15,000 men and orders to capture Villa "dead or alive." Although Carranza had agreed to let the American soldiers come, he did nothing to help them and soon showed an unfriendly attitude. To avoid further ill will, Wilson recalled Pershing early in 1917, leaving the Mexicans to deal with Villa.

The oil controversy begins.

Under old Mexican laws everything beneath the surface of the soil belongs to the nation: a landowner has no right to minerals found beneath his land. Díaz had paid no attention to this principle when he gave away most of Mexico's mineral lands to foreigners. In 1917 Mexico adopted a new constitution, declaring that oil pools and other mineral deposits belong to the nation. No action was taken except passage of a law which said the oil companies should no longer get their oil absolutely free, but should pay the government 5 per cent of the value of every barrel produced. The big American oil companies tried hard to get the United States government to interfere, but President Wilson steeled himself against them. "I have to remind myself," he said to his secretary, "that I am President of the United States and not of a small group of Americans with vested interests in Mexico." The question of who owned Mexico's oil pools came up again while Coolidge was President and still again in the time of President Franklin D. Roosevelt.

Reaction to our Caribbean policy.

As we have said, American interference in the affairs of the Caribbean republics produced fear and resentment throughout Latin America. Its people at times thought that the United States might be planning to get control of the entire hemisphere. They claimed that we were interpreting the Monroe Doctrine more and more broadly to suit our interests. They accused us of practicing *economic imperialism:* that is, of controlling industrially backward areas for the sake of American investors.

In spite of this Latin-American reaction, every American President from McKinley to Hoover thought it necessary to maintain a certain degree of peace and order in Caribbean lands. Our intervention generally brought benefits to these weak nations. They had less war, revolution, and financial chaos than they would have had if left to themselves. If "dollar diplomacy" did encourage American investments, that too was of value to these lands.

As you will read in a later chapter, relations between the United States and the other American republics improved during the presidency of Herbert Hoover and his successor, Franklin D. Roosevelt. The change was due to a number of factors: (1) the declaration (1928) that the Roosevelt corollary was no longer in effect; (2) our agreement (1936) that the Monroe

Doctrine was the concern of all the American republics and each should have a voice in helping to enforce it; (3) our willingness to stop intervening in the affairs of the Caribbean states; (4) greater concern for the welfare of native workers on the part of American companies; and (5) our financial and technical support of programs for improving the health and prosperity of some of the American republics. These changes proved that the United States wanted to be a Good Neighbor.

GENERAL PERSHING

FOR IDENTIFICATION

General Carranza	General Huerta
Porfirio Díaz	Korea
Col. George W. Goethals	Ferdinand de Lesseps
	Manchuria
Col. William Gorgas	Gen. John J. Pershing
Hay–Bunau-Varilla Treaty	Sakhalin
	Shantung
Hay-Pauncefote Treaty	Vera Cruz

FOR EXPLANATION OR DEFINITION

ABC powers	Good Neighbor policy
Boxers	indemnity
"dollar diplomacy"	protectorate
Drago Doctrine	territorial integrity
economic imperialism	"watchful waiting"
gentlemen's agreement	

FOR REVIEW

1. Explain how the Chinese Empire was carved into spheres of influence by the European powers and Japan.

2. What is meant by the Open Door policy? To what extent was it accepted?

3. (a) What was the Boxer uprising? (b) What action was taken by the interested powers? (c) What did the United States do with the Boxer indemnity?

4. What brought about the Russo-Japanese War? How did this war change our attitude toward Japan? Japan's attitude toward us?

5. List the provisions of the Root-Takahira agreement.

6. (a) How did immigration cause friction between Japan and the United States? (b) What were the terms of the gentlemen's agreement with Japan?

7. (a) When and how did Japan acquire the Shantung Peninsula and the Caroline, Marianas, and Marshall Islands? Of what value were they to Japan? (b) What was the purpose of Japan's twenty-one demands on China?

8. When did the United States become interested in digging a canal across the Isthmus of Panama?

9. What were the terms of the Clayton-Bulwer Treaty, 1850? What parts of this treaty were modified by the Hay-Pauncefote Treaty, 1901?

10. Describe the efforts of Ferdinand de Lesseps and the French Panama Company to dig the Panama Canal.

11. (a) What groups in the United States were interested in digging the canal? What groups were opposed? (b) Why did Congress decide to build the canal through Panama instead of Nicaragua?

12. (a) What terms did we offer Colombia for a strip of land through Panama? Why did Colombia refuse our offer? (b) How did President Theodore Roosevelt encourage the uprising in Panama? (c) How did the United States acquire the Panama Canal Zone? (d) What did the United States do to soften Colombia's resentment toward us?

13. How did Colonel William Gorgas make possible the building of the canal?

14. Describe the work of Colonel George W. Goethals in digging the canal.

15. What principles have determined the Caribbean policy of the United States?

16. (a) State the provisions of the so-called Platt Amendment to the Cuban constitution. (b) Why did the United States

send troops to Cuba at different times? (c) How did President Franklin D. Roosevelt implement the Good Neighbor policy with regard to Cuba?

17. How did President Theodore Roosevelt settle Venezuelan difficulties in 1902?

18. (a) What is the Drago Doctrine? (b) What is the Roosevelt corollary of the Monroe Doctrine? (c) How did Roosevelt apply his corollary to the financial difficulties of the Dominican Republic?

19. How did President Taft practice "dollar diplomacy" in Nicaragua?

20. What were the results of American occupation of Haiti?

21. What conditions in Mexico led to the overthrow of Porfirio Díaz in 1911? Who led the revolt?

22. (a) Why did President Wilson refuse to recognize General Huerta? (b) What was the policy of "watchful waiting"? (c) Why did Wilson send warships to Vera Cruz? (d) How did the ABC powers intervene to settle the dispute?

23. (a) Who was Pancho Villa? (b) What was the result of Pershing's expedition into Mexico?

24. Under Mexican law who owns minerals found beneath the surface of the soil? What happened when Mexico tried to enforce this law?

25. (a) What were the effects of our repeated intervention in Latin America? (b) When and why did our relations with Latin American countries improve?

FOR FURTHER STUDY AND DISCUSSION

1. Was the United States pursuing a policy of self-advantage when it championed the Open Door policy? Helpful source: Bemis, *Diplomatic History*, pp. 479–502.

2. Why was the Open Door policy approved in word and disregarded in action? Helpful sources: Morison and Commager, *American Republic*, Vol. II, pp. 350–354; Link, *American Epoch*.

3. What events in the early twentieth century show the development of a friendly American interest in China? What events in the same period tend to illustrate the development of tension between the United States and Japan?

4. What did England gain or lose by substituting the Hay-Pauncefote Treaty for the Clayton-Bulwer Treaty?

5. In the years 1900–25, how did the Monroe Doctrine become an economic policy?

6. Professor Bemis suggests that what has been called America's "Caribbean policy" might more appropriately be called America's "Panama policy." Give your reasons for accepting or rejecting this interpretation. Helpful source: Bemis, *Diplomatic History*, pp. 519–538.

FOR INDIVIDUAL OR GROUP ACTIVITIES

1. On an outline map, of the Far East locate: Korea, Shantung, Manchuria, Port Arthur, Formosa, Japan, Tokyo, Shanghai, Canton, Sakhalin, Hong Kong, Peking (Peiping), the Philippines, Manila.

2. On an outline map of the Western Hemisphere locate: Panama, Panama Canal Zone, Colombia, Venezuela, Nicaragua, New York, Havana, Key West, Vera Cruz, San Francisco, Rio de Janeiro, Buenos Aires, Valparaiso. Label approximate distances between key ports.

3. Collect statistics and prepare charts concerning the cost of operating the Panama Canal; the number of ships using it; the cargo tonnage carried through it. Helpful sources: *World Almanac, Information Please Almanac.*

4. Arrange an exhibit of pictures showing construction of the canal and present-day scenes along its route.

5. Report on the work of Colonel Gorgas.

6. Report on the details of American intervention in Haiti, Santo Domingo, Nicaragua. Helpful source: Beard and Beard, *Rise of American Civilization.*

7. List in parallel columns the main activities of Elihu Root and Charles Evans Hughes as Secretary of State. Summarize the diplomatic achievements of each man.

8. Write a short essay on the historical meaning and practical importance of Theodore Roosevelt's phrase, "Speak softly and carry a big stick." Helpful source: Bailey, *The American Pageant*, pp. 635–649.

> The world must be made safe for democracy. Its peace must be planted upon the tested foundations of political liberty.——Woodrow Wilson, 1917

36. THE UNITED STATES IN WORLD WAR I

The United States Joins the World Peace Movement

Peace conferences at The Hague.

In its new role as a world power the United States took part in efforts designed to promote international peace. When the Czar of Russia invited the nations of the world to a peace conference at The Hague in 1899, President McKinley sent an American delegation. The conference was called to discuss measures for reducing armaments and insuring world peace. The most important work done was to organize The Hague Permanent Court of Arbitration. Incidentally, the United States and Mexico were the first nations to submit a case to the court.

A second peace conference met at The Hague in June, 1907, in a marble peace palace built by Andrew Carnegie. The conference adopted a softened form of the Drago Doctrine (see p. 590), stating that nations should not use force to collect their debts unless the debtors refused to arbitrate. In addition, resolutions were adopted for better protection of the rights of neutrals and for the more humane conduct of war. An American proposal to limit naval armament was blocked by Germany, which had plans for a navy second to none.

Roosevelt wins Nobel Peace Prize.

President Theodore Roosevelt took the United States still farther from isolationism when he offered his services as a mediator in the Russo-Japanese war (see p. 582). A few months later T.R. again served the cause of peace when he arranged a meeting of French, British, German, and American representatives at Algeciras, Spain. This conference (1906) settled a dangerous dispute between France and Germany over trading privileges in Morocco. For these and other efforts toward world peace, Roosevelt was awarded the Nobel Peace Prize (1906).

Treaties of arbitration and conciliation.

Among methods for the peaceful settlement of disputes are arbitration [1] and conciliation. In 1908 and 1909 Roosevelt's Secretary of State, Elihu Root, concluded arbitration treaties

---

[1] By *arbitration* is meant the submission of a dispute for settlement to a group of disinterested parties. The parties agreeing to arbitrate are bound in honor to accept the decision, or award, of the arbitration committee. By *conciliation* is meant the reference of a dispute to a committee which will make suggestions for a settlement. The disputing parties are not bound to accept these suggestions.

with twenty-five nations. These pacts bound the signatory nations to submit to the Hague Court all disputes which did not "affect the vital interests, the independence, or the honor of the two contracting parties."

President Wilson's Secretary of State, William Jennings Bryan, negotiated thirty-one conciliation treaties in 1913 and 1914. These treaties said that *every* dispute between the United States and the other signatory party which the two could not settle peacefully should be submitted to an international commission. The signers agreed to a "cooling-off" period of one year while the commission was trying to bring about a settlement. Before the last of these treaties went into effect, Europe was plunged into the most terrible war the world had yet seen. Our country was drawn into it as well, despite the agreements which Americans had hoped would assure lasting peace.

World War I Engulfs Europe

Underlying causes of World War I.

Although most people in every country wanted peace, mighty forces were driving them toward war. The strongest of these were imperialism, nationalism, militarism, and alliances.

1. *Imperialism.* The desire for colonies and for control over backward areas was probably the chief cause of the war. Industrial nations thought they had to have colonies as markets, sources of raw materials, and places to invest surplus capital. Great Britain had the largest and richest empire. France also had a valuable empire, while Russia had a huge area of undeveloped land in Siberia. These three powers watched with alarm the rise of Germany, which was rapidly becoming the foremost industrial and military nation of Europe. Germany was eager to expand both her territory and her commerce. Italy and Japan were eager to expand as well. Imperialistic rivalries created one crisis after another, especially after 1900. Tension was greatest in the Balkans, a backward region just getting free from Turkey. Germany and Austria-Hungary wanted control of the Balkans, but Russia thought the area should be under her influence. The clash of interests in the Balkans led directly to World War I.

2. *Nationalism* ("my country first") was a second cause of war. Nationalism had brought about the unification of Italy and of Germany. (Unification was completed in both countries about 1870.) Wanting to be ranked among the first-rate powers, these nations built up their military strength and looked around for additional territory. Italy particularly wanted to annex the Italian regions of Trentino and Trieste, which were in the hands of Austria-Hungary. Nationalism in France was shown in a fervent desire to regain the "lost provinces" of Alsace and Lorraine, which Prussia had seized from her in 1871. Nationalism in Russia showed in the desire to control the waterways from the Black Sea to the Mediterranean and to win influence over the Slavic peoples in the Balkans.

3. *Militarism.* The years from 1871 to 1914 saw a frantic arms race among the great European powers. Germany built up the most efficient and powerful army in the world. France, Russia, Austria-Hungary, and Italy also had big standing armies. About 1905 Great Britain and Germany began a naval race. German naval officers drank toasts to *der Tag* (the day) when their fleet should take control of the seas from the British. Nations which saw they were falling behind in the struggle for military might became more and more frightened.

4. *Alliances.* Nations that feel insecure naturally seek allies. Germany,

KAISER WILHELM

Death of a Zeppelin

Austria-Hungary, and Italy formed the Triple Alliance in 1882. About ten years later, to balance the growing power of the Triple Alliance, France and Russia made a secret alliance. When Britain became fearful of Germany, she reached an understanding with her old enemy, France (1904), and with Russia (1907). The agreement between Britain, France, and Russia was known as the Triple Entente. The German Kaiser, Wilhelm II, insisted that the Entente was a plot to surround Germany with an "iron ring" and deprive her of a "place in the sun."

War breaks out.

Europe had become a powder magazine. In 1914 came the explosion. It was set off on June 28, when the heir to the throne of Austria-Hungary was assassinated by a Serbian patriot. Austria then made extreme demands on Serbia. While the Serbs were eager to make amends, they were not willing to become a puppet state. British and other diplomats urged that the dispute be arbitrated. Austria-Hungary de-

clined to arbitrate and instead declared war on Serbia (July 28). Thereupon Russia began to mobilize in order to protect Serbia. At once Germany came to the aid of Austria by declaring war on Russia (August 1). Three days later Germany declared war on Russia's ally, France. The Germans, violating a treaty that guaranteed Belgian neutrality, sent their armies across Belgium to attack France. The invasion of Belgium brought Great Britain into the war. Japan, which had been an ally of Britain since 1902, shortly joined the Allies (i.e., Britain, France, Russia, Serbia, and Belgium). Turkey and Bulgaria joined the Central Powers (i.e., Germany and Austria-Hungary). Italy hesitated until 1915, then went in on the side of the Allies. By 1917 every country in Europe had gone to war except Spain, Holland, Switzerland, Norway, Sweden, and Denmark. After the United States declared war in 1917, nine Latin American countries, China, and Siam (Thailand) joined the Allies.

The United States Tries to Remain Neutral

Wilson urges Americans to be neutral.

The outbreak of war in Europe came as a shock to the United States. The first idea here was to keep out of the conflict. "Peace-loving citizens of this country," said the *Chicago Herald*, "will now rise up and tender a hearty vote of thanks to Columbus for having discovered America." That was a joking way of saying, "Thank heavens we are not mixed up in the fight."

President Wilson issued a proclamation (August, 1914) saying that the United States would stay neutral. He urged Americans to be neutral "in thought as well as in action." This advice proved impossible to follow. "Only persons mentally paralyzed," said one editor, "could be neutral in thought."

Most Americans side with the Allies.

Americans could not help taking sides. From the outset the majority hoped the Allies would win. Cultural ties between the United States, Great Britain, and France were strong. Moreover, they were the three great democracies. All three had similar ideals of justice, liberty, and the rights of the individual. All three stood for the peaceful settlement of international disputes.

The Central Powers, on the contrary, were autocracies. Their rulers championed the divine right of kings, resisted their people's efforts to gain self-government, and oppressed the minority groups within their borders. Germany, moreover, had aroused our distrust by its ambitions in China, the East Indies, the Pacific, and Africa. Leaders of the Pan-German movement boasted that Germans were destined to dominate the world.

As the war went on, more and more Americans felt that the cause of Britain and France was our cause too. Thousands of our countrymen enlisted under the British and French flags. Hundreds of thousands contributed to

EUROPE IN 1914

Allied war relief. On the other hand, there were nearly nine million Americans of German birth or parentage, and they tended to support their fatherland. In addition, many Americans of Irish descent were ready to cheer any foe of their ancient enemy, the British.

Both sides tried to influence American opinion by means of propaganda. The Allies were far more effective in swaying Americans than were the Central Powers. This was partly due to British control of the cables which carried news from Europe. Even more important was the widespread sympathy here with the Allied cause. Propaganda succeeds best when people want to believe it.

The British interfere with our trade.

At the start of the war, the British drove enemy ships from the seas and declared a blockade of Germany. The Allies published a list of contraband articles which neutrals must not send to the enemy. In addition to munitions, the list included many things useful in modern war but not previously considered contraband, such as leather, cotton, wool, rubber, chemicals, and even foodstuffs. To get around the blockade American shippers sent cargoes to neutral countries on Germany's borders. The goods were then reshipped to Germany. British ships therefore began to halt American ships bound for Europe, take them into port, and search them for contraband. Our State Department sent note after note of protest to Great Britain, claiming that our neutral rights were being violated. Yet the British did not stop.

German submarine warfare.

Germany's answer to the blockade was the use of the submarine. The Germans proclaimed that the waters around the British Isles were a war zone in which submarines would destroy every enemy ship they found. Neutral ships might be sunk by mistake, and they were warned to keep out. The Germans also stated that they might be unable to provide for the safety of crew and passengers on destroyed vessels.

Under the rules of international law as accepted up to that time, any merchant ship could be stopped by a warship belonging to a nation at war. If found to be carrying contraband, the merchant ship could be seized and taken to port, or it could be sunk. Should the captain of the warship decide to sink the merchant ship, however, he must first provide for the safety of its passengers and crew. Germany insisted that these old laws of "visit and search" did not apply to the submarine. If it came to the surface near a hostile vessel, it might be rammed or sunk by a shell. By the submarine's very nature, it had to torpedo a hostile ship without warning. Furthermore, said Germany, it could not stop to save the lives of those on board.

From the start, the people of the United States were appalled by the savagery of submarine warfare. It was brought home to them when several Americans were drowned in the sinking of British freighters in the war zone. Then came an event which shocked the entire civilized world. On May 7, 1915, the British liner *Lusitania* was torpedoed off the Irish coast. The great ship sank in eighteen minutes. Of the nearly two thousand persons on board, some twelve hundred were drowned, among them over one hundred Americans. A wave of horror and anger swept the United States. In the East many voices urged a declaration of war.

President Wilson did not listen to those who called for war. Instead he sent a series of sharp notes to Germany. He protested against the sinking of passenger ships and asked that no merchant ship be sunk without warning.

THE WOMAN'S PEACE PARTY *urged a "cooling-off" period for heated emotions aroused by the preparedness campaign.*

Finally, in February, 1916, Germany said it was sorry for the loss of American lives in the *Lusitania* sinking and agreed to pay damages.

The next month, however, a German U-boat torpedoed another unarmed passenger ship, the *Sussex,* without warning. Three Americans were killed. The United States threatened to break off diplomatic relations with Germany unless it changed its methods of submarine warfare. Germany then made the famous *Sussex* pledge: that neither merchant nor passenger ships would be sunk without warning and without protecting the lives of their crews and passengers. Wilson's patience had won a temporary victory. That fall the slogan "He kept us out of war" impressed peace-loving Americans and the President was elected for a second term.

Wilson urges preparedness.

Early in the war, a number of Americans tried to rouse the country to the need of strengthening our armed forces. President Wilson gradually came to their way of thinking. In January, 1916, he toured the Middle West, urging preparedness. Six months later Congress passed the National Defense Act. This measure provided for increasing the regular army to 223,000 men in five years, establishing officers' training camps, and building a $20,000,000 plant to produce nitrates for munitions. Later, Congress authorized the building of warships costing $600,000,000. To make plans for the efficient use of the country's economic resources—its industries, farms, railroads, and merchant ships—in case of war, Congress established a Council of National Defense. Congress then created the United States Shipping Board to build up our merchant marine, which had been declining ever since the War between North and South.

The President tries to end the war.

From the start Wilson hoped that the war might be settled by negotiation. A complete victory for one side with a harsh peace for the other would, he felt sure, only sow the seeds for a future war. Early in 1916 Wilson sent his friend Colonel Edward House to Europe to sound out both sides. Colonel House discovered that neither the Allies nor the Central Powers were ready to discuss peace terms. Each side hoped to force the other to beg for peace.

Late in 1916 the President again tried to mediate. Again his efforts were not well received by either side. In January, 1917, in a speech to the Senate, Wilson outlined his ideas for a peace settlement. A peace worth guaranteeing and preserving, he said, should be based on certain principles: an international organization or league, reduction of armaments, freedom of the seas, the abandonment of entangling alliances, and the right of nations to liberty and self-government. Most of all, the world needed a *"peace without victory."* The truth of his words was to be proved in the years between the first and the second world wars. Perhaps World War II would not have occurred if in 1917 the warring powers had been willing to work out a "peace without victory." Instead, the Allies got victory without peace.

The United States Enters the War

Ruthless submarine warfare is resumed.

On the last day of January, 1917, the Germans announced that they would adopt all-out submarine warfare. They had decided to stake everything on winning an early victory. By sinking all ships, enemy or neutral, approaching the British Isles, the Germans expected to starve Britain within a few months and force it to ask for peace. They knew that the sinking of American ships would bring the United States into the war, but they were not afraid of that. The war would be over,

they thought, before we could raise, equip, and train a sizable force, let alone take it to Europe. Three days after the German announcement, President Wilson broke off relations with Germany. The Senate approved his action by a vote of 78 to 5.

Tension increases.

During the next two months the United States moved closer and closer to war. Every day the newspapers reported the toll of ship sinkings in the war zone. In February alone, two hundred ships, many of them neutral, went to the bottom. If Germany sank American ships, war could not be avoided.

Late in February the British gave our government a secret German dispatch they had intercepted and decoded. Written by the German foreign minister, Alfred Zimmerman, it proposed that in case the United States entered the war, Mexico should become an ally of Germany. In return Mexico could regain the territories lost in 1848. Japan was to be invited to abandon the Allies and join Mexico in attacking the United States. Publication of the note caused widespread anger here.

On March 12 a German submarine sank an unarmed American ship without warning. The next day Wilson ordered American merchant ships entering the war zone to carry guns and gun crews. Within a few days, four more unarmed American ships were sunk. Such actions made it clear that Germany was at war with us.

War is declared.

On April 2, 1917, the President went before Congress to ask for a declaration of war. In what is one of the greatest speeches in our history, Wilson stated America's war aims. Saying that we did not intend to seek revenge, territory, or indemnities, he called Americans to join in a crusade for democracy and a lasting peace. Public opinion had kept pace with the President, and Congress promptly voted for war. The Senate vote was 82 to 6; the House vote 373 to 50. The President signed the war declaration on April 6. The United States entered the war not as one of the Allies but as an "associated power." Thus we were left free to make a separate peace.

Why we went to war.

"It was clear from the first," writes the historian H. S. Commager, "that the United States could not tolerate a hostile power on the shores of the Atlantic and that it could not stand idly by while Britain and France went under." Wilson reached this conclusion very early in the war. In September, 1914, he told the British ambassador that a German victory would compel the United States to "give up its present ideals and devote all its energies to defense, which would mean the end of its present system of government." Most Americans came to agree with Wilson that a German victory would threaten our safety and would endanger democratic institutions everywhere.

President Wilson had an additional reason for taking the United States into the war. It would give us a place at the peace table, where we could use our influence to bring about a just peace. We could make sure that the peace terms gave millions of oppressed peoples in central and eastern Europe the right of self-determination. We could also encourage democratic elements in Germany and lend support to the new democratic government in Russia.[1] Even more important in Wilson's view was the opportunity, if we had a place at the peace table, to help set up an international organization to maintain peace. These things were in the national interest of the United States.

---

[1] The Czar had been overthrown in March, 1917.

A nation united but unprepared.

Now that war had come, the vast majority of Americans loyally supported the government. The nation was more firmly united than at the start of any previous war. Disloyal groups were fewer and weaker than in the War between North and South, and they were not able to interfere seriously with the war effort.

Although united, the country was far from ready to fight a well-armed enemy. We had fewer than 300,000 soldiers, including the National Guard (volunteer militia). Even the regular army was not trained for the sort of fighting demanded by the European war. There was a serious shortage of trained officers. In addition we were short of machine guns, planes, big guns, and a thousand other articles needed by a modern army. German experts ranked our military strength between that of Belgium and Portugal.

Most Americans were not troubled by our lack of preparedness. They thought the part of the United States in the war would be to furnish money, food, ships, and munitions to the Allies and to use our excellent navy to fight the submarine. Many thought that Germany was on her last legs and would soon be beaten. The President himself did not think our army would have to go to Europe.

Men, Resources, and Opinions Are Mobilized

We decide to send an army overseas.

A few weeks after our declaration of war, British and French leaders sent word that the Allies were in grave danger of defeat. German submarines were destroying Allied ships at a terrible rate. For three years there had been a powerful German army in northern France, and the Allied armies were not strong enough to drive it out. Germany had conquered Belgium, Serbia, and Rumania. Russia was going through a revolution, and her armies were close to collapse. Italy was tottering. The French army had suffered frightful losses and was losing heart. British and French statesmen begged Wilson to send at least a small force overseas at once. Its arrival, they said, would give their people courage to go on.

The President sent General John J. Pershing to France with 12,000 men. Arriving ahead of his troops, Pershing visited the tomb of Lafayette, an act which thrilled liberty-loving people everywhere. A few days later, on July 4, 1917, Pershing's little army paraded through Paris to thunderous applause and cries of "Vive l'Amérique!" (Long live America!)

Pershing decided that three million American soldiers were needed to defeat Germany. He at once set about preparing for their arrival. In the ports assigned for American use, channels had to be deepened and docks built. A thousand miles of railroads must be constructed to carry our men and supplies. A hundred thousand miles of telegraph and telephone lines had to be strung. Training camps, supply depots, and hospitals had to be established. It was a gigantic undertaking, and it was accomplished with a speed that amazed the Europeans.

We raise and train an army.

How should the United States recruit the millions of men needed for the army? Should it rely on a call for volunteers, or should men be drafted? Americans did not like the idea of drafting soldiers. The one time it had been tried, after two years of the War between North and South, riots had broken out. Even so, army leaders convinced President Wilson that a draft was necessary. He in turn persuaded Congress to pass the Selective Service Act.

Careful thought was given to ways of making the draft as democratic as possible. The whole procedure was carried out by civilians. All men of draft age were asked to register; no one was allowed to hire a substitute. A local board of civilians decided who should be excused from service because of dependents, physical disabilities, or home duties. Lots were drawn to fix the order in which men were called to duty. Over two million men were drafted before the war came to an end. The draft machinery worked well, with almost no disturbances.

Setting-up exercises for new recruits. Preparedness plans had come late, but the nation quickly united in an effort to get her men ready for war.

Not only did the recruits have to be trained, but first they had to be provided with quarters. With lightning speed thirty-two big camps were built. The average soldier spent six months in training before going overseas, where he had additional training. The training camps, which cost nearly as much to build as the Panama Canal, were torn down after the war.

Modern war is total war.

Modern war is not just a contest between opposing military forces. It is *total* war, in which victory goes to the

605

side with the greater war production and the better morale. Not only the men of fighting age but the whole population must be mobilized to make the largest possible contribution to the war effort. President Wilson had this fact in mind when he said: "It is not an army we must shape and train for war —it is a nation."

Our economy is geared for war.

Production of every kind of war goods—guns, planes, ships, chemicals, clothing, food—had to be increased with all possible speed. Basic raw materials, such as steel, copper, fuel, lumber, cotton, wool, and fats, had to be turned out to the limit of the nation's capacity. All this must be done in spite of the absence of almost five million men in the armed forces. To win the battle of production, businessmen accepted controls which they had never thought possible.

For the duration of the war Congress gave the President broad emergency powers, similar to those of a dictator, over the nation's mines, industries, labor, and food supplies. He carried out his wartime powers through such agencies as the War Industries Board, Emergency Fleet Corporation, Railroad Administration, War Trade Board, Fuel Administration, War Labor Board, and Food Administration. Hundreds of business leaders served on these boards without pay. They were known as "dollar-a-year men."

The War Industries Board, directed by Bernard M. Baruch, co-ordinated the nation's industries so that all war materials would be produced in sufficient quantities. Factories had to be converted from making things used in peace to those needed in war. Thousands of new war plants had to be built. Vital raw materials had to be allocated under a system of priorities. The board succeeded in raising the nation's industrial output by 30 per cent.

The Emergency Fleet Corporation seized eighty-seven German ships that were interned in American ports. It also bought neutral ships. It built four huge shipyards and contracted for the building of hundreds of vessels.

In December, 1917, the government took control of all the railroads. William G. McAdoo, Secretary of the Treasury, headed the Railroad Administration. He combined all the lines into one big system, ending wasteful competition. To make the railroads more efficient, large sums were spent to improve and modernize railroad equipment. The chief job of the railroads became the moving of soldiers and war supplies.

The War Trade Board took control of foreign trade. Unnecessary imports and exports were stopped. Trade with neutral countries was watched to prevent supplies from reaching the enemy.

The Fuel Administration brought about a 40 per cent increase in coal production. It introduced "daylight saving time" to curtail the use of fuel. Homeowners and landlords were asked to observe "heatless Mondays."

A shortage of labor developed. Women by the hundreds of thousands took jobs in war industries. More Negroes than ever before were hired for industrial jobs. Many Negroes came North to work in war plants. Labor leaders promised not to call strikes: in return the War Labor Board guaranteed the right to organize and to bargain collectively. The board allowed wages to rise as fast as prices. It insisted on equal pay for equal work regardless of sex. It encouraged employers to reduce hours to 48 a week. These wise labor policies were effective in keeping labor unrest to a minimum.

"Food will win the war!"

When the United States entered the war, Great Britain and France were close to actual hunger. So many of their ships had been sunk by submarines that none could be spared to bring food from distant Argentina and Australia. The United States, therefore, had to expand its production of food at the very time when much of the man power on its farms had gone into the army or into war industries.

Herbert Hoover was named Food Administrator. With remarkable energy and efficiency, he threw himself into his task. He appealed to farmers to plant more grain and raise more hogs. He asked every family in the nation to plant a war garden. He asked the people to use substitutes for meat, sugar, and wheat, to observe certain days of the week as "meatless" and "wheatless" days, and to avoid all waste of food. Everywhere, in newspapers and on posters, appeared the slogan, "Food will win the war!" The result of Hoover's program was the doubling of American food exports to Europe.

How we paid for the war.

From April, 1917, to April, 1919, the United States spent 32 billions for direct war costs, including 10 billions lent to the Allies. This was three times what the federal government had spent for all purposes between 1789 and the beginning of the war. The people accepted taxes far heavier than ever before. The income tax rose to 12 per cent on incomes of $4000 or more, with surtaxes reaching 65 per cent on incomes above $1,000,000. Corporations paid 12½ per cent on net incomes. They also paid an "excess profits" tax designed to capture war profits. Nearly every luxury bore a special excise tax.

The whole cost of the war, however, could not be raised through taxation. The sale of "liberty bonds" and "victory bonds" brought in 21 billion dollars. Over 20 million Americans—1 in every 5—bought bonds in the fourth war loan drive. This was an amazing record when we stop to consider that

before the war not more than 300,000 Americans were in the habit of buying stocks and bonds.

Opinion is mobilized.

In fighting total war, it is important to obtain the full co-operation of the people. George Creel, head of the Wartime Committee on Public Information, undertook to "sell" the war to the public. He asked the advertising men of the country to help make America war-conscious. He also enlisted 75,000 volunteer speakers, known as "four-minute men." They spoke in factories during the lunch hour, at restaurants, on trains, at theaters—everywhere, in fact, where they could find an audience. Creel recruited singers to lead patriotic singing, artists to make posters, and writers to explain the war effort. As a result the nation was stirred as it never had been before. The great majority of Americans were uplifted in the belief that the war was a crusade for democracy, a war to end wars, injustice, and oppression.

As enthusiasm for the war effort grew, so did intolerance toward everything German. The teaching of the German language was discontinued in many schools and colleges. Orchestras stopped playing music by German composers. All German-Americans found themselves under suspicion of disloyalty, and a few of them were mistreated. Yet on the whole, they were loyal to the United States.

Freedom of speech and press is curbed.

Since before the Revolution, freedom of discussion had been a principle of American life. Curbs placed on it by the Alien and Sedition Acts of 1798 caused so much anger that these acts were allowed to expire (see p. 192). During the War between North and South, although there were many people in each section who did not support the war, neither side passed a sedition act. The right to hold and to express a minority opinion, even in time of war, was generally respected.

In 1917 this fine tradition was set aside. Soon after declaring war Congress passed the Espionage Act. It provided severe penalties for anyone aiding the enemy, interfering with the operation of the draft, or attempting to incite disloyal acts. A year later Congress passed the Sedition Act, imposing the same penalties on anyone who used disloyal or abusive language in speaking of the government or the armed forces. Passage of these acts was inspired in part by actual incidents of sabotage and partly by the unreasoning fears of the time. About sixteen hundred persons were convicted under these laws and given prison sentences. Some were members of a small, radical labor organization, the Industrial Workers of the World. Most of them, however, were pacifists who said war was wrong, or Socialists who denounced the war as a capitalist enterprise. Very few were Germans or German-Americans. After the armistice many petitions were sent to Congress asking that those imprisoned under the Espionage and Sedition Acts be set free as victims of wartime intolerance. Congress did not act but some received a presidential pardon. Eventually—on Christmas Day, 1933—all those still in prison were pardoned.

American Armed Forces Contribute to Victory

The navy plays a big part.

As soon as we entered the war, our navy began to help the British and French in fighting submarines. By the end of 1917 the loss of ships to U-boats had been cut in half. Before the war ended U-boat sinkings had almost stopped. This victory was brought about by the use of the convoy system,

THE CHIEFS OF THE ALLIED FORCES, *1918.* (Left to right) *Marshal Joffre (France), Marshal Foch (France, Supreme Commander), General Weygand (France), Field Marshal Haig (Great Britain), General Pershing (United States), and Marshal Pétain (France).*

the newly invented depth bomb, and a mine barrier across the North Sea from Scotland to Norway. Laying the thousands of mines was a gigantic undertaking, carried out mainly by American ships. Our navy also took part in sweeping up enemy mines and attacking enemy submarine bases.

Our army goes to France.

The problem of getting American soldiers and their supplies to France was so hard that the Germans thought the United States never could solve it. To carry millions of men was difficult enough. Still more difficult was carrying the vast quantities of materials they had to have for living and fighting. When we entered the war, we did not have nearly enough ships for the task. The British and French too were short of ships, for submarines were sending their ships to the bottom two or three times faster than new ones could be built. The United States had started a vast shipbuilding program, but few ships could be produced until more shipyards were built and until hundreds of thousands of shipyard workers were recruited and trained. In view of these facts American military leaders thought they could not attempt large-scale operations in Europe until 1919.

As 1917 drew to a close, defeat stared the Allies in the face. Russia collapsed, releasing forty divisions of fresh German troops to fight in France. The Allies desperately needed more soldiers. America had less than 200,000 men in France, none of them yet in combat. General Pershing cabled:

The Allies are very weak and we must come to their relief this year, 1918. The year after may be too late. It is very doubtful if they can hold on until 1919 unless we give them a lot of support this year.

Making a tremendous effort, America speeded up the shipment of men. By June, 1918, nearly 300,000 men a month were going overseas. Before the fighting stopped there were 2,000,000 American soldiers in France. Half of these men went overseas in vessels that the British managed to spare from the work of carrying food to their people.

The troop ships sailed in formation, guarded by destroyers. At night every glimmer of light was hidden, and the ships speeded ahead in blackness. Lookouts watched the sea for the ripple of a periscope or the trail of a torpedo. To the "doughboys," packed in the crowded hold, the voyage meant homesickness and fear of sudden death. Fortunately less than two hundred soldiers bound for Europe were lost at sea.

The Germans take the offensive.

In the winter of 1918, with high hopes of victory, the Germans made ready to take the offensive. Late in March they began a strong attack on the British line. Within eight days they swept forward 32 miles, capturing ninety thousand prisoners and threatening to separate the British and French armies. The crisis forced the Allies for the first time to appoint a commander in chief, General Ferdinand Foch.

The German advance went on throughout April and May. The situation was so grave that Pershing postponed his plan for an independent American army and offered all his resources to Foch. American troops rushed to the front to serve with British and French units at weak spots in the line. Our men helped to halt the German advance less than fifty miles from Paris. On July 15 the Germans thundered across the Marne in another powerful drive. They were successful everywhere except when they ran into the fresh American divisions. American resistance was so stubborn that the German chief of staff complained, "The Americans appear inexhaustible." By July 18 the strength of the German attack was used up.

Full speed ahead, an AMERI-
CAN CONVOY *sweeps through
a submarine zone. This
photo was made from the
deck of a British dirigible
helping to guard the way.
These dirigibles were responsible for bombing and sinking many enemy subs.*

*Beneath the skeletons of
trees an American infantry
platoon advances inch-by-
inch on the entrenched Germans.*

France is cleared of the enemy.

The Allied counteroffensive began
on July 18 and continued until the signing of the armistice. In August, Pershing insisted that the time had come to
form a separate American army. It was
assigned to straighten out a dent in
the Allied front at Saint Mihiel. Over
half a million American soldiers took
part in this battle, which freed seventy
French villages from occupation.

In September, Foch ordered an attack along the entire Allied line. The
task of the American army, which by
this time included 1,200,000 men, was
to push the Germans out of the Argonne Forest. The sector was strongly
fortified. In addition its ridges and deep
ravines, all densely wooded, made it
hard to take and easy to defend. Fighting raged for forty-seven days, with
heavy losses on both sides. Step by step

During the last months of the war the ALLIED ARMIES *liberated many people who had known only German occupation for four years. This old French couple greet with smiles and tears of gratitude the men who have freed them.*

the Germans were forced back a distance of about thirty miles. The battle ended with the capture of Sedan, an important railroad center. Farther to the west the British and French armies also were advancing. Part of Belgium and nearly all of France had been cleared of the enemy. By the second week of November the German army was in danger of destruction.

The armistice, November 11, 1918.

To save Germany from invasion, the German high command asked for an immediate armistice based on Wilson's Fourteen Points (see p. 615). The armistice terms were set by Allied military leaders. They required Germany to give up occupied territory, prisoners of war, a great quantity of guns, tanks, freight cars, locomotives and trucks, all of her submarines, and nearly all of her fleet. Acceptance of these terms would amount to unconditional surrender. When the Kaiser's government received them on November 7, it protested that they were too harsh. However, Germany's allies had already surrendered. Revolution spread across Germany. On November 9 the Kaiser abdicated and fled to Holland. The new German republic then signed the armistice. On November 11, at eleven in the morning, firing ceased.

What did the war cost?

Both the human costs and the money costs of World War I were far greater than in any previous war. A total of 65 million men bore arms—a figure without precedent in history. The ratio of dead and wounded to the total number of men engaged was also the highest in history. In addition, there were millions of civilian deaths caused by hunger, cold, massacre, and revolution. Ten million families were driven from their homes, many never to return.

Compared to the loss of life in those countries which bore the brunt of the fighting for four years, our loss was not great. We had 112,000 soldier dead, of whom 50,000 died in battle or from wounds. Some 230,000 Americans were wounded, but nearly five sixths were restored to duty again.

The human cost of the war cannot be considered entirely apart from the material costs. For all the belligerents, the total direct cost of the war—that is, for war supplies and equipment and other military expenses—came to 186 billion dollars. Indirect costs—including property losses, the value of lives lost figured at the nominal sum of $2500 each, and loss of production due to the absence of workers in the armed services—came to nearly as much more. War costs left many countries so impoverished that they did not recover.

VOL. LXVIII. NO. 22,304   NEW YORK, MONDAY, NOVEMBER 11, 1918. TWENTY-FOUR PAGES.   TWO CENTS

ARMISTICE SIGNED, END OF THE WAR! BERLIN SEIZED BY REVOLUTIONISTS; NEW CHANCELLOR BEGS FOR ORDER; OUSTED KAISER FLEES TO HOLLAND

FOR IDENTIFICATION

Algeciras Conference
Allied Powers
Central Powers
General Ferdinand Foch
Herbert Hoover
Edward M. House
William G. McAdoo
Permanent Court of Arbitration
General John J. Pershing

FOR EXPLANATION OR DEFINITION

Armistice
Committee on Public Information
Emergency Fleet Corporation
Food Administration
Fuel Administration
imperialism
militarism
nationalism
Railroad Administration
Sussex pledge
"total war"
War Industries Board
Zimmerman note

FOR REVIEW

1. (a) What was the purpose of the first Hague Peace Conference (1899)? What did it accomplish? (b) What was accomplished by the second Hague Peace Conference?

2. How did Theodore Roosevelt promote the cause of world peace?

3. (a) Explain *arbitration* and *conciliation*. (b) What was the purpose of the Root treaties of arbitration? The Bryan treaties of conciliation? (c) What were the main differences between them?

4. How did imperialism promote tension among the European powers?

5. How did nationalism influence the foreign policy of the European powers?

6. Who were the members of the Triple Alliance? Who were the members of the Triple Entente?

7. (a) What started the chain of events that led to the outbreak of World War I?

612

(b) Why did Germany declare war on France? (c) What action of Germany precipitated England's entry into the war?

8. (a) Why, in spite of Wilson's proclamation of neutrality, did many Americans sympathize with England, France, and Russia? (b) Why did some Americans sympathize with the Central Powers? (c) Why was Allied propaganda more successful than that of the Central Powers?

9. How did England interfere with the rights of neutrals? How did Germany?

10. (a) Why did the sinking of the *Lusitania* precipitate a crisis in our relations with Germany? (b) What action did Germany take in response to Wilson's protests?

11. What preparedness measures did we adopt in 1916?

12. (a) What steps did Wilson take to settle the war by negotiation? (b) Explain what Wilson meant by urging a "peace without victory."

13. (a) Why did Germany decide to resume "ruthless submarine warfare" early in 1917? (b) What action did Wilson take?

14. What was the Zimmerman note?

15. (a) State some of the reasons the United States went to war with Germany. (b) Show that Wilson regarded America's participation in the war as a crusade or mission in a "war to end war."

16. (a) Why did the United States decide to send an army overseas? (b) What difficulties did we overcome to send the needed millions of soldiers to Europe?

17. Describe the Selective Service Act of 1917. What mistakes made in 1863 did it avoid?

18. (a) Explain Wilson's statement, "It is not an army we must shape and train for war—it is a nation." (b) Describe the work of the Emergency Fleet Corporation, the War Industries Board, the Fuel Administration, the Railroad Administration. (c) How did the United States manage to double its food exports to Europe after we entered the war? Explain the slogan, "Food will win the war."

19. How did the United States obtain money to finance the war?

20. How did George Creel and his Committee on Public Information mobilize public opinion?

21. Explain the Espionage Act of 1917 and the Sedition Act of 1918.

22. What part did the navy play in World War I?

23. Why did General Pershing plan not to attempt large-scale operations in France for 1918? What caused him to alter his plans? How did the United States respond?

24. (a) When did General Foch order the Allied offensive? (b) Describe the achievements of American forces at Saint Mihiel, the Argonne, and Sedan.

25. What forced Germany to agree to an armistice? Outline the armistice terms.

26. (a) Discuss the relative cost of World War I to the various belligerents—in lives, money, and property. (b) What are some of the hidden or indeterminable costs of modern war?

FOR FURTHER STUDY AND DISCUSSION

1. Distinguish between the fundamental and immediate causes of World War I. Helpful sources: Slosson, *The Great Crusade and After, 1919–1928*, pp. 1–31; Dulles, *America's Rise to World Power*, pp. 87–107; Link, *American Epoch*.

2. (a) Why did the United States find it difficult to maintain neutrality? (b) Criticize or defend Wilson's policies toward England and Germany. (c) Should the United States have gone to war with Germany after the sinking of the *Lusitania?* Helpful sources: Bailey, *Diplomatic History*, pp. 610–646; Bemis, *Diplomatic History*, pp. 590–616; Commager, *Documents*, Nos. 400, 405, 408, 409.

3. Compare the type of propaganda used to influence American opinion, 1914–18, with the type of propaganda used in the period 1937–41. Helpful sources: Bailey, *Diplomatic History*, pp. 740–776; Bemis, *Diplomatic History*, pp. 844–862.

4. Why were the Espionage Act (1917) and the Sedition Act (1918) passed? Were they necessary? Compare the acts and the reaction to them with the Alien and Sedition Acts of 1798.

1. Report on the use of each of the following in World War I: trench warfare, the airplane, the submarine, poison gas, camouflage, the tank, the long-range gun. Helpful sources: Hart, *Contemporaries*, Vol. V, pp. 719–808; Commager and Nevins, *Heritage of America*, Nos. 240, 241, 242.

2. Have a small committee select and arrange for dramatic reading and subsequent class discussion selections from Wilson's speeches. (Include his address to Congress, asking for a declaration of war.) Helpful source: Commager, *Documents*, Nos. 389, 400, 409, 416, 418, 423, 429.

3. Prepare a brief in defense or criticism of the theory that the chief reason for American entrance into World War I was to safeguard American loans to the Allies.

4. Collect and exhibit important poems and popular songs of World War I.

5. Arrange for an exhibit of cartoons, pictures, and posters on World War I.

At Belleau Wood, where the first United States offensive of the war was made. Only white crosses remain—symbols of the cost of war.

I can predict with absolute certainty that within another
generation there will be another world war if the nations of the world do not concert the method to prevent
it.——Woodrow Wilson

37. THE UNITED STATES REFUSES WORLD LEADERSHIP

The World Looks to Wilson for a Just and Lasting Peace

Wilson outlines his peace program.

Entrance into World War I gave the United States a position of leadership in world affairs. President Wilson wanted to use our influence (1) to promote democracy in Europe, and (2) to establish an association, or league, of nations to keep the peace. Just as communities have courts to settle disputes between individuals and to punish lawbreakers, he thought that nations should band together to have a world court and to see that quarrels between nations were settled justly and peaceably. In this way the nations could create a system of *collective security* in which even the smallest would be safe from attack.

The President made it plain that the United States had no selfish war aims. It desired no territory or war damages. It was not seeking revenge. It did not want to crush Germany, but only to destroy the undemocratic German government. "We have no quarrel," Wilson said, "with the German people." We were fighting, he repeated again and again, for a world order of peace and justice.

Wilson hoped to persuade the Allied leaders to accept the same war aims as the United States. Early in 1918 he outlined his program for a peace without revenge. There were fourteen points.

To abolish the causes of modern war, the first five points called for:

1. Open instead of secret diplomacy
2. Freedom of the seas in peace and war
3. The removal of barriers to world trade and the establishment of equal opportunities for trade among all nations
4. Reduction of armaments to the "lowest point consistent with domestic safety"
5. An impartial adjustment of colonial claims, with consideration for the needs of the native peoples

Eight points were intended to assure self-determination for the peoples of Europe:

6. Evacuation of Russia by German troops and the right of the Russians to determine their country's political development
7. Restoration of Belgium
8. Return of Alsace-Lorraine to France

9. Adjustment of Italian boundaries
10. Freedom for the minority peoples of Austria-Hungary
11. Restoration of Rumania, Serbia, and Montenegro
12. Freedom for minority peoples in the Turkish Empire
13. Poland to be an independent state

The last point was the one that Wilson thought most important:

14. A general association of nations, or world league, to enforce peace

Men had talked for centuries of an organization of nations to prevent war. Early in the war leading Americans of both parties formed an organization to work for a League of Nations to Enforce Peace. Former President William H. Taft became its head. Wilson made this project the keystone of his peace program.

"Words are weapons."

George Creel used Wilson's peace program as a weapon against the enemy. He showered Germany and Austria-Hungary with leaflets containing the Fourteen Points. A great many of the enemy were stirred by these leaflets. Peace on Wilson's terms looked so attractive that they began to wonder why they should go on fighting. In October, 1918, the government of Austria-Hungary crumbled. The unhappy minorities under its rule refused to fight for it any longer. Soon after, the Germans asked for peace based on the Fourteen Points.

The Fourteen Points were studied not only in the enemy countries but throughout the world. To millions of war-weary people they brought new hope—hope that a day was at hand in which the nations would live together in peace and justice. Wilson began to be thought of as a kind of world savior. In southern and eastern Europe the peasants put up pictures of Wilson beside images of the saints.

The Allies accept the Fourteen Points.

In the armistice agreement with Germany, the Allies promised to make a peace treaty based on the Fourteen Points. However, Great Britain refused to accept freedom of the seas in time of war. The Allies also insisted on a point of their own—that Germany should pay for the damage done by her armed forces to civilians and their property. With these very general ideas on how the peace treaty would be written, the war came to an end.

Wilson Takes Part in the Peace Conference

Importance of the conference.

The Peace Conference was called to meet in Paris on January 18, 1919. Delegates from thirty-two countries would be there but none from the Central Powers. The peace settlement therefore would not be "a peace of equals" but "a victor's terms imposed upon the vanquished." In their anxiety to prevent future aggression, some delegates wished to crush Germany so that it might never rise again.

The questions facing the Peace Conference were many and difficult. Border fights were still going on in eastern Europe. There was famine in the defeated countries, and communism was spreading among their people. Order must be restored with all possible speed. The boundaries of the new republics in eastern Europe must be fixed. The amount to be paid by Germany for war damages must also be considered. On the solutions found for these problems depended the future peace of the world.

Although no previous President had ever left American soil [1] during his term of office, Wilson announced

---

[1] President Theodore Roosevelt visited Panama "to see the dirt fly" while the canal was being dug.

that he would go to Paris. He believed that the American peace program would not be carried out unless the United States exerted all its influence. Since no American could speak with the authority of the President, Wilson thought he must take part in the conference in person. He told Congress (December 2, 1918):

The peace settlements which are now to be agreed upon are of transcendent importance both to us and to the rest of the world, and I know of no business or interest which should take precedence over them.

Wilson loses the support of Congress.

Wilson went to the Peace Conference under a serious handicap—the political tide at home had turned against him. Shortly before the midterm election the President had asked the people to elect a Democratic Congress, that he might "continue to be your unembarrassed spokesman in affairs at home and abroad." In spite of his plea, the Republicans had won control of both houses of Congress.

The election gave evidence of a postwar reaction. With victory at hand, Americans were losing interest in world problems. Isolationism was emerging. There were demands for ending wartime control of the economy, for lowering taxes, and for raising the tariff. In addition, conservatives hoped to reverse Wilson's domestic reforms. Taken together, these attitudes led to the Republican victory at the polls.

Without question, the 1918 election results made Wilson's task at the Peace Conference more difficult. The *New York Tribune* declared: "The President goes abroad a rebuked and discredited leader in his own nation." Theodore Roosevelt said that "our allies and our enemies" should know that the President had "no authority whatever to speak for the American people at this time."

Wilson's choice of peace commissioners did not please Republican leaders. Henry Cabot Lodge, a Republican and a bitter foe of the President, was the incoming chairman of the Foreign Relations Committee. Rather than have Mr. Lodge on the peace commission, the President did not include any senator. This omission might have been less disastrous had the commission included some other prominent Republicans.

(Left to right) SENATORS BORAH, LODGE, AND SMOOT, *the leaders of the fight against the League*

Yet Wilson chose only one Republican —Henry M. White, a former ambassador to Italy and France. White was an able man but without much political influence. The other delegates were Secretary of State Robert Lansing, General Tasker H. Bliss, and Wilson's "roving ambassador," Colonel Edward M. House.

Wilson is honored in Europe.

Although the President left for Paris in a storm of criticism from Republican newspapers, he received a wonderful welcome in Europe. He was the guest of honor at great celebrations in France, England, and Italy. Crowds cheered him wherever he went.

Wilson was deeply touched by the faith shown in him by the people of Europe. Yet he knew they expected too much. On the way to the Peace Conference he said to George Creel:

I am wondering if you have not unconsciously spun a net for me. It is to America that the whole world turns, not only with its wrongs but with its hopes and grievances. . . . Yet these ancient wrongs, these present unhappinesses, are not to be remedied in a day or with a wave of the hand. What I seem to see—I hope I am wrong—is a tragedy of disappointment.

Many compromises are necessary.

The seventy delegates to the Peace Conference divided into a number of committees. Each committee drew up recommendations for dealing with certain problems. The recommendations were then studied in secret sessions by the Big Four—President Wilson; Lloyd George, the British prime minister; Clemenceau, the premier of France; and Orlando, premier of Italy. The decisions of these four men formed the basis of the peace treaties.

Each member of the Big Four had to make compromises. Both Clemenceau and Lloyd George demanded that Germany be made powerless to start another war and that it be forced to pay heavy reparations. Wilson had to meet them part way in order to get their support for the League of Nations. The resulting peace terms for Germany were more severe than he wished. Nevertheless, he stood firm on many issues. He blocked a French plan to detach the Rhineland from Germany and to take permanent title to the Saar Basin. Although the Allies had promised Fiume to Italy in return for entering the war on their side, Wilson refused to consent. He kept Poland from getting all of East Prussia. He prevented Japan from securing permanent control of China's Shantung province, which Japan had seized from Germany.

The peace treaties.

A separate treaty was written for each of the Central Powers. The treaty with Germany was signed at Versailles. It declared Germany guilty of starting the war, forced her to disarm, stripped her of overseas colonies, and required her to pay reparations to the limit of her ability. The Saar Basin with its rich mines of coal was turned over to France for fifteen years, to make up for the destruction of French coal mines. Germany's Polish provinces went to the new Republic of Poland. Alsace-Lorraine was restored to France. Germany was ordered to surrender most of her navy; however, the surrender was not carried out because the crews sank the ships. The Germans protested that the treaty was unjust, but they had to sign. Actually, its terms were far less harsh than those Germany had imposed on Russia and Rumania in 1917.

Three important features of Wilson's peace program were placed in the peace treaties. These features were:

1. The principle of self-determination. In drawing the boundaries of the new republics in eastern Europe (Austria, Hungary, Czechoslovakia, Poland, Lithuania, Latvia, Estonia, and Finland), the Peace Conference tried to unite the people of a single nationality. The boundaries of several other countries—Yugoslavia (formerly Serbia), Greece, Rumania, Italy, Belgium, and Denmark—were enlarged to include land belonging to them earlier and inhabited by their people. Germany complained because some people of German blood were placed under the rule of Poland and Czechoslovakia. A perfect adjustment of boundaries was of course not possible.

2. Mandates, or trusteeships, under the League of Nations for all former German and Turkish colonies. The Permanent Mandates Commission supervised these mandates and tried to protect their people from exploitation.

The nation holding a mandate was supposed to teach the people living there to govern themselves. The former Turkish possessions—Palestine, Jordan, Iraq, Syria, and Lebanon—became independent after only a few years as mandates.

3. The covenant, or constitution, of the League of Nations, which was attached to the Versailles Treaty. Wilson thought the League would have power to correct any injustices or mistakes contained in the peace treaties. He hoped it would carry out those portions of the Fourteen Points, such as disarmament and the removal of trade barriers, which the Peace Conference had not provided for.

Before we can understand the fight that developed as to whether our country would join the League of Nations, we need to know something about the organization.

The League of Nations Is Founded

A design for collective security.

The purposes of the League were: (1) to enforce the peace treaties made at Paris, (2) to promote international co-operation, (3) to remove the causes of war, and (4) to prevent aggression. Membership was open to all self-governing nations. When the League began its work in 1920, it had 24 members. At the peak it had 62.

The League had three organs. (1) The Assembly, in which all members had an equal voice. It had the right to take up any matter concerning the peace of the world and to make recommendations to its members. On most questions the Assembly could decide

EUROPE IN 1919

nothing without a unanimous vote. (2) The Council, which acted as an executive committee for the Assembly. The covenant originally provided for five permanent members (France, Great Britain, Italy, Japan, and the United States) and four nonpermanent members chosen by the Assembly. (3) The Secretariat, or working force of officials and clerks, located at Geneva. One of the League's first tasks was to establish the Permanent Court of Justice, commonly known as the World Court. Although essential to the League's work, the World Court was designed to be entirely separate from its parent.

The League offered a system of collective security. Each member pledged itself not to interfere with the territory and independence of the other members and also *to defend them from attack*. This promise was contained in Article X of the covenant, which Wilson called the "heart of the League." Members also promised to place major disputes with other nations before the Council, the World Court, or a board of arbitration. In case one of the parties in a dispute should refuse to settle it peaceably and should go to war, it was to be considered an *aggressor*. Under Article XVI the members of the League were pledged to apply sanctions, or penalties, against an aggressor when asked to do so by the Council. The Council might, for example, ask all members of the League not to trade with the aggressor. If this failed to stop the fight, the Council might ask the members to use their armed forces. If members really lived up to their obligations under Articles X and XVI, any aggressor could be stopped.

It was obvious that in case a great power should attack another nation, the plan for collective security would be severely tried. Would the other great powers unite against the aggressor? The test came in 1931 when Japan invaded Manchuria, and again in 1936 when Italy attacked Ethiopia. In both cases the members of the Council shrank from taking any action that might involve them in war, even on a small scale. Had the United States been a member, and had it used its great influence to support Articles X and XVI, the story might have been different.

The League of Nations carries on.

Events proved that the main defect of the League was weakness. It settled a number of serious disputes among small nations, but could not force major powers to keep the peace. Yet until a new world war broke out, it accomplished a great deal of useful work.

Economic, as well as political, matters came to the attention of the League. It helped the nations to rebuild their economies after the war. Later it tried to check the depression of the 1930's. At times it gave assistance to small countries in economic difficulties. Through its affiliate, the International Labor Organization, the League sought better conditions for workingmen everywhere. Among the concerns of the I. L. O. were the security and health of workers, the length of the working day, and the question of child labor.

The League was noted for its humanitarian efforts in other fields too. Like the present-day World Health Organization, the League worked for the improvement of health all over the world. It promoted medical research, improved the training of public health workers, and organized international efforts to control epidemics. Members of the League agreed to limit the trade in harmful drugs.

The League tried to help groups of people who were downtrodden. It called for fair treatment of minorities. It aided millions of refugees to get a fresh start in life. Its Permanent Mandates Commission had the task of protecting natives in the former German and Turkish colonies. The League also took steps to check the slave trade and the use of forced labor.

The League held an endless chain of conferences on matters of international concern. It gathered information and published reports that were of value to leaders in many countries, including our own. Through the League the nations of the world gained experience in working together on some of their common problems. This experience proved the value of an international organization and led in time to the creation of a stronger one, the United Nations.

The Senate Rejects the Treaty and the League

The League had widespread support.

When President Wilson returned to the United States in July, 1919, he laid the Treaty of Versailles, including the League covenant, before the Senate. At that time a majority of the American people seem to have favored signing the treaty and thereby joining the League. Thirty-two state legislatures had gone on record in favor of it. Influential groups, such as the American Bar Association, the American Bankers' Association, and the Federal Council of Churches, endorsed it. A poll of newspaper editors showed that most of them believed we should join. In the Senate a majority was ready at that time to vote for the treaty and the League. A few senators, however, were against the League in any form; others wished to make changes in the covenant.

Lodge fights the League.

Senator Lodge, chairman of the Senate Committee on Foreign Relations, disliked Wilson. While Lodge had at one time supported the idea of a league to prevent war, he rejected the league designed at Paris. He made up his mind to take out of the covenant the very parts which Wilson thought most important. His committee proposed forty-five amendments or reservations. Most of them had to do with Articles X and XVI. After a long and angry fight, the Senate approved fourteen amendments known as the "Lodge reservations."

Wilson believed that the proposed changes would make the League helpless to prevent war. In September, against the advice of physicians, he went on a nationwide tour to explain the covenant to the people. Wilson knew the risk he was taking and said he would gladly give his life to save the League. After making nearly forty speeches, he collapsed (September 25, 1919). For the rest of his term he lay helpless in the White House, watching his enemies win the fight against the League.

The treaty is defeated.

In November, a few weeks after the President fell ill, the Senate was ready to vote on the treaty with the attached Lodge reservations. Wilson asked his supporters to vote "no." Accordingly, the treaty was voted down. An effort to have it ratified with mild reservations that were acceptable to the President also failed. Some blamed the result on Wilson's unwillingness to compromise. Some placed the blame on Senator Lodge, Theodore Roosevelt, and other Republican leaders who wanted to discredit the President.

In explaining the defeat of the treaty we must take account of several factors. Partisan politics and the feud between Lodge and Wilson are only part of the story. There was also pressure from German-Americans (who thought the treaty unjust to Germany), from Italian-Americans (who were angry over Fiume), and from Irish-Americans (who hated Great Britain). The Irish-Americans and others objected to the League because they thought Great Britain would have more influence in it than the United States. (Each British dominion had a vote in the Assembly.) Even more important was the fear that the League would involve us in the Old World's wars. Many thought it much safer to return to our traditional policy of nonentanglement with European affairs.

The election of 1920.

Wilson declared that the presidential election of 1920 would be a "great and solemn referendum" upon the League. The Democratic candidate for President, Governor James M. Cox of Ohio, and his running mate, Franklin D. Roosevelt, tried to make the League the central issue of the campaign. The Republican candidate, Senator Warren Harding of Ohio, did not take a clear-cut stand. He had voted against the League in the Senate, but now said vaguely that he favored an association of nations to keep the peace. On election day a landslide swept Harding into office. The popular vote was 16 million for Harding and 9 million for Cox.

The election of 1920 cannot be considered a vote on the League. The Republican victory was due to many causes, some of them going back to the beginning of Wilson's presidency, when he attacked big business. If the election meant anything, it meant that the voters were tired of Democratic rule and Wilsonian idealism. They wanted a change. Harding had sensed their mood when he said during the campaign:

America's present need is not heroics, but healing; not nostrums, but normalcy; not revolution, but restoration; not surgery, but serenity.

We return to isolationism.

The fight over the League was between two groups of Americans—the *internationalists,* who thought the United States should use its influence to establish a system of collective security, and the *nationalists,* or *isolationists,* who thought we could safely turn our backs on world affairs. The 1920 election convinced Harding that the isolationists spoke for the people. As President he had nothing to do with the League of Nations and did his best to isolate the United States from the rest of the world, especially from Europe.

Wilson warned the people that they had rejected

. . . fruitful leadership for a barren independence. They will now have to learn by bitter experience what they have lost. We had a chance to gain the leadership of the world. We have lost it and soon we shall be witnessing the tragedy of it all.

Twenty years later, when a second war, even greater than the first, raged over the world, men recalled Wilson's forecast. They wondered whether American leadership, exercised in the Council of the League of Nations, might have prevented the conflict.

League of Nations, Geneva, Switzerland

FOR IDENTIFICATION

Georges Clemenceau	David Lloyd George
James M. Cox	Henry Cabot Lodge
Fiume	Emanuele Orlando
Fourteen Points	Versailles Treaty
Warren G. Harding	World Court
International Labor Organization	

FOR EXPLANATION OR DEFINITION

aggressor	reparations
Big Four	reservations
collective security	sanctions
mandates	secretariat
normalcy	self-determination

1. What two great objectives did Wilson have in mind in planning his peace program?

2. (a) Name five measures included in Wilson's Fourteen Points intended to eliminate the causes of war. (b) Name eight specific measures to carry out the principle of "self-determination."

3. How did Wilson's Fourteen Points influence the people in enemy lands?

4. (a) Why did Wilson decide to attend the Peace Conference? (b) What did critics say about his decision? About his appointments to the Peace Commission?

5. How did the congressional elections of 1918 affect Wilson's leadership?

6. (a) How did the Peace Conference carry on its work? (b) What compromises did Wilson make? Why?

7. (a) State the chief terms of the Treaty of Versailles applying to Germany. (b) What principle was followed in adjusting boundaries in eastern Europe? (c) What new republics were created? (d) What was done with former German and Turkish colonies?

8. (a) What were the purposes of the League of Nations? (b) How was the League governed? (c) State the provisions of Article X and Article XVI of the League covenant. (d) Why did Wilson regard Article X as the "heart of the League"?

9. What important tests did the League face in 1931 and again in 1936?

10. Summarize the accomplishments of the League.

11. How did Senator Lodge undertake to prevent ratification of the League?

12. (a) Describe Wilson's speaking tour in behalf of the League, 1919. (b) Summarize the reasons for the defeat of the treaty in the Senate.

13. Who were the candidates and what were the issues in the presidential campaign of 1920?

14. Did Republican victory in 1920 mark a reversal in that party's attitude on the subject of isolation?

1. Was the presidential campaign of 1920 a "great and solemn referendum on the League"? Explain your answer.

2. Bismarck said, "Public opinion is the great enemy of efficient diplomacy." Wilson advocated "open covenants openly arrived at." Which concept of diplomacy do you favor? Why?

3. What were the implications of Wilson's appeal to the people to elect a Democratic Congress in 1918?

4. Why was the covenant of the League of Nations linked with the terms of the peace settlement? Was this a wise policy?

5. How may World War I be said to have marked the close of one era and the beginning of another?

6. Should the Vice-President assume the powers of the Presidency when the President is incapacitated as Wilson was in 1919–20? Who has the power to decide whether the President is capable of acting as President?

1. On an outline map of Europe indicate the territorial changes that resulted from World War I.

2. Prepare a radio broadcast describing Wilson's tumultuous welcome in Europe.

3. Dramatize a private meeting of the Big Four on a controversial issue at the Peace Conference.

4. Report on the Senate fight over the ratification of the Treaty of Versailles. On what terms might Wilson have secured ratification? Debate the question whether Lodge or Wilson was ultimately responsible for the rejection of the Treaty of Versailles. Helpful sources: Hofstadter, *American Political Tradition*, pp. 272–282; Hart, *Contemporaries*, Vol. V, Nos. 129–132, 191–193, 201–204; Sullivan, *Our Times*, Vol. V; Bailey, *Diplomatic History*, pp. 667–680; Bemis, *Diplomatic History*, pp. 643–670; Lodge, *The Senate and the League of Nations.*

5. Hold a panel discussion on the topic: "America's spurning of the League was tragically shortsighted."

623

HIGH POINTS

1

The Spanish-American War (1898) marks a turning point in our foreign relations. From that time the United States took an increasingly active part on the world stage. Americans saw that their country had become a great power with world-wide influence.

2

Before 1898 the United States had no overseas possessions except for some fifty tiny islands in the Pacific, which were used for harbors and coaling stations. The war with Spain brought us possession of Puerto Rico and the distant Philippines. The war also convinced Congress that we should annex the Hawaiian Islands. Thus the nation suddenly had to face the problems involved in ruling and defending colonies. For a time there was sharp debate over whether we ought to hold colonies at all. It soon became American policy to prepare our possessions for self-government.

3

In 1900, to prevent the dismemberment of China and to protect our right to trade there, the United States proclaimed the Open Door policy. From that time on we used our influence to preserve the independence of China. We let Japan know that we disapproved of the twenty-one demands (1915), which would have given it virtual control of China. As a result Japan backed down.

4

The Russo-Japanese War (1904–05) left Japan the strongest power in the Far East. From that time, our relations with Japan became less friendly. Japan resented our efforts to keep it from dominating China. Japan was offended also by laws passed in certain of our states that discriminated against Japanese immigrants.

5

Construction of the Panama Canal added to America's responsibilities as a world power. Protection of the canal became one of the leading aims of our foreign policy.

6

Since the First International Conference of American States in 1889, our government has tried to promote co-operation between all the republics of the Western Hemisphere. For a long time, however, Latin Americans were suspicious of the United States. During the first third of this century our interference in the affairs of several Caribbean countries, especially Theodore Roosevelt's treatment of Colombia, aroused resentment. In recent years, under the Good Neighbor policy, our relations with Latin America have greatly improved.

7

The United States took an active part in the world peace movement before World War I. Under Theodore Roosevelt, Taft, and Wilson, we made arbitration and conciliation treaties with many governments. The treaties pledged that the signatory nations would submit certain kinds of disputes to the Hague Court or to an international commission for peaceful settlement.

8

World War I broke out in 1914. Shortly, most of the European nations were drawn in on the side of either the Central Powers or the Allies. President Wilson tried to keep this country neutral. Violations of American neutral rights by Germany, particularly in submarine warfare, brought the United States to declare war (April 6,

1917). Even without these provocations we might have gone to war eventually, in order to save Britain and France from defeat. The Allies probably would have lost after Russia withdrew from the war, had we not thrown our strength against the Central Powers.

9

During the first World War the federal government took control of the nation to an extent few Americans had ever imagined possible. Man power, industries, and even the opinions of the people were mobilized. Freedom of expression was severely curbed; hundreds of dissenters were sent to prison. Although controls were relaxed after the war, some people thought that the damage to our traditional freedoms was permanent.

10

President Wilson hoped to use the influence of the United States to extend democracy in Europe and to establish a system of collective security. His statement of war aims—the famous Fourteen Points—helped to shorten the war. In order that these aims might be carried out in the peace settlement, Wilson went in person to the Peace Conference at Versailles. Although he had to make compromises, he succeeded in writing many of his ideas into the peace treaties.

11

The treaty with Germany, known as the Versailles Treaty, included the covenant of the League of Nations. For a time it appeared that the majority of Americans favored joining the League, but bitter partisan attacks turned public opinion against it. The Senate refused to approve the covenant without a long list of amendments, some of which Wilson felt would cripple the new organization. He advised his supporters to vote against these amendments.

Consequently the United States did not ratify the Versailles Treaty and remained outside the League of Nations.

QUESTIONS

1. (a) How did our absorption in the conquest of a continent during the nineteenth century influence our foreign policy? (b) When and how did the United States acquire Alaska, Samoa, and Hawaii? (c) Why did economic and industrial development in the last decades of the nineteenth century cause Americans to become interested in overseas trade and possessions?

2. (a) How did humanitarian and economic interests combine to influence both the cause and results of the war with Spain? (b) Explain how, in a war with Spain over Cuba, the United States acquired possession of the Philippines. (c) What were the indirect results of the war with Spain?

3. (a) What political and constitutional problems resulted from the acquisition of an overseas empire? (b) Has the United States solved "the problem of empire" in Alaska, Hawaii, Puerto Rico, the Philippines, and elsewhere?

4. (a) What were the reasons for Hay's formulation of the "Open Door" policy toward China? (b) Why did the powers approve the Open Door policy in principle, but disregard it in action? (c) What part did Theodore Roosevelt play in the Russo-Japanese War of 1904–05? (d) How did the Root-Takahira agreement of 1908 tend to ease the growing tension with Japan? (e) Why, in spite of this agreement, did tension continue to develop between the United States and Japan?

625

5. (a) Outline the steps by which the United States acquired the right to build a canal through Panama. (b) Describe the problems that had to be overcome in building the Panama Canal. (c) How did the construction of the canal add to our responsibilities as a world power?

6. What guiding principles have controlled American policy toward the Caribbean?

7. What was the "Platt amendment"? When and why was it abrogated?

8. (a) What was the "Roosevelt corollary" to the Monroe Doctrine? (b) What was the "Drago Doctrine"? (c) What is "dollar diplomacy"? (d) Explain the circumstances under which the United States intervened in Santo Domingo, Nicaragua, Haiti, and Mexico. (e) How did these actions affect our relations with South American countries?

9. (a) Outline the immediate and the fundamental causes for the outbreak of war in Europe in 1914. (b) What problems did the United States face as a neutral? (c) How did the United States deal with these problems? (d) Was World War I a war to make the "world safe for democracy"?

10. (a) What steps were taken to mobilize men, resources, and opinion during World War I? (b) How did President Wilson give purpose and direction to the war and to the peace that followed the war?

11. (a) Summarize Wilson's "Fourteen Points." How did they influence the armistice and the peace treaties? (b) What factors help to explain Wilson's failure to secure a "just peace"?

12. (a) Describe the organization of the League of Nations. (b) How did the League hope to achieve international peace and security? (c) Describe Wilson's efforts to secure Senate ratification of the Versailles Treaty. (d) Why did the United States fail to join the League of Nations? The World Court? (e) Why did the League fail to live up to the high hopes of its friends? (f) What aspects of the work of the League have been taken over and continued by the United Nations?

SUGGESTED READINGS

SOURCE MATERIALS, DOCUMENTS, AND MAPS

Adams, *Album*.

Amherst Series: *American Imperialism in 1898.*

Bartlett, R. J. (ed.). *The Record of American Diplomacy: Documents and Readings in the History of American Foreign Relations.* 3rd .ed. Knopf, 1954.

Commager, *Documents*.

° Commager and Nevins, *Heritage of America*.

Davidson, M. B. *Life in America.* Houghton Mifflin, 1951.

Hacker, Louis M., and Zahler, H. S. (eds.). *The Shaping of the American Tradition.* Columbia University Press, 1947.

Hart, *Contemporaries*.

Lord, *Historical Atlas*.

Plischke, Elmer (ed.). *International Relations: Basic Documents.* Van Nostrand, 1953.

GENERAL REFERENCES

Bailey, Thomas A. *Diplomatic History.*

————. *Woodrow Wilson and the Peacemakers.* 2 vols. Macmillan, 1947.

Beard, *American Civilization*, Vol. II.

Bemis, Samuel Flagg. *Diplomatic History.*

————. *Latin American Policy of the United States.* Harcourt, Brace, 1943.

Brebner, John B. *The North Atlantic Triangle; The Interplay of Canada, the United States, and Great Britain.* Yale University Press, 1945.

° Considine, Robert B. *The Panama Canal.* Random House, 1951.

Dulles, Foster R. *America's Rise to World Power, 1898–1954.* Harper, 1955. (N.A.N.)

° Dunne, Finley Peter. *Mr. Dooley at His Best.* Scribner, 1938.

Falk, Edwin A. *From Perry to Pearl Harbor.* Doubleday, 1943.

Faulkner, *Economic History*.

° Fish, Carl R. *The Path of Empire.* Yale University Press, 1919. (Y.C.S.)

Fleming, Denna F. *The United States and the League of Nations.* Putnam, 1932.

Griswold, A. Whitney. *The Far Eastern Policy of the United States.* Harcourt, Brace, 1938.

Kennan, George F. *American Diplomacy, 1900–1950.* University of Chicago Press, 1952.

° Latané, John H. *America as a World Power, 1897–1907.* Harper, 1907. (A.N.S.)

Link, Arthur S. *American Epoch.*

———. *Woodrow Wilson and the Progressive Era, 1910–1917.* Harper, 1954.

Millis, Walter. *The Martial Spirit: A Study of Our War with Spain.* Houghton, 1937.

———. *The Road to War: America, 1914–1917.* Little, Brown, 1935.

Morison and Commager, *American Republic*, Vol. II.

Munro, Dana G. *The United States and the Caribbean Area.* World Peace Foundation, 1934.

Paxson, Frederic L. *American Democracy and the World War.* 3 vols. Houghton, 1936–1948.

Perkins, Dexter. *Hands Off: A History of the Monroe Doctrine.* Little, Brown, 1941.

Pratt, Julius W. *American Colonial Experiment.* Prentice-Hall, 1950.

° Seymour, Charles. *American Diplomacy during the World War.* Johns Hopkins Press, 1934.

———. *American Neutrality, 1914–1917.* Yale University Press, 1935.

———. *Woodrow Wilson and the World War.* Yale University Press, 1931. (Y.C.S.)

Slosson, P. W. *The Great Crusade and After, 1914–1928.* Macmillan, 1930.

Sprout, Harold, and Sprout, Margaret. *The Rise of American Naval Power, 1776–1918.* Princeton University Press, 1946.

Stallings, Laurence. *The World War in Uncensored Photographs.* Garden City, 1934.

Stimson, Henry L., and Bundy, McGeorge. *On Active Service in Peace and War.* Harper, 1948.

Sullivan, Mark. *Our Times.* 6 vols. Scribner, 1926–1935.

Tansill, Charles C. *America Goes to War.* Little, Brown, 1938.

Wood, William, and Gabriel, Ralph H. *In Defense of Liberty.* Yale University Press, 1928. (Pageant)

BIOGRAPHY

Bishop, Joseph B., and Bishop, Farnham. *Goethals, Genius of the Panama Canal.* Harper, 1930.

Dennett, Tyler. *John Hay: From Poetry to Politics.* Dodd, Mead, 1933.

Dodd, William E. *Woodrow Wilson and His Work.* 4th ed. rev. Doubleday, 1920.

Garraty, J. A. *Henry Cabot Lodge.* Knopf, 1953.

Gibson, John M. *Physician to the World; The Life of General William C. Gorgas.* Duke University Press, 1950.

° Gorgas, Marie D., and Hendrick, B. J. *William Crawford Gorgas, His Life and Work.* Doubleday, 1924.

Jessup, Philip. *Elihu Root.* Dodd, Mead, 1938.

° Judson, Clara. *Soldier Doctor.* Scribner, 1942.

Simonds, Frank H. *They Won the War.* Harper, 1931.

° West, Richard S. *Admirals of the American Empire.* Bobbs-Merrill, 1948.

FICTION

° Abbott, Willis J. *Blue Jackets of 1918.* Dodd, Mead, 1921.

Cather, Willa. *One of Ours.* Knopf, 1922. (A Nebraska youth in the war)

° Driggs, L. L. *The Adventures of Arnold Adair, American Ace.* Little, Brown, 1918. (An American in the French Flying Corps)

° Ellsberg, Edward. *Pigboats.* Dodd, Mead, 1931. (Submarines)

Gerould, G. H. *Filibuster.* Appleton, 1924. (War in Canada)

° Haines, Donal H. *The Dragon-Flies.* Houghton Mifflin, 1919. (Aviation)

° Nordhoff, Charles B., and Hall, James N. *Falcons of France.* Little, Brown, 1929. (Lafayette Flying Corps)

Paine, Ralph D. *Ships Across the Sea.* Houghton Mifflin, 1920. (Battleships and submarines)

° Remarque, Erich M. *All Quiet on the Western Front.* Little, Brown, 1929. (An indictment against war)

° Rolt-Wheeler, Francis W. *The Wonder of War in the Air.* Lathrop, 1917. (Aviation)

° ———. *The Wonder of War on Land.* Lathrop, 1918. (Battle of the Marne)

° ———. *The Wonder of War at Sea.* Lathrop, 1919. (Naval engagements)

Walpole, Hugh. *The Secret City.* Doran, 1919. (Russian Revolution)

° Wells, H. G. *Mr. Britling Sees It Through.* Macmillan, 1917. (England and the war)

Werfel, Franz V. *The Forty Days of Musa Dagh.* Viking, 1934. (Armenian defense against Turkey)

TIME LINE

1920

1921	Harding inaugurated; Washington Conference on naval armaments
1922	Mussolini comes to power in Italy
1924	Johnson Immigration Act
1927	First coast-to-coast radio network; first talking movie; Lindbergh solos the Atlantic
1928	Kellogg-Briand Pact
1929	The depression begins; London Naval Conference

1930

1931	Japan invades Manchuria
1932	RFC established; Norris-LaGuardia Act passed; Lausanne Conference
1933	Prohibition repealed; Hitler comes to power in Germany; Twentieth Amendment ratified; F. D. Roosevelt inaugurated; the "Hundred Days" inaugurates sweeping laws to ease depression; U.S. recognizes Russia
1934	Reciprocal Trade Agreements Act; Securities and Exchange Commisssion established; Federal Communications Commission established; Platt Amendment repealed
1935	Social Security Act; Wagner Labor Relations Act; NLRB formed; CIO established; Neutrality Act
1936	Civil war in Spain; Rome-Berlin Axis formed
1937	Japan and China at war; FDR inaugurated for second term
1938	Munich Pact
1939	World War II begins

1940

1941	FDR inaugurated for third term; Atlantic Charter; Pearl Harbor
1942	First successful experiment in self-starting nuclear reaction
1943	Germans surrender in Africa; Battle of Stalingrad; Conferences of Allied leaders in Casablanca, Moscow, and Teheran
1944	June 6, D-Day; Dumbarton Oaks Conference

1945

| 1945 | FDR inaugurated for fourth term; Conferences at Yalta and Potsdam; Germany surrenders—V-E day; San Francisco Conference on U.N.; atomic explosions at Hiroshima and Nagasaki; September 2, Japan surrenders; World War II ends |

UNIT NINE

Prosperity, a Terrible Depression, and a Second World War

★ ★ ★ ★ The decade that followed World War I is sometimes spoken of as the "Incredible Era." It was a period of swift economic and social change. In the short space of ten years a revolution took place in the customary ways of travel, and America became "a nation on wheels." At the same time the radio and various other new products came into common use. Production climbed; hours of work were shortened; the end of poverty seemed to be in sight. In a spirit of reckless optimism a large number of people began to speculate on the stock market. They paid no attention to the plight of the nation's farmers and to other signs that the national economy was out of balance.

Suddenly the stock market crashed. As the 1930's opened, the nation entered the worst and longest depression in its history. Millions were jobless. Millions lost their homes. Hundreds of thousands of farmers lost their farms and became tenants or migrant workers. The whole economy slowed down until nearly half the nation was in want. President Hoover tried to halt the decline and for the first time the federal government stepped in to relieve suffering caused by a depression. When the decline continued, the nation voted for a "new deal" by electing the Democratic candidate for President, Franklin D. Roosevelt.

Relief, recovery, and reform were the three goals of the New Deal. Today we are interested mainly in the reforms. These strengthened the powers of the federal government, made the economy more stable, and renewed the nation's faith in democratic government.

While the nation was still absorbed in meeting its domestic problems, signs appeared that another war might break out in Europe. Congress passed laws intended to keep the United States neutral, regardless of what happened abroad. Germany and Italy formed a loose alliance known as the "Axis" and were later joined by Japan. The Axis nations soon started conquering their neighbors. After a time Americans began to realize that the whole world was threatened by the Axis. Gradually we shifted from our policy of neutrality. We supplied arms to the nations fighting the Axis. Then Japan attacked our bases in the Pacific and forced us to declare war. How the United States threw all its resources into the fight and how the tide finally turned against the Axis, is one of the great chapters in human history.

629

THE TWENTIES *ushered in a period of moral revolution. Old values were criticized, abandoned, or laughed at; rebellion was the aim of a whole generation. It was the adolescent spree of a nation, and, like adolescents everywhere, people had their heroes. Sinclair Lewis* (right) *spoke for those who felt confined by small-town restrictions and the narrow views of the middle class. Charles Lindbergh* (below) *was the embodiment of all that youth hoped to be—for he had done what his elders said couldn't be done. He had shown the worth of dreaming and the excitement of daring.*

In many ways the decade of the 1920's was one of the most amazing in American annals. Peering beneath the advancing prosperity and the rising standard of comfort, we perceive a confusion of ideas, an uprooting of ancient mores, and a revolution in ways of living.——Harold U. Faulkner

38. LIFE IN THE INCREDIBLE TWENTIES

Social Confusion Marks the Postwar Decade

The Incredible Era.

The years between the first World War and the Great Depression have been given various names—the "Mad Decade," the "Roaring Twenties," the "Golden Twenties," the "Era of Wonderful Nonsense," the "Jazz Age," and the "Incredible Era." As these names suggest, the period was unusual. Those who were young adults at the time still talk of how exciting it was.

It was a period of fast-moving social and economic change. The change from war to peace created difficulties—high prices, strikes, and in 1920–21 a depression. Then by 1922 business began to boom. A score of new industries developed rapidly as cars, radios, electrical appliances, cigarettes, silk stockings, and other new products came into common use. Many people made more money than ever before. A craze for speculating led to a land boom in Florida and to a spectacular rise on the stock market. The optimistic, or "bull," market in stocks was a reflection of the notion that good times would go on forever.

Most people seemed more interested in making and spending money than in public affairs. There was much lawlessness and political corruption. Crooked stock promoters fleeced the public of billions of dollars. Respectable citizens disobeyed the prohibition laws. Bootleggers and racketeers flourished. In some circles, cynicism became the fashion; there was a letdown in moral standards; and idealism was treated as a joke.

The nation turned its back on Wilsonianism and became strongly nationalistic. Nationalism was commonly expressed in such slogans as "America first" and "One hundred per cent Americanism." Nationalism caused the United States to remain outside the League of Nations and the World Court. It led to strict curbs on immigration. Nationalism also showed itself in distrust of foreigners and fear of radical ideas.

631

An American Communist party is born.

When the Communists, or Bolsheviks, seized power in Russia (1917), they called on workers everywhere to unite against the capitalistic system. Communist parties were formed in a number of countries. In 1919 the Communist International, or Comintern, was organized in Moscow. Its aim was to promote communism throughout the world. From the beginning the Comintern was controlled from Moscow and Communists everywhere followed the same "party line." Communists therefore were feared not only because of their revolutionary ideas but because they were suspected of serving the interests of the Soviet Union.

A Communist party was organized in the United States in 1919. Its members came chiefly from the left wing of the Socialist party and from the I.W.W. (see p. 608). Its membership grew very slowly and at its height in 1939 did not exceed 100,000. The American Communist party, however, had more influence than was shown by its small membership. At times a considerable number of American intellectuals were attracted by communism. Particularly after Hitler came to power in Germany (1933), they regarded communism as a bulwark against fascism and war. These Communist sympathizers later came to be known as "fellow-travelers." In the 1920's they were often spoken of as "parlor pinks."

Labor unrest creates a "red scare."

At the war's end communism spread in the defeated nations. Before it was stamped out, some leaders in western Europe and in the United States thought that a world-wide revolution was near. Their fears were built up by a period of intense labor unrest. The unrest was due largely to skyrocketing prices; many strikes were called to back up demands for higher wages. Employers, both in this country and in Europe, usually blamed the strikes on "reds." [1]

In the United States, the year 1919 brought a record number of strikes. Early in the year a general strike in Seattle paralyzed all but the most essential activities. Under pressure from high labor officials, who thought the strike a mistake, the workers returned to their jobs after five days. When John L. Lewis called 450,000 coal miners out of the pits, the federal government obtained an injunction ordering the men back to work. A strike of 350,000 steelworkers for union recognition, higher wages, and an end to the twelve-hour day lasted four months. It was stopped by the use of strikebreakers, but not until there had been outbreaks of violence. Unrest began to infect even city employees, for they had been hard hit by the rising cost of living. Most of Boston's policemen walked out (September, 1919) when the police commission refused to allow the men to form a union. The strike was quickly broken and the strikers lost their jobs. Altogether about 4,000,000 workers went on strike in 1919. Few of the strikes were successful.

The alarm caused by labor unrest was intensified by two events. Shortly before May 1, 1919, thirty-six bombs were found in the mails. The packages were addressed to public officials and business leaders involved in labor troubles. A month later a bomb exploded in the home of Attorney General Palmer. These crimes were thought to be the work of Communists. Thus they magnified the "red scare." Palmer ordered the arrest of several thousand persons suspected of being Communists. Eventually 550 of them were de-

---

[1] Strictly speaking, a "red" is a person who believes in violent revolution. The term has often been applied, however, to labor leaders, Socialists, pacifists, and others with unpopular views.

ported under a wartime act which gave the Secretary of Labor power to deport alien radicals without a court trial.

State governments also took action to suppress radicals. Many states passed laws that forbade writing or speaking words that might incite to violence in a labor dispute or might lead to the overthrow of the government. The effect was to outlaw membership in radical organizations. In certain states mere possession of radical literature could be punished. Years later the Supreme Court nullified some of these laws because they went too far in limiting the right of free speech, free press, and free assembly.

The "red scare" was at its height between 1919 and 1921. It led to many acts of intolerance. For instance in 1920, when the New York State legislature opened, five members were expelled simply because they were Socialists. The state bar association, led by Charles Evans Hughes, protested in vain that the action was not a proper way to defend democracy. Within a few years the fear of revolution died down. Liberals could again speak freely, and in many places radicals could voice their ideas without risk.

A new Ku Klux Klan sows discord.

An organization taking the title of "Ku Klux Klan" sprang up after the war to fight so-called "un-American ideas." Despite its name, the organization was more like the Know-Nothings of the 1850's than the Klan of Reconstruction days. It directed its activities mainly against foreigners, radicals, Roman Catholics, Jews, and Negroes. Using the flaming cross, tar and feathers, and the whip, white-hooded Klansmen spread terror over a large part of rural America. Where the Klan was strong, newspapers, politicians, and even business and professional men feared to speak against it. In 1925, at its peak, it claimed to have five million members.

At that time the Klan boasted that it controlled ten state governments.

In 1928 the Klan campaigned against the Democratic candidate for President, Alfred E. Smith, because of his religion. The Klan helped defeat him. Soon after, a congressional investigation exposed the scandalous grafting of Klan officials. Instead of a crusade, the movement was shown to be a "racket" for collecting initiation fees and dues and for diverting public funds into the pockets of Klan leaders. When these facts came out, the Klan lost most of its influence.

Immigration is drastically cut.

Another sign of the swing toward nationalism was the change in our immigration policy. In the decade before the war the United States received an average of a million immigrants a year. After the war the flood of immigration began again. Labor unions had long been asking Congress to curb immigration. Now the American Legion and other patriotic societies, claiming that it was difficult to "Americanize" so many newcomers, asked Congress to act. For the first time, employers too favored restrictions. Employers now had an ample supply of workers. Besides, they thought that immigrants often had radical ideas which led to labor unrest. Thus patriotic societies, employers, and labor unions joined in asking for a new immigration law.

Congress had already taken one step to reduce immigration when it voted in 1917 to require immigrants to pass a literacy test. The law was passed over President Wilson's veto. In 1921 the Emergency Quota Act was adopted. It cut the number of immigrants to be admitted from a given country in one year to 3 per cent of the number of foreign-born from that country living in the United States in 1910. The Johnson Act of 1924 made a further cut in immigration. It set up temporary quotas

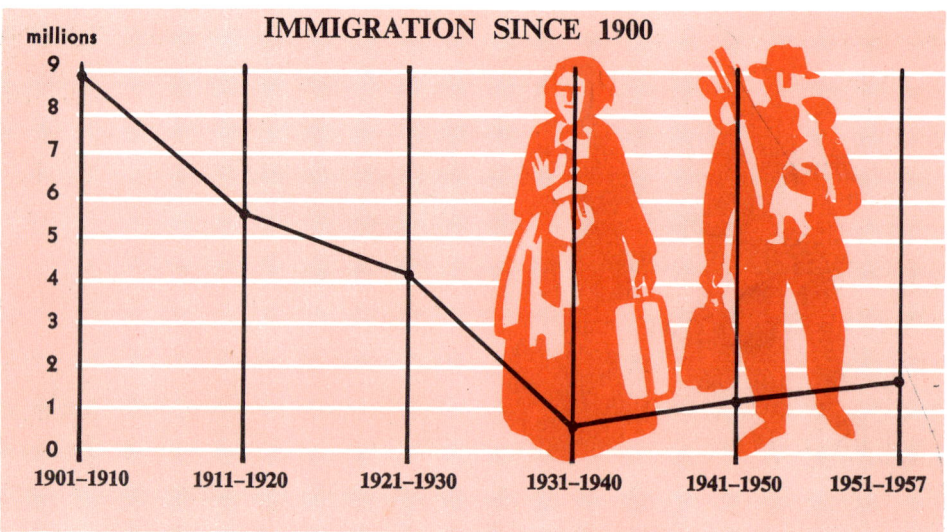

IMMIGRATION SINCE 1900

millions

9
8
7
6
5
4
3
2
1
0

1901–1910 | 1911–1920 | 1921–1930 | 1931–1940 | 1941–1950 | 1951–1957

equal to 2 per cent of the number of foreign-born from a given country living here in 1890. Selection of the date 1890 favored immigrants from the British Isles, Germany, and the Scandinavian countries (the so-called "old immigrants"), who made up the majority of our immigrants until close to 1890. Thus the Johnson Act discriminated against the so-called "new immigrants" from eastern and southern Europe, where living standards were lower and opportunities for education were more limited.

Congress included a "national origins" clause in the Johnson Act. It stated that after the Census Bureau found out the national origins of our population, permanent quotas should be worked out. The total number of quota immigrants who could be admitted in any year was set at 150,000. The minimum quota for any country outside of Asia was to be one hundred persons a year.

After much study the Census Bureau estimated that our white population at that time consisted of 50 per cent colonial stock, 35 per cent of "old immigrant" stock, 14 per cent of "new immigrant" stock, and 1 per cent of

French-Canadian stock. Adding colonial and "old immigrant" figures together, 85 per cent of our total white population had its origin in the British Isles, Germany, Holland, and the Scandinavian countries. The new quotas based on national origins went into effect in 1929.

The Johnson Act provided that immigrants from the Western Hemisphere should be admitted without a quota. As the number of immigrants from Europe fell, more people came here from nonquota regions—Canada, Latin America, Puerto Rico, Hawaii, and the Philippines. The greatest rise was in immigration from Mexico.

Although President Coolidge and Secretary of State Hughes objected, the Johnson Act excluded Japanese and other Asiatics entirely. The proud Japanese people regarded their exclusion as an insult. They thought Congress should have given Japan a quota of at least a hundred. In their resentment, many Japanese threw their support to a military party which was demanding a policy of "Asia for the Asiatics." This party eventually tried to drive the United States out of the Far East and so helped bring us into World War II.

Prohibition proves impossible to enforce.

One cause of social confusion in the postwar years was national prohibition. The Eighteenth Amendment, which went into effect in 1920, forbade the manufacture, sale, or transportation of intoxicating liquor. To provide for enforcement, Congress passed the National Prohibition Act, also known as the Volstead Act. Intoxicating liquor was defined in the act as any beverage containing more than ½ of one per cent alcohol. The definition pleased the extreme "drys," or prohibitionists, but it offended millions of foreign-born Americans who were accustomed to drinking wine and beer. Had the Volstead Act permitted the sale of light wine and beer the law would have been easier to enforce. President Wilson vetoed the act but Congress passed it over his veto.

In spite of the years of agitation for national prohibition, the nation in 1920 was not ready for it. While most rural dwellers and many city dwellers honestly wanted to end the liquor traffic, too many others were determined to have liquor, even at a high price. Profits from selling liquor illegally were so great, in fact, that sellers were willing to pay large bribes to the officers responsible for enforcing the law.[1] Almost every city of any size had "speak-easies," as the illegal drinking places were called, and numerous "bootleggers," or persons who sold or transported illegal liquor. Some of the liquor was brought in by smugglers, or rum-runners; some of it was made illegally within our borders. Much of this lawless business was in the hands of well-organized gangs of criminals. Often one gang stole liquor from another gang, this practice being known as "hijacking."

---

[1] Despite this, most prohibition agents were honest. However, one in twelve federal agents had to be dismissed for taking bribes.

In areas which had long forbidden the sale of liquor, state and local officials generally tried to enforce the federal law. But in many other sections state and local authorities winked at violations, leaving enforcement to federal agents. The federal Prohibition Bureau had about three thousand agents—far too few to cover the country. The Bureau could not hire more because it never received sufficient funds to do its work. Congress, it appears, had passed the Volstead Act partly to be rid of an annoying issue. The lawmakers were unwilling to appropriate the large sums needed to enforce prohibition. The discouraged head of the Prohibition Bureau testified in 1925 that only about 5 per cent of the liquor smuggled into the country was being stopped and that only about one in every ten illegal stills had been seized.

With all the shortcomings of enforcement, the "drys" claimed that prohibition had benefited the nation. Drinking among the poorer half of the population was greatly reduced. Employers noted a decline in absenteeism and inefficiency. Social workers reported that much money formerly spent for alcohol now went for food, clothing, and home furnishings. Several respected economists wrote articles saying that prohibition had contributed to the prosperity of the twenties.

Opponents of prohibition charged: (1) that it was making drinking fashionable, even among women; (2) that it was creating a contempt for all laws; (3) that it was responsible for much of the prevailing corruption in city government; and (4) that it was breeding gangsters and racketeers.

Gradually most of the friends of prohibition became discouraged. They began to think that perhaps it would be best to return the control of the liquor business to the states and to try, by education of the young, to solve the drink problem. Early in 1933 Congress submitted the Twenty-First, or Repeal, Amendment, to the states. It was ratified before the end of the year.

The underworld has a heyday.

In every large city criminal gangs grew rich from the illegal trade in liquor. As they gained power, they branched into other criminal activities, including various "rackets." In a typical racket, the gang forced small businessmen to pay for so-called "protection." A man who refused to pay soon met with costly "accidents." For instance, in the dry cleaning business a truck might be forced off the road and wrecked, acid might be thrown on a truckload of clothes, or a bomb might go off in the cleaning plant. A few incidents of this kind soon convinced all businessmen in the gang's territory that they must pay whatever the gangsters asked. Frequently racketeers got control of a labor union and forced both workers and employers to pay them tribute. The gangsters even managed to place their own men in strategic positions in local government. To maintain their power, gangsters murdered their opponents. In Chicago over five hundred gang killings took place in the 1920's. Scarcely any of the murderers were legally punished.

By the end of the decade racketeering had aroused the nation. Congress passed antiracketeering laws giving federal authorities new powers in criminal cases. Federal and state agencies co-operated in using new methods, based on laboratory science, to track down criminals. "G-men"—agents from the Federal Bureau of Investigation—waged a vigorous campaign against the racketeers. Some of the most notorious, among them Al Capone of Chicago, were placed behind bars, not for murder but for income tax frauds. The repeal of prohibition ended the gangsters' chief source of income. Yet they quickly shifted to other fields. The fight against organized crime, it was plain, could never be abandoned.

The excesses of a moral revolution were evident in the public admiration of lawbreakers. When Tony Lombardo, a Chicago gangster, was slain, floral wreaths worth thousands of dollars adorned his bier.

Prohibition meant profit for the rumrunners, but also danger. Here, a bootlegger dumps his load as a federal boat chases him.

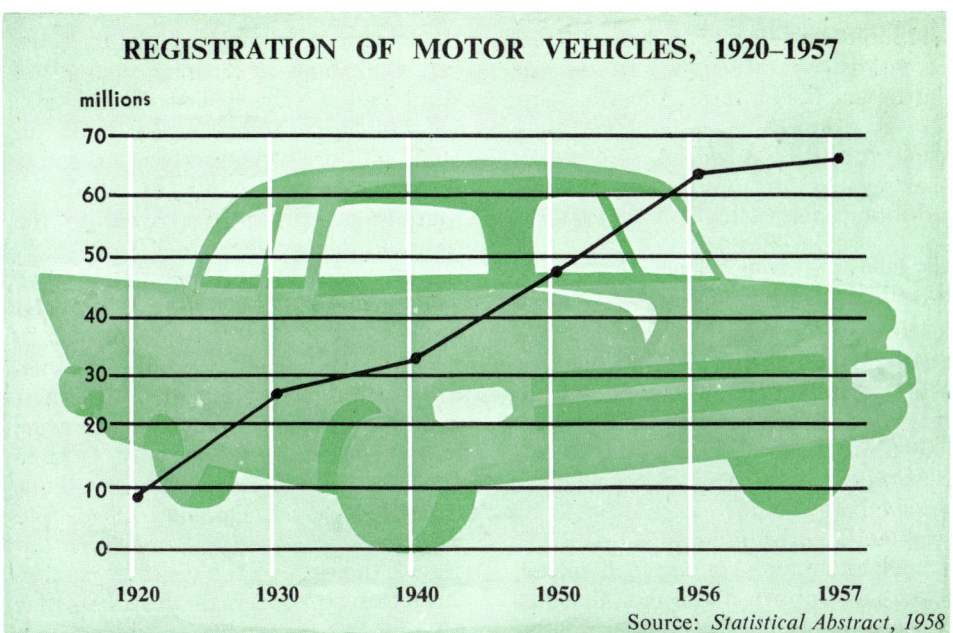

REGISTRATION OF MOTOR VEHICLES, 1920–1957

millions

70
60
50
40
30
20
10
0

1920　1930　1940　1950　1956　1957

Source: *Statistical Abstract, 1958*

The revolution in transportation and communication.

After the war a revolution took place in the field of transportation as millions of automobiles, busses, and motor trucks came into use. The automobile enabled people to move out of the cities into the suburbs. It also led them to do far more traveling than in the past. It closed up rural distances and ended the isolation of rural dwellers. It encouraged the consolidation of rural schools. It brought city and country people into close contact. In fact, the automobile transformed many aspects of life.

The changes due to the automobile were revolutionary enough. Yet while they were in progress, American life was being made over by the swift development of agencies for mass communication. The first tabloid newspaper appeared in 1919. Tabloids soon reached a host of readers, many of whom found the ordinary newspaper too difficult. Newspaper chains bought hundreds of local newspapers. A number of national magazines built up their circulation to a million or more. The motion picture became immensely popular. Radio broadcasting grew with unbelievable speed. The first regularly scheduled programs were broadcast late in 1920. Within three years, hundreds of stations were on the air. The first coast-to-coast network was achieved on New Year's Day, 1927. By the end of the decade one third of American homes had a radio. The influence of all these mass media of communication was enormous. New fashions in clothes, furnishings, foods, and manners sometimes swept the country almost overnight. Such rapid and continuous change was an important source of the confusion of the times.

Economic Changes Occur

A postwar depression is brief.

The wartime boom ended shortly after the armistice. The former servicemen and war production workers found that jobs were scarce. In 1921 there were five or six million unemployed. Farmers too suffered hard times. Farm production had been expanded to meet war needs. Now there were crop surpluses which cut farm prices in two. The farm depression lasted for twenty years, but the industrial slump was brief. By 1922 most of the unemployed had found jobs.

New industries create a boom.

From 1922 to 1929 many lines of business were prosperous. Profits were greatest in new industries, particularly in the manufacture and service of automobiles. The motorcar, it is said, pulled America out of the postwar depression. Production of motor vehicles trebled between 1919 and 1929. Since car manufacturers used huge quantities of steel, aluminum, copper, lead, nickel, plate glass, rubber, and upholstery fabrics, scores of other industries shared in the prosperity of the automobile industry. The construction industry boomed as a great road-building program was carried out. Thousands of gas stations, tourist cabins, inns, and roadside stands were built to service the motorists. By 1929 some 5,000,000 persons had jobs that depended, directly or indirectly, upon the motorcar.

Another expanding industry was electric power. The production of electricity more than doubled during the 1920's. While most of the electric current was used in factories, homes too were gradually gaining the benefits of electricity. As more and more houses were wired, the sale of electrical appliances climbed. By the end of the decade the manufacture of electrical equipment had become a major industry.

It was electricity that made possible two new forms of entertainment—the motion picture and the radio. In the twenties each of these grew into an important industry. The first movie that told a connected story, *The Great Train Robbery,* appeared in 1903. During the war full-length pictures had

their birth. After the war picture theaters were built in all but the smallest communities. The first successful talkie, *The Jazz Singer,* was shown in 1927. Within two years most theaters were wired for sound. By 1930 the number of persons who went to the movies in an average week equaled 82 per cent of the entire population. The growth of the radio industry was even more rapid.

Air transportation is another industry which developed in the 1920's. Airmail service began soon after the war. Many cities built airports. After Charles A. Lindbergh made a solo flight from New York to Paris in 1927, people were less afraid of air travel. By the end of the decade the air lines carried 3,000,000 passengers a year. At that time, however, very little of the nation's total travel was done by air.

Business grows bigger.

The consolidation of business, which had temporarily slowed down after passage of new antitrust laws in 1914 (see pp. 552-3), went on faster than ever after the war. The federal government was friendlier to big business than it had been during the Progressive Era. The Justice Department started very few antitrust suits. Besides, the Supreme Court handed down a series of decisions which made enforcement of the antitrust laws difficult. For example, the Court refused (1918) to dissolve the United Shoe Machinery Corporation, although at that time it made 90 per cent of all shoe machinery and leased the machines instead of selling them to customers.

Consolidation seemed especially rapid in such new industries as those making automobiles, chemicals, appliances, electric power, and motion pictures. Most of the nation's electric power lines and plants, for example, came under the control of but a dozen holding companies. Consolidation also took place in a number of old industries. Railroads continued to merge until a few large systems controlled most of the rail lines. Manufacturers of many kinds of packaged foods combined into a few large firms. Mergers of city banks and the rapid growth of chains of banks alarmed those who feared a "money trust." Chain stores strode ahead in the sale of drugs, tobacco, groceries, variety goods, and supplies for the motorist. By 1929 the largest grocery chain had 17,500 stores. In that year one fifth of the nation's retail trade was done by chain stores. Chains also bought most of the theaters, newspapers, magazines, and radio stations. By 1930, six hundred corporations owned half of all the corporate wealth in the country.

Productivity per man-hour goes up.

New techniques of industrial production came into wide use in the twenties. One of these, the assembly line, was developed by Henry Ford in

FORD HIGHLAND PARK PLANT, 1914. *This automatic assembly line, the first in the industry, produced more cars more quickly to satisfy a growing demand.*

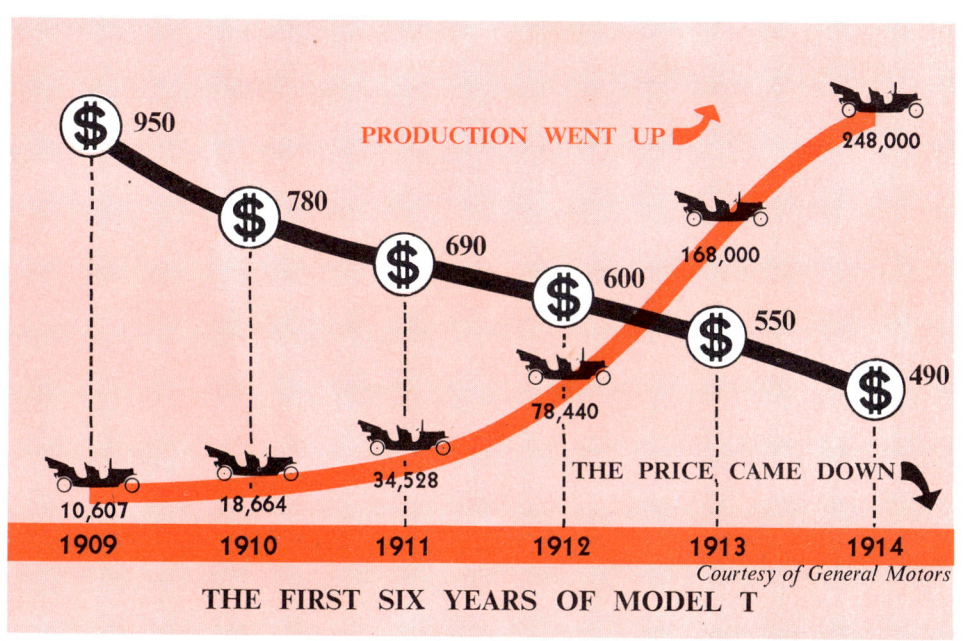

PRODUCTION WENT UP

THE PRICE CAME DOWN

1909	1910	1911	1912	1913	1914
$950	$780	$690	$600	$550	$490
10,607	18,664	34,528	78,440	168,000	248,000

Courtesy of General Motors

THE FIRST SIX YEARS OF MODEL T

the early years of the century. The assembly line consists of a giant conveyor belt that moves from one end of a factory to the other. A basic part, such as the chassis, is placed on the belt. Workers are stationed beside the belt, and each one adds a new part or carries out some other simple operation as the product goes by. Step-by-step planning of the work and the placing of all the needed parts and materials in readiness are, of course, essential. Engineers study the time and motions used in each operation, and every worker is taught the most efficient way to do his particular task.

It was soon found, however, that efficiency depended not only on skillful planning of the work to be done but on friendly relations between workers and management. Employers, therefore, began to pay more attention to good working conditions, safety devices, sanitation, lunchrooms, and facilities for rest and recreation.

Business seeks mass sales.

Mass-production industries need a wide market. They must sell to the great mass of people or else shut down. For this reason national advertising developed very rapidly. By 1929 two billion dollars a year was spent on advertising—five times as much as in 1915. Advertising quickly created a demand for the new comforts and luxuries. Every American family began to dream of owning a new car, a radio, electric appliances, and other conveniences.

To encourage people of ordinary means to buy expensive items like a car or a set of furniture, businessmen offered the "easy-payment," or installment, plan of buying. The buyer could pay for his purchase by the week or month. This form of consumer credit grew very fast during the 1920's. It fed the boom. In time, however, millions of families had spent their income so far ahead that they had to stop buying.

The resulting decline in the sale of cars and other durable goods helped bring about the 1929 crash.

Labor unions lose ground.

Membership in labor unions declined in the postwar decade. Several reasons may be given for the loss:

1. *The open shop drive.* Shortly after the war large organizations of employers launched a campaign in favor of the open shop, which they called the "American plan." The campaign was directed against the closed shop, in which employment is limited to union members. In the open shop, employment is supposed to be open to all—union as well as nonunion members. In practice, the open shop did not live up to its name, for employers often refused to hire union members.

2. *Unfavorable Court decisions.* A series of Supreme Court decisions took away from unions nearly all the protection given them by the Clayton Act of 1914 (see p. 552). The right to picket was greatly restricted. Boycotts were declared to be conspiracies in restraint of trade. The Court also upheld the free use of injunctions.

3. *Inability of unions to organize the mass-production industries.* In such industries as iron and steel, automobiles, rubber products, chemicals, electrical equipment, and food packing, efforts to start unions were fought in three ways: (a) employment of labor spies and strikebreakers, (b) propaganda charging that labor leaders were either racketeers or "reds," and (c) the organization of company unions or employee associations, which provided recreational facilities and other benefits at the employer's expense.

4. *"Welfare capitalism."* To develop a more loyal and efficient working force, certain companies adopted a policy known as "welfare capitalism." It was concerned with the health, safety, and security of the worker and his

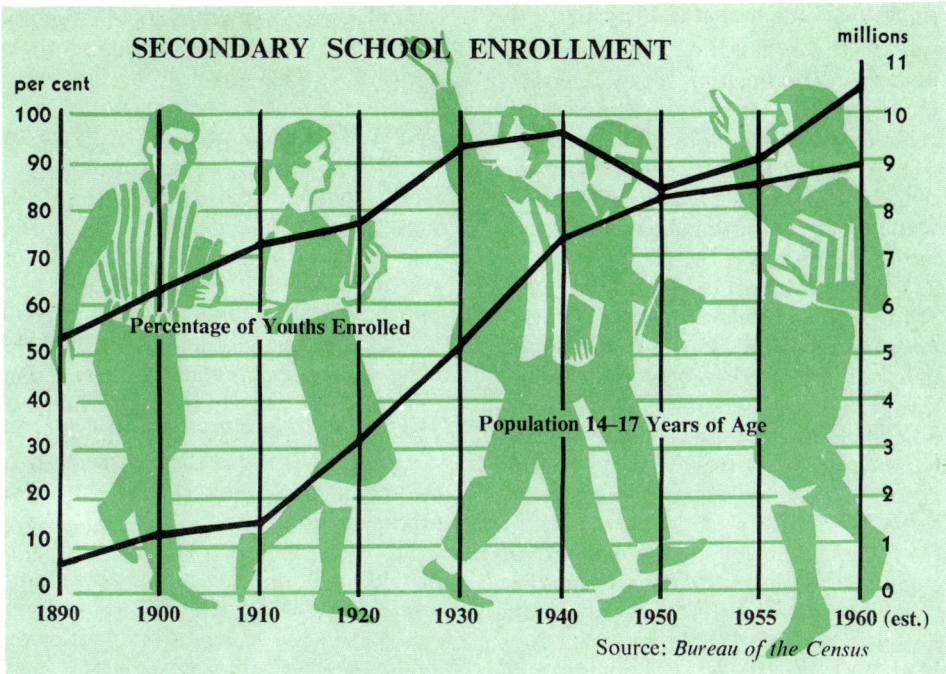

SECONDARY SCHOOL ENROLLMENT

per cent — millions

Percentage of Youths Enrolled

Population 14–17 Years of Age

1890 1900 1910 1920 1930 1940 1950 1955 1960 (est.)

Source: *Bureau of the Census*

family. A program of employee welfare might include some or all of the following: low-cost cafeterias in the plant, free medical service, vacations with pay, life insurance paid in whole or in part by the company, aid in the purchase of stock in the company, retirement pensions, and profit sharing. Where such benefits were offered, workers naturally looked to their employer rather than the union for the better things of life.

Some industries are "sick."

Despite the widespread prosperity of the twenties, certain industries suffered from low prices and lack of demand for their products. Among these were wheat and cotton farming; coal mining; the manufacture of cotton textiles, shoes, and leather goods; and shipbuilding. Railroads and trolley lines were hurt by the growing use of automobiles, trucks, and busses. As a result, most trolley lines and many branch lines on the railroads were abandoned. In addition, small businesses and small banks had hard sledding because of strong competition from larger rivals. When we hear of the "golden twenties" we should remember how uneven the prosperity really was.

Facilities for Education, Research, Health, and Recreation Expand

The prosperity of the postwar years was reflected not only in more motorcars and other luxuries but also in more schools and colleges, more public health work, more help for the unfortunate, and more parks and other recreational facilities. Cities and states taxed themselves to provide such public benefits. In addition much money was donated by private individuals. Both the wealthy and the average citizen gave money to private colleges and welfare agencies.

641

Educational opportunities increase.

By the end of the twenties the goal of universal education for all American children was at hand. More public schools were available and more children were attending school than ever before. Furthermore, the school year was longer and attendance more regular than it had ever been.

A movement to consolidate one-room rural schools was under way. It was helped along by the improvement of roads and the advent of the school bus. The use of school busses also enabled children with severe physical handicaps to get to school. The larger cities established special classes for these children.

The greatest educational expansion took place in the secondary schools. Between 1900 and 1930 the number of high school students doubled in every decade. While in 1900 only a few boys and girls had a chance to attend high school, by 1926 one half of the fourteen- to seventeen-year-olds were in school. Along with the climbing enrollment came changes in the curriculum. In 1900 over 50 per cent of the students took Latin, but in 1930 only 20 per cent did so. The percentage who studied algebra dropped almost as sharply. At the same time the number of high schools offering vocational subjects rose. In the larger high schools the program was enriched by adding art, music, dramatics, athletics, student government, and other activities. A few of the larger school systems introduced vocational guidance. City after city built magnificent high school buildings, equipped with laboratories, shops, libraries, auditoriums, gymnasiums, and lunchrooms. Admiring visitors from abroad described these high schools as "colleges for the common people."

Meanwhile, more high school graduates obtained a higher education. In 1930 one in eight young people of college age was in college or normal school compared with one in twenty-five in 1900. Since the beginning of the century, a new institution, the junior college, had made its appearance in the West. It provided the first two years of a college course. Like the four-year colleges, some junior colleges were supported by taxes and others by tuition fees and endowments. Junior colleges provided for only part of the rise in enrollment in higher education. The larger part of the rise was in colleges, normal schools, and universities.

The South makes educational strides.

The South was the last section of the country to approach the goal of universal education. After 1900, however, it made remarkable progress in providing public schools for both whites and Negroes. The movement was aided by Northern philanthropic agencies. The Julius Rosenwald Fund, for example, helped in building thousands of schoolhouses for Negroes. While the South had few public high schools in 1900, after that the number of high schools grew rapidly. By 1930 the larger Southern towns had a high school for Negroes, as well as one for whites.

Scientific research marches on.

Research was generously supported after the war. Big corporations established their own research laboratories. Universities sought and obtained gifts to build laboratories and conduct research. From the professional schools and universities came a growing number of well-trained young scientists.

During the postwar years Americans added to nearly every field of scientific knowledge. Chemistry made the swiftest advance, partly because of the German patents we had seized during the war. After 1918 we were able to produce numerous drugs and coal-tar dyes formerly made only in Germany. Various types of artificial silk, or rayon, were perfected and placed on the market. From the laboratories poured an endless stream of new or improved products. Chemistry was indeed opening the door to a new world.

The twenties were a memorable decade also in American medicine. From grim experience with wartime wounds came major advances in surgery. New uses were found for the x-ray. Better ways for treating severe burns were developed. An antitoxin for scarlet fever brought this dangerous disease under control. The use of insulin added years to the lives of millions of sufferers from diabetes. Research in nutrition showed the importance of a long list of vitamins, only two or three of which were known before the war. By adding appropriate vitamins to the diet, pellagra, scurvy, rickets, and other nutritional diseases could be cured.

Public health work expands.

The public health movement had been growing ever since the War between North and South. At first its main concern was the problem of water supply. About the turn of the century public health officials began to give special attention to the milk supply. One of the first steps was to require regular inspection of dairies. Another step was to require that all cows be tested for tuberculosis. A later step, taken in many places during the twenties, was to forbid the sale of raw milk.

The twentieth century saw steadily increasing attention to the health of babies and children. Baby clinics, where specialists give advice to needy mothers on the health of their children, increased from 20 in 1900 to 1500 in 1920. Most of these were provided by private agencies. After Congress passed the Maternity and Infancy Act (1921), federal grants encouraged the states and cities to provide prenatal and baby clinics.

Around 1900 cities began to provide for periodic medical inspection of school children by a nurse or doctor. Massachusetts made it compulsory throughout the state in 1906. By 1930 most schools provided for medical and dental examinations. Some also provided free inoculations and free dental service for needy children.

Deepening concern for the public health and welfare was shown also by the growing number of general hospitals, clinics, and institutions for the tubercular, the blind, the deaf, the mentally sick, and the mentally defective. Many of these institutions were supported largely from tax funds. Others received most of their support from religious and fraternal groups, service clubs, or from individual donors.

The profession of social work develops.

Voluntary organizations to help the needy were found in almost every American city. To carry on their varied activities a new profession arose—that of social work. It is concerned with helping people in difficulty to solve their problems and if possible to become self-sustaining members of the community. By the end of the twenties social work had broadened to include mental hygiene, the prevention and treatment of juvenile delinquency, counseling for disorganized families, vocational guidance, and medical assistance. Graduate schools of social work were established to prepare social workers for their profession.

Facilities for recreation expand.

The twenties brought more leisure time to nearly everybody. Some people were satisfied to use their leisure listening to the radio or watching movies and spectator sports, but others wanted a chance for active participation. To meet this need, large and medium-sized cities throughout the nation built parks, playgrounds, bathing

643

beaches, swimming pools, golf courses, tennis courts, and athletic fields. In 1930, however, most small cities still lacked any public facilities for recreation except perhaps a small park.

Churches and voluntary agencies helped to supply facilities for wholesome low-cost recreation. In the larger cities, Christian and Hebrew associations and other groups operated centers where young people could take part in athletic and social activities. Some churches had an extensive recreational program. Many of them provided a meeting place for Boy Scouts and Girl Scouts.

Scouting, which first came to the United States in 1910, soon spread over the nation. It helped awaken a new interest in camping. Thousands of camps sprang up in the twenties. Some of them were conducted by voluntary agencies at low cost. Others were run for profit. By the end of the decade about 3,000,000 boys and girls went to camp each season. Another development in outdoor recreation was the growing use made of our state and national parks and forest preserves. These areas began to attract millions of tourists, who reached them by car or bus.

City planning makes strides.

The need for public recreational areas and the growing congestion of city streets aroused an interest in city planning. The larger cities spent considerable sums for widening streets, developing their water fronts, and establishing motor parkways. In an effort to stop the growth of slums, cities of all sizes began to adopt zoning laws. Such a law divides the community into zones, within each of which only certain kinds of buildings and certain uses of land and buildings are permitted.

DAN BEARD, *founder of the Boy Scouts, instructs his scouts in woodcraft.*

644

For example, some areas are reserved for one-family houses, others for apartment buildings, still others for factories. Only 8 cities had a zoning law in 1916 but by 1929, 821 cities had zoning. This change showed that people were trying to direct the growth of their cities to make them more attractive, safe, and healthful.

Historic shrines are restored.

The twenties saw a great revival of interest in American history and in all things American. Museums displayed American antiques. Private collectors bought antiques. The study of local history became popular. Associations were founded to preserve or restore hundreds of neglected historical shrines. The costliest of all restoration projects was that at Williamsburg, Virginia. John D. Rockefeller, Jr., spent millions of dollars to restore this eighteenth-century capital of Virginia as a gift to the public.

Literature and the Fine Arts Flourish

Much distinguished writing is produced.

The postwar years proved stimulating to American writers. A large number of able novelists, poets, and dramatists tried to state their feelings about human existence. Most of the serious writers of this period expressed doubt about the accepted values of society. Many were hostile to religious dogmas and to social customs that they felt had repressed them in youth. They wanted society to give individuals more freedom. They wrote about the various aspects of life with new frankness. Some expressed scorn for the supposed vulgarity of a business civilization. Others sought escape from that civilization by going to live in Europe or by writing about an earlier period when society was more to their liking.

Fiction writers were influenced by a literary movement known as *naturalism*. Its aim is to portray society and the lives of men and women objectively, as a scientist might do. The characters are often from the lower class, and the hero and heroine usually represent the vices and weaknesses of a particular type or group. There is constant emphasis on the social environment of the characters and the way it shapes their actions and destinies.

Theodore Dreiser was a leading naturalist writer. His long novel *An American Tragedy* (1925) is a powerful psychological study. It tells of a young Midwesterner who tries to escape from poverty, is swept off his feet by contact with unaccustomed wealth, and is ruined by it.

Probably the most widely read novelist of the period was Sinclair Lewis. In *Main Street, Babbitt, Arrowsmith,* and other novels Lewis wrote caustically of middle-class materialism and hypocrisy. In 1930 he became the first American to receive the Nobel prize for literature.

One of the most brilliant novelists of the twenties was F. Scott Fitzgerald. His books picture the confusion, cynicism, and unhappiness of wealthy young people in the "Jazz Age." Among his novels are *This Side of Paradise* (1920), *The Great Gatsby* (1925), and *Tender Is the Night* (1934).

Other writers of naturalistic fiction who became known during the 1920's include Ernest Hemingway, Sherwood Anderson, William Faulkner, John Dos Passos, Ring Lardner, and Erskine Caldwell.

Great fiction dealing with an earlier day.

Not all the outstanding fiction writers of the twenties confined themselves to describing contemporary society. Edith Wharton wrote about New York's "best families" of the late nineteenth century. *The Age of Innocence*

(1920) won her the Pulitzer prize. Ellen Glasgow's novels told of contrasting social classes and social change in her native state, Virginia, over the past century. She was one of the first Southern novelists to write realistically of her section. Willa Cather, who grew up on the Nebraska frontier, was known for her stories of pioneers. *Death Comes for the Archbishop* (1927) is probably her most famous work. Thornton Wilder won the Pulitzer prize for *The Bridge of San Luis Rey* (1927), dealing with Peru in the early eighteenth century. Ole Edvart Rölvaag wrote realistic novels which bring us the hard life of Norwegian immigrants to Minnesota. The most famous is *Giants in the Earth* (1929). All five of these writers were expert craftsmen whose work is still read with delight. In telling us of characters whose lives were dignified by their devotion to love of home, religion, duty, unselfishness, and integrity, these authors were perhaps commenting on the materialism and lawlessness so prevalent in their own society.

A great dramatist appears.

The twenties also saw an unusual amount of good writing for the legitimate theater. Eugene O'Neill, hailed as our greatest dramatist, won recognition for his deep and moving psychological studies of American men and women. He experimented with various devices to show his characters' inward reactions, such as having them speak in asides or put masks on and off. Some of his plays dealing with moral decay shocked conservative viewers. O'Neill received the Pulitzer prize three times— for *Beyond the Horizon* (1920), *Anna Christie* (1922), and *Strange Interlude* (1928). The Nobel prize for literature was awarded to him in 1936.

A wealth of good poetry is written.

A revival of poetry, which had begun before the war, was evident in the

A scene from Ben Turpin's movie "Shriek of Araby."

EUGENE O'NEILL'S *bold experiments with technical devices and his introduction of themes from Greek tragedies gave his plays originality and depth and brought maturity to the American theater.*

"Sixth Avenue Elevated at Third Street," from a painting by JOHN SLOAN *in 1928*

The success of the realists in capturing city life on canvas inspired the work of the regionalist painters like GRANT WOOD, *who looks objectively at farm life in his "Dinner for Threshers."*

postwar years. We had not heard from so many gifted poets since the middle of the 1800's. Edwin Arlington Robinson of Maine laid bare the frustrated soul of modern man. "The world," he wrote, "is a kind of spiritual kindergarten where bewildered infants are trying to spell God with the wrong blocks."

T. S. Eliot expressed the postwar mood of futility. To him the America of his day was mechanical, vulgar, and intellectually barren. Accordingly, he went to England to live. In *The Waste Land* and *The Hollow Men,* he wrote of the spiritual emptiness in modern society where trust in science was replacing religious faith.

Robert Frost sang the simple joys of farm life and the changing seasons in New England. His serene *New Hampshire* (1923) won a Pulitzer prize. Carl Sandburg, a disciple of Walt Whitman, was the poet of the prairies and the prairie city, Chicago. Vachel Lindsay wandered from town to town, "trading his rhymes for bread" and expressing the feelings and experiences of the common people. Edna St. Vincent Millay wrote sensual lyrics celebrating love and the right of women to as much freedom as men. Her book *The Harp Weaver* (1923) won a Pulitzer prize. Stephen Vincent Benét's heroic narrative poem *John Brown's Body* (1928) is considered by some critics to be the best long poem in American literature.

Poetry was the medium chosen by a number of talented Negro writers. Their work filled an anthology compiled by James Weldon Johnson, *The Book of American Negro Poetry* (1922). Many of the poems dealt with the tragedy of the Negro in a white man's world.

Architecture advances.

The prosperity of the period led to much building, some of it of striking beauty. As in the past, many American architects found inspiration in classical and medieval models. The Lincoln Memorial in Washington was in the Greek style. New buildings erected at Yale, Princeton, West Point, and the University of Chicago made impressive use of a modernized Gothic style. The most distinctive American buildings were skyscrapers. Architects developed a new device, the setback, by which the building becomes narrower as it ascends. In this way, the upper floors do not cut off the light and air of lower floors. One of the most impressive skyscrapers in the world, the hundred-story Empire State Building in New York City, was erected in 1930–31.

The American architect best known outside the United States was Frank Lloyd Wright. He experimented boldly with new materials and tried to fit each building to its use and its setting. His "prairie houses" emphasized horizontal lines close to the earth and a wide expanse of windows.

Painters displease conservatives.

Turning away from traditional subjects early in the century, a group of New York and Philadelphia artists painted realistic scenes of life in a great city. Among their themes were machinery, laborers at work, crowds in public parks, prize fights, pushcart markets, barrooms, tenement buildings, and children in alleys strewn with ash cans. Although derided as the "ash can school," their work was admired by discerning critics.

The realists were followed by a group who might be described as "regionalists." We can mention only a few. Grant Wood painted the farms and the common people of Iowa. John Steuart Curry chose midwestern plains and southern cotton fields. Waldo Pierce painted the rugged Maine coast.

Still other artists, influenced by the French, experimented with strange new styles such as cubism, futurism,

648

expressionism, and surrealism. Conservative critics denounced the efforts of these artists as undisciplined and chaotic.

Jazz becomes popular.

The twenties are often called the "Jazz Age" because in those years jazz first became widely known. Jazz, which Negro bands developed by combining ragtime and the blues, was born in New Orleans shortly before the war. Paul Whiteman's band was the first to play it from fully scored parts (1920). Until that time jazz bands did not use written parts. In 1924 in New York Whiteman gave the first jazz concert ever held. Later, he and his band toured the United States and Europe with great success.

A number of American and European composers began to employ jazz rhythms and tunes in serious compositions. George Gershwin wrote several symphonic works in the jazz idiom. The most famous is *Rhapsody in Blue* (1923) for piano and orchestra. Gershwin's work brought a lull to the furious debate between those who consider jazz an unpleasant noise and those who consider it an important contribution to American art.

Frank Lloyd Wright's falling water house

FOR IDENTIFICATION

Bolshevik Revolution	Sinclair Lewis
Comintern	Eugene O'Neill
Eighteenth Amendment	Twenty-first Amendment
Johnson Act	Volstead Act
Ku Klux Klan	Frank Lloyd Wright

FOR EXPLANATION OR DEFINITION

assembly line	materialism
"bootlegger"	naturalism
chain stores	prohibition
"hijacking"	realism
installment buying	"speakeasy"
junior college	zoning laws

FOR REVIEW

1. Why was the postwar decade a period of lawlessness and political corruption?

2. How did the spirit of nationalism show itself in the postwar period?

3. (a) Why did a "red scare" sweep the country? (b) How did it manifest itself?

4. (a) Why was there an increased demand for the restriction of immigration during and after World War I? (b) What action did Congress take in 1917 in response to this demand? (c) How did the Emergency Quota Act of 1921 restrict immigration? (d) Why did the Johnson Act of 1924 use 1890 as the base year? (e) How was this law modified in 1929?

5. Describe the Ku Klux Klan movement of the 1920's.

6. (a) Why was it difficult to enforce the Prohibition amendment? (b) What were the arguments of those who urged its repeal?

7. Describe the racketeering and gangsterism of the 1920's. What was done to bring it under control?

8. Why was there a depression in 1920 and 1921?

9. How did the automobile industry help to pull America out of the depression?

10. What changes took place in the consumption of electric power? How did they help to stimulate a business boom?

11. (a) Why was there a new trend toward business consolidations in the 1920's? (b) In what industries was business consolidation especially marked?

12. Why was there increased productivity per man hour?

13. (a) How did mass production affect the advertising industry? (b) How were mass-produced commodities made available to the ordinary consumer?

14. (a) Why did labor unions lose ground during the 1920's? (b) Explain the meaning of the phrase "welfare capitalism."

15. (a) In spite of the general prosperity, why did some industries have serious difficulties? (b) Name industries that were referred to as "sick" during this period.

16. (a) Describe the expansion of educational facilities between 1900 and 1930. (b) What changes took place in high school enrollment and in the curriculum?

17. Why did scientific research make significant strides in the 1920's?

18. Name important advances in the fields of chemistry and medicine.

19. (a) Outline the development of public health work; of social work. (b) What was done to provide for low-cost recreation? (c) What advances were made in city planning?

20. (a) What are some of the characteristics of the literary output of the period? (b) Name three exponents of naturalism, and tell about the works they produced. (c) Name three writers of fiction who concentrated on describing earlier periods. (d) Name four poets who achieved fame during this period.

21. Describe the chief characteristics of the new architecture.

22. Explain the terms "realism" and "regionalism" as applied to modern art.

23. (a) Why is the decade of the 1920's sometimes referred to as the "Jazz Age"? (b) For what are Paul Whiteman and George Gershwin noted?

FOR FURTHER STUDY AND DISCUSSION

1. (a) What have been the outstanding contributions of the immigrant to American life and culture? (b) What economic interests have opposed and what interests have supported unrestricted immigration? Helpful sources: Cavanah, We Came to America; Wittke, We Who Built America; Orth, Our Foreigners (Chronicles).

2. (a) What were the reasons for the adoption of the Eighteenth Amendment, and the reasons for its repeal by the Twenty-first Amendment? (b) How do you account for the shift in public opinion indicated by the adoption of these amendments in the short space of fifteen years? Helpful sources: Merz, The Dry Decade; Hart, Contemporaries, Vol. V, Nos. 107, 108; Wish, Contemporary America; Hacker and Kendrick, The United States Since 1865, pp. 520–523; Allen, Only Yesterday.

3. Compare educational progress and changes in the decade of the 1920's and in the decade of the 1950's. Helpful sources: Wish, Contemporary America; World Almanac; and magazines of the periods.

4. How did the literature of the 1920's reflect the mood of the people? Helpful sources: Wish, Contemporary America; Kazin, On Native Grounds; Perry, The American Spirit in Literature (Chronicles).

FOR INDIVIDUAL OR GROUP ACTIVITIES

1. Prepare an exhibit to illustrate life during the 1920's. Include pictures of automobiles, electric appliances, fashions, advertising art, sports, newspaper headlines, popular songs, popular movies, political cartoons. Helpful sources: Davidson, Life in America; Adams, Album; old magazines.

2. Have a small committee select poems by authors mentioned in the text for reading to the class.

3. Prepare a book report on one of the novels or dramas mentioned in the text.

4. Have five different committees make special reports on each of the following: The "red scare" of the 1920's; the Ku Klux Klan movement; the development of the radio; the development of the motion picture industry; the development of jazz.

5. Arrange for panel discussions on some of the following topics: The repeal of the present quota law; the extension of the present quota law to the countries of the Western Hemisphere; and a desirable substitute for quota restrictions.

6. Study conditions in your own town or city and report on traffic congestion, automobile accidents, recreational facilities, and plans for future development.

> Confident of our ability to work out our destiny,
> and jealously guarding our right to do so, we
> seek no part in directing the destinies of the
> Old World. We do not mean to be entangled.
> ——Warren G. Harding, 1921

39. CONSERVATIVE REPUBLICANS CONTROL THE GOVERNMENT

A Period of Reaction Sets In

The Progressive Era ends.

During the Progressive Era many laws had been passed which restricted businessmen, especially the heads of big business. A reaction was bound to come. The progressive tide turned during Wilson's second term in the White House. From our entry into World War I in 1917 until the stock market crash in 1929, few reform laws were adopted by Congress or by state legislatures. In this period of a dozen years there were few reform mayors and governors, few reform congressmen, and no presidents who stood for reform.

The retreat from progressivism took place in both major parties. After 1912, when Theodore Roosevelt launched the Bull Moose party, progressives had little voice in Republican affairs. The Old Guard got back in the saddle in 1912 and stayed there. Progressives dominated the Democratic party until the war; after that their influence declined. In the 1920's the conservative wing of the Democratic party was stronger than the progressive wing.

Democratic leaders in Northern cities still depended on wage earners for votes, but in both North and South the party got most of its campaign funds from industrialists. Hence, leading Democrats were, on the whole, almost as conservative as their rivals in the Republican ranks.

President Harding takes office.

On March 4, 1921, the popular Warren G. Harding was sworn in as Chief Executive. Tall, dignified, and well-built, Harding looked "every inch a President." Yet by experience and temperament he was ill qualified for the office. For many years he had been owner-editor of a small-town Ohio newspaper. He called the policy of his paper "inoffensivism." He had also taken an undistinguished part in Ohio politics. Not a student or a deep thinker, he had only a slight knowledge of public affairs. His affable personality, "folksy" way of public speaking, and loyalty to regular Republican leaders in his state won him election to the

651

United States Senate (1914). An average sort of senator, he followed the dictation of party whips, or leaders. A Senate clique of Old Guard Republicans, led by Henry Cabot Lodge of Massachusetts, secured Harding's nomination to the Presidency. They wanted a man they could control. The clique was thoroughly tired of strong-minded and progressive presidents like Theodore Roosevelt and Woodrow Wilson.

Harding pleased his Senate backers and millions of voters by his campaign promise of "normalcy" (see p. 622). It voiced his desire, and theirs, to return to the "good old days" of McKinley conservatism. It meant both a retreat from foreign entanglements and the reversal of a number of domestic reforms adopted in the Progressive Era.

With the advice of party leaders, Harding chose the able Charles Evans Hughes to be Secretary of State. Hughes was the only member of the Cabinet who had ever been a progressive. He promptly displayed his qualities of leadership as chairman of the Washington Conference on Naval Limitation and Far Eastern Affairs (see pp. 659–61). Herbert Hoover, noted for his work as wartime Food Administrator and for his relief activities in Europe, became Secretary of Commerce. An engineer and businessman, he raised this usually inconspicuous Cabinet post to first-rate importance. Andrew J. Mellon, a wealthy industrialist and banker of Pittsburgh, took the post of Secretary of the Treasury. He constantly urged economy in government and relief for the upper-income taxpayers. Mellon held the Treasury position for twelve years. His strong influence in national affairs led a senator to quip, "Three Presidents served under him."

Like his appointments to the Cabinet, Harding's appointments to the Supreme Court were thoroughly conservative. In his three years in office there were four vacancies on the high bench.

For Chief Justice he chose former President William H. Taft. As associate justices he named George Sutherland, Pierce Butler, and Edward Sanford. While Chief Justice Taft sometimes sided with the liberal justices Holmes and Brandeis, Harding's other appointees always took the conservative side. Two of them remained on the bench until well into the 1930's and opposed a long series of New Deal reforms.

Congress raises the tariff.

Because of the war, the moderate Underwood Tariff of 1913 never had a chance to prove itself under normal conditions. It was unjustly blamed for the unemployment which followed the war. As soon as Harding took office he called Congress into special session to raise the duties. An emergency tariff law was passed, followed the next year by a more permanent measure, the Fordney-McCumber Act. The Fordney-McCumber Tariff boosted duties to the highest level yet reached. It contained one novel feature—a "flexible clause," permitting the President to raise or lower duties as much as 50 per cent. In practice the flexible clause was used chiefly to raise rates.

While the new tariff pleased most American manufacturers, it did not please those who made electric equipment, machine tools, and motor vehicles. These producers could hold the domestic market without tariff protection. They opposed the rise in duties because they wanted to increase their sales abroad. As they foresaw, our new tariff soon led other nations to retaliate by erecting barriers to American goods. To get around trade barriers, several large American companies then established branch factories abroad.

Economists also objected to the new tariff. They pointed out that during the war the United States had changed from a debtor nation to a creditor nation. Since our debtors had little or no gold, they expected to pay what they owed us by sending us goods. Our high tariff, however, shut out most of their products and made payment of their debts almost impossible. The *Wall Street Journal* called the Fordney-McCumber Act "one of the most selfish, short-sighted, and extravagant laws of the kind ever enacted."

Business is given a free rein.

Republican leaders believed the government should relax its controls over business. Repeal of the laws that business disliked might be difficult; however, these laws could be administered in a new spirit. Accordingly, President Harding and his successors, Presidents Coolidge and Hoover, filled federal offices with men who thought that "the business of the United States is business." All three Presidents appointed conservative judges to the federal courts, just as liberal Presidents have picked liberal judges. To the Federal Trade Commission and the Interstate Commerce Commission they appointed men friendly to the corporations they were supposed to regulate. The antitrust laws were used against labor unions but not against big business. Various state governments likewise relaxed their controls over business and even repealed regulatory laws. New Jersey, for example, repealed the sweeping program for business control which had been enacted under Governor Woodrow Wilson. Until the New Deal, practically nothing was done either on the state or federal level to check the rapid march of consolidation.

The policy of noninterference with business did not mean a return to strict laissez faire. For twelve years the federal government gave business all possible aid, direct and indirect. Under Secretary Hoover the activities of the Department of Commerce were greatly expanded. Commerce agents searched the entire world for opportunities for American traders and investors. Congress voted large subsidies to aviation companies and shipowners. It helped nationwide advertising by keeping the postal rate for magazines below the cost of shipment. Congress also subsidized inland water transportation by building new canals, dams, and locks. It helped the infant trucking industry, as well as every business connected with automobiles, by continuing to give federal aid for building roads. The policy of aid to business was expected to benefit the entire nation.

Congress also repeatedly reduced corporation taxes and taxes on individuals in the higher income brackets. Mellon vigorously defended this type of tax cut. He said that it encouraged wealthy people to invest their money in business rather than in tax-exempt bonds. Progressives, however, claimed that Congress merely was shifting the tax burden from the shoulders of the rich to those of the middle class and the poor.

ANDREW W. MELLON'S *magnificent collection of paintings, housed in the Mellon Art Gallery in Washington, D.C., was his gift to the nation.*

Corruption disgraces Harding's term.

Political corruption, although common in American cities, has rarely invaded high federal office. It did so under Harding. His administration set a new record for incompetence and dishonesty, worse even than that of President Grant. Like Grant, Harding was personally honest but a poor judge of men. He rewarded his friends and political helpers with important federal jobs, which they were not wise enough or honest enough to handle.

To Harding's campaign manager, Harry J. Daugherty, went the post of Attorney General. Daugherty and his friends, the "Ohio gang," grew rich by selling protection to bootleggers, appointments to office, pardons, paroles, and government contracts. Charles R. Forbes, director of the Veterans Bureau, in less than two years stole or squandered $250,000,000. The major scandal involved Albert B. Fall, Secretary of the Interior. Fall secretly leased oil lands reserved for the navy at Teapot Dome, Wyoming, and Elk Hills, California, to private interests. The leaseholders expected to make a profit of at least $200,000,000. For forgetting his duty to the nation, Fall received bribes amounting to a third of a million dollars. After the facts were disclosed by Senate investigators, the oil leases were canceled and Fall was sent to prison.

Death cuts short Harding's term.

In the summer of 1923 Harding left Washington on an extensive speaking tour. The scandals of his administration were known to insiders but had not yet become public. Harding was tired and worried. On the return trip he suddenly passed away. Death probably saved him from impeachment. So ended the Presidency of a man who was amiable but lacked ability and moral courage. Harding's one achievement through his personal efforts while in the White House was his persuading the big steel companies to end the twelve-hour day.

The Country Finds President Coolidge "Safe and Sane"

Calvin Coolidge succeeds Harding.

When news of Harding's death was brought to Vice-President Coolidge, he was asleep at his boyhood home in Plymouth, Vermont. Before daybreak, in the light of a kerosene lamp, Coolidge was sworn into office by his father, a justice of the peace.

Coolidge had more education than Harding and was made of sterner stuff. After graduating from Amherst College (1895) and reading law for two years in the small town of Northampton, Massachusetts, he turned to politics. Conscientious, honest, and of "sound" (i.e. conservative) views, he early won the support of the Republican leader of western Massachusetts, William Crane. With Crane's help Coolidge pushed his way up through local and state offices to the governorship. During the Boston police strike in 1919 (see p. 632), Governor Coolidge became nationally famous for his telegram: "There is no right to strike against the public safety by anybody, anywhere, any time." Although he had done nothing to prevent the police strike, his firm handling of it made him Vice-President.

Coolidge was conservative in the extreme. Distrustful of the whole progressive movement, he especially opposed government interference with business. At all times he stood for strict economy in government. Coolidge announced he would carry out the same policies as Harding. To the dismay of many citizens, for a time he even kept the same Cabinet. But Daugherty and the "Ohio gang" gradually disappeared from office. Thus Coolidge restored the reputation of his party.

A KU KLUX KLAN *initiation in New Jersey. The rebirth of this organization struck a severe blow at social reform.*

Congress rebuffs the new President.

Ever since the war Congress had shown a tendency to ignore requests and suggestions from the White House. Neither Harding nor Coolidge tried to exert strong presidential leadership. Coolidge showed during his first year in office that, except for an occasional veto, he would let Congress have its own way. Thus it is not surprising that when Congress passed an immigration act in 1924, it disregarded the President's advice and excluded Japanese immigrants (see p. 634).

The same year Congress passed the World War Adjusted Compensation Act over the President's veto. The measure provided a bonus to veterans of the World War at the rate of $1.25 a day for overseas service and $1.00 a day for service in the United States. The bonus was in the form of an endowment policy to mature in twenty years.

Congress also rebuffed the President by turning down his recommendation for selling the federal government's property at Muscle Shoals, Alabama, to private interests. This property consisted of two nitrates plants and a hydroelectric plant built during the war and now standing idle. Although Presidents Harding, Coolidge, and Hoover each in turn urged the sale of Muscle Shoals, the Senate refused to go along (see p. 693).

Coolidge and Dawes are nominated.

When the Republican convention met in 1924, Coolidge easily won the nomination for President. Charles G. Dawes, Director of the Budget, was nominated for Vice-President. Their platform called for rigid economy, further reduction of taxes, restriction of immigration, collection of war debts from the Allies, and membership in the World Court.

655

Democrats split over prohibition and K.K.K.

At the Democratic convention two issues ignored by the Republicans came to the fore. These were prohibition and the Ku Klux Klan. The great Democratic machines in the big cities of the North opposed both. In Governor Alfred E. Smith of New York, a Roman Catholic, they found a leader who dared to speak out boldly both for repeal of prohibition and against the Klan. With few exceptions Southern and Western delegates backed William G. McAdoo, a "dry" and a Protestant. After a hundred ballots, it was plain that neither Smith nor McAdoo could gain the necessary two-thirds majority. Both withdrew. John W. Davis, a native of West Virginia and a Wall Street lawyer, was then nominated. For second place on the ticket, the party chose Governor Charles W. Bryan of Nebraska, brother of William J. Bryan, the "Great Commoner."

In their platform the Democrats bore down heavily on corruption under Republican rule. They promised farm relief, collective bargaining, enforcement of the antitrust laws, and immediate independence for the Philippines. They suggested giving the people a chance to vote on whether the United States should join the League of Nations. A motion condemning the Klan, supported by William J. Bryan, failed to pass by a single vote.

La Follette runs as a Progressive.

Since the war's end farmers and organized labor had been bitterly discontented. A Farmer-Labor party appeared in 1920 but did not get much support. Its leaders helped to launch a new Progressive party in 1924. The Progressives named Senator Robert M. La Follette of Wisconsin (Republican) for the Presidency and Senator Burton K. Wheeler (Democrat) of Montana as his running mate. Leaders of the Railroad brotherhoods and of the American Federation of Labor endorsed the Progressive ticket. This was the first time in its history that the A.F. of L. had officially supported a presidential candidate. The Socialist party also backed the ticket, although La Follette was not a Socialist. The support of the Communists was turned down.

Among other reforms Progressives urged public ownership of railroads and hydroelectric power, protection of labor against injunctions, higher taxes on inheritances, and an amendment giving Congress power to override decisions of the Supreme Court.

The Republicans pictured La Follette as a dangerous radical. Ignoring Davis and his charges of corruption, they concentrated their attacks on La Follette. The election aroused little interest. Only 51 per cent of the voters went to the polls. Coolidge won 382 electoral votes; Davis, 136; and La Follette, 13. Beyond question the nation's rising prosperity limited the Progressive vote. The Progressives were further limited by having only $200,000 to spend on their campaign. Yet La Follette polled 17 per cent of the popular vote, chiefly west of the Mississippi.

Prosperity creates an "era of good feeling."

Throughout the six years of Coolidge's presidency (1923–29), business boomed. Taxes were reduced four times, but in spite of this the public debt was cut by one third. The policy of the Federal Reserve Board created

SENATOR ROBERT M. LA FOLLETTE

an abundance of easy credit and this encouraged gambling on Wall Street. The administration made no attempt to check the growing speculation on the stock market. Although the farmers clamored for relief, Coolidge did little about their problems. While he favored the World Court, he brought no pressure on Congress in regard to joining it. He seemed unconcerned with the problem of reparations and war debts. On the question of prohibition, he said nothing except that the laws should be enforced. Despite his inactivity, or perhaps because of it, he was one of the most popular Presidents we ever had. The discontent of the farmers was the only disturbing element in the Coolidge "era of good feeling."

Progressives attack the power trust.

A few voices could still be heard urging control of big business. They were most concerned about the rapidly growing power industry. The states could not bring the industry under control because so much electric power crossed state lines. The first feeble gesture toward federal control came in 1920 when Congress created the Federal Power Commission to license hydroelectric plants on public lands and navigable streams. But nine tenths of the nation's electricity was produced in plants using coal for fuel. Through the 1920's some congressmen tried in vain to get federal regulation of all power companies doing business across state lines.

Some congressmen urged government ownership as the only way to get low rates for small users. They pointed out that publicly owned hydroelectric plants in Canada were selling electricity to consumers at less than half the price charged by private companies in the United States. Senator George W. Norris of Nebraska was the leader of this group. For years he fought to keep Congress from selling the great power plant at Muscle Shoals. In 1928 he succeeded in getting Congress to pass a bill directing the government to operate the plant. Coolidge vetoed the Norris bill.

Herbert Hoover Defeats Alfred E. Smith

The Republicans nominate Hoover.

Since the public gave Coolidge credit for the prevailing good times, he could easily have had another term. But with his usual brevity he declared he did not "choose to run" again. In 1928 Herbert Hoover was named the Republican standard-bearer on the first

SENATOR GEORGE W. NORRIS, *independent Republican from Nebraska*

ALFRED E. SMITH

ballot. As Secretary of Commerce since 1921, Hoover had earned the confidence of businessmen. Under their leadership he was sure the country could expect continued prosperity. "We shall soon," he declared in his acceptance speech, "with the help of God, be in sight of the day when poverty shall be banished from this nation."

The Democrats nominate Alfred E. Smith.

In 1928 the name of Alfred E. Smith, the "Happy Warrior," was again placed before the Democratic convention. This time Smith was nominated on the first ballot. In four terms as governor of New York he had given the state clean and efficient government and had carried through a number of reforms. A warm, colorful personality, he was extremely popular among city wage earners in the Northeast. He was the first lifetime city dweller and the first Roman Catholic ever to be nominated by a major party.

Both parties promised to enforce prohibition. Yet Smith in his campaign speeches boldly advocated (1) a change in the Volstead Act to permit the sale of light wines and beer and (2) eventual repeal of the Eighteenth Amendment. He opposed the return of the saloon, however, and urged that liquor be sold only through state stores. While Smith's proposals made sense to many voters, he probably lost more votes on the liquor issue than he gained. Hoover, on the other hand, defended prohibition as "a great social and economic experiment, noble in motive and far-reaching in purpose."

Smith bid for the farm vote by endorsing the principles of the McNary-Haugen bill. He also favored the public operation of Muscle Shoals and other power sites. Hoover condemned both proposals. He said they would lead the country to state socialism. Declared Hoover: "You cannot extend the mastery of the government over the daily working life of a people without at the same time making it the master of the people's souls and thoughts."

False issues confuse the voters.

The campaign of 1928 was the first in which the radio played an important part. Millions who had never before heard a presidential candidate listened to Smith and Hoover over the air. Campaign expenditures reached a new high, and for once the Democrats had almost as much to spend as the Republicans. Excitement ran high. The public showed more interest in personalities than in the real issues. People talked about Mr. Smith's East Side accent, his immigrant parentage, and his religion. Millions of pamphlets, circulated chiefly in rural areas, played upon religious bias. This irresponsible campaigning was assisted by the Ku Klux Klan.

Hoover is elected.

Seventy-five per cent of the voters went to the polls, an amazing record. Smith received the largest popular vote that any Democrat had ever won up to that time. He polled 40 per cent of the votes cast. Yet Hoover carried forty states, including five states of the "Solid South." Four of these had never before been in the Republican column. In view of Republican gains in the South, news analysts said that the Democratic party could never again capture the Presidency except by a lucky chance like that of 1912.

Isolationism Is Mixed with Internationalism

After World War I most Americans were weary of international responsibilities. They did not want to be disturbed by events abroad. They found it easy to forget foreign affairs while Harding and Coolidge were in the White House. Neither of these Presidents gave much thought to the world outside our borders. During their administrations the United States reversed the trend toward greater participation in world affairs. Yet of course they did not entirely ignore the rest of the world.

Harding rejects the League.

In his inaugural address President Harding said that the United States sought no part "in directing the policies of the Old World." Shortly afterward he announced that his administration would not enter the League of Nations "by the side door, back door, or cellar door." At that time he undoubtedly expressed the feelings of some Democrats as well as of the majority of Republicans. These people thought the United States could have peace by turning its back on world affairs. It seemed to them that the nation could be self-sufficient, both in the economic and in the political realm.

Congress makes a separate peace.

Since the Senate had twice refused to ratify the peace treaties containing the covenant of the League of Nations, we had to make a separate peace with the Central Powers. In July, 1921, Congress adopted a resolution declaring the war at an end. Soon after, Washington signed peace treaties with Germany, Austria, and Hungary. Thus the United States avoided any responsibility for enforcing the Versailles peace terms. Knowing how shaky the peace settlement was, Woodrow Wilson denounced this policy as a retreat into "sullen and selfish isolation." He believed it would end in our having to fight another world war. Unhappily, his prediction came true when Hitler tore up the Versailles treaty bit by bit and brought about World War II.

The Washington Conference.

In 1921 our State Department was worried about Far Eastern affairs, particularly Japanese expansion. Japan had received a League mandate over all the former German-owned islands north of the equator (see p. 619). This had brought the Japanese flag south and east of the Philippines and not far from Australia. In Japan's possession also was the Chinese province of Shantung, though Japan promised to restore it to China in the near future. That this pledge would be carried out seemed doubtful, in view of Japan's Twenty-one demands on China in 1915 (see p. 583). China was weak and Japanese leaders wanted to establish a protectorate over the whole country. Furthermore, Japan was thought to have designs on eastern Siberia, where it had kept troops since 1918.

Another problem troubling our State Department was the Anglo-Japanese alliance, made under a treaty signed in 1902. This pact had a clause stating that the alliance could never be used against the United States. Yet we had always disliked it, as had the people of Canada, Australia, and New Zealand. London, seeking a graceful way to end the treaty, suggested a conference on Pacific problems.

At this same time the United States was carrying out a huge naval building program started during the war. The program would have given us the strongest navy in the world. Britain and Japan were also enlarging their navies. In fact, a naval building race had begun. In 1921 Congress asked President Harding to call an international conference on naval armaments. Accordingly, eight governments were invited to meet at Washington in November, 1921.

The purpose of this Washington Conference was to ease tensions in the Far East and to stop the naval race. Three important treaties resulted.

1. *The Four-Power Treaty* (United States, France, Great Britain, Japan). This pact replaced the Anglo-Japanese

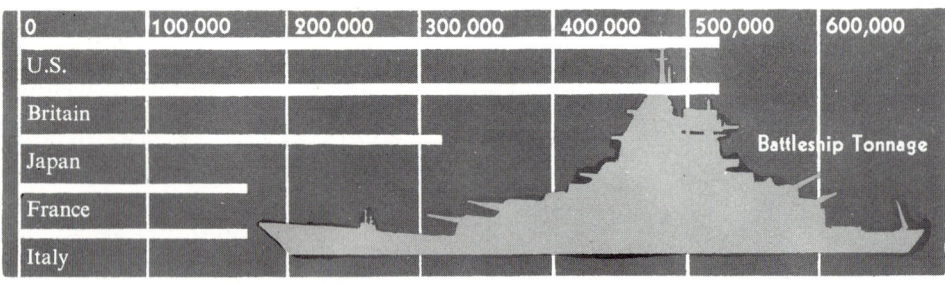

0	100,000	200,000	300,000	400,000	500,000	600,000
U.S.						
Britain						
Japan						
France						
Italy						

Battleship Tonnage

NAVAL LIMITS IMPOSED BY THE WASHINGTON CONFERENCE

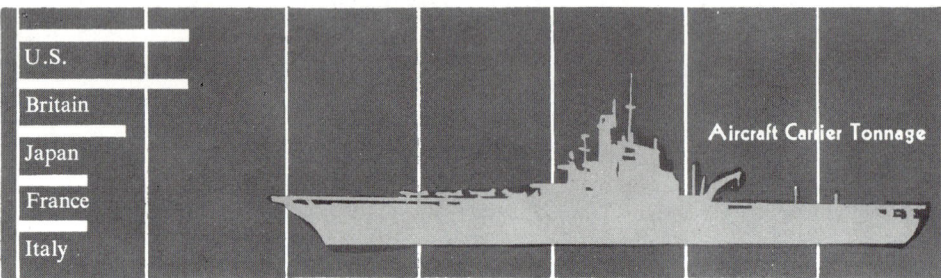

U.S.

Britain

Japan

France

Italy

Aircraft Carrier Tonnage

alliance. The signatory nations agreed to respect one another's possessions in the Far East and to confer if a dispute arose in regard to them.

2. *The Nine-Power Treaty* (United States, Belgium, China, France, Great Britain, Italy, Japan, the Netherlands, Portugal). The nine powers taking part in the conference included all those with an interest in China, except Russia. They agreed to support the principle of the Open Door—that is, to preserve equal commercial rights in China for all and to respect that nation's independence. In harmony with this treaty, Japan withdrew from Shantung and softened the Twenty-one demands made in 1915 (see p. 583). A democratic party came to power in Japan, and for a few years Japan followed a peaceful course.

The Nine-Power Treaty said nothing as to how it was to be enforced. It assumed that all the signatory powers would live up to their promises. Ten years later, when Japan resumed its aggressive policy toward China, the treaty was no obstacle.

3. *The Five-Power Naval Treaty* (United States, France, Great Britain, Italy, and Japan). This pact set limits on future naval building and provided for the scrapping of certain ships then being built. For ten years the signers agreed not to build any new capital ships (those of over 10,000 tons). In ships of this class the United States, Great Britain, and Japan agreed to keep their strength at the ratio of 5:5:3. France and Italy accepted the ratio of 1.67 each. Sixty-six battleships were to be scrapped, including 30 American ships and 36 British and Japanese ships. It was Secretary of State Hughes who proposed the ship scrapping. By this treaty the United States gave up a chance to become the world's greatest naval power, and with it the chance to act as guardian of the world's peace.

To get the Japanese to consent to limit their navy, the United States and Great Britain had to make a big concession. They agreed not to strengthen any of their fortifications and naval bases in the Pacific area from Singapore to Hawaii. This meant that the Japanese navy, though smaller in capital ships, would be supreme in Far Eastern waters.

At the time, the work of the Washington Conference was greeted with rejoicing. It was thought to be a triumph in the cause of peace. American and British taxpayers were especially pleased with the naval holiday, not foreseeing it would cost them a hundredfold when a new world war had to be fought. In reality the Washington Conference was a triumph for Japan. Since the treaty did not limit the building of cruisers, submarines, and other short-range vessels, Japan went on adding these to its navy. Soon it had an immense advantage in the seas washing the shores of the Dutch Indies, China, and the Philippines.

President Coolidge hoped to have the 5:5:3 ratio extended to all classes of ships. He called the signers of the Five-Power Treaty to a conference at Geneva in 1927. Nothing came of this meeting. A conference at London in 1930 was more successful.

We co-operate with the League.

Our government soon found that American interests required co-operation with the League. In 1923 the State Department began to send "unofficial observers" to meet with League committees concerned with nonpolitical matters, such as health regulations and commerce. The next year official American delegates were sent to a conference on the opium problem. After that the United States was represented at most League conferences of a nonpolitical nature.

We do not join the World Court.

Many Americans hoped that even if the United States would not join the League, it would join the Permanent Court of Justice. This organization, commonly called the World Court, was entirely separate from the League, although the League had founded it. Unlike the earlier Hague Court, the new court settled disputes not by arbitration but according to the principles of international law. The World Court could hear any case which the parties thereto might submit to it. It could also give an advisory opinion on any question referred to it by the Council or Assembly of the League. Five Presidents—Wilson, Harding, Coolidge, Hoover, and Franklin D. Roosevelt—urged that we join the World Court. But isolationists in the Senate succeeded in keeping us out.

The United States tries to "outlaw" war.

Although the United States did not join the League or the World Court, it did try to promote world peace. In 1928 we invited the nations of the world to sign the Kellogg-Briand Pact, also known as the Pact of Paris. This famous paper was drawn up by Secretary of State Kellogg and the foreign minister of France. It condemned war for the solution of international disputes and pledged the signers to settle all disputes by peaceful means. Since the pact made war illegal, it was said to "outlaw" war.

Unfortunately, the treaty had no teeth. Secretary Kellogg himself said, "The only enforcement behind the pact is public opinion." Yet many hailed it as a great forward step in the direction of world peace. They thought that somehow the pact would enforce itself. They did not discover for several years that the pact was only a gesture, an expression of the wish for peace.

War debts create hard feeling.

For many years after the war, relations between the United States and Europe were troubled by the question of war debts. During the war the United States government lent the Allies several billion dollars. Shortly after the war our government lent money to the new states formed out of Russian territory and out of Austria-Hungary.

Taken together these loans came to about ten billion dollars. Nearly all of the money was spent in the United States, with great benefit to American business.

Great Britain and France also had lent large sums to their allies. Much of the money could not be collected. European statesmen said that an all-round forgiveness of debts would prevent arguments, would encourage a revival of international trade, and would help their people to get back to work.

From the beginning, our government took the stand that the war loans were a business transaction and must be paid. If they were not paid, American taxpayers would have to make up the loss. Most Americans thought this would not be fair. People who borrow money should pay it back. President Coolidge expressed this attitude in the homely words—"They hired the money, didn't they?"

The United States made lenient arrangements with the debtor countries. They were to repay their debts over a period of sixty-two years. The original interest rate was cut substantially. When France and Italy had serious financial trouble in the mid-twenties, our government canceled a large part of the principal owed by these two countries. Despite these concessions, the French and Italians resented our refusal to cancel the entire debt. They felt we ought to consider our wartime loans as a contribution to the common cause—the defeat of the Central Powers.

The American people had little knowledge of international finance. They did not see that our tariff policy made payment of the war debts extremely difficult. There are only two ways by which one country can make payments to another: (1) by selling goods and services or (2) by sending gold. Our high tariffs shut out Euro-pean goods. We expected our debtors to pay in gold, not goods, yet there was not enough gold in all Europe for this purpose. Consequently, the countries which had large debts to the United States said they could pay us only what they collected from Germany in reparations.

In 1921 the amount of reparations to be paid by Germany was set at about thirty-three billion dollars. Germany protested it could not pay that much. Our debtors then suggested that if we would cancel their debts, they would forgive Germany an equal amount. The United States did not agree to this proposal. Germany got the money needed for reparations payments from funds which foreigners invested in German industry. Ironically, Americans supplied almost half these funds. When the depression came and investors stopped lending money abroad, Germany could no longer pay reparations. Our debtors then stopped making payments to us.

The debtors felt that the American attitude toward the war debts problem was selfish. Students of international affairs think it was short-sighted. They argue that (1) the attempt to pay war debts and reparations in cash caused grave economic troubles in Europe, and (2) the attempt gave fuel to the Nazi propaganda engine on which Hitler rode to power.

Relations with Caribbean America improve.

In the 1920's the United States still had to intervene at times to keep order around the Caribbean. The most disputed incident took place in 1927 when President Coolidge sent 5000 Marines to Nicaragua during a revolt. This action was sharply criticized by political foes of Coolidge and by Latin Americans. Coolidge then sent Henry L. Stimson to Nicaragua to arrange a truce. Stimson succeeded in getting

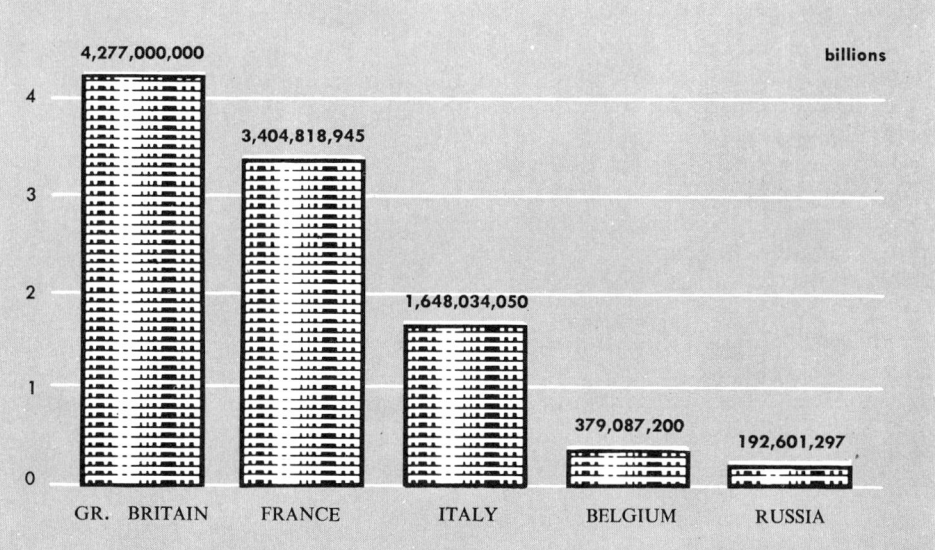

TOP FIVE ALLIED DEBTORS

billions

GR. BRITAIN 4,277,000,000
FRANCE 3,404,818,945
ITALY 1,648,034,050
BELGIUM 379,087,200
RUSSIA 192,601,297

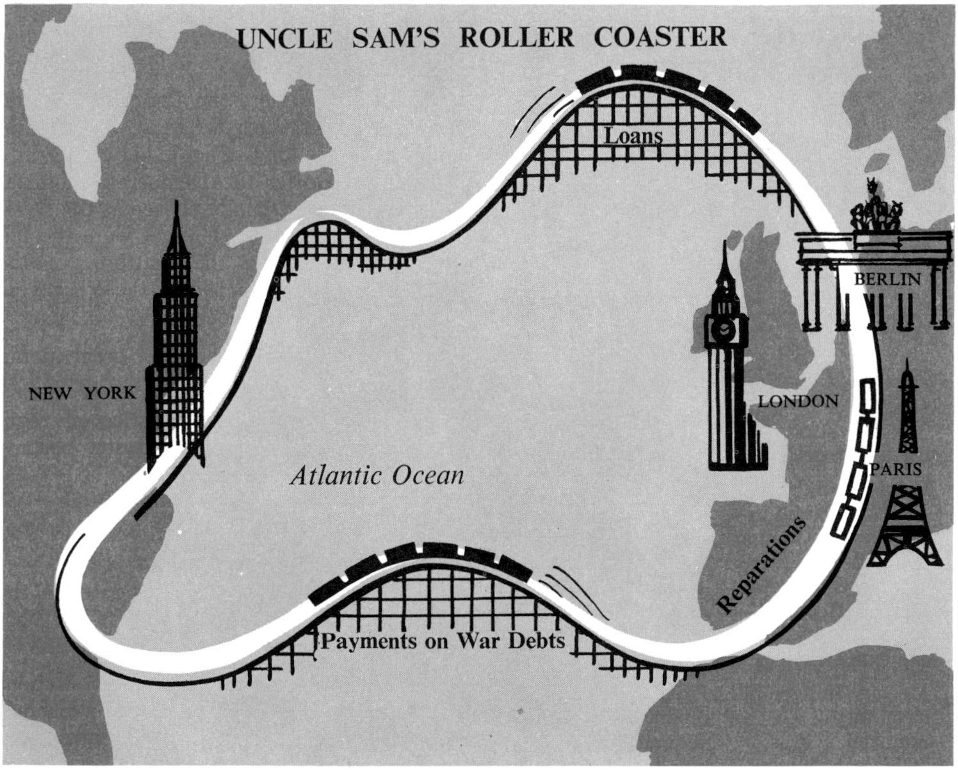

UNCLE SAM'S ROLLER COASTER

Loans

BERLIN

LONDON

PARIS

NEW YORK

Atlantic Ocean

Reparations

Payments on War Debts

the different parties to agree to a peaceful election under our supervision.

In the same year relations with Mexico took a turn for the better. There had been serious friction ever since 1917, when Mexico adopted a constitution saying that oil and other minerals found beneath the surface of the soil belong to the nation (see p. 594).

The war clouds lifted in 1927 when Coolidge chose Dwight W. Morrow to be ambassador to Mexico. Instead of threatening the Mexicans, Morrow tried to win their friendship. He was aided by the good-will tours of Charles A. Lindbergh, hero of the first solo flight across the Atlantic, and Will Rogers, the popular American humorist. Morrow worked out a compromise that settled the oil dispute temporarily. American oil companies were allowed to keep the subsoil rights they had bought prior to 1917. Thus the Coolidge presidency ended with signs of a new day in inter-American relations.

WILL ROGERS

FOR IDENTIFICATION

Calvin Coolidge	Charles Evans Hughes
John W. Davis	Kellogg-Briand Pact
Fordney-McCumber Tariff	Robert La Follette
	William G. McAdoo
Warren G. Harding	Andrew J. Mellon
Herbert Hoover	Alfred E. Smith

FOR EXPLANATION OR DEFINITION

McNary-Haugen bill	Progressive party
naval race	reparations
normalcy	veterans' bonus
"Ohio gang"	war debts

FOR REVIEW

1. What is the significance of Harding's promise of normalcy?

2. Who were the three strongest men in Harding's Cabinet?

3. (a) How did the Fordney-McCumber Tariff of 1922 differ from the Underwood Tariff of 1913? (b) What did the flexible clause in the 1922 tariff permit? (c) Why did some manufacturers object to this tariff? Why did economists object?

4. (a) What was the attitude of the Harding and Coolidge administrations toward the regulation of business? (b) In what ways did this attitude manifest itself?

5. On what grounds did Secretary of the Treasury Mellon defend the tax reductions of the 1920's?

6. What scandals are associated with the names of Charles R. Forbes, Harry J. Daugherty, and Albert B. Fall?

7. Describe briefly the career of Calvin Coolidge before he succeeded to the Presidency in 1923.

8. In what ways did Congress show its reluctance to follow Coolidge's leadership?

9. (a) Who were the Republican nominees in 1924? (b) What issues were involved in the long struggle between Smith and McAdoo for the Democratic nomination? Who were finally chosen as the Democratic nominees? (c) What were the important planks in the platform of the Progressive party in 1924? (d) What were the results of the election?

10. Account for Coolidge's great popularity.

11. (a) Why did the question of regulating the electric power industry become a national issue in the 1920's? (b) What was the policy of Senator George W. Norris toward the federal power plant at Muscle Shoals?

12. (a) Who were the candidates in the presidential campaign of 1928? (b) What were the chief issues in the campaign?

13. What were the chief considerations which led to the calling of the Washington Conference on Naval Disarmament and Far Eastern Affairs?

ease tension in the far east.

14. State the terms of the Four-Power Treaty. How did this treaty affect the Anglo-Japanese alliance of 1902?

15. What were the terms of the Nine-Power Treaty concerning China? *(handwritten annotation)*

16. (a) What were the terms of the Five-Power Naval Treaty? (b) Explain the phrase 5:5:3. (c) What concessions were made to Japan in return for Japan's promise to limit its navy? *(handwritten annotation)*

17. (a) How did the World Court differ from the Hague Court? (b) Why did the United States refuse to join the World Court?

18. What were the terms of the Kellogg-Briand peace pact?

19. (a) Why was it difficult for European nations to pay war debts? (b) How was the payment of war debts linked with the problems of reparations?

FOR FURTHER STUDY AND DISCUSSION

1. The scandals associated with the administrations of Presidents Grant and Harding are among the most shameful in the nation's history. Compare the two administrations, analyzing in some detail at least one scandal in each administration, and endeavoring to determine the basic causes of the scandals, and the role of each President. Helpful sources: Allen, *Only Yesterday;* Hopkins, *The Incredible Era;* Slosson, *The Great Crusade and After* (A.L.S.), pp. 91–100; Commager and Nevins, *Heritage of America*, No. 246.

2. Account for the relaxation of efforts to control big business during the 1920's. Outline some of the direct and indirect results of the hands-off policy.

3. Compare the Progressive party of 1912 with the Progressive party of 1924.

4. What is the significance of the long debate concerning Muscle Shoals? What is the relationship between this struggle and the creation of the Tennessee Valley Authority (TVA)? Helpful sources: Commager, *Documents*, No. 470; Hart, *Contemporaries*, Vol. V, No. 157; Wish, *Contemporary America*, pp. 371–374, 453–454; Lilienthal, *TVA, Democracy on the March.*

5. (a) Why was the Washington Conference ineffectual in checking naval expenditures? (b) Why was the United States willing to share naval equality with England but not with Japan? (c) In what ways were the Four-Power Treaty, the Five-Power Naval Treaty, and the Nine-Power Treaty interrelated? Helpful sources: Bailey, *Diplomatic History,* pp. 681–699; Wish, *Contemporary America,* pp. 391–394; Commager, *Documents,* Nos. 447–449; Bemis, *Diplomatic History,* pp. 690–697.

6. Explain the meaning of the following statements of President Coolidge: "The business of America is business"; "They hired the money, didn't they?"

7. What was the basic weakness of the Kellogg-Briand Pact to outlaw war as "an instrument of national policy"?

FOR INDIVIDUAL OR GROUP ACTIVITIES

1. Prepare charts to demonstrate the essential agreements of the Washington Conference.

2. Assume that you are a reporter assigned to cover the Democratic National Convention of 1924. Write an article interpreting the debates and final action of the convention in nominating John W. Davis.

3. Prepare outlines summarizing each of the following: Coolidge's veto of the McNary-Haugen bill; Hoover's veto of Muscle Shoals bill; and Hoover's defense of "rugged individualism." Helpful source: Commager, *Documents,* Nos. 462, 468, 470.

4. Write a book report on one of the following: Allen, *Only Yesterday;* White, *A Puritan in Babylon;* Adams, *The Incredible Era.*

5. Investigate and report on the efforts to secure American membership in the World Court. What part did Elihu Root play in formulating the statute of the Court? What controversy developed over "advisory opinions"? What was the "Root formula"? What was the attitude of Charles Evans Hughes toward the World Court? Helpful sources: Bailey, *Diplomatic History;* Bemis, *Diplomatic History.*

665

40. THE NATION SUFFERS AN ECONOMIC COLLAPSE

The Farm Crisis Deepens

Herbert Hoover becomes President.

On a rainy day in March, 1929, Herbert Hoover took the oath as President. His inaugural address was optimistic. We had, he said, "reached a higher degree of comfort and security than ever existed before in the history of the world." Our task was "to establish more firmly the stability and security of business and thereby remove poverty still further from our borders."

Hoover was a humanitarian, not a reactionary. When he praised rugged individualism, he was praising self-reliance, not indifference to the public welfare. A poor boy, he had worked his way through Leland Stanford University and made a sizable fortune before he was forty. Much of it he spent on good works. His sympathy for the suffering had led him to direct a mass relief program in Belgium, Russia, and central Europe during and after the war. In 1927 he took charge of the relief of flood victims in the Mississippi Valley. He was responsible for Harding's successful intercession (1923) in behalf of an eight-hour day for steelworkers.

Like Coolidge's, Hoover's personality was rather colorless. This was a handicap when he became President. So too was his lack of political experience. Until 1929 he had never held an elective office. He had, however, been extremely successful as a mining engineer and financial promoter. As Secretary of Commerce he had worked tirelessly to help business. Such help, he thought, would benefit the entire nation.

Hoover knew that the 1920's had been difficult years for the nation's farmers. During his campaign for election he promised to call a special session of Congress to take up the farm problem. Before we see what the special session did, let us see why farm prices were low and what action Congress had already taken.

Depression hits the farmers first.

Farm dwellers did not share the prosperity that so many Americans enjoyed in the twenties. The average income of farmers in 1929 was less than a third the income of nonfarmers. Every year during the 1920's thousands

666

of farms were foreclosed. Some of the dispossessed farmers became share-croppers. Others joined the ill-paid stream of migrants who harvest the crops. Still others moved to the city.

Farmers who grew grain, cotton, tobacco, and hogs had the hardest time in the postwar years. The slogan "Food will win the war" and the lure of high prices had led them to cultivate a larger acreage. Many bought land at several times its normal value, going into debt for it and for machines to work it. High prices for farm products did not last long enough for them to pay off their debts.

The market for farm staples shrinks.

The overproduction of staples was the main cause of the farm crisis. A large part of our wheat, hogs, cotton, and tobacco had always been sold in Europe. After the war, however, farmers in other parts of the world captured most of this market. Canada, Argentina, and Australia were exporting more grain and livestock; Japan and India, more tobacco; and Brazil, China, India, and Egypt, more cotton. These countries were less industrialized than the United States and had lower tariff walls. They would take European manufactured goods in exchange for farm products, and we would not. Our former customers in Europe therefore found it easier to buy from them.

At the same time the domestic market for staples also was shrinking. Americans were eating less grain, pork, and lard, and more milk, beef, poultry, eggs, fruit, and vegetables. Moreover, American women were wearing shorter and lighter clothing and were using more silk and rayon and less cotton. These changes naturally hurt the sale of cotton. The replacement of horses and mules by motor vehicles further cut the farmers' market. Millions of acres once used in growing fodder for work animals were no longer needed.

Migrants from the Oklahoma Dust Bowl arrive in California.

A day laborer's shack in Oklahoma

A Republican campaign ad in 1928

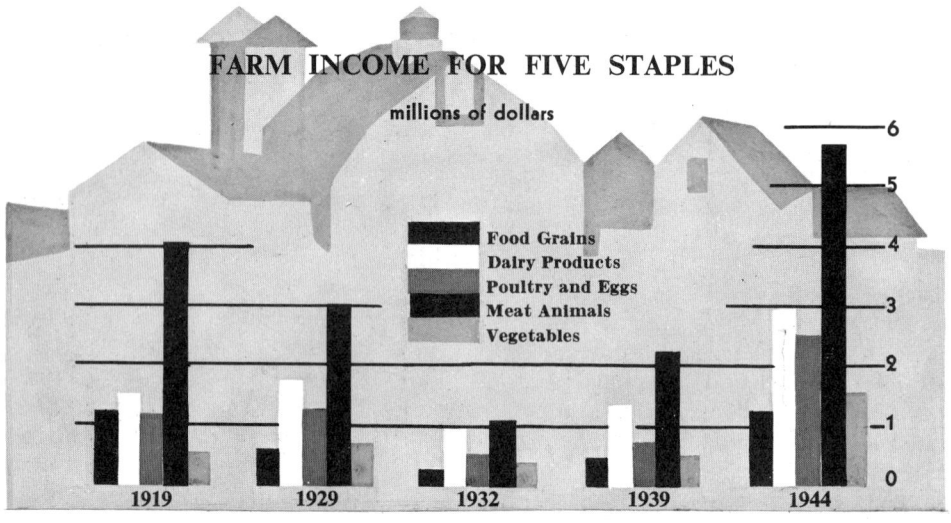

FARM INCOME FOR FIVE STAPLES

millions of dollars

Food Grains
Dairy Products
Poultry and Eggs
Meat Animals
Vegetables

1919 1929 1932 1939 1944

The "farm bloc" promotes aid to farmers.

A group of congressmen, chiefly from the Midwest, became known in the 1920's as the "farm bloc." Drawn from both parties, they joined in backing laws to help farmers. To aid the growers of staples, the farm bloc supported the McNary-Haugen bill. It called for fixing domestic prices and dumping surplus products abroad. Congress passed it in 1927 and 1928, but each time President Coolidge vetoed it. He believed price-fixing would lead to still more overproduction. He urged farmers producing staples to reduce the surplus by cutting their acreage. Few, however, felt they could afford to do this. Since they depended on a staple crop for the cash to meet taxes, interest, and living costs, they were afraid to cut down the amount they had for sale.

The Farm Board is set up.

Soon after his inauguration, President Hoover called a special session of Congress to consider farm relief. Stating that "no government agency should engage in buying and selling and price-fixing of products," he made known his opposition to the McNary-Haugen bill. He proposed instead that farmers be helped to set up their own marketing organizations. Accordingly, Congress passed the Agricultural Marketing Act of 1929. It provided for a Federal Farm Board with a revolving fund of 500 million dollars, to be loaned to co-operative marketing associations. The Board quickly organized several national marketing co-operatives to handle cotton, livestock, and other products not already sold through such organizations. Hoover hoped that the new co-operatives would be able to adjust supply to demand and thus obtain higher prices.

Within a year, unfortunately, world prices took another plunge. Our domestic prices fell by the same amount. Wheat dropped from $1.04 a bushel in 1929 to 32 cents in 1932, while cotton went from 17 cents to 5 cents. In 1930 and 1931, in a vain effort to raise prices, the Farm Board bought huge quantities of American wheat and cotton and placed them in storage. By 1932 the Board had used all its money, yet prices were lower than when it began its work. How to dispose of its wheat and cotton was a problem for which no solution was in sight. The Board's efforts to persuade farmers to grow less likewise failed.

Raising the tariff makes matters worse.

Upon taking office, President Hoover suggested minor tariff increases, mostly on farm products. Congress, however, raised the duties on all sorts of goods, until the average rate on nonfree items was 50 per cent higher than before. Senator Grundy of Pennsylvania pushed the new Hawley-Smoot tariff bill through by clever logrolling. Except among the Old Guard Republicans, the bill had few friends. Industrialists interested in foreign trade, bankers with foreign investments, and progressive congressmen from farm states all condemned the bill. Over a thousand of the nation's leading economists signed a letter urging Hoover to veto it. A large number of foreign governments expressed anxiety over its passage, saying it would force them to pass "defensive" tariffs. But the President signed it, praising the flexible clause which gave him the right to raise or lower duties as much as 50 per cent.

Critics of the new tariff law said it would be of no help to most farmers, since they needed to sell their surpluses abroad. In fact, they would be worse off because their sales abroad would fall. Foreigners could not buy American goods unless they had dollars to pay for them. But how could they get dollars if our tariff walls shut out what they had to sell? It was also argued that the new tariff would make it even harder for nations in Europe to pay us their war debts. These forecasts actually came true. Within a year twenty-five countries had passed laws to cut the import of American goods. If they had not done so, their entire gold supply would have come here to pay for their purchases. By 1932 our exports had fallen to a third of the 1929 figure. American farmers were among the first to suffer the consequences.

WALL STREET, *1929. In October the top-heavy pyramid of speculation toppled with a crash that was felt throughout the nation.*

The Nation Plunges into the Great Depression

The stock market soars.

In the years 1923–29, while Coolidge was President, large profits were made in industry. The stock market, which normally is a rough barometer of business conditions, rose without serious interruption. As prices climbed, more and more people entered the market. Many bought on margin—putting up only a fraction of the price and borrowing the rest. Gambling in stocks seemed an easy way to get rich quickly. Hundreds of thousands of Americans who had never before owned stock put their life savings into the stock market. Promoters took advantage of their ignorance to issue and unload vast quantities of almost worthless securities.

Warning signs are disregarded.

Signs that business was slowing up might have been detected early in 1929. Building was falling off. Steel and automobile production were slipping. About four million workers were jobless. Bank and business failures were increasing. Yet few leaders paid any attention to these warnings. President Coolidge and Secretary of the Treasury Mellon declared that all was well. Business tycoons talked of a new era of permanent prosperity.

Although President-elect Hoover was optimistic about business conditions, he asked Coolidge to do something to check the feverish speculation in stocks. Coolidge therefore allowed the Federal Reserve Board to raise the rediscount rate slightly in February. On March 6, two days after Hoover became President, he had the Federal Reserve Board shut off credit to banks making loans to stockbrokers. In May and again in June the rediscount rate was raised. These mild actions could no longer check the frenzy of speculation.

After Hoover's inauguration, stocks climbed faster than ever. Had he not been elected on the slogans, "Four more years of prosperity" and "Two cars in every garage"? In two days in March one bank stock rose $950 a share, and one investor made thirteen million dollars on this stock alone. Stories of such winnings started a new wave of gambling, which went on furiously until fall. Brokers' offices all over the country were crowded by men and women eagerly watching the changing prices on the board.

The fool's paradise ends.

Upon reaching a peak early in September, 1929, the stock market began to hesitate. We now know that European and American investors with large holdings were quietly selling stocks. On October 23, prices broke, dropping 18 points on the average. This started a stampede of selling. The bottom fell out of the market on October 29. That day representative stocks slumped 40 points on the average, and the total loss of stock values was fourteen billion dollars. The panic lasted for days. By the end of the year the loss in stock values came to forty billion dollars. For the next three years the market continued to coast downward.

A terrible depression, the longest period of hard times in our nation's history, began after the crash. The economy did not fully recover until we entered World War II. Let us try to understand the conditions that brought about this Great Depression.

Why was the depression so severe?

The causes of the Great Depression are complex. Economists continue to argue about them. Among the conditions which helped to produce the depression or to prolong it, the following are most often given high rank.

1. The stock market crash itself. Nobody knows how many Americans owned stock at the time of the crash. It is thought that one or two million people lost most of their savings in the panic. Some lost everything they had. All who had suffered in the crash reacted by spending less freely. The sale of luxury items tumbled, as did the sale of durable goods, such as motor cars and refrigerators. As consumer buying shrank, workers were laid off. Unemployment cut buying power and led to still more lay-offs, in a vicious descending spiral.

Without doubt, the crash is important in explaining the severity of the depression. Yet other factors were also at work.

2. The failure of purchasing power to keep up with expanding production. In the 1920's the nation's capacity to produce was greater than its capacity to consume. According to the best estimates we have, 60 per cent of the na-

PER CENT UNEMPLOYED, 1929–1943

Source: *Statistical Abstract of the United States* and *Historical Statistics*

tion's families in 1929 earned less than $2000 a year, while 20 per cent earned less than $1000 a year. Yet $2000 a year was barely enough at that time to supply a family with basic necessities. Had every family received an income of at least $2000, all the surplus goods could have been used and much more besides.

3. Poor distribution of the nation's income, which resulted in oversaving. A large proportion of the national income was going to a very small proportion of the population. Those in the upper income brackets could not spend all they received. They saved more than could be invested profitably in business. The excess savings flowed into foreign loans and into the stock market. Oversaving began as early as 1925.[1]

Idle savings were especially evident during the depression. Few people wanted to invest money to expand an old enterprise or to build a new one. Because of the scarcity of profitable

opportunities for investment, banks paid little or no interest on deposits. Yet deposits were large. Not until 1940, when idle money was put to work in defense industries, did prosperity return.

4. The farm depression. Throughout the twenties the farmers had little to spend. Since they made up a fourth of the nation's population, the shrinkage of their purchasing power was felt throughout the economy.

5. Technological unemployment. New machines and new processes were continually boosting the productivity of labor. It is estimated that such technological advances during the 1920's displaced about two million workers each year. Shortening the work week helped to spread the work but did not go far enough. New industries absorbed only part of the displaced individuals. In the years from 1922 to 1929 from 5 to 10 per cent of the labor force was unemployed at any one time. The crash did not stop the technological advance. On the contrary, it continued at a rapid rate throughout the 1930's.

---

[1] The statistics and conclusions are from reports of the Brookings Institution.

6. *Too much credit.* The "easy money" policy of the banks during the twenties promoted speculation. Easy credit also led millions of consumers to buy goods on the installment plan, pledging their income a long time in advance. By 1929 many consumers were so in debt that they had to curtail their spending. One result was a drop in the sales of automobiles and other durable goods.

7. *Weaknesses in the banking system.* Thousands of banks went to the wall in 1930, 1931, and 1932. Failure often resulted because of "frozen assets"—real estate, taken by the bank when mortgages were foreclosed, for which the bank could not find a buyer. When a bank failed, its depositors lost heavily and usually did less spending than before.

8. *Decline in our foreign trade.* As we have noted, American exports dropped almost two thirds between 1929 and 1932, since foreign nations could not buy American goods (see p. 669). Export industries laid off men by the thousand. At the same time farm surpluses kept piling higher, bringing a further drop in farm prices.

9. *Price-maintenance policy of big business.* In earlier depressions when warehouses filled with unsold goods, prices dropped until consumers could buy again. Lower prices started the wheels turning, provided jobs, and led to recovery. But in the Great Depression, prices of manufactured goods fell very little. Big business, which controlled more of the market than ever before, chose to cut output instead of prices. For example, between 1929 and 1933 the output of farm implements dropped 80 per cent and their price dropped only 6 per cent. The output of motor vehicles dropped 80 per cent and their price, 16 per cent. The price-maintenance policy resulted in grave unemployment and threatened to make economic recovery impossible.

The Federal Government Tries to Check the Depression

Hoover tries to restore confidence.

At first the President, like many others, thought the panic would quickly pass. The chief essential, he believed, was to restore confidence. From time to time he and other members of his official family made optimistic statements, suggesting that prosperity was just around the corner. Nevertheless, he also took positive action.

Within a month of the stock market crash Hoover called leaders of industry and labor to the White House. He asked the industrialists to maintain existing wage rates and to spread the available work as widely as possible among their employees. He called on the labor unions to avoid strikes and not to seek pay increases. Both industry and labor promised to co-operate. For two years there were few wage cuts. Many companies put their workers on part time rather than lay them off and leave them without any earnings.

Hoover also tried to stimulate the construction industry. Soon after the crash he urged businessmen to go on with their long-range building plans as if nothing had happened. He asked bankers to keep on lending money for construction. He telegraphed governors and mayors all over the country, requesting them to step up the construction of public works. In spite of these requests, both private and public construction declined rapidly.

When Congress met in December, 1929, the President asked for increased appropriations for public works. The number of persons employed on federal projects went up from 180,000 in 1929 to 760,000 in 1932. Had the depression been a mild one, this program of public works might have stimulated recovery. As it was, the program was far too small even to halt the decline.

The relief problem becomes desperate.

For about a year after the crash, relief for the needy was left to private charity. When this proved insufficient, city and county governments gradually had to take over most of the burden. Unfortunately, hundreds of small cities and scores of large ones, including New York, Chicago, Philadelphia, Detroit, Boston, and others, were close to bankruptcy. Tax receipts of all kinds had fallen until the cities could barely meet the ordinary expenses of government. In many places, therefore, relief was limited to a few cents a day for each person and took the form of a bread line. Persons evicted for not paying their rent moved in with relatives or built shacks out of waste material on vacant city land. To add to the misery of the poor, hospital and clinic budgets were cut and their services curtailed.

State governments found it necessary to share the relief load. They did not try to provide *work* relief, considering it to be too expensive. Instead they gave *direct* relief consisting of money or food. By 1932 most of the states were spending money for direct relief, yet in large sections of the country the relief available was of the scantiest sort. Some states were too poor to do any more. Both city and state officials claimed that the federal government ought to help carry the relief burden.

President Hoover objected strongly to this proposal. It would not only be expensive, he argued, but it might lead to political control of needy voters. Furthermore, he warned, it would undermine the American system of self-reliance and voluntary mutual aid.

Drought in the Plains states led to the first of many conflicts between the President and Congress on the question of relief. In December, 1930, Hoover asked Congress to vote 45 million dollars to be lent to drought-stricken farmers on good security to feed their livestock. He opposed a bill providing 25 million dollars additional for food for hungry farmers, saying human relief should be left to private organizations, such as the Red Cross. In the end he agreed to a bill under which farmers could borrow money for food.

Hoover differs with Congress on other issues.

As the depression deepened, the President's relations with Congress grew worse. In the winter of 1931 Hoover vetoed the Norris bill providing for federal operation of Muscle Shoals, saying it was socialistic (see p. 657). He turned down the Wagner bill for a federally aided system of state employment agencies, declaring it would weaken the responsibility of the states. He refused to sign the Bonus Act of 1931, allowing veterans to borrow up to 50 per cent on their federal endowment policies (see p. 655), because it would interfere with his efforts to balance the budget. Congress, however, passed this measure over his veto. Early in 1932, when a group of congressmen tried to force through a bill providing two billion dollars for public works, Hoover described it as a "pork barrel"—that is, a fund for political patronage.

Hoover takes steps to ease credit.

When Congress met in December, 1931, it was clear that conditions were getting worse. Unemployment was mounting; wages were being slashed; relief rolls were growing; foreclosures were taking place on a scale never seen before. A number of great banks, insurance companies, and railroad companies were close to bankruptcy. If they failed, the whole economy would be paralyzed. The President saw that strenuous federal action had become necessary. Acting on his recommendations, Congress passed three laws to ease credit:

1. The Treasury was authorized to buy 125 million dollars' worth of new

stock in the Federal Land Banks. The money would be lent to farmers who could qualify for Land Bank mortgages.

2. The Reconstruction Finance Corporation was established with a large revolving fund to lend to banks, insurance companies, mortgage and loan companies, and railroads. Critics called RFC loans the "millionaire's dole." Yet the loans helped the whole country by saving many a large financial institution and railroad from collapse. Six months later (July, 1932) Congress doubled the lending power of the RFC and authorized it to lend money to the states for self-liquidating, or income-producing, public works projects such as toll bridges. In addition the RFC was permitted to make temporary loans totaling 300 million dollars to states "absolutely unable to finance the relief of distress."

3. A system of Federal Home Loan Banks was set up. Since these, like the Federal Land Banks, could lend no more than 50 per cent of the value of a property, they did little business.

Congress proposes the "Lame Duck" Amendment.

For many years Senator Norris had urged a constitutional amendment to do away with "lame duck" sessions of Congress. "Lame ducks" were men who had been defeated for re-election in November yet served in Congress until the following March. In 1932 Congress at last approved an amendment directing the President, the Vice-President, and members of Congress to begin their terms in January instead of March. The Twentieth, or "Lame Duck," Amendment, was quickly ratified by the states and became law in 1933.

Congress passes the Anti-Injunction Act.

Progressives won an important victory with passage of the Norris–La Guardia Anti-Injunction Act (1932). It endorsed the principle of collective bargaining. It banned "yellow-dog" contracts, whereby a promise not to join a labor union is made a condition of employment. The act strictly limited the power of federal courts to issue injunctions. Henceforth injunctions would not be used to prevent joining a union, striking, paying strike benefits, assembling peaceably, or persuading others to do these things. The act stated that persons accused of violating an injunction are entitled to a jury trial. This measure, far more than the Clayton Act of 1914, deserves to be called the "Magna Carta" of organized labor.

THE UNEMPLOYED *line up for food and clothing.*

The Nation Votes for a "New Deal"

The country reaches rock bottom.

Throughout 1932 conditions got worse. Industry was operating at half its 1929 volume. Between ten and twelve million workers were unemployed. Most of those who still had jobs had taken wage cuts. In the Pittsburgh steel industry, for example, wages had dropped from $30 a week in 1929 to $15 in 1932. Salesclerks got as little as $3 a week, while servants and farm laborers often worked for their keep. Rural teachers in some places got only $15 a month. From such shrunken earnings, most people with jobs tried to help their unemployed relatives.

In the larger cities unemployed men sold apples on street corners. Bread lines and soup kitchens multiplied. At least 2,000,000 jobless men, including 200,000 boys, wandered from place to place looking for any kind of work. Meanwhile, the plight of the farmers was worse than ever. Between 1927 and 1932 one in every ten farms was sold at auction for nonpayment of taxes and debts. In rural areas thousands of dispossessed families squatted on abandoned or cutover land and tried to wring a subsistence from worn-out soil.

Some fear a revolution.

Although many people had lost everything, there was remarkably little disorder. Communist agitators claimed

GROUPS *of anxious depositors gathered in front of closed banks—business was at a standstill and the only thing to do was wait.*

675

that the only way to prevent depressions was to abolish capitalism, but they won few converts. American workers and farmers showed more interest in moderate proposals like unemployment and old age insurance and public works to create jobs. Yet in some circles there was fear of revolution. This fear led to one of the most controversial episodes of the Hoover administration.

In the summer of 1932, 11,000 unemployed veterans from all parts of the country hitch-hiked to Washington to ask for immediate payment of the entire bonus. Some brought their families. They settled down in tents and rude shelters along the Potomac River. Since they were penniless, they depended on charity for food. When Congress defeated the bonus bill and adjourned, most of the veterans went home. The rest were ordered to leave. When they did not go, they were driven out by troops and tanks and their camp was burned down. Veterans' organizations and many other people criticized strongly the harsh treatment given the "bonus army."

There were other disquieting incidents in 1932. Rebellious farmers in the Midwest sometimes banded together to stop auction sales or to see that foreclosed farms were sold for a dollar or two and returned to their former owners. In some places angry dairy farmers stopped milk trucks and emptied the milk on the road in protest at low prices. Yet there was no real danger of revolution. In the words of *Time* magazine:

Doubtless the most potent factor in keeping the country steady and averting even the threat of an armed uprising has been the certainty—such as exists in no other large country—that November, 1932, would in due constitutional order bring a presidential and congressional election.

President Hoover is renominated.

When the Republicans held their convention, they renominated President Hoover on the first ballot. They adopted a platform blaming the depression on world conditions and praising the President's policies. They promised to continue the gold standard and the high tariff and to support any sound and workable plan to raise the price of farm products. They called for a sharp cut in government spending and a balanced budget. A brisk fight took place in the convention over the prohibition issue. A so-called "wet-dry" plank was adopted, proposing an amendment to give each state the right to deal with the liquor problem, but promising federal protection to states wishing to remain dry.

The Democrats nominate Franklin D. Roosevelt.

No President except Monroe has ever won re-election during a depression. When the Democrats met at Chicago, they felt sure of victory. Passing over Alfred E. Smith, they nominated Franklin D. Roosevelt, the popular and progressive governor of New York. A conservative, John N. Garner of Texas, Speaker of the House, was named as his running mate. The platform was brief and definite. It called for a greatly expanded program of public works and unemployment relief, banking reform, regulation of stocks and commodity exchanges, a federal-state program of old age pensions and unemployment insurance, control of crop surpluses, repeal of prohibition, reciprocal trade agreements, independence for the Philippines, and membership in the World Court. The party's guiding principle was declared to be "the continuous responsibility of government for human welfare."

Roosevelt campaigns vigorously.

Roosevelt launched his campaign by flying to the convention and making a fighting acceptance speech. It concluded with these words:

I pledge you, I pledge myself, to a new deal for the American people. . . . Give me your help, not to win votes, but to win this crusade to restore America to its own people.

Roosevelt's close friends, knowing that he had to wear heavy braces on his legs, which made platform appearances difficult, advised a "front porch" campaign. But he insisted on traveling all over the country and giving hundreds of speeches. His speaking tour took him into nearly every state in the Union. Millions who saw him were won over by his famous smile and his infectious laugh. His optimism lightened the gloom that hung over the land. A reporter called his campaign a "laughing revolution."

Roosevelt won the support of progressives by advocating government operation of Muscle Shoals, laws to protect consumers and investors, and justice for the "forgotten man at the bottom of the economic pyramid." He criticized the Republican theory that aid to big business would cause prosperity to "trickle down" to the ordinary people. He said the Hawley-Smoot Tariff was a "ghastly jest." At the same time he tried to please conservatives by calling for a reduction of government expenses and a balanced budget.

Hoover fought back. Were the Democratic tariff proposals to be carried out, he said, "grass will grow in the streets of a hundred cities" and "weeds overrun millions of farms." The Democratic promise to put the jobless to work was cruel because it was "impossible of realization." The "new deal," moreover, would lead to regimentation and socialism. The campaign was "more than a contest between two men," he declared. "It is a contest between two philosophies of government. . . . Our opponents . . . are proposing changes . . . which would destroy the very foundations of our American system."

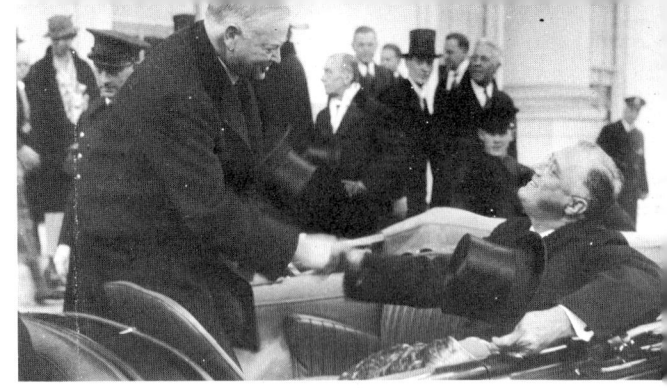

F.D.R. AND HERBERT HOOVER *shake hands as they leave the White House for Roosevelt's 1933 inauguration.*

The country goes Democratic.

The outcome of the campaign was never in doubt. Roosevelt carried 42 states and received nearly 7 million more popular votes than Hoover. Both houses of Congress went Democratic by a large majority. In addition the Democrats won 29 out of 34 contests for governor.

The leftist vote was slightly larger than in its previous peak years, 1912 and 1920. Yet it was still under a million. This showed that even in the depths of a terrible depression, the American people did not want radical economic changes. Norman Thomas, the Socialist candidate, got 885,000 votes. W. Z. Foster, the Communist candidate, got 103,000 votes. Doubtless many who voted for Socialist or Communist candidates did so only as a sign of protest.

Prohibition is repealed.

The final session of the Seventy-second Congress (December, 1932, to March, 1933) was the last in which "lame ducks" took part. About all it accomplished was to approve the Twenty-first amendment to repeal the Eighteenth. Special conventions met in the states during the summer and autumn, and by December, 1933, thirty-six had voted to ratify. Thus the twelve-year-old experiment with national prohibition came to an end.

677

The country is leaderless.

The last four months of Hoover's term were a nightmare for him and for the nation. The economic situation was growing worse day by day. By January, 1933, the entire banking system appeared close to collapse. Hoover felt it was useless to take steps which might soon be reversed by his successor. He asked Roosevelt to co-operate with him in handling the bank crisis and the war debt question. Although the two men met and discussed both matters, they could not agree. The nation was virtually leaderless, as in the four months before Lincoln took office.

Before we take up the story of the next administration and its efforts to cure the depression, let us see what Hoover accomplished in regard to foreign affairs.

As part of his GOOD-WILL TOUR *President Herbert Hoover visited President Gonzales Viquer of Costa Rica.*

President Hoover Tries to Promote World Peace

A believer in international co-operation.

Hoover was more interested in world affairs than Harding or Coolidge. He was also far better informed about world conditions. He wished deeply to promote international co-operation. In his inaugural address he promised that the United States would take "a practical part in supporting all useful international undertakings. We not only desire peace with the world, but to see peace maintained throughout the world." Hoover recognized the value of the League of Nations and co-operated with it as fully as he thought American public opinion would permit.

For Secretary of State, Hoover appointed the able Henry L. Stimson, then Governor General of the Philippines. Stimson, too, was an internationalist. He worked hard to find ways in which the United States could use its influence in the cause of peace.

Hoover seeks Latin American good will.

Soon after his election, Hoover sailed on the battleship *Maryland* for a visit to ten countries of Latin America. He said that the United States was eager that all the American republics should be "good neighbors." One of the main reasons for Hoover's visit was to stimulate trade with the United States. Latin Americans took his visit as a great compliment.

Many of the Latin American countries were hard hit by the depression and by our Hawley-Smoot Tariff of 1930. When several of them had to stop paying interest on their foreign debts, Secretary Stimson did not press for payment nor threaten to use force to collect what was due. The State Department said publicly it had given up the Roosevelt Corollary to the Monroe Doctrine under which the United States had claimed the right to interfere in such cases.[1] The following year Secretary of State Stimson declared that henceforth the United States would not concern itself with internal revolutions in Latin American countries. Arrangements were made to take the American Marines out of Nicaragua and Haiti (see p. 592). When revolution broke out in Cuba, our government did not intervene. This new policy of noninterference was a big step toward better relations with our southern neighbors.

The St. Lawrence Seaway.

In 1927 Canada sent its first minister to Washington. Thereafter Canada and the United States dealt with each other directly instead of through Great Britain. During Hoover's administration plans were worked out for joint action in deepening the St. Lawrence River all the way to the Great Lakes. Hoover sent the St. Lawrence Seaway Treaty to the Senate early in 1933. The treaty was opposed by our Atlantic seaports and the railroads serving the Northeast. Neither Hoover nor his successors could get the Senate to ratify it. The deadlock was broken in 1955, when Congress passed a bill authorizing the United States to take part in the St. Lawrence Seaway project.

The Paris Pact meets its first test.

Hoover and Stimson hoped that the Pact of Paris could be used to avert threats to world peace. Their first chance to try it came in the summer of 1929 when Russia and China quarreled over the Chinese Eastern Railway in North Manchuria. Fighting broke out

---

[1] The statement, known as the *Clark Memorandum* of 1928, said that the Monroe Doctrine was a guarantee of the independence and territorial integrity of the Latin American states. While self-preservation might require the United States to try to adjust the financial troubles of a weak neighbor, such intervention could not be justified by the Monroe Doctrine.

without a declaration of war. Since both China and Russia had signed the Pact of Paris, Secretary Stimson reminded them of their duty to settle their dispute by peaceful means. Great Britain, France, and Italy each sent a similar reminder. Moscow refused to accept mediation by any third power. It also rebuked the United States for giving advice to a government which it had never recognized. Chiang Kai-shek, the Chinese leader, was forced to give in by restoring Russia's former rights in North Manchuria. Thus the first test of the Paris Pact showed its weakness—the lack of any machinery to compel the signers to live up to their agreement.

Japan closes the Open Door.

Another crisis in Manchuria, which arose in 1931, showed still more clearly the weakness of both the Paris Pact and the League of Nations. In September, 1931, the Japanese army occupied southern Manchuria. China appealed to the League of Nations and the signers of the Paris Pact for help.

Secretary of State Stimson called Japan's attention to its obligations under the Paris Pact and the Nine-Power Treaty. At the same time he informed the League of Nations that the United States would co-operate with it to stop the war. The League Council then invited our government to send a delegate to take part in discussions on how the Paris Pact could be enforced. President Hoover named our consul at Geneva to represent us in the meetings.

Japan had no large stores of war materials and its war industries were weak. It is likely that Japan could have been stopped if the great powers had shut off trade and credits. Stimson, who believed in collective action to halt aggression, hoped that the League would impose economic sanctions. He knew, however, that the United States would not do so. President Hoover feared that sanctions might lead us into war with Japan, and he would not take the risk. Few Americans at that time would have been willing to fight even a short war to protect our interests in the Far East. The people of Great Britain, France, and the Netherlands, although they had important possessions in the Far East, were equally unwilling to risk war with Japan. The League Council merely appointed an investigating commission.

Stimson saw that he had no weapons to make Japan live up to its treaties except the force of world public opinion. In the words of an old Chinese saying, he was armed only with "spears of straw and swords of ice." He informed Japan that the United States would never recognize "any situation, treaty, or agreement" opposed to the Open Door policy or the Pact of Paris. Japan replied to this so-called "Stimson Doctrine" by setting up a puppet government in Manchuria and renaming the province "Manchukuo."

After a year of study the League investigating committee found that Japan had been guilty of aggression. Japan then resigned from the League (1933) and kept control of Manchukuo. Japanese military leaders got ready for new conquests. They made Manchuria, with its rich farm land, oil fields, and coal and iron deposits, a base for war industries.

The London Conference on Naval Disarmament.

President Hoover hoped to stop the rivalry in building light warships that had gone on since the Washington Conference. The naval conference of 1927 had been unsuccessful (see p. 661). Early in his term Hoover invited the British Prime Minister, Ramsay MacDonald, to come to Washington to discuss the problem. In 1930 the five nations that had signed the naval treaty of 1922 met in London. They agreed to extend the holiday on building capi-

tal ships to 1936. Three powers—Britain, the United States, and Japan—also agreed to limit the building of smaller vessels. While Japan had to accept the old ratio of 10:10:6 for capital ships, for lighter ones the formula of 10:10:7 was agreed upon. Also Japan was to be equal to any other power in submarines. The Japanese were dissatisfied with these concessions.

The World Disarmament Conference.

Hoover and Stimson wanted to promote general disarmament as well as the limitation of navies. In this aim they had the solid support of the American press. General disarmament had been one of the most popular of Woodrow Wilson's Fourteen Points. The great majority of Americans believed that disarmament was essential for world peace. They did not understand why France and other peace-loving nations failed to follow our example and reduce their armies to a skeleton force.

A League of Nations commission on disarmament had been meeting on and off since 1926. Presidents Coolidge and Hoover both sent delegates to take part in the commission's work. When the World Disarmament Conference met at Geneva early in 1932, the United States delegation had a major role. They transmitted Hoover's proposal that all *offensive* weapons be abolished. When the various nations could not agree on how to define offensive weapons, Hoover suggested that chemical warfare, bombing planes, heavy artillery, and tanks be outlawed. He also urged that all nations reduce their existing armaments by at least one third. The conference recessed in July without taking any action.

Although the Disarmament Conference was to meet again in 1933, the prospects that it could accomplish anything looked bleak. Every day France and its allies were becoming more afraid of Germany. That nation had

JAPAN'S SEIZURE OF MANCHURIA *ended a decade of treaty-making and relative peace.*

been disarmed at the close of World War I, and the Versailles Treaty had forbidden it to rearm. Yet the Nazi party in Germany already had a large private army of Storm Troopers and was demanding full-scale rearmament. Moreover, Japan had attacked the Chinese city of Shanghai while the conference was in session. European statesmen were further alarmed because they knew that Italy's Mussolini was making plans for conquests in Africa. Under these conditions, American proposals for disarmament seemed empty dreams.

The reparations–war debt problem again.

By 1931 the depression was worldwide. International trade had come almost to a standstill. American investors stopped lending money abroad. A financial crisis spread over many nations and was especially severe in Austria and Germany. If the Germans continued to pay reparations to the Allies, they could not meet their obligations to American investors. Moreover, economic distress in Germany was causing grave political unrest. Both the Nazi and the Communist parties were growing rapidly, and no one knew whether the German republic could survive.

President Hoover decided on a bold step. In June, 1931, he proposed a one-year suspension of payments on war debts and reparations. This suspension, known as the "Hoover Moratorium," was acclaimed in Europe. When Congress met in December it consented to the moratorium, but declared that none of the debts owed to the United States should be canceled or reduced.

By this time all European statesmen realized that the attempt to collect reparations was a grave mistake. It had filled the German people with bitterness, not only toward their conquerors but toward their own government. It had also made trouble between the former Allies. The Allies met at Lausanne (June, 1932) and agreed to cancel practically all further reparations. But the Lausanne Agreement was to go into effect only if the United States forgave its war debts. Our Congress, backed up by most of the American press, still insisted that the debts be paid. This insistence proved useless. Hitler's rise to power early in 1933 put an end to reparations payments. Very soon nearly all payments on war debts also came to a halt.

Depression wanderers

FOR IDENTIFICATION

Agricultural Marketing Act of 1929
Clark Memorandum
Federal Farm Board
Hawley-Smoot Tariff
Manchukuo

Reconstruction Finance Corporation
Henry L. Stimson
Twentieth Amendment
Twenty-first Amendment

FOR EXPLANATION OR DEFINITION

buying on margin
"farm bloc"
"frozen" assets
Hoover Moratorium
"lame ducks"
marketing co-operatives
national income

"pork barrel"
price-maintenance
revolving fund
self-liquidating project
St. Lawrence Seaway
"yellow-dog" contract

FOR REVIEW

1. Describe President Hoover's background and personality.

2. Why was there a farm depression during the "prosperity decade" of the 1920's?

3. Why did the export and domestic markets for farm staples decline?

4. Describe the membership and purpose of the farm bloc.

5. (a) How did the McNary-Haugen bill attempt to deal with the problem of overproduction of farm staples? (b) Why didn't farmers reduce production of farm staples? (c) How did the Agricultural Marketing Act of 1929 attempt to deal with the problem? (d) What did the Federal Farm Board accomplish?

6. (a) Why did Congress increase tariff rates in the Hawley-Smoot tariff? (b) Why did economists urge President Hoover to veto the bill? (c) How did European countries react to the new tariff?

7. (a) State some of the causes of the stock market boom in the 1920's. (b) List some of the warning signs in 1929 that business was slowing down. (c) What did Presidents Coolidge and Hoover do to check stock market speculation? (d) Why did Hoover's election and inauguration cause stocks to climb upward?

8. Describe the stock market crash of October, 1929, and its effects on individuals and on the country.

9. Tell what basic conditions helped to produce or prolong the Great Depression.

10. Explain the terms "expanding production," "purchasing power," "national income," "technological unemployment," and "oversaving."

11. What steps did President Hoover take to combat the depression?

12. Why were many city governments close to bankruptcy?

13. (a) What is the difference between "direct relief" and "work relief"? (b) Why did cities and states place emphasis on direct relief? (c) On what grounds did President Hoover object to spending large federal sums for public works? (d) What was his attitude toward the problem of relief?

14. (a) What steps did Hoover and the Congress take to ease credit? (b) Explain the work of the Reconstruction Finance Corporation.

15. What were the provisions of the Norris–La Guardia Anti-Injunction Act?

16. (a) Describe economic conditions in 1932. (b) What was the "bonus army"? How was it treated?

17. (a) What were the main planks of the Democratic platform of 1932? (b) What appeals to the voters were made by Hoover? By Roosevelt? (c) What were the results of the election?

18. (a) What steps did Hoover take to cultivate the good will of the Latin American nations? (b) What specific evidences of a change in attitude toward Latin Americans were given by Hoover and Secretary of State Stimson?

19. (a) What weakness did the quarrel between Russia and China in 1929 show

in the Paris Pact? (b) How did the Japanese occupation of Manchuria in 1931 test the League of Nations and the Pact of Paris? (c) What did the League of Nations do? (d) What was the Stimson Doctrine? (e) How did Japan react to these actions?

20. What decisions resulted from the London Conference on Naval Disarmament? Why was Japan displeased?

21. (a) What was the reason for the Hoover Moratorium on war debts and reparations? (b) What was the Lausanne Agreement among the European nations concerning reparations?

FOR FURTHER STUDY AND DISCUSSION

1. Explain the statement in the text that "Hoover was a humanitarian, not a reactionary."

2. Is the administration in power in any way responsible for good or bad times? Consider Cleveland and the Democrats in 1893, Coolidge and the Republicans in 1923–29, Hoover and the Republicans in 1929–32.

3. List the various forces, domestic and foreign, which influenced American agriculture in the period 1900–1930. Helpful source: Faulkner, *Economic History*, pp. 630–636.

4. What were the advantages and disadvantages of the increased mechanization of farms?

5. What were the purposes and accomplishments of the "farm bloc"? Helpful source: Link, *American Epoch*, pp. 263–267.

6. Find out more about the causes of the "Great Depression" and report on them to your class. Helpful sources: Faulkner, *From Versailles to the New Deal;* Wecter, *The Age of the Great Depression.*

7. Should the United States and the League of Nations have applied economic sanctions against Japan at the time of the Manchurian crisis?

8. Explain the Stimson Doctrine. Of what value was this statement of basic principle? Helpful source: Commager, *Documents*, No. 469.

9. Outline the story of the developments which led to the Hoover Moratorium and the Lausanne Agreement. Helpful sources: Bailey, *Diplomatic History*, pp. 700–705, 722–723; Bemis, *Diplomatic History*, pp. 704–719.

FOR INDIVIDUAL OR GROUP ACTIVITIES

1. Organize three or four special committees to study the effect of the Great Depression on your local community. Make oral reports to the class on such topics as unemployment, wages, rents, local industries, mortgage difficulties, local banks, charitable efforts, public works.

2. Prepare a book report on Allen, *Since Yesterday;* Chase, *Prosperity, Fact or Myth?* or Wecter, *The Age of the Great Depression.*

3. (a) Assuming that you are a newspaper reporter, write a news dispatch on the "bonus army." Read your article to the class. (b) On the basis of your article hold a class discussion on the merits of the veterans' actions and those of the government.

4. Select for reading to the class short excerpts from the writings or speeches of Hoover and F. D. Roosevelt which reflect the conflicting aims and points of view of the two men. Helpful source: Hofstadter, *American Political Tradition.*

5. Investigate and report on the Manchurian crisis, the action of the League of Nations, and the policy of Secretary of State Stimson. Helpful sources: Stimson, *The Far Eastern Crisis;* Stimson and Bundy, *On Active Service in Peace and War;* Bailey, *Diplomatic History*, pp. 723–729; Link, *American Epoch*, pp. 447–451.

6. "His [Hoover's] philosophy after the acute phase of the depression set in represents . . . a turning point, a transition toward a future characterized by a larger measure of federal leadership." Write a short essay in support of this interpretation of the administration of Herbert Hoover. Helpful source: Link, *American Epoch*, pp. 368–373, from which the quotation is taken; Hofstadter, *American Political Tradition* and *The Age of Reform.*

> Democracy ... must make men and women ... feel that it really cares for the security of every individual; that it is tolerant enough to inspire an essential unity among its citizens; and that it is militant enough to maintain liberty against social oppression at home and against military aggression abroad.
> ——Franklin D. Roosevelt, 1938

41. THE COUNTRY TRIES A NEW DEAL

F.D.R. Fearlessly Attacks the Depression

Franklin D. Roosevelt.

The new President, a distant cousin of Theodore Roosevelt, came from an old and well-to-do New York family. Like his cousin, he graduated from Harvard, studied law, and while still in his twenties was elected to the New York State legislature. His election was remarkable not only because of his youth but because he ran as a Democrat in a strongly Republican district.

In Albany the young senator led a successful revolt against the state political boss. The following year he helped manage Woodrow Wilson's successful campaign in New York State. In return he was appointed Assistant Secretary of the Navy. In 1920, as Democratic candidate for Vice-President, he carried on a vigorous fight for the League of Nations. When stricken with paralysis a few months later, his promising political career seemed to be over. For the next seven years he struggled to regain his health. Meanwhile he studied American history and government and exchanged letters with leading thinkers here and abroad.

In 1928, still crippled, Roosevelt was elected governor of New York. He fought for government control of public utilities and for public ownership of water-power sites. A keen interest in conservation led him to work for reforestation. In his travels about the state he saw for himself the suffering caused by the depression. He succeeded in persuading the legislature to establish old-age pensions and the first statewide system of unemployment relief in the country. He was re-elected in 1930 by the biggest majority in the state's history. His popularity in New York and the state's large number of electoral votes put Roosevelt in line for presidential nomination by his party.

Roosevelt takes office.

On March 4, 1933, when Franklin D. Roosevelt became President, the depression was at its worst. Throughout the country most of the banks were closed. Estimates of the number of unemployed varied from twelve to seventeen million. State and local relief funds were nearly exhausted. Many cities and towns were bankrupt, without money to pay schoolteachers and other public servants. Millions of farm families were penniless. Panic gripped the country.

Roosevelt's inaugural message renewed the nation's courage. Democratic government, he said, would endure; prosperity would return.

684

FDR *and part of his "Brain Trust" lunch at a CCC camp in Virginia.*

The only thing we have to fear is fear itself—nameless, unreasoning, unjustified terror which paralyzes needed efforts to convert retreat into advance. . . . Only a foolish optimist can deny the dark realities of the moment. Yet our distress comes from no failure of substance. . . . Plenty is at our doorstep but a generous use of it languishes in the very sight of the supply.

The President promised quick action to relieve want; to prevent foreclosure of small farms and homes; to put people to work; and to raise farm prices.

The first "Hundred Days."

The new President's first acts were to order the closing of all the banks in the country and to call Congress into special session on March 9. The hundred following days were unlike any in the history of Congress. With the aid of college professors and other experts—the so-called "Brain Trust"—the President had prepared a long series of bills to meet the emergency. He placed these before Congress one after another, and they were all passed. Even the Republican congressmen for the most part supported the President.

The Emergency Banking Relief Act was passed the day that Congress met. The President then gave his first "fireside chat" over the radio. He explained that all the banks were being examined and that, starting the next day, the sound ones would be allowed

685

...oon most of the banks were ...business.

Congress next passed an Economy Act, giving the President authority to slash the budgets of federal departments by 25 per cent, to cut federal salaries 15 per cent, and to reduce veterans' pensions and benefits. (Congress restored most of the cuts a year later.) Congress then gave the Reconstruction Finance Corporation more money and broader lending powers. Another act provided federal grants to help the states care for the needy. A record-breaking appropriation of over three billion dollars was made for public works to create jobs. Congress also established the Civilian Conservation Corps, which provided work for needy young men. To stop the flood of foreclosures and at the same time to relieve mortgage holders, Congress passed the Emergency Farm Mortgage Act and the Home Owners Refinancing Act. Before the end of this remarkable session Congress also created the Tennessee Valley Authority, passed the Agricultural Adjustment Act and the National Industrial Recovery Act, gave the President power to manage the nation's currency, and brought the sale of securities under federal control.

These hundred swift-moving days went far to restore the nation's faith in democracy. For the time being the President's program was approved by nearly every group in the country. Almost everyone hailed the President as a great leader.

"But above all, try something."

Roosevelt had a trial-and-error approach to the nation's problems. "It is common sense to take a method and try it," he said. "If it fails, admit it frankly and try another. But above all, try something." Much New Deal legislation was experimental. As time passed, some New Deal laws were improved and others discarded.

686

MOST IMPORTANT

The purposes of the New Deal.

From the outset the New Deal had three aims: relief, recovery, and reform. Relief involved feeding the hungry and preventing the loss of homes, farms, and businesses. Recovery meant restoring prosperity to agriculture and industry. Reform was necessary too if recovery was not to be merely temporary. Indeed, recovery from this, our worst depression, might be impossible without reform.

Roosevelt wished to preserve our economic system by making it work better. He thought production was out of balance with consumption and that the cure lay in raising the purchasing power of the poorer three fourths of the people. He was seeking "balance between agriculture and industry and balance between the wage earner, the employer, and the consumer." By giving the country vigorous leadership, Roosevelt believed he was saving it from the danger of revolution, either a Fascist one from the right or a Communist one from the left. In a fireside chat in 1938, he said:

Democracy has disappeared in several other great nations, not because the people of those nations disliked democracy, but because they had grown tired of government confusion and government weakness through lack of leadership. . . . Finally, in desperation, they chose to sacrifice liberty in the hope of getting something to eat. . . . History proves that dictatorships do not grow out of strong and successful governments, but out of weak and helpless ones.

The New Deal Helps Agriculture

The AAA seeks to restore "parity prices."

One of the most important laws passed at the outset of the New Deal was the Agricultural Adjustment Act. It aimed at raising the prices of certain basic crops to "parity" by reducing the supply. Parity prices were defined as those which would give growers the same purchasing power as they had enjoyed in the "normal" years from 1909 to 1914. (The "normal" years for tobacco were 1919–1929.) The act provided benefit payments to farmers who agreed to reduce their output of certain crops. The crops selected were those of which there was a large surplus—cotton, corn, hogs, wheat, and tobacco. After a year's trial Congress extended the program to include nine other crops. Money for benefit payments was obtained by taxing processors of the same farm products, who in turn passed the tax on to consumers.

Farmers co-operated well; in 1933 cotton farmers even plowed under a portion of the already planted crop. In 1934 and 1935 about forty million acres of farm land were taken out of cultivation. Farm prices rose. In addition, farm owners received benefit payments. Unfortunately, the reduction of crop acreage left almost a million Southern share croppers and farm laborers without any way to earn a living. Early in 1936 the Supreme Court declared that the processing tax was unconstitutional.

The Court said that it was not really a tax but part of a system for "coercing" farmers to reduce production and that the control of agriculture was a power reserved to the states. Congress then sought another solution to the farmer's problems.

The Soil Conservation Act.

In 1934 and 1935 a series of terrible dust storms swept the Great Plains. Dust covered the whole country and drew attention to the need for saving the nation's soil. In 1936 Congress passed an act creating the Soil Conservation Service and offering benefit payments to farmers who practiced soil conservation in co-operation with the Service. Co-operating farmers would be paid for reducing the acreage of soil-depleting crops (such as grain, cotton, and tobacco), provided they grew clover and other legumes instead. Legumes enrich the soil. They also have a soil-binding effect which prevents erosion of the valuable topsoil. The purpose of the new law was to conserve the soil, a power which Congress has, and indirectly to reduce crop surpluses. The money for benefit

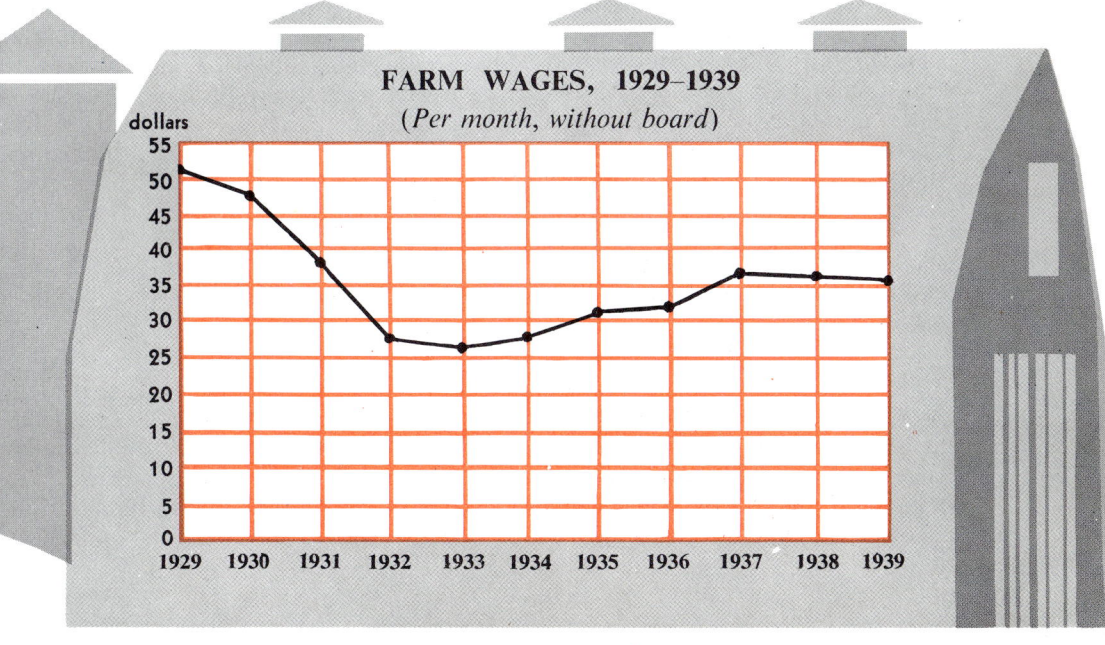

FARM WAGES, 1929–1939
(Per month, without board)

payments came from the general Treasury. Sharecroppers and tenants received part of the payments. The law raised farm income slightly and promoted soil conservation. Yet crop surpluses continued. With the growing use of machines, fertilizers, improved seed, and better methods, farmers increased their output in spite of cuts in acreage.

The second Agriculture Adjustment Act.

A more comprehensive measure to help the farmer became law in 1938. It continued the soil conservation program and the benefits paid for planting soil-conserving crops. It set up a system of price supports for major crops which is still followed. The system is based on acreage controls voted by the producers of each crop. It empowers the Secretary of Agriculture to establish a marketing quota (the proportion of his total crop a grower might send to market) if a surplus is produced. Farmers who abide by acreage controls (and marketing quota if any) are entitled to storage loans equal to the support price of their crop. Should the crop sell for less than the support price, the difference is made up to the grower out of federal funds. Although consumers grumbled and farmers complained of being "regimented," the new law helped to stabilize farm prices. By 1940, thanks to benefit payments and price supports, farm income was double what it had been in 1932. Yet on the whole farmers were less well off than farmers had been in the five years before 1914. Not until World War II, when everything farmers could produce was needed, did farmers enjoy prosperity.

Credit facilities are improved.

Ever since the early days of the Republic, farmers have clamored for easier credit. The New Deal did more to meet this need than had ever been done before. During the first "Hundred Days" Congress authorized new federal agencies to lend money to farm cooperatives and to farmers on their growing crops. In addition, the Federal Land Banks were instructed to sell two billion dollars' worth of bonds and to use the proceeds for refinancing farm mortgages. This action enabled many farmers to replace a short-term mortgage with one of long term, usually at a lower rate of interest.

In 1934 Congress went still farther to save farmers from losing their farms. It passed the Farm Mortgage Foreclosure Act, which enabled farmers to borrow federal money to recover property already foreclosed. This act and the Farm Mortgage Moratorium Act of 1935 practically stopped the loss of farms by foreclosure. Insurance companies and banks, as well as farmers, were relieved. Their funds, which had been "frozen" in unproductive farm mortgages or in foreclosed farms which they could not sell, became liquid again.

Small farmers and laborers need help.

About one third of the farmers produced 80 per cent of all farm products that were sold. It was this group who received most of the AAA benefit payments. The remaining two thirds produced so little for sale that their AAA benefits were little or nothing.

To help farmers not reached by the AAA, the Resettlement Administration was set up in 1935. It bought several million acres of inferior farmland for reforestation and relocated the displaced farmers on subsistence homesteads on better land. In 1937 the Resettlement Administration was replaced by the Farm Security Administration (FSA). A Farm Tenancy Act passed that year empowered the FSA to lend money to a limited number of carefully selected tenants and laborers for the purchase of small farms. In addition FSA worked with farmers on relief, advising them how to supply more of their own needs and lending them small sums to buy seed, tools, fertilizer, or livestock. FSA also built about a hundred camps where migratory laborers could live during the slack season. Appropriations for FSA were always small, partly because the larger farmers were unfriendly to its program. On the whole, Congress showed little interest in the tragic situation of the millions of sharecroppers, subsistence farmers, and migratory farm laborers. In 1947 FSA was abolished.

An aerial view of STRIP ROTATION, *a type of conservation plowing*

Trade agreements increase farm exports.

The Democrats did not repeal the Hawley-Smoot Tariff, which had cut our foreign trade to a trickle. Instead Secretary of State Cordell Hull persuaded Congress to pass the Reciprocal Trade Agreement Act (1934). Under its terms the President could make reciprocal trade agreements with other countries without submitting them to the Senate. He could lower tariff rates as much as 50 per cent for nations which made similar concessions to us. By 1939 Secretary Hull had worked out trade agreements with twenty-one countries. The net result of the treaties was to expand our exports more than our imports. Hull's program was especially helpful to American farmers and manufacturers who produce for export. It was strongly endorsed by the American Manufacturers' Export Association, which said that one third of all American wage earners were in some way dependent on the export-import business.

Other programs aid farmers.

Still other New Deal projects to help farmers should be mentioned. Starting in 1933 the Surplus Commodities Corporation bought surplus farm products and distributed them to the needy. Some of the food was used to provide low-cost school lunches. Some was given to charitable institutions. Between 1939 and 1943 much of it was distributed by means of the food stamp plan. Food stamps were given to families on relief. The stamps could be exchanged at grocery stores for any food then listed as a "surplus commodity." Thus new outlets for surplus products were created by enabling needy people to have more and better food.

Another agency that helped farmers, the Rural Electrification Administration (REA), was set up in 1935. At that time only 8 per cent of the nation's farms had electricity, because private companies did not find rural service profitable. The REA lent money to cooperative associations and to municipalities in rural areas for erecting generators and electric lines. The program was remarkably successful in bringing electricity to rural dwellers. It also opened up a huge market for electrical equipment.

The planting of trees in narrow strips, or "shelter belts," on the Great Plains was another interesting New Deal project. About twenty million trees of drought-resistant varieties were supplied to farmers. The shelter belts cut the force of the wind and helped to conserve water and soil. They also made farms on the Great Plains more attractive.

Beginning in 1938 Congress authorized the Department of Agriculture to offer crop insurance. This was a service desired by farmers, but private companies could not afford to take a chance on it. At first, crop insurance was limited to wheat growers in certain areas. In later years Congress extended the experiment to a few other crops.

Of course farmers benefited from all New Deal measures which stimulated the economy. As unemployment declined and wages went up, people spent more for food and clothing. As a result the demand for farm products rose. The federal public works program helped farmers by providing flood control and improved highways and waterways. Perhaps the greatest of all New Deal benefits to agriculture, however, was the nationwide program to conserve soil, water, and forests.

Regulation of Business, Banking, and Currency

NIRA and "industrial self-government."

The most spectacular measure adopted in the "electric spring of 1933" was the National Industrial Recovery Act (NIRA). It grew out of proposals by industrial leaders, who wished to stop the desperate price-slashing and labor-sweating tactics of small competitors. Trade associations, argued these leaders, should be allowed to stabilize prices and prevent cutthroat competition. The scheme was described as "industrial self-government."

NIRA suspended the antitrust laws for two years. It directed businessmen in every line to join in drawing up a code of fair competition for their industry. Besides putting an end to ruinous price-cutting and other unfair practices, each code was expected to ban child labor, reduce working hours, and raise wages. After a public hearing and approval by the President, the code would have the force of law and would bind all members of the industry. Violators would be subject to fine and imprisonment.

The most remarkable feature of NIRA was Section 7a, stating the right of labor to organize and bargain collectively through representatives of its own choosing. This section was intended to encourage labor to organize and to demand higher wages.

The National Recovery Administration (NRA), headed by the vigorous and colorful General Hugh S. Johnson, promptly went to work. With parades, speeches, and advertising, businessmen were invited to sign a temporary "blanket code." Upon doing so, they could display the Blue Eagle, symbol of national recovery. Within four months 96 per cent of the nation's places of business had Blue Eagle signs in the window.

The blanket code was gradually replaced by almost six hundred codes drawn up by separate industries. Most codes limited the work week to 40 hours and set a minimum wage of $13 to $15 a week in the North (a dollar or two less in the South). They banned child labor and various unfair methods of competition. They also fixed prices.

Enthusiasm for NRA soon gave way to complaints. Labor claimed that the codes did little to raise wages except among the lowest paid workers. Moreover, despite Section 7a, many employers refused to bargain with a labor union. Small businessmen protested that they were being strangled by the codes, which they said favored big business. The mounting criticism led General Johnson to resign, as he put it, "under a hail of dead cats."

As more and more businessmen ignored the rules they disliked, enforcement of the codes broke down. Few were sorry when the Supreme Court ended the experiment with industrial self-government. In a unanimous deci-

690

sion (*Schechter Poultry Corporation* vs. *United States,* May, 1935) the Court said that Congress had no right to delegate its lawmaking power to the President or to trade associations. Furthermore, the federal government had no right to determine wages, hours, and other matters in businesses not engaged in interstate commerce. To keep the labor provisions of the act, Congress soon passed other laws (see pp. 698 and 699).

Savers and investors receive protection.

The need of federal laws to regulate banks and stock exchanges had been brought out by a Senate investigating committee in 1932. The Pecora committee, as it was called, revealed how men prominent in the financial world had organized speculative pools to run up the price of a stock before unloading it on the unsuspecting public. Also they had formed holding companies to evade taxes or to "milk" operating companies of their earnings, and they had promoted the sale of worthless foreign and domestic securities.

The Banking Act of June, 1933, ordered commercial banks to stop selling securities. To prevent another speculative orgy like that in the late twenties, the act gave the Federal Reserve Board power to refuse credit to banks who lent too much money to speculators. The act also set up the Federal Deposit Insurance Corporation to protect savings bank depositors. A second banking act passed in 1935 gave additional powers to the Federal Reserve Board, renaming it the Board of Governors. The act brought each member bank more fully under the Board's control.

The Truth-in-Securities Act of 1933 attacked the old principle of selling securities, "Let the buyer beware." Instead, the act laid down a new principle, "Let the seller beware." Under this act no security may be offered to the public until it has been registered and all pertinent information about it made available. In 1934 Congress set up the Securities and Exchange Commission (SEC) to supervise the issuance of new securities and to regulate stockbrokers and security exchanges. In 1935 Congress gave the SEC power to regulate public utility holding companies.

The dollar is cheapened.

When Roosevelt took office he was under strong pressure from Congress to inflate the currency. If the dollar were cheaper, it was thought that prices would rise and debts would be easier to pay. Senator Wheeler of Montana revived Bryan's old demand for unlimited coinage of silver (see p. 505). The President used his influence to defeat the proposal. Instead Congress gave him wide power to manage the currency, including the right to cheapen the dollar.

The United States went off the gold standard in April, 1933. All persons owning gold bullion, gold coin, or gold certificates were asked to exchange these for other forms of money. Because United States bonds and the bonds of many private corporations had been issued with a promise that the holders should be paid in gold, Congress passed a joint resolution canceling the gold clause in these bonds. The fears of those who had considered the gold standard sacred proved false. The world's confidence in American currency was unshaken. The hopes that going off the gold standard would boost our foreign trade also proved false.

In October, 1933, the Treasury began to buy gold at a price well above the old standard of $20.67 an ounce. Early in 1934, the President set the price of gold at $35.00 an ounce. This action reduced the value of the dollar to 59 per cent of what it had been earlier. Yet the dollar still bought about as much inside the United States as it had before.

691

The currency was further inflated by the Silver Purchase Act of 1934. This measure, pushed through Congress by senators from the silver states, compelled the Treasury to buy the output of our silver mines at a price much above its value. The silver was paid for with paper money.

Whether New Deal monetary policies helped to stimulate economic recovery is in doubt. Prices rose somewhat, though less than the inflationists hoped. The index of wholesale commodity prices went up a third between 1933 and 1937, but by 1939 half this gain had been lost. How much of the rise was due to the devaluation of the dollar and how much to large-scale government spending is hard to say. Prices are determined chiefly by the demand and supply of goods. As we have noted (see p. 485), demand may be limited by a shortage of currency. When, however, the supply of money is ample, as it was in the 1930's, increasing it will raise prices only if the additional money goes into circulation and is spent. It is purchasing power, not mere quantity of money, which creates demand.

Controls over transportation increase.

In 1933 the nation's railroads were in serious financial trouble. Passenger and freight traffic had been dropping ever since 1920. The decline was due to several things: (1) the increasing use of automobiles, trucks, and busses, (2) the building of pipe lines for transporting oil, and (3) the steady growth of shipping on inland waterways and through the Panama Canal. In June, 1933, Congress passed an Emergency Railroad Transportation Act. It gave the Interstate Commerce Commission new power over railroad lines that were close to bankruptcy or already bankrupt. Financial reorganization was made easier and less disastrous to stockholders.

For years the railroads had been urging Congress to bring their competitors under control. Congress responded with the Motor Carriers Act of 1935. It gave the Interstate Commerce Commission (ICC) the right to regulate interstate busses and trucks. Three years later Congress created the Civil Aeronautics Authority to regulate the air lines. In 1940 Congress gave the ICC control over coastal and inland water carriers.

The Federal Communications Act.

Another step toward more government control was the passage of an act (1934) establishing the Federal Communications Commission (FCC). The new law did away with the Federal Radio Commission and strengthened federal control over broadcasting. The authority held by the ICC over telephone, telegraph, and cable companies was transferred to the Federal Communications Commission.

Gas and electric power are regulated.

The most bitterly fought of all New Deal measures was the Public Utility Holding Company Act of 1935. This law authorized federal regulation of companies sending electric power or natural gas from one state to another. Holding companies which own electric and gas companies were placed under the supervision of the Securities and Exchange Commission (SEC). Holding companies were forbidden to charge unreasonable prices for services they performed for companies under their control—a practice known as "milking." The SEC was given power to dissolve any "second degree" holding company if to do so appeared to be in the public interest. (A "second degree" holding company is one which controls another holding company.) Under this law many of the great holding company "pyramids" built up in the 1920's have been dissolved.

Regional Planning

Congress creates the TVA.

Early in 1933 Senator Norris took the President-elect to see the government dams at Muscle Shoals. Roosevelt was stirred by the needs and the possibilities of the Tennessee Valley. Here was a big rural region where most of the people lived in poverty. Only 3 per cent of the farms had electricity. Most of the forests had been cut down. Floods were a constant menace. The land was badly eroded. After every rain the streams ran brown with the topsoil they carried. In good times most of the Valley's young men and women went north in search of a better living. But since 1929 a large number of unemployed people had come back into the area. Roosevelt and Norris saw that cheap electric power, combined with a program to restore and develop natural resources, could transform the Valley.

In his first inaugural address Roosevelt asked for legislation to end "the continued idleness" of the Muscle Shoals development and "to enlist this project in the service of the people." He proposed the creation of a Tennessee Valley Authority—"a corporation clothed with the power of government but possessed of the flexibility and initiative of a private enterprise." Congress soon approved the plan.

The Tennessee Valley Authority (TVA) is a public corporation managed by three directors appointed by the President. Congress gave TVA the right to produce, distribute, and sell electric power; build dams, reservoirs, and power lines; improve navigation; control floods; and promote the social and economic welfare of the Tennessee basin. The basin includes parts of seven states—Alabama, Georgia, Kentucky, Mississippi, North Carolina, Tennessee, and Virginia.

TVA helps reconstruct the region.

TVA built sixteen dams and acquired five more. The dams not only produce electric power but control floods by storing water in large artificial lakes, or reservoirs. No river in the world is now so thoroughly controlled as the Tennessee. Flood control in the Tennessee Valley has helped to control floods on the Ohio and the Mississippi.

In harnessing the Tennessee, TVA provided 630 miles of navigable waterways. The waterways and the abundant electric power encouraged rapid industrial development of the region.

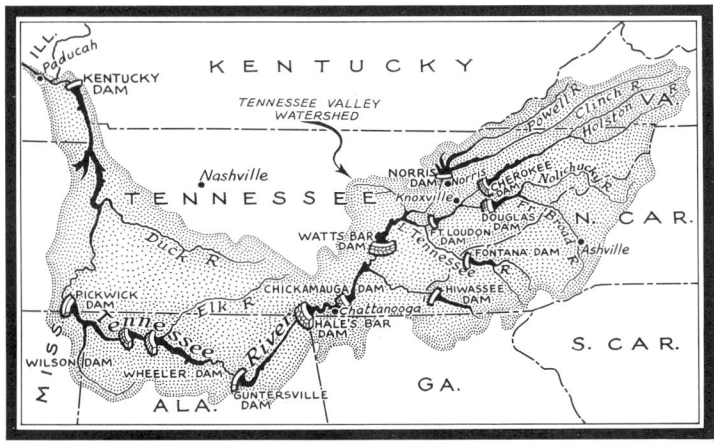

THE TVA

This in turn raised the per capita income 500 per cent in fifteen years.

From the start TVA co-operated with agricultural colleges and state agencies in a campaign for soil conservation and reforestation. Such a program was necessary to prevent TVA reservoirs from filling up with silt, as well as to save the Valley's natural resources from ruin. The soil conservation program depended on persuading farmers to practice such methods as contour plowing and the planting of soil-binding crops. Farmers who promised to follow the recommended conservation methods were supplied free fertilizer manufactured by TVA. Tree seedlings were given to landowners who agreed to plant them on cutover woodland and badly eroded farmland. Part of the reforested land is still privately owned. Part of it is in state and municipal forests established after TVA aroused interest in reforestation.

TVA built generators and about 5000 miles of power lines. The electric current it produces is sold at wholesale to private companies, municipalities, and electric co-operatives. As Congress directed, preference is given to municipalities and co-operatives, which take about half of the current produced. The use of electricity by farmers and homemakers in the region has grown faster than in any other part of the United States. This reflects two facts: (1) that the rates to small users are low and (2) that the Valley's standard of living has climbed since the TVA came there.

Objections to TVA.

Private electric companies already in the area objected to government competition and fought a long series of legal battles against the Authority. The Supreme Court upheld TVA on all major points. Thereupon several of the private companies sold their property to TVA or to municipalities. The largest corporation to sell out was a holding company, Commonwealth and Southern, whose president was Wendell Willkie. Mr. Willkie became nationally known for his vigorous attacks on TVA and ran for President in 1940.

TVA develops local participation.

The directors of TVA wished to encourage local initiative. They tried from the first to draw all the people of the region into making plans for and participating in the development of the Valley. No step was taken without the advice of state and local agencies, colleges, businessmen's associations, farm bureaus, and other interested groups. Wherever possible such local groups were asked to supply services needed by TVA under contract. For example, the Authority wanted traveling libraries for thousands of employees who were building dams in isolated spots. It contracted with the Tennessee Division of Libraries to send out bookmobiles. When TVA support was withdrawn, the legislature decided to continue the service for the benefit of the people of the state. In the same way the Authority stimulated the development of agricultural research, education, public health service, mosquito control, community food lockers, and local industries.

"Nobody Is Going to Starve"

The federal government helps the needy.

When Roosevelt took office the nation's most urgent problem was relief for the unemployed. During his campaign he had promised that no one was going to starve, but millions were close to it. The resources of many state and local governments were exhausted. As almost everyone agreed, the federal government would have to take over a big share of the relief load.

The Federal Emergency Relief Administration was set up in May, 1933.

694

Government experiments with SOIL ENRICHMENT

By the time it was discontinued two years later, it had granted three billion dollars to the states for their relief work. The states distributed the money as they chose, generally as direct relief in the form of cash, food, or clothing. Direct relief, also known as the "dole," is cheaper than work relief but it is costly in self-respect.

Unemployment was so severe as 1933 drew to a close that the Civil Works Administration (CWA) was hurriedly set up. During the winter of 1933–34 CWA distributed nearly a billion dollars to states, cities, and counties to put needy people to work. Projects were chosen practically overnight by local authorities and supervised by them. The work was not supposed to compete with private industry nor to cost much for material. Typical projects were: removing old streetcar tracks, building parking lots, building drainage ditches and levees, repairing roads, landscaping schoolyards, mending library books, and making garments for the needy. Some projects were poorly chosen or poorly carried out and had no lasting value. Because of widespread criticism, CWA was abolished in March, 1934. It had given jobs to about four million men and women for about three months at an average of 60 cents an hour. Besides helping a large number of the needy, CWA created buying power which tended to boost the whole economy.

The CCC puts young men to work.

One of the most tragic aspects of unemployment during the Great Depression was the inability of the unskilled and the inexperienced to find jobs. Each year several hundred thousand young people entered the labor market, and very few of them managed to obtain work. In their discouragement, many boys and some girls took to the road in a vain effort to become self-supporting. When Roosevelt took office perhaps half a million of these young hoboes were wandering over the country, and their number was growing.

Early in the "Hundred Days" Congress established the Civilian Conservation Corps (CCC). It was designed to give work and training to young men and at the same time to promote a nationwide program of conservation. Fifteen hundred camps were quickly built, mostly in state and national forests. By August, 1933, a quarter million men were enrolled in the Corps. Working for thirty hours a week, they made trails, cut fire lanes, planted trees, placed brush dams across gullies to check erosion, and built recreational facilities for the public. Besides food, clothing, and medical care, each man received $30 a month, of which $22 went to parents or other dependents. Before the CCC was discontinued in 1942, it had provided jobs for three million youths.

PWA provides jobs on public works.

The Public Works Administration (PWA) continued, on a much bigger scale, the emergency program of public works started under President Hoover. PWA made grants and loans to public agencies for construction of a permanent nature. Under the direction of Harold Ickes, Secretary of the Interior, strict standards were maintained for the use of PWA funds. Each project was closely supervised from start to finish. It has been said that "Never in American history has as much money been spent with so little graft or even rumors of graft." Nearly 34,500 projects were built, at a total cost of about four billion dollars. They included dams, bridges, schools, university buildings, hospitals, water works, sewers, highways, municipal electric plants, and low-cost housing. In hiring workers preference was given to union members and to veterans. For every two persons employed on PWA construction, it is estimated that five were employed in the building materials industry. The money spent by PWA stimulated the entire economy. It also created valuable facilities to serve the nation.

WPA provided work relief to millions.

Early in 1935 there were still some ten million unemployed, about half of whom were living on a meager dole. To relieve the suffering of these people and to "prime the pump" of the national economy, Roosevelt asked Congress for money to set up a broad program of work relief. The Works Progress Administration (WPA), directed by Harry Hopkins, soon became the nation's chief relief agency. Unlike the ill-fated CWA, which hired a good many "unemployables," WPA employed only the able-bodied people, 90 per cent of whom were drawn from relief rolls. WPA workers got less than those in private employment and were dropped after eighteen months to make way for others.

WPA projects could not compete with private business. It was barred from other fields because it had to depend on state or local governments to provide any materials it needed. In spite of these limitations, every effort was made to choose activities of real value and to find work for people of diverse abilities. Manual laborers were given jobs improving airfields, repairing public buildings, and building minor public works, such as sidewalks, playgrounds, and dirt roads. Women were employed at sewing, preparing school lunches, or as aides in schools, clinics, and hospitals. Thousands of nursery schools and kindergartens were established, partly to employ jobless teachers. Long-idle actors, writers, musicians, and artists received up to $94 a month for work using their special skills. WPA theatrical and musical groups gave thousands of programs every month. Artists hired by WPA decorated public buildings with paintings and sculptures. Writers collected local history, indexed historical papers, or prepared state and city guidebooks. Most of the time, until World War II wiped out unemployment, WPA had about two million workers on its rolls.

WPA was based on the belief that everyone has a right to useful work and to the self-respect that goes with earning his living. Opponents said that much of WPA activity was "boondoggling"—made work of little value. They also charged that relief jobs were used to buy votes for the Democrats. The most frequently heard charge was that the cost of work relief would bankrupt the federal government.

NYA helps needy students.

The National Youth Administration was a division of WPA. It gave part-time work to needy high school and college students in order that they might continue their education. They were employed chiefly by the institutions they attended. Earnings were limited to about $10 a month, yet even this small sum enabled many young people to remain in school.

The Social Security System is established.

President Roosevelt described the Social Security Act of 1935 as the "supreme achievement" of his administration. This law had a double purpose: (1) to help the states improve their services to the needy, and (2) to provide *social insurance* to protect workers and their dependents from want. Other in-

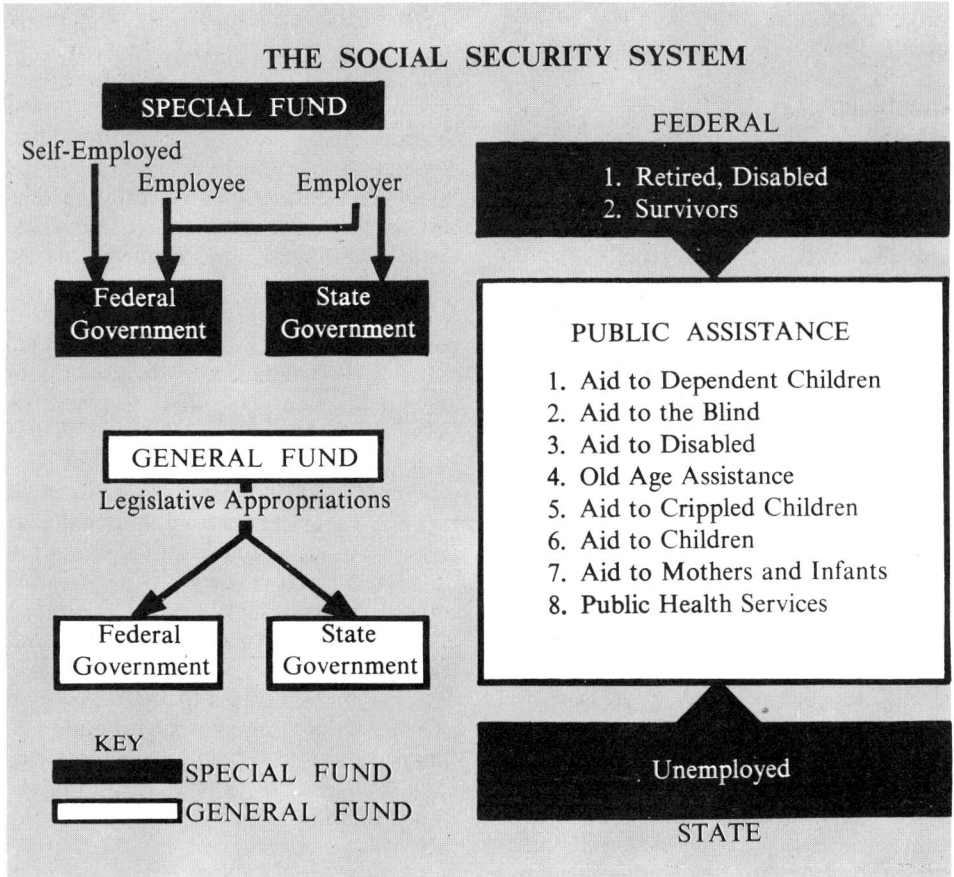

THE SOCIAL SECURITY SYSTEM

SPECIAL FUND

Self-Employed

Employee   Employer

Federal
Government

State
Government

GENERAL FUND

Legislative Appropriations

Federal
Government

State
Government

KEY

SPECIAL FUND

GENERAL FUND

FEDERAL

1. Retired, Disabled
2. Survivors

PUBLIC ASSISTANCE

1. Aid to Dependent Children
2. Aid to the Blind
3. Aid to Disabled
4. Old Age Assistance
5. Aid to Crippled Children
6. Aid to Children
7. Aid to Mothers and Infants
8. Public Health Services

Unemployed

STATE

dustrial nations had social insurance long before the United States did. The Great Depression convinced Americans that we needed it too.

Here are the main features of the Social Security Act:

1. General welfare services. The federal government offered to match funds set aside by each state to provide for: (a) the care and treatment of crippled children, (b) welfare work with homeless and delinquent children, (c) the rehabilitation of disabled workers, (d) aid to the needy blind, and (e) aid to needy mothers with dependent children. The new federal grants-in-aid encouraged all the states to do more for these needy groups, which had been sadly neglected in most

places. The act also made outright grants to the states for extending their public health work.

2. Old age and survivors insurance. The original act provided monthly payments to retired workers over 65. Survivors insurance was added in 1937 to protect widows and children. If a worker dies, his widow receives monthly payments after she reaches 65. If he dies leaving young children, his wife receives monthly payments until the youngest child is 18. The cost of old age and survivors insurance is met by a payroll tax. The worker and his employer are each taxed an equal percentage of his earnings. Under the original act about three out of five workers were covered. Today the proportion is much higher, for Congress has extended this protection to additional groups of workers, including those who are self-employed.

3. Old age assistance. When the Social Security Act was passed, twenty-eight states already had an old age pension system. In these states small pensions were given to needy persons over 65, if they had no relatives who could be required to support them. Under the Social Security Act, the federal government promised to pay half the cost of such pensions. With this encouragement every state set up an old age pension system (now known as old age assistance). We should keep in mind that unlike old age *insurance,* old age *assistance* is given only to those who can prove they are in need.

4. Unemployment insurance. In 1935 Wisconsin was the only state with compulsory unemployment insurance. The Social Security Act persuaded every state to adopt it. To pay for it the federal government collects a special payroll tax from employers. Ninety per cent of the money collected in a state is returned to it if it has a satisfactory program of unemployment insurance. Among other conditions to be met, the state must maintain free employment bureaus to help unemployed workers find jobs. Some groups of workers are not covered by unemployment insurance. When a covered worker becomes unemployed, he is entitled to a weekly benefit for a limited number of weeks. The maximum benefit, and the number of weeks it is paid, varies in different states.

The Social Security Act gave millions of families more peace of mind. The fear of having to go to the poorhouse in old age was banished. Widows left with young children could now keep the home together until the children grew up. The blind and certain other needy groups were also better provided for.

The Labor Movement Revives

The New Deal seeks to strengthen labor.

Labor unions had lost ground ever since the depression of 1921. By the beginning of 1933 there were only about three million organized workers. Many unions were barely able to stay alive. After passage of the National Industrial Recovery Act, unions began to grow, but a great many employers still refused to recognize them.

Senator Wagner and other New Deal leaders in Congress wished to strengthen the labor movement. They believed that strong labor unions were needed to offset in part the immense power of big business. Labor unions, they thought, could exert a counter-balancing force that would be healthy for the country. If labor had the power to get a larger share of the national income, the market for farm and industrial products would expand.

When the Supreme Court rejected the National Industrial Recovery Act, Congress quickly passed the Wagner Labor Relations Act (1935). This measure ordered employers to give up practices that interfered with the right of workers to organize free labor unions and to bargain collectively. The law prohibited company unions dominated or financed by the employer. A National Labor Relations Board (NLRB) was created to prevent practices unfair to labor. Workers could call on the NLRB to hold a secret election in the place where they worked to find out whether the majority wished to join a union. The Supreme Court upheld the Wagner Act in 1937.

The Wagner Act did more to support the rights of labor than any measure Congress had ever passed. It made collective bargaining the normal practice in labor disputes. Thus it tended to improve the relations of labor and management. Many employers thought the act was one-sided, since it said nothing about unfair practices by labor unions. In 1947, as we shall see, it was replaced by the Taft-Hartley Labor Relations Act (see p. 760).

The CIO competes with the A.F. of L.

Under the Wagner Act, labor unions grew rapidly. By 1939 they had eight million members. Most of the new members worked in mass-production industries which had never been organized before. Progress in organizing these industries began in 1935, when the heads of eight A.F. of L. unions formed the Committee for Industrial Organization (CIO). Its chairman was John L. Lewis, leader of the United Mine Workers. The CIO rejected the principle of a separate union for each craft. Instead it aimed to unite all the workers within a given industry, regardless of the sort of work they do, in one *industrial* union. President William Green of the A.F. of L. thought that the rise of industrial unions would injure existing craft unions. He had the CIO expelled from the federation.

The CIO had aggressive leaders. In 1936 they carried on a vigorous campaign to organize the steel and auto industries. Late that year auto workers at the General Motors plants at Flint, Michigan, hoping to get their union recognized, tried a new weapon— the "sit-down" strike. They did not leave the plants but remained near their machines. Their object was to prevent the company from operating the plants either with imported strikebreakers or with workers who did not choose to strike. The strike lasted forty-four days. Then General Motors recognized the United Auto Workers' Union. In the next few months there was an epidemic of sit-down strikes, in some of which force was used to evict the sit-downers. After the Supreme Court declared the sit-down strike to be an illegal seizure of property (Fansteel case, 1939), the practice stopped.

Meanwhile, in 1937, several big steel and auto companies recognized the CIO and signed agreements with it. That year the CIO's membership reached nearly four million. It changed its name to "Congress of Industrial Organizations." This was done to emphasize its independence from the A.F. of L. Eighteen years later the CIO and the A.F. of L. were merged (see p. 761).

Congress raises labor standards.

In 1936 Congress passed the Walsh-Healy Government Contracts Act. This act said that federal contracts would be given only to concerns that pay prevailing wages, have a work day of no more than eight hours and a work week of five days, and maintain fair labor conditions. The Secretary of Labor was to determine whether the conditions had been met. Since the federal government makes contracts with many concerns, enforcement of the act helped considerably to lift labor standards. For example, fear of losing government contracts led steel companies to bargain collectively with their workers for the first time in the industry's history.

In 1937 and 1938 Congress debated a bill to help workers who seemed incapable of effective organization—children, women, and the unskilled. The bill, which became the Fair Labor Standards Act, aimed to set a floor under wages, to end child labor in factories, and to put a ceiling over hours. Although it met strong opposition, the bill finally passed in 1938. It applied to industries whose products are sold across state lines. It prohibited the sale of products made by children, outside the state in which they are made. It set forty hours as the normal working week and said that "time and one half" must be paid for overtime.[1] It fixed 25

---

[1] In 1949 Congress raised the minimum to 75 cents an hour; in 1955, to a dollar an hour.

cents an hour as the minimum wage, to be raised gradually to 40 cents. The law benefited millions of workers in low-paid jobs.

The New Deal Wins

Opposition from both right and left.

At first, as we have said, there was little opposition to the New Deal. In 1933 almost everyone agreed that drastic action was needed to save the nation. But as soon as the emergency was over, conservatives in both parties attacked Roosevelt's program. Among these critics was the President's former friend, Alfred E. Smith, who said the New Deal was destroying personal liberty. Former President Hoover claimed that the New Deal was destroying the self-reliance of the American people and strangling private enterprise in a mass of governmental controls. Financial and industrial leaders echoed these charges and added others. It was often said that the New Deal was moving toward socialism or even toward communism. Roosevelt was accused of making himself a dictator, forcing Congress to do his bidding, and encouraging class hatred.

The President had many other critics who denounced him for not doing enough to help the common people. Father Charles Coughlin of Detroit, the "radio priest," spoke weekly to millions of listeners, demanding a "living annual wage" and cheaper money and calling Roosevelt a "double-crosser." Dr. Francis Townsend won a large following by advocating a pension of $200 a month for every person over 60. The millions of old people who enrolled in Townsend clubs were far from satisfied by the Social Security Act. Senator Huey P. Long, the self-styled "Louisiana Kingfish," led a "Share-the-Wealth" movement which called for providing every family with a homestead and a yearly income of $5000. Long stood for dictatorship of the Fascist type. He had a numerous following and planned to run against Roosevelt on a third party ticket. Until he was killed in 1935, Democratic national leaders thought him a serious threat. The Communists were another group who found the President entirely too conservative. In the early days of the New Deal they called Roosevelt a Fascist.

The Republicans nominate Landon.

When the Republicans wrote their 1936 platform, they charged that the American system of free enterprise was in peril. They accused the Democrats of "frightful waste and extravagance." They said the New Deal was prolonging the depression by frightening business. They promised economy. At the same time they said they favored unemployment relief, aid to farmers, and more generous social security benefits. They nominated Governor Alfred M. Landon, described as the "Coolidge of Kansas" because he had cut the state's expenditures.

The Democrats nominated President Roosevelt and endorsed his policies. Yet Alfred E. Smith and other prominent Democrats of conservative views said they would vote for Landon. Business leaders gave heavily to the Republican campaign fund. Two thirds or more of the newspapers joined the "stop-Roosevelt" movement. The *Literary Digest* poll, which sampled automobile owners and telephone subscribers, forecast a Republican victory.

Minor parties win few votes.

A new Union party entered the contest. It nominated Representative William Lemke, a North Dakota Republican, on a platform calling for cheap money, more aid to farmers, a ceiling on incomes and inheritances, and an end to monopoly. Lemke was backed by Father Coughlin, Dr. Townsend, and by Huey Long's successor, the rabble-rousing Gerald L. K. Smith. Some thought the Union party might take enough votes from the Democrats to insure the election of Landon. However, less than 900,000 votes were cast for Lemke, while the Socialists, Communists, and Socialist Labor parties together got about one third as many.

F.D.R. wins by a landslide.

The President had the support of labor, most of the farmers, and many small businessmen. A record-breaking number of people voted. Of the 46 million votes cast, almost 61 per cent were for Roosevelt. The Democrats carried every state but Maine and Vermont. Quipsters said the old slogan "As Maine goes, so goes the nation" should be changed to "As Maine goes, so goes Vermont." The Democrats increased their majority in both houses of Congress and elected Democratic governors in most of the states. The 1936 election was an impressive vote of confidence in the New Deal.

A Constitutional Revolution

F.D.R. tries to enlarge the Supreme Court.

Roosevelt's second inauguration took place on January 20, 1937, the date set by the Twentieth Amendment. In his inaugural speech he pointed out that the United States had means to provide a comfortable living for all its people, yet one third of the nation was "ill-housed, ill-clad, and ill-nourished." He pledged himself to go on fighting for reform. The Supreme Court, however, stood in the way of many of his reforms. It had already found a large number of New Deal laws to be unconstitutional. It would soon rule on cases testing the Wagner Labor Relations Act, the Social Security Act, the TVA, and other key New Deal measures. The nation expected that most, if not all, of these laws would be rejected. As the President pointed out, the Supreme Court had created a "twilight zone" in

FONTANA DAM, *in North Carolina, is TVA's highest dam, rising 480 feet over the Little Tennessee River.*

which neither the states nor the federal government could move. For example, it set aside state laws establishing minimum labor standards on the ground that these violated the Fourteenth Amendment. Federal laws for the same purpose were set aside because they invaded the powers of the states.

All the justices at this time had been appointed before Roosevelt took office. Most of them were elderly men. Four justices were very conservative and rarely approved of any law, state or federal, that affected the rights of property. Three—Brandeis, Stone, and Cardozo—were liberals. They accepted the principle that the law must adapt itself to the changing needs of society (see p. 555). The others, Chief Justice Hughes and Justice Roberts, sometimes lined up with the liberals, but more often with the conservatives. In most of its decisions, therefore, the Court split 6 to 3, or 5 to 4.

Early in his second term Roosevelt startled the country by proposing a reorganization of the federal courts. He recommended that when any federal judge passed the age of seventy without retiring, the President should have the power to appoint an additional judge to share his work. Under this plan the membership of the Supreme Court might be increased to fifteen.

Although in the past Congress had six times changed the number of Supreme Court justices, Roosevelt's proposal led to a storm of protests. Not only conservatives but others thought that it threatened the independence of the judiciary. The President was charged with planning to "pack" the Supreme Court. Critics of the Court replied that it was already packed, and the problem was to unpack it. The debate raged for months. Even the experts on constitutional law disagreed with one another about the President's proposal.

The Supreme Court changes its attitude.

Meanwhile, the Supreme Court began to take a more liberal view of the Constitution. In March 1937, by a 5 to 4 decision (*West Coast Hotel* vs. *Parris*), it upheld a Washington minimum-wage law, although a year earlier it had set aside a similar New York law. In April in another 5 to 4 decision (*NLRB* vs. *Jones and Laughlin, and others*), it upheld the Wagner Labor Relations Act. To do so, the Court changed the definition of interstate commerce that had led it to throw out the NIRA. In May the Court voted 5 to 4 to uphold the Social Security Act. In so doing it defined the national welfare as broadly as Chief Justice Marshall had done a century earlier. After this no important New Deal law was found unconstitutional.

Friends of the President felt he had won his battle over the Supreme Court, although Congress did not pass his reorganization plan. In any event, two conservative justices soon resigned and the President appointed liberals to replace them. By 1941 Roosevelt had been able to name seven of the nine justices. The decisions of the Court reflected the change in its membership. The Court was now inclined to approve social welfare laws, whether passed by a state legislature or by Congress. Historians have described the change in the Court's attitude as a "constitutional revolution."

The Threat of War Postpones Further Reforms

The reform program is interrupted.

By 1937 Roosevelt had become deeply concerned about the aggressive designs of the Nazis, Fascists, and Japanese. Events abroad forced him to give more and more attention to our foreign relations and to the strengthening of our national defense. Yet he still pushed for reform. Congress passed the National Housing Act of 1937 to improve housing conditions for families of low income. The Bituminous Coal Act of 1937 was designed to bring order into the chaotic soft coal industry. In 1938 a permanent AAA was created (see p. 688), the Fair Labor Standards Act was passed (see p. 699), and the Food, Drug, and Cosmetic Act strengthened the Pure Food Act of 1906.

When Congress met in January, 1939, the President for the first time since taking office proposed no new domestic reforms. Instead he stressed the dangers to democracy and world peace. Although Roosevelt's reform program was still incomplete, he felt that war was coming and he must use all his powers of leadership to prepare the nation for the new emergency.

Roosevelt wins a third term.

War was raging in Europe when the Republicans and Democrats met in 1940 to choose their candidates for President. The Republicans chose Wendell Willkie, a newcomer in politics. As head of a great Southern power company, he had won fame for his criticisms of the TVA. He insisted that private enterprise must be freed from governmental restraints and socialistic competition. It could then produce enough for everyone. The only way to give more people more of the good things of life, he argued, was to produce more. Willkie's forthright and friendly personality appealed to the public. He owed his nomination not to Old Guard leaders but to the rank and file of the party.

A large number of Democrats urged Roosevelt to run for a third term. Mainly because of the threat of war, he decided he would run again. The Democrats broke the two-term tradition to nominate him. Henry Wallace, Secretary of Agriculture, was nominated for Vice-President.

On questions of national defense and foreign affairs, Willkie differed little from Roosevelt. Both candidates promised to keep the United States out of the war unless we were attacked and to give all possible aid to Great Britain, short of war. The New Deal was the only real issue between them. Once more Roosevelt gained a substantial victory. He had 55 per cent of the popular vote and carried 38 states.

How shall we appraise the New Deal?

Since Roosevelt's third term was concerned mainly with war, this is a good place to evaluate the New Deal.

The New Deal did not solve the problem of unemployment. By 1939 business activity and industrial output were greater than ever before. Yet one in six of those able and willing to work still could not find jobs. Unemployment did not disappear until after the United States went to war.

The New Deal spent more than it collected in taxes. The average deficit in the 1930's was three billion dollars a year. About half of this was for useful public works and for loans that were eventually repaid. The remainder went chiefly for the relief of farmers and the unemployed.

On the other hand, the New Deal has many recognized achievements to its credit. It made great strides toward providing easy credit to farmers and home owners; conserving soil, forests, and water; developing hydroelectric resources; controlling floods; bringing order into the stock market; protecting small investors; and safeguarding depositors in savings banks. It made a lasting contribution to the welfare of working people and the underprivileged by establishing minimum wages and maximum hours; by ending child labor in interstate industries; by promoting collective bargaining; by launching the social security system; by encouraging the states to expand their services to the needy; by reducing farm tenancy; and by helping to clear slums.

As a result of the New Deal, Americans, on the whole, have accepted the idea that the government has much responsibility for the people's social and economic security—for their employment, health, and general welfare. In carrying out this principle the New Deal expanded the activities of both the federal government and the state governments. Yet our liberties did not suffer. Democracy was preserved here at a time when it was being lost in most of Europe.

JOHN L. LEWIS

FOR IDENTIFICATION

Agricultural Adjustment Acts
Civilian Conservation Corps
Fair Labor Standards Act
William Green
Cordell Hull
Alfred M. Landon
John L. Lewis
Huey P. Long
National Recovery Administration
Public Works Administration
Securities and Exchange Commission
Social Security Act
Works Progress Administration

FOR EXPLANATION OR DEFINITION

Brain Trust
codes of fair competition
company union
deficit financing
deposit insurance
devaluation of dollar
"Hundred Days"
industrial self-government
industrial union
migratory farm labor
"packing the Court"
parity prices
"prime the pump"
processing tax
reciprocal trade agreement
shelter belt
sit-down strike
subsistence farmer
surplus commodity

FOR REVIEW

1. What experiences helped prepare Franklin D. Roosevelt for the Presidency?

2. Describe economic conditions at the time of Roosevelt's first inauguration.

3. List the important laws passed during the "Hundred Days" of the special session of Congress. Distinguish between those that were temporary or emergency measures and those that were continuing features of the New Deal program.

4. What were the three basic purposes of the New Deal? Give examples of laws for each purpose.

5. (a) What were the provisions of the first AAA (1934)? What were some of its results? Why was it declared unconstitutional by the Supreme Court? (b) How was the Soil Conservation Act of 1936 a substitute for the first AAA? (c) What were the chief characteristics of the second AAA (1938)?

6. How did the New Deal improve credit facilities for farmers?

7. How did Congress help to save farmers from losing their farms?

8. What were the purposes of the Resettlement Administration?

9. Describe the work of the Farm Security Administration.

10. (a) What were the provisions of the Reciprocal Trade Agreements Act? (b) In what way did reciprocal trade agreements tend to help the farmer?

11. How did the Surplus Commodities Corporation help the farmer? The Rural Electrification Administration?

12. (a) What were the chief provisions of the National Industrial Recovery Act? Why was Section 7a included? (b) What were the chief criticisms of the NIRA? (c) On what grounds did the Supreme Court declare it unconstitutional?

13. (a) What important reforms in the banking system were made by the Banking Acts of 1933 and 1935? (b) What powers were granted to the Securities and Exchange Commission? (c) What steps were taken by the New Deal to cheapen the dollar?

14. (a) Why were most of the railroads of the country having serious financial difficulties? (b) What emergency and permanent measures of the New Deal

were designed to help the transportation industry?

15. What were the provisions of the Public Utility Holding Company Act of 1934?

16. (a) What broad powers did Congress give to the TVA? (b) What were the major purposes of the TVA? (c) What has TVA accomplished?

17. (a) How did the CWA (1933–34), and the CCC (1933–42) undertake to provide relief? (b) What limitations were placed on CWA projects? (c) What were some of the accomplishments of the CCC?

18. (a) What types of projects were carried out by the Public Works Administration? (b) How did the PWA help to improve economic conditions and relieve unemployment?

19. (a) What was the function of the Works Progress Administration? (b) How did it differ from the CWA? From the PWA? (c) What criticisms were directed against the WPA? (d) What was the purpose of the National Youth Administration?

20. (a) What was the purpose of the Social Security Act? (b) What general welfare services were assisted by the Social Security Act? (c) How does old age and survivors insurance differ from old age assistance? (d) Explain the unemployment insurance feature of the Social Security Act.

21. Outline the provisions of the Wagner Labor Relations Act of 1935. What effect did this law have upon the labor movement?

22. Explain the reasons for the development of the CIO. How did the CIO differ from the A.F. of L.?

23. (a) How did the Walsh-Healy Government Contracts Act help labor? (b) Outline the provisions of the Fair Labor Standards Act of 1938.

24. (a) What different groups criticized the New Deal? (b) Who were the candidates in the presidential campaign of 1936? (c) What were the results of the election? (d) What is significant about the date of Roosevelt's second inauguration— January 20, 1937?

25. (a) Why did President Roosevelt in 1937 propose to reorganize the Supreme Court? (b) Describe the composition of the Court at this time. (c) What arguments were made for and against President Roosevelt's Court proposals?

26. (a) What Supreme Court decisions in the spring of 1937 tended to weaken Roosevelt's criticism of the Court? (b) What was the outcome of the "Court battle"?

27. Why did President Roosevelt omit reference to domestic reforms in his annual message to Congress in January, 1939? What subjects did he stress in this message?

28. (a) What considerations probably prompted Roosevelt to seek a third term in 1940? (b) On what issues did Roosevelt and Willkie agree? Disagree? (c) What were the results of the election?

29. (a) Why did unemployment persist in spite of New Deal efforts? (b) How did the New Deal affect the national debt? (c) Summarize the main achievements of the New Deal.

30. What fundamental theory concerning governmental policy seems to have been established as a result of the New Deal?

FOR FURTHER STUDY AND DISCUSSION

1. (a) What defects in the banking system became apparent as a result of the boom and depression? How were they corrected by the Banking Acts of 1933 and 1935? (b) How does the Federal Deposit Insurance Corporation tend to centralize control over banking practices? Helpful source: Faulkner, *Economic History*, pp. 663–665.

2. (a) What steps toward inflation or "reflation" were taken by the Roosevelt administration? (b) How is an unbalanced budget a form of inflation? (c) How was the devaluation of the dollar expected to stimulate foreign trade? (d) Investigate and report on the actual effects of dollar devaluation as compared with arguments that were advanced for and against it at the time. Helpful source: Faulkner, *Economic History*, pp. 660–663, 687–692.

3. Why may the Reciprocal Trade Agreement Act be regarded as a partial retreat from economic nationalism? Helpful source: Faulkner, *Economic History*, pp. 694–698.

4. State the principles underlying the Agricultural Marketing Act of 1929, the Agricultural Adjustment Act of 1933, the Domestic Allotment and Soil Conservation Act of 1936, and the Agricultural Adjustment Act of 1938. As a long-time program, which of these measures provides the best approach to a solution of the farm problem? Helpful sources: Faulkner, *Economic History*, pp. 665–669; Amherst Series, *The New Deal, Revolution or Evolution?* Brogan, *The Era of Franklin D. Roosevelt*.

5. How did the Roosevelt farm program benefit others than farmers? How is the farm problem related to flood control, power development, and conservation?

6. (a) What is a public utility? Why have state and local governments regulated public utility companies? (b) Why did the federal government attempt to regulate public utility holding companies? (c) Give arguments for and against the policy outlined in the Public Utility Holding Company Act.

7. (a) Why is the TVA frequently referred to as a profoundly important "social experiment"? (b) Outline the advantages and disadvantages of organizing the country under the control of several regional authorities similar to the TVA. Helpful source: Lilienthal, *TVA, Experiment in Democracy*.

8. Debate the merits of Roosevelt's Supreme Court proposals. Helpful source: Amherst Series, *Franklin D. Roosevelt and the Supreme Court*.

9. It has been said that the New Deal borrowed heavily from populism, progressivism, and the New Freedom, but it advanced far beyond them, involving the direct intervention of the federal government to control the actual workings of the economic system. Indicate why you agree or disagree with this statement.

FOR INDIVIDUAL OR GROUP ACTIVITIES

1. Prepare short biographical sketches of Huey Long, Harry Hopkins, Cordell Hull.

2. Hold a panel discussion between those who argue that crop curtailment is economically unsound, stimulates imports of agricultural products, and imposes an extra burden on the factory worker, and those who contend that the economic distress of American farmers justifies a program of agricultural "planning." (Should American farming be subsidized? Relate your discussion of this topic to the tariff and to subsidies for a merchant marine.)

3. Investigate and report to the class the claims of public utility companies and the TVA concerning the value of the TVA as a "yardstick" to measure the reasonableness of the price charged consumers by private public power utilities.

4. Make a special study and report on the operation of the National Labor Relations Act of 1935 and the Fair Labor Standards Act of 1938. Helpful source: Amherst Series, *Industry-wide Collective Bargaining, Promise or Menace?*

5. Have a committee select key passages from Roosevelt's speeches which illustrate his political philosophy.

6. Investigate and report on the origin and development of the Congress of Industrial Organizations. Helpful source: Brogan, *The Era of Franklin D. Roosevelt*; Faulkner and Starr, *Labor in America*; Link, *American Epoch*; Wecter, *The Age of the Great Depression*.

7. Hold a panel discussion on these views concerning the New Deal: "A revolution was started by the New Deal—not a revolution in the violent, turbulent sense, but a revolution nevertheless." "We can see now (1945) that the 'Roosevelt Revolution' was no revolution, but rather the culmination of a half century of historical development." Helpful sources: Brogan, *The Era of Franklin D. Roosevelt*; Hofstadter, *The Age of Reform*; Amherst Series, *The New Deal, Revolution or Evolution?*

8. Have different committees report on Perkins, *The Roosevelt I Knew*; Sherwood, *Roosevelt and Hopkins*; Hofstadter, "Franklin D. Roosevelt, The Patrician as Opportunist" in *American Political Tradition*, pp. 315–353.

If we are to have a world in which we can breathe freely and live in amity without fear, the peace-loving nations must make a concerted effort to uphold laws and principles on which alone peace can rest secure.
——Franklin D. Roosevelt, 1937

42. ISOLATION PROVES IMPOSSIBLE

F.D.R. Follows the Good Neighbor Policy

The Good Neighbor policy.

In his first inaugural address (March 4, 1933), President Roosevelt stated the principle which guided him in foreign affairs:

In the field of world policy I would dedicate this nation to the policy of the good neighbor—the neighbor who resolutely respects himself and, because he does so, respects the rights of others.

To help make this policy a reality, F.D.R. chose Senator Cordell Hull of Tennessee to be Secretary of State.

Like the President, Cordell Hull was eager to promote international good will. He believed that world peace rests on sound economic relations between nations. At that time the channels of world trade were choked as they had never been before by high tariffs, exchange restrictions, and quotas which various nations had adopted in a frantic effort to protect their own economies. Hull regarded trade barriers as acts of economic war which hurt everybody. The Trade Agreements Act of 1934 gave him the chance to negotiate with other nations for the reduction of trade barriers (see p. 689).

Secretary Hull worked particularly hard to build up trade between the United States and Latin America. The reciprocal trade agreements he made with these countries helped our businessmen regain Latin American markets which they had been losing to Germany, Italy, and Japan. The Export-Import Bank, which Congress set up in 1934, made loans to Latin American countries so that they could buy more of our goods.

Special attention was given to improving our relations with the republics south of the Rio Grande. In 1933 for the first time the United States pledged itself not to intervene in another country's affairs. In 1934 Congress repealed the Platt Amendment, which had so long displeased Cuba (see p. 589). About the same time the last American Marines were called home from Haiti. In 1936 a new and more generous treaty was negotiated with Panama.

The contest for Latin America.

Throughout the 1930's Germany and Italy competed with the United States for the friendship of Latin America. Germany and Italy poured propaganda into the Latin American countries. To the countries south of Panama they sent millions of emigrants. Vigorous Nazi and Fascist organizations sprang up there. They stirred up hatred of the United States and glorified Hitler and Mussolini. Nazi and Fascist agents established or bought newspapers, radio stations, banks, utility companies, mines, and plantations. They built airports and operated air lines. The Nazis sold armaments to South American countries and sent military and naval officers to train their armed forces. If the Nazis and Fascists were to get control of Europe, their agents in the New World would be a grave threat to North and South America.

Roosevelt and Hull saw the danger and did what they could to offset it. In 1936, at the suggestion of President Roosevelt, a special Inter-American Conference met at Buenos Aires, Argentina. Roosevelt made the 7000-mile trip to be there in person.[1] He announced that the Monroe Doctrine was henceforth the concern of all the American republics. In case of a threat to

---

[1] This was the third time a President had left the United States during his term.

708

the Western Hemisphere from abroad, all the American republics, he said, should have a voice in deciding how to meet it. In 1923 the United States had claimed that the Monroe Doctrine was the concern of no American nation except itself. Now we meant to treat the other American republics as equals.

The oil dispute with Mexico is settled.

The Good Neighbor policy met one of its severest tests in Mexico when the reform-minded President Cárdenas made up his mind to break the power of the great oil companies. In 1938 he nationalized—that is, had the government take possession of—the property of seventeen British and American companies. As a result the British broke off diplomatic relations with Mexico. Our Secretary of State said that Mexico had acted within its rights provided that it paid a fair price for the property it had taken. Although the oil companies demanded that soldiers be sent to protect their holdings, the only pressure our government exerted on Mexico was to discontinue buying Mexican silver. After much argument over the value of the properties, Mexico and the oil companies worked out a settlement. The mild approach taken by our government looked altruistic, but it was also the only practicable approach. The State Department feared that if we prevented Mexico from solving the oil problem in its own way, we would nullify our efforts to unite Latin America against fascism and communism.

The United States recognizes Russia.

Ever since the Bolshevik revolution (November, 1917), the United States had ignored the Russian government. At first we did not recognize it because a civil war was raging in Russia and no one knew whether the Reds or the Whites would win. When the Reds were firmly in control, we did not recognize their government for two reasons: (1) It refused to pay debts owed to American citizens by former Russian governments. (2) It helped support the Communist International, or Comintern, which was founded in 1919 to encourage the spread of communism throughout the world.

By 1933 many Americans thought that the time had come to recognize Russia. It had 160 million people, covered one-sixth of the world's land area, and might become an important market for American goods. Besides, Russia wanted to block Japanese expansion and might help us maintain the Open Door in China. In addition, recognition would make for a friendlier spirit in world affairs.

On the invitation of President Roosevelt, Stalin sent Maxim Litvinoff to Washington to discuss recognition. Litvinoff brought the promise of the Russian government not to carry on propaganda in the United States and not to harbor any organization which aimed at the overthrow of our government by force. Moscow also promised to negotiate a debt settlement. Thereupon (November 16, 1933), the President announced that we were resuming diplomatic relations with the Soviet Union. This step did not, of course, imply that we approved of communism.

The results of the agreement were disappointing. Further negotiations failed to settle the debt question. Under the Debt Default Act of 1934 (see p. 711), the Soviets could not get credit to buy American goods. Trade between the two nations therefore increased only a little. In spite of the Kremlin's promise the Comintern and the American Communist party continued their propaganda. The Soviet government alleged that it had no direct control over the activities of either organization. In 1935 our State Department protested against a Comintern meeting in Moscow attended by leaders of the American Communist party.

The World Economic Conference fails.

When Roosevelt took office, plans had already been made for a World Economic Conference to meet in London in the summer of 1933. Its purpose was to discuss ways to halt the worldwide depression. Preparatory talks in which the United States took part had been going on for months. Many of the participating nations were eager to draw up an agreement to stabilize currencies. Many also wanted to discuss war debts. While the American delegation was on its way to London, Roosevelt sent word that it should confine itself to discussing reciprocal tariff treaties. However, France and four other European nations that were still on the gold standard refused to talk of tariff reduction until a plan was made for holding currencies to a stable value. Such a plan was being drawn up when the President announced that we would stay out of it. He wanted to be free to devalue the dollar (see p. 691). Thus, as he confessed later, he "torpedoed" the conference. Angry at Roosevelt's action, the delegates went home with hardly anything accomplished. F.D.R.'s decision to place American recovery ahead of world recovery turned out to be wrong. Devaluation of the dollar probably did little or nothing to restore prosperity in the United States (see p. 692). The continued violent fluctuations in currencies hampered world trade and drove the world farther toward extreme nationalism.

The Disarmament Conference collapses.

Contrary to his actions in regard to the economic conference, Roosevelt did his best to keep the World Disarmament Conference from failing. During the 1933 session the British offered a plan which called for reducing armies and limiting heavy artillery and airplanes. To satisfy the demand of France and her partners for security, the British proposed that all nations which had signed the Kellogg-Briand Pact should hold a conference to decide on ways to enforce it. Roosevelt urged acceptance of the British plan.

For months Germany had been secretly and rapidly rearming. In October, 1933, Hitler announced that Germany was withdrawing both from the Disarmament Conference and from the League. The announcement frightened Germany's neighbors. Since further talk of disarmament was useless, the conference broke up.

Germany, Italy, and Japan Defy the League of Nations

Fascism threatens world peace.

The first World War left Europe with a bitter heritage of poverty and unrest. In several countries the people were ready to follow a strong man who promised jobs and bread, especially if he also promised to gain the nation new territory and prestige. Thus Benito Mussolini and his black-shirted Fascists were able to seize control of Italy in 1922. Mussolini made himself an absolute dictator. He built up Italy's army and navy and boasted that he would revive the glories of the ancient Roman Empire. Similarly, Hitler rose to power in Germany by promising to restore that nation's prosperity, its empire, and its national pride. His Nazi party won the election early in 1933 and soon destroyed representative government. From then on Hitler ruled with an iron hand. He and his henchmen laid plans to bring most of the world under their control.

Japan was another discontented nation. Like Italy, its homeland was small and had few natural resources. Without foreign markets it could not buy needed raw materials and foodstuffs. Yet many countries had put up trade barriers which kept out Japanese goods. Japan had other grievances as well. The United States had blocked Japan's efforts to gain control of China (see p. 583). Moreover, the exclusion of Japanese immigrants from the United States in 1924 (see p. 634) was a severe blow to Japanese pride. The fact that a few of our states barred Japanese-Americans from owning land also caused bitterness (see p. 583). The military party in Japan harped on these affronts to their country's dignity and attacked liberal leaders friendly to the West. In 1932 the military party seized power. It hoped to make Japan the dominant nation of the Far East.

MUSSOLINI *and* HITLER *reviewing German troops*

The Japanese militarists, Italian Fascists, and German Nazis had much in common. All believed that war is glorious and "might makes right." They despised democracy as weak and decadent. They stood for *totalitarian* government, in which the individual has no rights which the government is bound to respect. A movement based on such ideas may be called "Fascist."

The "have-not" nations become partners.

Japan, Italy, and Germany felt that they had been deprived of their fair share of the world's resources. They called themselves "have-not" nations. They regarded the "have" nations, who possessed extensive homelands or valuable colonies, as their natural enemies. Since the "have" nations were satisfied with the way the world's territory and wealth were divided, they wished to maintain the *status quo*. They opposed the ambitions of the three Fascist nations to obtain more territory.

Japan, Italy, and Germany regarded the League of Nations as an instrument for the benefit of the "haves." The League also upheld the *status quo*. In 1933, when it adopted a report labeling Japan as an aggressor in Manchuria and refusing to recognize the puppet state set up there, Japan resigned from the League (see p. 680).

Mussolini had been rattling the sword for years. In 1935 his forces invaded and conquered the African kingdom of Ethiopia. When the League of Nations tried to restrain him by shutting off the shipment of war supplies, Mussolini took Italy out of the League.

Meanwhile, in defiance of the Treaty of Versailles, Hitler was building a huge air force and a mechanized army such as the world had never before seen. In 1936 he marched an army into the Rhineland, which had been demilitarized by the terms of the Versailles Treaty. France, Russia, and other neighbors of Germany were alarmed by Hitler's actions. Their fears deepened when Hitler and Mussolini entered a partnership known as the Rome-Berlin Axis. The same year Germany and Japan joined in the Anti-Comintern Pact, pledging them to work together to stamp out communism. Italy signed the pact in 1937. Observers regarded the Anti-Comintern Pact as an alliance against Russia.

Neutrality Laws Express American Desire for Peace

The Debt Default Act.

In 1933 nearly all the nations which owed war debts to the United States either failed to send the installment that was due or sent only a token payment. The American people, not realizing that payment in dollars or gold was impossible, felt that they had been cheated. They argued that nations spending large sums for arms could well afford to pay their just debts. Resentment over nonpayment led Congress to pass the Debt Default Act of 1934. It forbade Americans to make loans or give credit to any government that had defaulted on its debts to our government. Since token payments were considered a default, they too came to an end. Only Finland, whose debt was small, continued to pay. The war-debt muddle strengthened American isolationism.

"Stay out this time."

During the 1930's a good many Americans thought that the United States had made a mistake in entering World War I—that we had been tricked by bankers, munitions makers, and Allied propagandists into a war which was not our business. This notion was so strong that in 1934 the Senate appointed an investigating committee, headed by an arch-isolationist—Senator Nye of North Dakota. The committee's inquiry was not impartial. It popularized the idea that economic ties between the United States and the Allies had been one of the chief causes of our entry into the war.

A crop of magazine articles, books, and radio broadcasts denounced both the "merchants of death" who sold munitions, and the international bankers. Also many novels and motion pictures showed the horrors of war and suggested that all wars are evil. A number of pacifist organizations were formed; thousands of college students and other young people signed pledges not to go to war. Reflecting the popular desire for peace, Congress passed a series of neutrality acts intended to make sure we would stay out of another war.

Congress tries to legislate neutrality.

In 1933 both Hoover and Roosevelt had proposed a law giving the President the right to forbid the shipment of munitions whenever such shipments might encourage aggression. The proposal was based on the idea that our government ought to discriminate between an aggressor nation and its victim. Congress, however, was unwilling to give the President the power to discriminate. The Neutrality Act of 1935 forbade the sale or transport of munitions to *any* country at war. This law, said the columnist Walter Lippmann, was equivalent to announcing:

I see two thugs about to start an assault on my honest neighbor next door. As he may expect me to hand him a stick to help beat them off, I am signaling the thugs to go ahead and I'll keep clear. I am neutral.

Our arms embargoes help the Axis.

Late in 1935 Italy attacked Ethiopia. The President quickly enforced the Neutrality Act by forbidding the shipment of munitions to either country. He had no power to keep Americans from filling Italian orders for other materials important in war, such as cotton, copper, scrap iron, rubber, and oil. Roosevelt promised, however, that if the League of Nations chose to blockade Italy, the United States would not interfere. The League Council then considered asking Great Britain and France to use their fleets for a blockade. These nations, partly because they knew they could get no munitions from the United States if Italy attacked them, voted against the blockade. Italy then had no trouble conquering the unarmed people of Ethiopia. After this no weak country could expect protection from the League.

In the summer of 1936 civil war began in Spain. The rebels, led by General Franco, planned to set up a Fascist dictatorship to replace the republic. From the very first the rebels received powerful aid from Italy and Germany. Later the "Loyalists," those fighting the rebels, received aid from Russia. The Kremlin, though not able to give much material help, sent agents to Spain with the hope that the Communist minority would take over the government. Hoping to prevent a general war, France, Great Britain, and the United States agreed not to send arms to either side. To carry out this agreement, Congress then imposed an arms embargo on Spain. Since Franco continued to get all the arms he needed from Germany and Italy, the embargo assured his victory.

Congress strengthens the neutrality law.

The neutrality law was to expire in May, 1937. The administration fought in vain for a flexible bill which would allow it to shut off aid to aggressors without denying it to their victims. Instead, Congress, intent on isolating us from Europe, made the law even more rigid. The Neutrality Act of 1937 forbade the export of arms to belligerents whenever the President proclaimed the existence of a state of war (either civil or international). The act prohibited loans to either side. It barred travel by American citizens on the ships of countries at war. The President was given power to require that raw materials needed for war, such as oil, copper, and scrap iron, be sold on a "cash and carry" basis. Belligerents could then obtain these raw materials only if they paid cash and took them away on non-American ships.

This new law swept away the old principle of freedom of the seas for neutral trade. Thus it gave up the very rights for which we had fought in 1917. More important, it stopped the most powerful nation in the world, the United States, from contributing to collective security. As President Roosevelt said later, "Our arms embargo played right into the hands of aggressive nations." They were encouraged to attack their neighbors by the knowledge that their victims could not buy American arms after a declaration of war.

Japan Conducts an Undeclared War in China

Japan seeks markets in Asia.

After Japan resigned from the League, her military leaders went ahead with their plans for expansion in Asia. They led a propaganda drive throughout the Orient with the slogan "Asia for the Asians." The Japanese wanted to control the markets of China and Southeast Asia. Since trade barriers in Europe, the Americas, and the British Empire shut out most Japanese exports, especially after 1930, Asian markets had become all the more important to Japan. The Japanese also looked with longing eyes on the oil fields, rubber plantations, and other riches of Southeast Asia. If Japan controlled these lands, it would no longer need to depend on the United States, the British Empire, and the Dutch East Indies for vital supplies.

Japan advances in China.

Japan wanted to close the Open Door so as to have all of China's trade. For several years after taking Manchuria, Japanese army officers worked to get control of the five northern provinces of China proper. They tried to set up a puppet government which would allow Japan full control of the natural resources and markets of this rich area. They also wanted to stop the Chinese from making border raids into Manchuria and from stirring up disturbances there.

There was a strong Communist movement in China. In 1931 the Communists had proclaimed a People's Republic, but Chiang Kai-shek, head of the Nationalist government, succeeded in driving the Communists into the western provinces far from the coast. Japan feared the Communists, believing that they were dominated by its old enemy, Russia. Late in 1936 Japan allied itself with Germany in the Anti-Comintern Pact. About the same time Japan presented seven demands to China under threat of immediate invasion. The principal demands were: (1) joint action by Japanese and Chinese Nationalist troops to crush the Communists, (2) employment of Japanese advisors in all branches of government, (3) autonomy for the five northern provinces, and (4) reduction of the tariff.

The ultimatum had an unforeseen result. To agree to its terms would destroy China's independence. Chiang, instead of accepting Japanese help in driving out the Communists, joined with the Communists to resist Japan.

In July, 1937, Japan launched a full-scale attack on China. Before the year ended Japanese armies were fighting over a good part of northern and central China. They soon held the coastal region, containing most of China's railroads, industries, and large cities. As the Japanese advanced, they bombed and looted hundreds of mis-

GENERAL CHIANG KAI-SHEK *in 1936*

JAPANESE ADVANCES

sion schools, churches, and hospitals built and supported by American religious groups. The Japanese mistreated Americans and Europeans and shut out all but Japanese commerce from occupied areas. Even more disturbing to Americans was the great loss of life caused by the Japanese bombing of Chinese cities.

The crisis in the Far East put our neutrality law to a hard test. To enforce it would help Japan at the expense of China. Japan was far better equipped for war and could produce its own guns, warships, and airplanes, while China must buy them abroad. Besides, China needed American loans in order to buy arms. Roosevelt took advantage of the fact that no declaration of war had been made. He announced that the neutrality law would not be applied and that American merchant ships could take war supplies to China and to Japan at their own risk. This course seemed to meet with approval.

Roosevelt calls for a "quarantine."

While the President hated communism as much as fascism, he believed that the three Fascist powers had actually set out to conquer the world under the guise of fighting communism. At that time Russia was weak and divided; it was going through a series of "purges," and hundreds of its top military men had been executed. Therefore Roosevelt did not accept Japan's excuse that it was fighting communism in China and that Russia was the real enemy.

In Chicago, on October 5, 1937, Roosevelt made his famous "quarantine" speech, calling attention to Japanese, German, and Italian aggression. An era of lawlessness had set in, he said, which threatened the entire free world. The United States could not escape this menace. If it dallied, the Western Hemisphere would eventually be attacked. The United States should join with peace-loving nations to "quarantine" aggressors. The President did not say how the quarantine should be applied. This effort to awaken public opinion got very little support. The idea of collective security was no more popular in 1937 than it had been during Woodrow Wilson's time.

714

The height of isolationism.

American isolationism reached its peak in 1937 when Congress almost voted to submit the Ludlow Amendment to the states. If ratified, the amendment would have prevented Congress from declaring war, except in case of actual invasion of the United States, without first getting the approval of the voters in a national referendum. This extraordinary proposal had strong popular support. It was defeated in Congress only after a hard fight by administration forces.

The *Panay* incident was another sign of the wish for peace at almost any price. In December, 1937, some young Japanese officers deliberately shelled and sank the American gunboat *Panay* on the Yangtze River in China, along with three American merchant vessels. A number of Americans were killed outright. Several survivors were machine-gunned. When the Japanese government apologized and offered to pay damages, the American public thought no more about it. A Gallup poll in January, 1938, showed that 70 per cent of those questioned thought we should withdraw from the Orient.

Roosevelt calls for rearmament.

The London Naval Treaty (see p. 680) expired in 1936. Yet to save money, we had not built up our navy even to the strength allowed in the London Treaty. Besides, many of our ships were out of date. Roosevelt had been trying since he took office to get funds to strengthen the navy. If we should have to fight a war in distant waters, we were totally unprepared. In a special message to Congress in January, 1938, Roosevelt said that other powers were rearming at an alarming rate. He asked for big increases in our national defense. Congress saw no need for haste. After four months' delay, it authorized a billion dollars' worth of new ships, to be built over a ten-year period.

At the same time Congress turned down the President's request for a small appropriation to fortify the Pacific island of Guam. Naval experts said a fleet base there would deter an attack on the Philippines, but Congress was more eager to abandon the islands than to defend them. They were scheduled to have full independence in 1946 anyway. Many Americans felt that if we set the islands free at once, we would not have to go to their defense. The refusal of Congress to fortify Guam reflected the popular desire for isolation.

Totalitarian States Overrun Europe

Hitler seizes Austria and Czechoslovakia.

By 1938 Hitler was ready to carry out his plans for the domination of Europe. Events in China, Ethiopia, and Spain convinced him that the peace-loving nations would do nothing effective to interfere. Moreover, the United States seemed to be done with Europe forever. What then could stop the advance of the German "master race"?

Hitler had often said he had no desire to annex Austria and would not meddle in its affairs. In 1936 he even signed a treaty promising to respect Austria's sovereignty. Yet the ink was hardly dry before his agents were at work in Austria organizing a Nazi party and seeking to overthrow the government. On March 11, 1938, German troops occupied the country. Two days later Hitler announced the union of Austria and Germany.

Hitler next began a war of nerves against Czechoslovakia. He falsely charged the Czechs with mistreating the 3,500,000 Germans who lived in the Sudetenland. This narrow strip of mountainous land formed a rim around Czechoslovakia's western border. If Hitler seized the Sudetenland, the little country would be defenseless.

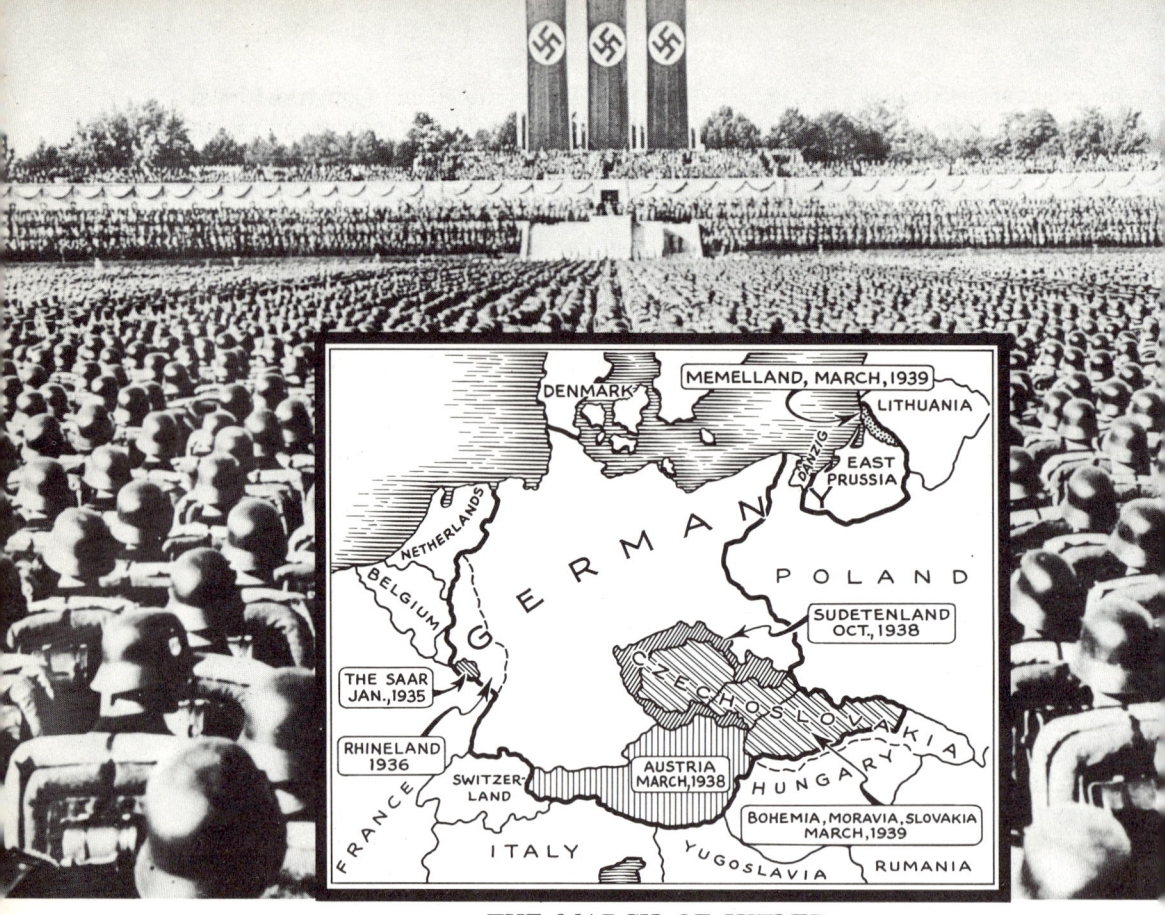

THE MARCH OF HITLER

Rather than yield the Sudetenland to Germany, the Czechs wanted to fight. Russia and Rumania offered help, but whether they could send much aid was doubtful. Russia's army was thought to be demoralized. Czechoslovakia's ally, France, was weak and divided. Great Britain, which had signed a treaty to aid the Czechs if France aided them, was by no means prepared for war. The British and French prime ministers therefore went to Munich (September, 1938) to beg Hitler not to touch Czechoslovakia. When he insisted on having the Sudetenland, they yielded rather than go to war. Hitler told them he wanted no further territory.

Like the United States, Great Britain had a large number of isolationists. They thought their nation could have peace if only their government would mind its own business. Ever since Hitler and Mussolini began their aggressions, British isolationists had favored "appeasement," which meant giving in to the dictators rather than risking war. After Munich the British saw that appeasement was a threat to their own safety. They quickly adopted conscription and set to work to strengthen their defenses.

Later events showed that Hitler never intended to keep the promises he made at Munich. In March, 1939, he took the rest of Czechoslovakia. Thereby he gained forty Czech army divisions and a large number of munitions plants. Britain and France were left without a single strong European ally.

716

Hitler and Stalin make a bargain.

The same month that Czechoslovakia fell, Hitler seized Memel from Lithuania. Shortly after that, he began to thunder at Poland for the return of Danzig and the Polish Corridor. Faced with the prospect of unlimited German expansion, Great Britain and France promised to help Poland in case it was attacked. In April Mussolini seized Albania. This event led Britain and France to guarantee the independence of Greece and Rumania. The British then tried to make a mutual aid pact with Soviet Russia, but the attempt was too late.

For years Hitler had been shouting his hatred of the Communists and the Soviet Union. Moscow in turn feared a German attack and, since Hitler's rise to power, had been seeking for allies. France entered an alliance with Russia in 1935, but at that time England was unwilling to join them. Conservative leaders in England feared communism more than fascism. After Hitler occupied Czechoslovakia, London awoke to the Fascist threat and began to talk with Moscow about a possible alliance. The talks got nowhere because, as we now know, Stalin had already decided to work with the Nazis. On August 23, 1939, the world listened in surprise to the news that Russia and Germany had signed a nonaggression pact. Stalin and Hitler had also come to a secret understanding by which Poland was to be divided between them, and Russia was to have control of Finland and the Baltic states.

World War II begins.

On September 1, 1939, Hitler suddenly ended his talks with Poland and hurled his forces across the Polish frontier. While German panzers (armored divisions) moved swiftly across the land, German aircraft bombed the cities and the throngs of fleeing refugees. Meanwhile, Russian forces invaded from the east. Although the Poles fought hard, the German _blitzkrieg_ (lightning war) soon compelled them to surrender. By the end of September the Germans had possession of the western half of Poland and the Russians the eastern half.

Britain and France declared war on Germany two days after Poland was invaded. Most of the British dominions also declared war. Yet neither the British nor the French could do much to aid the Poles. Their land forces were insufficient to attack Germany and their air forces were pitifully small. All they could do was blockade Germany by sea.

Congress revises the neutrality law.

When the Nazis invaded Poland, Roosevelt at once issued a proclamation of neutrality. As the Neutrality Act of 1937 required him to do, he shut off the export of arms to the belligerents. This did not hurt Germany, which was heavily armed, but it placed the democracies at Hitler's mercy. The President called Congress into special session on September 21, 1939, and urged repeal of the arms embargo.

For the next six weeks a stormy debate raged in Congress, in the newspapers, and over the radio. Isolationists argued that repeal of the arms embargo would surely cause the United States to be drawn into the war. Those favoring repeal argued that as long as the arms embargo was in force America was really helping Hitler. According to a Gallup poll, 56 per cent of the American people favored repeal. Early in November, Congress passed the Neutrality Act of 1939. It lifted the arms embargo and placed all trade with belligerents on a cash-and-carry basis. As long as belligerents had ready cash, they could buy in the United States anything they wanted. Loans to belligerents were forbidden. The new law also gave the President power to bar American ships and passengers from danger zones.

Russia attacks Finland.

Until World War I, Finland and the Baltic states—Estonia, Latvia, and Lithuania—had been part of Imperial Russia. In the peace settlement after the war they were given their independence. Now Stalin wanted them under his control. After occupying eastern Poland, he demanded bases in Estonia, Latvia, Lithuania, and Finland. The three Baltic states gave in, believing it useless to resist. Finland, which had better natural defenses, rejected the Russian demands. Russia invaded Finland on November 30, 1939. The heroic struggle of the Finns won world-wide admiration, but in March they had to surrender.

Hitler conquers western Europe.

For seven months after the conquest of Poland, there was little fighting on the western front. The French army was entrenched behind the heavily fortified Maginot Line, while the Germans sat behind their Siegfried Line. Newspapermen dubbed the war a "sitzkrieg." By April 9, 1940, Hitler was ready for a second round. Without warning, his troops poured into Denmark and took control of the country in a single day. On the same day the Germans attacked Norway. By occupying Denmark and Norway the Germans got valuable bases and made Sweden their prisoner.

On May 10, 1940, German panzers and paratroopers invaded the Netherlands, Belgium, and Luxemburg. These little countries soon had to give up. In Belgium the Nazis met British and French forces. To the horror of the free world, Hitler's armored columns won the battle. Some 330,000 Allied soldiers were trapped on the French side of the English Channel. In a heroic operation known as the "miracle of Dunkirk," British skippers rescued nearly all these men.

After mopping up the Low Countries, the swift-moving German columns

German armored divisions moving into PO-LAND *in September, 1939. This overt act was a direct challenge to the Anglo-French defense agreement with Poland, and prompted the Allied declaration of war.*

outflanked the Maginot Line and swept across northern France. On June 22, 1940, the French signed an armistice. Germany kept more than a million French prisoners of war and held two thirds of the country, including Paris. The remainder was turned over to a puppet government seated at Vichy. By leaving part of France under French rule, Hitler hoped to keep the French fleet and colonies from breaking away.

Italy jumps in.

Shortly before the French sued for peace, Italy entered the war, attacking

The first Allied encounter with the Germans ended in defeat and a near tragedy ON THE BEACHES OF DUNKIRK. *This painting by R. E. Eurich shows the helplessness of the soldiers while waiting for rescue. That so many men were saved is a tribute to the many English seamen who rushed to the aid of their countrymen with fishing boats, launches, and merchant ships.*

France from the southeast and detaching a small piece of territory. Mussolini next invaded Greece, using Albania, which he had conquered in 1939, as a base. Much to his chagrin, the Greeks soon drove his forces back to Albania. Meanwhile an Italian force sallied out of Libya to attack the British in Egypt. In the spring of 1941 Hitler sent Rommel's desert corps to Africa to help the Italians.

The British fight on.

After the fall of France, the British expected immediate invasion. Hitler's army stood on the shores of the English Channel less than twenty miles away. England had no land defenses worth mentioning. Her army was far smaller than the German army and had left all its equipment in France. Fortunately, England had found a great leader in Prime Minister Winston Churchill. Saying that he could offer nothing but "blood, toil, tears and sweat," he inspired his people to resist to the uttermost.

Let us therefore brace ourselves to our duties, and so bear ourselves that, if the British Empire and its Commonwealth last for a thousand years, men will still say, "This was their finest hour."

719

In the summer and fall of 1940 clouds of German bombers hammered at English factories and cities night after night. Although the Royal Air Force was outnumbered, it finally beat off the German *Luftwaffe.* By November the air offensive slowed down. Hitler decided to postpone the invasion of England, believing that submarine warfare would force the British to give up. Meanwhile, he got ready to drive toward the East. This meant tearing up his peace pact with the Soviet Union.

America Puts Its House in Order

The United States rearms.

For three years Roosevelt had been trying to awaken the United States to the Axis menace. Reports received by the State Department convinced him that Germany, Italy, and Japan had plans to control the entire world. However, when F.D.R. said that the United States was in danger, few Americans took him seriously. Not until the fall of France (June, 1940) did the average American think that our country had anything to fear.

In May, 1940, when the Nazis invaded France, President Roosevelt reminded our nation that a new era of air power had begun. We could no longer rely on the breadth of the Atlantic and Pacific oceans to protect North and South America. If the Nazis got control of French West Africa, only 1600 miles from the bulge of Brazil, they could easily launch an attack against Latin America. If the Japanese overran Alaska, they would be only four hours' flying time from Seattle and Portland.

By fall Congress had appropriated eighteen billion dollars for defense. The plans called for a two-ocean navy, a large army, and an air force second to none.

In September, Congress passed the Selective Training and Service Act, making all male citizens between the ages of 21 and 30 liable for a year's military training. This was the first peacetime draft act in the history of our country.

The American republics take action.

The outbreak of war in Europe opened a new chapter in inter-American relations. In September, 1939, the twenty-one republics sent their foreign ministers to a meeting in Panama. The ministers drew up a Declaration of Neutrality and formed an Inter-American Financial and Advisory Committee to sit in Washington for the duration of the war. This committee took steps to prevent economic breakdown in Latin America resulting from the loss of the European market.

The fall of Denmark, the Netherlands, and France in the spring of 1940 brought a new meeting of the foreign ministers at Havana, Cuba. The ministers had to decide how to prevent Hitler from getting control of the Danish colony of Greenland and of Dutch and French possessions in the Caribbean. The conference adopted the "Declaration of Havana," stating that colonies in the Western Hemisphere could not be transferred from one non-American nation to another. If any colonies should be handed over to the Axis the American republics would take them away.

Another urgent problem was what to do about Axis spies and fifth columnists. Just before the Havana meeting a plot to set up a Fascist government in Uruguay was uncovered. Hoping to prevent similar plots in other republics, the ministers arranged to exchange information about illegal activities of Axis agents. This exchange led most of the countries to take strong steps to stop such activities. But in several of the countries, the Axis still had influence.

The delegates took another step which showed that the Monroe Doctrine had become a policy of all the American republics, not of the United States alone. They declared that a threat by a non-American state against any one of the American republics should be regarded as an act of aggression against all of them. Thus the United States and the other American republics became military allies.

After this meeting, the Latin American republics strengthened their defenses. They bought war equipment with the aid of loans from the United States. Our army and navy officers helped train their fighting men. Many of their top officers came here to study our methods of defense and to consult with our military leaders. Brazil and Panama gave the United States air bases on their soil. In many ways most of our southern neighbors co-operated with us to meet the Axis menace.

Canada and the United States become allies.

In 1938 President Roosevelt had assured the Canadians of American help "if domination of Canadian soil is threatened by any other empire." This promise became extremely important to Canada after France fell and Hitler made ready to invade England in the summer of 1940. At that time Canada and the United States set up a Permanent Joint Board of Defense. Thereafter the two nations worked closely together for the defense of North America.

Destroyers exchanged for bases.

From the beginning of the war German submarines took a heavy toll. In July, 1940, some 400,000 tons of Allied shipping went to the bottom. If losses continued at this rate Great Britain could not hold out. To combat the U-boats, the British navy was in desperate need of escort vessels.

It happened that the United States had over a hundred old destroyers tied up in port. Built in World War I, they had been out of commission for years. We did not need them so long as the British navy controlled the Atlantic. Early in September, 1940, the President announced the transfer of fifty of these destroyers to Britain. In return we received ninety-nine year leases for eight bases on Newfoundland, Bermuda, and British islands in the Caribbean. We needed these bases for the defense of the Western Hemisphere. The arrangement was never submitted to Congress, but polls showed that the majority of Americans approved it.

By this time many people in the United States realized that the Western Hemisphere was safe only so long as the British fleet guarded the Atlantic. The United States had but a one-ocean navy and that was needed in the Pacific to safeguard our western coast and our Pacific outposts. American naval leaders were greatly relieved therefore when Churchill announced that if his country fell, the British navy would not surrender but would continue the fight from bases in the Western Hemisphere.

Interventionists vs. isolationists.

From the time that France collapsed until Japan attacked us, seventeen months went by. During that time Americans took part in the so-called "Great Debate" on foreign policy. One group, the "isolationists" or "noninterventionists," was against any action that might lead to American participation in the war. They had opposed membership in the League of Nations and now opposed Roosevelt's policy of aid to the Allies. They charged that such aid would drag the United States into a war that was not our concern.

Many organizations expressed the noninterventionist point of view. The most prominent was the America First

WENDELL WILLKIE *speaks before the Senate Foreign Relations Committee in support of the lend-lease bill in 1941.*

Committee. Some of its well-known members argued publicly that we could "do business with Hitler" if he conquered England and that it made no difference to us whether Germany or England won the war.

Opposed to the isolationists were a group whom their critics called "interventionists." The principal organization that spoke for them was the Committee to Defend America by Aiding the Allies (CDAAA). Its leaders included such prominent men as Stimson, Willkie, and Pershing. They believed that England was fighting for democracy. They also insisted that our best chance of staying out of the war was to help England. If England were defeated, they said, we would surely have to fight and would then face impossible odds. As early as September, 1940, a public opinion poll showed that a slight majority of Americans accepted this view, for they favored aid to England even at the risk of war.

The 1940 presidential election came in the midst of the debate. At the Republican convention in June the leading contenders for the nomination were all sincere isolationists. To the astonishment of professional politicians, the nomination went to Wendell Willkie. This was a victory for the interventionists, since Willkie's views on foreign policy were similar to Roosevelt's. By supporting Roosevelt's policy of all possible aid to England, Mr. Willkie helped to unify the nation.

The United States Abandons Neutrality

Congress passes the Lend-Lease Act.

In November, 1940, Roosevelt was re-elected for a third term. Sure of popular support, he pushed ahead vigorously with his program for strengthening national defense and aiding Great Britain. Late in December he said, "The United States is determined that the Axis powers are not going to win this war." Only an Allied victory would ensure the kind of world in which nations could live in security. "We must be the great arsenal of democracy," said the President, "to keep war away from our country and our people."

England's cash reserves were almost used up. She would soon be unable to pay cash for her heavy purchases in this country. If we lent her billions of dollars she could never repay us in money. The President suggested that we lend goods instead of dollars and expect repayment to be made in goods. Accordingly, a "lend-lease" bill was placed before Congress early in January, 1941. The bill would give the President power to lend defense materials and war equipment to foreign nations "whose defense the President deems vital to the defense of the United States."

The lend-lease bill was hotly debated up and down the land. The America First Committee claimed that the bill made Roosevelt a dictator and that it put us into the war against Germany. Willkie threw himself into the fight for the bill and it became law on March 11, 1941.

Passage of the Lend-Lease Act made us a nonshooting ally of Great Britain and the other nations fighting the Axis. By this time three out of four Americans were willing to enter the war "if it appeared certain there was no other way to defeat Germany and Italy." The question now was whether we should have to begin shooting.

We move closer to war with Hitler.

Since it would have been foolish to export war material that would only go to the bottom of the Atlantic, the President took steps to protect lend-lease cargoes. In April, 1941, our air force was ordered to patrol the North Atlantic as far as Iceland in order to warn British ships of the presence of enemy submarines. Soon after this the United States took Greenland and Iceland under its protection to prevent their use as Nazi bases.

Late in May a German submarine sank an American freighter, the _Robin Moor,_ in the South Atlantic. When news of this reached the United States, the President proclaimed an "unlimited national emergency." He froze all German and Italian assets in this country. Next he closed all German and Italian consulates, because they were carrying on illegal activities directed against our government. We were fast drifting into an open break with the Axis.

The "four freedoms."

Like Woodrow Wilson, F.D.R. believed "ideas are weapons." He wanted to make clear to the people of the United States and of the free world that democracy was worth defending. In his annual message to Congress in January, 1941, he said that a moral world order must be based on "four freedoms": freedom of speech and expression, freedom of religion, freedom from want, and freedom from fear. In later speeches he again called for a world consecrated to the four freedoms.

The Atlantic Charter.

In August, 1941, President Roosevelt and Prime Minister Churchill met secretly at sea. The two statesmen drew up a statement of "certain common principles" or aims. The Atlantic Charter, as the declaration came to be known, had eight points:

1. The United States and Britain seek no additional territory.
2. Territorial changes should only be made according to the wish of the population concerned.
3. All peoples should be allowed to choose their own form of government.
4. All nations should have access to the trade and raw materials of the world.
5. The United States and Britain will encourage international co-operation to improve labor standards and social security.
6. The peace should give all peoples freedom from want and freedom from fear.
7. The seas should be free to all in time of peace.
8. Aggressor nations should be forced to disarm, until a permanent system of international security can be established.

Like Wilson's Fourteen Points, the Atlantic Charter stirred the imagination of free people everywhere. It gave new hope to the conquered nations of Europe. It seemed to pledge the United States to the defeat of Hitler and Mussolini and the establishment of a just peace.

Hitler invades Russia.

Meanwhile, the Nazis were rapidly completing the conquest of all Europe. In the fall and winter of 1940–41, Hitler forced Hungary, Rumania, and

Bulgaria to join his "New Order." In April, when Yugoslavia and Greece refused to join, they were invaded and crushed. Hitler then drove the English from the island of Crete. Military experts guessed that he would next launch a drive to get control of the Suez Canal, the Red Sea, and the Near East. Instead, Hitler suddenly hurled his armies against Russia (June 22, 1941).

Only three powers stood between Hitler and the domination of the entire world—the United States, the British Empire, and the Soviet Union. Hitler wanted to smash Russia for three reasons: (1) to make sure her military power would not be turned against Germany, (2) to gain control of Russian raw materials, industrial strength, and man power for use in further conquests, and (3) to open a gateway to India.

The war in Russia raged along a front of 2000 miles. By the middle of November, 1941, the Germans had advanced over 500 miles and had conquered 500,000 square miles of Russian territory, or almost three times the area of Germany. Then the Russians stopped the German drive and slowly pushed the Germans back.

By posing as the leader of a crusade against communism, Hitler may have hoped to divide the people of the free world. If so, he was disappointed. Churchill said that whoever marched with Hitler was a foe, whoever fought him was an ally. Hard pressed as the British were, they sent war materials to Russia. The United States also sent aid. Without this help it is doubtful that the Russians could have held out against the Nazis.

More American ships are sunk.

During the summer of 1941 German and Italian submarines sank several freighters flying our flag or the flag of a Latin American nation. In September Roosevelt made a world-wide radio address announcing that our patrols would attack any Axis warship found within the waters considered vital to our defense. These waters included a broad area around the continents of North and South America. Roosevelt's speech meant that an undeclared naval war had begun. Within a few weeks one of our destroyers patrolling in the North Atlantic was damaged and another sunk by U-boats.

In November Congress passed an act permitting the arming of merchant ships as a defense against submarines. Congress also repealed parts of the Neutrality Act so that our ships could carry lend-lease cargoes to countries fighting the Axis. This was necessary because England was losing the Battle of the Atlantic and no longer had ships enough to carry lend-lease supplies. We appeared to be on the verge of war with Germany and Italy. To the surprise of most Americans, when war came, however, it was precipitated by the action of the Japanese.

Japan Attacks the United States

We use pressure on Japan.

After the shelling of the *Panay* in 1937 (see p. 715), Americans generally showed little interest in the Far East. If they thought about foreign affairs at all, it was Europe that troubled them. Nevertheless, the administration was greatly concerned about Japan. Not only was that nation still fighting in China, but it was building a larger navy.

During 1938 the State Department sent frequent notes to Japan, protesting its interference with American rights in China and condemning the bombing of Chinese civilians. Secretary of State Hull asked manufacturers not to sell airplanes and airplane parts to any nation which used planes to attack civilian populations. The following year he made a similar request of the manufacturers of high-octane gasoline. He also asked bankers not to extend credit to Japan. These requests might be described as a "moral" embargo, since they did not have the force of law. Finally, growing tired of writing notes of protest, Washington notified Tokyo (July, 1939), that the commercial treaty of 1911 would be terminated in six months. The United States would then be free to cut off exports to Japan.

The war in Europe seemed like a golden opportunity to Japan. South of China lay rich lands which were weakly defended—French Indo-China, British Malaya, Burma, and the Netherlands Indies. In June, 1940, Japan took advantage of the fall of France to move into French Indo-China. When Roosevelt asked for power to stop the shipment of war materials to aggressors, Congress passed the Export Control Act (July, 1940). The President then banned the shipment of aviation gasoline, machine tools, scrap iron, and steel to Japan.

Japan joins the Axis.

In September, 1940, Japan made an alliance with Germany and Italy. The three powers promised to come to one another's aid if any one of them should be attacked by any country then a neutral. This was clearly meant as a warning to the United States. Hitler hoped it would keep the United States from entering the war until Britain was defeated. In return for joining the Axis, Germany and Italy agreed that Japan should have a free hand in Southeast Asia and the South Pacific. Hundreds of German experts were promptly sent to Japan to assist in military preparations.

At the beginning of 1941 our intelligence had informed the President that Japanese militarists were preparing for all-out war. Roosevelt sent reinforcements to Hawaii and the Philip-pines and warned the 17,000 American citizens in the Far East to come home. He arranged additional loans to China. He kept adding to the list of war materials which it was unlawful to ship to Japan. Meanwhile, the military clique in Japan was growing bolder.

When Hitler invaded Russia on June 22, 1941, Japan no longer feared Russian interference. In July, Japan completed its occupation of French Indo-China and prepared to seize the Netherlands Indies. Our government froze Japanese assets in the United States, putting a stop to all trade between the two countries. Great Britain and the members of the British Commonwealth took the same step. We refused to resume trade unless Japan would give up its conquests.

Peace talks fail.

Meanwhile, Japan was apparently trying to reach an agreement with the United States. Between March and December, 1941, the Japanese ambassador in Washington, Admiral Nomura, had no less than sixty talks with Secretary Hull. Nomura wished for peace as much as did Hull. Unfortunately, his government went ahead on its program of expansion.

We know now that in April, 1941, Hitler and the Japanese foreign minister discussed plans for attacking the United States on both oceans. In August the Japanese fleet rehearsed its attack on Pearl Harbor. In October the warlike General Tojo became prime minister, and Tokyo decided that if peace talks with Washington did not succeed by November 29, the attack would take place on December 7. In mid-November, claiming that it was a last effort to maintain peace, Japan sent a veteran diplomat, Saburo Kurusu, to help Nomura. Kurusu brought Japan's offer to withdraw from Indo-China and to stop its advance in Southeast Asia if the United States would agree to

Japanese control of China. On November 26 our government gave its reply: Japan must withdraw all troops from Indo-China and also from China. In return the United States promised a liberal trade agreement with Japan.

The Japanese answer was given on December 7, 1941. It took the form of a sneak attack on the American naval bases at Pearl Harbor and Manila. On the following day Congress declared war on Japan. Germany and Italy then declared war on the United States.

WINSTON CHURCHILL

FOR IDENTIFICATION

Atlantic Charter	Cordell Hull
Chiang Kai-shek	lend-lease
Winston Churchill	Benito Mussolini
Debt Default Act	Neutrality Acts (1935,
Declaration of	1937, 1939)
Havana	Pearl Harbor
Dunkirk	Rhineland
Ethiopia	Sudetenland
Adolf Hitler	Vichy France

FOR EXPLANATION OR DEFINITION

appeasement	"have-not" nations
arms embargo	Ludlow Amendment
arsenal of democracy	Maginot Line
Axis powers	Nazi
blitzkrieg	*Panay* incident
Comintern	Rome-Berlin axis
fascism	Siegfried Line
four freedoms	totalitarian

FOR REVIEW

1. How did Secretary of State Cordell Hull endeavor to promote international good will?

2. What specific actions of the Roosevelt administration carried out the policy of the good neighbor?

3. What important interpretation of the Monroe Doctrine did Roosevelt announce at the Inter-American Conference at Buenos Aires in 1936?

4. Why did the United States refrain from recognizing Bolshevik Russia, 1917–1933?

5. What were the terms of the Litvinoff agreement under which the United States recognized Soviet Russia? To what extent has this agreement been honored?

6. (a) What was the purpose of the World Economic Conference of 1933? Why did it fail? (b) Why did the World Disarmament Conference of 1933 end in failure?

7. (a) What conditions in Italy prepared the way for Mussolini's rise to power in 1922? (b) What conditions in Germany prepared the way for Hitler's rise to power in Germany in 1933? (c) Why did militarists rise to power in Japan? (d) In what respects were developments in Italy, Germany, and Japan similar in the period from 1922 to 1935? In what respects were they dissimilar?

8. (a) Under what circumstances did Italy withdraw from the League of Nations? (b) What were the terms of the Anti-Comintern Pact between Germany and Japan?

9. Why did many Americans feel that their participation in World War I had been a mistake? (b) What incidents tended to mold public opinion in the direction of isolationism?

10. (a) What were the terms of the Neutrality Act of 1935? (b) How did this act influence the war between Italy and Ethiopia? How did it influence the attitude of Great Britain and France toward this conflict? (c) How did the Neutrality Act of 1935 influence the outcome of the Spanish Civil War of 1936?

11. What were the terms of the Neutrality Act of 1937? How did this law "play right into the hands of aggressive nations"?

12. (a) What were the economic reasons for the "expansionist fever" in Japan? (b) What steps did Japan take to secure control of northern China? (c) What demands did Japan make upon China in 1936? Why did China refuse to accept these demands?

13. (a) What success did Japan have in its attack upon China in 1937? (b) How did the war test our neutrality laws? (c) On what grounds did Roosevelt avoid the full application of our neutrality laws?

14. What ideas did Roosevelt champion in his "quarantine speech"? Why did they receive little popular support?

15. (a) What were the terms of the proposed Ludlow Amendment? (b) What was the *Panay* incident?

16. (a) What steps toward rearmament did the United States take in early 1938? (b) What rearmament proposals did Congress refuse to accept?

17. (a) How did Hitler take over Austria? What demands did Hitler make upon Czechoslovakia? (b) What were the reasons for the Munich Conference? (c) Why did Great Britain and France adopt a policy of appeasement toward Hitler?

18. (a) What aggressive actions were taken by Hitler and Mussolini shortly after the Munich Conference? (b) Why did England and France seek an alliance or understanding with Russia? Why did the Anglo-French negotiations with Russia fail? (c) What were the terms of the Stalin-Hitler nonaggression pact?

19. (a) How and when did World War II begin? (b) Why did England and France declare war on Germany?

20. How did the United States modify the Neutrality Act in 1939?

21. (a) What demands did Russia make upon the Baltic states? (b) What were the reasons for and the results of the Russo-Finnish war of 1939–1940?

22. (a) Describe Hitler's attack upon Norway, Denmark, the Netherlands, Belgium, and France. (b) What were the terms of the armistice with France, June, 1940? (c) When Italy entered the war in 1940 in what directions did she strike? (d) Describe the air warfare between Germany and England, 1940–41.

23. (a) How did the United States Congress respond to Roosevelt's plea for rearmament in 1940? (b) What were the provisions of the 1940 draft act?

24. What were the reasons for the Havana Conference? What were the terms of the Declaration of Havana?

25. What were the terms of the destroyer-naval base agreement of September, 1940?

26. (a) What were the arguments of the isolationists and the interventionists in 1940 and 1941? (b) What effect did the presidential campaign of 1940 have on the debate between the interventionists and the isolationists? (c) How did Roosevelt's victory in 1940 affect his policies?

27. (a) Explain the terms of the Lend-Lease Act of 1941. (b) What steps "short of war" did the United States take in 1941 to protect lend-lease cargoes?

28. (a) What purpose did Roosevelt have in announcing the "four freedoms"? Name them. (b) What were the terms of the Atlantic Charter? What was its purpose?

29. (a) Why did Hitler attack Russia in June, 1941? (b) Describe the German invasion of Russia.

30. (a) How did Roosevelt's policy lead to an undeclared naval war with Germany? (b) What actions of Congress brought us closer to war with Germany and Italy?

31. What were the provisions of the Export Control Act of 1940?

32. (a) Why did Japan, Germany, and Italy form an alliance in 1940? (b) What territorial gains had Japan made by the fall of 1941?

33. (a) What proposals did Japan make to the United States in November, 1941? What reply did the United States make to Japan? (b) Describe the Japanese attack upon Pearl Harbor.

FOR FURTHER STUDY AND DISCUSSION

1. Outline the reasons why efforts to find the road to peace and security after World War I ended in failure. Helpful sources: Dulles, *America's Rise to World Power;* Churchill, *The Gathering Storm.*

2. (a) Explain Hitler's rise to power. (b) Outline the actions taken by Hitler between 1933 and 1939 which led to World War II.

3. Explain Churchill's comment concerning the Munich Conference: "Britain and France had to choose between war and dishonor. They chose dishonor. They will have war." Helpful source: Bailey, *Diplomatic History*, pp. 747–749; Churchill, *The Gathering Storm*.

4. Compare the efforts of the United States to remain neutral in the periods 1807–1809, 1914–1917, and 1935–1939. Helpful sources: Bailey, *Diplomatic History*, pp. 754–764; Kennan, *American Diplomacy, 1900–1950*.

5. (a) Why has the Neutrality Act of 1937 been referred to as the high-water mark of American isolationism? (b) What developments within the United States help to explain the popular interest in the proposed Ludlow Amendment?

6. What seems to be the most satisfactory explanation of the Russo-German pact of 1939, and of Hitler's invasion of Russia in 1941? Helpful sources: Bemis, *Europe Since 1914*; Link, *American Epoch*.

7. How did the "four freedoms" speech and the Atlantic Charter tend to mobilize and direct public opinion? Compare with Wilson's "Fourteen Points." Helpful sources: Commager, *Documents*, No. 537, 540; Sherwood, *Roosevelt and Hopkins*, pp. 359–365.

FOR INDIVIDUAL OR GROUP ACTIVITIES

1. On an outline map of Europe indicate, with dates, the gains or thrusts made by the aggressor nations, Germany and Italy, in the period 1933–39.

2. On an outline map of the Far East, indicate the gains or thrusts made by Japan in the period 1930–41.

3. Prepare reports on the "miracle of Dunkirk" and the "Battle of Britain." Helpful sources: Churchill, *Their Finest Hour*, pp. 74–119, 319–381; Reynolds, *The Battle of Britain*.

4. Assume that you were the editor of a newspaper which had supported the Neutrality Act of 1937. Prepare an editorial on passage of the Lend-Lease Act.

5. Investigate and report on the "popular front" movement of the Communist party in the mid-1930's. Helpful source: Link, *American Epoch*, pp. 442–446.

December 7, 1941, PEARL HARBOR

The true goal we seek is far above and beyond the ugly field of battle. When we resort to force, as now we must, we are determined that this force shall be directed toward ultimate good as well as against immediate evil.

——Franklin D. Roosevelt

43. THE UNITED STATES FIGHTS FOR SURVIVAL

The United States Builds a World-wide Alliance

The United Nations Pact.

When the United States entered the war in 1941, we were far from ready for war. The conflict had been going on for two years. The military situation in Europe and Asia was extremely grave. It looked as if the Axis might win control of all Europe and Asia before the United States could throw its full strength into the fight.

American leaders saw that the best hope for victory lay in getting all the nations fighting the Axis to pool their resources and to co-ordinate their efforts. This was easier said than done. It involved continuous conferences between the officials of the nations and endless discussion. Although the democratic countries worked together pretty well throughout the entire war, Russia's co-operation was only partial.

A dramatic step toward building an effective alliance against the Axis took place in Washington on January 1, 1942. That day twenty-six governments then at war with the Axis, including a number of "governments-in-exile,"

signed a pact entitled "Declaration of the United Nations." In this pact they accepted the Atlantic Charter and promised not to make a separate peace. The United States became an ally of the other signers. Before the war ended, twenty-one more countries joined the alliance.

The lend-lease program was broadened into a system of mutual aid. Nearly all the Allies exchanged some aid with one another. The United States supplied fifty billion dollars' worth of lend-lease aid to its allies. They gave us nearly eight billion dollars' worth of "reverse lend-lease aid."

Anglo-American co-operation.

From the start Great Britain, Canada, and the United States shared all their military resources—men, material, ships, and knowledge. They set up joint planning boards in Washington to cover all phases of the war effort. Their military strategy was worked out by a group known as the Combined Chiefs of Staff.

729

Churchill flew to Washington for frequent conferences. Between visits, Churchill and Roosevelt were in constant touch by mail, cable, and transatlantic telephone. As General Marshall wrote later, the result was "the most complete unification of military effort ever achieved by two allied nations."

Latin America helps too.

The Japanese attack on Pearl Harbor awakened Latin America to its own danger. Nine of the Caribbean republics declared war on the Axis as soon as we did. Most of the other American nations broke off relations with the Axis within a few weeks. By August, 1942, two others had gone to war with the Axis. A number of Latin American countries took unusual steps to show their friendship for the United States. The Central American republics gave us bases for use in defending the Panama Canal. Colombia said that the United States might establish bases anywhere within its borders. Brazil and Mexico co-operated with us in every possible way. Argentina, however, remained friendly to the Axis until a few months before the end of the war.

The United States Mobilizes Its Resources

The armed services expand.

When we entered the war, we had 1,600,000 men in the armed services. The number grew rapidly as Congress authorized the drafting of millions more. At peak strength in 1945 our armed forces numbered 12,300,000, including about 200,000 women who enlisted for noncombat duty. Fifteen per cent of the entire population served in the armed forces at some time during the war. The training of these millions of "G.I.'s" was a huge task. Because the war was so highly mechanized, many men received a long technical training.

A labor shortage develops.

The drafting of millions of men and the employment of millions more in war industries resulted in a shortage of labor in other fields. The shortage was greatest in low-paid occupations, such as farming. To meet the scarcity, employers hired people who in ordinary times do not easily find jobs—housewives, inexperienced young people, the aged, and the handicapped. In December, 1942, the War Manpower Commission was set up to work for the wisest possible use of the nation's labor supply. Rules had to be made to prevent employers in war industries from grabbing one another's workers and to discourage the workers from shifting from one job to another. Steps were taken to persuade millions of women to become wage earners. As the labor shortage grew worse, President Roosevelt asked Congress to pass a law to draft workmen. Labor organizations were so strongly against the plan that Congress did nothing about it.

Industry goes to war.

Our economy was partly on a war footing when the Japanese struck at Pearl Harbor. American factories were already turning out huge quantities of arms. Once we entered the conflict, production expanded at a rate such as the world had never seen. A large number of new shipyards and armaments plants were built. Meanwhile, thousands of existing factories shifted wholly or partly to war production. For instance, automobile factories made army trucks, jeeps, and tanks instead of cars for civilian use. Additional plants for producing steel, aluminum, copper, aviation gasoline, and other basic materials had to be constructed. A huge synthetic rubber industry had to be created. To direct these changes in industry and to step up war production with all possible speed, the War Production Board was set up.

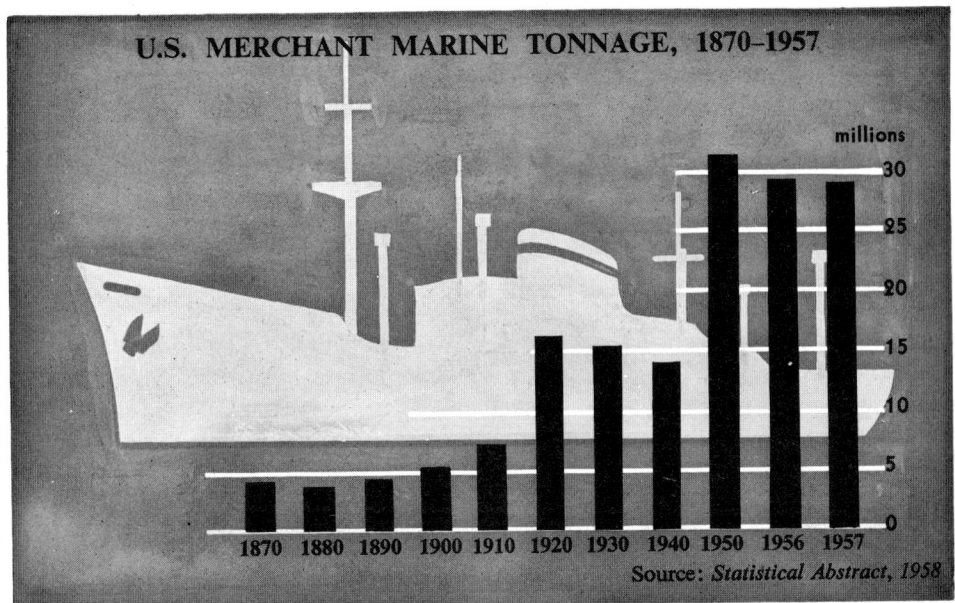

millions

30
25
20
15
10
5
0

1870 1880 1890 1900 1910 1920 1930 1940 1950 1956 1957

Source: *Statistical Abstract, 1958*

The United States became indeed the "arsenal of democracy." In the single year 1942 we produced more than 8,000,000 tons of ships, 48,000 planes, and 50,000 tanks. The following year the production of these items almost doubled. If modern war is a battle of supplies, then the struggle against the Axis was won in American shipyards, steel mills, mines, and factories.

Science goes to war.

More than in any earlier war the contestants made use of scientific research. The day after the fall of Paris, Roosevelt appointed a National Defense Research Committee. Soon after, a group of British scientists came here to give us the benefits of their knowledge in such fields as military medicine, radar, mine and submarine detection, rockets, explosives, and guided missiles. From that time on, British and American scientists worked together. Among them were a number of scientists who fled here to escape Hitler.

The most spectacular triumph of Allied science was the atomic bomb.

Before the war much preparatory research related to atomic fission had been done by physicists in Europe, Canada, and the United States. German scientists had gone farthest in this field. In 1939 Albert Einstein and other refugee scientists warned Roosevelt that Germany might produce an atomic bomb within a few years, and that with such a bomb it could rule the world. The President, acting in deepest secrecy, got the aid of the foremost British and American scientists in pushing atomic research. At first Roosevelt found money for the project in general funds. After Pearl Harbor he persuaded Congress to provide him with two billion dollars to be spent for an unspecified purpose. While research went on in university and government laboratories, huge manufacturing plants were built at Oak Ridge, Tennessee, and at Hanford, Washington. Scientists at the University of Chicago succeeded (December, 1942) in effecting the first self-sustaining nuclear chain reaction. This event was "the halfway mark on the road to the atomic bomb." By midsummer, 1945, the scientists were ready to set off the first experimental bomb. On July 16, in a remote part of New Mexico, the first man-made atomic explosion occurred.

While Nazi scientists failed to produce an atomic bomb before Germany was defeated, they did develop other important secret weapons. Three of these weapons, the V-2 rocket bomb, the jet fighter plane, and a faster submarine that could stay submerged for weeks, were used in the final months of the war. They might actually have turned the tide of battle had they been ready for mass production a little sooner.

The scarcity of raw materials.

The production of war supplies demanded huge amounts of rubber, metal, oil, and other raw materials. Early in the war, Japan cut us off from the places where we formerly got nearly all our rubber and tin. Many months went by before synthetic rubber relieved the shortage of natural rubber. Throughout the war we did not produce enough aluminum, copper, steel, leather, wool, fat, or pulpwood to meet the wartime need, nor could we import any of these in the quantity required. It was therefore necessary for the War Production Board to decide how our scant supplies of raw materials could best be used. A system of priorities was worked out by which the most important war industries had first call on any material. As a result many industries making goods for civilians had to use substitute materials or shift into war production.

Consumer goods are rationed.

Many kinds of goods wanted by civilians became scarce. Those that were most in demand, like shoes, sugar, meat, canned goods, butter, coffee, gasoline, and tires, were rationed so that the supply might be fairly divided.

Without rationing, scarce goods would have gone only to those able to pay the highest prices. The rationing system placed every consumer on his honor. Some, of course, tried to get more than their share by buying on the "black market." But the great majority of Americans accepted rationing good-naturedly and did not cheat.

War costs are huge.

The direct cost of the war to the United States came to about 330 billion dollars, or fifteen times the cost of World War I. This huge sum was equal to seven eighths of all the wealth possessed by the American people when the war began. It amounted to about $2400 for every man, woman, and child in the country. About one third of the money came from taxes, which were higher and more numerous than ever before. They fell heavily on all classes of the population. Besides paying taxes, everyone was asked to put at least a tenth of his income into war bonds. Employers helped millions of workers to buy bonds through a payroll savings plan. The total national debt had shot up by 1946 to the staggering sum of 280 billion dollars.

Prices and wages are controlled.

Even after paying high taxes and buying bonds, most Americans had more money to spend than ever before. Yet there was a shortage of nearly every kind of goods and services used by civilians. The combination of a small supply and a heavy demand caused prices to go up. The price rise started with the lend-lease program. In April, 1941, Congress established the Office of Price Administration (OPA) to keep prices in check. Early in 1942 Congress gave OPA power to fix price ceilings on all commodities except farm products and to control rents. A few months later Congress ordered that wages and salaries should be held steady.

The task of holding prices and wages down was difficult. Farmers, who had suffered so long from low prices, insisted that farm prices should be allowed to rise, and Congress listened to their pleas. As food prices went up, workers demanded higher wages. Manufacturers and storekeepers in turn complained that they must get higher prices to cover the increased cost of doing business. By the end of the war the cost of living had risen 31 per cent above the 1939 level. Yet it would certainly have risen much more had prices and wages not been regulated.

Preventing disloyal activities.

Organizations of Nazis and Nazi sympathizers, such as the German-American Bund and the Silver Shirts, had been active in the United States before the war. They continued their agitation after we entered the war until their leaders were rounded up and imprisoned. The Alien Registration Act, which Congress passed in 1940, helped the FBI to watch suspicious aliens. In compliance with the act, almost five million noncitizens residing in the United States were fingerprinted.

At the beginning of the war, many Americans in the Far West feared Japanese attacks by air and by sea. They also feared that Japanese-Americans, most of whom lived in the Pacific states, might be disloyal to the United States. To prevent race riots and as a precaution against possible disloyalty, the War Department persuaded the President to order all Japanese-Americans in the Pacific states removed to internment camps. Nearly two thirds of the 112,000 persons thus moved were American-born. There was no evidence that the Nisei (American-born Japanese) were disloyal, and liberals condemned their removal as unnecessary and unjust. One authority on constitutional law wrote that the relocation of the Japanese Americans was "the most drastic invasion of the rights of citizens of the United States by their own government that has thus far occurred in the history of our nation." Nearly all the Nisei were released from camp before the war ended. Thousands of them fought bravely for the United States. After the war all were allowed to return to their homes.

Apart from the internment of the Japanese, there was less interference with civil liberties than in World War I. Conscientious objectors were treated more tolerantly than in the earlier struggle. There was no interference with freedom of the press; newspapers adopted voluntary censorship and did not print news helpful to the enemy.

Germany Is Defeated

The Joint Chiefs of Staff decide our strategy.

The military aspects of our war effort were directed by the Joint Chiefs of Staff (JCS). The chairman was Admiral William D. Leahy, the personal representative of the President as Commander in Chief of the Armed Forces. The others were General George C. Marshall, Army Chief of Staff; General Henry H. Arnold, Chief of the Air Force; and Admiral Ernest J. King, Chief of Naval Operations. All were men of high ability and long experience. All had spent a lifetime in the armed services. The President kept in daily touch with the JCS. His excellent knowledge of military strategy enabled him to appreciate the advice of this devoted group of men.

"Stop Hitler first."

After the treacherous Japanese attack, millions of Americans wanted revenge against Japan. The President, guided by the Joint Chiefs of Staff, decided we must halt Hitler first. If instead we threw most of our strength against Japan, Hitler might subdue

(Above) *In recognition of services the* UNITED STATES JOINT CHIEFS OF STAFF *receive the British "Order of the Bath" from Lord Halifax in November, 1945. Left to right: General Arnold, Fleet Admiral King, Lord Halifax, General Marshall, and Fleet Admiral Leahy.*

(Below) *At an Eastern seaport in 1942, Allied ships, with precious cargoes of food and raw materials, gathered to form a convoy. Along the Atlantic sea lanes German planes and submarines were waiting to strike.*

AXIS CONTROL, NOVEMBER, 1942

At the CASABLANCA CONFER-
ENCE *(1943), Generals Gi-
raud and de Gaulle of
France meet with President
Roosevelt and Prime Min-
ister Churchill.*

both England and Russia. Then nothing could stop his pushing through the Middle East and India to join forces with Japan. The Western Hemisphere, with no allies left, would be at the mercy of the Axis. Therefore, the JCS thought it wiser to concentrate most of our effort on defeating Germany. After that, all the United Nations could join in the fight against Japan. A large segment of the American public, particularly in the Far West, criticized this strategy, but the President stood firm.

The U-boat war.

In the first year after we entered the war, Allied shipping losses were worse than ever. Japanese submarines raided shipping in the Pacific. German submarines were active in the Caribbean Sea, the Gulf of Mexico, and the North Atlantic. Italian submarines did great damage in the Mediterranean. On the average, thirty-six Allied ships were sunk each week in 1942. Furthermore, at the end of the year, Axis submarines were being built twice as fast as the Allies could destroy them. Unless ways could be found to defeat the U-boats, the United Nations would lose the war.

By the spring of 1943, more effective ways of fighting U-boats had been developed. Ship losses declined. By the fall of 1943 the Axis was losing submarines as rapidly as the Allies were losing merchant ships. But the Battle of the Atlantic was won by only a narrow margin. Shortly before Germany surrendered, it was ready to make large numbers of its remarkable "snorkel" submarine. Against the new U-boat our antisubmarine weapons would have been a feeble defense.

The Russian front.

During the winter of 1941–42 the Russians recovered some territory, but in May the Germans again took the offensive. Declaring that the war would

be decided on the eastern front, Hitler launched a furious drive toward the Caucasus. The drive had three objectives: (1) to capture the rich Caucasian oil fields, (2) to cut Russia off from the Black Sea, and (3) to open a pathway into Iran and the Middle East. The Nazis captured Odessa, the Crimea, and the great naval base at Sevastopol, all on the Black Sea. In August one army laid siege to Stalingrad in an effort to gain control of the Volga River. A second army pushed southeast and entered the Caucasus. The Nazis came in sight of the oil resources so vital to their success.

In the summer and fall of 1942 the outcome of the war hung in the balance. The Russians fought desperately and sustained a heavy loss of life. They begged their allies to open a second front in western Europe. To do so at that time was impossible. However, England and the United States sent huge quantities of war supplies to the hard-pressed Russians. The Combined Chiefs of Staff also decided to invade French-held North Africa. This action, which took place in November, 1942, was a compromise second front.

The Battle of Stalingrad ranks as one of the most decisive military engagements in history. In three months of fierce hand-to-hand fighting, September to November, 1942, the defenders hurled back one sledge-hammer attack after another. Then Russian reinforcements suddenly began to encircle the ruined city. When Hitler ordered his men not to retreat, they were trapped. The survivors gave up in February, 1943. The Nazis never regained the initiative in Russia. The Russians soon started an advance which went on, with few interruptions, until they entered Berlin over two years later.

The war in North Africa.

The German offensive of 1942 was not limited to Russia. In June, 1942, the

German Afrika Korps defeated the British in Libya and drove into Egypt. It appeared that the Nazis would soon get control of the Suez Canal. Then they could conquer the weakly defended Middle East and attack India. Tanks and planes from the United States and fresh British troops brought from the Middle East saved the Allies from a major disaster in Egypt. In October the Axis armored columns were stopped at El Alamein. In three months the Germans were driven from Egypt, across Libya, and into Tunisia.

Meanwhile, American forces and war materials were being concentrated in Great Britain. In November, 1942, in the biggest seaborne invasion ever made up to that time, American and British troops landed on the coast of Morocco and Algeria. Their commander was General Dwight D. Eisenhower. French colonial troops, under orders from the Vichy government, offered some resistance during the first five days. Vichy officials in North Africa then agreed to help the Allies. The Germans at once occupied all of France. They tried to take the French fleet, which lay at anchor in Toulon, but the French scuttled their ships rather than have them used by the Nazis.

In the winter of 1943 the Allied forces in North Africa made little progress because of rain, mud, and supply troubles. But once the Allies gained superiority in the air, they kept the Axis forces in Tunisia from getting supplies. In May, 1943, after a winter of hard fighting, these German and Italian armies surrendered. It was the greatest victory yet won by the Allies. They now held the whole of Africa. As a result they had three advantages: (1) The Mediterranean was open to their ships. (2) They could bring pressure on Spain and Turkey to shut off the sale of strategic raw materials to Germany. (3) From Tunisia they could strike at either Italy or the

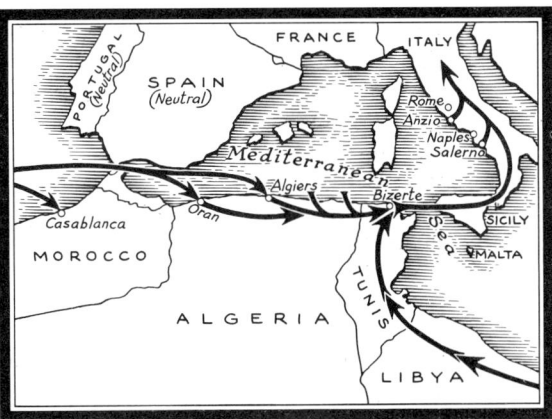

ALLIED THRUSTS IN NORTH AFRICA AND ITALY

Balkans—what Churchill called the "soft underbelly of the Axis."

The Casablanca Conference.

Meanwhile (January, 1943) Roosevelt and Churchill met at Casablanca, Morocco. Together with their military advisors they made plans to invade Sicily and Italy. They also decided to send forces to the Pacific for an offensive there. They announced that the United Nations would demand the "unconditional surrender" of their enemies.

The invasion of Italy.

As soon as fighting stopped in North Africa, Eisenhower got ready to move against Italy. In July and August, 1943, British and American troops occupied Sicily. Early in September they landed in southern Italy. Five days later a group of high Italian officials imprisoned Mussolini and announced their country's surrender. Soon after, the Italian fleet was turned over to the United Nations. Hitler rushed a large force into Italy, occupying the country as far south as Naples.

Although the Italian people were now out of the war, most of their country was in German hands. The Combined Chiefs of Staff had to make a hard decision. Should they conduct a large-scale offensive to drive the Germans out of Italy? Or should they use just enough men to pin down the twenty to thirty Nazi divisions Hitler had sent there? The American Joint Chiefs favored the second course, in order not to delay or weaken the coming cross-channel invasion of France. A compromise plan was adopted.

In October, 1943, the Allies captured Naples and moved up the Italian peninsula. Three months later they secured a beachhead at Anzio, thirty miles south of Rome. Hitler threw in strong reinforcements. On June 4, 1944, the Allied armies marched into Rome. The Nazis fell back, fighting all the way until they reached the Arno River. Here they entrenched themselves in the so-called Gothic Line. They held northern Italy until the end of the war.

The air front.

During 1941 Hitler used most of his air power in Russia and North Africa. Meanwhile England recovered from the bombings of 1940 and built up its air strength. By the summer of 1942 the British were able occasionally to send out as many as a thousand planes at once to raid Nazi industrial areas.

In the spring of 1943 the air war on Germany began to do heavy damage. By this time the United States had a large air force based in the British Isles. Five hundred to a thousand British and American planes could now attack Germany whenever the weather was suitable. In the last year of the war, as many as six thousand planes attacked European targets in a single day. Air raids went on around the clock, the Americans flying by day and the Royal Air Force by night. Bombing was directed chiefly at oil refineries, synthetic oil plants, and transportation facilities. The collapse of the German economy in the last few weeks of war was partly due to month after month of relentless bombing.

Conferences at Moscow, Cairo, Teheran.

Throughout 1942 and 1943 the Russian government kept up its demands for a full-scale second front. Stalin complained (with much truth) that his country was bearing the greatest losses in the fight against Hitler. He suspected that the United States and Britain wanted communism and fascism to destroy each other. Therefore he did not permit his allies to send military or economic observers to Russia. When Churchill and Roosevelt suggested sending an Anglo-American air force to the Caucasus, he made no reply. Nor did he accept other proposals for joint action.

In 1942, in an effort to attain greater co-operation, Churchill went to Moscow to see Stalin. Averell Harriman accompanied him to represent the United States. A year later our aged Secretary of State, Cordell Hull, made the difficult journey to Moscow. He spent nearly two weeks there conferring with the Russian, Chinese, and British foreign ministers. Hull and Eden promised that the invasion of western Europe would take place within a few months. A Joint Four-Nation Declaration stated that the four governments would act together in all matters concerning the surrender of the enemy.

In November, 1943, President Roosevelt, Prime Minister Churchill, and General Chiang Kai-shek met together for the first time. This historic meeting took place at Cairo, Egypt. The three leaders joined in the Declaration of Cairo, which said: (1) The three nations had no desire to expand their territory, (2) Japan must surrender unconditionally, (3) Japan would be stripped of all islands taken since 1914 and all territories stolen from China since 1890, such as Manchuria, Formosa, and the Pescadores, (4) Korea should become free and independent.

Directly after the Cairo meeting Roosevelt and Churchill flew to Tehe-

June, 1944. Into the hills of Normandy American soldiers march, headed for the front lines.

ran, the capital of Iran. Here they held their first joint conference with Stalin. The Russian leader promised to launch a new offensive against the Nazis from the east when the Allies landed in France. He also agreed to declare war on Japan once Germany was beaten. Plans for a new world organization to keep the peace were discussed. Although the Teheran Declaration said the three powers wanted to end "tyranny and slavery, oppression, and intolerance," it soon became clear that Russia had imperialistic designs for eastern Europe.

France is liberated.

Since early in the war British and American experts had been making plans for the invasion of western Europe (Operation Overlord). Soon after the landings in North Africa, the United States began to build up troops and supplies in England in preparation for "Overlord." Meanwhile, the air war went on relentlessly in an effort to "soften up" Germany. In the summer of 1943, the Combined Chiefs of Staff decided to invade France the following spring. The delay in starting this operation was partly due to the lack of ships. Most of the available shipping was being used on the long supply lines to Russia and to the South Pacific. Another reason for the delay was the knowledge that it would involve a heavy sacrifice of life. Hitler had made the channel coast of France into a fortress.

Since three fourths of the Allied Expeditionary Force (AEF) were to be Americans, Churchill agreed that an American should be in supreme command. General Eisenhower was chosen.

On D-Day, June 6, 1944, the Allies landed an army on the Normandy coast of France. The free world waited anxiously to see the outcome. Would the men wading ashore on those beaches get through the Nazi shore defenses—the underwater obstacles, the big guns

739

planted close together behind concrete ten feet thick, the miles of mine fields and tank traps, the jungles of barbed wire, the endless hedgerows lined with machine guns? Or would most of the soldiers perish in a heroic but useless attempt to establish beachheads?

For hours before the landings, an Allied fleet—the greatest ever assembled—blasted the Nazi defenses. Hundreds of planes dropped paratroopers behind the enemy lines to seize bridges and destroy communications. When the landings started, swarms of American and British fighter planes crossed the skies overhead to prevent German planes from interfering. Far behind the beachheads Allied bombers pounded bridges, railroad depots, and oil dumps in order to keep enemy reinforcements

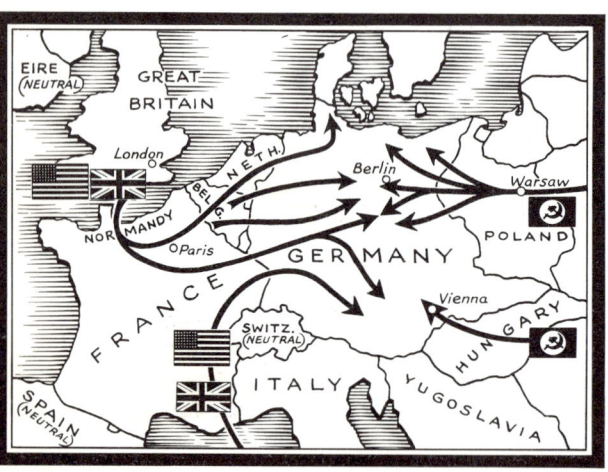

ALLIED VICTORY IN EUROPE

from reaching the battle area. These complicated operations were a success. By the end of a week the Allies held a narrow strip sixty miles long on the French coast. Within a month a million Allied soldiers had crossed the English Channel. After desperate fighting, they took Cherbourg and Caen, two seaports where heavy equipment could be landed. Then they broke through heavy

German defenses at the base of the Norman peninsula and swept eastward.

In mid-August the American Seventh Army landed in southern France. They quickly overcame a Nazi force, of which almost half were Russians, Czechs, and Poles, fighting only because they were forced to do so. Then the Americans raced up the Rhone Valley to join the Allies coming from Normandy.

Meanwhile the French Army of the Interior (the Maquis), which had been fighting underground since the fall of France, gave aid to the Allies. With arms dropped by Allied airplanes, they freed large areas of France from the Nazis. By early September the enemy was in headlong flight from France. Allied forces pursued them across Belgium and the Netherlands.

The Russian offensive of 1944.

While the Allies were fighting in France, Red forces drove the last of the Nazis from Russian soil. Then the Russians marched across eastern Poland. At the same time another Red army began an advance through the Balkans.

As the Soviet armies advanced, Moscow announced that it did not recognize the boundaries of prewar Poland and suggested that Poland's eastern boundary might be the line recommended by Lord Curzon in 1919. Adoption of the Curzon line would leave Russia in possession of the territory it had seized from Poland in 1939. The Polish government-in-exile protested. Thereupon Russia established a puppet government at Lublin, on Polish soil.

Churchill had long feared that Russia meant to control the Balkans. Late in 1944, as the Soviet armies fought the Germans in the Balkan states, Churchill acted to keep Greece from falling under Communist control. He sent British soldiers to free Greece from the Nazis.

740

The Yalta Conference.

The need for another conference between Churchill, Roosevelt, and Stalin was urgent. The Big Three leaders decided to meet at Yalta in the Crimea in early February, 1945. Roosevelt had just been inaugurated for his fourth term, having defeated Thomas E. Dewey in the November election.

The conference dealt with a great number of important questions, some of them military, some of them political. Stalin was a hard bargainer, and Roosevelt and Churchill have been sharply criticized for the concessions they made to him. Yet he had the power to do about as he pleased in eastern and central Europe. His armies were advancing through Poland and Hungary and would soon be ready to drive into Austria and Germany.

Roosevelt and Churchill consented to Russia's border claims in Poland "in principle." In return for the territory yielded to Russia, Poland was to have land taken from Germany. Stalin promised that in the countries of eastern Europe occupied by his armies, free elections would be held to set up permanent governments. Furthermore, the United States and Great Britain should help to oversee these elections. These promises were not kept.

The Big Three leaders agreed that Germany should be divided into three zones of occupation, and that Berlin should also be divided into zones of occupation. The occupation would last until peace treaties could be written.

The most controversial agreements had to do with the Far East. At the time of the Yalta meeting our military experts believed that two more years of bitter fighting lay ahead. General Marshall, strongly backed by General MacArthur, wanted to obtain Russian help in fighting Japan. Roosevelt and Churchill therefore felt obliged to pay Stalin's price. In return for entering the war against Japan, Russia was to get

German prisoners

southern Sakhalin, the Kurile Islands, Port Arthur, virtual control over Manchuria's chief port (it was to be internationalized), and joint control with China of the Manchurian railways. These concessions were made without consulting China.

The Battle for Germany.

At the end of February, 1945, while the Russians broke into Germany from the east, the other Allies launched a great drive from the west. General Eisenhower's troops reached the Elbe River in April, 1945. There, American and Russian advance guards greeted each other joyfully. The Supreme Command ordered the Anglo-Americans to halt their advance and allow the Russians to take Berlin.

On May Day a German radio station announced Hitler's death in his flaming capital. The next day all the German forces in Italy and Austria— over a million men—surrendered. Three days later a million German soldiers in Holland and Denmark laid down their arms. On May 7 the German High Command signed formal papers of unconditional surrender. The war in Europe was over after nearly six years of terror and destruction.

741

The Japanese Are Defeated

Japan advances in East Asia.

When the Japanese struck at Pearl Harbor, they crippled our main Pacific fleet. A few hours later they destroyed most of our air force in the Philippines. To deprive us of air and naval bases in the Pacific, they shortly seized Guam and Wake Island and invaded the Philippines. On January 2, 1942, they captured our naval base at Manila. General Douglas MacArthur, our Far East commander, withdrew his forces to Bataan Peninsula and the island of Corregidor at the entrance to Manila Bay. In March, acting on orders from President Roosevelt, MacArthur escaped to Australia to take charge of all Allied forces in the southwest Pacific. Within a few weeks the starving defenders of Bataan and Corregidor had to surrender. Japan now had possession of the Philippines. Forty thousand American and Filipino troops began the "Death March" to prison camps. Only half of them survived the terrible march and the imprisonment which followed.

The Japanese had meanwhile scored important victories in Southeast Asia. The day after Pearl Harbor, they sank two British battleships guarding Malaya. The Japanese fleet was now stronger than the Pacific fleets of the United States, Great Britain, and the Netherlands put together. Early in the winter the Japanese drove the British out of Hong Kong and the Malay peninsula. Then they attacked the great British naval base at Singapore from the land side. The loss of Singapore (February 15, 1942) was a terrible blow to our side, for it deprived the Allies of the best base in the South Pacific and opened the way for new Japanese conquests.

The Japanese invaded Burma before the fall of Singapore. Their object was to cut off the Burma Road, over which lend-lease supplies reached China, and to get bases for the invasion of India. By the end of April all Burma was in the enemy's hands, and Japanese planes began to bomb cities in India. India was saved from invasion only by the onset of heavy monsoon rains. Meanwhile, the enemy had invaded and conquered the entire Netherlands Indies, a rich source of oil, rubber, and other strategic materials. Japan now had all the resources it needed for a long war.

The threat to Australia.

The Japanese had already advanced southward into New Guinea, the Solomon Islands, and the Bismarck Archipelago. From these islands they threatened Australia and New Zealand. The United States sent every ship that could be spared to carry men and munitions to the lands "down under."

In May, 1942, a Japanese fleet appeared in the Coral Sea, just off the northeast coast of Australia. An American carrier force sank or damaged twenty enemy ships and drove the others off. It was the first big naval battle in history in which the fighting was done entirely by carrier-based planes. Surface ships neither saw one another nor exchanged gunfire. The Battle of the Coral Sea saved Australia from immediate invasion.

The threat to Alaska and Hawaii.

Early in June, 1942, the Japanese moved eastward. The thrust was two-pronged. A small fleet attacked Dutch Harbor in the Aleutians, probably to divert attention from the main attack on Midway. It was driven off. In retreat from Dutch Harbor the Japanese admiral left garrisons on three tiny islands at the end of the Aleutian chain. As a result of this attack, the Alcan Highway, linking the United States to Alaska, was rushed to completion. The highway improved the chances for stopping a possible invasion of Canada and the United States from the northwest.

In their main thrust, the Japanese hoped to take Midway. From this base they could control, or even occupy, Hawaii. On June 3 a large Japanese fleet was sighted 700 miles from Midway. It was attacked by bombers based on Midway and by planes from three American carriers. Our small fleet won a smashing victory. The Battle of Midway marked a turning point in the Pacific war. The Japanese navy was still powerful but was no longer master of the Pacific. The outcome of the war against Japan now depended on which side could build the most ships.

The Battle of Guadalcanal.

In July, 1942, the Japanese landed on Guadalcanal in the southern Solomons. They built an airfield which threatened our supply lines to Australia and New Zealand. American Marines seized the airfield in August and began a six-month campaign to drive the enemy from the island. In November a large Japanese naval force attempted to bring reinforcements. It was routed in a three-day battle. In February, 1943, the Japanese abandoned Guadalcanal. During the following eighteen months, Americans, Australians, and New Zealanders slowly pushed the enemy from the Solomons and from New Guinea. The gains were limited and won at great cost.

Island hopping begins.

Our Pacific fleet was rapidly growing in strength. Late in 1943 Admiral Chester Nimitz took the offensive in the central Pacific. In November he directed amphibious (land and water) operations in the Gilbert Islands. In February he took possession of the Marshall Islands. The capture of major islands in the Marianas during the summer of 1944 gave us valuable air bases about 1500 miles from Tokyo.

Before the end of that year giant superfortresses began pounding the Japanese homelands.

In October, 1944, after completing the conquest of New Guinea, General MacArthur headed for the Philippines with 600 ships and 250,000 men. He landed at Leyte Island. The Japanese sent their main fleet in a desperate effort to save the Philippines. In the great Battle of Leyte Gulf, suicide dive bombers, or *kamikaze,* were first used by the Japanese. The fight was perhaps the greatest naval battle of all time. It resulted in a decisive American victory. By the end of the year the bulk of the Japanese navy had been put out of action.

In January, 1945, MacArthur landed troops on Luzon, the largest of the Philippines. By July, all of the Philippines were in our hands. Meanwhile our Marines had taken Iwo Jima, a small island only 750 miles from Tokyo. Iwo, which fell in March, 1945, was needed as a base for fighter planes and a refueling station for bombers. In April our troops went ashore on Okinawa, one of the Ryukyu islands about 350 miles from Japan. As on Iwo Jima, a long and costly struggle followed. Okinawa fell in June. It provided a base for the expected invasion of Japan.

Japan is besieged by sea and air.

As 1945 began the Japanese empire started to crumble. Allied forces were advancing in Burma. Meanwhile the Japanese in the Dutch East Indies were being wiped out.

By the end of January, 1945, Allied convoys were once more moving over the Burma Road into China. The lend-lease supplies they brought ended the long stalemate in China. In the south the Chinese Nationalists, commanded by Chiang Kai-shek, resumed the fight against the Japanese. The Chinese Communists, led by Mao Tse-tung, fought the Japanese in North China

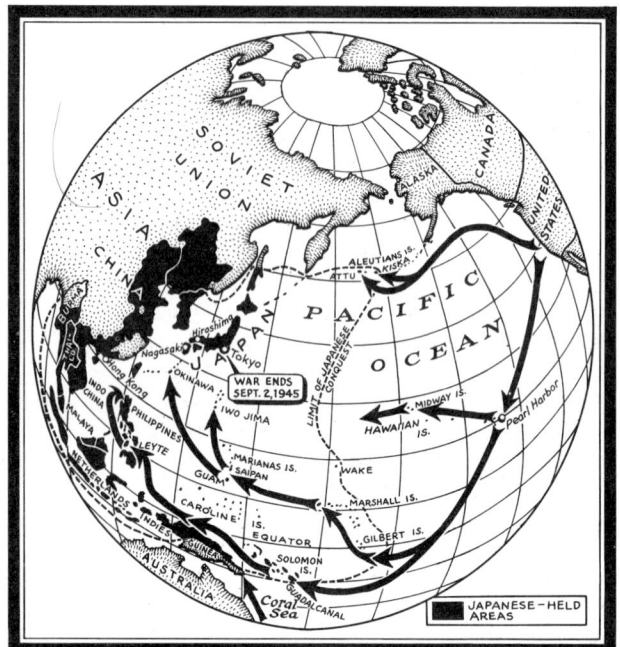

UNITED STATES THRUSTS IN THE PACIFIC

but did not co-operate with Chiang. Throughout the war the United States had vainly tried to get the two groups to work together.[1] However, Mao and Chiang seemed more anxious to fight each other than to fight the Japanese. Nevertheless, in 1945, Chinese forces cleared the enemy from some areas.

With the capture of the Philippines and Iwo Jima, bombing attacks on Japan's home islands grew fiercer. Hundreds of superfortresses took part in a single raid. Fire bombs destroyed large areas in about seventy of Japan's flimsy cities. Transportation facilities, airfields, and industrial plants were bombed day after day. Planes from British and American carriers joined the

---

[1] In those years the Chinese Communists apparently had little connection with Moscow. In 1945 Stalin actually made a treaty of alliance with Chiang's government. Our State Department tried to persuade Chiang to make much-needed reforms, believing that reforms were necessary to halt the spread of communism. Chiang, however, did not agree.

attack. In addition Allied warships bombarded coastal cities at will.

Japan's survival was also threatened by submarine attacks on its shipping. By the end of the war our submarines had sunk over half of Japan's merchant fleet. With the cutting off of imports, Japan suffered an acute shortage of food, raw materials, and aviation gasoline. For lack of fuel oil in the last months of the war, what was left of Japan's navy could not be sent to sea.

As the United States and Britain prepared for a large-scale invasion, Japan's leaders realized that defeat was certain. In May they secretly asked the Russian government to try to make peace between them and their opponents. This Moscow refused to do. Tokyo then asked for details on the meaning of "unconditional surrender."

Japan is forced to give up.

In mid-July a Big Three conference met at Potsdam, Germany. One of the questions taken up was how to hasten the surrender of Japan. It was decided to outline the peace terms and call on Japan to surrender or be destroyed.

JAPANESE LEADERS *come aboard the battleship* Missouri *to sign the surrender papers.*

battleship *Missouri* in Tokyo Bay. Thus World War II, the most terrible conflict in history, came to an end.

A New World Organization

Plans are made for world security.

The second World War convinced almost everyone of the need for a world organization to enforce peace. Every statesman knew that such an organization could not succeed unless the United States was a member. From the time that the United Nations pact was signed on New Year's Day, 1942, President Roosevelt hoped to make the wartime alliance the basis for a new world security organization. He and Secretary of State Hull, together with distinguished Americans in both parties, worked to win the necessary public approval.

Late in 1943 the powers taking part in the Moscow Conference and in the Teheran Conference pledged their support to a general international organization open to all peace-loving states. At about the same time the House of Representatives adopted the Fulbright Resolution and the Senate adopted the Connally Resolution to assure the rest of the world that the United States would participate in such an organization. The Connally Resolution passed by the overwhelming vote of 85 to 5. The vote proved that public opinion in the United States had undergone a great change.

In the late summer of 1944 representatives of the United States, the Soviet Union, Great Britain, and China met at Dumbarton Oaks, Washington, D.C. They prepared the outline for an organization similar to the League of Nations but much stronger. All members of the United Nations were asked to study the Dumbarton Oaks proposals.

When the proposals were published, the United States was in the

The terms were published on July 26. Japan promptly turned them down. The United States then made use of a secret weapon. On August 6, an atomic bomb was loosed on the Japanese city of Hiroshima, a military base. In one flash three fifths of the city was wiped out. The whole world was stunned by the news.

Two days later the Soviet Union declared war on Japan. For weeks Stalin had been moving men and supplies to the Manchurian border. Russian troops now quickly overran Manchuria and captured a large number of Japanese soldiers.

On August 9 American fliers dropped a second atomic bomb on Nagasaki. Most of the city was pulverized. A few hours later Tokyo agreed to accept the Potsdam terms if the emperor could stay in power. The Allies replied that the emperor must carry out the orders of the Supreme Commander of the Allied forces. Japan then gave up. General MacArthur took up residence in Tokyo as Supreme Commander. On September 2, 1945, the papers of surrender were signed on the

midst of a presidential election campaign. Many people waited anxiously to learn what position would be taken by the Republican candidate, Governor Thomas E. Dewey of New York. There were powerful isolationists in the Republican party, but Dewey endorsed the work done at Dumbarton Oaks. His statements did much to overcome the fear that a Republican victory might bring a return to isolationism after the war. On election day, however, Dewey was defeated and President Franklin D. Roosevelt was re-elected for a fourth term.

In February, 1945, Roosevelt, Churchill, and Stalin met at Yalta (see p. 741). Among other things, they decided to summon all the United Nations to meet at San Francisco in April for the purpose of writing the charter of the new world security organization. The countries invited to the San Francisco meeting were those which had declared war on Germany or Japan by March 31, 1945. "This time," said President Roosevelt, "we shall not make the mistake of waiting until the war is over to set up the machinery of peace."

The death of President Roosevelt.

Following the Yalta Conference the President worked on preparations for the meeting at San Francisco. Exhausted by his heavy wartime duties, he passed away on April 12, 1945, at Warm Springs, Georgia, where he had gone for a brief rest. Vice-President Harry S. Truman became President. Throughout the free world Roosevelt's death was mourned. To the peoples fighting the Axis, Roosevelt was the symbol of unity, justice, and freedom.

The U.N. Charter is prepared.

From April 25 to June 26, 1945, representatives of fifty anti-Axis nations met at San Francisco. They prepared a charter, or constitution, for a permanent organization to be known as the United Nations (called, for short, the U.N.). The preamble is a noble statement of democratic ideals:

We, the peoples of the United Nations

Determined to save succeeding generations from the scourge of war, which twice in our lifetime has brought untold sorrow to mankind, and

To reaffirm faith in fundamental human rights, in the dignity and worth of the human person, in the equal rights of men and women and of nations large and small, and

To establish conditions under which justice and respect for the obligations arising from treaties and other sources of international law can be maintained, and

To promote social progress and better standards of life in larger freedom, and for these ends

To practice tolerance and live together in peace with one another as good neighbors, and

To unite our strength to maintain international peace and security, and

To insure by the acceptance of principles and the institution of methods, that armed force shall not be used, save in the common interest, and

To employ international machinery for the promotion of the economic and social advancement of all people, have resolved to combine our efforts to accomplish these aims.

To fulfill the purposes set forth, the members promise to act according to the following principles:

1. The sovereign equality of all members,

2. The execution in good faith of the obligations assumed under the charter, including the obligation to help the United Nations organization in any action it may take to further the purposes expressed in the charter,

3. The settlement of international disputes by peaceful means,

4. Abandonment of force or threats of force against the territorial integrity or political independence of any state.

Structure of the U.N.

The United Nations has six major organs: the General Assembly, the Security Council, the Economic and Social Council, the Trusteeship Council, the International Court of Justice, and the Secretariat.

1. *The General Assembly.* This organ is made up of all the members of the United Nations. It meets at least once a year. Each member nation has one vote, although it may have five representatives. Decisions on important questions are taken by a two-thirds vote. The Assembly may make recommendations to the members on any problem related to world peace and the improvement of international relations.

2. *The Security Council.* This organ has the principal responsibility for preventing war. Representatives of its eleven members must be ready to meet whenever an emergency arises. The five permanent members are commonly referred to as the "Big Five." They include the United States of America, the United Kingdom of Great Britain and Northern Ireland, the Union of Soviet Socialist Republics, the Republic of China, and France. Six other members are elected by the Assembly for two-year terms. The Security Council may discuss any question which any

seven of its members wish to bring before it. But in order to take action on a matter of importance, seven members, including each of the Big Five, must vote "Yes." Thus, each of the Big Five has the right to veto any important action of which it disapproves.

3. *The Economic and Social Council.* This organ is a board of eighteen nations elected by the General Assembly. Its purpose is to help the entire world achieve better living conditions and thus to remove the economic and social causes of war. The Economic and Social Council has committees and commissions at work on various problems. A number of specialized agencies are affiliated with it, among them the World Health Organization (WHO), the International Labor Organization (ILO), the International Bank for Reconstruction and Development, and the United Nations Educational, Scientific, and Cultural Organization (UNESCO).

4. *The Trusteeship Council.* This organ supervises territories taken from the defeated nations after World Wars I and II. The country which is responsible for such a territory does not own it outright, but acts as a trustee, or guardian, for it. The charter says that the people in a trust territory may look forward to independence.

5. *The International Court of Justice.* This organ resembles the World Court established by the League of Nations. Like that court, it meets at The Hague. All nations may use this court and many, including the United States, have pledged themselves in advance to refer certain kinds of disputes to it. The Court hears only cases in which the parties agree in advance to accept the decision.

6. *The Secretariat.* This organ is the administrative staff of the United Nations. It is directed by a Secretary-General, who is nominated by the Security Council and elected by the General Assembly for a five-year term. The

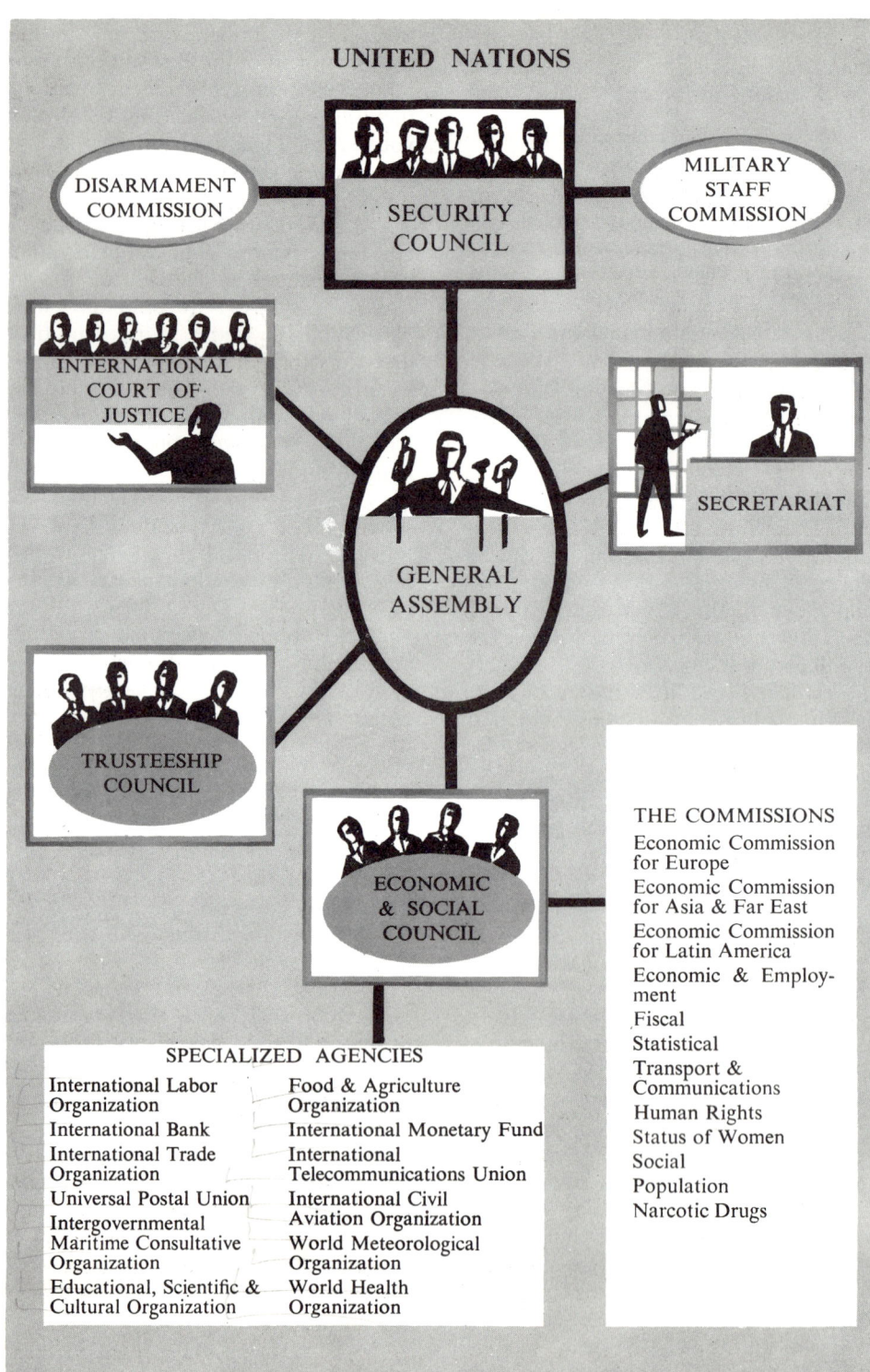

UNITED NATIONS

SECURITY COUNCIL

DISARMAMENT COMMISSION

MILITARY STAFF COMMISSION

INTERNATIONAL COURT OF JUSTICE

SECRETARIAT

GENERAL ASSEMBLY

TRUSTEESHIP COUNCIL

ECONOMIC & SOCIAL COUNCIL

SPECIALIZED AGENCIES

International Labor Organization

International Bank

International Trade Organization

Universal Postal Union

Intergovernmental Maritime Consultative Organization

Educational, Scientific & Cultural Organization

Food & Agriculture Organization

International Monetary Fund

International Telecommunications Union

International Civil Aviation Organization

World Meteorological Organization

World Health Organization

THE COMMISSIONS

Economic Commission for Europe

Economic Commission for Asia & Far East

Economic Commission for Latin America

Economic & Employment

Fiscal

Statistical

Transport & Communications

Human Rights

Status of Women

Social

Population

Narcotic Drugs

Secretariat includes more than three thousand workers from all parts of the world—economists, statisticians, stenographers, translators, and others.

The Senate ratifies the charter.

In appointing six delegates to the San Francisco conference, President Roosevelt had tried to avoid the mistakes made by Woodrow Wilson in regard to the League (see p. 617). He selected four congressmen, two from each major party. He also chose Harold E. Stassen, former Republican governor of Minnesota, and Virginia C. Gildersleeve, Dean of Barnard College.

One of the Senate's foremost Republicans, Arthur H. Vandenberg, was among the six American delegates. Vandenberg, who had been an isolationist before we entered the war, gave his full support to the charter. Speaking in the Senate, he said: "I shall support the ratification of this charter with all the resources at my command. . . . Peace must not be cheated out of its only collective chance." His influence counted heavily. Late in July, after a brief debate, the Senate approved the United Nations charter by a vote of 89 to 2.

The United Nations is launched.

By the end of 1945 fifty-one nations had ratified the charter. The General Assembly held its first meeting in London early in 1946. The Assembly decided that the headquarters of the U.N. should be in the United States.

The United Nations began to function in a confused and critical era. From the start the Assembly and the Security Council came to grips with serious problems. Disputes continually arose, and the exercise of the veto in the Security Council often blocked action. Students of world affairs thought that bringing the disagreements into the open was a good thing. But they pointed out that the success of the United Nations would depend in large measure on the Big Five. Unless they could agree on the basic principles of co-operation and justice, the plan for world security would remain a dream.

Trygve Lie, first Secretary General of the U.N.

FOR IDENTIFICATION

Declaration of United Nations
Economic and Social Council
General Assembly
International Bank
International Court of Justice
International Labor Organization
Iwo Jima
Douglas MacArthur
Chester Nimitz
Okinawa
Secretariat
Security Council
Stalingrad
Trusteeship Council
UNESCO
World Health Organization

FOR EXPLANATION OR DEFINITION

amphibious operation
beachhead
"Big Five"
Connally Resolution
D-Day
Dumbarton Oaks
island hopping
kamikaze
Maquis
Operation Overlord
rationing
War Production Board
War Manpower Commission

FOR REVIEW

1. State the purpose of the "Declaration of the United Nations." What effect did it have?

2. What was the task of the Combined Chiefs of Staff?

3. How did the United States obtain enough man power to supply both the armed forces and essential industries?

4. (a) How did war stimulate scientific research? (b) Name some of the notable achievements of science during the war.

5. What kinds of raw materials were particularly scarce in the United States? What was done to conserve these raw materials?

749

6. Why was rationing necessary? Was it a success?

7. (a) What was the approximate cost of the war in dollars? (b) How did the United States raise money to finance the war? (c) Why was price control necessary? Why was it difficult?

8. Why did the Joint Chiefs of Staff decide that the defeat of Germany should precede the defeat of Japan?

9. Describe the Battle of the Atlantic. What was its importance?

10. (a) Describe the German thrust into Russia and the Caucasus. (b) Why was the Battle of Stalingrad one of the most decisive engagements in World War II?

11. (a) Why was German success in North Africa in 1942 a serious threat to the United Nations? (b) What advantages did the Allies gain by their conquest of North Africa?

12. What were the results of the Allied invasion of Sicily and Italy in 1943?

13. Why did Russia keep urging Britain and the United States to open a second front in Europe? Why was the opening of a second front so long delayed?

14. What was decided at the Cairo Conference? The Teheran Conference?

15. (a) What was D-Day? (b) Describe the liberation of France.

16. What did the Russians accomplish in their 1944 offensive?

17. What decisions were reached at the Yalta Conference?

18. Describe the Battle for Germany.

19. (a) What immediate advantages did Japan have as a result of her surprise attack upon Pearl Harbor? (b) What gains did Japan make in the Pacific in 1942?

20. (a) What is the special importance of the Battle of the Coral Sea? (b) Why does the Battle of Midway mark the turning point in the war in the Pacific?

21. (a) What is the significance of the Battle of Leyte Gulf? (b)· What is the importance of the reconquest of the Philippines? Of the capture of Iwo Jima and Okinawa?

22. Describe Japan's situation just before atomic bombs were dropped on Hiroshima and Nagasaki.

23. What decisions were reached at the Potsdam Conference?

24. (a) When did Russia declare war on Japan? (b) When did Japan agree to surrender?

25. (a) What were the Dumbarton Oaks proposals? (b) When and where was the charter of the United Nations drafted?

26. (a) Name six organs of the United Nations. State the functions of each. (b) Name the permanent members of the Security Council. (c) Explain the principle of the veto in the Security Council. (d) Is the General Assembly more democratic in its procedures than the Security Council?

FOR FURTHER STUDY AND DISCUSSION

1. Report on the outstanding achievements of scientific research and development during the war. Helpful source: Baxter, *Scientists against Time.*

2. Should the United States have used the atomic bomb on Japan?

3. Explain the significance of Bataan Peninsula, MacArthur's escape to Australia, the closing of the Burma Road.

4. Why are the battles of Stalingrad and Midway regarded as decisive? Compare with El Alamein and the Battle of Leyte Gulf. Helpful sources: Pratt, *War for the World;* Churchill, *The Hinge of Fate,* pp. 238–255, 586–604.

5. What part did air power play in defeating Germany? Japan?

6. What part did American industry play in the outcome of World War II?

7. Describe the "consumer's front" and the "labor front" during the war.

8. What mistakes in strategy were made by Hitler? By Japan? By our side?

9. (a) Why was it thought desirable to establish a world security organization before the war ended? (b) Why was the United States willing to take part in it? (c) In what respects does the United Nations differ from the League of Nations?

10. Criticize or defend the principle of the veto in the Security Council of the United Nations.

FOR INDIVIDUAL OR GROUP ACTIVITIES

1. On an outline map of western Europe, indicate, with dates, the important military engagements which enclosed and led to the surrender of Germany. Helpful sources: Lord, *Historical Atlas;* Link, *American Epoch;* Eisenhower, *Crusade in Europe;* Pratt, *War for the World.*

2. On an outline map of the Pacific area, indicate, with dates, the important military and naval engagements which led to the defeat of Japan.

3. Select some military, naval, or air engagement in which you are especially interested. Prepare a three- or four-minute report to the class.

4. Organize a committee to prepare an exhibit of pictures which illustrate World War II. Helpful sources: Old magazines and Life, *Picture History of World War II.*

5. Prepare a table, with dates, of the conferences that were held by the leaders of the United Nations during the war. Indicate the important leaders present at each conference, and briefly state the major decisions reached at these conferences.

6. The conferences held at Teheran, Yalta, and Potsdam have been the subject of considerable criticism in the postwar period. Write a brief report on the nature of this criticism, indicating your own point of view. Helpful sources: Commager, *Documents,* Nos. 553, 554, 556, 560; Churchill, *Closing the Ring;* Sherwood, *Roosevelt and Hopkins;* Link, *American Epoch;* Amherst Series, *The Yalta Conference.*

7. Report on the part played by the countries of South America in World War II.

8. Compare Wilson's leadership in World War I and Roosevelt's leadership in World War II. Helpful source: Hofstadter, *American Political Tradition.*

HIROSHIMA *after the first atom bomb was dropped*

HIGH POINTS

1

The effects of World War I on American life and thought were profound. Among them were: (1) an enormous expansion of industrial and agricultural productivity, (2) the adoption of national prohibition, (3) increased nationalism, (4) cynicism about the reasons for entering the war, (5) a desire to avoid foreign entanglements, especially the responsibility for helping to enforce the peace treaties, (6) fear of Communists and other radicals, (7) the charge by a number of serious writers and artists that American society had become materialistic, (8) the stimulation of scientific research.

2

During the 1920's the majority of Americans had more leisure and a higher standard of living than formerly. They purchased cars and did far more traveling than before. The use of electric lights and appliances grew rapidly. For the first time mass media of communication reached nearly the whole population. Recreational and educational facilities were expanded. The number of high school and college graduates increased. Interest in literature and the fine arts grew.

3

For twelve years (1921 to 1933), the federal government was in the hands of conservative, or "Old Guard," Republicans. They wished to free private enterprise from government control and also to aid business in every way possible. The anti-trust laws were more often used against labor unions than against big business. The labor movement declined. Few business or political leaders gave thought to the need for raising the income of the lower and middle income groups in order to enlarge the market for mass production industries.

4

In the twenties few listened to the aging survivors of the Progressive Movement. However, after the Great Depression began in 1930, the country rang with demands for reform. The reform movement went into high gear in 1933, immediately after Franklin D. Roosevelt became President. The Federal Reserve System was strengthened. The stock exchanges and the sale of securities were placed under federal control. New protection was given to savings bank depositors. Farm incomes were raised, cheaper credit was provided for farmers, and a nation-wide program of soil conservation was established. The Tennessee Valley Authority was set up. Labor's right to collective bargaining received federal support. The use of injunctions in labor disputes was severely restricted. Of all New Deal reforms the most popular was the establishment of the Social Security system.

5

From 1930 to 1940 the nation tried a variety of measures to meet the problem of unemployment. By 1933 one third of the nation's labor force was unemployed. In spite of all its efforts, the New Deal only halved this figure. About one sixth of the labor force was jobless until the United States went to war again. Then unemployment quickly disappeared.

6

The nation's foreign policy between 1918 and 1940 wavered between complete isolationism and limited international co-operation. Congress and the general public usually moved toward isolationism. Such efforts as were made toward co-operation with other nations came from the executive branch of the government. Even

President Harding, who favored isolation, sent observers to certain meetings called by the League of Nations. Under Presidents Coolidge, Hoover, and Roosevelt the United States took an increasingly active part in many League activities of a non-political nature.

7

The Washington Conference called by President Harding in 1921 reduced tensions in the Far East and gave Americans a false sense of security. At that conference the United States abandoned plans for building a navy second to none and agreed that Japan's navy should be supreme in the Far East. In 1940, when we realized that Japan intended to establish control over a large part of Asia, Congress provided funds to double our navy. To avert war, Japan offered to withdraw from Indo-China but not from China. Our refusal to agree was followed by the Japanese attack on Pearl Harbor and Manila. That attack silenced American isolationists and led Congress to declare war.

8

Events in Europe since 1933 had caused Americans more anxiety than the events in the Far East. Beginning in 1935 Congress passed a series of neutrality laws forbidding the sale of munitions to belligerents. In the fall of 1939, when it appeared that France and England might fall under Hitler's yoke, public opinion caused Congress to lift the arms embargo. During the next two years, as Hitler brought all Europe under his heel and as Great Britain fought for its life, Americans gradually came to realize that the Western Hemisphere itself was in danger. The majority approved Roosevelt's policy of giving all possible aid to Great Britain even at the risk of war. Passage of the Lend-Lease Act early in 1941 made us a non-shooting ally of all nations fighting the Axis.

9

The struggle to defeat the Axis was the mightiest war in history. Our whole economy had to be reorganized for the maximum output of arms and food. Our armed forces took part in fighting all over the globe. For eighteen months Nazi U-boats were close to winning the crucial Battle of the Atlantic. Then the Anglo-American navies got the upper hand. In May, 1943, Anglo-American forces drove the Axis from North Africa and soon after invaded Italy. In June, 1944, the Allies landed in France. Eleven months later Germany surrendered.

In the Pacific the Allies had at first met with severe reverses. Singapore, Malaya, Burma, and the Philippines fell early in 1942. For some time Australia and Hawaii were in danger. Then we won several big naval battles. By the end of 1944, our Navy had control of the Pacific. Costly fighting gave us bases close to Japan's home islands, which were then bombarded from the sea and the air. Japan's surrender in August, 1945, was hastened by use of the atomic bomb and perhaps also by Russia's last-minute declaration of war.

10

Before final victory fifty countries met at San Francisco to frame the Charter of the United Nations. The new world security organization had bipartisan support and the charter was promptly ratified by the Senate. The action of the United Nations in selecting the United States as headquarters emphasized the fact that our people were at last accepting a leading part in world affairs.

QUESTIONS

1. Tabulate the chief social and economic characteristics of the postwar decade.

2. (a) Describe the "red scare" which developed in the years following the war. (b) What groups were referred to as "fellow-travelers"?

3. (a) Explain the term "quota immigrant." (b) What were the effects of the abrogation of the gentlemen's agreement with Japan?

4. Explain the conditions which led to the adoption of the Eighteenth Amendment (1919) and its repeal by the Twenty-first Amendment (1933).

5. Why may the term "revolution" be employed to describe the changes in transportation and communication in the postwar decade? What were the social and economic effects of these changes?

6. Why, for the most part, was the decade of the 1920's one of remarkable prosperity? What occupations failed to share in the general prosperity?

7. (a) How did educational and recreational facilities expand in the 1920's? (b) What notable gains were made in research and in public health?

8. What were the chief characteristics of the literature of the period? Of the art, architecture, and music?

9. (a) Why did progressivism give way to normalcy in the 1920's? (b) What actions of the Harding and Coolidge administrations indicated a drift toward conservatism?

10. Why did the regulation of the electric power industry become an important issue? What was the ultimate outcome of this controversy?

11. Describe the presidential campaign of 1928, listing the candidates, issues, and outcome.

12. (a) What were the reasons for the Washington Conference of 1921? (b) Outline the agreements reached at this conference. (c) How was the naval limitation treaty of 1921 modified by the London Naval Conference of 1930?

13. (a) Why did the question of the payment of war debts create friction between the United States and her wartime allies? (b) How was the payment of war debts related to the payment of reparations? (c) What was the Lausanne Agreement? The Hoover moratorium?

14. (a) Why was there a farm depression during the prosperity decade of the 1920's? (b) How did the Agricultural Marketing Act of 1929 endeavor to help the farmer? (c) Outline the provisions of the various New Deal laws designed to help the farmer.

15. Describe the Hawley-Smoot Tariff of 1930. Why did many economists object to this tariff?

16. (a) Why was there a stock market boom in the 1920's? (b) What did President Hoover do to check stock market speculation? (c) What were the reasons for the stock market crash of 1929?

17. (a) What did President Hoover do to stem the ravages of the depression? (b) Distinguish between "direct relief" and "work relief." (c) What controversies developed between President Hoover and Congress over the depression?

18. Explain the "Lame Duck," or Twentieth, Amendment.

19. Explain the Norris-LaGuardia Anti-Injunction Act of 1932.

20. Describe the presidential campaign of 1932, listing the candidates, the issues, and the results.

21. Tabulate and explain the measures of the New Deal designed to provide relief, to promote recovery, and to bring about major reforms.

22. Explain the Social Security Act of 1935. How has this act been amended and improved?

23. What were the provisions of the National Labor Relations Act of 1935? Of the Fair Labor Standards Act of 1938?

24. Why did President Roosevelt propose to reorganize the Supreme Court in 1937? How? What was the outcome?

25. (a) What did President Hoover do to inaugurate the "Good Neighbor" pol-

icy? (b) How did the dispute between Russia and China test the Pact of Paris? (c) What developments in the Far East caused Japan to ignore both the Pact of Paris and the League of Nations? (d) What was the Stimson Doctrine?

26. What were the circumstances and conditions under which the United States recognized Soviet Russia in 1933?

27. (a) Account for the rise of Mussolini to power in Italy; the rise of Hitler to power in Germany. (b) Outline the acts of aggression by Mussolini and Hitler which weakened the League of Nations and alarmed England and France.

28. What were the provisions of the Neutrality Acts of 1935 and 1937? Account for the reversal of American policy represented by these acts.

29. What were the reasons for the Munich Conference of 1938? The results?

30. (a) What were the terms of the Russo-German nonaggression pact of 1939? (b) How and when did World War II begin? (c) What changes in the Neutrality Acts were authorized by Congress? (d) Explain the provisions of the Lend-Lease Act of 1941.

31. Explain the significance of the Atlantic Charter, the Battle of Britain, the Battle of the Atlantic, and the Battle of Stalingrad.

32. (a) On an outline map indicate the gains made by Japan in 1942. (b) Explain the importance of the battles of the Coral Sea, Midway, and Leyte Gulf. (c) Describe the events leading to Japan's surrender.

33. (a) Describe the purpose and the organization of the United Nations. (b) How does the United Nations differ from the League of Nations?

SUGGESTED READINGS

SOURCE MATERIALS, DOCUMENTS,

AND MAPS

Amherst Series. *Franklin D. Roosevelt and the Supreme Court.*

————. *Industry-wide Collective Bargaining—Promise or Menace?*

————. *The New Deal—Revolution or Evolution?*

————. *Pearl Harbor—Roosevelt and the Coming of the War.*

————. *The Yalta Conference.*

Bartlett, R. J. (ed.). *The Record of American Diplomacy; Documents and Readings in the History of American Foreign Relations.* 3rd ed. Knopf, 1954.

Davidson, M. B. *Life in America.* Houghton, 1951.

Hacker, Louis M., and Zahler, H. S. (eds.). *The Shaping of the American Tradition.* Columbia University Press, 1947.

Langsam, W. C., and Egan, M. (eds.). *Documents and Readings in the History of Europe Since 1918.* Lippincott, 1951.

Plischke, Elmer (ed.). *International Relations: Basic Documents.* Van Nostrand, 1953.

GENERAL REFERENCES

* Adams, Samuel Hopkins. *Incredible Era: The Life and Times of Warren Gamaliel Harding.* Houghton, 1939.

* Allen, Frederick L. *Only Yesterday: An Informal History of the Nineteen Twenties.* Harper, 1931.

* ————. *Since Yesterday: The Nineteen Thirties in America.* Harper, 1940.

Bailey, Thomas A. *Diplomatic History.*

Baxter, James P. *Scientists against Time.* Little, Brown, 1946.

* Bliven, Bruce, *The Story of D-Day.* Random House, 1956.

Bradley, David J. *No Place to Hide.* Little, Brown, 1948.

* Brogan, D. W. *The Era of Franklin D. Roosevelt.* Yale University Press, 1950.

Burlingame, Roger. *Backgrounds of Power: The Human Story of Mass Production.* Scribner, 1949.

Churchill, Winston S. *The Second World War.* 6 vols. Houghton, 1948–53.

Dulles, Foster R. *America's Rise to World Power, 1898–1954.* Harper, 1955. (N.A.N.)

————. *Labor in America.* Crowell, 1949.

————. *Twentieth Century America.* Reynal and Hitchcock, 1945.

Eisenhower, Dwight D. *Crusade in Europe.* Doubleday, 1948.

Faulkner, Harold U., and Starr, M. *Labor in America.* Harper, 1949.

755

Feis, Herbert. *The Road to Pearl Harbor.* Princeton University Press, 1950.

Hersey, John. *Hiroshima.* Knopf, 1946.

Hicks, *American Nation.*

° Janeway, Eliot. *The Struggle for Survival.* Yale University Press, 1951. (Y.C.S.)

Kennan, George. *American Diplomacy, 1900–1950.* University of Chicago Press, 1952.

Langer, William M., and Gleason, S. E. *The Challenge to Isolation, 1937–1940.*

° Lawson, Ted, and Considine, Bob. *Thirty Seconds over Tokyo.* Random House, 1953.

Lilienthal, David. *TVA: Democracy on the March.* Harper, 1953.

Lindbergh, Charles A. *The Spirit of St. Louis.* Scribner, 1953.

Lord, Walter. *Day of Infamy.* Holt, 1957.

Lyons, Eugene. *Red Decade.* Bobbs-Merrill, 1941.

° Merz, Charles. *Dry Decade.* Doubleday, 1931.

Millis, Walter. *This Is Pearl! The United States and Japan, 1941.* Morrow, 1947.

Morgenstern, George E. *Pearl Harbor: The Story of the Secret War.* Devin-Adair, 1947.

° Nevins, Allan. *The New Deal and World Affairs.* Yale University Press, 1950.

° ——. *The United States in a Chaotic World, 1918–1933.* Yale University Press, 1951. (Y.C.S.)

° Pratt, Fletcher. *War for the World.* Yale University Press, 1950.

Pyle, Ernest. *Brave Men.* Holt, 1944.

——. *Here Is Your War.* Holt, 1943.

° Reynolds, Quentin. *The Battle of Britain.* Random House, 1953.

Schlesinger, Arthur M., Jr. *The Crisis of the Old Order.* Houghton Mifflin, 1957.

——. *The Coming of the New Deal.* Houghton Mifflin, 1959.

Sherwood, Robert E. *Roosevelt and Hopkins; An Intimate History.* Rev. ed. Harper, 1950.

Slosson, Preston W. *The Great Crusade and After, 1914–1928.* Macmillan, 1931. (A.L.S.)

Soule, George H. *Prosperity Decade; From War to Depression, 1917–1929.* Rinehart, 1947.

Stettinius, Edward R. *Lend-Lease; Weapon for Victory.* Macmillan, 1944.

Stimson, Henry L., and Bundy, McGeorge. *On Active Service in Peace and War.* Harper, 1948.

Stone, Irving. *They Also Ran.* Doubleday, 1945.

° Tregaskis, Richard. *Guadalcanal Diary.* Random House, 1943.

Wilson, Edmund. *The American Earthquake.* Doubleday, 1958.

BIOGRAPHY

Burns, J. M. *Roosevelt: The Lion and the Fox.* Harcourt, Brace, 1956.

Charnley, Mitchell V. *The Boys' Life of Herbert Hoover.* Harper, 1931.

Farley, James A. *Jim Farley's Story; The Roosevelt Years.* McGraw-Hill, 1948.

° Frank, Anne. *Diary of a Young Girl.* Doubleday, 1952.

Green, Thomas. *What Roosevelt Thought.* Michigan State University, 1958.

Hatch, Alden. *George Patton, General in Spurs.* Messner, 1950.

Josephson, Matthew. *Sidney Hillman; Statesman of American Labor.* Doubleday, 1952.

Lief, Alfred. *Democracy's Norris.* Stackpole, 1939.

° Moses, Belle. *Franklin Delano Roosevelt, the Minute Man of '33.* Appleton-Century, 1933.

° Nicolay, Helen. *Born to Command.* Appleton-Century-Crofts, 1945.

° ——. *MacArthur of Bataan.* Appleton-Century-Crofts, 1942.

Perkins, Frances. *The Roosevelt I Knew.* Garden City, 1951.

Pringle, Henry F. *Alfred E. Smith.* Macy-Masius, 1927.

Pusey, Merlo J. *Charles Evans Hughes.* Macmillan, 1951.

° Romulo, Carlos P. *I Saw the Fall of the Philippines.* Doubleday, 1942.

° ——. *I See the Philippines Rise.* Doubleday, 1946.

Roosevelt, Eleanor. *This I Remember.* Harper, 1949.

Smith, Alfred E. *Up to Now.* Viking, 1929.

Whitcomb, Edgar D. *Escape from Corregidor.* Regnery, 1958.

White, William Allen. *A Puritan in Babylon; The Story of Calvin Coolidge.* Macmillan, 1938.

White, William L. *Bernard Baruch, Portrait of a Citizen.* Harcourt, Brace, 1950.

FICTION

Adams, Samuel Hopkins. *Revelry.* Boni and Liveright, 1926. (Harding era)

Brown, Henry P. *A Walk in the Sun.* Knopf, 1944. (Invasion of Italy)

Gallico, Paul. *The Snow Goose.* Joseph, 1946. (Dunkirk)

Glasgow, Ellen. *Vein of Iron.* Cape, 1939. (Depression in the South)

* Hersey, John. *A Bell for Adano.* Knopf, 1944. (Military government)

Lansing, Elisabeth. *Ann Bartlett Returns to the Philippines.* Crowell, 1945.

* Lawrence, Josephine. *If I Have Four Apples.* Stokes, 1935. (The depression)

* ———. *Sound of Running Feet.* Stokes, 1937. (The depression)

Lewis, Sinclair. *It Can't Happen Here.* Doubleday, 1935. (Possible changes in American government)

* Meader, Stephen W. *Sea Snake.* Harcourt, Brace, 1943. (Submarines)

* ———. *Shadow in the Pines.* Harcourt, Brace, 1942. (Fifth column)

* Michener, James A. *Tales of the South Pacific.* Macmillan, 1947.

Pashko, Stanley. *Ross Duncan at Bataan.* Messner, 1950.

Rayner, Denys A. *The Enemy Below.* Holt, 1957. (Submarine warfare)

Schary, Dore. *Sunrise at Campobello.* Random House, 1958. (Roosevelt's early career)

Shiber, Etta. *Paris-Underground.* Scribner, 1943. (Occupied France)

Thomas, Dorothy. *The Home Place.* Knopf, 1936. (The depression)

Williamson, Thames R. *Beyond the Great Wall.* Bobbs-Merrill, 1936. (Japanese invasion of Manchuria)

BERLIN TODAY. *Out of the rubble and ruins of a bomb-devastated city has risen a modern Berlin.*

757

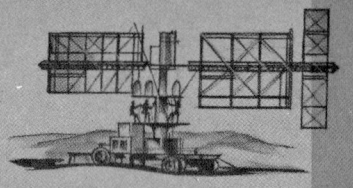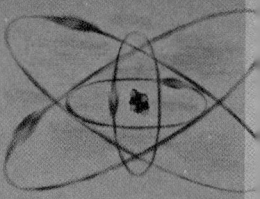

TIME LINE

1945	1945	Harry S. Truman succeeds to Presidency; World War II ends; San Francisco Conference on U.N.
	1947	Presidential Succession Act modified; Taft-Hartley Act passed; Truman Doctrine announced; Marshall Plan introduced
	1948	Universal Declaration of Human Rights adopted by U.N.
	1948–49	Berlin Crisis
	1949	Truman inaugurated; NATO organized
1950	1950	Internal Security Act passed; Korean War begins
	1951	Twenty-second Amendment ratified
	1952	SEATO organized; McCarran-Walter Immigration Act
	1953	Dwight D. Eisenhower inaugurated; Korean War ends
	1954	U.S. Supreme Court bans segregation in public schools
1955	1955	A.F. of L. and C.I.O. merge
	1957	Civil Rights Act; Dawn of Space Age
	1958	European Economic Community formed
	1959	Alaska becomes the 49th state; Hawaii statehood enacted by Congress
1960		

UNIT TEN

★ ★ ★ ★ The six years of World War II violently disturbed political, social, and economic arrangements throughout the world. Russia emerged from the war as the dominant industrial and military power in Europe, and within a few years became a powerful influence in Asia. Central and Eastern Europe also came under Russian influence. France and Italy were weak and torn asunder by factional quarrels. The British Empire was in decline. In the Far East, Japan had lost her position of power. In China, the Communists finally triumphed and forced the remnants of the Nationalist Army to seek refuge on the island of Formosa. Colonial populations in Asia and in Africa were restless and in revolt. There were rising new nationalisms. Everywhere there was a ground swell of demands for status in the world of nations.

During World War II the United States had become the strongest economic, industrial, and military power. After the war it hastened to return to peacetime pursuits, quickly demobilizing its armed forces, and converting to peacetime production of civilian goods. Foreign relations, however, overshadowed domestic affairs. Isolation had become impossible and the United States found itself with many international problems on which it could not turn its back.

The United States became a leader in world affairs. It took an active part in the United Nations. It helped the nations of western Europe to rebuild their ruined cities and industries. It adopted a "policy of containment" toward Russia and its satellites. It entered a military alliance with the countries of western Europe and supplied them money to strengthen their defenses. It intervened, on behalf of the United Nations, to repel a Communist attack on South Korea. By mid-century the democratic nations of the world were once again threatened by a combination of totalitarian powers seeking world domination. A "cold war" developed between the Communist nations and the Western powers. Three important geographic areas became the scenes of near-conflict: the Far East, the Middle East, and Germany. In dealing with the various crises of the cold war the United States has sought to develop a military strength greater than that of any other nation and has used all the nonmilitary means possible.

A mid-century survey of the United States shows that remarkable economic, scientific, and social progress has been made. Productivity has climbed. Prosperity has been widely distributed. If peace and stability in the world could be maintained, the United States should anticipate days of even greater accomplishment.

44. DOMESTIC AFFAIRS IN THE POSTWAR YEARS

The Nation Demobilizes

After the defeat of Japan, a mood of war weariness swept over the United States. Everyone was tired of wartime sacrifices and wartime restrictions. People wanted the men and women in the armed services to come home at once. They wanted an end of rationing and high wartime taxes. Business wanted price controls abolished. Landlords wanted an end of rent controls. As at the end of World War I, Americans longed for a return to "normalcy."

Demobilization is rapid.

Within a year after the end of the war, more than twelve million members of the armed services had returned to civilian life. Nearly all the troops who were overseas at the time of Japan's surrender were back in the United States. Within two years the air force was reduced from 85,000 to 9,000 planes, the army from 89 to 12 divisions, and the navy had withdrawn hundreds of ships from active service. Because of threatening events abroad, the country soon had to rebuild some of the military strength it had so quickly demobilized.

The Congress, in 1947, passed an act merging the army, navy, and air force under a Secretary of Defense.

This important official is a member of the Cabinet. The former Cabinet positions of Secretary of War and Secretary of the Navy were abolished. The merger of our military departments was undertaken in the belief that a united Defense Department would be more efficient than separate departments.

After World War II President Truman urged the adoption of a program of universal military training, often spoken of as UMT. The proposal was favored by military leaders and many veterans. The public generally opposed it. Congress took no action on the proposal for UMT. It did, however, authorize the maintenance of about two million men in the armed services. Hoping to obtain enough men by voluntary enlistment, Congress raised the pay of servicemen and took other steps to make military life more attractive. When enlistments still lagged, Congress in 1948 passed a peacetime draft law. It required the registration of all men between the ages of eighteen and twenty-six. Except during the Korean War, few men were drafted.

Veterans are helped.

Veterans found the change to civilian life made easier by the Servicemen's Readjustment Act, which Congress passed in 1944. Because of the generous benefits it provided, the act became popularly known as the "G.I. Bill of Rights." The G.I. Bill enabled many veterans to go into business, to become homeowners, to go to college, or to take apprenticeship training.

Civilians control atomic energy.

In 1946, less than a year after the first use of atomic weapons, Congress created the Atomic Energy Commission, a board of five civilians. The establishment of a civilian rather than a military board is in harmony with the democratic belief that final authority over the nation's military power should rest in civilian hands. The commission was instructed to carry out research on both the military and nonmilitary uses of atomic energy. The atomic energy law was revised in 1954 to permit the exchange of secret information with Allied governments and to permit the entry of private business into the field of nuclear power.

Industry reconverts.

In 1945, consumer goods were in short supply throughout the world. Furthermore, there was a scarcity of raw materials, fertilizer, steel, machinery, and railroad equipment which interfered with efforts to raise the output of consumer items. In the United States the supply of certain raw materials, especially lumber, wood pulp, oil, and steel, was not sufficient to meet even our own needs. Yet people in devastated areas throughout the world looked to us for help. For several years we exported more goods than we had ever before sent abroad in peacetime.

At the same time our own demand for goods was also larger than ever before. Billions of wartime savings were ready to be spent on homes, automobiles, radios, refrigerators, washing machines, and many other things that civilians could not purchase during the war. To satisfy the huge demand, our industries, which had done an amazing job in producing war materials, did an equally amazing job in converting rapidly to peacetime production. The widespread unemployment that was predicted did not develop. Returning veterans and workers discharged from war plants soon found jobs.

Labor is restless.

During World War II millions of workers earned more than ever before, largely because of the opportunities for overtime work, which was paid for as time and one half and sometimes as double time. The end of the war put a stop to nearly all this overtime work.

Labor grew restless. Most organized workers soon demanded higher hourly wage rates. They argued that wages must be increased because of: (1) the increased cost of living, (2) the loss of overtime pay, and (3) the necessity for maintaining the buying power of wage earners in order to prevent another depression. Employer reluctance to meet such wage demands led to strikes in the automobile, steel, coal mining, and other basic industries. Most unions won an increase in hourly wages and "fringe benefits."

The Eightieth Congress

Republicans gain control of Congress.

In the congressional campaign of 1946, the economic condition of the country strongly influenced politics. The Republicans promised to cut government expenditures, reduce taxes, hold prices in check, and restrain the "arrogant monopoly" of labor. They used the slogan "Had Enough? Vote Republican." The Republicans captured control of Congress. For the next two years President Truman had to deal with a Congress controlled by the opposition.

761

The Twenty-second Amendment.

The Eightieth Congress lost no time in sending the Twenty-second Amendment to the states for ratification. This amendment provides that "no person shall be elected to the office of President more than twice, and no person who has held the office of President, or acted as President, for more than two years of a term to which some other person was elected President, shall be elected to the office of President more than once." The necessary three fourths of the states had ratified this amendment by February, 1951.

The Presidential Succession Act.

In July, 1947, the Republican Congress, responding favorably to a suggestion of President Truman, modified the Presidential Succession Act of 1886. The old law provided that in the event of the death or incapacity of the President when there was no Vice-President, the Secretary of State should become President. The new law said that under the same circumstances the Speaker of the House of Representatives is to succeed to the Presidency. Next in line of succession would be the president pro tempore of the Senate and then the Cabinet members, beginning with the Secretary of State. The change was made in the belief that the President's successor should be an elected official.

The Hoover Commission reports.

Congress, that same year, created the Commission on the Reorganization of the Executive Branch. This bipartisan commission, under the chairmanship of former President Hoover, made extensive studies. It then published a series of recommendations for running the executive branch more efficiently. President Truman carried out a large number of the reforms recommended by the Hoover Commission. One that he approved—namely, the organization of a Department of Welfare—was rejected by the Senate. However, in 1953, Congress did create the Department of Health, Education, and Welfare.

The Taft-Hartley Act is controversial.

The numerous strikes after the war helped to create a demand for legislation to check the power of the unions and make them more fully responsible for their actions. Congress passed the National Labor Relations Act of 1947, better known as the Taft-Hartley Act. The new law amended the National Labor Relations Act of 1935 (the Wagner Act) and was strongly opposed by organized labor. Congress passed it over President Truman's veto.

The Taft-Hartley Act increased the membership of the National Labor Relations Board (NLRB) and enlarged its powers. While the Wagner Act condemned unfair employer methods, the Taft-Hartley Act condemns unfair union methods. It forbids labor unions to coerce either workers or employers in choosing a collective bargaining agency; to compel or persuade employers to discriminate against any worker; to refuse to bargain collectively; to fix excessive fees for admission to union membership; to engage in jurisdictional strikes and secondary boycotts; to adopt "featherbed rules" which require an employer to hire unneeded workers; to use union funds to influence elections to political office.

The Taft-Hartley Act forbids the closed shop—one which makes union membership a condition of employment. Yet it permits the union shop—one which requires a person to join a union after employment.[1] The law requires labor unions to file a notice of intention to modify or terminate a contract sixty days before its expiration. If

---

[1] Since passage of the Taft-Hartley Act a number of states have passed laws forbidding the union shop.

a strike should occur in a key industry, the President is given power to proclaim an emergency and to direct the Attorney General to ask the courts for an eighty-day injunction.

Under the Taft-Hartley Act, a labor union which desires to have the right to appeal to the NLRB must do certain things: (1) It has to file an affidavit from each of its officers saying he does not adhere to Communist principles. (2) A union is also required to file important information with the Department of Labor. It must report the names and compensation of officers; the amount of initiation fees, dues, receipts and disbursements; and the details of insurance benefits.

Labor leaders believed the Taft-Hartley Act was intended to check the spread of unions and to weaken existing unions. They attacked it as a "slave labor law." Under President Eisen-

hower, as under President Truman, Congress held hearings on proposed changes in the measure, but no agreement was reached.

Labor unions increase their influence.

Whatever the merits or defects of the law, labor unions were able to win repeated wage increases. Workers also obtained important "fringe benefits." Part of the gains made by labor appears to be due to a changed attitude on the part of management. "Scientific management" regarded a contented and well-paid worker as more efficient.

In 1955 the A.F. of L. and the CIO finally merged into one large federation of unions. George Meany became president of the new combination. Walter Reuther became vice-president.

The twentieth century has seen the emergence of powerful and responsible labor leaders. The rise of such men as

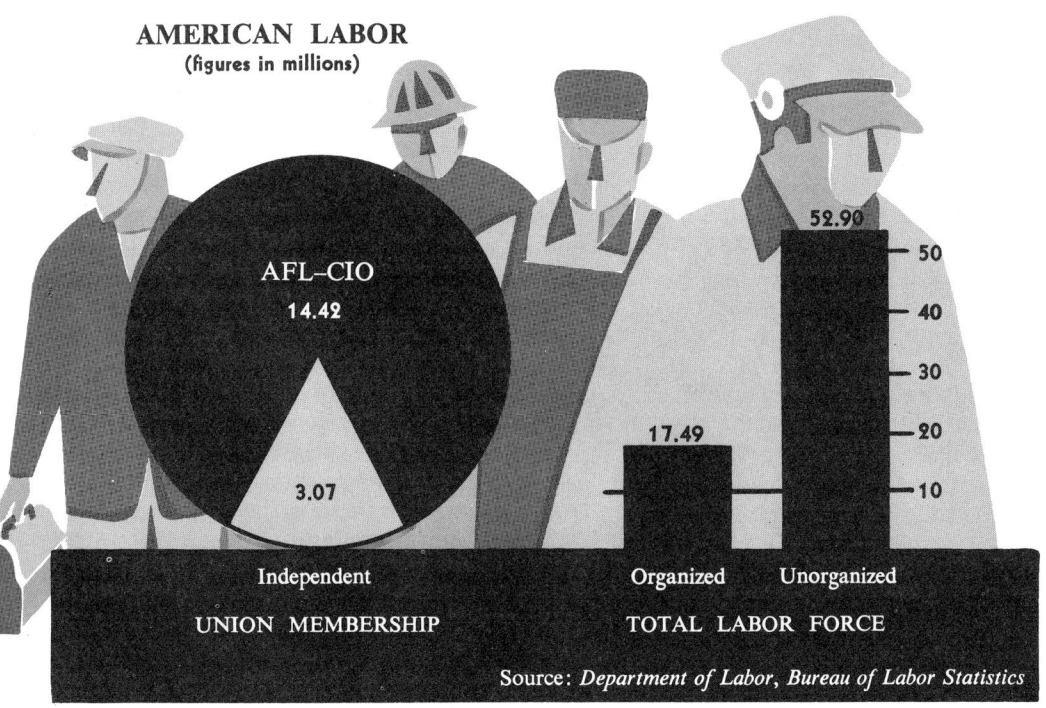

AMERICAN LABOR
(figures in millions)

AFL–CIO
14.42

3.07

Independent

UNION MEMBERSHIP

52.90

17.49

Organized   Unorganized

TOTAL LABOR FORCE

Source: *Department of Labor, Bureau of Labor Statistics*

an important force in politics is comparable to the rise in influence of the businessman in the nineteenth century. Some observers have referred to the mid-twentieth century as the age of "Big Business," "Big Labor," and "Big Government."

President Truman's Fair Deal

Truman surprises the country.

Because the Republicans had gained control of Congress in 1946, many leaders in the Democratic party believed that President Truman could not carry the party to victory in 1948. However, the Democratic convention of 1948 renominated the President and named Senator Alben W. Barkley of Kentucky for Vice-President.

A number of Southern Democrats, referred to as "Dixiecrats," bolted the convention because, at Mr. Truman's insistence, the platform contained a strong "civil rights plank." [1] Subsequently the "Dixiecrats" nominated Governor Thurmond of South Carolina for President. An extreme liberal faction of the party, led by Henry Wallace, also held a separate convention. This faction took the name "Progressive" and nominated Mr. Wallace for President. The Communist party endorsed Mr. Wallace; the Socialist party again nominated Mr. Norman Thomas.

The Republicans were confident of success. After a spirited contest, the nomination finally went for the second time to Governor Thomas E. Dewey of New York. Governor Earl Warren of California was nominated for the Vice-Presidency.

While the leaders in his own party did little to help, President Truman waged a vigorous campaign.

---

[1] It called for guarantees of the right of Negroes to (1) full and equal political participation, (2) equality of opportunity, (3) security of employment, and (4) equal treatment in the armed services.

Although all pre-election polls predicted the President's defeat, he emerged triumphant. The Democrats even recaptured control of Congress. Several factors account for the unexpected results of this "miracle" election —the great discontent among farmers, the failure of Mr. Wallace to lure many votes away from the Democrats, the relatively poor showing of the "Dixiecrats" in the South, the cautious campaign tactics of the overconfident Mr. Dewey, and the vigorous "whistle-stop" campaign of Mr. Truman. The electoral vote was Truman, 303; Dewey, 189; Thurmond, 39.

The "Fair Deal" replaces the "New Deal."

Upon taking office in January, 1949, President Truman gave the label "Fair Deal" to the program which he planned. He declared that "every segment of our population and every individual has the right to expect from his government a fair deal." To a large degree, the Fair Deal program was an expansion of the New Deal.

The Democratic party controlled the Eighty-first Congress (1949–50) and the Eighty-second Congress (1951–52), yet Mr. Truman could not get congressional approval for many of the measures he proposed. The President's steady support of civil rights legislation alienated many Southern Democrats. By means of a filibuster in the Senate, they blocked a federal anti-poll-tax bill and a fair employment practices bill. Enough Southern and conservative Democrats joined with Republicans to prevent the enactment of several other administration measures.

Congress failed to adopt the following items in the Fair Deal program: repeal of the Taft-Hartley Act; the creation of valley authorities, similar to the TVA, for the Columbia and Missouri river valleys; approval of the St. Lawrence Seaway project; the admission of Alaska and Hawaii as states;

provision for federal aid to education; a universal military training program; an improved farm support program; and a system of national health insurance. Congress also showed its independence by overriding the President's veto of the new McCarran-Walter Immigration Act and of the Internal Security Act of 1950.

Scandals are revealed.

President Truman was troubled by the unearthing of scandals which touched some members of his administration. The evidence revealed that businessmen often paid a fee of 5 per cent to individuals claiming to be able to get them government contracts or other favors. Corruption came to light in the granting of loans by the Reconstruction Finance Corporation. Investigation also revealed that a few officials in the Internal Revenue Bureau were guilty of wrongdoing in the handling of income tax cases.

The Fair Deal wins some success.

Despite these setbacks, Fair Deal accomplishments were substantial. The minimum wage rate set by the Fair Labor Standards Act of 1938 at forty cents an hour was raised to seventy-five cents. Federal rent controls were retained in modified form; the Reciprocal Trade Agreement program was continued. Urged on by the President, Congress corrected weaknesses in the Displaced Persons Act and doubled the number of persons to be admitted. Although the President's national health insurance program went down to defeat, Congress did appropriate funds for medical research, a National Science Foundation, and grants-in-aid to the states for hospital construction. Congress also provided subsidies for low-rent public housing. To encourage the private construction of houses, Congress authorized federal loans and federal mortgage insurance. One of the most notable achievements of the administration was the improvement of the social security system. Old age and survivors' benefits were increased. An additional ten million workers were made eligible for old age and survivors' insurance. The new act also provided assistance to needy persons who are totally and permanently disabled.

Early in 1952 President Truman announced that he would not be a candidate for re-election. The twenty-year period of Democratic control came to an end on January 20, 1953.

SENATOR ESTES KEFAUVER *of Tennessee won a national reputation as head of a special Senate committee to investigate crime in interstate commerce.*

Americans Become Concerned over Communism

Ever since the 1917 Bolshevik (Communist) Revolution in Russia many Americans have feared that communism would spread. In the 1920's and 1930's, through their state and city governments, they took various steps to restrict Communists and their activities. After World War II fear of communism became more intense. Congress and the state legislatures placed new curbs on Communists and their sympathizers. Communism was attacked as the enemy of democracy, religion, and liberty.

Karl Marx advocates communism.

The origin of modern Communist or Socialist theories can be traced to the writings of Karl Marx. He was a German scholar who lived in the nineteenth century. Two of his writings had great influence. One was a pamphlet, *The Communist Manifesto,* by Marx and Friedrich Engels, which appeared in 1847. The other was a three-volume work, *Das Kapital,* in which Marx set forth his ideas on capitalism and other economic systems.

Put very briefly, Marx argued that the private ownership of capital goods (the means of production and distribution, such as railroads, farms, machinery, factories) and the use of these goods for private profit were the basic causes of war, poverty, crime, and greed. Therefore, according to Marx, private ownership of the means of production and distribution should be abolished, and some form of social or governmental ownership substituted for it. Marx also argued that there is an *inevitable class war* between the owners of capital goods (the *bourgeoisie*) and the propertyless workers (the *proletariat*). Since no ruling class, said Marx, ever gives up its power and privileges voluntarily, the workers will have to use force in taking over the property of the capitalists. A dictatorship of the proletariat will then be established.

(Left) KARL MARX
(Above) NICOLAI LENIN

Communists and Socialists.

Marx did not invent the idea of a new social and economic system. It had been advocated in some form by visionaries for centuries. Followers of Marx called these forerunners "Utopian" Socialists and regarded themselves as "scientific" Socialists.

In time, many Socialists came to think that socialism could be brought about gradually and peacefully. They sometimes called themselves "Social Democrats" to emphasize their belief in democratic methods, not violent revolution. Social Democratic parties developed in every country in Europe and in many non-European lands. In Great Britain the group was known as the Labor party. In the United States the main group called itself the Socialist party, and its chief leaders were Eugene V. Debs and Norman Thomas.

In 1903 the Social Democratic party in Russia split. The majority, who were followers of Nicolai Lenin, took the name "Bolsheviks." They argued that revolution was near and that when it came a small, well-disciplined group should seize control and set up a dictatorship of the proletariat. The minor-

766

(Above) JOSEPH STALIN
(Right) MAO TSE-TUNG *and* NIKITA KHRU-SHCHEV

ity, who favored a more moderate program, were called "Mensheviks." When the Bolsheviks seized power in Russia in October, 1917, they adopted the name "Communists." In Russia the real power was kept in the hands of the Communist party, which, it is estimated, never included more than 3 or 4 per cent of the people. Hoping that the Communist regime would be overthrown and disapproving of its philosophy and policies, the United States did not recognize it until 1933.

Russia has a series of dictators.

Lenin remained in power until his death in 1924. Then Joseph Stalin, who was secretary-general of the Communist party, became the most powerful man in Russia. Stalin started a series of five-year plans to industrialize the country and make it secure against attack. To pay for this gigantic program of industrialization and armament, the standard of living of the people—always very low—was further reduced. The government became more and more powerful.

The people had even less liberty than they had enjoyed under the czar.

No criticism of the government was permitted. Those who opposed the government were executed or given long terms of forced labor. Even in the fields of literature, art, music, and science, individuals had to conform to the "party line." Both Lenin and Stalin "reinterpreted" Marx's ideas. Communists referred to their basic theories not as Marxism, but as Marxist-Leninist Stalinism. Every Communist was expected to be faithful to these ideas in even the smallest detail. "Deviation" from the party line was punished ruthlessly. At times even prominent party leaders were "purged" or "liquidated."

Under Stalin (1924–53) Russia entered World War II and emerged as a strong industrial and military power. Russia dictated the policies of several satellite countries in Europe. It helped communism triumph in China and extend its influence in other parts of the Far East. Stalin died in 1953, and in 1955 Nikita Khrushchev became the dominant party boss. The world was amazed in 1956 when Khrushchev and other party leaders in Russia openly denounced Stalin's leadership as brutal, tyrannous, and cruel.

767

International communism.

The Russian revolution, Lenin thought, would be the starting point for a world-wide revolution. To lead the Communist parties in different parts of the world, he organized the Communist International, or Comintern. The Comintern was controlled from Moscow. Communists everywhere followed the same "party line." The Communist party in Germany was suppressed when Hitler came to power in 1933. Elsewhere in Europe and in America communism attracted a small group of devoted followers and had the support of some intellectuals. The Comintern devoted considerable effort to stirring up revolutionary movements in the Orient. Colonial and semicolonial peoples were urged to struggle for independence.

Since Hitler made no secret of his desire to fight Russia, Communists throughout the world were ordered to emphasize the dangers of fascism. They urged a program of collective security to keep the Axis from carrying out its program of world conquest. The Soviet Union tried to have the League of Nations take action to prevent Fascist aggression in Ethiopia, Spain, and elsewhere. The Communists expressed a willingness to work with various groups in what came to be called a Popular Front against fascism. As a result, the Communists increased their influence in several countries which felt threatened by Hitler and Mussolini.

The 1937 and 1938 purges in Russia shocked many people and weakened the Popular Front movement. After the Soviet Union signed the treaty of non-aggression and friendship with Germany in 1939, the Popular Front movement was abandoned. During the war, in 1943, as a sign of good will to Russia's allies, Stalin dissolved the Comintern. He revived it in disguised form in 1947 as the Communist Information Bureau, or Cominform. This was dissolved in April, 1956.

768

The Communist party in America.

A number of former Socialists organized the American Communist party in 1919. They joined the Comintern and praised the Russian revolutionary program. In the years before the depression of 1929, they provided leadership in several strikes. They did not, however, capture control of any established union. In 1929, the Comintern directed the American Communists to start organizing new unions. This policy did not meet with much success, since few Americans were willing to join unions led by known Communists.

The Great Depression of the 1930's helped the Communists. They organized demonstrations by the unemployed. They boasted about Russian achievements under the first Five-Year Plan, claiming that Russia would soon surpass the American standard of living. Party membership in the United States increased from about 7500 in 1930 to 25,000 in 1934.

Communists "bore from within."

In 1935 the American Communists stopped trying to organize new unions. They set about to win influence in established unions by "boring from within." The party also worked hard, in many instances with success, to gain control of liberal organizations by planting in each a secret "cell" of Communists. The strategy of "boring from within" was based on a simple formula —the handful of Communists in the organization worked harder than the other members, always came to meetings, volunteered to do the difficult or unpleasant jobs that other members did not want to do, and stood for bold rather than timid policy. When an important matter was to be voted on, the Communists would often succeed in delaying the voting until most of the other members had gone home. Thus a few Communists could exert influence out of all proportion to their numbers.

During the 1930's, as part of the Popular Front movement, the party formed a number of organizations to promote special causes, such as minority rights, world peace, friendship with the Soviet Union, or adult education. These organizations had attractive names, and many non-Communists joined them. The name "transmission belt" or "Communist front" was applied to these organizations because they were under Communist control. Individuals who habitually supported Communist causes and fronts but did not join the party came to be known as "fellow travelers."

The Communist party membership in the United States has never been very large. Estimates have placed the largest actual membership at any one time at about 100,000. However, it has been revealed that a few Communists were not allowed to join the party because it was thought that their influence would be greater as nonparty members. Thousands drifted into the party for a short time and left it when they became dissatisfied with its methods, discipline, and shifting party line.

Fascist groups are organized.

The 1930's also saw the organization of many groups which had Fascist ideas. In general these groups voiced opposition to aliens, labor leaders, pacifists, liberals, Communists, Negroes, Catholics, and Jews. Some took patriotic names like "Defenders of the Constitution." Others frankly admitted their Fascist leanings and chose names like "Silver Shirts" and "Black Legion." Some of these organizations had a considerable following.

Committee on Un-American Activities.

The growth of un-American activities, both on the right and on the left, caused the House of Representatives in 1938 to set up the Committee on Un-American Activities. This committee conducted investigations to expose Communist and Communist-supported activities and agencies. Occasionally it also investigated Fascist organizations. Prior to and during World War II, little serious attention was paid to the committee's findings. Indeed, the committee was even ridiculed by many who regarded Communist agitation as not important. Others argued that the committee itself often used un-American methods and therefore should be discontinued.

After the war, however, public indifference toward communism and toward the activities of the House committee began to disappear. Events abroad, particularly in Poland, Czechoslovakia, Italy, Germany, and China revealed that Communist parties in foreign countries were in reality the agents of Moscow. American opposition to communism was strengthened by Russian foreign policy toward the United States, as well as by Russia's actions in the United Nations. A series of events in the postwar years confirmed the belief that Communist organizations were actually subversive.

1. It was found that a Communist spy ring in Canada had secured important secrets for transmission to Russia (1946).

2. A number of former American Communists testified in court about their activities. Two of them, Elizabeth Bentley and Whittaker Chambers, claimed to have acted as agents for collecting important information for Russia.

3. Acting upon evidence collected by the House committee and the FBI, the Attorney General in 1946 published a list of organizations which the Department of Justice described as subversive. Most of them were charged with supporting the Communist party line; others were Fascist organizations.

4. Some Communists or fellow travelers, it was revealed, had worked

their way into influential positions in the government, labor unions, the entertainment field, and the press. To check the loyalty of present and prospective employees of the federal government, in March, 1947, President Truman established a Loyalty Review Board. During the next few years, as a result of "loyalty probes," about two hundred and fifty federal employees were dismissed and about two thousand five hundred resigned while under investigation. In the meantime, labor unions "cleaned house." The A.F. of L. and CIO expelled Communist-dominated unions and got rid of officers who were regarded as Communists or Communist sympathizers.

5. Whittaker Chambers claimed that Alger Hiss had belonged to a Communist spy ring in 1938, while employed by the State Department. Chambers said Hiss had supplied him with official documents for transmission to Russia. During a series of investigations, Hiss denied the charges. Finally he was found guilty of perjury and sentenced to a five-year term in prison.

6. In 1949, the federal government tried eleven well-known Communists. They had been indicted on charges of violating the Smith Act of 1940, which made it a crime to teach or advocate the overthrow of the government of the United States by force. In their long trial, lasting from January to October, 1949, the government produced testimony based on the writings, speeches, and meetings of Communists over a period of years. Government witnesses included former Communists, as well as secret agents of the F.B.I. who had posed as Communists to gather evidence. The jury found the eleven guilty. Judge Harold R. Medina, at the conclusion of the trial, punished the defense lawyers for contempt of court for the delaying and disruptive tactics they had used during the long trial. Similar trials in other parts of the country led to the conviction of other Communist officials.

7. Early in 1950, Dr. Klaus Fuchs, a German-born scientist who had become a naturalized British citizen, was arrested in England as a Communist spy. Dr. Fuchs confessed that while working in America on the problem of atomic energy he had sent atomic secrets to Russia. A little later, a few Americans were arrested and either confessed or were found guilty of similar activities. Two Americans found guilty of espionage were executed.

These and other events finally convinced the great majority of Americans that the Communist party and its activities were a serious threat to the United States.

The Internal Security Act of 1950.

In September, 1950, Congress passed the Internal Security Act, also known as the McCarran-Wood Act. It provides that Communists or Communist-front organizations must register with the Attorney General, file financial statements, and properly identify their literature. Aliens who are members of Communist organizations may be deported, while Communists or members of any other totalitarian party may not enter the country. The law makes it unlawful to conspire to establish a totalitarian dictatorship or to conceal membership in Communist organizations when seeking government employment. The law also provides that in the event of an emergency proclaimed by the President, Communists may be placed in detention camps.

Congressional investigations create controversy.

In trying to find a satisfactory way of preventing Communist infiltration, the American people were equally interested in safeguarding the fundamental rights of free speech and free assembly. Consequently there was concern over the growing practice of demanding "loyalty oaths" from teachers, over the scrutiny of textbooks for "un-American" or unpopular ideas, and over the tendency of many persons to label ideas or proposals they do not like as "red," "Communistic," or "subversive." There was also considerable discussion of the fairness of applying the principle of "guilt by association" to those who had been members of various front organizations or who expressed sympathy for reforms that happened to have Communist approval.

Lawyers debated whether a person called before a congressional investigating committee was obliged to answer all questions asked. Some witnesses refused to answer questions concerning their past activities, pleading that under the Fifth Amendment one is not compelled to be a witness against himself. Even some who admitted former membership in the party pleaded the Fifth Amendment when asked to name others who may have been party members.

Senator Joseph R. McCarthy, Wisconsin Republican, was particularly vocal in claiming that a number of prominent people had been friendly to communism or sympathetic to Communist causes. He accused the Truman administration of not being vigilant in weeding out Communists. Because of the senator's methods of investigation, the phrase "McCarthyism" came into general use to describe reckless and unsupported charges of "guilt by association" or "sympathy" with communism.

Communist infiltration and McCarthyism were issues in the 1952 presidential campaign. Senator McCarthy was re-elected to the Senate and became chairman of the powerful Committee on Government Operations. He continued to claim that government officials were lax in dismissing individuals with Communist leanings. In 1954 McCarthy made charges against high army officers and even attacked Secretary of War Robert Stevens. The whole nation watched on television while a Senate subcommittee which included McCarthy held lengthy hearings on the charges. As a result of these hearings, the Senate voted to condemn Senator McCarthy for "conduct unbecoming a senator." His influence as a public figure had considerably weakened before his death in 1957.

In 1956 the Supreme Court by a vote of 6 to 3 ruled that the summary dismissal (without trial) of "security risks" in "nonsensitive" or noncritical areas was indefensible. The minority opinion stated, "We believe the Court's order has stricken down the most effective weapon against subversive activities available to the government." The Court minority argued that under the 1950 law the President was granted the power to make rules concerning the loyalty program and that the majority decision "so interprets the act as to intrude itself into Presidential policy making." The majority, however, claimed that it was difficult "to justify summary suspensions and unreviewable dismissals on loyalty grounds of employees who are not in sensitive positions, and who are thus not situated where they could bring about any discernible adverse effects on the nation's security." It would appear that the whole question of loyalty investigations had not yet been resolved.

The loading face of an atomic reactor

FOR IDENTIFICATION

Atomic Energy Commission	Karl Marx
	Joseph Stalin
Nikita Khrushchev	Harry S. Truman
Nicolai Lenin	Henry A. Wallace

bourgeoisie
civil rights
deviation
"Dixiecrats"
Fair Deal
"fringe benefits"
"guilt by association"
"McCarthyism"

Presidential Succession Act
proletariat
"security risks"
Twenty-second Amendment
universal military training

FOR REVIEW

1. (a) Why was there a drastic reduction in the armed services after the war? (b) How were the services reorganized shortly after the war?

2. What were the chief purposes of the G.I. Bill of Rights?

3. Why was control of atomic energy development given to a civilian board?

4. Why was there a rise in prices from 1945 to 1948? After 1950?

5. What was the purpose of the Hoover Commission?

6. (a) Why was labor restless in the postwar period? (b) What demands did labor make?

7. (a) State the purposes for the passage of the Taft-Hartley Act. Outline its chief provisions. (b) Why did labor refer to it as a "slave labor law"?

8. Why were the Republicans confident of victory in the presidential campaign of 1948? To what did they attribute their defeat?

9. What parts of the Fair Deal program did Congress adopt? What parts did Congress fail to enact?

10. (a) Summarize the main teachings of Karl Marx. (b) Differentiate between Utopian and "scientific" socialism.

11. Explain the purposes of the Comintern. Of the Cominform.

12. Explain what is meant by "boring from within," "transmission belt," "fellow traveler," the "popular front movement."

13. What is the history of the House Committee on Un-American Activities?

14. State the provisions of the Internal Security Act.

15. Explain how "McCarthyism" became an important issue. How did it lose its effectiveness?

FOR FURTHER STUDY AND DISCUSSION

1. Why was there anxiety about the possibility of a depression after World War II? What factors tend to explain the absence of a serious postwar depression?

2. In what respects was the Fair Deal based upon the New Deal? How did the Fair Deal differ from the New Deal?

3. What are the arguments for and against a guaranteed annual wage? A federal fair employment practices law?

4. Trace the history of the Communist party in the United States since 1919, emphasizing its tactics and strategy during the depression, during the war, and in the postwar period.

5. What methods were used by President Truman to prevent the employment of Communists by the federal government? By President Eisenhower?

FOR INDIVIDUAL OR GROUP ACTIVITIES

1. (a) Report on President Truman's veto of the Internal Security Act of 1950. (b) To what extent have events tended to support or refute the soundness of the reasons advanced by President Truman for his veto? Helpful source: Amherst Series, *Loyalty in a Democratic State.*

2. Hold a panel discussion on the functions and procedures of congressional investigating committees.

3. Prepare a report on Whittaker Chambers' book, *Witness;* on the publication of President Truman's Committee on Civil Rights, *"To Secure These Rights;"* on J. Edgar Hoover's *Masters of Deceit.*

4. Hold a panel discussion on the influence of the civil rights issue on the Democratic and Republican parties since 1945.

5. Report on the constitutional privilege against self-incrimination. Helpful source: *Annals* of the American Academy of Political and Social Science: "Internal Security and Civil Rights," July, 1955.

45. THE COLD WAR

Friction Develops among the Victors

World War II reduced the strong
nations of the world to two—the
U.S.S.R. and the United States. Each
possessed immense resources and military might. Each differed from the
other in its form of government, its
economic system, its moral and spiritual values, and its attitude toward human rights. Each became the leader of
other nations whose policies are consistent with its own. Yet the two governments might have got along peaceably except for the imperialistic ambitions of the U.S.S.R. and its use of
Communist parties throughout the
world to promote revolution.

For a long time Communist the-
orists had preached the doctrine that
a world revolution was inevitable and
that it would end in the triumph of the
Communist state and way of life.
Events in several countries strengthened the belief that the ultimate aim
of Russian foreign policy was to hasten
the world Communist revolution. The
continuing conflict between the United
States with its free world allies (the
West) and the U.S.S.R. with its allies
(the East) is referred to as the "cold
war."

Tension develops before the war is over.

Even before the war ended there
were signs of friction among the Allies.
Russia remained neutral in the Far
Eastern phase of the war until a few
days before Japan's surrender. Russia
also kept urging the opening of a second front in western Europe. As Russian armies advanced into Poland,
Moscow announced that it would not
recognize the prewar boundaries of
Poland. It indicated also the intent to
incorporate at least some parts of Poland within the Soviet Union. The
countries of eastern Europe—Rumania,
Bulgaria, Yugoslavia, Czechoslovakia,
Austria, and Hungary—were liberated
and occupied by Russian troops. American and British leaders soon had cause
to fear that Moscow intended to make
these countries into satellites and force
them to do its bidding.

During the war the Allies held
several conferences to reach agreement
on common war aims and to adjust differences among themselves. Two of
these wartime conferences sowed the
seeds of future discord: that held at
Yalta in February, 1945, and that at
Potsdam in the summer of 1945.

PRESIDENT TRUMAN *with* PRIME MINISTER CHURCHILL *and* PREMIER STALIN *at the* POTSDAM CONFERENCE

The Yalta Conference.

The Yalta (or Crimean) Conference, held February 4–11, 1945, was the second and last meeting of Roosevelt, Stalin, and Churchill. The declaration published at the close of the conference indicated that the "Big Three" had reached agreement on several points: military plans for the defeat of Germany, policies for enforcing the surrender terms, provision for changes in the boundaries of Poland, and the holding of a conference at San Francisco to draft a charter for the United Nations. After the war ended it gradually became known that the "Big Three" had reached other agreements at Yalta which were not made public at the time. (Not until March, 1947, did the State Department publish the full text of all the Yalta agreements.) These secret agreements dealt with the veto principle in the Security Council, details concerning reparations and occupation zones in Germany, and the price that Stalin demanded for Russian participation in the war against Japan. (See p. 741.) The Yalta Conference, and the secret agreements particularly, became the subject of bitter criticism and stout defense in the postwar years.

The Potsdam (Berlin) Conference.

The Yalta Conference was followed six months later by one at Potsdam, a suburb of Berlin.

The Big Three outlined principles that would control the peace settlements in Europe: (1) A Council of Foreign Ministers (China, England, France, Russia, and the United States) would draft peace treaties for Italy, Rumania, Bulgaria, Hungary, Finland. (2) Germany would be disarmed, discriminatory laws repealed, war criminals punished, and industrial equipment suitable for war destroyed or removed. (3) Germany would be divided into zones of occupation, with Russia occupying East Germany, and England, France, and the United States sharing in the occupation of Western Germany. Berlin, in the Russian zone of occupation, would be jointly occupied by all four nations. (4) Each nation would fill its own claims for reparations by taking German goods or equipment from its own zone of occupation. (5) Poland would receive Danzig and most of East Prussia, but Königsberg and a slice of East Prussia would go to Russia.

One week after the conference, August 8, Russia declared war on Japan, thus carrying out the agreement entered into at Yalta. Soviet armies quickly overran Manchuria and Korea. On August 14, Japan surrendered. Within the next few years nearly all of the agreements made at Potsdam became a source of friction.

The "iron curtain" descends.

The war had scarcely ended when differences between the western Allies and the Soviet Union became more open and more pronounced. In the summer of 1946, Winston Churchill called attention to Russia's unfriendly attitude. He said that Moscow was stretching an "iron curtain" around the little countries of eastern Europe. Friction between the great powers was also reflected in the following ways:

1. *The shifting party line.* While the war was in progress, Russia had given signs of abandoning the extremes

of Communist policy. In 1943 the rights and privileges of the Russian Orthodox Church were re-established. The Comintern was dissolved, and Moscow temporarily stopped its propaganda for a world-wide revolution of the proletariat. In the United States, the Communist party co-operated with "capitalistic democracy" in furthering the war effort. It announced that it would no longer function as a political party.

After the war, when Russia reverted to the fundamental Communist theory of promoting world revolution, Communists in the United States once more shifted the party line. They again took the form of a political party.

2. *Difficulties in negotiating treaties.* The Soviet Union repeatedly gave evidence of its intention to extend its territories and influence. At the end of the war it seized Latvia, Lithuania, Estonia, and parts of Poland and Rumania. Moscow justified the seizure on the ground that this territory had once belonged to Russia. That a majority of the people in any of these areas would have chosen annexation is very doubtful. Great numbers of those who protested against it were exiled to slave labor camps in Siberia.

Since Russia's aim was to extend communism far beyond its own boundaries, the writing of peace treaties was extremely difficult. After many conferences of the Council of Foreign Ministers, peace terms were agreed on for Italy, Hungary, Rumania, Bulgaria, and Finland. The treaties were signed at Paris early in 1947. After that, despite months of effort, the Council of Foreign Ministers made no progress. Late in 1947 they adjourned without setting a date for another meeting.

Years went by before agreement was reached on a peace treaty for Austria. Meanwhile the country remained under occupation. In 1955 Russia finally consented to a joint peace treaty with Austria. Moscow still refused to agree to a peace treaty for Germany or for Japan that was acceptable to the United States and Great Britain.

3. *Failure to agree on atomic weapons.* Shortly after atomic bombs were dropped on Hiroshima and Nagasaki, scientists pointed out that the principles involved in atomic fission were widely known. They said that only the technical "know-how" was secret and that any nation which wished to do so could develop atomic bombs within a few years. Great Britain, the United States, and Canada had worked together in producing the bomb. They announced that the method of manufacture would not be revealed until the new weapon was placed under international control.

The problem of control was referred to the United Nations. The U.N. set up an Atomic Energy Commission made up of all the members of the Security Council and Canada. Our representative, Bernard Baruch, announced the American plan for control of atomic weapons. This plan contained two essential features: (1) an international

RESEARCH SCIENTISTS *at Rensselaer Polytechnic Institute*

775

agency to license, operate, and supervise atomic energy developments in every country; and (2) a system of international inspection which would not be subject to veto. Mr. Baruch stated that when an effective International Atomic Authority was in operation, the United States would destroy all its existing bombs. We would then surrender to the Authority full information concerning atomic energy.

In 1948 the General Assembly of the United Nations recommended the adoption of the American plan by a vote of 48 to 6. Russia's counterproposal was defeated by the same vote. The deadlock over the control of atomic weapons could not be broken.

In September, 1949, President Truman made a startling announcement: "We have evidence that within recent weeks an atomic explosion occurred in the U.S.S.R." Thus it became known that Russia had learned the "secret" of the atomic bomb one or two years earlier than scientists had expected. A few months later the public heard that scientists thought they could produce a weapon many times more powerful than the atomic bomb. This new development in nuclear physics was referred to as a hydrogen bomb, or H-bomb, to distinguish it from the uranium-plutonium bomb, or A-bomb. The first H-bomb was tested late in 1952. Some nine months later Russia also tested an H-bomb.

Since then atomic research has made rapid progress. The Atomic Energy Commission built and supervised atomic energy plants, research centers, and laboratories in various parts of the country. Private industrial corporations were granted licenses to build atomic reactors to produce energy for peaceful commercial purposes.

Both the United States and Russia conducted tests with A-bombs and H-bombs. Whether or not governments should discontinue the testing of nuclear weapons became a subject of controversy. It was argued that the effects of radioactive "fall-out" were sufficiently dangerous for governments to stop testing nuclear weapons. In 1958 Russia announced that she would abandon future tests and urged the United States to do likewise. The United States proceeded with scheduled tests in the spring and summer of that year but indicated that it might be willing to enter into an international agreement concerning future tests.

A Policy of Containment

Not long after the war, as relations with the Soviet Union grew worse, the United States gradually adopted a new foreign policy, referred to as "containment." This new policy had three related aims: (1) to stop Soviet expansion, (2) to weaken the Communist movement in non-Communist lands, (3) to strengthen democracy and promote economic well-being in non-Communist lands.

The Truman Doctrine.

Our first strong effort to check Soviet expansion came in 1947, when we began to give military aid to Greece and Turkey. A civil war was going on in Greece. It seemed likely that the Communist rebels would seize the government. It was known that they were receiving aid from Bulgaria, Yugoslavia, and Albania. (Communists had seized control in these countries and also in Poland, Rumania, and Hungary.) Meanwhile, Russia was bringing pressure on Turkey for control of the Dardanelles, the straits that connect the Black Sea with the Mediterranean. If Communist designs in Greece and Turkey succeeded, the Soviet Union would dominate the eastern Mediterranean and could interfere with traffic through the Suez Canal. In March, 1947, President Truman told Congress that both Greece and Turkey had asked for economic and military aid from America. He requested $400,000,000 for this purpose, saying that "it must be the policy of the United States to support free peoples who are resisting attempted subjugation by armed minorities or outside pressures." This policy is known as the "Truman Doctrine."

After much debate, Congress voted the money which the President asked. American military missions were sent to Greece and Turkey to help in training their armed forces. The Greek and Turkish armies were supplied with modern equipment. A network of military roads was built in Turkey. Fighting in Greece came to an end in the summer of 1949. By that time the military and economic aid which we had given to Greece and Turkey amounted to one and a half billion dollars. It strengthened them and made them allies of the West.

The Marshall Plan.

In June, 1947, Secretary of State Marshall made a speech directing attention to the widespread misery in Europe and to the urgent need of a program to bring about economic recovery. He suggested that the European nations hold a conference to list their economic needs and resources, to work out a blueprint for aiding one another, and to decide how the United States could help them to help themselves.

Marshall's proposals led to the Conference for European Economic Co-operation, which met at Paris in July, 1947. Sixteen nations were represented. At first Russia acted as though it would take part in the conference. Then it withdrew and directed its satellites to do likewise. The conference worked out a four-year plan for economic recovery. The plan showed how the participating countries could help one another and the kinds of goods they

GEORGE C. MARSHALL

must have from the United States in order to feed their people and rebuild their basic industries.

In the fall of 1947, Congress appropriated 540 million dollars as "interim aid" to France, Italy, and Austria. Early the next year, Congress began debate on financing the European Recovery Program (ERP). Had it not been for the strong support of Senator Arthur Vandenberg, chairman of the Senate Foreign Relations Committee, and for the Communist *coup d'état* in Czechoslovakia (see p. 778), the measure might have been defeated. In April, 1948, Congress passed the Economic Co-operation Act, with an appropriation of 5.3 billion dollars for the first year of the program. Soon the Economic Co-operation Administration (ECA) was shipping large quantities of food, raw materials, and industrial and agricultural machinery to the co-operating European nations.

The ERP was remarkably successful in restoring industrial and agricultural production. Within a few years European industrial activity caught up with and surpassed that of the prewar years. The political effects of the Marshall Plan funds were equally important. This aid undoubtedly checked the spread of communism in western Europe.

Russia reacts to the Marshall Plan.

1. *The Cominform.* In September, 1947, Communist leaders from nine

777

countries met in Poland. They came from Russia, Poland, Hungary, Rumania, Yugoslavia, Bulgaria, Czechoslovakia, France, and Italy. The conference decided to establish a Communist Information Bureau, known as the "Cominform" (see p. 766). The Cominform declared war on the Marshall Plan, stating that it was a scheme by which the United States would undermine the independence of the nations taking part in it. Moscow proposed the "Molotov Plan" instead to encourage the exchange of goods between Russia and its satellites and to link them more firmly to the Soviet Union.

2. *The Berlin crisis, 1948–49.* Russian leaders turned down the proposal of France, Britain, and the United States to hold free elections in Germany. By 1948, therefore, the three western Allies were planning to merge their occupation zones in Germany and to establish a Federal Republic of West Germany. Shortly after these plans were announced, the Soviet Union, which controlled the roads and railroads leading out of Berlin, cut off all traffic to that city from the West. As an excuse for the blockade, Russian leaders said they objected to a proposed currency reform in Berlin. The real purpose, however, was to force the Western powers out of the city, and to make them abandon their plans for the West German Republic. Russia's aim was eventually to bring all of Germany under Communist control.

Berlin is about one hundred miles inside the Russian zone of occupation. The two million people in the American, French, and British zones of the city were dependent on imports from West Germany. The blockade meant that they would be without food, fuel, and other essentials. The United States and Great Britain declared that they would not be forced out of Berlin. They undertook to send necessary supplies to the city by air. The ingenious, daring, and costly "Berlin airlift" was a spectacular success. After it had continued for a year, Moscow decided to end the blockade.

3. *The Communist coup in Czechoslovakia.* The Communists in Czechoslovakia were a small but well-organized minority. In the early months of 1948 they executed a *coup d'état* and took over complete control of the government. Their seizure of power in Czechoslovakia helped to arouse people in other democratic lands to the menace of communism.

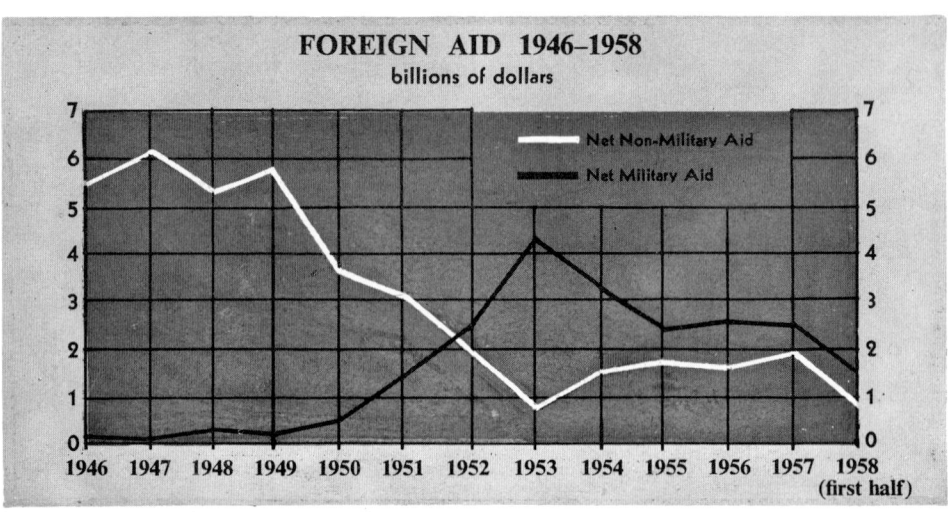

FOREIGN AID 1946–1958
billions of dollars

The United States supports "Titoism."

As a result of World War II, Communists under the leadership of Marshal Tito secured control of Yugoslavia. At first Yugoslav Communist leaders, like those in France and Italy, took part in the Cominform. As time passed, Yugoslav communism became nationalistic, and Marshal Tito refused to follow Russian dictates in all particulars. In June, 1948, Moscow denounced Tito as a "deviationist" and urged the Yugoslavs to oust him from power. Tito, however, remained in power and began to co-operate with the West.

"Titoism"—the effort of a Communist country to establish its independence from Russia—spread to other Red satellites in eastern Europe. Uprisings occurred, first in East Germany (1953), then in Poland and Hungary (1956). In each case Russia replied with armed force. The prolonged, heroic resistance of the Hungarians aroused the sympathy of the entire free world.

Economic aid to underdeveloped lands.

After the Marshall Plan had been in operation about a year, President Truman in his 1949 inaugural address declared: "We must embark on a bold new program for making the benefits of our scientific and industrial progress available for the improvement and growth of underdeveloped areas." Since this suggestion was the fourth point in his address, the program of aid to underdeveloped areas came to be known as the Point IV Program. After months of delay Congress appropriated about thirty-four million dollars to launch the program. The money was used on projects designed to increase the food supply and to fight disease in different parts of the world.

The United Nations in the meantime began to provide technical aid to countries wishing to improve their agriculture, industry, transportation, health, and education. The United Nations Technical Assistance program and our Point IV program are important agencies for improving the productivity and the health of underdeveloped areas. They are also effective weapons for fighting Communist propaganda in impoverished areas where the people might be misled into accepting communism as a way of improving their lot.

Mutual Security Agreements

The North Atlantic Alliance is formed.

The European Recovery Program was soon followed by diplomatic and military co-operation among the Western nations. The Berlin crisis of 1948–49 dramatized the danger that German Communists, with Russian support, would seize control of all Germany. If this happened, France and Italy, in each of which there was a large Communist minority, would probably soon find themselves in the Communist fold. The remaining countries of western Europe, under pressure from without and within, might then become Communist states. Great Britain and the United States believed that their own safety depended on saving western Europe from communism. Accordingly they proposed that the countries fringing the Atlantic join in a mutual defense pact. In the summer of 1948 the American Senate approved the Vandenberg Resolution declaring that the United States would give its support to such a pact. Encouraged by this action, diplomats worked out the details of the North Atlantic Treaty, which went into effect August 24, 1949.

The original signers of the treaty were the United States, Canada, Great Britain, France, Belgium, the Netherlands, Luxemburg, Norway, Denmark, Iceland, Italy, and Portugal. These nations agreed "to maintain and develop their individual capacity to resist attack." They also agreed to consider that an attack against any one of them is

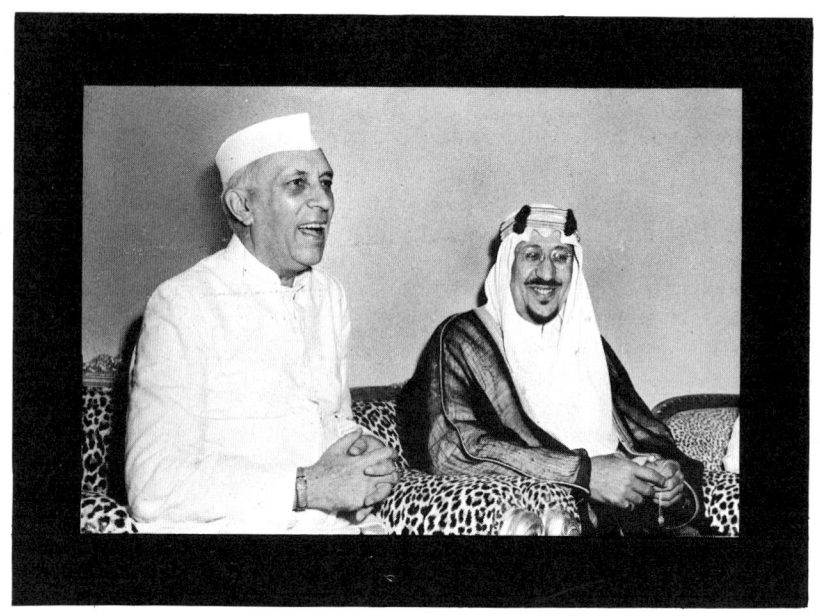

Prime Minister Nehru of India visits King Saud of Saudi Arabia.

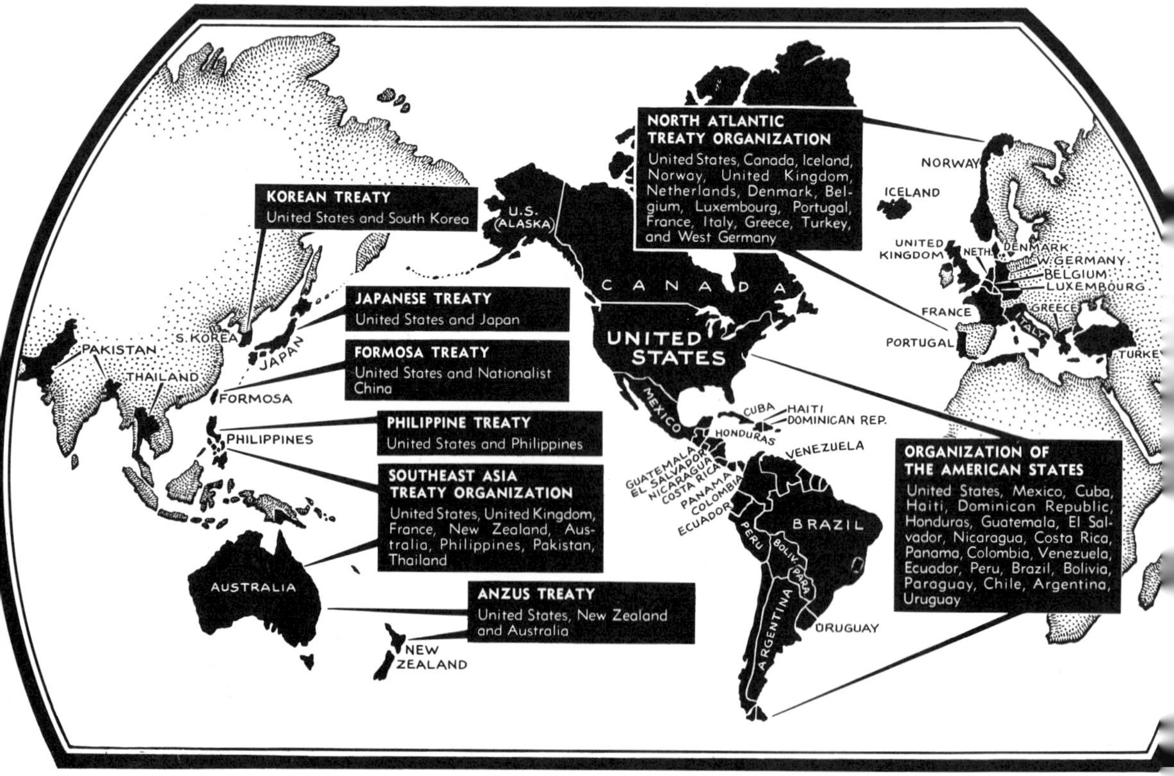

NORTH ATLANTIC TREATY ORGANIZATION
United States, Canada, Iceland, Norway, United Kingdom, Netherlands, Denmark, Belgium, Luxembourg, Portugal, France, Italy, Greece, Turkey, and West Germany
KOREAN TREATY
United States and South Korea
JAPANESE TREATY
United States and Japan
FORMOSA TREATY
United States and Nationalist China
PHILIPPINE TREATY
United States and Philippines
SOUTHEAST ASIA TREATY ORGANIZATION
United States, United Kingdom, France, New Zealand, Australia, Philippines, Pakistan, Thailand
ANZUS TREATY
United States, New Zealand and Australia
ORGANIZATION OF THE AMERICAN STATES
United States, Mexico, Cuba, Haiti, Dominican Republic, Honduras, Guatemala, El Salvador, Nicaragua, Costa Rica, Panama, Colombia, Venezuela, Ecuador, Peru, Brazil, Bolivia, Paraguay, Chile, Argentina, Uruguay
U.S. (ALASKA)
CANADA
UNITED STATES
MEXICO
CUBA
HAITI
DOMINICAN REP.
HONDURAS
GUATEMALA
EL SALVADOR
NICARAGUA
COSTA RICA
PANAMA
COLOMBIA
ECUADOR
VENEZUELA
BRAZIL
PERU
BOLIV.
PARA.
ARGENTINA
URUGUAY
NORWAY
ICELAND
UNITED KINGDOM
NETH.
DENMARK
W. GERMANY
BELGIUM
LUXEMBOURG
FRANCE
PORTUGAL
GREECE
ITALY
TURKEY
PAKISTAN
S. KOREA
JAPAN
THAILAND
FORMOSA
PHILIPPINES
AUSTRALIA
NEW ZEALAND

UNITED STATES ALLIANCES

"an attack against them all" and to assist the one attacked. They established the North Atlantic Council to make plans for joint defense. Greece and Turkey became members of the North Atlantic Treaty Organization—NATO—in 1952; West Germany became a member in 1955.

Western Europe rearms.

As soon as the treaty was signed, Congress made the first in a series of appropriations to help the NATO partners rearm. The North Atlantic Council worked out the details of the rearmament program. The United States established naval and air bases in several of the member countries. General Dwight D. Eisenhower was summoned from retirement to become the first Supreme Commander of NATO forces.

The European Defense Community.

In May, 1952, six European countries organized the European Defense Community (EDC), agreeing to form a six-nation army. The same countries organized the European Coal and Steel Community to unite all of their coal and steel industries into one free market. Neither agreement worked out as originally planned. However, the political and economic aspects underlying both led in 1958 to the formation of the European Economic Community (E.E.C.). This union of western European countries, known as the Common Market, looks toward political confederation with increased economic efficiency. How it will operate in the free world economy remains to be seen.

A "peace contract" with West Germany.

By 1949 it was clear that Russia would not agree to the unification of Germany unless a Communist government were established there. The United States, along with England and France, encouraged the organization of the West German Federal Republic.

Russia established in its zone the East German Democratic Republic. The first chancellor of the West German Federal Republic—also referred to as the Bonn government—was Dr. Konrad Adenauer. Under his leadership, West Germany achieved a fairly stable democratic government and made a remarkable economic recovery.

In spite of protests from Russia, the United States concluded a "peace contract" with West Germany. Congress ratified the contract in 1952. Two years later accords were reached which restored the sovereignty of West Germany and permitted limited rearmament.

The Cold War Extends to Asia

Meanwhile, other disturbing conflicts have flared up in different parts of the world. In Asia not only the "cold war" but the actual clash of armies has challenged the world leadership of the United States and the effectiveness of the United Nations.

Postwar changes in southern Asia.

Shortly after World War II, England gave up her dominant position in southern Asia. Burma withdrew from the British Commonwealth of Nations and became an independent nation. The great Indian subcontinent was divided into two self-governing dominions—India and Pakistan. Both remained within the British Commonwealth. Both appeared anxious to avoid entanglements and to concentrate their energies on domestic recovery. Prime Minister Nehru of India emerged as an important world figure. As time passed, he played the role of "neutralist" in the cold war. India, for example, did not join in the United Nations vote condemning Communist China as the aggressor in the Korean War. India was one of the first countries to recognize

(Above) GUM, *a government-owned department store in Moscow*
(Below) *University of Moscow*

the Communist regime in China. By cautious diplomacy Prime Minister Nehru endeavored to avoid taking sides in the dispute between East and West.

Fighting broke out in the East Indies when the Dutch returned there after the defeat of Japan. In 1949, through the good offices of the United Nations, the Netherlands finally recognized the independence of the rich and populous islands that make up the Republic of Indonesia.

In French Indo-China, a fertile land inhabited by some thirty million people, there was intermittent and bitter civil war for years. As in Burma, India, Pakistan, and Indonesia, the people wanted independence. In Vietnam, one of the provinces, the movement for independence was sponsored by an organization known as the Vietminh. The Vietminh was controlled by Communists and received supplies from Communist China. Although the United States provided financial aid and military supplies, France was unable to suppress the Communist uprising. After seven years of fighting France finally agreed (1954) to withdraw her troops from North Vietnam. This left the Communists in control of that area. South Vietnam and the provinces of Laos and Cambodia soon became independent republics but maintained economic and military agreements with the French Union. The United States gave economic aid to these regions and to the neighboring republic of Thailand. The money was used for roads, railways, and technical assistance.

A peace treaty with Japan is ratified.

Russia had a voice in the Far Eastern Commission which supervised the Allied Occupation of Japan. However, Russia had little influence, because the occupation troops were largely American. Moreover, General Douglas MacArthur exercised a vigorous and almost dictatorial authority in Japan. MacArthur disarmed the Japanese; lessened the power of the militarists, large landlords, and business leaders; secured a law for the distribution of land on easy terms to tenant farmers; and restored civil liberties. He sponsored a revised constitution for Japan, which reduced the authority of the Emperor and established a parliamentary government similar to that of England.

For a long time Russia opposed the writing of a Japanese peace treaty. In 1950 the United States announced that it would not tolerate a "perpetual veto." President Truman turned over the task of working out the treaty to John Foster Dulles. In September, 1951, at a conference in San Francisco, forty-eight nations agreed to the treaty, but Russia still protested against it.

The treaty reduced the territory of Japan to the home islands. Japan gave up Korea, Formosa, and many small islands formerly under its control. (In 1947 the Security Council of the United Nations had named the United States as trustee for the Marshalls, the Carolines, the Marianas, with the right to fortify them.) Japan was allowed to rearm for defensive purposes since it feared both Soviet Russia and Communist China. By a separate mutual security agreement the United States retained the privilege of keeping some troops and air bases in Japan.

The United States sponsors SEATO.

In addition to the mutual security pact with Japan, the Senate ratified two other mutual security pacts in 1952. One was with the newly independent nation of the Philippines; the other, with Australia and New Zealand (referred to as ANZUS). Two years later the United States and England succeeded in establishing the Southeast Asia Treaty Organization (SEATO). It includes the United States, France, England, Australia, New Zealand, the Philippines, Pakistan, and Thailand. All agreed to help one another to resist the subversive activities of international communism. Headquarters for SEATO were established at Bangkok.

The Communists acquire control of China.

When World War II ended, the Nationalists and Communists intensified their struggle for mastery of China. In 1946, the United States sent General Marshall as a special envoy to China. He attempted to get Nationalists and Communists to end their fighting and co-operate politically in a program of reform, but his mission failed. After that, the United States began to withdraw its support from the Nationalists. Many well-informed observers claimed that the Nationalist regime of Chiang Kai-shek was weakened by inflation, black market operations, graft, internal rivalries, and the failure to introduce long-needed agrarian reforms. Under the leadership of Mao Tse-tung, the Communists forced the Nationalists to abandon one stronghold after another.

In August, 1949, the Department of State published a White Paper, reviewing American policy in China. The White Paper declared that the United States had spent two billion dollars to support the Nationalists since the defeat of Japan without satisfactory results. Therefore, the report stated, it would be futile to spend any more.

Toward the close of 1949, Mao's military successes forced Chiang Kai-shek to withdraw the remnants of his Nationalist army—about 500,000 men— to the island of Formosa. Chiang Kai-shek claimed that the Nationalist government on Formosa was the real government of China. Yet Mao Tse-tung and the Communists were in actual control of China proper. India, England, Russia, and several other powers soon recognized the Communist government. But the United States refused to recognize it.

Russia protested the representation of Nationalist China, instead of Communist China, in the United Nations, where China is entitled to a permanent seat in the Security Council. To emphasize its protest, Russia refused to take part in the deliberations of the Security Council between January and August, 1950. (Russia was to regret its walkout when the Korean crisis came before the Security Council for decision. See p. 783.) In February, 1950, Russia and Communist China concluded a treaty that established close ties between them. Subsequent events brought about still closer collaboration.

Our "China policy" provokes controversy.

Even before the defeat of Japan, there was controversy both within and without the State Department over our China policy. Should we give more or less financial and military aid to Chiang Kai-shek? When Mao Tse-tung drove Chiang's forces into Formosa, some critics, including a so-called "China lobby," blamed the Truman administration for not giving Chiang more help. They claimed that pro-Communist sympathizers had played a part in shaping American opinion and policy. As the debate continued, it centered around the nature and purpose of the Marshall mission of 1946, the White Paper of 1949, the question of recognizing Mao Tse-tung, aid to the Nationalist forces on Formosa, and the possibility of armed intervention to protect them from Communist attack. Congressional investigations dealt with various aspects of the controversy. Our China policy aroused hot debate during the presidential campaign of 1952, and throughout President Eisenhower's administration.

The Korean War Tests U.N.

The Korean peninsula.

Japan secured control of Korea as one of the prizes of the Russo-Japanese

War of 1904–1905. At the Cairo conference in 1943 (see p. 738), Churchill, Roosevelt, and Chiang Kai-shek agreed that "Korea would become free and independent." When Korea was liberated from Japanese control at the war's end, it was divided into two zones along the 38th parallel. The northern zone was occupied by the Soviet Union, the southern zone by the United States.

In 1947 the United States asked the U.N. General Assembly to take steps to unite Korea under a democratic government. The General Assembly recognized Korea's claims to independence and set up a United Nations Korean Commission to supervise free elections. Russia refused to let the commission enter its zone. The commission supervised an election in the American zone, as a result of which the Republic of Korea was established. In North Korea, Russia set up a so-called People's Democratic Republic. Russia withdrew most of its occupation troops at the end of 1948 but left some of them to train the North Korean army. The United States completed its withdrawal from South Korea in June, 1949.

The Korean War begins.

A year later, on Saturday, June 24, 1950 (Eastern standard time and date), the armed forces of North Korea began a full-scale invasion of South Korea. The attack on the Republic of Korea was a challenge to the United Nations. If the U.N. did nothing, it would be powerless to stop any future aggression. At the request of the United States, an emergency meeting of the Security Council was held. The Council condemned the action of North Korea as a breach of the peace. It called for an immediate "cease fire" and the withdrawal of North Korean troops to the 38th parallel. It asked all members of the U.N. to give aid in carrying out its resolution. The Council was able to act

KOREA

only because at that time the Russian delegate was absent (see p. 782).

To save the Republic of Korea, fast action was necessary. In response to an appeal of the Security Council, President Truman quickly sent armed forces to Korea. He did this on his authority as commander in chief of our armed forces. At the time his decision won praise from the public and from Congress.

A few days after the outbreak of hostilities, General Douglas MacArthur was named Supreme Commander of the United Nations forces in Korea. During July and August the North Koreans forced United Nations troops into the southeastern corner of the peninsula. There a small beachhead around Pusan was maintained. In September the U.N. forces began to counterattack. As a result of a brilliant amphibious landing at Inchon (September 15), the United Nations recaptured Seoul, the capital of South Korea, and drove the enemy back to the 38th parallel. Red China threatened to intervene if North Korea were invaded, but General MacArthur and many diplomats at the U.N. regarded the threat as only a bluff.

GENERAL DOUGLAS MACARTHUR

Upended litters shelter the wounded.

After some debate, the General Assembly authorized MacArthur to move his troops northward. By late October the North Korean forces had been driven back almost to the Yalu River on the border between Korea and Manchuria.

Communist China intervenes.

Late in November, MacArthur ordered a general advance, hoping to crush all enemy resistance before Christmas. But with dramatic suddenness the war changed. A large army of Chinese Communist "volunteers" came to help the North Koreans. A powerful Chinese thrust split the U.N. forces in two. Many were taken prisoner. Within a few weeks the Chinese pushed the U.N. troops below the 38th parallel and recaptured Seoul. Then the U.N. forces checked the enemy attack and began a series of cautious advances. By the end of March, 1951, they had reached the 38th parallel for the second time.

Truman dismisses MacArthur.

At this point General Douglas MacArthur became the central figure in a controversy over the basic objectives of the Korean War and over the way it should be fought. When the Chinese entered the war in large numbers, MacArthur argued that the character of the war had changed. He wanted permission to bomb the enemy bases in Manchuria. He also wanted to blockade the China coast, and to allow the Nationalist forces on Formosa to attack China. President Truman, his advisors, and the leaders of other countries which had sent soldiers to Korea believed it would be unwise to carry the war outside of Korea. They feared that if China were attacked on its own soil, Russia might go to its defense and the Korean "police action" would become a global war.

On April 11, 1951, President Truman relieved MacArthur of his command, declaring that "We do not want to see the conflict in Korea extended. We are trying to prevent world war, not start one. . . . I have, therefore, considered it essential to relieve General MacArthur so that *there could be no doubt or confusion as to the real purpose and aim of our policy.*"

General MacArthur, who was greatly honored and admired by the American people for his many services, returned to the United States after an absence of fifteen years. He received a tumultuous welcome in several cities. On April 19, he was given the privilege of addressing a joint session of Congress. Here he outlined his point of view and stated, "In war there is no substitute for victory."

Armistice negotiations drag on.

A Senate committe held exhaustive hearings on MacArthur's dismissal. MacArthur testified at length. The Joint Chiefs of Staff also testified, explaining why they endorsed the policy of "limited war" in Korea. They stated that the moves MacArthur advocated would mean full-scale war with China, which might last a long time and exhaust our resources. The real enemy, they said, was Russia, which would probably assist China and might also overrun Europe while we were occupied in the Far East.

MacArthur was replaced by General Matthew Ridgway. Heavy fighting continued near the 38th parallel, but neither side gained much ground. In July, 1951, truce talks began. Discussion over the terms of a truce went on intermittently for more than two years. The principal stumbling block was the Red demand that all prisoners be repatriated, even against their will. About a third of the prisoners captured by the U.N. were unwilling to return to North Korea or China. U.N. negotiators insisted that no prisoner should be forced to return.

For several months after negotiations began there was a lull in the ground fighting. But later, when the armistice talks seemed to be getting nowhere, fighting was resumed. Both sides sought to hold onto or to capture strategic hills and ridges. The air war stepped up in intensity. More Russian-built planes entered the war than before. Jet-propelled airplanes, as well as other new weapons of attack and defense, were being tested by both sides.

The stalemate in Korea became a major issue in the presidential campaign of 1952. Before his inauguration President-elect Eisenhower made a brief inspection trip to Korea. The new administration let it be known that unless a truce were concluded in a reasonable time, it would resort to other means to end the stalemate.

Stalin died in March, 1953, and the new Russian leaders, temporarily at least, appeared to be more conciliatory toward the West. Within a few weeks a compromise agreement on the exchange of prisoners was worked out. The armistice was finally signed late in July, 1953, and the fighting ceased— three years after it began.

End of the Korean War.

Thus the costly Korean War ended in stalemate. In Europe and America there was satisfaction, but little rejoicing, over the signing of the truce. The war had devastated South Korea and inflicted over a million casualties. The financial cost of the war to the United States was estimated at more than twenty-two billion dollars.

The United Nations and the United States had fought for a limited objective. They achieved it. However, President Eisenhower warned the American people that they had "won an armistice on a single battleground, not peace in the world. We may not now relax our guard nor cease our quest."

Successes and Failures
of the United Nations

The "cold war" hampers the U.N.

The structure of the United Nations had been designed in the hope that the great powers which had been wartime allies would co-operate in maintaining peace throughout the world. Unfortunately, as we have seen, World War II was scarcely ended before friction began to develop between Russia and the West. This rivalry between East and West led to the development of what has been called a "Western, or United States, bloc," a "Communist, or Soviet, bloc," and a "neutral bloc."

The Soviet Union used its first veto in the Security Council in February, 1946. Since that time it has cast more than eighty vetoes. In addition, the Russian delegate has "walked out" of the Security Council on more than one occasion, as he did in 1950 in protest over the seating of representatives from Nationalist China.

Mainly because of Russian vetoes, the Security Council has been deadlocked over several important issues—disarmament, the control of atomic energy, and the admission of new states.

For a few years following the war the United States had hopes that the U.N. could function effectively in settling international crises. However, when Russia's excessive use of the veto prevented this it became necessary to adopt other measures. The United States sponsored the Truman Doctrine, the Marshall Plan, NATO, SEATO, and other mutual security pacts. Agreements such as these are permitted under the U.N. charter, which prescribes only that a nation's obligations to the U.N. take precedence over any other international agreements. However, the fact that various regional understandings have come into being does reflect a failure of the United Nations to bring peace to the world. The United States and other members of the "Western bloc"—and the "Soviet bloc," too—have held conferences to discuss mutual problems. All at times have pursued unilateral policies without reference to, or consultation with, the U.N.

The General Assembly grows in power.

While the Security Council has been plagued by vetoes, abstentions, and deadlocks, the General Assembly has grown stronger and more important. The representatives of the smaller nations have used the General Assembly as a forum to build up an international conscience which tends to hold aggression in check. One of the most significant actions of the General Assembly was the adoption in 1950 of a resolution known as "United Action for Peace." It was sponsored by the United States during the Korean War.

The United Action for Peace Resolution provides that if the Security Council, because of lack of unanimity of the permanent members, fails to deal promptly with a threat to peace, the General Assembly may consider the matter immediately. If the General Assembly is not in session, it may be called in a special emergency session within twenty-four hours on the request of any seven members of the Security Council.

In 1951 the General Assembly declared Communist China the aggressor in the Korean War. A little later, it recommended to the member nations an embargo on the shipment of war materials to Communist China and North Korea. Russia claimed that these resolutions were illegal and that the United Action for Peace Resolution was also illegal. However, the resolutions show that the General Assembly might break a deadlock resulting from the inability of the Security Council to take action.

Achievements of the United Nations.

In spite of setbacks the United Nations has achieved considerable success in preventing, postponing, or terminating disputes. Its success has come through public debate, the mobilization of world public opinion, and the persuasive power of moral leadership.

1. The U.N. was largely responsible for the withdrawal of Russian troops from Iran, and of British and French troops from Syria and Lebanon (1946).

2. The conflict between India and Pakistan over the province of Kashmir, which threatened to inflame the Indian subcontinent, was temporarily adjusted. Both sides agreed to a "cease fire" and to a plebiscite, or vote (1948). Agreements concerning a plebiscite were not reached and in 1957 Kashmir was incorporated as part of India.

3. The civil war in the Dutch East Indies was settled through the mediation of the Security Council. The islands became the Republic of Indonesia and were recognized as independent (1949) and admitted to the U.N. (1950).

4. The International Court of Justice has settled a number of legal disputes. The first case was referred to it by the Security Council in 1947 after England complained that its shipping had been damaged when Albania mined the Corfu Channel. The Court held that Albania must pay for the damage to British ships.

5. In 1947 Britain referred the problem of the future status of Palestine to the United Nations. The General Assembly's recommendation for partition into two states, one Jewish and one Arab, was accepted. The new state of Israel came into being in 1948. (The rest of Palestine was added to the Arab state of Jordan.) Israel was admitted to the United Nations in 1949. When fighting broke out between neighboring Arab states and Israel, the United Nations mediators established a truce and prepared the way for a treaty of peace. An American, Dr. Ralph J. Bunche, was the principal mediator. Sporadic outbreaks of violence between the Jews and Arabs continued, however, especially in the Gaza strip. In 1956, through the good offices of Secretary-General Dag Hammarskjöld, a temporary cessation of border incidents was again achieved. Late in 1956 Egypt took over control of the Suez Canal. Israeli troops invaded Egypt, and England and France sent troops to Egypt. The General Assembly obtained a cease-fire agreement and sent U.N. troops to police the Suez area.

6. The U.N., using troops from sixteen nations, succeeded after three wearisome years in checking the aggression against South Korea. The basic problem of uniting North and South Korea remains unsettled.

A genocide convention is adopted.

In 1948 the General Assembly of the United Nations adopted a convention declaring that genocide is a crime under international law. Genocide may be defined as the mass destruction of national, ethnic, racial, or religious groups. The convention characterizes the following as genocide: killing or inflicting mental or bodily injury on members of a group; imposing conditions on a group which will bring about physical destruction; imposing conditions which will prevent births within a group; forcibly transferring children from one group to another. Those guilty of genocide are to be tried and punished in the country where the crime is committed or by an international tribunal which has jurisdiction. As late as 1959 the United States had not ratified this convention.

Universal Declaration of Human Rights.

The General Assembly in 1948 also adopted a Universal Declaration of Human Rights. This declaration is a comprehensive statement of basic human rights and fundamental freedoms—political, social, economic, cultural—which each nation should seek to secure for all its citizens. Among these rights are the right to life, liberty, and security; the right to free speech, free assembly, and freedom of worship; the right to a fair trial, to freedom from arbitrary arrest, and to equal treatment before the law; the right to work, to free choice of employment, to freedom of movement, to join trade unions, to education, to own property; the right to the secret ballot; and the right to a nationality. The vote on this Declaration was 48 to 0, with the Soviet bloc of nations and the Union of South Africa and Saudi Arabia abstaining from voting. The Declaration has had wide influence—for example, in the drafting of the constitutions of the new nations, Israel and Indonesia.

An organization of wide activities.

The range of activities of the United Nations is vast and astounding — from care of refugees to public works projects, from the control of narcotics to a study of the conservation and utilization of the world's resources, from the work of the International Court of Justice to that of the World Meteorological Organization, from the work of the Technical Assistance Program to the drafting of a General Agreement on Tariffs and Trade (GATT). Not all U.N. activities capture spectacular headlines, but they contribute to the promotion of international co-operation and well-being.

In these early years, the United Nations established a record of accomplishment. It has become a new influence in the conduct of international affairs. To appreciate the progress it has made, we must realize the necessarily limited powers with which it works. Its first Secretary-General, Mr. Trygve Lie, made this pertinent comment about the United Nations:

> As a world organization, the United Nations must for a long time to come be an organization of clearly limited powers. How, otherwise, could the old nationalisms of Europe and the rising new nationalisms of Asia and Africa be contained within the same peaceful framework? How, otherwise, could people owing allegiance to different religions and different cultures, sometimes for thousands of years, be brought together on common ground?

FOR IDENTIFICATION

Konrad Adenauer	Mao Tse-tung
Ralph J. Bunche	Prime Minister Nehru
Chiang Kai-shek	Potsdam Conference
Formosa (Taiwan)	Marshal Tito
	Yalta Conference

FOR EXPLANATION OR DEFINITION

ANZUS	Point IV program
"China lobby"	"police action"
"containment"	Titoism
genocide	unilateral
"iron curtain"	Vandenberg Resolution
Nationalist China	Vietminh
NATO	

FOR REVIEW

1. Give some evidences of the friction between East and West before the end of World War II.

2. (a) What was the purpose of the Yalta Conference? (b) What Yalta agreements provoked controversy?

3. (a) What was the purpose of the Potsdam Conference? (b) What were the Potsdam agreements?

4. Explain what is meant by the phrase "shifting party line." Illustrate.

5. Why did difficulties develop in the negotiation of peace treaties?

6. (a) Outline the American plan for the control of atomic weapons. (b) What are some of the important developments in atomic energy since 1945?

7. (a) What conditions led the United States to give military aid to Greece and Turkey? (b) Explain the Truman Doctrine.

790

(Above) *The* GENERAL ASSEMBLY HALL
at United Nations headquarters

(Left) UNITED NATIONS HEADQUARTERS,
New York City

791

8. Who drew up the European Recovery Program? What did it cover?

9. (a) What were some of the direct results of Marshall Plan aid? Some indirect results? (b) How did Russia react to the European Recovery Program?

10. (a) Why and when did Russia blockade Berlin? (b) What did the other occupying powers do to break the blockade?

11. State the nature and purpose of the Point IV program.

12. (a) What conditions led Great Britain and the United States to propose the Atlantic alliance? (b) Why did Congress appropriate money to help the members of NATO rearm?

13. What was the policy of Great Britain and the United States in regard to West Germany? The policy of Russia?

14. (a) List some of the changes in southern Asia that resulted from World War II. (b) What events led to the partition of French Indo-China?

15. What were the terms of the Japanese peace treaty?

16. (a) What mutual security pacts did the United States enter into with countries in the Pacific? (b) Explain the purpose of the Southeast Asia Treaty Organization.

17. (a) Describe postwar developments in China. (b) What was the purpose of the Marshall mission to China? (c) What change in American policy toward China was indicated by publication of the White Paper?

18. Describe the actions of the United States and the United Nations in June and July, 1950, with regard to the invasion of South Korea.

19. (a) Explain President Truman's dismissal of General MacArthur. (b) What is the present status of the truce in Korea?

20. Explain the United Action for Peace Resolution adopted by the U.N. General Assembly.

21. List some major accomplishments of the United Nations and its agencies.

22. What is the purpose of the United Nations convention on genocide? The Universal Declaration of Human Rights?

FOR FURTHER STUDY AND DISCUSSION

1. What were the chief reasons for postwar rivalry between the East and West?

2. In what ways are the Truman Doctrine, the European Recovery Program, the Point IV Program, and the North Atlantic Treaty related to one another? Helpful sources: Schlesinger, *Modern America;* Dulles, *America's Rise to World Power.*

3. Outline the arguments for or against the termination of United States aid to China in 1949. Helpful source: Feis, *The China Tangle: The American Effort in China from Pearl Harbor to the Marshall Mission.*

4. State the arguments for and against the decision to wage a limited war in Korea as the situation existed in 1951. Helpful sources: Rovere and Schlesinger, *The General and the President;* Schlesinger, *Modern America.*

5. (a) What was the purpose of the European Defense Community? (b) What are some of the difficulties to be solved in achieving political federation or unity in western Europe?

6. Compare the Universal Declaration of Human Rights with the Declaration of Independence and our Bill of Rights.

7. Why has the United States hesitated to ratify the convention on genocide?

8. Summarize the main features of the policy of containment.

FOR INDIVIDUAL OR GROUP ACTIVITIES

1. Report on the following: the effects of radioactive explosions; the use of atomic energy in ships.

2. Report on postwar developments in each of the following: Egypt, Palestine, Indo-China, North Africa, Poland, Hungary, Malaya, Tibet.

3. On an outline map of the world indicate the spots where tension between the United States and Russia has developed.

4. Prepare charts which illustrate the cost of American military and nonmilitary help to the rest of the world. Include a chart on the current national budget for foreign aid.

We would do well to think of our accomplishments thus far as but the preface to what we may accomplish in the second half of the century if we can continue to invent, improve, and change —and can keep a good heart.

———Frederick Lewis Allen

DWIGHT D. EISENHOWER

46. THE REPUBLICANS RETURN TO POWER

Eisenhower Becomes President

The GOP turns from Taft to Eisenhower.

The outstanding Republican leader during the Truman administration was the able, courageous, and forthright Senator Robert A. Taft of Ohio. He became known as "Mr. Republican." Many political writers thought him the logical candidate for the presidential nomination in 1952. However, some Republican leaders, particularly in the East, disagreed with Taft's conservatism and with his views on foreign policy. Hence, they persuaded General Dwight D. Eisenhower to seek the Republican nomination.

"Ike" remained in Europe as Supreme Commander of NATO until a few weeks before the Republican convention. A newcomer to politics, "Ike" was genuinely popular at home and was greatly admired and respected abroad. He was nominated on the first ballot. The youthful Senator Richard M. Nixon of California was nominated for Vice-President.

The Democrats nominate Stevenson.

President Truman chose not to run again, although the Twenty-second Amendment, which limited a future President to two terms, did not apply to him. Senator Estes Kefauver of Tennessee began an early and active campaign for convention delegates. He was not acceptable to the Dixiecrats (see p. 764). Seeking a candidate who could unite all factions, the 1952 convention nominated Governor Adlai E. Stevenson of Illinois. Senator John Sparkman of Alabama was chosen for second place on the ticket.

Eisenhower is elected.

Both General Eisenhower and Governor Stevenson conducted vigorous campaigns. The general sought to take advantage of the friction between Northern and Southern Democrats. He became the first Republican presidential candidate to campaign in the South. At the same time he tried to

793

THE ROBERT A. TAFT MEMORIAL *located on Capitol Hill. The upper part of the structure houses a carillon.*

secure the support of the conservative admirers of Senator Taft. Democratic governors in some Southern states publicly announced that they would not support the Stevenson-Sparkman ticket. Governor Stevenson supported the Truman record and tried to avoid offending either the extreme liberal or the more conservative wing of his party.

The election resulted in an overwhelming victory for Eisenhower. In the largest popular vote ever cast, he had 33,900,000 votes and Stevenson 27,500,000. Eisenhower swept every section of the country except the South. Even there he captured the electoral votes of three states—Florida, Virginia, and Texas.

The election was an Eisenhower landslide, however, rather than a Republican landslide. Eisenhower generally ran ahead of the Republican candidates for governor, Congress, and local offices. The Eighty-third Congress (1953–54) was almost evenly divided between Republicans and Democrats.

The Eisenhower Administration Avoids Extremes

Twenty years of Democratic control end.

Eisenhower's inauguration on January 20, 1953, marked the end of twenty years of Democratic control of the national government begun with Franklin D. Roosevelt's inauguration in 1933. The election seemed to indicate, as the Republicans had argued during the campaign, that the people wanted a change. But the new Republican administration brought no drastic changes.

The social and economic adjustments resulting from New Deal and Fair Deal legislation on agriculture, labor, and welfare were well rooted and far-reaching. In these areas the Eisenhower administration did not attempt any basic changes. The nature of world affairs was such that the foreign policy developed by Roosevelt and Truman continued in its major outlines.

Nonetheless, the change meant new faces and a new team, determined to take a new but cautious look at national and international problems. The Eisenhower administration was committed to economy in government and a reduction in taxes. For these reasons, it was not sympathetic to heavy expenditures to finance the social welfare programs of its predecessors. Yet it did not scuttle these programs. As time passed the Republicans sponsored expenditures for housing, roads, education, and improvements in the social security program.

The Eisenhower administration indicated that it would examine carefully expenditures for foreign economic and military aid, with a view to balancing the budget and reducing taxes. There, too, the international situation was such that there were modifications and adjustments rather than abandonment of foreign aid programs. The budget was not balanced until 1956 and the Republicans made only minor adjustments in the tax burden. Probably one of the chief characteristics of the new administration was the determination to check, if possible, the tendency toward the centralization of economic and political power in the federal government.

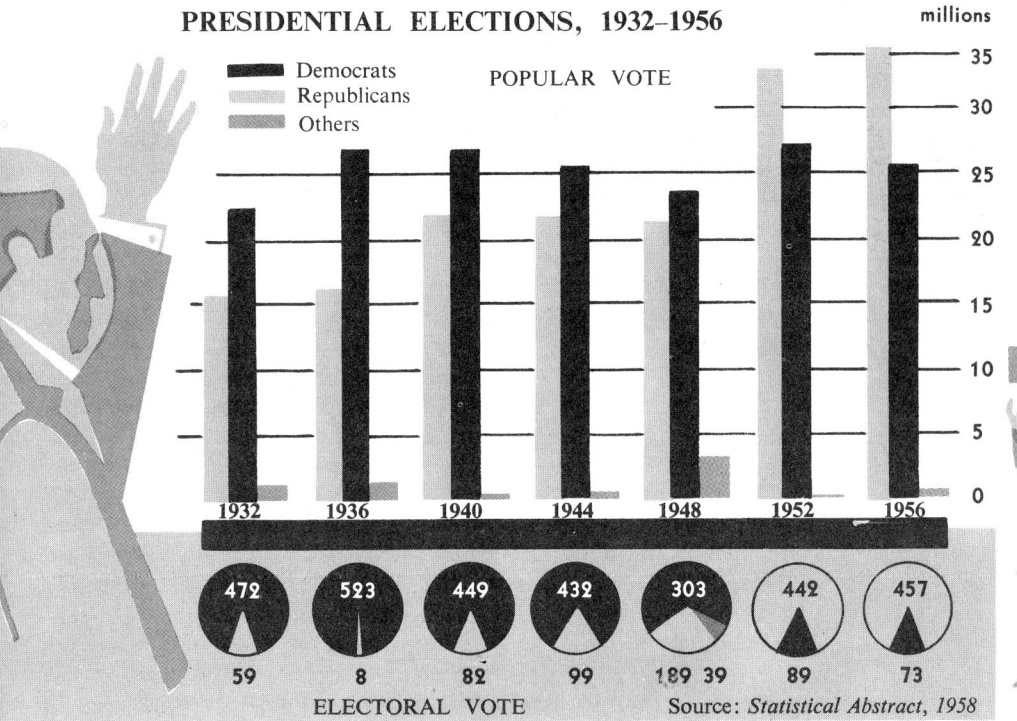

PRESIDENTIAL ELECTIONS, 1932–1956

millions

POPULAR VOTE

- ■ Democrats
- ▢ Republicans
- ▨ Others

| 1932 | 1936 | 1940 | 1944 | 1948 | 1952 | 1956 |

472 59 | **523** 8 | **449** 82 | **432** 99 | **303** 189 39 | **442** 89 | **457** 73

ELECTORAL VOTE

Source: *Statistical Abstract*, 1958

Contrary to precedent, the newly elected President before he took office named the men he intended to appoint to the Cabinet and to other important positions. With few exceptions they were men new to national politics. They were recruited for the most part from the fields of banking and industry. A few months later, when Congress created the Department of Health, Education, and Welfare, Mrs. Oveta Culp Hobby became its first Secretary.

Economic controls are lessened.

In February, 1953, wage controls were lifted. Gradually price controls were removed from various items. Rent controls were retained only in specified areas where there was a serious housing shortage. The Defense Production Act of 1950—enacted to strengthen the national economy for the effort to support the Korean struggle—was allowed to expire. The Reconstruction Finance Corporation, which had functioned throughout the depression, World War II, and the Korean War, terminated its activities. Congress created a Small Business Administration to aid small businesses by making loans and in other ways.

States gain control of offshore oil deposits.

Probably the most controversial law of the first months of Eisenhower's administration was one which gave the states control of offshore, or tidelands, oil deposits. President Truman had vetoed similar bills, and the matter had been an issue in the 1952 campaign.

The discovery of oil deposits in the area off the coast of California and some of the Gulf states had raised the question as to whether these offshore deposits belonged to the states or to the federal government. The states claimed ownership. They wanted to lease these deposits to private companies and use the royalties to reduce

795

OPENING THE ST. LAWRENCE SEAWAY. *In April, 1959, the first ships went through St. Lambert Lock, officially opening the Seaway for ocean-going vessels.*

taxes and to finance public improvements. Those who urged that these oil deposits belonged to the nation wanted them held as a national resource and as a reserve for navy use. In 1947 the Supreme Court had ruled that the federal government rather than the states had paramount rights to the three-mile coastal belt and "full control over the resources of the soil under the water area, including oil."

In 1953 Congress enacted a law to the effect that the states could lease and collect royalties on oil deposits within the "historic seaward boundaries" of the states. In the case of most states this phrase meant three miles out to sea. In the case of Texas and Florida, however, it meant ten and a half miles to seaward, because of agreements made when these two states were admitted to the Union. This same law gave Congress control of offshore oil deposits "beyond the historic boundaries of the states."

St. Lawrence Seaway and power project.

For a quarter of a century a plan to connect the Great Lakes with the Atlantic Ocean by way of the St. Lawrence River had waited for Congress to act. The proposed plan was to construct a seaway from Montreal to the Great Lakes. The project also involved the construction of hydroelectric power plants. The St. Lawrence Seaway would in effect convert such inland cities as Milwaukee, Chicago, Buffalo, Cleveland, Detroit, and Toledo into seaports and create a new 8000-mile seacoast.

In 1953, Canada announced its intention to proceed without American approval. President Eisenhower then persuaded Congress to give the state of New York the right to co-operate with the province of Ontario in building dams and hydroelectric power plants. The electric energy generated is to be divided between New York and Ontario, with the understanding that New York will make some of the energy

796

available to nearby states. Finally in 1954 Congress authorized the construction of the Seaway jointly by the United States and Canada.

TVA is the subject of political controversy.

From the beginning TVA has been the subject of controversy between those who support government-sponsored power projects and those who believe that the government should not compete with private power companies. In 1954 the question arose as to whether a steam-generated electric power plant should be built by TVA with money appropriated by Congress, or whether it should be built by private companies with the aid of a federal loan. In spite of strong Democratic criticism the Eisenhower administration awarded a contract—known as the Dixon-Yates contract—to private companies to build a steam plant at West Memphis, Arkansas. When the city of Memphis, Tennessee, announced that it would build the power plant, however, the Eisenhower administration cancelled the Dixon-Yates contract.

Other successes and failures.

In general, President Eisenhower pursued a middle-of-the-road policy. Frequently a combination of moderate Republicans and moderate Democrats gave the President the majority he needed. Thus, in spite of opposition from some members of his own party, Mr. Eisenhower succeeded in getting the Reciprocal Trade Agreements extended, first for one year, then for a three-year period, and finally (1958) for a four-year period into 1962. In the same way the number of people covered by the Social Security program was increased; so, too, were the benefits. In 1954 the minimum wage rate was raised to one dollar per hour. The insurance and mortgage features of the Housing Act were liberalized, and provision was made for the construction

of 45,000 housing units through 1956. On these and other welfare measures most of the argument in Congress had to do with the amount of money to be appropriated, not with the basic principle of whether there should be federal legislation in these fields.

Congress approved a gigantic appropriation for the construction of highways, but failed to appropriate funds to assist the states to build sorely needed schools. The Federal Highway Act of 1956 provided for the construction, during the next thirteen years, of a superhighway network. The network is expected to connect most cities with a population of 50,000 or more. The federal government will pay 90 per cent of the cost. To help pay for the program the federal gasoline tax was increased.

In 1952, Congress had passed the McCarran-Walter Immigration Act over the vigorous veto of Mr. Truman, who said the law was discriminatory. Under this law the total of quota immigrants that may be admitted each year is 154,000. No quota restrictions are placed upon persons born in the countries of the Western Hemisphere nor on the alien husbands and wives of American citizens. The following year the law was liberalized to permit the admission of 214,000 immigrants during the three-year period 1953–56, regardless of quota restrictions. This was done to provide for the admission of refugees from countries behind the "iron curtain." There were also a few minor amendments to the law in 1954, and a temporary increase allowed in 1957. That year the total immigration was almost 327,000.

Agricultural Distress Brings Compromise

Prosperity is general, except on farms.

President Eisenhower's first administration had four years of rather

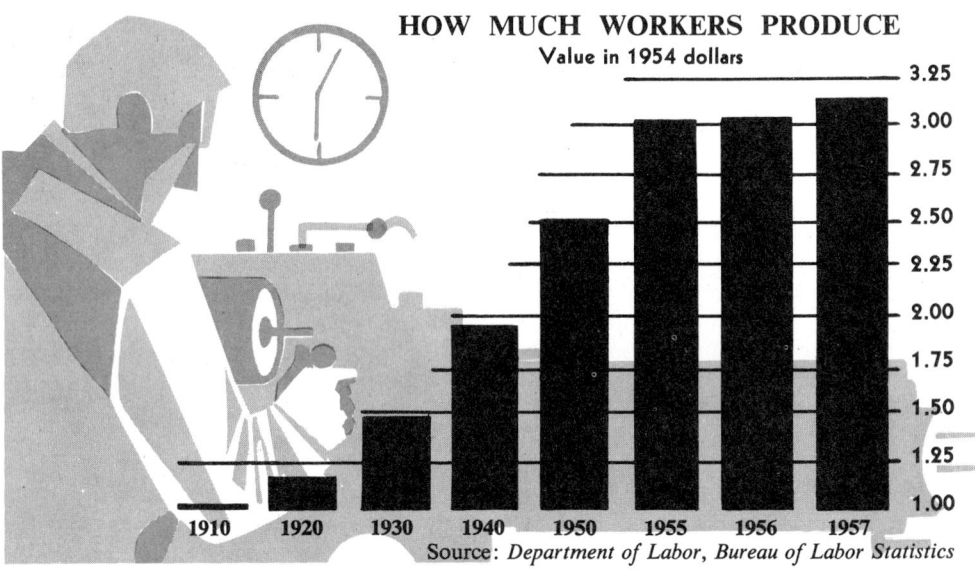

HOW MUCH WORKERS PRODUCE
Value in 1954 dollars

1910	1920	1930	1940	1950	1955	1956	1957

Source: *Department of Labor, Bureau of Labor Statistics*

general prosperity. There was a record number of employed persons; productivity levels in industry increased each year; wages remained high; and prices for most items tended to be somewhat stable. However, prosperity did not extend to the farmers. Farm prices and farm income declined.

How the price support program works.

The price support program to help farmers, begun in 1938, has continued ever since. Prices on certain crops are supported at a percentage of the "parity price" by means of storage loans. The system works as follows. The Commodity Credit Corporation lends money to farmers on crops they have placed in storage. The loan is equal to the support price. When a crop is sold, if the market price is greater than the loan, the farmer keeps the difference. If the market price is less than the loan, the government takes over the commodity at the support price. The CCC stores the crop and may sell it later at a profit or loss, depending on market conditions.

In the years after the Korean War, the CCC became the owner of more surplus agricultural products than it could store, sell, or distribute. The government gave food to subsidize school lunch programs; it sold food at a loss to needy countries all over the world; it also allowed large quantities of food to be spoiled or destroyed. Since food prices were high and the drain on the Treasury considerable, the whole support program came under attack.

Rigid vs. flexible price supports.

Under the agricultural acts of 1948 and 1949, price supports were fixed at 90 per cent of the parity price through 1954. After that, prices of some crops were to be supported at from 75 to 90 per cent of parity, and others at 60 to 90 per cent, depending on supplies. Whether price supports should be rigid or flexible became a matter of debate.

Mr. Benson, Eisenhower's Secretary of Agriculture, stoutly championed flexible supports. He argued that the 90 per cent parity program had been in effect too long. In 1954 the administration put price supports on wheat, cotton, corn, rice, and peanuts on a sliding scale of 90 to 75 per cent of parity. At the same time, under Mr.

Benson's leadership, wheat and cotton farmers voted to cut acreage sharply. In spite of these changes, however, farm prices and income continued to fall.

In the spring of 1956 Congress approved a compromise farm bill. This bill provided over a billion dollars to pay farmers for keeping certain acres out of production. The idle acres were described as a "soil bank." The bill retained flexible supports for wheat, corn, cotton, rice, and peanuts. It raised the price support on feed grains from 70 to 76 per cent of parity. It authorized the export of surplus cotton at a price below the world market price. Demands for higher price supports continued. Early in 1959 President Eisenhower estimated that during the first half of that year the government would invest more than 9 billion dollars in farm products.

Civil Rights Is an Issue

"To Secure These Rights."

In 1947 a committee was appointed by President Truman to study the treatment accorded minority groups. It made a significant report on civil rights entitled "To Secure These Rights." The report dealt with discriminatory practices of employers and labor unions and restrictions on voting and on the ownership of property. The committee showed that the problem of discrimination was not sectional but national in scope, and that it had many aspects. While various minority groups—Indians, Jews, Catholics, those of Oriental descent, and others—were subject to prejudice and discrimination, the unequal treatment of the Negro was the greatest problem. The report recommended a federal Fair Employment Practices Commission and laws against poll taxes and lynching.

Congress was slow to act on a program of civil rights legislation. While several civil rights bills passed the House of Representatives they did not pass the Senate. The chief argument used against such bills was the old one that federal legislation would be an unwarranted interference with the rights of the states. It was also argued that the problem of prejudice and discrimination can best be solved through education and persuasion.

Gains in securing civil rights.

There have been some notable gains throughout the country toward the goal of equality for all in the enjoyment of civil rights. During World War II, President Roosevelt by executive order set up a Fair Employment Practices Committee. The function of the FEPC was to provide for minority groups, especially Negroes, equal opportunities for work in factories having war contracts. Although the federal FEPC was discontinued when the war ended, several states and cities now have similar committees.

In more recent years there have been other steps toward more equal rights for all. Several states which formerly made payment of a poll tax a condition for voting no longer do so. The number of labor unions which exclude Negroes has been greatly reduced. The armed forces have moved rapidly toward the integration of whites and Negroes. In addition, various localities have taken steps to end discriminatory practices in schools, public conveyances, restaurants, and theaters. Public housing projects in some parts of the country are open equally to whites and Negroes.

Supreme Court rules on civil rights.

In recent years the Supreme Court has made several important decisions dealing with civil rights. One of these has to do with clauses in deeds prohibiting the sale of property to persons of a specified race. In the case of *Shel-*

ley vs. *Kraemer,* 1948, the Supreme Court ruled that such clauses, while not illegal, cannot be enforced by federal or state courts.

Since the war the Supreme Court has heard a number of cases dealing with segregation. The Court began to give careful scrutiny to a ruling made in 1896 in the case of *Plessy* vs. *Ferguson.* This old ruling said that a community could require segregation of races in schools and public conveyances if "equal facilities" were provided. In 1950 (*Sweatt* vs. *Painter*), the Court ruled that Texas could not exclude Negroes from the all-white University of Texas Law School, since the Texas State Law School for Negroes did not "provide separate but equal facilities." Here the Court took into consideration such factors as library facilities, scholarship funds, the number of students and teachers, and the prestige of the university. The Supreme Court also ruled in 1950 (*McLaurin* vs. *Oklahoma*) that the University of Oklahoma Graduate School could not assign special seats in the classroom, library, and cafeteria for the use of Negro students.

These decisions prepared the way for the historic decision on school segregation given by the Supreme Court in 1954. In a unanimous decision, the Supreme Court reversed the doctrine set up in *Plessy* vs. *Ferguson* and ruled that segregation itself violated the Fourteenth Amendment. The Court realized that its decision involved a drastic social revolution in several states and communities. It stated that it would accept briefs from interested parties as to when and how this decision should be carried out. A year later the Court ruled that states and communities should comply with the decision "within a reasonable time." It further directed that the lower federal courts should be used by interested parties in compelling compliance with the desegregation ruling.

As would be expected, some communities immediately began to plan for desegregation of their school systems. (The District of Columbia was one of these.) On the other hand, some states indicated that they would not comply with the decision. Several even threatened to abolish their public school system and to give financial support to private schools.

In 1957 Congress finally passed the Civil Rights Act. This law created a six-member commission on civil rights with power to investigate denial of the right to vote and of equal protection of laws because of race, color, religion, or national origin. The commission may obtain injunctions and start contempt proceedings in federal courts if the orders are disregarded.

The Crisis in Education

Education is a local and state function.

Throughout our history the control and financing of education has been the function of the local community. In each community there is a local school board which has wide powers. The state department of education tries to maintain uniform practices and standards throughout the state. Most states use their taxing powers to help local communities support their schools. State aid to schools is based on the assumption that poorer or sparsely settled communities need a share of state funds to maintain schools that will measure up to minimum standards.

Inadequate support for public education is an old problem. It is revealed in crowded, unsafe, and outmoded schools and in poorly trained and poorly paid teachers. In the postwar years the educational crisis became acute. The high birth rate of the 1940's and 1950's led to a marked rise in the number of children attending school. There was a shortage of classrooms and a shortage of teachers. Educational and civic leaders throughout the country believed that this deepening crisis could not be met without a broad program of federal aid.

The principle of separation of church and state enters the picture.

Alongside the public schools a large number of parochial and other private schools provided elementary and secondary education for an increasingly large number of children. The parochial schools are financed by various religious denominations. On the whole they conform to standards established by state departments of education; but in addition to the usual subjects they teach religion. Since parochial schools are privately financed, their existence, like that of other private schools, eases the financial burden of many states and communities. None of the federal aid proposals included direct financial help to private schools. Some did provide funds for auxiliary services, such as bus transportation and health services, to private school pupils. Ever since the 1930's the federal government has offered lunch subsidies to private as well as to public schools.

The policies of the individual states regarding financial assistance to pupils attending parochial schools are not uniform. Many states and local communities provide health services and free or reduced-fare transportation to all school children regardless of the type of school they attend. In 1947, in *Everson* vs. *the Board of Education,* the Supreme Court (5 to 4) ruled that the action of a New Jersey town in reimbursing parents for bus fares for children attending parochial schools did not violate the Constitution. In keeping with this decision, a compromise formula was suggested to Congress. It would permit each state to decide for itself whether federal funds would be used for auxiliary services in nonpublic schools. Congress failed to approve the measure.

Federal aid raises important problems.

At different times in the past the federal government has taken action to support *special* educational programs. Noteworthy instances are: the Morrill Act of 1862, under which land grants were given to colleges to provide instruction in agriculture and the mechanic arts; the Hatch Act of 1887, which established agricultural experiment stations in connection with land-grant colleges; and the Smith-Hughes Act of 1917, which granted federal funds for vocational education. Educational organizations in the 1940's and 1950's, however, pleaded not for *special* federal grants, but for *general* aid for schools. The demand for a *general federal aid program* raised a series of questions which are still hotly debated.

1. Would federal aid to education mean federal control of education?
2. Should the federal government allocate funds to states which maintain segregated schools?
3. What formula could be devised for the fair and satisfactory distribution of federal funds to the states?
4. Would the principle of separation of church and state, as expressed in the First Amendment of the Constitution, be violated if federal funds helped pay for transportation and other services to children going to church-supported private schools?

The plight of the schools grew progressively worse. The Eisenhower administration tried to obtain federal aid legislation which avoided the issues that had prevented action in the past. It proposed a bill allocating federal funds to help states and localities in the construction of sorely needed school buildings. This bill had bipartisan support. However, it failed to pass after an amendment was added providing that funds would not go to states which refused to "desegregate" in compliance with the Supreme Court decision.

American architecture today emerges from and serves our technological and social needs. It responds to several of our national characteristics—enjoyment of personal freedom, mobility, leisure, and the need for the functional. It combines structure with color and the arts of painting, sculpture, and decoration.

Casa Mañana musical arena theater in Fort Worth, Texas

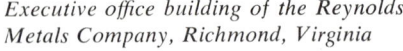

Executive office building of the Reynolds Metals Company, Richmond, Virginia

First Presbyterian Church, Ver Beach, Florida

Kellogg High School, Kellogg, Idaho

Northland Center for shopping, Detroit, Michigan

Living room of modern home in Massachusetts

Public disturbance over the condition of American schools and educational programs became pronounced. Russian scientific achievements continued to startle the world and arouse interest in Russian education. A number of American educators and political leaders visited Russia and observed its schools. Their reports to the American people were impressive. They told of the vast sums of money spent on educational programs. They described the rigid programs and the high scholastic standards demanded particularly of those students capable of advanced study in the sciences.

Public reaction to these reports increased the debate on American school programs and financial needs. There was no desire to pattern American education on the Russian system. However, serious consideration was given to the purposes and values of our educational programs and the extent to which these were being achieved.

In August, 1958, the National Defense Education Act was passed by Congress. This act was an attempt to strengthen some phases of American education considered weak. They include guidance and testing programs; instruction in mathematics, science, and languages; aid to needy college students; and development of graduate study programs. The act authorized $861,000,000 for expenditures during a period of four years. During the early months of 1959 the administration sponsored an additional plan concerned with helping certain areas in the construction of new schools.

The Cold War Troubles the Eisenhower Administration

During the Eisenhower administration, the cold war continued. There were new trouble spots and new crises, but the basic difficulties remained.

As we have already noted, an armistice, but not peace, was achieved in Korea; North and South Korea still were not united. The Communists had acquired control of North Vietnam. The question of admitting Red China to the U.N. was still unsettled. The Chinese Nationalists remained in control of Formosa. Yet in 1955 the possibility of hostilities in the area was so acute that President Eisenhower asked, and Congress authorized, the use of force to prevent the threatened invasion of Formosa by Red China.

Russia began to compete with the United States in extending economic and military aid and trade opportunities to certain countries, particularly those that were neutral in the cold war. Indeed, Russia used alternate threats and promises in its endeavor to woo the "neutralist countries" of the Far East and Near East.

Russian industrial and technical strength had made great progress. As time passed it became clear that the United States no longer had pre-eminent power in atomic weapons. Indeed there was some speculation that Russia was superior to the United States in air power and probably in some other areas of attack or defense. American complacency was rudely shattered in October, 1957, when Russia announced that a man-made moon had been successfully placed in orbit. Russia named its satellite *Sputnik*. The United States feverishly endeavored to recover its prestige, but did not succeed in placing a satellite in orbit until January, 1958. Russia's success clearly demonstrated that Russian scientists and technicians had triumphed in an area in which Americans had been led to believe they enjoyed pre-eminence.

In the Middle East, Russia tried to make the most of the continuing rivalry between the Israelis and the Arabs. As in other trouble spots, Moscow used the difficulties of France in North Africa to propagandize against the "imperialism and warmongering of the West." Russian propaganda was outspoken in criticizing the United States as the great enemy of the "people's democracies" and of peace.

Eisenhower advocates "Atoms for Peace."

Efforts to achieve agreement on the international control of atomic energy remained deadlocked. In 1953 President Eisenhower proposed an international atomic stockpile which would make nuclear materials available to all countries for research purposes. Congress, by the Atomic Energy Act of 1954, authorized the President to join with other nations in creating an international atomic pool for peaceful purposes. Without waiting for Russian participation, the United States gave fissionable materials to several nations.

To co-operate in peaceful atomic research several countries of western Europe joined in a mutual agreement popularly known as "Euratom." In 1955 an international conference on peaceful uses of atomic energy met at Geneva. Following this conference, plans were worked out for an International Atomic Energy Agency to promote peaceful use of atomic energy.

Three years later the United States and Euratom co-operated on a program for building several large nuclear power plants in western Europe. Under a revised United States Atomic Energy Act (1958) American and British scientists were permitted to exchange information on their research in nuclear physics.

A conference "at the summit" raises hopes.

Winston Churchill as early as 1953 strongly urged a face-to-face meeting of the heads of states engaged in the cold war. He believed that such a meeting might offer opportunities for easing world tension. The new Russian leaders accepted the suggestion and so finally did the United States. A meeting "at the summit," as it was called, was held at Geneva in July, 1955. President Eisenhower captured the imagination of the world by proposing that Russia and the United States exchange their military plans and permit mutual aerial inspection of each other's military installations. The President urged that the nations of the world should "substitute co-operation in human welfare for competition in the means of destruction."

The conference adjourned in apparent good spirits. Plans for the unification of Germany and the aerial inspection of military installations were left to a conference of foreign ministers. They met but accomplished little. It became known that while Russia was pretending to be interested in peace and disarmament, it was shipping munitions to Arab countries in the explosive Middle East.

Russian leaders attack the "cult of Stalinism."

Even though the "spirit of Geneva" failed to bring about any settlement of outstanding issues, there were signs of a change in Soviet strategy. Moscow apparently adopted a "soft policy," either to lure the West to let down its guard, or to win neutralists to its side. A few Russians were allowed to visit the United States; a few thousand foreigners were permitted to visit the Soviet Union. Soviet leaders made good-will tours to the countries of Southeast Asia as well as to its European satellites. At times Russian "smiles and wiles" puzzled the statesmen of the West.

Still more puzzling was the action of Khrushchev and other Russian leaders in openly criticizing Stalin's regime. Stalin's leadership of Russia was repudiated, and Stalin himself was painted as a brutal, bloody, and dictatorial tyrant. This shift in internal Communist strategy from almost devoted worship of Stalin to complete downgrading shocked the Communists in other countries. But the "faithful" accepted the "new party line," which said that all of the Kremlin's unpopular actions, both within and outside of Russia, should be attributed to the ruthless tyrant Stalin, and not to communism itself.

By 1958, Khrushchev had emerged as the undisputed boss in Russia. Those who had been permitted to share the limelight were demoted or removed. To all appearances Khrushchev had become another, if different, Stalin.

Eisenhower Serves a Second Term

The GOP depends on "Ike" for victory.

Republican party leaders, sensing the great personal popularity of "Ike," believed that their success in 1956 depended on having him head their ticket. They, as well as all citizens, were stunned in September, 1955, when the President suffered a heart attack. Everyone was pleased when he made a slow but steady recovery and announced early in 1956 that he would seek re-election. Republican leaders were worried again in June when Mr. Eisenhower had to undergo abdominal surgery. Nevertheless they felt confident that in spite of his two serious illnesses, the people would re-elect him.

The President's illness tended to center attention on Vice-President Richard Nixon. However, he did not have the whole-hearted support of some leaders in his own party. In the spring and summer of 1956 there was talk of selecting someone else for the Vice-Presidency. The President refused to suggest any other candidate. The Republican convention, meeting at San Francisco in August, renominated both Mr. Eisenhower and Mr. Nixon.

The Democrats select Stevenson and Kefauver.

As early as 1955 Adlai E. Stevenson announced that he would actively seek the Democratic nomination for a second time. Meeting in Chicago, the Democrats selected Stevenson as their presidential nominee. In a close contest with Senator John Kennedy of Massachusetts, Senator Kefauver won the convention's vote as Stevenson's running mate.

ADLAI E. STEVENSON

The presidential campaign of 1956.

Stevenson and Kefauver waged a vigorous campaign appealing to local interests in different sections of the country. Mr. Stevenson tried to arouse national enthusiasm by urging elimination of the draft and discontinuance of hydrogen bomb tests "as soon as practicable." These suggestions "boomeranged" in the last days of the campaign when developments in Hungary, Poland, and Egypt aroused fears that the cold war might become a hot one.

As in 1952, the election of 1956 was an overwhelming endorsement of Eisenhower, but not of the Republican party. The President's popular vote was approximately 35,000,000 as against 25,-600,000 for Stevenson. His electoral vote was 457, Stevenson's 74. In the South, Eisenhower won Florida, Virginia, Texas, Tennessee, and Louisiana. However, Eisenhower's landslide victory did not result in the election of a Republican Congress. The voters gave control of both houses of the Eighty-fifth Congress (1957–58) to the Democratic party.

The problem of presidential incapacity.

The illnesses of President Eisenhower tended to focus attention on the office of Vice-President. The constitutional question concerning the succession to the Presidency in the event of a President's incapacity has never been definitely resolved. Both President Eisenhower and President Truman have urged that the matter be clarified either by congressional action or by constitutional amendment. It is argued that the precise point where executive authority rests during a temporary or prolonged incapacity of the President is too important to be left to chance.

Eisenhower's second administration.

In domestic affairs the old issues remained. President Eisenhower had difficulty in getting Congress to vote approval of his large budget, and politicians talked hopefully of "slashing" the budget to prepare the way for a tax cut in 1958. Federal aid to education and civil rights were among the important topics debated in the first session of the Eighty-fifth Congress (see pp. 799–800). Charges of the misuse of labor union funds by a few labor leaders were aired before a Congressional investigating committee. Officials of the A.F. of L.–CIO undertook to "clean house."

An economic decline began in 1957 and continued through 1958. Layoffs in industrial plants made unemployment a serious problem. Creeping inflation added to the nation's economic woes. To check the economic down-turn the administration took steps to make credit more readily available, encouraged federal housing projects and private home building, extended weekly unemployment insurance benefits, and increased federal expenditures for defense. The administration refrained, however, from supporting the proposal of many business leaders for tax reduction. One exception in the economic

(Above) *The* Skipjack, *the Navy's fastest atomic submarine*

(Below) *How the X–15 rocket ship will be launched*

picture in 1957 and 1958 was the improvement in farm income.

During the early months of 1959, signs appeared that the economic recession had run its course. Unemployment was leveling off and the country seemed on the way to another period of prosperity.

National defense becomes an issue.

Criticisms of our defense program had been mounting for some time. However, during President Eisenhower's second administration the program became an issue of heated controversy. The reports of Soviet technological and military progress and of its future capabilities in intercontinental ballistic missiles (ICBM) provoked many pessimistic estimates of our own defense program.

FAIRBANKS, ALASKA, *has grown from a mining camp to a thriving center of transportation.*

In July, 1958, the Congress requested a reorganization of the Department of Defense. This was an attempt to increase the efficiency of the department and to obtain unified decisions faster. Vast sums were appropriated for defense purposes. Provision was made for the production of long-range bombers, nuclear-powered submarines, and new antisubmarine weapons. Money was provided for missiles and missile bases. High on the list was the provision for space projects.

In an effort to co-ordinate the various activities concerned with outer space, Congress established the National Aeronautics and Space Administration (NASA). This agency has research centers in several parts of the country. It works on nonmilitary programs of space research.

Alaska and Hawaii become states.

As territories of the United States both Alaska and Hawaii played important roles in our history. Both contributed to the material wealth of our country; both served as military outposts for defense. For several years bills had been introduced in Congress for the admission of these territories into the union as states. Finally, in 1958, a statehood bill for Alaska was passed by Congress and signed by President Eisenhower. Early in 1959 Alaska became the 49th state of the union. Following swiftly upon this action Congress enacted statehood for Hawaii. Thus, the United States had expanded its geographical boundaries and hastened its westward trend in population.

Trouble in the Middle East.

Foreign affairs attracted a great deal of attention during Mr. Eisenhower's second term. Many observers believed that in the struggle for world leadership the United States was losing ground to Russia, particularly in the Middle East, the Far East, and to some extent in South America.

Serious trouble developed in the Middle East, where Russian propaganda, along with financial and military aid, strengthened the leadership of President Nasser of Egypt. England withdrew troops from the Suez Canal area in 1956 and shortly thereafter Nasser announced that Egypt would nationalize the canal. Behind the nationalization of the canal was Nasser's desire to eliminate foreign influence in Egypt and to achieve leadership among Arab nations.

In spite of the Arab-Israeli truce there continued to be constant friction and border incidents. Egypt, for example, refused passage through the canal to Israeli ships. On October 25, 1956, Israeli troops invaded Egypt and quickly obtained control of the Sinai Peninsula. A few days later English and French military forces were dispatched to Egypt. Russia threatened to intervene on the side of Egypt. The United States, embarrassed by the actions of its friends, turned to the General Assembly of the United Nations and urged that the actions of Israel, England, and France be condemned. The United Nations then organized an international force to occupy the war zone. As U.N. forces moved in to maintain order, England, France, and Israel withdrew their troops.

The Eisenhower Doctrine.

In January, 1957, President Eisenhower asked Congress for authority to send troops to any nation threatened by international communism provided that the threatened nation or nations requested such help. After considerable debate Congress approved what has come to be called the Eisenhower Doctrine.

The situation in the Middle East remained tense and uncertain. Nasser organized the United Arab Republic, consisting of Egypt and Syria. As leader of the Arab nationalists he forged closer ties with the Soviet Union. Money, technical assistance, and a market for cotton were greatly needed by the Arab republics. The U.S.S.R. welcomed an opportunity to send such aid and to offer a market. For a while Russian propaganda was able to portray to the Arab peoples the picture of the Eisenhower Doctrine as a new imperialism. Consequently, the only government in the Middle East that dared accept the doctrine was the small country of Lebanon.

In July, 1958, a revolution in Iraq led to the assassination of the king and the establishment of a government friendly to the Arab nationalism of Nasser. Conditions soon looked as though the revolution would spread to nearby Lebanon and Jordan. Upon the request of the Lebanese president, the United States landed marines in Lebanon. England flew troops into Jordan. Nasser and Khrushchev accused the United States and England of armed aggression and demanded the immediate withdrawal of American and British forces. In an emergency session of the General Assembly President Eisenhower proposed that the U.N. should: (1) Take adequate measures to preserve peace in Lebanon and Jordan and halt indirect aggression from without, (2) undertake a program of regional economic development, and (3) prevent an arms race in the Middle East. The Arab states proposed a compromise, stating that they would accept the services of a U.N. observer team in the Middle East and would not resort to force to compel the withdrawal of American and British forces. For their part England and the United States agreed to withdraw their forces as soon as practicable. In October, 1958, this was accomplished.

United States stands firm in the Far East.

The Communist tactics of diverting world attention away from one crisis and toward a different scene of tension continued. In August, 1958, Chinese guns on the mainland began bombarding the island of Quemoy. Matsu and Quemoy are small islands a few miles off the China coast which are held by Chinese Nationalist forces under Chiang Kai-shek. The main stronghold of Nationalist China is the island of Formosa (or Taiwan). In 1955 Congress had approved the use of force to prevent Red China from invading Formosa. The shelling of Quemoy in 1958 was a threat to the security of Formosa.

The United States reaffirmed its support of Formosa. Secretary of State John Foster Dulles warned against any attempt to invade the offshore islands.

He declared that such action would be a "threat to the peace." He also let it be known that it might provoke a counterattack on the mainland. American warships were sent to help the Nationalists transport supplies to Quemoy. As the situation grew worse Secretary Dulles flew to Formosa for a conference with Chiang. Following their talks an announcement was made that the Nationalists would not attack the Chinese mainland. Communist China then announced that the offshore islands would be shelled on even-numbered days only. Thus, the crisis subsided.

The Free World works for international stability.

The unification of West and East Germany has been a continuing problem. During the years following the organization of the West German Federal Republic great gains were made in strengthening that government. West Germany, as a member of NATO (see p. 779), became more closely allied to the Western powers.

Communist East Germany made bids to the Western powers for the recognition of its government. At one point the U.S.S.R. proposed that the Potsdam Agreement (see p. 778) be canceled and that West Berlin be made a free city. Other Communist moves were made in trying to force the United States and its allies to recognize East Germany. The Western powers rejected these bids for recognition because of their accompanying terms.

The danger of military conflict over Germany was intensified in 1959. Early in the year Premier Khrushchev began sending notes on the German problem to the governments of the United Kingdom, France, and the United States. The notes accused the Western powers of blocking the reunification of the German people, of endangering the peace, and of preventing the signing of a peace treaty between West Germany and the U.S.S.R.

Premier Khrushchev seemed determined to force the Western powers out of Germany. In threatening tones he declared that a summit conference on the issues must be held by May 27, 1959, or the possibility of war would loom over all Europe. (Later he postponed this date.)

The United States and its allies had no intention of giving up their legal rights in West Germany. Furthermore, the experiences of the 1955 summit conference (see p. 803) had left them disillusioned. The probability of any constructive results coming from a summit meeting seemed remote.

In February, Britain's Prime Minister Harold Macmillan visited Moscow in an attempt to discover from Khrushchev the possible worthwhileness of a summit conference. On his return he reported to Chancellor Adenauer of West Germany and Premier De Gaulle of France his impressions of his talks with Khrushchev. In March he visited the United States to confer with President Eisenhower.

Speaking of the forthcoming summit conference, Macmillan declared, "It will be a tough task but one in which I believe we shall succeed."

President Eisenhower and his advisors did not share the Prime Minister's optimism. However, agreements were reached for holding a conference of foreign ministers in Geneva early in May, 1959. This meeting worked on the necessary preparations for the heads-of-government conference.

During the years following World War II the cold war has created a succession of tensions and crises. The free world has seen the Communist world become increasingly powerful. But it has also seen the development of strong alliances among free nations determined to resist Communist expansion. The eruption of trouble anywhere in the world has ceased to be considered an isolated problem. It has become part of the greater conflict. Yet, in spite of these eruptions, the determination of the United States and its allies to work for peace and stability in the world has continued.

JOHN FOSTER DULLES

FOR IDENTIFICATION

Ezra Taft Benson	Richard M. Nixon
John Foster Dulles	Adlai E. Stevenson
Estes Kefauver	Robert A. Taft

FOR EXPLANATION OR DEFINITION

"Atoms for Peace"	offshore oil deposits
Dixon-Yates contract	parity payments
Euratom	*Plessy* vs. *Ferguson*
Federal Highway Act	St. Lawrence Seaway
flexible price supports	"separate but equal
McCarran-Walter Im-	facilities"
migration Act	soil bank

FOR REVIEW

1. (a) Who were the Democratic candidates for President and Vice-President in 1952? The Republican candidates? (b) What were the main issues?

2. What inroads did the Republicans make in the Solid South in 1952? Why?

3. Why was the election of 1952 more a triumph for Eisenhower than for the Republican party?

4. State the provisions of the legislation concerning offshore oil deposits. What were some of the objections to this law?

5. Describe the St. Lawrence Seaway and power project.

6. What was the Dixon-Yates contract? Why was the contract canceled?

7. (a) How did the Eisenhower administration improve the Social Security program? (b) What were the provisions of the Federal Highway Act of 1956? Of the McCarran-Walter Immigration Act?

8. (a) Explain the principle of "parity payments." (b) What are some of the arguments for and against rigid and flexible price supports?

9. (a) What were a few of the findings and recommendations made by President Truman's Committee on Civil Rights? (b) What gains have been made in securing civil rights?

10. (a) Explain the effect of the decision of the Supreme Court in *Plessy* vs. *Ferguson* in 1896 concerning "separate but equal facilities." (b) What was the decision of the Supreme Court in May, 1954, concerning segregation in the public schools?

11. (a) What is the difference between "special" and "general" federal aid to education? (b) What were the purposes of the National Defense Education Act of 1958?

12. How did the policies of Khrushchev affect the "cold war"?

13. How is the principle of separation of church and state involved in the debate over federal aid to education?

14. What was Eisenhower's "Atoms for Peace" proposal?

15. What did Eisenhower propose at the "summit conference" at Geneva in 1955?

16. Describe the presidential campaign of 1956, indicating the candidates, the issues, and the results.

17. (a) Why did our national defense program become an issue of controversy in Eisenhower's second term? (b) What actions were taken to improve our defenses?

18. What trouble developed in the Middle East as Arab nationalism became intensified?

19. (a) Why did the United States send troops into Lebanon? (b) What were President Eisenhower's proposals to the U.N. General Assembly regarding this situation?

20. Describe the trouble in the Far East in 1958 over the islands of Quemoy and Matsu.

21. Why has the separation of Germany into East and West been a source of trouble?

FOR FURTHER STUDY AND DISCUSSION

1. What arguments might be advanced to support the idea that the "Solid South" may cease to exercise the political power that it once had? What events or trends support the idea that new political alignments are in process of development within the United States?

2. (a) State the problems involved in securing congressional approval for a program of general federal aid to education. (b) Outline the arguments for and against a program of general federal aid to education.

3. Have developments in the cold war or in the conduct of foreign affairs weakened or strengthened the United Nations? Weakened or strengthened NATO?

4. How would you have voted on (a) the bill concerning offshore oil deposits? Why? (b) the bill of 1956 proposing federal aid for the construction of school buildings? Why? (c) the National Defense Education Act of 1958? Why?

5. List recent developments in (a) the cold war; (b) labor-management relations and laws; (c) NATO; (d) the United Nations; (e) "Atoms for Peace"; (f) farm legislation; (g) civil rights.

6. (a) Trace the history of Alaska from its earliest association with the United States. (b) Do the same for Hawaii.

FOR INDIVIDUAL OR GROUP ACTIVITIES

1. (a) Using appropriate tables and charts, prepare a floor talk on the expenditures and revenues of the United States for a recent fiscal year. (b) Compare these expenditures and revenues with a fiscal year five years ago. (c) Discuss whether certain expenditures should be deleted or pruned in order to permit a reduction of taxes or to balance the budget.

2. Criticize or defend the present farm program of the federal government.

3. Select five major issues or problems which in your opinion will be matters of controversy five years hence. Write a short statement explaining the present status of each issue and why you think it will be debated for some time to come.

4. The Supreme Court has defended the right of parents to choose a nonpublic school for their children (*Pierce* vs. *the Society of Sisters*); has forbidden the use of school property for a religious purpose (*McCollum* vs. *the Board of Education*); has approved the release of time for religious instruction not conducted on school property (*Zorach* vs. *Clauson*). Report on these decisions. Helpful source: Commager, *Documents*.

5. On a map of the world mark the "hot spots" that have been the seats of world tension since 1945. Explain the causes of each crisis and give the outcome of each.

HONOLULU, *the capital of Hawaii, is an expanding commercial center. Here, too, is the cultural center of the Islands.*

The measure of the progress of a civilization is the progress of the people.——George Bancroft

47. AMERICA MOVES FORWARD

Industrialization Marches On

Productivity climbs.

At the end of the nineteenth century many Americans thought the Industrial Revolution was drawing to a close. It seemed to them that nearly all the possible improvements in production had been made. Yet, as we now know, even greater advances were to come. In fact, the Industrial Revolution gathered speed as it went on. Today its pace is more rapid than ever. Those who look back in the year 2000 may conclude that in 1900 our Industrial Revolution had barely got started.

The Industrial Revolution is marked by a rapid growth in productivity. Thus in the century from 1850 to 1950 output per ʼman-hour in the United States went up almost six times. Stated another way, the modern worker produces as much in ten minutes as his 1850 ancestor did in one hour. The difference is largely due to the use of power-driven tools and equipment. By 1950 the average American worker had the help of 5.5 horsepower, which is equal to the labor of 66 men. The use of muscle power, either human or animal, had almost ceased.

Productivity in the United States has been growing faster in recent years than ever before. Since 1940 output per man-hour has risen an average of nearly 3 per cent a year. This rate of growth is faster than that of most countries.

Total output rises.

With the remarkable gain in productivity has come a vast increase in the total volume of goods and services produced, that is, in the *gross national product* (GNP). Our GNP is the largest in the world. In 1958 it was 425.8 billion dollars.

At the mid-century we had only 7 per cent of the world's population, yet we were producing 50 per cent of the world's goods that are bought and sold. In 1957, Americans spent more than $284 billion on goods and services. These figures show why it is that Americans have the highest standard of living in the world.

Our material progress can be suggested by the rise in average income. Measured in dollars of constant purchasing power, our per capita income was about twice as high in 1950 as in 1900 and almost four times the 1850 figure. Today our per capita income is higher than in any other country and is probably five times the world average.

Occupational shifts occur.

Industrialization has also brought sweeping changes in the kinds of jobs by which Americans earn a living. For over a century the proportion of all workers employed in agriculture, forestry, and fishing has been declining. The proportion engaged in manufacturing and construction has risen. The proportion employed in most types of service occupations, including trade, transportation, communication, finance, and government service, also has risen. The over-all shift has been away from physical production and into what is referred to as "white-collar" work.

These occupational shifts mean that workers need more education and training today than formerly. There has been a marked drop in the employment of men and women who are unskilled; in 1950 those classified as unskilled made up only 6 per cent of the labor force. The demand for semiskilled and skilled workers has risen; together these two groups now make up about a third of the labor force. The demand for persons with technical or

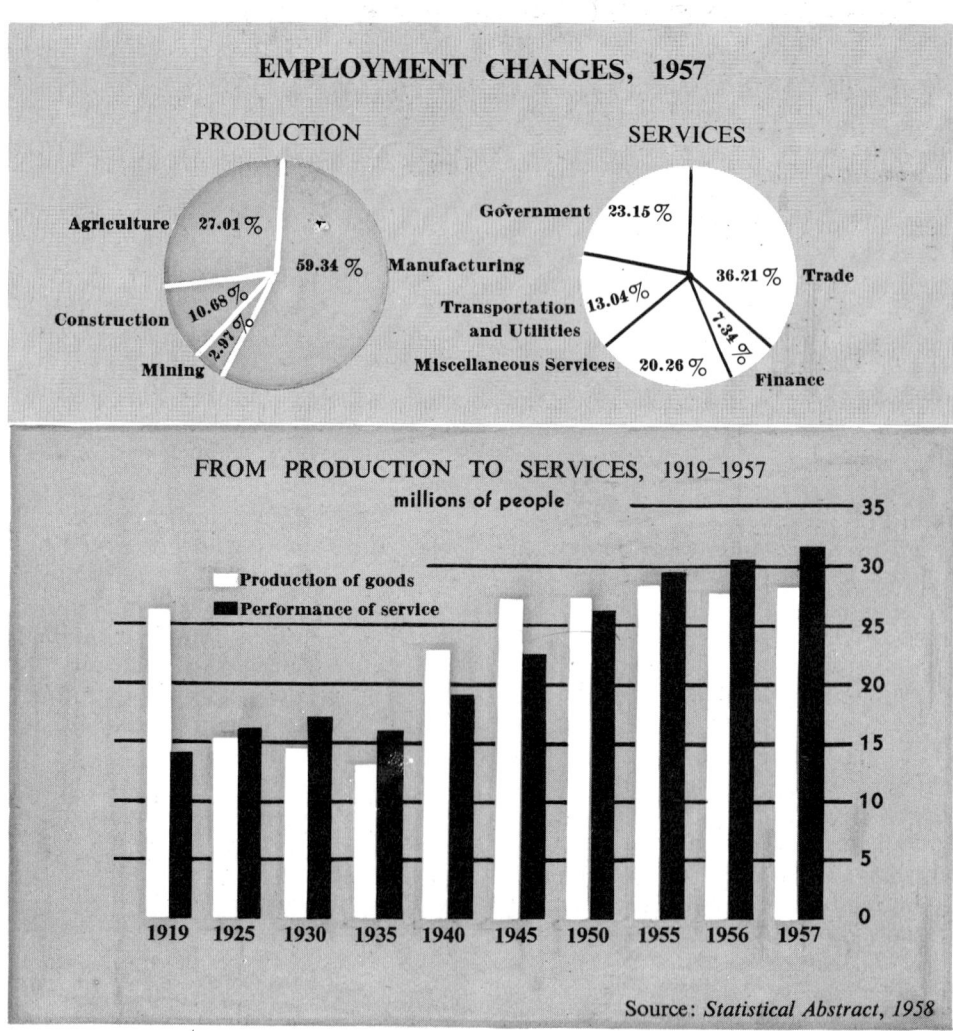

EMPLOYMENT CHANGES, 1957

PRODUCTION

Agriculture 27.01%
59.34% Manufacturing
Construction 10.68%
Mining 2.97%

SERVICES

Government 23.15%
36.21% Trade
Transportation 13.04%
and Utilities
Finance 7.34%
Miscellaneous Services 20.26%

FROM PRODUCTION TO SERVICES, 1919–1957
millions of people

☐ Production of goods
■ Performance of service

1919 1925 1930 1935 1940 1945 1950 1955 1956 1957

Source: *Statistical Abstract, 1958*

1900					
1920					
1940					
1950					
1956					
1957					
1960 (est.)					

millions 0   5   10   15   20   25

Source: *Statistical Abstract, 1958*

professional training has gone up sharply. To cite an example: in 1900 our industries employed one engineer for every 250 workers; today, they employ one engineer for every 60 workers. The employment of research workers, laboratory technicians, statisticians, and a long list of other workers with specialized education also has climbed.

More women work for pay.

The proportion of women with gainful occupations has more than doubled since 1870. In the 1950's about 3 in every 10 women were classified as "gainful workers." A Census Bureau report sums up the reasons for the shift of women from "nongainful" work inside the home to gainful employment:

This trend of women into gainful pursuits outside the home doubtless is closely associated with a number of other changes, such as smaller families, the transfer to the factory of much productive work formerly done in the home, the increase in laborsaving equipment and conveniences in the home, and the increasing desire of women for economic independence.

As late as 1900 a large proportion of gainfully employed women were farm laborers and domestic servants. This is no longer true. The largest group of women workers today (27 per cent) work in clerical occupations. The next largest group (19 per cent) are factory operatives. One in 8 women workers is engaged in professional or semiprofessional work.

The employment of married women is on the rise. About 1 in every 4 wives is now working for gain outside the home. Most of these working wives are childless or no longer have young children. The fact that women can earn their own living has vastly increased their personal freedom and economic independence.

Many workers leave the farm.

Industrialization has gone hand in hand with a revolution in agriculture (see p. 480). In 1820, before the agricultural revolution began, 72 per cent of all gainful workers were engaged in farming. By 1950 the figure was only 12 per cent. The length of the farmer's

815

FARM EMPLOYMENT

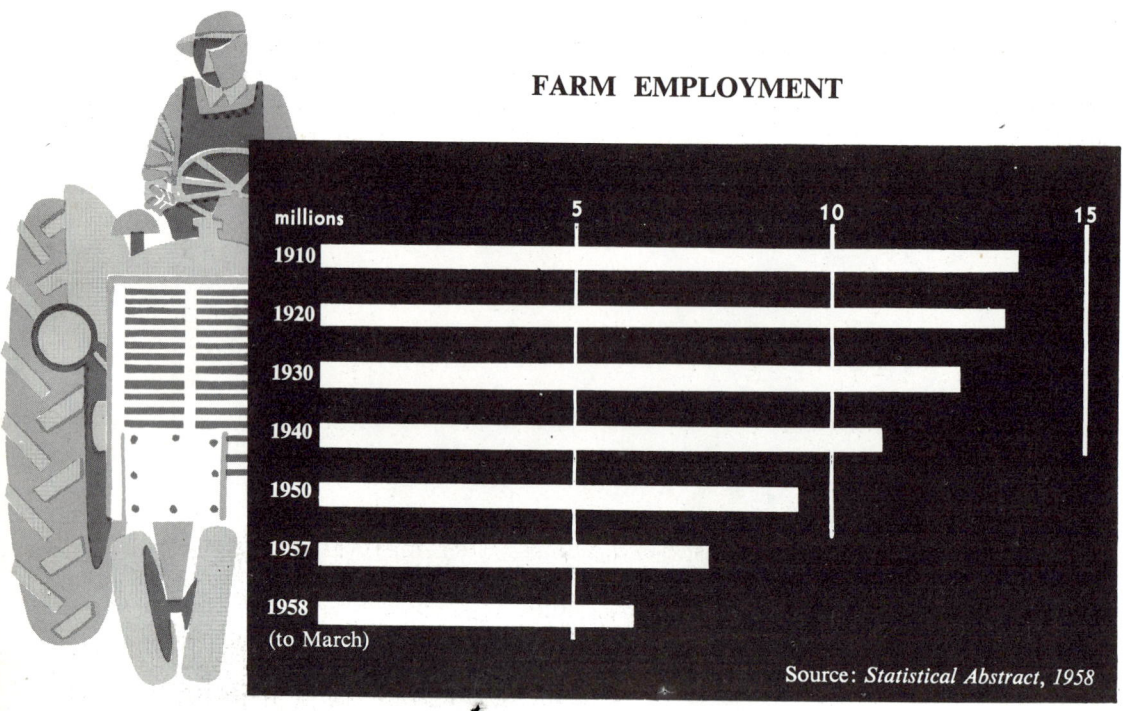

millions | 5 | 10 | 15

1910
1920
1930
1940
1950
1957
1958 (to March)

Source: *Statistical Abstract, 1958*

work week also dropped sharply. These changes were made possible by a great rise in farm output per man-hour.

The shift into nonagricultural work has gone on in every section of the country. In recent years it has been particularly noticeable in the South. In 1940 only 1 in 4 Southern workers held a nonfarm job; a decade later, 1 in 2 did so.

Opportunities for Negroes improve.

Industrialization has brought new opportunities to American Negroes. In 1900 nine tenths of them lived in the South, chiefly in rural areas. As a group, Southern Negroes were desperately poor. Nearly half were illiterate. Most of them worked as sharecroppers (p. 479) or as unskilled laborers. Those who could save up the railroad fare usually moved northward, where they could earn more. During World War I the northward migration swelled into a flood, as the war boom created a demand for unskilled workers in industry. Year after year the migration continued. When World War II broke out, more Negroes than ever before moved out of the South. In moving they generally shifted from farm work to industrial work, with a marked rise in their earnings.

Negroes are moving gradually into work that requires skill and education. As this shift continues, the gap between the average incomes of whites and Negroes will tend to close.

Urbanization increases.

Since the first days of the Industrial Revolution, Americans have been moving into cities. Urban centers have grown bigger and bigger. Today nearly two thirds of us live and work in 172 metropolitan areas. (A metropolitan area is defined by the Census Bureau as a central city of 50,000 or more, and the densely populated places nearby which house many of its workers and customers.) Evidence of the degree of urbanization we have reached is seen in these figures: 40 per cent of our population and 56 per cent of our manufacturing are concentrated in the forty largest metropolitan areas.

In recent years the suburbs have been growing faster than their central cities. The suburbs are residential areas inhabited chiefly by people who work in a large city and prefer to live where there is more open space. The electric trolley car launched the movement into the suburbs (see p. 433), and the automobile has extended it. Many suburbs are so crowded now that they have already lost their semirural character.

Industrialism Is Brought under Social Control

Signs that industrialism has been "tamed."

When the twentieth century began, thoughtful men in Europe and the United States wondered whether industrialism was a blessing or a curse. At that time mass production was creating great wealth for a few, yet the ma-

jority of industrial workers toiled long hours for meager wages and lived in poverty. Yet the captains of industry often had yearly incomes that ran into millions, and there was no income tax to pay. The gap between rich and poor was so wide that it threatened to make a mockery of democratic government. Socialists said the only remedy lay in public ownership of industry. Although socialism did not attract many followers in the United States, other reform movements were popular.

Ever since the days of the Grangers and the Populists, representatives of the people have sought ways to overcome the evils of industrialism while keeping its benefits. Today mass production is advancing faster than ever, but instead of making the rich richer and the poor poorer, it is narrowing the gulf between rich and poor. All classes of Americans are enjoying more leisure, better working and living conditions, and higher earnings. Even more significant, since 1940 the incomes of the poorer half of the population have risen faster than those in the richer half.

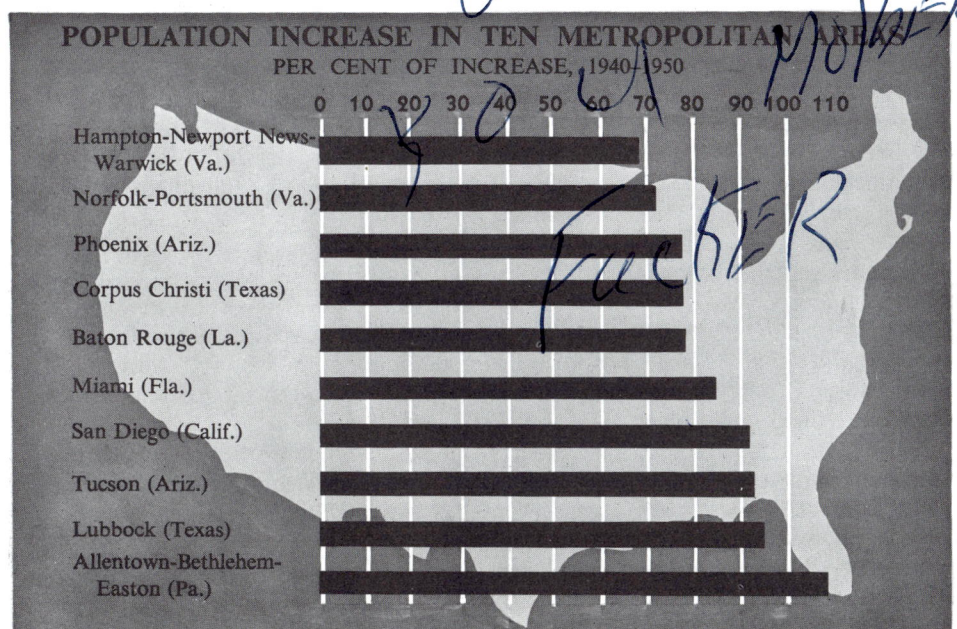

POPULATION INCREASE IN TEN METROPOLITAN AREAS
PER CENT OF INCREASE, 1940-1950

0 10 20 30 40 50 60 70 80 90 100 110

Hampton-Newport News-Warwick (Va.)
Norfolk-Portsmouth (Va.)
Phoenix (Ariz.)
Corpus Christi (Texas)
Baton Rouge (La.)
Miami (Fla.)
San Diego (Calif.)
Tucson (Ariz.)
Lubbock (Texas)
Allentown-Bethlehem-Easton (Pa.)

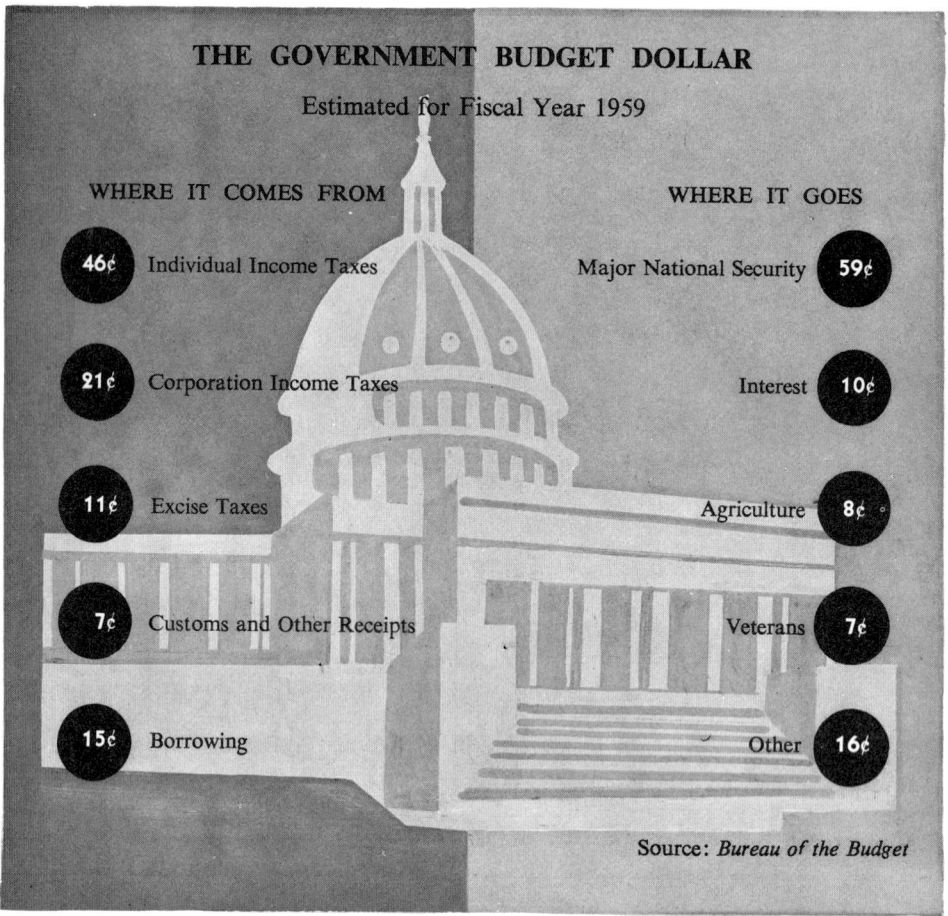

THE GOVERNMENT BUDGET DOLLAR
Estimated for Fiscal Year 1959

WHERE IT COMES FROM

- 46¢ Individual Income Taxes
- 21¢ Corporation Income Taxes
- 11¢ Excise Taxes
- 7¢ Customs and Other Receipts
- 15¢ Borrowing

WHERE IT GOES

- Major National Security 59¢
- Interest 10¢
- Agriculture 8¢
- Veterans 7¢
- Other 16¢

Source: *Bureau of the Budget*

Influences in "taming" industrialism.

The principal influences in harnessing industrialism for the public welfare are: (1) legislation, (2) union action, (3) the more responsible attitude of business managements, (4) the logic of mass production, and (5) progressive taxation.

1. *Legislation.* As we have noted, many state and federal laws have been passed for the regulation of business. Other measures are designed to protect consumers and to outlaw unfair methods of competition.

2. *Union action.* The growth of independent labor unions has reduced the once despotic power of employers to determine wages, hours, and condi-

tions of work. In some unionized plants almost every detail of labor-management relations is controlled by collective bargaining.

3. *Management's more responsible attitude.* The leaders of big business today have more sense of social responsibility than was true of leaders at the beginning of the century. Many of these men now believe that great corporations should operate not only for the benefit of the stockholders but for the benefit of their workers and the public. Today, for example, when a large company decides to close down an unprofitable plant, it considers what the effect will be on the employees and on the community. It may go so far as to help

the community attract some other company that can absorb the displaced workers.

A big business today cannot keep its affairs secret. It must send detailed reports to the Securities and Exchange Commission and other commissions, to the tax gatherers, and to its stockholders. Its affairs may be investigated at any time by the Federal Trade Commission or by a congressional committee.

4. *The logic of mass production.* In 1914, when the usual wage in the automobile industry was $2.40 for a nine-hour day, Henry Ford announced that he would pay his men a minimum of $5.00 for an eight-hour day. He wanted to improve the morale in his plant. He also felt that industry ought to pay higher wages in order to create a market for cars and other products. At the time most businessmen scoffed at his idea that wages should be higher and goods cheaper. Today, however, it is generally recognized that mass production depends on mass consumption. Mass consumption, in turn, depends upon the buying power of the lower- and middle-income groups.

The American worker could buy three times as much for an hour's work in 1950 as he could in 1900. Furthermore he could enjoy many things that were rare or unheard of in 1900, such as electricity, running water, central heating, automobiles, motion pictures, radio, television, and airplane travel. These material benefits were the direct result of the acceptance by American leaders of the logic of mass production.

5. *Progressive taxation.* The federal government and most of the states collect a graduated, or progressive, tax on incomes, estates, and gifts. These taxes help to pay the cost of government and all the services performed by government agencies. Many of these services, such as national defense, public health, education, research, and the building and care of highways, are of direct benefit to everyone. Other services, especially "welfare" services such as old age assistance, are designed to help the needy. Government expenditures for welfare have risen rapidly since 1929. Progressive taxation, by helping to make such payments possible, has raised the living standards of the very poor. At the same time, it has lessened the concentration of wealth in the hands of a small number of people.

A wider distribution of income.

One of the most important signs that industrialism has been tamed is the more equal division of the national income since 1940. During the 1930's the top 5 per cent of the population, income-wise, got 28 per cent of the total disposable income (that is, income after taxes). By 1945 their share had dropped to 17 per cent. Meanwhile, millions of families at the lower end of the income scale had risen from poverty to a point where they could enjoy a middle-class way of life. The improvement in their incomes was mainly due to higher wage rates, a high level of employment, and farm prosperity. In the 1950's prosperity continued to be widely distributed.

Growth of the labor movement.

The Wagner Act of 1935 established labor's right of collective bargaining (see p. 698). Thereafter the labor movement leaped ahead. In 1958 unions claimed 18 million union members. However, this number was less than a third of the total labor force. Nearly all production workers in big and middle-sized industry were organized. Unions of white-collar workers had been launched but their growth was slow.

The merger of the A.F. of L. and the CIO in 1955 brought together 140 national and international unions. These unions represented 68,000 locals

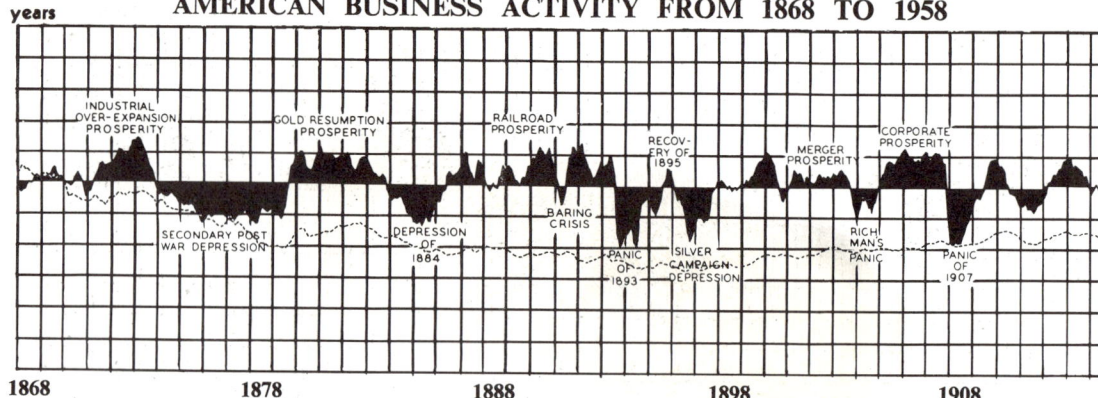

INDUSTRIAL OVER-EXPANSION PROSPERITY

GOLD RESUMPTION PROSPERITY

RAILROAD PROSPERITY

RECOVERY OF 1895

MERGER PROSPERITY

CORPORATE PROSPERITY

SECONDARY POST WAR DEPRESSION

DEPRESSION OF 1884

BARING CRISIS

PANIC OF 1893

SILVER CAMPAIGN DEPRESSION

RICH MAN'S PANIC

PANIC OF 1907

1868   1878   1888   1898   1908

with 15,000,000 members. Although some Americans feared that the combined AFL–CIO had too much power, its leaders pointed out that each national union was autonomous and would continue to run its own affairs. Furthermore, most of the local unions had individual contracts with employers, rather than contracts tied into industrywide agreements. The power to call a strike still rests in the local union.

Contracts are made by collective bargaining between representatives of the union and the employer. The contract states the rules as to working conditions, wage rates, seniority, the handling of grievances, and other matters. It may also provide certain "fringe benefits," such as holidays with pay, vacations with pay, life insurance, hospital insurance, and pensions. Until the 1940's, most industrial workers were not covered by fringe benefits. By 1958 some companies spent as much as 30 cents on fringe benefits for every dollar paid in straight wages.

Labor-management relations improve.

When the twentieth century began, labor was still thought of as a commodity to be bought as cheaply as possible. Few employers believed in collective bargaining. Even as late as the 1930's, efforts to destroy independent unions by means of violence, labor spies, and the bribery of union officials were common. Unions too were guilty of violence. Some of them felt they could get nowhere except by "class war."

Today industrial violence is rare. Collective bargaining is established in the major industries. The managers of these industries have a strong sense of responsibility for their employees, as shown by efforts to improve working and living conditions and the rapid increase in fringe benefits. Labor leaders too have taken a more responsible attitude. They see that industry must remain prosperous if labor is to prosper.

Efforts to control the business cycle.

Industrialism, as we have noted, brought the ups and downs in economic activity known as the business cycle. The Great Depression of the 1930's was the first in which the federal government took steps intended to stop the economic decline and to restore prosperity. At that time there was strong opposition to the idea that the government should try to control the business cycle. Today, however, this idea has been fully accepted. The only controversy has to do with how and when the government should act.

In 1946 Congress passed the National Employment Act, stating that the federal government had the responsibility to promote maximum employment, production, and purchasing pow-

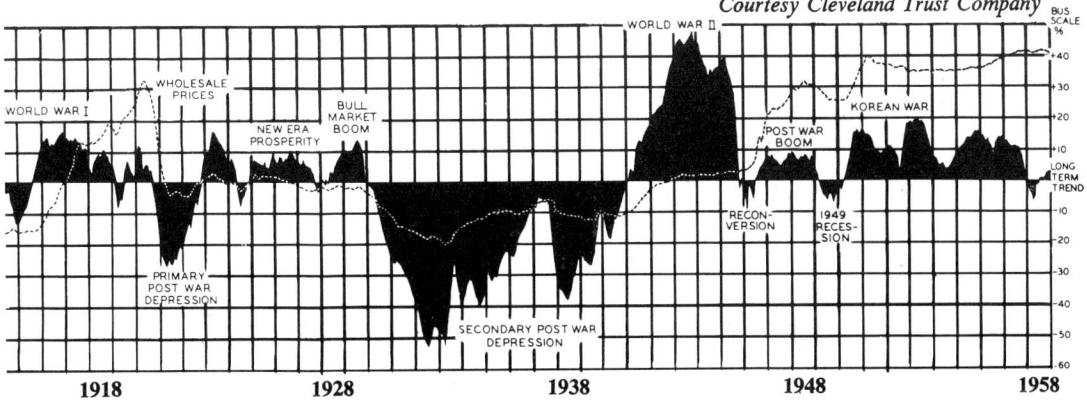

Courtesy Cleveland Trust Company

BUS SCALE %

WORLD WAR II

WHOLESALE PRICES

WORLD WAR I

NEW ERA PROSPERITY

BULL MARKET BOOM

KOREAN WAR

POST WAR BOOM

+40
+30
+20
+10
LONG TERM TREND
10
20
30
40
50
60

RECON- VERSION

1949 RECES- SION

PRIMARY POST WAR DEPRESSION

SECONDARY POST WAR DEPRESSION

| 1918 | 1928 | 1938 | 1948 | 1958 |

er. Under this act the President appoints three men to serve as a Council of Economic Advisors. They prepare frequent reports to the nation in regard to economic conditions and prospects.

From the close of World War II until 1957 there were a few brief periods of economic decline but they were relatively mild. In areas where unemployment became critical, federal, state, and local officials co-operated with businessmen to increase the number of jobs. For example, more defense contracts were awarded to manufacturers in these areas, and more public works were built there. The value of unemployment insurance was shown, for it helped to maintain consumer spending. Social security benefits acted as "built-in economic stabilizers."

The recession of 1957–58 proved to be more severe than any since World War II. However, the nation had more information about the state of the economy than ever before. The federal government issued reports on the number of unemployed, the number receiving unemployment compensation, the cost of living, and other information related to the recession. Congressional committees studied possible measures to stimulate the economy. The government then initiated a number of anti-recession moves. In 1959 many signs indicated that the downturn in business had been reversed.

Americans Enjoy Leisure, Health, and Cultural Opportunities

More leisure for all.

With the harnessing of industrialism for the benefit of the entire people has come more leisure for everyone. In 1900 the sixty-hour work week was the rule. By 1950 the forty-hour week was almost universal. In 1900 very few workers had a vacation with pay. Today most workers have one or two weeks of vacation with pay, and some have longer. There is a tendency, too, for employers to grant more holidays with pay. Homemakers too have leisure that would have amazed their grandmothers.

With more free time and higher income, the average American is enjoying leisure activities that once only the well to do could afford. Interest in travel and participation in hobbies, many of which require expensive equipment, and in outdoor sports, such as swimming, boating, fishing, and skiing, are growing.

The demand for recreational facilities and organized programs of recreation has been expanding for many years. Voluntary groups such as churches, community centers, country clubs, and organizations for young people

821

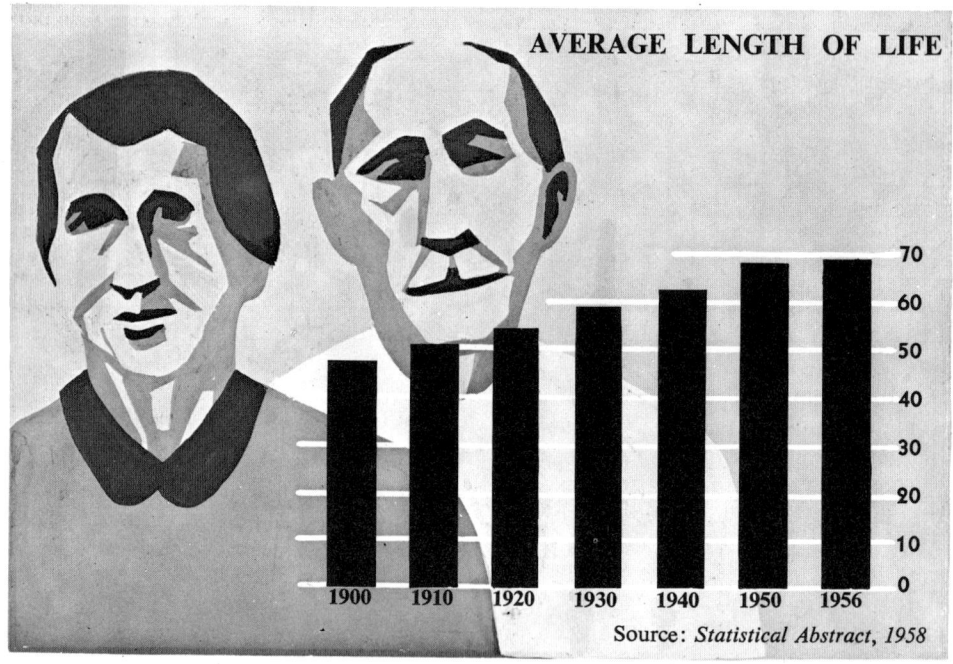

70
60
50
40
30
20
10
0

1900 1910 1920 1930 1940 1950 1956

Source: *Statistical Abstract, 1958*

meet the need in part. Government agencies, which provide parks, playgrounds, swimming pools, golf courses, and beaches, also help to meet the need. The importance of wholesome recreation has been recognized by big business, and many companies in recent years have provided recreational facilities for employees and their families. Labor unions too have begun to develop vacation places for the use of their members. All these activities, added to commercial amusements of all kinds, show that recreation is becoming an ever more important part of American life.

Americans live longer.

The twentieth century has brought more progress in conquering disease and prolonging life than was made in all the previous centuries since men appeared on earth. A child born in the United States today can be expected to live twenty-one years longer than a child born in 1900.

This impressive gain comes from advances in medical knowledge and medical training, in sanitation, and in public health measures; from greater popular understanding of the principles of health; and from a higher standard of living. Medical research has given us many useful drugs and treatments unknown a few years ago. More public clinics, health insurance benefits, and higher incomes have enabled a greater number of people to obtain expert medical care. Then, too, the average person today knows more about avoiding illness and caring for his health than did the average person of fifty years ago. Witness, for example, the change in eating habits which has taken place since the discovery of vitamins; today we eat more fruits, vegetables, meat, eggs, and dairy products than ever before.

The proportion of old people is rising.

The percentage of people over sixty-four years of age has doubled since 1900 and is still going up. Mean-

822

while, the proportion of old people who are employed has dropped from 50 per cent to less than half that figure. This change has come about with the decline in farming and other kinds of self-employment. While some old people enjoy the leisure that retirement brings, many others would far rather keep on working. Research concerning the problems of our older citizens has just begun.

More people gain an education.

We have already noted the rapid climb in the enrollment of high schools and colleges which took place from 1900 to 1930 (see p. 642). The rise went on during the 1930's, halted during World War II, then shot up again. By 1958, 85 per cent of the 14–17-year-olds and 32 per cent of the 18–21-year-olds were enrolled in educational institutions. The number of persons graduating from high school and college increased over tenfold from 1900 to 1958.

The most massive program of public aid to higher education in our history was authorized by Congress in 1944. Under the so-called "G.I. Bill of Rights," nearly eight million veterans of the second World War obtained additional training. Congress passed a similar law applying to Korean veterans, and nearly a million of them took advantage of it to obtain more education. In 1955 it was found that the average male veteran had completed over twelve years of schooling, or two years more than the nonveteran of the same age.

At the middle of the twentieth century the opportunity to obtain a college education was greater than the chances of a grammar school education a century ago. By 1955 we had nearly two thousand institutions of higher education. Enrollment in these institutions climbed so rapidly during the 1950's that before the end of the decade many were filled to overflowing. Not only was there a shortage of facilities for higher education, but also of teachers.

While formal education expanded at all levels from kindergarten through professional school, so did various kinds of adult education. Courses for adults were offered by more and more schools, colleges, and community organizations. Forums, discussion groups, and lectures—both face-to-face and broadcast—reached an ever greater number of listeners. In addition the 1950's brought an enormous rise in the sale of books, both fiction and nonfiction. By means of inexpensive paperback editions practically everyone could have at hand his own library of literature, history, science, and how-to-do-it information on every aspect of living. The nation had indeed made amazing educational gains since the beginning of the century.

Scientific research flourishes.

The twentieth century has seen the greatest scientific progress in all history. American scientists have had a leading part in this advance. By 1958 we were spending thirty times as much on research as in 1930. The share paid for by the federal government meanwhile jumped from a trifling figure to 50 per cent of the total.

In the last quarter century, spectacular discoveries have been made in three fields—physics, chemistry, and medicine. Easily the most sensational scientific discovery was the development of atomic power. This development was important not only for its potential destructive force in time of war, but as a source of unlimited power. By the late 1950's atomic energy had been harnessed for industrial use and as a source of power for ship propulsion. Scientists were at work applying nuclear power for many other peacetime uses.

An important branch of physics—electronics—made giant strides during

SPACE SUIT *to be worn by the pilot of the X–15 rocket ship. It is resistant to extremes of heat and cold and is pressurized to protect the pilot from accidents in flight.*

and after World War II. Among other things, research in electronics gave us television, frequency-modulation (FM) radio, electronic computers, the electronic microscope, and remarkable new devices to control machinery. Electronic controls have ushered in a new industrial era—the "automation revolution." Automation, or "push-button production," refers to the use of machines to run machines. It promises to make the manufacture of certain products, such as chemicals, plastics, rubber, and paper, completely automatic.

Research in chemistry has already given us a host of new products, including dyes, fabrics, plastics, paints, detergents, drugs, and many others. Nine in ten medicines prescribed by doctors today were unheard of in 1940. Four out of five present-day farm chemicals were unknown in 1945. Chemical research promises to bring us in the near future important new weapons against disease, synthetic foodstuffs, and substitutes for a number of scarce raw materials.

The exciting and startling experiences of the International Geophysical Year (I.G.Y.) introduced the Space Age. The I.G.Y. ran from July, 1957, to the end of 1958. Scientists from sixty-six nations co-operated in attempts to penetrate the mysteries of the earth and outer space. The organization of the project was a gigantic task. The thousands of scientists, equipped with the most advanced scientific instruments, gathered data on a vast number of the sciences—meteorology, oceanography, astrophysics, and related subjects.

American scientists were among the most active participants in the project. Congress appropriated $42,-500,000 to enable the National Science Foundation to carry through its part in the project.

Americans study their history and culture.

The new interest in Americana which appeared after World War I (see p. 645) is still evident. It has broadened to include every phase of America's history, folklore, and folk art. The study of Americana benefited from New Deal efforts to provide jobs that did not compete with private business. Unemployed writers and scholars were put to work gathering information for local histories and guidebooks, locating and cataloging old records, diaries, and other historical documents, preparing an index of American design, and collecting American folklore. During these years an enormous quantity of material useful in the study of America's past was made available for the first time. Today in many communities citizens have banded together to preserve their local historical houses, monuments, and the like.

Interest in music expands.

Public interest in music has developed at an incredible pace since World War I. A good deal of the credit goes to radio. The first network broadcast of a symphony orchestra was held in 1926. The Metropolitan Opera went on the air in 1931. Millions of people who had never heard good music expertly performed could now listen to it regularly. Many of them wanted to learn how to make music.

Thousands of schools and hundreds of colleges added bands, orchestras, and glee clubs to their activities. Community schools of music sprang up. So did music camps. Amateur choruses and orchestras were organized in many communities. In 1900 there were only a few symphony orchestras in the entire country, but by 1958 there were more than a thousand.

The introduction of microgroove, long-playing phonograph records after World War II revived record-playing in the home, which had declined with the coming of radio. The sale of records, both popular and classical, boomed. A new hobby developed—"hi-fi," or the construction and operation of high-fidelity phonographs.

The United States has a large number of gifted composers of music. Some are exiled European artists. Others were born in this country. Fine examples of every known style of music are being written here. Gian-Carlo Menotti, who came to the United States from Italy at the age of seventeen, ranks among the world's great operatic composers. Aaron Copland, to mention but one among many first-rate composers of instrumental music, has a world-wide reputation. Our popular music is, however, better known both here and abroad than the work of our more serious composers. Songs and light operas written by Victor Herbert, Jerome Kern, Cole Porter, Irving Berlin, Richard Rodgers, Sigmund Romberg, Vincent Youmans, and Oscar Hammerstein II bring pleasure to hosts of people in most parts of the world.

A wealth of American folk music is now being discovered and published.

It includes the songs and dances of American Negroes, Appalachian mountaineers, lumberjacks, miners, cowboys, canal boys, sailors, and other groups. Some of the most popular American dance music is heavily indebted to Negro folk music. Much of it contains passages with the distinctive rhythms and tonal quality of Negro ragtime and blues. George Gershwin used Negro musical themes in writing the folk opera *Porgy and Bess* (1935).

Interest in art expands.

Public interest in art was more evident in the 1950's than ever before. Each year, it was estimated, well over fifty million Americans visited art exhibits. A growing number of adults made a hobby of painting, sculpture, ceramics, or other fine arts. Still more of them bought reproductions of works of art. The demand for original works by American artists was also increasing and with it, the number of professional artists. Long-forgotten American painters were rediscovered. Many old-fashioned forms of folk art won admiration.

These developments could be traced to several influences: (1) The return to American soil in the early 1930's of many artists who had been living in Europe. (2) The gift of many private art collections to the public. (3) The establishment of the National Gallery of Art at Washington, D.C., through the generosity of Andrew W. Mellon. (4) The publication of articles on art, illustrated in full color, by pictorial magazines. (5) WPA federal art projects. During the 1930's many leading artists were on relief. The WPA put them to work making paintings for schools and other public buildings, teaching free art classes, indexing examples of folk art, and arranging traveling exhibitions of art works. (6) The study of art in schools and colleges. All these influences made the fine arts a living force in American life.

Architecture is modernized.

After 1945 the construction of houses, schools, factories, office buildings, and airports went forward at the greatest rate in our history. While the majority of buildings were put up with little thought of style, others were well designed. Leading architects followed an international style known as "functional modernism." This style, based on the idea that a structure's form should be determined by its function, was founded by three Americans—Louis Sullivan, Frank Lloyd Wright, and Albert Kahn. Buildings in this style are often starkly simple. Their beauty is found in straight lines and uncluttered flat surfaces; in a wide use of unadorned materials such as plate glass, aluminum, stainless steel, and panels of natural wood; and in the imaginative use of lighting and color.

American literature wins acclaim.

In the second quarter of the century distinguished poetry, fiction, drama, and biography continued to pour forth from American pens. Many writers specialized in portraying life in the region they knew best. The novelist John Steinbeck wrote of the Far West; James T. Farrell of the sordid life in the Chicago slums. In their novels, plays, and poems William Faulkner, Erskine Caldwell, Ellen Glasgow, Allen Tate, Thomas Wolfe, Tennessee Williams, Robert Penn Warren, and others pictured the changing South, often dwelling on the evil effects of industrialism. John P. Marquand's novels satirized the fading New England aristocracy.

Regionalists were not the only notable writers of the period. Sinclair Lewis warned his country of the danger of fascism in the novel *It Can't Happen Here* (1936). His *Kingsblood Royal* (1947) was an attack on racial prejudice. Ernest Hemingway's novel, *For Whom the Bell Tolls* (1940), pic-

tured the heroic struggle of the Loyalists in the Spanish civil war. Pearl Buck's *The Good Earth* (1931) told of Chinese village people with rare charm and sympathy. John Hersey's *A Bell for Adano, Hiroshima,* and *The Wall* related episodes in World War II. The poet Carl Sandburg created a noble six-volume biography of Abraham Lincoln.

A galaxy of gifted poets won attention, among them William Rose Benét, Karl Shapiro, Robert Lowell, Marianne Moore, and Wallace Stevens. There was also much creative writing for the stage. Eugene O'Neill, Thornton Wilder, Maxwell Anderson, Robert E. Sherwood, and Tennessee Williams were probably the best-known American dramatists of this period.

European critics showed more appreciation for American literature than in the past. Commencing with Sinclair Lewis in 1930, the coveted Nobel prize for literature was frequently awarded to an American. Eugene O'Neill received it in 1936, Pearl Buck in 1938, William Faulkner in 1949, and Ernest Hemingway in 1954.

Our country reaches cultural maturity.

When the twentieth century opened, it was already clear that Americans were well on the way to cultural maturity. By the mid-century the United States had scholars, artists, writers, musicians, and architects who ranked among the best in the world. In science, scholarship, and the fine arts even the most advanced nations could learn as much from us as we could learn from them. In another respect— the wide diffusion of education and the enjoyment of art among the people— we stood pre-eminent.

FOR IDENTIFICATION

Pearl S. Buck	Gian-Carlo Menotti
William Faulkner	National Gallery of Art
Ernest Hemingway	Eugene O'Neill
Sinclair Lewis	Frank Lloyd Wright

FOR EXPLANATION OR DEFINITION

automation
Council of Economic
   Advisors
electronics
"functional modernism"
gross national product
metropolitan area
progressive taxation
"regionalists"

FOR REVIEW

1. Compare the productivity of American industry today and in 1850.

2. Describe the "occupational shifts" brought about by industrialization.

3. (a) Explain why more women are employed in "gainful work." (b) How has the gainful employment of women tended to affect their status?

4. How has industrialization affected farming and the farm population?

5. How has industrialization affected the Negro population?

6. What are some of the signs indicating that industrialism has been "tamed"?

7. (a) Mention gains labor has made in recent years. (b) Why have labor and management relations improved? How?

8. What means are available to bring the ups and downs of the business cycle under control?

9. (a) In what ways has industrialism increased the amount of leisure time for all? (b) How do Americans tend to spend their increased leisure time?

10. What factors and conditions have increased the average life expectancy?

11. What are outstanding developments in American education at mid-century?

12. List some of the discoveries made in the fields of chemistry and physics in the last few years.

13. Give a few reasons for the increased interest in music. In art.

14. State some characteristics of modern architecture.

15. What are the evidences that our country has become culturally mature?

FOR FURTHER STUDY AND DISCUSSION

1. How does increased production per worker affect: (a) the volume of manufactured products; (b) wages; (c) employment? Helpful source: Lewis, *The Big Change*, chs. 13 and 15.

2. (a) What are the causes of the "spread of the city"? (b) What problems have resulted from growth of metropolitan areas?

3. Why has there been a marked shift in occupation and age groups throughout the United States? Helpful source: Hicks, *American Nation*, ch. 35.

4. Has the machine tended to displace workers, to create new jobs, or to do both of these things? Explain.

5. How was the I.G.Y. organized? Did its accomplishments achieve the goals of the project? Should there always be an unlimited international exchange of scientific information?

6. State the arguments for or against each of the following: (a) Literature reflects the spirit of an age; (b) Literature is an important factor in influencing political and social changes. Helpful source: Link, *American Epoch*, ch. 26.

7. Compare the 1950's with 1900 as regards: (a) life in cities; (b) recreation; (c) methods of transportation; (d) education; (e) scientific progress; (f) the status of women; (g) distribution of the national income. Helpful source: Lewis, *The Big Change*.

FOR INDIVIDUAL OR GROUP ACTIVITIES

1. Write a short essay on one of the following: The automobile, the motion picture industry, the radio, television. Helpful sources: Link, *American Epoch*, ch. 25; Seldes, *The Great Audience*.

2. Prepare a book report on Baxter, *Scientists Against Time*.

3. Report on developments in the peacetime uses of atomic energy.

4. Using old and current magazines, prepare a series of illustrations showing changes in art, housing, architecture, clothing, sports, and advertising in the last twenty-five years.

5. Hold a panel discussion on the influence of the radio and television on American education and culture. Helpful source: Seldes, *The Great Audience*.

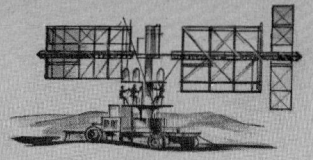

UNIT TEN REVIEW

HIGH POINTS

1

Following World War II, the United States demobilized rapidly. Congress put an end to most of the wartime controls over prices and production. American industries reconverted at astonishing speed and soon were turning out huge quantities of peacetime goods. Prices and wages went up. Inflation soon became a serious problem for which no solution was in sight.

2

In the mid-term elections of 1946 the Republicans capfured control of Congress. The controversial Taft-Hartley Act was passed in 1947, placing various controls on labor unions. The same year Congress submitted to the states the Twenty-second Amendment to prevent any President from serving more than two terms.

3

To the surprise of nearly all political forecasters, President Truman won re-election in 1948. His program, which he called the "Fair Deal," was an expansion of the New Deal. Only a part of it was enacted. Congress was inclined to assert its independence, as it had done after the War between North and South and after World War I.

4

World War II was hardly over before severe tension developed between the United States, Britain, and France on the one hand, and the Soviet Union on the other. Russia was believed to be encouraging Communist subversion throughout the globe. Hatred for Communists increased when Communist spy rings were uncovered in Canada, the United States, and Great Britain. Spies, it was learned, had transmitted many secrets to Russia. Congressional investigating committees found that a number of American Communists had infiltrated into labor unions, the press, the entertainment industry, and the civil service. In 1950 Congress passed the Internal Security Act, placing new and stronger curbs on Communist activities.

5

The writing of peace treaties revealed the sharp split between the Western democracies and the Soviet Union. In 1946, after months of wrangling, treaties were drawn up for Italy, Rumania, Bulgaria, and Hungary. Because Russia delayed so long in agreeing to take its troops out of Austria, that country had no peace treaty until 1955. Russia refused to agree to peace terms with Germany or with Japan that the United States and Britain could accept. The Western powers made a separate peace with Japan and with West Germany. East Germany remained under Soviet occupation; West Germany became an ally of the West.

6

Soon after the war many countries in eastern Europe became Russian satellites. In 1947 the United States began to give economic and military aid to Greece and Turkey in order to keep them from falling under Communist control. In the next four years the United States spent billions of dollars to promote economic recovery in sixteen European nations. This aid probably saved a number of these countries from communism. In 1952 all of them joined the United States in establishing the North Atlantic Treaty Organization (NATO). Congress voted large sums to help the NATO allies to rearm.

7

In its efforts to check the spread of communism, the United States was less successful in Asia than in Europe. In China the Nationalists were defeated despite a large amount of American aid. Chiang Kai-shek, the Nationalist leader, withdrew the remnants of his forces to Formosa.

Since the summer of 1950 they have had the protection of an American fleet. Largely because of our insistence, Nationalist delegates continued to represent China in the United Nations, although Red China demanded that its delegates be seated instead.

8

After the defeat of Japan, Korea was temporarily divided into two occupation zones. The Russians set up a Communist puppet government in North Korea, while the United Nations helped the people of South Korea to set up a government based on a democratic constitution. In 1950 the North Koreans invaded South Korea, intending to unite the country by force. The U.N. sent armed help to South Korea. When the U.N. forces, commanded by General Douglas MacArthur, drove the North Koreans into the extreme northern portion of their land, Red China sent in a large number of "volunteers." After months of bitter fighting, the war was brought to an end without victory for either side. Korea was still divided, but the independence of South Korea had been preserved.

9

From the start the United Nations was hampered by friction between the Soviet Union and the Western democracies. Russia used its veto again and again, blocking almost all action by the Security Council. The General Assembly, where there is no veto, gradually developed methods by which it could act to meet a threat to the peace when the Security Council was unable to act. The U.N. carried on a wide variety of activities of a nonpolitical sort, all of them contributing to international cooperation and well-being.

10

With the inauguration of Dwight D. Eisenhower (1953), the country had a Republican President for the first time in twenty years. His first administration tried without much success to reduce expenses for defense and foreign aid. There were few drastic changes in either foreign or domestic policy. During his second term of office Congress was controlled by the Democrats. While there was some opposition to the President's policies there was no great cleavage on major issues between the President and the Congress. Education became one of the critical national problems. In 1958 the National Defense Education Act provided limited federal funds to be used for the development of certain educational programs. Desegregation proceeded at a slow pace but some advances could be seen. An economic recession became a matter of grave concern but by the spring of 1959 had been controlled. The cold war became intensified. As one international crisis after another erupted, the nation was forced to expand its defense program and strengthen its alliances. Entering the Space Age stimulated increased attention on scientific experimentation.

11

In the years following World War II, the United States made great economic and cultural progress. As output climbed, all classes of Americans shared the benefits of higher earnings, better working conditions, and more leisure. One result was a tremendous expansion in the percentage of young people attending high school and college; another was increased popular interest in the fine arts. The nation supported more libraries, orchestras and art museums, and more centers for scientific research than ever before. Remarkable advances were made in every field of science. Many diseases were conquered. Americans were living longer and were living more fully. The great changes that began in Europe and produced the Modern Age were reaching a splendid fruition in the United

States. For the time being, at least, our nation had become the guardian of Western civilization. Whether this civilization could survive depended, in all probability, upon the courage, fortitude, and wisdom with which America exercised its position as the acknowledged leader of the West.

QUESTIONS

1. (a) Account for the great industrial productivity of the United States in the 1950's. (b) Summarize the important social, political, and economic effects of America's productivity. (c) In what respects has the attitude of Americans toward Big Business changed since the days of Theodore Roosevelt?

2. (a) Outline the differences between the Taft-Hartley Act and the Wagner Labor Relations Act. (b) What gains has labor made in the period since 1945? (c) What are some of the evidences of a different attitude by management toward labor? Of labor toward management?

3. (a) How have the following influenced education: television, industrialization, the G. I. Bill of Rights? (b) State the arguments for and against federal aid to education.

4. (a) Review the gains made by minority groups in the past quarter century. (b) Explain the 1954 ruling of the Supreme Court concerning "desegregation" in the schools. (c) What progress has been made in complying with the ruling of the Supreme Court?

5. Outline the present immigration laws of the United States.

6. Describe the St. Lawrence Seaway and Power Project: the Federal Highway Bill of 1956.

7. Account for Truman's "surprise" victory in the presidential campaign of 1948; for Eisenhower's success in 1952.

8. In what respects did the Republican administration of Mr. Eisenhower continue or modify the domestic program of the New Deal and the Fair Deal? The foreign policy of the Truman administration?

9. How did the Eisenhower administration endeavor to help the farmer?

10. (a) What legislative program did the President recommend to Congress in January, 1957? (b) What action did the 85th Congress take with regard to these recommendations?

11. List and explain briefly those issues or problems which in your opinion will continue to be of major concern to the American people in the next few years.

12. (a) Why did a "cold war" develop between the "East" and the "West"? (b) Prepare a chronological outline of the major events in the "cold war." (c) Outline the policy of the "West" and "East" toward Germany, Yugoslavia, Egypt and the Near East, Indo-China. (d) Explain the Truman Doctrine, the Marshall Plan, the Point IV Program.

13. (a) What special problems resulted from the rise of the Communists to power in China? (b) List the important political developments in the Pacific and Southeast Asia since 1945.

14. (a) How and when did the Korean War begin? (b) Was the Korean War a United Nations war or a United States war? (c) Why did President Truman relieve General MacArthur of his command? (d) What is the present situation in Korea?

15. (a) What is a "mutual security pact"? (b) Review and explain the mutual security pacts to which the United States is committed.

16. (a) How has the "cold war" affected the Security Council of the United Nations? The General Assembly? (b) Explain what is meant by "neutralism."

17. (a) Outline the major accomplishments of the United Nations. (b) Should the charter of the United Nations be re-

vised? If so, what changes should be made? If not, state the arguments against modifying the charter.

18. (a) Why was the United States deadlocked over the international control of atomic energy? (b) What is the present status of proposals for the international control of atomic energy? Of proposals for disarmament?

19. In what ways does our modern national defense program differ from past programs?

SUGGESTED READINGS

SOURCE MATERIALS, DOCUMENTS,

AND MAPS

Bartlett, R. J. (ed.) *The Record of American Diplomacy: Documents and Readings in the History of American Foreign Relations*, 3rd ed. Knopf, 1954.

Commager, *Documents*

Langsam, W. C. (ed.) *Documents and Readings in the History of Europe Since 1918.* Lippincott, 1951.

Lord (ed.) *Historical Atlas.*

Plischke, E. (ed.) *International Relations, Basic Documents.* Van Nostrand, 1953.

The Amherst Series: *Loyalty in a Democratic State; Education for Democracy; Industry-wide Collective Bargaining — Promise or Menace?* Heath.

GENERAL REFERENCES:

Allen, F. L., *The Big Change: America Transforms Herself, 1900–1950.* Harper, 1952.

° Arne, Sigrid, *United Nations Primer.* Rinehart, 1945.

Ashmore, H. S., *The Negro and the Schools.* rev. ed. 1954.

Bailey, T. A., *Diplomatic History.*

———. *America Faces Russia.* Cornell University Press, 1950.

Barth, Alan, *The Loyalty of Free Men.* Viking, 1951.

Bemis, *Diplomatic History.*

Budenz, L. F. *Men Without Faces: The Communist Conspiracy in the United States.* Harper, 1950.

Burlingame, R. *Backgrounds of Power: The Human Story of Mass Production.* Scribner, 1949.

Bush, Vannevar. *Modern Arms and Free Men.* Simon and Schuster, 1949.

Chambers, Whittaker. *Witness.* Random House, 1952.

Chase, E. P. *The United Nations in Action.* McGraw-Hill, 1950.

Cheney, M. *Modern Art in America.* McGraw-Hill, 1940.

Clay, L. D. *Decision in Germany.* Doubleday, 1950.

Curti, M. E. *The Roots of American Loyalty.* Columbia University Press, 1946.

Daniels, Walter M. *The Government and the Farmer.* H. W. Wilson, 1956.

De Toledano, R. and Lasky, V. *Seeds of Treason: The True Story of the Hiss-Chambers Tragedy.* Ryerson Press, 1950.

Dietz, D. *Atomic Energy in the Coming Era.* Dodd, Mead, 1945.

Dulles, F. R. *America's Rise to World Power, 1898–1954.* Harper, 1955.

———. *Labor in America.* Crowell, 1949.

Feis, H. *The China Tangle; The American Effort in China from Pearl Harbor to the Marshall Mission.* Princeton University Press, 1953.

Fischer, John. *Why They Behave Like Russians.* Harper, 1947.

° Galt, T. *How the United Nations Works.* Crowell, 1947.

Gitlow, B. *The Whole of Their Lives: Communism in America.* Scribner, 1948.

Goldman, Eric F. *The Crucial Decade; America, 1945–1955.* Knopf, 1956.

Gunther, John. *Inside U. S. A.* Harper, 1947.

———. *Inside Africa.* Harper, 1955.

———. *Behind the Curtain.* Harper, 1949.

Handlin, O. *The American People in the Twentieth Century.* Harvard University Press, 1954.

Hicks, J. D. *The American Nation.* Houghton, 1955.

Higgins, M. *The War in Korea: The Report of a Woman Combat Correspondent.* Doubleday, 1951.

Hoffman, F. J. *The Modern Novel in America, 1900–1950.* Saunders, 1951.

Kennan, G. F. *American Diplomacy, 1900–1950.* University of Chicago Press, 1951.

Kissinger, Henry A. *Nuclear Weapons and Foreign Policy.* Harper, 1957.

Lapp, Ralph E. *Atoms and People.* Harper, 1956.

Larkin, O. W. *Art and Life in America.* Rinehart, 1952.

Latourette, K. S. *The American Record in the Far East, 1945–1951.* Macmillan, 1952.

Lattimore, Owen. *Ordeal by Slander.* Little, Brown, 1950.

Leyson, B. W. *Atomic Energy in War and Peace.* Dutton, 1951.

Lilienthal, D. W. *Big Business: A New Era.* Harper, 1953.

———. *This I Do Believe.* Harper, 1949.

Link, A. *The American Epoch; A History of the United States Since the 1890's.* Knopf, 1955.

Marshall, C. B. *The Limits of Foreign Policy.* Holt, 1954.

Millis, W. (ed.) *The Forrestal Diaries.* Viking, 1951.

Mills, C. W. and Schneider, H. *The New Men of Power: America's Labor Leaders.* Harcourt, Brace, 1948.

Morison and Commager, *American Republic.*

Oliver, R. T. *Why War Came in Korea.* Fordham University Press, 1950.

Petrov, V. *My Retreat from Russia.* Yale University Press, 1950.

Philbrick, H. A. *I Led Three Lives.* McGraw-Hill, 1952.

President's Commission on Civil Rights. *To Secure These Rights.* Simon and Schuster, 1949.

Roosevelt, E. and Ferris, H. *Partners: The United Nations and Youth.* Doubleday, 1950.

Rovere, R. N. and Schlesinger, A. M., Jr. *The General and the President.* Farrar, Straus, 1951.

Schlesinger. *Modern America.*

Seldes, G. *The Great Audience.* Viking, 1950.

Spaeth, S. *The History of Popular Music in America.* Random House, 1948.

Spiller, R. E. and others. *Literary History of the United States.* Macmillan, 1953.

Welles, S. *Seven Decisions That Shaped History.* Harper, 1951.

Weyl, N. *The Battle Against Disloyalty.* Crowell, 1951.

White, T. H. *Fire in the Ashes: Europe in Mid-Century.* Sloane, 1954.

Wish, Harvey. *Society and Thought in Modern America.* Longmans, Green, 1952.

Wood, J. P. *Magazines in the United States.* Ronald, 1956.

For current developments consult the daily newspapers and weekly and monthly magazines, such as *Time, Life, U.S. News and World Report, Harper's, The Atlantic Monthly, Scholastic, The American Observer,* and others. *The Statistical Abstract of the United States, The World Almanac,* and *Information Please Almanac* are especially valuable. The Department of Public Information of the United Nations, New York, and the Superintendent of Public Documents, Government Printing Office, Washington, D.C., are helpful sources of information. Many pamphlets on topics of lively current interest are published by various organizations such as the American Association for the United Nations, Inc., 345 East 46 Street, New York; The Foreign Policy Association, 345 East 46 Street, New York; Public Affairs Committee, Inc., 22 East 38 Street, New York; The United Nations Information Center, 345 East 46 Street, New York. *Social Education,* published by the National Council for the Social Studies, Washington, D. C., provides important information on new books, pamphlets and audio-visual materials.

BIOGRAPHY

Bradley, Omar N. *A Soldier's Story.* Holt, 1951.

Donovan, R. J. *Eisenhower: The Inside Story.* Harper, 1956.

Gunther, John. *Eisenhower: The Man and the Symbol.* Harper, 1952.

Lee, C. G. and Henschel, R. *Douglas MacArthur.* Holt, 1952.

Martin, J. B. *Adlai Stevenson.* Harper, 1952.

Payne, R. *Mao Tse-tung: Ruler of Red China.* Schuman, 1950.

Truman, Harry S. *Year of Decision.* Doubleday, 1955.

———. *Years of Trial and Hope.* Doubleday, 1956.

FICTION

O'Connor, E. *The Last Hurrah.* Little, Brown, 1956.

Sterne, E. S. *Incident in Yorkville.* Rinehart, 1943.

Presidents and Vice-Presidents

No.	President	Years in Office	Political Party	Vice-President
1	George Washington	1789–1797	None	John Adams
2	John Adams	1797–1801	Federalist	Thomas Jefferson
3	Thomas Jefferson	1801–1809	Dem.-Republican	Aaron Burr
				George Clinton
4	James Madison	1809–1817	Dem.-Republican	George Clinton
				Elbridge Gerry
5	James Monroe	1817–1825	Dem.-Republican	Daniel D. Tompkins
6	John Quincy Adams	1825–1829	National-Republican	John C. Calhoun
7	Andrew Jackson	1829–1837	Democratic	John C. Calhoun
				Martin Van Buren
8	Martin Van Buren	1837–1841	Democratic	Richard M. Johnson
9	William H. Harrison	1841	Whig	John Tyler
10	John Tyler	1841–1845	Whig	
11	James K. Polk	1845–1849	Democratic	George M. Dallas
12	Zachary Taylor	1849–1850	Whig	Millard Fillmore
13	Millard Fillmore	1850–1853	Whig	
14	Franklin Pierce	1853–1857	Democratic	William R. King
15	James Buchanan	1857–1861	Democratic	John C. Breckinridge
16	Abraham Lincoln	1861–1865	Republican	Hannibal Hamlin
				Andrew Johnson
17	Andrew Johnson	1865–1869	Republican	
18	Ulysses S. Grant	1869–1877	Republican	Schuyler Colfax
				Henry Wilson
19	Rutherford B. Hayes	1877–1881	Republican	William A. Wheeler
20	James A. Garfield	1881	Republican	Chester A. Arthur
21	Chester A. Arthur	1881–1885	Republican	
22	Grover Cleveland	1885–1889	Democratic	Thomas A. Hendricks
23	Benjamin Harrison	1889–1893	Republican	Levi P. Morton
24	Grover Cleveland	1893–1897	Democratic	Adlai E. Stevenson
25	William McKinley	1897–1901	Republican	Garret A. Hobart
				Theodore Roosevelt
26	Theodore Roosevelt	1901–1909	Republican	Charles Fairbanks
27	William H. Taft	1909–1913	Republican	James S. Sherman
28	Woodrow Wilson	1913–1921	Democratic	Thomas R. Marshall
29	Warren G. Harding	1921–1923	Republican	Calvin Coolidge
30	Calvin Coolidge	1923–1929	Republican	Charles G. Dawes
31	Herbert C. Hoover	1929–1933	Republican	Charles Curtis
32	Franklin D. Roosevelt	1933–1945	Democratic	John Nance Garner
				Henry A. Wallace
				Harry S. Truman
33	Harry S. Truman	1945–1953	Democratic	Alben W. Barkley
34	Dwight D. Eisenhower	1953–*1961*	Republican	Richard M. Nixon

*35. John F. Kennedy 1961–196*3 *Democratic* — *Lydon B. Johnson*

Lyden B. Johnson 1964–68 Democratic

Humphrey

THE WORLD TODAY

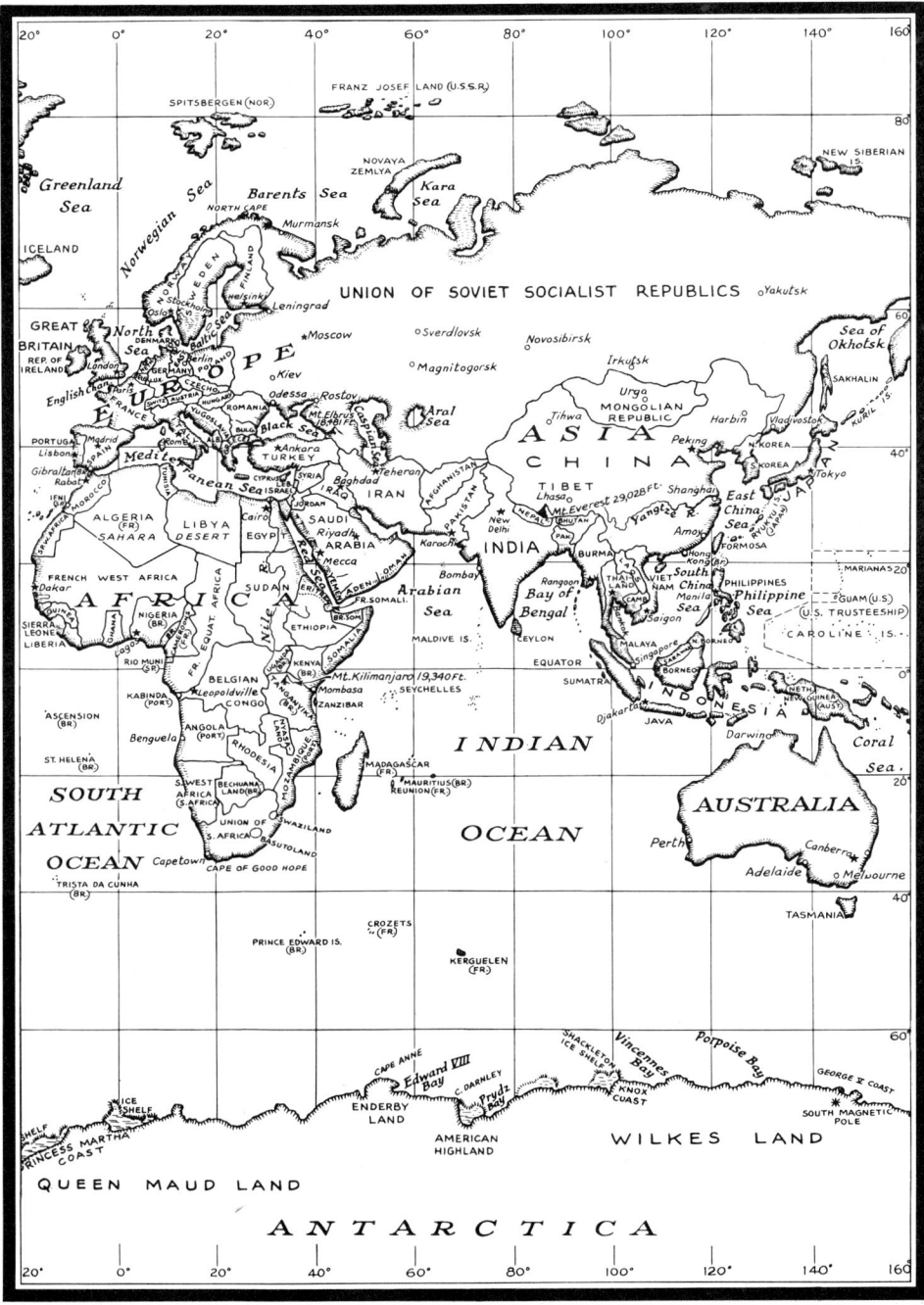

835

DECLARATION OF INDEPENDENCE

IN CONGRESS, JULY 4, 1776

A Declaration by the Representatives of the United States of America, in Congress Assembled

When, in the course of human events, it becomes necessary for one people to dissolve the political bands which have connected them with another, and to assume, among the powers of the earth, the separate and equal station to which the laws of nature and of nature's God entitle them, a decent respect to the opinions of mankind requires that they should declare the causes which impel them to the separation.

We hold these truths to be self-evident: That all men are created equal; that they are endowed by their Creator with certain unalienable rights; that among these are life, liberty, and the pursuit of happiness. That, to secure these rights, governments are instituted among men, deriving their just powers from the consent of the governed; that, whenever any form of government becomes destructive of these ends, it is the right of the people to alter or to abolish it, and to institute a new government, laying its foundation on such principles, and organizing its powers in such form, as to them shall seem most likely to effect their safety and happiness. Prudence, indeed, will dictate that governments long established should not be changed for light and transient causes; and accordingly all experience hath shown that mankind are more disposed to suffer while evils are sufferable, than to right themselves by abolishing the forms to which they are accustomed. But when a long train of abuses and usurpations, pursuing invariably the same object, evinces a design to reduce them under absolute despotism, it is their right, it is their duty, to throw off such government, and to provide new guards for their future security. Such has been the patient sufferance of these colonies; and such is now the necessity which constrains them to alter their former systems of government. The history of the present King of Great Britain is a history of repeated injuries and usurpations, all having in direct object the establishment of an absolute tyranny over these states. To prove this, let facts be submitted to a candid world.

He has refused his assent to laws the most wholesome and necessary for the public good.

He has forbidden his governors to pass laws of immediate and pressing importance, unless suspended in their operation till his assent should be obtained; and, when so suspended, he has utterly neglected to attend to them.

He has refused to pass other laws for the accommodation of large districts of people, unless those people would relinquish the right of representation in the legislature,—a right inestimable to them, and formidable to tyrants only.

He has called together legislative bodies at places unusual, uncomfortable, and distant from the depository of their public records, for the sole purpose of fatiguing them into compliance with his measure.

He has dissolved representative houses repeatedly, for opposing, with manly firmness, his invasions on the rights of the people.

He has refused, for a long time after such dissolutions, to cause others to be elected, whereby the legislative powers, incapable of annihilation, have returned to the people at large for their exercise; the state remaining, in the mean time, exposed to all the dangers of invasions from without and convulsions within.

He has endeavored to prevent the population of these states; for that purpose obstructing the laws for the naturalization of foreigners, refusing to pass others to encourage their migration hither, and raising the conditions of new appropriations of lands.

He has obstructed the administration of justice, by refusing his assent to laws for establishing judiciary powers.

He has made judges dependent on his will alone for the tenure of their offices, and the amount and payment of their salaries.

He has erected a multitude of new offices, and sent hither swarms of officers to harass our people and eat out their substance.

He has kept among us in times of peace standing armies, without the consent of our legislatures.

He has affected to render the military independent of, and superior to, the civil power.

He has combined with others to subject us to a jurisdiction foreign to our constitutions and unacknowledged by our laws, giving his assent to their acts of pretended legislation:

For quartering large bodies of armed troops among us;

For protecting them, by a mock trial, from punishment for any murders which they should commit on the inhabitants of these states;

For cutting off our trade with all parts of the world;

For imposing taxes on us without our consent;

For depriving us, in many cases, of the benefits of trial by jury;

For transporting us beyond seas, to be tried for pretended offences;

For abolishing the free system of English laws in a neighboring province, establishing therein an arbitrary government, and enlarging its boundaries, so as to render it at once an example and fit instrument for introducing the same absolute rule into these colonies;

For taking away our charters, abolishing our most valuable laws, and altering, fundamentally, the forms of our governments;

For suspending our own legislatures, and declaring themselves invested with power to legislate for us in all cases whatsoever.

He has abdicated government here, by declaring us out of his protection and waging war against us.

He has plundered our seas, ravaged our coasts, burned our towns, and destroyed the lives of our people.

He is at this time transporting large armies of foreign mercenaries to complete the works of death, desolation, and tyranny already begun with circumstances of cruelty and perfidy scarcely paralleled in the most barbarous ages, and totally unworthy the head of a civilized nation.

He has constrained our fellow-citizens, taken captive on the high seas, to bear arms against their country, to become the executioners of their friends and brethren, or to fall themselves by their hands.

He has excited domestic insurrection among us, and has endeavored to bring on the inhabitants of our frontiers the merciless Indian savages, whose known rule of warfare is an undistinguished destruction of all ages, sexes, and conditions.

In every stage of these oppressions we have petitioned for redress in the most humble terms; our repeated petitions have been answered only by repeated injury. A prince whose character is thus marked by every act which may define a tyrant is unfit to be the ruler of a free people.

Nor have we been wanting in our attentions to our British brethren. We have warned them, from time to time, of attempts by their legislature to extend an unwarrantable jurisdiction over us. We have reminded them of the circumstances of our emigration and settlement here. We have appealed to their native justice and magnanimity; and we have conjured them, by the ties of our common kindred, to disavow these usurpations, which would inevitably interrupt our connections and correspondence. They, too, have been deaf to the voice of justice and consanguinity. We must, therefore, acquiesce in the necessity which denounces our separation, and hold them, as we hold the rest of mankind, enemies in war, in peace friends.

We, therefore, the representatives of the United States of America, in General Congress assembled, appealing to the Supreme Judge of the world for the rectitude of our intentions, do, in the name and by the authority of the good people of these colonies, solemnly publish and declare, That these united colonies are, and of right ought to be, free and independent states; that they are absolved from all allegiance to the British crown, and that all political connection between them and the state of Great Britain is, and ought to be, totally dissolved; and that, as free and independent states, they have full power to levy war, conclude peace, contract alliances, establish commerce, and do all other acts and things which independent states may of right do. And, for the support of this declaration, with a firm reliance on the protection of Divine Providence, we mutually pledge to each other our lives, our fortunes, and our sacred honor.

CONSTITUTION
OF THE UNITED STATES OF AMERICA

(The headings in heavy type are inserted for the reader's convenience)

PREAMBLE

The people, voting by states, establish the Union. We the people of the United States, in order to form a more perfect union, establish justice, insure domestic tranquillity, provide for the common defence, promote the general welfare, and secure the blessings of liberty to ourselves and our posterity, do ordain and establish this CONSTITUTION for the United States of America.

Article I. Legislative Department

Section I. CONGRESS

Congress consists of two houses. All legislative powers herein granted shall be vested in a Congress of the United States, which shall consist of a Senate and a House of Representatives.

★ *See page 142, The "Great Compromise."*

Section II. HOUSE OF REPRESENTATIVES

1. The people elect their representatives. The House of Representatives shall be composed of members chosen every second year by the people of the several States, and the electors in each State shall have the qualifications requisite for electors of the most numerous branch of the State Legislature.

★ *"Electors" means "voters." The states set the "qualifications requisite" for their electors. Those persons allowed by the laws of their state to vote for members of the larger branch of their own state legislature are likewise entitled to vote for members of the House.*

2. Who may be representatives? No person shall be a Representative who shall not have attained to the age of twenty-five years, and been seven years a citizen of the United States, and who shall not, when elected, be an inhabitant of that State in which he shall be chosen.

3. Representation in the House is based on population. Representatives and direct taxes shall be apportioned among the several States which may be included within this Union, according to their respective numbers, which shall be determined by adding to the whole number of free persons, including those bound to service for a term of years, and excluding Indians not taxed, three fifths of all other persons. The actual enumeration shall be made within three years after the first meeting of the Congress of the United States, and within every subsequent term of ten years, in such manner as they shall by law direct. The number of Representatives shall not exceed one for every thirty thousand, but each State shall have at least one Representative; and until such enumeration shall be made, the State of New Hampshire shall be entitled to choose three, Massachusetts eight, Rhode Island and Providence Plantations one, Connecticut five, New York six, New Jersey four, Pennsylvania eight, Delaware one, Maryland six, Virginia ten, North Carolina five, South Carolina five, and Georgia three.

★ *The first sentence has been modified by the Sixteenth Amendment. "Other persons" refers to "slaves." See page 144. In 1911 the total number of representatives was set at 435. Apportionment under the 1950 census was one representative for every 350,000 people.*

4. Vacancies in the House are filled by election. When vacancies happen in the representation from any State, the Executive authority thereof shall issue writs of election to fill such vacancies.

5. The House selects its speaker; it alone has power to impeach. The House of Representatives shall choose their Speaker and other officers; and shall have the sole power of impeachment.

★ *The Speaker is one of the leaders of the political party holding a majority in the House.*

On "impeachment," see page 152.

Section III. SENATE

1. The Senate represents the states. The Senate of the United States shall be composed of two Senators from each State, chosen [by the legislature thereof,] for six years; and each Senator shall have one vote.

★ *This method of electing Senators was repealed in 1913 by the Seventeenth Amendment.*

2. **One third of the senators are chosen every two years.** Immediately after they shall be assembled in consequence of the first election, they shall be divided as equally as may be into three classes. The seats of the Senators of the first class shall be vacated at the expiration of the second year, of the second class at the expiration of the fourth year, and of the third class at the expiration of the sixth year, so that one third may be chosen every second year; [and if vacancies happen by resignation or otherwise, during the recess of the legislature of any State, the Executive thereof may make temporary appointments until the next meeting of the legislature, which shall then fill such vacancies.]

★ *The last statement was changed by the Seventeenth Amendment.*

3. **Who may be senators?** No person shall be a Senator who shall not have attained the age of thirty years, and been nine years a citizen of the United States, and who shall not, when elected, be an inhabitant of that State for which he shall be chosen.

4. **The Vice-President presides over the Senate.** The Vice-President of the United States shall be President of the Senate, but shall have no vote, unless they be equally divided.

5. **The Senate chooses its other officers.** The Senate shall choose their other officers, and also a President *pro tempore*, in the absence of the Vice-President, or when he shall exercise the office of President of the United States.

6. **The Senate alone has power to try impeachments.** The Senate shall have the sole power to try all impeachments. When sitting for that purpose, they shall be on oath or affirmation. When the President of the United States is tried, the Chief Justice shall preside: and no person shall be convicted without the concurrence of two thirds of the members present.

★ *See page 152.*

7. **Conviction may result in removal from office.** Judgment in cases of impeachment shall not extend further than to removal from office, and disqualification to hold and enjoy any office of honor, trust or profit under the United States: but the party convicted shall nevertheless be liable and subject to indictment, trial, judgment and punishment, according to law.

Section IV. ELECTION AND MEETINGS OF CONGRESS

1. **Regulation of elections.** The times, places and manner of holding elections for Senators and Representatives shall be prescribed in each State by the legislature thereof; but the Congress may at any time by law make or alter such regulations, except as to the places of choosing Senators.

★ *This is to keep Congress from naming the meeting places of the state legislatures.*

2. **Congress must meet once a year.** The Congress shall assemble at least once in every year, and such meeting [shall be on the first Monday in December, unless they shall by law appoint a different day.]

★ *This date was repealed in 1933 by the Twentieth Amendment. See page 253.*

Section V. ORGANIZATION AND RULES OF THE HOUSES

1. **Each House may refuse to seat a member.** Each house shall be the judge of the elections, returns and qualifications of its own members, and a majority of each shall constitute a quorum to do business; but a smaller number may adjourn from day to day, and may be authorized to compel the attendance of absent members, in such manner, and under such penalties, as each house may provide.

★ *A quorum means the number of members required for the transaction of business. In both House and Senate a quorum is a majority of the members.*

2. **Each House makes its own rules of procedure.** Each house may determine the rules of its proceedings, punish its members for disorderly behavior, and with the concurrence of two thirds, expel a member.

★ *Expulsion is the severest punishment that either branch may inflict upon its members. Seldom has it been found necessary by either branch to use this power. Since both House and Senate have control over the official conduct of their members, it follows that neither a Senator nor a Representative is subject to impeachment. See page 771.*

3. **Each House must keep and publish a record of its proceedings.** Each house shall keep a journal of its proceedings, and from time to time publish the same, excepting such parts as may in their judgment require secrecy; and the yeas and nays of the members of either house on any question shall, at the desire of one fifth of those present, be entered on the journal.

★ *The printed journal bears the title "The Congressional Record." It is issued daily when Congress is in session and contains an official record of all proceedings on the floor of both Houses.*

4. Both Houses must agree regarding adjournment. Neither house, during the session of Congress, shall, without the consent of the other, adjourn for more than three days, nor to any other place than that in which the two houses shall be sitting.

Section VI. PRIVILEGES OF AND PROHIBITIONS UPON CONGRESSMEN

1. Congressmen receive a salary from the United States and have certain privileges. The Senators and Representatives shall receive a compensation for their services, to be ascertained by law and paid out of the treasury of the United States. They shall in all cases except treason, felony and breach of the peace, be privileged from arrest during their attendance at the session of their respective houses, and in going to and returning from the same; and for any speech or debate in either house, they shall not be questioned in any other place.

★ *Members of Congress now receive a salary of $22,500 and a tax-exempt expense account of $2,500.*

2. A Congressman must not hold any other federal civil office. No Senator or Representative shall, during the time for which he was elected, be appointed to any civil office under the authority of the United States, which shall have been created, or the emoluments whereof shall have been increased, during such time; and no person holding any office under the United States shall be a member of either house during his continuance in office.

Section VII. METHOD OF MAKING LAWS

1. Money bills must originate in the House of Representatives. All bills for raising revenue shall originate in the House of Representatives; but the Senate may propose or concur with amendments as on other bills.

★ *Today the influence of the Senate in the passage of revenue bills is no less powerful than that of the House because of the Senate's power of amendment.*

2. The President has a veto power. Every bill which shall have passed the House of Representatives and the Senate, shall, before it become a law, be presented to the President of the United States; if he approve he shall sign it, but if not he shall return it with his objections to that house in which it shall have originated, who shall enter the objections at large on their journal, and proceed to reconsider it. If after such reconsideration two thirds of that house shall agree to pass the bill, it shall be sent, together with the objections, to the other house, by which it shall likewise be reconsidered, and, if approved by two thirds of that house, it shall become a law. But in all such cases the votes of both houses shall be determined by yeas and nays, and the names of the persons voting for and against the bill shall be entered on the journal of each house respectively. If any bill shall not be returned by the President within ten days (Sundays excepted) after it shall have been presented to him, the same shall be a law, in like manner as if he had signed it, unless the Congress by their adjournment prevent its return, in which case it shall not be a law.

★ *Neither branch of Congress is able to legislate independently of the other. Each house must agree separately upon all the terms of a bill before it may be presented to the President for his signature.*

3. All resolutions or votes go to the President for his approval. Every order, resolution, or vote to which the concurrence of the Senate and House of Representatives may be necessary (except on a question of adjournment) shall be presented to the President of the United States; and before the same shall take effect, shall be approved by him, or being disapproved by him, shall be repassed by two thirds of the Senate and House of Representatives, according to the rules and limitations prescribed in the case of a bill.

Section VIII. POWERS GRANTED TO CONGRESS

Congress has certain enumerated powers:

1. It may lay and collect taxes. The Congress shall have power to lay and collect taxes, duties, imposts, and excises, to pay the debts and provide for the common defence and general welfare of the United States; but all duties, imposts and excises shall be uniform throughout the United States;

2. It may borrow money. To borrow money on the credit of the United States;

3. It may regulate foreign and interstate trade. To regulate commerce with foreign nations, and among the several States, and with the Indian tribes;

4. It may pass naturalization and bankruptcy laws. To establish an uniform rule of naturalization, and uniform laws on the subject of bankruptcies throughout the United States;

5. It may coin money. To coin money, regulate the value thereof, and of foreign coin, and fix the standard of weights and measures;

6. It may punish counterfeiters. To provide for the punishment of counterfeiting the securities and current coin of the United States;

7. It may establish a postal service. To establish post offices and post roads;

8. It may issue patents and copyrights. To

promote the progress of science and useful arts by securing for limited times to authors and inventors the exclusive right to their respective writings and discoveries;

9. It may establish inferior courts. To constitute tribunals inferior to the Supreme Court;

10. It may punish crimes committed on the high seas. To define and punish piracies and felonies committed on the high seas and offences against the law of nations;

11. It may declare war. To declare war, grant letters of marque and reprisal, and make rules concerning captures on land and water.

★ *Letters of marque and reprisal are letters given to private citizens in time of war authorizing them to capture enemy ships.*

12. It may maintain an army. To raise and support armies, but no appropriation of money to that use shall be for a longer term than two years;

13. It may maintain a navy. To provide and maintain a navy;

14. It may regulate the Army and Navy. To make rules for the government and regulation of the land and naval forces;

15. It may call out the state militia. To provide for calling forth the militia to execute the laws of the Union, suppress insurrections, and repel invasions;

16. It shares with the states the control of the militia. To provide for organizing, arming and disciplining the militia, and for governing such part of them as may be employed in the service of the United States, reserving to the States respectively the appointment of the officers, and the authority of training the militia according to the discipline prescribed by Congress;

17. It makes laws for the federal district. To exercise exclusive legislation in all cases whatsoever, over such district (not exceeding ten miles square) as may, by cession of particular States, and the acceptance of Congress, become the seat of government of the United States, and to exercise like authority over all places purchased by the consent of the legislature of the State, in which the same shall be, for the erection of forts, magazines, arsenals, dock-yards, and other needful buildings; —and

Congress has implied powers:

18. It may make laws necessary for carrying out the enumerated powers. To make all laws which shall be necessary and proper for carrying into execution the foregoing powers, and all other powers vested by this Constitution in the government of the United States, or in any department or office thereof.

★ *See pages 145, 172.*

Section IX. POWERS DENIED TO THE UNITED STATES

1. The full control of Congress over immigration is postponed until 1808. The migration or importation of such persons as any of the States now existing shall think proper to admit shall not be prohibited by the Congress prior to the year 1808; but a tax or duty may be imposed on such importation, not exceeding $10 for each person.

★ *See page 144.*

2. Congress may suspend the writ of "habeas corpus" only in case of rebellion or invasion. The privilege of the writ of *habeas corpus* shall not be suspended, unless when in cases of rebellion or invasion the public safety may require it.

★ *See page 154.*

3. Attainders and "ex post facto" laws are forbidden. No bill of attainder or *ex post facto* law shall be passed.

★ *See page 154.*

4. Direct taxes must be apportioned according to the population. No capitation, or other direct, tax shall be laid, unless in proportion to the census or enumeration herein before directed to be taken.

★ *See page 154. Changed in 1913 by the Sixteenth Amendment.*

5. Export duties are forbidden. No tax or duty shall be laid on articles exported from any State.

6. Congress must not discriminate against any port in regulating commerce. No preference shall be given by any regulation of commerce or revenue to the ports of one State over those of another, nor shall vessels bound to, or from, one State, be obliged to enter, clear, or pay duties in another.

7. Public money may not be spent without an appropriation by Congress. No money shall be drawn from the treasury, but in consequence of appropriations made by law; and a regular statement and account of the receipts and expenditures of all public money shall be published from time to time.

8. Titles of nobility may not be granted. No title of nobility shall be granted by the United States: and no person holding any office of profit or trust under them, shall, without the consent of the Congress, accept of any present, emolument, office, or title, of any kind whatever, from any king, prince, or foreign state.

★ *For other powers denied to the United States see Amendments I–X.*

Section X. Powers Denied to the States

Absolute prohibitions on the states:

1. The states are forbidden to do certain things. No State shall enter into any treaty, alliance, or confederation; grant letters of marque and reprisal; coin money; emit bills of credit; make anything but gold and silver coin a tender in payment of debts; pass any bill of attainder, *ex post facto* law, or law impairing the obligation of contracts, or grant any title of nobility.

Conditional prohibitions on the states:

2. The states may not levy duties without the consent of Congress. No State shall, without the consent of the Congress, lay any imposts or duties on imports or exports, except what may be absolutely necessary for executing its inspection laws: and the net produce of all duties and imposts, laid by any State on imports or exports, shall be for the use of the treasury of the United States; and all such laws shall be subject to the revision and control of the Congress.

3. Certain other federal powers are forbidden the states except with the consent of Congress. No State shall, without the consent of Congress, lay any duty of tonnage, keep troops or ships of war in time of peace, enter into any agreement or compact with another State, or with a foreign power, or engage in war, unless actually invaded, or in such imminent danger as will not admit of delay.

★ *See pages 145, 154.*

Article II. Executive Department

Section I. President and Vice-President

1. The President is the chief executive. The executive power shall be vested in a President of the United States of America. He shall hold his office during the term of four years, and together with the Vice-President, chosen for the same term, be elected as follows:

2. The President is chosen by electors. Each State shall appoint, in such manner as the legislature thereof may direct, a number of electors, equal to the whole number of Senators and Representatives to which the State may be entitled in the Congress; but no Senator or Representative, or person holding an office of trust or profit under the United States, shall be appointed an elector.

★ *See pages 144–145.*

It requires a majority of the electoral votes to elect. [The electors shall meet in their respective States, and vote by ballot for two persons, of whom one at least shall not be an inhabitant of the same State with themselves.

And they shall make a list of all the persons voted for, and of the number of votes for each; which list they shall sign and certify, and transmit sealed to the seat of government of the United States, directed to the President of the Senate. The President of the Senate shall, in the presence of the Senate and House of Representatives, open all the certificates, and the votes shall then be counted. The person having the greatest number of votes shall be the President, if such number be a majority of the whole number of electors appointed; and if there be more than one who have such majority, and have an equal number of votes, then the House of Representatives shall immediately choose by ballot one of them for President; and if no person have a majority, then from the five highest on the list the said house shall in like manner choose the President. But in choosing the President the votes shall be taken by States, the representation from each State having one vote; a quorum for this purpose shall consist of a member or members from two thirds of the States, and a majority of all the States shall be necessary to a choice. In every case, after the choice of the President, the person having the greatest number of votes of the electors shall be the Vice-President. But if there should remain two or more who have equal votes, the Senate shall choose from them by ballot the Vice-President.]

★ *This section was changed in 1804 by the Twelfth Amendment. See page 187. See page 675 for the Twentieth Amendment.*

3. Congress decides the time of choosing electors. The Congress may determine the time of choosing the electors and the day on which they shall give their votes; which day shall be the same throughout the United States.

★ *Electors are chosen on the Tuesday after the first Monday in November of each "leap year."*

4. Who may be President? No person except a natural-born citizen, or a citizen of the United States, at the time of the adoption of this Constitution, shall be eligible to the office of President; neither shall any person be eligible to that office who shall not have attained to the age of thirty-five years, and been fourteen years a resident within the United States.

5. In case of the President's death or disability the Vice-President succeeds him. In case of the removal of the President from office or of his death, resignation, or inability to discharge the powers and duties of the said office, the same shall devolve on the Vice-President, and the Congress may by law provide for the case of removal, death, resignation, or inability, both of the President and Vice-President, declaring what officer shall then act as President, and such officer shall act accordingly, until the disability be removed, or a President shall be elected.

★ *See page 762, Presidential Succession Act of 1886 and the Twenty-second Amendment.*

6. The President receives a salary. The President shall, at stated times, receive for his services a compensation, which shall neither be increased nor diminished during the period for which he shall have been elected, and he shall not receive within that period any other emolument from the United States, or any of them.

★ *In 1949 the salary became $100,000 a year and an expense account of $50,000 plus a tax-free allowance of $40,000.*

7. The President takes an oath of office. Before he enter on the execution of his office, he shall take the following oath or affirmation: —"I do solemnly swear (or affirm) that I will faithfully execute the office of President of the United States, and will to the best of my ability preserve, protect and defend the Constitution of the United States."

Section II. POWERS OF THE PRESIDENT

1. The President has important military and civil powers. The President shall be commander in chief of the army and navy of the United States, and of the militia of the several States, when called into the actual service of the United States; he may require the opinion, in writing, of the principal officer in each of the executive departments, upon any subject relating to the duties of their respective offices, and he shall have power to grant reprieves and pardons for offences against the United States, except in cases of impeachment.

★ *The term "executive departments" implies a cabinet. See page 168.*

2. The President may make treaties and nominate officers of the United States. He shall have power, by and with the advice and consent of the Senate, to make treaties, provided two thirds of the Senators present concur; and he shall nominate, and by and with the advice and consent of the Senate, shall appoint ambassadors, other public ministers and consuls, judges of the Supreme Court, and all other officers of the United States, whose appointments are not herein otherwise provided for, and which shall be established by law: but the Congress may by law vest the appoint-

ment of such inferior officers, as they think proper, in the President alone, in the courts of law, or in the heads of departments.

★ *In making treaties the President takes the first step but the Senate has the power to ratify or reject a treaty. See pages 178, 621, and 749 as examples. Appointments require only a majority vote for ratification.*

3. The President may fill vacancies during the recess of Congress. The President shall have power to fill up all vacancies that may happen during the recess of the Senate, by granting commissions which shall expire at the end of their next session.

Section III. OTHER POWERS AND DUTIES OF THE PRESIDENT

Messages; extra sessions; receiving ambassadors; execution of the laws. He shall from time to time give to the Congress information of the state of the Union, and recommend to their consideration such measures as he shall judge necessary and expedient; he may, on extraordinary occasions, convene both houses, or either of them, and in case of disagreement between them, with respect to the time of adjournment, he may adjourn them to such time as he shall think proper; he shall receive ambassadors and other public ministers; he shall take care that the laws be faithfully executed, and shall commission all the officers of the United States.

★ *The responsibility for recommending "such measures" establishes the President as an important agent in the lawmaking process. His proposals often lead to the passage of new laws. Of historic interest see page 150 (Illus.), page 223 (Monroe), page 395 (Johnson), page 668 (Hoover), page 723 (F. D. Roosevelt).*

Section IV. IMPEACHMENT

Civil officers may be removed by impeachment. The President, Vice-President and all civil officers of the United States shall be removed from office on impeachment for, and on conviction of, treason, bribery, or other high crimes and misdemeanors.

★ *See pages 397–398.*

Article III. Judicial Department

Section I. UNITED STATES OR FEDERAL COURTS

The judicial power belongs to the federal courts. The judicial power of the United States shall be vested in one Supreme Court, and in such inferior courts as Congress may from time to time ordain and establish. The judges, both of the Supreme and inferior courts, shall hold their offices during good behavior, and shall, at stated times, receive for their services a compensation which shall not be diminished during their continuance in office.

★ *Congress cannot abolish the Supreme Court but may abolish the inferior courts. See pages 168–169 (federal courts).*

Section II. Jurisdiction (Authority) of the United States Courts

1. The kinds of cases which may be heard are listed. The judicial power shall extend to all cases, in law and equity, arising under this Constitution, the laws of the United States, and treaties made or which shall be made, under their authority;—to all cases affecting ambassadors, other public ministers and consuls; —to all cases of admiralty and maritime jurisdiction;—to controversies to which the United States shall be a party;—to controversies between two or more States;—between a State and citizens of another State;—between citizens of different States;—between citizens of the same State claiming lands under grants of different States, and between a State, or the citizens thereof, and foreign states, citizens or subjects.

★ *Controversies "between a State and citizens of another State" has been restricted by the Eleventh Amendment to suits by a state against citizens of another state.*

2. In certain cases the Supreme Court has original jurisdiction. In all cases affecting ambassadors, other public ministers and consuls, and those in which a State shall be a party, the Supreme Court shall have original jurisdiction. In all the other cases before mentioned, the Supreme Court shall have appellate jurisdiction, both as to law and fact, with such exceptions and under such regulations as the Congress shall make.

★ *"Original jurisdiction" means that a case must commence in the Supreme Court. "Appellate jurisdiction" means that a case must commence in an inferior federal court or a state court, from which it may be appealed to the Supreme Court.*

3. Trial for crime is by jury. The trial of all crimes, except in cases of impeachment, shall be by jury; and such trial shall be held in the State where the said crimes shall have been committed; but when not committed within any State, the trial shall be at such place or places as the Congress may by law have directed.

★ *See page 154. See pages 226–227 for the principle of judicial review.*

Section III. Treason

1. Treason is defined. Treason against the United States shall consist only in levying war against them, or in adhering to their enemies, giving them aid and comfort. No person shall be convicted of treason unless on the testimony of two witnesses to the same overt act, or on confession in open court.

2. Congress fixes the punishment for treason. The Congress shall have power to declare the punishment of treason, but no attainder of treason shall work corruption of blood, or forfeiture except during the life of the person attainted.

★ *See page 154.*

Article IV. Relations of the States to One Another

Section I. Credit to Acts, Records, and Court Proceedings

Each state must respect the public acts of the others. Full faith and credit shall be given in each State to the public acts, records, and judicial proceedings of every other State. And the Congress may by general laws prescribe the manner in which such acts, records, and proceedings shall be proved, and the effect thereof.

Section II. Duties of States to States

1. Citizenship in one state is valid in all. The citizens of each State shall be entitled to all privileges and immunities of citizens in the several States.

2. Fugitives from justice must be surrendered by the state to which they have fled. A person charged in any State with treason, felony, or other crime, who shall flee from justice, and be found in another State, shall on demand of the executive authority of the State from which he fled, be delivered up, to be removed to the State having jurisdiction of the crime.

3. Slaves and apprentices must be returned. No person held to service or labor in one State, under the laws thereof, escaping into another, shall, in consequence of any law or regulation therein, be discharged from such service or labor, but shall be delivered up on claim of the party to whom such service or labor may be due.

★ *"Persons held to service or labor" refers to slaves and apprentices.*

★ *Changed by the Thirteenth Amendment.*

Section III. New States and Territories

1. Congress may admit new states. New States may be admitted by the Congress into

844

this Union; but no new State shall be formed or erected within the jurisdiction of any other State; nor any State be formed by the junction of two or more States, or parts of States, without the consent of the legislatures of the States concerned as well as of the Congress.

2. Congress may regulate federal territory and property. The Congress shall have power to dispose of and make all needful rules and regulations respecting the territory or other property belonging to the United States; and nothing in this Constitution shall be so construed as to prejudice any claims of the United States, or of any particular State.

Section IV. Protection to the States

Congress guarantees to each state a republican government and protection against invasion and rebellion. The United States shall guarantee to every State in this Union a republican form of government, and shall protect each of them against invasion; and on application of the legislature, or of the executive (when the legislature cannot be convened) against domestic violence.

★ *See pages 156, 158.*

Article V. The Process of Amendment

The Constitution may be amended by either of two methods. The Congress, whenever two thirds of both houses shall deem it necessary, shall propose amendments to this Constitution, or, on the application of the legislatures of two thirds of the several States, shall call a convention for proposing amendments, which in either case shall be valid to all intents and purposes, as part of this Constitution, when ratified by the legislatures of three fourths of the several States, or by conventions in three fourths thereof, as the one or the other mode of ratification may be proposed by the Congress; provided that no amendments which may be made prior to the year one thousand eight hundred and eight shall in any manner affect the first and fourth clauses in the ninth section of the first article; and that no State, without its consent, shall be deprived of its equal suffrage in the Senate.

★ *See page 146.*

Article VI. General Provisions

1. The debts of the Confederation are taken over. All debts contracted and engagements entered into, before the adoption of this Constitution, shall be as valid against the United States under this Constitution, as under the Confederation.

★ *See pages 169–170.*

2. The Constitution and federal laws are the supreme law of the land. This Constitution, and the laws of the United States which shall be made in pursuance thereof; and all treaties made, or which shall be made, under the authority of the United States, shall be the supreme law of the land; and the judges in every State shall be bound thereby, anything in the Constitution or laws of any State to the contrary notwithstanding.

★ *See pages 156, 158.*

3. Federal and state officers are bound by oath to support the Constitution. The Senators and Representatives before mentioned, and the members of the several State legislatures, and all executive and judicial officers, both of the United States and of the several States, shall be bound by oath or affirmation to support this Constitution; but no religious test shall ever be required as a qualification to any office or public trust under the United States.

Article VII. Ratification of the Constitution

The Constitution is in force when conventions in nine states have ratified it. The ratification of the conventions of nine States shall be sufficient for the establishment of this Constitution between the States so ratifying the same.

★ *See pages 147–148 on ratification.*

Done in Convention by the unanimous consent of the States present, the seventeenth day of September in the year of our Lord one thousand seven hundred and eighty-seven and of the Independence of the United States of America the twelfth. In witness whereof we have hereunto subscribed our names.

[Signed by]   G⁰ Washington
Presidt and Deputy from Virginia

★ *Following George Washington's signature are the signatures of 38 other delegates. Of the 65 delegates chosen to go to the convention, 55 attended. Rhode Island did not send delegates. See pages 137, 139–140 on delegates. See page 146 on adjournment.*

AMENDMENTS TO THE
CONSTITUTION

★ *The first ten amendments were adopted in 1791. They are called the Bill of Rights. See page 169.*

Amendment I. Religious and Political Freedom

Congress may not interfere with freedom of religion, speech, meeting, and petition. Congress shall make no law respecting an establishment of religion, or prohibiting the free exercise thereof; or abridging the freedom of speech, or of the press; or the right of the people peaceably to assemble, and to petition the government for a redress of grievances.

Amendment II. Right to Bear Arms

The people may bear arms. A well-regulated militia being necessary to the security of a free State, the right of the people to keep and bear arms shall not be infringed.

Amendment III. Quartering of Troops

Soldiers may not be quartered on the people. No soldier shall, in time of peace, be quartered in any house without the consent of the owner, nor in time of war, but in a manner to be prescribed by law.

Amendment IV. Searches and Seizures

Unreasonable searches are forbidden. The right of the people to be secure in their persons, houses, papers, and effects, against unreasonable searches and seizures, shall not be violated, and no warrants shall issue but upon probable cause, supported by oath or affirmation, and particularly describing the place to be searched, and the persons or things to be seized.

Amendment V. Right to Life, Liberty, and Property

The individual is guaranteed certain rights when on trial and the right to life, liberty, and property. No person shall be held to answer for a capital, or otherwise infamous crime, unless on a presentment or indictment of a grand jury except in cases arising in the land or naval forces, or in the militia, when in actual service in time of war or public danger; nor shall any person be subject for the same offence to be twice put in jeopardy of life or limb; nor shall be compelled in any criminal case to be a witness against himself, nor be deprived of life, liberty, or property, without due process of law; nor shall private property be taken for public use without just compensation.

★ *A "capital" crime is one for which the penalty is death; an "infamous" crime, one for which the sentence is imprisonment for more than one year. "Twice put in jeopardy" means that a person may not be tried a second time for the same offence for which he had once before been tried and found not guilty. See pages 154, 156.*

Amendment VI. Protection in Criminal Trials

An accused person has important rights. In all criminal prosecutions the accused shall enjoy the right to a speedy and public trial, by an impartial jury of the State and district wherein the crime shall have been committed, which district shall have been previously ascertained by law, and to be informed of the nature and cause of the accusation; to be confronted with the witnesses against him; to have compulsory process for obtaining witnesses in his favor, and to have the assistance of counsel for his defence.

Amendment VII. Suits at Common Law

The rules of common law are recognized. In suits at common law, where the value in controversy shall exceed twenty dollars, the right of trial by jury shall be preserved, and no fact tried by a jury shall be otherwise reexamined in any court of the United States, than according to the rules of the common law.

Amendment VIII. Bail and Punishments

Excessive fines and unusual punishments are forbidden. Excessive bail shall not be required, nor excessive fines imposed, nor cruel and unusual punishments inflicted.

★ *See pages 155–156 on first eight amendments.*

Amendment IX. Concerning Rights Not Enumerated

The people retain their rights even though not here enumerated. The enumeration in the Constitution of certain rights shall not be construed to deny or disparage others retained by the people.

Amendment X. Powers Reserved to the States and to the People

Powers not delegated to the federal government are reserved to the states and the people. The powers not delegated to the United States by the Constitution, nor prohibited by it to the States, are reserved to the States respectively, or to the people.

★ *See page 156.*

Amendment XI. Suits against a State

The federal courts have no authority in suits by citizens against a state. The judicial power of the United States shall not be construed to extend to any suit in law or equity, commenced or prosecuted against one of the United States by citizens of another State, or by citizens or subjects of any foreign state. [Adopted in 1798.]

★ *This amendment changed Art. III, sec. II, clause 1.*

Amendment XII. Election of President and Vice-President

1. The procedure of the Presidential electors is changed. The electors shall meet in their respective States, and vote by ballot for President and Vice-President, one of whom, at least, shall not be an inhabitant of the same State with themselves; they shall name in their ballots the person voted for as President, and in distinct ballots the person voted for as Vice-President, and they shall make distinct lists of all persons voted for as President, and of all persons voted for as Vice-President, and of the number of votes for each, which lists they shall sign and certify, and transmit sealed to the seat of government of the United States, directed to the President of the Senate;—the President of the Senate shall, in the presence of the Senate and House of Representatives, open all the certificates and the votes shall then be counted;—the person having the greatest number of votes for President shall be the President, if such number be a majority of the whole number of electors appointed; and if no person have such majority, then from the persons having the highest numbers not exceeding three on the list of those voted for as President, the House of Representatives shall choose immediately, by ballot, the President. But in choosing the President, the votes shall be taken by States, the representation from each State having one vote; a quorum for this purpose shall consist of a member or members from two thirds of the States, and a majority of all the States shall be necessary to a choice. And if the House of Representatives shall not choose a President whenever the right of choice shall devolve upon them, before the fourth day of March next following, then the Vice-President shall act as President, as in the case of the death or other constitutional disability of the President.

2. The method of choosing the Vice-President is changed. The person having the greatest number of votes as Vice-President shall be the Vice-President, if such number be a majority of the whole number of electors appointed; and if no person have a majority, then from the two highest numbers on the list the Senate shall choose the Vice-President; a

quorum for the purpose shall consist of two thirds of the whole number of Senators, and a majority of the whole number shall be necessary to a choice. But no person constitutionally ineligible to the office of President shall be eligible to that of Vice-President of the United States. [Adopted in 1804.]

★ *See page 187. This amendment changed Art. II, sec. I.*

Amendment XIII. Slavery Abolished

Slavery is prohibited. 1. Neither slavery nor involuntary servitude, except as a punishment for crime whereof the party shall have been duly convicted, shall exist within the United States, or any place subject to their jurisdiction.

2. Congress shall have power to enforce this article by appropriate legislation. [Adopted in 1865.]

★ *See page 388.*

Amendment XIV. Limitations on the States

1. Negroes are made citizens. All persons born or naturalized in the United States, and subject to the jurisdiction thereof, are citizens of the United States and of the State wherein they reside. No State shall make or enforce any law which shall abridge the privileges or immunities of citizens of the United States; nor shall any State deprive any person of life, liberty, or property, without due process of law; nor deny to any person within its jurisdiction the equal protection of the laws.

★ *This defines citizenship. "Citizens of the United States and the State wherein they reside" is spoken of as "dual citizenship." The last part applies to the states the same prohibition against depriving any person "of life, liberty, or property without due process of law" as had formerly been applied against the federal government only by Amendment V.*

2. When a state limits the franchise, its representation shall be reduced. Representatives shall be apportioned among the several States according to their respective numbers, counting the whole number of persons in each State, excluding Indians not taxed. But when the right to vote at any election for the choice of Electors for President and Vice-President of the United States, Representatives in Congress, the executive and judicial officers of a State, or the members of the legislature thereof, is denied to any of the male inhabitants of such State, being twenty-one years of age and citizens of the United States, or in any way abridged, except for participation in rebellion, or other crime, the basis of representation therein shall be reduced in the proportion which the number of such male citizens shall bear to the whole number of male citizens twenty-one years of age in such State.

3. Certain persons who have been in rebellion are ineligible for federal and state office. No person shall be a Senator or Representative in Congress, or Elector of President and Vice-President, or hold any office, civil or military, under the United States, or under any State, who, having previously taken an oath, as a member of Congress, or as an officer of the United States, or as a member of any State legislature, or as an executive or judicial officer of any State, to support the Constitution of the United States, shall have engaged in insurrection or rebellion against the same, or given aid or comfort to the enemies thereof. But Congress may, by a vote of two thirds of each house, remove such disability.

4. Debts incurred in aid of rebellion are void. The validity of the public debt of the United States, authorized by law, including debts incurred for payment of pensions and bounties for services in suppressing insurrection or rebellion, shall not be questioned. But neither the United States nor any State shall assume or pay any debt or obligation incurred in aid of insurrection or rebellion against the United States, or any claim for the loss or emancipation of any slave; but all such debts, obligations, and claims shall be held illegal and void.

5. Enforcement. The Congress shall have power to enforce by appropriate legislation the provisions of this article. [Adopted in 1868.]

★ *See pages 395–396.*

Amendment XV. Negro Suffrage

Negroes are made voters. 1. The right of citizens of the United States to vote shall not be denied or abridged by the United States or any State on account of race, color, or previous condition of servitude.

2. The Congress shall have power to enforce this article by appropriate legislation. [Adopted in 1870.]

★ *See pages 398–399.*

Amendment XVI. Income Taxes

Congress has power to lay and collect income taxes. The Congress shall have power to lay and collect taxes on incomes, from what-

ever source derived, without apportionment among the several States, and without regard to any census or enumeration. [Adopted in 1913.]

★ *See page 375 for federal income tax during the War Between the States. See pages 503–504, "Supreme Court voids the income tax." Amendment XVI overruled the Court decision. See page 549.*

Amendment XVII. Direct Election of Senators

Senators shall be elected by popular vote. 1. The Senate of the United States shall be composed of two Senators from each State, elected by the people thereof, for six years; and each Senator shall have one vote. The electors in each State shall have the qualifications requisite for electors of the most numerous branch of the State legislatures.

★ *Changed Art. I, sec. III.*

2. When vacancies happen in the representation of any State in the Senate, the executive authority of such State shall issue writs of election to fill such vacancies: Provided that the Legislature of any State may empower the executive thereof to make temporary appointments until the people fill the vacancies by election as the Legislature may direct.

3. This amendment shall not be so construed as to affect the election or term of any Senator chosen before it becomes valid as part of the Constitution. [Adopted in 1913.]

Amendment XVIII. National Prohibition

The sale or manufacture of intoxicating liquors is forbidden. 1. After one year from the ratification of this article the manufacture, sale, or transportation of intoxicating liquors within, the importation thereof into, or the exportation thereof from, the United States and all territory subject to the jurisdiction thereof, for beverage purposes, is hereby prohibited.

2. The Congress and the several States shall have concurrent power to enforce this article by appropriate legislation.

3. This article shall be inoperative unless it shall have been ratified as an amendment to the Constitution by the legislatures of the several States, as provided by the Constitution, within seven years from the date of the submission thereof to the States by the Congress. [Adopted in 1919.]

★ *See pages 556, 635. Repealed by the Twenty-first Amendment.*

Amendment XIX. Woman Suffrage

Women are guaranteed the right to vote. 1. The right of citizens of the United States to vote shall not be denied or abridged by the United States or by any State on account of sex.

2. The Congress shall have power to enforce this article by appropriate legislation. [Adopted in 1920.]

★ *See page 556.*

Amendment XX. Presidential and Congressional Terms

Presidential and Congressional terms of office begin in January. 1. The terms of the President and Vice-President shall end at noon on the 20th day of January and the terms of Senators and Representatives at noon on the 3d day of January, of the years in which such terms would have ended if this article had not been ratified; and the terms of their successors shall then begin.

2. The Congress shall assemble at least once in every year, and such meeting shall begin at noon on the 3d day of January, unless they shall by law appoint a different day.

3. If, at the time fixed for the beginning of the term of the President, the President-elect shall have died, the Vice-President-elect shall become President. If a President shall not have been chosen before the time fixed for the beginning of his term, or if the President-elect shall have failed to qualify, then the Vice-President-elect shall act as President until a President shall have qualified; and the Congress may by law provide for the case wherein neither a President-elect nor a Vice-President-elect shall have qualified, declaring who shall then act as President, or the manner in which one who is to act shall be selected, and such persons shall act accordingly until a President or Vice-President shall have qualified.

4. The Congress may by law provide for the case of the death of any of the persons from whom the House of Representatives may choose a President whenever the right of choice shall have devolved upon them, and for the case of the death of any of the persons from whom the Senate may choose a Vice-President whenever the right of choice shall have devolved upon them.

5. Sections 1 and 2 shall take effect on the 15th day of October following the ratification of this article.

6. This article shall be inoperative unless it shall have been ratified as an amendment to the Constitution by the Legislatures of three-fourths of the several States within seven years from the date of its submission. [Adopted in 1933.]

★ *See page 674.*

Amendment XXI. Prohibition Repealed

The Eighteenth Amendment is repealed. 1. The eighteenth article of amendment to the Constitution of the United States is hereby repealed.

2. The transportation or importation into any State, Territory, or Possession of the United States for delivery or use therein of intoxicating liquors, in violation of the laws thereof, is hereby prohibited.

3. This article shall be inoperative unless it shall have been ratified as an amendment to the Constitution by conventions in the several States, as provided in the Constitution, within seven years from the date of the submission thereof to the States by the Congress. [Adopted in 1933.]

★ *See pages 635–636, 677.*

Amendment XXII. Limitation on Presidential Term

Presidential term is limited. 1. No person shall be elected to the office of President more than twice, and no person who has held the office of President, or acted as President, for more than two years of a term to which some other person was elected President shall be elected to the office of President more than once. But this article shall not apply to any person holding the office of President when this article was proposed by the Congress, and shall not prevent any person who may be holding the office of President, or acting as President, during the term within which this article becomes operative from holding the office of President or acting as President during the remainder of such term.

2. This article shall be inoperative unless it shall have been ratified as an amendment to the Constitution by the legislatures of three-fourths of the several States within seven years from the day of its submission to the States by the Congress. [Adopted in 1951.]

★ *This amendment did not apply to President Truman, who was in office at the time of its passage. See page 762.*

Figures in *italic* are pages on which illustrations appear.
Figures marked with a ° are pages on which maps appear.

Amusements: related to growth of cities, 435; kinds of shows, 435; commercialized sports, 436; *438*. *See also* Cities *and* Recreation
Anaconda mines, 470
Anarchism, and labor, 461
Anderson, Major, 370
Anderson, Maxwell, 826
Anderson, Sherwood, 645
Andros, Sir Edmund, 56
Anesthetics, early use of, 287
Anglican Church, 85, 129
Anglo-American relations, 221°. *See also* Foreign affairs *and* Great Britain
Anglo-French wars, 99. *See also* French and Indian War
Anglo-Japanese Alliance, 659
Annapolis Convention, 137
Anti-Comintern Pact, 711, 713
Antietam, Md., 378
Antifederalists, 147, 172
Antioch College, 310, *311*
Antisaloon League of America, 440
Antislavery societies, 130, 318
Antitrust laws. *See* Trusts; Monopolies; Big business; Competition
Anzio, 738
ANZUS, 781
Appalachians, 378, 541
Appomattox, Va., 385
Apprenticeship, system of, 67, 87
Arabs, 804, 809
Arbitration: of labor disputes, 517; of international disputes, 597
Arbuthnot and Armbrister, 221
Architecture, 285, 452, 648; skyscraper, 452, 648; functional modernism, *802*, 826
Argentina: 482, 590, 593, 607; and export of grain, 667; in World War II, 730
Argonne Forest, 610
Aristotle, 8
Arizona, 469, *469*, 470, 476
Arkansas: and cotton, 242, 250; and slaves, 252, 355; in Confederacy, 371, 380; frees slaves, 388; during reconstruction, 391; readmitted to Union, 398; mining in, 416
Arkansas River, 198
Armada, Spanish, 28, *29*
Armistice, World War I, 611
Arms embargo, and neutrality, 712, 713, 714, 717
Armstrong, Gen. Samuel, 446
Army: 373; and industrial expansion, 414; as strikebreakers, 461, *461*, 464, 496. *See also* U.S. Army

Army of the Potomac, 380, 381
Arno River, 738
Arnold, Benedict, 117
Arnold, Gen. Henry H., 733, *734*
Aroostook River, 270
Arthur, Chester A., 493, 496, 498, 535
Articles of Confederation: 130, 131; changes considered, 97, 137; displaced, 140; differ from Constitution, 143 (chart)
Arts, *see* Fine arts
Asbury, Francis, 289
Ashburton, Lord, 274
Ashley, William, 333
Asia, and the cold war, 781
Assemblies, power of, 52
Assembly line, *639*, 640
Associated Press, 422
Astor, John Jacob, *332*, 333
Astoria, *332*, 333
Astrolabe, 9
Atlanta, Ga., 297, 384
Atlantic Charter, 723, 729
Atlantic Monthly, 448
Atlantic Ocean: defense of in World War II, 721; submarines in, 736
Atomic bomb (A-bomb): 1st nuclear chain reaction, 731; Hiroshima, 745, *751*, 775; and Russia, 775, 804
Atomic Energy Act of 1954, 805; revised 1958, 805
Atomic Energy Commission, 761, 775
Attainder, bill of, 154
Audubon, John James, 286
Austin, Moses, 334
Austin, Stephen, 334
Australia: 659; and grain, 482, 667; and gold, 506; in World War I, 607; in World War II, 742; and ANZUS, *783*; and SEATO, 783
Australian ballot. *See* Secret ballot
Austria: 222, 618; and Hitler, 715; and the Russians, 741, 773; peace treaty with, 775; economic aid to, 777
Austria-Hungary, 598, 599, 616, 661
Automation, 824
Automobiles: and demand for roads, 555; social results of, 637, 667; manufacture of, 638, *639*; registration of, 637 (chart)
Axis, Rome-Berlin: 629, 711; joined by Japan, 725; alliance against, 729; advances by 1942, 734°. *See also* Germany *and* Italy
Aztecs, 20

Bacon, Nathaniel, 54
Balboa, Vasco, 13°, 16, 583
Balkans, 598, 737, 740
Ballot, short, 543
Baltic states, 717, 718
Baltimore, Md., 75, 212, 243, 297, 308
Baltimore and Ohio Railroad Co., 294, 297, 464
Bancroft, George, 279
Bangkok, 784
Bank of the U.S.: First, *173*, 209, 549; Second, 217; constitutionality of, 228; disapproved by South, 244; opposed by states, 265; cut off by Jackson, 267; advocated by Whigs, 268
Banking Act of 1933, 691
Banking system: revision advocated, 548; faults in, 549; Federal Reserve instituted, 550; near collapse, 678
Banks: national vs. state, 265, 267, 268, 414; failures of, 268, 672; National Banking Act, 413; and the farmer, 483, 549; instability of, 549; need for central bank, 549; mergers of, 639; and F.D.R., 685; regulation of, 691; international, 747
Baptists, 288
Bar Harbor, Me., 437
Barbary states, 193°
Barkley, Alben W., 764
Barnard, Henry, 309
Barnum, P. T., 436
Bartram, John, 89
Baruch, Bernard M., 606, 775
Baseball, 436, *436*
Bataan Peninsula, 742
Bayard, Thomas, 212
Beard, Dan, *644*
Beaumont, William, 287
Becknell, William, 333
Belgium: 599, 605, 611, 615, 618; and the Far East, 660; relief program in, 666; and the Nazis, 718, 740; and North Atlantic Treaty, 779
Bell, Alexander Graham, 422
Bell, John, 364, 365
Bell Act, 576
Bellamy, Edward, *447*, 449, 501, 518
Benét, Stephen Vincent, 648
Benét, William Rose, 826
Bennett, James Gordon, 282
Benson, Ezra Taft, 798
Bentley, Elizabeth, 769
Benton, Thomas Hart, 267
Berkeley, Sir William, 55
Berlin, Irving, 825
Berlin: zones of occupation, 741, 774; surrender of, 741; 1948 crisis, 757, 778, 779

852

Civil rights (*cont.*)
cies, 573; issue in 1948 election, 764; study of, 799
Civil Rights Act, 800
Civil Service: 495; and spoils system, 495; beginning of, 497, 520. *See also* Merit system
Civil War: *see* War between North and South
Civil Works Administration, 695
Civilian Conservation Corps, 686, 695
Clark, Gen. George Rogers, 122, *122*, 197
Clark, William, 197, 333, *335*
Clark Memorandum, 679
Classes, social: in feudalism, 7; after Industrial Revolution, 240; in power, 414
Classic style in architecture, 285
Clay, Henry: *205*, *333*, 350, 489; and Treaty of Ghent, 212; and tariff, 218; Speaker of House, 251; and Missouri Compromise, 253; as Secretary of State, 251, 253, 263, 264; candidate for President, 253, 266, 267, 337; and Whigs, 268, 270, 273; in Senate, 346, 347, 374
Clayton Antitrust Act, 425, 552; and labor, 553, 674
Clayton-Bulwer Treaty, 584, 585
Clemenceau, Georges, 618
Clemens, Samuel L. *See* Twain, Mark
Clermont, The, *292*, 293
Cleveland, Grover: 461, 464, *504*, 568; as President, 474, 493, 498; and conservation, 498; and pensions, 498; and tariff, 498, 503; second term, 502; and gold standard, 504; and Cuba, 569
Cleveland, Ohio, *128*, 304, 426, 434, 796
Clinton, DeWitt, 209
Clinton, George, 148
Clinton, Sir Henry, 122
Clipper ships, 298
Closed shop, 312, 458, 760
Clothing, of colonists, 81
Coal strike of 1902, 534
Coal trust, 533
Cobb, W. C., 252
Coeducation, 310
Cold war, 771, 810; and the United Nations, 786; and the Eisenhower administration, 804
Collective bargaining. *See* Labor unions
Collective security, 615, 620, 714

Colleges: for women, 310; land grants for, 446, 481; growth of, 642. *See also* Education
Collier's, 519
Collins, E. K., 298
Colombia, 584, 585, 586; and World War II, 730
Colonial policy, of Great Britain: problems involved, 102; Grenville Acts, 103; Townshend Acts, 104; Boston Massacre, 105; Intolerable Acts, 107; resistance to, 107; American ports closed, 111. *See also* Revolutionary War
Colonies, in America: the thirteen, 42°; royal, 50°; self-governing, 50°; life and customs in, 81, 82, 83; religion in, 84; education in, 85; superstition and witchcraft, 88; American character of, 89; union of, 97
Colorado: mining in, 468, 470; women's suffrage, 524
Colorado River, 537
Columbia River, 197, 334, 339, 537, 762
Columbian Centinel, 219
Columbus, Christopher: 4, 12, 13, 14, *14;* voyages of, 13°
Combined Chiefs of Staff, 729, 739
Commager, H. S., 604
Commerce: in Middle Ages, 5; in England, 28; in English colonies, 67; trading centers for, 67; relation to currency, 70; regulation of, in colonial times, 71; regulation of, by Congress, 144; vs. manufacturing, 241. *See also* Foreign trade *and* Industry
Commercial farming, 299
Commission on the Reorganization of the Executive Branch, 760
Committee for Industrial Organization, 699. *See* Congress of Industrial Organizations (CIO)
Committee on Un-American Activities, 769
Committees of correspondence, 106
Committee to Defend America by Aiding the Allies, 722
Commodity Credit Corporation, 798
Common Sense, 111
Communication: improvements in, 293; the telegraph, 297; increased need for, 417, 422; mass media,

637; federal control of, 692. *See also* Radio
Communism: fear of, 765, 769; international, 768, 773; and Fascism, 768; checked by Marshall Plan, 777; and the Eisenhower Doctrine, 809; growth of, 810
Communist China, 781, 804, 810
Communist Information Bureau (Cominform), 768, 777, 778, 779
Communist International (Comintern), 632, 709, 768, 775
Communist Manifesto, 766
Communist party: in Russia, 632, 767; in U.S., 632, 656, 709, 764, 775; and the Depression, 676, 677; and the New Deal, 700; in China, 713, 784; in Germany, 768, 779; in Greece, 776. *See also* American Communist party
Communists, in U.S.: trials of, 770; laws concerning, 770
Company towns, 456
Company unions, 640
Competition: threatened by big business, 424, 489; as regulator of economy, 524; protected from monopoly, 552; regulation of, 818
Composers, American, 825
Compromise of 1850, 331, 348, 358, 359
Comstock Lode, 469, 496
Conciliation, in international disputes, 597
Conciliatory Acts, 121
Concord, Mass., 109, 110, 279
Conestoga wagon, 246
Confederate States of America: 331; formed, 366, 371; advantages of, 373; currency in, 375; foreign relations of, 376, 377; war plans of, 378; surrender of, 385; and the 14th Amendment, 396
Confederation Congress. *See* Congress of the Confederation
Conference for European Economic Co-operation, 777
Congregationalists, 42, 85, 129, 288, 289, 334
Congress of Industrial Organizations (CIO): 699; joined to A.F. of L., 763, 819; and communism, 770
Congress of the Confederation: powers of, 131; weakness of, 132; and public land, 135; and government of territories, 135; and

Economic and Social Council, 747

Economic Co-operation Act, 777

Economic imperialism, 594

Economic recovery: and the Marshall Plan, 777; and the European Recovery Plan, 777

Economic sanctions, 679

Economy Act, 686

Eden, Anthony, 738

Edison, Thomas A., 435

Education: in colonies: 68–69, 85, 86, 86; colleges, 87; by apprenticeship, 87; in states: 135, 282; growth of public schools, 308, 442, 642; training of teachers, 309; for women, 309, 446; for handicapped, 310, 642; compulsory attendance, in 1880, 445*; in 1900, 445*; for Negroes, 446, 642, 800; growth of colleges, 446, 481, 641, 642, 823; vocational schools, 555, 642, 801; secondary, 641 (chart), 642, 823; international, 747; federal aid for, 765, 794, 800, 801, 807; parochial schools, 801; increased need for, 814; and G.I. Bill, 823; adult, 823

Egypt: and export of cotton, 479, 482, 667; and World War II, 719, 737; and Suez Canal, 790, 806, 808; invaded by Israel, 808; and United Arab Republic, 809

Einstein, Albert, 731

Eisenhower, Dwight D.: 150, 737; as Supreme Commander, 739, 741; as President, 761, 793, 794; as NATO Commander, 781, 793; and Korea, 787; administration of, 794, 796; and farm problem, 798; and educational crisis, 801; and atomic control, 805; and summit meeting, 805; second term, 806, 808; and national defense, 807; and foreign affairs, 795, 808, 809, 810

Eisenhower Doctrine, 809

El Alamein, 737

Elbe River, 741

Elections: provisions for, 129; presidential, in 1800, 184*; in 1912, 543*; 1932–1956, 795 (chart)

Electric companies: enfranchised, 416; regulated, 524; consolidated, 638

Electric power: in homes, 435; increased use of, 638; on farms, 689

Electronics, 823

Elevated railways, 433

Eliot, T. S., 648

Elizabeth I, Queen, 28

Emancipation, of slaves: early advocates of, 318; in Europe and Latin America, 319; in U.S., 387, 387*, 388

Emancipation Proclamation, 377, 378, 387

Embargo Act of 1807, 202

Emergency Banking Relief Act, 685

Emergency Farm Mortgage Act, 686

Emergency Fleet Corporation, 606

Emergency Quota Act, 633

Emergency Railroad Transportation Act, 692

Emerson, Ralph Waldo, 278, 280, 282, 288, 314, 317, 358

Empire State Building, 648

Employers' Liability Act, 536

Employment: shifts in, 814, 814 (chart), 815, 815 (chart); federal responsibility for, 820. See also Labor

Enclosures, as factor in colonization, 28

Engels, Friedrich, 766

England: exploration by, 15, 27*; defeat of Armada, 28; reasons for expansion, 28, 31; spirit of free enterprise, 31; rise of middle class, 28, 31; claims to North America, 31; colonization begun, 34; charters granted, 34; New Netherland seized by, 46. See also English colonies, Great Britain, and Revolutionary War

English colonies: 42*, 49*; civil liberties in, 35; religious unrest in, 39; political liberty in, 51; types of, 50*, 51; power of assemblies in, 52; free press in, 52; relations with Parliament, 54; attempts at union, 56; agriculture in, 60; products and resources of, 63*, 65, 66, 67; commerce with, 67; trade routes, 70*; population of, 75; education in, 85; and French and Indian War, 100

"Enumerated articles," 72

Ericsson, John, 375

Erie Canal, 245, 294, 353

Espionage Act, 608

Estonia, 618, 718, 775

Ethiopia, 618, 718, 775

Euratom, 805

Europe in 1914, 600*; in 1919, 619*

European Defense Community (EDC), 781

European Economic Community (EEC), 781

European Recovery Program (ERP), 777

Everson vs. the Board of Education, 801

Everybody's Magazine, 519

Expansionists, 337, 338, 342, 356

Exploration: early routes, 13*. See individual countries

Export Control Act, 725

Export-Import Bank, 707

Exports, and reciprocal trade agreements, 689. See also Tariff

ex post facto law, 154

Extraterritoriality, 357

Factories, growth of, 239, 240, 353; and child labor, 526

Fair Deal, the, 764, 794

Fair Employment Practices Committee (FEPC), 799

Fair Labor Standards Act, 699, 703, 765

Fall, Albert B., 654

Fall River, 240

"Fall-out," 776

Falmouth, Me., burning of, 111

Family life, in colonies, 83, 84

Fansteel case, 699

Far East: 357, 634; U.S. stake in, 572, 680; and trade, 576; and need for Panama Canal, 585; treaties concerning, 660; crisis in, 713, 714; and Yalta, 741; and communists, 809

Far Eastern Commission, 783

Farm employment, 816 (chart)

Farm Mortgage Foreclosure Act, 688

Farm Mortgage Moratorium Act, 688

Farm Security Administration, 688, 689

Farm Tenancy Act, 688

Farmer-Labor party, 656

Farragut, Admiral David, 379, 379, 385; statue of, 452

Farrell, James T., 826

Fascism: 632, 702; in Latin America, 708; defined, 711; in Spain, 712; opposed by Communism, 768; in U.S., 769

Faulkner, William, 645, 826

Federal Bureau of Investigation, 636, 733, 769, 770

International Atomic Authority, 776
International Atomic Energy Agency, 805
International Bank for Reconstruction and Development, 747
International Court of Justice, 747, 790
International Geophysical Year (IGY), 824
International Harvester Co., 423, 531
International Labor Organization (ILO), 620, 747
International law, provisions of, 601
Internationalism: U.S. rejection of, 659; partial acceptance, 678; United Nations ratified, 749
Internationalists, 622
Interstate commerce, regulation of, 542
Interstate Commerce Act, 424, 485, 500, 501, 524
Interstate Commerce Commission, 485, 536, 541, 653; and railroads, 692; and trucks and busses, 692; and air lines, 692
Interventionists, 722
Intolerable Acts, 107, 108
Inventions, and growth of industrialization, 415
Investment: and industrialization, 415; from abroad, 415; leading to empire, 568
Iowa, 501
Iowa, State University of, 310
Iran, 736, 790
Iraq, 619, 809
Ireland, 297
Irish: as immigrants, 304, 305; laborers on railroads, 420; in World War I, 601
Iron curtain, 774
Iron ore, 416
Ironclads, 376, 377, 382
Iroquois Indians, 99
Irrigation, and reclamation, 537
Irving, Washington, 277
Isabella, Queen, 12
Isolationism, 214, 565; and Monroe Doctrine, 223; growth of, after World War I, 617, 622, 659; and World Court, 661; and war debts, 711; and neutrality, 712, 715, 717, 721; threatened by air power, 720; after World War II, 746
Israel, 790, 791, 804; and Suez Canal, 808; and invasion of Egypt, 809
Italy: and early trade, 7, 12; and Venezuela, 590; and

imperialism, 598; in World War I, 599, 605, 616; in Ethiopia, 620, 711, 712; Rome-Berlin Axis, 629, 711; and Far East, 660; and disarmament, 660; and war debts, 662; and Mussolini, 681, 710, 719; and world trade, 707; and Spain, 712; in World War II, 719, 723, 774; and Japan, 725; in North Africa, 737; invasion of, 737, 738; and communism, 769, 779; peace treaty with, 775; economic aid to, 777; and North Atlantic Treaty, 779
Iwo Jima, 743

Jackson, Andrew: 259, 374, 480, 532, 546, 548; as Indian fighter, 212, 220; as favorite son, 237, 251, 253, 254; as President, 251, 258, 259, 260, 262, 263; U.S. under Jackson, 260°; and Bank of U.S., 264, 266, 267; 2nd term, 267, 270; and Van Buren, 271, 338; statue of, 284; and labor, 312, 456; and slavery, 320; and Texas, 337; and secession, 369
Jackson, Helen Hunt, 447
Jackson, Gen. T. J. ("Stonewall"), 378, 380, 380
Jacksonville, Fla., 400
James, Henry, 447, 448
James, William, 447
James I, King, 59
James Monroe, the, 297
Jamestown, Va., 35
Japan: 357, 567, 702; and Philippines, 576, 742; and China, 581, 659, 710, 713; Russo-Japanese War, 582; immigration from, 583, 634, 655; and World War I, 583, 598, 603, 618; and World War II, 583, 629, 732, 714°, 744, 745, 775, 783; and Manchuria, 620, 679, 680, 711; expansion of, 659, 681, 710, 713, 724; and naval disarmament, 660, 661, 680; exports from, 667, 707, 713; rise of military party in, 710; Panay incident, 715, 724; and the Axis, 725; Pearl Harbor, 726, 742; and Burma, 742; and Southeast Asia, 742
Japanese-Americans, relocation of, 733
Jay, John, 147, 178
Jazz, 649, 825
Jefferson, Joseph, 283

Jefferson, Thomas: 190, 220, 223, 251, 258, 264, 267, 300, 308, 318, 333, 414; as farmer, 62; and committees of correspondence, 106; and Declaration of Independence, 112, 130; and Statute of Religious Liberty, 129; and Democratic Republicans, 165, 173; as Secretary of State, 168, 171, 177; leaves Cabinet, 178; as Vice-President, 182; as President, 187, 190, 195; popularity of, 199; 2nd term, 199, 202, 205, 226; retirement of, 203; and Bank of U.S., 217; and the judiciary, 230; as architect, 285
Jet fighter planes, 732
Jewett, Sarah Orne, 448
Jews, as minority group, 799
Jingoism, 569
Joffre, Marshal, of France, 608
Johnson, Andrew: 397, 535; as Vice-President, 385; as President, 393, 395, 396, 397, 398, 493; impeached, 397, 398
Johnson, Hiram, 520
Johnson, Gen. Hugh S., 690
Johnson, James Weldon, 648
Johnson, Colonel R. M., 268
Johnson, Thomas L., 525
Johnson, Sir William, 98
Johnson Act of 1924, 633
Johnston, Gen. Joseph E., 384
Joint Chiefs of Staff, 733, 736, 737
Joint Four-Nation Declaration, 738
Joliet, Louis, 25
Jones, John Paul, 122
Jones, Samuel M., 525
Jones Act, 574, 578
Jordan, 619, 688, 809
Judicial review, 226
Judiciary: controlled by Federalists, 187; and legislative and executive branches, 227
Judiciary Act, 169, 192, 226
Julius Rosenwald Fund, 642
Juvenile delinquency, 643

Kahn, Albert, 826
Kaiser Wilhelm, 599, 612
Kalamazoo, Mich., 442
Kamikaze, 743
Kansas, 331, 359, 360; and shipping of cattle, 472; and Alliance, 501
Kansas City, Mo., 433
Kansas-Nebraska Act, 359, 359°
Kashmir, 790

and social legislation, 527; and Coolidge, 654

Massachusetts Bay Colony: 40, 283; Boston founded, 40; importance of religion in, 41, 42; education in, 42

Massachusetts Bay Company, 40

Maternity and Infancy Act, 643

Mathematics, and Byzantine culture, 9

Mather, Increase, *41*

Matsu, 809, 810

Maury, Matthew F., 286, *287*

Maximilian, Emperor of Mexico, 398

Mayans, *20*

Mayflower, the, *xvi*, 39

Mayflower Compact, 40

McAdoo, William G., 606, 656

McCarran-Walter Immigration Act, 765, 797

McCarran-Wood Act, 770

McCarthy, Joseph R., 771

McClellan, Gen. George, 378, 385

McClure's, 518

McCormick, Cyrus, 302

McCormick Harvester strike of 1886, 460

McCormick reaper, *301*

McCulloch vs. *Maryland*, 228

McIntire, Samuel, 285

McKay, Donald, 298

McKinley, William, 500, 504, 531, *571*, 652, 594; as President, 506, 568, 573, 597; and Populism, 504; and tariff, 500, 506; 2nd term, 531; and Cuba, 569, 571; and Philippines, 574

McKinley Tariff, 500, 503, 504

McLaurin vs. *Oklahoma*, 800

McNary-Haugen Bill, 658, 668

McReynolds, James C., 555

Meade, Gen. George, 381

Meany, George, 763

Meat Inspection Act, 537

Medical science, 287

Medicine: in colonies, 88; advances in, 643

Medina, Judge Harold R., 770

Mediterranean, 737; submarines in, 736; and Russia, 776

Mellon, Andrew J., 652, *653*, 825; as Secretary of the Treasury, 652, 653, 670

Melville, Herman, 282

Memel, 717

Memorial Day, 386

Memphis, Tenn., 379, 417, 797

Menotti, Gian-Carlo, 825

Mensheviks, 767

Mercantilism: theory of, 71; value of colonies, 71

Merchant marine, 731 (chart); conditions in, 554; building of, 602

Mergers, 425, 553

Merit system, 520, 541. *See also* Civil Service

Merrimac, the, 375, *382*

Merrimack River, 240

Metals. *See* Mining

Methodists, 288, 333

Metropolitan Museum, 449

Metropolitan Opera Company, 825

Mexican War, 331, 342; causes of, 340; campaigns in, 340*; settlement of, 341

Mexico: explored by Spanish, 22, 33; and Texas, 270, 335, 338, 342; trade with, 333, 708; and California, 339; Gadsden Purchase, 342; conquered by France, 398; civil war in, 592, 594; and oil, 594, 664, 708; and World War I, 603; immigration from, 634; and World War II, 730

Mexico City, 593

Michigan, 423

Middle Ages, close of, 5

Middle class, rise of, in England, 28

Middle East: and World War II, 736, 737; and Russia, 804, 805, 808; Arab-Israeli dispute, 808; United Arab Republic, 809

Middle West (U.S.), 353; industrialization of, 416; in literature, 448; and farm labor, 668

"Midnight judges," 187, 192

Midway Islands, 568, 742; Battle of, 743

Militarism, and World War I, 598

Millay, Edna St. Vincent, 648

Miller, Joaquin, 447

Milligan (a Copperhead), 375

Mills, Clark, 284

Milwaukee, Wis., 304, 449, 796

Miniatures, 284

Minimum wage laws, 700, 702

Mining: stimulated by industrialization, 414, 470; in South, 416; for resources, 426*; for gold and silver, 468, 469; for other minerals, 470; and child labor, 526; for coal, 534; safety in, 541

Minneapolis, Minn., 449

Minnesota, 427, 646

Minority groups. *See* Civil rights

Minutemen, 109

Missionaries, 289, 333, 357

Mississippi: 132, 250, 264, 316, 355, 366; in Civil War, 371, 378, 380*; readmitted to Union, 399; and T.V.A., 693

Mississippi River: 353, 432; explored and claimed by France, 25; contested by Spain, 132, 137, 178, 195; and Louisiana Purchase, 197; showboats on, 283; steamboats on, 293; in Civil War, 377, 379, 380; and floods, 666

Mississippi Valley: lost by France, 100

Missouri: 251, 252, 361; in Civil War, 378, 388; and reform, 520; and city government, 523

Missouri, the, 745, *745*

Missouri Compromise, 252*, 253, 331, 345, 359, 361, 362

Missouri Fur Company, 333

Missouri River, 198, 764

Mitchell, John, 89

Mitchell, John, 534

Mobile, Ala., 385

Modern age, birth of, 5

Molly Maguires, 459

Molotov Plan, 778

Money: medieval, 5; growing use of, 8. *See also* Currency

Money trust, 550, 639

Monitor, the, 375, *382*

Monopolies, 427; Standard Oil, 427; control of, 485, 500, 533; prevention of, 552. *See also* Big Business

Monroe, James: 165, *219*, 318; as envoy to France, 182, 195; as envoy to London, 202; as President, 218; 2nd term, 219, 222, 223, 253

Monroe Doctrine: 165, 223, 398, 568, 589, 590; principles of, 223; "Roosevelt corollary," 590, 592, 594, 678; and F. Roosevelt, 708; in World War II, 721

Montana, 469, *472*

Montcalm, Major General, *101*

Montenegro, 616

Monterrey, Mexico, 341

Montgomery, Gen. Richard, 117

Montgomery Ward & Co., 423

Monticello, 178, *200*, 203, 285
Montreal; founded by Champlain, 24; taken by Montgomery, 117; in War of 1812, 210; and St. Lawrence Seaway, 796
Moore, Marianne, 826
Moore's Creek, 117
Morgan, J. P., 534, *535*
Morgan, J. P., & Co., 428
Mormons, 288, 342
Morocco, 597, 737
Morrill Land-Grant College Act, 446, 801
Morrill Tariff Act, 413
Morris, Gouverneur, 53, 140, 190
Morristown, N.J., 119
Morrow, Dwight W., 664
Morse, Samuel F. B., 287, 297, *297*
Mortgages, farm: refinanced by New Deal, 688; federal insurance for, 765
Morton, Dr. W. T. G., 287
Moscow, 632; conferences in, 738, 745
Moslem culture, 9
Motion pictures, 637, 638; and sound, 638
Motley, John L., 279
Motor Carriers Act of 1935, 692
Motor vehicle registration, 637 (chart)
Mott, Lucretia, 317
Mount, William Sidney, 284
Mount Holyoke Female Seminary, 310
Mount Vernon, *136*, 175
Mount Vernon Conference, 136
Mountain Standard time, 421
Muckrakers, 519
Mugwumps, 498
Muir, John, *539*
Muller vs. *Oregon*, 527
Munich, 716
Munn vs. *Illinois*, 484
Murfree, Mary N., 448
Murray, John, 288
Muscle Shoals, Ala., 655, 657, 658, 673, 677, 693
Museum of Fine Arts, Boston, 449
Music: development of jazz, 649; increased interest in, 824
Musical societies, 286
Mussolini, Benito: 681, 708, 710, *710*, 723, 766; and Ethiopia, 711; and Albania, 717; and Greece, 719; and invasion of Italy, 737

Nagasaki, 357, 745, 775
Naples, 737, 738

Napoleon, 184, *189*, 195, 199, 205, 212
Napoleon III, 380, 398
Nashoba, 314
Nashville, Tenn., 258, 378
Nasser, Gamal Abdel, 808, 809
Nation, Carry, *523*
National Aeronautics and Space Administration (NASA), 808
National Banking Act, 413
National banks, 414; and the Federal Reserve, 550
National Child Labor Committee, 517, 525
National Conservation Commission, 537, 541
National conventions, first tried, 266
National Defense Act, 602
National Defense Education Act, 804
National Defense Research Committee, 731
National Employment Act, 820
National Gallery of Art, Washington, 825
National Guard, 604
National health insurance, 765
National Housing Act, 703
National Industrial Recovery Act, 686, 690, 698, 702
National Labor Relations Act: of 1935, 673, 698, 701, 702, 760; of 1947, 760
National Labor Relations Board, 698, 760
National Monetary Commission, 549
National origins, clause, 634, white settlers, 77*
National Progressive Republican League, 542; and T. Roosevelt, 543
National Prohibition Act, 635
National Prohibition party, 440
National Recovery Administration (NRA), 690
National Republicans, 254, 266; join Whigs, 268
National Science Foundation, 763, 824
National Youth Administration, 696
Nationalism: growth of, after Middle Ages, 5, 8; factor in English expansion, 30; influence of West on growth of, 135; in War of 1812, 214; of Republicans, 219; and Monroe Doctrine, 226; vs. sectionalism, 237, 254, 261; "new," 542; and World War I, 598; vs. internationalism, 631, 709

"Nationalism," founded by Bellamy, 449
Nationwide industry: replaces local plants, 422; chain stores, 423; mail-order catalogues, 423; new packaging in, 423
Natural resources: and industrialization, 415; minerals, 426*; and conservation, 537
Naturalism, in literature, 645
Naturalization Act, 184, 192
Nauvoo, Ill., 343
Navigation, 9
Navigation Acts, 72; enforcement of, 102
Navy: English, 115; American, 122; French, 122; in Tripolitan War, 193; in War of 1812, 210; in Civil War, 372. *See also* U.S. Navy
Nazi party, 710
Nazis, 681, 702; and armament, 681; in Latin America, 708; and pact with Russia, 717, 723; and secret weapons, 732; in U.S., 733. *See also* Hitler *and* Germany
Nebraska, 359, *475*, 483, 501, 646
Negroes: 244, 283, 356; and labor, 318, 459; and fear of slave uprising, 320; in Army, 372; under Reconstruction, 393, 394; made citizens, 395; and the vote, 396, 399, 401, 494; and education, 444, 642, 800; in literature, 448, 648; and World War I, 606, 816; as minority group, 799, 800; increased opportunities for, 816. *See also* Slavery
Nehru, Jawaharlal, 781, 782, 783
Netherlands: and Caribbean, 589; and Far East, 660, 680, 783; and Nazis, 718, 740; N. Atlantic Treaty, 779. *See also* Holland
Netherlands Indies, 725, 742, 783
Neutrality: in French-English war, 176; in World War II, 712
Neutrality Act: of 1935, 712; of 1937, 712, 714, 717; of 1939, 717, 724
Neutrals, rights of: 597, 713; in World War I, 601
Nevada, 469, 470
New Amsterdam, 45, *46*
New Brunswick (Canada), 270
New Deal, the: 527, 629, 677,

870

676, 677, 685, 735, 738; and Good Neighbor policy, 590, 594, 707, 708; and Mexican oil, 594; as candidate for Vice-President, 622; as President, 629, 661, 684, 685; as Governor of New York, 684; and the "Hundred Days," 685; and banking, 685, 691; and the farmers, 686, 688; and the dollar, 691, 692; and regional planning, 693; and relief, 694, 695, 696; and social security, 696; and the labor movement, 698; 2nd term, 701; and the Supreme Court, 701, 702; 3rd term, 703, 722; and foreign affairs, 712, 714; quarantine speech by, 714; and national defense, 715, 720, 731; and World War II, 717, 723, 730, 733; and the four freedoms, 723; at Casablanca, 737; at Cairo, 738, 783; at Teheran, 739; at Yalta, 741, 746, 774; 4th term, 741, 746; and international organization, 745, 746, 749; death of, 746

Roosevelt, Theodore: 260, 507, 515, 519, 530, 539, 548, 556, 617, 621; and housing, 525, 527; and the Rough Riders, 572; as Secretary of the Navy, 532, 571; as Vice-President, 531; as President, 531, 582, 585, 590; and Congress, 532; as trust buster, 533, 536, 552; 2nd term, 535; and conservation, 537; travels of, 542, 616; and Bull Moose Party, 542, 543, 544, 651; as arbitrator, 597; winner of Nobel Peace Prize, 597

Roosevelt Corollary, 590, 592, 594, 678

Roosevelt Dam, 537

Root, Elihu: and coal strike, 534, 535; as Secretary of State, 597

Root-Takahira Agreement, 583

Rosecrans, Gen. W. S., 381

Ross, John, 265

Rotation in office, 259

Rough Riders, 572

Royal Air Force, 738

Rumania: 605, 616, 618, 774; and Czechoslovakia, 716; independence guaranteed, 717; in "New Order," 724; and Russians, 773, 775, 776; peace treaty with, 775

Rural Electrification Administration, 689

Rural free delivery, 422

Rush, Alexander, 443

Rush, Benjamin, 130, 443

Rush-Bagot Treaty, 220

Russell, Jonathan, 212

Russia: relations with, 222, 226; and Alaska, 221, 398; grain from, 482; and the Far East, 581, 582, 679; and world disarmament, 597; and imperialism, 598; and World War I, 599, 604, 605, 615, 618; relief program for, 666; new government recognized, 709. See also Soviet Union

Russian-American Fur Co., 221

Russo-Japanese War, 582, 597

Ryan, Father John, 518

Ryder, Albert P., 452

Ryukyu Islands, 581, 743

Saar Basin, 618

Sacramento, Cal., 341, 343, 417

Saint-Gaudens, Augustus, 452

St. Lawrence, Gulf of, discovered, 24; in French and Indian War, 100

St. Lawrence Seaway, 679, 762, 796

St. Leger, Colonel, 120

St. Louis, Mo., 197, 245, 304, 333, 432, 471

Saint Mihiel, 610

Sakhalin, 582, 741

Salem, Mass., 88, 111, 285

Salt Lake City, 343

Samoan Islands, 568

San Antonio, Texas, 336

San Francisco, Cal., 221, 298, 347, 471, 583, 746, 774, 783, 806

San Jacinto, Battle of, 336

San Juan Hill, 572

San Salvador, 13

Sandburg, Carl, 648, 826

Sanford, Edward, 652

Santa Anna, Antonio López de, 336, 336

Santa Clara case, 485

Santa Fe, N.M., 333, 341

Santa Fe Railroad, 420

Santa Fe Trail, 333, 344

Santiago (Cuba), 572

Santo Domingo. See Dominican Republic

Saratoga Campaign, 120, 120*

Satellites: (dependent nations), 773; (in orbit), 804

Saud, King, 782

Saudi Arabia, 791

Savannah, Ga., 123, 297, 385

Savannah, the, 298

Savings banks, 691

Scalawags, 397, 399

Scandinavia, 634

Schools. See Education

Science: development of, 5, 8; predominance of natural history, 286; botany, 286; oceanography, 286; electromagnetism, 286; institutions founded, 287; pure vs. applied, 288; growth of, 411, 642; and spread of industrialism, 415; strengthened in land-grant colleges, 446; applied to farming, 480; chemistry, 642, 824; medicine, 643; physics, 823; in World War II, 731

Scotland, 609

Scott, Gen. Winfield, 270, 341, 350

Scouts, 644, 644

Sculpture, 284, 452

Seamen's Union, 554

Sears, Roebuck & Co., 423

Seattle, Wash., 632

Secession: early threats of, 263, 331, 337, 346, 354; by South Carolina, 365; causes of, 366; by other states, 371; states re-admitted to Union, 393

Secret ballot: advocated by Populists, 502; adopted, 521

Secretariat, of the U.N., 747

Secretary of Defense, 758

Sectionalism: growth of, after War of 1812, 237, 239; related to slavery issue, 252; and the tariff, 255, 256, 261

Secularization, 9

Securities, sale of, 691

Securities and Exchange Commission, 691, 692, 819

Security Council, of the U.N.: 747, 774, 783, 786; and Korea, 785; and the veto, 788; and Indonesia, 790

Sedan, 611

Sedition Act: of 1798, 184; of 1917, 608

Segregation: in education, 444, 642, 800; and the Supreme Court, 800

Selective Service Act, 605, 720

Seminoles, 264

Senators, direct election of, 515, 521, 541, 543

Seneca Falls Convention, 317

Seoul, 785, 786

Separatists, 39

Serbia, 599, 605, 616. See also Yugoslavia

Serfs, 5, 6

Servicemen's Readjustment Act, 761

Settlement houses, 440

Sevastopol, U.S.S.R., 736

of, 804; and summit meeting, 805; end of Stalinism in, 805; and the Arabs, 809; and division of Germany, 810. *See also* Russia

Space projects, 808

Spain: exploration by, 12, 14, 23*; and Balboa, 16; Magellan, 16; and the *conquistadores*, 19; de León, 19; Cortés, 20; Pizarro, 20; claims to North America, 22, 31; colonization by, 22; defeat of Armada, 28; war with England, 100, 121; hostility after the Revolution, 132, 137, 175, 178; Louisiana ceded to Spain, 195; Louisiana Purchase, 196; and Florida, 220; colonies of, in Latin America, 222; and Cuba, 356; and cattle raising, 471; war with, 506, 569, 571, 572; in World War I, 599; civil war in, 712, 768; in World War II, 737

Spalding, Archbishop John L., 518

Spanish-American War, 565, 572; fed by jingoism, 569; results of, 572

Spargo, John, 525

Sparkman, John, 793

Sparks, Jared, 279

Specie Circular, 267, 268

Specific powers, doctrine of, 172

Speculation: and issue of bank notes, 267; and depression of 1837, 268; and Federal Reserve System, 551; and stock market, 629, 631, 657, 670; and credit, 672

Spies, in World War II, 720

Spinning jenny, 239

Spoils system, 259, 495; opposed by Cleveland, 498

Sports, 436

Springfield, Ill., 392

Sputnik, 804

"Square Deal," the, 532

Squatters, 247

Stalin, Josef V., 717, 718, 738, 767, 785; at Teheran, 739; at Yalta, 741, 746, 774; and Chiang Kai-shek, 744; as dictator, 767, 768; at Potsdam, 774, *774*; death of, 787; criticism of, 805

Stalingrad, 736

Stalwarts, 496

Stamp Act, 106 (chart); Stamp Act Congress, 104, repeal of, 104

Standard of living, 813

Standard Oil Company, 423, 424, 427, 518

Standard Oil Company of Ohio, 426

Stanton, Edwin McMasters, 392, 397

Stanton, Elizabeth Cady, 317

Star routes, 497

Star-Spangled Banner, 212

Stassen, Harold E., 749

State banks, 267, 268

State governments: creation of, 128; powers of, 131, 145; quarrels among, 133; provisions for new, 136; problem for Constitutional Convention, 141; and residual powers, 151; relations among, 156

States' rights, 185, 213, 217; and judicial review, 227; upheld in South, 244; and the slavery issue, 252; and the tariff, 261; and Jackson, 263; and Democratic party, 274; and conscription, 374

Statute of Religious Liberty, 129

Steam locomotives, 294

Steamboats, 237, 293

Steel industry: and Bessemer process, 415; and Carnegie, 427; open-hearth process, 427; and labor, 461

Steffens, Lincoln, 518, *519*

Steinbeck, John, 826

Stevens, Colonel John, 294

Stevens, Robert, 771

Stevens, Thaddeus, 395

Stevens, Wallace, 826

Stevenson, Adlai E., 793, 794, 806, *808*

Stimson, Henry L., 662, 678, 679, 680

Stock exchange, regulation of, 691

Stockbrokers: and influence of telegraph, 422; regulation of, 691

Stockholders, 424

Stock market: in the 1920's, 669; and the crash, 670

Stone, Harlan F., 702

Stoughton, Mass., 286

Stowe, Calvin, 309

Stowe, Harriet Beecher, 358, *358*

Street railways, 433; regulation of, 525

Strikes: 312, 457, 459; railroad, 496; and T. Roosevelt, 534; and shortages, 534; after World War I, 632. *See also* Labor unions, *and* under names of particular strikes

Stuart, Gilbert, 283

Stuyvesant, Peter, 46

Submarines: 383; in World War I, 601, 603, 608; in

World War II, 721, 724, 732, 736; in Pacific, 744

Subsistence farms, 62, 299

Suburbs, development of: 433, 817; and development of trolleys, 433

Subversion, measures to combat, 374

Subways, 433

Sudetenland, 715, 716

Suez Canal, 584; threatened by Nazis, 724, 737; by Russians, 776; and Egypt, 790, 808

Suffrage: broadened, 129; male suffrage, 1830, 260*; women's, 523, 523*, 524, 543

Sugar: and Cuban rebellion, 569; and Philippines, 574

Sugar Act, 103, 106 (chart)

Sugar and Molasses Act, 72

Sugar trust, 533

Sullivan, Louis H., 452, 826

Summit meeting, 805, 810

Sumner, Charles, 360, 395, 494

Sunday schools, 290

Supreme Court: under Marshall, 226, 227; and right of judicial review, 226, 230; defied by states, 264; Dred Scott decision, 361; and right of trial, 375; and monopolies, 427, 533, 552, 638; and public utilities, 484; and income tax, 503, 504; and social legislation, 526, 527; on church and state, 528, 801; and child labor, 554; and empire, 573; and radicalism, 633; and labor, 640, 699; and the New Deal, 687, 691, 698, 701, 702; and subversion, 771; and offshore rights, 796; and civil rights, 799, 800

Surplus Commodities Corporation, 689

Surpluses, 688, 689

Sussex, the, 602

Sutherland, George, 652

Sutter's Mill, *343*

Sweatshops, 517, 546

Sweatt vs. *Painter*, 800

Sweden: 599, 718; settlements by, 45*

Switzerland, 599

Syria, 619, 790; and United Arab Republic, 809

Tabloids, 637

Taft, Robert A., 793, 794, *796*

Taft, William Howard, 515, 550, 552; as President, 540; and the tariff, 540; *541*;

Wall Street, 544, *699;* symbol of Big business, 501, 505
Wall Street Journal, 653
Wallace, Henry, 703; and Progressives, 764
Walsh-Healy Government Contracts Act, 699
Wanamaker, John, 423
War: humane conduct of, 597; attempts to outlaw, 661; evils of, emphasized, 712
War between North and South: causes of, 239; North and South in 1860, 373 (chart); beginning of, 370; secession of Southern states, 365, 371; events of, 378, 378*, 380, 380*, 381, 384, 384*; turning point of, 380; collapse of Confederacy, 385; magnitude of, 386. *See also* Confederate States *and* Lincoln
War debts, 657, 661, 663 (chart); moratorium, 681
War Hawks, 207, 208
War Industries Board, 606
War Labor Board, 606
War Manpower Commission, 730
War of 1812, 165, 208*; events leading to, 177, 207; causes of, 209; opposition to, 209; invasion of Canada, 210; Treaty of Ghent, 212; results of, 214
War of the Confederate States for Independence, 331. *See* War between North and South
War Production Board, 730, 732
War Trade Board, 606
Warm Springs, Ga., 746
Warner, Charles Dudley, 448
Warren, Earl, 764
Warren, Dr. John C., 287
Warren, Robert Penn, 826
Wartime Committee on Public Information, 607
Washington (state), *513,* 524
Washington, D.C., *171,* 191, 212, *213, 219,* 259, 285, 297, 349, 378; and arts, 449, 452; center of Pan American Conference, 588; and architecture, 648
Washington, Booker T., 446
Washington, George, 82, 89, 99, *99,* 111, 116, *145, 167, 175,* 219, 308, 548; in Revolutionary War, 117, 118, 121, 123, 132; at Mount Vernon, 136, *136,* 137; at Constitutional Convention, 139; as President, 148, *166, 167,* 168, 173; 2nd term,

175, 176, *180;* Farewell Address of, 179; statue of, 284; on slavery, 318
Washington Conference on Naval Limitation and Far Eastern Affairs, 652, 659, 660 (chart), 680
Water resources: well drilling, 474; droughts, 475
Water works: regulation of, 524; public ownership of, 525
Wayne, Gen. Anthony, 179, *179*
Weaver, Gen. James B., 501
Webster, Daniel, 227, 241, 261, *262,* 268, *272,* 374, 489; as Secretary of State, 273, 274; in Senate, 346, 348, 349, and Hawaii, 568
Webster-Ashburton Treaty, 274
Welfare, federal responsibility for, 819
Welfare capitalism, 640
Wells, Dr. Horace, 287
Wesleyan College, 310
West, the: 470*; as common national estate, 134; ordinances relating to, 135; growth of, 167, 244, 414, *473;* influence of improved transportation on, 194; growing political strength of, 237, 251, 258, 261, 270; growth of sectionalism in, 239; as market for manufactures, 241, 414; stages of settlement, 247; and states' rights, 263; and currency problems, 265, 550; religion in, 288; need for improved transportation to, 293, 296, 414; main routes west, 344*; growth of trade with East, 353; rapid growth of, after Civil War, 411; literature of, 447, 826; self-government in, 469; and women's suffrage, 524; and need for Panama Canal, 585
West, Benjamin, 283
West Florida, 220
West German Federal Republic, 778, 781; and NATO, 781, 810
West Indies: closed to American ships, 133; seizure of ships bound for, 177
West Memphis, Ark., 797
West Point, N.Y., 648
West Virginia, 371, 388
Western Lands Dispute, 131*
Western routes, before 1860, 344*
Weygand, Gen., *608*
Weyler, Gen., 569, 570
Whaling, 66, *66–67*

Wharton, Edith, 645
Wheeler, Burton K., 656, 691
Wheeling, W. Va., 245, 297
Whigs, 268, 338, 346, 349; and the bank issue, 269; and the campaign of 1840, 270, 271; end of party, 360
Whipple, Abraham, *117*
Whisky Rebellion, 170
Whistler, James, 449
White, Henry M., 617
White House, 191, 259, *283*
White Paper, 782
Whiteman, Paul, 649
Whitman, Marcus, 334
Whitman, Walt, *280,* 282, 648
Whitney, Eli, 240, 241, 242
Whittier, John Greenleaf, 279, *280,* 317
Wickersham, George, 541
Wilder, Thornton, 646, 826
Wilderness, the, 384
Willamette Valley, 334
Willard, Emma, 310, 317
William and Mary, College of, 87
Williams, Roger, 42, 95
Williams, Tennessee, 826
Williamsburg, Va., 57, 645
Willkie, Wendell, 694, 703, 722, *722,* 723
Wilmington (Fort Christiana), 46
Wilmot, David, 345
Wilmot Proviso, 345
Wilson, James, 140, 142
Wilson, Woodrow, 260, 413, 515, 519, 547, *554,* 618, 659, 723; as Governor of New Jersey, 546, 550; as President, 544, 548, 556, 591, 661, 635; and the "New Freedom," 547; and the tariff, 547, 548; and monetary reform, 550; and labor, 553; and Mexico, 556, 594; and the Caribbean, 592, 593; and World War I, 600, 601, 603, 604, 606; and ideas for peace, 603, 611, 615, 616, 618, 680, 723; at Peace Conference, 618; and the League, 619, 749
Wilson-Gorman Act, 503, 569
Winthrop, John, 40, 41, *41*
Wisconsin, 294, *559;* and Progressives, 520; and reform, 521, 698
Witches, belief in, 88; trial, *88*
Wolfe, Gen. James, 100, *101*
Wolfe, Thomas, 826
Women: rights of, 282, 316, 435; education of, 309, 446; Declaration of Sentiments, 317; increased leisure of, 435, 815; and labor movement, 459, 465, 699; pro-

ACKNOWLEDGMENTS

Grateful acknowledgment is made to the following sources for their kind permission to reproduce photographs in UNITED STATES HISTORY.

Page
iv   H. Armstrong Roberts
vii Phillips Andover Academy
xvi LIFE, Peter Stackpole
4   (top) U.S. Lines; (bot. r.) John Carter Brown Library
9   Royal Library, Brussels
11   Pan American World Airways
14   John Carter Brown Library
15   N.Y. Public Library
17   Addison Gallery of American Art, Phillips Academy
19   Photo Bulloz
20   Shostal

Page
21   (top) Shostal; (bot. l.) University Museum, Philadelphia; (bot. r.) Wide World
22   Ward Linton
24   N.Y. Public Library
25   Henry E. Huntington Library and Art Gallery
26   John Carter Brown Library
28   Frick Art Reference Library
29   National Maritime Museum
30   National Portrait Gallery
31   (top) National Maritime Museum; (bot.) National Portrait Gallery